WHERE *to* SKI

Edited by
Chris Gill
and
Dave Watts

B🌿XTREE

First published in Great Britain in
1994 by Boxtree Limited, Broadwall
House, 21 Broadwall, London SE1 9PL

10 9 8 7 6 5 4 3 2 1

ISBN 0 7522 1623 6

Editors Chris Gill and Dave Watts
Assistant editor Ian Porter
Editorial assistants Ian Stratford,
Mandy Crook, Dennis Shrives,
Nicola Cunningham, Seb Leber,
Alice Finlay
Production editors Kate Targett,
Christopher Madigan, Tom Crawley
Production assistants Joe Fox,
Adrian Taylor
Contributors Alan Coulson, Adam Ruck,
Nicky Holford, James Hooke,
Nick van Zanten, Chris Allan,
Katrina Moran, Jonathan Swinfen
Helena Wiesner, Tim Perry

Design by Fox and Partners
Photo credits: see page 4
Colour reproduction by
Monarch Lithogravure
Printed and bound in Portugal by
Printer Portuguesa

A CIP catalogue entry for this book is
available from the British Library.

Contents

Resorts in detail

*Each country section starts
with an introduction, and the
main ones include a road map*

4

Photo credits

p57 Badgastein – Gasteiner Bergbahnen Ag
p73 Ischgl – Tourismusverband Ischgl
p77 Kitzbühel – Tourismusverband Kitzbühel
p81 Lech – Verkehrsamt Lech
p93 Obergurgl – Lohmann Photo/Tourismusverband Gurgl
p105 St Anton – Tourismusverband St. Anton
p113 St Johann – Fremdverkehrsverband St. Johann
p125 Söll – Tourismusverband Söll
p133 Zell am See – Kurverwaltung Zell am See
p140 Alpe-d'Huez – NortonWood
p144 Les Arcs – Société des Téléphériques de l'Aiguille Rouge
p152 Avoriaz – OT Avoriaz
p153 Chamonix – OT Chamonix Mont-Blanc Franc
p165 La Clusaz – Maison du Tourisme, La Clusaz
p169 Les Contamines – Office du Tourisme, Les Contamines
p176 Courchevel – Christophoto, Courchevel
p177 Les Deux-Alpes – NortonWood
p192 Megève – J C Ligcon, OT Megève
p201 Méribel – Picture A – J M Goudard, OT Méribel; NortonWood
p220 La Plagne – NortonWood
p228 La Rosière – NortonWood
p237 Tignes – NortonWood
p241 Val-d'Isère – NortonWood
p248 Val-d'Isère – NortonWood
p252 Valmorel – P. Jacques/Service Presse/Jeanne Cattini
p257 Val-Thorens – F Gros, Val Thorens
p269 Cervinia – NortonWood
p272 Cortina d'Ampezzo – Foto Stefano Zardini, Cortina d'Ampezzo
p276 Courmayeur – Associazione Operatori Turistici Monte Bianco
p288 Sauze d'Oulx – IAT Sauze d'Oulx
p293 Selva – Consorzio Turistico Val Gardena
p311 Champèry – Office du Tourisme, Champèry
p320 Crans-Montana – Photo Deprez, Crans-Montana
p324 Davos – Kur- und Verkehrsverein Davos
p340 Gstaad – NortonWood
p344 Mürren – NortonWood
p353 St Moritz – Kur- und Verkehrsverein St Moritz
p361 Verbier – Clambin Productions Mark Shapiro/Office du Tourisme Verbier
p369 Wengen – NortonWood
p372 Zermatt – NortonWood
p377 Zermatt – NortonWood
p384 Aspen – Doug Child Photo, Aspen Skiing Co
p388 Aspen – NortonWood
p392 Breckenridge – Carl Scofield/Breckenridge Ski Resort
p393 Breckenridge – Bob Winsett/Breckenridge Ski Resort
p401 Jackson Hole – Bob Woodall/Wade McKoy/Jackson Hole Ski Corporation
p417 Park City – Lori Adamski-Peek/Park City Ski Corp
p424 Steamboat – Larry Pierce, Steamboat Ski and Resort Corp
p428 Taos – Robert Reck Photography/Taos Ski Valley
p432 Telluride – NortonWood
p433 Vail – Jack Affleck/Vail Photo/Vail Associates Inc
p441 Banff – Scott Rowed Photography, Ski Banff/Lake Louise
p448 Whistler – Whistler Resort Ass/Leanna Rathkelly

About this book

why Where to Ski?

This is a new guide to ski resorts. It sets out to help you pick the ideal resort – or at least the best resort – for your next skiing holiday, whether you are a beginner or an expert skier. It does one or two other very useful things as well, but that's a bonus. It is not the only such book on the market, but we are confident that it is the best.

Well, we would say that, wouldn't we? But we can support the claim with facts:

• It covers over 500 resorts – 250 of them in detail

• It has hard-hitting but user-friendly resort assessments – look at a resort chapter and you'll see that we give you four different ways to gauge the appeal of each resort:

    – comparative star ratings, assessing each resort on 11 key aspects
    – highly specific lists of pros and cons
    – our own overall verdict
    – separate one-line verdicts under 14 different headings

• It's up to date: most of the purely factual information in this book – new lifts, pass prices, package holiday programmes – is up to date for the 1994/95 ski season

• It's printed in colour – allowing us to include clear panoramic piste maps, and effective photographs

• It has a generous page size – allowing our designers to adopt a clear, multi-column layout; information is easy to find, not buried in reams of continuous text

• It has village plans – detailed full-colour street plans all specially drawn to a consistent scale to show how spread out the lifts are.

But that's only half the story. In the end, what you want from a guide book of any kind is reliable guidance. The information it presents must be detailed, comprehensive, accurate and up to date, as well as accessible; the descriptions must be accurate and vivid; perhaps most important of all, the judgements the editors have made must be sound.

On all these scores, we believe *Where to Ski* is ahead of the field. Judge for yourself. Pick a resort you know well, and see how accurately we describe it and how fairly we assess it. Pick a resort you don't know, and discover how thoroughly we have weighed up its merits and drawbacks.

We had to make *Where to Ski* the best because it doesn't have any laurels to rest on. It is competing with well established guides. If it isn't the best, it won't win readers and it won't survive.

We started with some advantages. Chris was founding editor of the Good Skiing Guide, generally recognised at birth (in 1985) as the best resort guide so far; he continued to edit the guide until 1992, when his ambitions for the guide diverged from those of the publishers. Dave contributed to the Good Skiing Guide from the beginning, and became one of its mainstays. For over a decade, we have been evaluating and comparing ski resorts – not simply writing entertaining magazine and newspaper articles about them. Between the two of us, we know a bit about this game.

We also know a bit about editing magazines and books. When the Good Skiing Guide was launched, Chris was editor of Holiday Which?, while Dave was editor of Which? itself. More recently, Dave has displayed his skills in developing Daily Mail Ski magazine. When he joined the magazine a couple of years ago it was already the biggest ski magazine in Britain; now, it's the most authoritative, too.

It won't escape your notice that *Where to Ski* carries advertisements. This is a fundamental part of our strategy for the book. Without the financial support of the ads, we could not meet the cost of printing our piste maps, village plans and photos in colour. We believe that in a world of colour holiday brochures and colour resort literature, it's time for a colour resort guide. We're grateful to the advertisers who have had the confidence to support this first edition, and we hope readers who approve of this new venture will in turn support our advertisers.

Most of the ads come from tour operators offering catered chalet holidays. We have accepted no advertising at all from ski resorts. So we are under no pressure to compromise our views on resorts, which is what this guide is all about. The chalet ads are laid out in a consistent way so as to look prominent without ruining the design of the book as a whole – and to make them easier for readers to use as a resource. To eliminate the possibility that they might be interpreted as editorial matter, they are clearly labelled as advertisements. We think these ads enhance rather than detract from the book.

Where to Ski has made a lot of use of reports from hundreds of holiday skiers. The 50 best have earned free copies of this edition. Next year, we plan to give away 100 – and, as this year, to offer all other reporters a hefty discount on the price of the book. Please help us to make the next edition even better than this one, by sending in a report this winter. There's more information on page 8.

In practice, anyone who goes skiing this winter can have a free copy of this edition. We've come up with an ingenious scheme which means you can get the cost of *Where to Ski* back when you book your 1994/95 holiday. It can be a package or an independent holiday, booked any time up to the end of April, for any number of people. Details are given on the facing page.

It's two years since we set about turning our ideas for *Where to Ski* into reality. We'll now be starting to plan improvements for next year. If you have any suggestions, we'd love to hear from you. Our address is on page 8.

Get your money back

Where to Ski comes free

You can reclaim the price of Where to Ski when you book a 1994/95-season skiing holiday. All you have to do is book the holiday through the specialist ski travel agency Ski Solutions. The price of the book will be knocked off your final payment.

Ski Solutions are Britain's longest-established and most respected ski travel agency. You can buy whatever kind of holiday you want through them, so you're not losing out on breadth of choice. Ski Solutions sell the complete range of package holidays offered by all the bonded tour operators in Britain, ranging from the smallest one-resort chalet operators (who otherwise sell directly by mail) to the mass-market operators who mainly sell through the brochure racks of high-street travel agents. Ski Solutions can also tailor-make holidays for independent-minded skiers who want to go their own way – whether it's a long weekend in Chamonix or an 18-day tour of the best half-dozen resorts in the Rockies.

Where to Ski has built strong links with Ski Solutions over the last couple of years, sharing staff and involving Ski Solutions clients in reporting on resorts. So we're delighted that we have been able to put together this special offer for readers.

Claiming your refund is easy. Right at the back of the book is a page which comprises two vouchers. When you make your definite booking, tell Ski Solutions that you want to claim a refund. Cut out the vouchers and send one to Ski Solutions and one to *Where to Ski* (the addresses are on the vouchers). That's all there is to it. When your final invoice arrives, it will show a refund of the price of the book.

Get next year's edition free

and help make it even better

There are too many ski resorts for us to visit them all every year, and there are too many hotels, chalets, bars, nightspots and mountain restaurants for us to hope to see them all in the resorts we do visit. So we are very keen to encourage more skiers to join our already healthy band of correspondents, who send in reports on their holiday experiences. To encourage readers, we'll be giving away 100 copies of next year's edition to the writers of the best reports.

If you reported on your holiday last year, we'll be sending you a new report form just before the season starts. If you didn't but would like a form, just drop us a line to the address below; no stamp is necessary. But we're always happy to receive reports, whether they are on the form or not – provided they are clearly set out in a structured way that we can handle. (Imagine sifting through a dozen rambling letters to see what people think of a particular ski school, and you'll understand why a clear structure is important.) Many reporters would rather use their word processor than struggle to write legibly, and we certainly want to encourage that.

The structure we favour is closely related to the structure of the resort chapters of the book – and indeed you'll find it helpful when compiling a report to have the relevant chapter to hand, to see what we've said in this edition. Here are the headings we'd like you to use:

HOW IT RATES
Give the resort marks out of five for:

The skiing
Snow
Extent
Advanced
Intermediates
Beginners
Convenience
Queues
Mountain restaurants
The rest
Scenery
Resort charm
Not skiing

OVERVIEW
Summarise the main pros and cons of the resort:

The resort
What did you like?
What did you dislike?
What surprised you?
Who does it suit?
The skiing
What did you like?
What did you dislike?
What surprised you?
Who does it suit?

DETAILED ASSESSMENT
Under each heading, summarise your view of the resort in as much detail as you can. Where appropriate (in the starred sections, probably) give your particular recommendations:

Snow reliability
For advanced skiers
For intermediate skiers
For beginners
For cross-country
Queues
Mountain restaurants*
Ski schools*
Facilities for children*
Choice of location*
Chalets*
Hotels*
Self-catering apartments*
Where to eat*
Après-ski*
For non-skiers*

Write to:
Where to Ski
NortonWood Publishing
The Old Forge
Norton St Philip
Bath
BA3 6LW

Introduction

the editors ramble

FIRST: SAFETY

Skiing is a risky business, everyone knows that. Well, actually, no – it isn't, on the whole. If perchance you are dipping into this book because you're toying with the idea of putting your limbs at risk on the ski slopes for the first time, let us immediately reassure you: turn to page 21, where you can read how much safer skiing is than activities you never give a second thought to. If, on the other hand, you are an experienced skier looking for challenges, turn to page 21 and read about the unnecessary risks that skiers face in some of the more challenging resorts in the Alps.

SNOW LOWDOWN

Last season was a pretty good one for snow in the Alps. On more than one occasion, our skiing plans were disrupted by an excess of the stuff rather than a shortage. But those who skied through the snow shortages of a few years ago will not easily forget them, and we believe that reliable snow is a high priority with British skiers, whose access to ski slopes is confined to a week or two booked long in advance. You'll find that we have given the matter a high priority ourselves, with a snow reliability rating at the start of each chapter and a section within each chapter discussing the resort's snow record in detail.

We're conscious that some of the information that resorts provide on snowmaking facilities is somewhat theoretical. It's one thing to have 20 mobile snowguns that can in theory deal with 10km of piste; but to do any good they have to be operated, and to do a lot of good they have to be moved around. Reports from readers on this particular aspect of resort operation are particularly welcome.

SKI SCHOOL BLUES

Another aspect of resorts which holiday skiers are uniquely well placed to assess is the performance of ski schools. For most schools in the Alps, it's fair to say that we get mixed reports, and only rarely do we get a clear picture. Sometimes it is of a school that is thoroughly well run, with entirely competent, professional and pupil-oriented teachers as well as efficient organisation; sometimes it is of a school that is in disarray. Last season the International school in Flaine seemed to fall into the latter category, particularly in its handling of children. One reporter was moved to write not only describing the problems but prescribing a solution, which we reproduce here:

'The arrangements made for our children by the Ski Ecole International were the worst aspect of our holiday. The whole thing was shambolic and unprofessional. There was complete chaos at the beginning – confusion about which class the children should be in, and instructors with no idea how many children they should have in their class. If a child fell off a lift it was often a long time before they were reunited with their class, if they ever were – our 7-year-old fell within the first five minutes on the first day, and lost his class. Had we not happened to pass him soon afterwards, I doubt he would have found the class again. When we found his teacher, she said "There are too many children in the class"; indeed there were – 18, in fact. We heard several other stories of children getting left behind by their class. One of the instructors with the older children swore and

shouted at them, and on one occasion hit a child with his ski pole. Many of the instructors seem to have little idea of how to teach children.
A few simple arrangements would improve things enormously:
1 Children should be registered into classes the evening before, or half an hour before the start of ski school on the first day, with a maximum of 10 in a class.
2 At the start of each day, each instructor should be issued with a list of children in his class, so that there is no excuse for losing any.
3 Children, at least younger ones, should be issued with arm-bands showing the class number (perhaps colour-coded) so that if they get stranded they can easily be spotted and reunited with their group.
Does that all sound too bureaucratic? I don't think it would be at all difficult or expensive to do this, and it would give parents much greater reassurance that their children are being looked after.
The basic problem with ski schools is that no one exerts any pressure on them. Most people are there for only six days and have no long-term interest. They can complain, but what does that achieve? People don't want to spend their holiday having a row with the ski school. The only people who have the clout to force changes are the tour operators. If all the British tour operators sending people to a resort like Flaine got together and demanded changes like these, I am sure they could get results.'

Having been alarmed on many occasions to see vast groups of children being led around at high altitude in French resorts, we have lot of sympathy for these suggestions. Reactions welcome – from other parents, tour operators and ski schools.

REPORTERS' FAVOURITES

We find it interesting to analyse where our reporters spend their skiing time, and we thought you might be interested to see the results. Here are last winter's top 13 resorts:

Méribel, France
Courchevel, France
Zermatt, Switzerland
Les Arcs, France
Val d'Isère/Tignes, France
Verbier, Switzerland
Alpe d'Huez, France
Val-Thorens
Cervinia, Italy
Obergurgl, Austria
Flaine, France
Morzine, France
Saalbach-Hinterglemm, Austria.

Quite apart from the inbuilt fascination of top-ten lists, we have another purpose in presenting this one if you ski in any resorts *other* than these this winter, we'd be especially grateful for a report. Of course, you'll be in with a chance of winning a free book whichever resort you report on (see page 8).

At the other extreme, we had isolated reports on Bivio, Cavalese, Formigal, Gotzens, Grimentz, Itter, Mont Sutton, Nôtre-Dame-de-Bellecombe, Smugglers Notch, St Wolfgang, Villaroger and Zinal. These, and dozens of other resorts you may not have heard of, are covered in *Where to Ski* either as part of longer chapters or in a short summary in the alphabetical Resort directory at the back of the book – starting on page 487.

We plan to expand our coverage of small resorts in future, so please keep these reports on out-of-the-way places coming.

EDITORS' FAVOURITES

You can't write about ski resorts without being asked the question: Where's your favourite resort? That's not to say you have to answer it, of course. It depends on the circumstances. But there are resorts that arouse a special kind of response – resorts that have what you might call the tingle factor. We're both adventurous skiers in that grey area between intermediate and expert; we both like a decent lunch on the mountain; we both appreciate mountain scenery and traditional architecture. Our personal top ten of resorts that we are always keen to go back to – for widely differing reasons – is:

> Val d'Isère
> Méribel
> Zermatt
> St Anton
> Mürren
> Chamonix
> Vaujany/Alpe d'Huez
> Cortina
> Whistler
> Aspen

VIVA ITALIA!

As we observe in the introduction to Italian resorts, Italy is enjoying something of a renaissance, and deservedly so. Even if you are not attracted by Italian prices, you might find that a week in the Dolomites or the Aosta valley makes a refreshing change from the Tarentaise or the Valais.

As our 'bestseller' list shows, only one Italian resort is notably popular with our reporters – Cervinia. It's not one of our favourite places, but if you like fast cruising on smooth pistes, there's nowhere to beat it. The one Italian resort on our list of personal favourites is Cortina; the skiing is amusing, but the scenery is the thing – it's heart-stopping. But we have a bit of a soft spot for lots of Italian resorts – including the infamous Sauze d'Oulx. Avanti!

OK BY US

There seems to be ample evidence now that North America is here to stay, as it were. Interest in crossing the Atlantic was first developed on a serious scale by a combination of high-pressure weather in the Alps and high-pressure marketing techniques, chiefly applied through the very effective mechanism of entertaining British skiing journalists in extravagantly luxurious style. (One well known hack has been known to spend entire winters in the Rockies.) But there are now enough British skiers with experience of skiing in the States for the market to have matured a bit. Most of those who go there like it. That's not to say they now ski there every year – it does cost a lot – but most first-timers come back with the intention of going again.

A more recent phenomenon is the development of interest in Canada. One of us is deeply sceptical of the merits of travelling to the west coast of Canada to ski a single resort close to the warm Pacific ocean and at an altitude of 650m – even if it does have North America's biggest vertical drop (1600m). The other of us has been to Whistler, and is besotted with it.

HIGH ON HORMONES

It was in a mountain restaurant at Serre-Chevalier that the notion first cropped up. It was a snowy day – a good day to be in that heavily wooded resort – and most unusually we had been persuaded by our companions to stop for something approaching a serious lunch. The place was busy, but before long we found a low table surrounded by low chairs in a sort of lobby area.

The waiter had a lot on his hands, and there was plenty of time to look around. Someone observed that there seemed to be a lot of people going up and down the stairs next to us. They weren't going to the loo – that was downstairs. They weren't going to some other dining-room, as far as we could tell. Where were they going? The answer, we soon discovered, was that they were going up to their bedrooms. We were awaiting our oeufs frites not in a mountain restaurant, but in a mountain restaurant-with-rooms.

The concept was not a new one. One of us had done a bit of mountain walking in summer, and was familiar with the notion of refuges where bedrooms and dormitories, as well as meals, were available to climbers and walkers. And we were vaguely aware of massive hotels accessed by mountain railways in Swiss resorts like Zermatt and Wengen. But here was something rather different: a simple chalet reached only by cable-car.

We resolved there and then to pay special attention to this aspect of skiing accommodation as we compiled *Where to Ski* – and the result is the 'Staying up the mountain' sections that you will find in many of the resort chapters of the book. We've found more possibilities than we ever expected, including much more comfortable options than most skiers would dream of.

We freely admit that these sections of our resort entries are based on very little first-hand experience; but we aim to put that right this winter with some deliberate exploration at altitude. Readers' reports on staying above resort level will also be very welcome.

Our quest for high-altitude lodgings is given extra spice by a bit of intelligence gleaned from the documentation distributed by the tourist office in Davos. This is a resort well known for its health and medical research facilities, and buried within the bumf they send around to impress journalists like us is the fact that increased altitude leads to increased production of testosterone, the male sex hormone. (They don't say whether there is a parallel increase in the production of oestrogens in women.)

Quite apart from explaining the reputation that ski instructors have long enjoyed, this discovery raises the possibility that lodging at altitude may bring benefits other than beating lift queues and giving spectacular views over breakfast. It adds an extra dimension to the appeal of high Alpine resorts such as Tignes and Val-Thorens – and, more particularly, of super-high resorts in the American Rockies such as Breckenridge, where the village is at 2925m.

Last time one of us was in Breckenridge, the chief effect was 24 hours of altitude sickness, so any libido enhancement was unlikely to manifest itself. But perhaps readers have been luckier. Can you shed any light on variations in sexual appetite (or indeed performance) at high altitude? All replies will be treated in the strictest confidence.

And where, we wonder, are the highest beds in the skiing world to be found? Vail's exclusive Trapper's Cabin immediately came to mind, but in fact it's not as high as Breckenridge. The base station at Arapahoe Basin is higher, at 3290m; but as far as we know it has no accommodation, and nearby Keystone is at 2835m. Telluride's Mountain Village? Nope: 2895m.

We were about to conclude that Breckenridge was the testosterone capital of the skiing world when an Alpine rival came to mind. And, sure enough, the Kulmhotel Gornergrat, at the top of Zermatt's mountain railway, takes the prize with an altitude of 3100m.

What's new?

lifts and snow for '95

AUSTRIA

Ischgl improves Swiss connection

Some of Ischgl's notorious queues will be relieved for next season. On the Swiss side, a new chair-lift will cut the long waits to get back home from Alp Trida and means you no longer have to take those long T-bars. And the T-bar from Alp Trida towards Visnitzkopf will also be replaced by a chair. On the Austrian side, the Hollspitz T-bar will be upgraded to a chair too.

Kitzbühel gets more snow

Kitzbühel belatedly installed artificial snow last season. This season sees more snow guns on the Hahnenkamm, bringing the total to 19, covering 13km of piste. This should improve the chances of the famous World Cup Downhill race being run each season, but won't do much to improve this large area's poor snow record for holiday skiers. The Silberstuben drag is being upgraded to a four-seater chair.

FRANCE

Courchevel bottlenecks eliminated

Two slow old chair-lifts which used to generate big queues at times are being replaced by high-speed quads for the coming season. One is the Chanrossa chair, which serves the excellent black run of the same name, as well as runs down to 1650. The other is the Coqs chair which goes from the main 1850 home run up to the Col de la Loze lift to Méribel. The lift also serves good black runs down to Le Praz and reds to La Tania.

New piste in Les Deux-Alpes

Les Deux-Alpes is turning the top part of the beautiful off-piste Les Gours run into a piste of about 700m vertical, with a new four-person chair back up to the 2600m mid-station. The ancient two-seater gondola from Venosc is being replaced by a new six-seater. And there's talk about having a snowcat link from the top lift over to La Grave's skiing.

Speedier access to La Plagne from Montchavin

The two successive drags out of Montchavin have been replaced by four- and six-seater chairs respectively, giving much quicker access to the higher slopes. This makes charming old Montchavin an even more attractive alternative to stay in than La Plagne's higher purpose-built 'villages'.

Megève gains a high-speed quad

A new high-speed quad will make getting to the good skiing of the Côte 2000 area much quicker this season.

Serre-Chevalier less of a drag

A new chair will replace the Orée du Bois drag-lift going up from Serre Ratier (the mid-station of the cable-car up from Chantemerle). Apart from being long and steep, the old drag was also a bottleneck.

Safer run home in Valmorel

Another 47 snow guns have been installed on the main Beaudin pistes back to the village (bringing the total to 97). All they need to do now is groom the slope more to stop slushy moguls building up.

St-Martin-de-Belleville's new magic carpet

A rolling carpet is being installed at the bottom lift station, which means the slow chair up into the Trois Vallées skiing can be speeded up a bit without the much higher cost of a detachable lift.

Alpe-d'Huez queues eased

A new chair from the Les Bergers area of the village to the mid-station of the main gondola at 2100m should ease queues at the bottom for both that lift and (more importantly) the smaller, queue-prone Sarenne gondola which also goes up from Les Bergers.

ITALY
Old lift news from Cervinia

The Furggen cable-car in Cervinia will be closed for the foreseeable future, putting the only steep slopes in the resort out of reach. So good skiers will find Cervinia's skiing even more boring than normal.

SWITZERLAND
Major new lift in Verbier may just shift the queues

Verbier is notorious for some of the worst queues in the Alps (see page 359). This season will see the Funitel – a new 2,000-people-per-hour jumbo gondola – replace the tiny cable-car from Les Ruinettes to Attelas. This will undoubtedly relieve the monster queues here, and should help the queues at resort level by persuading more people to catch the short gondola to Ruinettes rather than wait for the long one that goes all the way to Attelas. But don't worry folks – those hour-long queues at Tortin will still be there.

End of an era in Saas-Fee

The second stage of the Alpin Express jumbo gondola will open for this season. It will now go right up to Felskinn to link up with the Metro. This will mean the end of last season's mid-mountain scrum for the drag-lifts at the end of the first stage. It will also mean more people up the mountain, though, and may increase queues at other lifts. And it's goodbye to the Fee Chatz – the piste basher which used to double as a lift to take you from Längfluh across the glacier to the Felskinn skiing. They've managed to design a lift to replace it that can cope with the movement of the glacier it will be built on.

Grindelwald's First to the top

Grindelwald's smaller ski area of First (which has the highest skiing in the Grindelwald-Wengen ski area) has a new quad chair-lift replacing the old drag-lift from First to the summit at Oberjoch.

Drag-show at St Moritz shut down

St Moritz is replacing four of its drag-lifts with chairs. The Plateau Nair chair replaces the Paradis and Randolins drags. The Salastrains chair replaces the drag of same name. And the Piz Grisch chair replaces the Fuorcla Grischa drag. Not before time, say St Moritz's pampered clients.

USA
Aspen Highlands opens up

Aspen Highlands – taken into the Aspen Ski Company fold last year – has the biggest vertical drop in Colorado. This season two new high-speed quads will halve the time taken to get to the top to around 15 minutes. And 45 acres of new expert terrain is being opened up.

CANADA
Whistler storms ahead

Whistler will have three major new lifts for the coming season. The new eight-seater Excalibur gondola will go up Blackcomb Mountain from Whistler village, cutting out the need to go via the base of Blackcomb to get up the hill. The gondola will be met by a new high-speed quad chair to whisk you even higher. On Whistler Mountain itself, another new high-speed quad called Harmony will open up a huge amount of skiing in Whistler's famous top bowls that was previously accessible only by hiking.

Resort shortlists

The ratings and lists of pros and cons at the start of each resort chapter will help you spot resorts to suit you. But for a real shortcut, here's a list of the best (and worst). Most lists embrace European and North American resorts, but some we've confined to the Alps, because America has too many qualifying resorts (eg beginners) or because America does things differently, making comparisons invalid (eg off-piste).

RELIABLE SNOW IN THE ALPS
Alpine resorts with good snow records or lots of snowmaking, and high or north-facing slopes
Argentière, France p153
Cervinia, Italy p266
Courchevel, France p170
Hintertux, Austria p68
Lech/Zürs, Austria p80
Obergurgl, Austria p91
Saas Fee, Switzerland p348
Val-d'Isère/Tignes, France p241/235
Val-Thorens, France p255
Zermatt, Switzerland p372

OFF-PISTE SKIING
Alpine resorts where, with guidance, you can have the time of your life
Alpe d'Huez, France p137
Andermatt, Switzerland p307
Argentière/Chamonix, France p153
Davos/Klosters, Switzerland p321
La Grave, France p188
Lech/Zürs, Austria p80
St Anton, Austria p103
Val d'Isère/Tignes, France p241/235
Verbier, Switzerland p359
Zermatt, Switzerland p372

BLACK RUNS
Steep skiing within the safety of the piste network
Alta/Snowbird, Utah p382/419
Andermatt, Switzerland, p307
Les Arcs, France p144
Argentière/Chamonix, France p153
Aspen, Colorado p383
Jackson Hole, Wyoming p399
Taos, New Mexico p425
Telluride, Colorado, p429
Val d'Isère/Tignes, France p241/235
Zermatt, Switzerland p372

HIGH-MILEAGE PISTE SKIING
Extensive intermediate skiing
Alpe d'Huez, France p137
Davos/Klosters, Switzerland p321
Flims/Laax, Switzerland p328
Milky Way: Sauze d'Oulx (Italy),
Montgenèvre (France) p288/207
La Plagne, France p217
Portes du Soleil, France/Switz. p224
Sella Ronda/Selva, Italy p292
Trois Vallées, France p240
Val-d'Isère/Tignes, France p241/235
Whistler, Canada p447

MOTORWAY CRUISING
Long, gentle, super-smooth pistes to bolster frail confidence
Les Arcs, France p144
Aspen, Colorado p383
Breckenridge, Colorado p390
Cervinia, Italy p266
Cortina, Italy p271
Courchevel, France p170
Megève, France p190
La Plagne, France p217
La Thuile, Italy p300
Vail, Colorado p433

RESORTS FOR BEGINNERS
Alpine resorts with gentle, snowsure nursery slopes and easy runs to progress to
Alpe d'Huez, France p137
Les Arcs, France p144
Cervinia, Italy p266
Courchevel, France p170
Isola 2000, France p189
Montgenèvre, France p207
Pamporovo, Bulgaria p457
La Plagne, France p217
Saas Fee, Switzerland p348
Soldeu, Andorra p455

SKIING CONVENIENCE
Piste-side accommodation
Les Arcs, France p144
Avoriaz, France p149
Courchevel, France p170
Flaine, France p182
Isola 2000, France p189
Les Menuires, France p195
Obertauern, Austria p96
La Plagne, France p217
Valmorel, France p250
Val Thorens, France p255

WEATHERPROOF RESORTS
Alpine resorts with snowsure skiing if the sun shines, and trees in case it doesn't
Courchevel, France p170
Courmayeur, Italy p276
Flims, Switzerland p328
Montchavin/Les Coches, France p217
Schladming, Austria p114
Selva, Italy p292
Serre-Chevalier, France p230
Sestriere, Italy p299
La Thuile, Italy p300
Zermatt, Switzerland p372

BACK-DOOR RESORTS
Cute little villages linked to big, bold ski areas
Les Brevières (Tignes), France p235
Champagny (La Plagne), France p217
Falera (Flims), Switzerland p328
Leogang (Saalbach), Austria p97
Montchavin (La Plagne), France p217
St-Martin (Trois Vallées), France p240
Samoëns (Flaine), France p182
Stuben (St Anton), Austria p103
Vaujany (Alpe d'Huez), France p137
Villaroger (Les Arcs), France p144

SNOWSURE BUT SIMPATICO
Alpine resorts with high-rise skiing, but low-rise buildings
Andermatt, Switzerland p307
Arabba, Italy p292
Argentière, France p153
Ischgl, Austria p70
Lech/Zürs, Austria p80
Méribel, France p199
Obergurgl, Austria p91
Obertauern, Austria p96
Saas Fee, Switzerland p348
Zermatt, Switzerland, p372

RESORTS FOR FAMILIES
Accommodation surrounded by snow, not by traffic
Les Arcs, France p144
Avoriaz, France p149
Flaine, France p182
Isola 2000, France p189
Montchavin, France p217
Mürren, Switzerland p344
Saas Fee, Switzerland p348
Serfaus, Austria p119
Valmorel, France p250
Wengen, Switzerland p367

BUDGET SKIING
Cheap packages, cheap lifts, cheap drinks and meals
Bardonecchia, Italy p262
Arinsal, Andorra p454
Borovets, Bulgaria p458
Gressoney, Italy p281
Kranjska Gora, Slovenia (Directory)
Livigno, Italy p282
Poiana Brasov, Romania p467
Soldeu, Andorra p455
Sierra Nevada, Spain p462
Sauze d'Oulx, Italy p288

MOUNTAIN RESTAURANTS
Alpe d'Huez, France p137
La Clusaz, France p164
Courmayeur, Italy p276
Kitzbühel, Austria p75
Megève, France p190
Saalbach-Hinterglemm, Austria p97
St Johann in Tirol, Austria p110
St Moritz, Switzerland p353
Selva, Italy p292
Zermatt, Switzerland p372

DRAMATIC SCENERY
Banff, Canada, p445
Chamonix, France p153
Cortina, Italy p271
Courmayeur, Italy p276
Jungfrau resorts (Grindelwald, Mürren, Wengen), Switzerland p333/344/367
Lake Tahoe, California p408
Saas Fee, Switzerland p348
St Moritz, Switzerland p353
Selva, Italy p292
Zermatt, Switzerland p372

VILLAGE CHARM
Alpbach, Austria p54
Champéry, Switzerland p311
Courmayeur, Italy p276
Crested Butte, Colorado p396
Lech, Austria p80
Mürren, Switzerland p344
Saas Fee, Switzerland p348
Telluride, Colorado p429
Wengen, Switzerland p367
Zermatt, Switzerland p372

LIVELY NIGHTLIFE
Chamonix, France p153
Ischgl, Austria p70
Kirchberg, Austria p75
Kitzbühel, Austria p75
Saalbach, Austria p97
St Anton, Austria p103
Sölden, Austria p120
Soldeu, Andorra p455
Val d'Isère, France p241
Verbier, Switzerland p359

🎿 And finally ...

Some resorts you might want to leave off your shortlist.

SHAME ABOUT THE FAME?
Resorts that remain popular despite poor snow records
Gstaad, Switzerland p337
Kitzbühel, Austria p75
Megève, France p190
Söll, Austria p124
Wengen, Switzerland p367

INSUFFERABLE QUEUES
Argentière, France p153
Avoriaz, France p149
Kitzbühel, Austria p75
Mayrhofen, Austria p85
Verbier, Switzerland p359

HIDEOUS VILLAGES
Flaine, France p182
Les Menuires, France p195
La Plagne, France p217
Sierra Nevada, Spain p462
Tignes, France p235

by **Chris Allan**

Pounds, schillings and francs

the cost of skiing

There's no doubt that skiing is an expensive business. Even more so after the pound's decline against the currencies of the major Alpine nations. Only Italy's lira has plunged as much as the pound in the last few years – which makes Italy amazing value compared with the other countries. But costs can vary greatly depending on the country and upon the type of accommodation you choose. When you add on the costs of lift pass, equipment hire, ski school, eating, drinking and dancing, the differences become even greater.

You can pay a fortune for a skiing holiday if you try. Take a week's half-board package in the luxurious 5-star Badrutt's Palace in glitzy St Moritz, for example. Yours for a mere £2,264 per person in high season. You may get one of their north-facing rooms for that but will be glad to know that if you use the hotel's indoor pool, you can do so for no extra charge. At the other extreme, a week's half-board package to a 2-star hotel in Romania's Poiana Brasov will set you back just £219 in low season. That too includes free use of the pool, albeit the local municipal one.

Between the two you can move through hundreds of packages and resorts on the way down from the sublimely expensive to the ridiculously cheap. You may end up somewhere which doesn't quite match the glamour of St Moritz – but knocks it for six when it comes to the question of affordability. We've checked the cost of packages to some of the most popular destinations for Brits in Europe and North America. We've also compared the cost of lift passes, ski school, boot and ski hire. And, thanks to the hundreds of people who sent us price information, we've been able to get an idea of the costs of eating and drinking on the mountain.

EUROPEAN COSTS

We looked at the brochures of some of the major tour operators and worked out typical costs of 3-star and 4-star hotels, chalets and studios (including flights, transfers and half-board in hotels and chalets) for two people sharing a room for a week in high season. We chose a cross-section of resorts, from the top to the bottom of the market. On the next page, we list them in price order, based on the cost of 3-star hotel packages.

Once upon a time, Switzerland led the world by a mile in the race to be crowned as the most expensive country for skiers – but not any more. That's not to say that Swiss resorts have got any cheaper, it's just that some of the top French resorts have overtaken them. Of those we looked at, Courchevel is the most expensive by far, leaving Val-d'Isère and Zermatt trailing in its wake. Quite some distance behind them is a clutch of other resorts – Verbier, St Anton, Valmorel and Obergurgl. Italy is cheap – even top resorts like Courmayeur and Cervinia work out at around 40% cheaper than Courchevel. Andorra and Eastern Europe bring up the rear and are half the price of the three front-runners.

The same pattern emerges if you look at the costs of staying in a 4-star hotel. But the price of chalet holidays is much more evenly spread, making the top resorts much more affordable. All except Sauze d'Oulx and Söll are in the £440 to £530 range. With the expensive resorts, chalets work out very much cheaper than a 3-star hotel – and that's before you start adding your wine and bar bill on to the hotel cost. A studio works out even cheaper – but remember there's no food included in these prices.

Of course you can get much plusher chalets than the ones we looked at – these are likely to cost a bit more. And with studios and apartments, the way to keep costs down is to pack people in – the brochure prices normally assume four in a one-room studio, and we had to add on smallprint supplements to get the true prices. Why do tour operators assume we are all into four-in-a-bed orgies?

EUROPEAN PACKAGES	3★ Hotel £	4★ Hotel £	Chalet £	Studio £
Courchevel	780	1,120	500	480
Val-d'Isère	680	850	530	410
Zermatt	670	880	510	470
Valmorel	600	–	440	380
St Anton	590	690	500	490
Verbier	580	760	450	–
Obergurgl	570	670	–	450
Serre-Chevalier	540	–	480	340
Wengen	500	700	530	430
Courmayeur	490	700	480	380
Cervinia	470	630	–	330
Söll	410	480	390	–
Sauze d'Oulx	410	420	400	–
Soldeu	360	420	–	300
Poiana Brasov	320	–	–	–
Borovets	310	350	–	-

Notes: All prices are for February for two people sharing a room and include flights and transfers. Hotel and chalet prices are half-board. Not all types of accommodation were available in all resorts.

SWISS PRICE HIKE Switzerland is introducing VAT at the rate of 6.5% at the beginning of 1995. This will push up the costs of meals and drinks, and (we understand) lift passes, ski lessons and equipment hire too.

LIFT PASSES

Next, the cost of a six-day lift pass. The Swiss resume their traditional role, with Verbier and Zermatt most expensive. Surprisingly, St Anton and tiny Obergurgl in Austria are more expensive than the huge French ski areas of the Trois Vallées and Val-d'Isère/Tignes. Italy is a bit cheaper but, again, Andorra and Eastern Europe offer the real bargains – around 20% of the price in Verbier.

LIFT PASS PRICES

Verbier	£149	Serre-Chevalier	£96
Zermatt	£146	Söll	£95
St Anton	£130	Cervinia	£94
Obergurgl	£127	Courmayeur	£92
Courchevel	£125	Sauze d'Oulx	£86
Val-d'Isère	£117	Soldeu	£32
Wengen	£116	Poiana Brasov	£30
Valmorel	£107	Borovets	£29

SKI AND BOOT RENTAL

The same pattern emerges for ski and boot hire. Charges are highest in Switzerland. The top French resorts follow. Hiring equipment in Italy is around half the price charged in Wengen and Zermatt, and costs pretty much the same as in Andorra, Bulgaria and Romania.

BOOT & SKI HIRE PRICES

Wengen	£78	Serre-Chevalier	£47
Zermatt	£74	Cervinia	£40
Verbier	£68	Söll	£38
Courchevel	£66	Courmayeur	£36
Val-d'Isère	£57	Poiana Brasov	£36
St Anton	£53	Borovets	£35
Obergurgl	£50	Sauze d'Oulx	£32
Valmorel	£49	Soldeu	£30

SKI SCHOOL

Ski school fees are more difficult to analyse simply because the number of hours and days of tuition varies from resort to resort. We've included only those which operate for six full days. Yet again the top French and Swiss resorts lead the pack. A week's ski school in Val-d'Isère will cost nearly 60 per cent more than in St Anton.

SKI SCHOOL FEES

Val-d'Isère	£125	Serre-Chevalier	£94
Wengen	£118	Obergurgl	£92
Courchevel	£116	St Anton	£79
Zermatt	£108		

THE TOTAL BILL

If you add on the price of all the extras to the costs of staying in a resort and buying a lift pass, the differences are quite staggering.

For example, staying in a 3-star hotel, buying a lift pass, hiring equipment and going to ski school will cost you around £1,075 in Courchevel, £850 in St Anton. If you make the less straightforward comparison with resorts with shorter ski school hours – Sauze, for example – the differences are even more pronounced.

The costs don't stop there unless, of course, you lunch on tap water and digestive biscuits brought from home. How much more you'll spend will depend largely on how much you eat and drink. But again, where you go will make an enormous difference. From the information that so many of you sent us, the pattern is clear.

Top Swiss and French resorts are again by far the most expensive, with Courchevel and Méribel pretty much on a par with places like Wengen and Zermatt. The most expensive Austrian resorts (such as Lech and Obergurgl) aren't far behind, and are about as costly as Val-d'Isère and Verbier. Average price Italian resorts such as Selva and Bormio are likely to cost around half as much for lunch on the mountain as the top Swiss and French places – but Cervinia is much more expensive than you'd expect in Italy, and Sauze d'Oulx is a real bargain. Again Andorra is cheap, but Eastern Europe is rock-bottom – the cost of drinks and snack meals is literally negligible.

NORTH AMERICAN COSTS

At first glance, the brochure prices for North American resorts will look cheaper than those we've listed. That's because we've worked out what it would cost for two people sharing a room – brochure prices are normally based on four. When you compare prices with Europe, bear in mind that hotel costs exclude dinner, although you can eat out cheaply (or expensively if you like).

Hotel packages to Vail, Whistler and Breckenridge are on a par with half-board in the top French and Swiss resorts. Chalet holidays are much more expensive than European equivalents (but cheaper than US hotel holidays). Banff and Mammoth are relatively cheap.

NORTH AMERICAN PACKAGES		3★ Hotel £	4★ Hotel £	Chalet £	Studio £
Vail	1wk	790	880	730	720
	2wks	1,120	1,330	920	1,040
Whistler	1wk	710	730	–	710
	2wks	980	1,020	–	1,000
Breckenridge	1wk	680	800	720	750
	2wks	918	1,170	900	1,070
Banff/L. Louise	1wk	610	660	–	640
	2wks	760	800	–	830
Mammoth	1wk	520	560	–	–
	2wks	700	790	–	–

When it comes to lift passes, we're talking megabucks. Vail is more expensive than anywhere in Europe – the others aren't far behind and on a par with Europe's best resorts.

The costs of hiring equipment is also on a par with Europe's grandest. And ski school fees make Europe's priciest resorts pale into insignificance.

	Lift pass £	School fees £	Equipment hire £
Vail	156	267	72
Mammoth	140	152	64
Breckenridge	128	132	57
Banff/L.Louise	125	110	34
Whistler	124	163	63

Given the air fare costs and the problems of jet lag, it makes sense to go to North America for two weeks rather than one. But the price of a lift pass, equipment hire and ski school certainly bump up the costs. Of the resorts we looked at, Vail is particularly expensive – a lift pass and 3-star hotel, without dinner, will set you back around £1,430 for a fortnight. Mammoth works out at around £500 cheaper. And in Canada, two weeks in Banff costs around £200 less than in Whistler.

As far as the price of food and drink are concerned, North America compares quite favourably with Europe.

by **the editors**

Safety on the slopes

risks and responsibilities

Contrary to popular opinion, skiing is a relatively safe sport. Its tragedies tend to hit the headlines, giving people the wrong impression. However, it remains true that the mountain environment is inherently dangerous. If you stray off the marked pistes you ski entirely at your own risk; but if you stick to the pistes you should be safe from avalanches, cliffs, crevasses and the like. A few of the top resorts, however, have blurred the issue by taking the piste status away from their best black runs, putting their visitors at risk and plunging them into uncertainty about where they should and should not ski.

Last season's tragic accident, in which five British doctors and their guide were killed by an avalanche while skiing off-piste between Tignes and Champagny, generated huge amounts of publicity in the UK. The previous season, the main ski accident stories were of deaths caused by collisions and falls on the piste at a time of thin and icy snow cover.

But skiing is one of the safest sports around. At the National Ski Conference in October 1993, Dr Michael Turner, Chief Medical Advisor to the British ski teams, presented some fascinating statistics. Your chances of being killed during a day's skiing are less than one in eight million. In this respect, climbing is more than 60 times as risky, motorsport 12 times, watersport (such as windsurfing and canoeing) five times, and even riding getting on for three times as risky. And looking at injuries, you're even safer. Dr Turner says that a lot of minor skiing injuries go unreported. But even if you increase the skiing figure by four to allow for this, skiing still ends up around twice as safe as keep-fit, tennis and squash, five times as safe as cricket and ten times as safe as rugby.

So you can go skiing safely in the knowledge that you aren't putting yourself unduly at risk. But you are of course at risk to some degree (just as you are when crossing the road) and you should respect the mountains and take care not to behave stupidly and put yourself in real danger. On or off the piste you should obey the 'Skier's Highway Code' drawn up by the International Ski Federation – we reproduce these rules of the road in shortened form over the page. The rules cover rights of way and courtesy, and are designed to avoid collisions and promote enjoyable, safe skiing. The rules are binding in law and apply to both skiers and snowboarders.

On the piste, you should be safe from most of the natural dangers of the mountains.
Pistes are:
• marked with sticks or posts; how well they are marked (which matters during a white-out) varies a lot between resorts, but in principle there is a clear definition of where it is safe to ski
• graded for difficulty; in Europe, they are graded blue (easy), red (more difficult) and black (most difficult); in France there's also a green (very easy) grade; but grading can be very inconsistent both within and between resorts – some Val-d'Isère greens would be red in some Austrian and Italian resorts, for example
• checked against avalanche danger; if there is a danger, pistes are kept closed until the avalanche has been artificially triggered, or the snow has stabilised naturally
• patrolled so that injured skiers will be found (especially at the end

of the day when the runs are checked after they have been closed); patrolling should also mean that obstacles such as rocks and bare earth are marked.

Most greens and blues, many reds but few blacks are groomed regularly to keep the surface smooth and mogul-free.

The main danger on the piste will be from your own or other people's incompetence, or reckless behaviour resulting in collisions.

Off the piste, however, it's a completely different matter. You go off-piste completely at your own risk and should never do so without a competent guide. A perfectly innocent-looking slope may be lethal – there may be a high risk of triggering an avalanche (over 50% of all skiing deaths are caused by avalanches). There may be hidden cliffs or precipices (13% of all deaths are caused by them or crevasses). A guide should be able to steer you clear of the dangers, though even they can come unstuck. If you are injured in a lonely spot, you might never be found unless your companion can get help and tell them where you are. If you go off-piste you should do so in the knowledge that it is a risky thing to do and that you are accepting those risks yourself.

OFF-PISTE OR ON?

So that's clear then. On piste, the patrollers look after you and you're safe. Off-piste, your life's at risk and you accept the dangers.

Er, yes, almost. Except that some of the top resorts have changed the rules. Resorts such as Zermatt, St Anton, Lech and Verbier have removed 'piste' status from many of their best and toughest runs. They call them by a variety of names. The Zermatt piste map calls them 'Downhill Routes', says they are 'very steep' but tells you nothing else about their status.

St Anton and Lech divide their tough runs into two:
• 'Ski Routes' are marked but at less frequent intervals than pistes, protected from avalanches only in the immediate vicinity of the markers (so be careful where you stop!), groomed only occasionally in parts and not patrolled (so don't get injured on the last run of the day!). And 'It is recommended only to ski these routes having good Alpine experience or with a ski instructor.'
• 'High-Touring Routes' is the classification of St Anton's famous top bowls, together with many runs lower down near the resort. These are said to 'require expert guidance owing to the natural danger inherent to the Alpine area ... They are not marked, not protected from any dangers and not patrolled.'

In Verbier, many of the best difficult runs, including the main run to Tortin and the Col des Mines run back to Verbier, are classed as 'Ski-tours'. Now the former black run to Tortin from the Mont Fort area has been reclassified as a 'Ski-tour' too. The piste map says this means these runs are marked but not groomed, not patrolled and 'can be dangerous at any time'.

There are several interconnected problems here. First, there is an appalling lack of consistency and clarity in the information being given to skiers about these runs. If resorts want to create new categories of run, the least they can do is ensure that there is a clear, internationally accepted definition and that this is conveyed to the skiers who visit their resorts. Without this clear information, you don't know whether you are safe when you go along with the herd and ski these runs.

Secondly, attaching vaguely off-putting descriptions to runs that people have been cheerfully skiing as pistes for years encourages people to ignore warnings like this whenever they encounter them, and means they may be tempted to try much more dangerous terrain without guidance too.

THE SKIER'S HIGHWAY CODE

This is a shortened and simplified version of the ten Rules of Conduct that have been established by the International Ski Federation. The rules are binding in law and apply to both skiers and snowboarders.

1 Do not endanger or prejudice others.

2 Ski in control. Adapt your skiing and speed to your ability and the prevailing conditions of the terrain, snow and weather, as well as to the density of skiers on the slope.

3 The skier in front has priority. Leave enough space.

4 You may overtake to the left or right of the skier in front of you, but you must leave enough space to avoid a collision should the other skier make a voluntary or involuntary movement.

5 Look up and down the mountain before setting off to make sure the path is clear.

6 Only stop at the edge of the piste (and wherever possible, not in a narrow part) where you are clearly visible.

7 When climbing up or down, keep to the edge of the piste.

8 Obey all signs and markings – they are there for your safety.

9 If you come across an accident, provide what help you can and alert the rescue service.

10 Everybody involved in an accident, including witnesses, must exchange names and addresses.

Thirdly, categorising all the tough skiing in a top resort as off-piste is simply unrealistic. These runs form the bulk of the resorts' best skiing for good skiers, and thousands of people ski them every day without guidance. Either people will ignore the advice and ski the runs, or they will go elsewhere. Which do the resorts want? Do they really expect the young people who flock to Verbier or (even more so) St Anton to hire guides? The position the resorts have taken is indefensible.

Finally, skiing these runs may invalidate skiers' insurance cover for rescue and medical expenses. Some insurance policies exclude cover while you are off-piste – so not only might you be badly hurt on one of these runs, but also it will cost you a fortune in rescue costs and medical expenses.

Treating these tough runs like this may save the resort money by cutting their patrolling and avalanche protection costs, but at the same time they are putting their guests' lives at risk. In our report on St Anton, on page 104, we reproduce a longer quote from a long-standing St Anton regular who concludes: "There are some beautiful runs, but they are south-facing and prone to avalanches. It is outrageous that there is now no indication of whether I should ski them or not." We agree, and fear for many more skiers' safety if this and other leading resorts continue the disgraceful practice of abdicating responsibility for what were formerly straightforward, protected and patrolled black runs.

This abdication of responsibility contrasts strongly with the American attitude to these things. American resorts have 'ski area boundaries', usually marked by a rope. Within the boundary there are marked trails just like our pistes. But many resorts also have big 'off-piste' or 'bowl' areas within the boundary. These are often much steeper and hairier than any European piste, with avalanche risks that are just as severe. But they are strictly patrolled, protected from avalanche danger and closed when they are considered dangerous. So long as you stay within the ski area boundary, the resort accepts responsibility and most say there is absolutely no need for a guide. You know exactly where you stand.

As in so many other areas of their operation, we are left with the impression that American resorts have considered how best to give their visitors a satisfying holiday that they'll want to repeat, whereas the Alpine resorts we've identified have not.

One day all this is going to lead to a serious accident on one of the runs from the Valluga, or down to Tortin. The resort authorities will be able to point to the small print on their piste maps, and deny responsibility. They won't be able to escape the shame.

by **Katrina Moran** *and* **Jonathan Swinfen**

authors of The Ultimate Guide to Snowboarding, due for publication autumn 1995.

Let's go boarding now

come and be a goofy with me*

It's not by chance that the French call snowboarding 'Le Surf' – the sport has its roots in the California of Beach Boy days. Bored with the monotony of long winter months, American surfers picked up their boards and headed for them there hills. After various gravity-defying experiments, using surf boards on the snow, these beach refugees eventually hit on a successful formula. They began to have 'fun, fun, fun' and a whole new sport was born. Over the past 20 years or so, the growth of snowboarding has been phenomenal. And its popularity has by no means peaked – it is estimated that by the year 2000, one in three people riding the lifts will be a snowboarder.

Once you've been bitten by the boarding-bug, the chances are that you'll hang up your skis forever. Here's a guide to where you should be thinking of going, either for a first go, or for a more serious snowboarding holiday.

IDEAL FOR 'L' PLATES
Top resorts for beginners:
Austria: Lech, Seefeld; France: Alpe-d'Huez, La Plagne, Isola 2000, Val-d'Isère/Tignes; Italy: Cortina d'Ampezzo, Madonna di Campiglio; Switzerland: Adelboden, Davos, Leysin, Saas Fee; USA: Copper Mountain, Vail, Winter Park.

For a learner, good tuition is essential. Teaching standards vary enormously, so choose a resort which has a specialist school or one that can provide specialist instructors.

The USA, where snowboarding is still more popular than anywhere else, offers excellent tuition. Austria, France and Switzerland lead Europe in snowboard instruction and specialist schools. Surprisingly, in the cheaper destinations – Andorra, Bulgaria and Romania – good tuition is difficult to find.

Although Italy doesn't rank among Europe's snowboarding elite, the school at Madonna di Campiglio offers some of the best tuition you'll find this side of the Atlantic. And Cortina d'Ampezzo has the perfect slopes for beginners – wide open and uncrowded. The resort also has a good school.

If you can't bear the company of non-boarding addicts, you could try the Snowboardhotel Bolgenschanze in Davos – aimed solely at snowboarding clients.

HOT HALFWAY HAUNTS
Top resorts for intermediates:
Austria: Hintertux, Ischgl, Sölden, Zell am See; France: Avoriaz, Courchevel, Les Arcs, Méribel, Val-d'Isère; Italy: Courmayeur, Sauze d'Oulx; Switzerland: Arosa, Crans-Montana, Gstaad, Arosa, Villars; North America: Grand Targhee, Squaw Valley, Steamboat, Whistler.

We've chosen these resorts as top destinations for intermediates for a number of reasons. They have vast areas of wide, often tree-lined runs easily accessible to an intermediate snowboarder. There's also stacks of off-piste skiing. No need to be defeatist about this – even as an intermediate, you'll find powder much easier on a board than on skis. If you do go off-piste, always hire a guide. Finally, these resorts have good lift systems with few drag-lifts to the higher areas.

* 'Goofy' means you ride a snowboard with your right foot forward. 'Regular' riders lead with their left foot.

Austria has a very positive attitude towards snowboarding and Ischgl is no exception. You'll have the chance to see many professional boarders in action. If they inspire you, Ischgl has excellent freeriding and advanced courses.

Avoriaz is acknowledged as the capital of European snowboarding. It has some excellent runs and is exceptionally pro-snowboarding. Avoriaz has adopted a very American attitude: while giving boarders their own areas such as fun parks (where you can jump off picnic tables etc should the fancy take you), they've also managed to exercise good control of the sport and create a good relationship with skiers. Chalet Snowboard operate chalet holidays here specially for snowboarders.

The good lift system at Les Arcs makes the area very accessible. You'll find the best intermediate cruising pistes at Les Arcs 2000, but head for Les Arcs 1800 for good off-piste boarding. If you're comfortable in powder, you can't do better than try Le Fornet in Val-d'Isère, where the wide open slopes let you carve large turns to your heart's content.

Boarders were once banned at Squaw Valley – but the resort is now organised so that skiers and boarders co-exist in perfect harmony. There are some separate runs and good fun parks. Squaw, with challenging but accessible runs, is probably one of the best places for skiers who want to be snowboarders for a few days.

UTOPIA FOR SERIOUS BOARDERS
Top resorts for experts:
Austria: Axamer Lizum, St Anton; France: Argentière, Chamonix, Les Deux-Alpes, Tignes, Val-d'Isère, Val-Thorens; North America: Breckenridge, Jackson Hole, Mt. Batchelor, Stratton, Vail, Whistler

If you're an experienced boarder, then these resorts are for you. They provide the thrill of riding some of the most challenging off-piste runs in the world. There's also plenty of scope for trying out freestyle – halfpipes and snowboard parks are par for the course.

St Anton has steep, mainly off-piste runs but there are many good qualified guides and instructors who will keep you safe.

For excellent off-piste boarding and a good halfpipe, Les Deux-Alpes is a good choice. It also gives you the chance to explore the unpisted paradise of La Grave.

Chamonix has some excellent snowboard guides for off-piste. There are plenty of powder possibilities and extreme couloirs, especially above Argentière. A fun park is planned for Les Bossons. But Chamonix is the resort for the fully initiated boarder – a definite no-go area for learners. If you haven't mastered the sport, its jargon and dress etiquette, you could feel like a Cliff Richard fan at a Guns 'n Roses concert.

Jackson Hole has done a great deal for snowboarders and has attracted a huge following. If halfpipes are your scene, then Stratton in Colorado has one of the biggest. Many freestyle riders come here for the whole season purely to ride the pipe. Like Whistler, Stratton holds technique clinics. But Whistler is the place to go for summer camps, held on the Blackcomb glacier.

SNOWBOARD-FRIENDLY RESORTS
Top Ten all-round resorts: Austria: Ischgl; France: Les Arcs, Avoriaz, Tignes, Val-d'Isère; Italy: Madonna di Campiglio; Switzerland: Saas Fee; North America: Squaw Valley, Vail, Whistler.

These resorts make our Top Ten because they've made a concerted effort to attract and welcome snowboarders. They provide facilities such as specialist schools, parks, halfpipes and varied terrain.

by **Alan Coulson**

Adventure skiing

life beyond the lift lines

More and more British skiers are now discovering that there's more to skiing than piste-bashing. For many, the modern new lifts and perfectly groomed pistes which make the ski slopes accessible to millions of skiers each year have taken the thrill out of it. They go to the mountains to get away from the hordes, not to join them. They want to ski virgin unbashed snow, not artificially created corduroy. They want challenging terrain that will test them to their limits. Well, everything's possible, if you know where to look.

You can try out off-piste and ski touring (where you head off to peaks inaccessible from the lift system by attaching 'skins' to your skis and plodding up) at many of the Alps' top resorts. Val-d'Isère, Verbier, Zermatt, Chamonix and St Anton, for example, are all well organised to provide schooling and guidance in touring and the other off-piste arts.

Val-d'Isère would be a good place to get started and has a well established reputation for adventurous skiing as well as an amazing piste network. It has a handful of smaller independent schools (Top Ski, Mountain Masters, Evolution 2, Snow Fun and Alpine Experience) specialising in off-piste and powder skiing; you can join a group for a day or half-day, or sign up for longer expeditions – tours of the Tarentaise or a 'wilderness experience' which includes one night in a mountain hut. Many keen skiers go to Val-d'Isère and ski off-piste every day with one of the specialist schools.

Even at a resort that many skiers think of in terms of perfect grooming, such as Méribel, there's the opportunity to progress from the pistes via marked itineraires to genuine off-piste and ski touring; and still be back at the chalet for tea. The ESF here organises daily off-piste groups – as do the main ski schools in many resorts.

But Chamonix can legitimately claim to be the off-piste capital of the world. It's a real mountain town, much more than 'just' a ski resort, and it does attract many of the best skiers and most accomplished guides in the business. There's a strong British flavour too; some of the guides who operate in Scotland also run courses and tours from Chamonix, as do several specialist tour operators. Jewel in the crown for those wanting to go off-piste without climbing is the amazing Grands Montets at Argentière, where the off-piste opportunities are endless – and frequently extreme. Much less taxing is Europe's most famous off-piste run, the Vallée Blanche – 24km of stunning scenery across glaciers manageable even by an average intermediate (see page 155). Although it may well be the world's busiest off-piste route, when you're out there in amongst all that ice and thin air it still feels like a long way from home. The Haute Route, the classic high-level route from Chamonix to Zermatt, is a week's hard labour needing considerable stamina, good touring equipment and luck with the weather. It's one to aspire to, but not for the novice.

For many keen off-piste skiers, La Grave rivals Chamonix. It is certainly something very special – 2000 vertical metres of rough, tough mountainside that never sees a piste machine and all just a short walk away over the top from adjacent Les Deux-Alpes. It's the only resort with virtually no pistes (there are a couple of tame ones on the glacier right at the top).

OFF-PISTE SPECIALISTS

If you are keen on getting started by going on a proper organised course, rather than just trying off-piste or touring for the odd day as part of a largely-piste based holiday, there are a few tour operators who specialise in this area.

Fresh Tracks is probably the main specialist off-piste operator. They have a range of courses in Chamonix, La Grave, Verbier, Alpe d'Huez and Flaine, aimed at four different standards of skier ranging from off-piste novice through to powder expert. Powder Byrne also has Introduction to Powder courses in Klosters and Grindelwald, where you use the new Fat Boy skis – shorter and wider than normal skis, to make powder skiing a doddle. And they have Adventure courses for more accomplished off-piste skiers in Zermatt and Gressoney in Italy as well as their other two resorts. The Ski Club of Great Britain also runs a number of courses for off-piste skiers of varying standards.

This kind of off-piste skiing is usually aimed at finding and skiing powder snow – it's still resort-based and done on regular Alpine equipment but most of the action takes place away from the crowds. The concept of a ski safari is a newer idea that goes one step beyond the confines of a resort's off-piste terrain – most of the skiing takes place between resorts or at least between lodgings and transportation points. But most of the uphill work is still done using lifts. 'Soft' safaris can include luggage transportation between valley-based lodgings – Fresh Tracks offer a route from Tignes to Chamonix via Champagny, Les Arcs, Sainte-Foy and Courmayeur, with a finishing flourish down the Vallée Blanche. This safari involves some climbing on skins (using binding adaptors) but not much.

At the other end of the scale, you can try traditional touring –

carrying a hefty pack and doing a significant amount of climbing using proper touring skis. Skins – made of artificial fibres – attach to the base of your skis and the heel binding releases to allow the skis and skier to glide effortlessly uphill – or at least with less effort than it would be without them. On downhill stretches the skins are removed, the heel clicked back into place, and away you go.

Fresh Tracks organise full-scale tours, staying overnight in mountain huts, in both the Alps and Morocco's Atlas mountains. The Ski Club of Great Britain also has touring holidays. And even Inghams now feature an introductory ski touring package at Kühtai in the Austrian Tyrol – perhaps a sign of things to come.

SAFETY FIRST

One thing that is very different about skiing in areas other than on prepared and patrolled pistes is the degree of responsibility you assume for your own and other's safety. Skiing off-piste should never be treated casually: accidents happen even close to marked runs and within area boundaries. Avalanches are the biggest danger, and a constant threat on slopes of black-run gradient. Snow stability is influenced by many factors and only an experienced mountain guide who has done his homework can accurately judge how dangerous a particular slope is likely to be. There is only one safe rule: ski with a guide. Although mere ski instructors are allowed to take groups off-piste only fully qualified UIAGM (International Association of Mountain Guides) guides are authorised to guide groups on glaciers. They are trained to know where it's safe to ski and where there's crevasse danger – and will carry all the necessary rescue gear in case one of their party should be unlucky enough to tumble into one.

Whenever you venture off-piste your guide should give everyone in your party an avalanche transceiver and training on how to use it. This enables you to search for any of your group caught by an avalanche – it transmits and receives radio signals when the victim is within range; the resulting beeps become louder as you get nearer.

ADVENTURE IN THE USA

Never to be outdone when it comes to adventure time, the Wild West of the USA could be just the place for the budding off-pister with a penchant for the steeps. Many resorts there have reasonably accessible deep-snow skiing – often bowls and chutes beyond the groomed areas but within the area boundary and cleared of avalanche danger (so not 'off-piste' in the Alpine sense). These areas are usually challenging but rarely for crazies only.

Take the 'Extreme Experience' at Copper Mountain, for example. 350 acres of double-black diamond terrain – ungroomed bowls and glades where a guide accompanies you and there's a lift back up. Once a taste for this kind of stuff really develops it's time to head for Crested Butte – a lovely little western town in the middle of Colorado with good piste skiing and some tremendous lift-served off-piste that they call The Extreme Limits. The area's two highest lifts give access to masses of steep, exhilarating terrain – not for nothing is the US Extreme Skiing Championship held here. There are rocks to jump off, gullies to jump into and trees to avoid – and some routes of a less extreme nature.

The US version of ski touring, back-country skiing, tends to be big with the locals but of little interest to most visitors – perhaps because of all those express lifts and lack of queues in the resorts. The Utah Interconnect is a one-day tour from Park City to Snowbird that has proved popular – it takes in Brighton, Solitude and Alta and several stretches of genuine back-country. But it's nothing like the tours you can do in the Alps.

Off-piste skiing attracts people for many reasons – the thrills, the unpredictability, the solitude, the need to be different and, especially, the powder. If you're lucky the powder sometimes finds you, more often you have to look pretty hard to find it. Grand Targhee, Wyoming is one of those places, like Alta in Utah, with a big reputation for big dumps of the finest white stuff. So what they've done at Targhee is to reserve 'Second Mountain' for snowcat skiing. You climb in a snowcat and ride up the mountain. It drops you off and you ski down in a group with a guide – the snowcat meets you at the bottom and ferries you up again. It's a more affordable version of heli-skiing. Snowcat skiing is available at many US resorts – Irwin Lodge near Crested Butte is another specialist centre. And see page 385 of the Aspen chapter.

TAKE TO THE AIR

If it's powder that you're hungry for, and powder that hasn't previously been touched, rent yourself a helicopter.

You can do it in the Alps (not in France – though from places like Val-d'Isère and Chamonix you can go over the border to be dropped in Italy). The biggest operation is in Zermatt, with cheaper alternatives in Italy including the Courmayeur and La Thuile areas. But the great thing here is you can buy just one ride. For about £140, for example, you can fly to near the top of Zermatt's Monte Rosa at over 4000m and ski down with a guide through the glaciers to Furi – a spectacular morning's skiing. Powder Byrne organises courses including heli-skiing in Grindelwald and Zermatt.

There's heli-skiing too in the US and New Zealand, and even Gudauri in the Caucasus has had a go – sadly some accidents and political instability have removed it from the scene for the time being. But the place where it all started, and still the biggest and the best, is the Canadian Rockies – there's a huge amount of wilderness out there just made for heli-skiing. Two outfits with a long history in the business continue to dominate the scene – CMH and Mike Wiegele – and both have links to British tour operators. A typical week's heli-skiing package involves a stay at a smart lodge in the Rockies – the kind with restaurant, bar, hot-tubs and massages – about 100,000 vertical feet of powder skiing down the Cariboos or Monashees, and the removal of around £3,000 from your bank account. These lodge-based packages are also available to novice heli-skiers of at least good intermediate skiing standard. You use the special 'Fat Boy' skis which make powder skiing easy.

Skiing in deep powder is exhilarating but physically demanding. If you're not yet ready to commit to a full week of this it is possible to book locally in places such as Banff and Whistler for a day or even a half-day. It costs around £150 for a 3-run package; check out your insurance cover first.

Either way, the idea is that the helicopter drops about 10 of you, including guide(s), on a high snowy ridge in the middle of nowhere from where you ski maybe 1000 vertical metres through perfect powder; get picked up again by the helicopter; and so on until either body or finances are exhausted. There's no doubt that this is the best way to find consistently good powder snow – but it's not guaranteed, and the weather can curtail flying operations, especially December to February – just when the powder is likely to be at it's best.

So: everybody knows it's expensive, but is it good value? Well, you'll never know until you've tried it, but the fact that bookings start to fill up a year in advance and almost 70 per cent of heli-skiers are repeat customers does say something about its appeal.

by **Chris Allan**

Driving to the Alps

ski where you want to ski

Ask any skier to list three things that he or she likes best about their sport and most will include the sense of freedom that they get from it. Ask any motorist what they like most about having a car and the majority will reply that it's the freedom it gives them. All of which leaves us wondering why so many skiers choose to put shackles on their freedom by flying to the Alps rather than driving.

It can't be the attraction of long hours spent watching the clock tick round at the airport. It surely can't be the allure of the coach transfer up to the resort. And carting skis, boots and cases around can't appeal to many. In the summer season, it's almost impossible to travel a kilometre along a French autoroute or a German autobahn without seeing another GB plate – so why are they so Brit-free during the ski season?

Whatever the reasons, if you've never tried driving to the Alps, you don't know what you're missing. For starters, if you're taking your family or going self-catering, just think of all the extra things your can cram in that you'd otherwise have had to leave behind.

And just consider the flexibility that a car gives you. If the snow's bad in your resort, or if the lift queues are horrendous, you can try somewhere else. And a car will give you a perfect means of daily escape if it turns out that you don't like the resort you've booked into or find the skiing rather limited.

One of the most important plus-points as far as we're concerned is that we can add two extra days' skiing to a holiday while taking only one extra day off work. We catch an early ferry or hover on a Friday morning and return nine days later on the Sunday evening. That means we get a full day's skiing both Saturdays.

Of course that involves overnight 'stop-offs' but then variety is the much-needed spice of holiday life. On the trip down, you can ski for one or two days in a resort and then move on to your final destination. It's easy to combine resorts you might think of as being very far apart. You could stop off in Chamonix for a couple of nights before driving on to Courmayeur, Cervinia or La Thuile in Italy. You could stop off in Valmorel before going on to the Trois Vallées or Val d'Isère. And if you're going to Zermatt or Saas Fee, you could stop off and ski Wengen or Mürren before putting the car on the train for the half-hour journey through the Lötschberg tunnel, which takes you to the Valais. The possibilities are endless – all it takes is a couple of hours' drive.

After a full day's skiing on the final Saturday, if you drive for a few hours in the direction of home, you won't find Sunday's journey back to the port too demanding. In France, you'll be spoiled for choice as far as comfortable and reasonably priced hotels are concerned – particularly if you stay overnight in a city such as Mâcon or Strasbourg. You'll be able to enjoy a good, non-ski resort meal at good non-ski resort prices. And, what better way can there possibly be to round off the holiday than to enjoy a superb French Sunday lunch?

Over recent years, the substantial improvements made to the motorway networks in northern France and the Alps have certainly made life much easier for British drivers heading for the mountains. From Calais for example, you can cover the 900km (560 miles) to

Drive an Audi quattro and yo

Last year the snow in Davos, Switzerland, was so heavy that police stopped any car not fitted with snow chai
drive system. For more information call 0800 5856

on't get stopped by the police.

ever, an exception was made for Audi quattros, with their advanced four-wheel
have nothing to lose but your chains.

ISING YEAR 1: UNLIMITED MILEAGE MANUFACTURER WARRANTY AND YEARS 2 AND 3: DEALER WARRANTY UP TO 60,000
N-CALL RESCUE SERVICE. PRICES EXCLUDE DELIVERY AND NUMBER PLATES CHARGE OF £410. REF: SKI

Audi. Vorsprung durch Technik.

Chamonix in just nine hours plus stops – all but the final few miles is on motorways. The French Alps are the number one destination for most motoring skiers from the UK; some other areas of the Alps are less straightforward to get to, but the majority of resorts are within a day's driving range provided you take an early Channel crossing.

Taking a car means you can tailor your holiday to your needs. You can simply use it for the journey and then forget about it. You can enjoy day trips to other resorts or spend the week touring. It also enables you to escape far from the madding crowd.

DAY TRIPPER

If you fancy skiing in several resorts, you can use one as a base and make day trips to nearby places when the fancy takes you. If you do this you can still take advantage of the favourable accommodation prices offered by tour operators – and get a discount for driving. The discount varies from operator to operator and also depends on whether you go in high or low season – but you can expect to get from around £70 to £120.

The key to turning this kind of holiday into a success is to go for a resort which offers easy road access to others. A good choice is the Tyrol. The resorts to the east of Innsbruck offer many options to would-be day-trippers. Söll is a convenient base for exploring the other resorts in the Ski Welt area, as well as such resorts as Alpbach and Kitzbühel.

Further east, in Salzburg province, you can use Zell am See as a base for excursions to Badgastein and Saalbach, while Flachau is a convenient base for visiting the resorts covered by the Top Tauern lift pass, such as Schladming and Obertauern. Although western Austria is not ideal for this sort of holiday, you could use St Anton as a base and make day-trips to Lech, Zürs, Ischgl and Serfaus.

In the southern French Alps, Serre-Chevalier and Montgenèvre are ideal bases for day-tripping. If the extensive skiing offered in Serre-Chevalier isn't enough for you, Montgenèvre is within easy reach by car. It's at one end of the Milky Way ski area which includes Sauze d'Oulx and Sestriere in Italy – you can drive on to them or reach them on skis. On the French side of the border, a few miles south, there's Puy-St-Vincent. The major resorts of Alpe d'Huez and Les Deux Alpes are also within range. An added bonus is that these resorts share lift pass arrangements.

The Chamonix valley is an ideal destination for day-trippers. It offers a terrific amount of skiing covered by the Mont-Blanc pass – Chamonix, Megève, Les Contamines, Courmayeur plus a few more. Flaine and its satellites are also fairly accessible – so is Verbier if the Col des Montets and Col de la Forclaz are open.

You could consider resorts on the Swiss side of the Portes du Soleil, such as Morgins and Champéry, as a base for trips to such resorts as Verbier, Crans-Montana and those in the Chamonix Valley as well as skiing the Portes du Soleil circuit.

Because the resorts are so remote, Italy provides more of a headache for skiing day-trippers. Courmayeur is a notable exception – with quick access to La Thuile and, through the Mont-Blanc tunnel, to the Chamonix Valley and a slow trip to Cervinia. And in some parts of the Dolomites it's useful to have a car – to get from Cortina to the Sella Ronda circuit, for example.

Although eastern Switzerland provides more of a challenge to day-trippers, you might find that it's well worth the effort. Lenzerheide is about the best choice of base-camp. Flims, Arosa, Davos and St Moritz are all within striking distance. From St Moritz you could even go over to Livigno in Italy.

Audi

MAGICAL MYSTERY TOUR

If you've got really itchy skis and want to ski as much of the Alps as possible, then consider making a Grand Tour by car, moving every day or two to a different resort and enjoying the complete freedom of going where you want, when you want. Except in high season, there's no need to book any accommodation before you go. So you can leave your decision about which part of the Alps you want to visit to the last moment and go wherever the snow is best.

You may have the impression that if you take a touring holiday you'll be spending more time on the road than on the piste. This isn't the case – provided you plan your route carefully. And there's no need to eat into the skiing day. An hour's drive after the lifts have shut is all it takes to travel quite a distance.

Many of the areas that are great for day-trippers are also worth considering if you're going on tour. These include Western Austria, the Tyrol and the Chamonix valley. Take western Austria, for example; you can start with Lech, Zürs and St Anton, move on to Serfaus and Ischgl, then go down to Obergurgl, perhaps stopping at Sölden on the way. You can draw up the kind of schedule, albeit fairly hectic, for France's Tarentaise that the keen, expert skier would drool over. Imagine a week in which you could ski the Trois Vallées, La Plagne, Les Arcs, and Val d'Isère/Tignes.

Italy is far more suitable for tourers than day-trippers provided you're prepared to put up with some slow drives on winding passes. You can start in Livigno, drive to Bormio and then to the Dolomites, visiting Madonna di Campiglio and Selva, and finish your Italian expedition in Cortina.

Eastern Switzerland also offers a very attractive touring holiday. You can start in Davos/Klosters, take in Lenzerheide and Arosa and end up in Flims. You could even include St Moritz if you're prepared to put up with a little extra driving. Again in Switzerland, you can easily combine several resorts in the Bernese Oberland. You could, for example, ski in Gstaad, Adelboden, Grindelwald, Wengen and Mürren. But do remember that the last two are car-free so you'll have to leave your car in Lauterbrunnen.

There's no need to confine yourself to one country – why not sample more than one nation's skiing delights? You could imitate the famous Haute-Route by starting in Argentière in France and ending up in Switzerland's Saas Fee. On the way you could ski in Verbier and Zermatt and even Crans Montana if time permits.

The major thing that you'll have to watch out for with a touring holiday is the cost of accommodation. Checking into a resort hotel as an independent traveller for a night or two won't come cheap. You can save money by staying down the valley. Many places have excellent access to the main ski areas. For example, you can take the funicular from Bourg-St-Maurice to Les Arcs; a gondola links Brides-Les-Bains to Méribel. You can let the train take the strain in Lauterbrunnen for Wengen and Mürren; and Täsch for Zermatt.

ALONE ON A HILL

If you've ever been irritated in a lift-queue or restaurant by unavoidably having to listen to someone else's conversation about England's chances of regaining the Ashes, or the state of the NHS, you'll probably have wished you could have got away from it all rather more than you have done.

By travelling independently, you can boldly go where not too many Brits have gone before and explore new frontiers which British tour operators rarely or only occasionally offer. There are hundreds of resorts in the Alps to discover – and in many you'd be unlucky if you heard another British voice.

Most cars couldn'

The picture shows a standard, road going Audi 80 quattro, driving up a ski slope. Like every Audi quatt
All of which goes to show that there's nothing standard abo

rive down it.

...tantly monitors which axle has the most grip and distributes the power accordingly.
...dard Audi. For a brochure call 0800 99 88 77.

Audi. Vorsprung durch Technik.

THE COST OF A TICKET TO DRIVE

The cost of driving depends, of course, on how many passengers you cram into your car. If you're booking accommodation through a tour operator who offers a generous discount to drivers, you may find driving as cheap as flying even if there are only two or three of you. You'll pay from around £130 return to take your car with one passenger on a short channel crossing. Allow £100 to £200 for petrol, depending on where you're going and in what sort of car. Don't forget French motorway tolls – the trip from Calais to Albertville and back will cost around £90. And to use Swiss motorways you need a permit costing £15. In the Alps you can expect to pay for using many of the tunnels – for example, about £15 or £20 for a one-way trip through the Mont-Blanc tunnel (it depends on car size).

WHICH WHEELS?

A 4WD car is a great asset in the Alps. You'll have far more control when going downhill, as well as the ability to climb uphill. We've driven a lot in snow in 4WD cars with knobbly tyres and have never had to use snow-chains. Next best is a front-wheel drive car. The size and boot capacity of the car are clearly important. Four adults, plus luggage cooped up in a small family saloon for 700 miles doesn't make for a comfortable or harmonious journey. Special enclosed roof racks are available, capable of holding a lot of baggage as well as skis.

GETTING THE CAR READY

Alpine weather and roads are likely to make unusual demands on your car – it pays to make sure that:
• the tread on your tyres (including the spare) is up to scratch
• you test the battery if you suspect that it's dodgy
• the anti-freeze is strong enough to survive temperatures which could drop to -30°C overnight
• you have a similarly strong solution of winter screenwash
• you check the handbook to see if you need to do anything to adapt the car for cold weather; you may for example, have to adjust the engine air intake, or use a thinner oil
• you fit headlight beam deflectors; if they normally throw a lot of light upwards, fit special fog lights which will be a big help if you have to drive at night when it's snowing.

CAR COVER

Even if you have a fully comprehensive cover, it will often be downgraded to third party as soon as you leave the UK, unless you've made arrangements to extend it – allow at least a couple of weeks for this. Most companies don't charge for such extensions. Although it's no longer compulsory to carry a Green Card in other EU countries, it's a good idea to ask your insurance company for one.

If your car breaks down, you could face a big bill, lengthy delays and utter disruption to your holiday plans. You can buy peace of mind by taking out a breakdown insurance policy. National Breakdown's UK breakdown insurance also covers the Continent.

SAFE DRIVING

Except in severe weather, you're only likely to come across serious snow conditions on approach roads to fairly high resorts. Unless you've got a 4WD car you'll need chains on the car's driving wheels – not simply to keep you safe and mobile but also to stay on the right side of local laws. You can keep the chains on while you're driving on ordinary roads; but you'll have to drive very slowly and for a limited period only. The instructions should have information about this.

Audi

If you've never used chains before, it's well worth having a practice run at putting them on. The first time we had to fit them, we spent a very unhappy hour lying in the road-side slush as the snow came down and our fellow motorists cursed us in a variety of languages as they squeezed past us on a narrow mountain road.

Even if the road surface seems dry and free of ice, still take great care – there could be icy patches on shaded areas. You can't afford to relax in relatively warm weather – there's nothing more treacherous than ice that's melting. Be especially cautious when going downhill. If the road surface is slippery, keep your speed down and brake by using your engine – change down in good time. Brake on the straight, not on bends – otherwise the front wheels may lock and you'll slide straight on. If the back wheels slide and the car starts to spin, steer into the slide.

MOUNTAIN MOTOR MAINTENANCE

Your car will be in for quite a culture shock having, perhaps, left a nice warm garage for overnight temperatures way, way below freezing. So:
• overnight, park on flat ground and in a place where your car will be sheltered from the wind
• leave the car in gear with the hand-brake off; you could have problems if the hand-brake freezes in the 'on' position
• lift the wipers away from the windscreen
• if you're not planning any trips, it's worth taking the car out for short drives just to keep the battery ticking over.

RECOMMENDED ROUTES

From the Channel there are essentially only three 'gateways' into the Alps. For the French and some of the Swiss Alps, you go via the French motorways and **Mâcon**. For most of the Swiss and some of the Austrian Alps you aim for **Basel**. For all of the Austrian Alps you can go via **Ulm** – and for some Austrian resorts it's the only sensible route. Normally, once you've picked your destination you'll be able to see which gateway you need; our maps of Austria (page 52), France (page 136), Italy (page 261) and Switzerland (page 304) will help. Then you can concentrate on deciding how to get to that gateway from a particular port.

Where you have a choice of route, you may wish to bear in mind that German motorways are free, whereas French ones charge tolls that are not negligible (Calais to Albertville and back £90). German ones have no speed limit, making them potentially quicker but rather scary in wet weather. And their petrol stations rarely accept credit cards. To use Swiss motorways, you have to buy a sticker for your windscreen (£15 for a calendar year). These are sold at the border, and you're expected to buy one unless you have a pretty convincing route-plan involving no motorways.

DESTINATION: FRENCH ALPS

Wherever you're starting from, the gateway is **Mâcon** and the initial target is Beaune. If you're taking the short crossing to Calais, Boulogne or Dunkirk, the route is via Reims, Troyes and Dijon. From Le Havre or Caen your route sounds even simpler: the A13 to Paris then the A6 south. But you have to get through or around Paris. The most direct way around the city is the notorious périphérique – a hectic multi-lane urban motorway close to the centre, with exits every few hundred yards. But this is not the quickest if is jammed with traffic. The more reliable alternative is to take a series of motorways and dual carriageways through the south-west fringes of Greater Paris. The route (or one of the routes – there are a couple of

Audi

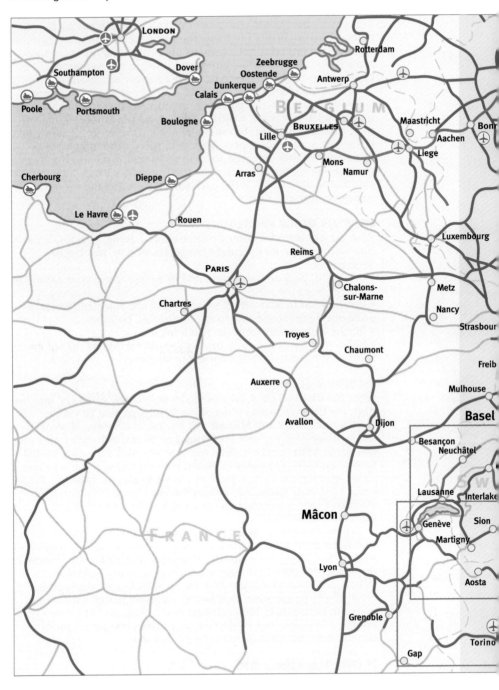

This map should help you plan your route to the Alps. As we've explained in the text, all the main routes from the Channel and all the routes up into the mountains funnel through three 'gateways', picked out on the map in larger type – Mâcon, Basel and Ulm. Decide which gateway suits your destination, and pick a route to it. Occasionally, different Channel ports will lead you to use different gateways.

Audi

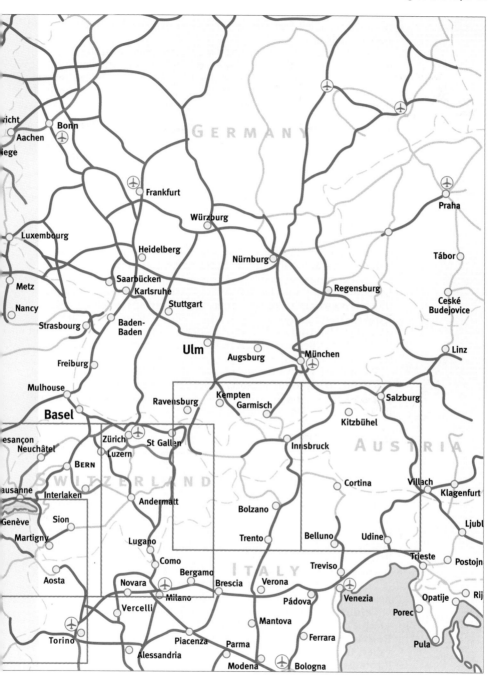

The boxes on the map correspond to the areas covered by the more detailed maps at the start of the main country sections of the book:
Austria page 52
France page 136
Switzerland page 304.
There is also a not-so-detailed map of the Italian Alps on page 260.

Audi

variants) is signed, but not easy to follow without a detailed map and a good navigator.

At Mâcon, the routes start to diverge; you go east on the A40 for **Geneva** to get to the northern resorts – Chamonix, the Portes du Soleil and so on; take the A43 off the Lyon bypass for **Chambéry** to get to the central Tarentaise mega-resorts; and take the A48 south off that road for **Grenoble** to get to the southern resorts.

DESTINATION: SWITZERLAND

There are two gateways for Switzerland. For the Valais resorts of Champéry, Verbier, Saas Fee, Zermatt and so on, and those in Vaud such as Villars and Les Diablerets, aim for **Mâcon** and then Geneva. Don't be tempted to aim for Lausanne, two-thirds of the way along lake Geneva – the route nationale from Besançon to the Swiss border via Pontarlier is slow going.

If you're going further east, the gateway is **Basel**. This presents more alternative routes than any other gateway. From Calais the obvious route is via Reims, Metz and Strasbourg, then across the border to the autobahn up the Rhine valley. But from ports further east, other routes are viable – via the Belgian motorways to Luxembourg and into France to pick up the Calais route; or Belgian motorways towards Cologne, then all the way up the Rhine valley. From the Normandy ports, you have a choice of going via Paris to join the Calais route at Reims or heading south, as if for Geneva, and turning left at Beaune. This is the better bet – slightly quicker, more scenic, and better equipped with good places for lunch.

From Basel, the routes diverge: you go on to **Bern** for the Bernese Oberland, to get to such resorts as Wengen and Grindelwald; to **Lucerne** for resorts in central Switzerland; and to **Zürich** for resorts in the Grisons – Davos, Flims and so on.

DESTINATION: AUSTRIA

For the Vorarlberg resorts in western Austria (notably Lech and Zürs) and for St Anton just inside the Tyrol, the best gateway may be **Basel** – particularly if starting from the Normandy ports. You drive through Switzerland, and cross into Austria at **Feldkirch**.

But for most purposes the gateway is **Ulm**, between Stuttgart and Munich. From the short-crossing ports there are several ways to get to it, but the basic choice is the same as those for Basel: via France and Strasbourg; via Belgium, Luxembourg and Strasbourg; or via Belgium and the Rhine valley. Our basic advice to those thinking of starting from the Normandy ports is: Don't.

From Ulm, routes diverge. For the Vorarlberg and Arlberg resorts, head south to cross into Austria at Bregenz and join the Basel route at **Feldkirch**. For Innsbruck and neighbouring resorts, branch south-east off that route, crossing into Austria between Füssen and **Reutte**, and then negotiating the low Fern pass to get to the Inn valley. For resorts further east, carry on through Munich and cross into Austria at **Kufstein** for resorts in the eastern Tyrol (Kitzbühel and neighbours) or **Salzburg** for resorts in Salzburg province (Zell am See, Badgastein), Styria (Schladming), and Carinthia (Badkleinkirchheim).

DESTINATION: ITALY

Italian resorts are spread out over the whole length of the Alpine range. They are reached by passes or tunnels from France, Switzerland or Italy. The possibilities are set out in detail in our introduction to Italian resorts on page 261.

Audi

by **Nick van Zanten**

Aspen or Vail?

the choice is a fine thing

If you're going all that way, you may as well go the whole hog and head for the best resort. That's the spirit in which many British skiers have approached the choice of a resort in America's Rocky Mountains. And for many, the automatic choice has been Vail – possibly the biggest, probably the smartest and certainly the smoothest of America's ski resorts. But it does have a rival as America's 'best' resort, although a much less popular one with Brits: Aspen. We sent bon viveur Nick van Zanten to Colorado to carry out an AB comparison.

The bathroom is the size of a village hall. The bath, not much smaller than an Olympic swimming pool. And just in case I hadn't noticed I was in one of America's top hotels, the porter showed me a dial on the bathroom wall.

"This is your floor temperature control feature," he said.

"My floor temperature control feature?"

"Yes, sir. It warms the marble on the floor so your feet don't get too chilly in the morning."

This is Vail, one of the swankiest ski resorts in the US. The hotel is the Sonnenalp, a place where pampering has been escalated to an art form. For those of us used to chalet parties with shared bathrooms in Méribel, the level of cosseting – and the high quality of the plumbing – comes as something of a shock.

Just 40 air miles away is Aspen, the world-famous playground of Hollywood superstars. Together, Aspen and Vail are known as the twin capitals of American skiing. The resorts that skiers dream about. The resorts that others emulate.

Both resorts are situated in the Rocky Mountains of Colorado. Each is clearly defined by the powerful mountains that overlook the respective communities. There is plenty of skiable mountain, lots of powder snow and each has a fiercely loyal clientele. But, despite these similarities and their close proximity, the skiing experience in Aspen and Vail is as different as chalk and cheese.

Aspen has been shaped by its previous life as a silver-mining boom town. It has beautifully restored 100-year-old Victorian homes, their clapboard sporting fresh coats of purple, blue and orange paint. It has red-brick buildings like the Wheeler Opera House, the hotel Jerome – the hotel to be seen at – and the Ute City Bank.

Vail is much newer. It's been built from scratch over the last 30 years. Its looks can best be described as mock Tyrolean; like a little bit of Austria plonked in the middle of the Rockies. Vail has names like the Gasthof Gramshammer, Tea Room Alpine Rose and the Sonnenalp. The staff at the Sonnenalp even dress in mock Tyrolean costumes. Although this may sound naff, it works, and is infinitely preferable to the big grey blocks of flats of many modern ski resorts.

Those who support Aspen will say that Vail is too fake (unkind critics call it `plastic Bavaria') and too nouveau riche. Those who support Vail will respond by saying that Aspen is too glitzy, too Hollywood.

Whatever the criticisms, the fact of the matter is that both resorts offer some of the best skiing in America.

Vail is big. Really big. Its seven-mile mountain has around 100 groomed trails (none seriously difficult). It's ideal for lazy skiers with a touch of class. Even the more direct fall-line runs invite you to linger in the turn, tips aimed straight downhill. Vail is great for beginners and intermediates. What sets Vail apart is its Back Bowls; seven huge ungroomed powder skiing areas which occupy the back side of the mountain. And just down the road it has the skiing at Beaver Creek – immaculately groomed blues, but steep, steep bump runs too.

Aspen Mountain – also known as Ajax – is Aspen's local hill. It doesn't have the all-purpose, something-for-everyone vastness that Vail has. Here the bumps and steep slopes call for adrenalin as well as grace. Periodically your knees will come up to your chest; the terrain will encourage you to dart and stretch and slip through the steep but open patterns – great for the more advanced skier, not much fun for the weak skier.

But Aspen has four distinct ski areas. As well as Aspen Mountain with its big bold runs, there is Aspen Highlands with Colorado's biggest vertical and an unusual mix of beginner and expert terrain. There is Snowmass – a vast intermediate playground (the biggest of the four mountains). And there is Tiehack, which used to be called Buttermilk – the name has been changed by the locals for being 'too wimpish'. It's a mountain tailor-made for beginners and children.

Vail is easy to get to from Denver and consequently attracts a huge day-skier crowd. At Vail, having 10,000 to 15,000 people on the mountain at once is not unusual; a huge crowd at Aspen is still under 6,000.

Aspen attracts screenplay writers, environmentalists, film stars and eccentrics. Vail attracts a broader cross-section including teen skiers from Denver, ski clubs from Ohio, Australians with back-packs, and Wall Street financiers. Both attract professionals – lawyers, pharmacists and doctors.

In Aspen you're more likely to see the hand-painted ski-suits and gold lame stretch pants. In Vail, the correct multi-layered North Face ensemble is more appropriate.

So for that once-in-a-lifetime trip to the Rockies, should you choose Vail or Aspen? It's a bit like asking a motoring correspondent to choose between a Mercedes and a Jaguar. Both will pander to your every whim. Both will be a superb driving experience. The difference between them is one of character, rather than technical excellence.

Vail is the Mercedes. It's a piece of high-quality, well engineered, teutonic efficiency. Aspen is the Jaguar – full of tradition, with plenty of enchanting quirks. The town has heated pavements, a real joy when walking around in the evening.

If pushed, and I had to choose to limit all my future skiing days to one of these two mountains, then – purely in skiing terms – I'd choose Vail. Vail's skiing has more dimensions, fills more space and is more liberating than Aspen's. But looking at the resorts all-round, and if I could visit only one Rocky Mountain ski town ever again, I'd have to pick Aspen – a less polished resort machine, but ultimately a more eccentric and far more stimulating place.

But I don't want to choose and I don't have to. I'll take them both. And that's just what the resorts seem to want their international guest to do – with their joint Premier Passport lift pass, which includes a free transfer between the resorts.

Choosing your resort

get it right first time

Most British skiers, unlike those lucky enough to live closer to the Alps, get to go skiing only once or twice a year. And then only for a week at a time in most cases. So choosing the right resort is crucially important. This book is designed to help you do just that. Here is some advice on how to use it to best effect.

Lots of factors need to be taken into account. And the weight you attach to each of them depends on your own personal preferences and on the make-up of the group you are going on holiday with. On page 15, you'll find shortlists of resorts which are outstanding in various key respects. For most people cost will be an important factor. That's why we've devoted a whole chapter to it – see page 17.

WHICH RESORT?
Each resort chapter is organised in the same way, to help you choose the right resort. This short introduction explains how they work.

We start off with a How it Rates section, in the margin, where we rate each resort from 11 points of view – the more stars the better. For major resorts we then give lists of the main good and bad points about the resort and its skiing, picked out with ✔ and ✘. These lists are followed by a summary in **bold type**, in which we've aimed to encapsulate the essence of the place and to weigh up the pros and cons, giving our view of who might like it. These sections should give you a good idea of whether the resort is likely to suit *you*, and whether you should read our detailed analysis of it.

You'll know by now whether this is, for example, a high, hideous, purpose-built resort with superb, snow-sure skiing for all standards of skier but absolutely no nightlife, or whether it's a pretty, traditional village with gentle wooded skiing ideal for beginners if only there was some snow.

We then look at each aspect of the resort in more detail.

THE RESORT
Resorts vary enormously in character and charm. At the extremes of the range are the handful of really hideous modern apartment-block resorts thrown up in France in the 1960s – step forward, Les Menuires – and the captivating old traffic-free mountain villages of which Switzerland has an unfair number. But it isn't simply a question of old versus new. Some purpose-built places (such as Valmorel) can have a much friendlier feel than some traditional resorts with big blocky buildings (eg Davos). And some places can be remarkably strung out (eg Vail) whereas others are surprisingly compact (eg Wengen).

The landscape can have an important impact – whether the resort is at the bottom of a narrow valley (eg Ischgl) or on shelf with panoramic views (eg Crans-Montana). Some places are working towns as well as ski resorts (eg Bormio). Some are full of bars, discos and shops (eg St Anton). Others are peaceful backwaters (eg Arabba). Traffic may choke the streets (eg Châtel). Or the village may be traffic-free (eg Mürren).

In this first section of each chapter, we try to sort out the character of the place for you. Later, in the Staying there section, we tell you more about the hotels, restaurants, bars and so on.

THE SKIING

The ski area Some ski areas are vast and complex, while others are much smaller and lacking variation. The description here tells you how the ski area divides up into different sectors and how the links between them work. You'll need to understand this to make the most of the descriptions of the skiing that come later. Read this section together with the piste map for the resort.

Snow reliability A crucial factor for many people and one which varies enormously. In some resorts you don't have to worry at all about there being no snow to ski on, while others (including some very big names) are notorious for treating their paying guests to ice, mud and slush. Whether a resort is likely to have decent snow on its slopes normally depends on the height of the skiing, the direction most of the slopes face (north good, south bad), its snow record and how much artificial snow it has (we list this figure in Ski Facts).

For advanced/ intermediate/ beginner skiers Most (though not all) resorts have something to offer beginners. But remarkably few will keep an advanced skier happy for a holiday. As for intermediates, whether a resort will suit you really depends on your standard and temperament. Places such as Cervinia and Obergurgl are ideal for those who want easy cruising runs but have little to offer intermediates looking for more challenge. Others such as Sölden and Val-d'Isère may intimidate the less confident intermediate who doesn't know the ski area well. We sum up the skiing for different grades of skier and describe outstanding runs or areas.

For cross-country We don't pretend that this is a guide for avid cross-country skiers. But if you or one of your group wants to try it our summary here will help you gauge whether the resort is worth considering or a wash-out. It looks not just at the amount of cross-country available but also its scenic beauty and whether or not the tracks are likely to have decent snow (many are at low altitude).

Queues Another key factor. Not only is standing in queues tedious – it also robs you of valuable skiing time. Most resorts have improved their lift systems enormously in the last ten years, and monster queues are largely a thing of the past. But there are notable exceptions – such as Verbier, Mayrhofen and Kitzbühel.

Mountain restaurants Here's a subject that divides skiers clearly into two opposing camps. To some, having a decent lunch in civilised surroundings – either in the sun, contemplating amazing scenery, or in a cosy Alpine hut, sheltered from the elements – makes or breaks their holiday. Others regard a prolonged mid-day stop as a waste of valuable skiing time as well as valuable spending money – they prefer a sandwich on the mountain top or a quick, cheap self-service snack. We are firmly in the former camp. We get very disheartened by places with miserable restaurants and miserable food (eg many resorts in America); and there are some resorts that we go to regularly partly because of the cosy huts and excellent cuisine (eg Zermatt).

Ski school This is an area where we rely heavily on your reports of your own or your friends' experiences. The only way to judge a ski school is by trying it. Reports on ski schools are always extremely valuable and frequently disappointing.

Facilities for children If you need crèche facilities don't go to Italy. In other countries, facilities for looking after and teaching children can vary enormously between resorts. We tell you what is available in each resort, including what's on offer from tour operators – often the most attractive option for British families, particularly those who like catered chalet holidays (explained later in this section). But, again, to be of maximum use we need reports from people who've used the facilities.

You don't have to ski alone
...to be an individual!

SKI
SOLUTIONS

*Britain's original
and largest specialist
ski travel agency*

SKI SOLUTIONS

The first and only place you need to call to book your ski holiday.

We are a ski travel agency as opposed to a ski tour operator. When you call us you immediately place at your disposal a choice of thousands of holidays offered by a wide variety of different reputable, fully bonded tour operators, both large and small.

By calling Ski Solutions first, rather than ringing round lots of ski tour operators, you can make *an instant short-cut to finding you ideal ski holiday.* To start the snowball rolling, simply ring us and give us a very rough idea of what kind of holiday you are seeking and when:

- **How many in your party?**
- **Are there any children? What ages?**
- **What levels of skier?**
- **Traditional or modern resort?**
- **Where, ideally, do you want to fly from?**
- **What standard of hotel, chalet or apartment?**

Our experienced staff will gently "cross-examine" you, asking what you did and didn't enjoy about past ski holidays and allowing you to reveal any personal preferences.

Acting on what you have told them, our staff will then research and compile a shortlist of appropriate holidays and will send this together with relevant brochures and other information. (If you're in a hurry, we can even fax these details to you.)

We do all the hard work for you by working out exactly what each option will cost with each operator, taking into account all the various complicated supplements and discounts. (Because they spend each day immersed in ski brochures, our staff are experts on the small print.) Without any financial obligation on your part, we can "hold" provisionally the holidays that

particularly interest you for a couple of days, giving you time to discuss things with any others involved.

After further discussions with you we will then book the holiday of your choice. The price of the holiday will be *exactly as in the brochure:* our service is absolutely *FREE*. Indeed, it actually saves you money in terms of time and phone bills.

If, by chance, we cannot find you a suitable holiday in one of the many brochures, then we are happy to tailor-make the perfect holiday for you through our A La Carte department, which works closely with many of the world's top ski resorts.

Between us the 12 staff of Ski Solutions have skied over 100 resorts on both sides of the Atlantic and we have a first-hand up-to-date knowledge of the hotels, chalets and apartments offered by most of the operators in these places.

Because we are primarily a travel agency and not a tour operator, we have the luxury of being able to sell you the holiday you want rather than the holiday we need to sell.

Discounts for *Where to Ski* readers
**Book through Ski Solutions and we'll refund the cost of this book
– see page 7.**

Call us now!
071 602 9900

84 Pembroke Road, Kensington, London W8 6NX
Facsimile 071-602-2882

STAYING THERE

In some resorts such as St Anton and Zermatt, choosing where in the resort to stay is very important – otherwise you might end up with long treks to and from the lifts or being woken at 2am by noisy revellers. We tell you what to take into account.

How to go The basic choice is between catered chalets, hotels and self-catering accommodation. Catered chalets remain a peculiarly British phenomenon. A tour operator takes over a chalet (or a hotel in some cases) staffs it with young Brits (or antipodeans), fills it with British guests, provides half-board and free wine with dinner, lets you drink your duty-free booze without feeling guilty and often provides free ski guiding to help you get the best out of the area. And we love it! It is a very economic way of visiting the top resorts – see our chapter on costs on page 17. And it makes for a very sociable holiday. Standards of accommodation and cuisine can vary a lot.

Hotels, as ever, can vary a lot but, especially in France and Switzerland, can work out very expensive. Apartments can work out the most economical way of going skiing but French ones, in particular, tend to be very small – it's not unusual for brochure prices to be based on four people sleeping in a one-room studio, for example. To be comfortable, find out the apartment size and put fewer people in than the number it is advertised for.

In this section we have looked at the accommodation of all three types that is available through British tour operators. For hotels and self-catering we also look at what's available for independent travellers who want to fix their own accommodation. With hotels we've given each a £££ rating – the more pound signs the pricier.

Staying up the mountain / down the valley If there are interesting options for staying on the slopes or in valley towns, we've picked them out. The former is often good for avoiding early-morning scrums for the lifts, the latter for cutting costs considerably.

Eating out The range of restaurants varies enormously between resorts. Even some big ones, such as Les Arcs, may have little choice because most of the clientele stay in their apartments and self-cater. Chalet-dominated resorts such as Méribel can also have a surprisingly limited choice. Others such as Val-d'Isère have a huge range available, including national and regional cuisine, pizzas, fondues and international fare. American resorts, in particular, generally have an excellent range of restaurants – everyone eats out.

Après-ski Tastes and styles vary enormously. Most resorts have pleasant places in which to have an immediate post-skiing beer or hot chocolate. Some then go dead. Others have noisy bars and discos until the early hours. And, especially in Austrian resorts, there may be a lot of events such as tobogganing and bowling that are organised by British tour operator reps. We've done our best to summarise what you'll find. But when we are touring around inspecting resorts, discos that don't get lively until midnight don't come high on our agenda. So we are largely dependent for this section on hearing from those of our reporters who are keen après-skiers. And we are very grateful to the several tour operators who have helped us put together this section for certain resorts.

For non-skiers Here's one area where, you might be surprised to hear, we are experts. That's because one of us is married to a dedicated non-skier who loves the mountains and has been on no fewer than 19 Alpine holidays while setting foot on skis just once. If you'd like any more specialised advice – eg which are the easiest resorts to get the Times in; which bar terraces get the sun first in Méribel, Zermatt, Wengen, Saas-Fee and Val-d'Isère; how to save mountain restaurant tables for ten for two hours in peak season – just write in.

Austria

Austria has traditionally been the favourite destination for British skiers. France now claims a similar share of the market – about a third – and the resurgence of interest in Italy is bound to harm the Austrians' business. But for a large number of Brits, Austria will remain number one. For beginners and cautious intermediates seeking reassuring surroundings rather than challenges, it's difficult to beat Austria's blend of friendly and often pretty villages and similarly captivating ski areas. Most of its ski areas, however, do lack the extent and/or the altitude that French resorts offer, and there are lots of experienced skiers who won't consider going to Austria except to visit steep, snowy St Anton or to ski one of the several excellent glaciers. The experienced skiers who take a different view are mainly those who like the lively nightlife that is a particular feature of Austrian resorts.

Austria is the heartland of the mainstream package ski holiday, sold over the counter by high-street travel agencies and based on hotel or guest-house accommodation. Austria has vast amounts of this reliably comfortable accommodation, distributed over a huge number of resorts, large and small – you can buy packages to over 100 Austrian resorts this winter. Chalet and self-catering packages are less widely offered.

Most of these resorts are real villages in valley bottoms, with skiing on the wooded slopes above them. They have expanded enormously since the war, but practically all the development has been in traditional chalet style; the German demand for summer holidays is as important to Austria as skiing, and the villages of the Tyrol have to look good without the snow that is the saving grace of many French and even some Swiss resorts.

The skiing is often quite limited. There are many Austrian resorts that a keen skier could explore fully in half a day. Those who start their skiing careers in such resorts may not be worried by this – and it certainly means that there is nothing to distract you from concentrating on learning to ski properly. But those who have developed a taste for travelling around on skis find that the list of acceptable Austrian resorts is quite a short one.

Unfortunately, several of the resorts on that short list bring you up against another problem – low altitude, and therefore poor snow conditions. Kitzbühel is at 760m, Söll at 700m, Zell am See at 755m. When considering altitudes, you do have to remember that in winter Europe gets colder the further east you go – so 700m isn't as low in skiing terms as 700m would be in France. But it's still low, and the top heights of Austrian resorts are relatively low too – typically 1800m to 2000m. And snowmaking is not as widespread here as in France, Italy or Switzerland.

The resorts of the Arlberg area, at the western end of the Tyrol – St Anton, Lech and Zürs, stand apart from these concerns, with excellent snow records and extensive skiing. And there are other resorts where you can be reasonably confident of good snow, such as Obergurgl and Ischgl, not to mention the reliable year-round skiing on glaciers such as those at Hintertux, Neustift and Kaprun. But for most other resorts our advice is to book late, when you know what the snow conditions are like.

Nightlife is an important feature of Austrian skiing for many regular visitors. It ranges from lively hotel bars selling large volumes of beer, through Tyrolean evenings and activities organised by the representatives of UK tour operators, to much more sophisticated discos and nightclubs in resorts such as Lech, Ischgl and Kitzbühel.

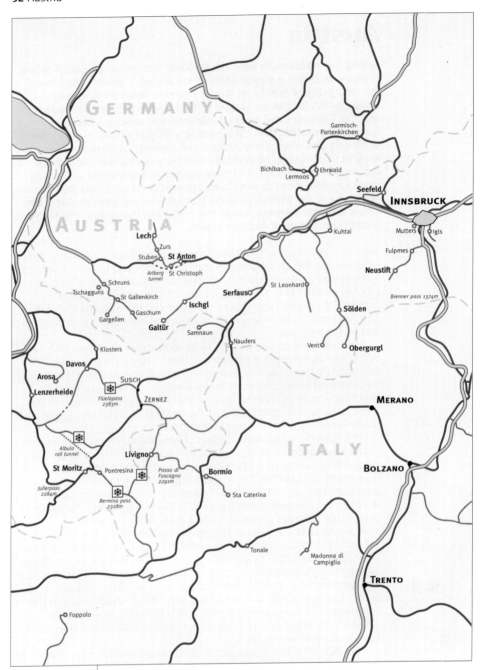

0   30

Scale in km

GETTING AROUND THE AUSTRIAN ALPS

The dominant feature of Austria for the ski driver is the thoroughfare of the Inn valley, which runs through the Tyrol from Landeck via Innsbruck to Kufstein. The motorway along it extends, with one or two breaks, westwards to the Arlberg pass and on to Switzerland.

The Arlberg – which divides Tyrol from Vorarlberg, but which is also the watershed between Austria and Switzerland – is one of the few areas where driving plans are likely to be seriously affected by snow. The east-west Arlberg pass itself has a long tunnel underneath it; this isn't cheap, and unless you're in a tearing hurry you may want to take the high road when it's clear, passing through Stuben,

St Christoph and St Anton instead of missing all three. The Flexen pass road to Zürs and Lech (which may be closed by avalanche risk even when the Arlberg is open) branches off just to the west of the Arlberg summit, and in snow it is best approached from the west.

At the eastern end of the Tyrol, the Gerlos pass road from Zell am Ziller over into Salzburg province (1628m) is occasionally closed. Resorts such as Bad Kleinkirchheim, over in Carinthia, are easily reached by motorway, thanks to the Tauern and Katschberg tunnels. There is the alternative of driving over the Radstädter Tauern pass through Obertauern (1739m), or of using the car-carrying rail service from Böckstein (just beyond Badgastein) to Mallnitz.

Alpbach 1000m

HOW IT RATES

The skiing

Snow	**
Extent	*
Advanced	*
Intermediates	**
Beginners	****
Convenience	**
Queues	***
Restaurants	***

The rest

Scenery	***
Resort charm	*****
Not skiing	***

SKI FACTS

Altitude	830m-2025m
Lifts	23
Pistes	45km
Green/Blue	15%
Red	70%
Black	15%
Artificial snow	2km

PACKAGES

Austrian Travel Service, Enterprise, Inghams, Made to Measure, Neilson, Ski Europe, Thomson

TOURIST OFFICE

Postcode A-6236
Tel 010 43 (5336) 5211
Fax 5012

Alpbach is an old British favourite – there is even a British ski club, the Alpbach Visitors. We go there in numbers partly out of habit, but also because it is exceptionally pretty and friendly – 'you are a guest, not a tourist,' says a recent visitor – and because its tiny ski area is not without interest, even for good skiers.

THE RESORT

Alpbach is a captivating place in summer and winter alike – one of the prettiest villages in a province that is renowned for them. It lies near the head of its valley, slightly elevated and looking south across the valley towards the Wiedersbergerhorn, where most of the skiing takes place. Traditional chalets crowd around the immaculate little church, and open fields (including the nursery slopes) are just yards away. The Inn valley is only a few miles to the north, and expeditions eastward to the Kitzbühel area or westward to Innsbruck and beyond are possible. The Hintertux and Stubai glaciers are within reach.

THE SKIING

Alpbach's **ski area**, on two flanks of the Wiedersbergerhorn, is small and simple. The main gondola goes up from the isolated roadside lift-station of Achenwirt (830m), a mile from the centre; slower alternatives go up from Inneralpbach (1050m), half-way round the mountain on its east side, and they all meet at Hornboden (1890m). Two recently built drags take the skiing up to 2025m. The small ski area down at Reith is on the ski pass.

Like most lowish resorts in Tirol, Alpbach cannot claim great **snow reliability**; but at least most of the skiing faces north. The village nursery slope has artificial snow, as does one of the runs down the top stage of the gondola.

Although Alpbach can't generally be recommended for **advanced** skiers, the reds and the two (short) blacks are not without challenge, and runs of 1000m vertical are not to be sniffed at. There are a couple of off-piste routes to the valley, short ski tours are also offered, and the ski schools make the most of the off-piste terrain.

The terrain is ideal for **intermediate** skiers; the problem is that there is not very much of it. This is a resort for practicing technique on familiar slopes, not for high mileage.

Beginners love the sunny nursery slopes, reassuringly close to the village centre, and higher slopes can be used when snow is poor. But this is not a resort for confidence-building: most of the longer runs are red.

There are pretty **cross-country** trails up the valleys beyond Inneralpbach (1050m); the most testing is 9km long and climbs 300m.

Serious **queues** are rare, thanks to the efficient gondola. But the resort does attract some weekend trade.

There are as many **mountain restaurants** as the small ski area can squeeze in. Hornboden now has a popular table-service restaurant as well as self-service. There is something to be said for descending to Achenwirt.

Alpbach and Alpbach Innertal are the two **ski schools**, and both operate ski nurseries; the former takes **children** from age 4, from 9.30 to 4.15. (They bring the children back on the ski-bus at the end of the day.) The non-ski nursery operates from 9.15 to 4pm (noon on Saturday).

STAYING THERE

Alpbach is a small village, so there's no need to worry about where you stay. But the very centre is undoubtedly most convenient, both for the ski-bus to Achenwirt and for après-ski. The backwater of Inneralpbach is convenient for skiing, and suits families.

There isn't much choice of **how to go** – hotels and pensions dominate UK package programmes. Of the three smart 4-star places with pools, the Alpbacherhof gets most votes. But most simpler places also get good reports. Haus Thomas, Haus Angelika and Haus Theresia are recommended. Some self-catering is offered.

Eating out means eating in hotels, or at least in restaurants attached to hotels. The Reblaus is recommended.

The **après-ski** scene is typically Tirolean, with a great deal of tea-time beer swilling – and noise – in the bars of central hotels such as the Jakober. In the evening there are organised events, and a couple of late-night bars and discos.

There is more to amuse **non-skiers** than you might expect, including swimming and curling (400m from the centre), pretty walks, and excursions to Innsbruck and beyond.

Bad Kleinkirchheim 1080m

Having local-boy-made-good Franz Klammer as its ski ambassador has helped to put Bad Kleinkirchheim on the international map. The old spa town has developed its ski area substantially in recent years, and now offers attractive intermediate terrain.

HOW IT RATES

The skiing

Snow	**
Extent	**
Advanced	*
Intermediates	***
Beginners	***
Convenience	***
Queues	*****
Restaurants	***

The rest

Scenery	***
Resort charm	***
Not skiing	***

SKI FACTS

Altitude	1080m-2055m
Lifts	32
Pistes	85km
Green/Blue	15%
Red	75%
Black	10%
Artificial snow	25km

PACKAGES

Alpine Tours, Sloping Off

TOURIST OFFICE

Postcode A-9546
Tel 010 43 (4240) 8212
Fax 8537

THE RESORT

Bad Kleinkirchheim is Franz Klammer's home town and is in the far south-east of Austria's mountains, away from the usual skiing destinations. To attract custom, 'BKK' has developed from a summer spa with a limited ski area into a fair-sized ski resort. The result is modern lifts and a positive attitude towards making improvements.

The drawback to having spa origins is that the village is laid out in a sprawling manner, less than ideal for skiers. The most convenient place to stay is close to the Priedröf and Maibrunnbahn lifts.

BKK has a sophisticated, relaxed feel, with superb spa facilities.

THE SKIING

The BKK and St Oswald **ski areas** are now linked by both lift and piste – the former has two-thirds of the skiing. Both are made up of mostly flattering intermediate runs. Two lifts – a quad chair and a long drag – service the skiing immediately above BKK. Those staying near the tennis centre have a gondola to whisk them up to the far end of BKK's area. Two short chair-rides take skiers from central BKK to the St Oswald skiing, while a little drag enables a speedy return.

Being east of the Tauern Pass, BKK can have completely different weather from the rest of Austria. In recent years **snow reliability** has been noticeably better at times and much worse at others. It is sufficiently distant from most other resorts to avoid a massive invasion when its conditions are better; portable snowmaking helps matters when the situation is reversed. However, it's essentially a low, sunny ski area where late holidays in particular are risky. The top of the skiing is only a little over 2000m.

This is not a resort for **advanced skiers**. The red from the top of the Lärchegg drag is a tough run when icy. The World Cup downhill course is surprisingly easy at 'normal' speed. The Franz Klammer run is better, but finishes with a walk to a bus stop.

The area is ideal for improving **intermediates**, the majority of runs

being long, wide and flattering, as well as nicely uncrowded. St Oswald's partly open skiing provides welcome variety to an area that can otherwise seem a little 'samey'.

St Oswald is best for complete **beginners**, with better nursery slopes and very easy runs at the top of the Nockalm. Near-beginners will enjoy the blue running parallel to the bottom part of the World Cup downhill course.

BKK takes **cross-country** seriously, keeping its 40km of trails well maintained. BKK has the largest loop, running around its golf course, but St Oswald has snowsure trails at the top of the Nockalm.

Queues are not a problem, though we have no reports of how the new St Oswald link works at peak periods.

Mountain restaurants are generally attractive, without any being really special. Waldratte, at the gondola mid-station, has a good ice-bar for drink-only customers.

St Oswald is good for **children**. There is a fine ski kindergarten and the Farmhouse apartments have a free nursery.

STAYING THERE

Good quality is the norm in BKK's **hotels**. Ronacher is well-placed, luxurious and has excellent spa facilities. Eschenhof is similar. Gasthof Weisses Rössl is a good-value 3-star. The Farmhouse village at St Oswald is a high-standard **self-catering** complex.

There is no need to pay a lot for quality when **eating out**. The cheap and cheerful Zirkitzerhof is popular. The Farmhouse has its own restaurant, but Gasthof Schneeweiss has perhaps the best food in St Oswald.

Apart from a good video-disco-bar, complete with chat-up phones on the tables, this is a quiet resort, with little of the usual jolly Austrian **après-ski**.

Superb spa facilities, with indoor and outdoor thermal pools, fitness centres, whirlpools, saunas and so on, make this a great choice for a certain type of **non-skier**. However, there is little else to do than take good walks. Those with cars can visit Villach (36km away) for a shopping spree.

Badgastein 1000m

✔ Extensive, varied ski area

✔ Rare opportunity to ski steep woodland runs

✔ Long runs above mid-station and liberal use of snowmaking make the area relatively snowsure by Austrian low-altitude standards

✔ Many good mountain restaurants

✔ Plenty of non-skiing facilities

✔ Cosmopolitan

✘ Lack of good nursery slopes and easy runs to progress to

✘ Awkward layout on a steep hillside, which means tiring walks to go skiing or après-skiing

✘ Infrequent crowded buses between valley lift stations; village buses are also erratic

✘ Unusual village that grew up as a spa resort, lacking Alpine atmosphere and now suffering from local traffic

✘ Sophisticated après-ski will disappoint those expecting something lively and informal

✘ Tedious number of T-bars, some uncomfortably steep

Despite its large and varied ski area, Badgastein has not really taken off on the British market. Neilson even had to take the unusual step of cancelling their advertised accommodation there prior to the start of last season, due to lack of interest. Perhaps this is because its pretentiously baroque hotels, sophisticated spa ambience and steep slopes are not what people expect of an Austrian resort. Badgastein loses out to other major Austrian resorts – Saalbach, Kitzbühel, Söll and Schladming – in terms of informal après-ski, Alpine charm, easy skiing and friendly hotels. But it also fails to attract the fans of high-altitude, high-mileage skiing; in places like Les Arcs, La Plagne and Austria's own Ischgl, they get more altitude, and more mileage.

Doubtless there are skiers for whom Badgastein is the ideal compromise. For us, a more attractive bet is down the valley: Bad Hofgastein is even less well known in Britain, but it is a more attractive resort, has direct (although queue-prone) access to the best intermediate skiing, and is well placed for excursions even further down the valley to the charming rustic village and friendly skiing of Dorfgastein.

ORIENTATION

The spa resort of Badgastein sits at the head of eastern Austria's Gastein valley. From the railway station above the resort centre, a gondola rises into the main ski area, which spreads north down the west side of the valley to Bad Hofgastein (8km by road) – a resort which gets less international attention but is about as big. The separate ski area of Dorfgastein (8km further north) is linked to Grossarl in the next valley to the east. 9km up the valley from Badgastein, beyond Böckstein (where cars bound for Italy must be loaded on to trains), is a separate area, small but high, at Sportgastein. Rail excursions to **Zell am See** and **St Johann im Pongau** are easy, while car drivers can also visit snowsure **Obertauern** and **Kaprun**.

🏠 The resort

Badgastein is an old spa that had its heyday many years ago; it has spread widely, but still has a compact core. Its central buildings are a bizarre combination (smart, modern, hotel-shopping-casino complex, baroque town hall and concrete multi-storey car park) and it has a cramped horseshoe layout in what is virtually a gorge, complete with waterfall crashing beneath the main street. The thick surrounding woods lend a degree of charm, and the fact that the main road and railway bypass the centre helps; but it is not an easy resort to like the look of.

Skiers feel more at home in the area up around the railway station and main lift departure point, where much of the recent expansion of the resort has taken place.

Badgastein is a formal resort. People tend to be smartly dressed for hotel evening meals, and the general ambience of the village is sophisticated, quiet and relaxed.

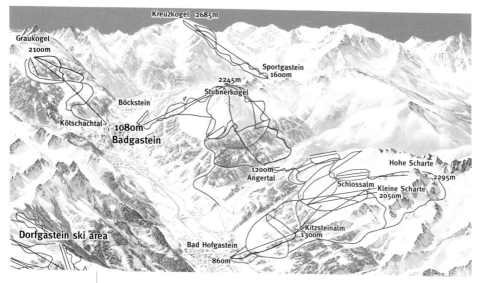

SKI FACTS

Altitude	840m-2685m
Lifts	49
Pistes	250km
Green/Blue	24%
Red	66%
Black	10%
Artificial snow	40km

SKI SCHOOL

94/95 prices in schillings

Badgastein
Manager Werner Pflaum
Classes 6 days
6hr: 10am-4pm, 1hr lunch; 3hrs: 1pm-4pm
6 full days: 1,650
Children's classes
Ages: up to 14
6 full days: 1,380
Private lessons
55 mins
450 for 55 mins; each additional person 120

Luigi
Manager Luigi Kravanja
Classes 6 days
5hr 15min: 10am-3.15 with 1hr lunch
6 full days: 1,350
Children's classes
Ages: 4 to 14
6 full days including lunch: 1,950
Private lessons
1hr or full-day
420 for 1hr; each additional person 100

 # The skiing

On the whole, this is an area that suits confident intermediates best; most of the skiing is graded red, and rightly so. Where there is a blue option, it is not always a very attractive one – and not always as easy as a timid intermediate might hope.

THE SKI AREA
Fragmented, but adds up to a lot
The main ski area is made up of two distinct sectors, above Badgastein and Bad Hofgastein respectively, linked mid-way between the resorts via the side-valley of Angertal.

From the upper part of Badgastein a gondola goes up to **Stubnerkogel**, from where you can ski back towards the resort or down to Angertal. This valley has lifts going up towards **Schlossalm** above Bad Hofgastein, from where a variety of pistes lead off in different directions. The runs back to Angertal are south-facing and low, but this section is well covered by artificial snowmakers.

The much smaller **Graukogel** area lies at the other side of Badgastein. This is a steep, straightforward mountain with just three lifts, which makes it ideal for 'yo-yo' skiing. Having a ski area here, set in broad swathes through the forest, is a great asset in bad weather.

High, wild **Sportgastein** has the best snow in the area, now served by a new eight-person gondola; but there are only a few pistes: red and blue variants of one long run down the narrow mountainside.

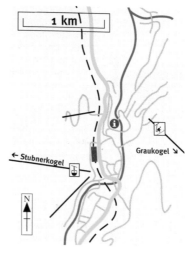

SNOW RELIABILITY
Good for a low-altitude resort
Although the area is essentially a typically Austrian low altitude one, there is a battery of snowmakers in crucial sections, and the higher sector of Sportgastein is an important fallback. This part of the Alps also has a good snow cover record in relation to its height, and there is a lot of skiing above mid-station height.

FOR ADVANCED SKIERS
Plenty of challenge for most
Although there are few super-tough runs in the area, these consistently steep mountainsides offer long, interesting pistes to challenge most advanced skiers. The Graukogel is the World Cup skiing area, and provides plenty of challenge on its upper slopes. The route between Stubnerkogel and Badgastein is steep,

LIFT PASSES

94/95 prices in schillings

Gastein Super Ski Pass

Covers all lifts in Gastein valley and Grossarl, and buses, trains and road tolls between the resorts.

Beginners Day- and points-tickets for baby-lifts.

Main pass
1-day pass 390
6-day pass 1,860
(low season 1,580 – 15% off)

Senior citizens
Over 65 male, 60 female: 6-day pass 1,580 (15% off)

Children
Under 14: 6-day pass 1,120 (40% off)
Under 6: free pass

Short-term passes
Single ascent on selected lifts, time card (2, 3 and 4 hours) and half-day passes available.

Alternative periods
5 or 10 days in one season.

Notes Discounts for students (under 26) and groups of over 20.

Alternative passes
Gastein Super Ski Pass only available for 3 days or more. Passes for shorter periods cover only Badgastein/Bad Hofgastein. Single ascent passes available for lifts in Dorfgastein and Sportgastein.

CHILDCARE

Both ski schools run ski kindergartens.

There is kindergarten at the Grüner Baum hotel, taking children aged 3 to 8, from 9.30 to 4pm. Skiing is available, with a special lift. A free shuttle bus is offered.

and often icy, with plenty of room for off-piste excursions on the open, top section. The direct route to Angertal is another tough run in this section.

Sportgastein is worth the trip, especially with the efficient new lift in place. There are off-piste possibilities on the front of the mountain, and a long off-piste trail off the back drops almost 1500m from Kreuzkogel to Heilstollen in the valley (on the bus route). Dorfgastein has some of the least demanding slopes in the area, but there is a fine black run down to the village.

FOR INTERMEDIATE SKIERS
Not for the leisurely cruiser
The area as a whole is uncomfortably challenging for early intermediates. But the Grossarl and Schlossalm sectors have less demanding pistes than other sectors, and the open bowl around the main cluster of restaurants at Schlossalm is reassuringly blue in gradient. Most intermediates will enjoy the network of red runs above Dorfgastein and Grossarl, as well as the whole Schlossalm sector.

Good intermediates will love the whole area. A particular delight is the beautiful 8km run, well away from the lifts, from Höhe Scharte down to Bad Hofgastein. The open north-facing slopes of Stubnerkogel down into Angertal are particularly good, in terms of both skiing interest and snow cover. The same can be said of the Graukogel runs. None of the skiing is boringly easy.

FOR BEGINNERS
Unsuitable slopes
Inadequate nursery slopes are dotted around. Only the good ski school makes this resort in any way suitable.

FOR CROSS-COUNTRY
Extensive, but low and fragmented
There is an impressive 90km of trails, but all are along the valley floor, making only the small loop at Sportgastein reasonably reliable for snow. Another drawback is the scattered nature of the loops. Bad Hofgastein is by far the best base for cross-country skiing, with long trails to Badbruck, just short of Badgastein itself.

QUEUES
Buses are the problem
In the past, Sportgastein has experienced queues when conditions are poor elsewhere, but this will presumably have been put right by the powerful new gondola opened last

season. Otherwise there are few problems outside the peak season in late February.

Morning queues for the Bad Hofgastein mid-station cable car are the worst in the area. Delays getting to the lifts are far more serious: the buses between villages are infrequent, and Badgastein's in-village transport (essential for some accommodation) is unreliable and erratic.

MOUNTAIN RESTAURANTS
One of the pleasures of this area
Numerous atmospheric, traditional huts are dotted around. Good value and good food are the norm. Badgastein's places are more expensive than those in the rest of the valley, but they are still cheap compared to most of the Alps.

Bad Hofgastein's smart Schlossalm has a large terrace, plus yodelling! The Aeroplanstadl on the 8km Höhe Scharte run, Hamburger Skiheim, at Schlossalm (with 'barbecue in the snow'), and Dorfgastein's Panoramastube are all jolly places, while the Wengeralm, also above Dorf, is a cosy, upmarket refuge with a good terrace. Two new restaurants were built last year at Sportgastein, as part of the new gondola construction.

SKI SCHOOL
English widely spoken
The two ski schools have good reputations. Most reporters have used the main Schi & Rennschule. Instructors are enthusiastic and English standards are generally good, especially if you get one of the Americans or Australians employed by the school! Optimal use of time and good division of abilities are other positive comments.

Class size seems to vary, which is not uncommon where English speakers make up only a small proportion of guests. It all depends on how many of the limited number of one's fellow Brits having tuition happen to be at your ability level when you are visiting. Group lesson prices are high for short courses – it's worth booking for the week. Schischule Luigi concentrates on guiding, touring, snowboarding and children.

FACILITIES FOR CHILDREN
Reasonable
Badgastein hardly seems an ideal resort for small children, but there are facilities for all-day care, of which the kindergarten at the Grüner Baum sounds the most inviting.

GETTING THERE

Air Salzburg, transfer 2hr. Linz or Munich, transfer 3½hr.

Rail Mainline station in resort.

PACKAGES

Club Europe, Crystal, Enterprise, Inghams, Made to Measure, Ski Miquel, Ski Partners, SkiBound

Bad Hofgastein
Austrian Holidays, Crystal, Enterprise, Inghams, Made to Measure

ACTIVITIES

Indoor Fitness centre (swimming, sauna, gym), thermal baths, squash, bridge, chess, tennis, bowling, indoor golf, darts, casino, museum, theatre, concerts
Outdoor Natural ice rinks (skating and curling), sleigh rides, horse-riding, ice climbing, toboggan runs, ski-bob, 35km cleared paths

TOURIST OFFICE

Postcode A-5640
Tel 010 43 (6434) 25310
Fax 253137

 # Staying there

Getting around Badgastein is not easy, so it is worth picking your location with care. For most skiing purposes, the best place to stay is in the upper part of town, close to the Stubnerkogel gondola station.

HOW TO GO
Packages limited to hotels
Although apartments make up nearly 15 per cent of the total beds available, British tour operators sell only hotel-based packages.
Chalets We don't know of any 'proper' chalets, but Ski Miquel's Tannenburg is something like a chalet-hotel. It offers good value for money – although wine is extra.
Hotels This is an upmarket spa resort, and it has lots of smart hotels with excellent spa facilities – almost as many 4-stars as 3-stars.
££££ **Elizabeth Park** Luxury hotel popular with British skiers looking for excellent facilities, style, comfort and formality. Unfortunately, poorly placed for skiing, but does run a courtesy bus.
££££ **Salzburger Hof** 4-star with excellent spa facilities, a longish walk from the village gondola.
££££ **Schillerhof** Reliable 4-star in good position, opposite Graukogel lift.
££££ **Wildbad** 4-star within reasonable walking distance of the main lift.
££££ **Grüner Baum** Splendidly secluded Relais & Châteaux place, tucked away in the Kötschachtal.
£££ **Mozart** Well placed for buses.
£££ **Alpenblick** Good value, less formal 3-star; well placed for skiing.
Self-catering We don't know of any apartments available through tour operators, but there are plenty available to those booking directly.

EATING OUT
Something for most tastes
There is a fair range of restaurants, including surprisingly fine Chinese and seafood places. The Bellevue Alm is one of the liveliest places to eat at, whilst the à la carte menus at the 3-star hotels Nussdorferhof and Mozart are good value.

APRES-SKI
Varied, but no oom-pah-pah
Despite its reputation for good, varied nightlife, Badgastein can disappoint in this department. Admittedly there are elegant tea rooms, numerous bars and discos, sophisticated dances, and casinos, but the general ambience is rather subdued.

This part of Austria has not imported the informal Tyrolean-style 'oom-pah-pah'; neither are there any lively bands. The tea-dance at the Bellevue Alm is the only real concession to Kitzbühel-style fun. The best tea-rooms are the Causerie, in the Elizabeth Park, Wiener, in the Salzburger Hof, the Weismayr and the Panorama. Eden's Bar and Manfreda's Bar are pleasant for a quiet drink. The Hexen Haüsl is a more informal little wooden schnapps bar.

Haggenblooms has live music and gets full of young Swedes out to have a good time. The Bunny Bar is more sophisticated than its name suggests. The various functions in the Grüner Baum are the most informal hotel entertainment, but the elegant Ritz and Felsen bars in the Satzburger Hof and the Elizabeth Park respectively are more typical of the scene later on. The Gatz and the Blockhaüsl are the main clubs. The casino gives you a generous amount of free chips, so those with will-power and/or luck can have a surprisingly inexpensive couple of hours there. Bowling and a casino trip are the only events likely to be organised by tour reps.

FOR NON-SKIERS
Great variety of things to do
Provided you don't mind the style of the place, Badgastein has a lot to offer non-skiers, whether active or not. The spa facilities are superb. 17 thermal radon springs originate in the town and are very well used – various baths, thermal mud, massage, underwater therapy, inhalation, 'drinking cures', and all sorts of regenerative, preventative and specific illness treatments are provided.

The Gastein Healing Gallery is a highlight – a train takes you down into an old gold-digging tunnel where you have the opportunity to lie on benches inhaling radon in steam-room-like heat and humidity for a couple of hours! The Rock Pool is a large indoor pool hewn out of the rock, heated naturally by hot springs.

Meeting up the mountain is no problem, although pedestrians can't easily get to the best mountain restaurants.

There are organised coach excursions to Kitzbühel, Salzburg and Goldegg Castle, and trains run to the towny ski resort of Zell am Zee and St Johann im Pongau.

Bad Hofgastein 860m

Bad Hofgastein is an attractive, sizeable old spa village set out spaciously in a broad section of the valley. It has an impressive old Gothic church, traditional style buildings, elegant hotels, narrow alleys and a babbling brook. Everything is kept in pristine order, in contrast to the peeling paint evident in Badgastein. Although rather sprawling, the village has a pleasant pedestrianised area which acts as a central focus. The relatively high proportion of part-time and non-skiers pottering about during the day, notably on or around the curling rinks in Kurpark, adds to the olde worlde winter holiday atmosphere. Several reporters have also emphasised how pretty the whole place looks in the evenings, under the soft glow of night lamps. The large public spa building, the Kurzentrum, is the only relative blot on the landscape, though it's not exactly an eyesore.

The best location to stay is in the pedestrian zone, which is relatively handy for most things including the slopes. Ski convenience is not generally a strong point, however. A high proportion of hotels are a long walk from the single village lift station, though many people simply catch the efficient inner-village ski-bus that stops close to most accommodation.

Buses to the other Gastein valley ski areas are far less frequent (half-hourly to Badgastein, hourly to Dorfgastein, twice daily to Sportgastein), and several reporters have found the timetable in Dorfgastein particularly difficult to decypher. Note the five o'clock bus home from there doesn't stop at the lift station as all other services do – you have to trek to the main road.

Bad Hofgastein's lift is a funicular that takes you up to a mid-station (1302m), above which most of the skiing takes place. Here, you have a choice between a cable-car and two-stage chair. The funicular ride is short, usually allowing the railway to get skiers up the mountain without undue delay, but long queues can form for the much lower capacity cable-car (up to 30 minutes in rush hour during peak season). At such times, the chair is an obvious alternative. There's a useful closed-circuit TV at the funicular base station which shows skiers the situation up at the cable-car.

Advanced skiers should head for the black runs on the Graukogel if they are looking for challenge.

Wonderfully long, mostly intermediate, runs head down from the 2300m top station back towards the village or across to the Angertal link with Badgastein.

Beginners are less well provided for, the limited nursery area being inconveniently sited over at Angertal, a longish bus ride from town.

Bad Hofgastein makes a fine base for cross-country skiers when its lengthy valley floor trails have snow.

Mountain restaurants are liberally scattered around the area, and are generally good (see Badgastein report for details). We have received complimentary reports of the two ski schools, both of whom have a fair number of English-speaking instructors. One is based at Angertal, and runs the village ski kindergarten over there, which can be very inconvenient for parents. Lack of many other English-speaking children to play with may be another drawback.

Bad Hofgastein is essentially a hotel resort. They tend to be large, good quality and many have their own fine spa facilities. Some are within easy walking distance of the funicular, a few others provide courtesy transport, and most of the remainder are close to a bus stop. A high proportion of the following places are available through tour operators.

The Palace Gastein is a luxurious 4-star with superb leisure facilities, including pool and thermal baths. The elegant Germania is similarly comfortable. The high quality Norica is atypically modern in design, but is well positioned in the pedestrian zone. The Alpina is another well located 4-star, five minutes from the slopes. The Astoria is well appointed but quite poorly positioned and doesn't supply courtesy transport. The old 3-star Alte must be one of Austria's best equipped 'Posts' but has retained its rustic charm. The Kaiser Franz also looks a real little charmer but has the distinction of being the only hotel in Bad Hofgastein about which we have received negative reporter comments. The Kürpark is much more popular, for its good food, service and location in the pedestrian zone. Gasthof Reiter is poorly positioned but provides a useful inexpensive, informal B&B.

Restaurants provide, between them, for most tastes and pockets, from cordon bleu to pizza, from Austrian to Chinese. Many of the hotels have good formal restaurants. Standards are pretty much in keeping with their respective gradings.

The Moserkeller is a nice, intimate specialist restaurant. The Pyrkerhöhe, on the slopes just above town, is worth an evening excursion. Pension Maier is one of the better informal places. The Tele Pizza Bar cooks outside on an open fire at lunchtimes in fine weather. It's also good inside in the evenings. One reporter rated it as having the best service he'd ever had in a ski resort. The Tschickeria and Da Dimo are good pizza and pasta places.

Après-ski is very quiet by Austrian standards. Some reporters have been disappointed; others have loved the peacefulness. There are, however, a few animated places around, but you have to find them. Adabei's is the best bar for youngsters, having loud pop music. Next door is Georgie's Club, which along with Sherwood's disco gets packed late. Francky's bar and the Sonia Pub are the only other places that can become lively at times.

Most of Bad Hofgastein's clientele prefer something more sedate. Café Weitmoser is a historic little castle popular for its cakes after skiing. The outdoor bar of the Ostereicher Hof is a pleasant spot to catch the last rays of the sun. Another civilised, atmospheric tea-time rendezvous is the Tennishalle. Later, the West End bar is a cosy place for a quiet drink in an alcove. The Glocknerkeller in Pension Zum Toni and the Rondo bar in Hotel Käruten have live music in a low-key ambience.

The Badgastein casino provides free taxis to and from town. A bowling evening is organised by tour reps. The Kurzentrum is the centrepiece of the things to do when not skiing, being arguably an even more impressive spa facility than that of Badgastein. It has an impressive thermal pool, and an Institute of Rheumatology, Rehabilitation and Sports Medicine. You name it this place does it – electrotherapeutics, curative massages, hydrotherapy, special baths, mud and so on. Other off-slope amenities include artificial and natural ice skating, indoor tennis, squash, sleigh rides. lovely walks and riding.

Dorfgastein 830m

Those who wish to ski the Gastein valley but would prefer not to stay in large, commercialised villages should consider Dorfgastein. It's a simple, unspoilt, typically Austrian little place surrounding a church square. Prices are lower, and the atmosphere more friendly and informal – something of a contrast to its rather cold setting sheltered from the sun.

The ski area is more suitable for inexperienced skiers than the steep slopes above Badgastein. Runs are long and varied, amid lovely scenery, and the area as a whole (shared with Grossarl, in the next valley) is extensive, making up a third of the whole valley's 250km of piste. Unfortunately the low-altitude nursery slopes can be cold and icy. Badhofgastein's funicular is 15 minutes away by bus (infrequent and sometimes crowded). Those not interested in venturing that far can buy a local pass costing 75 per cent of the Gastein Valley lift pass price.

For some, this rustic backwater may be too lacking in amenities. There are a few shops or après-ski haunts, a five- or ten-minute walk or short bus-ride from the slopes. Café St Ruperb is a nice village pizzeria. The Kirchenwirt and Romerhof are comfortable hotels. Pension Schihause is cheaper, does good food, and is next to the slopes. There is an outdoor heated pool with sauna-solarium, a bowling alley and a ski kindergarten.

Ellmau 800m

HOW IT RATES

The skiing

Snow	*
Extent	****
Advanced	*
Intermediates	****
Beginners	****
Convenience	***
Queues	****
Restaurants	**

The rest

Scenery	***
Resort charm	***
Not skiing	***

✔ Large, pretty, easy ski area

✔ Cheap by Austrian standards

✔ Quiet, charming family resort – more appealing than neighbouring Söll

✔ Excellent nursery slopes (but see minus points)

✘ Very poor snow record, yet limited snowmaking set-up

✘ Poor lift and bus connections to remainder of Ski-Welt ski area

✘ Queues can be a severe problem when snow is in short supply

✘ Lack of nightlife other than rep-organised events

✘ Little difficult skiing

✘ Nursery slopes vulnerable when snow is in short supply

Like nearby Söll, Ellmau gives access to the large, unthreatening ski area now known as Ski-Welt (though we still think of it as the Grossraum). From some points of view it is attractive. Ellmau is a pleasantly quiet alternative to Söll, but offers more holiday amenities than other neighbours such as Scheffau. Its nursery slopes and its main lifts are both more convenient than most in this area. But there are snags.

We have received quite a few holidaymakers' reports on Ellmau, and we have yet to receive one that does not mention the problem of a lack of snow, at least on the lower half of the ski area. To make matters worse, the links between Ellmau and the rest of the Ski-Welt ski area are poor, particularly when the snow-cover is less than perfect. And the alternative means of access to more snowsure slopes – the ski-bus service – is also exasperatingly feeble.

Ellmau is a likeable village; whether it makes a sensible base for a ski holiday booked well in advance is another matter. Skiers looking for a quiet, pretty Austrian village with a fair amount of reliable, hassle-free skiing have safer options available.

ORIENTATION

Ellmau sits at the north-eastern corner of the Ski-Welt ski area, on the road between St Johann and Wörgl. A funicular railway goes up from a large car-park on the edge of the village into the skiing. The Ski-Welt is ringed by valleys and roads, with lifts from several other resorts. **Going** and **Scheffau** (covered by this chapter) are nearby; **Söll**, **Itter**, **Hopfgarten** and **Brixen** are spread around the high-point of Hohe Salve. **Westendorf** is covered by the Ski-Welt pass, although its ski area is separate. **Kitzbühel**, **Waidring**, **Fieberbrunn** and **St Johann** are all within easy range for day-trips.

 ## The resort

Although a sizeable resort, and becoming more commercialised each year, Ellmau remains a quiet, pretty place, complete with traditional chalet-style buildings, welcoming bars and shops, and a picturesque old church. Unfortunately its Alpine charm is spoilt a little by the main road that runs along the edge of the village, and by its frequent lack of snow on the rooftops and streets.

By Austrian standards the nightlife is rather tame, and although non-skiing diversions have recently been improved, the village doesn't really amount to much more than a pleasant dormitory for skiers.

SKI FACTS

Altitude	810m-1555m
Lifts	90
Pistes	250km
Green/Blue	37%
Red	53%
Black	10%
Artificial snow	30km

The skiing

The Ski-Welt is reputedly the largest ski circus in Austria, but most of the time it hardly compares in size, and never in quality, to St Anton, Ischgl, Saalbach and the Gastein valley. Most of its runs are short, and not difficult.

THE SKI AREA

Slow links to the rest of Ski-Welt

At least Ellmau is close to the best skiing in the area, above Scheffau. The village funicular (served by a free shuttle bus which tours the village) takes skiers up to Hartkaiser, from where a fine long run leads down to Blaiken (Scheffau's lift station). A choice of gondola or two-stage chair then goes back up to Brandstadl, the start point for three varied and long alternatives back to Blaiken.

Immediately beyond Brandstadl, the skiing becomes rather bitty; an array of short runs and lifts link Brandstadl to Zinsberg. From there, excellent, long, south-facing pistes lead down to Brixen. A short bus-ride takes skiers from Brixen to Westendorf's pleasant separate ski area. Part way down to Brixen you can head towards Söll – either by the steep Hohe Salve or by circumnavigating the latter using a series of easy runs. Hohe Salve also provides access to a long, west-facing run down to Hopfgarten. If you want to include the fine long run down to Itter in your tour, it's best to do so before getting to Hochsöll.

LIFT PASSES

94/95 prices in schillings

Ski-Welt Wilder Kaiser-Brixental
Covers all lifts in the Wilder Kaiser-Brixental area, from Going to Westendorf, and the ski-bus.
Beginners Points cards for lifts available (25 point 70). Small drags are 5 points.
Main pass
1-day pass 330
6-day pass 1560
Children
Under 15: 6-day pass 890 (43% off)
Under 5: free pass
Short-term passes
Single ascent, half-day passes up to noon and from 11am, noon and 2pm to the end of the day.
Alternative periods
Passes available for 5 skiing days in 7, 7 days in 10 and 10 days in 14.
Notes Discounts for physically disabled skiers and children with a Kinderkarten (child's card) of 70%.
Alternative passes
Ellmau ski pass covers 13 local lifts (adult 6-day 1,335).

CHILDCARE

The lst Ski School has a playroom open from 9am. The Hartkaiser school opened a ski nursery last season. The Top-Ski school welcomes children and provides lunchtime care on request. There is also a village non-skiing kindergarten

Returning to Ellmau is a time-consuming business. Getting back to Blaiken via the Süd drag is quicker, but the buses from there to Ellmau are irregular.

Ellmau and Going share a pleasant little section of skiing on Astberg, slightly apart from the rest of the area and well suited to the unadventurous or for families. One piste leads to the funicular for access to the rest of Ski-Welt. The main Astberg chair is rather inconveniently positioned, midway between Ellmau and Going.

SNOW RELIABILITY
Very poor
Ellmau has a poor snow record. The north-facing Eiberg area above Scheffau holds its snow well, but is small and gets terribly congested when snow is in short supply. Ellmau skiers are better off getting a bus to St Johann at such times; changing at St Johann for Waidring's high Steinplatte area is even better.

FOR ADVANCED SKIERS
Not suitable
There's a steep plunge off the Hohe Salve summit, and a little mogul field between Brandstadl and Neualm, but the area isn't really suitable except for those prepared to seek out worthwhile off-piste opportunities.

FOR INTERMEDIATE SKIERS
For the unadventurous or families
Unfortunately most of the best runs are among the least snowsure. Good intermediates will enjoy the runs to Brixen and those on Hohe Salve. Skiers of mixed ability will enjoy a good variety of pistes above Blaiken, while moderate skiers have fine runs down to all the valley villages, including long ones alongside the Ellmau funicular. Ellmau is particularly well placed for timid skiers, with the quiet, easy slopes of Astberg on hand.

FOR BEGINNERS
One of the best Ski-Welt villages
Ellmau has an array of good nursery slopes – snow permitting. East of the village is a vast area of gentle slopes that spreads across to Going. The area next to the funicular station, west of the village, is smaller but still very satisfactory, with the Astberg chair opening up a more snowsure plateau at altitude. The Brandstadl-Hartkaiser area has another section of short, easy runs. Near-beginners looking for a rest from drag-lifts have a nice long piste running the length of the funicular.

FOR CROSS-COUNTRY
Plenty of valley trails
When there is snow, there are long and quite challenging trails along the valley towards St Johann and Kirchdorf, and an easier one to Scheffau and via Söll to Itter. But trails at altitude are lacking.

QUEUES
Few local problems
Again, snow-cover dominates the analysis. With good snow, the worst areas are quite distant from Ellmau. Hochsöll can be a bottleneck – particularly the Hohe Salve chair. The Blaiken gondola gets oversubscribed at weekends and when snow is poor elsewhere. At such times, everyone wants to head for Eiberg's reliable snow, and the higher lifts on and around Eiberg suffer bad queues.

The poor, valley bus service and the roundabout links between Hartkaiser and the rest of the Ski-Welt are more of a problem, causing greater delays in practice than any lift queues.

MOUNTAIN RESTAURANTS
Stick to the little huts
'Little huts good, big huts bad' is a simple but fairly accurate description. The smaller places are fairly consistent in providing wholesome, good-value food in pleasant surroundings, although perhaps only the one at Neualm deserves special mention. The larger self-service restaurants are rather functional and suffer queues. Going is a good spot for a quiet lunch.

SKI SCHOOL
Dual language can waste time
The school has a good reputation except that classes tend to be very large. The high number of Dutch in the village means dual language tuition is not uncommon, and this can waste a great deal of class time. As well as the main ski school there is a mountaineering school that organises daily tours in the Wilder Kaiser group as well as the Kitzbühel mountains.

FACILITIES FOR CHILDREN
Fine in theory
Ellmau is an attractive resort for families, and the kindergarten facilities seem satisfactory. We have no recent reports on how they work in practice.

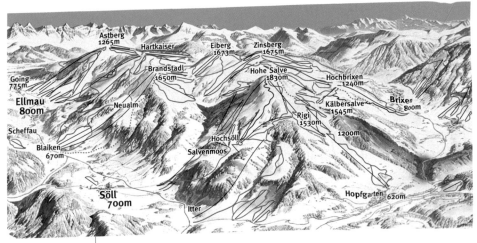

SKI SCHOOL

94/95 prices in schillings

1st Ellmau
Manager Friedl Fuchs
Classes 6 days
4hr: 10am-noon and 2pm-4pm
6 full days: 1280
Children's classes
Ages: 4 to 14
6 full days including lunch: 1830
Private lessons
Hourly or full day (4hr)
450 for 1hr; each additional person 200

Ellmau-Hartkaiser
Manager Dietmar Maier
Classes 6 days
4hr: 10am-noon and 2pm-4pm
6 full days (93/94): 1160
Children's classes
Ages: 4 to 14
6 full days including lunch (93/94): 1650
Private lessons Hourly or full day
450 for 1hr; each additional person 170 (93/94)

Top
Manager Hans Peter Haider
Classes 6 days
4hr: 10am-noon and 2pm-4pm

GETTING THERE

Air Salzburg, transfer 2hr.

Rail Wörgl (18km), St Johann in Tirol (14km), Kufstein (15km), bus to resort.

 # Staying there

Ellmau has a compact centre, but its accommodation is scattered. Hotel position is quite important: keen, experienced skiers will want to be close to the funicular. Après-skiers will want to be more central, close to the village facilities and up to 20 minutes' walk or a bus-ride from the railway. Near-beginners might want to be near the Astberg chair, half-way between Ellmau and Going. The main nursery slopes are also at the Going end of the village, beside the ski school, but there are some on the road to the funicular.

HOW TO GO
Lots of chalet-style hotels
Ellmau is essentially a hotel and pension resort, though there are plenty of private apartments that can be booked locally.
Chalets Crystal's converted little pension is pleasant, and convenient for intermediates but a trek from the village centre and nursery slopes.
Hotels Ellmau is typical of Austrian resorts that have expanded since World War II, with many comfortable, modern, chalet-style hotels, largely indistinguishable at first sight.
£££££ Bär Elegant but relaxed Relais & Châteaux chalet that seems almost out of place in Ellmau – twice the price of any other hotel.
£££ Hochfilzer Central, well equipped and described by a reporter as 'the best encountered in 22 years'.
£££ Christoph Large, comfortable, multi-facility place in secluded position on the outskirts – quite handy for the funicular.
£££ Sporthotel Similar in style to the Christoph, but opposite the ski school and main nursery slopes.

£££ Alte Post Pleasant and central, though not self-evidently 'alte'.
££ Pension Claudia Good bedrooms, next to the ski school.
£ Gasthof Au Cheapest place in town, five minutes from the funicular and ten from the centre.
Self-catering There is a wide variety. Basically you get what you pay for. The Bauer Annemarie is under the same management as the hotel Christoph and equally well placed for lifts. Conveniently close to the nursery slopes is Feyersinger Martin.

WHERE TO EAT
Hotel-dominated
Most people are on half-board so there are not many restaurants. The hotel Hochfilzer has a reputation for good food and is open to non-residents. The Lobewein and Buchingerstüberl are worth a visit. Café Bettina, midway between the funicular and town, is good for afternoon coffee and cakes.

APRES-SKI
Limited but varied programme
The rep-organised events include bowling, sleigh rides, Tyrolean folklore and inner-tubing, but there is little else. The Memory bar is lively, but not for those who hate passive smoking.

FOR NON-SKIERS
Excellent new sports centre
The Kaiserbad leisure centre, opened last winter, has made Ellmau much more appealing for active non-skiers. There are many excursions available, including Innsbruck, Salzburg, Rattenburg, Vitipeno or even Venice (six hours each way). St Johann in Tirol is a nice little town only a few miles away by bus. Other facilities are very limited. Valley walks are spoilt by the busy main road.

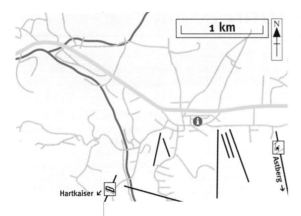

1 km

Hartkaiser

Astberg →

ACTIVITIES

Indoor Swimming pool, sauna, solarium, tennis, squash, bowling, golf, billiards, ski museum, theatre
Outdoor Winter hiking, natural ice rink, curling, toboggan run, sleigh rides, cleared walking paths, para-gliding, hang-gliding

PACKAGES

Airtours, Crystal, Inghams, Neilson, STS, Thomson
Scheffau Austrian Holidays, Crystal, Enterprise, Thomson

TOURIST OFFICE

Postcode A-6352
Tel 010 43 (5358) 2301
Fax 3443

Scheffau 745m

Scheffau is one of the most attractive of the Grossraum villages: a rustic little place complete with pretty white church, it is spacious yet not sprawling, and has a definite centre. It is tucked away a kilometre off the busy main Wörgl road, which increases the charm factor at the cost of ski convenience (the Grossraum lifts are at Blaiken, on the opposite side of the main road). The nursery slopes are in the village, however, and this makes Scheffau a poor choice for mixed-ability parties. When snow conditions are very good it is possible to ski down to the main road from the village. Ski convenience freaks have the option of staying in Blaiken, where there are several hotels.

A gondola and parallel two-stage chair give rapid and generally queue-free access directly to the Grossraum's best (and most central and snowsure) section of pistes. This makes Scheffau (or more accurately Blaiken) arguably the best place to stay for skiers who want to ski every run in Austria's largest ski area.

The pistes above Blaiken are some of the longest and steepest in the Grossraum, while nearby Eiberg is the place to go when snow is poor.

Links from Ellmau and Söll are awkward (or impossible) when snow is poor, which is another attraction of being based in Scheffau or Blaiken.

The village nursery slope is adequate when snow-cover allows it to operate. Higher skiing suitable for novices is an inconvenient and expensive distance away up the main mountain, though

there are plenty of options for improving beginners.

Given full snow-cover there are few queuing problems, but delays can be long when poor conditions elsewhere force Söll, Hopfgarten and Brixen skiers into the Scheffau section. At such times the two-stage valley chair can be a useful alternative to the oversubscribed gondola.

The ski school is quite well regarded by intermediates, but beginner class sizes can be far too big (around 15).

Hotels dominate the accommodation scene. The modern Alpin Tirol is one of the best, and has the only pool in town. Gasthof Weberbauer is a lovely, olde-worlde place at the centre of the village, and the Waldrand, of a similar standard, is popular. The Wilder Kaiser is the best hotel at Blaiken. Nearby are the good value gasthofs Waldhof (right next to the gondola), Aloisia and Blaiken.

There is a distinct lack of village restaurants, and those staying in B&B places are advised to book tables well in advance.

Scheffau après-ski is unlikely to draw Blaiken residents up the hill. Pub Royal is the only bar with much animation, though the Kaiseralm disco livens up at weekends. The usual rep-organised events such as bowling and tobogganing are available.

Walking apart, there is little for non-skiers to do. Tour operators organise excursions to Innsbruck and Salzburg.

Scheffau is a good family choice: both the ski kindergarten and non-ski nursery have good reputations.

Going 775m

Going is a tiny, attractively rustic village, well placed for the limited but quiet slopes of the Astberg and for the vast area of nursery slopes between here and Ellmau. Prices are low by Austrian standards, but it's not an ideal place for skiing the whole of the Ski-Welt on the cheap: the bus service to Ellmau is poor, and the skiing link depends on resort-level snow which is not reliable.

Going is ideal for families looking for a quiet time, particularly if they have a car for transport to Scheffau or St Johann when the Astberg's low runs lack snow.

Fieberbrunn 800m

SKI FACTS

Altitude	800m-1870m
Lifts	25
Pistes	50km
Green/Blue	34%
Red	50%
Black	16%
Artificial snow	7km

PACKAGES

Club Europe

TOURIST OFFICE

Postcode A-6391
Tel 010 43 (5354)
6304
Fax 2606

Beginners could do worse than try Fieberbrunn, with its good nursery slopes, pretty tree-lined skiing and jolly Tyrolean atmosphere. But any decent intermediate skier will soon tire of its limited and unexciting skiing.

THE RESORT

Fieberbrunn is a non-commercialised, atmospheric resort that is very attractive, despite the fact that it sprawls along the valley road for 2km. It has all the classic 'Tyrolean charm' elements: wooden chalets, pretty church, cosy little bars and coffee shops, sleighs, tea dances and friendly locals. Much of the village is also pleasantly set back from the road and railway, allowing peace interrupted only by church bells! Light sleepers can escape these by staying in one of two large hotels out near the main lift-station, served by a bus (regular but sometimes overcrowded) from the village. Beginners should stay in the centre, however, near the nursery slopes. The resort is very popular with the Dutch but has relatively few British visitors these days.

THE SKIING

The **ski area**, with its 34km of piste (50km including neighbouring St Jakob), is best suited to beginners and leisurely intermediates who like very pretty skiing. The tree-lined runs are attractive but don't offer much variety. Most of the skiing is on north-facing slopes which reach 1870m.

Fieberbrunn is in a snow pocket, which means better **snow-cover** than usual at this altitude. But its above-average snowfall record has led the village to rest on its laurels: there are few snowmakers. New for 1994, however, were snow-guns on the village nursery slopes. Nearby Waidring's Steinplatte (on the same lift pass) provides particularly snow-reliable skiing. There are few lift queues normally.

Fieberbrunn holds little attraction for **advanced skiers**, or indeed for good **intermediates**. Its prettiest runs are the easy Doischberg reds, which would be blue in many resorts. The Streuböden runs to the village are pleasant cruising territory, while the Reckmoos chair accesses steeper, open skiing. Some of the most popular runs can get very crowded at weekends. Guided off-piste excursions, including some towards Kitzbühel, are popular.

Beginners have broad nursery slopes conveniently close to the village centre. Graduation to the long, gentle Streuböden runs is comfortable.

Cross-country skiers have 40km of good trails.

Weekday **queues** are rare outside the peak morning ski school rush for the Streuböden lifts. But when the rest of the Tyrol, especially Kitzbühel and Söll, is short of snow, Fieberbrunn is often invaded by large numbers of skiers. Sunny weekends are also busy, though overcrowded pistes are a greater problem than queues.

Fieberbrunn's **mountain restaurants** are a little disappointing, though there are a couple of good ones at the Streuböden mid-station and at Reiteralm.

The **ski school's** reputation is high, though classes can be large.

Children's facilities include a ski kindergarten which takes children from the age of 4. There is no longer a non-ski kindergarten, but baby-sitting is available.

STAYING THERE

Fieberbrunn is essentially a hotel resort. The 4-star Fontana (very expensive) and 3-star Lindauhof (half the price) are the only hotels near the main slopes. On the other side of town, near the railway station, is Fieberbrunn's other top-quality hotel, Schloss Rosenegg, with a swimming pool complex. More central, cheaper places include the 3-star Metzgerwirt and Grosslehen and pensions Pirker and Mariandl.

Restaurants are mainly hotel-based. The candlelit Weinstubli in the Rosenegg is good for a splurge. Hotel Alte Post has a particularly pleasant restaurant. La Pampa is an excellent specialist Mexican establishment.

Après-ski is livelier at 4pm than after dinner. The Enzianhütte, Lindauhof and Siglu snow bar at the foot of the slopes are atmospheric; the first two have good tea dances. Later, the expensive Londoner Pub is popular but overloud – conversation is impossible. Riverhouse is classier, with quieter music and live shows.

For **non-skiers**, there are cleared walks, and the train station opens up excursion possibilities to Salzburg, Innsbruck and Kitzbühel.

Galtür 1585m

HOW IT RATES

The skiing

Snow	****
Extent	*
Advanced	**
Intermediates	***
Beginners	****
Convenience	***
Queues	****
Restaurants	**

The rest

Scenery	***
Resort charm	***
Not skiing	**

SKI FACTS

Altitude	1635m-2465m
Lifts	12
Pistes	40km
Green/Blue	20%
Red	65%
Black	15%
Artificial snow	3km

PACKAGES

Austrian Travel Service, Crystal, Made to Measure

TOURIST OFFICE

Postcode A-6563
Tel 010 43 (5443) 521
Fax 52176

Galtür stands in sharp contrast to its brash neighbour, Ischgl. It is a good base for a quiet, relaxing family holiday, with ideal and uncrowded intermediate pistes among splendid high-mountain scenery. If you want more extensive or challenging skiing, Ischgl is only a short bus-ride away.

THE RESORT

Galtür is a charming, peaceful, traditional village clustered around a pretty little church, amid impressive mountain scenery at the head of the Paznaun valley, beyond Ischgl. The valley is wider and sunnier here than at Ischgl. The local slopes are a short bus-ride away at Wirl, where there are also a couple of hotels. The more extensive skiing of Ischgl is a 20-minute bus-journey away and is covered by the lift pass.

THE SKIING

A high-speed quad whisks skiers into the heart of the **ski area**, opening up a spacious section of long runs towards a large lake. The scenery is impressive and all the steeper descents have easier variants. The pistes are wonderfully uncrowded, but there is a high proportion of drag-lifts.

The **snow reliability** is usually good, but there's not much snowmaking, so the lower pistes can suffer from thin cover at times.

There is nothing very challenging for **advanced skiers**: many runs are overgraded. The black descending the length of the Breitspitz chair to the lake is perhaps the most fun. There is also wonderful ski-touring from Galtür – guides can be arranged for both day and overnight tours. Otherwise a trip to Ischgl is recommended.

The black runs are ideal for good **intermediates**. Average skiers will be able to ski over most of the mountain, with the lake seeing the finish of some of the best runs. Less adventurous skiers will enjoy the overgraded runs, and the meandering blue down to the Wirl chair.

There are fine nursery slopes at Galtür itself and at Wirl, and though the piste map shows the area to be short of blue runs, there are in fact plenty of 'graduation' pistes for improving **beginners**. Galtür would be an excellent choice for a quiet family holiday with young children learning to ski and mum and dad not looking for anything too challenging.

Galtür has 60km of excellent **cross-country** trails, many of them at high altitude (ending at over 2000m).

Queues are very rare. Remarkably, few Ischgl visitors come to Galtür – no matter how bad the queues there.

The solitary **mountain restaurant** is adequate, but many prefer to ski down to the hotel Almhof at Wirl for lunch.

The **ski school** has a very high reputation, particularly for friendliness and small classes.

There is a non-ski nursery and ski kindergarten at Wirl, both taking **children** from 3 years old. Although lack of English-speaking tuition and supervision may be a problem, facilities are good and ski classes are fun. Lunchtime supervision of older children in ski school is also available.

STAYING THERE

Though small, Galtür has plenty of accommodation – around 3,500 beds. Most brochures only list top-of-the-range hotels, but there is cheaper accommodation. Position is not important within the compact village, but families may prefer Wirl.

The Almhof is a comfortable 4-star **hotel** at Wirl, with pool, sauna and jacuzzi. The Ballunspitz is a good-value 3-star on the edge of Galtür (you can pole home from Wirl). The cheapest place close to lifts is the Pension Gorfenhof. Good central hotels range from the 4-star Post to the Pension Cultura.

Self-catering accommodation is available; the Alp Aren apartments are good value and Gasthof Alpkogel has large apartments for groups.

Restaurants are mostly hotel-based. The Post, Rössle and Alpenhotel Tirol all have good food. Cheaper places for eating out are the Alpkogel and the Landle.

Nightlife is quiet and there is no evening bus service to the more energetic **après-ski** of Ischgl . The Wirlerhof (tea dancing) and Almhof are jolly between 4pm and 6pm. After dinner, the Tanz Café, Leo's Keller and the Igloo bar are the most animated nightspots (though not throbbing). The Post disco is very expensive.

Galtür has a superb sports centre with pool, tennis and squash. There is a natural ice rink, but otherwise off-slope facilities are limited. Attractive walks are in short supply, and the mountain restaurant is inaccessible to **non-skiers**.

Hintertux 1500m

Hintertux has one of the best glacier skiing areas in the world. It's popular with national ski teams for summer training. In winter, it provides guaranteed good snow even when the resorts of the nearby Zillertal are suffering badly.

HOW IT RATES

The skiing

Snow	*****
Extent	**
Advanced	***
Intermediates	***
Beginners	*
Convenience	**
Queues	***
Restaurants	**

The rest

Scenery	***
Resort charm	***
Not skiing	*

SKI FACTS

Altitude	1500m-3250m
Lifts	20
Pistes	86km
Green/Blue	35%
Red	55%
Black	10%
Artificial snow	none

THE RESORT

Hintertux is a tiny village set in a bleak position at the dead-end of the Tux valley. Surrounded by steep mountains on all sides except to the north, the village is in shade for much of the day in mid-winter. It consists of little other than a small collection of hotels and guest-houses. Its lifts lie a 15-minute walk away, across an enormous car park which gets filled with day-visitors' cars and coaches, especially when snow is poor in lower ski areas. There are more hotels near the lifts. The nearest bank, doctor and chemist are in Lanersbach, 5km down the valley (see separate chapter). Between the two villages are the hamlets of Madseit and Juns.

THE SKIING

Hintertux has a fair-sized **ski area**, with surprisingly challenging skiing for a glacier. The main chain of lifts rises in four stages up the eastern side of the north-facing glacier. A choice of gondola and chair go up to Sommerbergalm (2100m), then to Tuxer-Ferner (2660m); then it's fiercely cold chairs only to 3050m and finally to Gefrorene Wand ('frozen wall') at 3250m. There are links across to another 1000m-vertical chain of lifts below Grosser Kaserer on the west side of the glacier, and behind Gefrorene Wand is the area's one sunny piste, served by a chair. Back at Sommerbergalm is a small area of skiing below Tuxer Joch (2310m), start of an excellent off-piste run down a secluded valley to Hintertux.

The glacier area is of course snowsure, and the remaining skiing is high and north-facing, making for reliable **snow-cover**.

There is more to amuse **advanced skiers** here than on any other glacier, with runs of justifiably black grading on the west side, and skiing beneath glacier level that is consistently steep.

The whole area is particularly suitable for good or aggressive **intermediates**. The long runs down from Gefrorene and Kaserer are tests, while the off-piste route from Tuxer Joch to the valley is not difficult apart from the unnerving initial traverse. Moderate skiers love the glacier, and there is a pleasant tree-lined run to the valley from Sommerbergalm.

Novices have to take the bus to the nursery slopes at Madseit or Juns. There are a couple of fine near-**beginner** runs at the top of the glacier, but you need a full lift pass.

There are **cross-country** trails between Madseit and Lanersbach.

There are few **queues** until Hintertux is invaded by skiers from other, lower resorts, when there can be long queues at the bottom station and for some lifts up the mountain.

Queues for the inadequate glacier-area **mountain restaurants** can be even worse. The one at Tuxer Joch is less crowded, but still hardly a gourmet experience. Gletscherhütte, at the top of the mountain, has great views but is very expensive.

The **ski school** has a good reputation and English is surprisingly widely spoken. There's a **children's** section and Lanersbach has a nursery.

STAYING THERE

Most of the **hotels** are large and expensive and have spa facilities. But there's also a selection of pensions. For maximum ski-convenience, stay next to the lifts, not in the village. The 4-star Neuhintertux and 3-star Vierjahreszeiten are both close to lifts. Pensions Jörglerhof, Kössler and Willeiter are right in the heart of the village. There are no cheap places close to the lifts.

There are plenty of **apartments**. The 3-star Nennerhof is the highest quality and best-placed, in the centre.

Restaurants are hotel-based, so expensive. The Berghof has a very high reputation. The Vierjahreszeiten is pleasant and informal.

Lanersbach and Mayrhofen are within easy reach by car. Otherwise there is very little **nightlife**. The hotel Rindererhof, at the foot of the slopes, has a lively tea dance.

The spa facilities are excellent, but some walks are relatively uninspiring. In general, **non-skiers** would be much better off in Mayrhofen.

Skiing Hintertux from **Lanersbach** has its advantages, particularly for ski-drivers, who can reach the glacier lift station in 10 minutes and be better placed for ski excursions along the Ziller valley. Lanersbach has a wider variety of amenities – see Mayrhofen chapter on page 85.

PACKAGES

Juns Alpine Tours

TOURIST OFFICE

Postcode A-6293
Tel 010 43 (5287) 606
Fax 5287 624

Innsbruck 575m

British skiers are not inclined to think of Innsbruck as a ski resort. It is a sizeable city and a major Alpine crossroads. In summer it is an attractive tourist destination, with plenty of historic and cultural (as well as scenic) interest. But a ski resort? Well, yes. It is at the heart of a little group of ski areas that share a common lift pass, and has some skiing of its own right on the edge of the city. You have to travel by car or bus to most of the ski areas, but that is a bearable hardship if you like the idea of a civilised urban base.

INNSBRUCK

The Inn valley is a broad, flat-bottomed trench hereabouts, but Innsbruck manages to fill it from side to side. It is a sizeable city, with an excellent range of winter sports facilities (it has twice hosted the Winter Olympic Games) as well as a captivating medieval core. It has smart modern shopping areas, museums, concert halls, theatres and other attractions that you might seek out on a summer holiday but don't dream of when going skiing. It has 1200m vertical of skiing on the south-facing slopes of the Hungerburg, reached by cable-car from the suburbs; but for visitors, if not for residents, skiing at Innsbruck usually means skiing on the other side of the trench, to east or west of the side-valley that reaches southwards towards the Brenner pass and Italy. The Brenner road is a major pipeline for goods and tourists between Germany and Italy, and opens up the possibility of interesting excursions (skiing and non-skiing) to the Dolomites and beyond.

The Innsbruck ski pass covers the lifts in all the resorts described here, which are served by a free ski-bus. If there is insufficient snow for skiing locally, free buses run to the Stubai glacier beyond Neustift (described in a separate chapter, page 89).

IGLS

Igls (900m) is a resort in its own right, although a small one. It is a leisurely, even sedate little place that barely seems part of the modern skiing world; frankly, we find it difficult to imagine spending a whole week here – but people do.

The skiing consists essentially of a single run with slight variations on- and off-piste. It is an excellent, long, testing red of about 1300m vertical, which formed the men's Olympic downhill course in 1976 when Franz Klammer took ski racing (and the gold medal) by storm.

There is a ski school with all-day ski kindergarten, and a non-skiing kindergarten.

AXAMER LIZUM

Axamer Lizum (1600m) could scarcely offer a sharper contrast to Igls. It offers a much more varied and interesting ski area, and is the standard local venue for weekend skiers – hence the huge car park which is the most prominent feature of the 'resort'. You can stay up here (there's a 4-star hotel beside the lifts) but no one in their right mind would do so. If you're going to stay in a morgue-like skiing service station, you might as well stay in one with a lot more skiing to service than this.

The vertical drop on the main east-facing slopes back to the main lift stations is only in the order of 700m, which makes Igls look impressive. But there is much more variety here, on open red and blue runs below the peaks of Hoadl and Pleisen. From the latter, a long easy black run, well away from lifts and other intrusions, goes all the way to Axams on a shelf above the Inn valley at 880m – a great way to end the day. There is more accommodation here, and at Birgitz and Götzens nearby.

On the other side of the Axamer Lizum base station is a genuinely black slope served by a chair-lift, with a connection at the top to Mutters.

There are two ski schools, both with all-day ski kindergartens.

MUTTERS

Mutters (830m) is a charming, rustic village at the foot of a long, narrow ski area giving delightful easy cruising down from the link with Axamer Lizum to the village – a very respectable vertical of 900m.

TULFES

Tulfes (900m) gets overshadowed by Olympic Igls and Axamer Lizum, but has a very worthwhile ski area – red runs at the top, blue lower down – with the biggest local vertical of almost 1500m.

Also close to Innsbruck, but not covered by the lift pass, is Seefeld, dealt with separately on page 118.

Ischgl 1400m

✔ Old Tyrolean village which has grown quite large but retained much of its atmosphere and charm

✔ High ski area by Austrian standards, with reliable snow record

✔ Lots of good intermediate skiing

✔ Lively après-ski

✘ Lift queues can be a problem

✘ Quite a number of long T-bars

✘ Expensive, particularly initial package price

Ischgl is still little-known on the British market. That's strange, because it has most of the ingredients which make Austrian resorts so popular with British skiers. There's a traditional village, lively nightlife, choice of swish hotels or modest B&Bs and the chance of visiting nearby resorts. It has a better ski area than most – in terms of extent (it's one of Austria's biggest, and linked to duty-free Samnaun in Switzerland) and good, reliable snow.

So what's the problem? Apart from the lift queues, which can be very bad, we can't see it. The resort is dominated by Germans and Scandinavians and you won't find many Brits around – whether that's a good or bad thing depends on your point of view. It isn't cheap. But neither are many Austrian resorts these days. For a group of mixed-ability intermediate skiers, it's worth putting on your short-list. Because of the shortage of tour operators going there, many of our reporters made their holiday arrangements themselves.

ORIENTATION

Ischgl is tucked away down the long, narrow Paznaun valley south-west of Landeck.

Like the valley, it's a long, narrow resort at the foot of steep north-facing slopes.

Three gondolas go up into the skiing, two from the eastern end of town and one from the west. The main ski area starts at the top of these lifts and spans the border into Switzerland, where there's a cable-car back from the duty free village of **Samnaun**.

The Silvretta lift pass covers all this area plus the skiing of **Galtür** at the head of the valley and the smaller areas of **Kappl** and **See**. These areas are all linked by a rather infrequent bus service. If you have a car, visits to **St Anton** are easy.

 ## The resort

The village is set in a steep wooded valley and gets little sun in early season. We've had a report from one non-skier who went for a week in late January and found nowhere in the village where the sun stayed long enough to be able to sit out.

The main street is bypassed and almost traffic-free, making it a pleasant place to stroll in early evening. The architecture is a mixture of old original buildings, traditional Tyrolean-style hotels and shops, and more modern-looking recent additions. It's possible to walk from one end of the village to the other in ten minutes or so. It's far from flat though – and the ups and downs can be quite treacherous when there's snow or ice on the ground; we've seen quite a few nasty falls.

There's a good selection of bars, an excellent sports centre and a fair number of shops to stroll round.

 ## The skiing

Ischgl has a fair-sized, relatively high, snowsure ski area ideally suited to intermediates. Most of the pistes are red with very few black or easy blue runs. The opportunity of skiing over the border to duty-free Samnaun in Switzerland adds spice to the skiing.

THE SKI AREA
Cross-border cruising

Gondolas leave from both ends of the village and arrive at the sunny **Idalp** plateau at 2310m. Another arrives slightly above that at Pardatschgrat from where it's an easy ski down to the ski school meeting place at Idalp.

Lifts radiate from here leading to a wide variety of predominantly north-west- and west-facing runs. The top of the ridge at around 2760m is the border with Switzerland. If you drop down the other side you'll find south- and east-facing runs.

Just as the lifts on the Ischgl side are centred around Idalp, on the Swiss side the hub of the skiing is **Alp Trida** at 2265m. But from here you can't actually ski down to Samnaun, only to the hamlet of Compatsch, from which there is an infrequent bus to the cable-car back up at Ravaisch near Samnaun.

To ski to Samnaun itself you have to start from the **Palinkopf** area. The Samnaun run is very beautiful: it's away from all signs of lifts, down an unspoilt valley. It is not difficult skiing, but doesn't always have ideal snow conditions. The latter part of the run takes you by the road past Samnaun to the cable-car. If you want to pause in the village, there's a bus from there to the lift.

Freestyle snowboarders have a competition-standard half-pipe available to them.

SKI FACTS

Altitude 1400m-2870m
Lifts 40
Pistes 200km
Green/Blue 25%
Red 60%
Black 15%
Artificial snow 25km

LIFT PASSES

94/95 prices in schillings
VIP Skipass
Covers all lifts in Ischgl, Samnaun and Mathon and local buses.
Main pass
1-day pass 370
6-day pass 1800
(low season 1640 – 9% off)
Senior citizens
Over 60: 6-day pass 1320 (27% off)
Children
Under 15: 6-day pass 1115 (38% off)
Under 6: free pass
Short-term passes
Single and multi ascent passes for main cablecars; half-day pass from 11.30 (340), trial ticket from 2pm (205).
Alternative periods
5 skiing days in 7, 10 days in 14 and 10 days in the season.
Notes VIP skipass is only available to those staying in Ischgl, Samnaun or Mathon on presentation of guest card. Discounts for physically disabled and groups.
Alternative passes
Silvretta ski pass covers Ischgl, Samnaun, Galtür, Kappl and See (adult 6 days 2340), 68 lifts and use of ski bus, See is 15km away.

SNOW RELIABILITY
Very good

All the skiing except the runs back to the resort is above 2000m and much of it on the Ischgl side is north-west- or north-facing. So snow conditions are often good here even when they're poor elsewhere (which can lead to crowds when bus-loads of skiers arrive from lower resorts). The run from Idalp back down to Ischgl has artificial snowmaking facilities all the way, with most of the variants from the mid-station of the gondolas benefiting from artificial snow.

FOR ADVANCED SKIERS
Some attraction

Ischgl can't compare with nearby St Anton for exciting skiing, and many of the runs marked black on the piste map barely deserve their rating. But if you hire a guide, there is plenty of challenging and beautiful off-piste skiing to be found – and because there are fewer expert skiers around, it doesn't get skied as much as it would in a more 'macho' resort.

The steepest piste skiing is probably the run from Pardatschgrat down to the village. If snow conditions are poor near the bottom, you can ski the top half of this repeatedly by catching the gondola at the mid-station.

FOR INTERMEDIATE SKIERS
Something for everyone

Most of the skiing is ideal for intermediates. No matter what your standard, you should be able to find runs to suit you.

At the tough end of the spectrum our favourite runs are those from Palinkopf down to Gampenalp and on along the valley to the secluded and rustic restaurant at Bodenalp. From there you can catch a short drag-lift back up to the main ski area or carry on along the almost flat path to the gondola mid-stations. The top of these runs has been made more accessible and repeat skiable by a new chair-lift up from Gampenalp to Palinkopf. Sadly this has also meant the runs no longer have the attraction of being away from civilisation.

There are also interesting and challenging runs (some marked black) down the Hollenspitze drag and from both the top and bottom of the drag-lift from Idjoch.

For easier motorway skiing, try the Swiss side, where the runs from the border down to Alp Trida should prove ideal. So should the runs that take you back to Idalp on the return journey. There are frequent moans

from intermediates, however, about the runs back to Ischgl itself; none is easy, and conditions can be tricky despite the artificial snow. Most are marked red on the piste map but are at the tough end of the rating.

FOR BEGINNERS
Not ideal

There are good sunny nursery slopes and a short beginners' drag-lift at Idalp. But away from this area there are few runs ideal for the near-beginner. Better to learn elsewhere and come to Ischgl after getting two or three years' experience. If you want to stay in the Paznaun valley area, Galtür would be a much better choice.

FOR CROSS-COUNTRY
Plenty in the valley

There is 28km of cross-country track in the valley between Ischgl, Galtür and Wirl. This tends to be pretty sunless, especially early in the season, and is away from the main ski area, which makes meeting downhillers for lunch rather inconvenient. We've also seen people doing cross-country higher up along the path between the gondola mid-station and Gampenalp, though this isn't an official trail. Galtür would be a better cross-country skier's choice, with 60km of loops.

QUEUES
Some notorious bottlenecks

There can be lengthy waits at key lifts at peak times. The main Silvrettabahn gondola is often a problem during the morning peak, especially when people are being bussed in from other resorts. We've managed to avoid this on our visits by taking one of the gondolas at the other end of the village, but we're told this isn't always a foolproof method. Several reporters have remarked on gondolas being prone to closure because of wind.

The other notorious waits are for the cable-car out of Samnaun in the early afternoon and the long drag-lifts back up from Alp Trida after that. But the latter, at least, will be relieved by a new quad chair-lift up to Viderjoch due to open this winter.

MOUNTAIN RESTAURANTS
Mostly large and crowded

Ischgl isn't the place to go for either culinary delights or charming small mountain restaurants. The main restaurant at Idalp is a big self-service cafeteria, and there's a smaller crowded alternative nearby. The restaurant at the top of the Pardatschgrat gondola tends to be

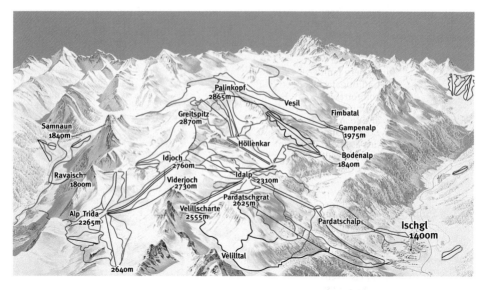

SKI SCHOOL

94/95 prices in schillings

Ischgl-Silvretta
Manager Edi Zangerl
Classes 6 days
4hr: 10.30-12.30 and 1.30-3.30
6 full days: 1400
Children's classes
Ages: from 5
6 full days including lunch: 1850
Private lessons Half-(2hr) or full-day (4hr) 1100 for half-day; each additional person 150

CHILDCARE

The childcare facilities are all up the mountain at Idalp. There's a ski kindergarten for children aged 3 to 5; from age 5 they go into a slightly more demanding regime in an 'adventure garden'; lunch is included in both arrangements, which are open 6 days a week. Toilet-trained children can be left at a non-ski nursery; lunch is available.

quieter. Our favourite place for lunch and beer breaks was the quiet rustic restaurant at Bodenalp, which is accessible for non-skiers who enjoy the walk from the mid-station of the gondola. Just above this is the lively Paznauer Taya, which often has a band playing on the large terrace.

They take Austrian schillings in the Swiss restaurants. But don't forget the prices are marked in Swiss francs – and aren't cheap. At Alp Trida the terrace is huge and sunny and has an outdoor bar and barbecue.

SKI SCHOOL
Language problems
The ski school meets up at Idalp and starts very late (10.30am to 12.30pm and 1.30pm to 3.30pm). We've heard from both supporters and critics of the school. There are few British skiers here, and the standard of English of the instructors is variable, so it's quite possible that you will end up in a mixed-language group. The instructor having to explain everything twice can slow things down, as can the large size of classes.

As well as normal lessons the ski school organises off-piste tours – this area is one of the best in the Alps for ski touring.

FACILITIES FOR CHILDREN
High-altitude options
Taking small children up the mountain with you rather than leaving them behind at village level is an unusual arrangement, and as yet we've had no reports on how it works in practice. (The ski kindergarten is a new facility that was opened only last season.)

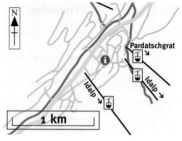

1 km

↑ Staying there

On or near the main street is the best place to stay. Both the main lift-stations are an easy walk from there and the nightlife is on your doorstep. Beware of accommodation set up the steep hillside (some roads are so steep that tour operators' coaches may not make it to the door) or across the bypass road at the far side of the valley floor from the main village – though this does have the advantage of getting more sun.

HOW TO GO
Expensive packages
As is the norm in Austria you pay for altitude. Much of the accommodation is expensive, particularly the mostly upmarket places sold through tour operators. There is, however, a big choice of cheaper little pensions.

Travelling most of the way by train is easy – the nearby town of Landeck has a main-line station.
Chalets There aren't any catered chalets run by tour operators.
Hotels Ischgl has a splendid selection of hotel and B&B accommodation,

GETTING THERE

Air Innsbruck, transfer 2hr. Zurich, transfer 5hr.

Rail Landeck (30km); frequent buses from station.

PACKAGES

Austrian Travel Service, Crystal, Inghams, Made to Measure

Samnaun Inghams

ranging from the luxurious and expensive to the plain but comfortable and good-value.

£££££ Madlein Convenient and quiet. Near the two quieter gondolas. Modern family-run chalet built in traditional style. Reportedly comfortable rooms. Facilities include swimming pool, sauna, steam room and solarium. Nightclub and disco.

£££££ Solaria Near the Madlein and just as luxurious. Splendid carved wooden ceiling to restaurant, and wood-panelled wine bar. Swimming pool, sauna, steam room, solarium, fitness room and squash courts.

££££ Goldener Adler Traditional 250-year-old hotel right in the middle of the village. Wood-panelled and painted restaurant. Sauna, steam room, jacuzzi and solarium.

££££ Sonne One of Ischgl's oldest hotels. Well modernised, but with some very small rooms. In the centre of the village. Lively stube, with traditional squeeze-box music. Sauna, steam room, jacuzzi, solarium.

£££ Astoria Comfortable B&B hotel that faces the main Silvrettabahn gondola.

£££ Christine Probably the best B&B in town. Right opposite the end of the main run down from Idalp. One of the liveliest cafés at the end of the day.

£££ Erna Small, central B&B. Firmly recommended by a reporter who has holidayed in Ischgl 20 times.

Self-catering New for 1995, Inghams have very attractive apartments with all mod cons – a bargain compared with hotel prices. Crystal also have good accommodation which, though expensive, books out early because of the popularity of this resort.

EATING OUT
Plenty of choice

Our favourite places for dinner are the traditional Austrian restaurants and stubes, of which there's a wide choice. The Goldener Adler probably serves the best food around and has a splendid traditional dining room. The Wippas stube in the Sonne is lively and serves good food. For pizza try the Trofana-Alm, which is as much a bar as restaurant, and for fondue the Kitzloch with its galleried tables overlooking the dance floor. La Bamba is the new kid on the block, a restaurant-bar serving Mexican specialities. The Grillalm, Salner and Tirol are also popular eateries.

APRES-SKI
Very lively

Ischgl is one of the liveliest resorts in the Alps, both immediately after skiing and after dinner.

At the end of the skiing day the Café Christine gets packed and does great coffee and cakes, as well as alcohol. If you get up to dance to the disco music, make sure someone is saving your seat for you, unless you're happy to join the stand-up crush for the rest of the time.

The Kitzloch at the bottom of the run down from Pardatschgrat is just as lively and a bit more rowdy – dancing on tables and communal congas are common. In good weather the ice bar of the Elisabeth hotel by the Pardatschgratbahn is popular. The Wippas stube at the hotel Sonne also gets crowded and has live music but no dancing. Other places for tea dancing include the Wunderbar of the hotel Madlein and the Trofana Alm.

Serious drinkers head for the umbrella-shaded outdoor bar of the Post hotel.

Most of these places are also popular later on, and there's no shortage of other joints to choose from. The Taja Bar and Seespitz are two of the most popular haunts.

All this action is, however, rather one-dimensional. Ischgl is popular with beer-swilling Germans and 'crazy' Swedes whose idea of a good time revolves around drinking. There are, for example, few stylish discos in which to strut your stuff. The main exception is the Wunderbar, which becomes a sophisticated nightclub in the evenings with international floor shows and disco nights.

FOR NON-SKIERS
Fair by high-village standards
Although the resort is best suited to keen skiers, there's no shortage of things for non-skiers to do. There are plenty of walks (24km of marked paths) and a splendid sports centre with an interesting pool and sauna, steam room and solarium. There's another sports centre in Galtür with swimming, tennis and squash.

It's easy to get around the valley and to Landeck by bus. But meeting skiers for lunch presents problems: the restaurants at the top stations of the gondolas are crowded and characterless. And if you stay in the valley you won't see much sun – certainly not in the early season.

STAYING DOWN THE VALLEY
Too far without a car
Ischgl is fairly isolated. We don't recommend staying down in the main valley unless you have a car and want a touring holiday. Landeck is the nearest big town. It has good shopping and is well positioned for trips to surrounding ski resorts, including Serfaus, Nauders, Sölden and St Anton.

You could consider staying up the valley instead, in Galtür. It is quieter, sunnier and considerably cheaper than Ischgl. It would be a good base for a quiet family holiday. But if you intend to ski Ischgl most of the time, bear in mind that the bus service isn't frequent. The last bus home is disappointingly early in the evening and tends to be a real crush. See report on page 67.

Samnaun 1840m
The main attraction of staying in Samnaun is to ski the Ischgl-Samnaun skiing without the worst of the queues. The village itself is nothing special and consists of not much more than a handful of shops and hotels. It is very quiet. Its duty-free status makes it a useful stopover for those who want to restock on duty-frees and then go back to Ischgl. If you're touring around in a car it's also a cheap place to fill up with petrol. Inghams have a hotel allocation here for the first time this year.

ACTIVITIES

Indoor Silvretta Centre (bowling, billiards, swimming pool, sauna, steam baths, solarium), museum, library, cinema, gallery, tennis courts
Outdoor Curling, skating, sleigh rides, hiking tours

TOURIST OFFICE

Postcode A-6561
Tel 010 43 (5444) 5266
Fax 5636

Kitzbühel 760m

✔ Vibrant nightlife

✔ Plenty of off-slope amenities, both for the sporty and the not-so-sporty

✔ Large, attractive, varied ski areas offering a sensation of travel to piste and off-piste skiers

✔ Beautiful medieval town centre (but see minus points)

✔ A surprisingly large amount of cheap and cheerful accommodation

✔ Jolly mountain restaurants

✘ Unreliable snow conditions, and a snowmaking installation that is still small relative to the ski area

✘ Peak-season and weekend lift and bus queues that are shockingly bad by today's standards

✘ Surprisingly little tough skiing

✘ Disjointed ski areas, with quite a lot of bussing to get around them

✘ Traditional charm spoilt by heavy traffic in and around the town

✘ Disappointing nursery area

✘ Crowded pistes

'Been there, skied it, bought the t-shirt'. Kitzbühel is an impressive name to drop in the pub when discussing ski resorts. Every Ski Sunday viewer knows that the Hahnenkamm downhill race is the most challenging on the World Cup circuit. And over the years the resort has successfully cultivated an international reputation as a rather special, even glamorous resort. But the Hahnenkamm race course is irrelevant to most skiers; it is specially prepared for the famous race, and is completely untypical of Kitzbühel's skiing, which is mostly easy. And there is nothing very special about standing in long lift queues, fighting for places on crowded buses and skiing on ice and slush. We have visited Kitz countless times over the years, and never found decent snow on the lower slopes of the main ski area. It does of course get good snow at times, and (at long last) the resort has recently made serious investments in snowmaking, but the spread-out nature and low altitude of the ski area mean that the problem is unlikely to go away.

Equally surprising to visitors impressed by the PR image of Kitz is the fact that the resort is very far from exclusive. It has its expensive, elegant hotels, but it also has a huge amount of hotel and pension accommodation that is quite inexpensive – and not surprisingly attracts quite a few low-budget visitors, many of whom are young and intent on a good time.

And yet the reports we receive on Kitzbühel are almost all from fans, most of whom are regular visitors. For them, its unique combination of historic town and extensive ski area outweighs other considerations.

ORIENTATION

Kitzbühel is a sizeable town in a broad valley, with its two local ski areas on opposite sides. The main Hahnenkamm area is reached by cable-car from quite close to the centre, or from an out-of-town gondola at Klausen, on the road to **Kirchberg**, another sizeable resort which shares the skiing. The smaller Kitzbüheler Horn ski area is reached by gondola starting some way from the centre. Nearby is a small chain of lifts above the village of **Aurach**.

A fourth ski area, just about accessible on skis from the Hahnenkamm, links the valley village of **Jochberg** to the high outpost of **Pass Thurn**.

Lots of resorts in the eastern Tyrol are accessible by car or public transport.

 ## The resort

Set at a junction of pretty valleys, Kitzbühel is a large, animated town, with a beautiful walled medieval centre – complete with quaint church, cobbled streets and attractively painted buildings – which is traffic-free during the day. But the much-publicised old town represents only a relatively small part of Kitz; the resort spreads widely, and busy roads girdling the old town reduce the charm factor markedly. Visitors used to peaceful little Austrian villages are likely to be disappointed by its essential urban nature. For those who like it, the sophisticated towny ambience is what 'makes' Kitz.

 ## The skiing

Snow and lift queues permitting, the skiing suits intermediate skiers well. Although more advanced skiers can find things to do, there are many better places for experts.

THE SKI AREA
Big but bitty

Kitzbühel has four ski areas, two of them just about connected. The **Hahnenkamm** is by far the largest, and the most accessible from the town. It is reached via a cable-car or two chair-lifts, from the top of which a choice of steep and gentle runs lead down into Ehrenbachgraben; from there several chair-lifts fan out in

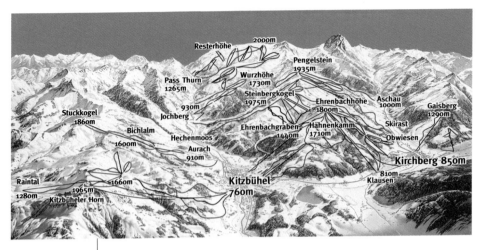

SKI FACTS

Altitude	760m-1975m
Lifts	64
Pistes	158km
Green/Blue	50%
Red	42%
Black	8%
Artificial snow	10km

LIFT PASSES

94/95 prices in
schillings
Kitzbühel
Covers all lifts in
Kitzbühel, Kirchberg,
Jochberg, Pass Thurn,
Bichlalm and Aschau,
linking buses, and
swimming pool.
Beginners Points
cards valid on 15
mainly drag-lifts
(adult 10 point card
150).
Main pass
1-day pass 370
6-day pass 1820
(low season 1640 –
10% off)
Senior citizens
Over 65 male, 60
female: 6-day pass
1460 (20% off)
Children
Under 16: 6-day pass
910 (50% off)
Under 4: free pass
Short-term passes
Single ascent tickets
for the major lifts;
hourly refunds on day
tickets; day tickets
can be bought in
hourly steps from
11am.
Notes 5% reduction
for groups of over 15
people. The season
pass is valid in
Gstaad and
Davos/Klosters.

different directions. One takes you to
the gentle peak of Steinbergkogel, the
high-point of the sector at 1975m.
Beyond is the slightly lower peak of
Pengelstein. On the far side of
Pengelstein several long runs lead
down to the valley to the west of the
ski area; ski-buses link their end-points
at Aschau and Skirast with Obwiesen,
Kirchberg and Kitz. From Obwiesen, a
slow series of lifts can take you up to
Ehrenbachhöhe, the focal point of the
whole Hahnenkamm sector.

Pengelstein is the start of the 'ski
safari' route to Kitzbühel's most
remote but most snowsure ski area,
Jochberg-Pass Thurn. The piste
finishes at Trampelpfad, a short walk
from the Jochberg lifts. A parallel piste
from Steinbergkogel appears on the
piste map, but Hechenmoos, where it
ends, is more than a walk from
Jochberg. Jochberg-Pass Thurn is a not
inconsiderable area, despite the
shortness of most of the runs. By local
standards they are high, and have the
best snow in the area – well worth the
excursion even when snow is
acceptably good lower down. Runs
lead to Pass Thurn, the terminus of
the ski-bus, where it is well worth
ending the day to ensure a seat.

The very small **Bichlalm** area is of
little interest except for getting away
from the crowds and working on your
suntan. When conditions are good,
the top station (Stuckkogel) accesses
an off-piste route to Fieberbrunn. A
train returns you to Kitz.

The **Kitzbüheler Horn** is equally
sunny, with repercussions for snow-
cover, but much of its skiing is above
the 1270m-high mid-station, accessed
by a modern gondola close to the
railway station. The second stage leads
to a sunny bowl at around 1660m, but
the alternative cable-car takes you up

to the summit of the Horn, from
where a fine, solitary east-facing piste
leads down into the Raintal on the far
side, with a chair-lift returning to the
ridge. There are widely spread blue,
red and black runs back towards town.

There is a timed slalom course on
the Kitzbüheler Horn.

SNOW RELIABILITY
Overdue improvements
Kitzbühel's skiing has one of the
lowest average heights in the Alps,
and when snow disappears from its
wealth of valley-bound pistes the ski
area is drastically reduced in size. Long
lift queues result, and many of the
mountain restaurants become
inaccessible. Such problems are sadly
common. The introduction of
snowmakers in recent years has
improved matters, notably on the
main Hahnenkamm piste early in the
season, but most of the area remains
unprotected. The best plan is to book
late when snow-cover is known to be
good. Otherwise, take a car for snow-
searching excursions (which may take
you far afield).

FOR ADVANCED SKIERS
Plan to go off-piste
Steep piste skiing is concentrated in
the ring of runs down into the bowl of
Ehrenbachgraben, the most direct of
which are challenging mogul fields.
Nearby the Streif red, which is the
basis for the downhill race-course, is
also good fun, particularly when ice
adds to the challenge. (Bravos are
prevented from throwing themselves
down the famous near-vertical
Mausfalle by a wicker fence.) When
conditions allow there is plenty of off-
piste potential, some of it safely close
to pistes, some requiring guidance.
(See Ski school section.)

SKI SCHOOL

Hahnenkamm
Manager Helmut Egger
Classes 6 days
4hr: 2hr am and pm
6 full days: 1200
Children's classes
Ages: up to 14
6 full days including lunch: 2280
Private lessons Half- or full day
1900 for 1 day; each additional person 250

Kitzbüheler Horn
Manager Wasti Zwicknagl
Classes 6 days
4hr: 2hr am and pm
6 full days: 1300
Children's classes
5 full days including lunch: 1780

Red Devils
Manager Rudi Sailer
Classes 6 days
4hr: 2hr am and pm
6 full days: 1350
Children's classes
Ages: 4 to 11
6 full days including lunch: 1830
Private lessons
Half- or full day
2100 for full day

Total
Manager Ernst Hinterseer
Classes 6 days
4hr: 9.30-11.30 and 1pm-3pm
6 full days: 1300
Children's classes
Ages: 4 to 11
6 full days: 1250
Private lessons
Half- or full day
2100 for full day

FOR INTERMEDIATES
Lots of alternatives

The Hahnenkamm area is prime intermediate terrain. Good intermediates will want to do the Streif run, of course, but the long 1000m-vertical red down to Klausen from Ehrenbachhöhe is equally satisfying. The long runs down to the Kirchberg-Aschau road make a fine end to the day; earlier, they are rather spoilt by the lack of return lifts.

The east-facing Raintal runs on the Horn are perhaps the best 'yo-yo' skiing in the whole area for good intermediates, though the long runs back to town from the ridge are disappointingly easy.

The runs above Jochberg are particularly good for mixed abilities, with plenty of varying routes from the top of the mountain down to Wirtsalm. Moderate skiers also have some fine runs either side of Pengelstein, including the ski safari route, and the Hieslegg piste above Aschau. The short high runs at the top of the Pass Thurn skiing are ideal for timid skiers. There are also easy routes down to both Pass Thurn and Jochberg. Much of the Horn and Bichlalm is also cruising territory, including very long glides down to town when conditions allow.

FOR BEGINNERS
Not ideal

The Hahnenkamm nursery slopes are no more than adequate and prone to poor snow conditions. The Horn has a high, sunny nursery-like section, and precocious learners will soon be skiing home from there on the long Hagstein piste. There are also plenty of easy runs to progress to.

FOR CROSS-COUNTRY
Plentiful but low

There are nearly 40km of trails dotted about, but all are at valley level and prone to lack of snow. When conditions are good, try the quiet Reith area.

QUEUES
A serious drawback

Although Kitzbühel has improved its lift system, it still lags behind other places of similar size and standing, and remains one of the worst resorts for queues. The Hahnenkamm cable-car has a capacity of an incredible 380 people an hour, so it's not surprising that queues are serious. There is the alternative of a slow chair (naturally, this gets busy too) or of going out to the Klausen gondola. Leaving town on the Horn or Jochberg buses can also involve long delays in peak season and at weekends. Overcrowded pistes are generally a greater problem than queues once up both the Horn and Hahnenkamm. The Silberstube drag-lift – the only way back to the Hahnenkamm from Pengelstein – has been a bottleneck, but is due to be replaced by a quad chair this season.

MOUNTAIN RESTAURANTS
A highlight

'One of the reasons we keep going back,' says one of our Kitz regulars. There are many restaurants, none of them marked explicitly on the resort piste map – though most of their names appear. So long as you keep to the smaller places, huts are generally good, both for food and service. Most of the Horn restaurants have their fans, the Hornköpfl particularly so

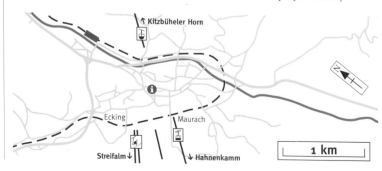

thanks to good food, reasonable prices, sunny terraces and few queues. The Alpenhaus is good for a lively lunch, the Gipfelhaus quieter. The Bichlalm in the next-door sector is also a good spot for a quiet lunch. In the Pass Thurn-Jochberg sector the Jägerwurzhütte and Trattenbachalm are recommended, and the new Panoramaalm has (surprise!) great views. The Ochsalm and Brandseit are two of the best in the Hahnenkamm sector – though there are lots of others, both close to town and further away on the west-facing slopes.

SKI SCHOOL
Off-piste guiding a bargain

There are now four ski schools, and at least one reporter says that the resort's increased teaching capacity – aided no doubt by the spur of competition – has put an end to the over-large classes that have long been a problem here. The original school, Rudi Sailer's famous Red Devils, runs regular off-piste guiding groups at normal class rates – an excellent way to explore outside the pistes without the usual expense of hiring a guide. In contrast to the 220-strong Red Devils, the other schools emphasise their small scale and personal nature. Ernst Hinterseer's Total school is the best-established of the newcomers – started in 1989/90 – and includes video analysis.

FACILITIES FOR CHILDREN
Not an ideal choice

Provided your children are able and willing to take ski instruction, you can deposit them at any of the four schools. The Total school has the advantage of post-skiing supervision until 5pm. But parents who have to hurry back to the resort can't make the most of the skiing day here.

↑ Staying there

The size of Kitz makes choice of location important. Staying in the old town has advantages other than aesthetic. It's reasonably equidistant from the two main lift stations either side of town, both being within walking distance. However, the Hahnenkamm is very much the larger (and more snowsure) of the two ski areas, and many visitors prefer to be as close as possible to its cable-car. Beginners should be aware that the Hahnenkamm nursery slopes are often short of snow, at which time novices are taken up the Horn.

The bus service around town is good, but the sheer weight of numbers wishing to use it, and the congested one-way system, often make journeys slow and uncomfortably crowded. Having a car is very useful for quick access to the rather distant Pass Thurn-Jochberg and Bichlalm ski areas and the Klausen gondola, which is relatively queue-free.

HOW TO GO
Mainly hotels and pensions

Kitz is essentially a hotel resort, and UK package offerings reflect this.

Chalets A few tour operators run chalet-hotels here. Crystal have a couple of plain but pleasant and very conveniently positioned places close to the Hahnenkamm slopes. Skibound run a characterful old coaching inn 8 minutes' walk from the main cable-car. Kings Club have a cheap and cheerful old place on the edge of town, five minutes by bus from Klausen.

Hotels There is an enormous choice, with 4-star and 3-star hotels forming the core of the resort.

££££££ **Tennerhof** Much-extended, luxuriously converted farmhouse in big garden with renowned restaurant. Beautiful panelled rooms.

££££££ **Schloss Lebenberg** Modernised 'castle' with smart pool, and free shuttle bus to make up for secluded but inconvenient location. Free nursery for kids aged 3-plus.

££££ **Goldener Grief** Historic inn, elegantly renovated; vaulted lobby-sitting area, panelled bar, casino.

££££ **Weisses Rössl** Smartly traditional, with a welcoming bar-sitting room area (open fire); food can be good, but one package holidaymaker calls it 'boring and badly prepared'.

£££ **Schweizerhof** Comfortable chalet in unbeatable position.

£££ **Maria Theresia** Big, comfortable modern chalet.

£££ **Hahnenhof** Small converted farmhouse retaining rustic charm.

£££ **Strasshofer** A favourite with one of our regular reporters – 'central, family-run, friendly, good food, quiet rooms at back'.

£ **Mühlbergerhof** Small, friendly pension in good position.

Self-catering Although there are plenty of apartments in Kitz, very few are available through tour operators. Many of the best (and best-positioned) places are attached to hotels. The 4-star Garni Ludwig and 3-star Garni Christophorus, Haselberger and Pension Hillebrand all have good apartments close to the cable-car.

CHILDCARE

All four ski schools cater for small children, offering lunchtime supervision as well as tuition on baby slopes – generally from age 3. There is no non-ski nursery, but babysitters can be hired.

GETTING THERE

Air Salzburg, transfer 2hr. Munich, transfer 2½hr. Innsbruck, transfer 2hr.

Rail Mainline station in resort. Postbus every 15 mins from station.

PACKAGES

Airtours, Austrian Holidays, Austrian Travel Service, Club Europe, Crystal, Enterprise, Inghams, Kings Ski Club, Made to Measure, Neilson, Ski Club of GB, Ski Europe, Ski Partners, SkiBound, Stena Sealink, Thomson, Timescape, Travelscene Ski-Drive

Kirchberg Crystal, Enterprise, Neilson, Ski Partners, Thomson, Timescape, Top Deck, Travelscene Ski-Drive

ACTIVITIES

Indoor Aquarena Centre (2 pools, sauna, solarium, mud baths, aerated baths, underwater massage – free entry with lift pass), indoor tennis hall, 2 squash courts, fitness centre, beauty centre, bridge, bowling, 2 indoor riding schools, local theatre, library, museum, chess club, casino

Outdoor Ice-rink (curling and skating), horse-riding, sleigh rides, wildlife park, toboggan run, ballooning, ski-bobs, guided excursions, flying school, hang-gliding, para-gliding, 40km of cleared walking paths

EATING OUT
Something for everyone

There is a wide range of restaurants to suit all pockets, down to good-value pizzerias and fast food outlets (yes, even MacDonalds). Some of the 4-star hotels have excellent restaurants; the Weisses Rössl and Maria Theresia are particularly recommended. But the Unterbergen Stuben vies with the Schwedenkapelle for the 'best in town' award. Good cheaper, less formal places include the Huberbräustube, Sportstüberl and Zinnkrug. Goldene Gams does a good fondue and provides live entertainment.

APRES-SKI
A main attraction

Nightlife is a great selling point of Kitz. There's something for all tastes from throbbing bars full of the young, free and single, to quiet little places popular with local workers, nice cafés full of calories and self-consciously smart spots for the fur-coat brigade to flaunt themselves.

Much of the action starts quite late; immediately after skiing the town is jolly without being much livelier than many other Tyrolean resorts. Cafés Praxmair and Pirchl are two of the most atmospheric tea-time places, where many a diet has been ruined by their cakes and pastries. Later the lively English-style Big Ben bar is a focal spot, while the quieter Seppi's and Glockenspiel are also popular. Das Lichtl, Royal Dancing, Grief Kellar, Drop In, and Take 5 are other lively nightspots. The Londoner Pub is the loudest, most crowded place in town. A downmarket facsimile of a British boozer, it's something of an acquired taste; one reporter described it as 'busy but with no atmosphere – lots of lads looking gloomy wondering where all the women were'.

Tour reps organise plenty of the usual events, and there's also a casino for more formal entertainment.

FOR NON-SKIERS
Plenty to do

The Aquarena leisure centre is very impressive, with two pools, sauna, solarium and various health activities, and there are lots of other diversions, including a surprisingly worthwhile museum. The railway also affords plenty of scope for excursions (to Salzburg and Innsbruck, for example) and there are a number of rep-organised coach trips available. Meeting skiers for lunch can be tricky, but Jochberg is one fairly convenient possibility.

Kirchberg 850m

Anyone going to Kirchberg expecting a quiet, rustic little haven from which to ski Kitzbühel will be sadly disappointed. Kirchberg is a large, crowded, lively, commercialised village very popular with young Brits, Scandinavians and Germans. It suffers the same traffic congestion and inconvenient layout of its famous neighbour, without its compensating medieval town centre. Nor are prices much lower here.

There is a choice of ski schools: here as in Kitz there is a Total school. Meeting points are spread about. Beginners, for example, start over on the Gaisberg mountain, on the opposite side of town from the main area. There are non-ski and ski kindergartens at Obwiesen, 2.5km out of town, near the Elisabeth-Zeinlach hotel complex. Total's Snow Adventure ski kindergarten will keep children until 5pm. The village Krabbelstube crèche accepts babies.

Like Kitz, Kirchberg is essentially a hotel-pension resort, with a wide choice of modern chalet-style places available. Choice of location is important. Beginners have slopes within walking distance of the village, but experienced skiers wishing to avoid crowded bus journeys should look for a hotel a couple of kilometres out of town near the Maierl chair

The 3-star Elisabeth and Zeinlach twin-hotel complex, even further out at Obwiesen, provides the best slope-side accommodation. They are particularly good for families, with shared games and playroom amenities, and kindergartens on hand (see above). Those preferring a central village location will appreciate the 4-star multi-amenity Tiroler Adler, which has a fine leisure complex and a bus stop right outside. The 3-star Landhaus Brauns is also comfortable and has a good position next to the nursery slopes.

Nightlife is very lively, to the point of rowdiness at times. The best bars in town for good, lively fun and atmosphere without getting silly are Le Moustache, Vis a Vis and Charlie's Club. Habitat is a cheaper, more basic place full of Brits. The Londoner is a raucous spot catering for rich teenagers. All the usual Tyrolean-style entertainment is available, plus rep-organised sleigh rides etc.

Kirchberg does not have as much to offer non-skiers as Kitzbühel, but still provides plenty to do – and has the same range of excursion possibilities.

TOURIST OFFICE

Postcode A-6370
Tel 010 43 (5356) 2155
Fax 2307

Lech 1450m

✔ Picturesque Alpine village

✔ Fair sized, largely intermediate piste network

✔ Excellent off-piste skiing

✔ Easy access to tougher skiing of St Anton and other Arlberg resorts

✔ Sunny ski area with excellent snow record and extensive snowmaking

✔ Lively après-ski scene

✔ Very chic resort, good for posing and people-watching

✔ Some captivating hotels and restaurants

✗ Very expensive

✗ Surprising dearth of atmospheric mountain restaurants

✗ Very little tough piste skiing

✗ Can be bad for queues

Lech is one of the most glamorous and expensive resorts in Austria. It shares a ski area with neighbouring and equally upmarket Zürs. The skiing could fairly easily be linked with that of neighbouring St Anton. The fact that it hasn't been emphasises the difference between Zürs' and Lech's rich and royal visitors and the hoi polloi of its equally famous neighbour.

Lech is for those who don't mind fur coats, do like well groomed, snowsure, easy piste skiing and are content to enjoy a comfortable winter holiday in pampered comfort and style in a traditional Alpine village. There is challenging skiing available (mainly off-piste) and the tough skiing of St Anton is only a short bus- or car-ride away. But it is the part-time skier, who enjoys the après and the strolling as much as the skiing, who will get the most out of the resort. It helps to have a deep pocket.

ORIENTATION

Lech is set towards the end (in winter) of a high valley leading off the main Switzerland-Innsbruck motorway near to St Anton. Its own main ski area is reached by a choice of chairs or cable-car from various points in town (the cable-car goes to Oberlech, a mini-resort 300m above Lech in the middle of the ski area). Another cable-car also goes up the opposite side of the valley to link up with the skiing of **Zürs**, which you pass through on the road into Lech. Zug is a tiny hamlet 3km up another dead-end valley. The Arlberg ski pass covers not only these two resorts but also **St Anton, Stuben** and **St Christoph**, all reachable by car or local bus.

 ## The resort

Lech is Austria's answer to glitz-and-glamour resorts such as Courchevel and Zermatt. People come here to be seen. The village offers cosy old-world Austrian charm, complete with onion-domed church and covered wooden bridge over the river, combined with every modern convenience. It lies in a small valley with good views of the mountains on all sides.

The main street is bordered on one side by the Lech, a gurgling river, and by enticing and pricey shops on the other. In good weather it is a picture of open air cafés, dancing in the street and a fashion show of fur coats and horse-drawn carriages.

While some of the best hotels are right in the centre, they are not obtrusive. There are no towering monstrosities in Lech and the village remains picturesque despite its growth and popularity. Recently it has become associated with Princess Diana's annual pilgrimage to the Arlberg hotel. She is Lech's best-known celebrity but there are many others. Princess Caroline of Monaco

goes to neighbouring Zürs.

The clientele is largely German and Austrian, with very few Brits. The fur coat count is one of the highest in the Alps. And it helps to be able to afford a helicopter transfer out if the high Flexen Pass on the road in and out is shut – which it can be for days on end after an exceptional snowfall. The top hotels are owned by a few families and have large numbers of regular guests who come back year after year.

The first settlers in Lech came from the Valais region of Switzerland in the 11th century. The village is named after the river Lech, originally the 'Licca' which means stonewater. Skiing started in the early 1900s. The Lech ski school was founded in 1925 and the first T-bar was built in 1939. Lech's most famous son is Patrick Ortlieb, Albertville Olympic Downhill champion in 1992. He was born and learned his skiing in Oberlech.

Oberlech is a small, traffic-free collection of hotels and chalets set on the piste above Lech and served by a cable-car which works until late at night, allowing access to Lech's much livelier nightlife.

Zug is a hamlet, 3km from Lech

which connects with the Lech-Oberlech ski area. The small amount of accommodation is mostly bed and breakfast with one 4-star hotel, the Rote Wand, which serves the best Kaiserschmarren (a delicious pancake and fruit desert) in the Arlberg. From Lech, Zug makes a good night out: you can take a horse-drawn sleigh for a fondue at the Rote Wand, Klosterle or Auerhahn, followed by a visit to the Rote Wand disco.

SKI FACTS

Altitude	1445m-2450m
Lifts	88
Pistes	260km
Green/Blue	30%
Red	40%
Black*	30%
Artificial snow	18km

* includes ski routes
– see text

 # The skiing

For such an upmarket resort the lift system is surprisingly antiquated and badly planned in many ways. But perhaps that reflects the fact that its clientele are there primarily for a relaxing and social winter break, rather than wanting to clock up as much ski mileage as possible between dawn and dusk. The runs are also designed to flatter leisurely skiers, with a lot of gentle wide blue and red runs.

THE SKI AREA
One-way traffic

Lech's main ski area centres on **Oberlech**, which can be reached from the village by chair-lifts as well as the cable-car. The wide open slopes are perfect for intermediates and the area, served by 16 lifts, also accesses off-piste for experts. **Zuger Hochlicht** is the highest point of this sector, at 2380m, and the views from here and Kriegerhorn below are stunning. As at St Anton, the toughest runs here are now classed as 'ski routes' or 'high-touring routes' rather than pistes, with all the confusion and added danger that involves (see St Anton chapter). The only official pistes back to the main skiing from Zuger Hochlicht are now gentle blues, and the only way down to Zug is a ski route.

To get to the Zürs ski area and the linked Lech-Zürs-Lech circuit, you take the **Rüfikopf** cable-car in the opposite direction from Lech's main ski area. This goes from the centre of town. From the top there are long cruisey pistes, via a couple of lifts, down to Zürs. The circuit can only be skied in a clockwise direction. This

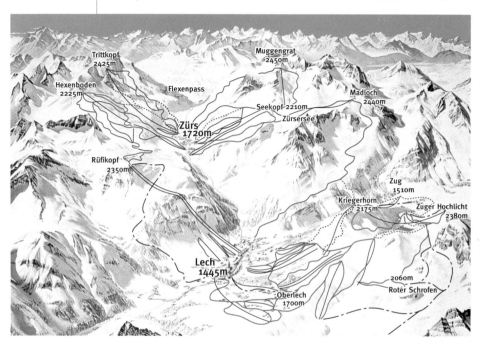

LIFT PASSES

94/95 prices in schillings

Arlberg Ski pass
Covers all St Anton, St Christoph, Lech, Zürs and Stuben lifts, but not the buses between them.

Beginners Limited day passes covering a few lifts; adventurous second-week skiers need an area pass.

Main pass
1-day pass 445
6-day pass 2140
(low season 1930 – 10% off)

Senior citizens
Over 65 male, 60 female: 6-day pass 1720 (20% off)
Over 80: free pass

Children
Under 15: 6-day pass 1280 (40% off)
Under 6: free pass

Short-term passes
Single ascent tickets on some lifts throughout Arlberg. Half-day tickets (adults 335) from noon, afternoon 'taster' tickets (180) from 3pm. Day tickets have by-the-hour reimbursement.

Notes Arlberg pass also covers Klösterle (10 lifts), 7km west of Stuben. Arlberg Special ski pass for passes of 6 days and over, reductions of about 200 if staying in Lech area and for children until 17.2.95. Snowman ticket (100) for children under 7 and adults over 80 covers whole season. Special reductions during wedel, firn and snow crystal weeks.

means that in school holidays and other busy periods the linking lifts and runs can get crowded.

All the skiing at Zürs is above the treeline. There are two areas on either side of the village. The more difficult runs are off the top of the **Trittkopf** (on the same side as the runs down from Lech).

On the other side of the valley, chairs go up to **Seekopf** and Zürsersee with intermediate runs down. There's a chair up to Muggengrat (at 2450m the highest point of the Zürs skiing) from below Zürsersee. This has a blue back under it and a lovely long red away from all the lifts back down to Zürs. But most people head for the Madloch-Joch chair. This accesses the long red run all the way back to Lech. You can peel off part way down and ski to Zug and the chair-lift up to the Kriegerhorn above Oberlech.

SNOW RELIABILITY
One of Austria's best

Lech and Zürs both get a lot of snow, but Austrian weather station records show a big difference between them despite their proximity. Lech gets an average of almost 8m of snow between December and March, almost twice as much as St Anton and three times as much as Kitzbühel, but Zürs gets half as much again as Lech. The altitude is high by Austrian resort standards and there is excellent snowmaking on Lech's sunny lower slopes.

This combination, together with excellent grooming, means that the Lech-Zürs ski area normally has good skiing from December until April. And the snow is frequently better here than on St Anton's predominantly south-facing slopes.

FOR ADVANCED SKIERS
Off-piste is main attraction

There are no black pistes on the piste map, only the two types of off-piste route referred to above. Skiing these with a guide is the official recommendation, though many ignore the advice. The truth is that good skiers will get a lot more out of the area if they do have a guide. There is plenty of excellent off-piste that isn't marked on the map, much of it accessed by long traverses. Especially in fresh snow, it can be wonderful.

Many of the best runs start from Zuger Hochlicht or the Steinmähder chair, which finishes just below it. Some routes involve a short climb to access bowls of untracked powder. From the Kriegerhorn there are shorter off-piste runs down towards Lech and

a very scenic long run down to Zug. There are also good runs from Salober Kopf at the northern end of the ski area. One of the problems with all these, however, is that most are south- or west-facing and can suffer from getting a lot of sun.

At the end of the season, when the snow is deep and settled, the off-piste off the shoulder of the Wöstertäli from the top of the Rüfikopf cable-car down to Lech can be superb. There are also good runs from the top of the Trittkopf cable-car in the Zürs sector, including a tricky one above the Flexen Pass down to Stuben.

Good skiers will also enjoy cruising some of the steeper red runs and will want to visit St Anton once or twice during the week, where they will find more challenging piste as well as off-piste skiing.

Heli-skiing is available from either the Kriegerhorn or the Flexen Pass.

FOR INTERMEDIATE SKIERS
Flattering variety for all

The piste skiing in the Oberlech area is nearly all immaculately groomed blue runs, the upper ones above the trees, the lower ones in wide swathes cut through them. It is ideal territory for leisurely skiers not wanting any surprises. And even early intermediates will be able to ski the circuit to Zürs and back, the only red run involved being the beautiful long (and not at all difficult) piste back to Lech from the top of the Madloch chair in Zürs.

More adventurous intermediates should take the Steinmähder chair to just below Zuger Hochlicht, or the cable-car all the way up, and from there take the scenic red run all the way to Zug (the latter part on a 'ski route' rather than a piste). If you want to record the speed of your schuss there is an electronic speed indicator at the Weibermahd chair-lift in Oberlech.

Zürs has much more interesting red run skiing, on both sides of the valley. We particularly like the west-facing reds down from the Trittkopf cable-car and the usually quiet run back to Zürs from the Muggengrat chair, which starts in a steep bowl.

FOR BEGINNERS
Easy skiing in all areas

The main nursery slopes are in Oberlech, but there is also a nice isolated area in the village dedicated purely to beginners. There are also good easy runs to progress to, both above and below Oberlech.

SKI SCHOOL

94/95 prices in schillings

Lech and Oberlech
Classes 6 days
4hr: 10am-noon and
1pm-3pm
6 full days: 1510
Children's classes
Ages: 3½ to 12
6 full days including
lunch: 1870
Private lessons
Full day
2100 for full day;
each additional
person 160

CHILDCARE

There are ski
kindergartens in Lech
(2161-0) and Oberlech
(3236) taking children
from age 3, from 9am
to 4pm.

GETTING THERE

Air Zurich, transfer
3hr. Innsbruck,
transfer 2hr.

Rail Langen (15km);
12 buses daily from
station, buses
connect with
international trains.

PACKAGES

Austrian Holidays,
Austrian Travel
Service, Bladon Lines,
Inghams, Made to
Measure, Ski Choice

Zürs Made to
Measure

FOR CROSS-COUNTRY
Picturesque valley trail
There are two cross-country trails in
Lech. The longer one is 15km; it
begins in the centre of town and leads
through the beautiful Zug valley,
following the Lech river and ending
up outside Zug. The other begins
behind the church and goes to
Stubenbach (another hamlet in the
Lech area). In Zürs there is a 3km track
starting at Zürs and going to the
Flexen Pass. This starts at 1600m and
climbs to 1800m.

QUEUES
Bad despite limit on skier numbers
Even early starters may well find
queues at the Rüfikopf cable-car as the
morning rush heads off towards Zürs.
Similarly the crucial Madloch chair at
the top of the Zürs area generates
queues of people going towards Lech.
The problem is that the circuit goes
only one way, so everyone is headed
in the same direction. Other
bottlenecks include the Zuger
Hochlicht lift, Trittkopf cable-car and
getting up from Zürs to Seekopf where
new chair-lifts still can't cope with the
volume in high season and holidays.
All this is despite the proud boast that
the region limits skier numbers to
14,000 a day for more enjoyable
skiing. The Oberlech region rarely
causes problems.

MOUNTAIN RESTAURANTS
Not enough
A lack of cosy Alpine restaurants sends
many frustrated lunchers back to the
resorts of Lech and Zürs to be sure of
an enjoyable meal. One of the best
mountain restaurants is Seekopf
(reached by the Seekopf chair-lift)
which has a lovely sun terrace. Also
popular is the self-service Palmenalpe
above Zug, but it does get very
crowded. There are a few good places
set prettily around the piste at
Oberlech but all get crowded; our
favourite is the Goldener Berg. For a
gourmet blow-out in Zürs, Chesa
Verde in the hotel Edelweiss and the
restaurant in the hotel Hirlanda both
feature in Gault-Millau but are not
cheap. The hotel Rote Wand in Zug
serves more casual fare. Café Schneider
in Lech serves good local dishes.

SKI SCHOOL
Excellent
The ski schools of Lech, Oberlech and
Zürs all have good reputations and we
have had no bad reports of them. But
in peak periods it might be as well to
book in advance as many of the

instructors are hired regularly every
year by an exclusive clientele. While
the instructors speak good English, as
they are used to foreigners, they may
not have picked up the typical British
sense of humour. Do not be surprised
if lessons become like a military
exercise. The days instructors ate for
free (as their commission) when
taking you to a restaurant appear to be
over. The new rule seems to be that
you pay for their lunch! Group lessons
are divided into no less than 12 ability
levels, which augurs well for optimum
use of time.

FACILITIES FOR CHILDREN
Oberlech's fine if you can afford it
We haven't got many reports on Lech,
and hardly any from families, who
presumably find it a rather expensive
destination. But Oberlech, in
particular, makes an excellent choice
for those who can afford it, and at
least one of the hotels there – the
Sonnenburg – has an impressive in-
house nursery.

 # Staying there

Lech is big enough for some of the
cheaper accommodation to be quite a
walk from the lifts. Unless you're
heavily into nightlife, staying up in
Oberlech is very attractive.

HOW TO GO
Luxury dominates
Chalets There are no catered chalets in
Lech itself, but Bladon Lines have a
little place in neighbouring Zug. It's
been highly praised by reporters, and
represents very good value by local
standards – book early.
Hotels There are several 5-star hotels,
and dozens of 4-star and 3-star ones,
but also countless more modest places
charging one-tenth of the 5-star rates.
££££ **Arlberg** A favourite with
certain royal(ish) persons. Elegantly
rustic chalet, centrally placed. Pool.
££££ **Krone** One of the oldest
buildings in the village, in a prime
spot by the river.
££££ **Tannbergerhof** Splendidly
atmospheric luxy inn on main street,
with outdoor bar and hugely popular
disco (tea-time as well as later). Pool.
££££ **Sonnenburg** (Oberlech) Big
luxurious chalet on the piste (popular
for lunch), with good children's
facilities. Pool.
££ **Haus Rudboden** Right by the
nursery slopes.
Self-catering There are no apartments
available through tour operators.

EATING OUT
Not necessarily expensive
There are over 50 restaurants in Lech with nearly all the hotels having dining rooms. For reasonably priced meals try the Montana, which has an excellent wine cellar, the Krone or the Post, which serves Austrian nouvelle-type food. The Madlochblick has a typically Austrian restaurant, very cosy with good solid food. For pasta and other Italian fare there is Pizza Charly. In Oberlech there a good fondue at Goldener Berg, a tavern built in 1432. In Zug the Rote Wand is excellent for fondues and a good night out. Also try the Alphorn, the Gasthof Alpenblick and the Klosterle.

APRES-SKI
In abundance
The umbrella bar of the Berg hotel at Oberlech is popular immediately after skiing. Then the 'beautiful people' head down to Krones ice bar, which has a lovely setting by the river, or to the outdoor bar of the Tannbergerhof.

Inside the Tannbergerhof, there's always a lively tea dance disco. Dancing in the streets is quite common. If you're looking for a disco there's the Arlberg hotel's Scotch Club, owned and run by former Olympic champion, Egon Zimmermann, and others in the hotels Almhof-Schneider and Krone. The latter's Side Step specialises in 60s and 70s music. The Pfefferkörnd'l is a good place for a drink, and is particularly popular for its after-skiing cocktails and gourmet snacks. You can also get a steak or pizza there until 11.30pm. For a change of scene after skiing, there's the champagne bar in Oberlech's hotel Montana, or later the Rote Wand in Zug has a disco.

FOR NON-SKIERS
Poseurs' paradise
Many visitors to Lech don't ski. If armed with a limitless credit card the shopping possibilities are enticing and the main street is often filled with fur-clad browsers. Strolz's plush emporium in the centre of town is a good place to up the rate at which you're spending schillings.

It's easy to get to Oberlech or Zug to meet skiers for lunch – or for them to come back to the village. The village outdoor bars make ideal posing positions – but make sure you are immaculately groomed or you'll feel out of place. An excursion to St Anton, to see how the other half live, is possible, though Lech clientele may feel more at home getting off the bus at chic St Christoph. For the more active there are 25km of walking paths and a variety of sporting activities.

Zürs 1720m
Ten minutes' drive towards St Anton from Lech, Zürs is almost on the Flexen Pass, with good snow virtually guaranteed. Zürs was a tiny hamlet used for farming during the summer only until (in the late 1890s) the Flexen Pass road was built and Zürs began to develop, entering the ski scene in the early 20th century.

The village is even more exclusive than Lech, with no hotels of less than 3-star standing, and a dozen 4-star and 5-star hotels around which life revolves. But the opulence is less overt here. There are few shops. Nightlife is quiet, though there are discos in the Edelweiss, Mara and Zürserhof hotels. There's also a piano bar in the Alpenhof and a good après-ski watering hole is Gerhard's Bar. Serious dining means the Zürserhof and the Lorünser – make sure you have a platinum credit card for these. For something cheaper try spaghetti in the basement of the hotel Edelweiss. Princess Caroline (who stays at the Lorünser) managed to get a plate of spaghetti here at 5am.

Zürs has its own ski school, but many of the instructors are booked for the entire season by regular clients, and more than 80% of them are hired privately. The resort has its own kindergarten.

ACTIVITIES
Indoor Tennis, squash, hotel swimming pools and saunas, cinema, museum, art gallery, bowling, hotel spas (massage and balneotherapy)
Outdoor 25km of cleared walking paths, toboggan run (from Oberlech), natural ice rink (skating, curling), sleigh rides, billiards, helicopter rides

TOURIST OFFICE
Postcode A-6764
Tel 010 43 (5583)
21610
Fax 3155

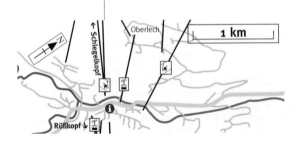

Mayrhofen 630m

✔ *Excellent children's amenities*

✔ *Lively après ski – but easily avoided if you prefer peace*

✔ *Wide range of non-skiing facilities*

✔ *One of the more snowsure ski areas in the Tyrol, with the added safety of the Hintertux glacier nearby*

✔ *Opportunity to try various nearby areas on the same lift pass, linked by free bus*

✔ *Easy road and rail access*

✘ *No skiing at village level, even for beginners*

✘ *Long queues for lifts up and down the mountain – though a major new lift is planned for this season*

✘ *Inconveniently situated lifts, some out of town, can mean walks and buses*

✘ *Sprawling, commercialised village*

✘ *Little difficult skiing*

✘ *Small, crowded local ski areas*

Mayrhofen is a British favourite which wears two distinctly different hats. Many young or youngish visitors like it for its lively nightlife. But it is also an excellent family resort: its amenities include highly regarded kindergartens, and a new fun pool with a special children's area. Fortunately, the liveliest of the nightlife is confined to a few very popular places, easily avoided by families in such a large resort.

But there are other considerations. Having skiing that is remote from the village is forgiveable; having remote skiing accessed by inconvenient and inadequate lifts is not. Some people, clearly, are not worried by the inconvenience of getting up and down Mayrhofen's mountain. We are, and we would be very wary of booking a holiday (particularly a high-season holiday) in Mayrhofen until the long-awaited new lifts are up and running.

The Zillertal pass covers all the resorts in the valley, including the excellent glacier at Hintertux (see page 68). If you're thinking of spending more than a day up there, there is something to be said for basing yourself closer to the glacier – perhaps at Lanersbach, a pretty, rustic village with a respectable local ski area, described at the end of this chapter.

ORIENTATION

Sitting in the flat-bottomed Zillertal, Mayrhofen is a cable-car ride from both its ski areas. Lifts also access the main area from **Finkenberg** and **Mühlbach**, villages either side of town. A frequent free bus serves several other resorts covered by the area pass, notably **Hintertux, Lanersbach** and **Gerlos**.

SKI FACTS

Altitude	640m-2250m
Lifts	30
Pistes	91km
Green/Blue	52%
Red	40%
Black	8%
Artificial snow	4½km

🏠 The resort

Mayrhofen is a large resort – big enough to be called a town, but not towny in character. It's essentially a traditional little village of a few bars, restaurants, hotels large and small, and sports shops – but multiplied twenty-fold. As the village has grown, architecture has been kept traditional, but the place is so sprawling and commercialised it can hardly be considered charming.

The main street is surrounded by almost every kind of tourist amenity – except ski lifts. Conservationists have thus far blocked attempts to build new lifts in the village, with the result that many visitors face long walks or bus-rides to the old ones.

Despite its 'lively' reputation, Mayrhofen is not dominated by lager louts. They exist, but tend to congregate in a few particular and easily avoided bars. The central hotels are mainly slightly upmarket places, and overall the resort has a pleasantly civilised atmosphere.

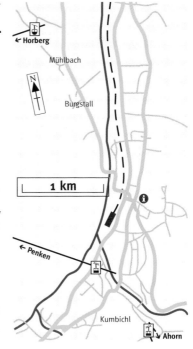

SKI SCHOOL

93/94 prices in schillings

Uli Spiess
Manager Uli Spiess
Classes 6 days
4hr: 10am-noon and 1pm-3pm
6 full days: 1370
Children's classes
Ages: 4 to 12
6 full days including lunch: 2090
Private lessons
Hourly and daily
450 for 1hr; each additional person 200

Manfred Gager
Manager Manfred Gager
Classes 6 days
4hr: 10am-noon and 1.30-3.30
6 full days: 1370
Children's classes
Ages: 4 to 14
6 full days including lunch: 2090
Private lessons
Hourly and daily
450 for 1hr; each additional person 200

SMT Mayrhofen Total
Manager Max Rahm
Classes 6 days
4hr: 10am-noon and 1pm-3pm
6 full days: 1370
Children's classes
Ages: 4 to 14
6 full days including lunch: 2090
Private lessons
Hourly and daily
450 for 1hr; each additional person 200

OTHER SCHOOLS
Mount Everest
Manager Peter Habeler

 # The skiing

Mayrhofen has two skiing mountains, one of which (Penken) is mainly suitable for intermediates, the other (Ahorn) only for beginners. Neither has much to offer advanced skiers.

THE SKI AREA
Highly inconvenient

Both skiing sectors are served by very queue-prone cable-cars, a bus-ride apart, which usually have to be ridden down as well as up. An unpisted run from **Ahorn** is the only trail from mountains to village. Needless to say, changing ski areas or meeting friends for lunch in the village is a serious waste of good skiing time. Access to the **Penken** is also provided by the gondolas a couple of kilometres either side of the resort at Hippach and Finkenberg. It is possible to ski back down to Finkenberg and Hippach when snow is good. The Finkenberg run is is only a path. The unpisted Hippach trail is the best run in the area for good skiers, but rarely has good snow cover.

SNOW RELIABILITY
Good by Austrian standards

Although the highest lift goes no higher than 2280m, the area is reasonably good for snow-cover because (apart from the unreliable valley runs) all of Mayrhofen's skiing is above 1580m. Mayrhofen is also fortunate in having one of the best glaciers in the Alps within day-trip range, at Hintertux.

FOR ADVANCED SKIERS
Go elsewhere

Mayrhofen is not a sensible base for good skiers unless aiming to go touring. The long unpisted run down to Mühlbach is the only worthwhile local skiing, and this is rarely skiable.

FOR INTERMEDIATE SKIERS
Problematic

Mayrhofen's ski area is sufficiently small to disappoint the avid piste basher, yet just difficult enough to be unappetising for the nervous intermediate. If you come between those categories, its short, mainly open runs spread across the Penken and next-door Gerent may suit you.

On the other hand, the Ziller valley is excellent for intermediates willing to travel. Each of the main ski areas covered by the valley pass is sufficiently large and varied to make an interesting day's skiing.

FOR BEGINNERS
Overrated: big drawbacks

Despite its reputation for ski teaching Mayrhofen is less than ideal for beginners. The Ahorn nursery slopes are excellent – high, extensive and sunny – but it's a tiresome journey to reach them. Overcrowded slopes and restaurant add to the hassle. The Penken nursery area is less satisfactory, and a short but irritating climb up from the cable-car.

FOR CROSS-COUNTRY
Go to Lanersbach

In theory there is a fine 20km trail along the valley to Zell am Ziller, plus small loops conveniently in, or close to, the village. But snow at 600m is not reliable. Vorderlanersbach has a much higher, more snowsure trail running to Madseit, a tiny hamlet just short of Hintertux.

QUEUES
Never-ending

Mayrhofen continues to be one of the worst resorts in the Alps for queues at the beginning and end of the day. The small Ahorn and Penken cable-cars are totally inadequate, even in January. A new, higher capacity Penken cable car is due to open for the 1995/96 season, which we suspect will reduce rather than eradicate delays. Beginners also have to put up with over-subscribed lifts. But intermediates, once away from the busy area close to the Penken cable-car, have surprisingly queue-free skiing. The buses to and from the out-of-town gondolas are often crowded, particularly the Finkenberg one, which also serves Hintertux.

MOUNTAIN RESTAURANTS
Penken good, Ahorn bad

The Penken is very well endowed with mountain restaurants, most of which are attractive and sunny and serve good-value food. The Ahorn has only one restaurant, which is inadequate for the hordes of beginners using it.

SKI SCHOOL
You name it, they do it – well

Mayrhofen's popularity is founded on its four ski schools, which between them provide a wide range of services. We have received positive reports on many of them, including the ordinary group and private lessons. There's also ski guiding around the Zillertal, and ski tours with the Mount Everest school to the Hoher Riffler and Rastkogel summits. Snowboarders are also well catered for, with their own specialist section of the Total school.

LIFT PASSES

94/95 prices in schillings
Mayrhofen/Zillertal
Coverage depends on period – see notes.
Main pass
1-day pass 330
6-day pass 1965
Children
Under 15: 6-day pass 1180 (40% off)
Under 6: free pass
Short-term passes
Half-day pass for Mayrhofen only.
Alternative periods
Zillertal pass available for 4 days skiing in 6, 5 days in 7, 6 days in 7 and 10 days in 14.
Notes 1- to 3-day pass covers Penken/Ahorn area only; 4-day and over includes all 154 Ziller valley lifts (including Hintertux glacier), 430km of piste, ski bus and railway.
Alternative passes
Zillertal pass without Hintertux glacier (6 days 1500 for adults, 900 for children).

CHILDCARE

All four ski schools run children's classes, and ski kindergartens where lunch is provided – Spiess at Ahorn, Gager at Penken, the other two at both ski areas. All take children aged 4 to 12 or 14, and appear to operate only until the end of ski teaching at 3.30.

Wuppy's Kinderland non-skiing nursery at the fun pool complex takes children aged 3 months to 7 years, 8.30am to 5pm.

The Sporthotel Strass has a playroom.

GETTING THERE

Air Salzburg, transfer 3hr. Innsbruck, transfer 1½hr.

Rail Local line through to resort; regular buses from station.

FACILITIES FOR CHILDREN
Excellent but inconvenient

Mayrhofen has put childcare at the centre of its pitch, and the facilities both for skiing and non-skiing children are excellent. However, we prefer to take our offspring to resorts where they don't have to be bussed around and ferried up and down the mountain.

 # Staying there

In such a large sprawling village, with two widely separated lifts, location is important. The original centre of the village, around the market place, church and bus/railway stations, is now on the periphery of things. The most convenient area is on the main street, as close as possible to the Penken cable-car.

HOW TO GO
Plenty of mainstream packages

There is a wide choice for package-buyers and independent travellers – except for chalet fans.
Chalets Equity Total Ski have the only catered chalet we are aware of. It's a traditional villa conversion, well located close to the Penken cable car, high street and swimming complex.
Hotels There is an enormous choice of hotels. There are dozens of cheap pensions, but most British skiers stay in the larger, better hotels. Most of the packaged hotels are centrally located in a good position for village amenities but a fair walk from the Penken cable-car, and a bus-ride from the Ahorn lift.
£££££ Elisabeth The resort's only 5-star hotel, an opulent chalet in a fair position near the post office.
££££ Manni's Well-placed, smartly done out; pool.
£££ Sporthotel Strass Best-placed of the 4-stars, very close to the Penken cable-car. Lively bar, disco, fitness centre, solarium, pool and children's playroom.
£££ Waldheim Smallish, cosy 3-star gasthof, close to the Penken lift,.
£££ St Georg Poorly positioned for amenities, but is ideal for those wanting a multi-facility quality hotel in peaceful surroundings.
£££ Jägerhof Another peaceful hotel with good facilities, midway between the two cable-cars.
£ Claudia, **Monika** Cheap little twin guesthouses in a good position.
£ Kumbichl, **Kumbichlhof** Adjoining pensions, right next to the Ahorn cable-car.

Self-catering Although there's a wide choice of apartments for independent holidaymakers, we are not aware of any packages on the UK market.

EATING OUT
Wide choice

Most Brits come here on half-board, but there is a large choice of restaurants catering for most tastes and budgets. The Hotel Rose has a particularly good but informal restaurant.

APRES-SKI
Lively but not rowdy

Nightlife is a great selling point. Mayrhofen has all the standard Tyrolean-style entertainment such as folk dancing, bier-kellers and tea dances, along with bowling, sleigh rides, tobogganing and several lively bars and discos. The Movie bar, Scotland Yard pub and the Sporthotel's Arena video disco are particularly rocking places to go. Although après ski is lively, it usually avoids becoming too rowdy; Mayrhofen is no 'Benidorm am Ziller'.

FOR NON-SKIERS
Good for all but shoppers

There's lots to do. The village travel agency arranges trips into Italy, while Innsbruck is easily reached by train. There are also good walks and sports amenities. Meeting skiers for lunch is not a problem; at least non-skiers can wait for the crowds to disperse before going up the mountain. Shopping is the one disappointment – just a lot of sports shops and souvenir places.

Finkenberg 840m

Finkenberg offers a welcome alternative to Mayrhofen, being a much smaller, quieter village with far better access to and from the Penken skiing. It is no more than a collection of traditional-style hotels, bars, cafés and private homes awkwardly dispersed along a steep section of the busy main road between Mayrhofen and Lanersbach. There are two distinct halves – the original village around the church, and a second cluster of buildings conveniently close to the gondola station, just over five minutes' walk away.

The gondola gives queue-free access to the Penken (Mayrhofen-based skiers tend to use the Hippach gondola rather than this one) and, importantly, a speedy ride home for beginners (and all other skiers when the Katzenmoos path is not skiable). Thus Finkenberg residents can be

PACKAGES

Airtours, Crystal, Enterprise, Equity Total Ski, Inghams, Made to Measure, Neilson, Ski Club of GB, Snowcoach Club Cantabrica, Thomson, Timescape

Finkenberg Crystal

ACTIVITIES

Mayrhofen

Indoor Bowling, 3 hotel pools open to the public, massage, sauna, jacuzzi, Turkish baths (in hotels, but open to non-residents), squash, 4 fitness centres, chess, indoor tennis centre at Hotel Berghof (3 courts, coaching available), indoor riding-school, pool and billiards, stamp-swapping, cinema.

Outdoor Natural skating-rink, curling, horse-riding, horse and dog sleigh rides and racing, 45km cleared paths, hang-gliding, para-gliding, tobogganing (2 runs of 2.5km)

TOURIST OFFICE

Mayrhofen

Postcode A-6290
Tel 010 43 (5285) 2305
Fax 411633

tucking into coffee and cake in their favourite café while Mayrhofen guests are freezing to death, queuing in the dark for their cable-car home.

Finkenberg has a nursery slope in the village which, given good snow, means that beginners do not need to buy the full lift pass. But it's a sunless spot, and good conditions are far from certain at this altitude.

Cross-country skiers have to get a bus up to Lanersbach.

There are two ski schools. The Klauss-Kroll school has a particularly good reputation.

Like Mayrhofen, Finkenberg prides itself on its ability to give children a good time. But it is not a resort for young tots: there is no non-ski crèche and the ski nursery doesn't take children under the age of 4.

All hotels are within walking distance of the gondola. The 4-star Margit is particularly well positioned in the new sector, and the equally comfortable Stock is close to the lift station, on the edge of the original village. The 3-star Gasthof Panorama is well placed in the new part. In the centre of the original village the 4-star Eberl, the 3-star Garni Austria and 2-star Pension Troppmair are six or seven minutes from the gondola.

Restaurants are mostly hotel-based. The Stock has one of the best and most expensive. The Neuwirt is a good mid-range place, while the Finkenberghof has an appetising cheaper menu.

Finkenberg is quiet in the evenings. The main après-ski spots are Pub Laternall and Cafe Zum Fink'n, and there are rep-organised events such as tobogganing and bowling. Mayrhofen is a short taxi-ride away and offers a far wider choice of evening action.

Swimming and ice-skating are available, but most non-skiers find themselves spending a lot of time down in Mayrhofen.

Lanersbach 1300m

Lanersbach is an attractive, spacious, traditional village spoilt only by the busy road up to Hintertux cutting through part of it, and passing the main lift station. The area around the pretty church is hidden away off the road, yet within walking distance of the lift. The village is small and uncommercialised, but it has all you need in a resort. And prices are low.

The Eggalm ski area, now accessed by a cable-car, has a high point of 2300m at Beil, and a small network of pleasantly varied mostly wooded pistes leading back to the village and across to the Rastkogel sector above nearby Vorderlanersbach. This sector (also accessed by its own modern gondola) goes higher (top station 2500m) but is not so pretty or interesting. The two sectors total 33km of piste. Snow conditions are usually good; by Austrian standards this is high skiing.

There are no pistes to challenge good skiers, but there is a fine off-piste route starting a short walk from the Lanersbach top station and finishing at the village. Intermediates should enjoy the wonderfully uncrowded, well-groomed runs. Lanersbach's nursery slope is rather small, and finding an English-speaking instructor can be a problem.

Lanersbach is the best base in the area for cross-country, with 23km of trails running to Madseit.

Lanersbach is essentially a hotel resort. The Lanersbachhof is a multi-amenity olde worlde 4-star close to the lifts but is also on the main road. The cheaper 3-star Pinzger and Alpengruss are similarly situated. The 3-star Bergkristall is central, but reasonably close to the cable-car.

Restaurants are mainly hotel-based. The Bergfried and Central hotels have good but expensive restaurants. Gasthof Jäger is a cheaper place with a charming restaurant.

Nightlife is quiet by Austrian standards, though the Mondschein Keller and Sporthotel Kirchler bar have plenty of atmosphere, and there is a disco which livens up at weekends.

Non-skiers are fairly well catered for considering the size of the resort. Some of the better hotels have facilities such as pools, jacuzzis and fitness rooms open to non-residents. Just outside the village is a tennis centre, plus squash and ten-pin bowling. Mayrhofen is a worthwhile excursion, while Salzburg is just within range.

The non-ski nursery takes children from age 2, the ski school from 4. Lanersbach is generally a child-friendly village, though a lack of English-speaking supervision, tuition and other children to play with could be a problem.

Neustift 990m

Neustift earns its prominent place here for a curious reason – the quality of the glacier skiing 20km away at the top of the Stubai valley. It has its own little ski area where unadventurous intermediates can potter happily about – but so have dozens of other little Tyrolean villages that we have relegated to a footnote at the back of the book. However, the Stubaigletscher is one of the best skiing glaciers in Austria, and that means one of the best in the world.

THE RESORT

Neustift is a very attractive, traditional Tyrolean village about half-way along the Stubai valley, south-west of Innsbruck. It is the closest large community to the glacier, but not the only village in the valley with ski-resort status. Down the valley towards Innsbruck, Fulpmes has a more extensive local ski area, and plenty of accommodation both in Fulpmes itself and in the satellite village of Telfes. Mieders, still further down the valley, has some skiing too. The Stubai valley lift pass covers all these resorts and the glacier lifts, as well as the ski-bus.

THE SKIING

Neustift's local **ski area** is a narrow chain of slopes and lifts – mainly drags – from Elferhütte at 2080m down to the village. With the exception of one short blue run at altitude, the skiing is all graded red. This main area is on the south-east side of the valley; there is also a nursery area at village level, on the other side.

The Stubai glacier is a much more extensive area of blue and red runs (and one short black) between 3200m and the first station of the main access lifts, at 2300m. The glacier is broken up by rocky peaks, giving more sense of variety in the skiing than is normal on a glacier. But the landscape is harsh and unattractive, with lots of moraine. The bus service to the glacier is sadly inadequate – 45-minute intervals between buses even at peak times, and insufficient capacity.

With one of the world's best glaciers at the top of the valley, **snow reliability** is not a problem. The local slopes face roughly north, but are of typically modest Austrian altitude. The village nursery slopes are sunny, and not reliable.

The local skiing does not have much to offer **advanced skiers**, and the glacier is not in the same league as Hintertux for challenge, but there are long runs to be done, including a 4km ski route down the east side of the glacier, and a splendid 10km ski route down a deserted bowl back to Mutterberg in the valley at 1750m.

For **intermediate skiers**, the local skiing rather falls between two stools: it is not easy, but it is not extensive – so its main appeal is to the confident intermediate who wants to practise technique rather than get around. The glacier is splendid intermediate territory, whatever your standard.

This is not a resort for **beginners**; the village nursery slopes are attractive, but too sunny – though they do have snowmakers.

There are 100km of **cross-country** trails in the Stubaital, including some trails at altitude reached by the lifts serving the Fulpmes and Mieders Alpine skiing. Mieders is the best base. There are trails on the glacier.

There can be serious **queues** for the access lifts to the glacier – worst, of course, when snow conditions lower down are poor.

The **mountain restaurants** in both sectors are no more than adequate – a mixture of primitive mountaineering huts and big impersonal cafeterias. There are great views to be had outside the tiny cabin at the top of the glacier, at Jochdohle.

There are **ski schools** both in Neustift itself and at the glacier. Guided ski tours are available. **Children** can be looked after all day.

STAYING THERE

If you fly into Innsbruck, you can be in the resort an hour after landing. There are lots of 4-star and 3-star **hotels**. The 3-star Tirolerhof is excellent – comfortable and relaxed, with good food. It has its own ski school and ski hire shop. The central 4-star Sonnhof is also recommended.

Most of the **restaurants** are hotel-based. There is some **après-ski** activity, focused apparently on the Romanstuben.

Neustift has quite a lot to offer **non-skiers**. There is skating, swimming, tennis, squash and bowling. The Stubaital looks like heaven for toboggan enthusiasts; all the villages have impressive runs – at Neustift, for example, there is an 8km run from the top of the main chair-lift. Innsbruck is only minutes away by bus.

Niederau 830m

HOW IT RATES

The skiing

Snow	*
Extent	*
Advanced	*
Intermediates	**
Beginners	****
Convenience	***
Queues	****
Restaurants	**

The rest

Scenery	***
Resort charm	***
Not skiing	**

SKI FACTS

Altitude	830m-1900m
Lifts	37
Pistes	42km
Green/Blue	65%
Red	30%
Black	5%
Artificial snow	none

PACKAGES

Alpine Tours, Crystal, Enterprise, Inghams, Neilson, Thomson

Auffach Alpine Tours

Mühltal Alpine Tours, Winterski

Oberau Enterprise, Inghams, Thomson

TOURIST OFFICE

Postcode A-6311
Tel 010 43 (5339)
8255
Fax 2433

An attractive, friendly resort with a small, quite varied ski area, that has a strong British following. Good for families and beginners, so long as there is decent snow. Sadly, this is far from guaranteed.

THE RESORT

Niederau is a popular example of what Austria does so well: the unspoilt, hassle-free, family ski village. It's more convenient than Waidring and Fieberbrunn, cheaper and prettier than Obergurgl, and less commercialised than Westendorf. It has a lovely setting in a pretty valley and is made up of pleasant chalet-style buildings – even if it does lack village atmosphere.

A cluster of restaurants and shops opposite the Markbachjoch chair-lift is the nearest thing to a focal point, but few hotels are more than five minutes' walk from one or other of the two main chair-lifts up into the skiing. The roads are quiet, except on Saturdays.

The resort is geared towards families looking for a friendly, unsophisticated but civilised atmosphere. Niederau has strong British connections, with a faithful following who return year after year.

The Wildschonau lift pass covers the higher ski area of Auffach, a bus-ride away in the next valley, and the nursery slopes in and around the pretty village of Oberau, on the col between the two.

THE SKIING

The small local **ski area** is spread over a broad, wooded mountainside which does not rise above 1600m. Mountain access is via two chairs, a few minutes' walk apart, in central Niederau. The Markbachjoch chair gives immediate access to a novices' plateau at 1500m and the area's steepest runs, back to the village. Easier runs to Niederau open up from the plateau. The other chair doesn't go so high, but is surmounted by a steep drag to the high-point of Lanerköpfl (1600m). A choice of red runs descend to the village.

A reliable half-hourly bus (free) goes to Auffach. Its sunny ski area is narrower, but taller (up to 1900m, with a vertical of 1000m). The main lift is a two-stage gondola. There are few **queues** in either area.

Snow reliability is a problem, made worse by a lack of snowmaking. When it is impossible to ski back to Niederau, its ski area is tiny. Because of its mid-station, Auffach is not as badly affected in such circumstances.

The few black runs don't have much appeal, and **advanced skiers** should go elsewhere.

Good **intermediates** may find the ungroomed gully black runs awkward rather than interesting and the whole ski area much too small to keep them interested for more than a day or two. Leisurely skiers have some interesting runs to enjoy; the long main Auffach piste is the highlight.

Niederau is suitable for **beginners** and moderate intermediates, but has surprisingly little for those in between. Excellent nursery slopes lie at the foot and top of the mountain, but the low ones lose the sun each afternoon.

There are 35km of **cross-country** trails along the valley, which are good when snow is abundant.

Mountain restaurants are scarce, causing lunch-time queues, and many return to the village for lunch.

The **ski school** has a good reputation but classes can be large.

Children are cared for from the age of 3 – in both ski kindergarten and non-ski nursery.

STAYING THERE

The Austria is the best hotel in Niederau, 50m from the Markbachjoch chair. Vicky and Schneeberger are well-placed 3-stars. Staffler is a lively, central 2-star. Pensions Bergwett and Lindner are basic, good-value B&Bs. Haus Jochum has spacious and comfortable **self-catering** accommodation positioned close to the Tennladen drag.

Hotels Alpenland and Wastlhof have reputations for good-value restaurants if you're **eating out**.

Niederau has a nice balance of **après-ski**, neither too noisy for families nor too quiet for the young and lively. Hotel Staffler's Cave Bar is the liveliest place in town, except when instructors take clients into the Sport Café for a yodel. A number of places have live music: hotel Vicky, the Sonnbergstuberl, the Starchenhof and the Alm pub.

For **non-skiers**, walks are limited and there is little to do except swimming and excursions to Salzburg, Innsbruck, Vienna and Rattenburg.

Obergurgl 1930m

✔ One of the most reliable resorts for snow in the Alps, especially good for a late-season holiday

✔ Excellent ski area for beginners, unadventurous intermediates and families

✔ Normally queue- and crowd-free

✔ Retains village charm despite modern development

✔ Jolly tea-time après-ski

✘ Small ski area with no difficult runs

✘ Very bleak setting, with little skiing possible in bad weather

✘ Few off-slope amenities except in hotels

✘ Quiet nightlife by Austrian standards

✘ Expensive

Cruising down the Festkogl on a sunny Sunday morning, with seemingly the whole piste to yourself, sending up plumes of powdery snow, Obergurgl can seem idyllic. Few places can rival it for trouble-free, snowsure skiing. When you add high-quality hotels, a civilised atmosphere and very jolly tea-time après-ski, Obergurgl becomes the perfect resort for a certain type of skier. This is borne out by the remarkably high proportion of Obergurgl regulars who have been going there annually for years. It's best to book early to avoid disappointment.

But the Obergurgl-Hochgurgl ski area is not for everyone. Our postbag confirms this. Reporters either love it or hate it. There's no other resort where views are so sharply divided.

So what's the downside? The ski area is small and almost entirely easy. It also lacks variety, making the skiing feel even more limited. Keen piste-bashers will have explored it all in a day or two. Its slopes are high, treeless and can be cold and bleak in early season and poor weather. The village itself is made up primarily of hotels, with little in the way of shops or a vibrant nightlife. Those expecting something even remotely akin to other high Austrian resorts such as Ischgl or Lech will be sadly disappointed.

ORIENTATION

Obergurgl lies in a remote, bleak spot at the head of the Ötztal beyond Sölden. A gondola from near the entrance to the village gives access to all the local skiing and a chair-lift from above the village centre to part of it.

The Hochgurgl ski area is a bus-ride away, usually reached by chair-lift from Untergurgl. There's some accommodation at Hochgurgl.

Sölden (short bus or car journey) and **Kuhtai**, a worthwhile high ski area near Innsbruck, (long car journey) are the main ski excursion possibilities. Much closer is the tiny ski-touring launch-pad of **Vent**.

 ## The resort

Obergurgl is small and based on a traditional old village, set in a remote spot, the dead end of a long road up past Sölden. It is the highest parish in Austria and is usually under a blanket of snow from November until May. The surrounding mountains are bleak, with an array of avalanche barriers giving them a forbidding appearance.

Once they have arrived, most people don't use their cars. Obergurgl has no through-traffic and few day visitors, so the village is usually traffic-free.

Despite its small size, Obergurgl is a village of parts. At the entrance to the resort is a cluster of hotels near the main gondola. The road then passes a second group of hotels around the ice rink, up the hillside to the left, before coming to the village proper. This starts with an attractive little square, complete with church and fountain (and the original village hotel, the Edelweiss und Gurgl).

Village atmosphere is jolly during the day and immediately after skiing,

but can be subdued at night when most people stay in their hotels. The resort is popular with British families and well-heeled groups of adults looking for a relaxing winter break.

Hochgurgl, a bus-ride away, is little more than a handful of hotels at the foot of its own ski area.

 ## The skiing

For a well-known and popular resort, Obergurgl's ski area is surprisingly small and lacking in interest and challenge to any who think of themselves as adventurous intermediates or better. You also don't get a sense of travelling anywhere on skis, as you do in most resorts. That's because you just ski up and down north-west facing slopes, without travelling from area to area or down into a valley and up the other side. There are, however, some good off-piste runs to explore with a guide.

The lift pass at S2,090 for six days is very expensive for the amount of skiing and number of lifts. We've had

SKI FACTS

Altitude 1795m-3080m	
Lifts	22
Pistes	110km
Green/Blue	32%
Red	50%
Black	18%
Artificial snow	1km

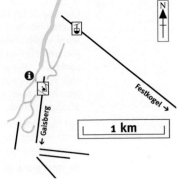

LIFT PASSES

94/95 prices in schillings

Obergurgl ski pass
Covers all lifts in Obergurgl, Untergurgl and Hochgurgl, and local ski-bus.

Beginners Lift pass or points card.

Main pass
1-day pass 420
6-day pass 2090
(low season 1840 – 12% off)

Senior citizens
Over 60: 6-day pass 1280 (39% off)

Children
Under 15: 6-day pass 1280 (39% off)
Under 5: free pass

Short-term passes
Half-day (from 11am, noon or 2pm).

several complaints about poor piste-marking, making life very tricky in white-outs. One worrying story told how 'One of our party went over the unmarked edge of the piste in poor visibility and broke her leg.'

THE SKI AREA
Fragmented cruising

The ski pass covers the two separate ski areas of Obergurgl and Hochgurgl. Adventurous skiers may prefer to leave their last day free for an excursion to Sölden – which unfortunately has no pass-sharing arrangements with Obergurgl.

The **Obergurgl** ski area is the smaller of the two. It is in two sections, well linked by piste in one direction, more loosely in the other.

The Festkogl gondola from near the village entrance takes you to the highest skiing area, served by two drags and two chairs, one of which reaches 3035m. From these runs you can ski back to the gondola base or over to the Gaisberg area, which has a high point of 2670m reached by a long, slow chair-lift. There are four other short lifts here as well as the chair-lift up to the area from just above the village square.

You can ski along by this access lift back to town and pole your way over to the Festkogl gondola to start the circuit again.

The regular and reliable free ski-bus service takes you to Untergurgl, a few minutes away. From there a chair-lift takes you to **Hochgurgl** (also reachable by car and the occasional bus – two or three times a day). Another chair-lift takes you from Hochgurgl to the heart of the skiing, which is served by four drags. Two alternative chair-lifts up from here take you to spectacular views of the Italian Dolomites and to the 3080m Wurmkogl summit. A single tree-lined run leads down from Hochgurgl to the bottom of the Untergurgl chair and the bus home.

SNOW RELIABILITY
Excellent

Obergurgl is arguably the most snowsure of Europe's non-glacier resorts. It has a justifiably popular mid-December white week and regular late-season visitors who book well in advance. The skiing is high, and there is virtually no tree-lined skiing. Wind and white-outs can shut the lifts and, especially in early season, severe cold can curtail skiers' enthusiasm.

FOR ADVANCED SKIERS
Not generally recommendable

There is a fair amount of enjoyable off-piste skiing to be found with a guide – especially from the Obergurgl ski area – and the top ski school groups often go off-piste when there is little avalanche danger. This is a well-known area for ski-touring .

The most challenging official piste is the Hohe Mut mogul field beneath the slow, old chair-lift at Gaisberg. But this is often irritatingly awkward rather than pleasurable, being icy, worn and difficult to follow in places. The other blacks are rather overgraded and there's little challenge for good skiers. Advanced skiers will soon tire of cruising the predominantly short runs, no matter how powdery the snow. Excursions by local bus to Sölden are possible.

SKI SCHOOL

94/95 prices in schillings

Obergurgl
Classes 6 days.
4hr: 10am-noon and
2pm-4pm.
6 full days: 1520
Children's classes
Ages: from 5
6 full days including
lunch: 2820
Private lessons
Half- and full day.
1400 (for half-day, for
1 to 2 people)

Hochgurgl
Classes 5 days.
4hr: 10am-noon and
2pm-4pm.
5 full days: 1490
Children's classes
Ages: from 5
5 full days: 1490
Private lessons
Half- and full day.
1350 (for half-day, for
1 to 2 people)

FOR INTERMEDIATE SKIERS
Good but limited

The ski areas have some perfect intermediate terrain, made even better by the normally flattering snow conditions. The problem is there's not much of it. Keen piste-bashers will quickly tire of skiing the same runs all the time and be itching to catch the bus to Sölden, down the valley.

Hochgurgl has the bigger area of easy runs. These make good cruising. For more challenging intermediate runs head over to the Vorderer Wurmkogellift, on the right hand side as you look at the mountain.

The run down from Hochgurgl to the bus at Untergurgl is about the only tree-lined skiing in the area, and the only run served by artificial snow. Less confident intermediates can find this tricky but necessary unless they want to wait for an infrequent Hochgurgl bus or take an expensive taxi back home.

The Obergurgl area has more red than blue runs but most offer no great challenge. The area served by chairs at the top of the Festkogl gondola is easy cruising. And there is a long enjoyable run down the length of the gondola, with a parallel, scenic off-piste route in the adjoining valley.

In the Gaisberg area, there are very easy runs in front of the Nederhütte and back towards town. The bottom drags here serve very short but sometimes tricky and bumpy runs.

FOR BEGINNERS
Good for first-timers or improvers

There is an adequate nursery slope above the village, and the Gaisberg run under the chair out of town can be completed as soon as a modicum of control is achieved.

Near beginners can ski from the top of the four-person Wurmkogel chair to Hochgurgl village (600m vertical) without any problems. The quality of the snow at Obergurgl makes the area a good (but expensive) choice for beginners compared with most lower Austrian resorts.

CROSS-COUNTRY
Limited but snowsure

Four small loops: two at Obergurgl, one at Untergurgl and another at Hochgurgl give a mere 13km of trail. They are, however, relatively snowsure and all pleasantly situated, the lower ones run alongside the river. Instruction is available.

QUEUES
No problems

Lift queues are rare. The resort is too remote to attract day trippers, and its authorities do not encourage 'bussing-in' when lower villages are struggling for snow.

MOUNTAIN RESTAURANTS
Little choice

Compared with most Austrian resorts, mountain huts are not very numerous and not very special. The Nederhütte at Gaisberg is one of the best value and jolliest, often with live music. David's at the bottom of the lowest drags is friendly and cheerful. The Schönwieshütte, a 10-minute walk

from the piste above here, is in a beautiful setting – as is the tiny hut at the top of the Hohe Mut chair. At Hochgurgl, the tiny hut at Wurmkogel has stunning views into Italy and basic food. Many skiers return to Obergurgl and Hochgurgl for lunch. Hotels Edelweiss and Jenewein in Obergurgl are particularly convenient, if expensive. Café Josl is a cheaper alternative. In Hochgurgl, hotel Riml has excellent reasonably priced food.

SKI SCHOOL
Good and bad

We've had good reports of the Obergurgl ski school, with reasonable class sizes of eight to ten and good English spoken. But Hochgurgl's school has its critics, with some suspicion that residents of the Hochgurgl hotel get preferential treatment. Class sizes of 14 or 15 are reported, along with a lack of interest and English on the part of instructors.

FACILITIES FOR CHILDREN
Check out your hotel

For a village with obvious appeal to families, Obergurgl doesn't seem to put itself out to cater for children. There is no ski kindergarten catering for tots who want to start early, and no special arrangements for lunchtime care of young children attending classes. Although both ski schools claim to run children's classes, one reporter found there were no specific facilities for children at Hochgurgl. The key factor would appear to be hotel facilities; many offer childcare of one sort or another, and the Alpina is particularly recommended.

⬆ Staying there

The Festkogl gondola area at the village entrance is the best place for getting into the skiing and for ease of access by car. However, it's a long walk or a ski-bus from the village centre and the nursery slopes.

Accommodation around the ice rink is perched above the village, with very steep, sometimes treacherous walks to and from other amenities. It's a very short ski to the chair-lift and a pole or ski to the Festkogl gondola.

Many of Obergurgl's mainly middle-aged clientele much prefer the convenience of staying in the village centre, being close to the Gaisberg lift and well placed for the ski-bus. Ski-drivers have underground parking bang in the centre of town.

HOW TO GO
Plenty of good hotels

Virtually all package accommodation is in hotels and pensions, but there are a number of comfortable apartments available to independent travellers. Demand for rooms in Obergurgl exceeds supply, and for once it is true that you should book early to avoid disappointment. Inghams have by far the largest allocation, including much-sought-after self-catering accommodation.

Hotels Obergurgl's accommodation is of high quality: most of its 30 hotels are of 4-star rating, and none is less than 3-star. Within each rating, hotels are uniformly comfortable. In our fat file of reports we have hardly any complaints. The main one comes from a young couple staying in the Deutschmann who came down to breakfast on the last day of their holiday to find that they were required to share their table with two *Where to Ski* researchers. How a 4-star hotel can treat its paying guests like this is a mystery to us.

££££ Edelweiss und Gurgl The focal hotel – biggest, oldest, among the most appealing; on the central square. Pool.

££££ Alpina Big, smart chalet with excellent children's facilities – kindergarten and playroom. Pool.

££££ Jenewein Recently refurbished, friendly staff, excellent food; good central position next to main lift.

££££ Gamper Best rooms very comfortable, good food; at far end of village, past the square.

££££ Crystal If you don't mind the ocean-liner appearance, one of the best hotels in Festkogl lift area.

£££ Fender Good all-rounder with friendly staff; central

£££ Wiesental Comfortable, well positioned, good value.

£££ Granat-Schlössl Amusing pseudo-castle, surprisingly affordable.

££ Alpenblume Good B&B hotel well-placed for Festkogl lift.

Hochgurgl has equally good hotels.

£££££ Hochgurgl The most luxurious in the area – the only 5-star. Pool.

£££ Laurin Well equipped, traditional rooms, excellent food.

Self-catering Inghams have an allocation in Lohmann, a high-standard large modern apartment block. It is well placed for the skiing, less so for the village centre below. Bookable independently, the 3-star Pirchhütte Garni has apartments close to the Festkogl gondola, while the Wiesental hotel has more central ones.

CHILDCARE

The ski schools at Obergurgl and Hochgurgl take children over the age of 5, but do not offer any special care arrangements.

The village kindergarten (305) takes children from the age of 2.

The Alpina and Austria hotels (among others) have in-house kindergartens.

PACKAGES

Austrian Travel Service, Crystal, Enterprise, Inghams, Made to Measure, Ski Club of GB, Thomson

Hochgurgl Austrian Travel Service, Inghams

GETTING THERE

Air Innsbruck, transfer 2hr. Salzburg, transfer 5hr. Munich, transfer 6hr.

Rail Train to Ötz; regular buses from station, transfer 1hr.

ACTIVITIES

Indoor Swimming pool (at Hotel Muhle, open to the public), saunas, whirlpools, steam baths, massage, bowling, pool and billiards, squash, table tennis, shooting range
Outdoor Natural skating rink (open in the evenings), curling, sleigh rides

TOURIST OFFICE

Postcode A-6456
Tel 010 43 (5256) 258
Fax 35377

EATING OUT
Wide choice, limited range
Hotel dining rooms and à la carte restaurants dominate. The commendable Pic Nic is the only independent restaurant, and hotel Madeleine has a good separate pizzeria. Hotel Alpina has a particularly good reputation for its food, while the restaurant at the Gasthof Gamper is pleasantly cosy.

APRES-SKI
Lively early, quiet later
Obergurgl is reasonably animated immediately after skiing, but things are pretty quiet later on. The Nederhütte mountain restaurant has an excellent tea dance three times a week, and the Umbrella Bar outside the Edelweiss hotel is popular when the weather is good.

Later on, the crowded Krumpn's Stadl barn is the liveliest place in town with live music on alternate nights. The Josl, Jenewein and Edelweiss hotels have atmospheric bars. Discos are uninspiring, but hotel Alpenland's bowling alley is popular.

Hochgurgl is very quiet at night except for Toni's Almhütte bar in the Olymp Sporthotel – one of three places in the resort which have live music. Hotel Hochfirst has a disco but it's difficult to believe much atmosphere is generated.

FOR NON-SKIERS
Very limited
There isn't much during the day. Innsbruck is over two hours by post-bus. Sölden (20 minutes away) has a leisure centre and shopping facilities. You can walk to the restaurants in the Gaisberg area to meet skiers for lunch. The Hochfirst hotel has a good health centre; be aware that it's mixed-sex and no clothes are allowed.

STAYING IN HOCHGURGL
Very quiet
The usual advantages of staying part way up a mountain are ski convenience, good snow and no queues. Obergurgl itself scores well in these, but Hochgurgl does have some good hotels, including the most luxurious in the area (the hotel Hochgurgl). It is even quieter than Obergurgl – great if you're looking for a quiet comfortable time with the easy skiing right on your doorstep.

Obertauern 1740m

Because of its excellent snow record, Obertauern is often chosen by skiers who are worried about conditions in lower Austrian resorts and don't mind the lack of tradition, charm and nightlife. It has a good intermediate circuit, plenty of beginners' slopes and some challenges for better skiers. But its trend-bucking snow means it can be overrun by skiers from less fortunate resorts.

HOW IT RATES

The skiing

Snow	****
Extent	**
Advanced	***
Intermediates	****
Beginners	*****
Convenience	****
Queues	****
Restaurants	***

The rest

Scenery	***
Resort charm	**
Not skiing	**

SKI FACTS

Altitude	1640m-2335m
Lifts	25
Pistes	120km
Green/Blue	50%
Red	35%
Black	15%
Artificial snow	10km

PACKAGES

Club Europe, Crystal, Inghams, Made to Measure, Neilson, Thomson

TOURIST OFFICE

Postcode A-5562
Tel 010 43 (6456) 252
Fax 515

THE RESORT

In the land of postcard resorts that have grown out of rustic valley villages, Obertauern is something of a sore thumb – a mainly modern development at the summit of the Tauern pass road. It's not a French-style blot, but is just as obviously functional and lacking in charm and village life. The resort straggles a long way along the pass, but there is a central focus of shops and bars.

THE SKIING

The Tauern pass road divides Obertauern's **ski area** into two unequal halves, well linked to make a user-friendly well-signed circuit that can be skied clockwise or anti-clockwise.

Most of the pistes are on the sunny slopes north of the resort: a wide, many-faceted basin of mostly gentle skiing, with a few steepish mogulled pitches punctuated by long schusses. The vertical range is rather limited, and skiers used to big areas will soon feel they have exhausted Obertauern.

The slopes on the other side of the road have Obertauern's highest and most difficult skiing. Even here, though, the top station is less than 600m above the resort.

The resort was developed to exploit the exceptional **snowfall** record of its high bowl. In the unlikely event of a shortage, there is plenty of snowmaking lower down.

Advanced skiers would naturally incline towards the Zehnerkar and Gamsleiten sectors to the south-west. There are some genuinely steep pisted and off-piste runs from the Gamsleiten chair, but it is prone to closure by wind and avalanche danger. For a greater challenge and longer descents you can join guided ski tours to peaks above the top lifts.

The biggest draw for **intermediates** is Obertauern's circuit. You can stay lower for easier pistes, or try some of the tougher runs higher up. The central point of the north area is Hochalm, from where the Seekareck quad and the Panorama chair take you to challenging, often mogully runs for better intermediates. The chair to Hundskogel leads to a choice between a red and a black. Over at the Plattenkar quad, there are two splendid 400m vertical reds.

Obertauern has very good nursery slopes, with three drag-lifts for **beginners** close to the village. After the first couple of lessons it's possible to go up the mountain, because the Schaidberg chair leads to a drag-lift serving a high-altitude beginners' slope and it is an easy run back home.

There is a 15km **cross-country** loop in the heart of the resort.

When neighbouring resorts don't share Obertauern's good snow, non-residents arrive by the bus-load. The lift system is impressively modern, so the horrendous **queues** you might fear do not materialise. But there is no escaping the crowded slopes.

The **mountain restaurants** are plentiful and good, especially the Kringsalm.

Of the several **ski schools,** most tour operators use the Krallinger – and its kindergarten. We have enthusiastic reports of both, despite classes as large as 15. But one regular visitor rates the Willi Grillitsch school 'much the best'.

STAYING THERE

Practically all of Obertauern's **accommodation** is in hotels (mostly 3-star and 4-star) and guest-houses. Location is not a major consideration. The 4-star Enzian is welcoming and comfortable, with good food and an outstanding wine cellar. The Edelweiss and Alpina are also recommended.

Eating out is mostly in hotels (the Enzian is recommended) and the busy après-ski bars at the foot of the north-side lifts. The Hochalm restaurant at the top of the quad chair sometimes serves early-evening meals. For an outing on a stormy day, Obauer at Pfarrwerfen (between Salzburg and Obertauern) is one of the finest restaurants in Austria.

Obertauern is not the hottest of Austria's **après-ski** resorts but there is music and dancing immediately after skiing at the Latschenstub'n. Later the main focus is the throbbing Taverne. Several visitors report high prices.

Non-skiers won't find much here beyond an impressive sports centre (with tennis). Salzburg is an easy trip.

Saalbach-Hinterglemm 1000m

HOW IT RATES

The skiing

Snow	★★★
Extent	★★★★
Advanced	★★
Intermediates	★★★★★
Beginners	★★★
Convenience	★★★★
Queues	★★★
Restaurants	★★★★

The rest

Scenery	★★★
Resort charm	★★★★
Not skiing	★★

✔ Large, well-linked, intermediate ski circuit with a good mix of open and tree-lined runs

✔ Little walking to the lifts from central accommodation

✔ Saalbach is a big but pleasant, affluent and lively village

✔ Both villages are now traffic-free in the centre

✔ Atmospheric mountain restaurants throughout the ski area

✔ Sunny skiing

✔ Large snowmaking installation and excellent piste maintenance

✔ Short transfers from Salzburg

✘ Large number of low, south-facing slopes that suffer from the sun

✘ Not much difficult skiing

✘ Nursery slopes in Saalbach are not ideal – sunny, and busy in parts

✘ Saalbach has now spread along the valley and some accommodation is far from central

✘ Expensive by Austrian standards – especially Saalbach

ORIENTATION

Saalbach and Hinterglemm, their centres 4km apart, have spread along a narrow dead-end valley floor to the point where they almost merge, and a few years ago they adopted a single identity. The ski area spreads across north- and south-facing mountainsides, with lifts and runs connecting the villages via both. **Leogang** is a quiet village in the next valley to the north, its long, north-facing ski area forming a spur from the main area.

Right at the eastern periphery of the Tirol, the resort is rather isolated from the rest of the province; but several resorts in Salzburg province are reachable by road – **Badhofgastein, Kaprun** and **Zell am See,** the last a short bus-ride away.

Traditional Austrian ski villages are charming by day and lively by night, but have a reputation for small ski areas, long walks or bus-rides to lifts (followed by queues), too many of the dreaded T-bars, and poor snow-cover, thanks to their low altitude. Saalbach-Hinterglemm answers all such criticisms.

Its ski circus is large by all but the highest French standards, much of the accommodation has something approaching ski-to-the-door convenience, the lifts are modern and, although it is quite busy, the ski area is free of any serious bottlenecks. There are snow-cover problems, particularly on the sunny side of the valley late in the season, but Saalbach's impressive snowmaking operation and its snow-pocket location provide conditions that are much better than the Tyrolean norm.

If you come to Saalbach as a step up the skiing ladder from Alpbach, you'll find it expensive. If you view it as a lively alternative to Megève or La Plagne, you won't.

 ## The resort

Saalbach is one of the most attractive ski villages in Austria. Wedged into a narrow valley, with skiable slopes coming right down to the village centre, its traditional-style buildings are huddled together around a classic onion-domed church.

Purists will point out that the old look is false, with practically all the buildings being modern reproductions – the main exceptions are the Post inn and the church. But the result is a close approximation to Austrian charm with French ski convenience.

Saalbach is quite upmarket. It has a number of large, expensive hotels, and few cheap and cheerful pensions. The attractive main street is lined with hotels, restaurants and ski shops, is festooned with fairy lights and comes complete with gigantic snowman. Thanks to the face-lift the resort got in readiness for the 1991 World Championships held here, the village

centre is now traffic-free; there is a completely pedestrianised zone and another area with car access only allowed for reaching hotels. A tunnel and underground car park hide the four-wheeled beasts. The valley road bypasses the village.

Hinterglemm is a more scattered and less appealing collection of hotels and holiday homes, but it has taken even greater strides recently, with another tunnel transforming the centre into a pleasantly traffic-free zone. It offers a cheaper, though by no means inexpensive, alternative to Saalbach, and has far better access to the north-facing slopes.

Despite the generally high prices of Saalbach in particular, it has a youthful, not over-sophisticated atmosphere. It attracts a cosmopolitan, brash clientele, particularly from Germany and Scandinavia. Whether you would call them rowdies is a matter of opinion, but they certainly like to drink a lot and know how to party.

SKI FACTS

Altitude 930m-2095m
Lifts   62
Pistes   159km
Green/Blue   54%
Red   37%
Black   18%
Artificial snow   17km

LIFT PASSES

94/95 prices in
schillings
**Saalbach-
Hinterglemm-Leogang**
Covers all the lifts in
Saalbach,
Hinterglemm and
Leogang, and the ski
bus.
Main pass
1-day pass 400
6-day pass 1840
(low season 1465 –
20% off)
Senior citizens
Over 65 male, 60
female: 6-day pass
1095 (40% off)
Children
Under 15: 6-day pass
1095 (40% off)
Under 4: free pass
Short-term passes
Day pass refundable
by the hour; day pass
price reduced hourly
from 11am; single and
return tickets on main
lifts.
Notes 6-day pass for
6-10 yrs 805. Special
rates for children over
Christmas (15% off
pass price) and Easter
(free passes for
accompanied
children).

✦ The skiing

The ski area is a 'circus' of almost
exclusively intermediate skiing, much
of it on lightly-wooded slopes. Few
runs are likely either to bore the
aggressive intermediate or to worry
the timid one. And there are sufficient
open sections and changes of pitch
and direction to give pistes
individuality and variety. There is
some genuinely black piste skiing, but
not much of it.

THE SKI AREA
User-friendly circuit
The complete circuit of the valley can
be skied only in an anti-clockwise
direction, there being no lift from
Jausern, at the eastern extremity, up to
the north-facing slopes. But a
truncated clockwise circuit can be
undertaken, crossing to the south side
of the valley at Saalbach itself. The
valley floor is very narrow, so there is
very little walking necessary when
changing hillsides.

The south-facing slopes have a good
deal of skiing above 1400m, albeit on
rather short runs. Five sectors can be
identified – from west to east,
**Hochalm, Reiterkogel,
Bernkogel, Kohlmaiskopf** and
Wildenkarkogel. The last connects
via Schönleitenhütte to the Leogang
skiing – a small, open area at altitude,
which leads to a long, narrow north-
facing slope down towards the village,
broadening towards the bottom. An
eight-person gondola brings you most
of the way back.

The connections across Saalbach-
Hinterglemm's south-facing slopes
work well: when traversing the whole
hillside you need to ski down to the
valley floor only once, whichever
direction you are going in. This occurs
at Saalbach itself, where a very short
walk across the main street is
necessary to get from the Bernkogel
piste to the Kohlmaiskopf piste and
vice versa. Both these runs are well
endowed with snowmakers to ensure
the link normally remains skiable, and
there is a choice of lifts going up –
chair-lifts, plus a multi-cabin cable-car
to Kohlmaiskopf .

The north-facing slopes are different
in character – two more distinct
mountains, with long runs from both
to the valley. Access from Saalbach is
by a solitary, queue-prone cable-car to
Schattberg. The high, open, sunny
slopes behind the peak will be served
by a new quad chair this season.

From Schattberg, long runs go down

to the village, to Jausern and to
Hinterglemm. From here, lifts go up
not only to Schattberg but also to the
other north-facing mountain,
Zwölferkogel. A new two-stage
eight-person gondola replaced the
parallel chair-lift here last season.
Drags serve open slopes on the sunny
side of the peak, and a little-used
gondola provides a link from the
south-facing Hochalm area.

SNOW RELIABILITY
Better than most of the Tyrol
The excellent condition of Saalbach's
slopes when hosting the 1991 World
Championships, at a time when
nearby Kitzbühel was really struggling
after two weeks of sun, testified to the
importance of Saalbach's array of
snowmakers, which cover two of the
main lower runs on the north-facing
side, as well as three on the south-
facing side.

The resort also claims 'snow pocket'
status, which may have something to
do with it. Superb piste maintenance
also helps to keep the slopes in the
best possible condition. But an
altitude range of 900m to 2100m is
only a slight advance on Kitzbühel
and, with 60 per cent of the runs
facing south, Saalbach inevitably
suffers when the sun comes out.

FOR ADVANCED SKIERS
Little steep stuff
There is little testing skiing. Off-piste
guides are available, but snow
conditions and forest tend to limit the
potential. The long (4km) run beneath
the length of the Schattberg cable-car
is the only truly black run, but even
this is far from really challenging.

Worthwhile runs are the 5km
Schattberg West-Hinterglemm red,
and the Zwölferkogel-Hochalm link.
Now that it is served by two gondolas,
Zwölferkogel is where better skiers are
likely to spend most of their time.

FOR INTERMEDIATE SKIERS
Paradise
This area is ideal for both the great
British piste-basher, eager to clock up
the miles, and the more leisurely skier.
The south-facing pistes have mainly
been cut through the pine forest at an
angle, allowing plenty of movement
across the ski area on easy runs.

For those looking for more
challenging skiing, the most direct
routes down from Hochalm,
Reiterkogel, Kohlmaiskopf and
Hochwartalm are good fun. All the
south-facing slopes are uniformly
pleasant and, as a result, skiers tend to

SKI SCHOOL

94/95 prices in schillings

Hannes Fürstauer
Courses start Sun or Mon
Classes 6 days.
4hr: 10am-noon and 1pm-3pm.
6 full days: 1500
Children's classes
Ages: from 5
6 full days: 1500
Private lessons
Hourly and daily.
500 for 1hr, for 1 to 2 people. Each additional person 100
Lift priority No

Wolfgang Zink
Courses start Sun or Mon
Classes 6 days.
4hr: 10am-noon and 1pm-3pm.
6 full days: 1500
Children's classes
Ages: from 6
6 full days: 1500
Private lessons
Hourly and daily.
500 for 1hr, for 1 to 2 people. Each additional person 100
Lift priority No

Willi Fritzenwallner
Classes 6 days.
4hr per day.
6 full days: 1500
Children's classes
Ages: from 6
6 full days: 1500
Private lessons
Hourly.
500 (for 1hr, for 1 to 2 people. Each additional person 100
Lift priority No

OTHER SCHOOLS
Hinterholzer
Schönleiten
Hinterglemm-Maria Lechner
Mitterlengau-Hinterglemm
Hinterglemm-Thomas Wolf

be fairly evenly distributed over them. Only the delightful blue from Bernkogel to Saalbach gets really crowded at times.

The north-facing area has some more challenging runs, and a section of relatively high, open skiing around Zwölferkogel which often has good snow. None of the black runs is beyond a competent intermediate, while the long pretty cruise from Limbergalm to Jausernalm is near paradise for people who like to get away from the lifts.

FOR BEGINNERS
Best for improvers

Saalbach's two nursery slopes are very well positioned for convenience, right next to the village centre. But they are both south-facing, and the upper one gets a lot of intermediate traffic taking a short-cut between the Kohlmaiskopf and Bernkogel areas. The lower one is very small, but the lift is free.

Alternatives are trips to the short, easy runs at Bernkogel and Schattberg. There is also a suitable little slope at the foot of the Schattberg but the ski school seem loath to use it, making it great for pottering about on your own at lunchtime. It's rather sunless and a little steeper than the other nursery areas but perfectly useable from day two or three.

Hinterglemm's spacious nursery area is separate from the main ski area. Being north-facing, it is much more reliable for snow later on in the season, but it consequently misses out on the sun in midwinter.

There are lots of easy blue runs to move on to, in all sectors of the area.

FOR CROSS-COUNTRY
Go to Zell am See

Trails run beside the road along the valley floor from Saalbach to Jausern and between Hinterglemm and the valley end at Lindlingalm. In midwinter these trails get very little sun, and they are in any case not very exciting. The countryside beyond nearby Zell am See offers more scope.

QUEUES
Busy, but only one long delay

The Schattberg cable-car is an obvious problem, with half-hour waits routinely encountered in the morning peak period. Otherwise, much depends on snow conditions. When all runs are in good shape there are few problems, other than small morning peak queues to leave Saalbach. When snow conditions are poor, the Bernkogel chair and the

following drag get very busy, as, obviously, do any lifts servicing the better snow.

Saalbach-Hinterglemm does not get as overrun at weekends as other Tyrolean resorts – it's less accessible for the Munich hordes than the Grossraum area and its neighbours.

MOUNTAIN RESTAURANTS
Excellent quality and quantity

The south-facing slopes are liberally scattered with attractive little huts that serve good food. And they do not simply rely on good weather; many have pleasant rustic interiors where an animated atmosphere is generated, sometimes with the assistance of music. (There is a tax on establishments that provide music, and this is passed on to the customer through higher prices.)

The Panorama on the Kohlmaiskopf slope and the Turneralm close to Bründelkopf serve particularly good food. The little Bernkogelalm hut, overlooking Saalbach, has a great atmosphere. The large hut above the main Saalbach nursery slope gets packed at 4pm, when ski-booted customers dance to disco music.

On the north-facing slopes there are relatively few places. The Gipfelhütte at Schattberg West is adequate. Ellmaualm, at the bottom of the Zwölferkogel's upper slopes, is a quiet sunny retreat with good food but suspect loos.

SKI SCHOOL
An excess of choice

We're all in favour of competition between ski schools but visitors to Saalbach-Hinterglemm may feel that they are faced with rather too much of this good thing. Two or three schools offers a choice; eight or nine begins to look like a recipe for confusion. It certainly makes life difficult for the editors of resort guides: the few reports we have are all on different schools, half of them not clearly identified. But we have a half-hearted endorsement of Wolfgang Zink (aka Ski Pro). Another report, which would be amusing if it did not have such worrying implications, tells of a Thomas Wolf instructor who admitted he and his class were lost.

FACILITIES FOR CHILDREN
Hinterglemm tries harder

Saalbach doesn't go out of its way to sell itself to families, although it does have a ski kindergarten. Hinterglemm, perhaps seeing itself as more of a family resort, has some good hotel-

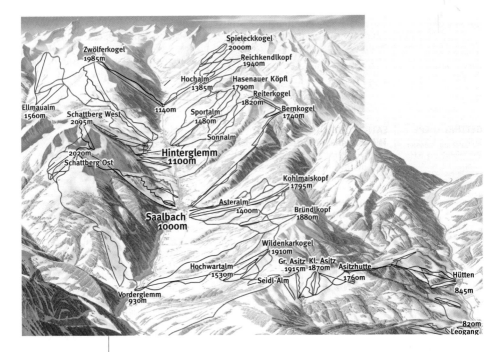

CHILDCARE

Some of the ski schools take children from age 4 or 5 and can provide lunchtime care – there are special ski areas in both villages.

Several hotels have nurseries, and some in Hinterglemm are open to non-residents, including the Egger, Glemmtalerhof, Lengauerhof and Theresia. The Glemmtalerhof is part of a group of 'Partner-hotels' which operate a shared nursery.

PACKAGES

Airtours, Club Europe, Crystal, Enterprise, Inghams, Kings Ski Club, Made to Measure, Mogul Ski, Neilson, STS, Ski Choice, Ski Europe, Ski Partners, SkiBound, Sloping Off, Thomson, Travelscene Ski-Drive

Leogang Mogul Ski, Ski Leogang

based nursery facilities – the one at the Theresia is reportedly excellent. Hotels in both resorts are identified in the resort literature as 'child-friendly' if they conform to a long list of requirements ranging from electric socket covers in bedrooms to provision of ice-skates.

 Staying there

The walk to lifts from Saalbach's central hotels is minimal. Unfortunately Saalbach has seen a fair amount of expansion in recent years, and many of the cheaper hotels used by British tour operators tend to be situated in the least convenient part of the village, along the road towards Hinterglemm. In Hinterglemm itself, position isn't so important. Most of the accommodation is near a lift.

HOW TO GO
Cheerful doesn't mean cheap
Chalets Crystal has the only catered chalets that we are aware of in the main resorts – in central Hinterglemm. It offers a relatively cheap alternative to the mostly expensive hotels.
Hotels There are a large number of hotels in Saalbach, mainly 3-star and above. Most of the more expensive ones have excellent positions in the village centre, whereas the cheapest places tend to be less conveniently placed along the road to Hinterglemm – or in Hinterglemm itself, which is

rather less ritzy than Saalbach. Be aware that some central hotels are affected by disco-noise
Saalbach
££££ **Alpenhotel** Luxurious, with a wealth of facilities, including an open-fire lounge, disco, pub and small pool.
££££ **Berger's Sporthotel** Liveliest of the top hotels, with a popular daily tea dance, good bar and disco. Good pool.
££££ **Kendler** Position second to none, right next to the Bernkogel chair.
££££ **Saalbacher Hof** Retains a friendly feel despite its large size.
£££ **Haider** Best-positioned of the 3-stars, right next to the main lifts.
£££ **König** Slightly cheaper 3-star, particularly well placed for ski school and nursery slopes.
Hinterglemm
££££ **Theresia** Hinterglemm's top hotel, and one of the best-equipped for families. Out towards Saalbach, but nursery slopes nearby. Pool.
£££ **Wolf** Small but well equipped 4-star that is home to the Wolf ski school, and part of the nursery-sharing scheme with the nearby Glemmtalerhof. 'Especially good' food, excellent position. Pool.
££ **Pension Austria** Half-way between the villages, and so good value by local standards for those who don't mind catching a bus every morning.
Self-catering There's an enormous choice of apartments for independent travellers, but we are not aware of any available on the package market.

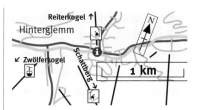

GETTING THERE

Air Salzburg, transfer 2hr. Munich, transfer 3½hr.

Rail Zell am See; hourly buses from station, transfer ½hr.

ACTIVITIES

Indoor Swimming pools, sauna, massage, solarium, bowling, billiards, tennis, squash (Hinterglemm)
Outdoor Floodlit tobogganing, sleigh rides, skating, ice hockey, curling, 35km of cleared paths

TOURIST OFFICE

Postcode A-5753
Tel 010 43 (6541) 7272
Fax 7900

EATING OUT
Wide choice of hotel restaurants

Saalbach-Hinterglemm is essentially a half-board resort, with relatively few non-hotel restaurants. Peter's restaurant, at the top of Saalbach's main street, is atmospheric and serves excellent meat dishes cooked on hot stones. The Auwirt hotel on the outskirts of Saalbach has an à la carte restaurant that is better than the hotel's 3-star status would suggest. The simple Hochleiten hotel in Hinterglemm also has a surprisingly good restaurant.

Otherwise general hotel standards and style are reflected in their restaurants.

APRES-SKI
Excellent but expensive

Après-ski is very lively immediately after skiing and late. In mid-evening the atmosphere is more subdued, as the majority of visitors tuck into large hotel meals.

There are a number of animated bars such as the Kuhstall (Saalbach) and Lumpi's Bla Bla (Hinterglemm), but after-dinner fun is often centred around rep-organised events such as tobogganing, sleigh rides and bowling (nine-pin skittles).

At tea time there are plenty of tea dances and lively bars with music to choose from. The Hintertag and Bauer's Schialm in Saalbach are recommended, as is Hinterglemm's Wedl-Stube.

There are several good but expensive discos, but they all take an age to get warmed up.

FOR NON-SKIERS
Surprisingly little to do

Saalbach is not a very entertaining place for non-skiers. There are few shops other than supermarkets and skiing equipment places, and meeting skiers for lunch isn't going to be easy unless you can persuade them to descend to one of the resorts. Walks tend to be restricted to the paths alongside the cold cross-country trails or along the Saalbach toboggan run to Spielberghs. But there are excursions by bus and train (or car) to Kitzbühel and Salzburg.

Leogang 800m

Leogang is an attractive, although rather scattered farming community-cum-mountain resort. The lack of any central focus has repercussions for skiers: many of the hotels are a long way from the main lifts, and the bus service is disappointingly infrequent.

Leogang is, however, a much less expensive alternative to Saalbach-Hinterglemm. It is also far quieter, smaller, less commercialised and more Brit-free than its neighbours. Situated on the St Johann-Bischofshofen road, and having a mainline railway station, Leogang is also better placed for independent travel access and for taking day excursions.

The link with Saalbach is fairly reliable: the gondola towards Asitz is followed by a couple of short pistes and lifts, with all the skiing above a lofty 1590m. These pistes are red, but not difficult. Less experienced intermediates can amuse themselves on the blue slopes served by the first stage of the gondola, or on the separate little ski area closer to the village centre.

Beginners have good nursery slopes, conveniently placed just above the village. If snow is poor, the higher slopes are not too steep, though icy conditions can be a problem for novices.

Leogang is the best of the local villages for cross-country. There are 25km of trails, with a connection to Saalfelden, plus a panoramic high-altitude course which links through to other resorts. Given good snow, trails are kept in fine condition.

The Leogang Altenberger ski school has a high reputation – good attitude and a surprising number of English-speaking instructors. But we've had a bad report of the smaller Schischule Diesenberger, complaining of mixed abilities and languages in the same class, with no English spoken. There is a non-ski crèche, and ski school starts at 4 years old.

Ski Leogang runs a catered chalet in a converted farmhouse in Hütten, a tiny hamlet west of Leogang, which is better positioned for the skiing than the main village.

There are convenient hotels in each price category. The luxury Krallerhof has its own nursery lift which can be used to ski across to the main lift station. The 4-star Salzburgerhof, and much simpler Gasthof Asiztstuberl, are the best-placed hotels, within a two-minute walk of the gondola. Gasthof Stockinggut is a fine 3-star, within reasonable walking distance of the main lift, and also has a good free minibus service to the slopes, driven by the hotel's 'nothing is too much trouble' manager. The informal Rupertus is better placed, right next to the gondola, and closer to the village.

Restaurants are hotel-based. The Krallerhof has the excellent food you would expect. The much cheaper Gasthof Hüttwirt has a high reputation for wholesome Austrian home cooking.

The rustic old farming chalet Kralleralm is very much the focal tea-time and evening rendezvous. Its atmosphere seems to please everyone, which is just as well, there being very little else available. The Stockinggut does, however, have an entertainment programme including a cow-milking competition!

Excursions to the pleasant nearby town of Saalfelden and the lovely city of Salzburg are the main attractions for non-skiers. Other facilities include swimming and tennis.

St Anton 1305m

✔ *Extensive ski area with good skiing for adventurous intermediate and advanced skiers*

✔ *Heavy snowfalls, backed up by snowmakers, generally give good snow-cover despite sunny slopes*

✔ *Much improved lift system has greatly reduced queuing problems*

✔ *Easy rail access, direct from Britain*

✔ *The liveliest, most varied après-ski around (but see minus points)*

✔ *Despite resort expansion, village retains distinct Tyrolean charm*

✘ *Skiing doesn't suit beginners or timid intermediates*

✘ *Pistes can get crowded*

✘ *Long walks or bus-rides to lifts from much accommodation*

✘ *All the tough skiing is off-piste*

✘ *Surprisingly little to amuse non-skiers*

✘ *Nightlife can get rowdy, with noisy drunks in the early hours*

St Anton has, along with Wengen and Mürren, a strong British tradition. From the 1920s, successive generations learned to ski here, adopting the distinctive 'feet together' style of the famous Arlberg ski school. Sir Arnold Lunn helped start the Kandahar race here in 1928. The resort remains popular with good British skiers (and for the last couple of seasons has been one of the sponsors of the British ski team).

It has also become one of the world's Meccas for ski bums. That's a reflection of the wonderful, tough skiing available in the bowls below the Valluga – the best that Austria has to offer. These are now all off-piste. In good snow conditions they are superb. Sadly, conditions are often less than perfect except just after a fall, because of their south-facing aspect. But if you are lucky with the snow you'll have the time of your life.

There's a lot to offer adventurous intermediate skiers too. As well as the generally challenging St Anton pistes, there is all the skiing of Lech and Zürs to explore, a short bus-ride away.

The ski bum ethos extends to the large number of late-night discos and bars. The resort is an ideal choice for the hard-drinking, disco-loving, keen skier who can stand the pace of getting to bed late and being up for the first lift.

 ## The resort

St Anton is a long, sprawling mixture of traditional and modern buildings crammed into a narrow valley, between a busy road and mainline railway. In terms of sheer size, you might call St Anton a town, but it lacks a 'lived in' feeling, being essentially just a very overgrown village full of tourism-related facilities.

It is an attractively bustling place, full of life, colour and noise, and positively teeming with a lively young international ski clientele, eager to sample the skiing and après-skiing

Although it is crowded and commercialised, St Anton is full of character, and its traffic-free main street retains Alpine charm and traditional-style buildings.

Most of the resort's ski slopes and lifts start immediately beyond the railway tracks.

 ## The skiing

St Anton vies with Val-d'Isère for the title of 'resort with most undergraded slopes'. There are plenty of red runs which would be black in many other resorts, and plenty of blues which would be red. It now has very few blacks because it has scrapped the grading for runs on the upper mountain and chosen to make them 'high-touring routes' – not marked, not groomed, not patrolled and not protected from avalanche danger. There are also some 'ski routes'. These have some markers, are groomed occasionally in part, but are not patrolled and are protected from avalanches only in 'the immediate vicinity of the markers'.

This has caused much confusion; one life-long St Anton fan has written to us to say, 'I started to ski as a five-year-old in St Anton in 1962 and skied

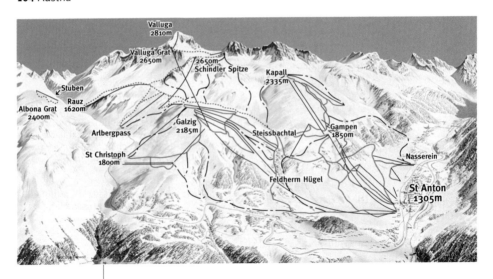

SKI FACTS

Altitude	1305m-2650m
Lifts	88
Pistes	260km
Green/Blue	30%
Red	40%
Black*	30%
Artificial snow	18km

* includes ski routes
– see text

there every year until 1981. Since then I have been back on four occasions. The resort has gone overboard on not marking what used to be black runs on the piste map. And now the indicators at the top and bottom stations do not show whether these runs are open or closed (or even that they exist). There are some beautiful runs, but they are steep, south-facing and prone to avalanches. It is outrageous that there is now no indication of whether I should ski them or not.'

The resort's answer to this would be that you shouldn't be thinking of skiing these runs without a guide. The policy is completely unrealistic, and widely ignored – most St Anton skiers couldn't afford to hire a guide, even if they were convinced they needed one.

THE SKI AREA
Large linked area
St Anton's ski area is made up of several sectors, all except one of which are linked, on a predominantly south-facing mountain.

Starting on the east, you have the choice of a four-person chair or ancient funicular up to **Gampen**. From there pistes lead back to St Anton and Nasserein, or in the opposite direction across to the links with the Valluga-Galzig ski area. Or you can go up higher to **Kapall** and ski down unmarked routes – ending up at the same places.

A four-person chair is the quickest link to **Galzig**. This brings you out just above the mid-station of the cable-car up from St Anton. From here you can ski in most directions, including back to town, down to St Christoph (from where there's a cable-car back up) or back to Feldherrn

Hügel. The blue pistes down from here are some of the most crowded we've come across at peak periods.

You can get up to St Anton's most famous skiing, the bowls below the **Valluga**, from Galzig in one of two ways. For the second stage of the cable-car, you can take a ticket which allocates you a place on a specific cable-car (the first available) and ski around locally until it's time for your ride. Or you can ski to the Schindlergrat three-person chair, which delivers you to the same height (2650m) but on a different peak. There's a tiny third stage of the Valluga cable-car which takes you up to 2810m, but this is mainly for sightseeing. The only way to ski from there is off the back, off-piste to Zürs. You are not allowed to take skis up the lift without a guide.

From both the second-stage of the cable-car and the Schindlergrat chair, you can ski down a long, beautiful ski route to Rauz, the western end of St Anton's own skiing.

From Rauz you can ski across the road and along to Stuben, where a slow two-stage chair-lift takes you to the predominantly north-facing **Albona** ski area.

The final ski area, **Rendl,** is separate and reached by gondola from just outside town (there are buses from the village, but if you don't happen to encounter one about to leave it's quicker to walk). Six lifts serve the west-facing runs at the top here, with a single north-facing piste returning to the gondola bottom-station.

LIFT PASSES

94/95 prices in
schillings
Arlberg Ski Pass
Covers all St Anton,
St Christoph, Lech,
Zürs and Stuben lifts,
but not linking buses.
Beginners Limited
pass covering
beginners' lifts.
Main pass
1-day pass 445
6-day pass 2140
(low season 1930 –
10% off)
Senior citizens
Over 65 male, 60
female: 6-day pass
1720 (20% off)
Over 80: free pass
Children
Under 15: 6-day pass
1280 (40% off)
Under 7: free pass
Short-term passes
Half-day from noon,
single and return
tickets on certain lifts,
also 'taster' passes
(180), starting 3pm.
Notes Arlberg pass
also covers Klösterle
(10 lifts), 7km west of
Stuben. Arlberg
Special pass for 6
days or longer,
reduction of about
200, available for
guests staying in St
Anton area and for
children until 17.2.95.
'Snowman' card for
under 7s, and senior
citizens over 80, 100
for season. Discounts
during wedel, firn and
snow crystal weeks.

SNOW RELIABILITY

Very good except late season

If the weather is coming (as it often is) from the west or north-west, the Arlberg gets it first, and as a result St Anton and its neighbours get heavy falls of snow. They often have much better conditions than other ski areas of a similar height. But many of the slopes face south- or south-east, causing icy or heavy conditions at times, particularly late in the season. It can be vital to time your runs off the Valluga to get decent conditions. The lower runs are now well equipped with artificial snowmaking, which ensures the home runs remain open as long as it's cold enough at night to make snow.

FOR ADVANCED SKIERS

One of the world's great areas

St Anton vies with Chamonix, Val-d'Isère and a handful of others for the affections of good skiers. It has one of the most consistently challenging large ski areas in the world.

The jewel in its crown is the variety of off-piste possibilities in the bowls accessed by the Valluga cable-car and Schindlergrat chair. You can see tracks going all over the mountain. No way (except the red ski route) is easy. Some descents look terrifying. In good snow this whole area is delightful for good skiers. There are two main high-touring routes down – both giving little respite during the long, steep, often mogulled descents. The Schindlerkar gully is the first you come to, and the steeper. For the wider, somewhat easier Mattun run, you traverse over further at the top. Both these feed down into the Steissbachtal gully where there are lifts back up to Galzig. The Schweinströge starts off in the same direction as the red ski route, but you traverse the shoulder of the Schindler Spitze and down a narrow gully.

Lower down the mountain, very difficult trails lead off in almost every direction from the Galzig summit. Osthang is an extremely tough, long mogul field that leads down to Feldherrn Hügel. Not much less challenging are trails down to Steissbachtal, St Christoph and past Maiensee towards the road. These lower runs can be doubly tricky if the snow has been hit by the sun.

SKI SCHOOL

94/95 prices in
schillings

Arlberg
Manager Richard
Walter
Classes 6 days
4hr: 2hr am and pm,
from 9.30
6 full days with guest
card: 1420
Children's classes
Ages: 5 to 14
6 full days with guest
card and including
lunch: 2210
Private lessons
Half- or full day
2050 for full day;
each additional
person 160)

St Anton
Manager Franz
Klimmer
Classes 6 days
4hr: 10am-noon and
1pm-3pm
6 full days with guest
card: 1300
Children's classes
Ages: 5 to 14
6 full days: 1800
Private lessons
Half- or full day
1800 for full day;
each additional
person 150)

The Kandahar men's downhill
course is a long run between Gampen
and town. There are countless
opportunities for off-piste skiing in the
Kapall-Gampen area, including the
beautiful Schöngraben unmarked
route to Nasserein.

The Rendl area across the road has
plenty of open space beneath the top
lifts and, with an accompanying
guide, there is some delightful skiing
off the back of this ridge.

The Albona mountain above Stuben
has north-facing slopes that hold good
powder and some wonderful, deserted
off-piste descents including beautifully
long runs to Langen (where you can
catch the train) and back to St Anton.

On top of all this, bear in mind that
many of the red runs on the piste map
are long and challenging too.

The ultimate challenge, though, is
perhaps to go with a guide off the
back of the third stage of the Valluga.
The initial pitch is very, very steep.
But once you have negotiated that,
the run down to Zürs is very beautiful
and usually deserted.

FOR INTERMEDIATE SKIERS
Some real challenges
St Anton is suited to good rather than
simply aggressive intermediates. They
will be able to try the Mattun run
from Vallugagrat for example (see
above). The red ski route from
Vallugagrat to Rauz is a very long,
tiring, varied run (over 1000m
vertical), which is ideal for good (and
fit) intermediates. Alternatively, you
can turn off from this part-way down
and take the Steissbachtal to the lifts
back to Galzig.

The Kapall-Gampen section is also
full of interest, with sporty bumps
among trees on the lower half. Skiing
from Kapall to town (over 1000m
vertical), keeping to the left of the
Kandahar funicular and ending up on
a piste called Fang, is a fun run.

Less adventurous intermediates will
find St Anton less to their taste. There
are few easy cruising pistes. The most
obvious are the blues from Galzig.
These are reasonably gentle but get
very crowded, particularly at peak
times when people ski them while
waiting their turn for the advance-
ticket Valluga cable-car. The blue to St
Christoph, served by drag-lifts, is
probably the best bet. The narrowish
blues between Kapall and Gampen
can have some challenging bumps.

Intermediates looking for easy
cruising will find the best by taking
the bus to Lech.

Mixed intermediate abilities are best
suited to the Rendl area. A good
variety of trails suitable for good and
moderate skiers criss-cross, including a
lovely long tree-lined run (over 1000m
vertical from the top) back to the
valley gondola station. This is the best
run in the whole ski area when
visibility is poor, though it has some
quite awkward sections.

FOR BEGINNERS
A lousy choice
St Anton has neither decent nursery
slopes nor easy runs for beginners to
progress to. Experienced skiers who
are desperate to ski the Arlberg but
are taking novices on holiday would
be better off staying in Lech or Zürs
and taking the bus to Rauz where
they want to ski St Anton. Pettneu is a
similar option. However, the bus
service from there to St Anton is
disappointing.

FOR CROSS-COUNTRY
A suitable valley
There are a couple of uninspiring trails
near town in the valley, another at St
Jakob 3km away, and a pretty trail
through trees along the Verwalltal to
the foot of the Albona ski area. There
is also an insignificant little loop at St
Christoph. Snow conditions are
usually good, but St Anton is not
really a cross-country resort. Total
trails 40km.

QUEUES
Improved, but still a problem
Queues are not the problem they
once were. But the same can be said
of virtually all resorts, and relative to
other resorts St Anton is below
average. The ticketing system for the
Valluga cable-car is intelligent, but
throws pressure on other lifts in the
area. The worst delays however are for
the Schindlergrat chair – 20 minutes is
quite common in peak season.

St Christoph's tiny cable-car is
another bottleneck. The infrequent,
crowded (and expensive) bus service
to St Christoph and Rauz provides
little motivation to avoid lift delays.

Overcrowded skiing on the Galzig
blue runs is now as much of a problem
as queues.

MOUNTAIN RESTAURANTS
Plenty of choice
Huts are generally quite good, though
there is a distinct difference between
the nice little table-service ones and
the characterless cafeterias. Two of the
best are just above town, the
Sennhütte and Rodelhütte. The Rendl
Beach and Kapall Grabli are others

worth a visit. The Mooserwirt serves typical Austrian food, and the Krazy Kanguruh burgers, pizzas and snacks.

Unfortunately, St Anton's best known hut, the Ulmer, on the way to Rauz from Valluga, tends to disappoint due to unfriendly service and overcrowding.

Having lunch in St Christoph or Stuben is also a useful idea. The St Christoph choices include the excellent but expensive Hospiz Alm, where you can sit in a slide which delivers you to the lavatories. Stuben's Gasthof Berghaus is particularly good and friendly.

SKI SCHOOL
Great for advanced skiers
The new St Anton ski school has brought much-needed competition to the Arlberg ski school, which had slipped, from its previously high standards, during the 1980s. Nowadays both schools come up with the goods, with classes kept at a reasonable level (8 to 10). Few schools are as well geared-up for teaching advanced skiers. Yet judging by the low proportion of our reporters that have used the schools, it would appear that British hot-shots consider lessons beneath them.

Hiring a guide to ski off the top of the Valluga appears more popular, and most reporters have been happy.

FACILITIES FOR CHILDREN
Getting better
St Anton might not seem an obvious resort to choose for family holidays, but there are no good reasons to avoid it if the skiing suits you, and the resort works increasingly hard to accommodate families' needs. The youth centre attached to the Arlberg ski school is excellent, and the special slopes both for tots (at the bottom) and bigger infants (up at Gampen) are well done. Reports from parents with practical experience of these facilities would be very welcome.

The big news for skiing families this year is that Mark Warner are opening a chalet-hotel with a crèche

↑ Staying there

The village itself is reasonably compact, but location is worth considering with a bit of care. Staying as close to the main ski-lifts as possible has obvious advantages, though noise in the streets may disturb light sleepers. Quite a bit of the accommodation 'in' St Anton is

actually in the quieter suburb of Nasserein, a bus-ride or 10- to 15-minute walk from the centre and the nightlife. It isn't too inconvenient for skiing when there is resort-level snow. A drag-lift and short ski takes you to the main lifts, and skiing home is possible from Gampen.

St Anton itself spreads up the hill to the west of the centre, towards the Arlberg pass. Places up here in and beyond Oberdorf can be up to 20 minutes' walk from the centre – but can be quite convenient for skiing, provided there is good snow-cover at resort level.

HOW TO GO
Austria's main chalet resort
St Anton has a very wide range of accommodation, from quality hotels to cheap and cheerful pensions and apartments. What sets it apart from other Austrian resorts for British skiers is the number of chalets. Practically all our reporters stayed in catered chalets.
Chalets Chalets are fairly expensive, though few are particularly luxurious and many are well away from the centre up the hill or at Nasserein.

There are chalets bang in the centre of things but these are apartment-based. Bladon Lines have a couple. They also have the comfortable Aitken and charming old hunting lodge Arlhof, both 5 minutes' walk up the hill. Ski Val's well furnished Baren is out at Nasserein, as are Ski Total's well liked modern chalets. Beach Villas have a good-value, central apartment. Crystal have a selection of places, including a pleasant small chalet out near the Rendl cable-car – particularly good for those who want to be a little removed from the noisy nightlife, but just an easy walk from the main lifts and village centre. Mark Warner have some of the nicest chalets in St Anton, close to the slopes on the hill west of the centre; the piste is close, but it's a taxi for nightlife. And this year they are reopening the central Rosanna as a chalet-hotel, with en-suite bathrooms throughout.
Hotels The market is somewhat polarised: there is one 5-star hotel, lots of 4-stars, rather fewer 3-stars (with and without restaurant); and then a great mass of cheaper B&B pensions spread around the valley.
£££££ St Antoner Hof Best in town, but its position on the by-pass is less than ideal except for curling (the rink is opposite) and motoring. Pool.
££££ Schwarzer Adler Centuries-old inn on main street. Widely varying bedrooms.

CHILDCARE
The kindergarten at the Jugendcenter (2526) takes toilet-trained children aged 30 months to 14 years, from 9am to 4.30. Ski tuition with the Arlberg school in a special snow-garden is available for children aged 5 (exceptionally 4).

PACKAGES
Austrian Holidays, Austrian Travel Service, Bladon Lines, Chalets 'Unlimited', Crystal, Enterprise, Inghams, Made to Measure, Mark Warner, Ski Beach Villas, Ski Choice, Ski Club of GB, Ski Equipe, Ski Europe, Ski Total, Ski Val, Ski Valkyrie, Ski West, Ski Wyatt, Thomson

Stuben Chalets 'Unlimited', Ski Total

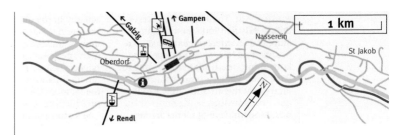

SKI TOTAL

helped us to compile the eating out and après-ski sections. Our thanks to them.

GETTING THERE

Air Innsbruck, transfer 1½hr. Zurich, transfer 3hr.

Rail Mainline station in resort.

ACTIVITIES

Indoor Swimming pool (also hotel pools open to the public, with sauna and massage), tennis, squash, bowling, museum, cinema in Vallugasaal
Outdoor 15km of cleared walks, natural skating rink (skating, curling), sleigh rides, tobogganing

TOURIST OFFICE

Postcode A-6580
Tel 010 43 (5446)
22690
Fax 25320

££££ Neue Post Comfortable if uninspiring 4-star at the centre of affairs, close to both lifts and nightlife.
££££ Grischuna Welcoming family-run place in peaceful position up the hill west of the town; close to the slopes, five minutes to the cable-car.
££££ Berghaus Maria Charmingly furnished, slightly further up the hill (hotel shuttle to lifts). Pool.
£££ Valluga About the cheapest of the 3 stars, but rather on the edge of things on the by-pass.
£££ Goldenes Kreuz A comfortable B&B hotel half-way to Nasserein, well positioned for skiing home.
Self-catering There are plenty of apartments available to independent travellers but package deals are few and far between. Inghams have reasonable standard places in Nasserein, while Beach Villas have ski-convenient apartments on the opposite side of town.

STAYING DOWN THE VALLEY
Nice and quiet
Beyond Nasserein is the more complete village of St Jakob – reachable on skis, but dependent on the ski-bus in the mornings. The Brunnenhof is an attractive little hotel with a highly regarded rustic restaurant.

Pettneu is a quiet little village further down the valley, with its own ski area that is best for beginners. It's best suited to skiers with a car.

EATING OUT
Mostly informal
People ski hard and eat hard in St Anton. Plain, filling fare is the norm, with numerous places serving healthy portions of traditional Austrian home-cooking, American, Italian and fondue. Several reporters on a budget have commented on the excellent value of the Bahnhof restaurant – 'a far cry from British Rail'. The fondue is particularly recommended. Dixies is the place for a lively meal in modern surroundings where American Western-style cuisine is enjoyed. The Reselehof is one of the best Tyrolean-style inns for Austrian cooking.

APRES-SKI
Throbbing till late
Every form of informal fun is available from karaoke to late discos; from 'English' pub-style bars to brash 'drunken Scandinavian' joints. Sophisticates are less well provided for. Most Brits find the infamous Krazy Kangaru an overcrowded, overpriced yawn these days. The Mooserwirt is now the main happening place for those looking for a post-skiing bop to live music. The Underground bar has a great atmosphere and live music, but gets terribly full. The Hazienda is equally lively and popular, and the Piccadilly pub is good for those who want a home from home. The Drop In disco throbs into the early hours. The rather inaptly named Chic Bar is the place for karoake. The Stanton is another popular place in the centre of town. One reporter complained of 'very few single females' – a drawback of skiing such a self-consciously 'macho' resort.

FOR NON-SKIERS
Not very relaxing
St Anton is a sprawling town, not especially attractive outside the centre, and with surprisingly little to offer the non-skier. Many of the most attractive mountain restaurants are not readily accessible by lift for pedestrians. The centre is lively with a fair selection of shops. Getting by bus to the other Arlberg resorts is easy but buses tend to run only early morning and late afternoon, so make excursions a long day. Lech would arguably be a better, if pricier, base for a non-skier, though St Anton's mainline railway station does at least allow easy access to Innsbruck.

St Christoph 1780m
A small, exclusive collection of hotels, restaurants and bars right by the Arlberg Pass and with drag-lifts and a cable-car into the ski area. Good place for a nice lunch. Expensive and deadly quiet place to stay. The most expensive hotel of all – much the most expensive in this whole area – is the huge Arlberg-Hospiz.

Stuben 1410m

Stuben is an interesting alternative to St Anton, quite the opposite of the large, noisy resort. Dating back to the 13th century, it's a small unspoilt village where personal service and quiet friendliness are the order of the day. Modern developments are kept to a minimum. The only concessions to the new ski era are a few unobtrusive hotels, a ski school, two banks and a couple of banks and a few little shops. The old church and traditional buildings, usually snow-covered, make Stuben a really charming Alpine village. The north-facing local slopes retain snow well, though the queue-free village chair can be a cold ride. Lech and Zurs are nearby, accessed by infrequent but timetabled buses. Stuben has sunny nursery slopes separate from the main ski area, but lack of progression runs make it unsuitable for beginners. Evenings are quiet, but several places have a pleasant atmosphere. Willie's Stubli is the most animated rendezvous. Hotels Mondschein and Albona have bars with dance areas. The S'Murmele and Gasthof Berghaus bars are quieter. buses and taxis are extortionate). Most people stay here on half-board, but the Sport Café is a good-value pizza place for those in B&B. The charming old Post is a very comfortable 4-star renowned for its fine restaurant (available through Ski Total, who also run a catered chalet operation). Haus Erzberg is a good pension. Kolerhaus is a simple, inexpensive B&B. Stuben doesn't have much to offer non-skiers.

Selected chalets in St Anton

St Johann in Tirol 650m

HOW IT RATES

The skiing

Snow	**
Extent	**
Advanced	*
Intermediates	***
Beginners	***
Convenience	***
Queues	***
Restaurants	****

The rest

Scenery	***
Resort charm	***
Not skiing	***

✔ Most accommodation reasonably close to lifts

✔ Slopes liberally endowed with restaurants

✔ Plenty of non-skiing activities and things to do in the evening

✔ Well placed for visiting neighbouring ski resorts

✔ Highly regarded ski school

✔ Few Brits by Tyrol standards

✔ Good snow record for height

✗ Very small ski area, with little to interest good skiers

✗ Busy town makes it unsuitable for families with small children

✗ Weekend crowds from Germany

✗ Can be especially busy when nearby ski areas with less reliable snow are suffering

In some ways St Johann falls between two stools. Its ski area is small and predominantly easy. Yet it is a far from ideal choice for families and others who traditionally turn to the Tyrol for 'small and friendly' resorts – the town is too busy to suit them. But with no fewer than 18 mountain restaurants, fairly convenient ski lifts and plenty of off-slope facilities, St Johann is a fine choice for leisurely, part-time skiers who like to spend as much time pottering about having coffee and lunch as they do actually skiing.

St Johann also suits the most energetic of skiers who want to tour around visiting surrounding ski resorts and have plenty of evening entertainment awaiting their return.

ORIENTATION

St Johann is ten minutes by car or train from **Kitzbühel**. The main gondola accesses its whole mountain. Lifts also go up from the hamlet of **Eichenhof**, on one side of the ski area, and the separate little village of **Oberndorf**, on the other. Other resorts surround the place – **Fieberbrunn** and **Waidring** share an area lift pass with St Johann. **Kirchdorf** is also close. **Leogang** and **Zell am See** are within reach, as is **Kaprun**'s glacier.

SKI FACTS

Altitude	650m-1700m
Lifts	18
Pistes	60km
Green/Blue	41%
Red	47%
Black	12%
Artificial snow	7km

 ## The resort

St Johann is a sizeable town with a life outside skiing. The compact centre is wedged between a railway track, main roads and converging rivers. It is fairly attractive, certainly atmospheric, and has retained some traditional character. The main street is full of old wooden chalet buildings housing hotels, restaurants, cafés and homely bars. The five-minute walk between centrally-placed hotels and the lift involves picking your way through town traffic and clambering over railway tracks.

St Johann has some growing and sprawling industrial and residential suburbs. Eichenhof to the east is convenient for the skiing (it has lifts starting there) but it is quite a trek along a busy road to the town centre.

The skiing

St Johann's small local skiing area is on the north-facing side of the Kitzbüheler Horn – the 'back' side of Kitzbühel's 'second' and smallest mountain. It would have been easy to link these two resorts' skiing, but up-market Kitzbühel appears to have no desire to mix with its poorer neighbour.

THE SKI AREA
Small and easy

The main access lift is a gondola which transports skiers to the top of the ski area at **Harschbichl** (1700m). From there, a choice of north-facing pistes lead back through the trees towards town.

Two chair-lifts and the mid-station of the gondola allow repeated skiing of the upper part of the mountain, and there are further chairs and drags on the lower part.

The top-station and one of the chairs also access a sunnier sector of west-facing pistes that lead down to a car park just above the hamlet of Oberndorf, served by another chair.

None of the skiing is particularly challenging and average intermediates could ski the whole area in a day.

SNOW RELIABILITY
Altitude problems

Lack of altitude is an obvious problem. But St Johann's skiing takes place on by far the snowier side of the Kitzbüheler Horn – its snow pocket location 'steals' some of Kitzbühel's snow. This, together with its largely north-facing slopes, means that St Johann often has better conditions than its famous neighbour (and the nearby Grossraum). Snowmakers also help when it is cold enough. They cover one piste from 1400m to town,

LIFT PASSES

94/95 prices schillings

St Johann lift pass
Covers all lifts and ski bus.

Beginners Points card, and half-day passes for nursery drags.

Main pass
1-day pass 320
6-day pass 1500
(low season 1375 – 8% off)

Children
Under 15: 6-day pass 795 (47% off)
Under 6: free pass

Short-term passes
Half-day (morning pass valid till 12.30, afternoon pass valid from 12.30), 'late sleeper' pass from 11am, 'try out' pass from 2pm.

Alternative periods
5 in 6 days and 11 in 13 days.

Alternative passes
Schneewinkl 6-day pass also covers Fieberbrunn, Steinplatte, Waidring and other small resorts (6 days 1650 for adults, 990 for children).

SKI SCHOOL

94/95 prices in schillings

St Johann
Manager Ulli Arpe
Classes 6 days
4hr: 10am-noon and 1.30-3.30
6 full days: 1280
Children's classes
Ages: from 4
6 full days including lunch: 1820
Private lessons
Hourly, half- or full day
450 for 1hr for 1 to 2 people; each additional person 110

Eichenhof
Classes 6 days
4hr: 10am-noon and 1.30-3.30
6 full days: 1300
Children's classes
Ages: from 4
6 full days including lunch: 1840
Private lessons
Hourly or full day
450 for 1hr for 1 to 2 people; each additional person 110

with both red off-shoots to the valley chair also endowed.

There are several nearby ski areas, such as Waidring's Steinplatte, that are also reasonably snowsure if St Johann is suffering. The glacier at Kaprun has guaranteed snow but gets very crowded when snow is scarce elsewhere. The Hintertux glacier and Obertauern are worth an hour's drive at such times.

FOR ADVANCED SKIERS
Totally unsuitable

There is nothing here to challenge a good skier. The long black run on the piste map is actually a moderate red – and it is often closed because it suffers the effects of the strong afternoon sun. Your best hope would be a solid week of snow, when you could practice your powder technique.

FOR INTERMEDIATE SKIERS
A small amount for all

The slopes are pleasantly varied, with something for everyone. Decent skiers have a fairly direct-running piste between Harschbichl and town (runs 1b and 2b), and the black mentioned above. There are some easier red runs, but the best of them (3a and 4b) are served by long drags. The Penzing piste (6a) is served by a more comfortable chair. Less adventurous skiers have plenty of options, with the long meandering run between the mid-station of the gondola and town completely covered by snowmakers.

FOR BEGINNERS
Good when snow is abundant

The main nursery slopes are excellent but have no snowmakers. The skiing served by the second stage of the chair out of town has much more reliable snow and is suitable for beginners who have a little dry slope experience. Near-beginners and fast learners have a fine easy run (2a) from the mid-station of the gondola back to the bottom.

CROSS-COUNTRY
Excellent valley trails

Given good snow St Johann is one of the best cross-country resorts in Austria. A wide variety of trails totalling 74km fan out from the cross-country centre just beyond the main road to Salzburg.

QUEUES
Good except when 'invaded'

Queues are relatively rare when St Johann is not hit by hordes from Germany and surrounding resorts.

At weekends, during 'Fasching' week (mid-February) and any time Kitzbühel is struggling for snow, the gondola can get long morning queues. The second stage of the Eichenhof drag is another bottleneck. But overcrowded pistes are a bigger worry at such times.

MOUNTAIN RESTAURANTS
Amazing array

With 18 restaurants spread over just 60km of piste, St Johann must have the densest array of huts of any sizeable ski area in Europe. Needless to say, most are pleasantly uncrowded and competitively priced. None is worthy of special mention, but many are very welcoming.

SKI SCHOOL
Good attitude

The St Johann and Eichenhof schools have a good reputation for English, tuition and friendliness, though large classes can be disappointing.

There's a specialist snowboard section, 'White Wave', which has its own half-pipe. (Three of the top performers in the world are based here.) There's a large cross-country set-up and off-piste guides are available.

FACILITIES FOR CHILDREN
Good resort and hotel amenities

St Johann is keen to attract families and provides first-class facilities for children. The village nursery, geared to the needs of workers rather than visitors, offers exceptionally long hours. We have no recent reports on how all this works in practice.

↟ Staying there

Most accommodation is central, but hotels beyond the railway track close to the lifts are better placed for the skiing. There is plenty of parking in this area, ski school is on the doorstep, and traffic noise is negligible. The railway is not far away, but not a problem; St Johann isn't exactly Clapham Junction. Cross-country skiers would be better placed at the other side of town, their trails being beyond the main road and river.

HOW TO GO
Plenty of hotel packages

British tour operators concentrate on hotels plus a few pensions but there are numerous apartments available to independent travellers.

Chalets We are not aware of any British-operated chalet parties.

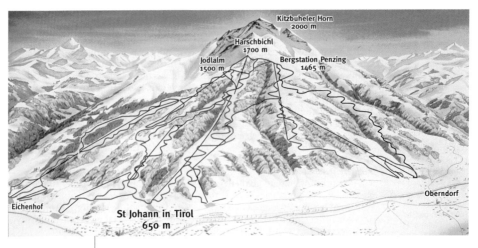

CHILDCARE

Both ski schools have special areas for children aged 4 or more to take lessons, and can provide lunch-time care. The St Johann school's kindergarten takes younger children from 9.30 to 4pm. It has a fairytale playground and a special Dwarfs' Express snowmobile lift.

The Krabbelstube Kunterbunt nursery (4903) takes children aged 12 months to 4 years, from 6.45am to 6.30pm. Lunch-time supervision is optional. Children's ski school starts at 4 years.

There's a free children's party at Café Rainer in the resort centre every Friday afternoon.

Hotels All the hotels are of 3-star or 4-star rating – about equally divided. Most of the best-placed hotels for skiing are 4-stars. Then there are dozens of B&B pensions.

££££ Brückenwirt Smartest in town, but wrong side for skiing.

£££ Fischer Central family-run 3-star, warmly recommended by a regular visitor.

£££ Goldener Löwe Vast, 200-bed 3-star in the centre of town. It has widely differing room standards, the simplest offering excellent value.

£££ Post House number one on the village plan: 13th century inn on the main street.

£££ Park Comfortable 4-star at the foot of the slopes.

£££ Sporthotel Austria Ditto, with more amenities including a pool.

£££ Sonne Cheaper, but comfortable place in the same area.

££ Moser Much smaller, cosier main-street hotel in the same price range as the Löwe's cheaper rooms.

££ Kaiserblick A modest B&B in a quiet spot, yet close to amenities.

Self-catering The Alpenblick (expensive), Gratterer (mid-range) and Helfereich (very cheap) are some of the best-situated apartments.

EATING OUT
Large range of options

There is a wide variety of restaurants, which stick mostly to good old-fashioned Austrian cooking. The Huber-Bräu is unusual in that it's a working brewery where you can taste the local beers before moving on to the surprisingly good food. The Bären, hotels Post and Park, plus the Rettenbachstuberl specialise in tasty local Tyrolean dishes. Serving international cuisine in addition to their Austrian fare, the Lemberg, Lowengrill and the Crystal and Fischer hotels have all been recommended by reporters. For a special meal, locals assure us the Ambiente is a fine establishment.

A couple of non-Austrian places recommended by locals are the Rialto for pizza, and the Hasianco for Mexican and pizza.

APRES-SKI
Plenty for all tastes

Ice bars and tea dancing greet you as the final run of the day is completed, and St Johann has plenty of evening animation without the rowdiness of some neighbouring Tyrolean resorts.

There is a good selection of lively, atmospheric bars. Bunny's Pub is perhaps the most popular, but Max's and Café Klausner also have their fans. Café Rainer has live music; Caprice and Ta Too are disco bars. Tirolerkeller is good for live accordion and zither music. Holzschuh and Caprice are quieter, cosy places. Two haunts popular with locals are the Jagglback and Platzl.

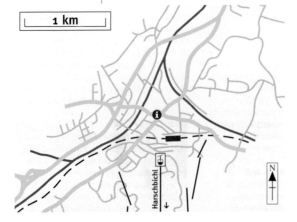

GETTING THERE
Air Salzburg, transfer
1½hr. Munich, transfer
2hr. Innsbruck,
transfer 2hr.

Rail Mainline station
in resort.

PACKAGES
Club Europe, Crystal,
Ski Europe, Ski
Partners, Thomson

ACTIVITIES
Indoor Swimming,
sauna, steam baths,
solarium, 2 indoor
tennis halls, fitness
centre, massage,
riding hall, bowling,
air-gun range
Outdoor Artificial
skating rink, curling,
sleigh rides, horse-
riding, floodlit
toboggan run, 40km
cleared paths,
ballooning, sight-
seeing flights

TOURIST OFFICE
Postcode A-6380
Tel 010 43 (5352)
2218
Fax 5200

Sleigh-ride, toboggan, Tyrolean and nine-pin skittles evenings are organised by tour reps.

The resort also has an entertainments programme, with something on most evenings. Some of the events you might see are: four o'clock snowboarding demonstrations followed by glühwein; floodlit ski-jumping or ski-acrobatics; after-skiing parties at the gondola base-station; and concerts at the festival hall.

FOR NON-SKIERS
A very good choice
There are plenty of things on offer, including an excellent public pool, indoor tennis, a new artificial ice-rink and 40km of cleared walks. There is also more worthwhile shopping in St Johann than is usual in a ski resort. Train excursions to Salzburg, Innsbruck, and to a lesser extent Kitzbühel, are interesting.

Waidring 780m
Anyone who wants to learn to ski in a traditional Tyrolean village, but baulks at the thought of long walks to lifts, poor snow and over-commercialised nightlife, should consider Waidring. This quiet, unspoilt, friendly place, complete with onion-domed church, has its nursery slopes right in the village, a stone's throw from most hotels, and has a good snow record for its height.

Most British visitors are couples or families on 'learn to ski' packages; it's not a place for action-seeking youngsters. Nightlife revolves around simple, organised fun – sleigh rides, bowling, tobogganing, Tyrolean folklore and a ski instructors' ball. The Keller Bar of hotel Post is good for a quiet drink, and Café Schneidermann has a civilised atmosphere.

The ski school employs English-speaking instructors from several countries who seem to go out of their way to make lessons enjoyable. Most of the week is spent on the nursery slopes before graduation to the main ski area, the Steinplatte (10 minutes away by bus). This is ideal for second-year skiers and nervous intermediates. The slopes are wonderfully uncrowded on weekdays, but Germans arrive en masse at weekends. However, the two newly-installed quad chairs ensure queueing is minimal even then, unless there's a shortage of snow in surrounding resorts. Mountain restaurants are pleasant. Try the Stellenalm on the piste back to the car park. Cafés Schneidermann and Weinstube are good for lunch in the village. Buses run to St Johann and Fieberbrunn (both on the area lift pass) and to Ellmau and Kirchberg. Cross-country skiers have 30km of trails.

The Waidringerhof is a central 4-star hotel with all mod cons, including indoor pool, which has been praised by reporters for good food and friendliness. The good-value Tiroler Adler is virtually next to the nursery slopes. Gasthof Brücke is less well placed but popular for good food, value and friendliness. The ski kindergarten is open all day and accepts children from 3 years old (younger if they can ski morning and afternoon). There's no nursery but baby-sitting can be arranged.

Kirchdorf 640m
Kirchdorf is very similar to Waidring – quiet and traditional, with nursery slopes on the doorstep. It's five minutes by bus from St Johann, 20 from the Steinplatte. You can buy a weekly pass that includes a day in Kitzbühel. Kirchdorf also has a new day-care centre that accepts children as young as 3 months. Both this and the ski kindergarten are open all day. There's a specialist cross-country ski school and 80km of trails.

Après-ski is livelier than in Waidring, with several bars and a good disco at the Wintersteller. We have a rave review of the restaurant in Gasthof Zur Mauth. Other good places are the Zehenthof and Giovanni's. The 3-star Wintersteller is one of the best hotels. The Tasma is comfortable, with leisure facilities and a bar with open fire. Gasthof Oberhabachhof is simple but handy for the slopes. Gasthof Marienstetten is poorly positioned but has a children's playground.

Schladming 745m

HOW IT RATES

The skiing

Snow	***
Extent	***
Advanced	**
Intermediates	****
Beginners	****
Convenience	**
Queues	****
Restaurants	****

The rest

Scenery	***
Resort charm	****
Not skiing	****

✔ *Large ski area by the standards of 'quiet and friendly' Austria*

✔ *Charming town with a life independent of skiing and tourism*

✔ *Excellent nursery slopes*

✔ *Very short airport transfer*

✔ *Excellent snowmaking operation and superb piste maintenance*

✔ *Very sheltered slopes, among trees*

✔ *Close to snowsure Obertauern and Dachstein*

✘ *Unconnected ski areas and infrequent buses between them*

✘ *Nursery slopes (at Rohrmoos) are inconvenient unless you stay beside them – and beginners are expected to pay for a full lift pass*

✘ *Little difficult skiing*

✘ *The skiing lacks variety – one mountain is much like the others*

To link or not to link, that is the question. Schladming gets rave reviews from most of its customers, in most respects. One constant whinge concerns the unconnected ski areas. But it may be this very inconvenience that keeps Schladming pleasantly unspoilt and uncrowded. If and when the projected linking lifts are put in place, Schladming will have a ski area to rival those of Kitzbühel and Söll in the Tyrol; but it may also come to suffer the same overcrowding and vulgarity.

Meanwhile, Schladming has another major plus-point. Its huge investment in snowmakers stands in stark contrast to the belated efforts of its Tyrolean competitors to give holiday skiers something other than grass, slush and ice.

ORIENTATION

Schladming sits at the eastern fringe of Austrian skiing (in Styria), in a broad valley running east-west. The main gondola into the Planai skiing starts close to the town centre; a drive out of town is the elevated suburb of Rohrmoos, where chair-lifts access the skiing on Hochwurzen. There are two further sizeable ski areas, reached from **Pichl** or **Gleiming** and from **Haus**.

The ski pass also covers a fifth area at Galsterbergalm, above **Pruggern**, and several other small ski areas at **Stoderzinken**, **Ramsau** and the **Dachstein** glacier. The glacier is a 45-minute bus-ride, and has only a handful of runs, but the views are superb.

The Top Tauern area pass also covers resorts such as **St Johann im Pongau**, **Flachau** and snowsure **Obertauern**.

 ## The resort

The old town of Schladming has developed both its skiing and mercantile interests without spoiling the charm of its attractive centre. A large woodyard, brewery and railway station are separated from town by a river, while the modern sports centre, tennis halls and Sporthotel, plus the lift stations, have also been consigned to the outskirts.

The main road also bypasses the town. The resort centre is compact, with most shops, restaurants and bars (and some of the most appealing hotels) gathered around the oblong main square.

 ## The skiing

All four of the hills local to Schladming have been developed for skiing; most of it takes place on the wooded north-facing slopes that line the main valley, with some runs down into the side valleys at higher altitudes. The skiing throughout is as consistent in standard as it is in its nature: most runs are easy reds, ideal for the intermediate majority. Although this may be an attraction for some skiers, many visitors would appreciate more variety.

THE SKI AREA
Series of poorly connected sectors

Planai, Reiteralm and Hauser Kaibling are the main sectors; Hochwurzen has less skiing, but has the main valley-level nursery slopes at its foot – at Rohrmoos.

Planai is accessed by gondola from the east edge of town. There is a little east-facing open section at the top, but otherwise all runs are typically village-bound through forest. One run branches off towards Rohrmoos at the foot of the **Hochwurzen** sector, but you have to get a lift down (then up and through a tunnel) to complete the link. A two-stage chair rises above Rohrmoos and its nursery slopes, to a cable-car which accesses the upper slopes on the mountain proper.

Hauser Kaibling, a bus-ride away, is accessed by a gondola and a cable-car from either side of Haus village. A small open section at the top has the only real off-piste in the whole area.

Rieteralm lies beyond Hochwurzen; it is accessed by a chair from Pichl, or the Gleiming gondola.

SNOW RELIABILITY
Excellent in cold weather

Schladming's impressive snowmaking operation is a real boon when lack of snowfall rather than high temperatures is the problem. Consequently, it is a particularly good

SKI FACTS

Altitude 745m-2015m
Lifts   79
Pistes   140km
Green/Blue   29%
Red   61%
Black   10%
Artificial snow   48km

LIFT PASSES

94/95 prices in
schillings
**Skiparadies
Dachstein-Tauern**
Covers all lifts in the
Dachstein/Tauern
region and ski bus.
Credit cards Yes
Main pass
1-day pass 355
6-day pass 1770
(low season 1645 –
7% off)
Children
Under 16: 6-day pass
885 (50% off)
Under 5: free pass
Short-term passes
Half-day from 11am,
noon and 1.30, 'trial'
ticket valid for 2½hr.
Alternative periods
1½- and 2½-day
passes.
Notes Discounts for
groups and senior
citizens on request.
Alternative passes
Day passes for
Ramsau/Dachstein
(excluding the
glacier),
Galsterbergalm and
Stoderzinken ski
areas only; Top-
Tauern Skicard covers
Dachstein/Tauern,
Obertauern, Lungau
and Sportwelt Amadè.

SKI SCHOOL

94/95 prices in
schillings
**WM Schladming
Classes** 5 days
4hr: 2hr am and pm
5 full days: 1300
Children's classes
Ages: from 4
5 full days including
lunch: 1900
Private lessons
1hr, 2hr or 4hr
450 for 1hr; each
additional person 200

choice for early holidays; for late
holidays it doesn't have the required
altitude, but the northerly orientation
of the slopes and superb piste
maintenance help keep the slopes in
good shape longer here than in some
neighbouring resorts. The run to Pichl
is not fully covered by snowmakers,
but is the only valley run in the whole
area without full artificial snow cover
– an impressive achievement.

FOR ADVANCED SKIERS
Strictly intermediate stuff
Schladming's status as a World Cup
downhill venue doesn't mean macho
skiing. The skiing is almost exclusively
gentle, the steep finish to the men's
downhill course being an exception,
and the moderate mogul slopes at the
top of Planai being another. Hauser
Kaibling's off-piste skiing can be good,
but it's a rather limited area. Excellent
piste grooming and quiet slopes at off-
peak times allow fast skiing. The
women's World Cup run is
particularly pleasurable in this respect.

FOR INTERMEDIATE SKIERS
Generally flattering runs
The two World Cup pistes, and the red
that runs parallel to the Haus
downhill course, are ideal for fast
intermediates. The open sections at
the top of Planai and Hauser Kaibling
also have some challenging slopes.
Moderate skiers have the whole area at
their disposal. Many concentrate on
Planai, but Reiteralm has some of the
best runs. Hauser Kaibling is the best
mountain for timid skiers, with a
lovely meandering blue running from
top to bottom and a quiet, easy little
section with good snow at the
summit. Unfortunately, skiing this
involves a long walk back to the main
ski area. Runs are so well-bashed that
intermediates will find Schladming's
slopes generally flattering.

FOR BEGINNERS
Good, particularly for improvers
Complete beginners start on the
extensive, but inconvenient and low-
altitude Rohrmoos nursery area – and
they are expected to pay for a full lift
pass. Another novice area near the top
of Planai is more convenient for most
people, has better snow, and superior
ski school. It is well worth novices
having a few pre-holiday dry slope
lessons so that they can start at Planai.

FOR CROSS-COUNTRY
Extensive network of trails
There is enormous scope, given
sufficient snow-cover, with 250km of

trails in the area. Schladming has
loops along the main valley floor,
beyond the furthermost reaches of
Alpine skiing, to Moosheim and
Mandling respectively. The Untertal
and Obertal valleys, between Planai
and Hochwurzen, have more trails.
Further afield there are more snowsure
trails at Stoderzinken, and the
Dachstein glacier has small loops with
spectacular views.

QUEUES
One or two bottlenecks
The Planai gondola can suffer 30-
minute delays on peak-season
mornings. The main Haus lift also
experiences short queues at such
times. However, there are alternatives
to these lifts and there are few other
problems. Surprisingly, given its
proximity to less snowsure resorts,
Schladming does not suffer too badly
from invasions when conditions are
generally poor. Those in search of
snow tend to go higher.

MOUNTAIN RESTAURANTS
Plenty of nice places dotted around
There are attractive restaurants in all
sectors, though Planai probably has
the edge – Mitterhaus at the extremity
of the piste system is particularly
pleasant, Onkel Willy's is popular for
its live music, open fire and large
terrace, and the newly refurbished
Schladmingerhütte at the top of the
Planai gondola has some of the best
food. The Knapphof at Hauser
Kaibling is also good, and particularly
interesting because it's owned by
Helmut Höflehner's family and has
many racing mementos on show. The
Imbisstube provides a good lunch if
you're in the Reiteralm area.

SKI SCHOOL
Satisfaction all round
There are two main schools, which
seem to impress reporters. Charly
Kahr's WM Schladming school, based
at Planai, is complimented for all
aspects of its operation, from
standards of English to friendliness
and organisation – and proudly claims
local boy Arnold Schwarzenegger as a
regular client. Beginners are
recommended to start at Rohrmoos,
where the Tritscher school has a
much-improved recent record. We
haven't heard anything recently about
the smaller Hoppl and Onkel Willy
schools – or about the two schools
based in Haus.

   Snowboarders are well catered for by
a specialist school. Ramsau is the best
place to get cross-country tuition.

Schladming-Rohrmoos/Tritscher
Classes 5 days
4½hr: 10am-noon and 1.30-4pm
5 full days (93/94): 1200
Children's classes
Ages: 4 to 14
5 full days including lunch (93/94): 1600
Private lessons
1hr (between normal course times), half-day or full day
400 for 1hr; each additional person 150 (93/94)

CHILDCARE

Huberta's Kinder-spiel-eck (22962) takes children aged 1 to 10, from 9.15 to 4.15.

At Rohrmoos, the Stocker nursery (61188) takes children from 18 months. There is also a Kinderwelt nursery (61301).

Children in ski school can be looked after from 9am to 5pm.

GETTING THERE

Air Salzburg, transfer 1½hr.

Rail Mainline station in resort.

FACILITIES FOR CHILDREN
Rohrmoos is the place

The extensive gentle slopes that make up the suburb of Rohrmoos could have been designed to build up the confidence of young skiers. Whether in the nursery or proper ski school classes, this is where we would head with children. That's the theory; reports on the practice welcome.

 # Staying there

Much of the accommodation is central, but some hotels and most apartments are on the outskirts. Staying on the east fringe of town is convenient for skiers, the Planai gondola being on that side. But the walk from central hotels to the lift is no great burden.

Rohrmoos has the advantage of doorstep skiing for beginners, and some like its peace and quiet, plus good-value hotels. But there is little else going for it. There is little to do but ski in the daytime and drink in the evenings – and Schladming is further away than tour operators using Rohrmoos would have you believe.

HOW TO GO
Packages means hotels

Packaged accommodation is in hotels and pensions, but there are plenty of apartments for independent travellers.
Chalets None that we know of.
Hotels Most of the accommodation is in modestly priced pensions – including some towny places in the centre, as well as the usual suburban chalets – but there are also a few more upmarket hotels. Staying at the resort entrance, near the Planai and Rohrmoos chairs, is good value. Hotels in this part of town are cheaper than

their centrally-placed opposition.
££££ Sporthotel Royer Big, smart, comfortable multi-amenity place, on the outskirts but within walking distance of the main Planai lift.
£££ Alte Post Characterful old inn with best position in town – on the main square, a few minutes from gondola. Very good food, but some rooms are rather small by 4-star standards.
£££ Stadttor Similarly priced, although less charming and well placed, but with more creature comforts. Special deals for families.
£££ Schladmingerhof Bright, modern chalet in peaceful position, a bus-ride from centre in Untere Klaus.
Self-catering The Plattner apartments are comfortable and reasonably well placed, eight minutes from the gondola. Ferienhaus Girik is cheaper and the best-positioned apartment house in town, close to the gondola.

EATING OUT
Plenty of choice

There is a wide choice of informal places. The Kirchenwirt hotel restaurant has excellent home-cooking. Giovanni's does the best pizza. Others worth a visit are the Vorstadtstub'n, Falbach and Lisi's. The Jaegerstubl in the hotel Neue Post is good, but more expensive, while the Alte Post is the place for a blow-out.

APRES-SKI
Pleasantly animated

Après-ski used to be quiet by Austrian standards, but seems to get livelier every year – without yet going overboard on the lederhosen that is such a feature of some major Tyrolean resorts. Numerous cafés and bars have a jolly atmosphere immediately after skiing. The ski-booted tea dance at the

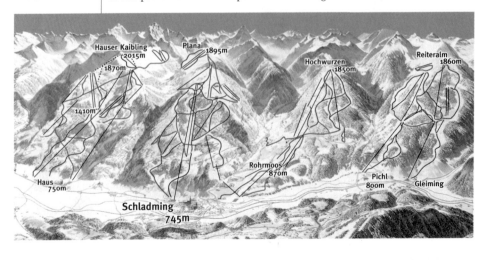

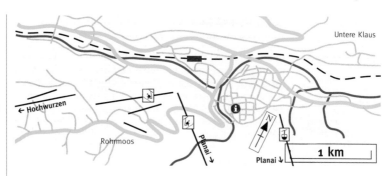

Touralm on Hochwurzen is great fun. Charly's Treff is the liveliest town bar. After-dinner revellers congregate in the Beisl, Hangl, Siglu or Porta bars. There's a weekly floodlit ski display, and tour reps organise toboggan and bowling evenings. The bowling alley has a karaoke night. Club Sonderbar is the livelier of the two discos.

FOR NON-SKIERS
Good for all but walkers
Lazy non-skiers should find adequate diversions. Some mountain restaurants are easily reached (though single gondola rides are very expensive). The town shops and museum are worth a look. Schladming has a railway station, making trips to beautiful Salzburg very easy. Buses run to the old walled town of Radstadt. For the more active, the public swimming pool and ice rink are supplemented by excellent sport facilities at Sporthotel Royer.

Haus 750m
Unlike Rohrmoos, Haus is a real village with a life of its own. It has a fair amount of accommodation plus its own ski schools and kindergartens.

The Hauser Kaibling lifts are a little peripheral, but the user-friendly nursery area is more handily placed between town and gondola station.

Haus is a railway stop, so excursions are easy, but non-skiers would be better off in Schladming. The same could be said of anyone looking for nightlife. It's a good choice for families looking for a quiet time, or those wishing to escape from their fellow Brits and experience a bit of the 'real' Austria – though Schladming itself isn't exactly over-commercialised or noisy.

Hotel prices are generally lower here. The Gurtl is a small, friendly, excellent-value hotel with good food. The Hauser Kaibling is a good, more upmarket place.

Seefeld 1200m

HOW IT RATES

The skiing

Snow	**
Extent	*
Advanced	*
Intermediates	**
Beginners	*****
Convenience	*
Queues	***
Restaurants	***

The rest

Scenery	***
Resort charm	****
Not skiing	*****

SKI FACTS

Altitude	1180m-2065m
Lifts	18
Pistes	25km
Green/Blue	75%
Red	25%
Black	0%
Artificial snow	10km

PACKAGES

Austrian Holidays,
Austrian Travel
Service, Crystal,
Enterprise, Inghams,
Made to Measure,
Thomson

TOURIST OFFICE

Postcode A-6100
Tel 010 43 (5212)
2313
Fax 3355

In a book called Where to Ski Cross-country, Seefeld would have one of the leading entries. There are better places in the Alps to wear skinny skis (St Moritz, Kandersteg) and there are better places than the Alps (Norway, classically), but Seefeld is one of the best. It is also one of the best mountain resorts in which to do things other than skiing – particularly curling, skating and swimming, for all of which its facilities are very impressive. For downhill skiing there are literally hundreds of better resorts in this book.

THE RESORT

In one competing publication that shall be nameless, we've seen Seefeld likened to Salzburg, Innsbruck and Kizbühel. A more misleading comparison would be hard to construct: there are parts of Seefeld that are of medieval origin, but they are far from typical. The village is a classical Tyrolean, post-war tourist development: modern, chalet-style, and with the warm glow of wood skillfully applied to interiors and exteriors alike. It attracts large numbers of well-heeled Germans of (or approaching) pensionable age; these people can afford to ski more or less where they like, so it is in a sense fashionable – and by Austrian standards rather expensive.

Seefeld sits on an elevated plateau to the north of the Inn valley, not far from Innsbruck, to which it is linked by railway. Ehrwald and Garmisch (over the nearby border in Germany) are also within easy reach.

THE SKIING

Seefeld's **ski area** consists of two main sectors, both on the outskirts and reached from most hotels by ski-bus. Gschwandtkopf is a rounded hill giving 300m vertical of intermediate skiing down two main slopes. Rosshütte is a more extensive but still very limited area. A funicular goes up to the main congregation area at 1800m, and a cable-car then goes up to 2100m. There is one main slope, served in addition by three drags. Runs go down from Rosshütte into the adjacent Hermannstal, with return by chair or the funicular. From Rosshütte another cable-car spans the Hermannstal to the shoulder of Härmelekopf at 2050m, whence there is an excellent red to the village.

With reasonable altitudes by Austrian standards and a serious snowmaking installation in both main sectors, **snow reliability** is not a serious problem. But most of the slopes are sunny in the morning or afternoon, affecting snow quality – particularly on Rosshütte.

The Rosshütte sector has some genuine challenges for **advanced skiers** – seriously steep off-piste routes, with and without climbing. These are great for skiers popping out from Innsbruck for the day, but no basis for a week-long holiday.

Only the most timid **intermediate skiers** should think of coming here. Gschwandtkopf is tiny, and Rosshütte is a two-run ski area.

This is an excellent resort for **beginners** – particularly those who are not dead set on becoming ace downhillers by the end of week one. The central village nursery slopes are broad and gentle; there is also a beginners' slope at Gschwandtkopf, but the slope and its lift get very busy.

The excellence of Seefeld's **cross-country** trails is one of the reasons why Innsbruck has been able to hold the Winter Olympics twice. More recently, the Nordic World Championships have been held here.

Queues are rarely a problem.

The **mountain restaurants** in both sectors are adequate, but most people east lunch in the village.

We lack reports on the **ski school**; **children** can be looked after all day, and there is a non-ski kindergarten.

STAYING THERE

The upmarket nature of the resort is made very clear by the range of **hotels**. There are no fewer than seven 5-star places, and almost 30 4-stars. To find anything less than 3-star standard, you have to look at pensions, and there are plenty of them. The Felseneck, not far from the sports centre, is one modest B&B that has been recommended.

Most of the **restaurants** are hotel-based. The lively **après-ski** scene also revolves largely around hotel bars, many of which have live music. Four hotels have tea-dancing.

Seefeld is great for **non-skiers**. The facilities are far too numerous to list, but include eight tennis courts, two skating rinks and 40 curling lanes. The public pool is superb, with special areas for non-swimmers and children.

Serfaus 1430m

Serfaus offers the charm and nightlife of a typical Austrian village but with a decent ski area, fairly reliable snow and the huge benefit of being largely traffic-free. The resort deserves to be better known on the British market.

HOW IT RATES

The skiing

Snow	★★★
Extent	★★
Advanced	★★
Intermediates	★★★
Beginners	★★★★
Convenience	★★★
Queues	★★★
Restaurants	★★★

The rest

Scenery	★★★
Resort charm	★★★★
Not skiing	★★★

SKI FACTS

Altitude	1430m-2685m
Lifts	20
Pistes	80km
Green/Blue	38%
Red	49%
Black	13%
Artificial snow	5km

PACKAGES

Made to Measure

TOURIST OFFICE

Postcode A-6534
Tel 010 43 (5476)
6239
Fax 6813

THE RESORT

Serfaus is an attractive and friendly village of traditional chalet-style buildings. It is largely traffic-free, with a big car park on the outskirts and a unique underground railway from there to the lifts, stopping off in the village en route. Few hotels are too far from one of the stations. This allows traditional charm to be preserved while reducing the effort of getting from one end of the long village to the slopes at the other end. A skating rink, sleighs and an old church add to the village charm.

Most visitors are well-heeled (though not particularly sophisticated) Germans and Dutch, who give the numerous bars and cafés a jolly atmosphere. Serfaus has few British visitors, but deserves more. The sunny shelf setting adds to the attraction.

THE SKIING

Though not as impressive a **ski area** as nearby Ischgl, Serfaus is far from negligible, served by lifts less prone to wind and queues. The 80km of sunny pistes spread westwards from the resort. The ski area is long and thin and reaches the respectable height of 2685m. Most of it is above the tree-line and served by drags.

The underground drops skiers at the main lift-station, from where a gondola and cable-car transport you to the mid-station. A second stage of the gondola rises to Lazid at 2350m. There are long reds from here back to the village and drags beyond lead to the highest Mindersjoch sector.

There's the skiing of neighbouring Fiss to explore too, linked in both directions. It's smaller than the Serfaus area, but is somewhat steeper.

The high average ski height, and snowmakers on four important pistes and the children's nursery area, make Serfaus reasonably **snowsure**.

There are few challenging slopes for **advanced skiers**, on- or off-piste, but it is a good area for ski-touring.

Good **intermediates** have a couple of short, steep runs between Lazid and the mid-station, while the most testing of the long runs is the pretty Alpkopf-village piste. Virtually the whole area has ideal runs for average intermediates. Less experienced skiers have wonderful long runs from Plansegg to the village, dropping gently almost 1000m vertical.

Both the village and mid-station nursery slopes are good, and there is ample opportunity for **beginners** to progress to longer runs. The **ski school** has a good reputation but there have been complaints about standards of English in group classes.

The 60km of **cross-country** trails are excellent and include some very pretty trails at altitude.

The replacement of the Lazid chair by a second-stage of gondola has improved the mid-station **queues**. The Scheid and Plansegg drags can be bottlenecks in the early morning and late afternoon respectively.

The seven **mountain restaurants** are adequate for the size of the ski area. The Masiner, on Mindersjoch, is atmospheric, and has a good ice bar. Skiing down the cross-country trail from Alpkopf is well worth it for a quiet lunch at Rodelhütte.

Facilities for **children** are excellent. The crèche takes children aged 2 to 7 all day. Ski kindergarten is available to 4-year-olds and above, and is also open all day. Our one concern would be the lack of English-speaking children to play with.

STAYING THERE

Most accommodation is in comfortable chalet-style **hotels**. Hotel Löwen is a charming old hotel with a tasteful modern wing and lots of facilities. The Alte Schmeide is closest to the slopes. The Post is an attractive, central 3-star. There are plenty of centrally-positioned pensions, too.

Restaurants are mainly hotel-based. Many hotels have a good 'farmer's buffet' once a week. Alte Serfaus is a jolly restaurant and bar.

Après-ski is lively and traditional. There are half a dozen dance bars. The most popular is Patschi's. The four discos liven up late.

There is not a great deal for **non-skiers**, though the better hotels have pools and sauna open to the public, and there are beautiful walks to enjoy. Going up the gondola to meet skiing friends for lunch is easy. For car-drivers several interesting excursions are possible – including St Moritz.

Sölden 1380m

✔ Good snow reliability by Austrian standards, with a high proportion of skiing above 2000m

✔ Glacier skiing in spring and summer

✔ Lively nightlife

✔ Ski convenience good from all package accommodation

✔ Short transfers from Innsbruck airport and Ötz railway station

✔ Very few T-bars for an Austrian resort

✘ Little challenging skiing

✘ Poor choice of resort for beginners and timid skiers

✘ Glacier skiing areas normally closed in winter

✘ Large village lacking much charm

✘ High-season queues can be bad

Sölden tends to disappoint. Its ski area is not as large, challenging or varied as most people expect. Many are also surprised to find the glacier lifts closed and, even when open, a bus-ride away.

This disappointment is partly the fault of tour operators. They tend to market Sölden as something akin to Ischgl or St Anton simply because, like those places, it is a big, lively, snowsure Austrian resort. However, it lacks the charm of the former, the tough runs of the latter and, most notably, the large, well-linked ski areas of both.

Sölden is, in fact, best suited to skiers who have enjoyed Mayrhofen's nightlife, intermediate runs and (usually) good snow, and who want to try an area that's more convenient, larger and slightly more challenging, with fewer queues – an area where they can start clocking up the miles.

ORIENTATION

Sölden sprawls for more than 2km along the Ötz valley floor, just before the road starts rising steeply towards Obergurgl. Lifts lead into the two linked ski areas from either end of town, the northern ones accessing Hochsölden. The road to Hochsölden and the separate glacier skiing area starts from the southern edge. Nearby **Obergurgl** and **Vent** and distant **St Anton** are reachable by public transport and the resorts around **Innsbruck** are all feasible car outings.

SKI FACTS

Altitude	1380m-3060m
Lifts	33
Pistes	101km
Green/Blue	42%
Red	44%
Black	14%
Artificial snow	10km

🏠 The resort

Sölden has mainly traditional Tyrolean-style buildings and it is set in a tree-filled valley. Yet, despite this, it lacks Alpine charm. It is a large, traffic-filled, rather characterless place which sprawls along both sides of a main road and river.

The geographical centre has a church and post office, but there is no real focus. There are numerous bars, cafés, hotels and typical touristy ski resort shops along its length.

The two main village lift-stations are at opposite ends of town, sufficiently distant from one another to make what is supposed to be 'central' accommodation a long walk or a bus-ride from both.

Sölden attracts a young, lively crowd – mostly made up of Germans – and is not a suitable resort for people looking for a quiet evening ambience. The bars and discos throb until the early hours.

Hochsölden, set over 700m above Sölden, is little more than a collection of fairly up-market hotels and is much quieter than its brash neighbour in the valley below. It's reachable by car, and served by day-time buses.

The skiing

Sölden's immediate ski area is made up of two similar-size sectors separated by a small valley. Both suit moderate-to-good intermediates. Sölden's two glaciers don't normally enter into the winter equation – see Snow reliability.

THE SKI AREA
Lacking variety

An impressive high-capacity two-stage gondola, at the southern edge of town, whisks skiers up to the top of the 3060m **Gaislachkogl**. From here a single piste runs down to Gratl, also reachable by the Innerwald chair and a further lift. This area is served by a number of chairs which allow you to reach **Gaislachalm** at the southern extremity of the ski area and Gampealm in its centre, from where a chair goes up to the other section of the ski area above **Hochsölden**.

Hochsölden can also be reached from the northern end of the village by a chair which goes right to it, and a gondola which finishes above it at Giggijoch. There is a network of runs above Hochsölden, served by chairs and drags. This section allows less

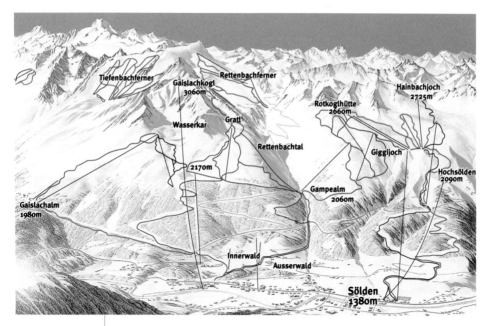

LIFT PASSES

94/95 prices in schillings

Ötztal Arena
Covers all lifts in Sölden, Hochsölden, Gaislachkogl and the Rettenbach and Tiefenbach glaciers (when open).
Beginners Points tickets, valid on lifts in Innerwald and Hochsölden areas.
Main pass
1-day pass 430
6-day pass 1980
(low season 1710 – 14% off)
Senior citizens
Over 65 male, 60 female: 6-day pass 1550 (22% off)
Children
Under 15: 6-day pass 1130 (43% off)
Under 6: free pass
Short-term passes
Half-day, 'hourly' cards refundable when you hand them in, single ascents for main cable-cars and chair-lift, only for non-skiers.
Alternative periods
Passes available for 5 days skiing in 7 and 10 days in 14.
Alternative passes
Separate passes for Vent (6 days 1,470 for adults, 1,020 for children).

horizontal movement, most pistes heading towards Hochsölden with lifts returning straight back. You can ski from near the top of this section back to Gampealm and catch a chair-lift into the Gaislachkogl-Gaislachalm sector of the skiing.

Both sectors have runs through trees to the village, and you can ski pretty much to any part of the village.

SNOW RELIABILITY
Good, but not that good
Sölden's two glaciers don't act as a snow guarantee in quite the normal way. They are generally not open in winter (the road up to the lifts is prone to avalanches) so you can't simply head for the glacier whenever you fancy skiing on perfect snow, as you can in Tignes, Hintertux or Zermatt, say. But if spring comes early, the glaciers are a very useful fall-back.

Similarly, the main area's top height of 3060m is deceptive: the lift serves only a single red piste. Most of the skiing is below 2700m. But most of it is also above 2100m – a decent height in Austrian terms – so it is reasonably snowsure. It faces east, so gets some sun, and the lower slopes depend heavily on snowmakers in late season.

FOR ADVANCED SKIERS
Don't believe the hype
Sölden has managed to gain a reputation for being suitable for good skiers but this simply isn't the case. Admittedly Sölden has little really easy skiing, but nor is there much to challenge the proficient.

None of the black runs is difficult. A steep plunge down the Gaislachkogl off-piste route is a highlight when conditions allow. Another good off-piste route is to ski from Gratl directly to the Mautstelle restaurant on the road up to the glacier. It's only a short walk to lifts.

Adventurers should note that there is a mountain guides' office in Sölden, and that at the top of the valley is one

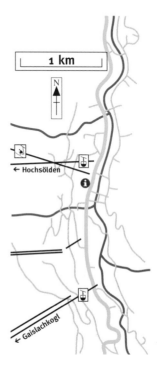

SKI SCHOOL

94/95 prices in schillings

Sölden/Hochsölden
Classes 6 days
4hr: 10am-noon and 1pm-3pm
6 full days: 1600
Children's classes
Ages: 4 to 13
6 full days: 1600
Private lessons
2hr or daily
1200 for 2hr

Total Vacancia
Classes 6 days
2½hr: 9.30-noon or 1pm-3.30
6 half-days: 1000
Private lessons Yes

CHILDCARE

As well as ordinary classes for older children, the ski schools run ski kindergartens for children aged 3 or more. The main school is open 9.30pm to 4pm, Total Vacancia 9.30 to 3.30. There are a couple of child-minders in the village – numbers from the Tourist Office.

GETTING THERE

Air Innsbruck, transfer 1½hr. Salzburg, transfer 4½hr.

Rail Ötz (30km); 12 daily buses from station.

---

of the premier ski touring areas of the Alps. Some of the tours launch off from the remote little hamlet of Vent, which comes under the Sölden marketing umbrella.

FOR INTERMEDIATE SKIERS
Something for all but the nervous
Nearly all of Sölden's skiing should really be classed as red run skiing, ideal for the average adventurous intermediate. Good intermediates have several easy black runs to try, but many may find the long, quiet piste down to Gaislachalm the most fun. It's ideal for fast skiing. The north-facing run beneath the Stabele chair is quite challenging in parts and tends to have good snow. It can be the second half of a fine 1000m vertical run from the Gaislachkogl summit.

The less experienced the skier, the further north they should head. The Giggijoch and Rotkogl sections above Hochsölden are good for moderate skiers, although the south-facing piste to Gampealm can get very icy. Immediately above Hochsölden is a small section of easy runs, but timid skiers are not really at home on Sölden's slopes.

Intermediates of all standards will enjoy a day out on the slopes of Obergurgl and Hochgurgl up the road.

FOR BEGINNERS
A poor choice
The only slopes for complete novices are inconveniently situated just above the village at Innerwald; they are prone to poor snow, yet no snowmakers are provided. These slopes are also dark and cold in mid-winter. Near-beginners can start at the top of the Giggijoch gondola, but Sölden is not a place for novices.

FOR CROSS-COUNTRY
Limited mileage
There are a couple of uninspiring loops at the back of town by the river, plus a small area at Zwieselstein. Total trails 16km. The one factor in its favour is Sölden's altitude.

QUEUES
They're getting there
Sölden is no longer one of the worst places for queues in the Alps, thanks to the upgrading of its lift system over the last six years. The notable improvements are the installation of the Gaislach gondola and Hainback four-person 'bubble' chair. But delays can still be lengthy when Sölden is full, during the morning peak at the gondola stations, especially the

---

Giggijoch. New Year is a bad time to visit, when overcrowded pistes add to the problems. Towards the end of the season there may be queues for the gondolas down at the end of the day, and for the glacier lifts (if open).

MOUNTAIN RESTAURANTS
Crowded
The restaurants tend to get very crowded and the quality of the food is nothing special. We like the two in the Gaislachalm area best. They are quieter than most, have good food, views and jolly accordion music. The Rauthalm at the bottom of the Mittelstation chair is rather low down the mountain but very welcoming, with good omelettes and Tyroler Gröstl (Rösti). There's a big terrace and outside bar at Gampealm.

The Rotkoglhütte has great top-of-the-world views. The atmospheric little Obstlerhütte, at the foot of the Rotkogl chair, is also worth a visit.

SKI SCHOOL
One or two problems
We haven't had many reports on Sölden's ski schools, and in particular we lack reports on the newish Total Vacancia school, which offers the distinct alternative of half-day tuition – 'the quickest road to success,' they say, and they may be right. Lack of spoken English has been a problem in the past (Sölden doesn't get huge numbers of British visitors). Beginners should be warned that the village nursery slopes are pretty sunless in midwinter.

CHILDREN'S FACILITIES
Half-hearted
Sölden doesn't go out of its way to cater for children; there is no proper day-care nursery, and the ski kindergartens keep rather short hours. The hotel Edelweiss up at Hochsölden has its own nursery, and this upper satellite resort has attractions for a family holiday.

 # Staying there

The two main lifts lying out at the edges of town make staying in the geographic centre inconvenient. The featureless nature of Sölden, and the similarity of its two linked ski areas, means there is no great advantage in staying at one end of the village in preference to the other. The impressive sports centre and pool is at the Giggijoch gondola (northern) end of town. Those near the Gaislachkogl

ACTIVITIES

Indoor Freizeit Arena sports complex (swimming, sauna, solarium, gym, bowling, tennis, shooting, badminton, billiards, cinema)
Outdoor Skating, curling, riding, toboggan run, para-gliding, sledging and sleigh rides

PACKAGES

Crystal, Inghams, Made to Measure, Sloping Off

Hochsölden Inghams

TOURIST OFFICE

Postcode A-6450
Tel 010 43 (5254) 22120
Fax 3131

gondola have slightly faster access to the top of the mountain each morning. Some accommodation is located just above Sölden, at Innerwald: useful for drivers as it has a large car park and marks the start of the glacier road.

Innerwald is also useful for those wishing to stay in a quiet area, but still have the bright lights of Sölden within walking distance. Ski convenience is good there too, a chair-lift taking skiers into the main area, and a returning piste allowing skiing almost to the door.

Hochsölden is good for those wanting a quiet time in a comfortable hotel.

HOW TO GO
Plush or basic?

Pensions and apartments dominate and independent travellers have a wide choice of cheap accommodation.
Chalets There are no catered chalets.
Hotels Most tour operators use Sölden's better hotels, rated 3-star or 4-star. All the hotels up at Hochsölden are 4-star.
£££££ Central Monster chalets make up the best and one of the biggest in town. Shuttle to the lifts. Pool.
££££ Tyrolerhof Big but friendly 4-star, well placed for the slopes and Giggijoch gondola.
££££ Regina Very comfortable 4-star right next to the Gaislachkogl lift.
££££ Edelweiss Large 4-star in Hochsölden with first-class leisure amenities including swimming pool. Satellite TV in rooms.
£££ Granat Best B&B hotel in Sölden, well placed off the road, yet close to the Giggijoch lift.
£££ Waldcafe Most attractive and best-positioned of Innerwald's hotels, 80m from the chair-lift.
££ Stefani Opposite the Waldcafe: pleasant good-value B&B pension.
Self-catering Some hotels have apartments. The Posthausl ones are good quality and well placed, though on the main road. Much cheaper and quieter are the Gerhard apartments opposite the Innerwald chair.

EATING OUT
Good range

There is a wide selection of restaurants. The good-value Café Hubertus does everything from snacks to full meals. The Nudeltopf and Café Corso vie for the title of 'best pizzas in town'. Other informal places worth a visit are the Pension Sonnenheim, Cafés Stefan and Philip, plus Dominic's. Of the many hotel restaurants the Birkenhof's is pleasantly traditional, and one of the best in town. The Kupferpfanne in the Tirolerhof and Otztaler Stube in the Central are also good.

APRES-SKI
Throbbing nightlife

Sölden is a happening place. There are a great number of lively piano bars, umbrella bars, discos and organised evenings. Café Philip at Innerwald is the liveliest post-skiing venue. Those skiing home from Rotkogl can have a similarly lively end to the day in the Obstlerhutte beneath Hochsölden. Taking the blue, rather than black, run home in the gathering darkness is advisable after a few glühweins.

A little later, the Après-Ski Club and Berglands keller bar are two of the most popular places. The glass-fronted Dominic's and the Hinterher on the main street get extremely crowded; they frequently have live bands later on. The Stamperl and Pfiff are other 'happening' bars. Madeus in the Alpenland hotel and the Centro Club are perhaps the best discos.

The toboggan evening is not the usual tame affair. Plenty of Dutch courage is built-up with drinking and dancing before an exciting 6km run back to town from the Gaislachalm mountain restaurant. And it takes place every night!

The Sonnblick Scene is the focus of the limited nightlife in Hochsölden.

FOR NON-SKIERS
Disappointing for a large resort

Given the size of Sölden there is surprisingly little to do. Buses run to Innsbruck and there may be an organised excursion to Igls. Walks are not particularly interesting. Mountain bikes are available and there is a large sports centre and swimming pool facility. The skating rink is merely a flooded, and frozen, tennis court.

Söll 700m

HOW IT RATES

The skiing

Snow	*
Extent	****
Advanced	*
Intermediates	****
Beginners	***
Convenience	**
Queues	***
Restaurants	**

The rest

Scenery	***
Resort charm	***
Not skiing	**

✔ Large, pretty, easy-intermediate ski area

✔ Lively (but no longer rowdy) nightlife

✔ Short airport transfers and easy road access

✔ Plenty of cheap and cheerful pensions for budget skiers

✔ Improved lift system has reduced queues

✔ Has the highest and steepest skiing in the Ski-Welt area

✘ Very poor recent snow record, and few snowmakers

✘ Long walks or inefficient bus to the lifts from most accommodation

✘ Little challenging skiing

✘ Local skiing is the most crowded in the Ski-Welt area

✘ Poor links to the most snowsure section of Ski-Welt area

✘ Mostly short runs in local sector

Söll has an image problem. In the 1980s it became known as prime lager-lout territory but, for some years now, the resort's reputation for rowdy behaviour has been undeserved, and it would doubtless have faded altogether but for the efforts of British tabloid 'journalists' to sustain it. Apart from anything else, the high value of the Austrian schilling has ensured that cost-conscious lager drinkers now prefer Eastern Europe and Andorra. Family skiers certainly need not avoid Söll, and young people bent on having a riotous time should not assume that they will find one.

There are other important considerations. Although it has pretty well solved its 1980s queuing problems by building new lifts, Söll has totally failed to deal with its most serious weakness, namely that it has no reliable snow. Whether the root problem is a lack of money, of will, of water or of permission, the end result is the same – there are no snowmakers on the local slopes. Sadly, the best snow in the Ski-Welt, above nearby Scheffau, is not easily accessible on skis or by bus. And only if you have a car can you hope to do much skiing in other, more snowsure ski areas further away.

With good snow, Söll is great for a lively holiday spent bashing undemanding pistes in pretty scenery – and all at modest cost. But skiers booking early should beware.

ORIENTATION

Söll sits in a wide valley, a few miles off the main road through the Tyrol. From a base station 1km out of the village, a gondola goes up to the mid-mountain junction of Hochsöll, from where the skiing spreads over to **Hopfgarten**, **Brixen**, **Scheffau** and **Ellmau**. The skiing of **Westendorf** is separate, but covered by the area lift pass.

Other resorts such as **Fieberbrunn**, **St Johann**, **Waidring**, **Kirchberg** and **Leogang** (for Saalbach) are easily accessible by car, much less so by bus.

🏠 The resort

Söll remains a small, friendly village, though a great deal of development has left it feeling rather cramped. But at least everything (except the skiing) is readily to hand, and the main new buildings have been designed to look attractively traditional. The pretty surrounding scenery adds to its charm, and the village benefits from being some way off the busy main road.

Unfortunately it is not well placed for skiing. Its lifts are a 15-minute walk from the village centre across the main road, and much further from some accommodation. What's more, the ski-bus service is poor. Staying in a central hotel at least means that you have the option of a lengthy walk as an alternative to the bus. The nightlife is not too wild, so you're unlikely to be woken up in the early hours.

🎿 The skiing

The Ski-Welt, or Grossraum as it used to be called, is supposed to be the largest completely linked ski area in Austria, but that doesn't make it a rival for the Trois Vallées. It's essentially a typically small, low, pastoral Austrian hill multiplied

1 km

↙ Hohe Salve

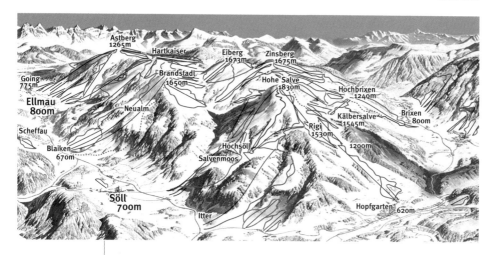

SKI FACTS

Altitude	620m-1830m
Lifts	90
Pistes	250km
Green/Blue	37%
Red	53%
Black	10%
Artificial snow	30km

LIFT PASSES

94/95 prices in schillings

Ski-Welt Wilder Kaiser-Brixental
Covers all lifts in the Wilder Kaiser-Brixental area from Going to Westendorf, and the ski-bus.

Beginners Points tickets (100 points 280). Most beginner lifts cost from 5 to 10 points.

Credit cards Yes

Main pass
1-day pass 330
6-day pass 1560

Children
Under 15: 6-day pass 890 (43% off)
Under 5: free pass

Short-term passes
Single ascent on some lifts. Day pass price reduces hourly from 11am.

Alternative periods
5 in 7 days, 7 in 10 days and 10 in 14 days.

Alternative passes
Söll only pass available (1335 6-day pass for adults, 755 for children), covers 12 local lifts.

several times. One section is pretty much like any other, with almost all the skiing best suited to intermediates. Runs are short and scenery attractive rather than stunning.

THE SKI AREA
Short run network
A gondola takes all but complete beginners up to the elevated shelf of Hochsöll, where there are a couple of short lifts and connections in several directions.

A two-stage chair rises to Rigi, from where you can ski to Hopfgarten or Itter, or get a further chair to the high point of Hohe Salve – also accessed directly by a long chair from Hochsöll. Hohe Salve is the start of runs down to Kälbersalve – steep at first, and south-facing – and then on down to Brixen or up by chair to Zinsberg, which in turn is an access point for Eiberg, the most snowsure section of the Ski-Welt. This rather protracted route is tiresome and crowded when snow is in short supply. Some years ago an alternative route from Hochsöll was created by the installation of a cable-car; this cuts out tricky Hohe Salve.

The excellent long runs from Brandstadl down to Blaiken are also accessed from Zinsberg.

No matter what route is chosen, in this rather amorphous area of rounded hills you're skiing very short runs. The few long pistes are the valley runs to Blaiken, Hopfgarten and Brixen.

SNOW RELIABILITY
Very poor
With a very low average ski height, and important links that get too much sun, Söll's lack of snowmakers is a real weakness. It is one of the least snowsure resorts in the Alps, and distant from more reliable resorts.

FOR ADVANCED SKIERS
Not a lot
The plunge straight off Hohe Salve towards Hochsöll and the black run alongside the Brixen gondola represent the only challenging piste skiing. There are further black runs in the Scheffau and Ellmau sectors, but most good skiers will need to seek amusement off-piste.

FOR INTERMEDIATE SKIERS
Something for everyone
The most direct of the runs between Brandstadl and Blaiken, the Hohe Salve red, and the pistes down to Brixen suit good intermediates. Moderate skiers have an enormous choice. With good snow, the lower woodland runs down to Söll, Hopfgarten and Itter offer some of the most interesting skiing in the area. The runs down to Ellmau are enjoyable, but it's a bit of a trek to get over there. Early intermediates have plenty of cruising terrain on the higher slopes between Hochbrixen and Brandstadl. The varied runs down to Brixen are good for groups of mixed abilities.

SKI SCHOOL

94/95 prices in schillings

Söll-Hochsöll
Manager Sepp Embacher
Classes 5 days. 2 hr or 4hr: 10am-noon and 2pm-4pm
5 full days: 1230
Children's classes
Ages: 5 to 14
5 full days: 1170
Private lessons
Hourly, or full day (4hr)
430 for 1hr; each additional person 170

Austria
Manager Hans Wohlschlager
Classes 6 days. 4hr: 10am-noon and 2pm-4pm
6 full days: 1200
Children's classes
Ages: 5 to 14
6 full days: 1150
Private lessons Hourly or daily
400 for 1hr; each extra person 200

CHILDCARE

The ski schools take children from age 5, starting them off in special snow-gardens. The Söll-Hochsöll school's is next to Gasthof Eisenmann, on the nursery slopes; while based here, children can be looked after from 9.30 to 4.15. Once they progress to Hochsöll, care has to be arranged with the instructor.

Next to the main ski kindergarten, the same school now operates a Mini Club for children aged 3 to 5 – fun and games, with skiing available. It is open 6 days a week, 9.30 to 4.30.

FOR BEGINNERS
OK when snow is good
The nursery slopes are between the main road and the gondola station, and are perfectly adequate when snow is abundant – gentle, spacious and uncrowded. Otherwise the Hochsöll area is used, though one of the most suitable runs is served by a chair rather than drag. Near-beginners and fast learners can ski home to the bottom station when the meandering blue from Hochsöll is not too icy.

FOR CROSS-COUNTRY
Neighbouring villages are better
Söll has 35km of local trails but they are less interesting than those between Hopfgarten and Kelchsau or the ones around and beyond Ellmau. Lack of snowcover is a big problem.

QUEUES
Much improved
New lifts have greatly improved this once queue-prone area. The Blaiken gondola is to be avoided on weekend mornings, and the tiresomely slow Hohe Salve chair can become over-subscribed. However, most delays are directly related to conditions: when snow is in short supply, the important linking lifts to and from Zinsberg and Eiberg get busy.

MOUNTAIN RESTAURANTS
Good, but crowded
Restaurants are generally pleasant, and there are quite a few jolly little chalets dotted about, but those at Hochsöll, in particular, can get very busy. The otherwise pleasant Stockalm, Kraftalm and Grundalm are also prone to crowds. The Alpenrose, near the top of Hohe Salve, has a good sun terrace, generous portions and reasonable prices. Further afield the Neualm, half-way down to Blaiken, is one of the best huts in the Ski-Welt.

SKI SCHOOL
The usual reservations
The two schools have fairly good reputations, though there are occasional reports of over-large classes and poor spoken English – more of a problem with the 'Red' Austria school than the bigger Söll-Hochsöll school, which is more widely-used by tour operators. With the latter, groups of five to eight can book an instructor for a set price of S2470 a day, but this works out much more expensive than ordinary classes even if there are eight of you.

FACILITIES FOR CHILDREN
Improved this year
The ski kindergarten of the Söll-Hochsöll school generally gets good reports, and this year is at last opening a proper day nursery for younger children who don't want to spend all day skiing. Reports welcome.

Staying there

Ski-convenience fans have a few options out near the lifts but most accommodation is in or around the village centre. Being on the edge of town nearest the lifts is the best bet for those who are prepared to walk to the slopes. The other side of town is better for those who prefer the bus, since you can board there before it gets too crowded. Be aware that some guest-houses are literally miles from the centre and lifts, and that the ski-bus does not serve every nook and cranny of this sprawling community.

HOW TO GO
Mostly cheap and cheerful gasthofs
There is a wide choice of simple gasthofs, pensions and B&Bs, and an adequate amount of better-quality hotel accommodation – mainly 3-star. As far as we know, none has a pool. There are apartments, too, but not through tour operators.
Chalets Crystal have a charming wood-clad chalet but it's poorly situated 7 minutes' walk from a ski-bus stop.
Hotels
£££ Greil The only 4-star – attractive place, but out of the centre on the wrong side for the lifts and pool.
£££ Postwirt Attractive and central old 3-star that is a hub of the nightlife.
£££ Austria Also central, and a bit quieter.
£££ Bergland Small 3-star, well placed mid-way between the village and lifts.
£££ Theresa Comfortable, 'superb' food, but a 10-minute walk out of the centre on the wrong side.
£££ Ingeborg Next to the lifts.
££ Feldwebel Central 2-star.
££ Schirast Next to the lifts.
££ Garni-Tenne B&B gasthof between centre and main road.
Self-catering We are not aware of any apartments available through tour operators, but there are plenty for independent travellers. The central Ferienhotel Schindlhaus has nice accommodation, though the best apartments in town are those attached to the Bergland hotel.

PACKAGES

Airtours, Crystal, Enterprise, Inghams, Neilson, Ski Choice, Ski Club of GB, Ski Partners, Stena Sealink, Thomson, Timescape

Hopfgarten Contiki, Ski Hillwood, Top Deck

Itter Crystal, Neilson

GETTING THERE

Air Salzburg, transfer 2hr hr. Innsbruck, transfer 1½hr.

Rail Wörgl (13km) or Kufstein (15km); bus to resort.

ACTIVITIES

Indoor Swimming, sauna, solarium, massage, bowling, rifle-range, squash **Outdoor** Natural ice rink (skating, curling), sleigh rides, 3km floodlit toboggan run, para-gliding, hang-gliding

TOURIST OFFICE

Postcode A-6306
Tel 010 43 (5333) 5216
Fax 6180

EATING OUT
A fair choice

Some of the best restaurants are hotel based. Hotels Greil and Postwirt are perhaps of the highest standard in town. Café Einstein and the Brunhof cook excellent pizzas, while other places worth a visit include the Dorfstub'n, Venezia and Al Dente.

APRES-SKI
Lively, but it's no Kitzbühel.

For a small village, there's a lot going on. Pub 15 is a crowded British-style bar with charts music. The ski bar of the Postwirt has a singalong that makes much use of double entendre, and the bar of the Austria hotel is popular for its live guitar music and atmosphere. The Mirabell is a much quieter alternative for a convivial drink. Every kind of organised evening event is available. The Whisky Mühle is a large disco which can get a little rowdy. The Klaus is a smaller nightclub, with a friendlier atmosphere, and is generally considered a better place to bop.

FOR NON-SKIERS
Not bad for a small village

The sports and leisure centre is Söll's pride and joy; it has an excellent main indoor pool with an outdoor area, a baby area and a sauna. There are numerous coach excursions, including trips to Salzburg, Innsbruck and even Vipiteno over in Italy. The local bus goes to Kufstein and St Johann. Walks are quite pretty.

Hopfgarten 620m

Hopfgarten is well worth considering as a base for skiing the Ski-Welt – an unspoilt, friendly and traditional resort tucked away several kilometres from the busy Wörgl road. Most hotels are within five minutes' walk of the queue-free chair that provides access to Rigi and Hohe Salve – the high-point of the Ski-Welt circus. The resort's great weakness is that you're unlikely to be able to ski down to 620m on the south-west-facing home slope. The village is a good size – small enough to be intimate, large enough to have plenty of off-slope amenities.

For a change of scene, and perhaps less crowded pistes, Westendorf (covered by the ski pass) is a short bus-journey away – see separate chapter.

When snow allows, the runs down to Hopfgarten and the nearby villages of Brixen and Itter offer some of the best skiing in the Ski-Welt. But the fine (and relatively snowsure) runs above Scheffau are irksomely distant.

There is a convenient nursery slope in the village, but it is sunny as well as low, so lack of snow-cover is likely to mean excursions up the mountain to the higher blue runs served by chair-lifts – at the cost of a lift pass.

Hopfgarten is one of the best cross-country bases in the area. There are fine trails to Kelschsau (11km) and Niederau (15km), and the Itter-Bocking loop (15km) starts nearby. Westendorf's trails are also close.

Although few British tour operators go to Hopfgarten, English is widely spoken in the two ski schools, thanks to the large number of Australians who take lessons via Contiki Travel.

Cheap and cheerful gasthofs, pensions and little, private B&Bs are the norm here. The exceptions are the comfortable but rather expensive hotel Hopfgarten and Sporthotel Fuchs, both of which are well placed for the main lift. Also centrally placed, and better value, are numerous little gasthofs such as the Krone and Oberbräu. The Lukas is one of the best-positioned B&Bs.

Après-ski is generally quiet, though a lively holiday can usually be ensured by booking through the Aussie-dominated Contiki Travel. Lift Stubl has a good tea-time atmosphere, while the Silver Bullet is the main rendezvous later. The ubiquitous Tyrolean evening is popular. Though most of the restaurants are hotel-based, there are exceptions, including a Chinese and a pizzeria.

The village has plenty of non-skiing amenities, including swimming, riding, bowling, ice-skating, tobogganing and parapenting. The railway provides excursion possibilities, including trips to Salzburg, Innsbruck and Kitzbühel.

Hopfgarten is a family resort, providing a fine nursery in the hotel Hopfgarten which is open to non-residents. Children are taken from 3 years. The ski kindergarten takes them from 4, and staff are friendly. The tour operator Ski Hillwood specialises in family holidays to Hopfgarten.

Itter 700m

Itter is a tiny village half-way around the mountain between Söll and Hopfgarten, with nursery slopes close to hand and a gondola just outside the village (reachable on skis) into the Ski-Welt via Hochsöll. There is one hotel, half a dozen gasthofs and a similar number of B&B pensions. There is a ski school and an associated ski hire shop, and when conditions are good it makes a good beginner's resort.

Brixen 795m

Brixen im Thale is a very scattered roadside village at the south-eastern edge of the Ski-Welt circus, close to Westendorf. Although one of the least aesthetically pleasing villages in the area, its queue-free, high-capacity gondola and the chain of snowmakers on its main piste give Brixen a more go-ahead feel than its neighbours. This is some compensation for the inconvenience of the place: its main hotels are clustered around the railway station, a bus-ride from the lifts.

When snow-cover is good, Brixen has some of the best skiing in the Ski-Welt. All three pistes leading down to the village lift station are fine runs in different ways: a black provides an interesting short cut from Hohe Salve; an unpisted route runs the length of the village gondola; and a much easier, prettier piste with artificial snow leads home from Holzalm. Another easy route home, strictly for the end of the day, is a lovely long, away-from-the-lifts run finishing close to the village centre. There is also a very small area of north-facing runs, including the nursery slopes, on the other side of the village below Kandleralm. A free bus runs to Westendorf every 45 minutes.

Brixen is a better base for good skiers than any other Ski-Welt resort. Two of the three runs to the village are challenging, and tend to be very icy. The Hohe Salve black is another test.

Good intermediates will find plenty to do, staying close to home and skiing the interesting runs down to Brixen, Hopfgarten and Itter, or going over to Scheffau's skiing. The less competent and the leisurely also have plenty of choice.

The nursery slopes are across the valley at the foot of the Kandleralm area – an inconvenient bus-ride from the village. They have the attractions of seclusion and shade, but meeting up with other skiers for lunch is a hassle. At the top of the gondola is some of the best terrain in the area for the improving novice. A special beginner's lift pass keeps costs down.

Brixen is one of the best cross-country villages in the Ski-Welt. There is a long trail to Kirchberg, and more leisurely loops that circumnavigate nearby Westendorf. Hopfgarten's trails are also nearby. A 5km loop up the mountain at Hochbrixen provides fine views, fairly reliable snow and a chance to meet up with Alpine skiers.

The surprisingly large ski school runs the usual group classes, and mini-group sessions for five to seven people, which are a third more expensive. Lack of English-speaking tuition can be a problem.

Brixen has plenty of hotels. The multi-amenity 4-star Alpenhof and Sporthotel, and the cheaper 3-star Hetzenauer are situated in the nearest thing to a village centre, some way from the lifts. The 3-star Gasthof Brixnerwirt and the less expensive Mairwirt are better placed for ski convenience, though still a lengthy walk from the gondola. Both are situated right next to the large white church, which has noise implications. Several little pensions are in an isolated position near the lifts, and are very inexpensive because they are out of town. These include Gästehaus Hofer and the Hubertus.

Restaurants are mainly in-house. Not surprisingly, the Sporthotel and Alpenhof have the best food in town. The Loipenstub'n and Brixner Thalhof are much less expensive, cosier places. The latter has a pleasant sun terrace.

Après-ski is very quiet by Tyrolean standards, but livelier Westendorf is a short taxi-ride away.

Non-skiers can play tennis, take excursions to Salzburg, Innsbruck and Kitzbühel or use the sports facilities of the Alpenhof and Sporthotel (both have a pool and fitness room).

Brixen is not as suitable for children as other Ski-Welt resorts, but it does have an all-day ski kindergarten with optional lunch-time supervision.

Westendorf 800m

HOW IT RATES

The skiing

Snow	**
Extent	*
Advanced	*
Intermediates	**
Beginners	****
Convenience	***
Queues	****
Restaurants	***

The rest

Scenery	***
Resort charm	****
Not skiing	**

SKI FACTS

Altitude	800m-1865m
Lifts	14
Pistes	40km
Green/Blue	38%
Red	62%
Black	0%
Artificial snow	8km

PACKAGES

Crystal, Enterprise, Inghams, Neilson, Thomson

TOURIST OFFICE

Postcode A-6363
Tel 010 43 (5334)
6230
Fax 2390

Westendorf is a small but lively resort that is part of the Ski-Welt pass-sharing arrangement (along with Söll, Ellmau, Brixen and others) but not part of the main skiing circuit. Its own slopes are not without interest, and the friendliness of the village wins many repeat visitors.

THE RESORT

The village is a small Tyrolean charmer, complete with attractive onion-domed church and sleighs. It attracts more Germans than Brits, and more Dutch than either.

THE SKIING

The local **ski area** is a small section of leisurely skiing. A two-stage gondola takes you to Talkaser (1760m), from where you can ski various north-west-facing runs back to the resort. There are short west-facing and east-facing runs below the two low peaks of Choralpe (1820m) and Fleiding (1890m), either side of Talkaser. A couple of red runs from Fleiding go down beyond the lifts to hamlets served by buses. The main Ski-Welt area is nearby at Brixen.

The **snow reliability** of Westendorf's slopes is slightly better than that of some other Ski-Welt resorts, but there are limits to what shade and good maintenance (with some snowmaking on the lower runs) can achieve at this altitude.

Essentially Westendorf is far from suitable for **advanced skiers**, but we have reports from some who have been happy pottering about off-piste. Leisurely **intermediates** have a fair amount of pretty, uncrowded skiing. Most pistes are of blue difficulty, whatever their official grading.

Second-year skiers and confident **beginners** have nice runs both between the mid-station and village, and alongside the Choralpe chair. The extensive nursery slopes are Westendorf's pride and joy.

There are 30 km of local **cross-country** trails, less than in many neighbouring resorts. One trail links up with the Brixen route to Kirchberg. Snow-cover is a big problem.

Given good conditions, **queues** are rare except at Fasching, and far less of a problem than in the main Ski-Welt area. If poor weather closes the upper lifts, queues do become long.

Mountain restaurants are adequate. Alpenrosenhütte is small and friendly; Brechhornhaus is quiet; Gassnerhof is good if you don't mind catching a bus back to town; and Talkaiser and Choralpe are both busy.

The two **ski schools** have quite good reputations, though classes can be over-large and may cram English and Dutch together.

Westendorf sells itself as a family resort and amenities are good. Both the crèche and the ski kindergarten are open all day. Ski school takes **children** up to the age of 15.

STAYING THERE

Although the village remains relatively compact, location is worth consideration. Staying in the centre puts you conveniently close to the village nursery slopes, and a five-minute walk from the lifts into the main ski area, on the edge of the village. But staying on the other side of the village, further from the lifts, may be preferable to putting up with the church bells at six in the morning.

There are a couple of central 4-star **hotels** – Jakobwirt and Schermer – and a dozen 3-star ones, but most reporters have stayed in more modest gasthofs and pensions. Pension Wetti is particularly popular, and distant from the church bells. Pension Ingeborg is highly recommended, and much more convenient – right next to the gondola. The Schermhof **apartments** are of good quality.

Most of the best **restaurants** are hotel-based – the Schermer, Mesnerwirt and Jakobwirt are good. A taxi to Berggasthaus Stimlach is well worth it, as is the sleigh ride to the Almaheuf restaurant. Something a little different is an excellent French place, Chez Yves.

The **nightlife** is quite lively, but it is a small place with a limited range of options. Kibo's Café is a pleasant tea-time place. Hausberger does the best coffee and cakes. Gerry's Inn is about the liveliest bar, and the main Dutch meeting place. The Post bar is the focus for Brits. There are also quieter, more mellow bars such as the Schermer and Sporer Stuberl. The discos liven up at weekends.

For **non-skiers** Westendorf is rather limited. There are excursions by rail or bus to Innsbruck, Salzburg and Kitzbühel. Walks and sleigh rides are very pretty. The ice rink is natural, and at this altitude unreliable.

Zell am See 755m

✔ Pretty, tree-lined skiing with good views

✔ Lively, but not rowdy, nightlife

✔ Charming old town centre with beautiful lakeside setting

✔ Lots to do off the slopes

✔ Enormous range of cross-country trails in the area

✔ Kaprun glacier skiing nearby

✔ Varied terrain including some genuinely black runs – though not many of them

✘ Sunny, low ski area often has poor conditions despite snowmakers

✘ Old-town charm spoilt somewhat by busy main road and development

✘ Trek to lifts from much accommodation

✘ Less suitable for beginners than most small Austrian resorts

✘ Kaprun glacier gets horrendous queues when it is most needed

Zell am See is an unusual resort – not a rustic village like most of its small Austrian competitors, but a lakeside town on an important through-route, with a charming old centre that seems more geared to summer visitors than to winter ones. It's a pleasant enough place, and the skiing has more variety than is normal in a small area, with more challenge. But we have some difficulty in spotting quite the sort of skier it suits for a week-long holiday.

One group of skiers the resort aims at is those concerned about snow reliability; the key is the resort's proximity to the Kaprun glacier. But Kaprun is within easy reach of many low-altitude resorts, all of which provide buses to the glacier when snow is in short supply. The result is horrendous queues (for buses as well as lifts) both to and from the glacier; you can wait up to four hours in mid-March. What's more, Zell's local skiing is excessively sunny, making reliance on the glacier more likely.

For skiers with a roving eye – especially (but not only) those with a car – Zell could be an attractive base from which to ski numerous resorts in Salzburgerland and the eastern Tyrol, and even Styria (Schladming).

ORIENTATION

Zell am See sits beside a large lake that virtually fills its broad valley. The skiing is on a horseshoe-shaped mountain, one arm of which approaches the town. A gondola goes up that arm from the edge of town, but other lifts are more remote – cable-cars 2km 'inland', and another gondola 3km away at **Schüttdorf**, beyond the southern end of the lake.

Kaprun is only 6km; **Saalbach** and **Bad Hofgastein** are easily reached by bus and train respectively; **Wagrain** and, at a push, **Obertauern** are car outings.

 ## The resort

Zell am See is a long-established, year-round resort town in a lovely setting between a large lake and a mountain. Its charming, traffic-free medieval centre occupies a flat promontory, and it's around this attractive core – with everyday towny shops as well as ones catering for summer tourists – that the resort has developed. Unfortunately, the result is a less than convenient ski resort; much of the accommodation is a long walk from the nearest lift, and separated from it by the busy road through the town. There is also accommodation out by the cable-car station, and on the road up to it.

Quite a number of British visitors stay in the satellite resort of Schüttdorf. Some of the accommodation here is quite close to the gondola, but the place is much less appealing than Zell itself, especially for après-skiers. It also has a very sunny home piste which, unlike the Zell ones, has no snowmakers.

 ## The skiing

Despite claims to the contrary, Zell has a fairly small ski area, best suited to good and timid intermediates, with little for moderate skiers. The fan-shaped ski area has easy runs along its horseshoe ridge, with steeper pistes heading down into the centre.

THE SKI AREA
Varied but limited

The town gondola rises to Mittelstation. From there you can ski to the double cable-car station at Sonnenalm via two runs, one easy, the other steep in places. Alternatively, a chair from this mid-station goes up to Hirschkogel, where it meets the lifts up from Schüttdorf. Continuing along the ridge via a couple of short lifts brings you to the Schmittenhöhe top station, also reached from Sonnenalm by cable-car. A gentle cruise and a single short drag-lift moves you across to Sonnkogel, from where several routes lead down to Sonnalm mid-

LIFT PASSES

94/95 prices in schillings

Europa-Sportregion Kaprun-Zell am See
Covers all lifts in Zell and Kaprun, and buses between them.

Beginners Points card or limited pass.

Main pass
1-day pass 390
6-day pass 1880
(low season 1760 – 6% off)

Senior citizens
Over 65 male, 60 female: 6-day pass 1692 (10% off)

Children
Under 15: 6-day pass 1170 (38% off)
Under 6: free pass

Short-term passes
Half-day pass from 11.30 for Zell only; reduces in price by the hour through the day.

Alternative periods
5 in 7 days and 10 in 14 days.

Notes Day pass valid on Zell am See, Schmittenhöhe and Thumersbach only.

Alternative passes
Zell am See only; Kaprun glacier.

CHILDCARE

All three ski schools take children from age 4 and offer lunch-time care. The Areitbahn school runs a snow kindergarten and play room for children from age 3, from 9am to 4.30. This is up the mountain at Areitalm (handy for Schüttdorf residents).

There are two village nurseries. Ursula Zink (6343) takes children from age 3, from 9am to 4pm; younger children looked after on an hourly basis. Feriendorf Hagleitner (7935) takes children from age 12 months, from 10am to 4pm.

station. A piste runs from here beneath the second of the cable-cars to Sonnenalm, and there is a choice of lifts back to the ridge.

SNOW RELIABILITY
Poor, despite artificial support
Zell am See has chosen to cover its north-east-facing pistes with snowmakers, while leaving its sunnier slopes in the hands of nature. This seemingly illogical approach is presumably designed to maximise the chance of continuous snow down to Zell; not much consolation to skiers based in Schüttdorf. Also, most of the slopes covered are the steeper ones, unsuitable for the moderate majority.

The Kaprun glacier is, of course, snowsure, but the queues when the glacier is in demand are horrendous.

FOR ADVANCED SKIERS
Limited
There is more steep skiing in Zell than in most ski areas of this size, but not enough to entertain a good skier for long. Off-piste opportunities are limited, too.

FOR INTERMEDIATE SKIERS
Bits and pieces for most grades
Good or aggressive intermediates have a choice of fine, long runs, but this is not a place for those keen on high mileage. Run number 1 from Breiteckalm is perhaps the best, but all pistes graded black are within their compass. Moderate skiers have a lovely run between Areit and Schüttdorf when conditions are good (not too often). Some of Sonnkogel's pistes are also suitable. Timid skiers can cruise around the ridge all day or ski past Mittelstation and cut across to the cable-car stations on an easy blue. The Hirschkogel runs are best for mixed abilities.

FOR BEGINNERS
Neighbouring villages are better
There are small nursery slopes at Sonnenalm and Schüttdorf, the former being covered by snowmakers. Near-beginners and fast learners have plenty of short, easy runs at Schmittenhöhe, Breiteckalm and Areitalm. Some of them are often used by complete beginners, due to poor snow conditions lower down, but it means buying a lift pass.

FOR CROSS-COUNTRY
Excellent if snow allows
The valley floor has extremely extensive trails, including a superb area on the Kaprun golf course.

Unfortunately, there is very little at altitude except a small loop (2km) at the top of the Zell gondola.

QUEUES
Not normally a problem
Zell am See doesn't have too many problems except at peak times, when the Schmittenhöhe cable-car is by far the worst spot, followed by the Hirschkogel chair. When snow is poor, Zell does not suffer too badly from queues during the day, because many residents are away queueing at Kaprun; but getting down by lift can involve delays.

MOUNTAIN RESTAURANTS
Plenty of little refuges
As well as anonymous lift-station places there are plenty of cosier, more atmospheric huts. Among the best are Glocknerhaus (just below Hirschkogel), Kettingalm, Areitalm and Brieteckalm. The Berghotel restaurant at Schmittenhöhe has good food and atmosphere and wonderful views, but is expensive.

SKI SCHOOL
Good attitude
The three schools (two in Zell, one in Schüttdorf) have quite good reputations. Standards of English, tuition and friendliness are all reported as high, though we lack very recent reports. Snowboarding seems to be enthusiastically supported. There are also specialist cross-country centres at Schüttdorf and at Kaprun.

FACILITIES FOR CHILDREN
Schüttdorf's the place
We have no recent first-hand reports on the workings of the childcare provisions, but staying in Schüttdorf has the advantage of direct gondola access to the Areitalm snow-kindergarten, and fairly convenient access to one of the two village nurseries (Ursula Zink is at Zeller-Moos, just outside Schüttdorf).

 Staying there

Choice of location is tricky, and will depend on your own priorities. Our three favourite strategies would be staying in a place with a beautiful lakeside setting, which also gets you on the ski-bus before it gets too crowded, or staying at the upper edge of the town centre within walking distance of the Zell gondola, or staying near the cable-car station at Sonnenalm.

SKI SCHOOL

93/94 prices in schillings

Schmittenhöhe
Courses start Sunday and Monday
Classes 6 days
Full day: from 9.30
6 full days: 1350
Children's classes
Ages: from 4
6 full days: 1350
Private lessons
Hourly or daily
450 for 1hr; each additional person 100

Wallner-Prenner
Courses start Sunday and Monday
Classes 6 days
Full day: from 9.30
6 full days: 1350
Children's classes
Ages: from 4
6 full days: 1350
Private lessons
Hourly or daily
450 for 1hr; each additional person 100

Areitbahn
Courses start Sunday and Monday
Classes 6 days
Full day: from 10am
6 full days: 1350
Children's classes
Ages: from 4
6 full days: 1350
Private lessons
Hourly or daily
450 for 1hr; each additional person 100

Before Zell improved its lift system it was well worth staying in Schüttdorf to avoid the queues. Perhaps it still is during peak season, but Schüttdorf is a characterless dormitory with little else going for it. Being closer to Kaprun is, perversely, a drawback unless you have a car. Trying to get on a glacier bus is tough, as they tend to be full when they leave Zell. Families wishing to use the Areitalm nursery and cross-country skiers stand to gain most from staying in Schüttdorf.

HOW TO GO
Choose charm or convenience
There is a very wide range of hotels or pensions and apartment accommodation, but tour operators have ignored the latter
Chalets Crystal have the only catered chalet operation we know of – in a good position on the edge of town.
Hotels There is a broad range of hotel and guest-house accommodation, with a slight upmarket bias – 4-star hotels outnumber 3-stars.
££££ Salzburgerhof Best in town – the only 5-star. Nearer the lake than the gondola, but with courtesy bus service. Excellent pool.
££££ Tirolerhof Excellent 4-star chalet in the old town, popular with Brits. It has a good pool, jacuzzi and steam room, superb food and friendly service. Breakfast starts at 5am when early starts for the glacier are needed.
££££ Eichenhof Poor position on the outskirts of town, some distance from the lifts and old centre. But popular and well run, with a minibus service, great food and lake views.
££££ Alpin Modern 4-star chalet next to the Zell gondola.

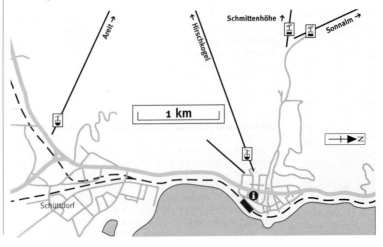

GETTING THERE

Air Salzburg, transfer 2hr. Munich, transfer 3hr.

Rail Station in resort.

PACKAGES

Airtours, Altours Travel, Austrian Holidays, Club Europe, Crystal, Enterprise, Equity Total Ski, Inghams, Made to Measure, Neilson, STS, Ski Choice, Ski Europe, Ski Partners, Thomson, Travelscene Ski-Drive

Kaprun Airtours, Austrian Holidays, Crystal, Enterprise, Inghams, Made to Measure, Neilson

Schüttdorf Airtours

ACTIVITIES

Indoor Swimming, sauna, solarium, fitness centre, spa, tennis, squash, bowling, museum, art gallery, cinema, lessons in self-defence and judo, library, massage, ice skating

Outdoor Riding, skating, curling, floodlit toboggan runs, plane flights, sleigh rides, shooting range

TOURIST OFFICE

Postcode A-5700
Tel 010 43 (6542) 2600
Fax 2032

££££ **Schwebebahn** Attractive 4-star in secluded setting by cable-cars.
£££ **Berner** 3-star by the Zell gondola.
£££ **Erlhof** Way out of town, in a completely peaceful setting across the lake: a rustic 4-star chalet with the best food in the area.
££ **Hubertus** B&B pension next to the Zell gondola.
££ **Margarete** B&B pension next to cable-car station.
Self-catering We don't know of any apartments available through tour operators. The budget Karger Christine apartments are well placed for the Zell gondola. Apartment Hofer is a mid-range place close to the Ebenberg lift (which links to the gondola). More comfortable places are the 3-star Diana and Seilergasse (both in the old centre) and the Mirabell, which is close to the Zell gondola.

STAYING UP THE MOUNTAIN
Widely spread choices
As well as the big hotel at the top of the Schmittenhöhe cable-car, there are a couple of more personal places – mountain restaurants with a dozen rooms. One is Breiteckalm, high up on the southern arm of the ski area, the other Sonnalm, at the mid-station of the lifts up to the northern arm.

EATING OUT
Plenty of choice
There is a good range of restaurants, with more non-hotel places than is usual in a small Austrian resort. The Ampere is a quiet, sophisticated place; Guiseppe's is a popular Italian restaurant with excellent food; and Kupferkessel and Traubenstüberl both do wholesome regional dishes. There are Chinese restaurants in both Zell and Schüttdorf. Car drivers could try the good value Finkawirt, across the lake at Prielau, or the excellent Erlhof (see Hotels).

APRES-SKI
Plenty for all tastes
Après-ski is lively and varied. Reps organise a full programme of the usual Austrian evening entertainments. Ice-hockey matches are lively; tea-dances and high-calorie cafés are popular at tea-time; and there are bars and discos a-plenty. The Pinzgauer Diele disco bar is arguably the liveliest place in town, followed by the cosmopolitan pub-style Craisy Daisy Pub. Liliput is cosier, and other popular spots include Sugar Shake, Evergreen, Taverne and the Lebzelter Keller. The Wunderbar cocktail lounge and Visage disco are the best places for people-watching.

NON-SKIERS
Spoilt for choice
There is plenty to do in this year-round resort. The train trip to Salzburg is a must, and Kitzbühel is also well worth a visit (for a detailed report on this resort, see page 75). Innsbruck is also just about in reach.

Walking across the lake to Thumersbach is often possible in early or mid-season.

Sports facilities are impressive, and include swimming, sauna, a fitness centre, tennis (Schüttdorf), skating and riding (Schüttdorf). Other activities include a museum, sleigh rides and flights.

Kaprun 785m

Kaprun is a spacious village with lots of Tyrolean charm. It is well-known for its glacier skiing, but this is a bus-ride away. There is a small, low-altitude ski area on the outskirts of the village, and a separate nursery area on the other side of town. Both ski areas are best suited to early intermediates.

Off-slope activities are good: these include a fine sports centre with a pool, and a tennis and squash centre. Summer ski visitors have a championship golf course. Nightlife is quiet, but there are numerous organised evening events. The Baum and Nindl bars are the liveliest places. There are plenty of good restaurants, including the Dorfstadl, the Schlemmerstuberl and the Bella Musica. Many of the hotels are large, comfortable places. The Orgler, Mitteregger and Tauernhof are three of the best. Good cheaper hotels include the Abendruh and Heidi. Haus Annelies is a pleasant B&B.

Zell am Ziller 575m

HOW IT RATES

The skiing

Snow	**
Extent	*
Advanced	*
Intermediates	***
Beginners	**
Convenience	*
Queues	***
Restaurants	***

The rest

Scenery	***
Resort charm	***
Not skiing	**

SKI FACTS

Altitude	930m-2410m
Lifts	25
Pistes	47km
Green/Blue	35%
Red	60%
Black	5%
Artificial snow	2km

PACKAGES

Neilson

TOURIST OFFICE

Postcode A-6280
Tel 010 43 (5282)
2281
Fax 2281-80

Although overshadowed by its near neighbour in the Zillertal, Mayrhofen, Zell has skiing of comparable scale and character, with similarly inconvenient lift arrangements. What it doesn't have is the vitality of the larger resort.

THE RESORT

Skiing seems rather incidental to Zell – partly because it is one of the main communities of the Zillertal and partly because the ski lifts at are some distance, and the pistes even further. Complete with ornately decorated church and brewery, it sits in the flat bottom of the Ziller valley, a few miles downstream of Mayrhofen. It is not an unpleasant place, but it does lack ski resort atmosphere.

THE SKIING

Zell's skiing is almost entirely for intermediates. It takes place on two mountains: Kreuzjoch and Gerlosstein. The main Kreuzjoch **ski area** is approached by gondola from Rohr, a short bus-ride across the valley to the east. It goes up to Wiesenalm (1310m); there is no piste back to the valley. The heart of the skiing, with runs above and below in every direction, is the sunny shelf of Rosenalm (1745m). One of the chairs from here goes to 2410m, the high-point of the skiing.

The Gerlosstein cable-car starts a longer bus-ride away away at Hainzenberg and gives access to a much smaller area – consisting mainly of two chair-lifts meeting at the peak of Arbiskogel (splendid views).

You have a choice of the local ski pass or the wide-ranging Zillertal pass, also covering valley trains and buses. The bus service to the local slopes is good, but geared towards skiing one area or the other all day. The service in the middle of the day is poor.

By Tyrolean standards the skiing is quite high, but the Kreuzjoch slopes get the afternoon sun, so **snow reliability** is better early in the season than late. Most of the Gerlosstein slopes are roughly north-facing, so snow is usually better.

Neither area has much to offer **advanced** skiers. The only black, from Arbiskogel at the top of the Gerlosstein area, is short and barely deserves its grading. There is off-piste skiing between the runs at Kreuzjoch.

Whether **intermediate** skiers will like Zell depends on how concerned they are about the inconvenient access to the skiing and the limited extent of it. There are essentially only half a dozen runs, and although the terrain is quite varied, the runs themselves are similar in character – with the exception of the secluded 3km red from Karspitz to Wiesenalm. Gerlosstein is worth visiting, especially for the red from top to bottom (900m vertical). The best skiing in this area, however, is at Gerlos, a bus-ride beyond Hainzenberg, where 50km of varied terrain awaits.

Although Rosenalm is an excellent nursery area (and there is another at Gerlosstein), the effort and cost of getting there mean that Zell is far from ideal for **beginners**.

The valley floor provides some long, flat **cross-country** loops, extending to Mayrhofen.

There are **queues** for the main gondola (downwards as well as up) at peak times, and for the nursery lifts below Rosenalm. The Gerlosstein cable-car copes, except when snow is poor at Kreuzjoch.

The **mountain restaurants** are adequate – mostly pleasant chalet-style self-service places.

There are two **ski schools** – Lechner and Pro Zell. Both have Rosenalm ski kindergartens and offer lunchtime care, and Pro Zell also runs a nursery.

STAYING THERE

The centre of Zell is quite compact, but the village now spreads across the valley towards the lift station and the foot of the Gerlos road. You can stay close to the Kreuzjoch lifts, or indeed the Gerlosstein ones (at Hainzenberg), but most visitors stay centrally.

Choice of how to go is pretty well confined to **hotels** and guesthouses. The 4-star Theresa and Zapenhof have pools, the latter open to the public.

Eating out is limited to traditional Tyrolean fare, largely in hotel-based restaurants, and a couple of pizzerias. Hotel Dörflwirt is well regarded.

There's a fair amount of informal **après-ski**. Café Reiter is a friendly place with a twice-weekly tea-dance, hotel Zellerhof has Tyrolean evenings; the Piccadilly bar is dark and cramped but popular for its live music; and the Tony Keller is a late-hours disco.

This is not an ideal resort for **non-skiers** but it is not without sports facilities, and it is well placed for interesting excursions.

France

France has the biggest linked ski areas in the world. For keen piste bashers who like to ski as many miles of piste in a day as possible, these are unrivalled. It also has some of the toughest, highest, wildest skiing in the Alps, and some of the longest, gentlest and most convenient beginner runs. In other words, French skiing takes some beating. French resort villages aren't quite so uniformly recommendable; but, equally, they don't all conform to the standard image of soulless purpose-built resorts thrown up without any concern for appearance during the building boom of the 1960s and 1970s.

Certainly France has its fair share of Alpine eyesores, such as Les Menuires, central La Plagne, Flaine, Tignes and Les Arcs. The redeeming features of places like this are the splendid quality of the skiing they serve, the reliability and quality of the snow and the amazing ski-in, ski-out convenience of most of the accommodation. But the French have learnt the lesson that new development doesn't have to be tasteless to be convenient – look at Valmorel, Belle Plagne and Les Coches, for example.

If you prefer, there are genuinely old mountain villages to stay in, linked directly to the big ski areas. These are not usually as convenient for the skiing, but they give you a feel of being in France rather than a skier-processing factory. Examples include Montchavin or Champagny for La Plagne, Vaujany for Alpe-d'Huez, St-Martin-de-Belleville for the Trois Vallées and Les Carroz or Samoëns (a short drive from the slopes) for Flaine. There are also old villages with their own ski areas, which have developed as resorts while retaining their ambience – such as Serre-Chevalier and La Clusaz.

And France has Alpine centres with a long mountaineering and skiing history. Chief among these is Chamonix, which sits in the shadow of Mont Blanc, Europe's highest peak, and is the centre of the most radical off-piste skiing there is.

France has advantages in the gastronomic stakes. While many of its mountain restaurants serve fast convenience food, it is generally possible to find somewhere to get a half-decent lunch. And in the evening most resorts have restaurants serving good traditional French food as well as regional specialities. And the wine is decent and affordable.

In general, especially at today's exchange rate (FF8 = £1 when we went to press), France is not a cheap place to ski. It can even work out more expensive than Switzerland, especially if you choose a hotel-based holiday in a smart resort in high season.

One good development over the last few years has been the end of the ski school monopoly of the Ecole de Ski Français. Most resorts now have at least one competing ski school, often aimed at non-French visitors, and this has raised teaching standards (and standards of spoken English and customer care) considerably.

France also helps beginners by using four grades of piste instead of the usual three. The very easiest runs are graded green and, except in Val-d'Isère, they are reliably gentle. (Under Ski facts in our major resort chapters we've lumped green and blue runs together – but bear in mind that some blues can be quite challenging.)

The one big drawback of many French resorts (though not all) is the lack of nightlife. But nightlife isn't important to many British skiers. Certainly, of the people who filled in questionnaires for us on their latest holidays in France, 90 per cent said they couldn't help us with the nightlife section because they skied so hard all day that all they wanted to do after dinner was to fall into bed.

0   30

Scale in km

GETTING AROUND THE FRENCH ALPS

Pick the right gateway – Geneva, Chambéry or Grenoble – and you can hardly go wrong. The only pass is on the approach to Serre-Chevalier and Montgenèvre – the 2058m Col du Lauteret. But the road is a major one, and generally kept clear of snow or reopened quickly after a fall. The tunnels into Italy present no difficulties other than expense and claustrophobia. Crossing into Switzerland involves two passes between Chamonix and Martigny that are not super-high but not reliably open – the Col des Montets (1461m) and Col de la Forclaz (1527m). When necessary, one-way traffic runs beside the tracks through the rail tunnel beneath the passes.

Alpe-d'Huez 1860m

✔ *Extensive sunny ski area, with excellent runs for all standards*

✔ *Efficient, modern lift system*

✔ *High skiing in stunning scenery*

✔ *Very little walking to and from most accommodation*

✔ *Well maintained pistes, including extensive snowmaking*

✔ *Some good rustic mountain restaurants*

✔ *Charming traditional villages in the valleys*

✗ *Little tree-lined skiing for bad-weather days*

✗ *Many of the runs can be icy early in the day in good weather*

✗ *Many of the tough runs rely on a high cable-car running*

✗ *Spread-out, charmless resort with a hotch-potch of architectural styles; seems to have developed without any real planning*

✗ *French holiday queues and crowded runs*

Alpe-d'Huez is one of France's best all-round resorts, with top-quality skiing for all and fine non-skiing facilities. It has some great tough runs (on- and off-piste) set amid spectacular, high mountain scenery – with glacier skiing from 3330m. Lower down it has extensive intermediate and beginner terrain too.

In good conditions, there are few places to rival Alpe-d'Huez for the extent and variety of the skiing – it's one of our favourites. It has a big British following too; the reporters who told us about their holidays there were almost unanimous in their praise. But in poor conditions it can be disappointing. The slopes get a lot of sun and can get icy. There's very little skiing in the trees – wind can shut the top lifts and falling snow can make skiing impossible. We have one report from someone very unlucky with the weather: the top runs were shut for the whole week.

Although Alpe-d'Huez isn't attractive, there are peaceful smaller villages which link with the skiing. Keen skiers should give the Alpe-d'Huez area a go.

🏔 The resort

Alpe-d'Huez is a large, amorphous resort. It has grown quickly in a seemingly unplanned way since being a venue for the 1968 Grenoble Winter Olympics. Its buildings come in all shapes, sizes and designs. There's even an amazingly futuristic building housing the church (which holds regular organ concerts). There's no real

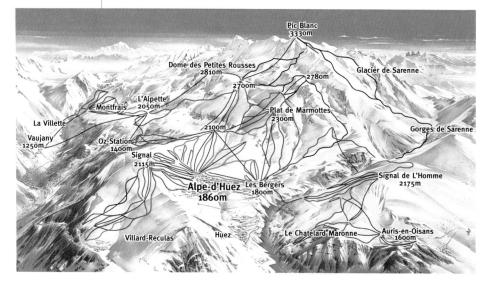

ORIENTATION

Alpe-d'Huez is a large village spread across an open mountainside, high above the Romanche valley, east of Grenoble. It lacks a definite centre – the lower end of town near the tourist office has a bucket-lift up to the main gondola station. And there's a cross-town chair-lift and a regular free bus. The main lift station at the top of the village has numerous lifts going in all directions, including the main high-capacity gondola. Another gondola heads up to the main skiing from the lower end of town (Les Bergers). And a chair from here goes to one of Alpe-d'Huez's three smaller ski areas. The slopes spread across and down to **Auris**, **Villard**, **Oz** and **Vaujany**, hamlets which all have accommodation and lifts back up.

Outings by road are feasible to other resorts covered on the lift pass, including **Serre-Chevalier**, **Les Deux-Alpes** (also linked by helicopter) and **Montgenèvre**.

SKI FACTS

Altitude	1350m–3330m
Lifts	85
Pistes	227km
Green/Blue	46%
Red	30%
Black	24%
Artificial snow	32km

central focus to the resort, though its main street is in the geographic centre and forms quite a main part of the village infrastructure. The swimming pool, ice skating and some of the shops, bars and restaurants are to be found there. The rest of the resort spreads out in a triangle, with lift stations close to all three apexes.

Many reporters have remarked on the surprising friendliness of the place, and in terms of ambience, this once quiet 'typically French' resort gets more animated and interesting each year. It now has an extremely good Palais des Sports, with lots of activities on offer, and 32 bars, 44 restaurants and three discos to choose from.

 # The skiing

Alpe-d'Huez isn't normally thought of as a ski area in the same class as bigger names such as Val-d'Isère, Méribel or La Plagne. But it deserves to be. It has extensive and varied skiing and as much to offer a group with mixed skiing abilities as any of those French giants. And the scenery is much more spectacular. If anything, Alpe-d'Huez's piste map understates the difficulty of its skiing. There are some red runs that would be black in other resorts and a few blues that would be red.

THE SKI AREA
Several well-linked areas
Changes in height mark fairly distinct ski areas. The tops of the mountains are rugged and steep, with black runs and steep off-piste runs only. The middle section is mainly tough reds and the lower section has the gentlest of blue and green runs.

The ski area can essentially be divided into four sectors. The biggest of these is accessed by the main gondolas out of the village. One of these (the biggest – with massive stand-up cabins) goes up in two stages to 2700m. The runs below its mid-station and below the top of the other gondola are the easy section. The big gondola delivers you to a cable-car which takes you up to the highest point of 3330m at **Pic Blanc**, from where there are endless steep options for good skiers. Above the mid-station, a couple of slow old chair-lifts serve a selection of long and difficult red runs. All the runs get a lot of sun because they face west or south.

The second sector can be accessed by skiing down black runs from the Pic Blanc or mid-mountain area, or by skiing down to the lower Bergers part

of the village. From here a spectacular chair-lift-ride down into the Sarenne gorge (where you can get one to return to the village) and up the other side brings you to more lifts up over the north-facing slopes of the **Signal de l'Homme** area. From the top you can ski back down towards the gorge, down south to Auris or west to the old hamlet of Chatelard.

The other end of town from Signal de l'Homme is the small **Signal** sector, reached by drag-lifts next to the main gondola or a chair lower down. Runs are down the other side to the old village of Villard-Reculas. The long drag-lift back is tricky in parts and sheds a fair number of its riders.

The fourth skiing sector is the **Vaujany-Oz** section of largely north-facing slopes. Oz can be reached by skiing straight down from the mid-station of the big gondola out of Alpe-d'Huez, underneath the gondola back up from Oz. Or you can go to the top-station of the Alpe-d'Huez gondola and take a beautiful run down along a shelf on the mountain towards Vaujany and the mid-station of the huge cable-car back up (at Alpette). You can ski down to Oz from here and a gondola brings you back up. Or skiing north from here leads you to the Vaujany sector of the skiing around Montfrais, where the gondola up from Vaujany arrives. Here there is a choice of five lifts, including one back to Alpette; from there you catch the second stage of the cable-car up to 2810m, and then can ski back to the top of the main Alpe-d'Huez gondola.

SNOW RELIABILITY
Good but...
The slopes get a lot of sun and the amount of skiing above 2300m is relatively limited. They can get icy in good weather (even at the top) and there have been occasions in recent seasons when nearby Serre-Chevalier, though lower lying, has had better conditions on its north-facing runs. However, under normal circumstances the runs are relatively snowsure. Moreover, the natural stuff is backed up by extensive snowmaking in the Vaujany and Oz sections as well as all the way down from the top of both of the Alpe-d'Huez gondolas. There are 385 snow cannon.

FOR ADVANCED SKIERS
Plenty of blacks and off-piste
This is an excellent resort for good skiers. Unlike so many ski areas, the black runs here are long. The run beneath the Pic Blanc cable-car is

LIFT PASSES

94/95 prices in francs
Grandes Rousses
Covers all lifts in Alpe-d'Huez, Auris, Oz, Vaujany and Villard-Reculas.
Beginners Premières Traces (First Steps) daily lift pass (65) covers 16 lifts in beginners' area, Moyenne Altitude (mid-altitude) daily pass covers 39 lifts (130) in Alpe-d'Huez, Villard-Reculas and Oz.
Main pass
1-day pass 195
6-day pass 935
(low season 748 – 20% off)
Senior citizens
Over 60: 6-day pass 842 (10% off)
Children
Under 14: 6-day pass 655 (30% off)
Under 6: free pass
Short-term passes
Passes from 12.30 (150) and 3.30 (80).
Notes Reduction for teenagers (14-18) 10% off (842 for 6-day pass).
Pass for 6 days or more includes one day's skiing at each of the Grande Galaxie resorts (Les Deux-Alpes, Serre-Chevalier, Puy-Saint-Vincent and the Milky Way).
Alternative passes
Passes for Auris only (15 lifts), Oz only (10 lifts), Vaujany only (10 lifts), Villard-Reculas only (8 lifts), Oz-Vaujany (19 lifts) and Moyenne Altitude (39 lifts).

SKI SCHOOL

94/95 prices in francs
ESF
Classes 6 days
5½hr: 9.45-12.45 and 2.30-5pm;
6 full days: 850
Children's classes
Ages: 3 to 12
6 full days: 700
Private lessons
Hourly
160 for 1hr, for 1 to 2 people

famous for its sudden plunge on exiting a tunnel through the mountain. Unfortunately this mogul field attracts a lot of macho intermediates who get in the way of good skiers as they struggle down. The run splits into three further blacks; all finish back at the cable-car station.

Another series of steep runs starts at Pic Blanc, including the longest black run in the Alps (16km with a vertical drop of almost 2000m). This starts off with a steep mogul field, but once you are off the glacier (which is open for summer skiing) it levels out and is pleasantly varied. There are stunning views on the upper part and the long lowest section (a gentle path) is beautifully set in a narrowing gorge by the side of a frozen river. There are several off-piste variants of this run, all finishing in the Sarenne gorge. Unfortunately, returning to Pic Blanc from here is a round about business.

Other very long off-piste routes that take skiers well away from the pisted area, and for which a guide is essential, lead all the way down from Pic Blanc to Vaujany, over 2000m vertical below.

Another series of steep runs starts at the top of the Clocher de Macle chair (the second of the slow chairs up from near the mid-station of the main Alpe-d'Huez gondola). These include a beautiful long, lonely black leading back to the village, with an option to ski across to the Signal de l'Homme access chair in the Sarenne gorge.

As well as the black runs, plenty of the upper red runs are tough enough to give good skiers a challenge. These include the Canyon and Balme runs accessed by the chair from the gondola mid-station. And there's off-piste on the lower half of the mountain that is excellent in good snow conditions, including lovely runs through scattered trees and bushes at the extreme northern edge of the skiing above Vaujany.

FOR INTERMEDIATE SKIERS
Much improved
Additions to the ski area in recent years have much improved the suitability of Alpe-d'Huez, increasing the number of runs between the tough and easy extremes.

Good intermediates now have a fine selection of runs all over the area. In good snow conditions the variety of the runs is difficult to beat. Every section of the skiing has some challenging red runs to test the adventurous intermediate. The most challenging are the Canyon and

Balme runs mentioned above. These would be graded black in many resorts. There are lovely long runs down to Oz and to Vaujany. The off-piste among the bushes and trees above Vaujany, mentioned above, is a good place to start your off-piste career in good snow. The Villard-Reculas and Signal de l'Homme sectors also have long challenging reds. The Chamois red from the top of the gondola down to the mid-station is beautiful but can get very crowded. Fearless intermediates should enjoy the long Sarenne black run, also mentioned above. After the first steep mogul field it's not at all difficult. But it is set in extraordinarily beautiful scenery – and you'll be able to say you've skied the world's longest black!

For less ambitious intermediates, there are usually blue alternatives, except from the top of Pic Blanc, the short top part of Signal de l'Homme and part of the run down to Villard-Reculas. The main Couloir blue from the top of the big gondola is a lovely run, well served by snowmakers, but it does get extremely crowded (and scary because of that) at times.

Early intermediates can get all the way over to Vaujany by taking the blue from the gondola mid-station to Oz, and then the gondola up from there to Alpette. From Alpette there's a very wide and gentle run to the Montfrais sector of great cruising runs above Vaujany. The blue down to the mid-station of the Vaujany gondola is picturesque and well-served by snowmaking. Early intermediates will also enjoy the gentle slopes leading back to Alpe-d'Huez from the main mountain, and the Signal sector.

FOR BEGINNERS
Good facilities
The large network of green runs immediately above the village is as good a nursery area as you will find anywhere. This is especially true because, from last season, the network of greens to the left of the main gondola (as you look at the mountain) has become a dedicated beginners-only area, and fast skiing there is banned. Add to this ski convenience, good tuition, a special lift pass covering 15 lifts, and usually reliable snow and Alpe-d'Huez is difficult to beat. The Signal and Petit Prince blues down towards Villard are suitable for quick learners, as is the run down to Huez. There's another good beginners' area with gentle green runs at the top of the Vaujany gondola – useful for Vaujany residents.

**International
Classes** 6 days
4¼hr: 2½hr am, 2hr
pm
6 full days
(93/94): 1010
Children's classes
Ages: 5 to 12
6 full days
(93/94): 845
Private lessons
Hourly
165 for 1hr, for 1 to 2
people (93/94)

CHILDCARE

The main schools
both run ski
kindergartens. The
ESF Club des
Oursons, at Les
Bergers and near the
main gondola
(76803182), takes
children from age 4,
ski school hours. The
SEI (76804277) runs
the Club des Mickeys
for children aged 3 or
4, the Club des
Marmottes for those
aged 5 to 12. The
Eterlous kindergarten
(76804327) has a
private ski area and
takes children aged 2
to 14 all day; it also
offers a child-minding
service (until 6pm) for
babies of 3 months or
more.

The Club Med nursery
takes children from 4,
with or without
tuition.

FOR CROSS-COUNTRY
High-level and convenient
There are 40km of trails, with two easy
loops and two more demanding
circuits, all around the 2000m mark,
and consequently relatively snowsure.
All trails are within the Alpine ski area.

QUEUES
OK except during French holidays
Outside French holiday periods and
busy weekends, the excellent modern
lift system ensures there are few
queues. The main delays are usually
for the Pic Blanc cable-car and Lièvre
Blanc chair from the main gondola
mid-station to the other area of
challenging skiing. These are
frustrating for good skiers. Queues can
also build up for the gondolas out of
the village. The main gondola is
usually quicker and takes you higher –
the right hand side of the queue is
quicker, so head for there. A new chair
from Les Bergers to the mid-station
should reduce the queues for 1994/95.
The bottom section of the Vaujany
cable-car never suffers from queues;
nor do the gondolas out of Oz.

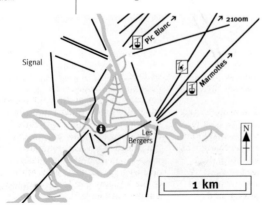

MOUNTAIN RESTAURANTS
Some excellent rustic huts
Mountain restaurants are generally
good and there are plenty of rustic
places you don't find in many French
purpose-built resorts. At Montfrais,
above Vaujany, Les Airelles is a rustic
hut, built into the rock, with a roaring
log fire, classical music and excellent
good-value food. The Chalet du Lac
Besson is a peaceful, rustic haven on
the cross-country circuit between
Alpette and the big gondola, with
good table-service food; getting there
is a bit of an adventure for
downhillers, easier for cross-country
skiers and walkers. The pretty Forêt de
Maronne hotel at Chatelard, below
Auris, is delightful and has a good
choice of traditional French cuisine.
The Combe Haute, at the foot of the
Chalvet chair in the gorge towards the
end of the Sarenne run, is very
welcoming. The Perce-Neige, just
below the Oz-Poutran gondola mid-
station, is so good it's permanently
packed. La Plage des Neiges is one of
the best huts available to beginners.
The Bergerie at Villard-Reculas is very
attractive, and has good views. The
Alpette and Super Signal places are
also worth a visit. Even the large self-
service places such as Marmottes, at
the top of the gondola from Les
Bergers, have above-average food.

SKI SCHOOL
Contrasting views of the schools
The sound reputation the ESF once
enjoyed here has been lost of late.
We've had reports of 14 or 15 people
in group classes and mixed views on
standards of English. In contrast, the
International School limits classes to
eight and standards of English are
reported high. It is linked to Ski
Masterclass run by a Brit, Stuart
Adamson. However, other reporters
have preferred the ESF, notably for
superior organisation and standards of
technical tuition. Ski évolutif is an
option. Instruction is also available in
off-piste, ski touring, mono and
freestyle. The Bureau des Guides has,
in contrast, a good reputation – very
useful for good skiers who want to try
the excellent off-piste.

FACILITIES FOR CHILDREN
Good reports
We haven't heard from many parents
about Alpe-d'Huez, but the reports we
have suggest that facilities are well
run, as do the more numerous
secondhand reports. Children who
need lunchtime care or breaks from
skiing must go to Les Eterlous.

GETTING THERE

Air Lyon, transfer 3hr. Geneva, transfer 4hr. Grenoble, transfer 1½hr.

Rail Grenoble (65km); daily buses from station.

Staying there

Staying close to one of the gondolas is useful, and most of the accommodation used by British tour operators is well placed for skiing. Les Bergers, at the entrance to the resort, has some of the available accommodation, and although convenient for skiing, including having its own nursery area, it is a trek to most of the other resort facilities. Being near the village bucket-lift is handy if you're not close to the slopes.

HOW TO GO
Something of everything

Chalets Skibound have a simple chalet on the slopes close to town. There are quite a few chalet-hotels. The best is the modern Bel Alpe (until recently an ordinary 2-star hotel) managed by Ski Miquel. It's quite comfortable, well run and conveniently located. Crystal run a decent chalet-hotel in the centre. Skiworld have a convenient, simple old hotel annexe at a bargain price. The hotel main building is also run as a chalet, by Neilson.

Hotels There are more hotels than is usual in a high French resort, providing 20% of the beds available. There is clear downmarket bias, with more 1-stars than 2- or 3-stars, and only one 4-star. There is a Club Med. **££££ Ours Blanc** Don't be put off by the ocean-liner looks. Stylish and luxurious inside, with lots of warm wood. Superb fitness centre. It's in the centre of the resort, so not especially close to lifts.
£££ Chamois d'Or Good facilities, modern rooms (some with balconies),

---

Selected chalets in Vaujany

PACKAGES

AA Ski-Driveaway, Airtours, Alpine Options Skidrive, Altours Travel, Club Med, Cresta Ski France, Crystal, Enterprise, Equity Total Ski, Fresh Tracks, Inghams, Kings Ski Club, Lagrange, Made to Measure, MasterSki, Neilson, Sally, Ski Ardmore, Ski Club of GB, Ski Europe, Ski Miquel, Ski Partners, Ski Valkyrie, Ski West, SkiBound, Skiworld, Stena Sealink, Thomson, Travelscene Ski-Drive

Vaujany Made to Measure, Ski Peak, Ski Valkyrie

ACTIVITIES

Indoor Artificial skating rink (skating and curling), sports centre (tennis, gym, squash, aerobics, body-building, climbing wall, sauna, jacuzzi), library, cinema, swimming pool, bowling, billiards, bridge **Outdoor** 30km of cleared paths, outdoor swimming pool, shooting range, hang-gliding, para-gliding, all-terrain carts, quad-bikes, ice climbing

TOURIST OFFICE

Postcode 38750
Tel 010 33 76803541
Fax 76806954

one of the best restaurants in town and well placed for main gondola.
£££ **Cimes** South-facing rooms with balconies, excellent food; close to cross-resort lift and pistes.
£££ **Grandes Rousses** Comfortable, excellent food, friendly staff; close to pistes and lifts.
£££ **Petit Prince** Pretty public rooms, sunny bedrooms; handy for the Grand Sure chair to Signal.
££ **Beau Soleil** The best-situated 2-star, offering good value.
££ **Les Gentianes** Close to the Sarenne gondola in Les Bergers; a wide range of rooms, the best of them comfortable.
Self-catering There is an enormous choice though most of the allocations held by British tour operators are in the same few, mostly simple, apartment blocks.

The Rocher Soleil (Inghams) are in a different class from most, offering unusually comfortable, spacious accommodation with good communal facilities including access to a heated outdoor pool. Their position, opposite the Sarenne gondola in Les Bergers, is good for ski convenience and those wanting a particularly quiet time away from the main village.

The Pierre et Vacances places (Inghams, Thomson, Neilson) are much more central, but are not up to the usual standards of the chain. They remain, however, better than some apartments in this resort.

The Residence Les Horizons d'Huez (Inghams, Enterprise) apartments are short on space but superior to the usual 'French box'.

EATING OUT
Good value
Alpe-d'Huez has 44 restaurants, many of which are good quality and good value by French purpose-built resort standards. Ancolie and Pomme de Pin are top of the range in quality and price. Cremaillere is highly recommended by one reporter for its excellent food; it gives aperitifs gratis and even lays on a free taxi home. Au P'tit Creux gets a similarly positive review for excellent food, ambience and value. L'Aquarium is a good French restaurant, though several reporters have commented on its excellent paella. Genepi is a nice old friendly place with good cuisine. Au Vieux Guide also has admirable food, though the animal skins used for decor are an acquired taste. Saint Huron, Fromagerie and Edelweiss are others worth a try. Oregano, Tremplin and Pizzeria Pinocchio have good wholesome Italian fare.

APRES-SKI
Variable according to season
The evening ambience varies a great deal according to season and time of the week. It can be pretty dead mid-week in January, extremely lively on peak-season weekends.

The Lincoln pub, complete with karaoke and Newcastle Brown, attracts many of the lively young Brit fraternity. The little Avalanche bar is often the liveliest thanks to its resident singer-musician who encourages audience participation. P'tit Bar takes some beating for atmosphere, and also has a fun singer. Sporting is a large but friendly French rendezvous which has a live band. Chamois, Menandiere and Charlies are other popular places with live music. Three discos liven up whenever the French are in town en masse. One of these, the Igloo, is wonderfully tacky. Most Brits prefer the Apples and Pears. English films are shown occasionally in the cinema, the ice rink is open till eleven, and the village swimming pool closes at seven.

FOR NON-SKIERS
Good by purpose-built standards
There is a wide range of facilities, including a new indoor pool, older open-air heated pools, Olympic-size ice rink and splendid sports centre. And there's a winter driving school. Shops are numerous, but limited in range. You can take helicopter rides to Les Deux-Alpes for the day with skiing companions. A car is useful for interesting excursions to Grenoble and Briançon. It's a shame that the better mountain restaurants aren't easily accessible to non-skiers.

Vaujany 1250m
Vaujany is a tiny rural village perched on the hillside opposite its own sector of the Alpe-d'Huez skiing. It has a giant 160-person cable-car (one of the biggest in the world) that whisks you, in two stages, to 2800m, from where you ski down a lovely red to the top of the main gondola up from Alpe-d'Huez and the bottom of the Pic Blanc cable-car. If you hate morning queues this is the place to be – no-one has ever seen the cable-car full. So time it right and you'll be right on and up the mountain in minutes.

The first stage gives you direct access to both the Oz and Vaujany sectors of the skiing. There's also a gondola from the village direct to the bottom of the Vaujany skiing and nursery slopes, with a mid-station at La Villette, an even smaller hamlet than Vaujany (just one tiny bar-restaurant). You can't normally ski back to Vaujany – only to the mid-station.

The cable-car and gondola are being paid for with the substantial income the community receives from a massive hydro-electric power project that it allowed to take place on its land (but which is very unobtrusive).

Vaujany has four simple hotels. The Rissiou is run by a British tour operator (Ski Peak). It has a popular bar (much used by locals, including the lift operators and ski instructors), pleasant dining room which serves excellent French cuisine (and has a good inexpensive wine list), and fairly basic bedrooms. The staff are friendly and the maitre d'hôtel is efficient and pleasantly eccentric. Ski Peak also has catered chalets in Vaujany and La Villette and some self-catering accommodation. It runs a minibus to ferry guests around.

The Cîmes, over the road and owned by the mayor, is less rustic but useful for a change of bar scenery. The Etendard, by the lift station, and Grandes Rousses, in the village above the road, are run by a Belgian tour operator and cater for a young, lively crowd – the Etendard bar gets noisy and packed at the end of the day.

There's a disco up in the old village, usually heaving with Belgians from the Etendard, and a nightclub run by the mayor's son, which is usually very quiet. There's an open-air ice rink, well-stocked sports shop, small supermarket, a couple of restaurants and a few chickens wandering the streets. And there's a bit of (tasteful) development going on up the mountainside. But essentially Vaujany is for those who want a quiet time and easy access to a big skiing area from a tiny, unspoiled French village.

Vaujany has its own ski school and ski kindergarten and a big, brand-new day nursery by the lift station.

Oz-Station 1350m

Oz is a purpose-built little place up in the heart of the main ski area, above the attractive original old village of Oz-le-Oisans. Its two large apartment blocks, which are the focus of the place, have been built in a sympathetic style, with much use of wood and stone. The village also benefits from being the only resort in the area with trees on all sides.

It has the basics required of a tiny, family ski resort – good access to the slopes, ski school, sports shops, nursery slopes, a couple of bar-restaurants and a supermarket.

A choice of gondolas move away in different directions, from where you can ski off to all points in double-quick time. The main run home is liberally endowed with snow cannon.

Auris 1600m

Auris is a series of wood-clad, chalet-style apartment blocks with a few shops, bars and restaurants. Beneath it is the original old village, complete with attractive, traditional buildings, a church and all but one of the resort's hotels. This is a pleasant base for those with a car. They can nip up to the upper village to start skiing locally, and also have speedy access to the valley for excursions to neighbouring resorts such as Serre-Chevalier. The upper village is quite pleasantly set close to the thickest woodland in the whole area. It's a fine, family resort, with everything close to hand, including a nursery that takes children from 18 months and a ski kindergarten for 4- and 5-year-olds. There's also a ski school.

Evenings are unsurprisingly quiet, with just four bar-restaurants to choose from. The Beau Site, an apartment block lookalike, is the only hotel in the upper village. Down the hill, the attractively traditional Auberge de la Forêt, hotel Emaranches and a selection of gîtes give you a feel of 'real' rural France. Over the hill, in a secluded spot, is a fourth hotel – the cosy open-fired Forêt de Maronne. A 'down and up' chair takes skiers over to Alpe-d'Huez, but there is a fair amount of skiing to explore on the local slopes, for which there is a special lift pass. This covers 45km of piste for just over half the cost of the full area pass. Most of the skiing is intermediate, though Auris is also the best of the local hamlets for beginners.

Villard-Reculas 1500m

Villard is a secluded little village, complete with an old church, set on a small shelf wedged between an impressive expanse of open snowfields above and tree-filled hillsides below. It's a farming community, with just the bare modern essentials of a 'resort' – one hotel, a few apartment buildings, a supermarket and a couple of bars and restaurants. Its local slopes are linked over the mountain to Alpe-d'Huez, and essentially have the skiing of the large resort in microcosm – good village nursery slopes and mostly steep, sunny intermediate runs. One surprise is the lack of snowmakers here, making for runs home that are often icy and patchy.

Les Arcs 1600m–2000m

HOW IT RATES

The skiing

Snow	****
Extent	***
Advanced	****
Intermediates	****
Beginners	****
Convenience	****
Queues	***
Restaurants	*

The rest

Scenery	***
Resort charm	*
Not skiing	*

✔ Skiing to and from the door of much of the accommodation

✔ Opportunity for beginners to learn by ski évolutif method

✔ Excellent children's facilities

✔ Few queues outside the 2000 area

✔ Plenty of tree-lined skiing as bad weather option

✗ Villages are purpose-built and lack charm

✗ Very quiet in the evenings

✗ Little for non-skiers to do

✗ Nearly all accommodation is in apartments; there's a lack of chalets and cheap hotels

At first sight Les Arcs has a lot going against it. Its architecture can at best be described as functional, at worst downright ugly. But look again and you'll find that the resort has too much going for it to be dismissed at first sight, especially by keen skiers who don't want much other entertainment. It has an unusual mixture of attractions.

There are some beautiful, long runs through the trees down to traditional rustic French villages. There's a splendid high area of tough runs with good snow above Arc 2000. Beginners can learn quickly using the ski évolutif method of starting on short skis and gradually moving up to longer ones. Intermediates will find plenty of cruising runs to keep them happy. And the lift pass covers days out in other major Tarentaise resorts if you want to explore further afield.

It's a very good resort for families. Its children's facilities are impressive, particularly for those who have the inclination and funds to stay in one of the several hotels having children's clubs – or at Club Med.

There are remarkably few Brits around outside 1800 – Les Arcs remains an essentially French resort.

ORIENTATION

Les Arcs is made up of three resorts linked by road, high above the railway terminus town of Bourg-St-Maurice in the Isère valley. 1800 is the focal spot, though all three villages have numerous lifts into different parts of the ski area. 1600 is linked directly to Bourg by funicular as well as road. 2000 is the newest and bleakest, but most convenient for the highest, best skiing.

At the perimeter of the ski area are a couple of old villages – Peisey-Nancroix-Vallandry on the west and Le Pré-Villaroger on the east. Both have links into the Les Arcs skiing.

Day trips are possible to **La Rosière** on the other side of the valley from Bourg, **La Plagne**, **Val-d'Isère-Tignes**, the **Trois Vallées**, **Pralognan-la-Vanoise** and **Les Saises**. The six-day lift pass gives unlimited access to La Plagne, plus a day per week in each of the others.

 ## The resort

Les Arcs has three villages, all fairly similar in many respects. All are purpose-built, relatively unattractive, apartment-dominated places, well positioned for doorstep skiing but lacking off-slope activities.

By far the largest of the three is 1800. It is also the central focus of the ski area with lifts in numerous directions. It has three sections. The 'battleship' architecture of giant apartment blocks and shopping arcades synonymous with Les Arcs dominates Charvet and Villards. More pleasant on the eye is Charmettoger at the periphery of the resort as a whole, with smaller, wood-clad buildings nestling among trees.

Charmettoger is also more consistently ski-convenient – some of the 'battleships' have been built at right angles to the slopes, falling away down the hillside on which the resort is built, and are so long that if you are unlucky enough to be staying at the far end of one, walks to lifts can be longer and more tiring than stated in the brochures.

If 1800 has a centre, it's the Hotel du Golf. Essentially where Charvet meets Villards, it's the focus of après-ski. The slopes and a couple of main lifts are just outside the door, and the village nursery and mini-club are nearby. The two arcades that house most of the shops, bars and restaurants are either side.

2000 is just a few hotels, apartment blocks and the Club Med huddled together in a bleak spot, with little to commend it but immediate access to the highest, toughest skiing.

1600 has the advantage of being at the top of the Bourg-St-Maurice

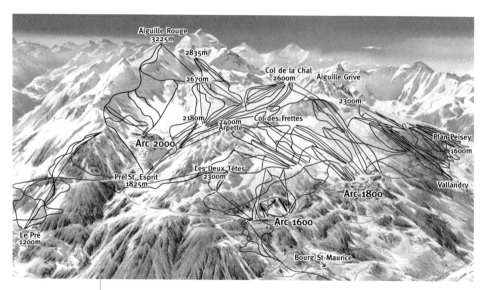

SKI FACTS

Altitude	1200m-3225m
Lifts	79
Pistes	150km
Green/Blue	54%
Red	32%
Black	14%
Artificial snow	12km

LIFT PASSES

93/94 prices in francs
**Massif Aiguille
Grive-Aiguille Rouge**
Covers all lifts in Les
Arcs and Peisey-
Nancroix, including
funicular from Bourg-
St-Maurice.
Beginners Included in
ski school beginners'
courses.
Main pass
1-day pass 200
6-day pass 915
Children
Under 12: 6-day pass
775 (15% off)
Under 7: free pass
Short-term passes
Half-day, 140.
Notes All passes
allow 1 day in La
Rosiere and La Thuile.
6-day pass and over
covers La Plagne for
duration of pass, and
one day each in
Tignes-Val d'Isère, the
3V, Pralognan-la-
Vanoise and Les
Saises; 10% reduction
on weekly pass for
families.

funicular, giving easy access to
'civilisation' for shopping, train
transfers and trips to other ski resorts.
It is set in the trees and has a friendly
feel to it; it enjoys good views along
the valley and towards Mt Blanc. It's
particularly user-friendly for families:
uncrowded, compact, set on even
ground and traffic-free. The road to
Bourg and the other villages bypasses
the resort, with the car park on the
outskirts. Things are even quieter at
night than they are during the day.
You might say 1600 combines the
functionality of Flaine with the
villagey feel of a more human place.

The skiing

Les Arcs' ski area is smaller than
neighbouring La Plagne's. But it has
more skiing suitable for good skiers
and a good mixture of high, snowsure
skiing and accessible low-level
woodland skiing ideal for bad weather.

THE SKI AREA
Well planned, and varied
The ski area is very well laid out and
moving around it is quick and easy.
All three villages are ski-in but not ski-
out places, having few runs
immediately beneath them. Each has a
number of lifts fanning out, none of
which are 'must-takes'. Virtually any
lift will do to gain height, after which
there is a plethora of runs criss-
crossing the mountainsides for access
to other sections.

   1600 and **1800** share a west-facing
mountainside with runs back to and
between both villages. At the southern
end of their skiing are runs down to

and lifts up from **Peisey-Nancroix**
and **Vallandry**. From the 1600 and
1800 skiing you take lifts up to a ridge
and ski down into the **2000** ski area.
On the opposite side of the bowl in
which 2000 is set, lifts take you to the
highest skiing of the area, served by
the **Aiguille Rouge** cable-car which
takes you to 3225m. As well as a
variety of steep runs back to Arc 2000
from here, you can take a lovely long
run right down to the hamlet of
Le Pré near Villaroger (over 2000m
vertical). This is arguably the longest
continuously interesting piste in the
Alps, with no boring sections as is the
case with runs claimed to be longer by
other resorts. This is at the extreme
opposite end of the ski area from
Peisey-Nancroix. You can also reach Le
Pré from below 2000, via a short drag-
lift. A chair brings you back up.

   All three resorts have a floodlit piste,
officially open twice a week.

SNOW RELIABILITY
Good – plenty of high skiing
A high percentage of the skiing is
above 2000m and a fair amount on
north-facing slopes. While the highest
skiing from Aiguille Rouge is more
suitable for good skiers, there are easy
north-facing runs starting from
2600m. There is limited artificial snow
on some runs back to 1600, 1800 and
Peisey, but none down to Le Pré.

FOR ADVANCED SKIERS
Challenges on- and off-piste
Although it does not have the macho
reputation of Chamonix, Verbier or
neighbouring Val-d'Isère, Les Arcs is
not a bad choice for advanced skiers.
There are a number of truly black runs

SKI SCHOOL

93/94 prices in francs
ESF
Classes 6 days
3hr: am or pm
6 half-days: 650
Children's classes
Ages: 3 to 13
6 half-days: 550
Private lessons
Hourly
180 for 1hr

International
Classes 6 days
5hr: 2½hr am and pm
6 full days: 760
Children's classes
Ages: from 4
6 full days: 760
Private lessons
Hourly
170 for 1hr

Virages
Classes 6 days
3hr per day
6 3hr days: 655
Children's classes
Ages: from 3
6 3hr days: 655
Private lessons
Hourly
185 for 1hr

Speed skiing on the Olympic slope

The 1992 Olympic speed skiing course is open to anyone mad enough to have a go! Actually, it's not too dangerous – you go from some way below the competition start at the top, and the stopping area is very wide, flat and immaculately groomed. The only deaths that have occurred have been from elite performers skiing blind, with head down for maximum streamlining, hitting the timing mechanism. You get a mini-medal for averaging 90kph between the timing posts, a bronze medal for 110kph, silver for 130kph, and gold for 150kph.

One run, including hire of special skis and glasses and the streamlining helmet (great for photos!), is FF60, or an all-day pass is FF160. It takes a long time to prepare the course after a snowfall (it's too steep for a piste-basher to get up or down), so don't be surprised to find it closed.

above Arc 2000, and a couple in other areas. The Aiguille Rouge cable-car is key for accessing several of the steepest runs, and when this is shut (as it often is in bad or windy weather) the area's interest for advanced skiers is severely limited. The Aiguille Rouge-Le Pré black, with a vertical drop of over 2000m, is superb, with remarkably varying terrain. There is also a great deal of off-piste potential, with powder skiing after a fresh snowfall among trees above 1600 and down towards Peisey, very difficult steep bowl skiing beneath Aiguille Rouge, and lovely runs on the outer edge of the ski area at Grand Col near the Le Pré black.

FOR INTERMEDIATE SKIERS
Plenty for all standards
One strength of the area is that most main routes have easy and more difficult alternatives, making it good for mixed-ability groups. There's lots to challenge, yet leisurely skiers are able to move around without getting too many nasty surprises. An exception is the solitary Comborcières black linking 1600 with Pré-St-Esprit. This long mogul field justifies its rating and can be great fun for strong intermediates, but too many near-novices attempt it, causing an overcrowded piste, which is exasperating for speedier skiers. Taking the Lac red is a more comfortable route to 2000.
   The woodland runs at either end of the ski area, above Peisey and Le Pré, and the bumpy Cachette red down to 1600 are also good for better intermediates. Those wishing to 'go for it' will like Peisey: its well-groomed runs are remarkably uncrowded much of the time – ideal for fast skiing. The over-confident should avoid the Le Pré black, due to a narrow section which

demands technical proficiency rather than guts. Better skiers will enjoy it all the way down.
   The lower section is good for mixed-ability groups, with a choice of routes through the trees. The red runs down from Arpette and Col des Frettes towards 1800 are quite steep but usually well groomed.
   Leisurely types have plenty of cruising terrain. Many of the runs around 2000 are rather bland and prone to overcrowding. The blues above 1800 are nice, though busy, motorways, whilst the easier of the pistes down to Peisey are pleasantly quiet. The pretty Mont Blanc run is a lovely glide.

FOR BEGINNERS
1800 best for complete novices
There are nursery slopes conveniently situated just above all three villages. The ones at 1600 (used for night skiing) are rather steep for complete beginners, while those at 2000 get crowded with intermediate through-traffic at times. The sunny, spacious runs at 1800 are best. Fast learners can take the gondola up to Col de la Chal at 2600m for 'top of the world' views and usually great snow on the easy runs down towards Arc 2000.

FOR CROSS-COUNTRY
Very boring locally
Short trails, mostly on roads, close to all three villages, is the extent of it unless you travel down to the Nancroix Valley, where there are 40km of pleasant trails.

QUEUES
2000 is the only problem area
There are few queues except at Arc 2000. Even when snow is good in other sections, too many skiers seem to make a bee-line for the runs above

CHILDCARE

The ESF branches in all three stations take children from 3. The International school's Club Poussin in 1800 starts at 4.

At 1600 the Baby Club at the hotel de la Cachette (79077050) takes children from 4 months to 12 years, from 8.30 to 6pm, with ski lessons available for those aged 3 or more.

At 1800 various arrangements are offered by the Pommes de Pin nursery (79415542). The nursery itself takes childrem aged 1 to 6, from 8.45 to 5.45. Children aged 3 to 9 can join the Mini-Mini club or Mini-Maxi club, which means morning and afternoon ski classes, with lunch by arrangement.

There are children's clubs at several hotels other than the Cachette – Golf (1800) ages 3 to 6, Aiguille Rouge (2000) 3 to 6, Latitudes (1800) 4 to 12, Eldorador (2000) 4 to 12 – this is one of their 'family villages'. The Club Med (2000) has comprehensive childcare facilities.

GETTING THERE

Air Geneva, transfer 3½hr. Lyon, transfer 3½hr. Chambery, transfer 2½hr.

Rail Bourg-St-Maurice; frequent buses and direct funicular to resort.

the highest village. The cable-car is a particular bottleneck. At holiday times overcrowded pistes can be as big a problem as queues, especially on some of the blue runs.

MOUNTAIN RESTAURANTS
Very little choice

Mountain restaurants are low in both quality and quantity. The large place at Pré-St-Esprit has a good sun terrace and cheap (by local standards) pizza and pasta. The older, smaller restaurant here, Chez Béliou La Fumée, has a rustic atmosphere and good food. The two refuges in the Planay area are attractive, but their food isn't. Chez Léa is perhaps the better of the two. The Poudreuse near the top of the Vallandry chair-lift is one of the best. The restaurant at the top of the Col de la Chal has fabulous views but lousy service.

SKI SCHOOL
Ski évolutif recommended

The ESF ski school is renowned for being the first in Europe to teach ski évolutif, where beginners learn parallel turns right from the start on short skis, cutting out snowploughs and gradually moving on to longer and longer skis. Such tuition is only available to the over 12s.

Tuition is also available in powder, mogul and racing techniques. We've had a couple of bad reports about the 1800 section of the school. One tells of being made to change classes three times in one day, with none of the instructors speaking any English. The 1600 section appears better organised. We lack reports of 2000.

In contrast to the ESF, we've had nothing but glowing reports of the other independent school in Arc 1800, the International, otherwise known as Arc Aventures – especially its private lessons.

FACILITIES FOR CHILDREN
Good reports

We have an enthusiastic report on the Pommes de Pin Mini-Mini club (1800) – with the slight reservation that advance bookings appear to be a waste of time. The mini-club at the Latitudes (1800) is also recommended – 'friendly, good English' – as is the one at the Eldorador (2000). We have no reports on the ski schools, but it is worth noting that the International school at 1800 claims to operate a maximum group size of six for children aged 4 and 5 – a welcome change from the French tendency to lead infants around in huge groups.

 # Staying there

Although essentially a consistently ski-convenient resort, self-caterers staying in 1800 can be unlucky (see page 144). Charmettoger is the best bet, but it has few facilities and is quite far from the children's facilities and ski school.

HOW TO GO
Geared towards self-catering

Although all the big tour operators come here, their accommodation is limited – mostly rough-and-ready apartments. The tour operator charter train to Bourg-St-Maurice is very convenient, with one of the shortest transfers to any resort. There is a Club Med 'village' at Arc 2000.

Chalets The only catered chalet available (Skiworld) in Les Arcs itself is a cheap and cheerful place on the piste among the trees above 1600. It offers great value compared to the expensive hotels and cramped apartments. It has a pleasant open-fired lounge, but bedrooms vary enormously – the spacious top-floor rooms are much the best.

Hotels The choice of hotels in Les Arcs is gradually widening, but they still seem rather ordinary and expensive – those in 1800 particularly so. All-in packages of full board accommodation and lift pass can be attractive.

£££ Golf (1800) A super-pricey 3-star; the best in Les Arcs, with recently renovated rooms, sauna, gym, kindergarten and covered parking.

£££ Trois Arcs (1600) Central.

££ Aiguille Rouge (2000) Daily free ski guiding.

££ Eldorador (2000) Comfortable, excellent food, regular entertainment ('some nights better than others').

Self-catering Over three-quarters of the resort beds are in apartments, mostly tight on space, so paying extra for under-occupancy is a sound investment. Given the lack of nightlife, atmosphere and off-slope facilities, cable TV may be worth considering, even if you wouldn't normally watch television on holiday. The Ruitor apartments (Inghams) are some of the best, in one of the smaller blocks at the foot of the slopes close to a lift. They are well equipped and nicely situated among trees between Villards and Charmettoger. The Nova residences in Villards, which house a kindergarten and Mini club, and the Pierre et Vacances places, the Arnoise and Grand Arbois (all Neilson), are about the best of the rest on the British market.

PACKAGES

AA Ski-Driveaway, Airtours, Chalets 'Unlimited', Club Med, Cresta Ski France, Crystal, Enterprise, Equity Total Ski, Finlays, Inghams, Kings Ski Club, Made to Measure, Neilson, Sally, Ski Club of GB, Ski West, SkiBound, Skiworld, Thomson, Travelscene Ski-Drive, UCPA

ACTIVITIES

Indoor Squash (3 courts 1800), Chinese gymnastics, saunas (1600, 1800), solaria, multi-gym (1800), bridge (1800, 1600), cinemas, amusement arcades, music, concert halls, fencing (2000), bowling (1800) **Outdoor** Natural skating rinks (1800 and 2000), floodlit skiing, luge run, speed skiing (2000), ski-jump, climbing wall (1800), organised snow-shoe outings, 10km cleared paths (1800 and 1600), hang-gliding, horse-riding, sleigh rides, helicopter rides to Italy

TOURIST OFFICE

Postcode 73706
Tel 010 33 79415545
Fax 79074596

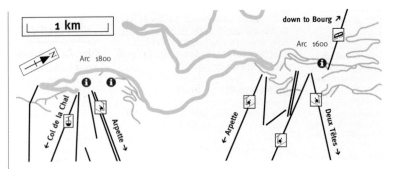

EATING OUT
Cook it yourself

Most people cook for themselves, which is pretty wise. Le Green restaurant in the Hotel du Golf has haute cuisine at sky-high prices. The Gargantus in 1800 is a welcome exception to the general mediocrity in the more informal places. L'Equipe specialises in Savoyard dishes. Casa Mia does good pizza and pasta.

APRES-SKI
Early to bed!

The Hotel du Golf in 1800 is the centre of very limited nightlife, with a jazz band and disco. The cinemas at 1800 and 1600 have English-language films once or twice a week. Otherwise it's make-your-own-atmosphere in one of the bars. Pub Russel, in 1800, is usually the most animated. The Blue Bar, an American-style cocktail joint, is the focus in 2000. It has occasional live music and stays open till late. 1600 is completely dead – there are a couple of cosy bars, one with an open fire, but they never seem to have more than a handful of punters in to give them any atmosphere.

FOR NON-SKIERS
Very poor

Les Arcs is not the place for a non-skier. There is very little to do off the slopes. It doesn't even have a swimming pool. A shopping trip to Bourg-St-Maurice, preferably on Saturday for the market, and a few walks are the main options available.

Bourg-St-Maurice 840m

Staying in Bourg-St-Maurice has its advantages. It's a real French town, without much charm, but with cheaper hotels and restaurants and easy access to other ski resorts for day trips. The funicular takes skiers straight to 1600 in seven minutes. However, those without a car will find the walk from town to the funicular a trek in ski boots.

Le Pré 1200m

A charming, rustic little hamlet with a chair-lift up to the Arc 2000 ski area. It has a few small bars and restaurants but not much more, and is a short drive from Villaroger on the road between Bourg-St-Maurice and Val-d'Isère. Finlays have a chalet here, recommended by a reporter. The Aiguille Rouge restaurant has been highly recommended for chalet girls' nights off.

Peisey-Nancroix 1350m

This small village dates back to AD1000, though its most striking feature is the fine baroque church. The other, mostly old, buildings house a small selection of shops, restaurants and bars, a short drive above the main Moutiers-Bourg road. The main tree-lined skiing of Les Arcs starts a five-minute gondola ride above the village, at Plan-Peisey-Vallandry. Skiing home off-piste is feasible.

Avoriaz 1800m

✔ Good position on the main Portes du Soleil ski circuit, giving access to a very extensive, quite varied ski area suitable for all grades of skier

✔ Avoriaz is the best base in the area for good skiers, and has the best snow

✔ Ski-from-the-door convenience

✔ Excellent family apartments

✔ Resort-level snow and ski-through, car-free village give an Alpine atmosphere

✔ Good children's facilities

✘ Bold architecture, not to the liking of traditionalists

✘ Disappointing number of lift bottlenecks, and some crowded pistes.

✘ Skiing doesn't go much higher than the village

✘ Portes du Soleil circuit involves some low-altitude links that are far from snowsure

✘ Unhelpful piste map system

✘ Little to do but ski

✘ Few alternatives to self-catering

✘ Pricey by local French standards

Avoriaz is not our favourite resort in the Portes du Soleil (that would be Swiss Champéry), nor is it that of our reporters, who go to Châtel and Morzine in much larger numbers. But it has clear attractions. In a low-altitude area where snow is not reliable, Avoriaz has the best there is – on relatively high, north-facing slopes of varying difficulty. The Linga sector of Châtel's skiing is also easily accessible. And the Hauts Forts sector facing the village offers much the most challenging terrain in the Portes du Soleil.

So, assuming you're set on the Portes du Soleil, why not choose Avoriaz? Several reasons. For us, the character of the village is the main problem. We don't mind sleeping in purpose-built ski stations in order to get instant access to high-altitude skiing, but there is no really high-altitude skiing here. The Portes du Soleil is mainly about pottering among attractive low-altitude villages, and we'd rather be based in one. Another factor that may clinch the decision for many is cost – Châtel and Morzine are cheap by French standards; Avoriaz is not. Queues, which can be a nuisance, are not a reason to stay away: they affect those skiing the Portes du Soleil from other bases just as much as they affect Avoriaz-based skiers – more so, in fact.

ORIENTATION

Avoriaz is perched high above the established valley resort of **Morzine**, to which it is linked by piste and lift. It is one of the main resorts on the Portes du Soleil ski circuit, and has good links to **Châtel** in one direction and **Champéry** in the other. Trips by car are possible to **Flaine** and **Chamonix**.

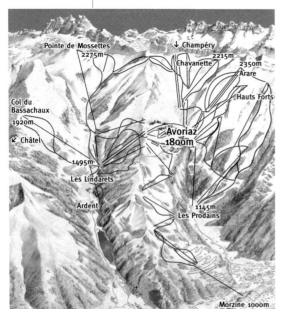

🏠 The resort

Avoriaz is a purpose-built resort perched impressively above a dramatic, sheer rock face. Cars and coaches have to stop at the edge of town, and a horse-drawn sleigh or snow-cat transports skiers and their luggage to the accommodation. The village is set on a considerable slope, but there are ski lifts in town and moving around on foot is straightforward except when pathways are icy (which is not uncommon).

Avoriaz usually has snow all over its byways, and being able to ski through it adds to the convenience of the place; it's also one of its great selling points. Pistes, lifts and off-slope activities are close to virtually all the accommodation. Skiing from the door is usually possible, but many of the pistes finish at the foot of town, a lift-ride away from home.

SKI FACTS

Altitude 1165m-2275m
Lifts   224
Pistes   650km
Green/Blue   54%
Red   33%
Black   13%
Artificial snow   11km

LIFT PASSES

94/95 prices in francs
Portes du Soleil
Covers all lifts in all
12 resorts, and
shuttle buses.
Beginners Reduced
price (and area) half-
day and day pass.
Main pass
1-day pass 190
6-day pass 863
Senior citizens
Over 60: 6-day pass
570 (34% off)
Children
Under 16: 6-day pass
570 (34% off)
Under 5: free pass
Short-term passes
Ascent and/or return
on the télépherique;
half-day pass (from
noon) 129.
Alternative passes
Pass covering the 35
lifts of Avoriaz only:
147 per day.

SKI SCHOOL

93/94 prices in francs
ESF
Classes 6 days
5hr: 2½hr am and pm
6 full days: 760
Children's classes
Ages: 4 to 11
6 full days: 600
Private lessons
1hr, 1½hr or 2hr
156 for 1hr, for 1 to 2
people; 3 to 6 people
190 per hour

L'Ecole de Glisse
Classes 6 days
2½hr, am or pm
6 full days: 850
Private lessons
Hourly
160 for 1hr

The village is composed of angular, dark, wood-clad high-rise buildings, mostly apartment blocks. Reactions to the architecture vary. But even critics must concede that the place has a distinct style, unlike the dreary cuboid blocks thrown up in the 1960s in Flaine and Les Menuires.

When snow-covered, the compact car-free village has an Alpine feel despite the architecture. It is also pleasantly cosmopolitan, with the numerous British joined by plenty of Scandinavians, Germans and Spaniards. The evenings are not ultra-lively, which is just as well since much of the accommodation is very close to the bars and nightclubs.

 # The skiing

The slopes closest to Avoriaz are mainly bleak and tree-less but relatively (note that word) snowsure. They suit all standards of skier, including advanced skiers, who also have quick access to the most challenging skiing in the Portes du Soleil, extending down into the trees below the resort.

The whole Portes du Soleil circuit can be done by moderately competent skiers. (The terrible piste maps give more cause for concern than the slopes!) The circuit breaks down at Châtel, where a bus or long walk is necessary, depending on the direction of travel (see below). The ski areas of Morzine and Les Gets are part of the Portes du Soleil network but are not actually on the core circuit. To get to them you have to get across to the far side of Morzine – most easily reached by skiing or riding the cable-car down to Les Prodains then taking the bus.

Avoriaz encourages snowboarding, and has a special area with half-pipe at the foot of the Hauts Forts sector.

THE SKI AREA
Short runs and plenty of them
The village has lifts and pistes fanning out in all directions. Staying close to Avoriaz assures the comfort of riding mostly chair-lifts – some other parts of the Portes du Soleil (particularly around Champoussin and Super-Châtel) have a lot of drags. Facing the village are the slopes of **Arare-Hauts Forts**; this is essentially short-run 'yo-yo' skiing, but when the snow conditions allow there is a long alternative down to Les Prodains. You ski down a little way to get to the lifts for this sector; you do the lifts off to the left making for the **Chavanette**

sector on the Swiss border – a broad, undulating bowl where you can ski anywhere. Beyond the border at the col is the infamous Swiss Wall – a long and impressive mogul slope with a tricky start, but not the terror it is cracked up to be unless it is icy (it gets a lot of sun). Lots of skiers doing the circuit (or returning to Champéry) ride the chair down, so don't hesitate to do the same. At the bottom of the Wall is the broad, open skiing of Planachaux, above Champéry, with links to the even broader open skiing around Les Crosets and Champoussin. There are several ways back from this sector, but much the most amusing is the chair up the Wall, with a grandstand view of skiers struggling down beneath you.

Taking a lift up from Avoriaz (or traversing from some of the highest accommodation) takes you to the ridge behind the village, where pistes go down into the **Lindarets-Brocheaux** valley, whence lifts and further runs in the excellent Linga sector lead eventually to Châtel. Getting back is basically a matter of retracing your steps, although there are several options from Lindarets.

Morgins is effectively the resort diametrically opposite Avoriaz on the circuit, and the state of the snow there may encourage you to ski anticlockwise rather than clockwise, so as to avoid the low, south-facing slopes down from Bec de Corbeau.

SNOW RELIABILITY
High resort, low skiing
Although Avoriaz is high, its skiing doesn't go much higher – and some parts of the Portes du Soleil circuit are much lower. Considering their altitude, the north-facing slopes between Hauts Forts and Avoriaz hold their snow particularly well. Chavanette also has fairly snowsure skiing. Elsewhere on the circuit, don't be surprised to find poor conditions.

FOR ADVANCED SKIERS
Several testing runs
The tough skiing tends to be rather dotted about. The challenging runs down from Hauts Forts to Prodains (including a World Cup downhill course) are excellent. There is a tough red, and several long, truly black runs, one of which cuts through trees – particularly useful in poor weather. Two chair-lifts serve for 'yo-yo' skiing on the lower runs, which newly-installed snow cannon help to keep open. The famous Swiss Wall at Chavanette will naturally be on your agenda, and Châtel's Linga sector is

CHILDCARE

Les P'tits Loups (50740038) takes children aged 3 months to 5, from 9am to 6pm; indoor and outdoor games, and so on.

The Village des Enfants (50740446) takes children aged 3 to 16, from 9am to 5.30, combining ski tuition with lots of other activities.

The Club Med in Avoriaz is one of their 'family villages', with comprehensive childcare facilities.

GETTING THERE

Air Geneva, transfer 2hr.

Rail Cluses (35km); bus and cable-car to resort.

PACKAGES

AA Ski-Driveaway, Airtours, Chalet Snowboard, Chalets 'Unlimited', Club Med, Cresta Ski France, Crystal, Enterprise, Inghams, Lagrange, Made to Measure, Neilson, Sally, Ski Chamois, Ski West, Stena Sealink, Thomson, Travelscene Ski-Drive

well worth the trip. It's not a great area for off-piste adventures, but there is plenty of skiing just outside the pistes in all of these sectors.

FOR INTERMEDIATE SKIERS
Virtually the whole area
Although some sections lack variety, the Portes du Soleil is excellent for all grades of intermediates when snow is in good supply. Timid skiers not worried about pretty surroundings need not leave the Avoriaz sector; Arare and Chavanette are gentle, spacious, 'ski anywhere' areas. To ski the long cruise between Chavanette and Les Brocheaux, you can take a short chair down to avoid the initial steep mogul field. The pretty run to Ardent via Les Lindarets is also quite easy. Champoussin has a lot of easy skiing, reached without too much difficulty via Les Crosets and Pointe de l'Au. Better intermediates have virtually the whole area at their disposal. The runs down to Pré-la-Joux and L'Essert on the way to Châtel, and those either side of Morgins, are particularly attractive. The long, sunny runs down to Grand-Paradis near Champéry are also a must when snow conditions allow; they offer tremendous views. Good intermediates will no doubt want to take on the Wall.

FOR BEGINNERS
Convenient and good for snow
The nursery slopes seem small in relation to the size of the resort, but are adequate because such a high proportion of skiers are intermediates. The slopes are convenient for accommodation and restaurants, they are sunny, yet good for snow, and they link well to longer, easy runs.

FOR CROSS-COUNTRY
Varied, with some blacks
There is a good variety of trails, mainly between Avoriaz and Super-Morzine, with other fine trails down to Lindarets and around Montriond. There are 45km of trails in total, a third graded black. The only drawback is that several trails are not loops, but 'out and back' routes.

QUEUES
Long at peak times
There are a disappointing number of bottlenecks. In mid- and late-season, long queues form to get out of Avoriaz at morning and afternoon peaks, and to get to the top of the village in the early evening. Both the Arare and Chavanette sectors get long weekend

queues in season. Going to Arare and skiing across to the Chavanette drags saves time in the mornings. Things are better in January and early February, though weekends are still a problem.

MOUNTAIN RESTAURANTS
Good choice over the hill
Avoriaz has a poor reputation for mountain restaurants because of the mediocre places close to the village, but there are plenty of good places only slightly further afield. The chalets in the hamlets of Les Lindarets – surely one of the great concentrations of mountain restaurants in the Alps – and Les Marmottes are generally charming. Others worth a visit are at the top of the Chavanette chair, Pré-la-Joux and Super-Châtel.

SKI SCHOOL
Good, but watch the queues
The ESF ski school has quite a good reputation, although classes can be large and queues may cut down the tuition time.

The newly-formed Ecole de Glisse provides useful competition. Their group tuition prices work out double those of the ESF, but classes have a maximum of six. They also offer more options for adventurous skiers. Both schools have progressive snowboarding sections.

FACILITIES FOR CHILDREN
Looking good
The central 'children's village', run by Annie Famose, is a key part of the appeal of Avoriaz for many French families. Its facilities are excellent – a chalet full of activities and amusements as well as special slopes complete with Disney characters. The management pride themselves on their 'original method', based on an 'appropriate' atmosphere, but we lack recent reports on how this goes down with British children. Children aged 7 to 16 can be looked after for a whole week without parental involvement – sounds marvellous.

The car-free village must be one of the safest in the Alps for children, but there are still sleighs, skiers and snow-cats to watch out for.

 # Staying there

The main consideration when choosing where to stay in the quite steeply sloping village is your evening habits. By day you can get around with the help of ski-lifts. If you plan to be out on the town every night,

ACTIVITIES

Indoor Health centre 'Altiform' (sauna, massage, solarium, gym, aerobics, jacuzzi), squash, turkish baths, volley-ball, cinema, bowling
Outdoor Para-gliding, hang-gliding, snow-shoe excursions, dog-sleigh rides, walking paths, sleigh rides, skating, curling, snow-scooter excursions, quad-bikes, helicopter and light aircraft flights

remember that what goes down must later come back up.

The resort is nominally divided into half a dozen 'villages'. The Village-de-la-Falaise is the most recent area of development; it is quite separate from the rest and is close to the entrance car parks and reception facilities.

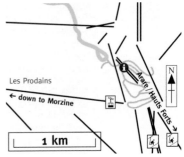

Les Prodains

← down to Morzine

1 km

HOW TO GO
Self-catering dominates
Alternatives to apartments are few.
Chalets There are several available, all of them comfortable and attractive but designed for small family groups. Neilson and Crystal both offer chalet accommodation.
Hotels There are only two 3-star hotels and a Club Med 'village', which is near the top of the resort.
£££ Dromonts The original Avoriaz construction. In the middle of the resort, reasonably well placed for skiing and après-skiing.
£££ Hauts-Forts Close to the bottom of the village, so you can walk up to it after skiing.
Self-catering We are unaware of any particularly comfortable apartments; most tend to be cramped if the full allocation is taken up. Many of the better ones are in the new Falaise area, by the resort entrance, reasonably convenient for most things. The Elinka & Malinka (Inghams, Crystal) is better equipped than most. The other Falaise apartments featured by Inghams are simple but slightly more spacious. The Thomson allocation in Falaise is of a fair standard. Up at the top of the resort – good for views and skiing from the door but little else – the Sirius apartments (Thomson, Neilson) are reasonable.

EATING OUT
Good; booking essential
There are numerous restaurants. The hotel Dromont's Bistro has some of the best French cuisine in town. Booking is essential. L'Igloo is also very good, but expensive. L'Ortolan, in the Elinka & Malinka complex, is friendly and good value (by local standards). There are the usual cheaper Italian places: Pizzeria Barbara is one of the best, Tex Mex and brunch in US One are also good value.

APRES-SKI
Lively, but not much choice
Nightlife lacks variety, but a few bars have good atmospheres. Le Chouca and The Place are lively and have bands, the Succa is popular, and La Taverna, Le Taraillon and Bar Fantastique are worth a visit. Happy hour in US One (also open late) is popular, as is the Midnight Express nightclub (free entry, pricey drinks).

FOR NON-SKIERS
Not much at the resort
Non-skiers are advised to go to Morzine for shops, sports facilities, riding and plenty of good walks.

TOURIST OFFICE

Postcode 74110
Tel 010 33 50740211
Fax 50741825

Chamonix 1035m

ORIENTATION

See page 156

HOW IT RATES

The skiing

Snow	★★★★
Extent	★★★
Advanced	★★★★★
Intermediates	★★
Beginners	★
Convenience	★
Queues	★★
Restaurants	★★★

The rest

Scenery	★★★★★
Resort charm	★★★★
Not skiing	★★★★

✔ A lot of very tough skiing, especially off-piste

✔ Access to arguably the most famous off-piste ski route of them all – the Vallée Blanche

✔ Amazing views of the Mont Blanc massif and surrounding glaciers

✔ Ancient mountain town, steeped in history and Alpine traditions

✔ Unforgettable cable-car ride to the Aiguille du Midi

✔ Well-organised and extensive cross-country trail system

✔ Plenty for non-skiers to do

✔ Easy access by road, rail and air

✘ Ski areas completely separate from each other

✘ Virtually no ski-in, ski-out accommodation

✘ The extent of the piste skiing in most areas is quite limited

✘ Runs down to the valley floor are often closed due to lack of snow

✘ Popularity and too many old lifts mean crowds and queues

✘ A car is very useful to get the best out of the area

✘ Mixed-ability groups will find it difficult to stick together and keep everyone happy

Chamonix could not be more different from France's well-known, purpose-built ski resorts. There is no huge area of well-connected lifts and groomed pistes. Unless you are content to ski one mountain and pick your place to stay accordingly, you have to drive or take a bus each day to your chosen ski area. There is all sorts of terrain, but it offers more to interest the good skier than anyone else; to make the most of the area you need a mountain guide rather than a piste map. Chamonix is neither convenient nor conventional, but it is special and – understandably – a Mecca for advanced skiers.

Both the skiing and the scenery are dramatic – the Chamonix valley cuts deeply through Europe's highest mountains and glaciers. The views are stunning and the skiing is everything really tough skiing should be – not only steep, but high and long. If you like perfectly manicured pistes accessed by queue-free bubbles, stick to the Trois Vallées; but if you like your skiing and your scenery on the wild side, give Chamonix a try. But be warned: there are those who try it and never go home – lots of them.

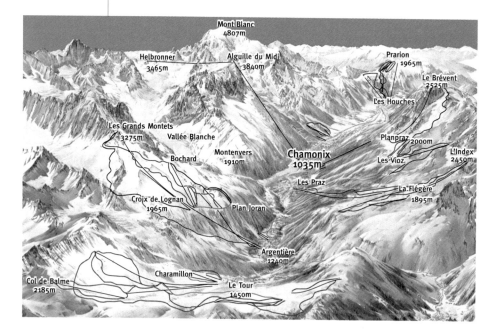

SKI FACTS

Altitude 1035m-3840m	
Lifts	52
Pistes	140km
Green/Blue	35%
Red	45%
Black	20%
Artificial snow	4km

LIFT PASSES

94/95 prices in francs
Ski pass Mont Blanc
Covers lifts in 13 resorts in the Mont Blanc region (plus Courmayeur in Italy 4 days out of 6) and ski buses in each resort, except the Grand Montets cable-car.
Beginners Points tickets or pay by the ride on nursery lifts.
Main pass
6-day pass 900 (low season 765 – 15% off)
Senior citizens
Over 60: 6-day pass 645 (28% off)
Children
Under 12: 6-day pass 645 (28% off)
Under 4: free pass
Short-term passes
Half-day passes for limited areas; single and return tickets on most lifts.
Notes Day passes only cover individual areas (Les Houches, Le Brévent, La Flégère, etc). Grands Montets cable-car costs extra (30 for 1 ascent, 460 for 20).
Alternative passes
Passes available for all the individual areas (Le Brévent, La Flégère, Balme, Les Houches, Les Grands Montets, Argentière and Le Tour).

 # The resort

Chamonix is a busy little town with hundreds of hotels and restaurants, visitors year-round, a lively Saturday market and generally lots of bustle and business.

The centre of town is full of atmosphere, with cobbled streets and squares, beautiful old buildings and a fast-running river. Sadly, unsightly modern buildings have been built on to its periphery (especially in the Chamonix Sud area near the Aiguille du Midi cable-car station) and some of its lovely old buildings have been allowed to fall into disrepair. But the views of the mountains of the Mont Blanc massif on one side and the Aiguilles Rouge on the other more than make up for that.

Vantage points in the town and, even better, in some of the ski areas, offer a spectacle of mountains and glaciers so impressive that it is almost overwhelming. The town squares and pavement cafés are busy most of the day, and especially on sunny afternoons, when skiers, shoppers and sightseers sip their drinks and stare at the glaciers pouring down the mountainsides. It all makes for a very agreeable and distinctively French atmosphere.

The shops in Chamonix cover the range from those dealing in high-priced, high-tech ski equipment to some surprisingly tacky souvenir shops completely full of rubbish. But it remains essentially a town for mountain men rather than poseurs.

 # The skiing

Once you get over the initial impression that the place is hopelessly disconnected and awkward to ski, you come to realise that there is actually a reasonable variety of skiing available, though seldom in the same place. There is excellent tough skiing on the pistes at Les Grands Montets and Le Brévent and some classic off-piste routes, many over the glaciers that dominate much of the higher terrain. Some of these routes suit intermediate, but confident and guided skiers quite well and some are best reserved for those with outrageous hairstyles and a 'bad' attitude. Intermediate skiers are best served at La Flégère, Le Tour and Les Houches. Several of the beginners' areas need snow-cover down to the valley floor to be operational.

THE SKI AREA
Very fragmented

For those who really like getting about a bit, the Mont Blanc ski-pass covers 14 resorts, 25 ski areas, over 200 lifts and 700km of piste. The resorts covered extend far beyond the Chamonix valley – including St-Gervais, Megève, Les Contamines and even Courmayeur in Italy.

The ski areas within the Chamonix valley – and there are a dozen of them – are either small, low, beginners' areas or are restricted to a patch of suitable terrain on the valley side with cable-car or gondola access from the valley floor. The modern 6-seater gondola for **Le Brévent** departs a short but steep walk from the centre of town, and the cable-car above it takes you to the summit at 2525m. At **La Flégère**, like Le Brévent, the skiing is mainly between 2000m and 2500m and the views across to Mont Blanc are themselves worth the price of the lift pass. There have recently been improvements to the system at **Les Grands Montets** above Argentière but the top cable-car to the 3300m summit is still relatively low-capacity. The area above Les Houches is served by a cable-car to **Bellevue** and a gondola to **Prarion**; there's no skiing above 2000m but there are links over to St-Gervais. The skiing at **Col de Balme**, above Le Tour, is mostly at opposite ends of a wide, sunny bowl reached by the almost-parallel gondola and chair-lift.

SNOW RELIABILITY
Good high up; poor low down

The top runs on the north-facing slopes above Argentière are almost guaranteed to have good snow-cover, and skiing normally lasts well into May. Finding the top lift shut because of the weather is more of a worry. The Col de Balme area above Le Tour doesn't have the highest skiing but has a snowy location and a good late-season record. The largely south-facing slopes of Brévent and Flégère and the low-altitude slopes of Les Houches can suffer in warm weather and runs to the resort are frequently closed. Snowmaking is restricted to two of the small, beginner areas.

FOR ADVANCED SKIERS
Head for the Grands Montets

Les Grands Montets above Argentière is justifiably renowned for the amount of tough, exciting skiing that this seemingly not very large area provides. A supplement is charged for each ride on the top cable-car. If you've got the

SKI SCHOOL

94/95 prices in francs

ESF
In both Chamonix and Argentière
Classes 6 days
4½hr: 9.45-noon and 2.15-4.30
6 full days: 660
Children's classes
Ages: 4 to 12
6 days (9am-5pm) including supervised lunch: 1100
Private lessons
1hr, 2hr, half- or full day
200 for 1hr, for up to 4 people

legs and lungs, climb the steep metal steps to the observation platform at the top and take in the stunning views and stimulating air. Bear in mind that it's a long way down again – 200 more steps once you are down to the cable-car before you hit the snow.

The black pistes – Point de Vue and Pylones – start with a narrow and lumpy section and are then long and exhilarating. The Point de Vue sails right by some dramatic sections of glacier, with marvellous views of the crevasses. The off-piste routes from the top are numerous and often dangerous; the Pas de Chèvre joins with the Vallée Blanche, but only after a fairly epic journey, and there's a scenic route through the Argentière glacier. From the Bochard covered chair-lift, you can head down the Combe de la Pendant bowl for 1000m vertical of wild, unpisted

mountainside. The continuation down the valley side to Le Lavancher is equally testing and suffers frequently from lack of snow on the steep sections. To get the best out of the area you really need to have a local guide. Without one you either stick to the relatively small number of pistes or put your life at risk.

At Le Brévent there's more to test good skiers than it might first seem from the map – there are a number of variations on the runs down from the summit; some are steep and icy and the couloir routes are very steep and very narrow. The skiing in the Col de La Charlanon is uncrowded and includes one marked red run and lots of excellent off-piste. At La Flégère there are several good off-piste routes flanking the main skiing area and a pretty tough run back to the village when snow-cover permits. Le Tour

---

The Vallée Blanche

This is a trip you do for the stunning views and glacial scenery rather than the skiing, which is easy and well within the capability of the average intermediate. It is a classic tour, not to be missed by anyone who is there when conditions are right.

Go in a guided group – despite the ease of the skiing, dangerous crevasses lurk to swallow those not in the know – and prepare for extreme cold at the top. It does get extraordinarily busy at times – going early on a weekday gives you the best chance of avoiding the worst of the crowds.

The cable-car is a stunning ride that takes you to 3790m. There are snack-bars and the '3842' restaurant, if time allows. Across the bridge from the arrival station on the 'Piton Nord' is the 'Piton Central' and the highest point of the Aiguille du Midi – the view of Mont Blanc from the summit terrace should not be missed.

A tunnel through the rock and ice of the 'Piton Central' delivers skiers to the top of the infamous ridge-walk down to the start of the skiing. Many parties rope up for this walk and a fixed guide-rope provides further security. You might still feel envious about those strolling nonchalantly down in crampons – you may wish you'd stayed in bed.

After that the skiing seems a doddle; mostly effortless gliding down gentle slopes with only the occasional steeper, choppy section to deal with. So stop often and enjoy the surroundings fully – no written description or amateur photography can do it justice. The views of the ice, the crevasses and seracs, are simply mind-blowing.

There are many variants on the classic route, all of which are more difficult and more hazardous – the 'Vraie Vallée' is for experts only and the 'Envers du Plan' is a direct descent down to the Refuge du Requin – the mountain hut where everyone takes a break and admires the recently-negotiated ice fall. Snow conditions may well not allow skiing the full 24km route back down to Chamonix, in which case the station at Montenvers (1910m) is the target. A short gondola links the edge of the glacier to the station where everyone piles onto the train for Chamonix.

Book your guide the day before at the Maison de la Montagne or other ski school offices. You can join a group for FF300, or have your own guide for FF1,100 (up to four skiers – then FF100 extra per additional skier).

ORIENTATION
Strung out for 20km along the Chamonix valley are several ski areas, some with attached villages – from Les Houches at one end to **Argentière** and **Le Tour** at the other. Chamonix is at the centre of it all, with a cable-car soaring up from the southern fringe to the Aiguille du Midi and the famous Vallée Blanche run, and lifts from the northern fringes up to Le Brévent and La Flégère.

The ski areas around **Megève** are covered by the lift pass, as is **Courmayeur** in Italy, a short drive through the Mont Blanc tunnel. Swiss resorts such as **Verbier** are also within reach over the Col des Montets.

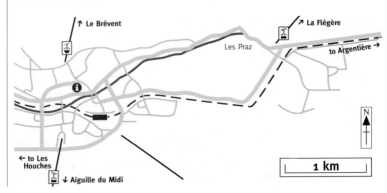

Selected chalets in Chamonix and Argentière

boasts little tough skiing on-piste but there are good off-piste routes from the high points back to the village and over the ridge into Switzerland.

FOR INTERMEDIATE SKIERS
It's worth trying it all
For early or less-confident intermediates, the best areas are at the two extreme ends of the Chamonix valley skiing. The slopes of the Prarion-Bellevue system above Les Houches weave gently through the trees and are the least likely to intimidate anyone. The area is good for intermediate skiers wanting to build confidence.

Likewise, the Col de Balme area above Le Tour is good for easy cruising. A trip to Courmayeur in Italy one day makes an interesting change of atmosphere and more cruising skiing. Try it when the weather's bad in Chamonix – the sun is often shining on the other side of the Mont Blanc tunnel.

More adventurous intermediates will also want to try the other three main areas, though they may find the Grand Montets tough going. The bulk of the skiing at Le Brévent and La Flégère provides a sensible mix of blue and red runs; at Brévent the slopes have been redesigned to achieve this. If the weather is good then you shouldn't miss a guided trip down the Vallée Blanche, perfectly within a competent intermediate's capability

FOR BEGINNERS
Best if there's snow in the valley
If there is snow low down, the nursery lifts at La Vormaine, Les Chosalets, Les Pelerins and Le Savoy are fine for teaching first-timers; learners will not be bothered by faster skiers. The Planards and Glacier du Mont Blanc lifts both benefit from snowmaking and also provide some progression from the nursery areas. But beginner-skiers would really be better advised to learn elsewhere, and come to Chamonix when they can appreciate the tough high-mountain terrain that is its hallmark.

FOR CROSS-COUNTRY
A good network of trails
Most of the 42km of prepared trails lie along the valley between Chamonix and Argentière. There are green, blue, red and black loop sections and the full tour from Chamonix to Argentière and back is 32km. All these trails are fairly low and fade fast in spring sun.

GETTING THERE
Air Geneva, transfer 1½hr. Lyon, transfer 3½hr.

Rail Station in resort, on the St-Gervais-Le Fayet/Vallorcine line.

QUEUES
Some notable blackspots
The upper cable-car and the Bochard lift at Les Grands Montets access some of the best skiing and, not surprisingly, can provide some serious queues. It can also get busy at the end of the day when runs to the valley have been closed – the cable-cars at Les Houches and La Flégère suffer more from this than the gondolas at Col de Balme and Le Brévent. The only significant amount of skiing to benefit from shelter among the trees is at Prarion-Bellevue, and in poor weather this is where the crowds go.

Chamonix
Le Tour

MOUNTAIN RESTAURANTS
Stunning views
The Panoramic restaurant at the top of Brévent enjoys the best views and also does a six-course 'gastronomic' menu at FF200. The food's fine but the place is dull. The Altitude 2000 is a straightforward self-service joint with a sunny terrace, as is the bar-restaurant at La Flégère.

The Grands Montets is well off. The new restaurant at Plan Joran serves good food and has a table- as well as self-service section. And the Chavannes, just down from the Croix de Lognan lift station, is a great place for a long lunch, whatever the weather.

At Le Tour, the Col de Balme refuge needs a bit of uphill work to get there, but it wouldn't be as nice if it didn't. The restaurants in the Prarion-Bellevue area are pleasant and good value.

SKI SCHOOL
The place to try something new
All the ski areas can provide traditional lessons with the ESF, but the schools here are particularly strong in some specialist fields – off-piste, glacier and couloir skiing, ski touring, snowboarding and cross-country. English-speaking instructors are plentiful. At the Maison de la

CHILDCARE

The ESF runs ordinary classes for children aged 6 to 12. For children aged 4 to 6 there are lessons in a snow-garden. And children in either category can be looked after all day (and amused when not skiing) from 8.45 to 5pm.

The day-care centre at the Maison pour Tous (50531224) takes children aged 18 months to 6 years from 8.15 to 6.30.

The Panda Club takes children aged 3 months to 12 years. For those up to 18 months there is a crèche in Chamonix (50558612). Older babies are taken here or in Argentière (505404760), where the club has its own skiing area, open to children aged 3 or more.

Some of the more expensive hotels will provide child-minding – the Alpina is one. Club Med has comprehensive in-house arrangements – their place here is one of their 'family villages', with a crèche taking babies from 4 months.

ACTIVITIES

Indoor Sports complex (sports hall, weight training, table tennis), indoor skating and curling rinks, ice hockey, swimming pool with giant water slide, saunas, 2 indoor tennis courts, 2 squash courts, fitness centre, Alpine museum (open school holidays), casino, 3 cinemas, library, 10-pin bowling
Outdoor Ski-jumping, snow-shoe outings, ice-driving circuit, mountain biking, hang-gliding, para-gliding, flying excursions, heli-skiing

Montagne in Chamonix, there is the main ESF office and also the HQ of the Compagnie des Guides de Chamonix Mont Blanc, which has taken visitors to the mountains for 150 years.

Competition is provided by a number of smaller, independent guiding and teaching outfits such as Stages Vallençant and Yak and Yeti Services. And there are many internationally-qualified British guides who base themselves in Chamonix.

FACILITIES FOR CHILDREN
Better than they were
The Panda Club is used by quite a few British visitors. In the past it has come in for some criticism, but recent reports are enthusiastic.

 ## Staying there

The obvious place to stay is in Chamonix itself – it's central, has all the amenities going and some of the skiing is close at hand. For those with a clear preference to do most of their skiing either at Argentière, Les Houches or Le Tour, it would be sensible to look for accommodation nearby. Whatever the choice, no location is convenient for everything so be prepared for some commuting – a car is a big advantage; the Chamonix bus runs frequently between Chamonix and the different ski areas, but only till about 7pm. It's free to holders of the Mont Blanc ski-pass.

HOW TO GO
Pile into the car and drive
There is currently a reasonable choice of packages to both Chamonix and Argentière. Given the value of having a car in the resort and the good road links to Chamonix, a ski-drive package should be considered.
Chalets Many are run by small outfits that cater for this specialist market. Quality tends to be quite high and prices relatively low, making for great value. Bladon Lines are new in the resort this year, with a choice of places. The Ski Company Ltd have the one very expensive place in town (featured in Tatler's World's Top 50 Villas to Rent!). Bigfoot also have an upmarket operation. Collineige have the largest selection – all of them very comfortable. Cheaper places are offered by Ski Olympic, Huski and several of the big tour operators, including Inghams, who have one chalet that's run by its owners rather than the tour company. Childcare specialists Ski Esprit also have a place.

Hotels The place is full of hotels, many of them modestly priced – several available through packages from the UK – and a few rather pricey. Practically all are small, with fewer than 30 rooms. If you have a car, location isn't crucial apart from the usual considerations about traffic. There is a Club Med 'village'.
££££ Albert 1er Smart, expensive, traditional chalet-style hotel with much the most ambitious food in town (Michelin star).
££££ Auberge du Bois Prin A small modern chalet with a big reputation; great views; bit of a hike to the centre; a shorter one to the Brévent lift.
££££ Mont Blanc Central, luxurious.
££££ Jeu de Paume (Lavancher) Alpine satellite of a chic Parisian hotel: a beautifully furnished modern chalet half-way to Argentière.
£££ Alpina Much the biggest in town: modernist-functional place just north of centre; child-minding available.
£££ Labrador (Les Praz) Scandinavian-style chalet close to the Flégère lift.
££ Sapinière Solid, traditional hotel run by long-established Chamonix family; reasonable site on the Brévent side of town.
££ Richemond Lovely old building and nice grounds, near the centre.
££ Vallée Blanche Smart low-priced 3-star B&B hotel, handy for centre and Aiguille du Midi cable-car.
££ Pointe Isabelle Not pretty, but central location; friendly staff, good plain food, well equipped bedrooms.
££ Roma Simple but satisfactory B&B hotel in hassle-free location on south side of centre; friendly patron.
£ Faucigny Cottage-style; in centre of Chamonix; cheap.
Self-catering There are hundreds of properties for renting throughout the valley – chalets, apartments and rooms (some on a B&B basis). Those that find their way into UK package brochures are typically in large purpose-built blocks, usually in Chamonix Sud – convenient but charmless. The Jardins du Mont Blanc – used by Inghams – look much better and they are well situated. The Splendid & Golf apartments in Les Praz have been created from the tasteful restoration of the old hotel of that name – the Flégère cable-car is nearby.

EATING OUT
Plenty of quality places
The good hotels all have good restaurants – the Eden at Les Praz and Bois Prin in Chamonix are first-rate – and there are many other good places to eat. The Sarpe is a lovely 'mountain'

PACKAGES

AA Ski-Driveaway, Airtours, Bigfoot, Bladon Lines, Chalets 'Unlimited', Club Med, Collineige, Cresta Ski France, Crystal, Enterprise, French Impressions, Fresh Tracks, HuSki, Inghams, Jean Stanford, Lagrange, Made to Measure, Neilson, Sally, Ski Addiction, Ski Club of GB, Ski Esprit, Ski Savoie, Ski Valkyrie, Ski Weekend, Snowline, Stena Sealink, The Ski Company Ltd, Travelscene Ski-Drive, Ultimate, White Roc

Argentière Bigfoot, Chalets 'Unlimited', Collineige, Crystal, Jean Stanford, Peak Ski, Poles Apart, Ski Club of GB, Ski Esprit, Ski Valkyrie, Snowline, Trail Alpine, Ultimate, White Roc

Le Tour Bigfoot, Poles Apart

Les Houches Bigfoot, Chalets 'Unlimited', Ski Savoie, Ultimate

TOURIST OFFICE

Postcode 74400
Tel 010 33 50530024
Fax 50535890

restaurant and The Impossible is rustic but smart and features good regional dishes. The Monchu and the Sanjon are good for Savoyarde specialities, and along the Rue des Moulins there are several more pleasant places to choose from. There are a number of ethnic restaurants – Mexican, Spanish, Japanese, Chinese etc – and lots of brasseries and cafés. The Grand Taverne is a lively grill-brasserie that stays open late, as does Poco Loco – possibly the narrowest eating-place in the Alps but good for a quick burger or something in a baguette. For something completely different try the restaurant of the catering college – the students get to practise and you get good food at a knockdown price; ambience not included.

APRES-SKI
No shortage of venues
Many of the bars around the pedestrianised centre of Chamonix get busy for a couple of hours at sundown. La Terrasse is a good spot for a glass of wine or coffee, and the Cheval Rouge, nearby, has good draught beer and Eurosport on TV. Later on, the likes of Chambre 9, Choucas video bar and Jekyll and Hyde get going – they're usually loud and busy and not suitable for oldies. Disco fun is provided by the Pele and the Refuge and there are also 'bars de nuit' which have a similarly young crowd – the Blue Night is occasionally jazz- or country-flavoured. The casino features both English and French roulette – and if you don't know the difference, you shouldn't be there.

FOR NON-SKIERS
An excellent choice
There's more for non-skiers to do here than in many resorts, and in spring it's a very pleasant place for a stroll by the river or a cable-car trip to admire the scenery at closer quarters. Scenic flights offer superb all-round views but are not for the nervous flier. Excursion possibilities are numerous – Annecy, Geneva, Courmayeur and Turin are within striking-distance and the St-Gervais-Martigny railway line runs through the valley. The Alpine Museum is an interesting diversion and there are good sports facilities.

Argentière 1240m
The old village is in a lovely setting towards the head of the valley – the Glacier d'Argentière pokes down towards it and the Aiguille du Midi and Mont Blanc still dominate the scene down the valley. There's now a

fair bit of modern development spread around the main street but it still has a certain cachet that brings people back year after year. Many of the winter residents these days are young, happy and broke, but there's also a good smattering of more seasoned Alpine visitors – Brits included. The small village of Le Tour, just beyond Argentière, is quiet and picturesque, and the place most likely to have snow in the streets.

Jean Stanford and Collineige both have comfortable catered chalets, and Snowline and childcare specialists Ski Esprit are also represented.

A number of the hotels are simple, inexpensive and handy for the village centre – less so for the skiing. On the main street are the Couronne and the Dahu – popular with weekenders.The Grands-Montets is a large chalet-style building, right next to the skiing and Panda Club for children. The Montana is in a pleasant location but neither in the centre nor at the skiing.

Restaurants are informal and inexpensive. The Dahu Brasserie does an excellent fixed-price menu and decent wine by the jug – probably the best value in town. The Fis, attached to the hotel Couronne, is almost as good. Chez Luigi claims 'Ici nous faisons vraie pizzas'; they're certainly good and the wine list is a lot better than you'd expect. The Samoyède is a bistro with Mexican dishes and occasional cheap beer. The R'mize à Ravanel outside the village specialises in mountain dishes.

The Office is the happening place in Argentière, from breakfast till late. The Trace video bar has games, a big collection of ski-videos, some cool customers and sometimes good music. The Eschoppe is in an unpromising location but plays the best music. The Stone bar is good for late drinking.

Les Houches 1010m
Les Houches sprawls along a busy main road. Views of Mont Blanc are impressive, but the shadow of the massif makes it a dark, cold place. There are packages to be had from Ski Savoie – hotels, apartments and a small, catered chalet run by the local owners. The 3-star Mont Alba is perhaps the best hotel, with good rooms, a pool and a gym. The Beausite is comfortable, the Bellevarde, Cottage and Peter Pan inexpensive. The best food is at the pricey Barberine; Peter Pan is good value. Après-ski is very quiet; the Perce Neige is the focal bar.

Ski and non-ski kindergartens are available.

Châtel 1190m

HOW IT RATES

The skiing

Snow   **
Extent   *****
Advanced   ***
Intermediates   ****
Beginners   **
Convenience   **
Queues   ***
Restaurants   ***

The rest

Scenery   ***
Resort charm   ***
Not skiing   **

ORIENTATION

Châtel lies near the head of the wooded Dranse valley, at the north-eastern limit of the French-Swiss Portes du Soleil ski circuit (see page 224).

Directly above the village, reached by gondola, is the outpost of Super-Châtel, with skiing links to **Morgins** and **Champéry** in Switzerland, and to **Torgon**. Morgins is also reached by road over a low pass. The other main French Portes du Soleil resorts – **Avoriaz** and **Morzine** – are quite easily reached on skis, but not by road. A few kilometres down the valley is **La Chapelle-d'Abondance**.

✔ Very extensive, pretty, intermediate ski area – the Portes du Soleil

✔ Wide range of cheap and cheerful, good-value accommodation

✔ Easily reached – close to Geneva, and one of the shortest drives from the Channel

✔ Pleasant, lively, French-dominated old village, still quite rustic in parts

✔ Local skiing relatively queue-free

✔ Good views

✘ Low, with no local snowmakers

✘ Inconvenient nursery slopes

✘ Time-consuming journey to Avoriaz to get to the best snow (and best tough skiing) in the area

✘ Queues can be a problem on the Portes du Soleil circuit

✘ Over-subscribed bus services

✘ Congested village traffic, especially at weekends

✘ Not much nightlife

Like neighbouring Morzine, Châtel offers a blend of attractions that is uncommon in France – an old village with plenty of facilities, cheap accommodation by French standards, and a large ski area on the doorstep. Châtel's original rustic charm has been largely eroded in recent years, but some of it remains, and the resort has one obvious advantage over smoother Morzine: it is part of the main Portes du Soleil ski circuit.

The circuit actually breaks down at Châtel, but this works in the village's favour. Whereas skiers doing the circuit from other resorts have the inconvenience of waiting for a bus mid-circuit, Châtel residents have the advantage of being able to time their bus-rides to avoid waits and queues. Skiers mainly interested in the local slopes should also consider Châtel. For confident intermediate skiers, Châtel's Linga has few equals in the Portes du Soleil, while the nearby Torgon section has arguably the best views. The Chapelle d'Abondance slopes are pleasantly uncrowded at weekends, when many other sections are crowded. Châtel is not, however, ideal for beginners – the nursery slopes are up at Super-Châtel.

🏔 The resort

Châtel is a slightly tatty, overdeveloped, but nonetheless attractive old village. Although there is a definite centre, the village sprawls along the road in from lake Geneva, and the diverging roads out – up the hillside towards Morgins and along the valley towards the Linga ski lifts at L'Essert. Lots of French and Swiss holidaymakers take cars and use them, and the centre gets clogged with traffic during the evening rush-hour. It's even worse at weekends, because the resort is easily accessible to day-trippers from Geneva.

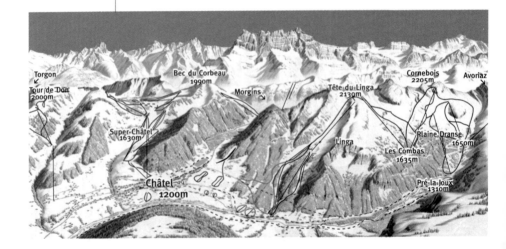

SKI FACTS

Altitude 1200m-2200m
Lifts 224
Pistes 650km
Green/Blue 54%
Red 33%
Black 13%
Artificial snow 11km

LIFT PASSES

94/95 prices in francs
Portes du Soleil
Covers all lifts in all
12 resorts, and
shuttle buses.
Main pass
1-day pass 190
6-day pass 863
Senior citizens
Over 60: 6-day pass
570 (34% off)
Children
Under 16: 6-day pass
570 (34% off)
Under 5: free pass
Short-term passes
Morning and
afternoon passes for
the Portes du Soleil
(both 133), and for
Châtel only (morning
75, afternoon 89).
Alternative periods
5 non-consecutive
days pass for Châtel
only available (adult
544).
Notes Discounts for
holders of the Carte
Neige (5%), families
(15%) and family
Carte Neige (22%).
Carte Neige gives
insurance cover and
discounts at ESF, ice
rink and some shops.

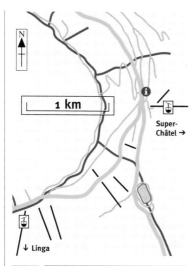

 ## The skiing

The Portes du Soleil as a whole is
classic intermediate skiing, and
Châtel's local slopes are very much in
character. Confident intermediates, in
particular, will find lots to enjoy in the
Linga sector.

THE SKI AREA
The PdS circuit breaks down here
Châtel sits between two sectors of the
Portes du Soleil circuit, linking the two
with a frequent but not entirely
adequate ski-bus service. **Super-
Châtel** is directly above the village –
an area of open and lightly wooded
easy skiing where beginner classes take
place, accessed by a choice of gondola
or two-stage chair from the top of the
village. From here you can ski over to

the quiet little Torgon sector or move
clockwise around the Portes du Soleil
circuit, crossing the Swiss border to
Morgins and then Champoussin and
Champéry, before crossing back into
France above Avoriaz.

The **Linga** sector starts a bus-ride
out of the village, and leads more
directly to Avoriaz. For competent
skiers Linga has some of the most
interesting skiing in the Portes du
Soleil, though the best of it leads back
in the direction of Châtel and is
therefore not skied by those in a hurry
to reach Avoriaz or do the complete
anti-clockwise circuit. If time is of the
essence it is quicker to avoid Linga
altogether by staying on the bus to
Pré-la-Joux. From here it's a short lift
and schuss to the hamlet of Plaine
Dranse; then a single lift and run to
Les Marmottes, where there is a choice
of final lifts towards Avoriaz

SNOW RELIABILITY
Poor – the main drawback
The main runs on Linga and down to
Pré-la-Joux are north-facing, but a lot
of the skiing around Châtel is sunny,
the altitudes hereabouts are low, and
there are virtually no snowmakers. So
snow is not entirely reliable. When it
is in short supply, the bus to and from
Pré-la-Joux is terribly oversubscribed
by people heading for Avoriaz (itself
not absolutely snowsure), and you
have to take a chair at Crête des
Rochassons because there is no
artificial snow on the crucial south-
facing piste to Les Marmottes. The
sunny Morgins-Champoussin area
struggles badly at such times, and its
Portes du Soleil link closes.

Alternative passes
Châtel pass covers 50 lifts in Châtel, Linga, Super-Châtel and Barbossine (adult 6-day pass 638).

SKI SCHOOL

93/94 prices in francs

ESF
Classes 6 days
2hr am; 2½hr pm
6 afternoons: 480
Children's classes
Ages: 5 to 16
6 afternoons: 425
Private lessons
1hr or 1½hr
158 for 1hr, for
1 to 3 people

International
Classes 6 days
3hr: 9am-noon or
2pm-5pm; 2hr: noon-2pm
6 mornings: 580
Private lessons
1hr or 2hr
165 for 1hr; each
additional person 15

Stages Henri Gonon
Courses including accommodation and pass

CHILDCARE

The ESF runs a ski kindergarten for children aged 5 or more, with lunch provided.

Le Village des Marmottons (50733379) takes children from age 14 months to 10, from 8.30 to 5.30, with ski tuition for those aged 3 or more.

FOR ADVANCED SKIERS
Avoriaz might suit you better
It's a long way from here to Les Hauts Forts above Avoriaz and the 'Swiss Wall' between Avoriaz and Champéry. There's a genuine black mogul field between Cornebois and Plaine Dranse, but the best local skiing is beneath the Linga gondola and chair – a pleasant mix of open and wooded ground follows the fall line fairly directly. An unpisted trail from Super-Châtel towards the village is also fun.

FOR INTERMEDIATE SKIERS
Some of the best runs in the PdS
When conditions are right the Portes du Soleil is an intermediate's paradise. Good intermediates need not venture far from Châtel; Linga has some of the best red runs in the whole area. But the Champéry-Avoriaz sector also beckons. Moderately good skiers can do the whole circuit without any problems, and will particularly enjoy the runs around Les Lindarets and Morgins. Even timid skiers can do the circuit, provided they take one or two short-cuts and ride chairs down the trickier bits.

Leaving aside attempts to complete the whole circuit in both directions, there are rewarding out-and-back expeditions to be made clockwise to the wide open snowfields above Champoussin, beyond Morgins, and anticlockwise to the Hauts-Forts runs above Avoriaz.

FOR BEGINNERS
Inconvenient slopes
The nursery slopes are fine, but they are in an inconvenient position up at Super-Châtel. Near-beginners not wanting tuition have some nice runs around Super-Châtel and nearby Tour de Don, and there's some gentle skiing above Pré-la-Joux.

FOR CROSS-COUNTRY
Pretty, if low, trails
There are plenty of pretty trails along the river and through the woods on the lower slopes of Linga (42km), but snow-cover can be a problem.

QUEUES
Lots of bottlenecks can occur
Queues vary enormously according to conditions and time of year. Given good snow in January, there are no problems apart from a couple of bottlenecks in Avoriaz. Poor conditions from February onwards can cause major delays. Beginners can face bad queues to get down from Super-Châtel, and skiers getting to and from Avoriaz face constant delays en route. Pré-la-Joux is a particular black spot.

MOUNTAIN RESTAURANTS
Variable
There are atmospheric chalets to be found, notably a couple at Plaine Dranse (Chez Crépy is recommended for cold days – there is a wood fire next to the bar) and further afield in the Marmottes-Lindarets section close to Avoriaz. The Perdix Blanche down at Pré-la-Joux scarcely counts as a mountain restaurant, but is nevertheless an attractive spot for lunch. Beginners have the very pleasant, if pricey, Chalet Neuf at Super-Châtel.

SKI SCHOOL
Diminishing complaints
Ski teaching in Châtel seems to be settling down, after a period in which the local schools seemed to be putting more effort into undermining British ski instructors working here than on the more productive business of raising their own standards.

FACILITIES FOR CHILDREN
Increasingly sympathetic
The Marmottons nursery has good facilities including toboggans, painting, music and videos. It used to have a reputation for harshness that British clients found difficult to come to terms with, but to judge by recent reports the increasing level of British business in Châtel has led to a softening of the regime – and good English is said to be spoken.

⬆ Staying there

Frequent free ski buses link the two valley lift stations. The Super-Châtel station is close to the village centre and can be reached on foot from much of the accommodation. The Linga gondola is a bus-ride for even the most determined of walkers. Snow conditions permitting, it is possible to ski back to town from Super-Châtel and Linga. The most convenient place to stay is close to the Super-Châtel lifts. The nursery slopes are served by these lifts, and timid intermediates are likely to prefer the skiing towards Morgins. A central position also has its advantages for skiers aiming for the more challenging skiing of Linga and Avoriaz: getting on the navette here may add a few minutes to your journey, but at least you get a seat before the bus gets overcrowded.

GETTING THERE

Air Geneva, transfer 1½hr.

Rail Thonon les Bains (42km).

PACKAGES

Alpine Expressions, Chalets 'Unlimited', Enterprise, Freedom, French Impressions, Made to Measure, MasterSki, Ski Addiction, Ski Club of GB, Ski Partners, SkiBound, Sloping Off, Snowise, Thomson, Trail Alpine, Travelscene Ski-Drive

ACTIVITIES

Indoor Swimming pool, bowling, cinema, mini-golf, library
Outdoor Skating rink, para-gliding, horse-drawn carriage rides, helicopter rides, dog-sledding, snow-shoe excursions

TOURIST OFFICE

Postcode 74390
Tel 010 33 50732244
Fax 50732287

HOW TO GO
A wide choice, including chalets

Although this is emphatically a French resort, the days are long gone when packages from Britain were difficult to track down.

Chalets Although a fair number of operators have places here, most are one-chalet operations, often not well positioned and fairly simple. Thomson have one of the best places, though it's rather modern. A more traditional and comfortable chalet is run by the Ski Club of GB. Ski Addiction have the best-positioned chalet available, five minutes from the village centre and the Super-Châtel gondola. Skibound have a similarly simple place. A small chalet-hotel is available through Freedom, with en-suite facilities in every room.

Hotels Practically all of the hotels are 2-stars, mostly friendly chalets, wooden or at least partly wood-clad, and none of the trio of moderate 3-stars is particularly well placed.

££ Macchi Modern chalet, most central of the 3-stars.

££ Fleur de Neige Well maintained and welcoming old chalet on edge of centre; Grive Gourmande restaurant does about the best food in town.

£ Kandahar One for peace-lovers: a Logis, down by the river, a walkable distance from the centre.

Self-catering Many apartments here are privately-owned summer retreats, and standards vary even within one operator's allocation. Many of the better places are available through self-drive specialists. French Impressions have a good selection of traditional-style chalets. Two of the best are the Gelinotte – out of town but close to the Linga lifts and children's village, and Les Erines – central and close to the Super-Châtel gondola. Travelscene and Snowise also have a fair selection. The Thomson and Enterprise apartments are more simple and not so well positioned.

EATING OUT
Fair selection

There is an adequate number and range of restaurants. The Vieux Four has good nouvelle cuisine served in a pleasant traditional atmosphere, the Bonne Ménagère is a modest, good-value place, the Fiacre does good pizza, and out-of-town the Kitchen is worth the taxi ride for superb raclette in cosy surroundings. The Fleur de Neige hotel has a good restaurant.

APRES-SKI
All down to bars

Châtel is fairly lively at tea-time but gets quiet at night. Busy bars supply some atmosphere; the most popular place is the Isba video bar. The unsophisticated Slalom is another Brit haunt. La Godille – close to the Super-Châtel gondola and popular at tea-time – has a more French feel. Otherwise there's a bowling alley, and one of the cinemas shows English-language films a few times a week. The Dahu disco, just out of town on the road to Morgins, livens up at weekends.

FOR NON-SKIERS
Morzine is much better

Those with a car have some entertaining excursions available: Geneva, Thonon and Evian. Otherwise there is a little to do but take some pleasant walks along the river. The Portes du Soleil as a whole is less than ideal for non-skiers who like to meet skiing companions for lunch: skiers will probably want to have theirs in a different country.

La Chapelle-d'Abondance
1010m

This unspoilt, rustic farming community, complete with old church and friendly locals, is 5km along a beautiful valley from Châtel. It's had its own quiet little north-facing ski area of easy wooded runs for some years, but has recently been put on the PdS map by a new gondola and three chair-lifts that now link it to Torgon and, from there, Super-Châtel. This new section remains essentially only a spur of the PdS circuit. But, taken together with Chapelle's own little area, it is worth exploring – good at weekends when Châtel gets crowded.

Lack of English-speaking instructors is reported to be a big drawback to using the local ESF ski school, which also runs a ski kindergarten for 4-year-olds. There is no non-ski nursery. Nightlife is virtually non-existent: just a few quiet bars, a cinema and torchlit descents. However, there are a number of good, reasonably-priced restaurants, notably the Cornettes and the Alpage.

Enterprise have dropped this resort for the 1994/95 season; most accommodation has to be booked independently. The hotel L'Ensoleillé has been recommended. The Cornettes, Alpage and Chabi are other hotel options. Ski La Côte run a comfortable catered chalet in an old farmhouse. The Airelles apartments have received a favourable report.

La Clusaz 1100m

ORIENTATION

La Clusaz has one of the shortest transfer times from Geneva: it is only 50km away.

The resort is rather sprawling, with accommodation along a winding road as well as in the village centre. Lifts serve the several separate skiing sectors from different points, with pistes back to most areas of the village. Les Etages is a much smaller accommodation centre where two of the sectors meet. The lift pass also covers **Le Grand-Bornand**, a ten-minute bus-ride away. If the Col des Aravis is open, a day-trip by car to **Megève** is possible.

✔ Traditional mountain village, with character retained despite development into fairly major resort

✔ Fairly large, interesting ski area, best suited to beginners and intermediates

✔ Very French atmosphere

✔ Prices low by French resort standards

✔ Very short transfer time from Geneva and easy to reach by car from UK

✔ Attractive mountain restaurants

✘ Snow conditions unreliable because of low altitude

✘ Not enough challenges to keep good skiers happy for a week

Few other major French ski resorts are based around what is still, essentially, a genuine mountain village rather than a purpose-built resort. It exudes Gallic charm and atmosphere, despite its expansion in recent years. It is proud of its skiing heritage, the latest manifestation of which is local boy Edgar Grospiron, who won gold for bumps skiing at the Albertville Olympics.

Combine that with a fairly large, spread-out, mainly intermediate ski area with five separate interlinked sectors and you've got a good basis for an enjoyable, relaxed week, especially if you're a Francophile.

La Clusaz has one big problem – its height, or rather the lack of it. Together with a lack of substantial snowmaking facilities, this means that its lower slopes are often bare or in poor condition. Snowmaking was installed for last season, but the high natural snowfall meant that it wasn't tested to see how it will cope in poor conditions.

🏔 The resort

Until a few years ago La Clusaz was frequented almost entirely by the French. But it has now developed into a major international resort – for both summer and winter seasons.

The village is built at the junction of a number of narrow wooded valleys, which mean that it has had to grow in a rather rambling and sprawling way. But it has retained the charm of a genuine French mountain village and the planners have successfully avoided the monstrous architecture that has been inflicted on many other French resorts. The village has been developed around the original old stone and wooden chalet buildings and, for the most part, the new buildings have been built in similar style and blend in

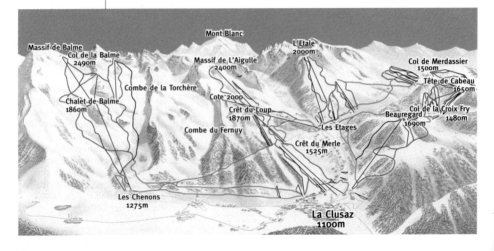

SKI FACTS

Altitude	1100m-2490m
Lifts	56
Pistes	130km
Green/Blue	71%
Red	25%
Black	4%
Artificial snow	1km

LIFT PASSES

94/95 prices in francs
La Clusaz pass
Covers all lifts in La Clusaz.
Beginners Points cards cover all lifts (60 points 97).
Main pass
1-day pass 135
6-day pass 680
Senior citizens
Over 60: 6-day pass 530 (22% off)
Children
Under 13: 6-day pass 530 (22% off)
Under 4: free pass
Short-term passes
2hr pass, half-day passes from 9am to 1pm and from 11am or 12.30 to the end of the day.
Notes Pass covers 40 lifts of Le Grand Bornand (6km away). Reductions for families, groups and holders of the Carte-Neige La Clusaz, which provides insurance cover and reductions in some shops.

well. The centre comes complete with large old church, fast-flowing mountain stream and a sympathetically designed modern shopping centre. Around this, narrow roads and alleys run in a confusing mixture of directions.

La Clusaz has a very friendly feel to it. The villagers welcome visitors every Monday evening in the main square with vin chaud and the local Reblochon cheese. There's a regular weekly market, and there are several typically French bars, ranging from the type you'd expect in any rural French village to modern ones with loud rock music.

For much of the season La Clusaz is a quiet and peaceful place for a holiday. But in peak season and at weekends the place can get packed out with French and Swiss families and the singles crowd. It is one of the most accessible resorts from Geneva – good for short transfer times but bad for crowds. And when the locals arrive in force, traffic and parking can be a problem.

✈ The skiing

Like the village, skiing at La Clusaz is rather spread out – which makes it all the more interesting. There are five main areas, each interconnecting with at least one of the others.

THE SKI AREA
Five interlinked areas

Several points in the village have lifts giving access to the predominantly west- and north-west facing slopes of the **Aiguille** mountain. From there you can ski to the **Balme** area on a choice of off-piste trail or easy green track. La Balme has the resort's highest skiing (normally the best snow) and a speed skiing track. From La Balme there are more woodland tracks which, perhaps with a bit of poling, take you back to the village.

Going the other way from L'Aiguille leads you to the **Étale** area via another choice of easy runs and the Transval cable-car, which has been built to shuttle skiers between the two areas in both directions. From the bottom of L'Étale, you can ski back along another path to the village and the cable-car up to the fourth skiing area of **Beauregard** which, as the name implies, has splendid views and catches a lot of sunshine.

From the top of Beauregard you can link via yet another easy piste and a two-way chair-lift with the fifth ski area of **Col de la Croix-Fry/Col de Merdassier/Manigod**. You can ski from here to L'Étale.

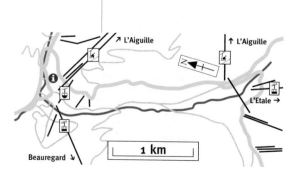

SKI SCHOOL

94/95 prices in francs

ESF
Classes 6 days
4hr: 9am–11am,
3pm–5pm
5 full days: 730
Children's classes
Ages: 5 to 12
5 full days: 527
Private lessons
Hourly
170 for 1 to 3 people;
220 for 4 to 5 people

CHILDCARE

The ESF runs a ski
kindergarten for
children aged 3 to 5,
at normal class hours.

The two all-day
kindergartens operate
8.30 to 6pm. The
Club des Mouflets
(50025060) offers
creative activities and
indoor games for non-
skiing children aged 8
months to 4 years,
with the babies
looked after in a
special section. The
Champions' Club
(50026092) takes
children aged 3 to 6
for indoor and
outdoor games, with
the option of skiing in
the ESF kindergarten
or (if over 5) in a
proper ESF class.

SNOW RELIABILITY
Poor on lower slopes

Most of the skiing is west or north-
west facing and tends to keep its snow
fairly well. That's fortunate because
most of it is below 2000m and there
are only three mobile snow cannon.
The best snow is usually at La Balme
where the north-west-facing slopes
reach over 2400m. The resort itself is
only just over 1000m and the runs
back can be tricky or bare when snow
is poor. The main lifts down from
Beauregard and Crêt du Merle will
carry skiers down as well as up.

FOR ADVANCED SKIERS
Limited

The best piste skiing for good skiers is
at La Balme, where a number of fairly
challenging runs lead from the top
lifts back down to the top of the
gondola. But the only black in the
area is the speed skiing piste which
leads right back down to the bottom.

On L'Aiguille, there are a couple of
good off-piste itineraires – the Combe
du Fernuy towards La Balme and the
Combe de Borderan towards Les
Etages. There's a black run down the
face of Beauregard that can be tricky
in poor snow conditions. And the red
run from the top of Étale is fairly steep
at the top.

Other than that, good skiers will
find La Clusaz skiing pretty tame.

FOR INTERMEDIATE SKIERS
Good if snow is good

Most intermediates will love La Clusaz
if the snow conditions are good. Early
intermediates will delight in the
gentle slopes at the top of Beauregard
and over on La Croix-Fry, where
there's a network of gentle tree-lined
runs. And they'll be able to travel all
over the area on the gentle green
linking pistes, where poling or walking
is more likely to be a problem than
any fears about steepness.

L'Étale and L'Aiguille have more
challenging but wide blue runs. The
best snow is usually on the top half of
the mountains here.

More adventurous intermediates will
prefer the steeper red slopes and good
snow of La Balme, from the top of
which there are wonderful views. This
is a fairly substantial area with good
lifts (a high-capacity gondola from the
bottom linking to a fast quad chair).

FOR BEGINNERS
Splendid beginner slopes

The best nursery slopes are up the
mountain at the top of the Beauregard
cable-car and at Crêt du Merle. The
Beauregard area has lovely gentle
green runs to progress to, including
one long run round the mountain
right back to the village.

FOR CROSS-COUNTRY
Excellent

La Clusaz has much better cross-
country facilities than many resorts,
with a total of 70km of loops of
varying difficulty. The main area is
near the lake at Les Confins, reached
by bus. There's also a lovely area at the
top of the Beauregard cable-car.

QUEUES
Not a problem

Except on peak weekends or if the
lower slopes are shut because of snow
shortage, lift queues aren't a problem.
The worst bottleneck used to be the
top half of La Balme. But the slow old
chair was replaced by a fast quad for
last season.

MOUNTAIN RESTAURANTS
High standard

Mountain restaurants are one of the
resort's strong points. There are lots of
them and, for the most part, they are
rustic and charming, and serve good,
reasonably priced – often Savoyard –
food. The Vieux Ferme at Merdassier is
charming and excellent value. The
Vieux Chalet, just above the top of the
gondola from the village, serves
excellent food and is very civilised and
quiet but expensive. The Crêt du
Merle restaurants are atmospheric and
good. The Crêt du Loup is less so but
has good vin chaud and splendid
views. The restaurant by the cross-
country circuit at Beauregard is sunny
and peaceful, with good food and
views.

SKI SCHOOL
Mixed reports

There are tales of large classes and
poor instruction in group lessons, but
we've heard from some satisfied
customers too – especially those who
took private lessons.

FACILITIES FOR CHILDREN
Excellent – in theory

The childcare arrangements seem
carefully considered, but we lack first-
hand reports. The resort is one where
families can feel at home – provided
they keep away from the traffic.

GETTING THERE

Air Geneva, transfer 1½hr. Lyon, transfer 2½hr.

PACKAGES

French Impressions, Made to Measure, Martin Brodier, Over the Hill, Sally, Silver Ski, Ski Aravis, Ski Valkyrie, Ski Weekend, SkiBound, Stena Sealink

Le Grand-Bornand
Headwater

ACTIVITIES

Indoor Various hotels have saunas, massage, jacuzzi, weights room, aerobics, sun beds and swimming pools **Outdoor** Para-gliding, hang-gliding, micro-light flights, snow-shoe excursions, snowmobile rides, winter walks

TOURIST OFFICE

Postcode 74220
Tel 010 33 50026092
Fax 50025982

 # Staying there

Much of the accommodation is a fair walk from an access lift to the skiing and the bus system is somewhat erratic. It's best to stay close to the start of one of the main access lifts near the centre of town.

HOW TO GO
Decreasing choice of packages

If you're set on La Clusaz, book early: last season's good snow led to demand for packages far outstripping supply. And Enterprise and Crystal have recently dropped the resort, severely reducing the choice of packages, particularly if you're going by plane or train (drivers have a wider selection). A car is useful around the resort, and the drive from the Channel is a relatively short one.

Chalets Ski Aravis have a high-standard farmhouse conversion with all mod cons, including en-suite rooms, well located close to the village centre and lifts. A cosy open-fired, exposed-beamed old chalet is available through Martin Brodier. The Silver Ski chalet is on the slopes and offers good value; it's not well placed for the village but is ski-convenient if there is resort-level snow. Towards the bottom end of the market, SkiBound have a place that is well positioned for the nursery slopes.

Hotels Small, friendly 2-star family hotels are the mainstay of the resort.
£££ Beauregard Best in town – comfortable, big by local standards; on the fringe of the village. Pool.
£££ Croix-Fry In a peaceful spot with good views, just beyond the col of the same name, on the fringe of the ski area – a rare French example of a really cosy, rustic chalet.
£££ Alp'Hôtel Comfortable modern chalet close to the centre, with one of the better restaurants. Pool.
£££ Alpen Roc Big but stylish, central and comfortable, with excellent well equipped bedrooms. Pool.
££ Vieux Chalet In a splendid piste-side setting overlooking the village, this is a favourite spot for lunch and dinner and has a handful of pleasant rooms. The food is probably the best in town.
££ Christiania Traditional, simple family hotel in the centre. Quiet, small rooms, and decent food.
Self-catering Martin Brodier have a very old chalet sold as a single booking to self-caters. It's fairly simple but charming and very well placed – just off the main square close

to the village gondola. French Impressions also have little self-catering chalets; one sleeps four. The one out near the Etale cable car, 2km from town, is best: spacious, open fire, views, garage, and pine-clad.

EATING OUT
Good choice

There's a wide choice of restaurants in town, with a number of others a short drive away, including the Vieux Chalet, which probably does the best food in the resort – traditional and modern. La Caleche and St Jacques are also good. L'Ecuelle is the place to go for good seafood, or steak that you cook yourself on a little brazier on the table. The Beau Site and Val d'Or hotels and La Dent Creuse are other mid-range restaurants worth a try. Chez Georges, La Cordee and L'Outa are unpretentious places that have been recommended for their great value for money. At the other end of the price scale is the fairly formal Symphonie restaurant in the hotel Beauregard.

APRES-SKI
Very quiet except at weekends

La Clusaz is a typically quiet French family resort during the week, but weekenders liven it up appreciably. Le Pressoir is a focal bar, popular for its skiing videos and draught Guinness. The Salto and Montmartre bars are other animated haunts. L'Ecluse disco has a gimmick that brings in the customers despite its very high prices: the glass dance-floor has a floodlit stream running beneath it. (There is no early evening entrance reduction.) The other two discos are cheaper but by no means inexpensive.

Other entertainments include floodlit skiing and ice-skating, and there's a cinema.

FOR NON-SKIERS
Quite good

The village is a pleasant enough place for strolling around, though the traffic can be quite annoying. It's easy to get to several different mountain restaurants for lunch. There are good walks along the valleys and a day in Annecy is a pleasant excursion.

STAYING UP THE MOUNTAIN
Cheap and panoramic

The Relais de l'Aiguille at Crêt du Loup has five adequate bedrooms that are about the cheapest in the resort.

Les Contamines 1160m

✔ *Traditional unspoilt French village*

✔ *Fair-sized intermediate ski area*

✔ *Very good snow record for its height and position*

✔ *Mont Blanc lift pass covers several other nearby resorts, easily reachable by road*

✘ *Limited local skiing for experts and beginners*

✘ *Not for nightlife lovers*

✘ *Ski area a bus-ride from main village*

✘ *Can be some lengthy queues*

Les Contamines is an unspoilt, traditional, typically French village complete with pretty wooden chalets, ornate church and reasonable prices (typical of rural France rather than upmarket international ski resorts). There is an interesting selection of local as well as tourist shops and a weekly market in the village square. Its local ski area offers substantial, surprisingly-snowsure intermediate terrain. It is included in the Mont Blanc area lift pass, which also covers neighbouring resorts such as Chamonix, Megève and Courmayeur. A good base for Francophiles, especially those travelling by car.

ORIENTATION

Les Contamines is set towards the end of a dead-end valley up from **St-Gervais** and just over the hill from the **Megève** ski area. The old village is separated from its ski area and a small newer development by a river and a lengthy walk or short bus-ride. The main gondola goes up from Le Lay, and a further one from Le Pontet a little further up the valley.

The resort

The village is compact, stretching 300m along the 'dead-end' valley road. Unfortunately the lifts are a long walk or short bus-ride out of the centre at Le Lay. There is some accommodation next to the main lift at Le Lay, but staying in this uninspiring spot seems to defeat the purpose of choosing charming Les Contamines for a holiday. Having a car is useful for getting to the lifts and to the other Mont Blanc resorts. The Mont Blanc lift pass does, however, give free access to the local ski bus (otherwise FF8 a trip) and the buses to other resorts.

The skiing

A reasonably efficient ski bus connects Les Contamines with its main lift-station, from where a two-stage gondola climbs up to the **ski area** above a small, narrow, wooded section of pistes returning to the valley lifts. Another gondola leads from a little

further up the valley. Above these, a sizeable network of open, largely north-facing pistes fans out from Le Signal. You can drop over the ridge at Col du Joly (2000m) to a series of south-facing runs. When these pistes are skiable, the ski area totals a respectable 120km. In bad weather, head for St-Gervais because there are few trees in the Les Contamines ski area except on the paths home.

A high proportion of the runs are above 1800m and north- or north-east-facing, and the mass of Mont Blanc is said to trigger heavy snowfalls, making for reliable **snow conditions**. People are often bussed in to here when neighbouring resorts such as Megève are short of snow. The lower pistes have had snowmakers installed.

The steep western section has a number of black runs which are enjoyable but not terribly challenging for **advanced skiers**. And some south-facing pistes are heavily moguled. But the main attraction of the local area is the substantial off-piste potential in good snow conditions – do take a guide, though.

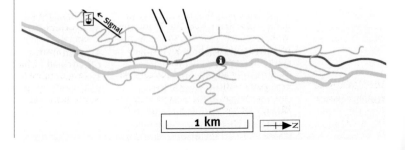

SKI FACTS

Altitude	1165m-2487m
Lifts	26
Pistes	120km
Green/Blue	37%
Red	40%
Black	23%
Artificial snow	3km

SKI TOTAL

helped us to compile the eating out and après-ski sections. Our thanks to them.

PACKAGES

Bigfoot, Chalets 'Unlimited', Ski Total, Superski

TOURIST OFFICE

Postcode 74170
Tel 010 33 50470158
Fax 50470954

You also have the other resorts covered by the Mont Blanc lift pass to explore – the Chamonix area has some of the most demanding skiing in Europe. The black runs are perfectly manageable for good **intermediates**. Much of the rest of the skiing is ideal for average intermediate skiers. The easiest of the runs are probably those down from the top-station to the mid-station of the gondola, but most of the red runs higher up the mountain have blue alternatives.

Given good snow, the nursery area in the village itself is adequate for **beginners**. There are other small areas, with short, beginner lifts, at the mid-station and top of the gondola. But there are no long greens to progress to.

There are **cross-country** trails of varying difficulty totalling 29km.

Queues can be a problem at times – especially when skiers are being bussed in from other resorts. The wait for the gondola up at the morning peak (and down at the end of the day when snow is poor on the lower runs) can be considerable. Some of the drags and chairs higher up can have queues, but these are being reduced by the introduction of more fast quad chairs, with another arriving this season.

There are some lovely rustic **mountain restaurants**, the best of which the lift company wickedly leaves off the piste map because it doesn't own them. La Ferme du Ruelle on the south-facing slopes is a jolly barn with good Savoyard food. Chalet du Col du Joly has panoramic views and friendly service. L'Etape at the mid-station of the gondola is in a pleasantly wooded spot, doubles as a hotel and has a children's play area. Best of all are two tiny, cosy chalets – the Roselette and the Buche Croisée.

We have had mixed reports on the organisation and standard of English in the **ski school**. One or two parents have thought their children's classes too strict and overcrowded. Excursions are organised each week to other resorts, including a guided group to do the famous Vallée Blanche down to Chamonix.

There is a non-ski nursery open all day for **children** aged 1 to 7, and the ski school takes children from the age of 4. The youngest have a pleasantly-sheltered kindergarten area conveniently adjacent to the main ski area's mid-station. At least one interested observer rates these facilities highly, but the standard of English is probably unreliable.

↑ Staying there

The only operator running **chalets** in Les Contaminas is Ski Total. They feature two separate, good-value chalet units within the one rustic building and provide a free shuttle bus to the slopes.

There are a dozen modest **hotels**, with only the Chemenaz, just 200m from the lifts, managing 3-star status. The Chamois is a popular 2-star, with a ski-bus stop outside the door and a sauna and jacuzzi. Good-value cheaper places include the Christiana, the

Moranches and Gai Soleil (a Logis).

The Hameau du Lay **self-catering** apartments are pleasant and are close to the lifts.

Après-ski is quiet. There are several very French bars and restaurants. As well as Savoyard specialities such as fondue and raclette, there are good pizzas, crêpes and classic French cooking. Locals assure us that the Bohème, the Husky and Colombaz are good restaurants. We've also had recommended to us the Trabla, the Air du Temps and the Op Traken. At tea-time Ty Briez is an atmospheric little crèperie, and it becomes a drinks rendezvous later. Brasserie de Rhodos is a pleasant spot for early evening jazz. The Tetras Pub and the Saxo, both at the gondola base station, are popular with the young crowd at tea-time. Later, the Cressoua is one of the more animated bars. The Igloo is the livelier of the two discos.

Options are limited for non-driving **non-skiers**. There are good walks and a natural ice-rink, but St-Gervais (10 minutes away by bus), Megève (25 minutes) and Chamonix (40 minutes) have a lot more to offer. You can take a train ride up from St-Gervais on the Mont Blanc tramway.

Courchevel 1300m–1850m

HOW IT RATES

The skiing

Snow	****
Extent	*****
Advanced	****
Intermediates	*****
Beginners	*****
Convenience	****
Queues	****
Restaurants	****

The rest

Scenery	***
Resort charm	**
Not skiing	***

✔ Very extensive, varied local skiing for all grades, as well as being part of one of the biggest linked ski areas in the world; unequalled easy runs for near-beginners

✔ Very impressive lift system; few queues, and easy links to other areas

✔ Excellent piste maintenance, and widespread use of snowmakers

✔ Wooded lower slopes give useful options in bad weather

✔ Ski-in ski-out convenience for much of the accommodation

✘ Generally characterless villages

✘ Lack of après-ski and atmosphere except for 1850

✘ Expensive, particularly the ultra-pricey 1850

✘ Little to do but ski

Courchevel is chic, pricey and the favourite place of the Paris jet set, who fly directly in to its own airport. But unlike many other smart places, it has excellent skiing. Its slopes are the most extensive, varied and immaculately groomed of the whole Trois Vallées. Many who visit are content to ski the Courchevel sector alone. It has everything, from gentle greens to narrow couloirs, with plenty of blues, reds, black mogul fields – and tree-lined runs for bad weather too.

Courchevel also has good access to the rest of the Trois Vallées skiing; getting to Val-Thorens at the opposite end can be almost as quick as it is from Méribel. Only Mottaret is better placed, in the centre of the lift system.

The downside is the resort itself. Only in certain points, away from the centre, is it pleasant to behold. And there's surprisingly little night-time animation.

ORIENTATION

Courchevel consists of four satellite villages (five if you include newly-built La Tania) widely scattered around the lower fringes of the north-eastern end of the Trois Vallées. The resorts are named after the altitudes at which they are set. A road connects 1850 with 1300 via 1650 and 1550. 1850 is the focal resort, having direct lift and piste links with 1300 and 1550, though all five centres have gondolas up into the main area. 1650 lies at the periphery, from where the skiing spreads west above the other villages to the link with **Méribel** and **Mottaret. St-Martin-de-Belleville, Les Menuires** and **Val-Thorens** are reached on skis via the Méribel-Mottaret valley. **Champagny** (La Plagne ski area) and **Valmorel** are easy road outings.

🏠 The resort

Courchevel is made up of four villages known by their altitudes (and nearby La Tania). They are sufficiently different from one another to make choosing the correct resort quite important. **1850** is by far the largest, and is very much the focal point of the area. It is certainly the place to stay if you're looking for nightlife or what few non-skiing facilities are available. 1850 is self-consciously très chic, with some of the highest prices in the Alps. Style is radiated by the rich clientele rather than the village itself, which is a messy sprawl that has surprising amounts of traffic and associated fumes.

A number of chalets and hotels are pleasantly sited among the trees that surround the village – ideal for skiing to the door but making evening trips into town a bit of a trek. The most convenient place to stay is close to the main lift station and the new Forum sports and accommodation complex.

1650 is less pleasant on the eye, and has little in the way of facilities. It is the most remotely sited of the villages.

This has pros and cons. It is not as convenient for skiing the Trois Vallées as 1850, but early intermediates and beginners will love the quietness of the local ski area. A bus service offers a useful link to 1850, giving access to nightlife and removing the need to catch the 1650 access lifts at the end of the day. The village is so small that all accommodation is close to the lifts.

1550 is a very quiet, featureless resort, a gondola ride or short ski beneath 1850. It has the advantage of having essentially the same position in the ski area as 1850, with much cheaper accommodation and restaurants. However, once skiing is finished, the village is isolated from 1850. Although small, it's a scattered place, with some accommodation a fair way from the gondola.

1300 (often called Le Praz) is the most attractive of the resorts. It's a traditional village set amid woodland, although the charm factor has been undermined by recent expansion triggered by the Olympics, including the building of the Olympic ski jump. It's still a quiet place with good links into the skiing above 1850, and has the advantage of tree-lined slopes on

SKI FACTS

Altitude 1300m-2740m
Lifts   200
Pistes   600km
Green/Blue   49%
Red   37%
Black   14%
Artificial snow   60km

LIFT PASSES

94/95 prices in francs
Three Valleys
Covers all lifts of
Courchevel, Méribel,
Les Menuires,
Val-Thorens and
St-Martin-de-Belleville
and buses in
Courchevel only.
Beginners 13 free lifts
in the Courchevel
valley.
Main pass
1-day pass 210
6-day pass 1010
(low season 910 –
10% off)
Senior citizens
Over 60: 6-day pass
760 (25% off)
Over 80: free pass
Children
Under 16: 6-day pass
760 (25% off)
Under 5: free pass
Short-term passes
Half-day pass (from
12.30) covers 66 lifts
in Courchevel valley
only.
Notes Over 70s get a
50% discount on
main pass price.
6-day pass and over
valid for one day each
in Tignes-Val-d'Isère,
La-Plagne-Les Arcs,
Pralognan-la-Vanoise
and Les-Saises.
Alternative passes
Premières Neiges
covers Courchevel
and Méribel for first 2
weeks of the season
(6 day pass 649).
Vallée de Courchevel
(6 day pass 827)
covers 66 lifts in
Courchevel.

its doorstep for bad-weather skiing. 1300 does not have a ski school, unlike the other villages, and being at the foot of quite steep, often icy slopes is not suitable for beginners.

The new accommodation centre of **La Tania** is nearby, and essentially has the same pros and cons as 1300 without any pretension to traditional village charm – it's purely a quiet, small, purpose-built base with lower prices than Courchevel.

⛷ The skiing

There are three sections to the local ski area, though everywhere is so well linked that it is essentially just one big network. The central 1850 section is suitable for all, the wooded 1300 area is best for good skiers, while 1650 has mainly very easy skiing. It is possible to ski back to all the villages, but the runs to 1300 can close due to lack of snow. Courchevel's skiing is a high-class operation. Piste maintenance is superb, snowmakers abundant and lifts modern, fast and comfortable. The ski area is also very well laid out. The main complaint we've had is that many people find the piste map hard to follow because it is too small.

THE SKI AREA
Highly interesting

The **1850** section is the largest, with a great network of lifts and pistes spreading out from the village, which is very much the focal point. The Verdons gondola, followed by a very efficient cable-car, transports skiers rapidly up to **La Saulire** (2740m), one of the two setting-off points for Méribel and all points to Val-Thorens. It is also possible to take several routes from here to the 1650 section.

The second of the Méribel departure points is **Col de la Loze**, reached by gondola and chair-lift from 1850. The top of the gondola is also the access point for the La Tania skiing and runs down to 1300.

The wooded area above **1300** is splendid when snow is in good supply, but unfortunately all but one of the lifts on this part of the mountain are of the bottom-to-top variety with no mid-station. Consequently, when runs to 1300 and La Tania are incomplete, the only pistes remaining open are those serviced by the Bouc Blanc drag.

The **1650** area is the most isolated; getting from 1650 to the Méribel or the woodland skiing above 1300 and La Tania is a round about business.

In some ski areas – for example Verbier or the Portes du Soleil – skiers need to check their watches constantly when skiing far afield. This isn't such a problem here: as long as you make the last gondola up from Méribel, you can ski all the way home from La Saulire to 1850, 1550 and 1330. 1650 skiers need an extra five minutes to make the Chanrossa or Roc Mugnier chairs.

A new piste has been built this year especially for snowboarders, between Renards and Verdons.

SNOW RELIABILITY
Very good

Courchevel's snow is often much better than neighbouring Méribel's because many of its slopes are north- or north-east-facing. The combination of this, its height, an abundance of snowmakers and excellent piste maintenance usually guarantees reliable skiing down to at least the 1850 and 1650 villages, and Bouc Blanc (1680m) above La Tania.

FOR ADVANCED SKIERS
Some black gems

Tough runs make up only a small proportion of the skiing. It's certainly not in the same league as Chamonix, Val-d'Isère or St Anton for steep expert terrain. But there is plenty to interest good skiers. The Saulire cable-car gives access to Courchevel's three famed couloirs which, though not terrifyingly narrow or very long, are certainly steep – especially the Téléphérique. Running parallel to these is a fine black from La Vizelle to Les Verdons. The Vizelle gondola also accesses the Suisses black. The quite difficult Chanrossa run is also nearby. For a change of scene, a couple of long blacks cut through trees from the top of the Chenus gondola to 1300.

The best off-piste is close to the black runs, in both the Chanrossa and Chenus areas. However, it's not an area for real powder hounds. You are never far from a piste, and new snow gets quickly and heavily skied.

Good skiers also have the rest of the Trois Vallées to race around.

FOR INTERMEDIATE SKIERS
Paradise for all levels

All grades of intermediate skiers love Courchevel. Less experienced skiers have wonderful long runs above 1650 in the Pyramide-Grand Bosses areas. Pralong, close to the airport, also has fine easy runs.

Average skiers can negotiate most of the red runs without too much

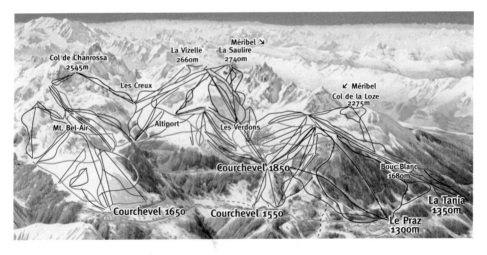

difficulty. Our favourite is the long, sweeping Combe de la Saulire run down from top to bottom of the cable-car. This is especially pleasant first thing in the morning, when it is immaculately groomed and free of crowds. The Bouc Blanc runs through the trees towards La Tania are also particularly attractive. This section also has fine red runs down to the 1850 area, with easier blues running alongside. The Marmottes and Creux area behind La Vizelle have some of the most challenging intermediate pistes, which can get quite bumpy – and crowded with ski school groups.

Excursions to Méribel and the rest of the Trois Vallées can be undertaken by all intermediates. Less adventurous skiers should go via Col de la Loze.

FOR BEGINNERS
Great graduation runs

There are excellent nursery slopes above both 1650 and 1850. At the former, lessons are likely to begin on the short drags close to the village, but quick learners will soon be able to ski from close to the top of 1650 area all the way down to the village. The Pralong area, near the altiport, is another fine nursery area. An easy green links this area with the skiing above 1650, so adventurous novices have the opportunity to move far afield. The green runs down into 1850 from various directions are also fun but, being important linking runs, tend to get crowded. 1550 has a tiny nursery area, but a gondola swiftly transports skiers up to 1850.

Selected chalets in Courchevel

Selected chalets in Courchevel

SKI SCHOOL
94/95 prices in francs

ESF in 1850
Classes 6 days
5hr: 9.30am-noon and
2.30-5pm; 2½hr: am
or pm
6 full days: 935
Children's classes
Ages: from 4
6 full days: 725
Private lessons
2½hr morning, 2hr
lunchtime, 2½hr
afternoon, 7hr full day
1400 for full day, for
1 to 4 people

ESF in 1650
Classes 6 days
4½hr: 9.30am-noon
and 2.45-4.45; am
(2½hr) or pm (2hr)
6 full days: 840
Children's classes
Ages: from 3
6 full day: 670
Private lessons
2½hr morning, 2hr
lunchtime, 2hr
afternoon, 7hr full day
1400 for full day, for
1 to 6 people

ESF in 1550
Classes 6 days
3hr: am or pm
6 mornings: 680
Children's classes
Ages: from 3
6 mornings: 590
Private lessons
3hr morning, 3hr
afternoon, 7hr full day
1300 for full day, for
1 to 6 people

Ski Academy
New French ski school

Ski Masterclass
British-run ski school

FOR CROSS-COUNTRY
Long wooded trails
All the villages have some cross-country, but 1300 is by far the most suitable, with trails through the woods towards 1550, 1850 and Méribel. Given sufficient snow there are also several loops around the village.

QUEUES
Superb lift system copes well
Even at New Year and Easter, when 1850 in particular positively teems with skiers, queues are minimal thanks to the excellence of the lift system. Only the huge La Saulire cable-car (for which the queue moves very quickly) is likely to have any delays. The Verdons gondola has had its capacity doubled, alleviating this old bottleneck. However, Courchevel skiers should remember that the lift home from Mottaret at the end of the day can become over-subscribed.

MOUNTAIN RESTAURANTS
Very expensive
Mountain restaurants are plentiful by French purpose-built resort standards, though prices are high. Snacks, chips and drinks are particularly expensive. The plat du jour tends to be better value if your budget can stretch to it. The self-service restaurant at the airport is good value by local standards, with good food and a fine terrace well placed for watching aircraft. The Verdon restaurant is in a pretty situation, serves good value food and is well placed for skier watching. Le Casserole, above 1650 at the foot of the Grandes Bosses drags, is a good self-service place. The Chalet de Pierre, on the Verdons piste above 1850, has been highly commended by several reporters for serving some of the best French food in the area, albeit at a very high price. A trip down to the Bistrot du Praz at 1300 is recommended for a gourmet blow-out on a bad-weather day.

SKI SCHOOL
Masterclass praised
The Courchevel ESF is the largest ski school in Europe, with bases at 1850, 1650 and 1550. With 480 instructors, it is not surprising that classes are usually small. The 1850 school has a mixed reputation for group lessons due to the poor English of many of its instructors. In contrast, the 1550 school is well liked for providing exclusively English-speaking classes in the afternoon.

We've had rave reviews about Masterclass – a ski school run by British instructors. 'Probably the best around ... anywhere' is a typical comment. Lessons are short (two hours) but intensive, and appear best suited to intermediates who want to push themselves. However, even this school had a few poor reports, mostly from beginners stuck in with second years when the school was short of instructors due to sickness.

Leisurely skiers may prefer Ski Academy, which one reporter states are more into fun-orientated lessons. Both they and the ESF in each village also provide special courses such as moguls, wedelling, style, off-piste and Trois Vallées tours.

FACILITIES FOR CHILDREN
British families don't use them?
None of our reporters has tried the resort ski kindergartens and children's ski classes; an in-house chalet crèche with British nannies is an alternative that many families have found more attractive. The Simply Ski operation in 1300 has been recommended, and in 1850 there is Ski Scott Dunn. Bladon Lines are also in 1850, and lay on free private nannies to groups booking whole chalets (eight or more beds) out of high season – first come, first served. Family specialists Ski Esprit have several chalets and two crèches in 1300, and this year are introducing their own Ski Sprites ski classes – specially contracted instructors, and a class size limited to eight children.

 Staying there

All the resorts are convenient for the skiing. So the choice of which to go for depends on how much importance you attach to nightlife (1850 best), charm (1300 best) or the quality and price of your accommodation.

HOW TO GO
Value chalets and apartments
Huge numbers of British tour operators go to Courchevel, with a wide choice of accommodation.
Chalets There are plenty of chalets available. Though some are expensive, few are particularly luxurious. You're paying for the privilege of staying in a top resort. However, chalets represent good value compared to the very expensive hotels.

Simply Ski's exceptionally smart Ancolies, in 1850, is elegantly furnished, and comes with numerous mod cons and cordon bleu cooking. It's initially sold as a single booking to groups, but can be available by the

GETTING THERE

Air Geneva, transfer 3½hr. Lyon, transfer 3½hr. Chambery, transfer 2½hr. Direct flights to Courchevel altiport from London at weekends only (contact tourist office for details)

Rail Moûtiers (24km); transfer by bus or taxi.

PACKAGES

Airtours, Alpine Expressions, Bigfoot, Bladon Lines, Chalets 'Unlimited', Cresta Ski France, Crystal, Enterprise, Finlays, FlexiSki, French Impressions, Go Worlds Apart, Inghams, Lagrange, Le Ski, Lotus Supertravel, Made to Measure, Mark Warner, Neilson, Powder Byrne, Sally, Silver Ski, Simply Ski, Ski Activity, Ski Equipe, Ski Esprit, Ski Les Alpes, Ski Olympic, Ski Savoie, Ski Scott Dunn, Ski Val, Ski West, Ski Wyatt, SkiBound, Stena Sealink, Superski, Travelscene Ski-Drive

La Tania Crystal, Enterprise, Inghams, Neilson, Stena Sealink

CHILDCARE

There are kindergartens in 1850 (79080847) and 1650 (79083584) which take children from age 2, until 5pm. The ESF branches in all three main parts of the resort have ski kindergartens; minimum age is 3 in 1550 (79082107) and 1650 (79082608) and 4 in 1850 (79080772).

room as a late booking. The same company also have a selection of much cheaper but very attractive places in 1850 and 1300.

FlexiSki offer a couple of contrasting places in 1850. There's a spacious luxury duplex a stone's throw from the main lift station, and a classic little wooden hut, full of character, among the trees on the Bellecôte piste into town.

Lotus Supertravel have one of the biggest and best selections, with all nine of their chalets well positioned and comfortable. We've had a particularly complimentary report of their Maisonnée apartment-based chalet. Ski Scott Dunn have several expensive chalets full of creature comforts.

Bladon Lines also have a good selection a little lower down the market. The cheapest, best-value places are in the lower villages.

Le Ski have a fine selection in 1650, most of which we've heard good things about. Finlays have a good reputation in 1550; Crystal have places in all parts, with particularly cheap options in 1300; Neilson and Crystal provide very good value in La Tania. All the chalets of family specialists Ski Esprit are in 1300.

There are also plenty of chalet-hotels available. Ski Val and Ski Activity share the superbly positioned, cheap and cheerful Tournier. Their Ski Lodge is rather rough and ready but offers an important budget option in 1850. Party animals should consider Ski Olympic's Avals in 1650. One reporter raves about the evening entertainment, which included fancy dress and even Sumo!

Hotels There are nearly 50 hotels in Courchevel, mostly at 1850. Three-quarters of these are graded 3-star and above, though some would have lower ratings in other countries.

££££ Chabichou (1850) The only French ski resort hotel with two Michelin stars. Big, beautiful bedrooms to match.

££££ Grandes Alpes (1850) In pole position, on the piste right next to the main lifts.

£££ Courcheneige (1850) Pleasantly informal, large chalet on the piste above the resort.

£££ Ducs de Savoie (1850) Pleasant, wood-built; well placed in the trees for skiing to the door, but only five minutes' walk from the village.

£££ Sivoliere (1850) No beauty, but charming and comfortable inside and pleasantly set among pines.

£££ Golf (1650) Pleasant, good value

3-star, in a superb position on the piste next to the gondola station.

££ Chanrossa (1550) This attractive 2-star is a friendly, well placed hotel.

££ Peupliers (1300) Well placed and cheap by local standards.

Self-catering There's a large selection of apartments, though high-season packages can get sold out early. Neilson have an allocation of above-average apartments in the superbly positioned new Forum complex, some of which are very large. Inghams have good apartments at the foot of the slopes in 1650, perfect for families.

Ski Val's accommodation in 1850 is basic but has a great position – at a bargain price. Crystal have good, attractively priced places in La Tania.

EATING OUT
You pay for quality

Restaurants are, in the main, high in quality and super-high in price. Self-caterers on a budget may be forced to cook for themselves when they want to or not! A raclette shared between two is one of the better-value meals.

Among the best, and priciest, restaurants are the Michelin 2-stars Chabichou and Bateau Ivre in 1850. The Bercail also has a high reputation, notably for good seafood, but many staying in the big resort venture to the other villages in search of lower prices. The Chanrossa hotel restaurant and the Cortona pizza place in 1550 are good value by local standards. Also recommended are the Lizard and the Plouc (for eat-in or take-away pizza) at 1650. Bistrot du Praz in 1300 is pricey but excellent.

APRES-SKI
1850 has it

If you want nightlife, it's got to be 1850. There are some exclusive night clubs, such as the Dakota, L'Equipe, New-St-Nicholas, Bergerie and Grange, with top Paris cabaret acts and sky-high prices. Jacques, L'Arbe and the basic, but inexpensive by local standards, Potinière are the most popular bars. The Chabichou piano bar is good for a quiet drink.

The Croisette cinema has a couple of English-language films each week. Concerts take place from time to time.

The lower villages are fairly dead, though buses run late enough for cinema and bar excursions to 1850, and the 1650 scene has improved in recent years. Its Signal bar is friendly, full of French and renowned for its views at the back and its incredibly strong Mutzig. Le Plouc is an intimate,

ACTIVITIES

Indoor Artificial skating rink, bridge, chess, squash, swimming and saunas (hotels), gymnasium, health and fitness centres (swimming pools, sauna, steam-room, jacuzzi, water therapy, weight-training, massage), bowling, exhibitions (galleries in 1850 and 1650), cinema, games rooms, billiards, language courses
Outdoor Hang-gliding, para-gliding, flying lessons, parachuting, floodlit skiing, ski jumping, toboggan runs, snow-shoe excursions, snowmobile rides, dog-sleigh rides, 35km cleared paths, 2½km toboggan run, curling, ice-climbing, flight excursions

TOURIST OFFICE

Postcode 73122
Tel 010 33 79080029
Fax 79083354

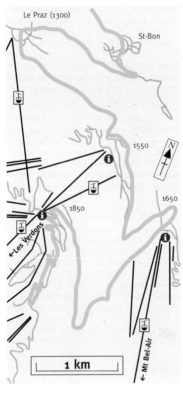

welcoming French bar with good music. Even the uninspiring Green Club livens up occasionally these days.

FOR NON-SKIERS
1850 isn't bad
A pedestrian ski pass for the gondolas and buses in the Courchevel and Méribel valleys (costing FF210 for six days) makes it easy to meet skiers for lunch and·get around the area. A fair amount of strolling around and posing goes on in 1850. And the new Forum sports centre in 1850 is an asset. You can take flights from the altiport around the area.

Les Deux-Alpes 1650m

ORIENTATION

Les Deux-Alpes is a narrow village spread along a long main street, sitting on a high, remote col. Access is from the Grenoble-Briançon road to the north or by gondola from Venosc. The main ski area is on the eastern side of the street with a small, unlinked area to the west. The main lift up to the east is the 20-person Jandri Express gondola from near the centre. The smaller Diable gondola leaves from the southern end. The newest development is Le Village, in an isolated position above the resort entrance. This has a chair-lift to the skiing.

From the top, you can get to the experts' resort, **La Grave**. The six-day pass covers a day in each of **Alpe-d'Huez**, **Serre-Chevalier**, **Puy-St-Vincent** and the Milky Way resorts from **Montgenèvre** to **Sauze d'Oulx**. All are easily reached by car, road conditions permitting.

✔ High, snowsure skiing including an extensive glacier area that's normally open winter and summer

✔ Attractions for both beginners and advanced skiers

✔ Efficient, modern lift system

✔ Animated village with lively, varied nightlife

✔ Rare opportunity for those who like hotels to find good value in a modern French resort

✗ Piste network much smaller than many skiers expect

✗ Ski area even more limited when runs to resort are incomplete, and/or glacier lifts closed

✗ Very congested skiing in places

✗ No easy runs back to the resort – slopes are steep, and snow conditions often poor

✗ Virtually no woodland skiing, so little skiing possible in bad weather

✗ Long, straggling village, not especially ugly but busy with traffic

✗ Poor mountain restaurants

Les Deux-Alpes is very different from most modern French resorts. In comparison with scores of medium-sized resorts, Les Deux-Alpes has a perfectly adequate ski area. But the place tends to be sold on the British market as a member of the big boys' league – and in that company its skiing (or its piste skiing, at least) can't compete. Anyone expecting another Alpe-d'Huez, La Plagne or Val-d'Isère will be disappointed. Whatever your standard of skiing, you need to be content to ski the same runs repeatedly if you're staying for a week.

In some other respects, Les Deux-Alpes is streets ahead of most high-altitude French resorts. It may not be a pretty village, but it is much more appealing in the evening than many of its rivals, thanks to the unusually large number of lively and varied bars and discos – many of which remain busy until the early hours. It's not a particularly smart resort either, so bar and restaurant prices – as well as hotel prices – aren't prohibitively high.

The resort

Les Deux-Alpes is a large, sprawling collection of hotels, apartments, bars and shops, most of which line the long, busy main street. Although there is no centre as such, and lifts are spread fairly evenly along the village, a couple of focal points are evident.

The resort has grown up haphazardly over the years – it is very far from being purpose-built – and there is a wide range of building styles, from old chalets, through monstrous 1960s blocks, to more sympathetic recent developments. Fans point out that it looks better as you drive out than as you drive in, because all the apartment buildings have their balconies facing the remote southern end of the resort.

The village is unusually lively for a French resort, which helps the general ambience. Bars, restaurants and nightclubs that originally catered for young French weekenders now

generate a suitable atmosphere for the growing lively Brit contingent. The resort is popular with Italians too, especially at weekends.

Traffic flows along a one-way system and can be heavy at times, making Les Deux-Alpes less than ideal for families.

SKI FACTS

Altitude 1300m-3570m
Lifts	64
Pistes	200km
Green/Blue	62%
Red	28%
Black	10%
Artificial snow	4km

LIFT PASSES

93/94 prices in francs
Super ski pass
Covers all lifts in Les Deux-Alpes, entry to swimming pool and skating rink.
Beginners 2 free lifts; 'Première trace' pass (covers 19 lifts).
Main pass
1-day pass 170
6-day pass 850
(low season 765 – 10% off)
Senior citizens
Over 60: 6-day pass 638 (25% off)
Children
Under 13: 6-day pass 638 (25% off)
Under 4: free pass
Short-term passes
Half-day 170
Notes Main pass of 2 days or more includes one day's skiing in La Grave. 6-day pass includes one day's skiing in Alpe-d'Huez, Serre-Chevalier, Puy-Saint-Vincent, and the Milky Way.
Alternative passes
3 limited area passes: 'Ski première trace' covers 19 lifts (78 per day), 'Ski sympa' covers 27 lifts (100 per day), 'Grand ski' covers 39 lifts (130 per day).

 # The skiing

There are two ski areas, one either side of the village. The main one has three distinct sections, each of which has different characteristics making it suitable for different types of skier. Consequently, while the area as a whole has skiing suitable for all grades, there are few places good for mixed-ability parties.

For a big resort, Les Deux-Alpes has a disappointingly small ski area; although extremely long and tall (it rises almost 2000m) it is also very narrow, with just a few runs on the upper part of the mountain, served by a few long, efficient lifts. Intermediate skiers and confident beginners, in particular, should beware. Many of the higher blue runs are easy and crowded – incredibly so at times – and most of the red runs immediately above the resort are steep and, especially in poor snow conditions, tricky. In good weather, at least, the skiing has considerable attractions for advanced skiers (largely off-piste, including excursions to La Grave over the top of the ski area). For novices there are very easy green runs on guaranteed good snow on the glacier, as well as good village nursery slopes; but it's a long ride up and down – and very cold, especially in early season.

Helicopter trips to Alpe-d'Huez are easily arranged and good value at FF330 return.

THE SKI AREA
Long, narrow and fragmented
The western **Pied-Moutet** side of Les Deux-Alpes' skiing is relatively little-used. It is served by lifts from various parts of town but reaches only 2100m. As well as the short runs back to town which get the morning sun, there's an attractive, longer north-facing run off the back which goes down through the trees to the small village of Bons. This is one of only two tree-lined runs in Les Deux-Alpes. The other drops down to Mont-de-Lans and is the only piste in the resort which can be skied directly from both ski areas. These runs are worth knowing about in poor visibility.

On the main, **eastern side** of the valley, the broad, steep slope immediately above the village offers a series of relatively short, testing runs, with a number of nursery slopes interspersed among them at the bottom of the hill.

The middle section above the first ridge, where most of the lifts from the

village finish, is made up primarily of blue cruising runs and is very narrow. At one point there is just a single run down the mountain, which all piste skiers have to use. As a result this area gets very congested. There are various chair-lift-served diversions you can take from the main channel.

The top **Glacier du Mont-de-Lans** section, served by drag-lifts and the warmer Funi Dôme Express underground funicular, has some fine, very easy runs which afford great views and are ideal for beginners and less adventurous skiers. Good skiers can trek across to neighbouring La Grave's challenging slopes.

SNOW RELIABILITY
Excellent on higher slopes
The snow on the higher slopes is normally very good, even in a poor winter – one of the main reasons for Les Deux-Alpes' popularity. Above 2200m most of the skiing is north-facing, and the top glacier section has summer skiing and guaranteed good winter snow. At Les Deux-Alpes you should worry more about bad weather shutting the lifts, or extremely low temperatures high up, than about snow shortage.

But the runs just above the village face west, so they get a lot of afternoon sun and can be icy at the beginning and end of skiing. Artificial snow on some of the lower slopes helps keep them skiable.

FOR ADVANCED SKIERS
Off-piste is the main attraction
With good snow and weather conditions, the area offers wonderful off-piste skiing. A particular attraction is La Grave, reached by a drag-lift (to 3570m) and a trek from the top of Les Deux-Alpes' skiing at Dôme de la Loze. From there it's a vertical drop of over 2000m to La Grâve. (See separate entry on page 188.) The downside is that in bad weather the link is often closed.

Back on the Les Deux-Alpes side, there are several good off-piste runs, including a number of variations from underneath the top stage of the Jandri Express down to the Thuit chair-lift. The best-known ones are now marked on the piste map. Off-piste skiers may regret that one of these runs, down the gunbarrel of Les Gours, will become a piste this season, with the installation of a new quad chair-lift.

The Tête Moute chair-lift, from the top of the Diable gondola, serves the steepest black run around. The brave can also try off-piste variations here between the rocks.

SKI SCHOOL

93/94 prices in francs

ESF

Classes 6 days
3hr: am; 2½hr: pm
6 mornings: 655
Children's classes
Ages: 6 to 12
6 mornings: 540
Private lessons
1hr over lunchtime or
full day Sunday
165 for 1hr, for 1 to 3
people

**International
St-Christophe**
Classes 6 days
3hr: am; 2½hr: pm
6 mornings: 575
Children's classes
Ages: 6 to 12
6 mornings: 450
Private lessons
1hr over lunchtime
180 for 1hr, for 1 to 3
people

CHILDCARE

Both ski schools run
kindergartens on
more-or-less identical
terms – taking
children aged 4 to 6
until 5pm. The ESF
(76792121) is slightly
more expensive and
does lunch only on
request, but starts at
9.15am whereas the
ESI de St Christophe
(76790421) starts at
9.30pm. The Crèche
du Village offers an
excellent service for
babies from 6 months
to 2 years, from
8.30am to 5.30pm.

Most of the runs back down to the resort are marked red on the piste map, but they deserve a black rating. They are usually mogulled and often icy early on because they get the afternoon sun. Some of these runs used to be black (and still have black piste markers) but were downgraded a few years ago – perhaps because the resort was worried that so many black runs marked would reduce the number of visitors.

FOR INTERMEDIATE SKIERS
Limited cruising
Les Deux-Alpes can disappoint intermediates. A lot of the skiing is either fairly tough or boringly bland. The steep runs home put off many. As one of our reporters (who classes himself as an 'advanced' skier) said, 'I myself fell from top to bottom. I was lucky. A girl in the "Tour of the Pistes" broke her back. You cannot afford to be complacent getting back.' There is a green zig-zag trail home but this is narrow in places and can be icy. It is also crowded at times.

The runs higher up generally have good snow, and aggressive intermediates can enjoy great, fast cruising, especially on the mainly north-facing pistes served by the chair-lifts off to the sides. You can often pick gentle or steeper terrain in these bowls as you wish, but avid piste-bashers will ski all there is to offer in a couple of days. Most of our keen skier reporters made use of their lift passes to take excursions to Alpe-d'Huez and Serre-Chevalier.

Less confident intermediates will love the quality of the snow and the gentleness of most of the runs. Their problem might lie in finding the pistes too crowded, especially if snow is poor in other resorts and people are bussed in. At the end of the day, the worst of the crowds and the steep lower slopes can be avoided by taking the Jandri Express down from the mid-station.

FOR BEGINNERS
Good slopes, shame about crowds
Les Deux-Alpes has great potential for beginners. The nursery slopes beside the village are spacious and gentle. The glacier has a fine array of very easy slopes. Unfortunately the weather can be hostile, not just on the glacier, but over a ravine high above which the glacier access lifts have to travel. Consequently glacier skiing is far from assured. The run below chair 37 (Séa) is the only other piste at altitude suitable for beginners, but it does get very crowded.

FOR CROSS-COUNTRY
Need very low altitude snow
There are three small, widely dispersed areas. Le Petite Alpe, near the entrance to the village, has a couple of snowsure if insignificant trails but, given good snow, Venosc (950m), reached by a gondola down, has the only worthwhile picturesque ones. Total trail distance is 20km.

QUEUES
Can be a problem
Les Deux-Alpes has a great deal of hardware to keep queues minimal since the village is large in relation to its ski area. But, especially in mid- and late-season, peak morning queues can be long for the Jandri Express and Diable gondolas. The Jandri queue moves quickly and, if you are headed for the top, it is worth joining to avoid further queues for the second stage.

Problems can also occur when skiers are bussed in from neighbouring resorts when snow is in short supply. At such times the lower slopes at Les Deux-Alpes are likely to be out of action too, causing even longer queues for the Jandri Express. The top lifts are prone to closure if it's windy, putting pressure on the lower lifts.

MOUNTAIN RESTAURANTS
Dreary
Mountain restaurants are scarce (there are only six) and generally pretty poor. La Pastorale, at the top of the Diable gondola, is the best, but it can have huge queues for the loo. The Panoramic at 2600m is fairly friendly and worth a try. Reasonable intermediates and above might consider skiing back to the village for lunch. Le Bimbo is well placed for the slopes, next to the ice rink.

SKI SCHOOL
One of the better ESFs
There are two ski schools, both of which have good reputations for standards of tuition and English, although class sizes can be large. Guiding services for excursions to La Grave are reportedly good. The School of Adventure section will take you to nearby resorts on the lift pass.

FACILITIES FOR CHILDREN
Fine for babies
Babies can safely be entrusted to the village crèche and Bladon Lines offer free nannies to groups booking whole chalets (eight or more beds) out of high season. But there are many better places for older children, whether skiers or not.

GETTING THERE

Air Lyon, transfer
3½hr. Grenoble,
transfer 2hr.
Chambery, transfer
3hr. Geneva, transfer
4½hr.

Rail Grenoble (75km);
4 daily buses from
station.

PACKAGES

Airtours, Alpine
Options Skidrive,
Bladon Lines, Chalet
Freestyle, Chalets
'Unlimited', Crystal,
Enterprise, Inghams,
Kings Ski Club,
Lagrange, Made to
Measure, Neilson,
Sally, Ski Partners,
Ski Valkyrie, Ski
White Knights,
SkiBound, Skiworld,
Stena Sealink,
Thomson, Travelscene
Ski-Drive, UCPA

 # Staying there

Alpe de Venosc, at the southern end of town, has many of the nightspots and hotels, the most character, the fewest cars and the best shops. It also has immediate access via the Diable gondola to the tough skiing around Tête Moute, but getting elsewhere is a roundabout business compared with going up the Jandri Express.

The geographical centre has a popular outdoor ice rink, some good restaurants and bars, and a variety of ways up the mountain, including the Jandri Express. The village straggles north from here, becoming less convenient the further you go. 'Le Village' consists of a cluster of apartments, a sports centre, a chair-lift, and little else, and is an inconvenient distance from the rest of town.

There's no doubt that staying near to the Jandri Express or the Diable gondola is the best place to be, especially for early risers, who can then avoid any queues.

HOW TO GO
Wide range of packages
Les Deux-Alpes has something for most tastes, including that rarity in high-altitude French resorts, good inexpensive hotels.

Chalets There are a number of 'catered chalet' packages available, but some use cramped apartments rather than real chalets. If you don't mind this, consider Ski White Knights, personally run with great enthusiasm by proprietor Robin Dann. Thomson has some good-looking real chalets on the northern edge of town, a bus-ride from the lifts. Skiworld's Tête Moute is much more central but rather basic. Its other places are even simpler. Bladon Lines has more comfortable but expensive chalets. Tessa is the best-situated. Crystal also have a large selection, including the comfortable, well positioned Chantal.

Hotels There are over 30 hotels, of which the majority are 2-star or below.

£££ Bérangère Smartest in town, with Michelin-starred restaurant, although dreary to look at; on-piste, but at less convenient north end of resort. Lots of facilities, including pool.

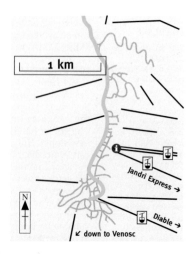

ACTIVITIES

Indoor 3 sports centres; Deux-Alpes tonic centre (sauna, steam bath, jacuzzi, aerobics and stretching), Club Forme (squash, swimming pool, sauna, jacuzzi), Tanking Centre (floatation chambers, physiotherapy, pressotherapy, sauna, jacuzzi, turkish baths, swimming pool, ice-rink)
Outdoor Hang-gliding, para-skiing, para-gliding, heli-skiing, quad-bikes, curling, skating, climbing wall, snow-shoe excursions

TOURIST OFFICE

Postcode 38860
Tel 010 33 76792200
Fax 76790138

£££ Farandole Better placed for nightlife and shopping, and within comfortable walking distance of the Diable bubble and east-facing slopes.
££ Chalet Mounier Attractive modern building. Good reputation for its food, and well placed for the Diable bubble and nightlife.
££ Souleil'Or Looks like a lift station, but appearances are deceptive. Pleasant and comfortable, and well placed for the Jandri Express gondola.
££ Edelweiss Good value, and popular with British clients.
££ Brunerie Cheap and cheerful large 2-star with plenty of parking for ski drivers, and quite well positioned.
Self-catering Many of the apartments are stuck out at Le Village at the north end of the resort, so it is well worth shopping around for more centrally situated ones.

STAYING DOWN THE VALLEY

If we were planning to spend a week skiing Les Deux-Alpes it would be with the intention of staying in the lively resort. But staying down the valley has great attractions for anyone thinking of travelling around to Alpe-d'Huez, La Grave and Serre-Chevalier – cutting travelling time as well as costs.

Close to the foot of the final ascent to Les Deux-Alpes are two near-ideal places, both Logis de France. At Le Freney, on the N91 Grenoble-Briançon road, is the cheerful 13-room Cassini. Nearby at Mizoën, just north of the N91, is the even more appealing 10-room Panoramique, with excellent food and friendly owners as well as the advertised views.

EATING OUT
Plenty of choice
The village restaurants are much better than those up the mountain. The Bérangère has a Michelin star and Chalet Mounier has the reputation for some of the best food in town. Le Petit Marmite has good food and atmosphere at reasonable prices.

Booking is essential. Bimbo is excellent. Brugi, Palate and Crêpes à Gogo are all worth a visit. Visitors on a budget can get a relatively cheap Italian meal at either Vetrata or the Spaghetteria. Crèperies are generally good for after-skiing snacks.

APRES-SKI
Unsophisticated fun
Les Deux-Alpes is one of the liveliest of French ski resorts, with plenty of bars to choose from. The Rodeo has a mechanical bucking bronco which attracts great numbers of rowdy après-skiers, many of them Brits. Mike's (which tour operators use a lot for quiz nights) and the Windsor are other noisy British enclaves. Smokey Joe's is recommended for its FF10 dice throwing – what you throw determines what drink you get! Bar Brazillienne is recommended for 'great music and tremendous atmosphere'.

There are plenty of quieter places around too. Most of the discos are expensive and take an age to warm up. La Casa, at the northern edge of town, is our favourite: it gets going at a reasonable hour and isn't too expensive – except coat checking, which is compulsory and pricey.

FOR NON-SKIERS
Not recommended
Les Deux-Alpes is not a particularly good choice for inactive non-skiers. It is quiet during the day, the shopping is uninspiring and the village is rather cut off, with little public transport for excursions. The pretty village of Venosc is well worth a visit, and you might be tempted to take the helicopter flight with skiing friends to Alpe-d'Huez for the day. For the active there are plenty of sports facilities.

Given the standard of mountain restaurants, competent skiers ought to be quite happy to return to the resort to meet non-skiers for lunch, but in practice this will depend on how icy the lower slopes are.

Flaine 1600m

HOW IT RATES

The skiing

Snow	****
Extent	****
Advanced	***
Intermediates	*****
Beginners	****
Convenience	*****
Queues	****
Restaurants	**

The rest

Scenery	***
Resort charm	*
Not skiing	*

✔ *Big ski area*
✔ *Reliable snow cover*
✔ *Most accommodation very convenient for the skiing*
✔ *Excellent facilities for children*
✔ *Short airport transfer*

✘ *Ugly architecture*
✘ *Very little nightlife*
✘ *Not a place for non-skiers*
✘ *Worrying reports on one of the ski schools*

So long as you don't care about the monstrous architecture or lack of lively evening ambience, Flaine has a lot going for it. Many keen skiers, especially families, love it.

There is some very pleasant and convenient accommodation. For families it theoretically wears the crown – if you want to spend a holiday with your kids, there is everything to help you. Whether families will be so happy in practice may depend on how well the ski schools perform – one school has prompted some alarming reports.

Flaine has slopes that intermediates will love, and it has kilometre upon kilometre of them. With its links to Samoëns, Morillon and Les Carroz, the Grand Massif is one of the big ski areas of France. Flaine caters masterfully for beginners too, with free access to nursery slope lifts. Advanced skiers can find some challenges. Above all, Flaine usually boasts excellent snow. It gets more than its fair share, and because many of its slopes are north- or north-west-facing, the snow stays in good condition for a long time after a snowfall.

ORIENTATION

Flaine is set at the foot of a bleak, largely tree-less bowl and reached by a long winding road up from Cluses in the valley below. It is only 70km from Geneva and has a very short airport transfer (around 90 mins). Flaine Forum is the main centre, with all the hotels and the two main gondolas into the skiing. Flaine Forêt lies above Forum and can be reached via a pair of funicular lifts. It has chair- and drag-lift access to the skiing, or you can ski down to Forum. The new development of Hameau-de-Flaine is a good 15-minute walk or short bus-ride from the skiing.

Flaine shares the Grand Massif ski area with the lower resorts of **Les Carroz, Samoëns 1600** and **Morillon**. Expeditions to **Chamonix** and neighbouring resorts are possible.

 # The resort

In our unofficial vote for Ugliest Resort in the Alps, Flaine was narrowly beaten by Les Menuires. Like 'Les Manures', it has a nickname based on how horrid it looks: 'Phlegm'. The concrete massifs that are its buildings were conceived in the sixties as 'an example of the application of the principle of shadow and light'. Hmm. They look particularly shocking the first time you see them from the approach road way above – a mass of blocks set nestling at the bottom of a beautiful snowy bowl. The one good thing about them is that from the ski slopes you can hardly see them – they do blend into the grey rocks.

In recent times, in common with other French Alpine carbuncles, efforts have been made to improve Flaine's looks. A striking example is the installation of a huge statue version of Picasso's 'A Woman's Head', which dominates the Forum.

The new development of Hameau-de-Flaine is built in a much more attractive chalet style – but is inconveniently situated a good 15-minute walk or a short bus-ride from the slopes. On a smaller scale, the interiors of much of the accommodation are now looking pretty classy.

Whatever the aesthetic problems of Flaine, when it comes to having an easy holiday, the planners made no mistakes with the layout. There is supermarket and speciality food shopping (you'll find good charcuterie and cheese available) close to all the Forum and Forêt accommodation; ski hire shops are a short hop away; the lifts are easy to get to and trips to organise ski passes, school and so on are no problem.

There are children all over the place, and they are catered for with play areas and, supposedly, by the resort being traffic-free. This has become pretty lax, in fact, and there is an uncomfortable amount of traffic buzzing around.

There are two main parts to the main resort. All the hotels, and some apartments, are set down in Forum. The focus of this area is a three-sided snow-covered square, with the fourth side being the piste back from the slopes. Watch out for skiers when you're strolling from the hotels on one side to the bars and shops on the other. Flaine Forêt has its own bars and shops and most of the apartment accommodation. Neither centre is very lively at night.

SKI FACTS

Altitude 700m-2480m
Lifts 80
Pistes 260km
Green/Blue 39%
Red 46%
Black 15%
Artificial snow 5km

LIFT PASSES

94/95 prices in francs
Grand Massif
Covers all the lifts in Flaine, Les Carroz, Morillon, Samoëns and Sixt.
Beginners Four free lifts. Ski pass for beginners covers 3 more lifts (80 per day for adults, 65 for children).
Main pass
1-day pass 160
6-day pass 760
Senior citizens
Over 60: 6-day pass 540 (29% off)
Children
Under 16: 6-day pass 540 (29% off)
Under 5: free pass
Short-term passes
Half-day from 11.30.
Alternative passes
Flaine area only
(1 day pass 140 for adults, 105 for children).

The skiing

THE SKI AREA
A big white playground

With its 260km of pistes, the Grand Massif claims to be the third largest ski area in France (behind the Trois Vallées and Espace Killy, arguing that the Portes du Soleil's 650km involves bus-rides and is partly in Switzerland so doesn't count). This long-running French ding-dong is difficult to judge, but whatever the truth, Flaine provides a comfortably spacious playground for the skier.

The skiing day for most begins at the **Grandes Platières** high-capacity stand-up gondola, which speeds you a single long stage up the north face of the Flaine bowl to the 2480m high-point of the Grand Massif. From here, in good weather, you can take in the view of Mont Blanc and the Aiguille du Midi, before choosing your route.

Most of the runs are reds (but there are some blues), curling away to the right as you look down the mountain and offering alternative tracks down the barren, tree-less, rolling terrain back to Flaine and to chairs in the middle of the wilderness that will take you back to the summit. On the far right, a difficult traverse leads to the Styx black that runs alongside the drag above Lac-de-Gers.

The alternative is to head left down the long red Méphisto (all the reds in this area have diabolic names – Lucifer, Belzebuth etc) to the **Aujon** area. This opens up another sector of the bowl, again mostly red runs but with some blues further down. The lower slopes here are much used as slalom courses. The Aujon sector is also reachable by gondola from below Forum at Flaine-Front-de-Neige.

The pistes in the Flaine bowl are mostly punchy medium-length runs. For a collection of longer cruises, head for the Grands Vans chair. To reach the chair from Forum you need to hop on the back of a 'milk float', the télébenne behind the Grandes Platières télécabine. From the top, you go over the edge of the bowl and have a choice of three different resorts to head towards, each with its own lifts and skiing.

In good snow there is a choice of blues and reds winding down to Les Carroz (1140m) or Morillon (700m), the latter with a half-way point at 1100m – Morillon Grand Massif.

There are only blacks and reds down towards Samoëns 1600, which tend to

be pretty mogully. You cannot reach the pretty old town itself – the furthest you can get on skis is to Vercland on the outskirts. Most of the lifts are centred around Samoëns 1600, a prime French weekenders' spot.

Getting back to Flaine is the important thing to think about. Reaching the crucial link – the Grand Vans drag – can be complicated, so don't leave it too late. And inexperienced skiers should leave enough time to fall off and have another go. In a premier league ski area like this, it's disappointing that that the only connection between the subsidiary ski areas and the main centre is a tricky button-lift.

Arrival back in Flaine can cause a problem on your first day: some reporters have complained that it's difficult to ski between the top of the resort and Forum. The trick is not to attempt to find a direct route down but to loop round away from the buildings and approach from under the gondola.

SNOW RELIABILITY
Usually keeps its whiteness

The main part of Flaine's skiing lies on the wide north- and north-west-facing flank of the Grandes Platières. Its direction, along with a decent height, means that it keeps the snow it receives. And in recent seasons this area of the Alps has enjoyed good snowfalls, providing a good run of powder days. The runs down to Samoëns 1600 and towards the Morillon area are north-facing too, but the low altitude means the lower parts are frequently unpleasant or unskiable. The Les Carroz runs are west-facing and can suffer from strong afternoon sun. However, the lower slopes of the Grand Massif have some snowmaking.

FOR ADVANCED SKIERS
Red run fun

Although the Grand Massif covers a large area, travelling around is not the attraction for advanced skiers that it is in, say, the Trois Vallées. Yes, you can thread your way down blacks towards Samoëns or explore possibilities in the trees above Les Carroz and Morillon, but it is in the bowl of Flaine itself that the real fun is to be found.

Although Flaine is a family resort, there are plenty of steepish reds coming off the top of the télécabine. You can usually cruise the groomed runs at a fair pace if they aren't too crowded. And there are a number of good bumpy gullies to bounce

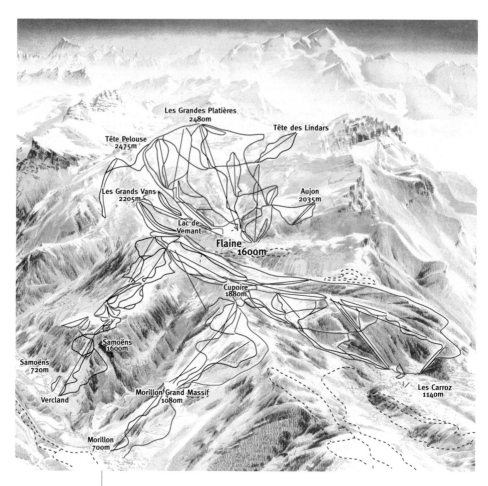

through, particularly on the long Faust run back to town. The best black mogul run is Diamant Noir, which starts under the télécabine, but the opening steep pitch can be overcrowded with skiers who fancied the challenge when they saw it from the lift but have changed their minds – choose your moment carefully if you want to build up a rhythm.

The Gers drag-lift serves expert-only terrain that offers excellent off-piste opportunities after a fresh snowfall. The open nature of the Grandes Platières and the frequently enticing powder make cutting away from the piste very alluring. But there have been some tragic cases of off-piste skiers coming across nasty surprises in the Flaine ski area. One incident a few years ago led to a British skier falling to his death down a gully only yards from the piste. So do not be tempted to leave the pistes without a qualified mountain guide.

Ski touring is a possibility in the Desert de Platé area, reached from the top of the Grandes Platières.

FOR INTERMEDIATES
Something for everyone

Flaine is ideal for all levels of intermediate, as you can almost always find a suitable piste on any area of the mountains. The 'devil' reds of the bowl are not really as hellish as their names imply – they tend to gain their status from steep sections rather than overall difficulty, and they're great for improving technique. If you prefer a gentler cruise, there is Cristal, to take you to the Perdrix chair back up to the top, or Serpentine all the way home. One of the attractions of Flaine for intermediates is the usually reliable quality of the snow.

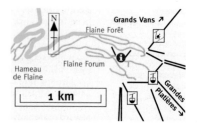

SKI SCHOOL

94/95 prices in francs

ESF

Classes 6 days
4hr: 10am-noon and
2.30-4.30
6 full days: 670
Children's classes
Ages: 3 to 12
6 full days: 570
Private lessons
1hr, 2hr or 6hr
185 for 1hr, for 1 to 2
people

International
Classes 6 days
4hr: 9.30-11.30 and
2.30-4.30
6 full days: 655
Children's classes
Ages: 4 to 12
6 full days: 525
Private lessons
1hr, 2hr or full day
170 for 1hr

Flaine Super Ski
Advanced skiers only

CHILDCARE

Both schools operate
ski kindergartens. The
ESF's Rabbit Club
(50908100) takes
children aged 3 to 12,
until 5pm. The SEI's
Club de la Souris
Verte (50908441)
takes children aged 4
to 12, until 5pm. The
hotel Les Lindars
(50908166) has a
nursery for babies
aged 3 months to 2
years, and a snow
garden for children up
to 7. Both schools
will pick up children
from Les Lindars for
lessons, and deliver
them at the end of
the class. There is
also an independent
nursery, the Petits
Loups (50908782).

In the Aujon sector, the snow is
often not so good, and though there is
a pair of partly tree-lined blues off the
Aujon drag, intermediates of all levels
might prefer the wider reds around the
top of the gondola. All intermediates
will enjoy the long, tree-lined runs
down to Les Carroz, as long as the
snow is good. You can choose between
red routes or slightly easier blues, one
of which constantly underpasses and
flies over the road out of Flaine,
allowing races between skiers and
coach drivers!

A trip to Morillon Grand Massif will
yield some pleasure for those who
want to clock up the kilometres; the
journey to Samoëns 1600 is suited
more to the better intermediate who
likes the odd dose of moguls.

FOR BEGINNERS
Very good
There are excellent nursery slopes
right by the village, served by free lifts
which make a pass unnecessary until
you can go higher up the mountain.
There are no long green runs to
progress to, but some gentle blues.

CROSS-COUNTRY
Very fragmented
The Grand Massif as a whole claims
64km of cross-country tracks but little
of it is around Flaine itself and none of
it lies at great altitude. Two 3km loops
lie just below the resort and a 600m
practice loop is found off the road to
Les Carroz near the mountain
restaurant at Chalet-de-Molliets.

There are extensive tracks over the
mountain between Morillon and Les
Carroz that involve some tough uphill
sections. And Samoëns 1600 has its
own tracks.

But the majority of the cross-
country is on the valley floor –
dependent on low snow. In a good
winter, it would make sense for cross-
country enthusiasts to be based in the
beautiful town of Samoëns rather than
up the hill.

QUEUES
Few real problems
You may choose Flaine for the very
reason many French do at holiday
weekends: it is quick and easy to get
to. There are three obvious crush
points when the resort is full. The
main one is the Grandes Platières
gondola at the start of the day, but
even the queue there moves quickly
because the cabins take large batches
of skiers at short intervals. It's just
that, as one reporter complains, it feels
like the Northern Line at rush hour.

The other bottlenecks – again only
at holiday times – are the chair over to
Samoëns and the twin drags back.

MOUNTAIN RESTAURANTS
Relatively scarce
Between Grandes Platières' summit
and the upper outskirts of Flaine there
is not a knife and fork in sight. The
'white desert' is very well named:
frozen water everywhere yet not a
drop to drink.

The Desert Blanc at the top-station
is a run-of-the-mill, two-room self-
service snackery, with a terrace
overlooking Mont Blanc. The Blanchot
at the bottom of the Serpentine run is
popular and rustic but has basic food.
The Chalets du Michet, near the foot
of the main gondola, is welcoming
and comfortable, with very good
Savoyard food and table-service. The
Eloge, in the same location, has
friendly self-service but 'plastic' food.
In Forêt, Chalet Bissac has a good
atmosphere, traditional decor, a huge
warming fire, self-service and 'great
chips'. The Cascade is self-service,
modern and clean, but with
inconsistent quality – all reporters talk
of amazing hi-tech loos. Over the
hills, the Oasis, above Morillon, is
recommended.

SKI SCHOOLS
ESF the best
The International school has a mixed
reputation, centring not around its
instruction, which most agree to be
good, but on those two key issues –
language and class size. Reporters have
given rave reviews when in a small
class with a good English-speaking
instructor. Others have called the
school a disaster because of 20-strong,
predominantly British classes run by a
non-English-speaking teacher. The
point is, it shouldn't be the luck of the
draw. There are several small specialist
schools, of which Flaine Super Ski is
one. Another does snowboarding.

FACILITIES FOR CHILDREN
Parents' paradise? Up to a point
Flaine prides itself on being a family
resort. The Rabbit Club has a
reputation for caring, and for good
English. Even very young children get
a good deal of ski instruction. But
experiences of the International
school's handling of children are less
reassuring. One disturbing report tells
of children being lost on the slopes
because the class was too big. That was
a class of 18; we also have a report of a
class that started the week with 30.
The parental mind boggles.

GETTING THERE

Air Geneva, transfer 1½hr.

Rail Cluses (30km); regular bus service (Mont Blanc Bus).

PACKAGES

Airtours, Bladon Lines, Chalets 'Unlimited', Cresta Ski France, Crystal, Enterprise, Fresh Tracks, Inghams, Made to Measure, Neilson, Over the Hill, Sally, Ski Choice, Ski Club of GB, Ski Safe Travel, Ski West, Stena Sealink, Thomson, Travelscene Ski-Drive

Les Carroz Lagrange, Mogul Ski, Winterski

Morillon Mogul Ski, Winterski

Samoëns Mogul Ski, Ski Europe

TOURIST OFFICE

Postcode 74300
Tel 010 33 50908001
Fax 50908626

The place to stay if you have children is hotel Les Lindars, designed specifically as a parents' hotel, with nursery, all-day crèche (open to non-residents, but residents have priority), ski school pick-up and drop-off service, a children's dining-room, in-house babysitters in the evening, even an automatic nappy-dispenser! Some other accommodation units, including the Forêt, have children's clubs.

 # Staying there

As a purpose-built resort, Flaine does not spark off much discussion of location – everywhere is convenient, except Hameau-de-Flaine. That is a good 15 minutes' walk or quick bus-ride away from the skiing.

HOW TO GO
Plenty of apartments
Accommodation is overwhelmingly in self-catering apartments. These are mostly based on the Forêt level and linked by lift to Forum, where more shops are located.

Chalets The few catered chalet options all offer very good value compared with the expensive hotels. Crystal have a couple of attractively traditional Scandinavian-style huts in Hameau, offering a good degree of comfort. They can be booked as part of a charter train package if required. Airtours have some unusual, simple accommodation packaged chalet-style with half-board and wine: an allocation of rooms in the Cascade mountain restaurant-cum-hostelry. It's on the slopes, but the village is within walking distance. The lounge has satellite TV which is very useful in this après-ski graveyard.

Hotels There are just four hotels, all around Forum.

£££ Totem Easily the best hotel in Flaine, recently renovated; modern, stylish, great views of Aujon skiing, nouvelle cuisine food is excellent (and plentiful!).

££ Les Lindars Great hassle-free holidays for families: free children's facilities, modern, smart and pleasant public rooms, functional bedrooms.

££ Flaine Somewhat boxy rooms, good substantial food. Being renovated for this season.

£ Aujon Large and impersonal, but rooms are comfortable; 'insufficient food, temperamental lifts, unhelpful management' says a reporter.

Self-catering Flaine is one purpose-built resort that's got self-catering right – realising that people choose this option on price grounds, not because they like cooking and cleaning. So they offer convenient facilities to help, such as a pizza and morning bread and croissant delivery.

Most favoured by the many Brits visiting Flaine is Forêt. Apartments are attractive, as French self-catering blocks go – the predominance of wood is a welcome relief from the concrete outside. This is one of the most recently renovated in Flaine's ongoing face-lift. It also boasts hotel facilities such as a restaurant, bar and kindergarten. A similar set-up which is almost as popular is the Grand Massif. Both are right next door to the Forêt shopping centre.

Along with the many apartments at Forêt, Flaine-Front-de-Neige has some accommodation, down through the trees from Forum, at the resort's edge.

Out at Hameau, various tour operators have allocations in high-standard, spacious apartments. These are more comfortable than anything in the main village.

EATING OUT
Mostly fast food
Most people eat in their apartments or hotels (Totem and Lindars take outside bookings). The bulk of the eateries are downmarket pizzerias and burger bars. For a more refined meal, the Perdrix Noire in Forêt is a meat and fish restaurant, busy and friendly. The Chalets du Michet (see Mountain Restaurants) is as good in the evening. In the mid-range, Trattoria is a good Italian, Chez la Jeanne is the best pizza restaurant. Chez Daniel offers crêpes and Savoyard specialities.

APRES-SKI
Hello! Anybody there?
You see a few parents snatching a quick demi in the bar, then it's back to the child-minding. After dinner there's little happening.

Earlier, the White Grouse pub is boisterous: extreme ski videos compete with rock music and British punters trying to get pints in before the end of happy hour.

Later, the more French Cîmes Rock is the only really lively joint, with live bands on towards midnight. Flaine's two nightclubs, the expensive Shelby and the 'seedy' Diamant Noir are not worth losing sleep over.

ACTIVITIES

Indoor Top Form centre (swimming pool complex with sauna, solarium, gymnasium, massage), arts and crafts gallery, cinema, auditorium, indoor climbing wall **Outdoor** Ice-rink, snow-shoe excursions, hang-gliding, para-gliding para-skiing, helicopter rides, snowmobiles, snow scooters, high mountain outings, ice-driving car circuit, all-terrain carts and motorbikes (in spring)

FOR NON-SKIERS
Curse of the purpose-built

As with most purpose-built resorts, there is little to recommend Flaine to non-skiers. There are few walks and no old town to explore. You could get a great thrill from a helicopter-ride around the Grand Massif, or even over Mont Blanc. Or try the ice-driving course. On a more sedate level, there is a cinema that shows English-language films, and an art gallery. Flaine often has arts festivals, including a jazz week.

Les Carroz 1140m

This is a spacious, sunny, traditional, family resort where life revolves around the village square with its pavement cafés and array of interesting little shops. It's a popular summer, as well as winter, resort and has a 'lived-in' feel, with much more animation than Flaine.

The queue-free gondola and chair-lift take you straight into the Grand Massif ski area – but there's a steep 300m walk from the village centre. The main hotel, the 3-star Serrages, is opposite the lift-station. The 1-star Airelles is in a good spot, half-way between the centre and the lifts.

The Croix de Savoie (2-star) and Sapins (1-star) are in quiet, secluded areas on the outskirts of the village. The Belles Pistes hotel (currently being graded) is bang in the village centre. It's British-owned and well-liked for good French cuisine.

Apartments make up a high percentage of the beds available. Self-drive specialists Sally Holidays have centrally-positioned studios.

The village centre has a pleasant after-skiing atmosphere, and the ski school's torchlit descent is something of a highlight – it's preceded by fireworks and concludes with vin chaud and live jazz in the village square. The Marlow and Squatt bars have regular live music, the latter becoming a disco after 11pm. The other two discos only liven up at weekends.

Other resort amenities include tobogganing, snowmobiles, floodlit skiing, ice skating, a cinema (weekly films in English), a health club, a kindergarten, banks and parapenting. There's also horse-riding if the valley is free of snow.

The local skiing is best suited to competent intermediates, the wooded lower runs of the Grand Massif tending to be steeper than the open slopes above Flaine.

The kindergarten has a good reputation, though we suspect that lack of English-speaking supervision and children to play with could be a problem.

Les Carroz is probably best for self-drivers who want to stay in a genuine village while having the snow reliability and family skiing components of Flaine just a short drive away.

Samoëns 720m

This is probably the most beautiful ski resort in France. It's certainly the only one to be listed as a 'Monument Historique'. Medieval fountains, rustic old buildings, an ancient church – it's all there.

In the centre of the village is an impressive 8.5 acre botanical garden with thousands of plants from around the world. The traditional-style bars and restaurants give you a feel for 'real' rural France.

The ski slopes are a bus-ride away, but most people here have their cars with them.

We've had very positive reports of the hotels Sept Monts (3-star) and Drugères (2-star). Other possibles are the Neige et Roc and Glaciers (both 3-star) and Gai Soleil (2-star). There are numerous good restaurants, mostly specialising in regional dishes – the 19th century Tornatta is certainly worth trying.

The centre for four o'clock cocktails is the Cheminee Café Bar, while later the Café is the main rendezvous. The Louisiana disco livens up at weekends.

Samoëns has its own ski school, ski kindergarten and nursery (taking children from 6 months). But English-speaking care and tuition is unlikely in this French resort.

Skiers may like to use their cars to visit the Portes du Soleil, only 30 minutes away. It takes longer to reach Flaine by lift and ski.

La Grave 1450m

HOW IT RATES

The skiing

Snow	***
Extent	**
Advanced	*****
Intermediates	*
Beginners	*
Convenience	***
Queues	****
Restaurants	**

The rest

Scenery	****
Resort charm	***
Not skiing	*

PACKAGES

Chalets 'Unlimited', Fresh Tracks, Ski Challenge, Ski Club of GB, Ski Weekend

SKI FACTS

Altitude 1450m-3550m
Lifts 4
Pistes 5km
Green/Blue 100%
(This figure relates to pistes; practically all the skiing is off-piste)
Artificial snow none

TOURIST OFFICE

Postcode 05320
Tel 010 33 76799005
Fax 76799165

La Grave is the Alps' best-kept secret. Its skiing is almost exclusively, tough, off-piste stuff in spectacular scenery, with a vertical drop of 2100m. Good skiers who love off-piste and don't need 4-star comfort should give it serious consideration. It ranks with top resorts such as Val-d'Isère, Chamonix and St Anton for off-piste skiing, but comes at a fraction of the price, and includes the rustic charm of a traditional Alpine village dating back to the 12th century.

THE RESORT

La Grave is a remarkably unspoilt old mountaineering village set on a steep hillside against impressive glacial scenery that is dominated by the majestic 4000m Meije, the last major European peak to be conquered by mountaineers. The drab local stone and busy main road which separates the village from the ski area reduce the charm somewhat, but it still has a genuinely rustic feel. Prices are more in line with rural France than with the exorbitant levels normally charged in ski resorts, but there isn't much there – a handful of small hotels, sports shops, food shops and bars. The single lift is conveniently close, but a car is useful in case poor weather closes the skiing. Les Deux-Alpes, Serre-Chevalier and Alpe-d'Huez are all around 30 minutes' drive away; Les Deux-Alpes can also be reached on skis over the top of the mountain.

THE SKIING

A three-stage gondola ascends into the **ski area** and finishes at 3200m. A few drag-lifts above here take you up to 3550m and serve the flat glacier terrain and the link over to Les Deux-Alpes. But the reason that people come here is to ski the legendary off-piste slopes back down towards La Grave. There are no marked or patrolled pistes back down at all. Various itineraires are marked on the map (the Itineraires des Vallons de la Meije and Itineraires de Chancel), but none should be attempted without a guide because of the danger from crevasses and cliffs, quite apart from the risk of losing your way or being caught by an avalanche.

Obviously this resort is best visited when **snow** is known to be good. Incomplete cover not only reduces the size of the ski area – if there's no snow above the village, you can only ski down to one of the gondola mid-stations – it also means less-than-satisfactory powder.

Advanced skiers are the only people who should contemplate a stay in La Grave. The variations in the routes you can take down are enormous: some end up in neighbouring villages or on roadsides where you can be picked up by taxi or bus; others take you right back to the village.

Intermediates and **beginners** should go elsewhere. There are small local areas nearby which provide some suitable slopes but a 'normal' resort with proper pistes would be much better. Don't be tempted to stay in La Grave with the intention of skiing Les Deux-Alpes most of the time – the link is often shut by poor weather.

La Grave has a couple of **cross-country** loops (total 12km); the longer one goes to the neighbouring hamlet of Les Freaux. A further 18km are available near Villar d'Arene.

There are short **queues** only at weekends – at the bottom station first thing in the morning and at the mid-station later.

The **mountain restaurants** at mid-station and Chancel are quite good. At the top station there's a basic old climbers' hut with a terrace. The **guiding** service is good, and inexpensive by French standards.

Children's baby-sitting can be arranged through the tourist office.

STAYING THERE

There are no luxurious **hotels**. The Edelweiss is a comfortable, friendly, family-run 2-star with good home cooking. The Chaumine Skiers Lodge (Freephone: 0800 893601) is run by a small British company. It provides guides and has mini-buses for trips to other resorts.

Self-catering studios are bookable through the tourist office.

Most people **eat** in their hotels. The Lou Ratel bar-restaurant does raclettes, while the Candy snack bar serves hamburgers and crèpes. The Candy has music too, but most people are too tired to venture out for any **après-ski**.

Non-skiers will probably find La Grave much too small and quiet. The interesting towns of Briançon (35km) and Grenoble (75km) are within reach if you have a car.

Isola 2000

A scheduled flight and a short (90km) transfer from Nice, with some decent from-the-door skiing, Isola is high on convenience as well as altitude. Like many purpose-built French resorts, it has been extended in a sympathetic, traditional style. But its original buildings are irredeemably block-like.

THE RESORT

Isola is one of the many small, high, purpose-built resorts in the French Alps, but differs from the rest in its extreme southern location, with access via Nice. One reporter says, 'On very clear days you can see the sea.'

Built by a British property company in the late 1960s, Isola aimed itself squarely at the family market. Front de Neige is a complex of apartments, shops, bars, restaurants and a couple of hotels that makes up the core of the resort, with nursery slopes and lifts on the doorstep.

Various owners have since worked hard to glamourise the image of the resort with new hamlets of more luxurious, wood-clad apartment blocks. But the main complex has become tatty at the same time, with shops closing down.

THE SKIING

According to the piste map, there are three **ski areas**, St Sauveur, Pélevos and Levant. Really it is one linked area in a horseshoe shape around the resort. Due to the great base height of Isola – the lowest skiable point is at 1840m – most of the skiing is above the tree-line. The main access point is the gondola from the centre of the complex to Pélevos at 2320m, and from there all three areas can be accessed more or less directly.

Isola can get different weather from other major French resorts. Sometimes it has masses of **snow** when the rest of the French Alps have none; at other times it misses out. Reporters who visit year after year say that although they never find all the lifts open, there is always snow – and plenty of strong southern sun. The north-facing slopes of St Sauveur and Pélevos tend to keep their snow well.

Advanced skiers head for St Sauveur, which has Isola's longest, most challenging runs and its best off-piste skiing. There are good blacks here – and from the chair to Mont Mené. The Pélevos area is a cluster of **intermediate** red and blue runs where you can take your pick of difficulty. The more adventurous can try the challenging St Sauveur sector, where there is a choice of steep reds

and blacks. The south-facing slopes below the Col de la Lombarde, in the Levant sector, are also intermediate.

There are excellent nursery slopes for **beginners** right in the heart of the resort, and an easy progression to greens, then blues, nearby.

There is a 4km loop just above the village, but little else to recommend Isola to **cross-country** enthusiasts.

Because it is the only central main lift, the gondola is prone to **queues** at peak times. And weekends see the arrival of day-trippers from Nice, causing further bottlenecks.

There is only a handful of **mountain restaurants.** The best is the excellent Génisserie at the foot of St Sauveur's skiing.

The ESF **ski school** has a good reputation for its English and its teaching – both in the traditional way and ski évolutif – but, as ever, class size is a gripe among reporters.

Isola has an all-day crèche, and a snow garden for **children** starting out on skis. English is widely spoken.

STAYING THERE

Accommodation is largely in **self-catering** apartments; the newer, better-appointed Bristol and Les Adrets complexes are recommended (the latter in a Neilson package).

There is one excellent luxury hotel (at a price), the Diva, with wonderful cuisine. The other **hotels** (in the original building) are Le Druos, Pas du Loup and Le Chastillon. The last two are available through Neilson, who offer weekends as well as the usual weekly packages.

The number of British operators serving Isola 2000 has declined and, with it, the vitality of the **après-ski** scene outside high season and weekends, when skiers from the Riviera arrive. That's the time to go to L'Equateur and La Tanière.

Despite its new Aquavallée leisure centre, Isola is hardly the place for a **non-skier** to spend a week: the resort name does mean 'island', after all. However, you could top up your tan and then treat yourself to the £300 package that helicopters you to Monte Carlo for a night, with dinner at the Café de Paris and entry to the Casino.

Megève 1100m

HOW IT RATES

The skiing

Snow	*
Extent	****
Advanced	*
Intermediates	****
Beginners	***
Convenience	**
Queues	***
Restaurants	*****

The rest

Scenery	***
Resort charm	***
Not skiing	****

✔ *Large, very pretty, intermediate-oriented ski area*

✔ *Gourmet mountain lunches in attractive surroundings*

✔ *Excellent area for cross-country skiing*

✔ *Plenty of things to do other than skiing*

✔ *Charming old village centre*

✘ *Often poor snow, yet no snowmakers*

✘ *Disjointed ski areas, inconveniently distant from town centre*

✘ *Nursery slopes unreliable for snow; little English spoken in ski school*

✘ *Traditional, rustic charm spoilt by bad traffic congestion around town*

✘ *Not a lot of challenging skiing*

Megève used to be France's most fashionable ski village, popular with its chic clientele for its gentle, woodland skiing, rustic charm, pretty scenery, attractive mountain restaurants, lovely walks, sophisticated nightlife and friendly locals. It has certainly lost that title now to Courchevel: it no longer boasts a single restaurant with Michelin stars; Courchevel has two.

The problem is that Megève's facilities are past their sell-by date. Its rustic charm is marred by severe traffic problems and its several ski areas are set inconveniently apart, and far from the centre of town. Worst of all, it has a poor recent snow record, very little skiing above 2000m and no artificial snow. That means the skiing is unreliable, to say the least.

The solution is to add to the traffic problems and take a car, use the local coaches, or find a tour operator who will transport you to neighbouring resorts in times of snow shortage. The area lift pass covers the relatively snowsure skiing of several nearby resorts, including Chamonix, Les Contamines and Courmayeur in Italy. Of course, if you happen to hit good snow, you'll find the local skiing delightful for gentle intermediate cruising – and for gourmet lunching. You'll also find that Megève still attracts its fair share of Beautiful People, complete with fur coats and fat wallets. But many of them are there as much for the posing as the skiing.

ORIENTATION

Megève sits in a pretty, sunny setting by the main Albertville-Chamonix road that bypasses only the medieval centre of town. It's one of France's largest resorts, surrounded on three sides by a sprawl of ever-expanding suburbs.

Lifts lead up into three different ski areas from opposite ends of town. There are also access lifts further from town. **St-Gervais** and **Le Bettex** share Megève's main ski area. And the Mont Blanc lift pass covers many other resorts, including the **Chamonix** valley and **Courmayeur** in Italy.

SKI FACTS

Altitude	915m-2350m
Lifts	58
Pistes	238km
Green/Blue	30%
Red	45%
Black	25%
Artificial snow	2km

 ## The resort

Megève is very much a tale of two cities. It is in a lovely setting and has a beautifully preserved traditional old centre, which is pedestrianised and comes complete with open-air ice rink, horse-drawn sleighs, cobbled streets and fine church. There are lots of smart clothing, jewellery, food, antique and gift shops.

Megève has expanded enormously and is surrounded by a strangulation of modern roads and traffic. Thankfully the main road bypasses the centre, and there are expensive underground car parks. But the cars are a problem – especially at weekends when the crowds arrive and at the end of the day when people are driving back from skiing excursions.

The clientele is mainly well-heeled French couples and families, who come here as much for an all-round winter holiday and for the people-watching potential as for the skiing. The nightlife is, as you'd expect for such a resort, lively and varied.

 ## The skiing

Megève's skiing is predominantly easy intermediate cruising, much of it prettily set in the woods. But there are tough runs to be found.

THE SKI AREA
Fragmented and low

There are three separate ski areas, two of them linked by cable-car – but not by pistes. The two linked areas are Rochebrune and Mont d'Arbois. A gondola within walking distance of central Megève serves both areas. From the mid-station, you can catch the cable-car, followed by a gondola, up to Mont d'Arbois (1840m), or you can carry on up the gondola to Rochebrune (1750m).

Rochebrune can also be reached directly by an ancient cable-car from the southern edge of town. From Rochebrune you can go up to Alpette (1880m), the starting point for Megève's historic downhill course. A network of gentle, wooded, east-facing slopes served by drag-lifts (and a high-

LIFT PASSES

94/95 prices in francs
Rocharbois-Mont Joly
Covers all lifts on
Rochebrune, Côte
2000, Mt d'Arbois,
Megève, St-Gervais,
Mt Joux and Mount
Joly.
Beginners Pay by the
ride.
Main pass
1-day pass 148
6-day pass 764
(low season 630 –
18% off)
Senior citizens
Over 60: 6-day pass
634 (17% off)
Children
Under 12: 6-day pass
634 (17% off)
Under 5: free pass
Short-term passes
Half-day pass
available morning or
afternoon.
Alternative passes
Mont Blanc Evasion
pass covers all lifts in
Megève, St-Gervais,
St-Nicolas and
Combloux, available
for 1 day or season,
(1-day pass 155 for
adults, 129 for
children). Mont Blanc
ski-pass covers all
lifts in the 13 resorts
of the Mont Blanc
area (700km of piste
and 190 lifts) and the
buses between them
plus Courmayeur in
Italy 4 days out of 6
(6 days 900 for adults
and 645 for children).
Jaco pass valid for Le
Jaillet, Christomet and
Combloux.

speed quad, new this year) takes you across to Côte 2000 – the sector's furthest and highest point, at 2015m.

Mont d'Arbois is Megève's largest and most interesting ski area. It's also accessed by another gondola starting at Princesse, way out to the north-east of town. From the top you can ski on north-facing slopes to Le Bettex and on down to St-Gervais at around 900m. Yet another two-stage gondola returns skiers to Mont d'Arbois, with its mid-station at Le Bettex. You can work your way over to Mont Joux and Megève's highest (2350m), most snowsure skiing – a small area.

The third, and quietest, area is **Le Jaillet**, accessed by gondola from just outside the northern edge of town. Above the top of the gondola (1600m) are predominantly easy east-facing pistes. The high-point is Christomet to the west, served by a two-stage chair. In the other directions a series of long tree-lined runs and lifts serve the area above Combloux.

SNOW RELIABILITY
The area's worst feature
The slopes are low (the resort map contains hardly any height information), sunny and not served by artificial snow. Need we say more? You only need to look at the snow reports in the newspapers each day to see how often Megève's lower slopes are bare or in poor condition, and how often it rains there when it's snowing on the slopes of higher resorts. The relatively snowsure Mont Joly and Le Bettex sections are very small – though new investment in snowmaking is starting to pay off here. You should be prepared to travel for good snow. Les Contamines, Chamonix and Courmayeur are covered by the Mont Blanc area lift pass and all have reliable snow. And Flaine is nearby and worth a visit.

FOR ADVANCED SKIERS
Limited interest
The Mont Joly and Mont Joux sections offer the steepest skiing. The top chair here serves slopes of a genuinely black 33°, and the slightly lower Epaule chair has some steep runs back down and also accesses some good off-piste, as well as pisted, runs down to St-Nicolas-de-Véroce. There is an off-piste route down to neighbouring Les Contamines from here too.

The steep area beneath the second stage of the Princesse gondola can be a play area of powder skiing among the trees. Côte 2000 has a small section of steep skiing, including some off-piste.

FOR INTERMEDIATE SKIERS
Superb if the snow is good
Good intermediates will enjoy the Mont d'Arbois area best. The black runs below the Princesse gondola are perfectly manageable. The runs served by the Grand Vorassel drag and the most direct route between Mont d'Arbois and Le Bettex are also interesting. Similarly testing are the steepest of the Jaillet sector pistes above Combloux. Nearby, the Christomet bowl is a fine area for mixed abilities, the same lift giving access to three widely differing runs.

Moderate skiers are particularly well suited to Megève. A plethora of comfortable reds lead down to Le Bettex and Princesse from Mont d'Arbois, while nearby Mont Joux accesses long, similar-standard runs to St-Nicolas. Alpette and Côte 2000 are other suitable sections.

Timid skiers can get a great deal of mileage in. All main valley-level lifts have easy routes down to them (although the Milloz piste to the Princesse mid-station is a little steep). Particularly good, long, gentle cruises are available between Mont Joux and Megève via Mont d'Arbois. But whichever sector you go to, you'll find easy, well-groomed blue runs – the main problem you are likely to encounter is the poor quality or thin snow-cover.

FOR BEGINNERS
Snow problems again
The large amount of very easy skiing makes Megève a good choice for near-beginners. And there are plenty of nice little nursery areas dotted around at the base of most ski areas. Unfortunately all of them are prone to poor snow conditions – in which situation you're better off going up to Jaillet or Mont d'Arbois.

FOR CROSS-COUNTRY
An excellent area
There are 75km of varied trails, spread throughout the ski area, some of which are at reasonable altitude (1300m–1550m). Meeting up with Alpine skiers or walkers at one of the many mountain huts is a particular attraction of this area.

QUEUES
Much improved
Megève has improved its lift system of late, and nowadays is relatively queue-free during the week, except at peak holiday time. But school holiday and sunny Sunday delays can be long at times, especially for the Petite

Fontaine and Lanchettes lifts in the Rochebrune sector and at the mid-station of the Princesse gondola.

Overcrowded pistes at Mont Joux and Mont d'Arbois are a problem at busy periods. Queues are noticeably genteel, a far cry from the push and shove of more macho resorts.

CHILDCARE

There are four kindergartens dotted around the sprawling resort, all offering skiing. Age limits and hours vary. Alpage (50211097), next to the Mont d'Arbois gondola: ages 3 to 6, until 5.30. Caboche (50589765) at the Caboche gondola station: ages 3 to 10, until 5.30pm. Meg'Loisirs (50587784) is a comprehensive nursery: ages 1 to 6, until 6pm or even 7pm. Princesse (50930086), out at the Princess gondola: ages 3 to 6, until 5pm.

MOUNTAIN RESTAURANTS
The long lunch lives

Megève is one of the great skiing gourmet venues, but prices are very high. The Mont d'Arbois area is particularly well endowed with mountain restaurants.

Several of the little old chalets around St-Nicolas have both great charm and fine food, while L'Alpage at Les Communailles beneath Mont Joux is worth a visit, and is particularly recommended for good salads and the plat du jour. The Club House at Mont d'Arbois is a nice place, but popular with the Megève poseurs with dogs and fur coats.

Self-service places are cheaper and less leisurely, but still reasonably good quality. Chez Tartine is a very friendly self-service spot at the Princesse mid-station. Le Rosay on Mont Joux is also friendly and generally quite good. The Igloo has both self-service and table-service sections; the staff in both are helpful and it has wonderful views of Mont Blanc.

Further afield, Côte 2000 is popular for its atmosphere, friendly service and good quality, while La Caboche is handily placed for an end-of-day drink. Forestier and Alpette are other recommended spots.

SKI SCHOOL
Adventurous

The two ski schools both have broad horizons, offering expeditions to the Vallée Blanche and heli-skiing (in Italy) as well as conventional tuition. The International school also advertises outings to the Grands Montets at Argentière.

FACILITIES FOR CHILDREN
Language problems

A comfortable low-altitude resort like Megève attracts lots of families who can afford day-care. The facilities seem impressive – all four kindergartens offer a wide range of activities as an alternative to skiing. Lack of English-speaking staff (and companions) could be the main drawback, and many parents of pre-skiing children will prefer the more predictable crèche services of Ski Esprit, who have chalets here (see following section).

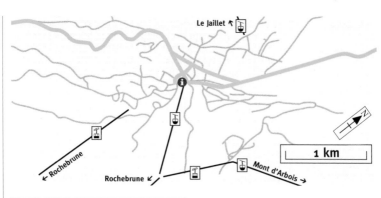

GETTING THERE

Air Geneva, transfer
1½hr. Lyon, transfer
3hr.

Rail Sallanches
(13km); regular buses
from station.

 # Staying there

Staying in the traffic-free centre of town gives you the best atmosphere and puts you within walking distance of the Rochebrune gondola.

HOW TO GO
Few packages
Relatively few British tour operators go to Megève. Although it's a chic resort with five 4-star hotels, there are plenty of simpler, charming hotels and good-value chalets available. Apartments tend to be expensive but of a good standard.

Chalets With Jean Stanford reducing their operation here from three to one chalet last year, there isn't a lot of choice these days. Their existing Sylvana chalet-hotel is a simple place, but well located for the skiing, close to the Rochebrune cable car. The family specialist Ski Esprit has a charming old villa with lots of personal touches and an exceptionally comfortable traditional-style modern chalet (all bedrooms have en-suite bathrooms). Both are pleasantly located away from the town congestion, 10 minutes' walk out of the centre. Ski Barrett-Boyce has a cosy open-fired place five minutes' walk from the centre. Ski Campus have a good-value chalet-hotel on the slopes at Le Bettex.

Hotels Megève may not be France's smartest resort any longer, but it still attracts enough affluent visitors to sustain some exceptionally stylish and welcoming hotels.

££££ Loges du Mont Blanc Megève's traditional leading hotel – elegant and fashionable. Right in the centre, and therefore close to the main gondola.

££££ Chalet du Mont d'Arbois Prettily decorated former Rothschild family home in a secluded position between the two gondolas.

££££ Fer à Cheval French rustic-chic at its best, with a warmly welcoming wood-and-stone interior. Excellent food, and a fitness centre to redress the balance. Close to the centre.

Selected chalets in the Megève area

PACKAGES

Alpine Expressions, Chalets 'Unlimited', French Impressions, Jean Stanford, Lagrange, Made to Measure, Ski Ardmore, Ski Barrett-Boyce, Ski Campus, Ski Esprit, Travelscene Ski-Drive, White Roc

St-Gervais Altours Travel, Ski Barrett-Boyce, Ski Europe, Snowcoach Club Cantabrica

ACTIVITIES

Indoor 'Palais des Sports' (climbing wall, swimming pool, sauna, solarium, skating, gym, golf driving), judo, classical and contemporary dance classes, music lessons, bridge, tennis, yoga, archery, language classes, museum, library, cinemas, pottery, casino, concert and play hall, body-building hall, table-tennis, tennis
Outdoor 50km of cleared paths, snow-shoe excursions, skating rink, riding, sleigh rides, plane and helicopter trips, para-gliding, curling, horse-riding, rock-climbing, mountaineering

TOURIST OFFICE

Postcode 74120
Tel 010 33 50212728
Fax 50930309

££££ Grange d'Arly Wrong side of the road, but still quite close to the centre – a beautifully furnished chalet.
£££ Ferme Hôtel Duvillard Smartly restored farmhouse, perfectly positioned for skiing, at the foot of the Mont d'Arbois gondola.
£££ Alpina Small, central.
££ Sapins Comfortable logis on edge of town, close to the main gondola.
££ Idéal-Mont Blanc At Combloux: a Relais du Silence with a great view of Mont Blanc and a pool.
Self-catering The weekend specialist White Roc has expensive but comfortable apartments within easy walking distance of the main gondola. Chalet operator Jean Stanford will also put together a self-catering package, using local contacts for apartments.

EATING OUT
Very French
Megève is a très chic French town whose restaurants are mainly high-quality, if expensive. Michel Gaudin is probably the best in town and does very good-value set menus. The Fermes de Marie, Chalet du Mont d'Arbois and Mont Joly are not far behind in quality but much more expensive. The Tire Bouchon and Sapinière are two of the best value, Vieux Megève is a delightfully cosy grill, Le Chamois cooks the ubiquitous fondue very well and Côte 2000 is an intimate candlelit place. The Pizzeria del Mare is good value, and the Phnom-Penh serves food rather different from normal French cuisine.

APRES-SKI
Plenty to try
Nightlife is lively, and less formal than it used to be. The Chamois and Sapinière bars are animated tea-time places. The Puck is an atmospheric locals' bar, Club des Cinque Rues is a very popular jazz club-cum-cocktail bar, while the Cocoon video bar is an informal rendezvous popular for its wide range of beers, a weekly live band, karaoke and satellite TV. Village Rock and the Enfants Terribles are other lively spots.
   The bar at the chalet-hotel Sylvana is a good place for a quiet, inexpensive drink in a friendly atmosphere. Senso is the liveliest disco. The fur and poodle brigade frequent Le Rols Club. The Esquinade Club (with casino) is another jet-set spot. The weekly broomball match, on the open-air ice rink, between the British and French is a good chance to let your hair down.

FOR NON-SKIERS
There are lots around
There is something for most tastes, with an impressive sports centre, a central outdoor ice rink, plenty of outdoor activities and a weekly market. Excursions to Annecy, Chamonix and even Courmayeur are possible. Walks are excellent outside town, with 50km of marked paths, much at high altitude. Meeting skiers up the mountain for lunch is easy.

STAYING IN OTHER RESORTS
A couple of places a car-drive away
Praz-sur-Arly (1035m) and Notre-Dame-de-Bellecombe (1130m) are much cheaper options for independent car travellers.
   Praz is a small, quiet place, but has hotels, restaurants, bars, sports club, ski school and ski kindergarten. It has a fair-sized ski area of its own, with short, mainly easy north-facing runs.
   Notre-Dame is a little further along the road past Praz, a pleasant enough village with mainly apartment accommodation, some simple hotels, and several bars and restaurants – L'Equipe is the most popular. Notre-Dame has its own varied, pretty ski area, with attendant ski school.

St-Gervais 850m

St-Gervais is a handsome 19th-century spa town set in a narrow river gorge, half-way between Megève and Chamonix, at the turn-off for Les Contamines. It has direct access to the Mont d'Arbois skiing via a 20-person gondola from the centre of town. At the mid-station is Le Bettex (1400m), a small collection of hotels, private chalets and new apartments, more conveniently situated for the skiing but with little evening animation.
   You can go up in the opposite direction from St-Gervais, towards Mont Blanc on a rack and pinion railway, which takes you to the Les Houches skiing. The only way back to St-Gervais from here on skis is off-piste, and there's frequently not enough snow. St-Gervais and Le Bettex both have their own ski schools.
   Its position makes St-Gervais a very convenient base for touring the different ski resorts of the Mont Blanc region. It also makes it fairly full of traffic much of the time.
   In St-Gervais, the Val d'Este hotel is conveniently situated in the town centre, while the chalet-style Carlina on the outskirts of town has a swimming pool, gym, sauna and table tennis. In Le Bettex, the Arbois offers stylish accommodation and a jacuzzi.

Les Menuires 1850m

HOW IT RATES

The skiing

Snow	****
Extent	*****
Advanced	****
Intermediates	*****
Beginners	***
Convenience	*****
Queues	****
Restaurants	***

The rest

Scenery	***
Resort charm	*
Not skiing	*

✔ Part of the biggest linked ski area in the world

✔ Some great local skiing for good skiers

✔ Swift access to both the Méribel and Val-Thorens ski areas

✔ You can ski directly to and from nearly all accommodation

✔ Extensive artificial snow facilities mean snow-cover is rarely a problem

✔ Probably the cheapest place to stay in the Trois Vallées area

✗ Main intermediate and beginner slopes into town get a lot of sun and snow deteriorates rapidly in warm weather; artificial snow turns into artificial slush

✗ The ugliest resort in the Alps

✗ Nursery slopes are busy as well as over-exposed to the sun

Les Menuires' big problem is its looks. Frankly, it's hideous. However, you can rent an apartment here for much less than you'd pay in the more chic Trois Vallées resorts.

It has good access to the Trois Vallées skiing. With 200 lifts and 600km of pistes plus endless off-piste possibilities, no keen skier will be bored in a fortnight here. Local skiing on La Masse is some of the best in the Trois Vallées for good skiers, with usually excellent snow. Many Courchevel- and Méribel-based skiers overlook it because it is set apart somewhat from the main circuit.

If you want to stay in a quiet, traditional Savoyard village, nearby St-Martin-de-Belleville – which was linked into the skiing in the late 1980s – is worth considering as a base.

ORIENTATION

Les Menuires now spreads up the valley towards Val-Thorens, with the building of two new satellites – Reberty and Les Bruyères.

A slow, old, two-stage gondola is the main lift out of the main resort. From its top you can ski direct to **Val-Thorens** and **Méribel** (and from there, on to **Courchevel**). The chair-lift alternatives are often quicker, and the quickest lift up to the link with Val-Thorens and Méribel is the two-stage high-capacity Les Bruyères gondola. On the other side of the valley a fast two-stage gondola now takes you to the top of La Masse.

Lift passes for six days or more also give you a day in **Val-d'Isère/Tignes** and **La Plagne** or **Les Arcs, Les Saisies** and **Pralognan-la-Vanoise**. But it's quite a drive to get to these resorts – Les Menuires is a long way up its valley.

The resort

Despite being 'smartened up' for the 1992 Winter Olympics (the men's slalom was held here), Les Menuires still manages to win our coveted Ugliest Resort in the Alps award, narrowly beating Tignes and Flaine. The original resort, the centre of which is known as La Croisette, is particularly horrendous.

Its newer outposts of Reberty and Les Bruyères are built in a somewhat more pleasing style. But, taken as a whole, the motley collection of mainly huge apartment blocks, varyingly wildly in design, make a disjointed blot on the Alpine landscape. The main advantage of most accommodation is its ski-in, ski-out convenience.

The new outposts have their own shops and bars. The main centre has an indoor shopping complex which is very dark and feels claustrophobic. However, there are some pleasant bar and restaurant terraces facing the main slopes into the resort.

The skiing

Les Menuires' skiing has two main attractions: La Masse, and the swift links to the skiing of the rest of the Trois Vallées. It suits all standards except complete beginners. But local skiing for intermediates and beginners is spoilt by the orientation of the main slopes, which get the full force of the afternoon sun; despite considerable artificial snowmaking facilities, in warm weather these local slopes – especially the lower ones – can be icy early in the day and heavy later.

THE SKI AREA
A good base for the Trois Vallées
Les Menuires and St-Martin-de-Belleville share a local ski area with 120km of runs and 50 lifts. The west-facing slopes have the vast bulk of the skiing. The main gondolas take you up to the **Mont de la Chambre** (2850m), from where you can ski back towards the resort or down to Val-Thorens or the Méribel skiing. Chairs and drags serve the local slopes, and you can work your way north by piste and lift, and ski down to the charming old village of St-Martin-de-Belleville.

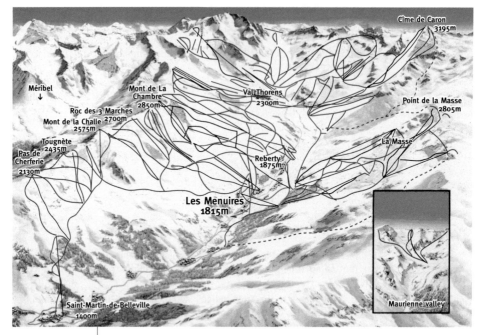

Cîme de Caron 3195m
Méribel ↓
Mont de La Chambre 2850m
Val-Thorens 2300m
Point de la Masse 2805m
Roc des 3 Marches 2700m
Mont de la Challe 2575m
La Masse
Tougnète 2435m
Pas de Cherferie 2130m
Reberty 1875m
Les Menuires 1815m
Maurienne valley
Saint-Martin-de-Belleville 1400m

SKI FACTS

Altitude	1400m-2850m
Lifts	200
Pistes	600km
Green/Blue	49%
Red	37%
Black	14%
Artificial snow	60km

SKI SCHOOL

94/95 prices in francs

ESF
Classes 6 days
5½hr: 3hr am, 2½hr pm; half-day am or pm
6 full days: 895
Children's classes
Ages: up to 15
6 full days: 750
Private lessons
Hourly
170 for 1 or 2 people

International
Classes 6 days
2½hr am or pm
6 half-days: 609
Children's classes
Ages: up to 15
6 half-days: 535
Private lessons
Hourly
175 for 1 or 2 people

The north-east-facing slopes of **La Masse** (2805m) are now served by a splendid two-stage high-capacity stand-up gondola that starts a short ski from the resort centre, and the snow on the top half is usually excellent.

SNOW RELIABILITY
Cover guaranteed but not quality
La Masse's height and orientation ensure good snow for a long season.

The opposite, west-facing slopes are supplied with abundant artificial snow (the resort boasts 277 snow cannon). But although cover there is guaranteed – so long as the weather is cold enough to make snow – the quality of the snow is often found wanting, especially on the lower slopes.

FOR ADVANCED SKIERS
Hidden treasures
La Masse has some of the steepest and least well-known piste skiing in the Trois Vallées – most skiers doing the 'circuit' skip it. Long reds and blacks come down either side of the top stage of the gondola. Other steep blacks, usually mogulled, are served by the Dame Blanche and Lac Noir chairs.

From the top there are also some marvellously scenic itineraires. The wide, sweeping, but not too steep, Lac du Lou takes off down towards Val-Thorens. Others lead off in the opposite direction to various villages from which you need transport back, but the Les Yvoses run takes you back into the Les Menuires lift system.

The easy access to the rest of the Trois Vallées skiing means that good skiers are spoilt for choice. Within an hour of leaving your door you can be skiing the steepest slopes of Méribel or Val-Thorens. Courchevel won't take much longer.

FOR INTERMEDIATE SKIERS
600km of pistes to choose from
The Trois Vallées is an intermediate skier's paradise. Virtually everywhere you go you'll find a blue or red piste to suit your tastes.

Les Menuires' local skiing is virtually all blue and red. But because of the west-facing aspect of most of the skiing the snow is often better elsewhere. In good snow, however, you may find little reason for leaving the local area. There's plenty of opportunity for playing on the chairs and drags here.

There are both pistes and itineraires down into Méribel, and five different peaks you can approach it from. Even a second- or third-time skier should have no problem cruising from valley to valley. In poor snow conditions the attractions of Val-Thorens become evident, and there's blue-run access via the Montaulever drag as well as red runs from the top of the mountain.

FOR BEGINNERS
Try elsewhere
Although there are wide and gentle slopes for beginners, we think you'd be better off for your first ski holiday in a resort which offers more of a real

LIFT PASSES

94/95 prices in francs
Three Valleys
Covers all lifts in
Courchevel, Méribel,
Les Menuires, Val-
Thorens and St-
Martin-de-Belleville.
Beginners Points card
for some ski lifts (25
points, 74).
Main pass
1-day pass 210
6-day pass 1010
(low season 910 –
10% off)
Senior citizens
Over 60: 6-day pass
760 (25% off)
Over 80: free pass
Children
Under 16: 6-day pass
760 (25% off)
Under 5: free pass
Short-term passes
Half-day pass from
12.30 for Les
Menuires and St-
Martin (adult 125).
Half-day pass from
12.30 for La Masse
area (adult 100).
Notes 6-day pass and
over valid for one day
each in Tignes-Val-
d'Isère, La Plagne-Les
Arcs, Pralognan-la-
Vanoise and Les
Saisies. Reductions
for families, students.
Alternative passes
Vallée des Belleville
pass covers 78 lifts
and 240km piste in
Les Menuires, St-
Martin and Val-
Thorens (adult 6-day
945). Les Menuires
and St-Martin pass
covers 48 lifts and
120km of piste (adult
6-day 830).

CHILDCARE

The ESF-run Village
des Schtroumpfs
(79006379) takes
children aged 3
months to 7 years. It
has a nursery for
babies, a Baby Club
for toddlers and a
leisure centre for
older children, with
indoor and outdoor
activities and ski
lessons for children
aged 2½ or more.

At Reberty-les-
Bruyères, the
Marmottons offers
similar facilities, and
the SEI runs a ski
kindergarten.

Alpine atmosphere and is easier on the eye. Good skiers can get away from Les Menuires and into beautiful Alpine scenery. Beginners are stuck with it in view all day.

Apart from that, the snow quality is a worry. We've seen beginners struggling on ice first thing and in thick slush in the afternoon – not the ideal introduction to skiing. The blue slopes immediately above the resort can also get extremely crowded.

FOR CROSS-COUNTRY
Valley hike
There are 28km of prepared trails along the valley floor between St-Martin and half-way between Les Menuires and Val-Thorens.

QUEUES
Can be bypassed
La Masse used to be queue-prone but that has been solved by the new high-capacity gondolas. The one remaining problem is the slow, four-person Mont de la Chambre gondola towards the Méribel skiing. But it can be avoided by heading to the high-capacity Bruyères gondola. Alternatively, take the high-speed Combes chair, then the slow Allamands chair up to Roc des Trois Marches.

MOUNTAIN RESTAURANTS
Have lunch in St-Martin
The restaurant at the top of the first stage of the La Masse gondola is fairly pleasant. And Le Panoramic at the top of the second stage has, as its name implies, great views. But a lot of people prefer to head for the restaurants of the old village of St-Martin-de-Belleville. The Bouite in nearby Saint-Marcel is also worth a visit. It's at the bottom of an itineraire from La Masse and you can get a taxi, hitch a lift or walk (2km) to the St-Martin lifts afterwards. The restaurant at the foot of the second chair up from St-Martin is also worth visiting. Locals tell us that Le Petit Savoyard, Le Necou and Chalet 2000, dotted around Reberty and Bruyères, are worth trying.

SKI SCHOOL
Overcomes language barrier
Reporters are full of praise, despite English not being widely spoken. Parents, in particular, were pleased that their children enjoyed themselves so much in multi-national classes. One mum states, 'My daughter, who is quiet and shy at times, loved every minute and preferred to ski with the school rather than me!'

Classes are usually small, by European standards, with a guaranteed maximum of ten. There are numerous interesting ski clinics on Thursdays, either half- or full-day, such as Moguls, Three Valleys Off-piste, Powder Technique, Ladies' Day, Snowboarding and Video Analysis.

FACILITIES FOR CHILDREN
All embracing
This is very much a family resort, and the childcare arrangements seem well organised. We have one recent report on the ESF ski kindergarten which is very enthusiastic, despite the fact that the child was the only English-speaker in the class – 'On departure day our four-year-old was crying, "Daddy, I want to go to school".'

 # Staying there

Despite the fact that the resort is designed for the convenience of skiers, you may wish to think quite hard about location. The central area around La Croisette is best for shops and après-ski.

HOW TO GO
Cheap, rough-and-ready packages
Most of the big, but few of the small, tour operators go to Les Menuires. They have a fair selection of both hotels and apartments. Les Menuires is essentially for those who want to ski the Trois Vallées from a good position, as cheaply as possible, and don't mind putting up with fairly sub-standard accommodation. Apartments are the norm, and there are, perhaps surprisingly, no catered chalets. Hotels are fairly thin on the ground too.

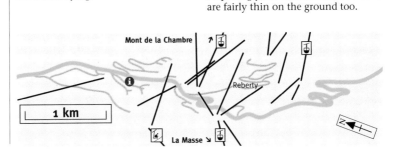

GETTING THERE

Air Geneva, transfer 3½hr. Lyon, transfer 3½hr. Chambery, transfer 2½hr.

Rail Moûtiers (27km); regular buses from station.

PACKAGES

AA Ski-Driveaway, Airtours, Club Med, Crystal, Enterprise, Inghams, Kings Ski Club, Made to Measure, SkiBound, Stena Sealink, Travelscene Ski-Drive

St-Martin-de-Belleville ABT Ski, Chalets de St Martin, Headwater, Poles Apart, Ski Total, Ski West

ACTIVITIES

Indoor Sports club, gym, body-building, table tennis, library, games room, theatre, 3 cinemas, gymnastics
Outdoor 2 outdoor heated swimming pools, plane and microlight rides, hang-gliding, guided walks, snow-scooters, artificial skating rink, snow-shoe excursions, para-gliding

TOURIST OFFICE

Postcode 73440
Tel 010 33 79007300
Fax 79007506

There is a Club Med above Reberty.
Hotels It comes as a slight surprise to find that there are some quite smart hotels here – although none above 3-star grading, and none with a pool.
££££ Latitudes Best in town, on the lower fringe of Les Bruyères.
££ Menuire Neat, well equipped new place on southern fringe of the resort.
££ Ours Blanc Wood-clad chalet on the slopes above Reberty 1850.
Self-catering Apartments are cheap but not so cheerful. It's a classic 'French box' resort, so paying extra for under-occupancy is an astute move. L'Oree des Pistes (Enterprise) and Residence Le Villaret (Inghams) are among the least objectionable, and the latter has a communal lounge with open fire, and a TV/video room. The Pierre et Vacances places (Inghams, Enterprise, Travelscene) are not up to the usual standard of the chain, but are still better than some other apartments in the resort.

EATING OUT
Good authentic French cuisine
Though some restaurants lack atmosphere at times, there's no shortage of good food. Savoyard specialities and 'real' French food are the order of the day. Reporters have recommended the Chaudron, Ruade and Bouquetin, but locals assure us that La Marmite du Geant is the best in town. Others we have liked are the Auberge de Lanau and Belle Epoque.

APRES-SKI
Improving but still very limited
The young people who are attracted here by low prices have done their best to bring a spark of life to the nightlife scene, but it's still pretty quiet. There are just enough bars to allow a half-way reasonable 'crawl'. The Pub is a gathering point for Brits, and other possibles are Pop 2000, Osian and the Calgary. It's all, however, very one-dimensional – there's little else to do but drink, though you can have an expensive bop at the uninspiring Liberty disco.

FOR NON-SKIERS
Forget it
Les Menuires is a resort for keen skiers who want to ski the world's most extensive ski area on a budget. It's not the place for non-skiers, though there are some pretty walks and a good open-air swimming pool.

St-Martin-de-Belleville 1400m
St-Martin is a traditional Savoyard village, complete with old church, small square and old wooden and stone buildings. It is the administrative centre for the whole of the Belleville valley (which includes Les Menuires and Val-Thorens).

In 1950 it didn't even have running water or electricity. In the 1960s and 1970s the nearby purpose-built ski resorts were developed. St-Martin became a bit of a backwater. But in the late 1980s a couple of slow chair-lifts were built linking it to the Trois Vallées skiing. It is now well worth considering as a quiet alternative to the mega-resorts.

The main disadvantages are the slow, cold 30-minute ride up into the skiing each day and the run back which doesn't survive if it's too warm for snowmaking. At least the chair-lift is to be slightly upgraded for the 1994/95 season. A rolling carpet is being installed at the base station so that the lift can be run at higher speed, cutting the ride by five minutes.

A new Grangeraies district has been built to extend the accommodation at the foot of the slopes. It blends in well, in contrast to its neighbours up the valley. There are a few hotels – the Alp-hôtel and the Edelweiss are traditional-style 3-stars – and a good variety of apartments. The few tour operators cover all styles of accommodation. Ski Total and Chalets de St Martin have several chalets, and ABT Ski a recently built chalet-hotel, convenient for skiing. Headwater package the main hotels. Ski West offer self-catering in the nearby hamlet of Villarabout, with minibus to the slopes.

There are a few restaurants and bars. The Pourquoi Pas piano bar is the most popular with tourists. There's a pizzeria as well as more traditional restaurants.

The ski school is said to have some instructors with poor English, and was so quiet in low season that there were only two classes – beginners and everyone else, leading to very different standards in the second group. There's a ski kindergarten of which we've had a good report.

Méribel 1400m–1700m

ORIENTATION

Méribel occupies the central valley of the Trois Vallées system. It consists of two main villages. Mottaret is around 200m higher and ten minutes further up the valley than the original resort of Méribel (now known as Méribel Centre), which is built along a winding road and has several 'centres' with shops and restaurants. Both resorts are served by lifts which take you quickly up to the ridges leading to **Courchevel, Val-Thorens** and **Les Menuires** as well as Méribel's own skiing.

Lift passes for six days or more also give you a day in **Val-d'Isère-Tignes** (just over an hour away), **La Plagne** or **Les Arcs** (30 and 45 mins respectively), **Les Saisies** (an hour) and **Pralognan-la-Vanoise** (45 mins).

For the Olympics, a new gondola was built from Brides-les-Bains, an old spa town way down in the valley, which served as the Olympic Village for the games, up to Méribel Centre. There's a mid-station at the old village of **Les Allues**, which has put the place back on the map as a possible place to stay.

✔ In the centre of the biggest linked ski area in the world

✔ Ideal for intermediates who love covering as many miles as possible

✔ Plenty for advanced skiers

✔ Modern, constantly improved lift system means little queueing and rapid access to all ski areas

✔ Good piste maintenance and artificial snowmaking facilities mean reliable snow

✔ Village purpose-built in pleasing chalet-style architecture

✔ Some accommodation convenient for skiing (most at Mottaret)

✘ Not the place to go if you want to get away from fellow Brits

✘ Main village spread out, straggling along a long, winding road that is mostly well away from the slopes

✘ Expensive

✘ Satellite resort of Mottaret is rather lifeless

For keen piste-bashers, Méribel is difficult to beat. It is slap in the middle of the Trois Vallées – the biggest inter-linked ski area in the world. With 200 lifts and 600km of pistes, and endless off-piste possibilities, no keen skier will be bored in a fortnight here. Méribel's local skiing is probably the least interesting in the region. But that is still good by any standards.

If you don't like skiing with hordes of Brits, be warned: more British tour operators go here than any other resort except Val-d'Isère. And it's not cheap. Indeed, the 1992 Olympics (the women's downhill and the ice hockey took place here) seem to have prompted the resort to move significantly upmarket. Several very comfortable and expensive hotels were built for the Games, and others were renovated, and food and drink prices have hit Swiss resort heights. But one of us learned to ski here, the other visited it on his second trip, and we both go back whenever we can.

 ## The resort

Méribel was founded by a Brit, Peter Lindsay, in 1939. It has retained a strong British presence ever since.

The original village of Méribel-les-Allues (now known as Méribel Centre) has grown enormously over recent years and is built each side of a road which winds its way up from the village centre at about 1400m to the Altiport (an airport with snow-covered runway and little planes with skis at) at around 1800m. All the buildings are wood-clad, low-rise, chalet style. It is one of the most tastefully designed of French purpose-built resorts.

Méribel-Mottaret started life in the early 1970s. It looks modern, with wood-clad apartment blocks built alongside the piste. But even Mottaret is much more attractive than many French resorts which have been purpose-built for ski convenience.

Méribel Centre rises from just above the main lifts, along the side of the main piste. Although some accommodation is right on the piste, much of it is a fair hike away.

There are a couple of concentrations of shops and hotels on the way up to Altiport. The main one is Belvedere, an upmarket enclave separated from the rest of the resort by the main home piste. Before that there is Altitude 1600, with a fair collection of shops and restaurants. The hotels and apartments of Altiport itself are rather isolated but beautifully set, in the woods. Lifts leave from here up towards the Courchevel skiing.

At Mottaret, the original village is set beside the piste on the east-facing slopes. New development has since taken place on the other side of the valley. Both sides are served by lifts for pedestrian access – the gondola up the original village stops at 7.30pm and it's a long, tiring walk after that if you're staying near the top. Mottaret has many fewer shops and bars and less après-ski than Méribel Centre.

SKI FACTS

Altitude	1450m-2950m
Lifts	200
Pistes	600km
Green/Blue	49%
Red	37%
Black	14%
Artificial snow	60km

The skiing

The main attraction of Méribel is the skiing of the immense Trois Vallées region, so read the entries for Courchevel, Les Menuires and Val-Thorens as well as this one.

It's keen piste-bashers who will get the best out of what Méribel has to offer. The grooming of the slopes is about the best in the Alps, which means there is endless cruising to be had – as well as more challenging skiing. And the lift system is so efficient that decent skiers can travel to the far end of the ski area and still be back in time for a late lunch. The Méribel valley tends to have rather inconsistent grading of runs, with some reds trickier than some blacks and others easier than some blues.

THE SKI AREA
Highly efficient lift system
The Méribel valley runs north–south. On the eastern side gondolas leave both Méribel and Mottaret for **La Saulire** at around 2700m. From here you can ski back down towards either village or down the other side in a choice of directions to join the Courchevel skiing.

From Méribel Centre a gondola rises to **Tougnète**, on the western side of the valley, from where you can ski down to Les Menuires or St-Martin-de-Belleville. You can also ski to Mottaret from here. From there a chair then a drag take you to another entry point for the Les Menuires skiing.

The Mottaret area has seen rapid mechanisation over the last decade.

The **Plattières** gondola rises up the valley to the south, ending at yet another entry point to the Les Menuires skiing. To the east of this a totally new ski area was opened up a few years ago by the building of a big stand-up gondola to the top of **Mont Vallon** at nearly 3000m. A high-speed quad from near this area goes south up to **Mont de la Chambre**, giving direct access to the skiing of Val-Thorens, as well as Les Menuires.

All the Méribel skiing, like the skiing throughout the Trois Vallées, interconnects without having to walk.

SNOW RELIABILITY
Great piste-maintenance
The Méribel skiing isn't the highest in the Trois Vallées, and snow conditions are often better elsewhere. But the grooming of the runs is excellent and the lower runs now have a substantial amount of snowmaking. So lack of snow here is very rarely a problem, though ice or slush low down at the end of the day can be.

At the southern end of the valley, towards Les Menuires and Val-Thorens, a lot of the runs are north-facing and keep their snow well, even when snow is in generally short supply.

It's the west-facing La Saulire side, which gets a lot of sun in the afternoon, and where snow conditions deteriorate first – but then you can always ski over the other side in Courchevel, and the north-east-facing slopes above Altiport generally have decent snow.

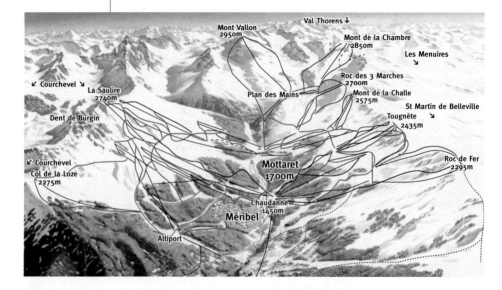

LIFT PASSES

94/95 prices in francs

Three Valleys
Covers all lifts in
Courchevel, Méribel,
Les Menuires, Val-
Thorens and St-
Martin-de-Belleville.

Beginners One free
lift in Mottaret and
one in Méribel;
reduced price lift pass
with beginners'
lessons.

Main pass
1-day pass 210
6-day pass 1010
(low season 910 –
10% off)

Senior citizens
Over 60: 6-day pass
760 (25% off)
Over 80: free pass

Children
Under 16: 6-day pass
760 (25% off)
Under 5: free pass

Short-term passes
Half-day pass (from
12.30) available for
Vallée de Méribel
(adult 125).

Notes 6-day pass and
over valid for one day
each in Tignes-Val-
d'Isère, La Plagne-Les
Arcs, Pralognan-la-
Vanoise and Les
Saisies.

Alternative passes
Vallée de Méribel
pass covers 120km of
runs in Méribel and
Mottaret (adult 6-day
827, child 6-day 580).

FOR ADVANCED SKIERS
Exciting choices
The extent of the skiing in the Trois
Vallées means that advanced skiers are
well catered for and shouldn't get
bored. In the Méribel valley one of the
most enjoyable runs is the very long,
steep, mogulled Combe de Vallon run
down the right hand side of the Mont
Vallon gondola. This is marked red on
the map but deserves a black grading.
There are wonderful views from the
top of the gondola of the unspoilt
nature reserve area behind, where
skiing is banned.

The newish chair-lift up towards
Val-Thorens has seen the conversion
of parts of the old itineraires into
official red runs, which are often
crowded. Though sadly less isolated
now, this remains one of our favourite
valleys: there is still plenty of
opportunity for skiing off-piste in the
wide open bowls on the way back
from Val-Thorens and Les Menuires.

A good mogul run is down the side
of the double drag-lift which leads
from half-way up the mountain at
Mottaret to Mont de la Challe. And
there is a steep black run all the way
down the gondola from Tougnète
back to Méribel Centre. Apart from a
shallow section near the mid-station,
this is unrelenting most of the way.

At the northern end of the valley
the new La Face run was built for the
women's downhill in the 1992
Olympics. Served by the two-stage
Olympic Express high-speed quad, it
makes a splendid cruise for a good
skier when it is freshly groomed, and
you can terrify yourself just by
imagining what it must be like to go
straight down.

On the La Saulire side, there are a
couple of black runs marked on the
piste map. But neither is as steep or
demanding as those on the opposite
side of the valley.

Throughout the area there are good
off-piste opportunities. The ESF runs
guided groups. We tried one last
season and had a wonderful day.

FOR INTERMEDIATE SKIERS
Paradise found
Méribel and the rest of the Trois
Vallées is a paradise for intermediate
skiers. There are few other resorts
where a keen piste-basher can cover as
many kilometres in as short a period
of time. Virtually all the pistes on both
sides of the Méribel valley will suit
advanced intermediates. Most of the
reds are on the difficult side.

For less adventurous intermediates,
the run from the second station of the
Plattières gondola back to Mottaret is
ideal, and used a lot by the ski school.
It is a gentle, north-facing, cruising
run which is well groomed and
generally has good snow.

Even second-year skiers should find
the runs over into Les Menuires and
Courchevel well within their
capabilities, opening up further vast
amounts of intermediate skiing.

This section on intermediate skiing
may seem short. That's because
virtually every piste in the Trois
Vallées region is ideal intermediate
terrain. To describe them all would
take a book in itself. If you're an
intermediate skier, don't miss it!

SKI SCHOOL

94/95 prices in francs

ESF
In Méribel and
Mottaret
Classes 6 days
4¼hr: 9.30-noon and
2.45-4.45
5 full days: 840
Children's classes
Ages: 5 to 12
5 full days: 662
Private lessons
1hr to 2½hr,
lunchtimes only
185 for 1hr

International
In Méribel and
Mottaret
Classes 6 days
4¼hr: 9.30-noon and
2.45-4.45
5 full days: 840
Children's classes
Ages: 5 to 12
5 full days: 662
Private lessons
1hr to 2½hr,
lunchtimes only
185 for 1hr

Ski Cocktail
Classes 6 days
2hr am or 3hr pm
6 mornings: 695
Children's classes
Ages: 6 to 12
6 full days: 945
Private lessons
2hr, 3hr, 4hr or full
day
430 for 2hr, for 2
people

Magic in Motion
English-speaking
school with course
maximum of 7
people.

CHILDCARE

The ESF runs P'tits
Loups kindergartens
at both Méribel and
Mottaret, with snow
gardens for children
aged 3 to 5 and
proper lessons for
older ones. Open 9.15
to 5pm.

Club Saturnin in the
tourist office building
in Méribel takes
children aged 2 to 8,
with skiing available
for those aged 3 and
ESF lessons for those
aged 4 or more.

FOR BEGINNERS
Not ideal
Méribel isn't an ideal resort for
beginners. But it has some good green
runs to progress to.

The resort lacks good nursery slopes
set apart from the main skiing. There
is a small one at Rond Point, mainly
used by the children's ski school.

But the best area for beginners is at
Altiport above Méribel Centre, now
accessible direct from the village at
Altitude 1600 by chair-lift. There is a
gentle out-of-the-way area here which
can be treated as a nursery slope. And,
once you can take a drag-lift, there are
two which lead to one of the best and
most attractively situated beginner
pistes we have seen. It is very gentle,
wide, beautifully set with trees on
both sides and has little through-
traffic of better skiers because it is a
dead end.

FOR CROSS-COUNTRY
Scenic routes
The main area is in the woods near
Altiport. There is about 17km of
prepared track here, which gives a very
pleasant and undemanding
introduction to those who want to try
cross-country for the first time.

There is also a track round the
frozen lake at Mottaret, and for the
more experienced there is an 8km
itinerary from Altiport to Courchevel.

QUEUES
Virtually non-existent
The huge investment in lifts that has
been made consistently over the years
has paid off in making the area
virtually queue-free despite the huge
numbers of skiers. If you do come
across a queue, there is generally an
alternative route available.

The old four-person gondola from
Mottaret to La Saulire can generate
queues, especially from mid-afternoon
onwards, with skiers going back to
Courchevel. But this can be avoided
by taking the gondola from Méribel
Centre or the chair from the Altiport
to Col de la Loze.

The Plattières gondola at Mottaret
can also get crowded at ski school
time, when the school gets priority.
Simply avoid the peak period.

MOUNTAIN RESTAURANTS
Places you won't want to leave
There is lots of choice by the standards
of most French purpose-built resorts.

The Pierres Plates, at the top of the
La Saulire gondolas, has magnificent
views and you can watch hang-gliders
taking off, though the food is nothing

special. Chardonnet, at the mid-
station of the Mottaret gondola, has
table-service and excellent food but is
expensive. Rhododendrons, at the top
of Altiport drag, has a modern but
atmospheric wooden dining room.
The Altiport hotel has a great outdoor
buffet in good weather and the 'best
tarts in town', but again is expensive.
Les Crêtes, below the top of the
Tougnète gondola, is one of smallest
mountain restaurants in the Trois
Vallées. La Sittelle, above the first
section of the Plattières gondola, has
decent food and magnificent views
towards Mont Vallon. Les Castors, at
the bottom lift station, has the best-
value food and excellent spaghetti
served in individual copper pots.

SKI SCHOOL
No shortage of instructors
The three main schools all have plenty
of English-speaking instructors and
we've had good reports on them.

The ESF is by far the biggest, with
over 300 instructors. It has a special
International section with instructors
speaking good English and run by Pat
Graham who also runs his own ski
clinics in the resort). Classes can,
however, be over-large, and one
reporter failed to get group lessons in
high season because they were fully
booked.

Reports on Ski Cocktail were
generally more encouraging; for
example: 'Good tuition. Well
organised, punctual, conscientious,
friendly instructors with a good sense
of humour.' They appear to keep class
sizes down to reasonable numbers too.

As well as standard group and
private lessons, there are some
interesting alternatives. For example,
the ESF runs full-day off-piste guided
tours, and Magic in Motion will
arrange heli-skiing from Italy.

FACILITIES FOR CHILDREN
Lots of choice
Despite our fat file of reports on
Méribel, none deals first-hand with
the childcare facilities. Two observers
have remarked on instructors shouting
at tearful tots. Several chalet operators
run their own crèches, with British
nannies. Snowtime devote a floor of
one chalet (Tronchet) to theirs. Mark
Warner have a crèche in their chalet-
hotel, and the option of a nanny
service for those taking over other
chalets completely. Crystal offer a
nanny service in their chalets Martine
and Marcelle. Meriski run a crèche in
its own chalet. Ski la Vie offers a
nanny service and after-skiing care.

GETTING THERE

Air Lyon, transfer 3½hr. Geneva, transfer 3½hr. Chambery, transfer 2½hr.

Rail Moûtiers (18km); regular buses to Méribel.

Staying there

The choice here is enormous. From the skiing point of view, Mottaret is hard to beat. It offers ski-in, ski-out convenience and the quickest access to the other valleys.

For those who prefer chalet accommodation, a more villagey ambience and a greater choice of shops, bars and restaurants, the best place would be around or just above the village centre of Méribel. The main thing to check is how far your accommodation is from the piste. Rond Point and Belvedere, for example, both have accommodation right on the piste. Many tour operators run their own minibus services to and from the lift station – a big plus point because the local bus is expensive (a big complaint of many reporters).

HOW TO GO
Huge choice but few cheap options
Package holidays with all types of accommodation are easy to find both with big tour operators and smaller Méribel specialists. There is a Club Med, occupying the swanky new Aspen Park hotel at Rond-Point. Unusually, the deal here does not include ski pass and tuition, broadening the appeal of the Club Med package somewhat.
Chalets Méribel has more chalets dedicated to the British market than any other resort. Some fair-sized chalet companies operate only in Méribel. The range of possibilities is vast. Here are just a few of the options available.

Meriski have an excellent selection of places at the top end of the market. All but one are sufficiently comfortable for position within the resort to be the main factor to consider. The exception is Refuge Corbey. Hermits with a feel for history (or ski convenience) will like this cheap and cheerful, piste-side ex-Resistance safe-house stuck way up the mountain, with luggage taken up by chair-lift and nightlife strictly DIY.

Mark Warner also have an interesting range of comfortable places, including a beautiful barn conversion with exposed beams and all mod cons at a bargain price for anyone not concerned about proximity to the slopes. It's in the original hamlet of Allues, a lift- or minibus-ride from Chaudanne. Their chalet-hotel Bellevue is cosier and smarter than many such places. Bladon Lines have a wide selection

across the price, comfort and convenience range. The Eden is good for those looking for a large chalet close to the main lifts.

Snowtime have a fine range, including a well-above-average chalet-hotel (the Parc Alpin), which benefits from having en-suite facilities, a small pool and an in-house crèche. Several reporters have praised this operation.

Crystal have a large choice, from ski-convenient 'real' chalets, far from town, to centrally located apartment conversions. Ski Activity have a small allocation of good-value, well-positioned accommodation.

Mottaret chalets tend to be towards the lower end of the Méribel market. Beach Villas, Olympic and Skiworld have cheap and cheerful places here, most of which are more ski-convenient than many of their Méribel Centre counterparts.

Hotels Méribel has some excellent hotels with reputations for high-quality accommodation and food. But they don't come cheap. A lot of renovation and repositioning went on at the time of the Olympics, and there are now lots of smart hotels with health and fitness facilities.

£££££ Antares Best in town; beside the piste at Belvedere. Ambitious cooking. Pool, fitness room etc.

£££££ Chalet Luxurious, beautifully furnished wooden chalet at Belvedere, with lovely rooms and all mods cons – outdoor pool, fitness room etc.

££££ Grand Coeur Our favourite almost-affordable hotel in Méribel. Just above the village centre. Welcoming, mature building with plush lounge. Magnificent food. Huge Jacuzzi, sauna, etc.

££££ Altiport Modern and luxurious hotel, isolated at the foot of the Altiport lifts. Convenient for access to Courchevel, not for Val-Thorens.

££££ Mont Vallon The best hotel at Mottaret, with a reputation for good food, and excellently situated for the Trois Vallées skiing. Pool, sauna, jacuzzi, squash, fitness room, etc.

££££ Chaudanne One of the oldest Méribel hotels, but completely renovated with a new sports centre – pool, and the rest. Excellent food.

£££ Grangettes Near the lift station. Good food; friendly staff.

£££ Adray Télébar Welcoming piste-side chalet with pretty, rustic rooms and popular sun terrace.

£££ Oree du Bois Just off the piste at Rond Point, convenient for skiing but not for nightlife. Old hotel offering good value for money. Sauna, steam room and jacuzzi.

Selected chalets in Méribel

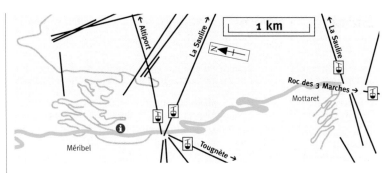

PACKAGES

AA Ski-Driveaway, Airtours, Alpine Expressions, Alpine Options Skidrive, Bladon Lines, Chalets 'Unlimited', Club Med, Cresta Ski France, Crystal, Enterprise, French Impressions, Inghams, Jean Stanford, Lotus Supertravel, Made to Measure, Mark Warner, Meriski, Neilson, Sally, Silver Ski, Ski 3000, Ski Activity, Ski Experience, Ski La Vie, Ski Les Alpes, Ski Peak, Ski Valkyrie, Ski West, Ski Wyatt, SkiBound, Skiworld, Snowcoach Club Cantabrica, Snowtime, Stena Sealink, The Ski Company Ltd, Thomson, Top Deck, Ultimate, White Roc

Brides-les-Bains
Alpine Options Skidrive, Crystal, Equity Total Ski, Kings Ski Club, STS, Sally, Ski Partners, Stena Sealink

££ Roc A good value B&B hotel, in the centre, with a bar-restaurant and crêperie below.

Self-catering There are a huge number of apartments and chalets to let in both Méribel Centre and Mottaret. Take care to make sure that the place you book is conveniently situated – see above. You also need to shop around to avoid 'French boxes'.

Ski Peak act as agents for a four-bedroomed apartment, and Snowtime offer many variations, from studios to a self-catered chalet.

Inghams have apartments that are owned by 3-star hotels, and as a result benefit from having access to numerous facilities such as an open-fire lounge, swimming pool and health centre.

Bladon Lines have some good accommodation which books out very early. Their Brimbelles apartments are particularly comfortable, and well positioned, close to the main lifts and the village square.

EATING OUT
Fair choice

There is a reasonable selection of restaurants, from ambitious French cuisine to fairly cheap pizza and pasta. For the best food in town, in plush surroundings, there is nothing to beat the top hotels – the Antares, Grand Coeur, Allodis and Chaudanne. Other top restaurants include Chez Kiki, for expensive but good charcoal-grilled food. The Jardin d'Hiver has great, if expensive, fish platters, and Les Castors is another fine place.

But our favourite is down in Les Allues, where the Croix Jean-Claude serves excellent-value French cooking in a pretty dining room.

Down the price scale, try the Galette, the Glacier and the Refuge. There's plenty of choice for local cuisine, including the Cave, Plantin and Cro Magnon, all of which are particularly popular for raclette and fondue. At Altitude 1600 try the Snowtime-run French Connection (where the ribs are particularly good) or the pizza restaurant. One reporter recommended the Crocodile restaurant in the Hameau at Mottaret.

Ski Crystal
T 081 399 5144 F 081 390 6378

Our choice of 9 chalets in Méribel includes beautiful chocolate box style chalets built mainly in local wood and stone, with a further 5 in the more modern Mottaret complex. There is an excellent range to suit all needs, budgets and group sizes, from the apart-chalet sleeping 6, to the larger traditional chalet accommodating up to 30 people. All chalets provide convenient access to the Three Valleys ski areas, many with skiing virtually to and from your door.

← Chalet Marcelle

OTHER CHALET HIGHLIGHTS
Chalets Martine and Marcelle offer **Nanny Service** all season, where qualified nannies will look after children aged between 6 months to 5 years, for either five full or half days between 9.30 and 4.30.
Premier Service is available in all chalets when a group books the entire chalet, and provides many extra comforts over and above the standard services. One week prices start from just £259 per person, including return flights.

ACTIVITIES

Indoor Parc des Sports Méribel (skating rink, swimming pool), Club Forme Mottaret (spa, sauna, solarium, gym), library, bowling, billiards, video club, bridge, fitness centres, jacuzzi, planetarium, 2 cinemas, concert hall
Outdoor Flying lessons and excursions, snow-mobiles, snow-shoe excursions, para-gliding, hang-gliding, 10km of cleared paths, motor-trikes, sleigh rides

MERISKI

helped us to compile the eating out and après-ski sections. Our thanks to them.

TOURIST OFFICE

Postcode 73551
Tel 010 33 79086001
Fax 79005961

APRES-SKI
Méribel has come to life

Méribel's après-ski scene used to be dead. It has improved beyond all recognition in the last few years. The liveliest places are in Méribel Centre rather than Mottaret and tend to attract a lot of British revellers.

Immediately after skiing, the Rond Point bar (also known as Yorkies after the previous owner) is usually packed and sometimes has live music. The focal spot at 1600 is the French Connection. Down in Centre, the Refuge is a French favourite, while the Capricorne is ever-popular. The Rock Café is louder and livelier, and vies with the Pub for the younger crowd. Jack's, at the Tremplin, is a new bar that's popular with resort staff (possibly because they get a 50 per cent discount). Later on, live music brings in the crowds at the Pub, Artichaud, French Connection and Rond Point. There is late dancing at Les Nuits Blanche and Scott's (run by Mark Warner). Les Saints-Pères, a cave-style disco on the fringe of town, attracts more of a French crowd.

In Mottaret the bars at the foot of the pistes get packed after skiing – especially the terraces on a sunny day. The Rastro and DownTown are the most popular, though reporters inform us that Zig Zag has lower prices. Later on, Plein Soleil sometimes has live music, and the Rastro disco is the main haunt for late revellers.

Both villages have a cinema which shows new Hollywood films in their English-speaking version up to three times a week.

FOR NON-SKIERS
Flight of fancy

Méribel is essentially a keen skier's resort. It attracts nothing like the number of poseurs that go to Courchevel. But as purpose-built French resorts go, Méribel is one of the most attractive architecturally, and not a bad choice for the non-skier.

Méribel Centre is the best choice to stay for non-skiers. There is a good public swimming pool near the lift station. You can also take joy-rides in the little plane which operates from the Altiport. The cinema often shows films in English.

The non-skier's pass covers all the gondolas, cable-cars and buses in the Méribel and Courchevel valleys and makes it very easy for non-skiers to get around the mountain and meet skiing friends for lunch.

STAYING DOWN THE VALLEY
The old village and a revived spa

If you want a quiet time, some tour operators have places in the old village of Les Allues down the road from the resort and connected by the gondola up from Brides-les-Bains. There are a couple of bars and a good-value hotel which serves some of the best food in the area and has been well renovated, La Croix Jean-Claude. Rooms are small, however, and we've had one complaint about poor service from a half-board guest.

Brides-les-Bains itself is an old spa town which served as the Olympic village in 1992 and is now trying to turn itself into a winter as well as summer resort. It's cheap and has some simple hotels and a casino. But reporters who've stayed there say it's dead. And the long gondola ride to Méribel is tedious, and not covered by the lift pass. If you are driving, it makes a good base for visiting other resorts as well as the Trois Vallées, and the car would be useful for getting to and from Méribel or Courchevel and into the lift system proper.

Further down the valley is the rather dull town of Moûtiers, which has a handful of hotels at less than half the price of those in Méribel. It would be fine for a couple of nights on a touring holiday, but pretty miserable for a whole week. The hotel Ibis is probably the most reliable.

From Moûtiers by car you can get reasonably quickly to not just the Trois Vallées resorts but also to Valmorel, La Plagne and Les Arcs.

Montgenèvre 1850m

HOW IT RATES

The skiing

Snow	★★★
Extent	★★★★
Advanced	★★
Intermediates	★★★★
Beginners	★★★★★
Convenience	★★★★
Queues	★★★★
Restaurants	★★

The rest

Scenery	★★★
Resort charm	★★★
Not skiing	★

✔ *Good, convenient nursery slopes, with easy progression to longer runs*

✔ *Few queues on weekdays*

✔ *Doorstep skiing from some accommodation; a short walk from the remainder*

✔ *Reliable snow on local north-facing slopes*

✔ *Attractive old village centre tucked away off main road*

✔ *Great potential for car-drivers to ski large intermediate ski areas*

✗ *Expensive compared to neighbouring Italy*

✗ *Poor base for skiing the Milky Way*

✗ *Slow lifts, short runs and continual pass-checking can be irritating*

✗ *Main road and tatty bars reduce village charm; former also reduces convenience and family appeal*

✗ *Virtually nothing for non-skiers*

✗ *Little to challenge good skiers*

Montgenèvre has a number of things going for it, but being a suitable base from which to ski the Milky Way is not one of them. The village is situated at one uninteresting end of the large ski area, a time-consuming trek from much of the best skiing, and lift pass arrangements make regular visits across the border an expensive business – you pay a daily supplement.

Unfortunately, the more central Milky Way villages have other drawbacks. Expensive Sestriere is a characterless place in a bleak setting; brash Sauze d'Oulx is not to everyone's taste; while little Sansicario and Clavière are really glorified lift base-stations with accommodation. Consequently, Montgenèvre is likely to remain a popular Milky Way base. Serious skiers should consider driving to the resort. This allows quicker access to the Milky Way's best skiing, prevents problems when the skiing links are shut because of poor snow, and simplifies day-trips to other French resorts. If you want to ski around the Milky Way a lot, pop over to Italy on day one and buy a weekly pass for the whole area.

ORIENTATION

Montgenèvre is a roadside village set in a high pass only 2km from the Italian border, relatively close to Turin. Its two facing ski areas are accessed from opposite sides of the narrow village. On each side the major lift up is a gondola. The skiing spreads east across the Italian border, via Clavière, Cesana and Sansicario to **Sauze d'Oulx** and **Sestriere** in the ski region known as the Milky Way. **Serre-Chevalier**, **Alpe-d'Huez** and **Puy-St-Vincent**, all with lift pass sharing arrangements, are easily reached by car.

 The resort

Perceptions of Montgenèvre as a village can vary enormously. This is understandable. At first glance it appears a dour, inhospitable place – a small, apparently purpose-built village of tatty-looking bars and restaurants set on a high, sometimes windswept and often busy, main road. The observant will also spot that the main ski lifts are inconveniently placed on the other side of the main road from the accommodation.

Appearances are, however, deceptive. Tucked away off the main road is a charming old village, complete with quaint church and friendly natives. Being covered in snow for much of the season accentuates the charm factor, as do the pleasantly wooded mountains either side of the village. Ski convenience, though far from ideal for families, is good. Other than crossing the road, there is little walking to be done in this compact village, where all accommodation is less than five minutes from a lift. Furthermore, the underrated Chalvet area is on the same side of the road as the village. For their part, the cheap and cheerful cafés and bars add an animated atmosphere sometimes missing from French resorts. The lack of a bank is a nasty surprise. There's a limited post office exchange service and hotel rates are reported extortionate.

 The skiing

Montgenèvre's local skiing is best suited to leisurely intermediates, with lots of easy cruising on blues and greens, both above and below the tree-line. The local upper slopes are particularly bland, but the skiing gains in interest further afield. Average intermediates and better will want to ski the whole of the Milky Way (see the chapters on the Italian resorts of Sestriere and Sauze d'Oulx).

SKI FACTS

Altitude 1850m-2580m
Lifts	23
Pistes	65km
Green/Blue	48%
Red	33%
Black	19%
Artificial snow	12km

SKI SCHOOL

94/95 prices in francs

ESF
Classes 6 days
5hr: 9.15-11.45 and
14.15-16.45
6 half-days: 500
Children's classes
Ages: Up to 12
6 half-days: 470
Private lessons
Hourly or daily
160 for 1hr, for 1-2
people

THE SKI AREA
Slow going
Lifts serve north-facing slopes in the
Les Anges-Le Querelay sector across
the main road from the village and
the south-facing slopes of **Le
Chalvet**, which lead straight up from
the village. The north-facing slopes
have a high altitude link to **Cesana**
and the rest of the Milky Way skiing,
or you can ski a network of runs above
and back down to Montgenèvre itself.
The Cesana link involves a long drag-
lift with a 200m walk at the top,
followed by an often-unbashed mogul
field – making the route a chore for
less able skiers. The Chalvet area's link
with the Milky Way skiing is easier but
lower, via **Clavière**, just across the
Italian border and down the road from
Montgenèvre.

Getting to the best of the Milky
Way's skiing is time-consuming. From
Clavière you have to go through
Cesana and up to **Sansicario** (at least
six lifts) before you hit a worthwhile
network of pistes; you can access
either **Sestriere** (probably the best
skiing of the Milky Way region) or
Sauze d'Oulx (also good).

It's a long day out on skis to and
from these areas, often made more
difficult by a lack of snow in the
Cesana area. Getting back to Cesana
from the top of the Sansicario skiing is
a single long run (actually several
connecting pistes). Things slow up
again after Cesana, with a three-stage
chair and drag making for a long spell
without skiing, before you cruise
down to Clavière and get a chair-lift to
the home run. You often get the

feeling you are doing a lot of
travelling without much skiing. A car
is helpful to speed up the journeys to
and from the best skiing.

SNOW RELIABILITY
Milky Way links can be a problem
The high, north-facing local slopes
have a fine snow record. The south-
facing area is obviously less reliable,
particularly late-season, but like the
north-facing area is supplemented by
artificial snow on its main village-
bound piste.

Sestriere is also snowsure, thanks to
its altitude and huge snowmaking
installation, but getting between the
two areas on skis is difficult at times of
snow shortage. The pistes either side
of the connecting Cesana valley are
often bereft of snow.

FOR ADVANCED SKIERS
Limited, exept for skiing powder
This is very little challenging piste
skiing in the Montgenèvre-Clavière-
Cesana sectors. Many of the runs are
overgraded on the piste map, with
none of the blacks being much more
than tough reds in reality. There is,
however, ample opportunity for off-

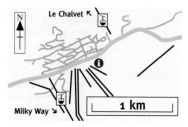

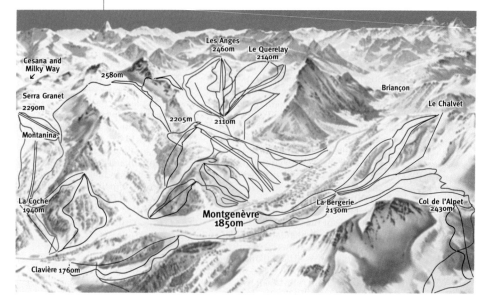

LIFT PASSES

93/94 prices in francs
Montgenèvre
Covers Montgenèvre lifts only.
Beginners One free drag-lift. Petit Réseau day pass covers 7 lifts (75).
Main pass
1-day pass 110
6-day pass 580
(low season 480 – 17% off)
Senior citizens
Over 60: 6-day pass 435 (25% off)
Children
Under 12: 6-day pass 435 (25% off)
Under 5: free pass
Short-term passes
Single ascent for foot passengers of Le Chalvet (25). Half-day pass from 1pm (80).
Notes 6-day pass and over allows free days at Alpe-d'Huez and Les Deux-Alpes. Extensions available at a supplement for Puy-St-Vincent and Serre-Chevalier. Reductions for families.
Alternative passes
Montgenèvre-Mont de la Lune (Clavière) (adults 125 per day, children 95). Voie Lactée (Milky Way) covers Montgenèvre, Clavière, Césana, Sansicario, Sauze d'Oulx, Grangesises, Borgata, Sestrières, (adults 170 per day, children 145).

CHILDCARE

The Halte Garderie takes children aged 1 to 4, from 9am to 5.30. Meals are not provided.

The ESF's kindergarten takes children aged 3 to 5.

piste excursions when conditions are right. There's a lonely north-east-facing bowl on the Chalvet side of Montgenèvre, served by a drag-lift from below the gondola mid-station, that is superb in good snow and has a black and red run too, with a chair to bring you back up. On the opposite side, both the runs from the top drag-lift on the Franco-Italian border can be fun. Unfortunately, there is no returning lift from the Italian side to allow repeated skiing in that direction (you get back to Montgenèvre via lower lifts, just above Clavière). The open section between Montanina and Sagna Longa on the Italian side is another good powder area. Drivers should visit Sestriere for the best challenging skiing.

FOR INTERMEDIATE SKIERS
Plenty of cruising terrain
The overgraded blacks are just right for adventurous intermediates, though none holds the interest for very long. The pleasantly narrow tree-lined runs down to Clavière from Plan del Sol, the steepest of the routes down in the Chalvet sector (including the lonely bowl mentioned for advanced skiers above), and the Montquitaine-Clavière piste (by the chair linking Clavière with Montgenèvre) are all fine in small doses. The Sagna Longa blacks are particularly uninteresting. Tours to the rest of the Milky Way are very rewarding, offering a real sensation of getting around the mountains on skis.

Average intermediates will enjoy many of the red runs, though most are rather short. The longest ones are down from the top of the Chalvet sector and from the Franco-Italian border at the top of the ski area opposite.

Skiing to Cesana via the lovely sweeping red starting at the top of the Coche drag and skiing home from La Coche via Plan del Sol is easier than the red gradings suggest, and these can be tackled by less adventurous intermediates, who also have a wealth of cruising terrain high up at the top of the north-facing Anges and Querelay slopes above Montgenèvre. These are served by several upper lifts, but you also have the option of continuing all the way down to the village. These long, gentle slopes are every bit as flattering as the famous motorways of Courchevel and Cervinia.

Further afield, skiing down to Clavière from the top of the Coche drags on the Italian border is a beautifully gentle cruise.

FOR BEGINNERS
Excellent for novices and improvers
There is a fine selection of convenient nursery slopes with reliable snow at the foot of the north-facing area. Progression to longer runs could not be easier, with a very easy green starting at Les Anges (2460m) and finishing at the roadside far below.

FOR CROSS-COUNTRY
Having a car widens horizons
Montgenèvre is the best of the Milky Way resorts for cross-country enthusiats, but it's useful to have a car. There are just two trails locally, totalling 20km, but a further 30km of track starts 8km away in the Clarée valley. One village trail is an easy loop that takes you parallel to the road, through the golf course, to the border post just outside Clavière; the other is a steeper route that climbs through woods in the opposite direction.

QUEUES
No problems most of the time
The ski area is wonderfully uncrowded during weekdays, when surrounding resorts have snow. At weekends and when nearby Bardonecchia is snowless, some lifts become oversubscribed. However, the improved links between Sauze d'Oulx and the impressive artificial snow of Sestriere now make bussing in from the former less likely.

MOUNTAIN RESTAURANTS
Head for Italy
These are in very short supply. Most local area skiers travel back to the village for lunch. The Ca del Sol café-bar does a good pizza. Milky Way skiers have several nice spots in Italy. Tucked away in the trees at Sagna Longa is the excellent Lo Scoiattola – atmospheric, friendly, cheap, and great pasta and antipasta.

SKI SCHOOL
Very varied reports
Comments on the school vary greatly, from very good to very poor. They tend to push pupils hard, which suits some but not others.

FACILITIES FOR CHILDREN
Lack of English likely to be problem
The intrusive main road apart, Montgenèvre would seem a fine family resort, yet none of our numerous reporters appear to have had a child in tow. We doubt whether much English would be spoken (by fellow inmates or supervisors) in the nursery.

GETTING THERE

Air Turin, transfer 2hr. Grenoble, transfer 3hr. Lyon, transfer 4½hr.

Rail Briançon (10km) or Oulx (17km); 3 or 4 buses per day from station.

PACKAGES

Chalets 'Unlimited', Enterprise, Kings Ski Club, Made to Measure, Ski Ca Va, SkiBound, Thomson

Clavière Equity Total Ski, Neilson, Ski Europe

ACTIVITIES

Indoor Library, cinema **Outdoor** Natural skating rink, curling, hang-gliding, para-gliding, snow-scooters, sledge runs

TOURIST OFFICE

Postcode 05100 Tel 010 33 92219022 Fax 92219245

Staying there

There are hotels, chalets and apartments available, all of which are cheap and cheerful places. Luxury-lovers should not stay here. Location is unimportant, as Montgenèvre is such a small place.

HOW TO GO
Limited choice

Tour operators concentrate their operation on catered chalets, though a few apartments are also available and one or two operators now package hotels as well.

Chalets Ski Ça Va Montgenèvre have arguably the best places in town, with a choice between a wooden hut and an old stone house, the latter in the attractive old village centre. The basic Bois de Sestriere and Boom chalets (Thomson) are popular for providing good value, ski-convenient accommodation, but neither are suitable for light sleepers. Reporters state that the former has been cheaply converted, and its thin walls fail to keep out early morning noise from the main road on which it is positioned. Boom has a disco attached, which reporters moan has inadequate sound-proofing. Enterprise also have a couple of cheap and cheerful places.

Hotels There are a handful of simple places, even the priciest of them offering good value.

££ Valérie Rustic old 3-star in the village centre.

££ Napoléon 3-star on the roadside.

£ Chalet des Sport About the cheapest hotel rooms in the Alps.

Self-catering Résidences La Ferme d'Augustin (Enterprise) are simple, ski-to-the-door apartments on the fringes of the main north-facing slopes, five minutes' walk (across the piste) from town.

EATING OUT
Cheap and cheerful

There are a dozen places to choose from, mostly pizzerias. Reporters have recommended the Ca del Sol and the Tourments. A reasonable pizza can be had in the Estable, Napoli or Transalpin. Chez Pierrot and the Jamy are the classiest places in town – and arguably the only ones to have much of an authentic French feel. The 3-star Napoleon is the only hotel with a restaurant open to non-residents, but it's yet another pizzeria! A trip over the border to Clavière is well worthwhile – the cheaper prices will pay for the taxi fare – and the Pian Del Sole hotel is a pleasant place to sample 'real' Italian food.

APRES-SKI
Mainly bars, but fun

Although the range is limited, the mainly like-minded 20- to 35-year-old clientele generate quite an atmosphere in a couple of bars. Le Graal is a friendly, unsophisticated place with satellite TV and occasional live entertainment; the Ca del Sol bar is a cosy old place with an open fire and a twice-weekly guitarist who sings slightly bawdy songs. Stevie Nick's is the better of the two discos, and livens up quite well at weekends. The Refuge and the Jamy are the focal café-bars at tea-time.

FOR NON-SKIERS
Very limited

There is very little to do. There is a weekly market and you can walk along the cross-country routes, but the main attraction is a bus-trip to the beautiful old town of Briançon.

STAYING IN OTHER RESORTS
Only for the dedicated skier

Cesana and Clavière are small, not particularly attractive villages with little in the way of resort infrastructure, and Cesana has the disadvantage of being a 15-minute walk from its lifts. Clavière has been introduced onto the 'Learn to ski' tour operator market by Neilson. Its nursery slope is small and steep but nicely uncrowded and snow-reliable, and there are plenty of longer runs suitable for progression. Both resorts are for dedicated intermediates who want to make the most of the Milky Way skiing and want a quiet time, without much après-ski.

Morzine 1000m

✔ *Part of the vast Portes du Soleil lift network*

✔ *Larger local ski area than other Portes du Soleil resorts*

✔ *Good nightlife by French standards*

✔ *Quite attractive old village – a stark contrast to Avoriaz*

✔ *One of the easiest drives from the Channel (a car is very useful here)*

✔ *Few queues locally (but see minus points)*

✘ *Avoriaz queues limit access to Portes du Soleil circuit*

✘ *Bus-ride or long walk to lifts from much accommodation*

✘ *Very poor recent snow record, with few snowmakers*

✘ *Low altitude or very inconvenient nursery slopes*

✘ *Very little for good skiers if Avoriaz Prodains runs are closed*

✘ *Weekend crowds*

Morzine is a long-established French resort, popular for its easy road access and gentle tree-filled ski area, where children do not get lost and bad weather rarely causes problems. Most British visitors, however, seem not to be families in search of a quiet time but keen skiers wanting to 'do' the Portes du Soleil. Some are graduating from Austria's smaller but similarly friendly ski areas, while others come in order to compare the Portes du Soleil with the Trois Vallées. For such skiers, the main drawback to staying in Morzine is the strong possibility of poor local snow conditions, and the frustration involved in getting to, and through, queue-prone Avoriaz.

Such problems can, however, be avoided by taking a car. A little-used gondola awaits at Ardent, a short drive from Morzine; from there you can ski the circuit clockwise via Châtel, missing out Avoriaz. There are buses, but not frequent ones. If snow is poor, Avoriaz is normally the first thought – but it's everyone else's first thought too. If you have a car, you have the alternative of visiting nearby Flaine, a resort far better than Avoriaz at coping with crowds looking for snow. Morzine is one of the easiest ski resorts to drive to from the Channel – there is a motorway from Calais to nearby Cluses.

ORIENTATION

Morzine is a large year-round resort village that sprawls on both sides of a river and on several levels. Its local skiing is shared with higher, smaller Les Gets. Lifts go up from the village into the Pléney sector, and from La Grangette, 2km from the centre, into the Nyon sector. The area is part of the Portes du Soleil lift-pass region, but is only tenuously linked to the main circuit: a gondola from the opposite side of the resort is the first in a series of lifts towards **Avoriaz**, which is on the main circuit along with **Châtel, Morgins** and **Champéry**. Car outings to **Flaine, Chamonix** and even **Courmayeur** are also feasible.

 ## The resort

Morzine is a large, traditional, towny mountain resort which sprawls amorphously on both sides of a river gorge and on several levels. Under a blanket of snow, its chalet-style buildings look charming, and in spring the village quickly takes on a spruce appearance. But at this altitude in France, the blanket of snow often gives way to slush and mud, which is less appealing. Perhaps because the French share our view that the resort suits car drivers, there are lots of them, and the resort suffers.

At the foot of this road, next to the river, is the old centre of Morzine, but most resort amenities are clustered up the hill around the Le Pléney lifts.

Accommodation is widely scattered, and a good bus service operates on six routes around the town, giving access to outlying lifts (though not linking them very cleverly).

Morzine is essentially a family resort. Consequently village ambience tends to be fairly subdued.

 ## The skiing

The local skiing, like that of the main Portes du Soleil area, suits intermediates well, with excellent slopes for beginners and near-beginners too.

THE SKI AREA
No need to go far afield
Morzine may not be an ideal base for skiing the Portes du Soleil circuit, but it has an excellent local ski area.

A cable-car and parallel gondola rise from the edge of central Morzine to **Le Pléney**, where numerous routes return to the valley, including a run down to Les Fys – a quiet junction of chairs which access **Nyon** and, in the opposite direction, the ridge separating the Morzine from the **Les Gets** skiing. Nyon is also accessed by cable-car, situated a bus-ride out of Morzine. The Nyon sector is also connected to the skiing of Les Gets higher up the valley that separates the two, with a lift up from Le Grand Pré to Le Ranfolly.

SKI FACTS

Altitude	975m-2020m
Lifts	224
Pistes	650km
Green/Blue	54%
Red	33%
Black	13%
Artificial snow	11km

SKI SCHOOL

94/95 prices in francs

ESF

Classes 6 days
5hr: 9.30-noon and
2.30-5pm; 2½hr: am
or pm
6 half-days: 500
Children's classes
Ages: Under 12
6 full days including
lunch: 1170
Private lessons
Hourly
200 for 1 to 2 people

The Nyon sector has two peaks – Pointe de Nyon and Chamossière – accessible from Nyon and Le Grand Pré respectively.

Connections between Pléney and Nyon are not easy for the uninitiated, owing to an inaccurate piste map and poor piste directions. Returning from Les Gets has to be via Le Ranfolly, from where you can ski home to Morzine without using a lift, via a path to central Morzine.

Beyond Les Gets is another small sector, chiefly of interest to Les Gets residents, on the front and back of Mont Chéry. The walk across the resort from the bottom of the Chavannes sector is a bearable one.

A third ski area starts at **Super Morzine**, accessed from town by gondola. A series of pistes and lifts transport skiers to Avoriaz. This section is very much an access route, used mainly by Morzine clientele moving to and from Avoriaz in the morning and afternoon respectively. The alternative is a bus-ride or short drive to Les Prodains, from where you can get a cable-car to Avoriaz or a chair-lift into the **Hauts Forts** skiing above it .

By bus or car you can also move swiftly to Ardent, from where a gondola accesses **Les Marmottes**. From here you can ski towards Châtel or get a lift up to Avoriaz.

SNOW RELIABILITY
Very poor

Morzine has a very low average ski height, and when snow disappears from the valley, both main ski areas become very small and unconnected. At such times, queues to and from Avoriaz are long. Snowmakers have at last been introduced – most noticeably on the two main runs to the valley from Nyon – but many more are needed.

FOR ADVANCED SKIERS
Limited; better than many in area

The run down from Pointe de Nyon is challenging, but the cable-car at Les Prodains is the place to head for, leading up to Avoriaz. The Hauts Forts blacks, including the World Cup downhill course, are excellent. Unfortunately, these runs are often closed due to lack of snow. The far end of the Chamossière section occasionally has good off-piste.

FOR INTERMEDIATE SKIERS
Something for everyone

Good intermediates will enjoy the challenging blacks down from Chamossière and Pointe de Nyon, the former also accessing a fine long red to Blanchots. Mont Chéry – remote from Morzine on the far side of Les Gets – has some fine steepish runs which are worth skiing over to. Moderate skiers

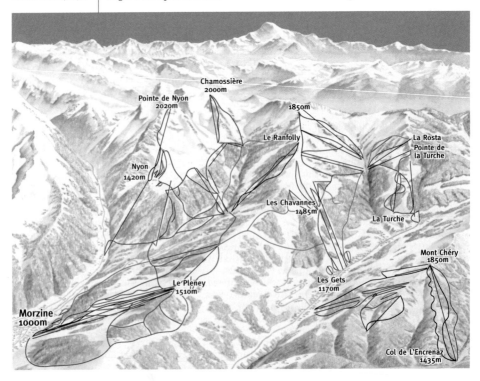

Chamossière
2000m

Pointe de Nyon
2020m

1850m

Le Ranfolly

La Rosta
Pointe de
la Turche

Nyon
1420m

Les Chavannes
1485m

La Turche

Mont Chéry
1850m

Le Pléney
1510m

Les Gets
1170m

Morzine
1000m

Col de L'Encrenaz
1435m

have a great number of runs to choose from, though most are rather short.

Le Ranfolly accesses a series of moderate runs on the Les Gets side of the ridge, and a nice piste back to Le Grand Pré. Le Pléney has a compact network of pistes that are ideal for groups with mixed abilities: mainly moderate intermediate runs, but with some easier alternatives for the timid, and a single challenging route for the aggressive skier. Nyon's skiing is rather bitty for those not up to at least Chamossière runs.

Timid skiers have plenty of options on Le Pléney, including a snow-gun-covered cruise from the summit back to the main lift station. Skiing from Le Ranfolly to Le Grand Pré is another nice run. Skiing down to Les Gets from Le Pléney is very easy when conditions allow (the run is south-facing).

FOR BEGINNERS
Good for novices and improvers
The village nursery slopes are quite good: wide, flat and convenient, and benefiting from snow guns. Fast learners have the inconvenience that the slightly longer, steeper runs are over at Nyon. However, precocious novices also have the option of easy pistes around Le Pléney. Near-beginners can ski over to Les Gets via Le Pléney, and return via Le Ranfolly. The skiing at Les Gets suits near-beginners well.

Selected chalets in Morzine and Les Gets

LIFT PASSES

Portes du Soleil
Covers all lifts in 12 resorts, and shuttle buses.
Beginners Limited area passes in Avoriaz, only half-day or day passes available for Morzine-Les Gets area.
Main pass
1-day pass 190
6-day pass 863
Senior citizens
Over 60: 6-day pass 570 (34% off)
Children
Under 16: 6-day pass 570 (34% off)
Under 5: free pass
Short-term passes
Half-day passes available for the Portes de Soleil (adult 129), Avoriaz only (adult 115) and Pléney-Nyon-Les Gets only (adult 102).
Notes Discounts for groups of 13 or more and holders of the Carte Neige.
Alternative passes
The Pléney-Nyon-Les Gets pass covers 85 lifts in the vicinity of Morzine and Les Gets (6 days 675 for adults, 507 for children); 6-day pass including 5 days in Pléney-Nyon-Les Gets and 1 day in Portes du Soleil (730 adults, 550 children).

CHILDCARE

The Halte Garderie l'Outa (50792600) takes children aged 2 months to 4 years, from 8.30 to 6pm. From age 3 they can have one-hour introductory ski lessons. The Centre de Loisirs takes children aged 4 to 12, ferrying them to and from ESF lessons.

FOR CROSS-COUNTRY
Good variety
There is a wide variety of cross-country trails, not all at valley level. The best section is in the pretty Vallée de la Manche beside the Nyon mountain. The Pléney-Chavannes loop is pleasant and relatively snow-reliable. A network of trails runs between Super-Morzine and Avoriaz, and around Montriond lake.

QUEUES
Few problems when snow is good
Queues are not a problem in the local area. The Nyon cable-car and Belvédère drag (Le Pléney) are weekend bottlenecks. Queues to and from Avoriaz are much improved, but are still bad when snow is in short supply. Bottlenecks in Avoriaz make skiing the Portes du Soleil circuit a rushed affair for those without a car.

MOUNTAIN RESTAURANTS
Within reach of some good huts
The nice little place at the foot of the d'Atray chair is perhaps the best of the local huts. The Chavannes self-service is good for lunch in the Les Gets area. Les Lindarets, Les Marmottes and Plaine Dranse are not too far and have some of the best restaurants in the whole Portes du Soleil. The restaurant at the top of the Zore chair, above Super-Morzine, is good, but most skiers pass it by in their haste to get to or from Avoriaz.

SKI SCHOOL
Children's classes get good reports
Most British visitors to Morzine appear to be intent on skiing the Portes du Soleil rather then taking tuition, and consequently we lack feedback on adult schools. The ESF children's classes have a good reputation.

FACILITIES FOR CHILDREN
Stick to Ski Esprit
We have always been quite impressed by the facilities of the Outa crèche, but a reporter who took his two-year-old there last January tells of unfriendly staff, little spoken English and a worrying staffing ratio of one to seven or eight children. Ski Esprit's facilities for children here are comprehensive, with three in-chalet crèches, an afternoon Snow Club for children attending morning ski school and their own Ski Sprites tuition scheme, using specially contracted instructors. But one reporter complains that sometimes less than half the morning lesson was spent on the slopes.

 # Staying there

As the extensive network of bus routes implies, Morzine is a town where getting from A to B can be tricky. It is well worth making sure that your accommodation is near the lifts that you expect to be using, which for most visitors means the gondola and cable-car to Le Pléney.

HOW TO GO
Good-value hotels and chalets
The tour operator market concentrates on cheap and cheerful hotels and chalets. Independent travellers have a wider choice, notably of apartments.
Chalets There's a wide choice, with something to suit all tastes. Position varies enormously: you can be in the centre of town or on the slopes with skiing to the door; many are on the outskirts, however, without either convenience.

The Ski Company Ltd have two chalets. One is a delightful 200-year-old farmhouse in Essert-Romand, a hamlet just outside Morzine, well placed for starting the day at Ardent, using the operator's minibus. It featured in Tatler's World's Top 50 Villas to Rent. The other, not far away on the outskirts of Morzine, is a modern Scandinavian-style affair.

Morzine specialists Ski Moose have one of the best selections, most convenient for the Pleney lifts and the town centre; one is close to the Super Morzine gondola. Trail Alpine have the ultimate place for Portes du Soleil ski convenience, at the Prodains cable-car station. A minibus provides access to Morzine.

Childcare specialists Ski Esprit have in-house crèches in three chalets. The central Gourmets – formerly a 1-star hotel – is arguably the best positioned. The Beach Villas chalet Mandarin is one of the least-expensive well-located town chalets – a converted 19th-century hayloft next to the Morzine lift. The Ski Chamois chalet-hotel is even cheaper, but it's up the mountain at the top of the Nyon cable-car – convenient for the skiing but very isolated. However, its DIY après-ski and value for money make it popular with reporters.

Thomson have a basic, badly positioned place, but it's cheap and could suit those with a car. Crystal's Coralie is perhaps the best chalet available through a big operator. Top Deck have one of their best places in Morzine, not well positioned but good for a lively holiday.

GETTING THERE
Air Geneva, transfer
1½hr. Lyon, transfer
3½hr.

Rail Cluses or Thonon
(30km); regular bus
connections to resort.

PACKAGES
Alpine Expressions,
Chalets 'Unlimited',
Crystal, Enterprise,
French Impressions,
Made to Measure,
Neilson, Ski Beach
Villas, Ski Chamois,
Ski Choice, Ski Esprit,
Ski Moose Chalet Co,
Ski Valkyrie, Ski
Weekend, SkiBound,
The Ski Company Ltd,
Thomson, Trail Alpine,
White Roc

Essert Romand Made
to Measure, The Ski
Company Ltd

Les Gets AGD Travel,
Alp Active, Chalets
'Unlimited', Fantiski,
French Impressions,
Made to Measure, Ski
Famille, Ski Hillwood,
Ski Total, Sloping Off

ACTIVITIES
Indoor Skating,
curling, bowling,
cinemas, sauna,
massage, gym, table
tennis, fitness track,
swimming pool
Outdoor Horse-riding,
sleigh rides, para-
gliding, snow-shoe
classes, artificial
climbing wall, tennis

TOURIST OFFICE
Postcode 74110
Tel 010 33 50790345
Fax 50790348

Hotels The range of hotel
accommodation is wider than it at
first appears – the handful of 3-star
hotels includes some quite smooth
ones. But the core of the resort is its
modest accommodation – dozens of 2-
stars and quite a lot of 1-stars. If there
is a resort with more hotels in the
Logis de France group (14 at the last
count), we have yet to find it.
££££ Dahu Best in town: upmarket 3-
star, complete with comfortable,
elegant public areas and good
restaurant and pool complex. Some
distance from all lifts and public buses
except the Ardent route, but with
private shuttle. Pool.
££££ Airelles Central 3-star close to
Pléney lifts and both Prodains and
Nyon bus routes. Good pool.
££££ Champs Fleuris Comfortable 3-
star right next to Pléney lifts. Pool.
£££ Tremplin Slightly simpler, but
just as close to the lifts.
£££ Bergerie Rustic, old-fashioned
chalet with a few rooms and many
more studios, in centre.
££ Côtes Simple, upwardly mobile 2-
star, with more studios than rooms.
Recently installed pool compensates
for poor position on the edge of town.
££ Equipe One of the better 2-stars,
superbly placed next to the Pléney lift.
Self-catering Trail Alpine offer packages
using the Eterlou apartments. They are
well equipped and good value but
their poor position makes them best
suited to self-drivers. The Télémark
apartments offer high quality
accommodation, and are close to the
Super-Morzine gondola.

EATING OUT
A fine choice across the price range
Morzine is a gourmet's resort. The
expensive La Chamade has high-
quality French cuisine, Café Chaud is
an atmospheric place that does good
fondue, Les Airelles has a fine
restaurant known for its hot buffets
and is open to non-residents, and Le
Dahu also has good food. L'Etale and
Le Varnay are worth visiting.

APRES-SKI
One of the livelier French resorts
Nightlife is good by French standards,
though far from wild. Dixie's
(occasional live music) and Le Bowling
(videos) are two of the most animated
bars. Boppers head for Opéra Rock or
Laury's and teenagers for Le
Wallington, a ten-pin bowling alley-
cum-disco bar. There are also two
cinemas.

FOR NON-SKIERS
Quite good; excursions possible
There is a fine sports centre with a
large ice rink and, although there is no
public pool in Morzine, Les Gets has
one and some of the hotels have their
own pools. Buses runs to Thonon,
which is a useful shopping excursion,
and car owners can drive to Geneva,
Annecy or Montreux. There are lots of
very pretty walks, and other amenities
include horse-drawn sleigh rides,
horse-riding, saunas and parapenting.

Les Gets 1170m
Les Gets is not a sensible base for
skiing the Portes du Soleil circuit, but
its local ski area has a far larger, denser
array of pistes than any of the resorts
on the circuit, and is perfectly
adequate for many intermediates. The
good children's facilities, pleasant
trees, French ambience, ski
convenience, nice village restaurants,
fine nursery slopes and reasonable
prices make Les Gets an excellent
choice for families and others looking
for a civilised, atmospheric ski holiday
venue. Weekend crowds are a
drawback, but lack of snow is a more
serious one. Snowmakers would
greatly improve the appeal of Les Gets.
    Les Gets is a little old village of
mainly traditional chalet buildings,
6km from its much larger neighbour,
Morzine. Although the village has a
scattered appearance, most of the
facilities are conveniently close to the
main lift station. Les Gets is on a
through road (Cluses-Morzine to
Avoriaz), but it does not intrude too
much, by-passing most of the village.
There is a fair amount of nightlife but
most places are quiet except at
weekends. The atmosphere becomes
more chic at weekends.
    As well as the ski area shared with
Morzine, Les Gets has skiing on Mont
Chéry, on the either side of the
village, accessed by gondola and
parallel chair from the edge of the
resort, with a further chair leading to
the summit. Much of this section gets
too much sun, but at least most of it is
reasonably high. Beyond Mont Chéry
summit is Les Gets' steepest skiing,
down the back of the mountain. These
are 'yo-yo' runs served by a solitary
returning chair.
    The quite good village nursery
slopes are convenient for most
accommodation, but Chavannes has
better and more snow-reliable ones.
Progression to pistes is simple, with a
very easy run between Chavannes and
the resort, and a couple of nicely
meandering routes from La Rosta. Easy

SKI TOTAL

helped us to compile the eating out and après-ski sections in Les Gets. Our thanks to them.

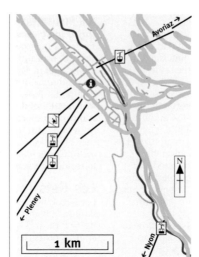

pistes between Le Ranfolly and Les Chavannes, and down to La Turche, mean precocious beginners can get a lot of mileage in without getting any lifts in a downward direction.

Keen cross-country skiers would be better off in Morzine, which has an excellent array of trails. But Les Gets has a good variety of loops on Mont Chéry and Les Chavannes – a total of 46km.

There are three ski schools, reports of which have been generally favourable. Group sizes can be large, though Ecole de Ski Plus guarantee classes of no more than nine. Beginners should shop around if conditions are less than perfect, looking for lessons at Chavannes.

The Ski Alpin pass covers all Les Gets, Nyon and Pleney lifts. The local ticket saves approximately £20 on the cost of a Portes du Soleil pass, and is well worth considering for moderate or timid skiers if snow conditions are good.

Many visitors stay in private chalets, quite a few of which are now on the British market in catered form. Most are pleasant, comfortable no-frills places. There are surprisingly few hotel beds and apartments available.

All the hotels are 3-star and below, mostly cheap and cheerful old 2-stars.

The Crychar is one of the best hotels in town, at the foot of the slopes, 100m from central Les Gets. The Ours Blanc is also comfortable and central, and known for its good food. The Labrador, of similar standard, is closer to the edge of town, though still an easy walk from the Chavannes chair.

The Praz Du Soleil and Bouillandire are simple, but pleasant good-value apartments five minutes from the main lifts.

After skiing, the hotel Bellevue at the bottom of the slopes is the natural rendezvous point. The English-run Prings and Irish-run Irlandaise also attract some trade.

Les Gets has a surprisingly wide variety of restaurants. Most of the hotels have worthwhile restaurants, including the Alpages, which does good fondues. The Tirol is perhaps the best of the pizza places. The Schuss and the Stade are others. The Vieux Chene is a very popular rustic place doing Savoyarde specialities. The Flambeau and Tourbillon are also recommended. El Rapido is a Mexican cantina, of all things!

Nightlife is quiet, particularly on weekdays. The Irlandaise and Prings bars can get quite lively. Magnetic Theatre is a very style-conscious piano bar, sometimes with other live music. The Igloos is a small disco, popular with the locals. The Jeckyll & Hyde is a less crowded alternative. Tour ops organise evening events, including bowling at the good two-lane alley.

Morzine is a better choice for non skiers, although Les Gets has a good fitness centre with swimming, saunas, massage, weights and so on, and an artificial ice rink. Outings to Geneva, Lausanne and Montreux are possible.

There is a non-ski nursery for children aged 3 months to 2 years, and two ski-kindergartens. The 'Ile des Enfants', run by the Ski Espace school, is reputedly the better of the two, and is open from 8am to 6pm, taking children from 3 years old. The ESF run Club Fantaski has been criticised for inattentive supervision and having a roadside slope used by other skiers.

La Plagne 1800–2100m

HOW IT RATES

The skiing

Snow	****
Extent	*****
Advanced	***
Intermediates	*****
Beginners	*****
Convenience	*****
Queues	***
Restaurants	**

The rest

Scenery	***
Resort charm	*
Not skiing	*

✔ *Extensive ski area, best suited to intermediates*

✔ *Excellent nursery slopes*

✔ *High snowsure skiing, including a glacier area*

✔ *Ski-in, ski-out convenience in the high, purpose-built resort units*

✔ *Some attractive traditional valley villages are connected to the skiing*

✔ *Wooded runs of lower resorts good for poor-weather skiing*

✔ *Good cross-country trails*

✗ *Few sustained challenging runs*

✗ *Lower villages often suffer from poor snow conditions*

✗ *Unattractive architecture in some of the higher resort units*

✗ *Some long queues during peak season*

✗ *Nightlife very limited*

La Plagne has one of the biggest areas of consistently intermediate skiing around. And above the main purpose-built resorts it is high, snowsure skiing. There's mile after mile of motorway cruising, usually with some more difficult options. There are also pretty runs down through the trees to traditional and quasi-traditional connected villages. These are, in general, more attractive but less convenient for the skiing than the seven separate higher purpose-built centres. Taken as a whole, La Plagne has considerable attractions for all skiers except those after the steepest pistes.

 ## The resort

La Plagne is one of the most disjointed ski resorts we know. There are no fewer than 11 separate 'villages'; seven are purpose-built at altitude on or above the tree-line and linked by road, lifts and pistes; the other four are widely spaced in the valleys below.

Even the resorts built up the mountain vary considerably in architectural style and character. The first to be built, in the 1960s, was Plagne Centre, at around 2000m – still the focal point for shops and après-ski. Typical of its time, it consists of big ugly blocks and dark, depressing passageways which house the shops, bars and restaurants.

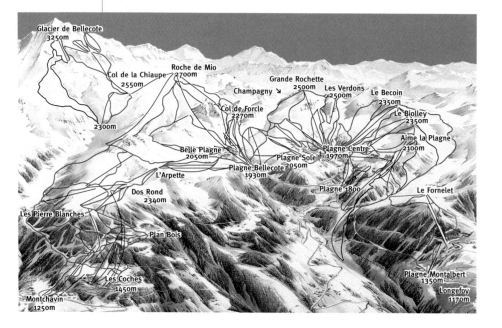

ORIENTATION

La Plagne is a big and complex ski area containing 11 identifiable resorts and seven interlinked sectors of skiing. La Plagne itself consists of seven resort units dotted around a high, fragmented bowl, above the tree-line. On lower wooded slopes outside this bowl are four satellite villages – **Champagny-en-Vanoise** to the south, Montalbert to the west, Montchavin and Les Coches to the north.

Day-trips to **Les Arcs** are easy, to **Val-d'Isère, Tignes** or the **Trois Vallées** more time-consuming.

SKI FACTS

Altitude	1250m-3250m
Lifts	113
Pistes	210km
Green/Blue	66%
Red	28%
Black	6%
Artificial snow	3km

Above it, and linked by cable-car, is the even more obtrusive Aime la Plagne – a single great apartment block in the shape of a giant chalet. Below these two, and somewhat out of the way, is Plagne 1800, a more tasteful chalet-style development.

A short walk above Plagne Centre is the newest incarnation of La Plagne, Plagne Soleil, still as yet small but with its own shops and very convenient for the slopes.

Plagne Village is an attractive collection of small-scale apartment and chalet developments built in traditional Savoyard style and around 50m higher than Plagne Centre. Again, it is very convenient for skiing.

The large apartment buildings of Plagne Bellecôte, on the other hand, are built an inexplicably awkward walk below the local lifts.

Belle Plagne, as its name suggests, is built in a pleasing style, with something of the Disneyesque neo-Savoyard look of Valmorel. It is very convenient for the lifts up towards the glacier area.

Accommodation in all these developments on the mountain is largely self-catering, and popular with French families, who pack the resort during peak season weeks. In low-season it can be eerily empty. There are some hotels in Plagne Centre.

Then there are the lower resorts in the valleys – the old villages of Montchavin and Champagny, on opposite sides of the ski area, and the newly developed villages of Les Coches (near Montchavin) and Montalbert. For a description of each, see the end of this chapter.

 ## The skiing

La Plagne is an ideal resort for intermediate skiers of all descriptions. There are wide motorways for early intermediates and long excursions for the more adventurous. Beginners are well catered for by good ski schools that operate on easy, accessible nursery slopes.

THE SKI AREA
Multi-centred; can be confusing
La Plagne boasts 210km of pistes over a wide terrain that can be broken down into seven distinct but inter-linked sectors. From Plagne Centre you can take a lift up to **Biolley,** from where you can ski back to Centre, to Aime la Plagne or down gentle runs to **Montalbert,** from which you ride several successive lifts back up. But the

main lift out of Plagne Centre leads up to **Grande Rochette**. From here there are good sweeping runs back and an easier one over to Plagne Bellecôte, or you can drop over the back into the predominantly south-facing **Champagny** skiing (from which a lift arrives back up at Grande Rochette and another brings you out much further east). From the Champagny sector there are great views over to Courchevel, across the valley.

From Plagne Bellecôte and Belle Plagne, the main gondola heads up to **Roche de Mio**, from where runs spread out in all directions. You can ski back down towards La Plagne proper, or down towards Champagny in one direction and **Montchavin** in the other. Montchavin can also be reached by taking a chair from Plagne Bellecôte. If you change gondolas at Roche de Mio, you go down to the mid-station at Col de la Chiaupe (there's no skiing down to it in that direction) then up again to the **Bellecôte glacier**. The easy glacier skiing here is open only in summer, but the gondola gives access to some of the steepest winter skiing in the area. You have to catch the gondola at the mid-station to get back up to Roche de Mio.

SNOW RELIABILITY
Good except in low-lying villages
In general, the bulk of La Plagne's skiing is very snowsure, with much of it being between 2000m and 2700m on the largely north-facing open slopes above the purpose-built centres. The Bellecôte glacier drags are normally shut in winter.

The runs down to the valley resorts can cause more problems, and you may have to take the lifts home at times. This is particularly true of the Champagny sector, where the two home runs are both south-facing and quickly lose their snow in warm weather. The lower runs down to Montchavin and Les Coches are north-facing and now have artificial snow, so are much less of a problem.

FOR ADVANCED SKIERS
A few good blacks and off-piste
There are two exceptional black runs leading down from the Bellecôte glacier, both of which take you away from the lift system and are beautiful long runs with a vertical drop of over 1000m. A chair-lift takes you back to the mid-station of the glacier gondola. The other main black run is the Emile Allais down from above Aime la Plagne through the forest, finishing at

LIFT PASSES

94/95 prices in francs
La Plagne
Covers all lifts in
La Plagne and
Champagny-en-
Vanoise.
Beginners Free baby-
lift in each centre.
Main pass
1-day pass 205
6-day pass 940
(low season 705 –
25% off)
Senior citizens
Over 60: 6-day pass
705 (25% off)
Children
Under 16: 6-day pass
705 (25% off)
Under 7: free pass
Short-term passes
Half-day pass (149).
Single ascent on
inter-area links.
Notes 6-day pass and
over covers Les Arcs
for duration of pass,
and one day each in
Tignes-Val d'Isère, the
Three Valleys,
Pralognan-la-Vanoise
and Les Saisies.
Reductions for
groups.
Alternative passes
Limited passes
available in the main
areas (La Plagne,
Champagny,
Montchavin).
'Discovery' passes in
each area.

1400m, with a couple of drag-lifts taking you back up. This is surprisingly little-skied, north-facing and very enjoyable in good snow.

The long, sweeping Mont de la Guerre red run, with a 1250m vertical drop down from Grande Rochette-Les Verdons to Champagny, is also a beautiful run in good snow – a rare event because of its orientation.

There are other good long reds to cruise around on. But good skiers will get the best out of La Plagne if they hire a guide and explore the vast off-piste potential. There are very popular off-piste variants from the Bellecôte glacier black run down to the restaurant at Les Bauches (a drop of over 1400m), from where you can ride chairs back to the main skiing above Les Pierres Blanches, or cruise down to Montchavin. You can also head down off-piste to Peisey-Nancroix and the lifts up to the Les Arcs skiing.

Another beautiful and out-of-the-way off-piste run from the Bellecôte glacier is over the Col du Nant glacier and down into the valley of Champagny-le-Haut.

Unfortunately, especially in the early part of the season, the glacier gondola can be closed by high winds or poor weather. This greatly reduces the area's interest for good skiers.

In fresh snow, skiers who enjoy picking their way through woods in search of fresh light powder will not be disappointed by the forests above Montchavin and Montalbert.

FOR INTERMEDIATE SKIERS
Great variety: a chance to improve
Virtually the whole of La Plagne's ski area is a paradise for intermediates, with blue and red runs wherever you look. Your main choice will be whether to settle for one area for the day and explore its skiing thoroughly, or just cruise around the pistes that form the main arteries of the network.

For early intermediates there are plenty of gentle blue motorway pistes in the main La Plagne bowl, and a long, interesting run from Roche de Mio back to Belle Plagne which includes a long, dark (and often very cold) tunnel. In poor weather the best place to be is in the trees on the gentle runs leading down to Montchavin-Les Coches or to Montalbert. The easiest way over to the Champagny skiing is from the Roche de Mio area rather than Grande Rochette.

Better intermediates have lots of delightful long red runs to try. Roche de Mio to Les Bauches is a drop of 900m. There are challenging red

mogul pitches down from the glacier to the mid-station of the gondola at Col de la Chiaupe. And the main La Plagne bowl has enjoyable reds in all sectors. The Champagny sector has a couple of tough reds – appropriately called Kamikaze and Hari Kiri – leading from Grande Rochette. The long Mont de la Guerre red, mentioned in the advanced skiers section above, is a satisfying run for adventurous intermediates.

FOR BEGINNERS
Excellent facilities for the novice
La Plagne is a good place to learn to ski, with generally good snow and above-average facilities for beginners, especially children. Each of the main centres has nursery slopes on its doorstep and a good number of green or easy blue runs for the beginner confident enough to graduate away from such areas.

CROSS-COUNTRY
Open and wooded trails
There are close to 100km of prepared and marked cross-country pistes in La Plagne and its surrounding satellites. The most beautiful of these are the 35km set out in the Champagny-le-Haut valley. Here the pistes loop and wind through wild countryside, often in good sunny conditions. The north-facing areas have more wooded trails that link the various centres. There is a 12km route around Les Coches-Montchavin and a longer, 25km route that begins low down at Longefoy (1350m) and winds up through Montalbert to Plan Bois at 1700m. The resorts of Plagne Bellecôte, Belle Plagne and Plagne Villages are similarly linked by a less arduous, 24km route.

QUEUES
Bottlenecks in high season
When the resort is full there can be big queues to get out of the high-altitude purpose-built villages at the start of the day. The old gondola from Plagne Bellecôte via Belle Plagne to Roche de Mio is still a bad bottleneck, despite the alternative more roundabout ways now available. The higher gondola can also get very oversubscribed when snow is poor lower down (and the return pistes can get very crowded). The gondola from Plagne Centre to Grande Rochette can also generate fair-sized queues (after lunch as well as first thing). In low season, things are much better.

Queues for the lifts in the lower satellite villages are rarely a problem.

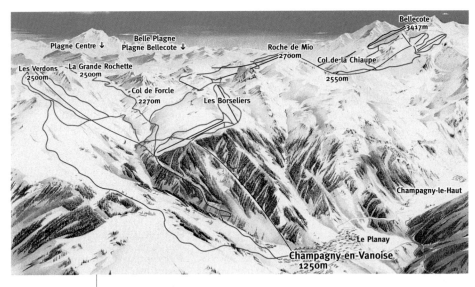

SKI SCHOOL

93/94 prices in francs

ESF
Schools in all centres. Prices do vary; those given here are for Plagne Centre

Classes 6 days
2½hr, 3hr, 5hr, 6hr, depending on centre and time of day and season
6 full days: 700

Children's classes
Ages: Up to 14
6 full days: 590

Private lessons
Hourly
175 for 1hr

Eric Laboureix
New ski and mountain sports school in Belle Plagne

Oxygène
Private school in Plagne Centre

MOUNTAIN RESTAURANTS
Functional; lacking in charm

Mountain restaurants are numerous, varied and seldom crowded, as many skiers prefer to descend to their resort at the end of the morning. The British-run Lincoln in Plagne Soleil and the Grange in Plagne Bellecôte get good reports. For skiers based in the central resort units, skiing over to Montchavin or Champagny for lunch is an attractive option.

There are the usual large self-service restaurants. Particularly popular are the two on the Roche de Mio and Grande Rochette summits. There are smaller quieter alternatives for those who prefer more leisurely rest-stops. One ideal restaurant refuge in poor weather is Le Sauget, above Montchavin, which serves sensibly priced local Savoyarde dishes in a pleasant family-run setting. We also liked the restaurant at the top of the Champagny gondola – friendly staff, both table- and self-service, beautiful views from the terrace over to Courchevel, good basic cooking and free schnapps with the bill if you linger as long as we did!

SKI SCHOOL
Adequate for all levels

Each centre has its own ESF ski school which is generally well run and offers classes for all standards. Groups tend to be large (between 10 and 15) in peak season but shrink during the off-season. Instructors speak English of varying standard, according to reporters. Generally, our most positive reports have been of Plagne Centre; the most negative are of 1800. Belle Plagne has received mixed reports: good tuition but a lack of English speakers (surprising, because it is a popular base with British tour operators). Ski évolutif is popular. More popular still are the snowboarding and monoski lessons.

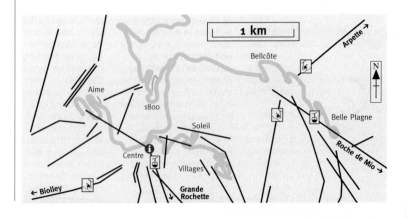

Selected chalets in La Plagne

Ski Amis — T 0233 732187 F 0233 732769

Chalet Danielle and Les Gavins
2 purpose-built, traditional chalets with spectacular south-facing views. Managed by their owners, the chalets offer a high standard of accommodation with excellent cuisine in a warm and friendly, relaxed atmosphere. Family and twin rooms plus a flexible approach ensures that most requirements can be met. Direct access to the extensive area of La Plagne yet quiet location above Montalbert at 1650m, offering skiing to suit all abilities.

SKI AMIS OFFERS:
PARTIES UP TO 20

- 7 day catering
- Free Ski Guiding
- Nanny Service
- Travel & Insurance
- Ski to door
- Bonded by ABTOT
- COLOUR BROCHURE

Ski Beat *The La Plagne specialists* — T 0272 557361 F 0272 412099

Chalet Perrier SLEEPS 12/13
Set among the trees above Plagne 1800, Chalet Perrier was designed especially for Ski Beat. The spacious living room is both elegant and comfortable; the views from the vast French windows, breathtaking. Four bedrooms have full en suite bathrooms and two share a bathroom. The chalet is 375m from a chairlift and the independent ski school in Plagne Centre offers a free taxi service from the chalet to your lessons.

OTHER HIGHLIGHTS IN LA PLAGNE:
Chalet Beryl SLEEPS 10
Arguably the most attractive chalet in 1800. Doorstep skiing.
Chalet Marine SLEEPS 14/16
En suite in all rooms, well-located for 1800 ski school.
Chalet Charmant SLEEPS 12
A charming, rustic chalet. En suite in all rooms.
Chalet Almach SLEEPS 8/9
Dramatic position overlooking 1800. 350m from chairlift.
Chalet Arpette SLEEPS 8
Modern & stylish. Doorstep skiing. Opposite ski school.

Ski Crystal — T 081 399 5144 F 081 390 6378

← Chalet Les Circes

There is an impressive variety of chalets in La Plagne with **16** featured in 4 of the best centres of this famous resort. All needs, budgets and group sizes are catered for, from the small – sleeping 6 to 7, to the larger chalet which can accommodate up to 20 people. From modern apart-chalets to beautiful chocolate box properties, furnished in traditional local materials, all providing convenient access to the ski areas and village amenities.

OTHER CHALET HIGHLIGHTS
Chalets Rose and Nikita offer **Nanny Service**, with a dedicated crêche (also available for use by guests with children staying in other chalets) where qualified nannies will look after children aged between 6 mths. to 5 years, for either five full or half days between 9.30 & 4.30. **Premier Service** is available when a group books the entire chalet, and provides many extra comforts. One week prices start from just £269 per person including return flights.

CHILDCARE

There are ESF ski kindergartens in all the high resort units, generally taking children from age 3. The ESF also runs all-day nurseries in most of the villages, mostly taking children aged 2 to 6. In Centre, the independent Marie Christine nursery offers much the same service.

The arrangements in the outlying satellite villages are similar, except that in Montchavin and Les Coches very young skiers are handled by the Nursery Club, the ESF taking children aged 4 and 5.

GETTING THERE

Air Geneva, transfer 3½hr. Lyon, transfer 3½hr. Chambery, transfer 2½hr.

Rail Aime (18km); frequent buses from station.

FACILITIES FOR CHILDREN
Good choice
Children seem to be well looked after throughout La Plagne's network of resorts. We have only one first-hand report, on the nursery at Belle Plagne – 'excellent, with good English spoken'. The Club Med at Aime la Plagne is one of their 'family' villages. La Plagne and its satellites are fast becoming the chalet-crèche capital of the Alps. Nannies are provided by: Ski Esprit in Montchavin and Les Coches; Simply Ski in Montchavin; Ski Amis in Montalbert; Crystal in Plagne 1800 and Les Coches; and Ski Beat in 1800.

 Staying there

Door-to-door skiing is the norm in the high altitude resorts. This means that, unless you miss a crucial linking lift, you can nearly always ski home. There is, however, an efficient bus system linking the resorts, which runs until after midnight and might tempt you to explore the après-ski in different areas. Most people, however, are happy to use the après-ski facilities most immediately accessible.

HOW TO GO
Plenty of packages
For a resort which is very apartment-dominated, there are a surprising number of attractive chalets available through British tour operators. There are few hotels, but some attractive, simple 2-stars in the lower villages. There is a Club Med 'village' at Aime

la Plagne. Accommodation in the outlying satellite resorts is described at the end of the chapter.

Chalets There's a large number available, though many are of a similar standard, type and position – fairly simple, small and in 1800. We've had several good reports of the Ski Beat chalets in 1800 (one has a crèche), and Ski West have a welcome new addition nearby. Of the big tour operators, Crystal have the biggest and best selection, with comfortable places in 1800 and Belle Plagne. Skiworld have simple chalets that are difficult to beat for price. Silver Ski offer a good selection of comfortable places in Centre and Plagne Villages.

Hotels There are very few, all of 2-star or 3-star grading. Probably the most comfortable place, if you're looking for a package, is Club Med, up at Aime la Plagne.

££ Graciosa Well-run 14-room hotel in Plagne Centre.

££ Eldorador 'Excellent' hotel in Belle Plagne – spacious rooms, generous buffet breakfast.

Self-catering La Plagne is the ultimate apartment resort, but many of the blocks are similar in standard. In-house communal facilities such as lounges, restaurants and the like are not as commonplace here as in most French purpose-built resorts. Fortunately, many tour operators have allocations in the above-average Pierre et Vacances apartments in Belle Plagne. The same chain also has reasonable places in Les Coches (Crystal, Travelscene). Crystal have

---

Try the Olympic bobsleigh run

If the thrills and spills of the slopes aren't enough, you can try the 1992 Winter Olympic bobsleigh run. The 1.5km run drops 125m, has 19 bends and you can go in a proper four-man bob or in a special bob raft.

With the bob, you are one of two passengers wedged between the driver and brakeman. You reach a maximum speed of 100-105kph and the pressure in some turns can be as high as 2-3g. The ride lasts for 50 seconds and is not recommended for people suffering from heart, vascular or back problems, or for pregnant women. It costs FF430 a go.

The bob raft is padded and mounted on 20cm wide skids. The good news is that it goes slower – a mere 75-80kph and takes around one and a half minutes. The bad news is it has no professional driver or brakeman – just four terrified punters crammed in together. It costs FF160 a go.

For both, the price includes the ride itself, the loan of a helmet and a diploma. Additional insurance is available (yours may not be valid).

The course is generally open to tourists from Tuesday to Sunday from 5pm to 8pm (from 2pm on Tuesday and Friday) from Christmas to mid-March – though the season may be shorter if it's not cold enough.

PACKAGES

AA Ski-Driveaway, Airtours, Alpine Options Skidrive, Altours Travel, Chalets 'Unlimited', Club Med, Cresta Ski France, Crystal, Enterprise, Inghams, Kings Ski Club, Lagrange, Made to Measure, Mogul Ski, Neilson, Sally, Silver Ski, Simply Ski, Ski Beat, Ski Club of GB, Ski Partners, Ski West, Ski Wyatt, SkiBound, Skiworld, Stena Sealink, Thomson, Travelscene Ski-Drive, UCPA

Champagny France des Villages, Made to Measure, Sally

Les Coches AA Ski-Driveaway, Crystal, Made to Measure, Simply Ski, Ski Esprit, Ski Olympic, Travelscene Ski-Drive

Montalbert Ski Amis

Montchavin Made to Measure, Simply Ski, Ski Esprit

ACTIVITIES

Indoor Swimming pool (Plagne Bellecôte), sauna and solarium in most centres, skating (Plagne Bellecôte), squash (1800), fitness centres (Belle Plagne, Plagne 1800, Plagne Centre, Plagne Bellecôte), cinemas, bowling
Outdoor Bob-sleigh (La Roche), 30km marked walks, para-gliding, skidoos, rafting, climbing, skating, hang-gliding, snow-shoe excursions, helicopter rides

TOURIST OFFICE

Postcode 73211
Tel 010 33 79097979
Fax 79097010

some mostly quite simple places in many of the other main villages. Inghams and Skiworld join them in Plagne Soleil and 1800 respectively. The latter's Maeva allocation is good if you are looking for a studio.

EATING OUT
Emphasis on convenience.
Throughout the resort there is a good range of restaurants, with something to suit most pockets and tastes, but the emphasis is on less expensive pizzeria-style dining which suits the self-catering family. Some satellite villages cater more for the diner interested in the regional dishes: raclette and Savoyard fondue restaurants are popular (La Ferme in Plagne Bellecôte is recommended). Le Bec Fin in Plagne Centre is a popular choice for traditional French cuisine in a more formal setting, as is Le Matafan in Belle Plagne. Hotel Les Glières, in Champagny, serves good Savoyard food in friendly rustic surroundings.

APRES-SKI
Nothing exclusive or original
La Plagne has a wide range of après-ski amenities catering particularly for the younger crowd who still have energy at the end of a day's skiing. Each centre produces a weekly events bulletin listing special forthcoming events, particularly those run by the hotel 'animateurs'. There is an ice rink and outdoor heated pool at Plagne Bellecôte, ten pin bowling and electronic golf at Belle Plagne, and most large hotels or apartment blocks have games rooms. Tom's Bar at Plagne 1800 is a favourite for the beery British crowd, and there are bars and discotheques a-plenty.

FOR NON-SKIERS
OK for the active
Non-skiing activities have evolved throughout La Plagne to offer the visitor a strong alternative to bashing the pistes. As well as the sports and fitness facilities, winter walks along marked trails during the March and April sunshine are particularly pleasant. It's also easy to get up the mountain on the gondolas, which both have restaurants at the top. The Olympic bobsleigh run is a popular evening activity. Excursion possibilities are limited.

STAYING IN OTHER RESORTS
A good plan
Montchavin is a relatively unspoilt old farming community where rustic timber haybarns and cowsheds are much in evidence. Restaurant terraces set in orchards at the foot of the slopes add to the scene. There are adequate shops, a kindergarten and a ski school. Reaching the main high La Plagne skiing is a roundabout affair of three chairs and a drag. The local slopes are well-endowed with snowmakers, a cheap local lift pass covers 30km of mostly easy, pretty, sheltered skiing, the nursery slopes are conveniently placed, and the village restaurants provide a good lunch. Those who do venture further afield can return from Roche de Mio (2,700m) in one lovely long swoop. Après-ski is quiet, but the village doesn't lack atmosphere and has a couple of nice little bars. Simply Ski and Ski Esprit both have chalets with crèches. The Bellecôte is a well-run modest hotel with a decent restaurant, the Boule de Neige.

Les Coches is a sympathetically designed modern resort that several reporters have liked for its 'small, quiet and friendly' feel. It has its own ski school and kindergarten, and skiing arrangements are much the same as at Montchavin. Ski Esprit and Crystal have chalets with crèches.

Montalbert is a traditional village with quicker access into the main skiing, notably the five runs above and below Aime and 1800. The local slopes are easy and wooded – a useful insurance against bad visibility. Remoteness from the Bellecôte glacier is a drawback for good skiers. The Ski Amis run two chalets with a nanny service. The Aigle Rouge is a simple hotel.

Champagny-en-Vanoise is a charming old village in a pretty wooded setting. The south-facing local slopes mean you often have to get a gondola home at the end of the day, but Champagny is better placed than any of the other outlying villages for access into the main area. There are routes from the gondola station to summits above Centre and Bellecôte, the former being a particularly speedy affair using just one further lift. Given good snow, there are lovely runs home from above Centre (2,500m). There are several hotels, of which the two best are both Logis The Glières is a rustic old hotel with varied rooms, a friendly welcome and good food. L'Ancolie is smarter, with modern facilities.

Portes du Soleil

The Portes du Soleil vies with the Trois Vallées for the title of World's Largest Ski Area, but its skiing is very different from that of Méribel and neighbours. It is spread out over a much larger area, most of which forms part of a central circuit straddling the French-Swiss border; smaller areas branch off from that circuit. The skiing is great for keen intermediate skiers who like to travel long distances in a leisurely fashion. There are few of the tightly packed networks of runs that encourage you to stay put in one area.

The main resorts and the skiing are described in four chapters – Avoriaz, page 149, Châtel, page 160, Morzine and Les Gets, page 211, and Champéry (and the other small Swiss resorts), page 311.

Purpose-built **Avoriaz** has the most snowsure skiing. Its main slopes face north and are the highest in the area – though still low by French standards. It also has the most densely packed section of runs, ski-in, ski-out convenience and good lift links to Champéry, Châtel and Morzine. Prices are high for this normally modest area.

The other villages are generally attractive but less snowsure – and those in France are noticeably cheaper. Staying in one of them and travelling to the better snow of Avoriaz would seem a shrewd move. But beware: many of the important links around the circuit are low, sunny and distressingly short of snowmakers.

Morzine is the closest and best-linked. It's a summer as well as a winter resort – a pleasant, bustling little town with a sizeable, pretty ski area of its own. All the pros and cons of a town are there – good shops and restaurants, traffic, lots of walking to the lifts, plenty to do. The local skiing is shared with unspoilt user-friendly **Les Gets**.

The other main French resort is **Châtel**. It's on the main circuit, and given good snow has some of the best skiing in the area. Although an old village, it's a busy, traffic-jammed place.

Champéry is the obvious choice for those looking for something more peaceful and attractive. It's a classic Swiss charmer, linked by cable-car to the main circuit. A lack of village nursery slopes may be a drawback for families and other beginners.

Morgins, in contrast, has excellent village slopes – but its local skiing is otherwise very limited. **Champoussin** and **Les Crosets** are purpose-built mini-resorts between Champéry and Morgins, with extensive slopes all around – and excellent links to Avoriaz.

Risoul 1850m

HOW IT RATES

The skiing

Snow	***
Extent	***
Advanced	**
Intermediates	****
Beginners	****
Convenience	****
Queues	****
Restaurants	**

The rest

Scenery	***
Resort charm	**
Not skiing	*

PACKAGES

Airtours, Crystal, Enterprise, Inghams, Neilson, Thomson

TOURIST OFFICE

Postcode 05600
Tel 010 33 92460260
Fax 92460123

Reasonable prices, ski-convenience, good snow, few queues and a large ski area: Risoul has a lot going for it, particularly for intermediates, beginners and families. And it's one of the more attractive purpose-built resorts.

THE RESORT

Risoul, opened only in 1977, is now featured by all the big British tour operators, but remains a relatively undeveloped, quiet, apartment-based resort, popular with families. Set among the trees, with excellent views over the Ecrins National Park, Risoul is made up of wood-clad chalet-style buildings, small restaurants and open-air cafés, which give it a friendly feel. The village lacks many resort amenities – a pool, for example – and the ski area is seriously short of comfortable, fast lifts and mountain restaurants. Watch out for long transfers from Turin airport.

THE SKIING

The sunny **ski area** is shared with neighbouring Vars and is the biggest in the southern French Alps, offering 170km of pistes. The slopes leading back into Risoul are attractively wooded and good for bad-weather skiing. Above them are open slopes set in a big sunny bowl.

The top of the skiing above Vars reaches 2750m and the Vars skiing is accessed by a long drag, which has the advantage that wind is unlikely to close the link. Returning from Vars over the top is via some of Risoul's steeper skiing, though there is an easier route via Col de Valbelle. New lifts are planned, which will improve the area, particularly for better skiers.

Risoul's skiing is entirely above 1850m, so despite its southerly position (only 300km north of Nice) and sunny aspect, **snow reliability** is reasonably good. The nursery area has snow-cannon back-up.

Risoul does not yet offer much to interest **advanced skiers**. The main top stations access a couple of steepish descents, and there are six black runs in all. There are some good off-piste opportunities if you have a guide, especially in the trees. The whole area is best suited to **intermediates**, with some good long reds and blues in both the Risoul and Vars sectors. Virtually all Risoul's runs head towards the village, making it difficult to get lost in even the worst of weather. So intermediate children can be let off the leash with the minimum of worry.

Beginners have good, convenient, autonomous nursery slopes and a free lift. Graduation to longer pistes is straightforward.

There are a couple of short **cross-country** loops, including a snowsure and scenic trail along the top ridge of the Alpine ski area.

Risoul has arguably the quietest large ski area in France. **Queues** are very rare except in the French school holidays – even then delays are short.

There are more **mountain restaurants** than it appears from the piste map. But many people prefer to ski down to Vars or return to the village for lunch.

We have extremely conflicting reports of the **ski school**. Small classes are a consistently positive feature, lack of good English a similarly ever-present negative comment. Hopefully, the latter will change as more and more Brits visit, many on 'Learn to Ski' packages which guarantee English-speaking instruction.

Risoul is very much a family resort. It provides an all-day nursery for **children** over 6 months. The ski kindergarten takes children aged 3 to 5, and children's ski school starts at 6 years old.

STAYING THERE

Nearly all Risoul's visitors stay in apartments. **Hotels** are in short supply. The Dahu is used by some British tour operators but we have had complaints about poor food and a noisy disco. **Chalets** are becoming more widely available, and most of the operators who go there now offer them. The Mélèzes, Christiana and Belvedere **self-catering** units are good by French standards, though they can vary.

There's plenty of choice for **eating out**, from pizzerias to good French food, and it's mostly good value. More expensive are the Traderidera, Oasis and Assiette Gourmande.

Après-ski is limited to a few quiet bars. The best are the Licorne, Cimbro, Chérine, l'Eterlou, Thé 'n Thé and L'Ecureuil. The Dahu disco, for all its noise, is uninspiring. Risoul is not recommended for **non-skiers**.

La Rosière 1850m

✔ Fairly big area of intermediate skiing, linked to La Thuile in Italy

✔ Quiet, pleasant resort built in traditional style

✔ Convenient for visiting other resorts of the Tarentaise

✔ Splendid view across the Tarentaise valley towards the Les Arcs ski area

✘ South-facing slopes can mean poor snow conditions in good weather

✘ Little in the way of tough piste skiing

✘ Not much nightlife

La Rosière, like La Thuile in Italy with which the skiing is linked, is not well known on the British market. For beginners and intermediates it deserves consideration. It's also a good choice for families and those wanting a quiet, relaxing week. Unlike many French purpose-built resorts, it has been built in traditional style, with chalets tucked away in the woods and no hideous high-rise buildings. And its prices are much lower than in the better-known (and nearby) Tarentaise resorts.

The south-facing aspect of most of the slopes means it is very sunny – handy in early-season cold weather but a drawback in warm weather when the snow can deteriorate. However, you can always ski over to Italy where the north-facing slopes usually remain good.

ORIENTATION

The resort is set along a winding road, with lifts at the top end just above the centre of town. From here a chair- and drag-lift take you up into the skiing. From the outlying district of Les Eucherts, another drag-lift goes up to mid-mountain. The skiing spreads right along the flank of the largely south-facing mountain and goes up to a high point of 2400m. It also extends below La Rosière to 1150m in Les Ecudets.

The skiing is linked to that of **La Thuile** in Italy. On the French side, **Les Arcs** is on the opposite side of the valley and easily reached by funicular from Bourg-St-Maurice. **La Plagne**, **Val-d'Isère-Tignes** and the **Trois Vallées** are all within easy reach by car.

 ## The resort

La Rosière has been built in traditional chalet style beside the road which zig-zags its way up to the Petit St Bernard pass to Italy from Bourg-St-Maurice and Seez in the valley. In winter the road ends in a snow bank at the top of the village, by the lifts. This is also home to some friendly St Bernard dogs, usually eager to pose for photos.

The village makes a pleasant contrast with the stark architecture of resorts such as Les Arcs and La Plagne across the valley. All the buildings are attractive and many are dotted around discretely in the woods. But there really isn't that much there other than accommodation and a few shops. Expect peace, quiet and friendly locals but not a lively nightlife.

Also expect few British, as La Rosière hasn't been discovered by many tour operators yet.

 ## The skiing

The first lift was built in 1962 and the resort has developed gradually since. The link with Italy means it has a big ski area for such a little-known resort.

THE SKI AREA
Best for intermediates and novices
The skiing is on the largely south-facing flank of the mountain above the resort. Most runs, especially those back to the resort, are well groomed and make for easy cruising.

The chair and drag out of the village take you into the heart of the skiing, from where a series of drags and chairs spread across the mountain take you up to **Col de la Traversette** (2400m). From there you can ski over the ridge and ski to the lifts which link with **Italy** at Belvedere (2640m). These top lifts are prone to being closed by wind in poor weather.

SNOW RELIABILITY
Surprisingly good
Despite its south-facing direction, relatively low height (most of the skiing is between 1850m and 2400m) and most of the area's artificial snow being on the Italian side, La Rosière has a remarkably good snow record. But in warm weather expect the snow to be better on La Thuile's slopes.

FOR ADVANCED SKIERS
Little excitement
Advanced skiers will find little to keep them amused in La Rosière. The steepest skiing is on the lowest slopes, going down the Marcassin run to Le Vaz (1500m) and Ecudets or Eterlou to Les Ecudets (1150m). Even these aren't especially steep but probably deserve their black ratings because of the poor snow conditions you may encounter at these heights.

Other than that there are some good off-piste itineraires to be explored with a guide. And you can go heli-skiing by

LIFT PASSES

93/94 prices in francs
Domaine International
Covers all lifts in La
Rosière and La Thuile.
Beginners 2 free lifts.
Points card (50 points
260, lifts cost from 3
to 7 points).
Main pass
1-day pass 160
6-day pass 786
Senior citizens
Over 60: 6-day pass
519 (34% off)
Over 70: free pass
Children
Under 12: 6-day pass
519 (34% off)
Under 4: free pass
Short-term passes
Half-day pass 12.30-
5pm (adult 107). Half-
day 9am-1pm and
12.30-5pm La Rosière
only (adult 80).
Alternative periods
6-day (non-
consecutive) pass
available (adult 708).
Notes Passes of 6
days and over allow 1
day in Les Arcs.
Alternative passes
La Rosière-only pass
covers 18 lifts (6-day:
adult 611, child 397).

CHILDCARE

The Village des
Enfants takes children
aged 1 to 10, with ski
lessons available for
those aged 3 or more.

SKI SCHOOL

93/94 prices in francs
ESF
Classes 6 days
5hr: 9.15-11.45 and
2.30-5pm
6 full days: 590
6 half-days 390
Children's classes
Ages: 4 to 12
6 full days: 560
6 half-days 340
Private lessons
Hourly
135 for 1 or 2 people

---

skiing over into Italy for the
helicopter. This is reputed to be the
cheapest heli-skiing in Europe.

FOR INTERMEDIATE SKIERS
Cross-border delight
On its own La Rosière would be
nothing special. But taking account of
all the linked La Thuile skiing too,
there's a big area to explore.

Apart from the lowest runs down to
below the main village, the bottom
half of La Rosière's local skiing area is
mainly gentle, open blue and green
runs, ideal for early intermediates to
brush up their technique. The top half
of the mountain, however, below Le
Roc Noir and Col de la Traversette
boasts somewhat steeper and more
interesting red runs.

The red over the ridge from Col de
la Traversette has good snow and
views, but is narrow for its top section.
Weaker intermediates can avoid it by
taking the Chardonnet chair down.

FOR BEGINNERS
Good for families
La Rosière has good nursery slopes and
short beginner lifts at the main slopes
above the village and at the altiport,
near the cross-country tracks.
Combine that with the resort's quiet
and friendly ambience and you've got
a good combination for a family's first
skiing holiday.

FOR CROSS-COUNTRY
Pretty setting
La Rosière has four trails totalling
12km, prettily set around the tree-line
in the altiport area, with good views
over the valley.

QUEUES
A good reputation
La Rosière has a reputation for being
queue-free. But when we were there
last February we found it much busier
than on the Italian side and
encountered a couple of substantial
queues, especially for the Les Eucherts
and Plan du Repos lifts back up to
mid-mountain from the eastern sector
of the skiing.

MOUNTAIN RESTAURANTS
In short supply
The only real mountain restaurant is
the Plan du Repos, at mid-mountain.
This is a pleasant self-service place
with decent food and a huge sunny
terrace. But it can get very crowded,
with long queues at peak times.
Combine that with La Thuile's basic
fare and you can see that gourmets
won't find the ski area to their liking.

There are also a couple of tiny bars
near the top which are fine for picnics.
Many people ski down to the village
for lunch. Toni's Bar in the Relais du
Petit St Bernard at the foot of the
pistes is convenient and has good food
and service.

SKI SCHOOL
Mixed reports
Reporters were divided in their views.
One said, for example, 'Instructor was
very keen on jumping over rocks.
Started with six people, ended with
two! Also poor English.' Another
thought, 'Very good and safety-
conscious, worked hard; friendly.' One
general good point appears to be small
classes, and one couple had an
excellent private lesson with a British
instructor from the ESF.

FACILITIES FOR CHILDREN
Apparently good
Many reporters have observed the
caring and patient supervision that
children get in the snow garden of the
Village des Enfants, although we lack
first-hand reports. Ski Olympic can
arrange a nanny service, given enough
notice and enough demand.

 # Staying there

The most convenient accommodation
is in the main village, near the lifts, or
just below in Le Gollet or Vieux
Village. There is also some by the
other main lift up, in Les Eucherts,
and more in rural old hamlets further
down the mountain, though you need
a car to make the most of staying
there. The free ski-bus is efficient –
and every 15 minutes at peak times.
But it stops at 6pm. And one reporter
complained of arduous walks from
chalet to bus and bus to lifts.

HOW TO GO
Not a lot of choice
As far as we know, Ski Olympic are
once again the only operators selling
packages here – in two chalets.
Chalets Ski Olympic has a couple of
cheap places well liked for everything
except their position, a bus-ride or
very long walk to the lifts.
Hotels There are half a dozen 2-star
places. Prices are low.
££ Relais Petit St-Bernard The main
hotel, at the top of the village, where
the road terminates in winter.
££ Solaret Out of the village, at the
satellite hamlet of Les Eucherts.
££ Belvédère Welcoming family-run
place 6km down towards Bourg.

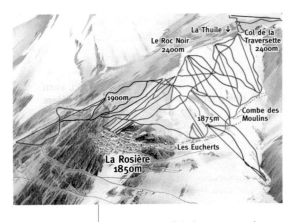

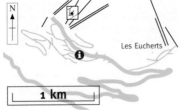

GETTING THERE

Air Geneva, transfer 3½hr. Lyon, transfer 3½hr.

Rail Bourg-St-Maurice (23km); frequent buses to resort.

PACKAGES

Ski Olympic

ACTIVITIES

Indoor Fitness Club (body-building, aerobics, sauna, Turkish baths, jacuzzi, Californian baths, hammam, massage) cinema, museum, library, table tennis
Outdoor Para-gliding, cleared paths, husky walks, floodlit skiing, luge run, ski jump, flights over Mont Blanc, heli-skiing, toboggan run for the children, 3 km of marked walking paths

TOURIST OFFICE

Postcode 73700
Tel 010 33 79068051
Fax 79068320

Self-catering Enterprise has pulled out of La Rosière this year, and we are unaware of any other tour operators with apartments here. There are a number of self-catering places bookable independently, including some ski-to-the-door ones in the upper part of the village.

STAYING DOWN THE VALLEY
Only if skiing other resorts

There are some ancient hamlets where you can rent gîtes, or you can stay in the valley village of Seez or the bigger town of Bourg-St-Maurice – both are connected to the ski area by post bus, though it's infrequent and expensive (FF44 Bourg–La Rosière). If you did this, however, it would make sense to ski some other resorts too – particularly Les Arcs, which is directly connected to Bourg by funicular.

EATING OUT
Good for a small resort

There's a surprisingly wide choice of restaurants, many of which have been praised in reports. The Eterlou, Pitchounette, Christophi, Plein Soleil and Toni's Bar Pizzeria are all well liked. The classiest place in the area, however, is perhaps the Chaumière, down in nearby Montvalezan – a popular old atmospheric farmhouse with excellent food.

APRES-SKI
Limited

La Rosière is essentially a quiet family resort, though the two main bars in town, Toni's and the Yeti, can be lively at tea-time. Later, the former becomes a cosy place for a quiet drink in front of any open fire, while the Yeti remains fairly animated. One reporter also recommends the Neige et Chocolat for a friendly break immediately after skiing.

FOR NON-SKIERS
Not much of interest

Non-skiers will find La Rosière very limited. They'll soon get bored of admiring the St Bernards (although if you're very nice they may be allowed to take you for a walk!). There are scenic flights and a cinema. Walks are good while they last, but there's only 3km of them marked.

Sainte-Foy 1550m

HOW IT RATES

The skiing

Snow	***
Extent	*
Advanced	***
Intermediates	***
Beginners	**
Convenience	***
Queues	*****
Restaurants	*

The rest

Scenery	***
Resort charm	***
Not skiing	*

SKI FACTS

Altitude	1550m-2620m
Lifts	5
Pistes	25km
Green/Blue	23%
Red	54%
Black	23%
Artificial snow	¼km

PACKAGES

Ski Arrangements

TOURIST OFFICE

Postcode 73640
Tel 010 33 79069170
Fax 79069509

This small ski area in the Tarentaise has been developed only since 1990. The millions who flock to the nearby mega-resorts never give it a thought. But those in the know are well rewarded. It is truly an undiscovered, uncrowded gem with some wonderful skiing for advanced and intermediate skiers.

THE RESORT

There isn't one; that's the charm of this place; it's skiing without the frills and some good skiing to boot. Ste-Foy is a tiny mountain hamlet of a few buildings – the latest addition is the largest, and houses the ticket office, ski shop and café. It's set in surroundings which are pleasant – though not outstandingly pretty – and there's a satisfying feeling of the area being undefaced by ski-lifts and skiers.

It's set up a turning off the main road between Val d'Isère and Bourg-St Maurice.

THE SKIING

Rumoured to be 'where the Val d'Isère instructors ski on their days off', Ste-Foy's skiing is an undiscovered, often deserted gem. If you are staying in one of the nearby well-known Tarentaise resorts such as Val, Tignes or Les Arcs, do take a day off to give Ste-Foy a try, especially after a fresh snowfall.

The **ski area** spreads over the mountainside directly above the village and on both sides of the three chair-lifts which rise, one above the other, from village level (1550m) to the Col de l'Aiguille (2620m). The top lift – the Aiguille – gives access to almost 600m vertical of skiing above the tree-line and to off-piste routes on the back of the mountain. The lower two chairs serve a number of pleasant green, blue and red runs through the trees and back to the base station. There are plans to cut some steeper trails alongside the lower lifts, and these should prove their worth when weather conditions on the open upper slopes are poor.

Most of the slopes are north-facing, so **snow reliability**, certainly on the upper slopes, is good. And because of the lack of crowds, a fresh fall of powder is skied out much less quickly than in the nearby larger resorts; you can make fresh tracks days after the latest storm.

Advanced skiers can pass many a happy hour on Ste-Foy's upper slopes, and although there are currently only two marked black runs, there's lots of scope for challenging skiing all around the Aiguille chair. The off-piste and touring routes on the back of the mountain require guides – pick-up and return to Ste-Foy can be arranged through the ESF.

Intermediate skiers should have a field-day at Ste-Foy. There's 1000m vertical of uncrowded red runs – ideal for confidence building, for sharpening technique or just for clocking up the miles. The higher slopes are the more difficult ones – the Aiguille run is a superb test for confident intermediates.

For complete **beginners** there is a small drag-lift near the base station; after which it's a case of getting on the Grand Plan chair and looping down on the Plan Bois trail – a pleasant, gentle run through the trees and the only real beginners' run.

There are no prepared **cross-country** trails, but you can lay some original tracks through the woods.

The three chair-lifts are all quads, and there are never any **queues** – it's not unusual for the highest chair to be so quiet that it's only started up when someone needs a ride.

There are two rustic **mountain restaurants** at the top of the first chair, both converted from barns and serving good food. The café adjacent to the ticket office serves pizzas, meals and snacks, and has a large terrace overlooking the valley. There is one other bar-restaurant, housed in an improbable-looking ruin nearby, which locals recommend highly for both food and ambience.

There is a **ski school** and a very good chance that any classes will not be too large. There are no special facilities for **children.**

STAYING THERE

It may be possible to rent a room in one of the few houses or farms nearby. Hotel Monal in the village of Ste-Foy, down at the turn-off in the valley, is clean and well-run, and serves wonderful food. There's a wider choice of accommodation in Bourg-St-Maurice, and there's a limited bus service from there to the skiing. But most people will want to stay in one of the major resorts and take a day trip to Ste-Foy, so having a car is handy.

On a busy day there may be a short-lived **après-ski** scene at Ste-Foy – the bar in the ruin is likely to be livelier than the main café.

Serre-Chevalier 1350m–1500m

HOW IT RATES

The skiing

Snow	****
Extent	****
Advanced	***
Intermediates	****
Beginners	****
Convenience	***
Queues	****
Restaurants	***

The rest

Scenery	****
Resort charm	***
Not skiing	**

ORIENTATION

Serre-Chevalier is made up of a string of villages – 13 in all – set on a valley floor running roughly east-west below the predominantly north-facing ski slopes. The three main villages are Monêtier (Serre-Chevalier 1500) at the western end, Villeneuve (Serre-Chevalier 1400) in the middle and Chantemerle (Serre-Chevalier 1350) at the eastern end, spread over a distance of 5km and linked by regular ski buses. Chair-lifts go up into the linked skiing from Monêtier, gondolas and cable-cars from the other two.

All the villages have charming old hamlets as well as modern new development areas.

The skiing connects with the lift up from the medieval walled town of **Briançon**, 5km further down the valley.

The six-day area lift pass also covers a day's skiing in each of **Les Deux-Alpes**, **Alpe-d'Huez**, the **Milky Way** ski area and **Puy-St-Vincent**.

✔ Fairly big ski area ideally suited to intermediates, with lots of blue and red cruising runs

✔ Interesting mixture of wooded skiing (ideal for poor visibility, white-out conditions) and open bowl skiing above the tree-line

✔ Predominantly north and north-east facing slopes mean snow remains in good condition, at least on the upper slopes

✔ One of the few big French ski areas with old, picturesque villages as the main bases for the skiing

✔ Good-value and atmospheric old hotels, restaurants and chalets

✔ Good bus system links all the villages, making getting home easy no matter where you end up

✔ Lift pass covers several other major resorts easily reached by car

✗ A lot of indiscriminate new building at the foot of the lifts, creating unattractive first impression

✗ Piste skiing limited for advanced and expert skiers

✗ Limited nightlife

✗ Little to keep non-skiers occupied; certainly not the place to go if you want to mix with the jet set and idle your time away in expensive shops

Serre-Chevalier is one of the less well known of the major French resorts to British skiers. It deserves better. If you love old French villages with a genuinely French atmosphere and traditional restaurants, hotels and crêperies, try it. It is one of the few resorts with the sort of ambience that you might choose for a summer holiday – a sort of Provence in the snow.

And the skiing is equally likable. Although there is skiing on only one side of the long valley, it is split into different segments, so you really feel you are travelling around as you tour them on pistes and lifts. Intermediates will appreciate the skiing most, but in good snow conditions there are excellent off-piste opportunities to keep good skiers happy too. What really sets it apart from the French norm is the amount of woodland skiing, making Serre-Chevalier one of the best places to be when snow is falling (though there's plenty of open skiing too).

 The resort

Monêtier is the smallest and most unspoilt of the main villages, with a distinctly Provençal feel to its narrow streets, stone buildings with shutters and small square with a fountain. New building, in sympathetic style, has taken place on the other side of the main road, near the lifts into the skiing. A quiet place without animation or much in the way of bars or restaurants, Monêtier isn't for those in search of lively après-ski.

Villeneuve has three major gondolas out of the village. The central area of new development near the lifts is modern and fairly charmless. But the hamlet of Le Bez is peaceful and traditional, with old small stone chalets and barns. Across the main

road and river the old village of La Salle is an enticing traditional village of stone houses, hotels, bars, restaurants and crêperies.

Chantemerle has more tasteless modern buildings in the centre and along the main road. But there's another old sector a couple of minutes' walk from the lifts with a lovely old church and most of the restaurants, bars and small hotels.

As spring approaches, the charm of these old villages is diminished by the usual curse of French Alpine scenery – corrugated iron roofs.

Briançon is not strictly Serre-Chevalier. But it is now linked into the same skiing area and offers a fair amount of accommodation. It feels like a town – it is the highest in France, in fact – rather than a ski resort. The modern part of town is in

SKI FACTS

Altitude 1325m-2780m
Lifts 77
Pistes 250km
Green/Blue 42%
Red 46%
Black 12%
Artificial snow 13km

LIFT PASSES

93/94 prices in francs
Grand Serre-Chevalier
Covers all lifts in
Briançon, Serre-Che
and Le Monêtier.
Main pass
1-day pass 155
6-day pass 775
(low season 580 –
25% off)
Senior citizens
Over 60: 6-day pass
600 (23% off)
Over 80: free pass
Children
Under 16: 6-day pass
600 (23% off)
Under 4: free pass
Short-term passes
Morning (up to 1.15)
and afternoon pass
(from 12.30) (adult
115). Half-day passes
available for each
area.
Alternative periods
8 non-consecutive
day pass available
(adult 1,010).
Notes Further
discounts for children
aged 4 to 8 and
senior citizens aged
70 to 79. Passes of 6
days or more give
one day in each of
Les Deux Alpes, Alpe
d'Huez, Puy-St-
Vincent and Voie
Lactée (Milky Way).
Reductions for
families.
Alternative passes
Passes covering
individual areas of
Serre-Che (adult 6-day
675), Briançon (adult
6-day 500) and Le
Monêtier (adult 6-day
550).

the valley surrounding the lift station, with a wide selection of shops, bars, hotels and restaurants. Higher up is the fortified old town with narrow cobbled streets, well worth an excursion even if you are staying elsewhere. Many of the best restaurants are also in the old town. The other dominating aspect of Briançon is the profusion of barracks, reflecting the town's historic role as guardian of the link between France and Italy.

🎿 The skiing

Serre-Chevalier's skiing is ideally suited to intermediates, with miles of easy cruising blues and reds, both above and below the tree-line. Trees cover almost two-thirds of the mountainside; the runs here are very pretty and offer some of France's best wooded skiing if the weather is poor.

THE SKI AREA
Interesting, fragmented and pretty
Serre-Chevalier's 250km of pistes are spread in four main sectors above the Grenoble-Briançon highway.

From **Monêtier** in the west two chair-lifts take you to mid-mountain and further lifts to the highest point in the Serre-Chevalier ski area (2780m), from which you can link with the other sectors. Skiing from Monêtier towards Villeneuve, the main link is a red piste which is much more interesting than the narrow, flattish tracks you take when travelling between the sectors in the other direction.

Villeneuve and **Chantemerle** both also have a choice of major lifts into the skiing, and a network of chairs and drags makes skiing between these sectors easy. This area forms the heart of the Serre-Chevalier skiing.

From the area above Chantemerle a pair of drag-lifts takes you to the link with the **Briançon** skiing. From there you can ski all the way down to the edge of town – a long run with great views of the valley and the town of Briançon itself.

SNOW RELIABILITY
Good – especially the upper slopes
Most of the slopes face north or north-east and therefore hold their snow well, especially high up (and much of the skiing is above 2000m). Runs down into all the main villages are served by artificial snow-making, with Monêtier's operation being somewhat less substantial than the rest.

FOR ADVANCED SKIERS
Little challenging piste skiing
There are few steep pistes. About the best is the beautiful Tabuc run which takes you away from the lifts, around the side of the mountain, through woods to Monêtier. This is generally narrow and in places genuinely steep, but levels out towards the bottom. When we skied it last season the snow was good and it had just been groomed. In poor snow and with big moguls it can be very tricky.

The top bowls above Villeneuve and Chantemerle have a few black runs – especially good are the two from the top of the Eychauda drag and the wide Balme run. And there are a couple of blacks down to Chantemerle and Villeneuve which are fun if you go down the fall line.

Apart from the above, the main interest for advanced skiers is the off-piste, both above and through the trees. In good snow this can be superb, but you will need a guide to get the best from the area (and to ski off-piste in safety).

For good, adventurous skiers, the highlight of a week should be an excursion (with a guide) to La Grave – the off-piste skier's Mecca, back along the road towards Grenoble.

FOR INTERMEDIATE SKIERS
Ski wherever you like
Serre-Chevalier's skiing is ideally suited to intermediates, who can buzz around from piste to piste and area to area without worrying about coming across anything too surprising or challenging. Looking at the piste map it might appear that red runs far outnumber blues. But most of the reds are at the easy end of the grading scale, and even nervous intermediates should have no problems with most – especially in the light of the intensive grooming that goes on.

There's plenty to challenge the more adventurous intermediate though. Many of the runs are wide enough to be able to choose a faster pace. The Cucumelle run in the Fréjus sector is a beautiful long red run with a challenging initial section. In the bowls, you can normally pick your own route – to offer as much challenge as you are looking for. And many of the runs down to the valley, including the Olympique down to Chantemerle and the Grande Gargouille towards Briançon, have steep pitches.

The runs either side of the little-used Aiguillette chair in the Chantemerie sector are quiet, enjoyable fast cruises.

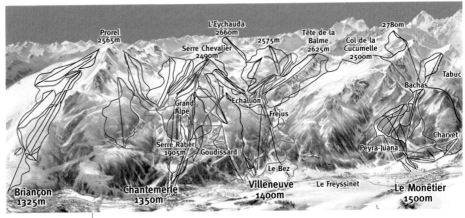

Prorel
2565m

L'Eychauda
2660m

2575m

Tête de la
Balme
2625m

Col de la
Cucumelle
2500m

2780m

Serre Chevalier
2490m

Tabuc

Bachas

Grand
Alpe

Echallion

Charvet

Fréjus

Serre Ratier
1905m

Goudissard

Peyra-Juana

Le Bez

Le Freyssinet

Briançon
1325m

Chantemerle
1350m

Villeneuve
1400m

Le Monêtier
1500m

CHILDCARE

Each of the three main villages has its own non-ski nursery that takes children all day (9am to 5pm) or for a half-day. At Villeneuve, Les Schtroumpfs (92247095) caters for kids from age 6 months; meals not provided. At Chantemerle, Les Poussins (92240343) takes them from age 8 months; meals provided. At Monêtier, Garderie de Pré-Chabert (92244575) takes them from age 18 months (6 months out of school holiday times); meals not provided.

SKI SCHOOL

93/94 prices in francs

ESF
In all centres
Classes 6 days
5hr: 3hr am and 2hr pm; half-day am or pm
6 full days: 760
Children's classes
Ages: Up to 12
6 full days: 640
Private lessons
Hourly
160 for 1 to 2 people

International
Group lessons and special courses

FOR BEGINNERS
Good at Villeneuve
All the villages have nursery areas at the bottom of the slopes – except Briançon, where they are at the mid-station of the gondola. Villeneuve is the best choice for beginners, with good nursery slopes served by artificial snow and excellent green runs to progress to above the tree-line at the top of the Fréjus gondola. The Chantemerle sector is less suitable, but also has some easy high skiing. Both these sectors have green runs that wind down from mid-mountain. All of Monêtier's easy skiing is at resort level, next to the excellent nursery slopes – handy, but not snowsure.

FOR CROSS-COUNTRY
Excellent if the snow is good
There are 45km of tracks along the valley floor, mainly following the gurgling river between Monêtier and Villeneuve and going on up towards the Col du Lautaret.

QUEUES
Generally not a problem
For the number of skiers on the mountain, the lift system is more than adequate. The lift out of Briançon is a high-capacity 10-person gondola. All the other main bases have a choice of lifts out. And once you are up the mountain the choice of lifts and routes means you can avoid queues.

Serre-Chevalier isn't a popular weekend resort, being just a bit too remote to attract the crowds from Grenoble and Turin. Even at Easter last season, we found no queues.

MOUNTAIN RESTAURANTS
Few, but quite good
For such a traditional French resort and large ski area, mountain restaurants are relatively thin on the ground, especially in the Briançon

sector. The Bachas, above Monêtier, is small, rustic and self-service, and has a good sun terrace. There's a choice at both Serre Ratier, above Chantemerle, (where Jaques is an excellent self-service choice) and at Echaillon, above Villeneuve. But our favourite is the Pai Mai in the hamlet of Fréjus, just off the beaten track of the Cucumelle run down from the Col above Villeneuve: it has a welcoming atmosphere and table service – but it is expensive. The restaurant at the bottom of the Monêtier lifts is to be avoided.

SKI SCHOOL
Good reports
There's an International ski school as well as the ESF. Both seem to have relatively small classes and reasonable English. People in classes seemed to be having fun. We've had no bad reports at all on them.

FACILITIES FOR CHILDREN
Facilities at each village
We don't have many reports on childcare, and they all come from skiers staying in Villeneuve – but they are enthusiastic, speaking of 'endlessly patient' instructors and 'excellent staff with good English' at Les Schtroumpfs. The ski school will take children from the age of 4.

 # Staying there

The central resorts of Chantemerle and Villeneuve are more convenient for getting in to the main skiing than the two extremities, Monêtier and Briançon. And the link between the Monêtier and Villeneuve skiing relies on high chair-lifts that can be closed by wind. But frequent buses run along the valley, so location isn't crucial.

Perhaps more important to the feel of your holiday will be whether you

GETTING THERE

Air Turin, transfer 2½hr. Grenoble, transfer 2½hr. Lyon, transfer 4hr.

Rail Briançon (6km); regular buses from station.

PACKAGES

Airtours, Alpine Options Skidrive, Altours Travel, Bladon Lines, Chalets 'Unlimited', Club Europe, Cresta Ski France, Crystal, Enterprise, Hannibals, Inghams, Kings Ski Club, Lagrange, Made to Measure, Neilson, Sally, Ski Ardmore, Ski Club of GB, Ski Miquel, Ski Partners, SkiBound, Thomson, UCPA

Briançon Alpine Options Skidrive, Alpine Tours, Sally

---

stay in an 'old' or 'new' part of the resort. What makes Serre-Chevalier different from so many of the competing French resorts (with similar-sized ski areas) is the old-world charm and genuinely French ambience of the traditional hamlets and villages of which it is comprised. If you are a Francophile, go for accommodation in one of the rustic areas, not in a modern adjunct.

HOW TO GO
A good choice of packages
There's a surprisingly wide choice of package operators for a resort which is still rather off the British beaten track. **Chalets** Bladon Lines have a good selection of rustic chalets in Le Bez and Villeneuve, ranging from the beautifully furnished, highly recommended Montalembert to a cheap, simply furnished old farmhouse. Ski Miquel have an interesting new addition in Monêtier. Crystal have a range of good-value places in Villeneuve and Chantemerle. The Jerome is one of the best, with an open-fire lounge and a sunny terrace with good views, but it is a tiring uphill walk from the lifts. The old Yeti (ex-Kings Club) has been taken over by Neilson this season – a cheap and cheerful chalet-hotel at the entrance to the old part of Chantemerle, a stone's throw from the lifts.

Hotels One of the features of this string of little villages is that it has a range of attractive, modest hotels. Monêtier:

£££ Auberge du Choucas Smart wood-clad rooms, and a stone-vaulted restaurant with good food.
Villeneuves:

££ Lièvre Blanc Former coaching inn, with a large stone-vaulted bar. Being steadily improved by British owners; popular with UK operators; has its own ski guide and ski hire shop.

££ Christiania Traditional hotel on main road, crammed with ornaments.

££ Vieille Ferme Stylish conversion – wood, tiles and white walls – on edge of village.

££ Cimotel Modern and charmless, but next to the piste and close to a main lift. Good food.

£ Le Chatelas Prettily decorated simple chalet right on the river (once a sawmill); small, cheap rooms.
Chantemerle:

££ Le Clos 200-year-old family-run chalet; good reputation for food.

££ Plein Sud Modern; pool and sauna.

££ Boule de Neige Comfortable 2-star in the old centre.

£ Ricelle Charming, but tucked away in Villard-Laté on the other side of the valley from the skiing.

Self-catering There are plenty of modern apartment blocks in the new parts of Villeneuve, Chantemerle and Briançon. Few appear to have great charm. Our pick would be Mélèzes in Chantemerle, offered by Crystal, and Moulins de la Guisanne in Villeneuve, available through Enterprise.

STAYING UP THE MOUNTAIN
Worth considering
The chalet-hotel Serre Ratier, at the mid-station of the cable-car out of Chantemerle, does full board at reasonable rates.

EATING OUT
Unpretentious and traditional
In Monêtier, the Auberge du Choucas (see Hotels) has the best sophisticated eating. The Alliey is more of a family French restaurant, and it has an excellent wine cellar.

In the old part of Villeneuve, La Pastorale has an open-fire grill and good-value menu. The Marotte is a tiny stone building with classic French cuisine. The Noctambule specialises in fondue and raclette. And there are a couple of good crêperies – the Bretonne and the Petit Duc.

In Chantemerle, Amphore has good pizzas and grills. The Couch Ou is good value for fondue and raclette and has a pizzeria upstairs. The Crystal is candlelit, and is the smartest (and most expensive) place in town. Clos has a wide choice of food and Kandahar is a charming little pizzeria.

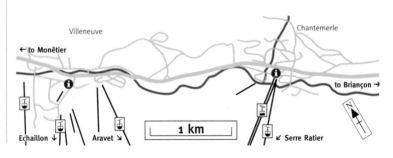

ACTIVITIES

Indoor Swimming pool, sauna, fitness centres, cinemas, bridge
Outdoor At Chantemerle: skating rink, ice driving circuit, para-gliding, cleared paths, snow-shoe walks. At Villeneuve: horse-riding, cleared paths, para-gliding, snow-shoe walks. At Monêtier: skating rink, cleared paths. Also hang-gliding, husky dog-sleigh rides

TOURIST OFFICE

Postcode 05240
Tel 010 33 92247188
Fax 92247618

APRES-SKI
Quiet streets and few bars

Serre-Chevalier isn't the place to go for wild nightlife. The village streets are usually deathly quiet, and having a car is handy of you want to try the scattered bar scene.

In Villeneuve the Lièvre Blanc is popular with Brits, and L'Iceberg is a pub-style bar frequented mostly by teenagers. Both are preferable to the only other animated place in Villeneuve, the Frog – a cramped, uninspiring tour rep joint. In Chantemerle the Yeti is focal for everyone, particularly its atmospheric cellar bar, which has live music twice a week. The bar in the Clos hotel is better for a quiet drink. Both villages have discos which rarely come to life except at weekends. The Baita in Villeneuve is perhaps the pick of them. Even Chantemerle's karaoke bar fails to attract customers most evenings.

FOR NON-SKIERS
Nothing special

Serre-Chevalier doesn't hold many attractions for non-skiers except its genuine French ambience and villages, and it's certainly not the place for avid shoppers. But the old town of Briançon is well worth a visit – for skiers and non-skiers alike. And there are plenty of activities on offer. A swimming pool in the hotel Sporting in Villeneuve is open to non-residents from 3pm to 9pm.

Briançon 1325m

The highest town in Europe, Briançon has recently been linked by gondola to the Serre-Chevalier ski area. It has a lovely 17th-century upper quarter, complete with impressive fortifications, narrow cobbled streets and typically French provincial restaurants, auberges and patisseries. However, the area surrounding the lift station, at the opposite and lower end of town, is an ugly urban sprawl, full of busy roads, large car-parks and petrol stations. Briançon suits car drivers best: they can stay in or close to the old part and make good use of the low prices, off-slope facilities and road connections of the town.

The gondola, followed by a choice of short lifts, brings you to the link to the rest of the Serre-Chevalier skiing. The east-facing local slopes (all intermediate) are the sunniest in the area, but a battery of snowmakers ensures that the main pistes down to the gondola mid-station (1625m) stay open throughout the season, and the run to town remains complete for much of it.

The ski school is reputed to be one of the best in France, though the lack of English speakers is a drawback. The nursery and ski kindergarten care for children all day if required, the former accepting them as young as 6 months.

Packages are mostly geared towards car-driving self-caterers, but independent travellers have plenty of hotels available. These are generally cheaper than their Serre-Chevalier equivalent, and very inexpensive compared to similar accommodation in French purpose-built resorts. The Vauban is a very comfortable 3-star; La Chaussée de Paris a central 2-star; Mont Brison is a good B&B. The Signal du Prorel apartments are next to the gondola, with the ski kindergarten close by. The Relais de la Guisaine apartments are also nearby. Both are fairly simple but not as cramped as many in French resorts.

There are numerous restaurants; some of the best are in the old part. One reporter gave the Auberge de la Paix a rave review for quality and value. Le Passe Simple, Le Péché Gourmand and L'Entrecôte are worth a try. The old town itself is the main off-slope attraction – there are wonderful views if you climb up through the ramparts. There is ice-skating and swimming, and Grenoble is a worthwhile excursion.

Tignes 2100m

✔ *One of the best ski areas in the world for off-piste skiing*

✔ *Huge ski area with ideal skiing for all standards of intermediate and for good skiers*

✔ *Good snow guaranteed for a long season*

✔ *Good lift system with swift access to skiing of Val-d'Isère*

✔ *Can ski directly to and from most accommodation*

✗ *One of the ugliest resorts in the Alps*

✗ *Can be cold and bleak in poor weather; little skiing below the tree-line*

✗ *Limited après ski*

✗ *Poor mountain restaurants*

If what you want from a ski holiday is Ski, Ski, Ski ... Sleep ... Ski Ski Ski ... Sleep, and you don't want much nightlife or care about high prices, finding attractive places for long lunches or the aesthetic appeal of where you are staying, Tignes is one of the best choices you can make.

Tignes and Val-d'Isère together form the enormous L'Espace Killy and share a lift pass. The area is a Mecca for expert skiers, and ideal for adventurous intermediates. Whereas Val-d'Isère has a huge British presence, Tignes is much more French. Set at 2100m it is one of Europe's highest resorts. The skiing goes up to 3500m and up there lasts all year round. The height guarantees good snow right back to the resort for most of the season.

Access to the highest skiing was greatly improved last season by the opening of a fast underground funicular and fast quad chairs almost to the top. Queues are now much less of a problem, and the amount of skiing you can get through each day is vastly increased.

If you want to stay in a pretty place or rave the night away, other resorts would be a better choice.

ORIENTATION

Tignes has two main centres: Tignes-Le-Lac and Val-Claret.

Tignes-Le-Lac has a high-capacity gondola linking it directly with the Val-d'Isère skiing on one side and a choice of chairs up the other.

Val-Claret is linked on skis and is a few minutes by bus. It has a slow chair direct to the Val-d'Isère skiing, drags, a chair up the other side and a fast quad chair and underground funicular to the Grande Motte glacier ski area.

The old villages of Tignes-Les-Brévières and Les Boisses are linked by lift and piste. And numerous other resorts are within an hour's drive. A six-day pass covers a day in several other resorts, including **Les Arcs** or **La Plagne** and the **Trois Vallées**.

 ## The resort

It's a shame the French didn't discover the acceptable face of purpose-built resorts – such as Valmorel, Mottaret and Belle-Plagne – before they started on Tignes. The only way of describing the two main centres of accommodation – Tignes-le-Lac and Tignes-Val-Claret – is 'ugly'. And that's what most of our reporters think too.

Large concrete blocks, some wood-clad, some not, set beside a conspicuous road, don't make for an aesthetically pleasing holiday base. But they are very convenient for the skiing. And there's an extremely reliable and frequent free ski-bus that links Le Lac, Val-Claret and all the accommodation which is not ski-in, ski-out. Both resorts have their own shops, restaurants and bars.

Some tour operators have allocations in Le Lavachet, a little place 10 minutes' walk from Le Lac. It's more villagey, with a compact horseshoe of small restaurants. It also has the best bar in Tignes. The accommodation is pretty much ski-in, ski-out.

Down the valley are two smaller settlements linked by the skiing and very different in style. Tignes-les-Boisses is quiet and set in the trees near a military camp. Tignes-les-Brévières is set at 1550m, the lowest point of the Tignes skiing, and is a renovated old Savoyard village.

 ## The skiing

The skiing of L'Espace Killy has few rivals for the attention of advanced and expert skiers. There is almost limitless off-piste as well as on-piste challenge. Intermediates too will have a great time here, with mile after mile of cruising pistes linked by an efficient lift system.

Tignes has all-year-round skiing on its 3500m Grande Motte glacier. And the resort height of 2100m generally provides good snow-cover right back to base for most of the long season.

SKI FACTS

Altitude	1550m-3500m
Lifts	102
Pistes	300km
Green/Blue	62%
Red	29%
Black	9%
Artificial snow	24km

The main drawback of the area is, as with most high resorts, that it can become unskiable during bad weather. There's no tree-line skiing except down towards Tignes-les-Boisses and Tignes-les-Brévières – a tiny fraction of the total ski area.

THE SKI AREA
High, snowsure and varied
Tignes' biggest asset is the **Grande Motte** glacier, especially now that access to it has been speeded up hugely by the long-awaited opening of the underground funicular from Val-Claret. (This was originally intended to be open for the 1992 Olympics but eventually started operating in Spring 1993.) It whizzes you up to 3000m in a few minutes and has cut out the enormous queues that used to form for the old gondolas. It feels just like riding the London tube system – mainly strap-hanging and with curved sides and ceiling.

The snow up here, with a cable-car taking you up a further 500m, is always good, even on the warmest spring day. There are chairs and drags to play on, as well as beautiful long runs back to the resort and a link over to Val-d'Isère.

Lifts from both Val-Claret and Tignes-le-Lac take you up to **Tovière**, from where you can ski back to the village or down into Val-d'Isère's skiing. Going up the opposite side of the valley takes you to an area of predominantly east-facing runs which are splendid for early morning sun. You can travel either way across the mountains here. They also mark the starting point of some delightful off-piste runs down the other side to the La Plagne and Les Arcs ski areas. From the **Aiguille Percée** peak (2765m) you can ski down on blue, red or black runs to the old village of Tignes-les-Brévières, from which there's now an efficient gondola back.

SNOW RELIABILITY
Difficult to beat
Few resorts can rival Tignes for reliably good snow-cover. The whole region, not just the glacier area, usually has good cover from November to May. The sunniest lower slopes now have substantial snowmaking facilities as a back-up.

FOR ADVANCED SKIERS
An excellent choice
There's no lack of challenge here for good skiers. On piste, our favourite run is the very beautiful Vallon de la Sache black from Aiguille Percée down to Tignes-les-Brévières. This is long

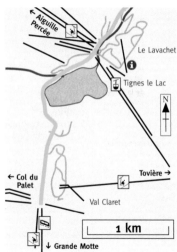

LIFT PASSES

94/95 prices in francs
L'Espace Killy
Covers all lifts and
resort buses in Tignes
and Val d'Isère.
Beginners Free lifts
on all main nursery
slopes; special
beginners' half-day
pass.
Main pass
1-day pass 205
6-day pass 940
Senior citizens
Over 60: 6-day pass
790 (16% off)
Over 80: free pass
Children
Under 13: 6-day pass
660 (30% off)
Under 5: free pass
Short-term passes
Half-day pass from
12.30 (adult 140).
Single ascents to
Palafour.
Alternative periods
14 non-consecutive
days (adult 2,385).
Notes 1-day pass and
over valid for one day
in La Plagne-Les Arcs.
6-day pass and over
valid for one day each
in the Three Valleys,
Pralognan-la-Vanoise,
Les Saisies and
Valmorel. On 3- to 15-
day passes, pass
reimbursed if all lifts
are shut due to bad
weather. Discount on
new passes on
presentation of
previous season's
pass. Extra discount
for senior citizens
aged 70 to 79.

and takes you down a secluded valley
with beautiful views right away from
the lift system. It isn't particularly
steep or narrow except for a couple of
short pitches. It is manageable by
adventurous intermediates. There are
also off-piste variants, for which you
should have the help of a guide.

The other long black run, from
Tovière to Tignes-le-Lac, is steep and
heavily mogulled at the top and
bottom but has a long easy section in
the middle. Parts of this get a lot of
afternoon sun.

But it is the off-piste possibilities
that make Tignes an excellent ski area
for good skiers. Go with one of the off-
piste guided groups that the ski
schools organise and you'll have a
wonderful time.

One of the big adventures is to ski to
Champagny (linked to the La Plagne
ski area) or Peisey-Nancroix (linked to
the Les Arcs ski area) – very beautiful
runs, and not too difficult. Your guide
will organise return transport. It was,
sadly, on the route to Champagny
that the well publicised tragedy
occurred last season when a group of
British doctors and their guide were
caught in an avalanche after a fresh
snowfall. But thousands of other
groups skied the same route during
the season in perfect safety.

Another favourite descent of ours is
the Tour de Pramecou, from the
Grande Motte glacier. After some
walking and beautiful away-from-it-all
skiing, you end up on a steep, smooth
north-facing slope which takes you
back to Val-Claret. There are other
descents across the glacier to the
bottom of the two Leisse chairs, which
take you back up to the arrival-point
of the funicular.

Then there's the whole of Val-
d'Isère's skiing to sample too.

FOR INTERMEDIATE SKIERS
One of the best
Only the Trois Vallées has
intermediate runs in greater quantity
than L'Espace Killy. But there's more
than enough here to keep even the
keenest intermediate happy for a
fortnight. And, in the unimaginable
event that you did get bored,
remember that a six day or more pass
covers a day in the Trois Vallées and a
day in La Plagne or Les Arcs too.

Tignes' local skiing is ideal
intermediate terrain. The red and blue
runs on the Grande Motte glacier
nearly always have superb snow. The
glacier run from the top of the cable-
car is a very gentle blue. The Leisse red
run down to the double chairs can get
very mogulled but has good snow. The
long red run all the way back to town
is a delightful long cruise – so long as
it isn't too crowded – and has a lot of
snowmaking guns on the lower
section to ensure good cover.

From Tovière, the Campanules red
and the blue 'H' run to Val-Claret are
both enjoyable cruises and generally
well groomed. But again, they can get
very crowded, especially at the end of
the day when skiers are returning from
Val-d'Isère. The direct way down from
the top to Tignes-le-Lac is a steep
black mogul field, but there are red
and blue alternatives.

On the other side of the valley, we
particularly like the Ves red run from
the top of the Col de Ves chair – the
highest point of Tignes non-glacier
skiing at 2845m. After an initial
traverse the run becomes an
interesting undulating and curvy

SKI SCHOOL

94/95 prices in francs

ESF
Classes 5 full days
9am-12noon and 1.45-
4.45 or half-days am
or pm
5 full days: 900
Children's classes
Ages: 4 to 12
5 full days: 800
Private lessons
Hourly or daily
165 for 1hr

Evolution 2
Classes 5 days
am or pm
5 half-days: 450
Children's classes
Ages: 5 to 14
5 half-days: 390
Private lessons
Hourly or daily
140 for 1hr

OTHER SCHOOLS
International
Henri Authier
Ski Action

SPECIALIST SCHOOLS
Stages 2000
Assoc. 9 Valleys
Kebra Surfing
Ski Fun

CHILDCARE

The Petits Lutins
kindergartens in Le
Lac and Val-Claret
(79065127) take
children aged 3
months to 6 years.

The Marmottons
kindergarten in Le Lac
(79065167) takes
children from 2 to 14,
with skiing for those
aged 3½ or more.

GETTING THERE

Air Geneva, transfer
4½hr. Lyon, transfer
4½hr. Chambery,
transfer 3½hr.

Rail Bourg-St-Maurice
(25km); regular buses
or taxi from station.

cruise, usually with good snow and a few moguls. It's never crowded because of the low capacity of the double chair which serves it.

The runs down from Aiguille Percée to Tignes-les-Boisses and Tignes-les-Brévières are also scenic and enjoyable. There are red and blue options as well as the beautiful black Vallon de la Sache which is easily skiable by an adventurous intermediate (see For Advanced Skiers, above). Brévières is a good place for a mid-morning break, especially if you need to recover from the Sache run.

The runs down from Aiguille Percée to Le Lac are gentle, wide blues. The Bluets red from the top of the Aiguille Rouge chair is a more interesting and challenging alternative.

FOR BEGINNERS
Little attraction

The nursery slope in Le Lac is convenient, snowsure and gentle, and is kept nicely autonomous from the main area by a man-made bank of snow. There are, however, no green runs at all to progress to, and the blues near both main villages get fairly crowded with skiers hurtling through to the lift stations. In poor weather, because of the height and lack of trees, beginners could find it cold and intimidating. We really think beginners would be better off going elsewhere.

FOR CROSS-COUNTRY
Interesting

L'Espace Killy has 44km of cross-country trails. There are tracks on the frozen Lac de Tignes, along the valley between Val-Claret and Tignes-le-Lac, at Les Boisses and Brévières and up the mountain on the Grande Motte.

QUEUES
Very few

The new Grande Motte funicular and parallel high-speed chairs have removed the worst bottleneck. But there can still be hordes of people waiting for the funicular. If there are, it's often quicker to take the chair. The worst queues now are usually for the cable-car above the funicular. Half-hour waits here are still common, especially when lower snow is poor. In late afternoon, queues can build up for the slow Tovière chairs to return from Val-d'Isère. A shrewd alternative is to take the Col de Fresse drag instead.

MOUNTAIN RESTAURANTS
Neither delightful nor cheap

Surprisingly, Tignes boasts few mountain restaurants. And reporters found them all expensive. The most popular was the one at the bottom of the Grande Motte. The one at the top of the funicular has great panoramic views and a huge terrace but is expensive and the terrace is invaded every few minutes by the next funicular-full of skiers clumping across to the piste.

The Chalet du Bollin restaurant, at the top of the short Bollin chair from Val-Claret, was the best we found, with table-service and a good plat du jour. The restaurant just above the mid-mountain lift junction going up to Col du Palet is again expensive but has a big terrace.

If you are in Les Brévières it's much cheaper to walk round the corner into the village than eat at one of the two places by the piste. Les Boisses has the best restaurant in the area in La Cordée (open for dinner too).

There was a huge cry of protest from reporters about the increasingly common practice of charging even big-spending customers of mountain restaurants FF2 for using the toilet.

SKI SCHOOL
Enormous choice

There are no fewer than nine schools. The ESF and Evolution 2 are the main ones, with sections in both resorts. They provide every form of tuition, including off-piste, moguls, racing and inter-resort (the Nine Valleys) off-piste excursions. Reports of the usual style group lessons are mixed, so it may be worth trying one of the smaller companies that concentrate on such classes plus private lessons – International, Henri Authier and Ski Action. Based in Le Lac, Stages 2000 specialises in off-piste tuition; Association 9 Valleys does mostly inter-resort circuits and extreme skiing; Kebra and Ski Fun are specialist snowboarding schools, one in each resort. A British ski instructor guru, Ali Ross, runs week-long ski clinics, bookable through Ski Solutions. One happy reporter tells us that with Ali's help he 'overcame problems that were 30 years old'.

FACILITIES FOR CHILDREN
Apparently good

We lack first-hand reports on the kindergartens, but observers from the side-lines are impressed with the Marmottons, remarking that there seemed to be 'only happy faces'.

PACKAGES

Airtours, Alpine Options Skidrive, Altours Travel, Bladon Lines, Chalets 'Unlimited', Club Med, Cresta Ski France, Crystal, Enterprise, Fantiski, French Impressions, Inghams, Kings Ski Club, Lagrange, Made to Measure, Neilson, Sally, Ski Arrangements, Ski Beat, Ski Choice, Ski Club of GB, Ski Esprit, Ski Europe, Ski Olympic, Ski Valkyrie, Ski West, SkiBound, Skiworld, Stena Sealink, The Ski Company, Thomson, Travelscene Ski-Drive, UCPA, Ultimate

ACTIVITIES

Indoor 'Vitatignes' in Le Lac (balneotherapy centre with spa baths, sauna etc), 'Espace Forme' in Le Lac, Fitness Club in Val-Claret (body-building, aerobics, squash, golf practice and simulation, sauna, hammam, Californian baths, jacuzzi, swimming pool, massage), cinema, covered tennis court, bowling, climbing wall, 'La Banquise M and M's' for children (ice skating, snow sliding, solarium, snow activitues, climbing activities)
Outdoor Natural skating-rink, hang-gliding, para-gliding, helicopter rides, snow-mobiles, husky dog-sleigh rides, diving beneath ice on lake, heli-skiing

TOURIST OFFICE

Postcode 73320
Tel 010 33 79061555
Fax 79064544

 # Staying there

There's little to choose between the two main resorts. Tignes-le-Lac has swifter access to Val-d'Isère, Val-Claret to the Grande Motte glacier.

HOW TO GO
Disappointing range of options

Although all three main styles of accommodation are available through tour operators, there isn't a lot of choice in any category, especially for those who like their creature comforts.
Chalets The choice is very limited in comparison to Val-d'Isère, or many other major French resorts for that matter. Many chalets are also surprisingly inconvenient for the skiing, and tend to be of a fairly similar standard to one another – reasonably comfortable but far from luxurious. We particularly like Skiworld's good-value Les Martins in Le Lac – cosy, eight minutes from the large gondola, ski-to-the-door off-piste. New in Le Lac this year is a Ski Olympic chalet on the lakeside, well placed for the lifts. Ski Beat and Bladon Lines have places on the outskirts of Val-Claret, a short bus-ride from the lifts. Bladon Lines have also taken over the cosy Alpaka hotel this year, and will be running it as a chalet-hotel.
Hotels The few hotels are small and simple, or (in a couple of cases) small and quite luxurious.
££££ Ski d'Or Smooth little Relais & Châteaux hotel; a modern chalet in Val-Claret, with the best food in town.
£££ Curling Tastefully renovated for the Olympics; in Val-Claret.
£££ Campanules Big modern chalet in Le Lac, with well equipped rooms.
££ Terril Blanch Well run place next to the lake.
££ Neige et Soleil Excellent family-run place in Le Lac – central, clean, cosy, comfortable, with good food.
£ Lavachey Very friendly, plain B&B place with 'very pleasant bedrooms with balconies', next to Tovière lift in Le Lac.
Self-catering In upper Val-Claret, close to the Toviere chair, the Residence Le Boursat (Inghams, French Impressions) apartments are about the best on offer – not too cramped, are reasonably well equipped and have a communal lounge.

The Chalet Club in Val-Claret (French Impressions) is a collection of simple studios, but has the benefit of free indoor pool, sauna and in-house restaurant and bar.

The self-drive specialists Stena Sealink have sizeable Val-Claret apartments which are spacious for those paying to under-occupy.

EATING OUT
Good places dotted about

Le Lavachet has a cluster of quite nice places. We particularly liked the Tex-Mex at the Cavern, and have received complimentary reports of L'Osteria. Finding anywhere with some atmosphere is difficult in Le Lac, though some of the food is good. L'Arbina has a high reputation and La Tocade has also been praised. The Bouf'Mich and Winstub (Alsatian cooking) are two of the better places in Val-Claret. Budget skiers here should try the Italian at Le Stelvio or Pignatta. But La Cordée in Les Boisses is a must if you have a car – unpretentious surroundings, great traditional French food and cheap. The most ambitious food in town is found at the hotel Ski d'Or.

APRES-SKI
Early to bed

Tignes is desperately quiet at night, though Val-Claret has some early evening atmosphere. The Wobbly Rabbit is popular with Brits – good for happy-hour jugs of margarita. It also serves Mexican and Thai food. The Corniche is more cosmopolitan and has live music. The Playboy and Marilyn Pub are other bars.

Le Lac is stone dead, even immediately after skiing. Late revellers head for Harri's in Lavachet, the most animated bar in town, though it's quite large and takes some filling before it warms up. The satellite TV here is popular with sports fans.

FOR NON-SKIERS
Forget it

Tignes is a resort for keen skiers. It's not the best choice for non-skiers. But there are plenty of other activities.

STAYING DOWN THE VALLEY
Only for visiting other resorts

See entry for Val-d'Isère. The same considerations apply broadly to Tignes. But bear in mind that there are rooms to be had in simple hotels on the edge of the Tignes skiing. The most comfortable is the 2-star Melezes at Les Boisses, but there are even simpler alternatives in the same hamlet (the Cordée and Marais) and in Les Brévières (the Perdrix Rouge and the Génépy).

Trois Vallées

Despite competing claims, notably from the Portes du Soleil, the Trois Vallées is in a league of its own. There is nowhere like it for a serious piste basher who wants to cover as much mileage as possible while rarely skiing the same run repeatedly. And it has a lot to offer every standard of skier from beginner to expert.

The skiing of the three valleys and their resorts are described and evaluated in four chapters – Courchevel, page 170, Méribel, page 199, Les Menuires, page 195, and Val-Thorens, page 255.

None of the resorts is cheap. **Les Menuires** is the cheapest but it is also by far the ugliest, and lacking in decent accommodation. It does, however, have some of the best steep piste skiing in the Trois Vallées on its north-facing La Masse mountain. Its near neighbour, **St-Martin-de-Belleville**, is a small, attractive, traditional village and offers good-value accommodation. The lifts into the skiing are slow, and the run home is south-facing.

Val-Thorens, set at 2300m, is Europe's highest ski resort and has the Trois Vallées' highest skiing. The snow here is pretty much guaranteed to be good, and there are two glaciers to choose from. But the setting is bleak, and skiing can be limited in bad weather; and the purpose-built resort isn't to everyone's taste.

Méribel's purpose-built satellite, **Mottaret**, is the best-placed of all the resorts for getting to any part of the system in the shortest possible time. **Méribel** itself is 200m lower, and has long been a favourite for British skiers, especially those going on chalet holidays. It is probably the most attractive of the main Trois Vallées resorts, built in chalet style beside a long winding road up the hillside, with some inconveniently situated accommodation.

Courchevel 1850 is the most expensive and fashionable of all the Trois Vallées resorts. The other satellites (1300, 1550 and 1650) are somewhat less pricey but don't have the same choice of nightlife and restaurants. The skiing around Courchevel is thought by many to be the best in the Trois Vallées, with runs to suit all standards and some of the most immaculately groomed slopes you'll find anywhere. The snow tends to be better than in neighbouring Méribel because many of the slopes are north-facing.

La Tania is a small place built for the 1992 Olympics and it still has very few facilities and very little evening animation. It is another good-value option, though.

Val-d'Isère 1850m

HOW IT RATES

The skiing

Snow	*****
Extent	*****
Advanced	*****
Intermediates	*****
Beginners	***
Convenience	***
Queues	****
Restaurants	**

The rest

Scenery	***
Resort charm	***
Not skiing	**

✔ Huge ski area linked with Tignes, with runs for all standards

✔ Some of the best lift-served off-piste skiing in the world

✔ High altitude means snow is more-or-less guaranteed, even in a poor season

✔ Choice of six ski schools for on- and off-piste lessons and guiding

✔ Wide range of chalets, hotels and self-catering offered by dozens of UK tour operators

✔ For a high, keen skier's resort, the town is attractive, and very lively at night

✘ Piste grading understates the difficulty of many runs, and piste grooming verges on the negligent

✘ You're quite likely to need the ski-bus at the start or end of the day – perhaps both

✘ British visitors and residents can be dominant in low season

✘ Not much skiing to do when the weather is bad

✘ Lifts and runs get crowded if snow is poor in lower resorts, and some key lifts at altitude need improvement

✘ Disappointing mountain restaurants

ORIENTATION

Val-d'Isère spreads along a remote valley which is a dead-end in winter. On your way in you pass the modern apartments of La Daille, from where a funicular goes to the Bellevarde skiing. The centre is 2km further on, where a road goes up a side valley, passing under the nursery slopes to Val's main lift station from which two cable-cars and parallel high-speed chairs head up in different directions into the Bellevarde and Solaise sectors. This side-valley road goes to the resort's main area of recent development. The valley road continues 3km to the old hamlet of Le Fornet, where a cable-car serves a fourth sector.

The ski area links with that of **Tignes**. A six-day lift pass gives a day's skiing in **Les Arcs** or **La Plagne**, plus the **Trois Vallées** – easily reached by car. Other resorts nearby are **Ste-Foy** and **La Rosière**.

More keen British skiers choose Val d'Isère than any other ski resort. And they aren't wrong: for adventurous skiers of any standard, there are few places to beat it. The key attractions are simple: the snow normally comes early (and stays late) even in a poor winter, and there is an enormous amount of wonderful skiing to suit all standards. The extent of lift-served off-piste skiing naturally attracts advanced skiers in particular. But you don't need to be an expert to enjoy Val – both the editors of this guide have recently had successful holidays there with mixed family groups. At the same time, the undergrading of pistes and relatively relaxed attitude to grooming mean that early intermediates must be steered to the right runs if their confidence is to be built up rather than demolished.

The list of drawbacks above may look long, but it's a list of mainly petty complaints. For some visitors, dependence on the ski-bus may matter, even though the free service is one of the most efficient in the Alps. The bus is necessary partly because of the rather strung-out nature of the place but ironically it has become more important recently because of lift improvements: lots of people based in central Val now start their day with a bus-ride to the super-quick funicular at La Daille.

The village is not exactly pretty, but it was improved enormously in appearance and ambience in the years leading up to the 1992 Olympics. One of our main reservations is its domination by the British – not just holiday skiers but also the hundreds imported each season to staff the chalets, shops and bars, plus of course the ski bums a resort like this pulls in. But for others this is a plus-point, and there's no denying that it results in a vibrant après-ski scene in which Brits can feel perfectly at home. And in high season, when the French arrive in numbers, the effect is much less pronounced.

🏠 The resort

Val-d'Isère is classic ribbon development. As you drive in from La Daille, the apartments and chalets lining the road increase in density, and then give way to shops, bars, restaurants and hotels. As you approach the centre the legacy of the 1992 Olympics becomes more evident: new wood- and stone-cladding, culminating in the tasteful pedestrian-only Val Village complex between the central T-junction and the nursery slopes.

Despite the fact that the valley is a dead-end in winter, there is a lot of traffic around, making the centre feel a bit towny, rather than villagey.

La Daille is a complex of high-rise apartment blocks – convenient for skiing, but hideous. Locals insist that they blend in superbly with the mountain environment in the summer.

🎿 The skiing

For good skiers, there are few areas to rival the skiing offered by L'Espace Killy (as the linked ski areas of Val d'Isère and Tignes are known). Its attractions are as much its splendid off-piste runs as its groomed runs. But there are significant on-piste challenges too. Intermediates of all standards will find enough to keep them interested for several successive visits. And, contrary to popular opinion, there are some great areas for novices too.

THE SKI AREA
Vast and varied
Val-d'Isère's skiing divides into three main sectors.

Bellevarde (2770m) is the mountain which is home to both Val-d'Isère's famous Men's Downhill courses – the OK piste, which opens each season's World Cup programme in early December, and the Face de Bellevarde Olympic course, which made such spectacular viewing in 1992 but which costs so much to prepare that it may never be used again. You can reach Bellevarde by the funicular from La Daille or by cable-car or high-speed chairs from Val.

From the top you can ski back down to the main lifts, play on a variety of drags and chairs on the top half of the mountain or take a choice of lifts to get over to the Tignes skiing.

Solaise is the other mountain accessible directly from the centre of Val-d'Isère. The Solaise cable-car was Val's first major lift – begun illicitly during the Occupation in 1940 and finished in 1942. The parallel high-speed quad Solaise Express chair-lift takes you a few metres higher. Once up, a short drag takes you over a plateau and down to a variety of chairs which serve this very sunny area of predominantly gentle pistes.

From near the top of this area you can catch a drag or chair over to the third main skiing area, above and below the **Col de l'Iseran** (with skiing going up to 3300m on the Pissaillas glacier), which can also be reached by cable-car from Le Fornet in the valley. The chair-lift is spectacular and – for the faint-hearted – nerve-wracking, because it climbs over a narrow ridge and then drops suddenly down the other side. You can also ride the chair-lift back if you don't want to catch the bus from Le Fornet. The drag-lift isn't the easy option, though. It's short and steep. At the top you ski through a low, narrow tunnel leading to an awkward black run which is often closed. The skiing you reach is predominantly easy, with spectacular views and access to the most beautiful off-piste runs in the region.

SNOW RELIABILITY
Unbeatable
In years when lower resorts have suffered, Val-d'Isère has rarely been short of snow. Its height of 1850m means you can almost always ski back to the village, especially because of the snowmaking facilities on the lower slopes of all the main routes back to town. Last season we skied the resort at the end of April in temperatures of 20°C to 30°C and still had wonderful spring snow and no bare patches all the way back to the resort.

Much of the skiing is north-facing (or northish) and a substantial amount is between 2300m and 3000m, even ignoring the higher glacier skiing. The pistes would be in even better condition if the resort took piste grooming as seriously as they do in Méribel and Courchevel.

FOR ADVANCED SKIERS
One of the world's best
Val-d'Isère is one of the top resorts in the world for good skiers. The main attraction is the huge range of beautiful off-piste possibilities. There are lots of well-known and well-skied runs which have their starting points marked on the piste map. And there are many more which aren't marked.

SKI FACTS

Altitude	1550m-3500m
Lifts	102
Pistes	300km
Green/Blue	62%
Red	29%
Black	9%
Artificial snow	24km

LIFT PASSES

94/95 prices in francs

L'Espace Killy
Covers all lifts and resort buses in Tignes and Val d'Isère.

Beginners 7 free beginners' lifts on main nursery slopes.

Main pass
1-day pass 205
6-day pass 940

Senior citizens
Over 60: 6-day pass 790 (16% off)
Over 80: free pass

Children
Under 12: 6-day pass 660 (30% off)
Under 5: free pass

Short-term passes
Half-day pass from 12.30 (adult 140).

Alternative periods
14 non-consecutive days (adult 2,385).

Notes 1-day pass and over valid for one day in La Plagne-Les Arcs. 6-day pass and over valid for one day each in the Three Valleys, Pralognan-la-Vanoise, Les Saisies and Valmorel. On 3- to 15-day passes, pass reimbursed if all lifts are shut due to bad weather. Discount on new passes on presentation of previous season's pass.

Don't be tempted to launch off on these runs without a guide. The runs are not marked once you're on them, and we've seen some horrific accidents through skiers who didn't know the terrain hitting rocks and skiing over precipices.

But the runs are normally quite safe with a guide. And a guide needn't cost a lot: several schools run guided groups you can join for a modest fee to see what the area has to offer.

Two of our favourite off-piste runs are outstandingly beautiful and not at all difficult. The Tour de Charvet starts from the top of the Grand Pre chair-lift in the Bellevarde sector, with a long traverse into a big bowl, then wends its way though a narrow gorge before the ski out to the bottom of the Manchet chair up to Solaise.

The Col Pers starts with a traverse from the top drag or chair-lift on the Pissaillas glacier and opens up into a huge open bowl with glorious views. There are endless variants on the way down. Most bring you out just below the source of the Isère river, where you drop down into the very beautiful, narrow Gorges du Malpasset and ski on top of the frozen Isère back to the Le Fornet cable-car. This is a good area for spotting chamois grazing in the sun on the rocky outcrops above you.

There is excellent piste skiing for good skiers, too. Many of the red and blue runs – even one or two greens – are steep enough to get mogulled, so the small number of blacks is not the limitation it might seem.

On Bellevarde the famous Face run is the main attraction – mogulled from top to bottom, but not worryingly steep. Epaule is the sector's other black run – where the moguls are hit by long exposure to sun and can be slushy or rock-hard too often for our liking. On Solaise the main attractions for bump enthusiasts are the runs back down under the lifts to the village. There are several ways down: all steep, though none fearsomely so.

Quite apart from all this, there's the Tignes skiing to explore – which offers as much again.

FOR INTERMEDIATE SKIERS
Quantity and quality

Val-d'Isère has as much to offer intermediates as it does good skiers. But timid skiers should be aware that many runs are under-graded.

In the Solaise sector is a network of gentle blue cruising runs ideal for building confidence. And there are a couple of beautiful runs from this area down through the woods to Le Laisinant, from where you catch the bus – these are ideal for bad weather, though prone to closure in times of avalanche danger.

The runs in the Col de l'Iseran sector are flatter and easier – ideal for early and hesitant intermediates. Those marked blue at the top of the glacier could really be graded green.

Bellevarde has a huge variety of runs ideally suited to intermediates of all standards. From Bellevarde itself there is a big choice of green, blue and red runs of varying pitch. And the wide, varied runs from Tovière normally give you the choice of groomed pistes or a mogul route.

A snag for early intermediates is that runs back to the valley can be testing. The easiest way is to ski down to La Daille, where there is a green run – but it should be graded blue (in some resorts it would be red) and gets very crowded and mogulled at the end of the day. None of the runs from Bellevarde and Solaise back to Val itself are really easy.

The blue Santons run from Bellevarde takes you through a long, narrow gun-barrel which often has people standing around plucking up courage, making things even trickier.

On Solaise there isn't much to choose between the blue and red ways down – they're both mogulled and narrow in places. At the top, there's no option other than the red mogul run in full view of the lifts. It's just a question of choosing how big you want your moguls – the largest are on the right as you go down. Many early intermediates sensibly choose to ride the lifts down – take the chair for a spectacular view.

FOR BEGINNERS
OK if you know where to go

Val-d'Isère has a superb nursery slope right by the centre of town. What's more the lifts serving it are free – no coupons, never mind a lift pass.

Once you get off the nursery slopes, there are some excellent easy runs, but you have to know where to find them; many of the greens would be blue, or even red, in other resorts. One experienced Val-d'Isère instructor, who wanted to remain anonymous, admitted: 'We have to have plenty of green runs on the piste map, even if we haven't got many green slopes – otherwise beginners wouldn't come here.'

The best place for your first real runs off the nursery slopes is the Madeleine green run on Solaise. The Col de l'Iseran runs are also gentle and wide;

they're less easily accessible but the snow is normally the best around.

As explained above, there are no really easy runs back to the valley.

FOR CROSS-COUNTRY
Limited
There are a couple of loops near the road towards La Daille and another going from behind the village centre out past Le Laisinant. Much more picturesque is the one going from Le Châtelard (on the road up the side valley past the main cable-car station) to the Manchet chair. But keen cross-country skiers should go elsewhere.

QUEUES
Few problems
Queues to get out of the resort have been pretty much eliminated by the building of the funicular and high-speed chair-lifts up the mountains as alternatives to the two main cable-cars. The slow Manchet chair-lift was replaced last season by a high-speed quad that has alleviated the serious queues that used to be found here.

The main outstanding problems arise mainly at peak periods and include two bottlenecks towards the end of the day: the chair back from Col de l'Iseran to Solaise and the two slow double Tovière chairs, taking visitors from Tignes back home.

Returning from Val-Claret at the end of the day may involve a lengthy wait for the Tufs chair, but there are no further lifts necessary to get home, so there's no risk of being stranded.

MOUNTAIN RESTAURANTS
Disappointing for a major resort
The mountain restaurants mainly consist of big self-service places with vast terraces at the top of major lifts. The best are in the Bellevarde sector, on the runs down to La Daille.

Until our latest visit, we'd have said the best food was at the Crech'Ouna just across the slope from the funicular station at La Daille. We've had countless excellent meals here. Sadly, on our last visit the food was appalling – and locals confirmed it had gone off. Let's hope it recovers; it's a charming and civilised place. It's great for a long lunch if the weather's poor; strangely, there's no outside terrace for sunny weather.

Selected chalets in Val-d'Isère

SKI SCHOOL

94/95 prices in francs

ESF

Classes 6 days
5½hr: 3hr am, 2½hr pm
6 full days: 1010
Children's classes
Ages: from 4
6 full days including lunch: 1490
Private lessons
1hr, mornings, afternoons, or whole day
175 for 1hr

Snow Fun
Classes 6 days
3hr am and 2½hr pm
6 mornings: 580
Children's classes
Ages: up to 13
6 full days: 920
Private lessons
Hourly or daily
170 for 1hr

Top Ski
Specialise in small off-piste guiding groups (max 6)
Classes 4 mornings (9am-1pm): 920
4 full days (9am-1pm, 2pm-4pm): 1280
Other courses
On-piste tuition including slalom and mogul clinics
Children's classes
Ages: 7 to 16
4 mornings on-piste: 720; off-piste: 920 (tuition and safety)
Private lessons
am (8.45-1pm), pm (2pm-4.30) or full-day (8.45-4.30)
750 for 2½hr pm; full-day (1,650) or am (1,250)

Alpine Experience
Specialise in courses for small groups (max 6)

YSE
helped us to compile the eating out and après-ski sections. Our thanks to them.

Other recommendations: Le Tufs, just below Crech'Ouna – a newer table-service restaurant, terrace, good pizzas and Savoyard fare; Trifollet, around halfway up the La Daille gondola – relatively new, table-service, terrace overlooking the men's downhill piste, good food; La Folie Douce, at the top of the gondola – recommended by several reporters for excellent food and service with a smile; Marmottes, in the middle of the Bellevarde bowl – not unpleasant, and handy for mixed groups to meet at.

An alternative is to ski down to town, to one of the restaurant terraces overlooking the nursery slopes. Our favourite is the big terrace of the Brussels. The restaurant near the cross-country course at Le Châtelard is also worth trying. When skiing at the Col de l'Iseran – especially on a wintry day – much the most pleasant plan for lunch is to descend to the rustic Arolay at Le Fornet.

SKI SCHOOL
A very wide choice
There are six ski schools plus several private instructors to choose from. ESF and Snow Fun are the two biggest, with a full range of group and private lessons – we've had recent good reports on them both.

Top Ski, Evolution 2 and Alpine Experience all specialise in taking skiers off-piste in small groups which they put together – excellent for good skiers who want to make the most of Val-d'Isère's vast off-piste possibilities. We've had great days off-piste with both Top Ski and Alpine Experience (started a couple of years ago by some of Top Ski's best guides). But we have to say – and this is a seriously unfashionable view, which will win us no friends – that we have found Top Ski's tuition rather less impressive.

Mountain Masters has a reputation for 'inner skiing'-type teaching methods, and has small classes, video analysis and native English-speaking instructors.

All the schools have teachers who speak good English – in many cases it's their native language. In peak periods it's best to book in advance, especially with some of the off-piste schools who have only a handful of teachers each.

Heli-skiing can be arranged – you are dropped in Italy because heli-skiing is banned in France.

FACILITIES FOR CHILDREN
Good tour op possibilities
The two resort crèches are small, and get booked up early; they also don't cater for children under two. So it's not surprising that tour operator facilities tend to be more important to British visitors. Mark Warner's Cygnaski jumbo-chalet (see below) has been the basis of an excellent family holiday for one of us; it has a spacious nursery in the basement – actually at ground level, so pleasantly light.

We have personal experience of the incompetence and indifference of the ESF ski nursery; stay away.

 # Staying there

The location of your accommodation isn't crucial. Free shuttle buses run along the main street linking the main lift stations. It is one of the most efficient bus services we've come across; even in peak periods, you never have to wait more than a few minutes. But in the evenings frequency plummets and it may be quicker to walk. Dedicated après-skiers will want to be within walking distance of the central T-junction – most of the bars and restaurants are here, around the main street. The recent development up the side valley beyond the main lift station is mainly attractive, and no more than a pleasant stroll from the centre.

HOW TO GO
Lots of choice
More British tour operators go to Val-d'Isère than to any other resort. The choice of chalets and chalet-hotels, in particular, is vast. There is a Club Med 'village'.

Chalets There is everything from budget chalets to the most luxurious you could demand. The resort has a fair number of chalet operators who don't go anywhere else, of which YSE has quickly become the most prominent. This year they have turned the simple hotel Les Lauzes, next to the church, into a chalet. YSE and the very upmarket Ski Company Ltd have the best chalets in town, notably their respective luxurious mountain lodges.

Lotus Supertravel have a good selection of small, very comfortable places. The jewel in the Finlays crown is the central, beautifully appointed Squaw Valley chalet. Bladon Lines have a large range, from intimate little places to several chalet-hotels, including the 68-bed Fôret. Silver Ski has a good-value little chalet in central

CHILDCARE

Garderie Isabelle (79411282) at La Daille takes children from age 2, from 8.30 to 5.30. The Petit Poucet (79061397) in the Residence les Hameaux at Val takes children aged 3 to 8, from 9am to 5.30. Both provide indoor and outdoor activities and delivery to and collection from ski school .

Snowfun's Club Nounours takes children aged 3 to 6 for lessons of 1hr30, 2hr or 3hr. Older children can be left in classes all day.

The ESF runs a ski nursery for aged 4 up, with rope tows and a heated chalet.

ACTIVITIES

Indoor Swimming pool, sports hall (basketball, volleyball, table tennis, badminton, trampoline and gymnastics), library, bridge, health centres in the hotels Christiania, Brussel's and Sofitel (sauna, hammam, jacuzzi, body building, massages, solarium etc), cinema, fitness club (body building, step, aerobics, sauna, massage, solarium) **Outdoor** Walks in Le Manchet valley and Le Fornet, natural skating rink, curling, hang-gliding, quad bikes, all-terrain karts, ice driving, snow-mobiles, para-gliding, shoe-snow outings, heli-skiing, microlight trips, bungee jumping

Val. Le Ski have a brand-new place this year, in the Joseray area – handy for the cable-cars. The big operators have struggled to acquire chalets here. Their catered 'chalet' holidays are exclusively in apartment conversions.

There is quite a choice of chalet-hotels. At the bottom of the price range is Ski Val's Tarentaise. YSE's Crêtes Blanches is much the most comfortable, verging on the luxurious. Bladon Lines' recently renovated Fjord is stylishly simple, and its Grand-Nord and Forêt have bars that are among the liveliest in town. Mark Warner's absolutely central Moris is possibly even livelier; in contrast, the family-oriented Cygnaski, half-way to La Daille, is much quieter – plain but comfortable.

The best-value chalets tend to be away from the centre, at Le Fornet, Le Châtelard and Le Laisinant. Le Ski , Ski Olympic and Ski Activity offer a wide range between them in these hamlets. **Hotels** There are 39 to choose from, mostly 2- and 3-star, but for such a big international resort surprisingly few are notably attractive. Don't overlook the wide choice of hotel-style accommodation run on chalet lines, described under chalets.

££££ Christiania Recently renovated big chalet, probably best in town. Traditional-chic, with friendly staff. Has a sauna.

££££ Latitudes Modern but stylish. Piano bar, nightclub. Leisure centre with sauna, steam room, whirl-pool and massage.

££££ Blizzard Renovated for Olympics. Indoor-outdoor pool behind. Convenient .

£££ Grand Paradis Excellent position. Good food.

£££ Brussels Excellent position. Large terrace, which is popular for lunch. Leisure centre.

£££ Savoyarde Rustic decor. Leisure centre. Good food. Rooms a bit small.

££ Sorbiers Modern but cosy bed and breakfast hotel.

££ Kern Basic, but good value, food and welcome.

££ Vieux Village Traditional old hotel. Good value.

££ Samovar In La Daille. Traditional hotel with good reputation for food.

Self-catering There are thousands of properties to choose from. UK operators offer lots of them, but they tend to get snapped up by early-booking ski-drivers. Local agency Val d'Isère Agence has a particularly good brochure showing its wares. As in all French resorts, most apartments are small – but you can find bigger places

if you scour the brochures.

The Rocher Soleil apartments are widely recognised as the best in town; with their satellite TVs, heated outdoor pool, leisure centre, lounge, bar and restaurant (with takeaway service), they resemble American condominiums – but don't expect American spaciousness. Inghams has an allocation.

Finlays has a good selection, most of which are bang in the centre. Other recommendable apartments: Rond Point des Pistes (lounge – Inghams), Jardins de la Balme (lounge, free parking), Châtelard (remote but comfortable, lounge – Crystal, French Impressions), Hauts de Rogonay (open-fire lounge – French Impressions), Jardins de Val (simple, not too cramped – Inghams).

EATING OUT
Plenty of good, affordable places

Restaurants here have to satisfy the still predominantly French market, so standards are high and prices lower than in London. Although there are, among the seventy-odd restaurants, some which specialise in Italian, Alsatian, Tex-Mex and even Japanese food, most stick to proper French dishes, from simple savoury Breton pancakes at the Brasserie des Sports to 'grande cuisine'.

You can get a good meal for less than £15 in numerous very pleasant places, such as the very popular Perdrix Blanche (everything from Savoyard to Sushi), Lodge and Taverne d'Alsace (due to re-open in new premises this season). Less well known but equally good value are the Olympique, Florence, Au Bout de la Rue (English-owned, excellent French cooking) and 1789. We'd also have recommended the Crech'Ouna until our last visit there (see Mountain restaurants).

The best restaurants in town are the Solaise, Grande Ourse or the hotels Savoyard and Tsanteleina.

Those on the tightest budgets should try the pizzas in Chez Nano, next to Dick's T-bar, or the Pacific, next to the Moris pub, which serves generous portions of pasta and seafood. G-Jay's and the Pavillon are recommended for breakfast.

APRES-SKI
Very lively

Nightlife is surprisingly energetic, given that most people have spent all day skiing hard. After skiing there are lots of bars to fall into, most offering happy-hour prices. The famous Dick's

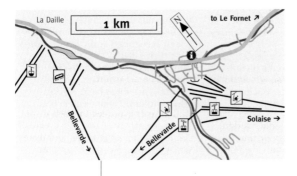

PACKAGES

AA Ski-Driveaway,
Airtours, Alpine
Options Skidrive,
Altours Travel, Bladon
Lines, Chalets
'Unlimited', Club Med,
Cresta Ski France,
Crystal, Enterprise,
Fantiski, Finlays,
French Impressions,
Inghams, Kings Ski
Club, Lagrange, Le
Ski, Lotus
Supertravel, Made to
Measure, Mark
Warner, Neilson,
Sally, Silver Ski, Ski
3000, Ski Activity, Ski
Arrangements, Ski
Choice, Ski Club of
GB, Ski Europe, Ski
Olympic, Ski Savoie,
Ski Val, Ski Valkyrie,
Ski Weekend, Ski
West, Ski Wyatt,
SkiBound, Skiworld,
Stena Sealink, The
Ski Company Ltd,
Thomson, Travelscene
Ski-Drive, UCPA,
Ultimate, YSE

GETTING THERE

Air Geneva, transfer
4½hr. Chambery,
transfer 3½hr. Lyon,
transfer 4½hr.

Rail Bourg-St-Maurice
(33km); regular buses
from station.

Tea Bar and the much smaller G-Jays are run by Brits for Brits; Bananas, Bar Jacques and the Perdrix Blanche bar are 'entente cordiale' places; and Brasserie des Sports, Boubou's and the Saloon are pretty much French-only enclaves.

There are lots of late bars, many with late music and dancing into the early hours. For those that hate such things or have skied themselves to a standstill, there are quiet hotel bars, piano bars and cocktail lounges. Dick's becomes the busiest disco in town late evening, often with a queue outside, but it has several little alcoves where those whose age exceeds their Continental shoe size can have a civilised chat. Dick's is, however, so British you may think it lacks the cosmopolitan, slightly chic and trendy feel of French places, such as Club 21. The same could be said of its main rival, Playbach. Other good bars are the Alsace, Couleur Café, Café Face and the aforementioned early-evening haunts. Try the 10-drink cocktail special at Bar Jacques! Live music can often be found at the Forêt, the

Aventure, Brussel's, Café Face, Pavillon, Pacific and Club 21.

Several British-run chalet hotels have bars that get very lively at times including Forêt, Grand Nord and Moris. The Forêt has karaoke nights.

FOR NON-SKIERS
Not good, except for sporty types
Val is primarily a skier's ski resort. Inactive non-skiers won't find many diversions, and may have trouble getting their skiing companions to commit themselves to a pedestrian-accessible lunchtime rendezvous.

The best walks are up the Manchet valley. The range of non-skiing activities is quite wide, including adventurous stuff like bungee-jumping. But the mainstream facilities are surprisingly poor: the swimming pool building is small and showing its age. They could really do with a smart new sports centre.

STAYING DOWN THE VALLEY
Not a great idea
Val-d'Isère is a long way up its dead-end valley. If you're driving out to the Alps you could consider staying half an hour away in rustic Ste-Foy (which has its own delightful and deserted ski area – see page 229) or even further away in Bourg-St-Maurice. But if you do that you'll really want to consider skiing different resorts each day rather than just Val-d'Isère.

TOURIST OFFICE

Postcode 73155
Tel 010 33 79060660
Fax 79060456

Valloire 1430m

HOW IT RATES

The skiing

Snow	**
Extent	***
Advanced	**
Intermediates	****
Beginners	****
Convenience	***
Queues	***
Restaurants	**

The rest

Scenery	***
Resort charm	****
Not skiing	**

SKI FACTS

Altitude	1430m-2600m
Lifts	33
Pistes	150km
Green/Blue	49%
Red	34%
Black	17%
Artificial snow	10km

Little-known on the British market, Valloire offers a surprisingly extensive ski area, ideally suited to intermediates. It also has a rustic French feel to it and retains a life as a farming community, as well as a ski resort.

THE RESORT

Valloire is an unspoilt, old, working village, tucked away above the Maurienne valley. Despite having developed into a significant-sized ski resort, it has retained a feeling of 'real' France, complete with impressive old church, crêperies, fromageries, reasonable prices, villagey atmosphere and friendly locals.

THE SKIING

The 150km of piste are spread over three similar-sized, lightly wooded **ski areas** – Sétaz, Valmeinier and Crey du Quart. The skiing is almost entirely intermediate, Les Karellis (a 45-minute drive) being better for more taxing runs (and for superior snow and scenery). A gondola leads up towards Sétaz and a chair towards Crey du Quart and the link with the skiing of next-door Valmeinier.

Reliable **snow-cover** is not a strong point, though Valloire does have a better recent snow record than similar but lower 'real' French ski villages such as La Clusaz, Morzine, Châtel and Megève. Important links are too low, sunny and lacking artificial snow to ensure the whole area is always skiable. The main piste down to the village is fully served by snow cannon, whilst the Valmeinier area holds snow particularly well.

There is not much to challenge **advanced skiers**, though the Cascade and Olympiques pistes are fun. The mogul field down to Valmeinier 1500 represents the greatest challenge.

Valloire is very much an **intermediate** area. Several of the pistes towards Valmeinier, and the JBM run to Valloire, are suitable for good intermediates, but average skiers have the widest choice of runs, with plenty of options in all three sections. A variety of pistes head to and from Valmeinier, making mixed-ability excursions a straightforward affair. The Crey du Quart section is particularly good for easy skiing.

The limited village nursery areas are adequate in low season when snow cover is good. Otherwise there are good nursery slopes up the mountain, at the top of the Sétaz gondola, but a full lift pass is needed to reach them. There are plenty of easy pistes suitable for improving **beginners**, and there are 40km of **cross-country** trails.

There are long delays when the Italians hit town en masse, but thankfully this is not a common occurrence. Otherwise there are few **queue** problems when snow-cover is complete. The Lac de la Veille (Crey) drag and Valmeinier 1500 chair can become oversubscribed when it is not. Understandably, the village gondola gets busy for a short period when ski school starts.

Mountain restaurants are in very short supply but are good quality. The Thimel is perhaps the best.

Recent reports suggest that the **ski school** has lapsed badly of late – large classes and poor organisation.

The nursery, which takes **children** from 6 months old, has a good reputation. The ski kindergarten is for 3- to 7-year-olds, but is open mornings only.

STAYING THERE

There's a fair choice of hotel and apartment accommodation. SkiBound have the rustic Timelets **chalet**. The Grand (3-star) and Christiania (2-star) are the best **hotels**, and both are well placed. The Centre is shabbier and noisier, but its food and position are good. Plein Sud is an adequate SkiBound club hotel which is well placed, though the cheapest rooms are extremely basic. The Rocher St Pierre **apartments** are good by French standards. The simple Val d'Aurea accommodation is well placed.

Most of the **restaurants** are pizza and fondue joints. The Crêperie and Asile des Fondues are perhaps the best of these. The Gastilleur has the best French cuisine in town.

Après-ski is quiet, though far from dead. The hotel bars of the Touring and Plein Sud, and American Dodgers, are lively. Piano Bar has live music. The Mammoth and Swell discos warm up at weekends.

There are few amenities for **non-skiers**, and Valloire feels somewhat cut off from civilisation. In the last week of January a large ice sculpture competition takes place.

PACKAGES

Enterprise, SkiBound

TOURIST OFFICE

Postcode 73450
Tel 010 33 79590396
Fax 79590966

Valmorel 1400m

HOW IT RATES

The skiing

Snow	✱✱✱
Extent	✱✱✱
Advanced	✱✱
Intermediates	✱✱✱✱
Beginners	✱✱✱✱✱
Convenience	✱✱✱✱✱
Queues	✱✱✱✱
Restaurants	✱✱

The rest

Scenery	✱✱✱
Resort charm	✱✱✱✱
Not skiing	✱✱

✔ Fairly large ski area provides something for everyone

✔ Probably the most tastefully designed of all French purpose-built resorts

✔ Excellent ski convenience

✔ Beginners and children particularly well catered for

✔ One of the most accessible of the Tarentaise resorts by road and rail

✔ One of the cheapest of the French resorts widely available from UK tour operators

✘ Limited challenging skiing

✘ Fairly low ski area, so good snow not guaranteed

✘ Little variety in accommodation and in restaurants and bars

✘ Some frustrating bottlenecks mar a good lift system

ORIENTATION

Valmorel, a short drive from Moutiers, is the main resort in 'Le Grand Domaine' – a ski area that links the Tarentaise with the Maurienne, by way of the Col de la Madeleine. The skiing stretches over to Saint-François and Longchamp on the Maurienne side. Chair-lifts and a gondola from the compact village provide access to all the main sectors of the skiing.

All the mega-ski areas of the Tarentaise are within reasonable driving distance – the **Trois Vallées, La Plagne, Les Arcs** and even **Val-d'Isère-Tignes**. An off-piste tour through a number of these resorts starts from the Col du Gollet above Valmorel.

This is the purpose-built resort where they got it right. Built from scratch in the mid-1970s, Valmorel was intended to look and feel like a mountain village: a traffic-free main street with hamlets grouped around it, low-rise buildings and traditional Savoie stone and wood materials throughout. The end-result is an attractive, friendly sort of place, even if it does have a 'Disney World' feel to it. There is easy access between the accommodation, the village centre and the skiing.

The ski area is large, by most standards – though it can't rival its huge neighbours, the Trois Vallées or Val-d'Isère-Tignes. But with good snow conditions and the whole system open, there's enough skiing to keep most grades of skier happy. As the snow conditions deteriorate, the variety of available skiing reduces rapidly and the flaws in the lift system can start to show through.

Unashamedly aimed at the middle-ground (intermediate skiers, families and mixed-ability groups), it does have considerable appeal to those groups because it has been so well put together.

 ## The resort

Happily for Valmorel and its visitors, the place was built with more than just convenience in mind – it also manages to look pretty good. Bourg-Morel is the heart of the resort – a traffic-free street where you'll find most of the shops, the restaurants, visitor information – just about everything – in a 200m stretch. It's pleasant and usually lively, with a distinctly family feel. And the skiing is right at hand, with the main pistes back and chair-lift out meeting at the end of the street. Nearby is an information board showing lift and piste status, and what's on locally.

Dotted around the hillside, but not very far from the Bourg-Morel centre, are the six 'hameaux' which contain most of the accommodation. Most of it is self-catering and of a reasonably high standard, without ever being very flash – which is pretty much a reflection of the sort of people who like Valmorel!

 ## The skiing

Beginners and intermediates will take to it. Those looking for more of a challenge will find it more limited. Variety is provided by a number of sectors of quite distinctive character, and the system is big enough to provide interesting, if hardly epic, exploratory trips to its farthest boundaries. Some visitors find the piste map inadequate, especially for the Longchamps sector, and there are a couple of long, awkward drag-lifts.

THE SKI AREA
A big system in miniature
The 48 lifts and 163km of piste spread out in an interesting arrangement over a number of minor valleys and ridges either side of the Col de la Madeleine, with Valmorel at the eastern extremity of the system and runs coming down into the village on three sides.

The most heavily used route out of the village is via the **Beaudin** chair which takes you over the main pistes

SKI FACTS

Altitude	1200m-2550m
Lifts	48
Pistes	163km
Green/Blue	69%
Red	19%
Black	12%
Artificial snow	8km

LIFT PASSES

94/95 prices in francs
Le Grand Domaine
Covers all lifts in
Valmorel and St-
François Longchamp.
Beginners One free
drag lift. Limited area
lift pass covers
beginner lifts and
runs.
Main pass
1-day pass 160
6-day pass 864
(low season 684 –
21% off)
Senior citizens
Over 60: 6-day pass
739 (14% off)
Children
Under 13: 6-day pass
739 (14% off)
Under 4: free pass
Short-term passes
Half-day from 11.30
(139) and 12.30 (119).
Saturday morning
until 1pm.
Alternative passes
Valmorel Domaine
covers 24 lifts in
Valmorel only (6 days
824 for adults, 695
for children).

back. From the top of the chair a
network of lifts and pistes takes you
over to the **Col de la Madeleine** and
beyond that to Lauzière (the highest
point of the ski area at 2550m) or the
slopes of **Saint-François** and
Longchamp at the far western end of
the ski area.

The Pierrafort gondola for the
Mottet sector and the Crève-Cœur
chair for the **Gollet** area take off from
Hameau-du-Mottet at the top end of
the village. Both areas have their own
runs back towards the village, or good
skiers can work their way over to the
Beaudin and Madeleine sectors (tough
runs down only). There's an easy link
in the other direction.

Adjacent to the village there are
nursery areas with good easy runs.

SNOW RELIABILITY
Sort of average
With a top station of 2550m and
much of the skiing below 2000m,
good snow conditions are not
guaranteed. Lower runs are frequently
closed, and even Lauzière, which has
the system's high point but faces
south, and Gollet can suffer quite
quickly during sunny spells. Mottet is
north-facing and usually has the best
snow. Artificial snowmaking covers
the almost 600m vertical from
Beaudin down to village level.

FOR ADVANCED SKIERS
Better than you might think
Although not renowned for its tough
skiing, there are challenging runs.
Gollet is usually a good place for
moguls – plenty of them but not too
big and not too hard. There are steep
black runs below the top section of
the Mottet chair and some interesting
off-piste variants. From the drag-lift up
towards the Madeleine sector, there
are a couple of fine runs (one off-piste
but indicated on the piste map).

The Lauzière chair can seem a bit of
a trek, but once there you'll probably
find it under-used and a lot of fun,
provided it hasn't suffered too much
sun. There are three marked runs and
plenty of acreage in which to pick
your own route – there are some steep
pitches and often some big bumps.

Ski-touring is a very popular activity
in the region, and trips such as the
Nine-Valley safari can be organised
from Valmorel.

FOR INTERMEDIATE SKIERS
Plenty to keep you busy
Lots of scope, though many skiers
seem to mill around Beaudin and the
Arenouillaz drag and Biollène chair –

the adjacent runs are quite friendly.
The runs down into the Celliers valley
are more testing, particularly the two
reds served by the Madeleine chair,
which are too difficult for early
intermediates to cope with
comfortably. The main thoroughfare
back to the village – from Beaudin
along the line of the snow cannons –
is graded blue then red, and the red
stretch can be quite daunting at the
end of the day. The artificial snow
tends to pile up in surprisingly large
heaps, as do tired beginners.

For a day out, the slopes around
Saint-François-Longchamp are within
easy striking distance, and form a big
area of mainly broad, flattering runs.
The Côte drag, which can be reached
on the return trip, is little used and
serves two pleasant runs with some
good terrain for practising off-piste.

The red route from the top of Mottet
is outstandingly boring on the upper
half – more push-and-walk than skiing
– but the views are some
compensation, and the lower half is
much better. The runs back to the
village, served by the Pierrafort
gondola, are graded blue but are long,
interesting and in parts tricky. The
adjacent Gollet slopes also provide
plenty of scope for good intermediates
to amuse themselves.

FOR BEGINNERS
An excellent choice
Valmorel suits beginners – there are
dedicated learning areas right by the
village for both adults (at Bois de la
Croix) and children (in the snow
garden of the children's club), and lots
of expertise among the instructors.
The terrain does not allow extensive
nursery areas in the valley, so progress
from novice to beginner usually sees
the children heading for the top of the
Pierrafort gondola and the adults for
the Beaudin sector. The lifts accessing
these areas can be used to return to
the village. If the snow-cover is
complete, there is a very pleasant
green run through the trees down to
Combelouvière.

FOR CROSS-COUNTRY
Inconvenient and not extensive
Valmorel is not the place for
aficionados; more for those giving it a
try. Trails adding up to 23km, at a
number of different locations in the
valley (and therefore likely to have a
limited season only), can be reached
by special bus from Valmorel itself.

SKI SCHOOL

94/95 prices in francs

ESF
Classes 6 days
2½hr am or pm
6 half-days: 550
Children's classes
Ages: 4 to 12
6 half-days: 510
Private lessons
Hourly
160 for 1 or 2 people

CHILDCARE

Saperlipopette
(79098445) provides
care for children aged
from 6 months to 7
years, from 8.30 to
5pm. Those aged 18
months to 3 are given
'a gentle and amusing
first experience with
the snow.' Those
aged 3 to 7 have
indoor activities as
well as ski classes
(divided into three
levels), and there is a
snow play area for
those who do not
wish to ski.

QUEUES
Occasional (avoidable) problems
Queues build up for the Beaudin chair
at ski school times. These can be
avoided by using the alternative
Lanchettes chair. Once into the skiing
area, there are only two bottlenecks to
worry about – the Madeleine chair,
which provides the only access to the
Saint-François and Lauzière side, and
the Frêne drag, almost as critical to the
return journey. Simply avoid using
them at peak times.

MOUNTAIN RESTAURANTS
Fair to middling
There are six of them: none is
appalling nor wonderful. At least a
couple of them do deserve more of a

mention: the Altipiano, below the
Mottet chair, and the Deux Mazots, at
Col de la Madeleine (and which
doubles as a roadside café in summer),
provide table-service, good food, and
some ambience, without charging silly
prices. Le Prariond, most of the way
down from Mottet, is, depending on
your point of view, either a fun place
to have a drink at the end of the day
or just plain loud.

SKI SCHOOL
Good, especially for first-timers
We've had several good reports (and
only one bad report) on the ski school.
Instructors generally speak good
English and are enthusiastic and
imaginative. The main criticism is the
familiar one that classes can be too
large. Teaching for first-timers and for
children is something of a speciality of
the resort, and likely to produce good
results.

FACILITIES FOR CHILDREN
First-rate but book early
Saperlipopette is a comprehensive
childcare facility – one of the few in
the Alps that gives the impression of
having been thought out as
thoroughly as those in America.

A satisfied parent sums up what it is
about: 'At the start of the week the
children came back from their lessons
in tears. By the end of the week they
could ski, and thought their teacher
was wonderful.' All the instructors
speak English.

Prices vary with the seasons.
Advance booking is essential except
for very quiet times.

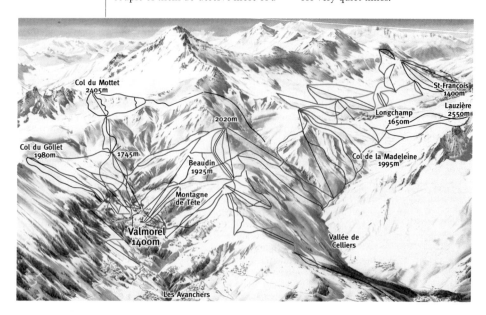

GETTING THERE

Air Geneva, transfer 3½hr. Lyon, transfer 3½hr. Chambery, transfer 2½hr.

Rail Moûtiers (6km); regular buses from station.

PACKAGES

Airtours, Altours Travel, Chalets 'Unlimited', Cresta Ski France, Crystal, Enterprise, Equity Total Ski, French Impressions, Inghams, Made to Measure, Neilson, Sally, Simply Ski, Ski Europe, Stena Sealink, Thomson, Travelscene Ski-Drive

Staying there

Athough it is basically a traffic-free resort, there are convenient drop-off points for all the accommodation. At the bottom end of Bourg-Morel is the base station of the Télébourg, a cross-village lift providing access to the 'Hameau-du-Mottet'. Between the other hameaux and Bourg-Morel, walking is usually the best bet. No walks are far – but some of the pathways should be graded red. Hameau-du-Mottet probably wins the hamlet convenience contest – it has the Télébourg, and access to the main lifts and from the return runs is good.

A car is of no use in the resort but very handy for trips to other resorts of the Tarentaise.

HOW TO GO
Take a package for value

Self-catering packages are the norm in Valmorel, though there seem to be more catered chalet deals available every year. There are few hotels in Valmorel, but tour operators have an allocation in most of them. If you're travelling independently and prefer more traditional suroundings, Les Avanchers is a possibility.

Chalets Though there are more on the market each year, their range isn't wide – most are simply catered apartments.

Neilson and Crystal offer a selection of such places, all of which are fairly cheap and cheerful. For those looking for a 'proper' chalet, it's got to be Simply Ski. The traditional-style chalet

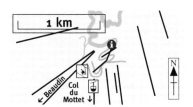

Penagos has received plenty of complimentary remarks from reporters. It's well placed for almost everything, including the skiing, though one beginner thought it a bit of a trek in ski boots to ski school. The same company also has small apartment-chalets, ideal for a family or small group looking for sole use.

Hotels There are only three hotels, and only the central hotel du Bourg expects casual callers – the others, up the hill a little way, basically cater for people staying the week on half-board. But we weren't turned away last time we rolled up at the Planchamp.

£££ Planchamp Best in town, with a rather pretentious restaurant.

££ Hotel du Bourg Neat, simple place in the middle of Bourg-Morel.

££ La Fontaine Across the piste from the Planchamp.

Self-catering Most people do – 8,500 apartment beds are distributed throughout the six hamlets and they are generally well-equipped. While it's entertaining having a view right over the piste, the downside of certain locations in Mottet and Planchamp is the proximity of some very powerful and noisy snow guns: sound-proofing is good but probably not good enough for light sleepers.

Selected chalets in Valmorel

ACTIVITIES

Indoor Keep-fit club, sauna, gym, cinema
Outdoor Snow-shoe outings, 12km of prepared walks, tobogganing, floodlit skiing, para-gliding

SIMPLY SKI

helped us to compile the eating out and après-ski sections. Our thanks to them.

The Creve-Coeur apartments (Thomson, Neilson) are among the most comfortable and best placed. They are in the Spie Loisirs sector, at the foot of the nursery slopes, next to the crèche and ski kindergarten, with good connections to the centre. The Hameau Planchamp apartments (Neilson) are less comfortable but better than some, and well positioned for the skiing.

EATING OUT
Good enough but rarely thrilling

You can check out the menus of most of Valmorel's restaurants in 15 minutes wandering up and down the main street. The pattern soon emerges – pizzas, pasta, fondues and a smattering of Savoie fare. There's also couscous and galettes available; not a huge variety but enough, and you're likely to get decent food and fair value. Many of the places need to be booked for any chance of a seat at a reasonable time.

Grill le Creuset is a bit smarter than most, for that special meal. The restaurant of hotel Planchamp is the other relatively upmarket place with prices to match. The Vadrouille does local dishes and has a lively atmosphere. The Pierrade and the Petit Savoyarde are mid-range places recommended by reporters. The Grenier in Mottet offers a bit of everything, in a slightly different location. Locals also recommend the similar standard the Galette and the Perce Neige. A pizza or sharing a fondue in the popular Chez Albert or the Petit Prince is the best bet if you're on a tight budget.

APRES-SKI
Unexciting

Immediate après-ski is centred on the outdoor cafes at the end of Bourg-Morel and Le Grenier. Both are lively spots, particularly while the sun shines. The after-dark activities are,

like everything else, concentrated around that main street. The Vadrouille is a pleasant and lively bar, Café de la Gare has live music, Ski Roc and Petit Prince are popular with locals, while the Perce-Neige frequently gets packed and boisterous. Cocktails can be enjoyed in more polished surroundings at the Shaker in hotel La Fontaine. There's one disco, Jeans, which is often neglected but occasionally buzzes.

You may catch the occasional musical event at the village hall, or a street parade (there's a Mardi Gras with medieval costumes and fireworks). Once a week there's floodlit skiing and the ski instructors generally turn out to race each other. A two-screen cinema and a wine-tasting evening are other possibilities.

FOR NON-SKIERS
Pleasant but boring

Its not a great place to hang around if you're not skiing – there are some marginal activities which, together with the usual café-based pastimes, can help to pass a few days. There are some cleared walks around the village and at the top of all the main lifts; and there's a pretty baroque church and some good lunch venues in Les Avanchers. Several mid-mountain restaurants are accessible to non-skiers, and it's also quite a practical proposition for skiers to return to the village for a lunchtime meet.

Snow-shoe treks and dog-sleigh trips can be organised – you can even learn to 'mush' the dogs.

STAYING DOWN THE VALLEY
Appealing

There are three small hotels in Les Avanchers – handy enough if you fancy Valmorel's skiing but prefer the ambience of the old village, and you have a car. They are the Cheval Noir, the Charmette, and the Crey.

TOURIST OFFICE

Postcode 73260
Tel 010 33 79098555
Fax 79098529

Val-Thorens 2300m

ORIENTATION

Val-Thorens is built high above the tree-line on a west-facing mountainside at the head of the Belleville valley, with pistes going past virtually all the accommodation. You can ski from your door to a variety of lifts that link to all the main ski areas.

A gondola takes you from the top of the village down and then up to the huge Caron cable-car, which goes to the area's highest point (3200m). Or you can ski down to the gondola's mid-point to join it. A number of chair-lifts lead up into the main north-facing Val-Thorens skiing. Or a 25-person gondola will whisk you east to the Péclet glacier.

From the resort centre and its western edge, chair-lifts lead up towards the skiing of the **Méribel** valley. You can also ski to **Les Menuires** from the top here.

SKI FACTS

Altitude	2100m-3300m
Lifts	200
Pistes	600km
Green/Blue	49%
Red	37%
Black	14%
Artificial snow	60km

✔ Part of the biggest linked ski area in the world, the Trois Vallées

✔ The highest resort in the Alps, with north-facing slopes guaranteeing good snow for a long season

✔ Local ski area good for all standards of skier

✔ Swift access to the Méribel and Les Menuires ski areas

✔ Can ski directly to and from nearly all accommodation

✘ Purpose-built style doesn't suit all tastes, although efforts to make the village more attractive have improved the ambience

✘ Can be cold and bleak in bad weather – no skiing below the tree-line

✘ Limited après-ski

Val-Thorens' great attraction is its height and the north-facing direction of most of its slopes. It has the highest skiing in the Trois Vallées (up to 3200m). That more or less guarantees good snow conditions for a long season – October to May. There are also a couple of glaciers and a summer skiing area.

On top of all this you have the skiing of the rest of the Trois Vallées on your doorstep. For the keen skier looking for the best snow, it's difficult to think of anywhere better.

The resort is purpose-built and opened in the early 1970s. When we first visited it, we thought it very ugly and unfriendly. But recent efforts to smarten the place up have paid off: it's now car-free; small trees have been planted; and the compact design, with friendly squares, makes it feel rather more pleasant than some other French purpose-built resorts.

⛵ The resort

Val-Thorens is a classic purpose-built resort, with skiing from many of its doors. But it is not as hideous as many such resorts – notably Les Menuires, just down the road. The buildings are mainly medium-rise and wood-clad, and the more recent ones in particular are distinctly stylish. The village streets that are now largely traffic-free, rather than just pedestrian zones, which also helps. There are indoor and outdoor shopping arcades, a fair choice of bars and restaurants, and a good sports centre. Despite the northerly orientation of the slopes, the village is quite sunny.

⛷ The skiing

When you take account of its abundance of high slopes, the extent of its local skiing and the easy access to the other resorts of the Trois Vallées, the attraction of Val-Thorens to keen skiers becomes clear. The main disadvantage is the lack of trees. Val-Thorens can be bleak and cold in bad weather – and heavy snowfalls can make skiing impossible.

THE SKI AREA
High and snowsure

The resort has a wide piste going right down the front of it and leading, in turn, to a number of different lifts out. The biggest is the enormous Funitel de **Péclet** gondola, each with a 25-person cabin, and an amazing base-station which includes a small exhibition centre and an escalator up to the gondolas. This takes you to one of the two glacier areas, with its own lifts and runs.

You can also ski from here to the larger **Montée du Fond** ski area, which can be reached directly from the resort too. From the top of a network of ideal intermediate runs you can also ski down into the relatively new 'Fourth Valley' of the **Maurienne** (it's a bit of a plod to the start of the run and back again from the top of the returning lift). Don't go past the welcoming restaurant at the bottom of the only chair-lift back, though, otherwise you face a long walk back up or an expensive taxi ride home via Albertville (£100 or more).

The 150-person **Cîme de Caron** cable-car to the highest lift-served point in the Trois Vallées, at 3200m, can be reached from the Montée du Fond area or by taking a gondola or

LIFT PASSES

94/95 prices in francs

Three Valleys
Covers all lifts in Courchevel, Méribel, Les Menuires, Val-Thorens and St Martin-de-Belleville.
Beginners 2 free lifts in Val-Thorens.
Main pass
1-day pass 210
6-day pass 1010
(low season 910 – 10% off)
Senior citizens
Over 60: 6-day pass 760 (25% off)
Over 80: free pass
Children
Under 16: 6-day pass 760 (25% off)
Under 5: free pass
Short-term passes
Half-day pass from 12.30 for Val-Thorens lifts only (adult 120).
Notes 6-day pass and over valid for one day each in Tignes-Val d'Isère, La Plagne-Les Arcs, Pralognan-la-Vanoise and Les Saisies. Reductions for families.
Alternative passes
Val-Thorens pass covers 32 lifts (6 days 740 for adults, 515 for children); Vallée des Belleville pass covers 78 lifts and 240km piste in Les Menuires, St-Martin and Val-Thorens (adult 6-day 945, child 745).

the fast four-person Boismint 2 chair.

Going the opposite way up from the resort leads you to the **Méribel** skiing via a couple of chair-lifts. **Les Menuires** can be reached using these lifts too, or by skiing the easy Boulevard Cumin which runs along the valley floor.

SNOW RELIABILITY
Difficult to beat

Few resorts can rival Val-Thorens for reliably good snow cover – accounted for by its altitude and the north-facing direction of most of its slopes. It even has two summer skiing areas on glaciers. The only place where you are likely to find poor snow is on the south-facing runs on the way back from an excursion to the rest of the Trois Vallées, and on the south-facing run down into the Maurienne valley.

FOR ADVANCED SKIERS
Few big challenges on-piste

Val-Thorens' local skiing is primarily intermediate terrain. But you'll certainly enjoy racing down the good snow on predominantly red runs. The runs down from the Cîme de Caron cable-car are probably the most challenging – with the red around the side narrower than, and almost as steep as, the black down the face. The Cascades run back into town from the Péclet direction is also worth trying. The Marielle Goitschel run down from the connection with Méribel is one of the easiest blacks we've come across – but its snow suffers from being south-facing and from the weight of traffic of skiers travelling to Val-Thorens.

There are three good itineraires. Two lead to the bottom of the chair in the

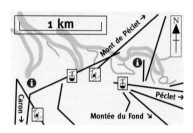

Maurienne valley. And the long Lac du Lou itineraire leaves from the summit of the Cîme de Caron and joins the run from the La Masse area of Les Menuires. There is also a great deal of unmarked off-piste skiing, for which you will need a guide.

FOR INTERMEDIATE SKIERS
Unbeatable quality and quantity

Although Val-Thorens is not in the centre of the Trois Vallées, it will take a decent intermediate only 90 minutes or so to get to Courchevel at the far end, if not distracted by the endless skiing opportunities on the way. You could be there for a mid-morning beer and back for a late lunch. The scope for intermediates throughout the Trois Vallées is enormous.

The local skiing in Val-Thorens itself is some of the best intermediate terrain in the region. The majority of the pistes are easy cruising reds and blues, made even more enjoyable by the usually excellent powdery snow.

The snow on the red Col run is always some of the best around. The blue La Moraine run below it is very gentle and popular with the ski schools. In general the runs on the top half of the mountain are steeper than those back into the resort.

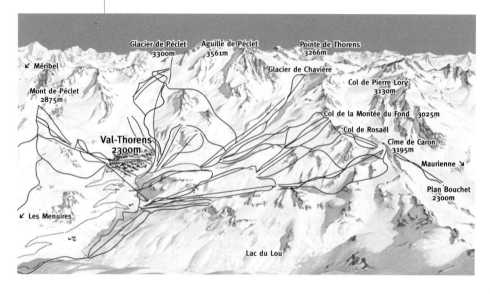

SKI SCHOOL

94/95 prices in francs

ESF

Classes 6 days
5hr 15min: 9.15-noon
and 14.15-16.45
6 full days: 870
Children's classes
Ages: 2½ to 12
6 full days: 735
Private lessons
Hourly
170 for 1 to 2 people

International
Known as Ski Cool
Classes 6 half-days
3hr, am or pm 680
(beginners only)
5 half-days: 600
Children's classes
Ages: up to 12
5 mornings: 520
Private lessons
Hourly or daily
190 for 1hr, for 1 to 2
people

CHILDCARE

Marielle Goitschel's
Children's Village
(79000047) takes
children aged from 3
to 16, from 9am to
5.30, 7 days a week.
The ESF can provide
all-day care and offers
classes for children
from age 2½. It also
runs Mini club crèches
in two locations, at
the top and bottom
of the resort, taking
children from age 3
months.

The Montée du Fond 1 and 2 lifts
serve a good variety of cruising red
runs. And adventurous intermediates
shouldn't miss out on the Combe du
Caron black run underneath the cable-
car: it is very wide and usually has
good snow.

FOR BEGINNERS
Good late-season choice
The slopes at the foot of the resort
itself are very gentle and provide
convenient, snowsure nursery slopes.
However, there aren't ideal long green
runs to progress to, though the blues
back into town are very easy. And
because of the resort's height and
bleakness, beginners can find it cold
early in the season and intimidating
in bad weather.

FOR CROSS-COUNTRY
Try elsewhere
Val-Thorens is a poor base for cross-
country, with only 4km of local trails.

QUEUES
A few bad lift bottlenecks
Val-Thorens has a very modern lift
system, offering choices of routes. This
means that queues are, for most of the
area, not a problem most of the time.
The biggest queues we've come across
have been at the slow, old two-person
Col chair (now fed by a high-speed
quad, so it's not surprising queues
build up) and for the Cîme de Caron
cable-car – we've heard of 45-minute
queues here, but the most we've
experienced has been 20 minutes.
There can also be long queues for
the 3 Vallées 1 and Plein Sud chair-
lifts back towards Méribel in mid-
afternoon, and for the short village lift
at the end of the day.
Reporters who've been here in high
season when snow has been in short
supply elsewhere tell us that queues
can become a significant problem,
particularly if people are bussed in
from lower resorts.

MOUNTAIN RESTAURANTS
Lots of choice
Moutière, just below the top of the
chair of the same name, is one of the
more reasonably priced of Val-
Thorens' mountain huts (which are
generally thought by reporters to be
expensive). We liked the Chalet de
Génépi, on the run down from the
Moraine chair. It has an open fire,
good soup and on a mid-morning stop
on the terrace, we enjoyed the medley
of sixties hits.
The Plan Bouchet refuge in the
Maurienne valley is very popular and

welcoming, but bar service can be
slow. You can stay the night there too.
On the other side of the valley the
Chalet Plain Sud, just below the chair
of the same name, has excellent views
from the sunny terrace.

SKI SCHOOL
Plenty of courses
There are two main schools, the ESF
and the International school (known
as Ski Cool), which between them
offer a wide range of options. Reports
of the ESF are mixed, but one reporter
was impressed with a private lesson.
As well as the usual group lessons, the
ESF have shorter duration, smaller-
class sessions (two hours for five days,
with a maximum of eight skiers). They
also have a Trois Vallées group for
those who want to cover a lot of
ground while receiving tuition. This is
available by the day or the week, and
can include off-piste if required. Ski
Cool also offers numerous courses,
with the added benefit of ordinary
class sizes guaranteed not to exceed
ten. They specialise in teaching
beginners, who get an extra day's
tuition (six instead of five), and offer
an 'Evoluski' package that includes
equipment hire and lift pass. Beginner
tuition is ski évolutif, so skiers start on
short skis and work their way up. Ski
Cool also have off-piste courses. There
are several specialist guiding outfits.

FACILITIES FOR CHILDREN
The childcare arrangements are
comprehensive and well-run. The ESF
crèche at the top of the village is
recommended for everything except
its inconvenient location. Classes for
very young children may not
materialise, but private lessons with an
instructor called Bernard who
specialises in children get rave reviews.
Children who have reached third-star
standard in ski school can go off in
guided groups around the Trois
Vallées led by Fabienne Pandier.

GETTING THERE

Air Geneva, transfer 3½hr. Lyon, transfer 3½hr. Chambery, transfer 2½hr.

Rail Moûtiers (35km); regular buses from station.

PACKAGES

AA Ski-Driveaway, Airtours, Alpine Options Skidrive, Altours Travel, Cresta Ski France, Crystal, Enterprise, Equity Total Ski, Inghams, Kings Ski Club, Lagrange, Made to Measure, Neilson, Sally, Ski Club of GB, Ski Valkyrie, Ski West, Skiworld, Stena Sealink, Thomson, Travelscene Ski-Drive, UCPA

ACTIVITIES

Indoor Club Pierre Barthes (tennis school, squash, golf practice and simulator, swimming pool, saunas, jacuzzi, gym), games rooms, music recitals, cinema, beauty centre, sports centre (climbing wall, volleyball, football, hockey, turkish bath, whirlpool, gym, weight training)
Outdoor Walks, snowmobiles, hang-gliding, flying school, snowshoe excursions, para-gliding, microlight flights

TOURIST OFFICE

Postcode 73440
Tel 010 33 79000808
Fax 79000004

 # Staying there

Everywhere is fairly ski-convenient, but there are two quite distinct parts of the village, with a nursery slope separating the two. Both have a shopping centre, but there is more animation in the upper section, Péclet, than in the lower part, Caron, which is dominated by apartments. It is not a big place, so walking from one part to the other is no problem.

HOW TO GO

Surprisingly high level of comfort

Accommodation tends to be of a higher standard than in many French purpose-built villages, and there's plenty of choice too.

Chalets These are exclusively catered apartments, and many are quite comfortable. Thomson and Crystal have well appointed places; Neilson have a new operation in the smart Val Chavière complex, and budget-price Skiworld have an interesting new allocation for this season.

Hotels There are a dozen hotels, mainly 3-stars. Most of those listed are grouped around the nursery slope that almost divides the resort in two.

£££££ Fitz Roy Swanky but charming Relais & Châteaux place with lovely rooms and about the best food in town. Pool. Well placed, just in the upper part of the resort.

££££ Val Thorens Very welcoming and comfortable; next door to the Fitz Roy.

£££ Sherpa Highly recommended for pleasant atmosphere and excellent, substantial food. Less-than-ideal position at the top of the resort.

£££ Bel Horizon Small, friendly, family-run 3-star with good food and south-facing rooms. On piste near bottom of resort, well-placed for skiing.

Self-catering There is a wide range of options, including apartments of a much higher standard than is the norm in France. Chalet le Val Chavière (Inghams) in Péclet and Residence Montana (Thomson, Inghams) in Caron are luxurious by French standards. They have comfortable furnishings, lots of mod cons and a wealth of communal facilities. The brand new Balcon de Thorens complex (Neilson), in an elevated position above Péclet, claims

to be of a similarly high standard.

Most of the other good places on the British market are in Caron. Les Temples du Soleil (Thomson, Neilson) are the nicest of the Pierre et Vacances apartments in the Trois Vallées, and have plenty of in-house amenities. Other places recommended to us are Cheval Blanc and Silveralp, both of which are in a number of brochures. The only really critical report we have received was of the Residence les Olympiades, which apparently has tiny rooms.

EATING OUT

Surprisingly wide range

Val-Thorens has something for most tastes. At the top of the range, gourmets will enjoy the Fitzroy hotel and Chalet des Glaciers. Sherpa is another hotel with fine cuisine. Several reporters have recommended the Montana in Caron. Tavern le Scapin du Lou is a nice brasserie. Matafan, El Gringo's Café and the Temples du Soleil pizzeria are informal places worth a try. One family made special mention of how child-friendly all the restaurants were.

APRES-SKI

Limited but improving

Although things are not exactly throbbing, Val-Thorens seems to be determined not to be another Tignes or Flaine when it comes to nightlife. Each season another bar seems to become sufficiently popular to be added to any list of worthwhile haunts. Champagne Charlie's, the Frog and Roast Beef, and the Lincoln Pub are focal bars for Brits. Ski Rock Café and the Malaysia cellar bar are more cosmopolitan places.

Having three discos is a bit of overkill: one good atmospheric place that everyone went to would be preferable. The Calypso is a shabby, outrageously expensive joint that relies on videos to attract customers. The intimate little Agora is better, but also very pricey.

FOR NON-SKIERS

Forget it

Val-Thorens is a resort for keen skiers. It's not the ideal place for non-skiers. But there's a good sports centre and plenty of outdoor activities, and you can get up to some of the mountain restaurants, but not the best, by lift.

Vars 1850m

HOW IT RATES

The skiing

Snow	★★★
Extent	★★★
Advanced	★★
Intermediates	★★★★
Beginners	★★★
Convenience	★★★★
Queues	★★★★
Restaurants	★★

The rest

Scenery	★★★
Resort charm	★★
Not skiing	★★

SKI FACTS

Altitude	1660m-2750m
Lifts	56
Pistes	170km
Green/Blue	56%
Red	40%
Black	4%
Artificial snow	4km

PACKAGES

Ski Europe

TOURIST OFFICE

Postcode 05560
Tel 010 33 92465131
Fax 92465654

Vars is a not very attractive purpose-built resort in the southern French Alps, which has the more interesting section of the fair-sized intermediate ski area that it shares with neighbouring Risoul.

THE RESORT

Vars is a sizeable resort, most of which has been purpose-built. It is bigger and has far more in the way of shops, restaurants, hotels, nightlife and other amenities such as squash, saunas and the like than Risoul, and it is equally ski-convenient and reasonably priced. Village architecture is unattractive, but Vars is not a complete eyesore thanks mainly to surrounding woodland. There are two centres: the original and geographic one, which has most of the accommodation and shopping, where the main gondola starts, and Point Show – a collection of bars, restaurants and shops, surrounding a main lift station, 10 minutes' walk from central Vars. The resort is very French, and locals are friendly to those making at least some attempt at the native tongue. Neighbouring Ste-Marie is a hamlet well linked to the skiing; being a popular summer resort, it actually has more hotels than Vars.

THE SKIING

Vars has the larger and more varied section of the **ski area**'s 170km of piste, with many more options for better skiers. There is also a good mix of open and wooded skiing on mountains either side of the village. The Peynier area is much the smaller and reaches only 2275m. The main skiing is the other side of the valley, with direct links to the skiing of Risoul. The two local areas are linked via a shortish walk across Ste-Marie, or by a two-stage gondola that rises up both mountains from just outside the village. The link to Risoul can be made in two places – near the top of the ski area, above 2500m, and lower down at the Col de Valbelle. Vars has very little skiing above 2500m and its slopes get a lot of sun, but there is virtually no skiing below village level (1850m), and the main pistes down to the village have artificial snow – so **snow reliability** is not bad.

There is little of challenge for **advanced skiers**, though the Crête de Chabrière top section accesses some off-piste, an unpisted route and a tricky couloir at Col de Crevoir.

The smaller of the two mountains, Peynier, is useful for better **intermediates**, having the only

black run of any length in the whole area, and some uncharacteristically long reds down to Ste-Marie. The remainder of the skiing is mainly comfortable reds, ideal for average skiers. There is a good network of easy pistes throughout the central section, with a comfortable route to Risoul available via Col de Valbelle.

Beginners have a nursery area of free lifts conveniently close to central Vars, with plenty of 'graduation' runs throughout the area. Precocious learners will be able to ski over to Risoul by the end of the week.

There are **cross-country** trails that start at the edge of town, but those above Ste-Marie are more extensive. **Queues** are rare outside the French holidays, and even then Vars is not overrun as some family resorts are.

The area is short of **mountain restaurants**, so many skiers return to the village or visit Risoul for lunch. The atmospheric Zizanie and Heureux Geleski are the best.

At the **ski school**, the lack of English-speaking tuition is an obvious problem. The well-equipped crèche takes **children** aged 18 months to four years. Ski school also has a nursery and a ski kindergarten.

STAYING THERE

With only a handful of hotels, Vars is dominated by **apartment** accommodation. Of the **hotels**, Le Caribou is the smartest place in town (with a swimming pool). L'Ecureuil is a modern, chalet-style 2-star. The Franou is no beauty, but its restaurant has a good reputation and it is well-positioned. Le Vallon is right next to the gondola station in Ste-Marie.

The range of **restaurants** is impressive, with numerous pizzerias, crêperies and fondue places, together with some more formal haunts. Chez Plumet has fine French cuisine; Pepito's and Chez Robert are good-value pizza joints; and Escondus is an elegant pricey establishment.

Après-ski is quite animated at tea-time, but less so after dinner, except during holidays and weekends, when the Look and the more glitzy Lem discos warm up. There is a cinema.

Non-skiers' amenities are disappointing, given the size of Vars.

Italy

Italy is on the up – and about time too. British skiers used to go there in large numbers, attracted mainly by modest prices but also by the Italian way of doing things. Then, during the 1980s, we rather lost interest. Prices weren't low enough to compete with Andorra and Eastern Europe for the custom of low-budget beginners, while more experienced skiers were seduced by the ever-expanding lift networks of the French Alps. One or two particular British favourites, such as Sauze d'Oulx, were hit by snow shortages before the Alps in general started to suffer from erratic weather at the end of the 1980s.

The tide has been turned, no doubt, mainly by exchange rates. Last winter, Italy was a bargain, and lots of British skiers took advantage of it. Having done a fair bit of skiing in Italy in the last two winters, we predict that the revival will be sustained. Lift systems have been modernised; snowmaking – something that the Italians were early to catch on to – is now very widespread; piste grooming and resort organisation in general are improved.

The Italian approach to skiing is a relaxed one; the Italian approach to visitors is a friendly one; and the Italian approach to food and wine is an enthusiastic one. No other country offers quite the same mix. And there's a bonus: many Italian resorts enjoy splendid settings – in the Dolomites the scenery is simply stunning.

Although there aren't huge numbers of them (on the international market, at least), Italian resorts vary as widely in characteristics as they do in location – and they are spread along the length of the Italian border, from Sauze and neighbours across the French border from Montgenèvre, all along the Swiss border to the Dolomites, an area that used to be part of Austria. There are high, snowsure ski-stations and charming valley villages, and ski areas that range from one-run wonders to some of the most extensive skiing in the world.

On our recent tours of resorts in north-east and north-west Italy, we've been struck by several things. As we've noted above, Italian resorts have pulled their socks up in recent years; most are no longer lagging in the new-lift stakes. And we'd forgotten how impressive the scenery is (something the brochures tend to overlook).

A lot of Italian skiing seemed flatteringly easy. This was partly because the piste grooming in the resorts we visited was immaculate, and also because piste grading in Italy seemed to overstate difficulty. Nowhere was this clearer than in La Thuile (in Italy, despite its French-sounding name). Its ski area connects (just) with that of La Rosière, across the valley from Les Arcs, and skiing from one to the other was like moving from the shelter of harbour to the open sea. Red runs on the La Thuile side were virtually motorways; at La Rosière, they offered challenging moguls.

We were also struck by the extent to which Italian skiing continues to be weekend-oriented. Except in the Dolomites, which depend largely on German custom, resorts are quiet as the grave during the week, especially in low season, and come to life on Friday night or Saturday morning when the weekenders from Italy's affluent northern plain arrive. If, like us, you quite like having the hotel bar to yourself (not to mention the pistes), this is a real advantage. If you're looking for a social whirl, you'll be disappointed.

In general, Italians don't take their skiing too seriously. Lifts may close for lunch, and mountain restaurants are generally welcoming places serving satisfying food, encouraging leisurely lunching. And at current exchange rates, prices in most resorts are noticeably low (though not in all – see our feature on the costs of skiing).

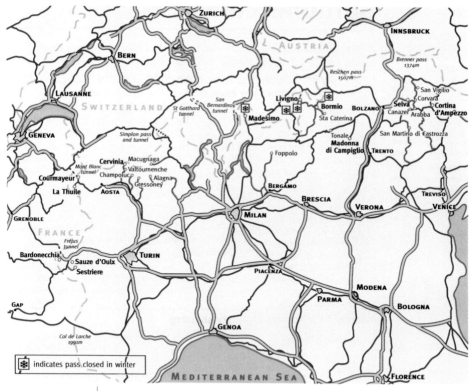

⊛ indicates pass closed in winter

0   80

Scale in km

DRIVING IN THE ITALIAN ALPS

There are four main geographical groupings of Italian resorts, widely separated (our map is drawn to a much smaller scale than those of the other Alpine countries, because it has to cover much more ground). Getting to some of these resorts is tricky, and getting from one area to another can involve very long drives.

The handful of resorts to the west of Turin – Sauze d'Oulx, Bardonecchia and neighbours – are easily reached from France via the Fréjus tunnel from Modane, or via the good road over the pass that the resort of Montgenèvre sits on.

Further north, and about equidistant from Milan and Turin, are the resorts of the Aosta valley, Courmayeur and Cervinia the best-known among them. Courmayeur is the easiest resort to reach from Britain, thanks to the Mont Blanc tunnel from Chamonix in France. The road down the Aosta valley is a major thoroughfare carrying heavy goods traffic, but the roads up to some of the other resorts are quite long, winding and (at least in the case of Cervinia) high. The Aosta valley can also be reached from Switzerland via the Grand St Bernard tunnel. The approach is high, and may require chains.

To the east is a string of scattered resorts, most close to the Swiss border, many in isolated and remote valleys involving long drives up from the nearest Italian cities, or high-altitude drives from Switzerland. The links between Switzerland and Italy are more clearly shown on our Switzerland map on page 304. The major routes are the St Gotthard tunnel between Göschenen, near Andermatt, and Airolo – the main route between Basel and Milan – and the San Bernardino tunnel reached via Chur.

Finally, further east still, are the resorts of the Dolomites. Getting there is easy, over the Brenner motorway pass from Innsbruck, but getting around the intricate network of valleys linked by narrow, winding roads can be a slow business.

Bardonecchia 1310m

A fairly extensive ski area worth considering as a base for touring other nearby French and Italian resorts. The local slopes, and the town itself, tend to be fairly quiet during the week, but lots of weekenders pour in from Turin.

HOW IT RATES

The skiing

Snow	**
Extent	***
Advanced	*
Intermediates	***
Beginners	**
Convenience	**
Queues	***
Restaurants	***

The rest

Scenery	***
Resort charm	*
Not skiing	**

SKI FACTS

Altitude	1290m-2750m
Lifts	26
Pistes	140km
Green/Blue	55%
Red	41%
Black	4%
Artificial snow	13km

PACKAGES

Chalets 'Unlimited', Crystal, Equity Total Ski, Neilson

TOURIST OFFICE

Postcode 10052
Tel 010 39 (122) 99032
Fax 902266

THE RESORT

Bardonecchia is a sizeable old railway town, set in a beautiful wide valley, at the entrance to the Fréjus road tunnel that links France and Italy. It has two separate ski areas either side of town, both a bus-ride away.

This description could almost be of Chamonix, but Bardonecchia is a far from similar resort. It's a middling sort of place, with reasonable prices, moderate nightlife and a useful ski area. The resort lacks classic mountain charm, but has a traditional market-town character. But the frequent lack of resort-level snow and the intrusive railway rather detract.

Valfréjus, Valloire, the Milky Way resorts (Sauze etc) and Serre-Chevalier are reachable by car.

THE SKIING

The two **ski areas** are different in some ways. The larger one is a wide section of low (little above 2000m), tree-lined, north-facing pistes above three valley lift stations – Campo Smith on the edge of town, Les Arnauds and Melezet. Jafferau is a tall, thin mountain of long, partly open, west-facing runs. Chairs are generally antiquated and there are no bottom-to-top lifts. Jafferau is the less popular area, yet it has sunnier skiing, and is certainly preferable at weekends when the Torinese hit town. All runs lead back to the town chair-lift, the top-to-bottom piste descending an impressive 1460m from the high-point of 2750m.

Although the area doesn't have a particularly good record for **snow reliability**, there is plenty of relatively snowsure skiing above the middle stations,and the main pistes above Campo Smith have snowmaking on them. South-west-facing Jafferau quickly loses snow below mid-station.

In the Campo Smith-Melezet sector, the highest run, which can have moguls, and a medium-length black from Pra Magnan are the most interesting for **advanced skiers**. There is some off-piste in the trees when conditions allow. Jafferau is worth a visit for the long top-to-bottom reds.

Virtually the whole 140km is suitable for **intermediates**. Good intermediates should head for Jafferau, where a network of fine runs finishes at the mid-station. There is a wealth of reds in the other area – skiing quickly down the tree-lined red from the top station to Campo Smith is great fun. There are plenty of leisurely cruises.

Campo Smith and Melezet have nursery areas, but the inconvenience of Bardonecchia, lack of special lift pass and the paucity of English spoken by some instructors are obvious disadvantages for **beginners**.

A varied, valley-level **cross-country** trail goes for many miles in both directions from just above Campo Smith; Melezet is a starting point for other long excursions.

Although the lift system is antiquated there are few **queues** during the week. Campo Smith is a weekend bottleneck.

Mountain restaurants are generally pleasant and uncrowded. All but one are prettily sited in trees.

The large **ski school** has a good reputation, except for over-large classes and unreliable English.

For **children**, there is a non-ski nursery and an all-day ski kindergarten at Campo Smith.

STAYING THERE

Accommodation is almost exclusively in **hotels**. The Tabor is a small, well-run 3-star. The chef and owner prides himself on the home-made cooking. The Park Hotel Rosa (4-star) is 10 minutes' walk from both the town centre and Campo Smith.

The Ronco **apartments** are inexpensive and only a couple of minutes' walk from Campo Smith.

There are numerous **restaurants** and pizzerias but some of the best places are in hotels (eg the Tabor). Loc Cá Fiore, at Campo Smith, is handy for Ronco-dwellers.

Being very much a working town, Bardonecchia lacks the usual **après-ski** atmosphere. A number of bars are good for a quiet drink among the locals, and become quite animated at weekends. Tour op reps organise some events. Only one disco.

For **non-skiers,** the town holds little interest except for its weekly market – though there are good sports facilities, including tennis and skating.

Bormio 1225m

HOW IT RATES

The skiing

Snow	★★★
Extent	★★
Advanced	★
Intermediates	★★★
Beginners	★★
Convenience	★★★
Queues	★★★
Restaurants	★★★★

The rest

Scenery	★★★
Resort charm	★★★★
Not skiing	★★★★

ORIENTATION

Bormio sits in a remote part of Lombardy at the foot of the Stelvio pass, close to the Swiss and Austrian borders. Tirano is the nearest town, 40km away.

Airport transfers are long (four to five hours). A gondola and cable-car leave from the southern edge of town to the main ski area. A second area lies on the other side of town served by lifts at Oga, Le Motte or Val di Dentro, all a bus-ride away.

Santa Caterina (20mins) and **Livigno** (40km but 1½hr on a poor road) are accessible by bus, their lifts covered by the Valtellina lift pass, which also gives one free day a week in **St Moritz** (3hr away). The **Passo Tonale** glacier is also within easy reach by car.

SKI FACTS

Altitude	1225m-3010m
Lifts	28
Pistes	62km
Green/Blue	36%
Red	46%
Black	18%
Artificial snow	7km

✔ Upgraded lift system and opening of new area has improved skiing in last few years

✔ Good mix of high snowsure pistes and woodland runs with artificial snow

✔ Several good neighbouring ski resorts on same lift pass

✔ Interesting, attractive town centre

✔ Good mountain restaurants

✘ Not suitable for beginners or experts

✘ Surprisingly small ski area for such a large, well-known resort

✘ Long airport transfers

✘ Queues and overcrowded pistes on Sundays

✘ Ugly urban sprawl outside centre

Bormio is unjustly neglected by British skiers. One look at the size of the town in relation to its small ski area and most keen skiers would assume the resort's reputation for queues still holds good. But Bormio is an old spa town with many of its inhabitants earning a living outside skiing. The disadvantage of this is the hassle involved in reaching the lifts, not waiting for them. The queues of the 1970s and 1980s were due to a poor lift system. The recent improvements seem to have gone unnoticed – a shame, because Bormio has a lot to offer, including some of Europe's longest runs.

 ## The resort

Bormio began life as a Roman spa and the thermal bathing facilities remain. It has a wonderfully preserved 17th-century town centre, complete with cobbled streets, markets with washing troughs, and old façades for today's shops, restaurants and cafés. Fortunately the town has escaped the dreariness and formality of many European spas. It's a colourful place where promenading is an important part of the evening scene.

Between the town centre and the ski lifts, over the other side of the river, lies a characterless urban sprawl. There are plenty of hotels in this area, and though they aren't situated in the prettiest locality, they are nearer the lifts and can save a 15-minute walk or a bus-ride. The ski-bus is reliable but not frequent. Most people walk. Although atmospheric, Bormio is not as lively as, say, Courmayeur.

The skiing

Bormio has good (but limited) skiing for intermediates who like long runs, with a nice mix of high, snowsure pistes and lower wooded slopes. Beginners and the advanced are less well provided for.

Both the piste map and the piste marking could do with some substantial improvement.

THE SKI AREA
One-dimensional

The main ski area is tall (1800m vertical drop) and narrow, with virtually all the pistes facing north-west and heading down towards town. The two-stage **Cima Bianca** cable-car goes from bottom to top (3010m) of the skiing via the mid-station at **Bormio 2000**. The **Ciuk** gondola goes up to 1620m. Drag- and chair-lifts above it serve all the runs including those from the very top. This alternative route is especially useful at busy periods and on windy days when the cable-car may not run. The gondola means little skiing is lost when runs to the resort have no snow and you have to take a lift down.

New lifts above **Oga** and **Val di Dentro** have made this once insignificant ski area, a short bus-ride out of Bormio, a useful addition to Cima Bianca. The area is now large enough to merit a day-trip. Half the runs are east-facing and not high, but some are north-facing and the mainly tree-lined skiing is very pleasant.

Day-trips further afield (see Orientation section) add greatly to the interest of a skiing trip to Bormio.

SNOW RELIABILITY
Good above mid-station

The runs above Bormio 2000 are usually snowsure, and the snowmaking facility on the lower slopes is impressive. The high, shaded, north-facing slopes of Santa Caterina

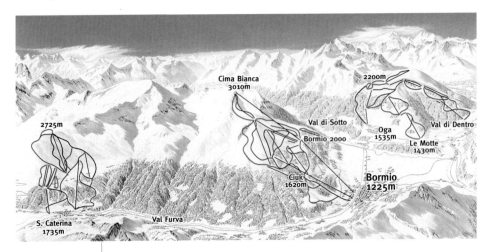

LIFT PASSES

94/95 prices in lire
Alta Valtellina
Covers all lifts in Bormio, Valdisotto, Valdidentro (all in local area), Santa Caterina (12km away) and Livigno (40km away) plus one free day in St Moritz.
Main pass
1-day pass 44,000
6-day pass 205,000 (low season 180,000 – 12% off)
Senior citizens
Over 65: 6-day pass 140,000 (32% off)
Children
Under 14: 6-day pass 140,000 (32% off)
Notes Day pass price covers Bormio lifts only.
Alternative passes
Up to 3-day pass for Bormio only (adult 3-day pass 120,000).

CHILDCARE

Children's ski classes are offered by some of the ski schools, but there are no special arrangements for all-day care, and no non-ski kindergartens.

GETTING THERE

Air Bergamo, transfer 4hr.

Rail Tirano (40km); regular buses from station.

(1735m to 2725m) usually have good snow, and are not far away. However, the summer ski area at Passo Stelvio is not open in winter.

FOR ADVANCED SKIERS
Rather limited

There is little challenging skiing in Bormio's small ski area. Long, steep off-piste routes between Cima Bianca and the Ornella drag to the west are feasible when conditions allow. Otherwise there are a couple of short black runs. Despite this, Bormio is one of Franz Klammer's favourite ski areas. However, it was the length of the runs, not their difficulty or extent, that impressed him.

FOR INTERMEDIATE SKIERS
A few options for all grades

The men's 1985 World Championship downhill course starts with a steep plunge but otherwise is no more than a tough red, which makes ideal skiing for strong intermediates. The Stella Alpina run down to 2000 is another fairly steep piste.

Many of the runs are less tough, ideal for average skiers. The longest is a superb top-to-bottom cruise, excellent for the less aggressive skier. The Oga area is similarly suitable for early intermediates. The runs beneath Ciuk in the main area and above Le Motte in the other, can get quite icy at times. Santa Caterina has good intermediate skiing too.

FOR BEGINNERS
Many better Italian resorts

There are small, inadequate nursery areas at both Ciuk and 2000, but novices would be better off at nearby Santa Caterina or Livigno. Near-beginners have a nice, quiet little area beneath 2000 using the Ornella drag.

FOR CROSS-COUNTRY
Go to Santa Caterina

There are some trails either side of Bormio, towards Piatta and beneath Le Motte and Val di Dentro, but cross-country fans would be better off at snowsure Santa Caterina.

QUEUES
Much improved

Bormio has had a reputation for queues. But recent improvements to the lift system, and the opening of Oga-Le Motte area have greatly improved matters. Both sections of the cable-car suffer delays in the morning peak period and on Sundays. When the lower slopes are incomplete, queues form to ride the gondola down at the end of the day. Otherwise there are few problems except at Carnival week (end of February).

MOUNTAIN RESTAURANTS
Good fare everywhere

The nice thing about the mountain restaurants is that they are uniformly good for value and food. Even the efficient self-service at 2000 has a good choice of dishes. La Rocca, just over halfway down to Ciuk from Cima Bianca, is cosier. Cedrone, at 2000, has a good terrace plus a play area for

CRYSTAL HOLIDAYS
helped us to compile the Eating out and Après-ski sections. Our thanks to them.

SKI SCHOOL

93/94 prices in lire

Bormio 2000
Classes 6 days
2hr: 9am-11am, 11am-1pm or 2pm-4pm
6 2hr days: 140,000

Nazionale
Classes 6 days
2½hr: 10am-12.30 or 2pm-4.30
6 2½hr days: 120,000
Private lessons
Daily
40,000 per hour; each additional person 5,000

Sertorelli
Italian-speaking instructors only.
Classes 6 days
2½hr
6 2½hr days: 170,000

Anzi
Small school offering package of accommodation and instruction.

Capitani
Italian-speaking instructors only.

Alta Valtellina
Cross-country specialists.

PACKAGES

Crystal, Enterprise, Inghams, Thomson

Santa Caterina
Airtours, Enterprise, Thomson

ACTIVITIES

Indoor 2 museums, library, thermal baths, squash, swimming pool, sauna, massage, sports hallXating rink
Outdoor Ski-bobX, toboggan run, horse-riding, walks in the Stelvio National Park

TOURIST OFFICE

Postcode 23032
Tel 010 39 (342) 903300
Fax 904696

children. Ciuk also has a pleasant refuge. The new Oga area has two huts, one of them set among trees on the way down to Val di Dentro.

SKI SCHOOL
Short lessons

There are six schools – three in town, two at 2000 and one at Ciuk. Most Brits get sent to Scuola Italiano Bormio 2000 by their tour operators, but we've had some negative reports of their group tuition, including classes of 15 last January. Classes were also considered too short (note the lack of all-day tuition), with not enough English-speaking instructors. The Nazionale private lessons received much more enthusiastic reports.

FACILITIES FOR CHILDREN
Typically Italian – limited

There is no crèche or ski kindergarten. But the Sertorelli and Bormio 2000 schools, at least, seem to make some effort to cater for children. The latter has a roped-off snow garden at its mid-mountain chalet.

 # Staying there

Bormio is big enough for location to be of some importance. The basic choice is between convenient locations on the ski-lift side of the river, and the vitality of the town.

HOW TO GO
Probably on a hotel package

Bormio is not a chalet resort, but there are plenty of apartments available. However, hotels dominate the package holiday market.
Hotels Most of Bormio's 40-plus hotels are 2-star and 3-star places, though there are a handful of 4-stars.
££££ Palace Only luxurious place in town, but poorly positioned.
£££ Baita dei Pini Best placed of top hotels: on the river, equidistant from lifts and centre. Excellent food, good facilities, fitness room and a piano bar.
£££ Posta Central hotel, rated a 4-star but with some 'pretty basic' rooms.
££ Nevada Comfortable 3-star, very well placed for the cable-car.
££ Alu Ditto.
££ Ambassador Chalet Welcoming place close to the gondola.
££ Derby Large, attractive 3-star.
£ Piccolo Mondo Small, basic but friendly B&B place with good breakfasts, close to Ciuk lift.
£ Genzianella Cheap, well positioned for the gondola.
£ Dante Good-value central 2-star.

Self-catering The only packaged apartments we know of are from Inghams, in the plain modern Residence Jolly, close to the centre.

EATING OUT

There is a wide selection of restaurants. The atmospheric Taulà does excellent nouvelle cuisine with great service. The Kuerc is popular but also pricey by local standards due to its prime location in the main square. The Primo Piatto in the Piccolo Mondo hotel, Vecchia Combo and the Caminetto are other places worth a try. The Jap, Gramola and Cristall are three of the best pizzerias in town. A taxi takes you to the Barona for a special night out.

APRES-SKI
Tea-time promenading

Nightlife is fairly subdued. Many people just like to do a bit of early evening promenading and visit the elegant Mozart tea-room which has classical music. A more hectic tea-time pursuit is to stop off at the Rocca mountain café for a 'Bombardino' (hot advocat, brandy, whiskey and cream) and then ski down in the gathering darkness. Bar Cristallo is then a popular rendezvous at the bottom of the piste. Just around the corner is the relaxing terrace of the Jolly Bar. Bar Nevada is another option, next to the cable-car station. Clem's Pub and the Piano Bar are two of the livelier after-dinner spots. Shangri-La is a friendly bar. La Terra is the karaoke joint. The Kings Club, the only disco, gets busy at weekends – free entry for Brits.

Every Wednesday there's a floodlit ski race open to all. Tour reps organise a trip to the Roman baths, skidoo rides and a quiz evening.

FOR NON-SKIERS
Take in the thermals

The town itself is very interesting but there are also plenty of other amenities, including thermal baths, riding and walks in the Stelvio National Park. St Moritz is a popular excursion, and duty-free shoppers will also appreciate the trip to Livigno.

STAYING UP THE MOUNTAIN
Possible on a package

The modern Girasole, up at Bormio 2000, is simple but well run, with a warm welcome and lots of organised events to counter the isolation. (In fact, it's not quite as isolated as you might think – there's a road up from the town.) What's more, you can buy packages from Inghams.

Cervinia 2050m

HOW IT RATES

The skiing

Snow	*****
Extent	***
Advanced	*
Intermediates	****
Beginners	*****
Convenience	***
Queues	***
Restaurants	***

The rest

Scenery	****
Resort charm	**
Not skiing	*

ORIENTATION

Cervinia is at the head of a long valley up from the Aosta valley on the Italian side of the Matterhorn. It is fairly compact with a lot of accommodation near the centre, at the foot of the nursery slopes. A series of drag-lifts from here takes you into the ski area. But the main gondola and cable-car up are an awkward uphill walk away. There is more accommodation further out at the Cielalto complex and on the road up to it.

The skiing links to **Valtournenche** further down the valley (covered by the lift pass) and **Zermatt** over in Switzerland (daily supplement payable). Day trips by car are possible to **Courmayeur, La Thuile** and the Monte Rosa resorts of **Champoluc** (you can ski there off-piste) or **Gressoney**.

✔ *Extensive, easy skiing area; ideal early intermediates' resort*

✔ *High, sunny, snowsure slopes amid impressive scenery*

✘ *Very little worthwhile skiing for good or aggressive intermediates and above – especially since the Furggen cable-car closed*

✘ *Almost exclusively above-the-tree-line slopes, with little skiing possible in bad weather*

✘ *Lifts prone to closure by wind, particularly early in the season*

✘ *Expensive by Italian standards*

✘ *Village not unpleasant in the centre, but an eyesore in general*

✘ *Tiresome amount of walking between lifts*

✘ *Few off-the-slopes amenities*

What brings skiers to Breuil Cervinia (as the resort now styles itself) is what brought climbers to the original village of Breuil in the 19th century: altitude. For climbers, it was a launch-pad for assaults on the nearby Matterhorn (Monte Cervino). For skiers, it offers an unusual combination: slopes that are gentle as well as extensive, and sunny as well as snowsure.

For skiers who like to cover the miles without worrying about the slopes being too steep, there is nowhere like it. But better skiers should steer clear. They'll find the slopes tame and the link with Zermatt disappointing because it doesn't access Zermatt's best skiing.

 ## The resort

When the old climbing village of Breuil made the transition to international ski resort sixty years ago, it boasted smart hotels and equally impressive lifts. Unfortunately, neither the village nor (until recently) the lift system kept pace with the times.

The village was allowed to develop in a rather haphazard way with no consistent style to the architecture. The result is an uncomfortable hotch-potch, neither pleasing to the eye, nor as offensive to it as some of the worst of the French purpose-built resorts. The centre is pleasant and traffic-free. But the surrounding apartment blocks and hotels, some quite a hike up the hill above the cable-car, make the village feel less friendly and welcoming. As one visitor told us, 'The architects must have been on drugs at the design stage.'

As well as the usual ski shops there are some very smart Italian clothes shops and jewellers, with upmarket Italian prices to match. The resort fills up with day-trippers and weekenders from Milan and Turin at peak periods. As well as their money they bring

their cars with them, making the village surprisingly traffic- and fume-ridden at times.

Though the resort is expensive by Italian standards, Cervinia is no longer a resort of the rich and trendy. It attracts a lively, young clientele, and a high proportion of Brits.

There are surprisingly few off-slope amenities, such as kindergartens, marked walks and swimming and spa facilities. And for those staying out of the centre there's no bus – though some hotels have courtesy buses.

 ## The skiing

Cervinia's main skiing is on a high, large, open, sunny, west-facing bowl. It has Italy's highest skiing and some of its longest runs (13km from Plateau Rosa down to Valtournenche – with only a short drag-lift part-way). Nearly all the runs are accessible to all standards of intermediate skier. More of a problem for skiers than steepness is the weather. If it's bad, the top lifts often close because of high winds. And even the lower slopes may be unskiable because of poor visibility. There is little woodland skiing.

SKI FACTS

Altitude 1525m-3480m
Lifts   36
Pistes   96km
Green/Blue   40%
Red   48%
Black   12%
Artificial snow   7km

LIFT PASSES

94/95 prices in lire
Breuil-Cervinia
Covers all lifts on the
Italian side of the
border including
Valtournenche.
Beginners Points
tickets in Cretaz area
only (150 points
145,000).
Main pass
1-day pass 48,000
6-day pass 225,000
Short-term passes
Half-day from noon
for Cervinia. Single
and return tickets on
some lifts.
Notes Daily extension
for Zermatt lifts
around Klein
Matterhorn and
Schwarzsee (34,000).
Alternative passes
Limited area passes
for Carosello (4 lifts)
and Cretaz (8 lifts).
Day pass covering
Cervinia, Zermatt and
Valtournenche
(63,000). Valle
d'Aosta ski pass
covers all lifts in
Courmayeur, La
Thuile, Gressoney,
Alagna, Champoluc,
Pila, Cervinia and
Valtournenche (adult
6-day 238,000).

THE SKI AREA
Very easy skiing

Cervinia has the biggest, highest, most snowsure area of easy skiing we've come across. A newish gondola and ancient cable-car leave from above the village centre , though it's a steep climb up to them. These take you to the main mid-mountain base of **Plan Maison** (2555m). From there a further gondola and cable-cars go up to **Plateau Rosa** (3480m) and the link with Zermatt.

From Plateau Rosa you can go left on a blue run to a large network of drag- and chair-lifts serving Cervinia's easiest skiing and linking back to Plan Maison again. Don't miss the sign to Italy and left turn near the top, otherwise you'll end up on the **Zermatt** lift system – paying the daily supplement. This area can also be accessed by drags from the village centre and you can ski back there or to the gondola and cable-car station.

If you go right at Plateau Rosa you ski down the splendid wide Ventina run, which you can take all the way down to Cervinia (8km). Or you can branch off left down towards **Valtournenche**. The skiing here is served by a number of lifts above the initial gondola from Valtournenche to Salette at 2245m. The top of the Ventina run can be skied repeatedly by taking the giant 140-person cable-car. And there's a chair to play on – but no other lifts serve this sector and you can't ski back to Plan Maison (though you can take the gondola down to there if you like).

There is also the small, little-used **Cieloalto** area, served by three lifts to the south of the cable-car at the bottom of the Ventina run. This can be very useful in bad weather as it has the only trees in the area.

From Plan Maison a cable-car used to go up to **Furggen** (3490m) and access Cervinia's steepest skiing. But this old lift has been closed down, and it's not known when a replacement will be built.

Plans for the return of floodlit skiing just above the village have also been shelved for the time being.

SNOW RELIABILITY
Superb

The ski area is one of the highest in Europe and, despite getting a lot of afternoon sun, can usually be relied upon to have good snow conditions. Lifts being closed due to wind is a bigger worry. The village nursery slopes and bottom half of the Ventina run have snowmaking facilities.

FOR ADVANCED SKIERS
Forget it

This is not the resort for good skiers. There are several black runs dotted about but most of the these would be graded red elsewhere. The beautiful, long, lonely piste from Furggen was the only worthwhile run, and with the cable-car out of action that is no longer accessible.

Good skiers paying the expensive Zermatt supplement in search of tough runs will be disappointed. The Trockener Steg-Schwarzsee area close to Cervinia has a great deal of easy skiing and only a few challenging pistes. Getting to and from the other, more challenging ski areas on a day trip isn't practical. And the link to Zermatt is often closed because of high wind.

FOR INTERMEDIATE SKIERS
Plenty of motorway cruising

Virtually the whole area can be skied comfortably by average intermediates. And if you are the sort of skier who thrives on wide, easy, motorway pistes, you'll love Cervinia's skiing. It has more long, flattering runs than any other resort. The high proportion of red runs on the piste map is misleading: most of them would be graded blue elsewhere.

The easiest skiing is on the left hand side as you look at the mountain. From top to bottom here, there are gentle blue runs and almost equally gentle reds in the beautiful scenery at the foot of the south face of the Matterhorn.

On the right, as you look at the mountain, is the best area for more adventurous intermediates. The Ventina run is a particularly good fast cruise. The long run down to Valtournenche is easy for most of its length. Good intermediates will be able to ski the black runs.

The trip over to Zermatt will bring you first of all to even gentler motorways than on the Cervinia side, but then to some more challenging pistes around Schwarzsee.

If you want to have a look at the village of Zermatt, allow plenty of time. The run down can be tricky, the lifts back time-consuming.

There's also the bonus of even more spectacular scenery. The view of the Matterhorn is the classic one you see on all the pictures (you wouldn't recognise it from the Cervinia side), and the view of the glacier below when you ride the Klein Matterhorn cable-car to Europe's highest piste skiing is breathtaking.

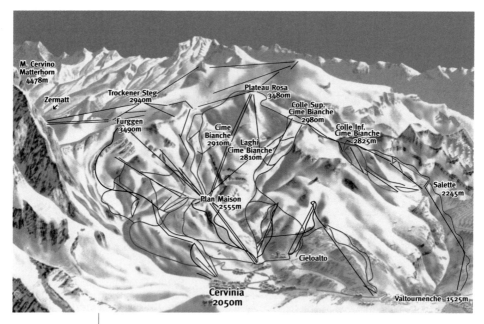

FURGGEN

The cable-car to Furggen has been taken out of commission. We understand that the resort intends to replace it, but the timing is unclear.

FOR BEGINNERS
Pretty much ideal

Complete beginners will start on the good village nursery slope, and should graduate quickly to the fine flat area around Plan Maison and its gentle green runs. Fast learners will be able to cover a great deal of ground by the end of the week, and end up skiing the blue run all the way from the top to the bottom of the mountain. The very easy runs down to Salette, on the way to Valtournenche, are a must.

FOR CROSS-COUNTRY
Hardly any

There are a couple of short trails, but this is not a cross-country resort.

QUEUES
Can still be problems

Although much improved recently, the lift system still has drawbacks. Access to the Plan Maison mid-station is crucial for most skiers, with the result that the two main access lifts get oversubscribed in peak season and at busy weekends – even though they jointly carry 2,850 skiers an hour. The alternative is a roundabout sequence of drags and chairs.

Plateau Rosa, at the top of the mountain, is another important junction that in the past has had serious access problems.

But the inadequate cable-cars from Plan Maison have had some of the pressure taken off them by a new gondola to Laghi Cime Bianche with a capacity (2,400 skiers an hour) three times that of the two cable-cars

combined. Above that is a big modern cable-car that shifts crowds quickly.

There can be queues for the lower lifts when the upper lifts are shut because of high wind.

MOUNTAIN RESTAURANTS
Good but pricey

The food in mountain restaurants is generally good, wholesome stuff, and helpings are liberal. But prices are high and the toilet facilities are primitive.

The restaurants are also not marked on the piste map, except on the Valtournenche side, where they are cheaper and less crowded – and, in our experience, serve good food. The one at the bottom of the Roisette chair has great views and a good platter of local salami and cheeses. The Motta, at the top of the drag-lift of the same name, has an excellent local speciality (Suppa di Valdostani – bread, cheese and vegetable soup). Back on the Cervinia side, the Etoile on the Roc Nere piste has good food and atmosphere. Baita Cretaz, near the bottom of the Cretaz

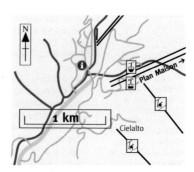

SKI SCHOOL

93/94 prices in lire

Cervino
Classes 6 days
2hr 50min: 10am-
12.50
6 days: 165,000
Children's classes
Ages: any
6 days: 165,000
Private lessons
Hourly
45,000 for 1 or 2
people; each
additional person
5,000

CHILDCARE

The ski school runs a
snow garden with
mini-lift at the foot of
the Cretaz slopes, but
there are no all-day
care arrangements.
Nor is there a non-ski
kindergarten.

GETTING THERE

Air Turin, transfer
2½hr. Geneva,
transfer 2½hr.

Rail Châtillon (27km);
regular buses from
station.

PACKAGES

Airtours, Crystal,
Enterprise, Inghams,
Thomson

pistes, is good value and has excellent
service and presentation. The British-
run Igloo, at the top of the Bardoney
chair just off the Ventina piste, is
popular and apparently does 'amazing'
chicken sandwiches – but gets mixed
reviews. Les Clochards, on the edge of
town, has tasty pasta. The Bontadini
da Lombard, on the blue run back
from Plateau Rosa, has good main
courses – but reporters recommend
against its puddings and house wine.

SKI SCHOOL
Varied reports
Cervinia has one main ski school, the
Cervino. We've had good and bad
reports about both the standard of
tuition and the quality of instructors'
English. One reporter said their group
asked the teacher to repeat his
instructions in French because that
was easier to understand. Classes tend
to be large. There is a separate school
up at the satellite of Cieloalto.

FACILITIES FOR CHILDREN
Do-it-yourself
The ski school children's classes is
about it. The ski area, with its long
gentle runs, should suit families.

Staying there

Most visitors to Cervinia accept that
it's not a very convenient resort and
put up with some walking. Central
hotels are quite convenient for the
Cretaz drags, but not for the main
gondola station. There are more
convenient hotels, some of them
mentioned below.

HOW TO GO
Plenty of hotel packages
Most of the big tour operators come
here, providing between them a wide
selection of hotels, though other
accommodation is thin on the
ground. A lot of the accommodation
out of the main village is private,
some of it time-sharing.
Chalets There are no catered chalets.
Hotels There are 44 hotels, mostly 2-
star or 3-star, with half a dozen 4-stars.
£££££ Cristallo The only 4-star which
is in any way luxurious; pool, sauna,
massage. Up the hill towards the
Cielalto lift.
££££ Hermitage Small, smartly
furnished chalet just out of the village
on the road up to Cielalto. Pool.
££££ Bucaneve Central, comfortable,
reasonably priced 4-star.

££££ Punta Maquignaz Captivating
chalet-style 4-star, recently opened, in
centre near Cretaz lifts.
£££ Neiges d'Antan Family-run chalet
in peaceful setting 4km down the road
in Perreres, with charming rustic
furnishings.
£££ Excelsior Planet Pleasant, central
3-star with a pool.
£££ Astoria Slightly down-at-heel, but
right by the main lifts, with friendly
staff and 'excellent' dinners.
£££ Furggen Modern hotel above the
resort on the Cretaz slopes, with skiing
from the door.
££ Breithorn Good food. One of a
number of good-value (by local
standards) 2-stars.
££ Marmore Clean, warm, with
'substantial' food; mid-way between
the lift stations.
Self-catering There are many
apartments in the resort but few are
available through British tour
operators. The Cristallino apartments
(Crystal) are fairly simple but guests
have use of the fine facilities of the
Cristallo next door. The Residence La
Pineta (Inghams) is of a similar
standard, five minutes from the
gondola and cable-car.

CRYSTAL HOLIDAYS

helped us to compile the eating out and après-ski sections. Our thanks to them.

ACTIVITIES

Indoor Hotel with swimming pools and saunas, bowling, casino, fitness centre
Outdoor Natural skating rink (until March), bob-sleigh run, horse-riding, para-gliding, hang-gliding, mountaineering, walks, heli-skiing

TOURIST OFFICE

Postcode 11021
Tel 010 39 (166) 949136
Fax 949731

EATING OUT
Expensive for Italy

Cervinia's 49 restaurants allow plenty of choice, though the range of food isn't vast. It helps if you like pasta, pizza or polenta-based meals. Prices are uniformly high. Some of the best hotels have good, but expensive, restaurants open to non-residents.

The Chamoix and Matterhorn are excellent, but are particularly pricey. The Grotta belies its unfortunate name with good food. Casse Croute serves probably the biggest, and best, pizzas in town. The Pania is good for local specialities. KL has traditional home cooking. The simple Dau is one of the best places for a relatively cheap meal.

APRES-SKI
Disappoints many Brits

Plenty of lively Brits come here looking for action but there isn't much to do but tour the mostly fairly ordinary bars. Things are particularly quiet after skiing, when most people quickly disappear into their hotels.

The Underground Kellar Bar, with Irish music, is the only animated early-evening joint. The characterless Dragon Bar is a major congregating spot for Brits looking for a 'home from home', but it simply gets crowded rather than atmospheric. Satellite TV, videos, Fosters lager and karaoke are provided. The Pellissier Bar and Yeti Pub are other downmarket haunts full of Brits trying, often without success, to have a lively time. More cosmopolitan bars that can have atmosphere are Lino's, Pippo's and Café des Guides. The Scotch Club has occasional live music, but it doesn't really get going till after midnight.

There are three discos, which liven up at weekends. Brits seem to prefer the Chimera. Blow Up and the Princess are more Italian in atmosphere. There are several tour-rep-organised events such as bowling, snowmobiling, quiz nights and various meals – with fondue, pizza and local specialities.

FOR NON-SKIERS
Little attraction

There is little to do. The pleasant town of Aosta is reached easily enough, but it's a four hour round trip. Village amenities include hotel pools, fitness centre and large natural ice rink. The walks are disappointing. The mountain restaurants reachable by gondola or cable-car have little going for them.

STAYING UP THE MOUNTAIN
To beat the queues

Up at Plan Maison, the major lift junction 500m vertical above the resort, Lo Stambecco is a 50-room 3-star hotel ideally placed for early nights and early starts. Available through Inghams.

Less radically, the Cime Bianche is a rustic 3-star chalet on the upper fringes of the resort (in the area known as La Vieille).

STAYING DOWN THE VALLEY
Great home run

Valtournenche, 9km down the road, is cheaper than Cervinia, has a genuine Italian atmosphere and a fair selection of simple hotels, of which the 3-star Bijou is the best. Except at weekends (when a lot of day-trippers arrive) the gondola is a queue-free way into the Cervinia skiing, though the drag-lifts above mean it takes time. And the exceptionally long run back down is a nice way to end the day. (It involves a short drag, so you can't leave it too late.) The main street through the village is very busy with cars going to and from Cervinia.

Cortina d'Ampezzo 1220m

✔ Magnificent Dolomite scenery, perhaps the most dramatic of any ski resort

✔ Marvellous nursery slopes and good long cruising runs, ideal for nervous intermediates

✔ Access to the vast amount of skiing on the Dolomiti Superski pass (easiest for those with a car)

✔ Attractive although rather towny resort, with lots of upmarket shops

✔ Good off-slope facilities, as you might expect of an Olympic venue

✗ Several separate ski areas, inconveniently spread around all sides of the resort

✗ Expensive by Italian standards

✗ Gets very crowded during Italian holidays but rather quiet at other times

Nowhere is more picturesque than chic Cortina, the most upmarket of Italian resorts. Dramatic pink-tinged peaks rise sheerly from the top of the slopes, giving picture-postcard views from wherever you are. (Those amazing shots in the movie Cliffhanger were filmed here.) As many people come for the views as for the skiing.

Cortina's skiing is fine for its regular upmarket visitors from Rome and Milan, many of whom have second homes here and enjoy the strolling, shopping, people-watching and lunching as much as the odd leisurely excursion onto the slopes. For complete beginners and leisurely intermediates, the splendid nursery slopes and long easy runs are ideal. But for keen piste bashers Cortina can be frustrating. For good skiers the skiing is limited, with few tough runs and most of those liable to poor snow conditions because of their south-facing aspect. And for everyone, the skiing is fragmented, with separate areas dotted around, most a bus-ride from much of the accommodation.

ORIENTATION

Cortina is a town, rather than a village, spreading across a broad valley. The main valley runs north-south, but minor roads go off to east and west, and give access to some of the skiing. The two main areas are reached by cable-cars on opposite sides of the town. **San Cassiano** is not far away to the west, with skiing links from there to **Corvara** and the other Sella Ronda resorts.

 ## The resort

In high season, you'll find almost as many non-skiers (or very part-time skiers) in Cortina as you will real skiers. It attracts the rich and wealthy from the big Italian cities, many of whom have second homes here. Fur coats and glitzy jewellery are the norm.

The resort itself is spread widely around the town centre, with exclusive chalets scattered around the woods and roads leading off into the surrounding countryside. The centre is the traffic-free Corso Italia, full of chic shops and a hive of activity in early evening, when everyone parades up and down window-shopping and people-watching. The cobblestones and picturesque church and bell tower add to a thoroughly Italian atmosphere.

Unlike the rest of the Dolomites, Cortina is pure Italy. It has none of the Germanic traditions of Selva and the Sud Tirol.

Surrounding the centre is a horrendous one-way system, often clogged with traffic and stinking of exhaust fumes. This makes an unpleasant contrast with the stunning scenery on view wherever you look. Few places can claim to match Cortina for the beauty of its setting. We first arrived in the dark. The next morning, walking down to breakfast, we noticed a painting with stupendous views on the wall of the hotel staircase. By the end of breakfast we'd woken up, and when we walked back to the room we realised the 'painting' was in fact a window, and the view was of the Cristallo peak at the back of the hotel – no artist could have imagined anything more stunning.

 ## The skiing

Cortina first leapt to fame when it hosted the 1956 Winter Olympics, for which many of its existing facilities were built. At the time, it was one of the most modern resorts around. Now it feels distinctly behind the times. Its widely spread ski areas are as different from the classic modern French purpose-built resorts as you can get.

SKI FACTS

Altitude 1225m–2930m
Lifts	52
Pistes	140km
Green/Blue	53%
Red	42%
Black	5%
Artificial snow	25km

LIFT PASSES

94/95 prices in lire
Cortina d'Ampezzo
Covers all lifts in
Cortina, San Vito di
Cadore, Auronzo and
Misurina, and ski-
buses.
Main pass
1-day pass 47,000
6-day pass 231,000
(low season 201,000
– 13% off)
Senior citizens
Over 60: 6-day pass
185,000 (20% off)
Children
Under 15: 6-day pass
162,000 (30% off)
Short-term passes
Half-day pass from
1pm (4,200).
Notes Discount prices
for senior citizens and
children for 2-day
passes and over only.
Alternative passes
Dolomiti Superski
pass covers 464 lifts
and 1180km of piste
in the Dolomites
(adult 6-day 243,000).

THE SKI AREA
Inconveniently fragmented
Cortina has several smallish separate
ski areas, each a fair trek from the
centre of town. The largest is the
Socrepes area, accessed by chair and
drag-lifts a bus-ride from town. This
interlinks with Cortina's highest
skiing area of **Tofana**, reached by a
two stage cable-car from just outside
the centre of town.

On the opposite side of the valley
from the cable-car is the tiny **Mietres**
area. Another cable-car from the
eastern side of town leads to the
Faloria area, from which you can ski
down to the long slow chairs that lead
up into the limited but dramatic
skiing beneath the **Cristallo** peak.

There are several other tiny separate
ski areas, each with two or three lifts
reachable by road. The most
worthwhile of these is a cable-car from
Passo Falzarego (at 2150m) up to
Lagazuoi (2750m) from where there is
a beautiful sweeping red run down to
Armentarola. A car would be a great
asset if you want to make the most of
the Sella Ronda and the other skiing
covered on the Dolomiti Superski pass.

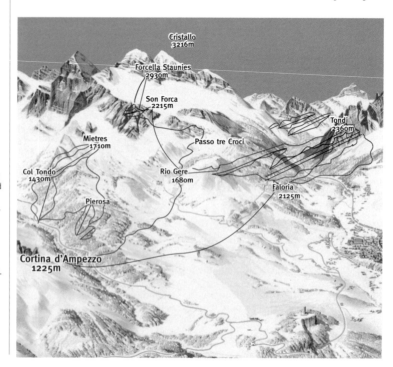

SKI SCHOOL

94/95 prices in lire

Cortina
Classes 6 days
2½hr: 9.30am-noon;
2hr: noon-2pm
6 2½hr days: 250,000
Children's classes
Ages: under 15
6 full days (9.30-3.30)
including lunch:
760,000
Private lessons
Hourly
55,000 for 1hr; each
additional person
15,000

Azzurra Cortina
Classes 6 days
3½hr: 9.15am-1pm;
3hr: 1pm-4pm;
6½hr: 9.15-4pm
6 3½hr days: 420,000
Private lessons
Hourly
56,000 for 1hr; each
additional person
14,000

SNOW RELIABILITY
Good, with plenty of artificial help

As in most of the Dolomites, Cortina has invested heavily in artificial snowmaking, so expect good cover on the main Socrepes slopes and on the south-facing runs of the Cristallo area. The record of natural snowfalls is an erratic one – the snow here can be good when it's poor on the north side of the Alps.

FOR ADVANCED SKIERS
Limited

There are a couple of challenging short runs but nothing like enough to keep a good skier happy for a week.

The run down from the second stage of the Tofana cable-car at Ra Valles goes through a gap in the rocks, and a steep, narrow, south-facing section gives you wonderful views of Cortina deep down in the valley below. This isn't as precipitous as it looks from the cable-car, but is often tricky because of poor snow conditions.

The same is true of Cortina's other steep run, from the top of the Cristallo area at Forcella Staunies. The top chair-lift takes you to a steep, narrow, south-facing couloir. This is frequently shut because of either avalanche danger or poor snow.

Other than that, good skiers will have to be content with cruising the many long red runs in the area, or exploring the Superski region.

FOR INTERMEDIATE SKIERS
Fragmented and not extensive

Skiers who enjoy cruising runs among beautiful scenery and don't mind skiing the same runs repeatedly will get the most out of Cortina. But don't expect a huge interlinked ski area.

The red runs at the top of the Tofana area are short but normally have the best snow. The skiing here goes up to over 2800m and is mainly north-facing. But be warned: the only way down is by cable-car or the often tricky black run described above.

The reds from the linked Pomedes area are longer and offer good fast cruising, served by three chair-lifts.

The Faloria area has a whole string

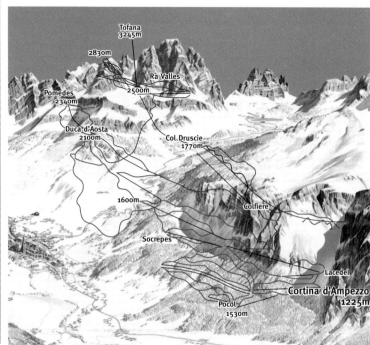

CHILDCARE

Both schools offer all-day classes for children – the Cortina school from 9.30 to 3.30, the Azzurra school from 9am to 4pm.

The Mini Club at the Socrepes lifts (860942) takes children aged 2 to 8, from 8.30 to 8pm. Comprehensive care arrangements are offered by an outfit called Natural...Mente (5086), which takes children from age 12 months, from 8am to 6pm.

GETTING THERE

Air Venice, transfer 3hr.

Rail Calalzo (30km) or Dobbiaco (32km); frequent buses from station.

PACKAGES

Crystal, Powder Byrne, Superski

---

of fairly short north-facing reds. And the Cristallo area that you can ski to from here has just one long red run from below the top couloir back down, served by slow old chairs.

FOR BEGINNERS
Wonderful nursery slopes
The Socrepes area has some of the biggest nursery slopes and best progression runs we have seen. Unfortunately we have had few reports on the ski school so we can't recommend it conclusively as an ideal beginner resort.

And some of the forest paths marked blue can be icy and intimidating for a novice skier. But if you stick to the main pistes, you'll find ideal gentle terrain.

FOR CROSS-COUNTRY
One of the best
Cortina has 74km of prepared trails, mainly in the woods to the north, towards Dobbiaco. There are also trails beneath the Cristallo ski area.

QUEUES
No problem for early birds
Most Cortina holiday-makers rise late, lunch lengthily and stop skiing early. That makes for few lift queues and generally uncrowded pistes. And out of the peak Christmas-New Year and February high seasons, the resort can be extraordinarily quiet. One lone skier found 'disconcertingly deserted pistes' which could be 'intimidating when descending steep slopes in total solitude'. But another reporter says that peak-season, peak-time queues can be 'chaotic'.

MOUNTAIN RESTAURANTS
Good but expensive
Lunch is a major event for many Cortina visitors. At weekends you often need to book to make sure of a table. Many of the restaurants can be reached by road, and non-skiers arrive mid-morning to sunbathe and admire the views. Prices are high, and some menus (and wine lists) tempting. We had one of the most expensive lunches ever at El Camineto, at the bottom of the main Pormedes lifts, where white-jacketed waiters minister to your needs.

The Socrepes sector has several hotels along the road going up its south-eastern edge – and close to the bottom of the slopes is the best restaurant in the resort, the Michelin-starred Tivoli.

SKI SCHOOL
Few reports
With such an upmarket Italian clientele, we'd expect tuition here to be good, but we have no reports on the standard of English spoken. We suspect it may be poor, as it generally is in this emphatically Italian area. There is a separate guiding school, the Gruppo Guide Alpine, which offers off-piste, ski-touring and special high altitude weeks. Snow-boarding also has its own section.

FACILITIES FOR CHILDREN
Better than average
By Italian standards the childcare facilities are outstanding, with a choice of all-day care arrangements for children of practically any age. Given the very small number of British visitors, you can't count on good spoken English.

Staying there

There's a wide range of hotels both in the centre and scattered around the outskirts. Wherever you stay it's unlikely to be convenient. To get the most out of the town, staying in the centre and resigning yourself to being a bus-ride from the lifts is probably the best bet. If you have a car, your choice is quite a bit wider.

HOW TO GO
Now with more packages
British tour operators have no catered chalets or self-catering allocations, but hotel packages are increasingly widely available. Upmarket Powder Byrne are in the resort this year for the first time, offering a choice of five hotels.
Hotels There's a big choice, especially at the luxury end, where there are two 5-star and fifteen 4-star hotels. But the resort is not literally exclusive: there are cheaper places – down to 1-and 2-star pensions at a fraction of the price of the top end.
£££££ Miramonti Spectacularly grand hotel in extensive grounds, 2km south of town. Pool.
££££ Poste Reliable 4-star, at the heart of the town in more ways than one.
££££ Parc Victoria Elegantly rustic 4-star, at Faloria end of town centre.
£££ Menardi Welcoming roadside inn, a long walk from centre and lifts.
££ Trieste Neat roadside chalet, not quite such a long walk from the centre and lifts.
Self-catering There's a wide choice of chalets and apartments available for independent travellers.

CRYSTAL HOLIDAYS

helped us to compile the eating out and après-ski sections. Our thanks to them.

ACTIVITIES

Indoor Swimming pool, saunas, museums, art gallery, cinema, indoor tennis court, public library **Outdoor** Olympic ice-stadium (2 rinks), curling, ice hockey, sleigh rides, horse-riding school, ski-bob run, olympic ski jump, 6km walking paths, toboggan run, heli-skiing

TOURIST OFFICE

Postcode 32043
Tel 010 39 (436) 3231
Fax 3235

EATING OUT
Huge choice

There's an enormous selection of places, both in the town centre and a little way out, doing mainly Italian food. The very smart and pricey El Toulà is in a beautiful old barn, just on the edge of town. Many of the best restaurants are further out – such as the Tivoli (which gets a Michelin star), Meloncino (a charming chalet), Leone e Anna, Rio Gere and Baita Fraina. Good central restaurants include: the Passetto, Ariston, Buca Dell' Inferno, Cazzetta, Croda and Ra Stua. Harry's Grill is one of the few good restaurants not specialising in Italian food.

APRES-SKI
Lively in high season

Cortina is a lively social whirl in high season, with lots of well-heeled Italians staying up very late (which is why the slopes are so quiet). But in low season, it can be very quiet – one reporter found it 'difficult to find a bar open after 10.30pm'.

Don't go if the sight of fur coats upsets you: during the early evening walkabout, every other person will be wearing one.

Bar Lovat is one of the most popular tea-time spots, notably for its home-made pastries. Bar Embassy is yet another place with a high calorie count, serving freshly made 'Krapfen' – a jam and cream speciality. The new Bar Bellevue, with its large terrace overlooking the pedestrian zone, has

become the 'in' place. Bar Cristallino is an elegant spot where young and old rub shoulders. The Enoteca is a wine bar popular with locals after skiing. Later the hotel de la Poste is a 'must' for observing the rich and glamorous over an aperitif. Terrazza Viennese, attached to hotel Ancora, is another fashionable spot. The Orange American Bar has good music. In peak season there are enough customers to give all the numerous discos a great atmosphere. Some of the best are the Metro, Hyppo, Belvedere and Limbo.

FOR NON-SKIERS
Classic resort for non-skiers

Along with St Moritz, Cortina rates as one of the leading resorts for non-skiers and essentially part-time skiers.

The setting is stunning, the town attractive, the shopping extensive, the mountain restaurants easily accessible by road (a car is handy) and there are plenty of other activities to keep you occupied.

There's ice skating, major ice hockey matches and even an ice disco on the Olympic ice rink. If you're there at the right time you can watch sleds careering down the Olympic bobsleigh run. There's horse jumping and polo on the snow occasionally.

Cortina is also a cultural centre, with several museums and art galleries, including the Mario Rimoldi, which has the largest private collection in Italy of painting and sculptures by leading modernists.

Courmayeur 1225m

✔ Stunning views of Mont Blanc massif

✔ Pleasant range of intermediate runs

✔ Much of the ski area is served by artificial snowmaking

✔ Good mountain restaurants

✔ Charming, traditional village, with car-free centre and some stylish shops

✔ Lively, but not rowdy, evening atmosphere and nightlife

✔ One of the shortest, easiest drives from the Channel, and short airport transfers

✘ Lack of good nursery slopes and easy runs for beginners to progress to

✘ No tough piste skiing

✘ Relatively small ski area, with mainly short runs

✘ Slopes get very crowded at weekends

✘ Tiresome walk and cable-car journey to and from the skiing (except from Dolonne)

✘ Not much for active non-skiers to occupy themselves with

ORIENTATION

Courmayeur is just on the Italian side of the Mont Blanc tunnel, by the main route down the Aosta valley.

The skiing is separate from the village. You get up to it via a huge cable-car from the edge of town, and come back the same way. There's some accommodation on the same side of the valley as the skiing, in Dolonne, from where a gondola goes to the ski area. Those with a car can drive to another cable-car a few kilometres towards Mont Blanc at Entrèves. From La Palud, a little further away, another cable-car takes you up to the off-piste skiing of the Mont Blanc massif, including the Vallée Blanche down to **Chamonix** in France (also an easy drive through the tunnel), covered by the lift pass. **La Thuile** is an easy drive the other way and **Cervinia** is reachable.

Courmayeur is very popular, especially at weekends, with the smart Italian set from Milan and Turin. It's easy to see why: not only is it very easy to get to, thanks to the road up to the Mont Blanc tunnel, but it is certainly the most captivating of the Val d'Aosta resorts, with splendid scenery as well as abundant village charm and a relaxed but stylish après-ski scene.

The scenery, the charm and the nightlife must weigh heavily with the many British skiers who go there too. Certainly, the ski area is unlikely to be the main attraction, given its limited range of difficulty, its inconvenient location across the valley from the village and, particularly, its limited size. A keen piste-basher will ski Courmayeur's runs in a day, then be wondering what to do for the rest of the week.

Courmayeur makes a good day trip from Chamonix (the weather on the southern side of Mont Blanc can be quite different from that on the northern side) or a jolly week for those who want to party as much as ski. It also appeals to a quite different kind of skier, who wants to explore the spectacular Mont Blanc massif with the aid of a guide and local peaks with the aid of a helicopter.

 ## The resort

Courmayeur is a traditional old mountaineering village which, despite construction of the nearby Mont Blanc tunnel road and proliferation of modern hotels, has retained much of its old-world charm. (The road passes close to the village, but generally has surprisingly little impact on it.)

The village has a charming traffic-free centre of cobbled streets, attractive shops and well-preserved old buildings, the most impressive of which is the church. An Alpine museum and a statue of a famous, long-dead mountain rescue hero add to the historical feel of the place. The potential that cobbles have for treacherous walking when icy is well appreciated – the streets are well maintained.

There is great atmosphere in the village centre, the focus of which is

Selected chalets in Courmayeur

SKI FACTS

Altitude	1295m-2755m
Lifts	28
Pistes	100km
Green/Blue	50%
Red	40%
Black	10%
Artificial snow	15km

the Via Roma. Immediately after skiing, lots of skiers fill up the numerous atmospheric bars, which include some of the most civilised places we have encountered. Others wander in and out of the many varied small shops, which include a salami specialist and a good bookshop. At weekends people-watching is part of the evening scene, as ski jackets are outnumbered by the fur coats of the Milanese and Torinese.

The village extends away from the centre in several directions, including southwards to the area around the cable-car station. Dolonne, across the valley, is a quiet suburb – inconvenient for the nightlife.

 # The skiing

The main ski area suits intermediates, with few difficult or easy runs, but it is surprisingly small for such a well known, large resort. The pistes are varied in character if not in gradient, and pretty. Piste marking could be improved.

THE SKI AREA
Small but interestingly varied

The ski area is separate from the village: a cable-car ride is necessary at the start and end of the day. This, the only lift from Courmayeur itself, transports skiers to the bottom of the skiing at **Plan Checrouit** (where you can store your skis and boots).

The ski area has two distinct sections, both almost entirely for intermediates. The north-east-facing Checrouit area catches the morning sun, and has open, above-the-tree-line skiing. The 25-person, infrequently running Youla cable-car goes up to the top of Courmayeur's piste skiing at 2625m. There is a further cable-car to Cresta d'Arp (2755m). This serves only long (and apparently beautiful) off-piste runs. But in our several visits we've never seen this cable-car open.

Skiers tend to follow the sun over to the north-west-facing slopes down towards **Val Veny** in the afternoon. These are interesting, varied and tree-lined. Connections between the two areas are good, with numerous alternative routes.

LIFT PASSES

94/95 prices in lire
Courmayeur Mont Blanc
Covers all lifts in Val Veny and Checrouit, and the lifts on Mont Blanc up to Punta Helbronner.
Beginners Free nursery lifts at Plan Checrouit and top of Val Veny cable-car (which can be paid for by the ride).
Main pass
1-day pass 44,000
6-day pass 220,000 (low season 190,000 – 14% off)
Short-term passes
Single ascent on some lifts and half-day pass (adult 30,000) available.
Notes Passes of 6 or more days are valid for one day in the Chamonix valley.
Alternative passes
Valle d'Aosta area pass covers all lifts in Courmayeur, Gressoney, Alagna, Champoluc, La Thuile, Pila, Cervinia and Valtournenche (adult 6-day 238,000). Mont-Blanc ski region pass covers all lifts in 13 resorts around Mont Blanc.

Apart from the main ski area, you can take a cable-car up to the shoulder of **Mont Blanc**. This should only be done with a guide, as all the skiing here is off-piste and on glaciers. You can do the famous Vallée Blanche down to Chamonix from here without the horrific initial ridge walk you encounter if you take the cable-car up from Chamonix.

SNOW RELIABILITY
Good except late season
Courmayeur's skiing is not high – mostly between 1700m and 2250m. But much of it faces north or north-west, and there is virtually blanket coverage of artificial snow on the main runs.

FOR ADVANCED SKIERS
Off-piste is the only challenge
Courmayeur has little challenging piste skiing. The only black run is not difficult, and few moguls form anywhere else. However, some of the red runs are sufficiently steep to test advanced technique, especially if they're icy. The classic off-piste runs from Cresta d'Arp go in three different directions – a clockwise loop via Arp Vieille to Val Veny, with close-up views of the Miage glacier; eastwards down a deserted valley to Dolonne or Pré St Didier; or southwards through the Youla gorge to La Thuile. But don't count on the cable-car running.

On Mont Blanc, the Vallée Blanche is not a challenge (though still recommended for its beautiful views as well as sheer length), but the Toula glacier route on the Italian side from Punta Helbronner to Pavillon most certainly is, often to the point of being dangerous. There's also heli-skiing available on the peaks above the Val Ferret, north-east of the resort.

FOR INTERMEDIATE SKIERS
Ideal gradient but limited extent
The whole area is suitable for most intermediates. But it is small. The avid piste-basher, who doesn't like to ski the same run twice in a day, will find it very limited.

The open east-facing Checrouit section is pretty much ski-anywhere territory, where you can choose your own route and make it as easy or difficult as you like. The blue runs here are about Courmayeur's gentlest. The red pistes running the length of the Bertolini chair are more challenging and very enjoyable, with several off-piste excursions possible. If you ski past the bottom of the chair, you link in with the pretty, wooded

slopes heading down to Zerotta. This whole north- and west-facing area has great views of Mont Blanc and the Ghiacciaio della Brenva.

The Zerotta chair dominates the area, with numerous alternatives starting at its top. It's a good area for mixed abilities, with runs of varying difficulty meeting up at several places on the way down to Zerotta.

The Vallée Blanche, reached from La Palud, has truly spectacular scenery. Although off-piste, the skiing is easy enough for an adventurous intermediate to try. But you should ski with a guide because the routes aren't marked and there are always crevasses to be wary of.

FOR BEGINNERS
Consistently too steep
Courmayeur is not well suited to beginners. There are several nursery slopes but none is ideal. The area at the top of the main cable-car from Courmayeur gets crowded with more experienced skiers and there are few easy runs for the near-beginner. The small area served by the short Tzaly drag, just above the Entrèves cable-car top station, is the most suitable beginner terrain, and it tends to have good snow.

FOR CROSS-COUNTRY
Beautiful trails
There are good trails dotted around Courmayeur. The best are the four covering 20km at Val Ferret, to which there is a bus service. Dolonne also has two short trails, and a skiable path runs from Entrèves to Zerotta, which is useful for meeting up with Alpine skiers for lunch. Total trails 35km.

QUEUES
Weekend cable-car black spots
The lift system is generally excellent. The Checrouit and Val Veny cable-cars suffer queues only at weekends, and even these can be beaten with an early start. Skiers also show remarkable patience in waiting long periods for the infrequently running Youla cable-car. Otherwise, no problems. Overcrowded slopes at the weekends, particularly those running down to Zerotta, are a greater problem.

MOUNTAIN RESTAURANTS
Lots – some of them good
The small ski area is lavishly endowed with 27 establishments ranging from rustic on-piste huts to larger self-service places at main lift stations. There is a large gap in quality between snack bars and fully fledged

restaurants. Some snack bars sell little more than uninspiring hard sandwiches and cardboard pizza. They also rely on good weather, having better terraces than interiors. Most of the restaurants serve delicious pizza and pasta.

One of the better snack bars is at the top of Dzeleuna chair. Several restaurants are excellent. Château Branlant, next to the Chiecco drag at Plan Checrouit, is recommended for good food, atmospheric interior, friendly service and good views of beginners struggling up the drag and down the piste. Maison Vieille, at the top of the chair of the same name, has a rustic dining room and good food. The rather neglected restaurant, poorly positioned for trade just above and to the right of the bottom of the Pra Neyron chair, is good value, with staff eager to please.

Ristorante Zerotta is expensive, but has good food and a sunny terrace well placed for people-watching. The Petit Mont Blanc, in the same sector, is also recommended.

SKI SCHOOL
Not a strong point
Reports on the ski school vary widely, with some recent criticism of chaotic organisation at the start of the week. Standards of English seem erratic, which is very disappointing given Courmayeur's large number of British customers. There is a thriving guides' association ready to exploit the area's off-piste potential.

FACILITIES FOR CHILDREN
Mark Warner have a crèche
Although the resort's childcare arrangements are well ahead of the Italian norm, most parents will be more attracted by the crèche at Mark Warner's chalet-hotel in Dolonne, which takes children from 4 months.

🔼 Staying there

The cable-car station is on the southern edge of town, a fair distance from much of the accommodation. There is no ski-bus alternative to walking. Once up the mountain, a further short walk is necessary from the cable-car to the other lifts before you can start skiing.

Having accommodation close to the cable-car is obviously advantageous. But don't stay too close to the Mont Blanc road, which can be very noisy. However, having this major route on the doorstep does afford particularly

easy access for ski-drivers. Most hotels have some parking spaces. Parking at the village cable-car is very limited, but drivers can go to Entrèves, a few kilometres away, where there is a large car-park at the foot of the Val Veny cable-car. Buses, infrequent but running to a timetable, link Courmayeur with La Palud, just beyond Entrèves, for the Punta Helbronner-Vallée Blanche cable-car.

HOW TO GO
Plenty of hotels
Courmayeur's long-standing popularity ensures a wide range of packages, mainly in hotels.
Chalets Courmayeur isn't a major chalet resort, but Bladon Lines have three simple, cheap units here. Lamastra is a complete house, above the town at Villair, 15 minutes from the cable-car. Donzelli and Marconi are in one larger chalet, with their good central location reflected in slightly higher prices. Mark Warner have a comfortable chalet-hotel in Dolonne – the Telecabine, sharing a building with the gondola base station. It has an in-house crèche (see Facilities for children).
Hotels There are nearly 50 hotels in Courmayeur, evenly distributed between the star ratings.
££££ Pavillon Charmless 4-star, unrivalled for its combination of comfort and convenience, with one of the two pools in town. Friendly staff.
££££ Royal Large well positioned hotel, with the other swimming pool.
££££ Palace Bron Small but tall, elegantly furnished chalet above the town at Plan Gorret.
£££ Cristallo Well placed 3-star, just off via Roma; attractively furnished, well equipped rooms, 'excellent' food.
£££ Grange Rustic, stone-and-wood farmhouse at Entrèves.
££ Edelweiss Friendly, cosy, good-value place close to the centre.
££ Lo Scoiattolo Good rooms, good food, shame about the position – at opposite end of town from cable-car.
Self-catering Inghams has simple apartments in a pleasant chalet building, well placed for the cable-car, less so for the village centre. Bladon Lines have a welcome new addition, with well appointed studios suitable for couples and small families. They aren't particularly well placed, 10 minutes above town, but have a communal lounge and sauna. There is much more self-catering accommodation available for independent travellers. The tourist office staff speak good English.

SKI SCHOOL
94/95 prices in lire
Monte Bianco
Classes 6 days
3hr: 10am-1pm
6 half-days: 170,000
Children's classes
Ages: over 6
6 half-days: 170,000
Private lessons
Hourly
47,000 for 1 to 2 people; each additional person 5,000

CHILDCARE
The Kinderheim at Plan Checrouit (845073) takes children from age 6 months, from 9.30 to 4pm. They can join ski school classes from 10am to 1pm.

GETTING THERE
Air Geneva, transfer 2hr. Turin, transfer 2hr.
Rail Pré-St-Didier (5km); regular buses from station.

PACKAGES
Bladon Lines, Collineige, Crystal, Enterprise, Inghams, Interski, Mark Warner, Ski Weekend, Ski West, Thomson, Ultimate

Entreves

Pre de Pascal

1 km

La Saxe

N

Villair

La Villette

La Villette

← Plan Checrouit

Dolonne

EATING OUT
Jolly Italian evenings

There is a great choice of restaurants.
Many of them make up for what they
lack in quality by serving enormous
portions. The touristy but very jolly
Maison de Filippo in Entrèves is for
gluttons – its speciality is a fixed-price,
36-dish menu. Further out, at Val
Ferret, Chalet Proment (Floriano's) is
attractively rustic, with a warm
welcome. K2 in Villair appears to have
deteriorated. A better bet for a serious
meal out is the central Pierre Alexis,
which has good food, service and
value. The Pizzeria Tunnel serves
enormous pizzas, and is very popular,
so book well in advance is advisable.
The Turistica is one of the cheapest,
good-value places in town. Again

booking is advisable. La Petite Bouffe,
at Dolonne, has a good set meal, the
price of which includes Clochard disco
entrance.

APRES-SKI
Stylish bar-hopping

Courmayeur has a lot of evening
atmosphere. Après-ski is centred on
lively bars and a couple of discos that
do not liven up till late. Ziggy's and
Steve's are popular bars. The American
49 is another, although this gets so
crowded that only a one-drink visit is
advisable. The Red Lion is worth a
visit if you're missing English pubs.
Our favourites are the Roma and the
back room of the Posta, both with
comfy armchairs to collapse in. The
Abat Jour disco plays 70s pop, whilst
Dolonne's excellent Clochard night
club has the latest sounds.

FOR NON-SKIERS
Very limited for sporty types

Inactive non-skiers will find the village
pleasant and may find the shops
diverting. There are also some
interesting excursions – by cable-car
up to Punta Helbronner and by bus to
Aosta or Chamonix. It's easy to go up
the main cable-car to Plan Checrouit
to meet skiers for lunch up the
mountain. But, considering the size of
the resort, there is surprisingly little
for sporty non-skiers to do.

STAYING UP THE MOUNTAIN
Why would you want to?

The idea of visiting Courmayeur and
not making the most of the charming
village seems perverse – if you're that
keen on getting onto the slopes in the
morning, this is probably the wrong
resort. But there are simple, cheap
rooms to be had at the Christiania at
Plan Checrouit.

Gressoney 1640m

Monterosa is Italy's answer to the Trois Vallées. Not surprisingly, the skiing of this little-known area is less extensive; it is also mostly easy. But it offers the same sensation of travelling around on skis, amid impressive scenery and a relaxed atmosphere. For piste skiers it is actually a two-valley system; for off-piste skiers this region has more to offer.

HOW IT RATES

The skiing

Snow	***
Extent	***
Advanced	**
Intermediates	****
Beginners	**
Convenience	****
Queues	****
Restaurants	**

The rest

Scenery	****
Resort charm	***
Not skiing	*

SKI FACTS

Altitude	1640m-2970m
Lifts	30
Pistes	70km
Green/Blue	31%
Red	63%
Black	6%
Artificial snow	12km

PACKAGES

Crystal

Champoluc Crystal

TOURIST OFFICE

Postcode 11020
Tel 010 39 (125)
366143
(125) 307876

THE RESORT

Gressoney la Trinité is a quiet, neat little village in a rather enclosed setting at the heart of the three-valley Monterosa ski area, east of Cervinia. It sits a couple of miles from the head of the narrow central valley, which runs roughly north-south. Gressoney St Jean, a more substantial and appealing village 5km (and 250m vertical) down the valley, has its own ski area, separate from the main system.

The main resort in the eastern valley is Champoluc; in the western valley it is Alagna. Expeditions by road to Cervinia, La Thuile and Courmayeur are possible.

THE SKIING

The Monterosa **ski area** is relatively extensive, and very scenic. The piste skiing is almost all easy (and very well groomed). The terrain is undulating and fragmented; runs are attractively varied, but many of the lifts serve only one or two defined pistes. The lift system is impressively modern, with several high-speed chair-lifts. There are lifts out of the village, but the main linking lifts are at the head of the valley, at Stafal.

La Trinité's local ski area is centred on the sunny shelf of Gabiet (2300m). Chairs and drags serve the area below it, and above it a long 12-person gondola goes up to Passo dei Salati (3000m). From here, a serious off-piste run makes the link with the pistes of the Alagna valley. You can descend to Orsia or Stafal (both in the Gressoney valley), where chair-lifts go up towards the Colle Bettaforca (2705m), the link with the Champoluc valley.

The area's **snow reliability** is good, thanks to altitude and extensive snowmaking on west-facing runs.

There is not much to interest **advanced skiers**, apart from one black of 700m vertical (most blacks on the badly printed piste map turn out to be blues). At Alagna there is a long black run (roughly 7km for only 850m vertical) from the top of the cable-car at Punta Indren (3260m). But there are great off-piste possibilities from the high points of the lift system in all three valleys, and some excellent heli-drops. Powder Byrne are running an adventure skiing course here this year.

For **intermediate** skiers who like to cover a bit of ground, the area is fine, with long runs from the ridges down into the valleys.

Beginners are adequately catered for on the lower slopes at La Trinité, but Champoluc's sunny area at Crest (1950m) is better.

There are long **cross-country** trails around St Jean, and shorter ones up the valley; but Brusson, in the Champoluc valley, has the best trails.

Only at weekends, when the Italians arrive, are there **queues**.

The **mountain restaurants** are adequate, no more; the Lys mountain refuge at Gabiet (with very simple food) is the most captivating.

The **ski school** doesn't get much chance to practise its English. As far as we know, there are no special facilities for **children**.

STAYING THERE

For keen skiers who don't mind isolation, **accommodation** at Stafal, at the head of the valley, is the best choice. The best hotel is the 4-star Monboso – a big modern chalet. At La Trinité, the main accommodation for skiers is half a mile outside the village, at the foot of the slopes.

Eating out possibilities are limited. **Après-ski** is very quiet; some discos may open up at weekends.

Non-skiers should go elsewhere.

STAYING IN THE OTHER VALLEYS

Champoluc is another attractive, quiet chalet-style village with a handful of hotels and only a couple of sports shops. Access to the Gressoney valley involves taking a series of lifts and runs across the mountainside to Colle Bettaforca – and much the same in reverse at the end of the day. The hotel Villa Anna Maria is a captivatingly creaky wooden chalet, tucked away amid trees a short walk from the lifts.

Only good skiers with plans to go off-piste should base themselves in **Alagna**. The piste skiing is very limited, and it does not include the connection to Gressoney.

Livigno 1815m

✔ Excellent snow record, and good snowmaking set-up

✔ Large choice of beginners' slopes

✔ Few lift queues

✔ Cheap by Alpine standards

✔ Cosmopolitan, friendly, informal resort

✔ Long, snowsure cross-country trails

✔ Improving lift network

✗ No difficult skiing

✗ Long airport transfers

✗ Skiing links across the valley depend on buses

✗ Peak-time buses overcrowded

✗ Very few non-skiing amenities

✗ Bleak setting – not a good place in bad weather

✗ Lack of really comfortable hotels bookable through tour operators

✗ Nightlife can disappoint– it's not as lively as many expect

Livigno may not be the most convenient of ski resorts, its history of internal politics having produced the most ill-conceived of ski areas, but it consistently pleases its clientele. This is because few resorts in Europe can rival Livigno for cheap and cheerful holidays that are also snowsure.

Livigno's duty-free status is an obvious attraction, but don't get the wrong idea: booze may be cheap in the shops, but they don't give it away in the bars, and the resort discourages rowdy behaviour (and remains relatively free of lager-louts). More important to its fans is Livigno's snow record, far superior to those of downmarket rivals such as eastern Europe, the Pyrenees and the smaller resorts of Austria's Tyrol. To supplement nature, Livigno has made an investment in snowmaking.

Lifts have been improved over the years too.

ORIENTATION

Livigno is an amalgam of three villages; the centres of the two peripheral ones, Santa Maria and San Rocco, are 4km apart, their fringes merging with central San Antonio. They sit in a wide, remote valley close to the Swiss border. The ski area spreads evenly over mountains either side, with lifts into both sections from San Antonio, and just the westerly half from San Rocco.

The area lift pass covers **Bormio** and **Santa Caterina**, an easy drive away to the south-east if the high pass is open, and a 6-day pass covers a day in **St Moritz** to the south-west, which is more reliably accessible. A road tunnel to the north gives reasonably easy access from Zürich and Munich.

SKI FACTS

Altitude	1815m-2795m
Lifts	29
Pistes	100km
Green/Blue	42%
Red	46%
Black	12%
Artificial snow	4km

 The resort

Livigno is a continuous string of hotels, bars and supermarkets lining a single secondary road running along a valley that is rather inconveniently wide for skiers.

The original hamlets of Santa Maria and San Rocco mark the 'village' boundaries, with the old San Antonio community between them being the nearest thing Livigno has to a centre. Here a cluster of banks, petrol stations, restaurants and shops surround a small church mid-way between the Mottolino and Costaccia lifts.

Buildings are a mixture of old and modern. Fortunately, construction controls have ensured that recent development has not produced any particular blots on the landscape. This allows Livigno a fair amount of Alpine charm.

The main road, a through-route, is constantly busy, and although it by-passes San Rocco it becomes intrusive in San Antonio and Santa Maria. Germans arriving in Livigno for duty-free shopping as well as skiing add to traffic nuisance.

 The skiing

The skiing appeals mainly to beginners and intermediates. There is quite a lot of it, at least in comparison with the other cheap and cheerful destinations that Livigno competes with.

THE SKI AREA
Improved links
There are three ski areas, all suitable for moderate and leisurely skiers. Thanks to a new lift last season, two of them are now reasonably well-linked.

The ridge of **Mottolino** is reached by a 12-person gondola (replacing a famously cold drag-lift) from Teola, a tiresome walk or a short bus-ride from San Antonio. As well as north-west-facing runs back towards Livigno from Monte della Neva, the high point at 2660m, there are north-east-facing pistes and lifts on the other side of the ridge above Trepalle. On the other side of the valley, closer to town, chairs in the middle of a row of nursery slopes take you up to **Costaccia** (2370m), where a long high-speed quad chair-lift was opened last season along the

LIFT PASSES

94/95 prices in lire
Alta Valtellina
Covers all lifts in Livigno, Bormio (40km away, but 1hr 30min by a very poor road), Valdidentro (30km away) and Santa Caterina (5km away) plus one free day in St Moritz (6-day pass+).
Main pass
1-day pass 42,000
6-day pass 205,000 (low season 180,000 – 12% off)
Senior citizens
Over 65: 6-day pass 140,000 (32% off)
Children
Under 13: 6-day pass 140,000 (32% off)
Short-term passes
Afternoon pass for Livigno only 30,000.
Notes Day pass price is for Livigno lifts only.
Alternative passes
Livigno only pass for up to 2 days (adult 2-day 80,000).

SKI SCHOOL

94/95 prices in lire
Livigno
Classes 6 days 2hr: 9am-11am or 11am-1pm
6 2hr days: 100,000
Children's classes
Ages: from 5
6 2hr days: 95,000
Private lessons
Hourly 40,000 for 1hr; each additional person 6,000

Livigno Inverno-Estate
Classes 6 days 2hr: 9am-11am or 11am-1pm
6 2hr days: 100,000
Children's classes
Ages: from 5
6 2hr days: 95,000
Private lessons
Hourly 40,000 for 1hr; each additional person 6,000

OTHER SCHOOLS

Livigno Italy
Azzurra Livigno

ridge towards the **Carosello** sector. (Unbelievably, this long-awaited new lift did not find its way on to the resort's piste map.) Route-finding on the linking run beyond this lift – to the mid-station of the Carosello gondola – is not easy. The Carosello skiing is usually accessed by the optimistically named Carosello 3000 gondola at San Rocco, which goes up to 2750m. Most of the runs return towards the valley, but there are a couple of runs on the back of the mountain and the option of a gentle cruise along the ridge to Costaccia.

New quad and triple chair-lifts are planned for this winter in the Carosello sector, replacing existing drags. And there are less-certain plans to replace the long Sponda drag at Mottolino with an even longer quad.

SNOW RELIABILITY
Very good, despite no glacier
Livigno's ski area is high (you spend most of your time skiing around the 2500m mark), and with snowmakers backing up nature on the lower slopes of Mottolino and Costaccia, the valley has one of the longest of ski seasons.

FOR ADVANCED SKIERS
Unsuitable
The piste map shows a few black runs but these are not difficult. Nor is the off-piste.

FOR INTERMEDIATE SKIERS
Flattering slopes
Few pistes follow the fall line directly, and consequently good intermediates looking for a challenge are liable to be disappointed. Learning to ski off-piste may be their best option. The runs on the back of Carosello down to Federia are more challenging than most, and bumpy at times. Moderate skiers have virtually the whole area at their disposal. The long run beneath the Mottolino gondola is one of the best. Leisurely types have several long cruises. Passo d'Eira-Teola, Monte della Neve-Sponda drag, and Costaccia's easy skiing are all enjoyable. The run from Vetta Blesaccia to Livigno must be one of the longest motorways in the Alps.

FOR BEGINNERS
Excellent but scattered slopes
An array of nursery slopes along the sunny lower flanks of Costaccia and other slopes dotted around the valley make Livigno an excellent novices' resort. There are lots of longer runs suitable for fast learners and near-beginners – see above.

CROSS-COUNTRY
Good snow, bleak setting
Long snowsure trails (50km in total) follow the valley floor, making Livigno a good choice, except that the scenery is bleak and the road not usually far away from the trail. Staying in Santa Maria is best, being close to a nicer trail along the Val Federia. There is a specialist cross-country school. The resort organises major cross-country races.

QUEUES
Few problems these days
Lift queues are not usually a problem; the Mottolino gondola relieved the major bottleneck. There may be a short delay for the Carosello gondola on holiday mornings. Overcrowded pistes at Mottolino, particularly at weekends, are a greater problem, as are queues for buses and mountain restaurants.

MOUNTAIN RESTAURANTS
Neither good nor bad
Whilst there are few great culinary delights by the standards of some Italian resorts, many reporters have commented on the consistent adequacy of huts. No restaurants attract particularly negative remarks. The self-service places at the top of Mottolino and Carosello, for example, are perfectly acceptable, and there are some more charming places lower down. One of the best is not marked on the piste map – Mama's at Passo d'Eira, at the low point of the Mottolino ridge. The welcoming Tea del Vidal is in the same sector, making Mottolino the best bet for serious lunchers, though Costaccia's Tea del Plan is also pleasantly rustic and sunny, with good food. When skiing Carosello, lunch in the valley at the hotel Sporting (close to the gondola station) is also a popular option – excellent cheap pizza.

SKI SCHOOL
Short lessons a drawback
There are several schools, all with a good reputation, except for a tendency toward large classes. Many visitors consider the two-hour-per-day lessons too short.

FACILITIES FOR CHILDREN
Bring your own
The schools run children's classes, but there are no special arrangements for all-day care, with or without ski tuition.

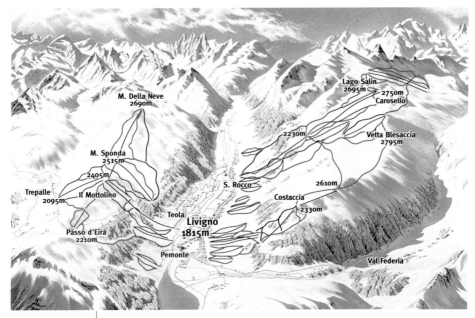

PACKAGES

Airtours, Crystal, Enterprise, Inghams, Panorama, Thomson

CHILDCARE

There are no all-day care facilities.

 # Staying there

In such a long village with fragmented skiing, location of accommodation can be important. The position of your hotel can come as a surprise. Tour operators tend to be a little vague at times, stating that a particular hotel is 'close to the lifts'. Which lifts?

Beginners should avoid staying in San Rocco (the Carosello lift end of town), because your ski school is likely to meet a bus-ride away in San Antonio. The latter is the best all-round location now that there is lift access from Costaccia to the Lago Salin sector – though it will still be quicker (and warmer, in January) to take a bus out to the Carosello gondola. Much of the nightlife is in San Antonio.

HOW TO GO
Lots of hotels, some apartments
Livigno has an enormous range of hotels and a number of apartments.
Chalets Crystal are the only tour operator with catered chalets here. They have a couple of simple, good-value apartment conversions – one pleasantly rustic, the other newly built – 5 minutes from the Carosello gondola.
Hotels Most of the hotels are small 2- and 3-star places, with a couple of 4-stars out of the centre.
£££ Intermonti Huge, modern 4-star with all mod cons (including a pool); above the village – reachable off-piste from Mottolino.

££ Europa One of the better 3-stars, within walking distance of the Mottolino gondola and village centre.
££ Bivio Bang in the centre of things, close to ski school and lifts; the only hotel in central Livigno with a pool.
££ Steinbock Nice little place only five minutes' walk from some nursery slopes.
££ Montanina Good 2-star in the village centre.
££ Sporting Basic but satisfactory little hotel, close to Carosello gondola.
££ Camana Veglia Charming old wooden chalet with popular restaurant, well placed in San Antonio.
£ Silvestri Well liked by several reporters, reasonably handy for lifts, ski school and nightlife
Self-catering All the big tour operators that come here have apartment options. Most are similarly cheap and cheerful, position being perhaps the most important thing to consider. The Primavera apartments (Inghams) are more comfortable than their rustic exterior suggests, and well placed for Costaccia. Thomson's Bait da Bark are reasonably well appointed, and convenient for the Carosello gondola. Airtours have basic places well located for nightlife and the Mottolino gondola. Panorama have cheap, very simple apartments.

EATING OUT
Value for money
Livigno has an appetising range of good (though mainly simple) restaurants, many hotel-based. Hotel Concordia has some of the best

CRYSTAL HOLIDAYS

helped us to compile the Eating out and Après-ski sections. Our thanks to them.

ACTIVITIES

Indoor Sauna, gym, body-building, games room, indoor golf and tennis club
Outdoor Cleared paths, skating rink, snow-mobiles, sleigh rides, para-gliding

TOURIST OFFICE

Postcode 23030
Tel 010 39 (342) 996379
Fax 996881

cooking in town, and the Camana Veglia restaurant is superior to the hotel's 2-star rating. Mario's has one of the largest menus in town, serving seafood, fondue and steaks in addition to the ubiquitous pizza and pasta. The Bellavista is a charming little restaurant. Bait dal Ghet has excellent pizzas, the Rusticana wholesome, cheap food. The Vecchia Lanterna, Ambassador and Mirage are others worthy of mention.

APRES-SKI
Lively but disappoints some
Many reporters have expressed disappointment in the nightlife. It's not that there isn't plenty of action, but simply that the scene is quieter than anticipated – given the hype about Livigno's duty-free status. In fact it's this very status that has tended to restrict the après-ski scene. It's largely given over to drinking, with few alternatives. Another drawback is that the best places are rather dotted about, leaving the village as a whole rather lacking atmosphere. The San Rocco end of town is particularly quiet, and ideal for those looking for peaceful surroundings.

There's not much of a four o'clock scene. Most skiers return to their hotels for a quiet drink. Galli's pub in San Antonio (not to be confused with the Galli in San Rocco) is popular with lively Brits at such times. Most after-dinner nightlife doesn't really get going till after 10pm. Galli's is again popular, notably for its music, games and karaoke.

Foxi's cellar video bar is more Italian and stylish. Mario's is another good video bar with an organist (livelier than it sounds!). The Underground pub is a cheap and cheerful, noisy place. The Cielo is a chic and

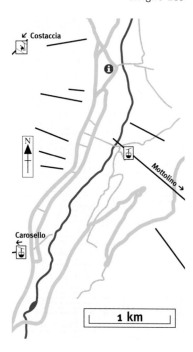

expensive nightclub with live music, popular with Italians. Brits tend to prefer the less sophisticated Koleodis disco. Other après-ski is limited to a few tour-rep-organised events such as early evening snowmobiling and a party night with games.

FOR NON-SKIERS
Disappointing but improving
Livigno is not a good place for non-skiers. Walks are uninspiring and there is no sports centre or public swimming pool. The few hotel pools are kept for the exclusive use of guests. Excursions to Bormio and St Moritz are the most popular things to do, although snowmobiling, ice skating and a new indoor golf and tennis centre may keep a few people happy.

Madesimo 1545m

Madesimo falls between stools – its steep skiing is too tough for some, too limited for others. The village is old but lacks real charm. The nursery slopes are good, but there are few easy runs to progress to. But Madesimo is gaining fans, due primarily to low prices.

THE RESORT

Madesimo sits in a remote, pretty side valley a two- to three-hour drive north from Bergamo which ends in a dramatic hairpin bend ascent to the resort. The village claims 17th-century origins and has old farm buildings to prove it, some of them converted into bars and restaurants. But the remainder of the village is a random assortment of piecemeal modern development. Pitched roofs and timber are evident, but so too is concrete. The delightful old church, narrow streets and little shops in its centre are overlooked by what appears to be a hideous airport control tower (the hotel Torre).

THE SKIING

A two-stage cable-car is the primary lift into the **ski area**, with chair and drag alternatives to the first section. Most runs return straight back towards the village, but the top station accesses pistes on the far side of the mountain. The altitude is respectable, but most of the slopes get too much sun for the **snow** to be particularly reliable.

Advanced skiers need the upper section to be open so that they can take on the famous Canalone runs – a long, consistently steep black gunbarrel which keeps its snow well and is therefore not usually as terrifying as its reputation suggests.

The best **intermediate** runs also start from the top station, dropping down into the beautiful Valle di Lei area, separate from the rest of the skiing. The reds descending from the cable-car mid-station are also very pleasant, passing through pretty woodland. Some of the easier runs have steeper sections that could prove awkward for nervous or inexperienced skiers. The nursery slopes are fine, but improving **beginners** have few really easy pistes to graduate to.

There's plenty of **cross-country** skiing dotted around the area, but you need a car to reach most of it.

There are weekend **queues** for the cable-car, but otherwise there are few lift delays.

The **mountain restaurants** are not particularly appealin.

Having been popular with British school groups, Madesimo has plenty of **ski school** instructors who speak some English. Tuition is reportedly good and classes not too large.

There are no public **children's facilities**, but the Cascata et Cristallo 4-star hotel has a Mini club for children aged 4 or more. Madesimo is, however, better suited to families with older children who can ski quite well.

STAYING THERE

The village centre is a tight cluster of buildings with both main lift stations a short walk away. A 500m strip of ribbon development finishes at the nursery slopes.

A fair choice of **hotels** is available through tour operators. The Emet is the more traditional of the two 4-stars. The Cascata et Cristallo is a large, modern, multi-amenity place. The Ferrè is highly recommended: a small modern 3-star hotel in the centre with 'first-class service, good-sized rooms and excellent food'; it has a popular après-ski bar. The Liro and the Soldanella are small, simple 2-stars in a central position. Inghams offer well-equipped but poorly positioned **self-catering** apartments.

Eating out is one of Madesimo's delights. Taverna Verosa is atmospheric, good value and popular for pizzas cooked over an open fire. Osteria Vecchia is a charming, traditional place with some of the best and most expensive food in town. Dogana Vegia is one of the original 17th-century village buildings, and serves tasty local specialities. Go to La Clessidra for good fondue. Tec de L'Urs is also good-value.

Après-ski is fairly quiet. There are several pleasant cafés for a tea-time cappucino and cakes. Later the log-cabin-style Cantinone bar in the hotel Andossi has a good atmosphere. The piano cellar bar in the Meridiana and the Ferrè are other focal spots. The Facsimile Videoteque and Queen's are discos that liven up at weekends. Tour reps organise several events.

It's not a place for **non-skiers**, unless they just like walks and excursions. The nearby medieval town of Chiavenna, and a trip to St Moritz, are highlights.

Madonna di Campiglio 1520m

HOW IT RATES

The skiing
Snow	★★★
Extent	★★★
Advanced	★★
Intermediates	★★★★
Beginners	★★★★
Convenience	★★★
Queues	★★★
Restaurants	★★★★

The rest
Scenery	★★★★
Resort charm	★★★★
Not skiing	★★

SKI FACTS
Altitude	1520m-2505m
Lifts	49
Pistes	150km
Green/Blue	43%
Red	41%
Black	16%
Artificial snow	40km

PACKAGES
Crystal, Inghams

Folgarida Equity Total Ski

Marilleva Winterski

TOURIST OFFICE
Postcode 38084
Tel 010 39 (465)
42000
Fax 40404

Madonna is a sort of poor person's Cortina – an attractive village amid splendid Dolomite scenery, with an almost exclusively Italian clientele. Folgarida and Marilleva, with which it shares quite an extensive ski area, have a history of British group and school package business. Madonna is a rather more upmarket and rounded resort that many intermediates would enjoy.

THE RESORT
Madonna is a pleasant, traditional village that has spread widely across its wooded valley beneath the impressive Brenta Dolomites. It is on a through-road, but most of the traffic is local and the road bypasses the focal Piazza Brenta Alta. There is another area of development about 1km to the south, and between the two a frozen lake that is used for skating and other diversions.

The resort attracts an affluent Italian clientele, with almost as many 4-star hotels as 3-stars, and the kind of smart clothes shops that you also find in Courmayeur and Cortina. A high proportion of Madonna's customers potter about the village during the day, and promenading is an important ritual in the early evening.

THE SKIING
The skiing, like that in other Dolomite areas, provides short runs of mainly intermediate difficulty. There are three **ski areas** around Madonna itself, each with a handful of lifts and runs. Cable-cars from the edges of the village serve Cinque Laghi to the west and Pradalago to the north, and a rather more peripheral gondola accesses Monte Spinale to the east. Just outside the village and 130m vertical above it, another gondola serves a fourth sector, Passo Groste – the highest area, reaching 2505m. This is also reachable from Spinale. Pradalago is linked by lift and piste to Monte Vigo (2180m), where the ski areas of Folgarida and Marilleva meet.

Although many of the slopes are sunny, they are at a fair altitude and all three resorts have invested heavily in snowmakers. As a result, **snow reliability** is reasonable.

Madonna's status as a World Cup racing resort should not lead **advanced skiers** to expect a lot. Even the 3-Tre race-course is no more than a steep red. Pista Nera is a good mogul field in the Folgarida section, and the Spinale and Groste sections can provide good off-piste skiing.

Cinque Laghi, Madonna's racing mountain, is ideal for good **intermediates**. Moderate skiers will love the area, and will have no difficulty exploring virtually the whole network. The tree-lined runs above Folgarida are particularly lovely pistes. Groste and Pradalago have long easy runs for the less experienced, although the former can get crowded.

It's a good resort for **beginners**, provided they don't mind taking a bus out to the main nursery slopes at Campo Carlo Magno. There are excellent long runs to progress to.

Madonna is big on **cross-country** quality if not quantity. The 30km of trails are very pretty, running through the woods over the pass towards Folgarida. There is a specialist school.

Except at Christmas and New Year, there are few **queues**. The Spinale cable-car is the only real bottleneck.

The **mountain restaurants** are a highlight, serving good food in civilised settings, with lovely views.

Adult **ski school** classes are disappointingly short – two hours – and little English is spoken. Tuition in snowboarding is commonplace here.

STAYING THERE
There is a wide choice of **hotels**, and although there is a ski-bus it's best to think first about location. The 4-star Miramonti takes some beating for all-round convenience. The Spinale Clubhotel (with pool) is close to the Spinale gondola. Hotel Bellavista is an excellent 2-star right by the Pradalago lift; it has friendly staff, but has four storeys and no lift. Some self-catering accommodation is sold by tour ops.

There are 20 **restaurants** to choose from, limited to mainly Italian dishes. Belvedere da Lele, Le Roi and Stube Diana are recommended.

Chalet Laghetto is the most atmospheric immediate **après-ski** place. Later, Des Alpes has a large dance bar, Bar Suisse is a popular place for poseurs, and the Stork Club has a an American bar and disco. The best disco is Contrasto.

For **non-skiers**, Madonna is quite limited. Window-shopping and beautiful walks are the most popular things to do. Otherwise there are excursions to Lake Garda, Verona, Venice and Innsbruck.

Sauze d'Oulx 1510m

✔ Large and uncrowded ski area suitable for most abilities

✔ Linked into Milky Way

✔ Mix of open and tree-lined runs provides skiing in all conditions

✔ Entertaining nightlife

✔ Some scope for off-piste adventures

✔ One of the cheapest major resorts there is

✘ Brashness and Britishness of resort will not suit everyone

✘ Antiquated lifts in some areas, causing peak-time queues

✘ Lack of challenging piste skiing for good skiers

✘ Poor snow reliability in late season

Sauze d'Oulx is still living down the reputation that it had in the early 1980s of being prime lager-lout territory. Its nickname – 'Suzy does it' – only served to increase the expectations of those who went there. Then it faded from the British package holiday scene – partly because it had serious snow problems before the rest of the Alps. Now, it's back, but in slightly reconstructed form. The village still has something of the feel of a Spanish summer resort relocated to the Alps, with bars and shops conspicuously aimed at the British. But it's no longer fair to liken the place to Benidorm; the resort's nightlife is lively, but the extreme behaviour of previous years has been curbed and deliberate attempts are being made to solicit more respectable customers. There always were two sides to the resort – the downmarket package hotels and brash bars alongside the comfortable second homes and one or two smart restaurants catering for affluent Italians. The two now seem much more in balance.

The ski area offers little to challenge the more advanced skier, but it is attractively varied and prettily wooded, and its size and good ski school make it a good choice for improving skiers who wish to get some kilometres under their belts with the minimum expense.

People looking for an affordable combination of serious skiing and animated nightlife, not just wild nights, could do a lot worse than Sauze. And those for whom nightlife matters little – families, for example – need not stay away.

ORIENTATION

Sauze d'Oulx sits on a gentle mountain shelf facing north-west across the Valle di Susa. Chair-lifts go up from the top of the village and from two points on its fringes. There is also a chair-lift into the skiing from the nearby, lower hamlet of **Jouvenceaux**.

The area is part of the extensive 'Milky Way' region, with easy access to the slopes of **Sestriere** and **Sansicario**. **Claviere** and **Montgenèvre** (just over the French border) are part of the same network, but a longer trek, and more quickly reached by car than on skis.

Excursions by road are possible beyond Montgenèvre to **Briançon** and **Serre-Chevalier**, and to **Bardonecchia**.

SKI FACTS

Figures relate to the whole Milky Way area

Altitude	1390m-2825m
Lifts	97
Pistes	400km
Green/Blue	12%
Red	67%
Black	21%
Artificial snow	65km

The resort

Although it's not immediately obvious, Sauze has an attractive old core, with narrow, twisting streets and the occasional carved stone drinking fountain; houses have huge stone slabs serving as roof slates.

Most of the resort, however, is modern and undistinguished, made

up of block-like hotels, relieved by the occasional chalet, spreading down the steep hillside from the foot of the ski slopes to the village centre and beyond. Despite the shift in clientele, the centre is still quite lively at night, with late-closing bars that are usually quite full, as well as a handful of discos that do most of their business at the weekend.

Out of the bustle of the centre, where most of the bars and nightclubs are located, there are quiet wooded residential areas full of secluded apartment blocks, and a number of good restaurants are also tucked out of the way of the front line.

Traffic roams freely through the village, which can become congested both in the mornings and in the evenings as cars vie for the most convenient parking spaces and the quickest ways out of town respectively. This can also lead to the roads becoming slushy and dirty during the day and icy and

LIFT PASSES

94/95 prices in lire
La Via Lattea
Covers all lifts in
Sauze d'Oulx,
Sestriere, Sansicario,
Cesana and Clavière.
Beginners Points
book (85 points
95,000), with lifts
costing from 1 to 12
points.
Main pass
1-day pass 39,000
6-day pass 215,000
(low season 195,000
– 9% off)
Children
Under 13: 6-day pass
193,000 (10% off)
Under 8: free pass
Short-term passes
Some single ascent
passes and afternoon
pass (27,000).
Notes Includes one
free day in each of:
Alpe d'Huez, Les Deux
Alpes, Serre-Chevalier
or Puy-St-Vincent.
One day extension for
Montgenèvre 17,000.
One day extension for
Pragelato 10,000.
Alternative passes
La Via Lattea VIP card
also covers
Montgenèvre and
Pragelato.

treacherous at night – a hazard in a resort with few pavements. As the snow withdraws up the mountain later in the season, the dirt stays behind, and one reporter complained of the streets being particularly dusty.

The area is surrounded by trees, and on a good day the views across the Valle di Susa, to the towering mountains forming the border with France, can be quite spectacular.

 # The skiing

Sauze's skiing is excellent intermediate terrain. The piste grading fluctuates from year to year if you believe the resort's map – and we're not sure we've caught up with the latest changes from blue to red and red to blue. Never mind: there is plenty of skiing for intermediates of any shade, and not much to amuse better skiers.

The same might be said of the whole extensive Milky Way area, of which Sauze is one extreme.

THE SKI AREA
Big and varied enough for most
Sauze's local skiing is spread across a broad wooded bowl above the resort, ranging from west- to north-facing.

The main lifts are chairs up to **Clotes** from the top of the village and up from the western fringes to **Sportinia**. This is a mid-mountain congregation area in a sunny clearing in the woods, with a ring of restaurants and hotels (see Staying up the mountain, page 291) and a small nursery area.

The high-point of the system is **Monte Fraiteve**. From here you can ski westwards down to Sansicario and on down to chair-lifts near Cesana Torinese that link with the skiing of Claviere and then Montgenèvre, in France – the opposite end of the Milky Way. You can also ski southwards to Sestriere, though this is more often done from the lower point of Col Basset. And you can ski back towards Sauze, on some of the steepest terrain in the area.

As in so many Italian resorts, piste marking, direction signing and piste map design are not taken very seriously, and finding your way can be tricky at times.

The linked skiing of Sestriere and Montgenèvre is dealt with in separate chapters.

SNOW RELIABILITY
Poor in late season
Sauze's very poor snow record in the mid-1980s was mainly to do with a lack of snowfall. In normal winters, a bigger worry is that many of the slopes get a lot of afternoon sun. At these modest altitudes, late-season conditions are far from reliable. There is snowmaking on a couple of slopes, notably the key home run from Clotes to the village.

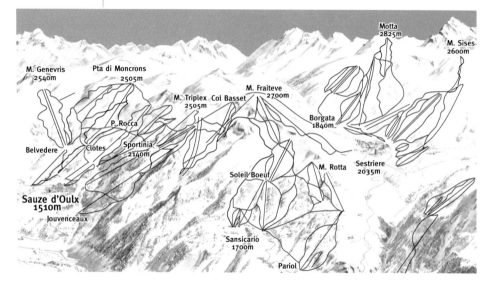

SKI SCHOOL

94/95 prices in lire

Sauze Sportinia
Classes 6 days
3hr: 10am-1pm
6 3hr days: 160,000
Children's classes
Ages: from 6
6 3hr days: 160,000
Private lessons
Hourly
41,000 for 1hr

Sauze d'Oulx
Classes 6 days
3hr: 10am-1pm
6 3hr days: 170,000
Children's classes
Ages: from 4
6 3hr days: 170,000
Private lessons
Hourly
42,000 for 1hr

Sauze Project
Italian-speaking
school only

CHILDCARE

The village
kindergarten (858396)
has English and
Italian staff and takes
children aged from 6
months to 6 years,
from 9am to 5pm.
You have to provide
lunch, but it can be
heated up.

PACKAGES

Airtours, Crystal,
Enterprise, Inghams,
Neilson, Ski Partners,
SkiBound, Thomson
Jouvenceaux Neilson
Sansicario Equity
Total Ski, Neilson

GETTING THERE

Air Turin, transfer 2hr.

Rail Oulx (5km);
frequent buses.

FOR ADVANCED SKIERS
Head off-piste

Very little of the piste skiing is
challenging. Virtually at opposite ends
of Sauze's local area are the best slopes
– a high, north-facing run from the
shoulder of M Fraiteve, and the sunny
slopes below M Montcrons. The main
interest is in going off-piste. There are
plenty of minor opportunities within
the piste network, but the highlights
are long, top-to-bottom descents of up
to 1300m vertical from M Fraiteve,
ending (snow permitting) at villages
dotted along the valleys. The best-
known of these runs (which were until
recently marked on the piste map) is
the Rio Nero, down to the road near
Oulx. When snow low down is poor,
some of these runs can be cut short at
Jouvenceaux or Sansicario.

FOR INTERMEDIATE SKIERS
Splendid when there's snow

Practically the whole area is skiable by
confident intermediates. For less
confident skiers there is plenty of
scope, though the piste grading
doesn't help by picking out only the
very easiest runs in blue.

At the higher levels where the slopes
are open, the terrain is interestingly
lumpy, allowing a choice of route.
Lower down are pretty runs through
the woods, where the main
complication can be route-finding.
The mountainside is broken up by
gullies, and pistes that appear to be
quite close together may have no easy
connections between them.

FOR BEGINNERS
A reasonable choice

Sauze is not ideal for beginners: its
village-level slopes are a bit on the
steep side and the main nursery area is
up the mountain at Sportinia. But
there is easy skiing to progress to, and
a good ski school in a cheap and
cheerful resort is a formula that rightly
appeals to many.

FOR CROSS-COUNTRY
Severely limited, even with snow

There is very little cross-country
skiing, and it can't be considered
reliable for snow.

QUEUES
No real problems

There may be 10-minute waits at
Sportinia when ski school classes are
setting off or immediately after lunch,
but otherwise the system has few
bottlenecks. Many lifts are ancient
(the recently installed high-speed
quad up to Sportinia is a conspicuous

exception), and breakdowns on drag-
lifts may be a bigger nuisance than
queues.

MOUNTAIN RESTAURANTS
Some pleasant possibilities

The hotel Capricorno at Clotes is one
of the most civilised and appealing
lunch-spots in the Alps. It is not
cheap, though. There are more modest
restaurants at the mid-mountain lift
stations across the mountainside, with
the main concentration at Sportinia,
where deck chairs come free with a
drink or meal.

SKI SCHOOL
Good reports

This is one Italian resort where a lack
of English in the ski schools is not
likely to be a problem. Equally
importantly, reports suggest that
tuition is enthusiastic and effective.
Even in a class of 12 – not excessive,
but hardly ideal – one reporter says
'everyone got great value'. Classes are
only half-day, but at least they give
three hours' tuition.

FACILITIES FOR CHILDREN
Consider Neilson

As well as the resort kindergarten
(which has from some English staff),
there is the possibility of plugging into
the arrangements Neilson offer at the
hotel des Amis down in Jouvenceaux:
a crèche for children aged 6 months to
2 years, and a children's club for those
aged 3 to 8.

 # Staying there

The resort spreads quite widely, but
most of the hotels are reasonably
central and location would be fairly
unimportant were it not for the short
but steep hill that separates the central
area from the foot of the slopes. As it
is, staying near the slopes is the best
bet. There is a ski-bus, and many
hotels need it, particularly for getting
to the Sportinia chair; it runs fairly
regularly but not frequently (every 20
minutes) and gets very crowded in the
morning peak.

HOW TO GO
Packaged hotels dominate

All the major mainstream operators
offer hotel packages here, but there are
also one or two chalets offered by
those same operators.
Chalets As well as the Crystal chalet
(see Staying up the mountain),
Neilson have a simple chalet, with log
fire, 1km outside the village.

CRYSTAL HOLIDAYS

helped us to compile the eating out and après-ski sections. Our thanks to them.

ACTIVITIES

Indoor Bowling, cinema, sauna, massage
Outdoor Artificial skating rink, floodlit tobogganing, torchlit descents, heli-skiing from Sestriere

TOURIST OFFICE

Postcode 10050
Tel 010 39 (122) 85009
Fax 85497

Hotels Simple 2-star and 3-star hotels form the core of the holiday accommodation, with a couple of 4-stars and some more basic places.
£££ Capricorno At Clotes – see Staying up the mountain.
££ Hermitage Neat chalet-style hotel in about the best position for skiing – beside the home piste from Clotes.
££ Gran Baita Comfortable place in quiet, central back-street, with 'excellent' food and good rooms, some with spectacular sunset views from their balconies.
££ Biancaneve Recommended despite 'smallish' rooms; close to centre.
££ Villa Daniela Pleasant chalet with popular restaurant, on main piazza.
££ Des Amis Down in Jouvenceaux, but close to bus stop; small, simple hotel run by Anglo-Italian couple, with childcare facilities offered through Neilson.
Self-catering There are apartments and chalets available locally, but none as far as we know through UK tour operators.

EATING OUT
Caters for all tastes and pockets
Typical Italian banquets of five or six courses can be had in the upmarket Don Vincenzo and U Cantun restaurants. The Italian chef at the Del Falco cooks a particularly good three-course 'skier's menu'. In the old town, Del Borgo serves perhaps the best pizza in town, and has a very friendly atmosphere. Nearby is La Griglia, which is full of character and does a good steak. U Lampione's is the place to go for 'pub grub' – good-value Chinese, Mexican and Indian food.

APRES-SKI
Suzy does it with more dignity
Once favoured almost solely by large groups of youngsters, some of whom were very rowdy, Sauze now attracts middle-aged skiers, families, couples and more sober young people, and has the appropriate nightlife for them. But it's still in a different league from places over the border in France.
The Assietta terrace bar is popular for catching the last rays of the sun after skiing. The more discerning then move on to the pleasant Scotch Bar, while nearby, the once famous Andy Capp's Pub still attracts punters looking for a 'home from home'. Other early-evening places include the Max Bar, popular for its satellite TV, the small cocktail bar Moncrons, and the U Lampione Pub in the old town.

After dinner, more places warm up. Those who like to rub shoulders with the locals should try the small Cotton Club bar for a chic aperitif. Gossips is popular with both nationalities thanks to its band, which plays six nights a week, covering everything from Frank Sinatra to Bon Jovi. Torinese weekenders pack it out on Saturday nights. The Derby Bar has some fun games such as nail bashing. Gran Trun is a downmarket relic of the 'old Sauze', popular for its pool table. The two discos are quite different: Newlife is a large club which has special promotions, theme nights and so on; Schuss is an intimate little place.
Tour reps organise various activities, including torchlit descents, bowling and 'broomball' on the ice rink. There's also a karaoke bar, mostly frequented by locals; once a week it's taken over by Brits for a quiz and party night.

FOR NON-SKIERS
Go elsewhere
Sauze is not a particularly pleasant place in which to while away the days: the shopping is limited, all the lifts are chairs, and there are few non-skiing activities.

STAYING UP THE MOUNTAIN
You pays your money . . .
In most resorts, staying up the mountain is an amusing thing to do and is often economical – but usually you pay the price of accepting simple accommodation. Here, the reverse applies. The 4-star Capricorno, up at Clotes, is one of the most comfortable hotels in Sauze, certainly the most attractive and by a wide margin the most expensive. It's a charming little chalet beside the piste with a smart restaurant and terrace (a very popular spot for a good lunch on the mountain) and only eight bedrooms.
Not quite in the same league are the places up at Sportinia, of which the best is the 3-star Monte Triplex. Crystal offer packages to the hotel's annex, the Turistico. They also have a chalet here, with access to the facilities of the Monte Triplex.

Sansicario 1700m
If any resort is ideally placed for exploration of the Milky Way, it is Sansicario. It is a smart, purpose-built, self-contained resort mainly consisting of apartments linked by monorail to the little shopping precinct. The 40-room Rio Envers is a comfortable, quite expensive hotel.

Selva/Sella Ronda 1565m

HOW IT RATES

The skiing

Snow	****
Extent	*****
Advanced	***
Intermediates	*****
Beginners	****
Convenience	***
Queues	***
Restaurants	****

The rest

Scenery	*****
Resort charm	***
Not skiing	***

✔ Enormous, beautiful ski area, particularly well suited to intermediate skiers

✔ Very impressive snowmaking set-up – the most extensive in Europe

✔ Attractive, panoramic mountain huts with good food

✔ Much improved lift system with few bad bottlenecks

✔ Good nursery slopes

✔ Best nightlife in the Sella Ronda

✔ Excellent value

✘ Small proportion of tough runs

✘ High proportion of short runs, few long ones

✘ English not universal in ski school

✘ Not the most attractive of the Dolomite ski villages

✘ Erratic snow record; and heavy dependence on artificial snow and modest top heights make skiing vulnerable to warm weather

The skiing of the Sella Ronda has been revolutionised over recent years by heavy investment in both the lift system and artificial snowmaking. Both are now among the best and most extensive in Europe. Combine that with extraordinarily picturesque Dolomite scenery, a lift pass which covers over 460 lifts and 1100km of runs, cheap Italian prices and jolly mountain refuges, and you have a compelling case for going on a skiing holiday there.

Only expert skiers who find the lack of challenging skiing frustrating will be disappointed. If what you want is a feeling of travelling around on skis, there's little to beat the Sella Ronda – a trip around the Gruppo Sella massif that is easily skiable in a day by an average intermediate. On the way round you will hit many separate ski areas that have local areas well worth spending time on.

If you don't want to stay in Selva there are plenty of smaller, quiet, attractive places on the circuit to base yourself in.

ORIENTATION

Selva is the biggest of the linked resorts that encircle the enormous Gruppo Sella massif, making up the Sella Ronda ski circus. It straggles along a road which follows the Val Gardena, and is now virtually merged with the next village of Santa Cristina. Gondolas rise in two directions. One heads east from the top of the nursery slopes towards Colfosco and Corvara and the clockwise route round the Sella Ronda. The other heads south from the village itself to Ciampinoi and the anti-clockwise route. Spreading far afield, the skiing takes in numerous villages, including **Colfosco, Corvara, Arabba, Canazei, Ortisei** and **San Cassiano. Cortina** is an easy excursion if the roads are open. Its ski area, like many others reachable by car, is covered by the Dolomiti Superski pass.

The resort

Selva is a long roadside village which suffers from traffic but retains a fair level of charm. It has traditional-style architecture, with an attractive central church. And it enjoys a lovely setting among trees beneath the impressive pink-tinged walls of the Gruppo Sella massif and Sassolungo.

Despite its World Cup fame (it's known as Val Gardena, the name of the valley) and animated atmosphere, Selva is neither upmarket nor brash. It is essentially a good-value, lively but civilised family resort with none of the fur coats, poseurs, trendies or ski bums of some large, well-known places. The quite newly available short transfer from hassle-free Verona airport is another plus point.

The area is famous for its wood carvings and you'll find them everywhere – on lamp-posts, doorways, interiors and for sale in shops. The locals have their own Ladino dialect, which has resisted being absorbed into either German or Italian. The main language, however,

is German – as are most of the visitors. Place names are normally given in both German and Italian. Selva is also known as Wolkenstein and the Gardena valley as Gröden. For many years the area was under Austrian rule and the influence is still strong.

The skiing

There really is a vast amount of skiing here, all amid stunning scenery and practically all of it ideally suited to intermediate skiers who don't mind shortish runs. You can set off for the day, pick an area that takes your fancy and explore the local skiing. Or you can set off on the trip round the Sella Ronda circuit.

THE SKI AREA
High mileage piste excursions
A gondola and parallel-running chair go up from Selva to **Ciampinoi**, from where several pistes spread out across the mountain and lead back down to Selva, **Santa Cristina** and **Plan de Gralba**. These include the famous World Cup downhill run which takes

SKI FACTS

Altitude 1230m-2520m
Lifts	86
Pistes	175km
Green/Blue	29%
Red	57%
Black	14%
Artificial snow	78km

place in mid-December each year. From Plan de Gralba, you can head off towards **Passo Sella**, **Canazei** and the rest of the Sella Ronda.

Across the valley from the Ciampinoi gondola is a short chair which links with the Dantercëpies gondola. This accesses the Sella Ronda in the opposite direction or you can ski back down the Ladies downhill to Selva. From the top you ski straight down to **Colfosco**, then lifts link with **Corvara** and from there to **Arabba** and the rest of the Sella Ronda.

Throughout the Sella Ronda there are diversions you can take to ski areas not directly on the circuit. The biggest is the **Alta Badia** area to the west of Corvara, from which you can ski down to **San Cassiano** and **La Villa**.

Local to Selva is the **Seceda** area, accessed by a gondola a bus-ride from town. You can ski back down to the bottom of here or to **Ortisei**. And from Ortisei a cable-car goes up the other side of the valley to **Alpe di Siusi** and its virtually flat plateau of easy skiing, cross-country and walks.

SNOW RELIABILITY
Excellent when the weather is cold
The skiing in the area is not high. There's very little above 2200m. Most is between 2000m and 1500m. And

the Dolomites miss out on many of the snowstorms which affect the Alps to the north. That was why the area invested so heavily in snowmaking machinery after a series of lean snow years. It now has the biggest snowmaking capacity in Europe, covering 78km of runs. Only the high Arabba, Passo Sella and Pordoi sections lack cannons. All other areas have snowmakers on at least the main runs to resorts, and almost all Selva's local pistes are liberally endowed.

The only problem therefore arises in poor snow years when temperatures are too low to make snow. Late season is obviously more of a risk than early season as night-time temperatures are more likely to be above freezing.

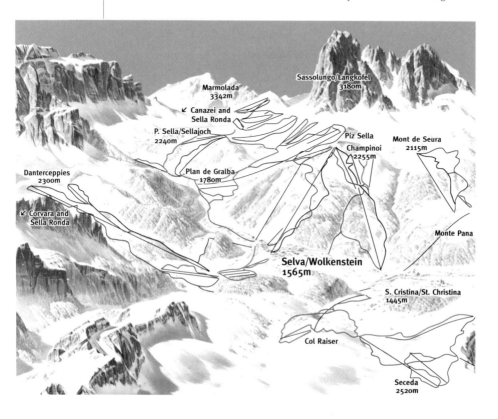

LIFT PASSES

94/95 prices in lire
Val Gardena
Covers all lifts in Selva, S Cristina, Ortisei and Castelrotto, and ski-bus between Selva and Ortisei.
Beginners Points card with 520 points for 40,000 (93/94 price).
Main pass
1-day pass 45,000
6-day pass 223,000 (low season 194,000 – 13% off)
Senior citizens
Over 60: 6-day pass 178,000 (20% off)
Children
Under 14: 6-day pass 156,000 (30% off)
Under 6: free pass
Alternative periods
10 days skiing in 14 pass available.
Alternative passes
Dolomiti Superski pass covers 464 lifts and 1180km of piste in the Dolomites, including all Sella Ronda resorts (adult 6-day 243,000).

FOR ADVANCED SKIERS
Staying in Arabba is better
Arabba has the best steep skiing, though it's rather distant from Selva with a lot of bland skiing en route. The north-facing black and red runs from Porta Vescovo back to Arabba are served by an efficient high-capacity gondola and are great fun. The Val Gardena World Cup piste, the 'Saslonch', is one of several steepish runs between Ciampinoi and both Selva and Santa Cristina. Unlike many World Cup pistes it is kept in racing condition, for Italian team practices, but is open to the public much of the time. It's especially good in January, when it's not too crowded. The unpisted trail from the top of the Saltaria chair on Alpe Di Siusi down to Santa Cristina is not difficult, but pleasantly lonely.

There is also some exciting off-piste to be explored with a guide. The run from Sass Pordoi (the highest point in the region at 2950m) to Colfosco finishes in the spectacular narrow descent through the Val Mezdi. The ski schools arrange group trips here. But overall, off-piste is limited because of the sheer-drop nature of the tops of the mountains in the Dolomites.

In general, advanced skiers might find the region as a whole too tame, especially if they are looking for a lot of steep challenges.

FOR INTERMEDIATES
A huge network of ideal runs
The Sella Ronda region is renowned for its easy skiing. The runs down from Dantercëpies to Colfosco and Corvara, and across the valley from there in the Alta Badia are superb for early or unadventurous intermediates – it is a big area of confidence-boosting runs. These are easily reached from Selva, though returning home from Dantercëpies may be a little daunting. Riding the gondola down is an option. Nearer to Selva itself, the runs at the top of Ciampinoi and those of the Plan de Gralba area are nice and gentle. The Alpe di Siusi runs above Ortisei are likely to prove too flat, with too much poling involved for even the most nervous skier.

Average intermediate skiers have an extraordinarily large network of suitable pistes, though there are few long runs. The beautiful swoop down the far side of the Seceda massif from Cuca to Ortisei is perhaps the best long run. The Mont de Seura above Santa Cristina is very pleasant, but skiing both to and from it involves tackling unpisted trails. The Plan de

Gralba area, the runs either side of the Saltaria chair, and the main pistes down to La Villa and San Cassiano are other particularly nice spots.

The runs back down to the valley direct from Ciampinoi are a bit more challenging, as are the descents from Dantercëpies to Selva.

As long as the better skiers in a party can resist schussing off into the distance every time one of the many very easy runs is negotiated, the Sella Ronda circuit is ideal for mixed abilities wishing to do day-long excursions together. There are no awkward sections that have to be taken, and when there are no queues most intermediates can complete a circuit in five hours (and any stops).

FOR BEGINNERS
Great slopes, but...
Near-beginners have numerous runs, and the village nursery slopes are excellent – spacious, convenient, and kept in good condition by snow cannons. But we have reservations about the ski school – see opposite.

FOR CROSS-COUNTRY
Beautiful trails
There are over 70km of trails all enjoying wonderful scenery. The 12km trail up the Vallunga-Langental valley is particularly attractive, with neck-craning views all around. The largest section of trails (40km) has the advantage of being at altitude, running between Monte Pana and Seiseralm, and across Alpe di Siusi.

QUEUES
Much improved: few problems
New lifts have vastly improved this once badly queue-prone area. Bottlenecks are no longer apparent and, except for peak times and German holidays, delays are now virtually non-existent.

In busy periods some of the Sella Ronda lifts can have delays. The Bec De Roces chair out of Arabba towards Corvara can be a problem.The drags from Colfosco to Selva are another possible delay. The Plan de Gralba cable-car on the Selva to Passo Sella road can also have a queue, but there is a chair alternative. In general, the efficient lifts deal well with crowds.

MOUNTAIN RESTAURANTS
Wide range of attractive refuges
There are plenty of them, generally very good in quality, atmosphere and value for money. As well as restaurants, there are lots of snow bars to stop off at for a quick grappa.

GETTING THERE

Air Verona, transfer 3hr. Innsbruck, transfer 3hr.

Rail Chiusa (27km); frequent buses from station.

SKI SCHOOL

94/95 prices in lire

Selva Gardena Classes 6 days
4hr: 9am-1pm or 1pm-5pm; 2hr: 11am-1pm
6 4hr days: 200,000
Children's classes
Ages: 4 to 12
6 6hr days: 360,000
Private lessons
Hourly
47,000 for 1hr for 1 person; each additional person 5,000

CHILDCARE

The ski school runs a kindergarten for children aged 1 to 4, with skiing available for the older children. Those attending proper ski school classes can be looked after all day.

The little place at Piz Sorega above San Cassiano is called a 'ski bar' but it is also a fine restaurant. The Panorama is a small, cosy, rustic sun-trap at the foot of the Dantercëpies drag. The Scoiattolo, at the bottom of the Dantercëpies gondola, alongside the nursery area, is very atmospheric, particularly at four o'clock on Fridays, when it hosts a tremendous tea dance.

On the way down to Plan de Gralba from Ciampinoi, the Vallongia Rolandhütte is renowned for its apple strudel, but is actually a fine all-round restaurant – watch out for the huge St Bernard dog. Nearby the Gran Paradis is good for watching racers but gets rather busy. The Clerchütte at Ciampinoi is a very lively place, with a wonderfully tacky stuffed badger wearing mock Ray Bans next to the fireplace. The triumvirate of little huts above Colfosco – Forcelles, Edelweiss and Pradat – are all very pleasant.

Way over at Lagazuoi, beyond San Cassiano, the Scotoni restaurant is worth the excursion, serving some of the best food in the area, including spit-barbecued pig. Capana Alpina is another one to try in this area.

Those skiing the Alta Badia should try the excellent Cherz above Passo di Campolongo. The Gamsbluthütte above Santa Cristina is a major sunbathing spot. Lupo Bianco, at the bottom of Val Zalei between Passo Sella and Canazei, is a notable rendezvous point and sun-trap. Capanna Bill, on the far side of Arabba beyond Passo Padon, is well worth a visit for stunning views of the Marmolada glacier.

SKI SCHOOL
Don't count on English

Selva claims to have 30 English-speaking instructors, but many of them have only a perfunctory knowledge of our language. The relative lack of Brits in the resort also makes getting a group lesson exclusively in English fairly unlikely. If you are lucky enough to get a good English-speaker or understand German or Italian, the lesson is likely to be useful. Selva has a good reputation for standards of tuition.

FACILITIES FOR CHILDREN
Good by Italian standards

There are comprehensive childcare arrangements, but given the lack of British visitors it would be surprising if English were routinely spoken.

 # Staying there

Selva is the biggest and liveliest of the places actually on the Sella Ronda circuit at which to stay. Ortisei is the administrative centre of the Val Gardena – pretty, and more of a complete community – but it is not so conveniently situated for the skiing. For a brief description of the other villages on or near the circuit, see the end of this chapter.

In Selva itself, the most convenient position to stay is near one of, or between, the two main gondolas. But there is a free, regular bus service throughout the valley until early evening, so position isn't that crucial.

HOW TO GO
Surprisingly few packages

Selva and the Sella Ronda area has made a comeback in a few British tour operators' programmes after being dropped for several years.

Chalets There is now quite a wide choice of catered chalets, with three operators in the resort; and some of the properties are of good quality, with en-suite bathrooms.

Enterprise have the attractive, modern Splendid, on the edge of the village, 500m from the Ciampinoi lifts. Their Elise is a smaller apartment-based chalet in a superb position opposite the Ciampinoi gondola. Crystal have several chalets, most close to the centre and lifts. The new Salvan is particularly comfortable. Bladon Lines and Crystal both have floors of the Vanadis, and Bladon Lines also have the simpler and less convenient Wiesenheim.

Hotels There are 10 4-stars, over 30 3-stars and numerous lesser hotels. Few of the best hotels are well positioned.
£££ Gran Baita Large, luxurious sporthotel, with lots of mod cons including indoor pool. A few minutes' walk from centre and lifts.
£££ Aaritz Best-placed of the 4-stars, opposite the gondola.
££ Astor Family-run chalet in centre, below nursery slopes. Good value.
££ Olympia Well positioned, central 3-star, highly recommended by reporters.
££ Solaia 3-star chalet, superbly positioned for lifts and slopes, recommended by reporters.
Self-catering There are plenty of apartments but we are unaware of any available through tour operators. The 3-star Rondula apartments are in a pretty chalet building just out of town near the Ciampinoi chair.

PACKAGES

Bladon Lines, Crystal, Enterprise, Inghams, Ski Beach Villas

Arabba Ski Beach Villas

Campitello Enterprise, Thomson

Canazei Crystal, Enterprise, Simply Ski

La Villa Ski Beach Villas

Pozza di Fassa Crystal

San Cassiano Enterprise

Vigo di Fassa Crystal

ACTIVITIES

Indoor Swimming, sauna, solaria (in hotels), bowling alley, squash, artificial skating rink, ice hockey, curling, museum, indoor golf, concerts, cinema, billiards, tennis
Outdoor Sleigh rides, torch-light descents, horse-riding, extensive cleared paths around Selva and above S Cristina and Ortisei, ski-bob

TOURIST OFFICE

Postcode 39048
Tel 010 39 (471) 795122
Fax 794245

EATING OUT
Plenty of good-value choices

Selva offers the best of both Austrian and Italian food at prices to suit all pockets. The higher-quality restaurants are mainly hotel-based. The Antares and Laurin have particularly good menus while the Olympia is renowned for its fondues. The Freina specialises in traditional Austrian food and large meals suitable for two or three people to share (good value). Da Rino has some of the best pizzas in town, whilst the Ciampinoi pizzeria serves excellent pasta and Austrian dishes in a lively atmosphere.

APRES-SKI
Above average for a family resort

Nightlife is lively and informal, though the scattered nature of the village means there is little on-street atmosphere. The Luisl, Speck and Laurin kellers are the liveliest bars in town. The Sun Valley and Savoy nightclubs have live bands. Hotel Stella has an atmospheric bar but its disco can lack atmosphere except at weekends. The Médel disco is just out of town, but worth the taxi-ride. Tour operators organise a lively bowling evening. The Friday tea dance at the Scoiattolo mountain hut is a must – oompah, yodelling etc.

FOR NON-SKIERS
Good variety

Excursions are difficult without a car, but otherwise there is a fair amount to do. The lovely walks are the highlight. The charming town of Ortisei is close by and well worth a visit for its large hot-spring swimming pool, shops, restaurants and lovely old buildings. Numerous good mountain restaurants, nicely scattered around the different sections of ski area, can be reached by gondola or cable-car from the village or nearby. Car-drivers have Bolzano and Innsbruck within reach.

Ortisei 1235m

Ortisei is a charming market town that has a life outside skiing. It's full of lovely old buildings, pretty churches

and pleasant shops. The lift station that accesses the south-facing side of the skiing is conveniently central, but skiers wishing to start on the north-facing Alpe di Siusi slopes have to negotiate the busy main road that skirts town. The nursery area, ski school and ski kindergarten are at the foot of these slopes, but families have a fair range of accommodation available to them on the piste-side of the road. The fine public indoor pool and ice rink are also here. A central hotel is equidistant from both lift stations. The south-facing Seceda slopes give the fastest access to Selva.

There is hotel and self-catering accommodation to suit all tastes and pockets, but we are not aware of any available through tour operators. Many of the more expensive hotels have good pool and health facilities. The 4-star Adler is very central. The unfortunately named hotel Hell is close to the Alpe di Siusi lifts. If you have a car, the out-of-town Perla and Rodes, both 3-stars, take some beating for value. Inexpensive, central places include the 2-star Beleval, Garni Dr. Senoner and the Pra Palmer B&B. The best apartments are clustered around the Seceda chair. The Stella Rondula places are examples. The simpler Aquila-Kirchmayr and Oswald apartments are close to the centre and north-facing slopes respectively.

There are many good restaurants, mainly specialising in local dishes. The Grien is expensive but very good. Villa Emilia and Dolimiten Madonna are both worth a try. The immediate après-ski atmosphere is quite jolly, but things are fairly subdued later. The Cosmea bar is the place to go if returning from the north-facing slopes at the end of the day; the Albergo Sureghes taverna has live music; the Posta has a Tyrolean-style stube.

Non-skiing facilities are plentiful. Apart from exploring the town, there are good indoor swimming, tennis and ice skating centres, squash, bowling, sauna and tobogganing. There are lovely walks, and some mountain restaurants are within reach by cable-car.

Colfosco 1645m

Colfosco is a smaller, quieter version of Corvara, 2km away. It has a fairly compact centre with a sprawl of large hotels along the road towards Selva. It's connected to Corvara by a horizontal-running chair-lift. In the opposite direction, a series of irritatingly short lifts head off to the Passo Gardena and on to Selva.

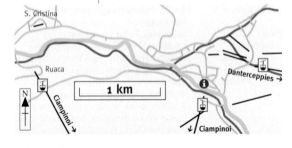

There are several large hotels that between them provide plenty of services. The top-class Cappella and Kolfuschgerhof hotels both have indoor pools and provide most of what little nightlife there is. The Centrale is a cheaper place to stay. The rustic, cramped Garni Peter bar is the one lively après-ski haunt; it often has live music and a tea dance. Restaurants worth a try include the Stria, Tabladel and Matthiaskeller.

Corvara 1570m

Corvara is the most animated Sella Ronda village east of Selva, with plenty of hotels, restaurants, bars and sports facilities. It's well positioned within the ski area, with village lifts heading off in different directions towards the reasonably equidistant Selva, Arabba and San Cassiano. The main shops and some hotels are clustered around a small central piazza, but the rest of the place sprawls along the valley floor.

Hotel Sassongher is perhaps the best hotel in town, but it's not particularly well placed for the skiing. The Posta is a more central, quality hotel. The Eden is a good, cheaper option. The Pradat is an attractive pension, well placed for the lifts, which has the only babysitting service in town. Ardent après-skiers should visit the Posta Zirm, which has great tea dances. It becomes a nightclub later, when its main rival is the Sassongher keller bar. The Arabesque bar is best for a quiet drink. There are a number of good-value restaurants: the Adler, Perla and Panorama are examples.

There's a ski kindergarten but English is not widely spoken, and there's no nursery. Non-skiers have an indoor pool, bowling, squash, indoor tennis and an ice rink.

San Cassiano 1530m

San Cassiano is a pretty little village, set in an attractive, tree-filled valley. It's a very quiet, slightly upmarket resort, full of well-heeled Italian families and comfortable hotels, but little else. The local skiing, the Alta Badia, though sizeable and fully linked, is something of a spur of the main Sella Ronda circuit. Moving further afield is a tiresome business for adventurous skiers who want to do the circuit.

Enterprise has a couple of quite different catered chalets. One is a large, comfortable pension-conversion. The other is a smaller, more basic, rustic place. Among the best hotels in each category are the Rosa Alpina (4-star), Tyrol (3-star),

Alexander (2-star), Plang (1-star) and Jasmin (B&B). The Ciasa La Ro and Ciasa Ulli are good apartments.

The Pitscheiderhof is perhaps the best restaurant in town, and others worth a try are the Diamant, La Stüa, Frohsinn and Antersies. The Ski Bar at the base of the village chair is the main après-ski spot.

The tea dance in Corvara's Posta Zirm is a must for those wanting something lively. Ski there at the end of the day, taxi home afterwards. Later nightlife is very limited. The Rosa Alpina hotel has dancing and there's a bowling alley in the Diamant hotel. Walking in the pretty scenery is the main non-skiing activity. Swimming is the other. There is no nursery or ski kindergarten.

La Villa 1435m

La Villa is similar to neighbouring San Cassiano in most respects – small, quiet, pretty, unspoilt – but is slightly closer to Corvara, making it rather better placed for the main Sella Ronda circuit. Beach Villas has a large, good-value catered chalet here. La Bercia Pizzeria is recommended for chalet girls' nights off. Village amenities include pool, bowling, ski kindergarten (no nursery), and ice skating on a frozen lake.

Canazei 1440m

Canazei is a sizeable, bustling, pretty, roadside village of narrow streets, rustic old buildings, traditional style hotels and nice little shops, set in the Sella Ronda's most heavily wooded section of mountains. It has reasonably animated nightlife and plenty going on generally. It is not, perhaps, an ideal choice for some British families due to the busy road and lack of English spoken in the ski school and nursery facilities.

A cable-car is the only mountain access point, but it's not as queue-prone as one might imagine. A single piste back to the village is linked to runs returning from both Selva and Arabba. The village nursery slope is inconveniently located, but it's unlikely to be used after day one. The local Belvedere slopes are uniformly easy and particularly well endowed with mountain restaurants.

Crystal have an apartment-based catered chalet in Canazei, ten minutes from the cable-car. There are no luxury hotels, but the 3-star Croce Bianca offers elegant comfort and old-world charm. It's also central and close to the cable-car. The much cheaper Diana is a charming place, five minutes from the village centre.

The Palace Dolomiti is another hotel with a touch of class, and particularly popular for its cuisine and central position. The Astoria is another good choice available on the British market.

There are numerous restaurants. The Stala, Principe, Rosticceria Melester and Te Cevana are all worth a try. Nightlife is fairly jolly, if limited in scope. Two happening places dominate – the Montanara bar and Gatto Nero bar disco.

There's a fair amount to do for non-skiers. Walks are beautiful, clothes shopping worthwhile. There's a good pool, sauna, Turkish baths, and ice skating in neighbouring Alba. There is an all-day nursery and ski kindergarten available.

Campitello 1445m

This is a smaller, quieter village than neighbouring Canazei but, with the exception of Selva, is the most prominent of the Sella Ronda resorts on the British package market. It remains, however, very unspoilt, with little English spoken.

By the high standards of the Sella Ronda, the village is nothing special to look at, particularly when there's little snow – which is much of the time – but it's still pleasant. It's remarkably quiet during the day, having no slopes to the village.

A cable-car takes skiers up into the Sella Ronda circuit. If you don't wish to return by lift at the end of the day, skiing down to Canazei and catching a bus back is an option.

The Rubino is an elegant 4-star hotel well placed close to the cable-car. The good 3-star Sella Ronda is also very convenient for everything. The 3-star Enrosadira is less well positioned, a tiring uphill walk from the cable-car. Pension Festil is similarly placed but offers a useful cheap and cheerful B&B

option. Campitello is short on après-ski and general amenities but Canazei has both, and the neighbouring village of Pozza has ice skating and night skiing.

Arabba 1600m

Arabba is a small traditional village, uncommercialised to the point where basic resort infrastructure is in short supply. But the lifts into the Sella Ronda in both directions make it very convenient. It is much more of a serious skiers' resort than its sunny, family-oriented neighbours. The high north-facing slopes have the best natural snow in the Dolomites, and the nearby Marmolada glacier opens in February (for a supplement).

Apartment-conversion chalets and self-catering accommodation are available through Beach Villas. The chalets are cheap, comfortable and close to the lifts. The self-catering apartments are in the same building as some chalet accommodation.

Hotels are available to independent travellers. The 4-star Sport is the best. The Porta Vescovo is a large, comfortable, multi-amenity 3-star with the only pool in town. The Evaldo is a simpler 3-star. Albergo Pordoi is a 2-star with character, and Garni Erika is a pleasant 1-star.

Venues for eating out are limited. Al Forte, 3km out of town, is best. Al Tablé, 7 Sass and Ru De Mont are cheap and cheerful pizzerias.

The après-ski is also very limited. The Al Fegole bar is the smartest place in town. Bar Peter, and the bars of Pension Erika and Albergo Pordoi, are others worth a try. The Delmonego family's bar-caravan, at the bottom of the piste, is the tea-time rendezvous.

Non-skiers are marooned and children's facilities are non-existent.

Sestriere 2000m

Sestriere was built for snow – high, with north-west-facing slopes. It now also has some of the most extensive snowmaking facilities in the Alps. A lot of smart Italians patronise the place, but not many British – perhaps because the village (unlike Sauze, over the hill) is not what we look for in an Italian resort.

THE RESORT

Sestriere was the Alps' first purpose-built resort. It sits on a broad, sunny and windy col at 2000m. Neither the site nor the village looks very hospitable, though the buildings have benefited from renewed investment in recent years – a process that has gained impetus from the resort's successful bid to hold the World Championships in 1997.

THE SKIING

The local **ski area** has two main sectors: Sises, directly in front of the village, and Motta, above Borgata – a satellite village 2km away to the north-east and 150m lower. There is a further ski area at Pragelato, 8km down the same valley.

Drag- and chair-lifts predominate on the local north-west-facing slopes. The chair-lift link on the other side of the resort to Monte Fraiteve has been taken out of action as part of the preparations for the World Championships. For the moment, access to Sansicario and the rest of the Milky Way is via the gondola from Borgata to Col Basset at the top of the Sauze d'Oulx skiing, and a drag-lift back up to Monte Fraiteve.

With most of the local slopes facing north-west and ranging from 1840m to 2820m, it is fair to expect them to have **snow-cover** for most of the season, even without snowmaking that is on practically all of the Sises sector and about half of Motta.

There is a fair amount to amuse **advanced skiers** – steep pistes served by the drags at the top of both sectors, and off-piste opportunities in several directions from here and from the lifts on Monte Fraiteve.

Both sectors also offer plenty for **intermediate skiers**, who can also expect to explore practically all of the Milky Way areas, time permitting. The terrain is excellent for **beginners**, with several nursery areas and the gentlest of easy runs down to Borgata. There are two **cross-country** loops covering 15km of ground.

Queues for the main lifts occur at the weekends and holidays. The lifts from Borgata to Sestriere inevitably become crowded at the end of the day,

as everyone skiing Motta or returning from Sauze via Col Basset has to use this link.

The local **mountain restaurants** are fair – the one at Sises is best – but there are better ones further afield.

Lack of English-speaking tuition can be a problem in the **ski school**.

An all-day crèche takes **children** between 3 and 6 years.

STAYING THERE

Sestriere is not the most convenient of purpose-built resorts, but choice of location is not crucial. Most of the **accommodation** is in apartments, but there are a dozen hotels, practically all of 3-star or 4-star status.

The central 4-star Grand Hotel Sestriere is an ugly low building, but is comfortable and well placed. Just out of the village (but not far from a lift, and with courtesy transport) is the luxurious Principi di Piemonte. The Savoy Edelweiss is a central, attractive 3-star. The cheaper 3-star Bianca Neve is on the edge, equidistant from both main lifts. The distinctive round towers of the Torre and Duchi d'Aosta are occupied by Club Med.

The comfortable Residence Bellavista apartments at the entrance to the resort, are equidistant (10 to 12 minutes' walk) from the main lifts, though skiing from nearby is possible.

The numerous 3- and 4-star hotels offer plenty of options for **eating out**. For example, the Grand has good local specialities. The Gargotte, I Tre Rubinetti and the Last Tango grill have good Italian and French food across the price range. The Pinkey is perhaps the best of the bars that double as pizzerias or snack joints.

Après-ski is lively at weekends, quiet at other times. The Prestige and Palace are just two of the many little bars that liven up. The Rendezvous is a cosy piano bar. The Black Sun piano-bar-cum-disco and the Tabata club are great fun at weekends.

There is a fair amount for active **non-skiers** to do, but it is not a very attractive place in which to while away the days, despite some smart shopping. It's remarkable that such a sizeable resort with so many quality hotels has no indoor swimming pool.

La Thuile 1450m

✔ Fair-sized, very quiet ski area linked to La Rosière in France

✔ Excellent beginner and easy intermediate skiing

✔ Unusual mix of modern purpose-built accommodation at foot of slopes and more villagey atmosphere of the old town, a ten-minute walk away

✘ All the seriously tough piste skiing is low down, and most of the low tree-lined skiing is tough

✘ Mountain restaurants very disappointing

✘ Not the place for lively après-ski

La Thuile is surprisingly little known on the British market. It deserves better. It has a fair-sized ski area of its own as well as being linked with La Rosière in France (they have a shared lift pass). The skiing best suits beginners and intermediates in search of little challenge, but it is not devoid of interest for good skiers, particularly if the snow conditions are good, when there is the choice of venturing off-piste above the Petit St Bernard pass between France and Italy (closed in winter) or skiing the short but serious blacks through the trees above the village. It has an excellent lift system and uncrowded runs.

The resort itself is an unusual mixture of old and new, with both a modern, purpose-built complex at the foot of the slopes and an old, partly restored mining village over the river.

ORIENTATION

La Thuile consists of two quite distinct parts. An old mining village sits across a river from a new purpose-built resort at the foot of the lifts. A fast chair and a gondola speed you up the mountain with further high-speed chairs to the top.

The skiing links with **La Rosière**, over the border in France. **Courmayeur** is within easy reach by road, **Chamonix** is just through the Mont Blanc tunnel and **Cervinia** is about an hour's drive away.

 The resort

At the foot of the lifts is a modern purpose-built complex, with accommodation, splendid leisure centre, bars, restaurants and shops. It looks and feels much like a typical French purpose-built resort such as La Plagne or Tignes, but with a distinctly Italian atmosphere.

Cross the river and things are completely different. La Thuile started life as a mining town but became depopulated, and large parts of it fell into disrepair until the skiing area was developed and boom times returned.

Much of the old village has been restored and new buildings tastefully added around it. But parts remain in ruins, with a slight 'ghost town' feel to them. There's a reasonable selection of restaurants and bars, but not much in the way of shopping other than food and ski gear.

 The skiing

For a little-known resort, La Thuile offers a surprisingly large amount of skiing. And it is normally very uncrowded, with quiet pistes and no lift queues. Beginners and early intermediates will get the most out of it, although most of the lower runs in the woods are seriously steep. Although many of La Thuile's runs are

marked red, they often deserve no more than a blue rating. The ski area has a reputation for being very cold, especially early in the season – many of the runs are north-facing.

THE SKI AREA
Big and gentle

The lifts out of the village take you to **Les Suches** (2200m), with black runs going back down directly to the village through the trees, and reds taking a more roundabout route. From here chairs and drags take you to the top of the mountain and a number of different gentle bowls accessed from **Chaz Dura** (2580m). You can also drop down over the back from here to the Petit St Bernard road.

The link with **La Rosière** in France is via Belvedere (2640m) and the Col de Traversette (2400m) and is quite a tiresome journey. In contrast with La Thuile's mainly north- and east-facing runs, La Rosière's skiing is largely south-facing and, although the runs in France tend to be steeper, the snow in Italy tends to be better.

SNOW RELIABILITY
Good

Most of La Thuile's skiing is north- or east-facing and above 2000m. So the snow generally keeps in good condition. There's also a reasonable amount of snowmaking both above the tree-line and on a couple of the runs home.

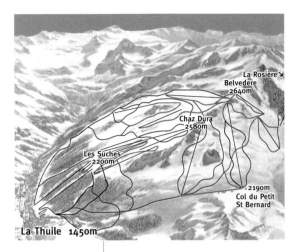

La Thuile 1450m

the trees back to the resort.

The red runs on the other side of the top ridge, down towards the Petit St Bernard road, offer a greater challenge for more adventurous intermediates. But La Thuile's skiing really suits less ambitious intermediates best.

FOR BEGINNERS
Good, but not much English
There are nursery slopes both at village level and at Les Suches. There's a good gentle green run above Les Suches to progress to, and some shallow blues too. But none of these are segregated from the main ski area. The main problem for beginners is likely to be the lack of English in the ski school (see next page).

FOR CROSS-COUNTRY
Varied choice
La Thuile has 16km of tracks of varying difficulty on the valley floor.

QUEUES
Very rare
The resort has a very effective lift system for the number of skiers it attracts, starting with an exceptionally powerful gondola and parallel high-speed chair up to Les Suches. You can usually walk straight on to any of the lifts; it's only at peak weekends that you might find queues.

MOUNTAIN RESTAURANTS
Very disappointing
La Thuile was the only resort last season in which we failed to have a decent lunch up the mountain. And the locals recommend skiing back to town for lunch.

Although there are several ristorantes marked on the piste map, most serve little more than sandwiches and snacks. If you are coming to Italy for the pasta, you'd be better off going elsewhere. The biggest facility is the self-service cafeteria at Les Suches which lacks atmosphere but serves good home-made Italian

LIFT PASSES

94/95 prices in lire
Dominio Internazionale
Covers all lifts in La Rosière and La Thuile.
Beginners One baby-lift in village. Points tickets (50 points 60,000).
Main pass
1-day pass 43,000
6-day pass 202,000
(low season 175,000 – 13% off)
Children
Under 4: free pass
Short-term passes
Half-day from 1pm.
Notes Discount of 10% for groups of 25 or more.
Alternative passes
Valle d'Aosta pass covers La Thuile, Courmayeur, Gressoney, Champoluc, Alagna, Cervinia, Valtournenche and Pila (adult 6-day 238,000).

SKI SCHOOL

94/95 prices in lire
Rutor
Classes 6 days
2½hr: 10am-12.30;
2hr: 1pm-3pm
6 2½hr days: 147,000
Children's classes
Ages: from 6
6 2½hr days: 147,000
Private lessons
Hourly
47,000 for 1 or 2 people; each additional person 5,000

FOR ADVANCED SKIERS
Rather limited
The only steep pistes are those down through the trees from Les Suches back to the resort. The steepest of these, the Diretta, is serious stuff. What's more, because they are low (below 2000m) these runs can suffer from poor conditions and become very tricky indeed.

The rest of the skiing is tame by comparison. The best of it, for good skiers, is the area above the Petit St Bernard road, served by the San Bernardo and Fourclaz chairs, where there is some genuinely black terrain and plenty of opportunity to venture off-piste. You'll find many of the other red runs seem overgraded.

An added attraction of La Thuile, for those who can afford it, is its heli-skiing. This includes drops on the Ruitor glacier, with a 20km run into France, ending at La Rosière.

FOR INTERMEDIATE SKIERS
Something different
La Thuile has some good intermediate skiing, and its link with La Rosière in France adds a sense of adventure as well as doubling the extent of the skiing. Together, the two resorts offer a large and varied ski area, with over 130km of runs. However, timid intermediates are better off staying on home ground: the route back from La Rosière involves a short but tricky red right at the start, and most of the terrain at La Rosière – particularly on the top half of the mountain – is fairly challenging.

On the Italian side, the bowls above Les Suches have numerous gentle, groomed blue and red runs, ideal for easy cruising and practising your technique. There are also long roundabout red runs down through

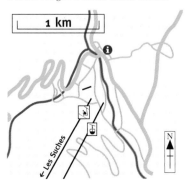

1 km

food. Just below there's a pleasant hut.

Many of the on-slope places operate the typical Italian system of paying before you collect your food.

SKI SCHOOL
Good but foreign
Several of the reporters we've heard from praise the ski school for reasonably-sized classes and fair instruction. Repeatedly the biggest reservation is the lack of instructors who speak good English.

FACILITIES FOR CHILDREN
Very poor
La Thuile doesn't seem to cater much for children (or, perhaps more accurately, their parents). There is no kindergarten or crèche. Ski school starts at six years.

 # Staying there

Undoubtedly the most convenient place to stay for the skiing is in the modern purpose-built Planibel complex at the foot of the slopes. But many people find this rather soulless and prefer to stay in the old town over the river (served by a free bus service) or in one of the more traditional buildings nearer the slopes.

HOW TO GO
Some choice of packages
The number of tour operators going to La Thuile is gradually increasing.
Chalets Bladon Lines have the only catered chalet in town, an apartment conversion in a ramshackle old block, but is reasonably comfortable by the standards of such places. It offers good value and books out very early.
Hotels The choice is between the swanky but characterless 4-star Planibel, three 3-stars and 10 simpler places.
££££ Planibel American-style 'resort hotel' with all mod cons, including covered driveway for unloading your trunk, and underground parking. Right at the base of the lifts. Pool and other facilities.

£££ Eden Comfortable modern hotel in traditional wood and stone style, conveniently close to the lifts and Planibel centre.
££ Chalet Alpina Simple place with the atmosphere of a catered chalet, on outskirts of the resort.
Self-catering The Planibel apartments (Neilson and Enterprise) have received nothing but praise from a number of our reporters. They're spacious, well-equipped, ski-convenient and offer great value for money. Not surprisingly, they book out early.

EATING OUT
Limited range, consistently good
There are only eleven restaurants in La Thuile but we've received positive reports on most of them. The Bricole and Marmottes both serve excellent traditional Italian food. Lisse also has authentic Italian fare at cheaper prices. The always-busy Lo Creton, Relais and Grotta vie for the title of Best Cheap and Cheerful Pizzeria. The Maison de Laurent and Tufeja are also popular.

Booking at all the above is advisable if you want to eat at popular times.

APRES-SKI
Early to bed
A few of the bars fill up after skiing, notably the Buvette and Bon Chon in the Planibel complex, but most of the evenings tend to be taken up by a leisurely meal, after which people retire for the evening. The Rendezvous bar has karaoke but the Bricolette and Bricole have more atmospheric bars. The Bricole and Paradiso discos warm up at the weekend.

FOR NON-SKIERS
Not the best choice
La Thuile has little to attract non-skiers. The Planibel complex has an excellent range of leisure facilities including a huge swimming pool and indoor ice rink. But there's little in the way of attractive walks or shopping. Excursions to Courmayeur and Chamonix can be organised. Meeting at the top of the gondola for lunch is easy, but not terribly enticing.

CHILDCARE
There are no all-day childcare arrangements

GETTING THERE
Air Geneva, transfer 2½hr. Turin, transfer 2½hr.

Rail Pré-St-Didier (10km); regular buses to resort.

PACKAGES
Bladon Lines, Crystal, Enterprise, Interski, Neilson, Ski Valkyrie

ACTIVITIES
Indoor Skating rink, 2 swimming pools, gymnasium, 10 pin bowling, solarium, sauna, jacuzzi, massage, amusement arcade, billiards, squash
Outdoor Winter walks, heli-skiing

TOURIST OFFICE
Postcode 11016
Tel 010 39 (165) 884179
Fax 885196

Switzerland

Switzerland is home to some of our favourite ski resorts. For sheer charm and spectacular scenery, the 'traffic-free' villages of Wengen, Mürren, Saas Fee and Zermatt take some beating. Many resorts have impressive ski areas too – including some of the biggest, highest and toughest skiing in the Alps. For fast, efficient, queue-free lift networks, Swiss resorts rarely come up to French standards – and the worst are positively abysmal. But there are compensations: the world's best mountain restaurants, for example. Prices in resorts and up the mountain are high; but what you get for your money is first-class.

Downhill skiing in its modern form was invented in Wengen and Mürren, which were persuaded to open their summer railways in winter to take their British guests up the mountain to ski. They remain firm favourites with their regular British visitors, who return every year to savour the special atmosphere of these tiny villages and their awesome views of the Eiger, Mönch and Jungfrau.

While France is the home of the purpose-built ski resort, Switzerland is the home of the traditional mountain village which has transformed itself from farming community into year-round holiday resort. Many of Switzerland's most famous ski resorts are as popular in the summer as in the winter, or more so. This creates resorts with a much more lived-in feel to them and a much more stable local community. Many of the resorts are still run and dominated by a handful of families who were lucky or shrewd enough to get involved in the early development of the resorts.

This has its downside as well as advantages. The ruling families are able to stifle competition and prevent newcomers from taking a slice of their action. New ski schools, competing with the traditional school and pushing up standards, are much less common than in other countries, for example. And in many resorts, British tour operators are severely restricted in the amount of ski guiding they can offer their guests – a popular service which the ski schools see as taking business away from them.

Swiss resorts have a reputation for efficiently relieving you of your money. And the reputation is well earned: it is undoubtedly true that Switzerland is an expensive place in which to ski. Nothing is cheap; but the quality of the service you get for your money is generally high. Swiss hotels are some of the best in the world. The trains run like clockwork to the advertised timetable (and often they run to the top of the mountain, doubling up as a ski-lift). The food is almost universally of good quality, and much less stodgy than in neighbouring Austria. Although it is expensive, there are fashionable resorts in France that can cost you even more. And in Switzerland it is generally true that you get what you pay for. Even the cheapest wine, for example, is not cheap; but it is reliable – duff bottles are very rare.

Although reliable standards are among the key features of Switzerland, there are exceptions. Two notable examples are Verbier and Wengen. Verbier has Europe's most expensive lift pass. In return, you get the right to stand for hours in queues for inadequate and badly planned lifts – see page 359. Wengen and Grindelwald share an excellent intermediate ski area which has suffered a series of very poor years for snow-cover. And yet they have been painfully slow to invest in artificial snowmaking facilities, which means that they are falling way behind the standards of service that keen skiers now expect – and the service provided by many less prestigious resorts such as those in the Italian Dolomites.

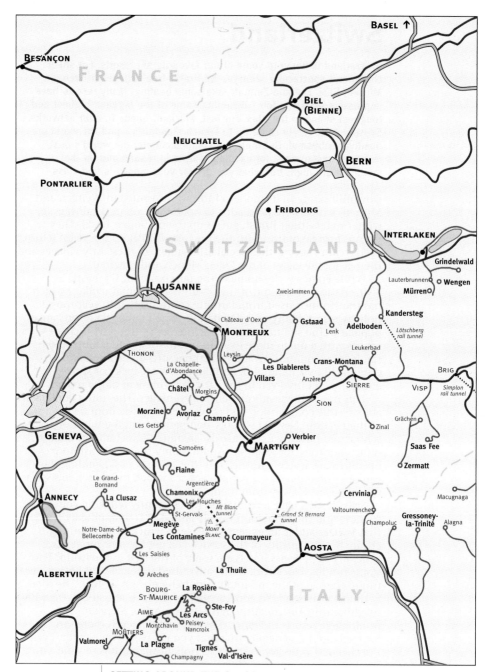

GETTING AROUND THE SWISS ALPS

Access to practically all Swiss resorts is fairly straightforward when approaching from the north. Many of the high passes that are perfectly sensible ways to get around the country in summer are closed in winter, which can be inconvenient if you are moving around from one area to another. There are car-carrying rail tunnels beneath the passes either side of Andermatt (Furka leading westwards to Brig, and Oberalp leading eastwards to Sedrun, Flims and Chur).

St Moritz is more awkward to get to. The main road route is over the Julier pass. This is normally kept open, but at 2284m it is naturally prone to heavy snowfalls that can shut it for a time. The

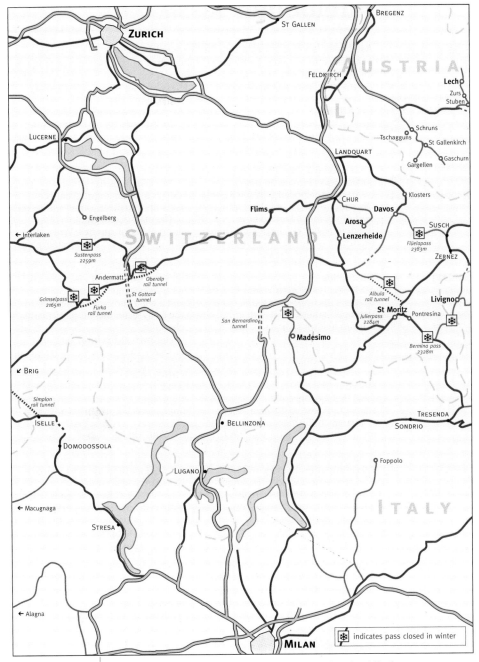

Scale in km

0   30

fall-back is the car-carrying rail tunnel under the Albula pass.

These car-carrying rail services are painless unless you travel at peak times, when there may be long queues, particularly for the Furka tunnel from Andermatt, which offers residents of Zürich the shortest route to the Valais. Another rail tunnel service that's very handy for skiers is the Lötschberg tunnel, linking Kandersteg in the Bernese Oberland with Brig in the Valais. There's no quicker way from Wengen to Zermatt.

There is a car-carrying rail tunnel linking Switzerland with Italy – the Simplon. But most of the routes to Italy are kept open by means of road tunnels. See the Italy introduction for more information.

Adelboden 1355m

HOW IT RATES

The skiing

Snow	**
Extent	***
Advanced	**
Intermediates	***
Beginners	****
Convenience	***
Queues	***
Restaurants	**

The rest

Scenery	***
Resort charm	****
Not skiing	****

SKI FACTS

Altitude	1070m-2355m
Lifts	50
Pistes	130km
Green/Blue	48%
Red	44%
Black	8%
Artificial snow	1km

PACKAGES

Inghams, Kuoni, Made to Measure, Plus Travel, Swiss Travel Service

Lenk Made to Measure, Swiss Travel Service

TOURIST OFFICE

Postcode CH-3715
Tel 010 41 (33) 732252
Fax 734252

Adelboden is unjustly neglected; for intermediate skiers who attach more importance to relaxing, pretty surroundings than to ski convenience, it has a lot of appeal. It will never be a convenience resort, but its investment in lifts over recent years has been heavy, and has produced great improvements.

THE RESORT

Adelboden comes quite close to the chocolate-box image of the Swiss mountain village: old wooden chalets with overhanging roofs line the quiet main street (cars are discouraged), and 3000m peaks provide an impressive backdrop. Adelboden is in the Bernese Oberland, a couple of valleys to the west of the much better-known Jungfrau resorts (Wengen etc). These resorts are within day-trip range, as is the Gstaad area to the west.

THE SKIING

Adelboden's **ski area** is split into six sectors. Lifts from close to the main street take you to three of them. Schwandfeldspitz, directly above the village, is now reached by a cable-car-gondola hybrid. The main gondola to nearby Hochsthorn and more remote Geils-Sillerenbuhl starts below the village at Oey (where there is a car park), but a connecting mini-gondola starts from close to the main street. This is much the biggest sector, with long, gentle runs (and some short, sharp ones) from around 2200m down to around 1450m, back towards the village and over the ridge towards Lenk in the next valley. The single drag up Fleckli (1860m) remains unlinked; so does Engstligenalp, a flat-bottomed high-altitude bowl reached by cable-car, 4km south of the resort; and the even more remote, but slightly more extensive, Elsigenalp.

The skiing doesn't go very high – most of it is below 2000m – so **snow reliability** is not a strong point. But it could be worse: much of the skiing is above 1500m and north-facing. There is very little snowmaking.

For **advanced skiers** there are some genuine blacks beside the chairs at Geils, where there are also off-piste possibilities down towards both Adelboden and Lenk (though there are protected forest areas). Engstligenalp has off-piste potential too – and is a launching point for ski tours on and around the Wildstrubel.

All six areas deserve exploration by **intermediate skiers**. At Geils, there is quite a lot of ground to be covered – and expeditions across the valley to Lenk's gentle Betelberg area (covered by the lift pass) are possible.

Beginners are well catered for. There are good nursery slopes in the village and at the bottom of nearby sectors. At Geils there are gloriously long, easy blue runs to progress to.

The **cross-country** trails along the valleys towards Engstligenalp and Geils are extensive, varied and scenic.

The main access gondola is not entirely free of **queues**. When snow low down is poor, the Engstligenalp cable-car cannot cope.

There is an adequate network of pleasant **mountain restaurants** with terraces and immaculate loos, and a good choice of such places in the Geils sector. Aebi is particularly charming.

The Swiss **ski school** gets good reports – 'caring, conscientious, good English, good approach'. For **children** aged 4 to 6 there is a 'very good' ski nursery (9.15 to 4pm); for those aged 2 to 6, a day nursery (9am-5pm). Several hotels have nurseries.

STAYING THERE

The village is compact, and there are efficient buses to the outlying areas; the ideal location for most people is close to the main street.

The choice of **how to go** is now quite wide: several UK operators, lots of locally bookable chalets and apartments, 30 pensions and hotels (mainly 3-star and 4-star, generally recommendable). The central 3-star Adler Sporthotel is one of the prettiest chalets, and is recommended. The little Bären is a classic wooden chalet – simple but captivating.

Eating out possibilities are quite varied, and include one or two mountain restaurants, including Aebi.

The **après-ski** is traditional, based on bars and tea-rooms (tea dancing at the Viktoria Eden hotel, 'great cakes' at Schmidt's). The Alte Taverne is a lovely, but pricey, old chalet with live music. Alpenrose is the cheapest bar.

There is a fair amount for **non-skiers**, and easy access to a couple of mountain restaurants. The Nevada-Palace hotel has a pool open to the public. There are indoor and outdoor curling and skating rinks. Excursions to Interlaken and Berne are possible.

Andermatt 1445m

Andermatt used to be a firm favourite with the Brits, but as other ski areas developed it got left behind. It's now an atmospheric old village with a small and outdated lift system giving access to some great, steep off-piste skiing.

THE RESORT
A familiar name among pre- and immediately post-war British skiers, Andermatt is now terra incognita to all but a few of the old brigade and a sporty minority of committed off-piste skiers. Historically an important Alpine thoroughfare, it has been sidelined since the opening of the Gotthard tunnel. Its primary livelihood now is not tourism but the army, whose barracks are the first buildings you see on your arrival and whose national servicemen are out in force in the bars and on the slopes.

But Andermatt is an attractive old village, with old wooden houses lining the dog-leg main street, which runs from railway to cable-car stations via a hump-backed bridge that many an unchained car fails to conquer. The heart of the village gets very little sun in the depths of winter.

SKI FACTS
Altitude	1445m-2965m
Lifts	13
Pistes	56km
Green/Blue	29%
Red	42%
Black	29%
Artificial snow	none

THE SKIING
For off-piste skiers Andermatt is one of the most inviting resorts in the world, thanks to a combination of suitable terrain, abundant snowfalls and retarded lift and piste development.

The main cable-car serves magnificent, varied skiing on the open, usually empty, slopes of the Gemsstock, and there are three more ski areas along the valley: Nätschen, Winterhorn (above Hospental) and Realp. The railway along the valley provides the only link between sectors, and offers tempting connections with resorts to the east (Davos, St Moritz) and west (Zermatt and other Valais resorts). You can put your car on some trains.

Andermatt is most definitely a resort for **advanced skiers**, with the Gemsstock boasting two superb long blacks in the north-facing bowl beneath the top cable-car, and another from mid-mountain back to the village. Much of the rest is 1500m vertical of challenging off-piste. Andermatt has plenty of guides for off-piste adventure and safaris, and heli-skiing.

Unfortunately the Gemsstock cable-car can take a while to get going after a heavy snowfall, but Winterhorn and Nätschen both provide black runs and off-piste opportunities while you wait.

Intermediates needn't be put off

approaching the Gemsstock: a fine long red run, the Sonnenpiste, can be tackled, and there are a couple of short lifts mid-mountain serving intermediate runs. Winterhorn's deceptively modest lift system offers ways down the 900m vertical of all standards, while Nätschen's south- and west-facing slopes are mostly open pistes perfect for finding your ski legs again.

There is an isolated nursery slope at Realp, along the valley towards the Furka pass, and the lower half of Nätschen has a good, long easy run back to the village. But essentially this is not a resort for **beginners**.

There is a 20km **cross-country** loop between Andermatt and Realp.

An antiquated lift system may provide plenty of off-piste opportunity, but it also means weekend **queues** when a heavy snowfall is followed by sunshine.

There are few **mountain restaurants** and none is very special. Lunch is for wimps, of course.

Over the years the **ski school** has had some good English-speaking instructors. And native-English-speakers have run some excellent off-piste courses here. Sadly, Canadian John Hogg has now gone back to British Columbia.

There are no special facilities for **children**; but there is skiing they can handle at Nätschen.

STAYING THERE
Accommodation is free if you're a 20-year-old Swiss male – the drawback is that you can't go home after a week. Otherwise Andermatt's beds are in small, cosy hotels and chalets.

The central Gasthaus Sternen is an attractive old wooden chalet with a popular and lively restaurant and bar. The 3-star Sonne, between the centre and the cable-car, is welcoming and comfortable. The Aurora is the closest to the cable-car, and the Monopol, on the station side of the centre, has a pool. The 2-star Bergidyll, next door, is a British favourite.

Après-ski revolves around a few cosy local bars and restaurants (including the Tell and the Adler) and there are a couple of places that have dancing.

Andermatt has little for **non-skiers**.

TOURIST OFFICE
Postcode CH-6490
Tel 010 41 (44) 67454
Fax 68185

Arosa 1800m

✔ Peaceful, quiet, sunny ski area

✔ Classic all-round winter holiday destination, with excellent non-skiing and cross-country facilities

✔ Very good children's facilities

✔ Good village transport compensates for scattered nature of the place

✔ Easy access by train, including packaged airport transfers

✘ Very limited skiing by large-resort standards

✘ Virtually no tree-lined runs, so little skiing feasible in bad weather

✘ Slopes face mainly south and east, and can get icy

✘ Some ugly, square, grey buildings in Obersee

✘ Lack of evening atmosphere

The classic image of a winter sports resort is perhaps an isolated, snow-covered Swiss village, surrounded by big, beautiful mountains, with skating on a frozen lake, horse-drawn sleighs jingling through the streets, and people in fur coats strolling on mountain paths. Arosa is just that.

Skiing is just one of its attractions – and not an important one for many of its visitors. It's not keen skiers that Arosa aims to attract. It's people who want a relaxing time in the mountains and, maybe, want to ski a little too.

Accommodation is mainly in quiet hotels. Most people who come here don't want lively nightlife. But they do want comfort, and they don't mind paying for it. It's a pity that many of the hotels that are so comfortable within are eyesores, dating from times when pitched roofs were out of fashion.

ORIENTATION

Arosa is in a high, remote setting at the end of a very long winding approach road from Chur. Rail access is easier. It is made up of two main centres, which are almost separate villages, Obersee and Innerarosa. Obersee, the first you come to, is the main centre and has a cable-car, chair and drag into the skiing. Innerarosa is about 1km further along and has a chair, a drag and (some way below the main focus) a gondola. Some accommodation is a long walk from the lifts, but there's a frequent, free ski-bus.

Outings by public transport or car are possible, notably to **Davos-Klosters, Flims** or **Lenzerheide**, the latter also reachable off-piste.

 ## The resort

Arosa is set in a sheltered basin at the head of a beautiful wooded valley, in contrast to the open mountainside on which the skiing takes place. The centre of the resort, Obersee, is a drab collection of Edwardian buildings – though its lakeside setting adds some charm. The remainder of Arosa is scattered over a wide area, with a substantial hill separating Obersee from the older, prettier Innerarosa.

Despite its wealth of activities, and a fair amount of traffic, Arosa is a quiet place. Its relaxed ambience attracts an unpretentiously wealthy clientele of families and older people.

 ## The skiing

For such a well known and long-established resort, Arosa's ski area is tiny and lacking in any real challenge. Don't be surprised by the number of pedestrians and tobogganists you'll find around the ski area.

THE SKI AREA
Small and friendly
The slopes are spread fairly widely over two main sectors. The **Weisshorn** skiing faces mainly south and south-east. Tschuggen, half-way up the Weisshorn peak, is the major

lift junction, reachable from both Obersee and Innerarosa. An inconveniently sited gondola below Innerarosa is the main access to the east- and north-east-facing slopes of the **Hörnli** sector.

Drags and chair-lifts allow skiing either way between the two sectors. Skiing around the area is straightforward for moderate skiers, with easy routes possible between all main points. It is also not an area where you have to keep an eye on the time. There are no potential dead-ends and it is possible to take the ski-bus home from wherever you end up.

Arosa has a US-style free ski host service every Sunday to help new arrivals get to know the slopes.

SNOW RELIABILITY
Quite good, despite sunny aspect
Although there is no very high skiing, and the slopes get a lot of sun, Arosa has a relatively good reputation for snow-cover. All the more interesting south-facing pistes are above 2000m and the shadier Hörnli slopes usually hold their snow well. A cannon for covering worn patches is the only artificial back-up to nature.

FOR ADVANCED SKIERS
A few off-piste options
Arosa isn't the resort for a keen advanced skier. There is a small section of steep skiing, both on- and

SKI FACTS

Altitude	1740m-2655m
Lifts	16
Pistes	70km
Green/Blue	45%
Red	45%
Black	10%
Artificial snow	1km

GETTING THERE

Air Zürich, transfer 3hr.

Rail Station in resort (Obersee); regular bus service.

SKI SCHOOL

94/95 prices in
Swiss francs

Swiss
Classes 5 days
4hr: 9.45-11.45
and 2.15-4.15
5 half-days: 125
Children's classes
Ages: 4 to 12
5 half-days: 115
Private lessons
Hourly or daily
120 for 1hr

CHILDCARE

The ski school runs
ski kindergartens for
children from age 4 to
6, from 9.45 to 4.15,
at Innerarosa and
behind the hotel Eden
at Obersee.

The two 5-star hotels
have their own
kindergartens, as do
some others – the
4-star Hof Maran,
Seehof and Valsana,
and the more modest
Eden.

off-piste, at the top of the Weisshorn.
But the most interesting opportunity
is to ski off-piste to and from
Lenzerheide via Hörnli. It's a scenic
but not difficult run.

FOR INTERMEDIATE SKIERS
Best for leisurely types
This is a good area for those who want
to take it easy and aren't looking for
high mileage or much challenge. Keen
piste-bashers will ski it all in the first
day. Even the interesting Weisshorn-Carmenna run,
is within the scope of good
intermediates. Average skiers will
particularly enjoy the long Hörnli-Innerarosa pistes. Less ambitious skiers
have some lovely long cruises, the
highlight of which is the Bruggerhorn-Pratschi motorway, well away from
the lifts. The only woodland run of
any note is one of the steeper blues.

FOR BEGINNERS
Very good beginner slopes
The Tschuggen nursery slopes are
excellent and usually have good snow,
but get other skiers passing through.

Innerarosa has a quieter but more
limited area usually reserved for
children. Quick learners will soon be
able to ski all the way to Innerarosa,
where there's a chair-lift straight back
to Tschuggen. There are other easy
runs for beginners to try too.

FOR CROSS-COUNTRY
High-quality trails
Although it lacks the sheer length of
trails of many resort, Arosa (with
29km) has some of the best, varied
loops in the Alps. Guided excursions
and instruction are widely available,
and buses serve the scattered areas.

QUEUES
Few problems
With so many part-timers and non-skiers, and a well laid out lift system,
Arosa does not suffer many queues.
There can still be waits for the recently
improved Weisshorn cable-car. The
Hörnli drag is the worst bottleneck
and is due to be replaced by a new
quad chair for the 1994/95 season.

MOUNTAIN RESTAURANTS
Excellent but crowded
Some of the mountain restaurants are
very good, but there are too few of
them, particularly considering the
number of non-skiers walking around
the slopes. Consequently they get
crowded. Most have table-service and
are expensive. Tschuggenhütte, near
the mid-station of the cable-car, is an
attractively rustic little refuge with a
nice sun terrace, but soon gets
crowded (from 11am according to one
Arosa regular). Hörnlihütte, at the top
of the gondola, has good food.
Carmennahütte, at the junction of the
main Hörnli and Weisshorn pistes has
a particularly pleasant interior. The
Weisshornsattelhütte, at the top of
Bruggerhorn on the periphery of the

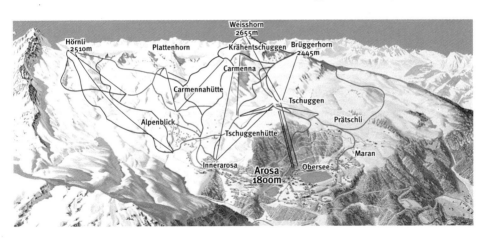

LIFT PASSES

94/95 prices in Swiss francs

Arosa area
All lifts in Arosa ski region.

Beginners Free baby-lifts at Innerarosa and Obersee. Tschuggen area ski-pass (am, pm or full-day) covers 7 beginner area lifts (adult 1-day 30).

Main pass
1-day pass 52; 6-day pass 219 (low season 186 – 15% off)

Senior citizens
Over 65 male, 62 female: 6-day pass 186 (15% off)

Children
Under 16: 6-day pass 110 (50% off)
Under 6: free pass

Short-term passes
Single ascent tickets for pedestrians on some lifts. Day-pass with refund when handed in early (58). Afternoon pass reduces by the hour, from 39 at noon to 27 at 3pm.

Alternative periods
4 days in 7: 187
7 days in 14: 309

Notes Discounts for students and groups.

ACTIVITIES

Indoor Hotel facilities open to non-residents (swimming, sauna, massage, tennis, squash), golf, bridge, chess, bowling, fitness centre, cinema, concerts, museum
Outdoor 3 skating rinks (2 artificial), 1 covered artificial rink, ice-hockey, curling, sleigh rides, 35km cleared paths, hot-air ballooning, horse-riding, ski-bob, toboggan runs, snow-shoe walks, para-gliding, hang-gliding, flying school

PACKAGES

Inghams, Kuoni, Made to Measure, Plus Travel, Ski Choice, Ski Club of GB, SkiGower, Swiss Travel Service

TOURIST OFFICE

Postcode CH-7050
Tel 010 41 (81) 311621
Fax 313135

ski area, is rarely crowded and has good food. Alpenblick, above Innerarosa on the easier of the two long red runs from Hörnli, is arguably the best restaurant, serving huge portions of good food in a friendly atmosphere.

SKI SCHOOL
Plenty of English speakers
There's a big ski school and a lot of demand for private lessons from the affluent Arosa guests. Practically all instructors speak at least some English, and we have had good reports which confirm the school's high reputation. However, one reporter 'had a great time for two days in a high-level off-piste group' but thought the teaching 'fairly non-existent'.

FACILITIES FOR CHILDREN
Accommodating hotels
Arosa seems a good choice for a family holiday, with its low-pressure approach to skiing and lots of alternative things to do. Observers have been impressed by the ski kindergartens, but we lack first-hand reports. Bear in mind that several hotels have kindergartens.

 # Staying there

It's a spread-out place, but location of accommodation is not unduly important as the resort has an excellent ski-bus service supplemented by hotel courtesy transport. But for skiers (as opposed to skaters), Innerarosa is preferable, with lifts into both sectors of the skiing.

HOW TO GO
Plenty of hotels, few packages
Part of Arosa's charm is that it is not big on the British market; but a few operators go there.
Hotels Arosa is essentially a hotel resort, with a high proportion of them 3- and 4-stars. Most reporters stayed in 4-stars. They are mainly block-like buildings, unpleasant to behold but enjoying excellent views.
£££££ Kulm Smart, luxurious; in splendid position at Innerarosa. Pool.
££££ Sporthotel Valsana Well equipped place on eastern side of Obersee. Pool, kindergarten.
££££ Hof Maran Comfortable retreat, up at Maran. Children's facilities, natural ice rink; particularly well placed for cross-country skiers.
££££ Bellevue On the road just below Innerarosa. Very good refurbished rooms and excellent food.

££££ Hohenfels Non-ideal position above the road between Obersee and Innerarosa, but runs a courtesy bus and is recommended for excellent food and attentive staff.
£££ Seehof Quiet family hotel, ten minutes' walk below Obersee; supplies courtesy bus. Good, varied food.
££ Eden Reliable place in central position in Obersee. Kindergarten.
££ Hold Good-value chalet across the road from the Kulm at Innerarosa.
Self-catering Holiday flats are widely available in the resort, but few are bookable as a package through British tour operators. The Promenade studios are a simple, modern block reasonably well placed on the main street just outside Obersee.

EATING OUT
Good, if formal
Although Arosa restaurants share a good variety of menus, they tend to be rather lacking in style range. Most are hotel-based, and there is a disappointing shortage of little rustic stublis. The Bellevue has a good reputation for food, and the Cristallo in central Obersee has a particularly attractive restaurant. The Hohenfels, Eden and Post hotels are others well worth considering. The jolly Waldbeck serves good local dishes.

APRES-SKI
Animated early; quiet later
Nightlife is fairly varied, but most is geared to pre-dinner activity. The Rondo is a good-value, lively bar with music, while the young and trendy congregate at the Barosa. Kaisers is an atmospheric tea-room. Otherwise the highlight of the week is the torchlit descent from Weisshorn followed by the fireworks. A number of the 'non-skiing' facilities are available in the evenings, and there's ice hockey, curling and floodlit cross-country skiing. But most people stay in their hotels after dinner, so the village streets are quiet. The two discos liven up at weekends.

FOR NON-SKIERS
A Swiss classic
Non-skiers have their own lift map and pass, with a number of mountain restaurants reachable via an array of cleared, marked walks (35km). The boutiques and jewellers are worth a look, though prices are likely to dull the interest. Sleigh rides (some go up into the skiing) are beautiful.

Champéry 1050m

✔ *Charming rustic village with impressive mountain views*

✔ *Very extensive ski area, linking with Avoriaz and Châtel in France*

✔ *Quiet, relaxed place – yet plenty to do off the slopes*

✔ *Easy access for independent travellers – car, train, plane/train*

✘ *Local slopes suffer from the sun – facing south-east, with no snowmakers*

✘ *No skiing back to the village – and often none back to the valley*

✘ *Beginners face the hassle and expense of getting up to Planachaux, which is not as gentle as it could be*

✘ *Not much difficult skiing nearby*

Champéry is one the prettiest of ski villages, with narrow streets, pleasantly rustic wooden buildings, informal cafés, nice little shops, and a friendly atmosphere – certainly the most appealing place from which to ski the main Franco-Swiss Portes du Soleil circuit. It is also one of the least reliable of Switzerland's ski resorts for snow, with sunny slopes mainly lying between 1600m and 2200m, and no local snowmakers to compensate.

With good transport links and sports facilities, Champéry is great for part-timers and non-skiers, or for families looking for a quiet time in a lovely place, especially if they have a car. But it also deserves consideration by skiers who simply put character before convenience. The north-facing slopes of Avoriaz, just across the French border, are only four lift-rides away – and we have skied fresh powder there when Champéry's lower slopes were bare and its upper ones slushy.

ORIENTATION

Champéry sits on the side of a valley separated from its ski area by a steep, fragmented mountainside. A cable-car goes up into the skiing from the railway station at the bottom of the village, and Grand Paradis, 2km further up the valley, has ski slopes down to it. The skiing is part of the main Portes du Soleil circuit, spreading north (anti-clockwise) and west (clockwise) into France and taking in **Avoriaz, Les Crosets, Champoussin, Morgins** and **Châtel**, the last four also easily reached by car.

Possible outings further afield are **Verbier, Chamonix** and **Les Diablerets**.

The resort

Champéry is the stuff of traditional picture-postcards. The main street that runs the length of the village is lined with attractive old wooden chalets that house most of the hotels, bars and restaurants, liberally adorned with large Swiss flags.

An attempt has been made to provide the facilities demanded by today's holiday-makers without spoiling the old-world charm. Down a steepish hill, somewhat removed from the main street, is the modern development of sports centre and large cable-car station – and a convenient new terminus for the narrow-gauge railway that comes up from the mainline town of Aigle.

The village has a friendly, relaxed atmosphere; it would be ideal for families if there was more convenient skiing available.

The skiing

Champéry's local skiing is as friendly and relaxing as the village, at least for intermediate skiers. It is far from ideal for absolute beginners, and experts have a choice of covering vast amounts of ground on the Portes du Soleil piste circuit, or exploring the considerable off-piste possibilities reachable from the resort.

THE SKI AREA
Extensive and sunny

The village of Champéry is not quite part of the main Portes du Soleil circuit (see overall summary on page 224) but its skiing is – the sunny bowl of **Planachaux**, way above the village, with a couple of runs leading down to the valley at **Grand Paradis**, a short bus-ride from Champéry. There is no piste skiing to Champéry itself, though on rare occasions local conditions allow off-piste trips. Planachaux is rather featureless, and most skiers quickly move on – at least as far as next-door Les Crosets. You can explore the Portes du Soleil by travelling west towards Avoriaz or north-east to Champoussin, Morgins and Châtel.

There are three ways to ski to Avoriaz – via a chair-lift from the eastern side of the Planachaux bowl to Chavanette (check out the infamous 'Swiss Wall' mogul field as you ride up) or via one of two lifts from Les Crosets. Care should be taken to allow plenty of time to return from Avoriaz. Queues can form at some lifts, and getting up to the top of the Champéry cable-car to ride down (when it's not

LIFT PASSES

94/95 prices in
Swiss francs
Portes du Soleil
Covers all the lifts in
12 resorts.
Beginners Points card
(adult 50-point card
30)
Main pass
1-day pass 45
6-day pass 204
Senior citizens
Over 60: 6-day pass
135 (34% off)
Children
Under 16: 6-day pass
135 (34% off)
Under 7: free pass
Short-term passes
Half-day pass to and
from noon (adult 32).
Notes Reductions for
families.
Alternative passes
Half-, 1- and 2-day
passes available for
35 lifts and 100km of
piste in Champéry,
Les Crosets,
Champoussin and La
Foilleuse (Morgins);
(adult 1-day 35).

possible to ski to Grand Paradis) is a
roundabout business. The run home is
usually either closed or made awkward
by poor snow conditions.

The easy runs of Champoussin are
most directly reached by walking
across the Les Crosets car park,
followed by a chair-lift to Pointe de
l'Au. From here there is a network of
short runs and lifts to Champoussin
and Morgins.

For more on skiing Avoriaz see page
149; for Châtel see page 160.

SNOW RELIABILITY
Very poor
Champéry gets a big thumbs down for
lack of snowmakers. Even the little ski
kindergarten in the village relies on
helicopter deliveries of the white stuff
when it's in short supply. The
Champoussin and Morgins runs are
also low and sunny, and getting to the
north-facing slopes of Avoriaz when
conditions are poor can be unpleasant
for moderate skiers.

FOR ADVANCED SKIERS
Few local challenges
Champéry is not well placed for
reaching the Portes du Soleil tough
runs. The Swiss Wall, on the
Champéry side of Chavanette, is an
intimidatingly long, steep slope, but
not nearly as terrifying as its various
names suggest; the main difficulty is at
the very top, which can be icy when
snow is in short supply or may have
moguls the size of small cars when it is
in abundance. There's a limit to how
many times you will want to ski the
Wall, and it's quite a trek to the Hauts
Forts above Avoriaz – the main black-
run sector in the Portes du Soleil.
There's lots of scope for off-piste at
Chavanette and on the broad slopes of
Les Crosets and Champoussin.

FOR INTERMEDIATE SKIERS
Wonderful if snow is good
Confident intermediates have the
whole of the Portes du Soleil at their
disposal. Without straying across the
border there is a huge amount of
intermediate skiing to be enjoyed.

The runs home to Grand Paradis are
as good as any when conditions allow,
and enjoyable by all grades of
intermediate. It's not worth dwelling
too long around the bland Planachaux
area, but Les Crosets is a junction of
several fine runs. The pistes down
from Pointe de Mossete and Grand
Conche are good direct running runs
ideal for competent, or simply
confident, skiers. The runs back from
Pointe de l'Au also hold the interest.
The Champoussin section is a network
of short, easy pistes ideal for leisurely
cruising. Skiers 'doing the circuit' tend
to find these runs uninteresting and
time consuming, and as such
circumnavigate them, leaving this
section nicely uncrowded and perfect
for nervous performers. Beyond, the
runs down to Morgins are delightful

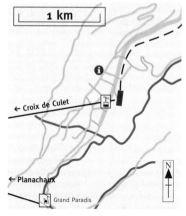

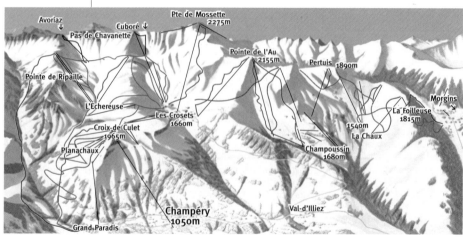

SKI SCHOOL

94/95 prices in
Swiss francs

Swiss
Classes 5 days
3hr: 9.15-12.15
5 days (15hr): 120
Children's classes
Ages: from 6
5 days (15hr): 110
Private lessons
Hourly or daily
45 for 1hr

CHILDCARE

The ski school runs a
ski kindergarten for
children aged 4 to 7,
from 9.15 to 4.30.

There are two non-ski
kindergartens, both
taking children aged
6 months to 5 years,
from 9am to 5pm –
Garderie Snoopy
(791969) and Maison
des Schtroumpfs
(741066).

tree-lined meanders for average skiers,
and certainly the place to head for in
poor visibility. If need be, you can ski
from Planachaux to Morgins by use of
just two lifts.

FOR BEGINNERS
Go elsewhere if you have a choice
Despite its good ski school, Champéry
is far from ideal for beginners. An
expensive cable-car ride takes novices
to the steepish Planachaux runs, on
the shortest of which they receive
tuition. Beginners with a car can reach
the far more suitable Champoussin
slopes reasonably quickly.

FOR CROSS-COUNTRY
Very poor
A 7km loop is advertised, but it's
very unreliable for snow and not well
maintained.

QUEUES
Few local problems
The cable-car comfortably copes with
the village's quite small ski
population. When snow is good,
weekend crowds can be a problem –
the car park opposite the cable-car
station is not there by accident – but
queues at Avoriaz are a greater
concern.

MOUNTAIN RESTAURANTS
Wide choice, some highlights
The local area is very good in terms of
numbers of mountain restaurants,
though few are particularly
memorable. Chez Coquoz at
Planachaux is recommended for its

traditional atmosphere and good
cheesy specialities. Chez Marius (or
Clavets) is a pleasant halt on the way
down to Grand Paradis. Further afield,
the refuges across at Marmottes-Les
Lindarets are worth heading for (see
Avoriaz chapter, page 149).

SKI SCHOOL
No worries
The few reports on the ski school that
we've had are free of criticisms and tell
of a surprising number of instructors
who speak good English.

FACILITIES FOR CHILDREN
Plenty of options
As well as the ski kindergartens and
two non-ski ones, there is the
alternative of half-day or all-day care
with the upmarket chalet operator Ski

Selected chalets in Champéry

GETTING THERE

Air Geneva, transfer
2hr.

PACKAGES

Chalets 'Unlimited',
Kuoni, Made to
Measure, Piste Artiste,
Ski La Vie, Ski Les
Alpes, Ski Scott Dunn,
Ski Weekend,
Snowline, Swiss
Travel Service

Champoussin
Snowline, Swiss
Travel Service

Morgins Chalets
'Unlimited', Kuoni, Ski
Morgins, Snowline

ACTIVITIES

Indoor Swimming
pools, ice skating and
curling rink, Sunfit
fitness centre (sauna,
solarium, body
building,
physiotherapy)
Outdoor Curling,
para-gliding

PISTE ARTISTE

helped us to compile
the eating out and
après-ski sections.
Our thanks to them.

TOURIST OFFICE

Postcode CH-1874
Tel 010 41 (25) 791141
Fax 791847

La Vie, who have a crèche staffed by
their own trained nannies for children
aged up to 6. Piste Artiste offers a ski
kindergarten and nanny services.
Older children wanting to go to ski
school for a half-day can spend the
rest of the day in the Snowflake club.

 # Staying there

Although only a small village, much
of the accommodation is not
particularly well located for skiers. The
new cable-car station has been
consigned to the outer fringes, some
way from many hotels; one or two
chalets are stuck on hillsides at the
periphery of things. The result,
surprisingly for a small resort, is that
the ski-bus is quite important –
fortunately it is fairly efficient – and
that having your own transport can be
an advantage.

HOW TO GO
Limited packages available
There's a limited range of hotels and
catered chalets available through tour
operators. Champéry is one of the
easiest resorts to get to – by car, train
or plane.
Chalets There are a number of chalets
available, mostly very small – ideal for
families. Piste Artiste have a couple of
well equipped chalets that, unusually,
are available by the part-week. Ski la
Vie have a traditional chalet and a
couple of smart modern chalet-
apartments. Ski Scott Dunn have a
selection of traditional, creaky old
places with lots of nice touches.
Hotels Champéry is essentially a hotel
resort, with a good spread of
accommodation from 4-star to B&B.
Prices are low by comparison with
many smarter Swiss resorts.
£££ Champéry Biggest and best in
town, but hardly in the luxury bracket
despite 4-star rating – a pleasantly
comfortable chalet on the main street.
£££ Suisse Rival adjacent 4-star.
£££ Beau Séjour Comfortable,
traditional 3-star at the southern end
of the main street.
££ National Classic Swiss villa-style
hotel on the main street, with neatly
renovated bedrooms.
££ Paix Creaky old chalet near the
Beau Séjour.
££ Alpes Ditto, but in a slightly
inconvenient position.
£ Souvenir Central 1-star which does
the cheapest half board you'll find.
Self-catering There are some
apartments but none are packaged on
the British market.

EATING OUT
A fair choice
Two of the best places are just outside
the village. Cantines des Rives, on the
other side of the valley, is a taxi-ride
away. It's a beautiful traditional chalet
specialising in fondue and raclette.
Similarly distant is the Grand Paradis.
It serves excellent, if expensive, local
specialities. A drawback for some may
be the use of stuffed animals to
decorate the place!
  Victor Hugo and 4 Saisons are
impressive gourmet restaurants in the
hotel Suisse. Good, less expensive
places are the Vieux Chalet and the
restaurants of the hotel des Alpes and
hotel National. For a less formal
ambience it's best to try the local
specialities of the Farinet, Café du
Centre or hotel du Nord, and the pizza
at Cime de l'Est.
  Once a week the restaurant at the
top of the cable-car is open in the
evening with special departures from
and to the base-station. Piste Artiste
organise post-skiing meals at the
mountain hut Chez Marius, followed
by a torchlit descent.

APRES-SKI
Something for everyone
Champéry has a convivial atmosphere
at tea-time, but things are fairly sedate
later in the evening. The Pub is the
liveliest place in town, with noisy
jukebox music earlier before a disco
starts in the basic little downstairs bar
around midnight. It's frequented
mostly by resort workers and locals.
  Far cosier places are the pleasantly
informal bars in the hotel Suisse. The
Bar des Guides is a pre-dinner
watering hole with interesting relics
and photographs of pre-war skiing.
The Mines d'Or is a cellar bar, mainly
frequented by ski instructors, that's
good for a mellow late drink.
  The Farinet is a spacious cellar
night-club with upstairs restaurant
which is good fun when there are
enough people to give it atmosphere –
mostly at weekends. Most Brits prefer
it to the simpler Levant disco, which is
more of a locals' haunt.

FOR NON-SKIERS
Excellent for the energetic
The Portes du Soleil has a general
drawback for non-skiers, which is that
skiers other than beginners are very
unlikely to want to hang around (or
return to) the local skiing for lunch.
That aside, Champéry is very
attractive for the non-skier who does
not insist on a lot of animation in the
village. Walks, particularly along to

Val d'Illiez, are very pleasant, and the narrow-gauge railway allows excursions to Montreux, Lausanne and Sion. There is a good range of things to do in this small village, thanks to the excellent sports centre.

Les Crosets 1660m

Les Crosets has a prime position within the Portes du Soleil, but to stay there you would have to be very keen. It's little more than a multi-lift station and car-park, with a couple of hotels and restaurants supposedly making it a mini-resort. It could be recommended only to car-driving hermits who might find it a useful base with the option to visit Champéry if they get bored. Hotel Télécabine is a homely British-run place with reputedly good evening meals.

Champoussin 1580m

Champoussin is, theoretically at least, a good choice for a family looking for a quiet, user-friendly base – no traffic, ski-in, ski-out convenience, enough altitude to have snow in the village often, no noisy late-night revellers, rustic-style buildings and the comfortable Ambassador hotel with all mod cons. It appears to lack just one thing – a helpful attitude – if one very bitter reporter is anything to go by. Her family's holiday was spoilt by problems with a poorly-run, impersonal ski school and a children's Mini club where kids spent much of their time standing around, no English was spoken and the unpleasant supervisor was seen shaking a small child. They fared little better at their swish hotel; it had variable food and a shortage of staff, making for almost non-existent service, and the accommodation they'd booked was not available. And all this was supervised by an unrepentant Basil Fawlty. Perhaps it was just a bad week, but is it worth the risk of finding out?

Morgins 1350m

Morgins can disappoint. Attracted there by visions of a quiet little Swiss village with a great ski area on its doorstep, visitors are surprised to find a scattered resort where some accommodation is a fair walk from one or both of the Portes du Soleil lifts. Although reasonably attractive, the village is not in the same league as Champéry for charm, and even those looking for peace and quiet may find too much of a good thing here. The bland local slopes lead skiers to look further afield; but with poor snow conditions affecting links, an irritating series of short lifts, and lack of public transport to Châtel, this is often easier said than done. Those expecting typical Swiss efficiency are also surprised to find poor local piste grooming and marking.

Morgins is best suited to those with a car. They can drive to Les Crosets for the highest and best of the Swiss Portes du Soleil skiing, or to the Linga gondola at Châtel.

Skiers not interested in 'doing the circuit' have the option to buy the cheaper Evasion lift pass which covers a still substantial area – Morgins, Champoussin, Super-Châtel, Torgon and La Chapelle-d'Abondance. Cross-country enthusiasts have 20km of pleasant trails.

The large 3-star Bellevue is a modern hotel, but built in traditional style, and has been praised by reporters for its friendliness and comfort. There are a couple of worthwhile restaurants – Café du Valais has good grill specialities and the Bergerie serves interesting French cuisine. The Bazot is the place for a four o'clock coffee. The Crystal bar is the only place with any atmosphere later. Off-slope amenities are indoor tennis, horse riding and a natural ice-rink.

Crans-Montana 1500m

✔ Large ski area suitable for all but black-run skiers

✔ Fair amount of woodland skiing – good for bad weather

✔ Modern, well designed lift system, with few queues except for top lifts

✔ Splendid wooded setting with magnificent panoramic views

✔ Golf course provides excellent, gentle nursery slopes

✔ Very sunny skiing (see minus points)

✔ Excellent cross-country trails – above, at and below resort level

✘ Towny resort centres composed partly of big chalet-style blocks but mainly of dreary cubic blocks – and therefore entirely without Alpine atmosphere

✘ Long, uphill walks to lifts from much of the accommodation

✘ Snow badly affected by sun except in early season

✘ Not much challenging skiing

✘ Long queues for the only lift going above 2500m – due to be replaced, but not until 1995/96

When conditions are right – clear skies above fresh, deep snow – Crans-Montana takes some beating. The mountains you bounce down with the midday sun full on your face are charmingly scenic, the slopes broken up by rock outcrops and forest. The mountains you gaze at – Zermatt's Matterhorn instantly recognisable among them – are mind-blowing. When conditions are right, mountain-loving skiers will forgive Crans-Montana almost anything – in particular, its inconvenient, linear layout and the ugly, towny style of its twin resort centres.

Sadly, conditions are more often wrong than right. Except in the depths of midwinter, that strong midday sun quickly bakes the pistes. For the typical British skier booking six months ahead, this is enough to keep Crans-Montana off the short-list. For intermediate skiers who can time a visit according to the weather – and who are content to avert their eyes from the architecture – the resort is worth serious consideration.

ORIENTATION

Crans-Montana is an amalgam of two villages, their centres a mile apart and their fringes now merging. They sit on a broad shelf facing south across the Rhône valley, reached by good roads as well as a funicular railway from Sierre. Gondolas go up into the main ski area from both villages. The skiing spreads east across the mountainside, with further lift base-stations (and accommodation) at Les Barzettes and Aminona.

Anzere is to the west, but the skiing is not linked. Outings by road or rail are possible, notably to **Zermatt** and **Verbier**. The smaller resorts of **Grimentz** and **Ovronnaz** are also worth bearing in mind.

 The resort

Crans-Montana celebrated its centenary as a resort in 1993, but is far from being a picturesque Swiss chocolate-box village. It is strung along a busy road, and its many hotels, villas, apartments and smart shops are mainly ugly blocks with few concessions to Alpine traditions.

Fortunately, the resort's many trees help to hide some of the architectural excesses, and give some areas a positively attractive appearance. And its wonderful south-facing balcony setting means you get a lot of sun as well as superb views to the great mountains beyond the Rhône. The balcony accommodates several small lakes and two golf courses, one of them home to the Swiss Open tournament.

The resort depends heavily on summer conference business and this rather sets the tone even in winter. Hotels tend to be formal, quiet and comfortable, village facilities wide-ranging but daytime-oriented, and the visitors middle-aged and dignified. In the evenings, the place lacks the Alpine-village atmosphere that many of us look for.

Crans is the more up-market village, with expensive jewellery shops, a casino, and a correspondingly high fur-coat count. It is well situated for the pretty golf course area, which has baby lifts for complete beginners, a cross-country trail and lovely walks. Montana has cheaper restaurants and bars, the main ice rink, and the station for the funicular from Sierre.

 The skiing

Although it has recently achieved some prominence in ski-racing – hosting the world championships in 1987 and the climax of the World Cup series in 1992 – Crans-Montana is not a bravo's resort. Its skiing suits intermediates well, containing few challenges and no nasty surprises. Beginners are well catered for.

SKI FACTS

Altitude	1500m-3000m
Lifts	39
Pistes	160km
Green/Blue	37%
Red	50%
Black	13%
Artificial snow	3km

LIFT PASSES

94/95 prices in
Swiss francs

**Crans-Montana-
Aminona**
Covers all lifts in
Crans-Montana and
Aminona and the
ski-bus.

Beginners
Points card

Main pass
1-day pass 47
6-day pass 215

Senior citizens
Over 65: 6-day pass
107 (50% off)

Children
Under 16: 6-day pass
129 (40% off)
Under 6: free pass

Short-term passes
Half-day from 11.15
(adult 37) or 12.30
(adult 32); 2hr
afternoon pass from
2pm (adult 27).

Alternative periods
8 non-consecutive
days (adult 311)

THE SKI AREA

Interestingly fragmented

Crans-Montana's 160km of piste are
spread over three well-linked areas, all
equally suitable for intermediates of
varying abilities and persuasions.

Cry d'Err is the largest sector – an
open bowl descending into patchy
forest, directly above Montana. Cry
d'Err itself is the meeting point of
many lifts and the starting point of
the cable-car up to the sector high-
point of Bella Lui (2545m). Cry d'Err is
served directly by two gondolas – one
carrying 2,200 people per hour from
just above central Montana, the other
carrying less than half that number
from just above Crans. Both have mid-
stations; the one above Montana
delivers beginners to the high-altitude
nursery slopes served by the twin

Verdets drags. A third gondola goes up
from the west side of Crans to
Chetzeron, with a drag above going
on to Cry d'Err.

The next sector, reached directly
from Les Barzettes by another
2,200p/h gondola, is focused on Les
Violettes, starting point of the lift up
to the Plaine Morte glacier. There are
three linking routes from Cry d'Err to
the **Violettes-Plaine Morte** sector.
One, starting at Bella Lui (or, strictly,
from Col du Pochet, a short run and
drag beyond) is officially 'for
experienced skiers only' because it is
off-piste; but it is largely a traverse,
made awkward only by wave-like
bumps and narrowness in places. Bella
Lui is also the start of the Men's
Downhill race course (Piste Nationale),
which passes Cry d'Err and finishes at

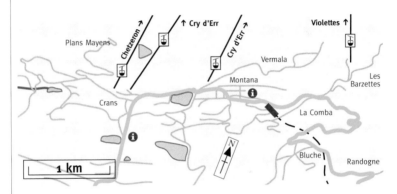

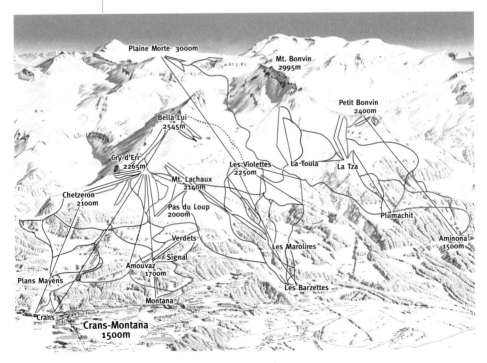

Les Barzettes. The third option is to take an easy path across from the Verdets drags, near the bottom of the Cry d'Err sector. Even this route is high enough to reach the low mid-station of the Violettes gondola.

The third sector is above **Aminona** at the eastern-end of the skiing. This is linked in both directions to Les Violettes and there's a gondola up from the valley.

SNOW RELIABILITY
The resort's main drawback
Crans-Montana's skiing goes up to glacier level at 3000m, but this impressive fact is misleading. The solitary run down from the Plaine Morte glacier, served by a cable-car prone to long queues and closures due to wind or avalanche danger, does not make this a snowsure ski area.

Little of the other skiing is above 2250m; on a south-facing mountain, this makes for icy, patchy conditions whenever the sun hits the pistes for long. Artificial snow is available in only three small areas – at the bottom of the Piste Nationale, and on short runs beneath Les Violettes and Cry d'Err. One reporter recommends a day-trip outing to Grimentz, across the Rhône valley, when the slush at Crans is no longer bearable.

FOR ADVANCED SKIERS
Lacks challenging piste skiing
There are few steep pistes. The only moguls worthy of the name are found on the short but usually quiet run served by the Toula lifts. Plenty of off-piste is available in all sectors, but particularly beneath Chetzeron and La Tza; guides are usually easy to book.

The Piste Nationale course is far from daunting taken at 'normal' speed, but has some enormous jumps just above Les Marolies. The direct run from La Tza to Plumachit is fairly testing in places, especially when icy.

FOR INTERMEDIATE SKIERS
Lots of attractive, flattering runs
Crans-Montana is particularly well suited to intermediates. Pistes are mostly wide and, although red dominates the map, many of the red runs don't justify the grading. They also tend to be uniform in difficulty from top to bottom, having few nasty surprises for the nervous. Avid piste bashers enjoy the length of many runs, plus the fast lifts and good links that allow a lot of varied mileage to be clocked up.

The 11km run from Plaine Morte down to Les Barzettes is a fine, varied piste, starting with superb top-of-the-world views and powder snow, and finishing among pretty woods. There are several truly contrasting variants of the bottom half from Les Violettes. But many skiers love the top half so much they 'yo-yo' ski it (see Queues).

The short runs from Bella Lui to just below Cry d'Err have some of the best snow and quietest skiing in the area, and provide fine views of awesome Montagne de Raul. The Piste Nationale is a good test of intermediate technique, with plenty of bumps but also lots of room. The quietest area, and a good one for groups of varying intermediate standards, is the Petit Bonvin sector above Aminona. Three long runs of varying difficulty take skiers from La Tza down to Aminona, while there are also drags up at Petit Bonvin which serve short, easy runs over good snow.

A surprising number of skiers are very unadventurous, tending to linger in the unremarkable area beneath Cry d'Err, content with short runs down to Merbé and Pas du Loup.

FOR BEGINNERS
Plenty to offer the first-timer
There are three nursery areas, all excellent in their own way, with slopes of varying difficulty. Complete beginners have very gentle slopes as an option, on the golf course next to Crans. Cry d'Err has an area of relatively long, easy runs, which have the advantage of up-the-mountain views and atmosphere as well as better snow. But the runs are also used by other skiers, and do require investment in a full lift pass. The Verdets-Grand Signal run is steeper, and lazy liftmen can let the drag-lift get terribly icy. For the near-beginner, the little run served by a drag at Plaine Morte is worth trying – powder snow and great views.

FOR CROSS-COUNTRY
Excellent high-level trails
There are 17km of pretty, easy trails (skating-style as well as classic) on and around the golf course. But what makes Crans-Montana a particularly good cross-country resort is the high-level route, in and out of woods, across the whole mountainside from Plans Mayens to beyond Aminona – a 15km round-trip. Plaine Morte has a further 12km available in the summer.

You must purchase a vignette, costing SF5 a day or SF35 for the season (valid in all other Swiss resorts too). It gets you a 50% discount on the lifts up to Plaine Morte.

CHILDCARE

The Montana ski school runs a kindergarten with skiing available up at Signal (4180540) for children aged 3 to 6, from 9am to 4.45.

There are several other kindergartens. In Crans, Bibiland (418142) takes children from age 2. In Montana, Fleurs des Champs (412367) takes children aged 2 months to 12 years; and Les Coccinelles (412423) takes children aged 3 to 16.

GETTING THERE

Air Geneva, transfer 3hr.

Rail Sierre (15km), Sion (22km); regular buses to resort.

PACKAGES

Inghams, Kuoni, Made to Measure, Ski Club of GB, Ski Esprit, Ski Europe, Ski Les Alpes, Travelscene Ski-Drive

SKI SCHOOL

94/95 prices in Swiss francs

Swiss
Classes
5 days
3hr: 9.30-12.30
5 days (15hr): 160
Children's classes
Ages: from 3
5 days (15hr): 160
Private lessons
Hourly
50 for 1hr

QUEUES
Imminent transformation
Access to the glacier – and, more importantly, the excellent red run of over 1000m vertical back down – can involve long waits. Even in January, if snow low down is poor, hour-long queues are not unknown. An impressive stand-up gondola with four times the capacity of the old cable-car is planned, but won't be ready until 1995/96. Minor irritations include short queues for the Barmaz chair-lifts up to Les Violettes from La Toula, and sometimes at Cabane des Bois. Delays become longer when snow lower down is in poor condition. On the other hand, the low-capacity gondola to Merbé becomes over-subscribed when wind closes the other major lifts. Crans-Montana does not get overrun at weekends.

MOUNTAIN RESTAURANTS
Disappointing for a smart resort
Mountain restaurants are generally undistinguished, but at least they tend to provide table-service. They are expensive, with main meals better value than snacks. Only the Cry d'Err sector offers much choice. The Merbé restaurant, at the Crans-Cry d'Err gondola mid-station, is the most attractive, with table-service of good food in a pleasant setting just above the tree-line. Bella Lui's terrace (with service) offers good views. The Chetzeron eatery allows 'picnics' provided a drink is purchased.

Petit Bonvin has perhaps the best of the self-service places, with superb views. The Plumachit restaurant, towards the bottom of the sector, has a large sun terrace in a pretty setting. In the Violettes sector there is not much choice; but there is a small hut 50m from the main cafeteria at Violettes itself, and a welcoming little hotel opposite the bottom station.

SKI SCHOOL
Not much to report
Both local branches of the Swiss ski school generally attract favourable comment, although class sizes can be excessive. Meeting places vary according to the standard of the class, but Cry d'Err is a common rendezvous spot. Note the unusual hours (see margin); no weekend tuition means no lessons are missed regardless of when you arrive, but also means that beginners arriving on Saturday waste the Sunday. Private lessons are easily booked, both for on- and off-piste.

FACILITIES FOR CHILDREN
Ski Esprit have moved in
The resort facilities for children are adequate, particularly in Montana. But what will attract British families is the news that Ski Esprit have opened a small chalet at Les Barzettes (see Staying there).

 # Staying there

Crans-Montana is quite a sprawling place. The free ski-bus service links the villages and satellite lift-stations during the day, but there is no evening service. Buses run (on several overlapping routes) to a timetable and are fairly frequent during peak periods, less so at other times. Buses can get very crowded at the end of the day, but are generally an effective way of travelling between sectors. They do not cut out walks. The gondola-stations are perched above the main road, a sufficiently tiring, and often icy, walk from many hotels to warrant paying for ski and boot storage.

The best choice of location for most people would be within a short walk of the powerful Montana gondola. But if you want to beat the queues up to Plaine Morte, you'll want to be out at Les Barzettes, at the base station of the Violettes gondola.

HOW TO GO
Much more choice on your own
The independent traveller to Crans-Montana has a wide choice of hotels and apartments. Package holidays are not widely sold in Britain.

Chalets Crans-Montana is not a major chalet resort. Childcare specialists Ski Esprit are now the only operator in town, with a simple, traditional-style chalet (with in-house crèche) at Les Barzettes, 500m from the Violettes lift.

Hotels Not surprisingly, this conference resort has a great number of mainly large, comfortable, expensive hotels. 42 of the 52 hotels are of 3-star or higher standard.

£££££ Crans-Ambassador Huge luxy place with distinctive 'chalet' roof-line, well placed for the Montana gondola. Pool.

££££ Hauts de Crans Smart modern hotel in excellent position up above Montana. Pool.

££££ Aïda Castel Beautifully furnished in chic rustic style, with hand-painted furniture and pine panelling. Between the two resort centres. Outdoor pool.

££££ Le Green Well placed near the Crans lifts; small, modern and chic.

ACTIVITIES

Indoor Hotel swimming pools, tennis, fitness centre, bowling, bridge, squash, concerts, cinema, casino
Outdoor Skating, curling, toboggan run, ski-bob, dog-sleigh rides, horse-riding, golf on snow

£££ La Foret Highly recommended hotel almost, but not quite, at Les Barzettes, with minibus to lifts. Pool in adjacent self-catering block.
£££ National Perfectly placed for the Crans-Cry d'Err gondola; 'quiet, comfortable, good food'.
£££ Au Robinson B&B only; well placed near the National, in Crans, with friendly service.
£ Petit Paradis Five minutes from Montana in Bluche, a family-run auberge with a welcoming restaurant.
Self-catering The number of visitor beds available in apartments outnumbers hotels five to one. Of course, not all those beds are available to rent, and very few find their way on to the British package market. Start with the Inghams brochure. Supermarkets in Montana are surprisingly cheap by resort standards.

EATING OUT
Plenty of alternatives
There is a good variety of restaurants from French to Chinese and Lebanese, although prices tend to push British self-caterers into pizzerias or supermarkets. Almost all the less expensive restaurants are in Montana. Most places do good rösti, which is relatively cheap and filling. The Carnozet has been recommended for excellent fondue. The Au Robinson hotel restaurant is good, reasonably priced by local standards, and open to non-residents. The Gréni is a welcoming restaurant on the western fringe of Montana. The Cervin up at Vermala is unusually rustic.

APRES-SKI
Can be ritzy, but otherwise quiet
The resort boasts plenty of après-ski amenities, but its clientele seems loath to use them; the nightspots (of which there are several) and the impressive ice rinks often lack animation. The Pub Georges & Dragon is by far the liveliest, most crowded bar; surprisingly, given its location in Crans, it has the cheapest beer in town. For peace and quiet, there are quite a few piano bars. The two cinemas change films every couple of days, and some play in English. Ten-pin bowling (not Austrian-style skittles) is about the only rep-organised nightlife. Swimming is available in about a dozen hotels, at about SF10; those wanting a sauna as well will find the Hauts de Crans hotel good value. Bridge is played from 3pm in the Aïda-Castel.

FOR NON-SKIERS
Excellent, but little charm
There is plenty to keep non-skiers busy. There are lovely walks through and around the golf course, in and among novice downhill and cross-country skiers. Restaurants have sun terraces. Lots of activities are available.
Sierre is only a funicular ride away for serious shopping, while the larger town of Sion is only a few minutes further by rail. Montreux is also within reach. The mountain restaurants are mainly situated at the gondola and cable-car stations, which allows beginners and non-skiers to meet others for lunch at altitude.

TOURIST OFFICE

Postcode CH-3962
Tel 010 41 (27)
413041
Fax 417460

Davos 1550m

✔ *Huge amount of skiing*

✔ *Some superb long and mostly easy runs away from the lifts, particularly in the Parsenn area*

✔ *Lots of off-piste skiing, with a wide choice of marked itineraries and some well-known short ski-tours*

✔ *Good cross-country trails*

✔ *Excellent sports facilities*

✔ *Some captivating mountain restaurants above Klosters*

✔ *Klosters is attractively villagey*

✗ *Dreary block-style buildings of Davos spoil the views*

✗ *Davos is a towny resort, rather plagued by traffic and lacking Alpine atmosphere*

✗ *Skiing is spread over six or seven essentially separate ski areas*

✗ *Some access lifts are inefficient, leading to queues, and antique T-bars are common*

Once popular with British skiers, Davos is a rather specialised taste these days. Few resorts in the world have a ski area more extensive, or that offers more for all grades of skier. But it has its drawbacks: it is split into five or six unlinked sectors, and relatively ancient lifts serve many of them. Skiers who are prepared to accept such drawbacks normally do so as the price of staying in a captivating Alpine village. But Davos is far from that.

Whether you forgive the flaws and fall for the resort as a whole depends on how highly you value three plus-points: the distinctive, long intermediate runs of the Parsenn area; the ability to ski a different sector every day; and the considerable off-piste potential. We like all three, and this is one of the ski areas in the Alps we always look forward to visiting.

But you don't have to stay in Davos to enjoy its skiing: Klosters offers a much more captivating alternative. Despite its royal connections, it is not an exclusive village – on the contrary, it has some exceptionally welcoming places to stay. It is rather less well placed than Davos for exploration of all the ski areas, but just as handy for the all-important Parsenn – in some ways, even handier.

Despite the early involvement of the British, Davos now attracts relatively few Brits; practically all the foreign visitors are German.

ORIENTATION

Davos shares its skiing with **Klosters**, its smaller and 350m lower neighbour. Set in a broad, gently sloping valley running north-east to south-west, with skiing mountains either side. Davos has two main centres roughly 2km apart; the road and railway from Klosters come first to Dorf, where a funicular railway goes up into the main Parsenn ski area, and then to Platz, where lifts go up in opposite directions to the Strela and Jakobshorn ski areas. The Rinerhorn area starts about 6km further down the valley at Glaris, the Pischa area 5km up a side valley. North of Klosters is the Madrisa area, start of easy tours to Gargellen in Austria.

Excursions by road or rail to **St Moritz** and **Arosa**, or by road to **Flims** and **Lenzerheide** are possible.

🏔 The resort

Davos was one of the places in the Alps where skiing first blossomed as a leisure activity (a process in which Brits, including Conan Doyle, were much involved). And arguably it was the very first to develop skiing as a business. The railway up the Parsenn was one of the first to be built for skiers (in 1931), and the first drag-lift was built on the Bolgen nursery slopes in 1934. But by then Davos was already well developed as a health resort, and many of its present-day luxury hotels are converted sanatoriums.

Sadly, converted sanatoriums are just what they look like. No one goes to Davos because they like the look of the town – and it is a town, not a village. It is often said to be the highest town in Europe, and probably is. It is sometimes said to be

Switzerland's biggest ski resort, but certainly is not – in terms of beds, at least. Crans-Montana is much bigger, and Verbier is slightly so.

Conferences are big business – from the annual World Economic Forum at one extreme, to the Zurich Master Plumbers' convention at the other. But the health business lives on, in the shape of several specialist clinics.

SKI FACTS

Altitude 810m-2845m
Lifts 55
Pistes 315km
Green/Blue 27%
Red 53%
Black 20%
Artificial snow 1km

LIFT PASSES

94/95 prices in
Swiss francs
Rega area
Covers all Davos and
Klosters, the railway
in the whole region
and buses between
the resorts.
Beginners Single and
return tickets on main
lifts in each area.
Main pass
1-day pass 52
6-day pass 259
(low season 207 –
20% off)
Senior citizens
Over 65 male, 62
female: 6-day pass
207 (20% off)
Children
Under 16: 6-day pass
155 (40% off)
Under 6: free pass
Short-term passes
Half-day passes, up
to and from 12.30,
for each area
(Jakobshorn, adult
35).
Alternative periods
Passes for 8 days
(Rinerhorn, adult 230)
and 15 days
(Rinerhorn, adult 377)
in the season, but
only for limited areas.
Notes Day pass price
is for Parsenn, Pischa,
Schatzalp, Strela and
Gotschna only.
Alternative passes
A confusing array of
passes covering
limited areas
(Jakobshorn,
Rinerhorn, Pischa,
Schatzalp and Strela,
and other
combinations).

⃛ The skiing

The skiing here has something for
everybody, although experts and
nervous intermediates need to choose
their territory with care.

THE SKI AREA
Vast and varied

It's a common trick, when describing a
ski area, to say how long you could
stay in the resort without skiing the
same run twice. But in Davos you can
spend a week without skiing the same
mountain twice – that is, you can ski a
different mountain every day. In
practice, you don't: the minor areas
tend to be neglected by most visitors –
but they are worth checking out, and
are all the better for their neglect.

The Parsennbahn funicular from
Davos Dorf takes you to the major lift
junction of Weissfluhjoch (2660m), at
one end of the **Parsenn** skiing. At the
other is Gotschnagrat, reached by
cable-car from Klosters. Between the
two is the wide, open bowl of the
Parsenn. From Davos Platz, another
funicular takes you up to Schatzalp, at
the base of the **Strela** skiing. A cable-
car from the top of this sector offers a
back-door way to Weissfluhjoch.

Across the valley, **Jakobshorn** is
reached by cable-car from Davos Platz.
Rinerhorn and **Pischa** are outlying
areas reached by bus or (in the case of
Rinerhorn) train.

Beyond the main part of Klosters, a
cable-car goes up from Klosters Dorf to
the sunny **Madrisa** area.

SNOW RELIABILITY
Good, but not the best

Davos is quite high by Swiss standards.
Its ski areas go respectably high too –
though not to glacial heights. Not
much of it faces directly south, but
not much of it faces directly north
either – mainly the long runs on the
back of the Parsenn. So snow
reliability is no more than fair. The
south-east-facing pistes down to Dorf
from Weissfluhjoch are the ones most
at risk. There is some artificial snow in
each main sector, but not much.

FOR ADVANCED SKIERS
Plenty to do, on- and off-piste

A glance at the piste map may give the
misleading impression that this is an
intermediate's resort. Blacks are
confined largely to the wooded lower
slopes of several sectors, which means
excellent skiing when snow is falling,
and rough skiing when snow is
needed. But there are two exceptions:

the trio of runs at the southern
extremity of the Strela area and the
runs from Gotschnagrat directly down
towards Klosters, on and around the
infamous Gotschnawang slope. The
Wang run, starting south of the peak,
is formally a piste, but it is not
marked; there are various ways down,
all seriously steep. Drostobel, starting
to the north, is less scary, though the
overall gradient is little different.

The main appeal of the area,
however, is that it is excellent for off-
piste adventures and short ski-tours.

Practically all the sectors of the
skiing now have at least one marked
off-piste itinerary to the valley – an
excellent arrangement which allows
good skiers to escape the crowds
without paying for guidance. The
exception is Rinerhorn – but that has
an excellent black piste of 1000m
vertical that amounts to much the
same thing.

Arosa can be reached much more
quickly on skis than by road or rail,
but requires a return by rail via Chur.
From the Madrisa sector, you can
make tours to Gargellen in Austria's
Montafontal. This involves an
exhausting one-hour uphill walk on
seal skins on the way back.

FOR INTERMEDIATE SKIERS
A splendid variety of runs

For intermediate skiers of any
temperament or tendency, this is a
great ski area. But its greatest appeal is
to the skier who likes to get around,
with long runs to the valleys and the
stimulating prospect of skiing several
different areas.

The epic runs to Klosters and other
places (described in the box opposite)
pose few difficulties for a confident
intermediate or even an ambitious
near-beginner (one of the editors did
the run to Klosters on his third day on
skis). And there are one or two other
notable away-from-the-lifts runs to the
valley that are more than just
woodland paths. In particular, you can
ski from the top of Madrisa back to
Klosters Dorf via the beautiful
Schlappin valley.

FOR BEGINNERS
Platz is the more convenient

The Bolgen nursery slope is adequately
spacious and gentle, and a bearable
walk from the centre of Platz. But
Dorf-based beginners face more of a
trek out to Bünda.

There is no shortage of easy runs to
progress to, and they are spread
around all the sectors. The Parsenn
sector probably has the edge, with

SKI SCHOOL
94/95 prices in
Swiss francs

Swiss
Classes 5 days
4hr: 2hr am and pm
5 full days: 190
Children's classes
Ages: 4 to 16
5 full days: 154
Private lessons
Half-day or full-day
145 for half-day

CHILDCARE
The ski school runs
the Pinocchio nursery
at Bünda, on the
outskirts of Davos
Dorf, taking children
from age 3, from 8.30
to 4.30. Children can
stay in the nursery,
play about on skis or
take proper ski school
classes.

The Berghotel
Schatzalp has its own
ski nursery – see
Staying up the
mountain. The hotel
Derby in Dorf has an
indoor kindergarten.

long, easy runs in the main Parsenn
bowl, as well as in the valleys running
down from Weissfluhjoch.

FOR CROSS-COUNTRY
Long, scenic valley trails
Davos may not be in the first division
for langlaufers, but it can't be far
outside, with a total of 75km of trails
running in both directions along the
main valley and reaching well up into
Sertigtal and Dischmatal. There is a
cross-country ski centre and special ski
school on the outskirts of the town.

QUEUES
Still a problem in places
The Parsennbahn was generating
queues when we first visited Davos 20
years ago, and it is still generating
queues today. The Schatzalpbahn –
the alternative, roundabout way into
Davos' main ski area – suffers too.
Other access lifts present fewer
problems. In Klosters, queues for the
Gotschna cable-car have been much
reduced by a doubling of its capacity,
but can still be a problem at weekends.

MOUNTAIN RESTAURANTS
Stay low down
The main high-altitude restaurants are
dreary self-service affairs, but there is
compensation in the charm and
satisfying food of some of the lower
places – notably the Conterser
Schwendi and Serneuser Schwendi in
the woods on the way down to the
Klosters valley from the Parsenn.

These are great places to end up as
darkness falls – the Klosters Schwendi,
at least, sells wax torches to illuminate
your final descent to the village.
Elsewhere, descent right to the
valley can be the best bet; there are
peaceful restaurants at or near the
bottom of the Pischa, Jakobshorn and
Rinerhorn sectors.

SKI SCHOOL
Don't count on English
Our most recent reporter tells us that
better skiers, at least, are likely to find
themselves in a German-dominated
group – scarcely surprising, given the
small number of British visitors that
Davos attracts these days.
The 'deep snow' classes guarantee a
maximum of six skiers, with half a day
per week given over to avalanche
rescue techniques and understanding
the behaviour of deep snow. Seniors
and teenagers can both enroll in
classes aimed at them. Snowboarders
have a keen specialist school.

FACILITIES FOR CHILDREN
Not ideal
Davos is a rather spread-out place in
which to handle a family – and indeed
the ski school nursery is in a slightly
isolated spot at Dorf's Bünda nursery
slope, inconvenient for dropping off
and picking up. We lack readers'
reports on the nursery. Our instinct, if
the budget will stand it, would be to
stay at the Berghotel Schatzalp (see
Staying up the mountain, below).

The Parsenn's super-runs

The runs from Weissfluhjoch that head north, on the back of the mountain,
make this area special for many skiers. The pistes that continue northward to
Schifer and then to Kublis, Saas and Serneus, and the one that curls around
the mountain to Klosters, are graded red but are not difficult. What marks them
out is their sheer length (10–12km) and the sensation of travel they offer.

Until 1987, only the very top 2.5km and 400m vertical of this enormous ski
field could be skied repeatedly; once below Kreuzweg, you skied on down to
the valley and caught the train home. Usually, you did it towards the end of
the day, dawdling in the rustic restaurants in the woods on the lower reaches.
The long Schiferbahn gondola changed all that – you can now ski 1100m
vertical as often as you like. Some long-standing visitors regret the change, but
there is the added advantage that the lower runs, below the Schifer gondola
station, are quieter.

The longest runs are the marked but unpatrolled routes to Fideris and Jenaz,
the latter being 18km from Weissfluhjoch, according to official figures. Start at
the Weissfluh summit and you can add another kilometre, as well as another
200m vertical. But these are not continuous runs: they require skins for a
couple of short ascents, and payment for the use of the lifts at Fideriser
Heuberge on the way.

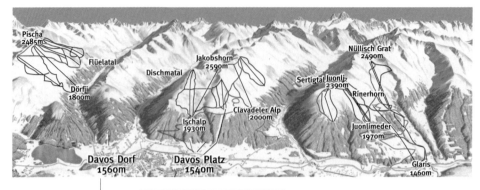

PACKAGES

Inghams, Kuoni, Made to Measure, Plus Travel, Ski Choice, Ski Les Alpes, Ski Weekend, SkiGower, Swiss Travel Service, White Roc

Klosters Kuoni, Made to Measure, Plus Travel, Powder Byrne, Ski Club of GB, Ski Les Alpes, Ski with Julia, SkiGower, The Ski Company Ltd, White Roc

↑ Staying there

Davos is a big, spread-out resort and although transport is good, with buses around the town as well as the railway linking Dorf and Platz to Klosters and other villages, choice of location is important. Dorf has direct but queue-prone access to the Parsenn; Platz has lifts up to the Jakobshorn and Strela sectors, the big sports facilities and the smarter shopping.

HOW TO GO

Hotels dominate the package scene
Although the bulk of the bed spaces in Davos is in apartments, hotels dominate the UK package market.
Chalets There are no catered chalet packages in Davos, but upmarket Powder Byrne have a couple of comfortable little places, sold as single bookings, in Klosters.
Hotels A dozen 4-star and about 30 3-star places form the core of the Davos hotel trade, though there are a couple of 5-stars and quite a few cheaper places, including B&Bs.
£££££ Fluela The more atmospheric of the two 5-star hotels, in central Dorf, and quite well placed to beat the Parsenn queues. Pool.
££££ Golfhotel Waldhuus As convenient for winter langlaufers as for summer golfers. Quiet, modern,

tasteful, with 'first-rate cuisine' and 'unusually attentive' staff. Pool.
£££ Parsenn What Davos needs is more hotels that look like this attractive chalet, directly opposite the Parsenn railway in Dorf.
£££ Davoserhof Our favourite: small, old, beautifully furnished, with excellent food, well placed in Platz.
££ Alte Post Traditional, cosy, central in Platz.
££ Hubli's Landhaus 5km out at Laret, towards Klosters. Quiet country inn with sophisticated food.
Self-catering The Allod Park apartments (Inghams) are in a dreary block, but are reasonably comfortable, and in a happy medium position, midway between the Parsenn and Strela lifts.

STAYING UP THE MOUNTAIN

Especially appealing for families
The Berghotel Schatzalp, on the tree-line about 300m above Davos Platz and reached by funicular (free to guests), is a 4-star hotel to rival any in the resort, complete with pool and sauna. The Strela skiing immediately above has something for everyone, but what makes the Berghotel especially interesting is that there is a nursery slope right next to it – and the hotel runs its own crèche (evenings as well as daytime) with ski tuition available. Schatzalp is also the start of the local toboggan run, a mini-Cresta.

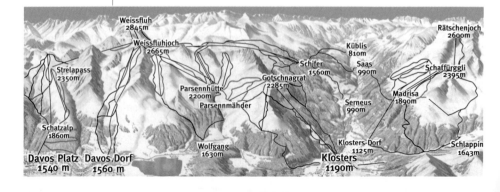

ACTIVITIES

Indoor Artificial skating rink, fitness centre, tennis, squash, swimming, sauna, cinema, museums, galleries, libraries
Outdoor Over 80km of cleared paths (mostly at valley level), natural skating rink, curling, toboggan run, horse-riding, hang-gliding, sleigh rides, para-gliding

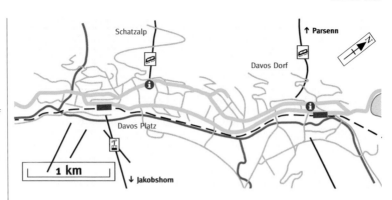

EATING OUT
Wide choice, mostly in hotels

Most of the better restaurants are in hotels. The Davoserhof's restaurant is one of the best in town , both for food and ambience. Chinese food is trendy here – the lavish Zauberberg restaurant in the Central and the Golden Dragon in the Terminus, are two of the best in this category. The Fluela has a highly regarded grill room. The Derby is good for an intimate dinner dance. Sharing a fondue in the Gentiana is rather pleasant. Pizzeria Padrino and the National are two good informal places.

The Mona Lisa and Da Elio, both Italian joints, are other possibles for those not wanting to spend too much.

An evening excursion for dinner out of town is popular. Prices are lower and restaurants less formal. Teufi, Schatzalp (reached by funicular), Laret, Islen, Wolfgang and Frauenkirch all have good places. Our favourite would have to be the wholesome local fare in the basic old Landhaus in Frauenkirch.

APRES-SKI
Lots on offer, but quiet clientele

There are plenty of bars, discos and nightclubs, but we're not sure how some of them make a living. Davos guests tend to want the quiet life. The non-ski activities and numerous cafés and bars give Davos a pleasant tea-time atmosphere, but things are subdued after dinner. High calories are consumed with enthusiasm after skiing at cafés Weber and Schneider. A civilised drink can be had at several hotels – the Derby's attractive Paluda bar; the Corner bar of the Post Morosani; the piano bars in the Central and Europe. The liveliest place in town is the rustic little Chämi bar. Its taped pop music and strange decor is popular with the young crowd. It's one of the few spots to retain a spark of life late in the evening. La Bohème, which also has music, is another. Nightclubs tend to be sophisticated, expensive and lacking atmosphere outside of weekends. The most popular are the Cabanna, Pöstli and

Selected chalets in Klosters

Europe. The intimate little Jakobshorn disco is more informal and less expensive.

FOR NON-SKIERS
Fine apart from the buildings
If only it were a better-looking resort, Davos would be unreservedly recommendable for non-skiers. As it is, it suits many non-skiers very well. The towny resort has shops and other diversions, and transport along the valley (covered by the tourist tax) and up into the skiing is good – though the best of the mountain restaurants are well out of range. For the energetic, the sports facilities are excellent; the natural ice rink is said to be Europe's biggest, and is supplemented by artificial rinks both indoor and outdoor. Spectator sports include speed skating as well as hockey. And there are lots of marked walks up in the ski areas as well as along the valleys.

The new winter sports museum may be of more interest to skiers than others; reports welcome.

FOR SNOWBOARDERS
Surprisingly, this staid old resort seems to have decided to cultivate snowboarders' custom. Not only is there a dedicated school, there is even a dedicated Snowboard Hotel, conveniently close to the Jakobshorn (the official Davos Fun Mountain).

Klosters 1190m
In a word association game, Klosters would normally trigger 'Prince of Wales'. The world's TV screens have shown him skiing there countless times. In 1988 he was almost killed there in an off-piste avalanche that did kill one of his companions, and now the enlarged cable-car to Gotschna – a quick way into the Parsenn skiing shared with Davos – is named after him.

Don't be put off. We don't know why HRH likes to ski in Klosters particularly, but it is certainly not because the place is the exclusive territory of royalty and aristocracy. It's a comfortable, quiet village with a much more appealing Alpine flavour than Davos, despite its lower altitude. Klosters Platz is the main focus – a collection of upmarket, traditional-style hotels around the railway station, at the foot of the steep,

TOURIST OFFICE
Postcode CH-7270
Tel 010 41 (81) 452121
Fax 431770

wooded slopes of Gotschna.

The village spreads along the valley road for quite a way before fading into the countryside; there's then a second concentration of building in the even quieter village of Klosters Dorf, from where a gondola goes up to the Madrisa ski area.

Although there are some nursery lifts at valley level, the sunny slopes of Madrisa are more appealing. There is a ski kindergarten up there. The hotel Vereina has a non-ski kindergarten, taking very young children on request.

Klosters' upmarket image is reinforced by UK tour operators. Powder Byrne have been here for some years, and this year they are joined by the even more exclusive chalet operator, The Ski Company Ltd. Powder Byrne are providing a nanny service here for the first time.

There are some particularly attractive hotels. The central Chesa Grischuna is irresistible, combining traditional atmosphere (carved wood everywhere) with modern comfort – and a lively après-ski bar. The less central Wynegg is a favourite with British visitors, with a warmly welcoming panelled dining room and good-value rooms.

The evenings are by no means lifeless. The Chesa Grischuna is a focus of activity from tea-time onwards, with its piano bar, bowling and expensive but popular restaurant. The Wynegg is also popular immediately after skiing, and for more affordable dinners. An alternative for eating out is the Walserhof (a rival to the Chesa Grischuna) and there are other more modest places. There is a Mexican place at the hotel Kaiser, and a pizzeria under the hotel Vereina with a famously vociferous tenor for a chef. A short taxi or sleigh ride out to Monbiel takes you to the Höhwald, a cosy stubli with good fresh fish.

In the late evening the bars of the hotels Kaiser and Vereina are popular. The Casa Antica is a small but popular disco. The Kir Royale, under the hotel Silvretta Park, is bigger and more brash. The Funny Place, under the Piz Buin, is more grown up and expensive.

Klosters is an attractive base for walking and cross-country skiing, but has little else to offer non-skiers. The hotels Pardenn and Sport have pools, and there is curling.

Engelberg 1050m

HOW IT RATES

The skiing
Snow   ★★★
Extent   ★★
Advanced   ★★★
Intermediates ★★★
Beginners   ★★
Convenience   ★
Queues   ★★★
Restaurants   ★★★

The rest
Scenery   ★★★
Resort charm ★★★
Not skiing   ★★★

SKI FACTS

Altitude	1050m-3020m
Lifts	25
Pistes	50km
Green/Blue	40%
Red	58%
Black	2%
Artificial snow	5km

PACKAGES

Kuoni, Made to Measure, SkiGower, Swiss Travel Service

TOURIST OFFICE

Postcode CH-6390
Tel 010 41 (41) 941161
Fax 944156

Engelberg makes a great retreat for the residents of Lucerne, less than an hour away. It attracts few British visitors, despite impressive mountains offering one of the biggest verticals in the Alps. The ski area is rather unusual, with its main mountain slopes broken up by balconies.

THE RESORT

Engelberg is one of Switzerland's longest-established year-round resorts – a bustling, rather towny village, home to an impressive 12th-century monastery, surrounded by spectacular mountains. Much of the old-world charm of the original village has been diluted by modern development. But it remains a pleasant enough place, and away from the town the valley is very scenic. Engelberg is rather isolated from other resorts, but it is possible to get to Andermatt and to the Jungfrau region.

THE SKIING

There are two contrasting **ski areas** either side of the village, their widely separated lift stations served by a regular ski-bus.

Very much the main area is Titlis, which rises an impressive 2000m from the valley floor. A two-stage gondola goes up to the shelf of Trübsee (1800m). Above this a two-stage cable-car rises to over 3000m, the second stage having the novelty of the world's first revolving cabin, allowing superb views of glacial scenery. Below the summit are some short drags; descent to Trübsee is via a single steep piste, with easier slopes lower down. Across the frozen Trübsee, a separate set of lifts serve good red runs below Jochstock (2565m). There is a roundabout run back to the valley.

The Brunni area, accessed by a gondola from the edge of town, has a small network of sunny pistes between Schonegg (2040m) and Ristis (1600m), and occasionally a run back to town.

The high, north-facing Titlis has good **snow reliability** (the high drags stay open into June); but the resort as a whole is not particularly reliable.

For **advanced skiers**, the big attraction is off-piste – the famous Laub. This is a steep wall dropping 1000m from the shoulder of Titlis, which must be superb when conditions are right, and very dangerous when they are not.

There is quite a lot of skiing for confident **intermediates**, at least if snow is good below Trübsee. But there is not much very easy skiing.

There is an adequate **beginners'** slope at the Titlis gondola mid-station and another at Trübsee, but the lack of easy runs to progress to is a drawback.

Engelberg is well regarded by **cross-country** skiers, with five trails totalling 30 km amidst lovely scenery up at Trübsee and along the valley.

There are no **queue** or overcrowded piste problems except at weekends and, particularly, holiday times – New Year crowds from Lucerne can create queues measured in hours.

There is plenty of choice of **mountain restaurants**, and most are friendly and inexpensive by Swiss standards. The Titlis restaurant is good but the overcrowded, poor-value snack bar is best avoided. The cosy Sporthotel Trübsee has a vast sun terrace overlooking the frozen lake.

Unusually, the Swiss **ski school** faces competition in the form of the Neue Schischule. Both have all-day care for **children**. Hotels Regina Titlis and Edelweiss have supervised crèches.

STAYING THERE

Most package **accommodation** is in hotels, although there are lots of chalets and apartments to rent locally. The 4-star Sporthotel (less packed with amenities than its claimed 'mini-resort' status would suggest) lies up the mountain at Trübsee. The Hess is a low-key 4-star with nice rooms and good food. Among the 3-stars, Edelweiss is poorly placed but has good children's facilities, and the Crystal and Engelberg are central.

Eating out is mostly in hotels. The excellent Tudor-Stübli in the Hess does particularly good lamb. Bänklialp, Europe and Spannort are worth trying. The Engel's Stübli is cheaper.

Après-ski is good, particularly at weekends. The hotel Alpenclub's Spindle cellar disco draws the crowds. The popular Club Carmena has live music. The Caribbean Dream Life and Peter's Pub are quieter places.

Engelberg provides plenty of options for **non-skiers**, with good sports facilities as well as excursions to nearby Lucerne and Zurich – worth taking at weekends, when the village is jam-packed with day-trippers coming in the opposite direction.

Flims 1100m

✔ Extensive, varied, beautiful ski area suitable for all but experts

✔ Fair amount of skiing above 2000m offsets effects of sunny south-east-facing slopes

✔ Large amount of wooded skiing for bad-weather days

✔ Virtually queue-free on weekdays

✔ Plenty to do off the slopes

✘ Sunny orientation can cause icy pistes and close runs to the resort; most lack snowmaking

✘ Buses or long walks to lifts necessary from much accommodation

✘ Very subdued in the evenings

✘ Village very spread-out, which detracts from its charm

✘ Weekend crowds

Flims remains a Swiss gem undiscovered by the British. With a large, sunny ski area set above a wooded shelf, it's reminiscent of Crans-Montana – but is superior in some ways, notably in the amount of high skiing available. It also has important advantages, in skiing terms, over other Swiss resorts more widely marketed on the British scene, such as Villars, Arosa and Lenzerheide. While the likes of Kitzbühel and Wengen remain popular despite their poor snow records, Flims stays well outside the list of top resorts.

The village was for many years a summer beauty spot that had only a moderate amount of skiing available in the winter. After winning a war with local conservationists in the 1970s, Flims and nearby Laax opened up a vast new network of lifts serving an impressive 220km of pistes. Yet it remains essentially a quiet place in winter, given the spark of life only by Zürich and Chur weekenders.

Flims has some excellent, very beautiful, high skiing ideally suited to intermediates. It deserves to be better known. If the village had a bit more character we'd be recommending it even more highly.

 ## The resort

Flims is made up of two villages, over a kilometre apart. Dorf is by far the larger and more animated, sprawling along a busy main road which houses most of the shops, hotels, restaurants and bars. Waldhaus is a sedate, sophisticated huddle of hotels – some of them quite grand – attractively set among trees. Both resorts have stuck to the traditional look, with almost all hotels being of the wooden chalet variety.

Dorf is better placed than Waldhaus for skiers, having the village lifts on its western outskirts. Given the spread-out nature of the resort, it's surprising there is no ski-bus. Waldhaus residents rely on hotel courtesy buses and the infrequent post buses. There are Dorf hotels close to the lifts, but the majority are a long walk away.

Although it's quiet, Flims has a pleasant cosmopolitan atmosphere – Germans, Dutch, Swedes, Belgians and Americans come here. Dorf is popular with fashionable families, while Waldhaus has an older, even more affluent clientele.

 ## The skiing

Flims has a big, underrated ski area, with varied skiing, including woodland and open runs, some long runs and high skiing which includes a small glacier area. Because of its sunny aspect, the lower runs deteriorate quickly and it's not uncommon to be unable to ski back to the villages.

THE SKI AREA
Impressive and well planned
The beautiful ski area has essentially four sections, each suitable for all grades but expert. The skiing has been well planned, and moving in either direction across it is straightforward, although one or two links do have inherent weaknesses.

The **Cassons** sector above Flims Dorf is the smallest sector, particularly so when runs to the village are incomplete. This is reached by the chair from the village, then a further chair or drag to the cable-car to the peak (2675m).

You can ski from here to Startgels, which is also the top of the gondola from the village. Lifts from here link

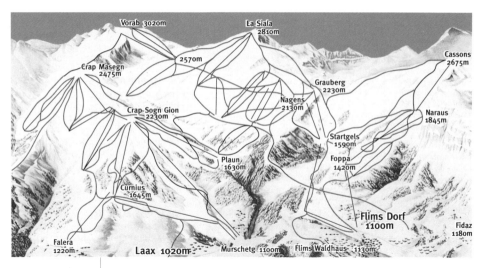

in with the middle sector, **La Siala**, which is served by chairs and drags and reaches 2810m. The linking lifts cross an exposed ravine that can be windy.

Skiing across to the **Vorab** glacier (where the top lift reaches 3020m) from the top of La Siala is a simple matter except when La Siala's high chair is inoperative. In that case, all three routes via Plaun involve skiing short black sections of piste.

From Vorab you can ski to the biggest section of the skiing, served by eleven lifts, around **Crap Mesegn** and **Crap Sogn Gion**. The lift up from Plaun also arrives at Crap Sogn Gion. From there you can ski down to Murschetg, Laax or Falera.

SNOW RELIABILITY
Poor lower down, good higher up
Due to its sunny aspect, Flims is far from snowsure top to bottom, with snowmaking confined to two runs from Crap Sogn Gion – the black race-course down to Murschetg and a red to Plaun. But even if you have to ride the lifts down the lower sections, there is a lot of skiing above 2000m which usually enjoys decent snow except in late season.

FOR ADVANCED SKIERS
Bits and pieces
There is a fair amount of challenging skiing but it's rather dotted about, with the added frustration that some of it is on short sections of otherwise easy pistes. The toughest run is the

Selected chalets in Flims

LIFT PASSES

White Arena
Covers all lifts and buses between Flims, Laax and Falera.
Beginners Half-day (25) and full-day (32) mini pass (8 lifts)
Main pass
1-day pass 55
6-day pass 270
Children
Under 16: 6-day pass 135 (50% off)
Under 6: free pass
Short-term passes
Half-day from 12.15 (adult 40)
Alternative periods
Passes for 8 non-consecutive days (adult 396)
Notes Day pass cost increases by 4 on weekends and bank holidays.

SKI SCHOOL

Swiss
Classes 5 days
4hr: 2hr am and pm
5 full days: 175
Children's classes
Ages: up to 12
5 full days: 175
Private lessons
Half- or full-day
130 for half-day

steep, unpisted Cassons black from the top of the cable-car near the village. An off-piste excursion from the Cassons summit looks tempting but don't even think about it without a guide. You could go over a cliff.

One of the great pleasures of the whole area is the men's World Cup downhill course from Crap Sogn Gion to Murschetg. It's so long (1000m vertical) and pretty that skiing it repeatedly using the Murschetg cable-car doesn't get boring – and it is not so vulnerable to the sun now that it is equipped with snowmakers. The Nagens-Startgels run is short but steep.

Off-piste skiing is generally between pistes, but in such an extensive area there is plenty of such terrain. Ruschein, at the western extremity of the ski area, is the best sector. And the long Sattel piste from Vorab – see below – is a good and beautiful starting point.

FOR INTERMEDIATE SKIERS
Paradise for all
A superb area, though less confident skiers have to watch out for some easy runs that have short steep sections (normally marked black on the map). The two lower links between Siala and Dorf (Platt 'Alta and Stretg) and the run from the bottom of the Grisch drag down to Plaun (Sogn Martin) are examples.

When conditions allow, the area immediately above Flims is splendid for easy cruising. But the real highlight for early intermediates is skiing to the Vorab glacier and back on blue runs. On the way back you can take the cable-car down from Grauberg to Startgels to avoid the awkward runs in this area.

More adventurous intermediates have most of the area to choose from, though the narrow little Scansinas runs to Plaun are best avoided. The easier of the two descents from Cassons is a lovely run along the shoulder of the mountain down into a valley and on to Startgels, a 1000m vertical trip. Skiing from Crap Sogn Gion to Larnags via Curnius is also great fun.

Good intermediates will enjoy the superb Sattel black run from the glacier to Ruschein on the extreme western edge of the ski area. It starts with a challenging mogul field but develops into a fast cruise and is one of the longest and most beautiful runs in the whole area.

The Crap Sogn Gion to Plaun routes along a valley are interesting, being quite steep, sheltered, and some of the few runs not to be almost directly facing the sun. The large amount of tree-skiing available, both at Flims and Laax, is useful in poor weather.

FOR BEGINNERS
Plenty of options
There is a good nursery area in Dorf, with an alternative at Startgels when snow is in short supply. Moving further afield is not a problem for quick learners. Getting the bus to the lovely easy runs above Falera is a good option. Although not a 'British' resort, there is plenty of tuition in English.

FOR CROSS-COUNTRY
One of the best
An excellent choice. There are 60km of beautiful well marked, mainly forest trails. Loops range from 3km to 20km The specialist cross-country ski school, centred at Waldhaus, has a good reputation, and gets sufficient numbers of customers to organise group classes. 3km of trail are floodlit. The only drawback is the possibility of poor snow.

QUEUES
Few problems
There is little queuing during the week. Flims customers will not be affected by the early morning delays for the Laax cable-car. The resort is much busier at weekends, but delays to get out of Flims in the morning are rarely more than ten minutes and you can choose between the gondola and chair. The Grisch drag towards La Siala can become a slight problem if Plaun has run out of snow. Treis Palas (below Masegn) is an obvious bottleneck, but it's an autonomous little sector, with no need to ski there at busy periods.

MOUNTAIN RESTAURANTS
Good, wide selection
Mountain restaurants are numerous and generally good, if expensive. The large cafeterias at Sogn Gion and Vorab are clean, efficient and serve good wholesome food. Nagens has another good high-altitude place, but the nicest refuges are lower down. The Spaligna below Foppa, the Tegia at Larnags, and the Runcahöhe where the Stretg piste flattens out as it crosses the path down from Startgels, are among the best.

SKI SCHOOL
Plenty of English tuition
The ski school has a good reputation. Being a cosmopolitan resort, it makes wide use of English as the international language.

CHILDCARE
The ski school runs ski kindergartens taking children from age 4 – in Flims from 9am to 4.30, in Laax from 8.30 to 4.30. Childcare in Falera is 'on request'.

Several hotels claim special facilities for children. The Park Hotel Waldhaus has its own crèche, and an independent crèche may be operating in the Adula.

GETTING THERE
Air Zürich, transfer 3hr.

Rail Chur (17km); regular buses to resort.

PACKAGES
Made to Measure, Plus Travel, Powder Byrne, Ski Weekend, Swiss Travel Service

Laax Made to Measure, Plus Travel

ACTIVITIES
Indoor 5 hotel swimming pools open to public, saunas, 2 indoor tennis courts, covered hall with 4 skating rinks, bowling, fitness centres (including Prau La Selva)

Outdoor 60km of cleared paths, riding, natural skating rinks, curling, sleigh rides, toboggan runs, ski-bob, para-gliding, hot-air ballooning

TOURIST OFFICE
Postcode CH-7018
Tel 010 41 (81) 391022
Fax 394308

FACILITIES FOR CHILDREN
Powder Byrne for babies
Not surprisingly, given the small number of British visitors, we lack reports on the resort childcare arrangements. If you want pre-skiing children to be looked after, your choice is to stay at the very expensive Park Hotel Waldhaus or go with Powder Byrne, who have a well-established nanny service here.

 # Staying there

Although it might seem best to stay near the lifts in Dorf, in practice most of the better hotels in Waldhaus (and the remote bits of Dorf) run efficient courtesy buses to and from the slopes. These satisfy most of their guests, especially as they don't often venture out after dinner. Don't overlook the possibility of staying in Laax, Murschetg or Falera.

HOW TO GO
Few tour operators
Only a handful of tour operators feature Flims.

Chalets Upmarket Powder Byrne have a small, attractive, well positioned chalet bookable by a single party.
Hotels Flims has over 30 hotels, the majority of which are either 3-star or simple B&B places, the latter tending to be booked out long in advance. Of the six top-notch hotels, five are in Waldhaus. Grading of hotels is accurate – you get what you pay for.
£££££ Park Enormous and very comfortable, but rather institutional, 5-star in wooded grounds at Waldhaus; the courtesy bus is essential in the mornings, but you can ski home. Pool.
££££ Crap Ner The only 4-star in Dorf, but well away from the lifts and just as inconvenient for skiers as Waldhaus. But it's a friendly hotel with spacious, well decorated rooms and superb food. The hotel's courtesy bus is very efficient. Good pool.
££££ Adula Big, highly recommended 4-star in Waldhaus. Good pool.
£££ Grischuna Pretty little 3-star just outside Dorf, and close to the lifts.
£££ Curtgin Attractive place in quiet position on edge of town, quite well placed for the lifts.
£££ Albana Sporthotel Modern 3-star beside lifts, with focal après-ski bar.
£££ Waldeck Neat 3-star place in Waldhaus, with pleasant restaurant.
Self-catering The Minerva in Waldhaus is by far the nicest of the limited apartments available.

EATING OUT
Varied options
Flims offers a wide variety of restaurants for different tastes and budgets – Italian, Chinese, local specialities and nouvelle cuisine are some of the main choices on offer. Most restaurants are in hotels. The good value (by local standards) Chesa does a nice fondue, and has a lovely open fire. The Meiler hotel restaurant also has a good reputation. Something a bit different is going up to the Spaligna mountain restaurant for a meal, with a toboggan run home. Little China is a good new Chinese restaurant. The Alpina Garni (Waldhaus) has some of the cheapest food in town – good pizzas.

APRES-SKI
Not a strong point
Flims is very quiet après-ski. The Spaligna trip mentioned under Eating out is the highlight of the week. The Stenna-Bar, opposite the Dorf base-station, has a tea dance, while just across the road the Albana Pub is popular with a young crowd. Later on, the focal spot is also in Dorf, at the hotel Bellevue's Caverna, an atmospheric old wine vault. Locals assure us the Iglou bar is also popular. The Park hotel is the centre of limited action in Waldhaus, having an old cellar with entertainer, plus the Chadafo bar which has dancing to live music. The Segnes and Bellavista bars are quiet. The sophisticated Viva Club comes to life at weekends.

FOR NON-SKIERS
Lots to do
There are plenty of things to do. The enormous sports centre has a huge range of activities, including shooting. And Flims has some of the best walks (60km) of any ski resort. Chur is an historic old town a short bus-ride away. Other good excursions are to the impressive church at Zillis, and to Rhine Canyon, which is nature at its best. Catching the Glacier Express train from Chur to Andermatt takes you through some wonderful scenery.

STAYING UP THE MOUNTAIN
Space station St John
Even though there are entire resorts that are higher, the prospect of staying 1100m above Murschetg in the ultra-modern 3-star Crap Sogn Gion, is an exciting one. It has all mod cons, including a pool. You can also stay above Flims in the more traditional Berghaus Nagens – it has dormitories as well as comfortable double rooms.

Laax 1020m

Laax is a quiet, spacious old farming community which has retained a lot of its original character; much of its modern development has taken place a short bus-ride away at Murschetg. This soulless complex has been built around the ski lifts and has its own hotels, shops and restaurants for those who want ski convenience above all else. Though the oldest house in Laax dates from 1615, and the setting is pleasant enough, the village is no more than routinely charming. Those looking for a traditional little gem would prefer Falera (see below).

The Murschetg cable-car (which generates peak-time queues) gives speedy access to Crap Sogn Gion, the main mid-station of the whole area. A gondola, followed by a chair, is an alternative route up the mountain. Runs lead back to Murschetg from Sogn Gion and Curnius; the routes converge at Larnags, where the village gondola has a joining station – useful for rides down when snow is becoming patchy.

Cross-country skiers visiting the area should stay in Laax. A fine trail network of 60km starts nearby.

Laax has its own ski school and ski kindergarten, run by the well known downhill racer Conradin Cathomen.

Most of the hotels are in the 3-star and 4-star categories. Although a few are large and modern, some semblance of traditional style has usually been attempted, and the thick pine forest which surrounds Murschetg also helps to hide the worst architectural excesses. The Vallarosa and Signina are Murschetg 4-stars – very user-friendly and comfortable. The 4-star Arena Alva is a more attractive building in the old village, with its own transport to the lifts. The Bellaval is a pretty, traditional 3-star in the village centre. We've enjoyed staying at the charming, central old Posta Veglia, with its lively stubli and piano bar. A good central B&B is the Cathomen.

Restaurants are mostly hotel-based. The Laaxer Bündnerstuben in the Posta Veglia is the best bet for a meal in traditional surroundings. The

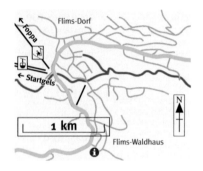

limited nightlife scene is centred around the Bistro Bar in the Capricorn hotel, live music in the Vallarosa bar, and the ubiquitous Posta Veglia.

As at Flims, there's a fair amount to do for non-skiers. The 60km of cleared walks are one highlight. Other facilities include a riding academy, curling and skating on a nearby lake or artificial rink, sleigh rides, indoor pool, squash and a little museum.

Falera 1220m

Along the road from Flims, beyond Laax, lies the attractively rustic village of Falera. It's a traditional, quiet little place, complete with two lovely old churches, and benefits from being traffic-free (parking is free at the entrance to the village). Sitting on a sunny plateau, it has good views over three valleys. Everything is close to hand, including the single village lift, ski slopes, ski school and ski kindergarten (by arrangement). Unfortunately, the old village chair-lift takes an age (15 minutes) to rise the 400m vertical to Curnius, but movement into the heart of the ski area is then rapid.

Accommodation is mostly in apartments, but the two hotels have plenty of beds between them. La Siala is a large 4-star with pool and sauna. It also has apartments. The Encarna is a much simpler, atmospheric place.

La Siala's Spielkeller is the only real nightspot.

Café La Punt is good for tea-time cakes. The Alpenblick is an appealing restaurant, and the Aurora and Casa Seeli are other possibles for a meal.

Grindelwald 1035m

✔ *Dramatically set in gorgeous scenery beneath the towering north face of the Eiger*

✔ *Large ski area, ideal for intermediates*

✔ *Traditional mountain village with long mountaineering history*

✘ *Village gets very little sunshine in early season*

✘ *Little challenging piste skiing for good skiers*

✘ *Long journey to top of skiing and inconvenient for visiting Mürren*

✘ *Not ideal for beginners – village nursery slopes often short of snow*

✘ *Snow cover unreliable, with little artificial help*

✘ *Queues for railway and gondola can be bad, especially when weekend visitors flock in*

Grindelwald is a much expanded, traditional mountain village, set at the bottom of some of Europe's best climbing terrain with the north face of the Eiger towering dramatically above. The main ski area is shared with Wengen and has stunning views – unmatched except perhaps by those from Mürren.

When conditions are good, the skiing matches the scenery – at least for intermediates. Experts will find the piste skiing unexciting, and beginners may find the snow on the lower slopes poor or non-existent. That's one of Grindelwald's main drawbacks. The ski area is low, there's virtually no artificial snow on the Grindelwald side of the ski area, and the region has suffered a series of poor years for snowfall – even last year saw a shortage relative to the bumper year of most other resorts.

But it has a loyal following of people for whom skiing is only one part of a winter holiday. It is best suited to leisurely skiers who aren't too fussed if conditions are less than ideal. Most reporters rated it highly for an all-round mountain holiday for the middle-aged and for visitors with young children. Many emphasised that it wasn't really ideal for teenagers or child-free people in their 20s and 30s.

Then there's the question of whether to stay here or in Wengen. On balance, we'd go for Wengen. Its 'traffic-free' village is prettier and more relaxing. And it has much quicker access to Mürren and its more exciting skiing.

ORIENTATION

Grindelwald is spread out along a narrow valley with mountains rising sheerly above it. The main Kleine Scheidegg-Männlichen ski area is shared with **Wengen**. Kleine Scheidegg is reached by cog railway from Grund, near the western end of town; the station for this railway is itself served by railway from the village. Männlichen is reached by gondola, also from Grund. The other ski area is First, on the opposite side of the valley, reached by a three-stage gondola from just to the east of the village centre.

Outings to other resorts are not very attractive, but you can get to **Gstaad** by rail and road, and **Adelboden** by road.

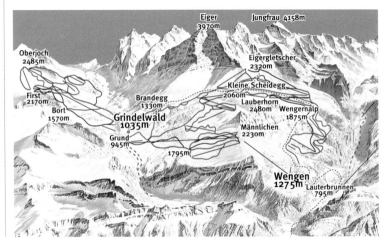

SKI FACTS

Jungfrau region –
including Wengen and
Mürren

Altitude	945m-2970m
Lifts	45
Pistes	183km
Green/Blue	32%
Red	52%
Black	16%
Artificial snow	10km

LIFT PASSES

94/95 prices in
Swiss francs
**Jungfrau Top Ski
Region**
Covers all lifts in
Wengen, Mürren and
Grindelwald, trains
between them and
Grindelwald ski-bus.
Beginners Points card
(adult 100 points 46,
lifts cost 4 to 10
points).
Main pass
1-day pass 52
6-day pass 232
Children
Under 16: 6-day pass
116 (50% off)
Under 6: free pass
Short-term passes
Single ascent tickets
for most lifts. Half-day
pass for First (adult
38), Kleine Scheidegg-
Männlichen (adult 40)
and Mürren-Schilthorn
(adult 38).
Notes Day pass price
for Kleine Scheidegg-
Männlichen area only
(98km of piste, 21
lifts), as Jungfrau Top
Ski Region pass is
only available for
3 days or over.
Discounts for
teenagers 16 to 21 (6-
day 186) and groups.
Alternative passes
1- and 2-day passes
available for First
(50km of piste, 11
lifts) (adult 2-day 90),
Mürren-Schilthorn
(adult 2-day 90) and
Kleine Scheidegg-
Männlichen (adult 2-
day 95, child 48).

 # The resort

Grindelwald is a traditional
mountaineering resort set either side
of the road along the foot of a narrow
valley. The buildings are primarily
traditional Swiss chalet style, with a
few grander buildings such as the
stone-built Grand Hotel Regina.

It can feel claustrophobic because of
the towering mountains rising sheerly
from the valley floor, and can be dark
in early season, when it gets no, or
very little, sun.

There is a splendid sports centre to
which entrance is now free with a
Visitor's Card. And it can feel very
jolly at times, such as during the ice-
carving festival in January, when large
and beautiful tableaux are on display.

At weekends, though, it can get very
crowded – or at least the train and the
gondola can – with coachloads of
people, especially from Germany, who
may well be staying cheaply in
Interlaken and Wilderswil.

The village tends to be more
animated at night than the other
Jungfrau resorts of Wengen and
Mürren. There's live music in several
bars and hotels, though it certainly
isn't the place for those who want to
bop every night until dawn.

The skiing

See Wengen (page 367) for a general
description of the main ski area. As
well as that, there is the separate First
ski area, now served by a three-stage
gondola which has replaced what used
to be the oldest chair-lift in the world
– you rode it sideways. The First area's
skiing is almost entirely south-facing.
So while it can be marvellous after a
fresh snowfall, the snow here
deteriorates rapidly in warm weather.
It's primarily intermediate terrain.

SNOW RELIABILITY
Poor
Grindelwald has had a succession of
relatively poor snow years. Its low
altitude – the skiing goes down to
below 1000m and little of it is above
2000m – and the lack of significant
amounts of artificial snow (it's limited
to the run down the short Aspen
beginners' drag) mean we've crossed
Grindelwald off the list of resorts for
which we'd be prepared to make a
firm booking months in advance. And
it's not the place for a late season
holiday.

FOR ADVANCED SKIERS
Very limited
See the chapter on Wengen. The main
interest for good skiers is off-piste, and
Powder Byrne runs holidays to
Grindelwald which include off-piste
courses with mountain guide Ueli Frei.
On-piste, there's little of interest,
especially on the Grindelwald side of
the ski area shared with Wengen. The
black run marked on the piste map
from Männlichen back to Grindelwald
must qualify as one of the most overgraded runs in the world. The black
run on First which runs beneath the
gondola back to town is tougher,
especially when the snow has suffered
from too much sun. Getting to the
tougher, higher skiing of Mürren is a
lengthy business unless you've got a
car – Wengen is a much better base in
that respect.

FOR INTERMEDIATE SKIERS
Ideal intermediate terrain
Again, see the chapter on Wengen for
a description of the ideal intermediate
slopes which the two resorts share. In
good snow conditions the whole area
is perfect for intermediate skiers,
especially those who don't like
unexpected surprises.

First has some very gentle slopes
right at the top, served by a couple of
drag-lifts. This is is the highest part of
Grindelwald's ski area, reaching
2485m – a few metres higher than the
Lauberhorn lift takes you. There's a
lovely long red run all the way back to
Grindelwald on the extreme eastern
side of the First ski area. In good snow,
First is a splendid intermediate
playground, and worth spending a day
or two on, although many skiers
ignore it and head straight for the
main ski area.

FOR BEGINNERS
In good snow, wonderful
Grindelwald's gentle slopes make ideal
beginner territory, with a splendid
gentle blue run through the trees to
progress to once you are off the
nursery slopes. It goes right from the
top of the train at Kleine Scheidegg
down to Grund. But you can just do
parts of it by getting off or catching
the train up at the intermediate stops
such as Brandegg and Alpiglen.

If the snow is poor, it's not good to
be a beginner in Grindelwald. The
main nursery slopes are at low altitude
at the foot of the sunny First ski area.

SKI SCHOOL

94/95 prices in
Swiss francs

Swiss
Classes 6 days
4hr: 10am-noon and
2pm-4pm
5 full days: 192
Children's classes
Ages: 3 to 14
5 full days: 192
Private lessons
2hr, 2½hr or 5hr
139 for 2hr

GETTING THERE

Air Zürich, transfer
3hr. Bern, transfer
1½hr.

Rail Station in resort.

CHILDCARE

The ski school takes
children aged 3 to 14,
and they can be
looked after at
lunchtime in the
Children's Club
kindergarten at the
Bodmi nursery slopes.
This takes children
from age 3, from 9.30
to 4pm. It apparently
ceases to function if
snow shortage closes
the nursery slopes.

In February there is
an organised
programme of
activities for
children of secondary
school age.

FOR CROSS-COUNTRY
The best in the Jungfrau region
The tourist office says that there are
between 25km and 32km of prepared
tracks, depending on snow conditions.
Almost all of this is in the valley floor
at around 1000m, so in good snow it's
delightful. In poor snow there may be
little more cross-country here than in
the rest of the Jungfrau region (where
there is hardly any).

QUEUES
Can be dreadful at weekends
The queues at Grund, for both the
gondola and the train, can be
substantial, especially at busy
weekends when all the day visitors
tend to enter the skiing via
Grindelwald rather than taking the
slower Lauterbrunnen-Wengen route.
The queue for the train, in particular,
was found by one reporter to be 'Just
like being in a cattle pen; very
disconcerting, with orders being
barked at you over loudspeakers in
German. And even once you're on it,
there may be standing-room only, and
it takes 50 minutes to get to the top.'
Another reporter tells of 'Waits of up
to one and a half hours to get on the
gondola after 8.45am'.
If the whole ski area is open, lift
queues higher up are not a problem.
But if snow is short on the lower
slopes, queues build up higher up.

MOUNTAIN RESTAURANTS
More choice on the Wengen side
See the Wengen chapter for restaurants
in the main ski area. On the First side,
the restaurant at Bort does extremely
good rösti. One of our reporters was
lucky enough to see chamois grazing
just below here – but there's no
guarantee of this!

SKI SCHOOL
One of the better Swiss schools
Reports suggest standards are high,
with small classes and good English
spoken. There are plenty of special
courses such as powder and seniors'
weeks, and there's a special section for
people with impaired vision.

FACILITIES FOR CHILDREN
Good reports
One reporter who has put four
children through the Grindelwald mill
has nothing but good words for the ski
school – not only caring instructors
and effective instruction but
'peppermint tea at 11am that our
5-year-old always remembers.'

 # Staying there

The most convenient place to stay for
the skiing is at Grund. But this is out
of the centre and rather charmless.
There's a wide range of hotels in the
heart of the village, which is handy
enough for everything else, including
the First ski area, at the foot of which
are the nursery slopes, ski school and
kindergarten.

HOW TO GO
Limited range of packages
Although tour operators offer a
reasonable selection of hotels, they
tend to concentrate on the upper end
of the market. Traditional little B&B
pensions and self-catering apartments
are, however, widely available to
independent bookers.
Chalets We are not aware of any
catered chalets run by tour operators.
Hotels There is one 5-star hotel, a
dozen 4-stars, and a good range of
more modest places.
££££ **Regina** The one 5-star. Big and
imposing; right next to the railway
station. Nightly music in the bar. Pool.
££££ **Schweizerhof** Beautifully
decorated 4-star chalet at west end of
centre, close to station. Pool.
££££ **Bodmi** New little chalet right on
the village nursery slopes.
£££ **Hirschen** Excellent family-run
3-star in central position at foot of
nursery slopes, mid-way between First
gondola and railway station.
£££ **Fiescherblick** Hospitable chalet
on eastern fringe of village, five
minutes from the First gondola.
£££ **Derby** Popular, modern 3-star
right on the station.
££ **Tschuggen** Modest chalet in
central position below nursery slopes.
£ **Wetterhorn** Cosy, simple chalet way
beyond the village, with great views of
the glacier.
Self-catering Inghams have comfortable
new apartments in a pleasant wooden
chalet in the main street. One
independent reporter recommends the
apartments of the hotel Hirschen for
comfort and spaciousness.

EATING OUT
Hotel based
There's a wide choice of good hotel
restaurants, but pizzeria-style places
are in short supply. The only one we
know is the Latino, which specialises
in home-made Italian cooking. Among
the more attractively traditional places
are: the Gepsi in the Eiger; Schmitte in
the Schweizerhof; Challi-Stubli in the
Kreuz; and the Alte Post.

PACKAGES

Inghams, Kuoni, Made to Measure, Plus Travel, Powder Byrne, Ski Choice, Swiss Travel Service, Thomson

ACTIVITIES

Indoor Sports centre (swimming pool, sauna, solarium, massage), indoor skating rink, curling, bowling, cinema **Outdoor** 80km of cleared paths, train rides to Jungfraujoch, tobogganing, snow-shoe excursions, sleigh rides

TOURIST OFFICE

Postcode CH-3818
Tel 010 41 (36)
531212
Fax 533088

The Kirchbuhl is good for vegetarians, the Bahnhof in the Derby for fondue and raclette. Hotel Spinne has a good restaurant for almost all tastes – the Mercato for Italian; Mescalero for Mexican, a Chinese place; and one of the best places in town for a special romantic meal, the candlelit Rôtisserie. Hotel Belvedere has a gourmet French restaurant.

APRES-SKI
Relaxed

It's a fairly subdued scene, though there's no shortage of live music. The Regina has a sophisticated dance band every evening, and the Derby has live entertainment, including rather incongruous country and western. The Spinne has reputedly the best of the two village discos. There is also a cinema, and ice hockey and curling matches to watch.

FOR NON-SKIERS
Plenty to do, easy to get around

There are 50km of cleared paths with magnificent views and a splendid sports centre.

It's easy to get around the mountain and meet skiing friends for lunch using both the train and gondola, and there's a special (though expensive at SF150 for five days) non-skier's lift pass. An excursion by train to Interlaken is easy, and Bern possible. Day trips to Mürren are surprisingly long-winded because you have to change three times, with a lengthy wait at the first change.

STAYING UP THE MOUNTAIN
Several possibilities

Grindelwald, like Wengen, gives easy rail access to Kleine Scheidegg, where there are quite pricey rooms at the Kleine Scheidegg hotel and cheap dormitory space above the station buffets. There are also dormitories at the nearby Grindelwaldblick. The Bort, at the gondola station in the middle of the First area (1570m), is perhaps the most attractive of all.

Gstaad 1050m

ORIENTATION

Gstaad sits at a broad junction of valleys, with skiing on three mountains reached by lifts from the fringes of the village. One of these sectors spreads west to **Rougemont**. A separate fourth sector of skiing is accessed from **Schönried**, **Saanenmöser** and **St Stephan**. The skiing of **Zweisimmen** comes between the last two but is not linked.

Château d'Oex, a few km to the west (reached by train, bus or car) is covered by the area lift pass. So is the skiing on and down from the **Diablerets** glacier, 15km to the south. And so is **Lenk**, up valley from St Stephan, and the linked resort of **Adelboden**.

✔ Surprisingly unspoilt, unpretentious, traditional village

✔ A wide variety of après-ski in January and February

✔ Plenty of off-slope amenities

✔ Large, pretty ski area, mainly of intermediate difficulty but with off-piste possibilities

✔ Few queues, given snow-cover

✔ Excellent descents from Diablerets glacier

✗ Very poor recent snow record, yet no snowmakers

✗ Several widely separated ski areas, none of which is convenient to the village (though most are served by good public transport)

✗ Little steep piste skiing to challenge good skiers – token black runs on the piste map don't mean much

✗ Nursery slopes less than ideal – though some smaller resorts nearby are better equipped

✗ No inexpensive hotels in the main resort village

✗ Diablerets glacier itself is of rather limited appeal, and certainly doesn't compensate for Gstaad's local snow record

Gstaad is renowned as a jet set resort – one of the places that's always trotted out when soppy magazines want to do a piece on where celebs ski. And it is one of the few resorts in the Alps where there is no cheap and cheerful accommodation at all – you have to go to outlying villages to find a hotel of less than 3-star standard.

But if you think this makes Gstaad another St Moritz – that is, another glitzy, self-consciously 'international' resort, you're wrong. The grandest of the hotels are tucked away in secluded grounds, and at first glance the resort still has the air of a country village, even if it is an obviously affluent one. Look again, and you see that the winding high street is lined with famous-name jewellers and designer boutiques.

For 'ordinary' holiday skiers Gstaad offers a civilised, crowd-free atmosphere, unspoilt rustic charm, beautiful scenery, high quality hotels and excellent non-skiing facilities. Those who attach a high priority to convenience, reliable snow or value for money should stay away – although there are smaller villages in Gstaad's inappropriately named White Highlands ski area that improve on the main resort in all three respects.

Rougemont, over the line into French-speaking Switzerland, is a particularly captivating and modestly priced village with a lift into the biggest of the three ski sectors that surround Gstaad. Schönried and Saanenmöser have lifts into another extensive area, away from Gstaad, that links with St Stephan.

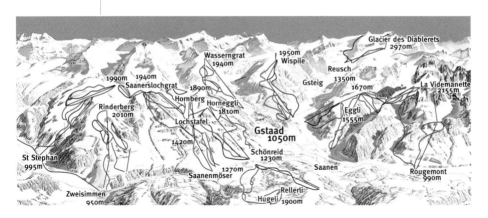

SKI FACTS

Altitude 950m-1950m
Lifts	69
Pistes	250km
Green/Blue	60%
Red	30%
Black	10%
Artificial snow	2km

LIFT PASSES

94/95 prices in Swiss francs

Gstaad Super Ski Region
Covers all lifts in Gstaad, Schönried, Saanenmöser, Zweisimmen, St Stephan, Lauenen, Gsteig, Reusch, the Glacier des Diablerets, Rougemont, Château d'Oex and Les Moulins, and the train, local buses and swimming pool.

Beginners Coupon booklet covers all lifts.

Main pass
1-day pass 46
6-day pass 233

Children
Under 16: 6-day pass 121 (48% off)
Under 6: free pass

Short-term passes
2hr (adult 32), 3hr (adult 35), 4hr (adult 38) and 5hr (adult 41) passes available.

Alternative periods
Any 6 days in the season.

Notes Passes of 4 days or more are also valid in Adelboden-Lenk and Les Diablerets-Villars. Discounts for teenagers 16 to 20 and for families.

 # The resort

Gstaad is an attractive, traditional, long-established, year-round resort in a spacious, sunny setting surrounded by a horseshoe of gentle wooded mountains where several valleys converge.

Life revolves around the bustling main street, which is lined by chalet-style buildings housing hotels, shops and cafés. This is also a through-route, with a fair amount of local traffic, which detracts from what is otherwise a pleasant and relaxing village. The Montreux-Oberland-Bernois (MOB) railway, which accesses numerous surrounding ski villages, loops in and out of the village on its way from Montreux to Berne; the station is conveniently positioned, close to much of the accommodation.

 # The skiing

The skiing is mostly pretty, intermediate stuff, with steeper slopes available to those who venture off-piste. This season the Ski-Data lift pass system is being introduced, as in Courmayeur and other Italian resorts – you can have a programmable wrist watch instead of a conventional pass.

THE SKI AREA
Fragmented and scattered
The local topography has implications for skiers. On each of the hills separating the surrounding valleys, unconnected ski areas have evolved. They would be awkward to link in any circumstances; in such a strong conservation area, the prospect can be discounted altogether.

The three local lift stations are disposed around the southern end of the village, just too far out to be reached on foot. A ski-bus links them and the village every 15 minutes; another line, running every 30 minutes, takes in Saanen as well.

To the east is **Wasserngrat**, a small 'yo-yo' skiing area, accessed by a gondola from the eastern side of Gstaad. To the south, **Wispile** is very similar. To the west is a more complex and extensive area, **Eggli**. There is another lift into this sector from north-east of Gstaad, at Rübeldorf. And you can ski via the Chalberhöni valley to lifts up to **Videmanette**, also reached by gondola from Rougemont. From here a steep, narrow off-piste route goes down beneath the second stage of the gondola, with

pistes leading down to Rougemont from the mid-station. There is also a much easier pisted route between Videmanette and Rougemont. Finishing the day here is not a bad plan. The train is nearby and an après-ski drink while waiting for it is very pleasant in this lovely village.

The closest access point to the fourth and largest sector, spreading east from the nearby peak of **Hornberg**, is a short train trip away from Gstaad – an enclosed chair-lift at Schönried. Slightly further east, at Saanenmöser, is the major access lift – a gondola up to the higher point of Saanerslochgrat. From Saanerslochgrat a couple of short lifts and pistes lead to Parwengesattel, the top station above St Stephan, the furthermost village in the local area. Although further from Gstaad, these departure points at Schönried and Saanenmöser are not appreciably less convenient than Gstaad's local lift stations; you just need to study the timetables of the MOB and the ski-bus Line 3, and time your day accordingly. Schönried also has a lift on the sunny side of its valley, up to **Rellerli**.

The Zweisimmen ski area on **Rinderberg** is strangely bypassed by the lifts and runs linking Saanenmöser and St Stephan. Off-piste routes linking the areas are possible, though rarely skiable.

SNOW RELIABILITY
Poor, despite the nearby glacier
A lack of both altitude and snowmakers has obvious repercussions for snow-cover, but at least all the ski sectors have a fair amount of north-facing skiing above the lift mid-stations, which are at altitudes ranging from around 1350m to around 1600m. The Diablerets glacier is snowsure, but is a limited area (not in the Hintertux-Stubai-Kaprun league); nevertheless, when snow is scarce it can suffer horrendous queues.

FOR ADVANCED SKIERS
Few options
Most of the piste skiing is easy; the blacks rarely exceed red difficulty, and some should be blue. There are off-piste possibilities in all the sectors, and sometimes steep ones – particularly on the wooded flanks of Wispile and on Eggli. When skiable, the run under the top gondola above Rougemont must be a challenge. The Diablerets glacier itself lacks challenge, but the black runs on the flanks of the mountain, above the Col du Pillon certainly do not. The run

SKI SCHOOL
94/95 prices in
Swiss francs

Swiss
Classes 6 days
3¼hr: 10am-2.45, 1hr
for lunch
6 full days: 195
Children's classes
Ages: Any
6 full days: 195
Private lessons
Hourly or daily
55 for 1hr for 1 to 4
people

CHILDCARE
The ski kindergarten
takes children from
age 3, from 10am to
3pm.

GETTING THERE
Air Geneva, transfer
2½hr.

Rail Station in resort.

described below, from the glacier to
Reusch, is worth an hour of anyone's
time. Not surprisingly in this very
affluent resort, heli-skiing is available.

FOR INTERMEDIATE SKIERS
Plenty for everyone dotted about
Good intermediates will find the
Wispile and Wasserngrat reds and
blacks entertaining for a while, but
'yo-yo' skiing has its drawbacks. A
better series of options lies in the
Hornberg sector above Schönried. The
moguls either side of Saanerslochgrat
and at Hornberg itself, plus the
steepest of the runs above St Stephan,
are all good fun.

Moderate skiers will like the long
runs down to Rougemont, the Wispile
and Wasserngrat reds, and the fine
pistes down to St Stephan. Leisurely
types have plenty of choice above
Saanenmöser, including long cruises
to the village from Saanerslochgrat
and Hornfluh. The Chalberhöni valley
area is good for mixed abilities, with
parallel-running pistes of varying
difficulty.

Adventurous intermediates should
not fail to make an outing to the
Diablerets glacier, not for the flat
glacier skiing but for the splendid run
down from it. After a slightly tricky
start, this develops into a glorious
swooping run of no great difficulty,
down a deserted valley which keeps its
snow very well. At the 'end' of the
valley, lifts take you up to Oldenegg
(the mid-station of the cable-car up to
the glacier) and you then resume your
descent, through pretty woods to
Reusch and the bus home.

FOR BEGINNERS
Château d'Oex is better
Nursery slopes at the bottom of
Wispileare are no more than adequate
and are prone to poor snow
conditions. A small area at the top of
the Wispile is fairly snowsure, but La
Braye, above Château d'Oex, has the
best nursery area in the region.
Unfortunately, it's rather a trek from
Gstaad. Saanenmöser has plenty of
suitable runs for precocious learners.

FOR CROSS-COUNTRY
Good when snow allows
The 60km of trails are very pretty, and
the trains and buses mean you don't
have to retrace your steps. But
virtually all of the trails are at valley
level, and prone to loss of snow. There
are slightly higher trails at Schönried,
and 25km much higher at
Sparenmoos near Zweisimmen.

QUEUES
Few delays
There are few queues in the main ski
area except at weekends and the peak
February weeks, and even then they
are easily avoided when there is resort-
level snow. Time lost on buses or
trains is a greater problem.

MOUNTAIN RESTAURANTS
Excellent, leisurely lunches
There is no shortage of restaurants and
most are attractive, if expensive. Many
have table-service, which can make for
longish waits at peak times. The
Chemi-Stube, with great views towards
Lenk, is a particularly nice place above
St Stephan. The hut at the top of the
Eggli gondola is another excellent spot
for lunch. But Berghaus Wasserngrat –
a small chalet with a big terrace – is
the most captivating of all.

SKI SCHOOL
English-speaking tuition
Although few Brits frequent it, Gstaad,
is an international resort, with plenty
of Americans among its clientele. So
English is more widely spoken in this
ski school than in many others in Brit-
free zones. It has a good reputation
too, though we lack recent reports.

FACILITIES FOR CHILDREN
Surprisingly poor
The limited hours offered by the ski
kindergarten mean that parents can
forget any ideas of escaping their
responsibilities for a whole day's
skiing. The only nursery appears to be
in the Palace hotel.

 # Staying there

For skiing, hotel position is relatively
unimportant; you're unlikely to be
close to a lift, and unlikely to be far
from a bus stop. Some hotels are close
to the Wispile lifts, but poorly placed
for everything else – including the
other lifts. Best to put aside thoughts
of skiing convenience and stay in the
heart of the charming village.

HOW TO GO
Easy to reach independently
Gstaad is certainly exclusive, with over
three quarters of its accommodation
in private chalets and apartments, and
the remainder of its beds in 3-star
hotels and above. It is one of the
easiest of ski drives from the Channel
and has good train links to Geneva
airport via Montreux. But you'll
probably prefer to fly directly to
Gstaad-Saanen airport, which now has

PACKAGES

Alpine Expressions, Inghams, Made to Measure, Neilson, SkiGower

Château d'Oex Kuoni, Neilson, Ski Valkyrie

Rougemont The Ski Company Ltd

immigration and customs facilities. About time, too.

Chalets We don't know of any catered chalets in Gstaad itself.

Hotels There aren't many hotels by usual ski resort standards – half a dozen 4-star, half a dozen 3-star and two 5-star.

£££££ Palace Extravagantly swish place overlooking the village from secluded grounds.

££££ Bernerhof Large, centrally placed 4-star with all conceivable facilities. Pool and playroom.

££££ Christiania Small, cosy 4-star, centrally placed.

££££ Gstaaderhof Large 3-star, centrally positioned but peaceful.

££££ Olden Exceptionally charming, small, family-run, prettily painted chalet, right in the centre of things, with locals' bar as well as upmarket restaurant.

£££ Posthotel Rössli Wooden chalet, close to the Olden in every way.

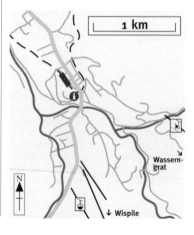

£££ Victoria Comfortable place, well placed for station.

£££ Rütti Cheapest hotel in Gstaad, close to Wispile gondola, 10 minutes from village centre.

Self-catering There is a wide choice of apartments for independent travellers. The Utoring has been recommended to us as a high-quality establishment , but it's not for budget skiers seeking to stay in Gstaad 'on the cheap'. The Christiania has luxury serviced apartments within the hotel and Ludi-Haus, Selini and Bel Horizon are well positioned places in the upper price range. Less expensive, but equally central, are Sunbeam, Blum, Burn and Hänsel.

EATING OUT
You pays your money ...
Restaurants are mainly hotel-based, and expensive. Hotel Bellevue's Chez Fritz is famed for its high-quality cuisine, although the elegant Chesery is perhaps the best in town. The Rialto restaurant bar is known for pasta and fish. The rustic (but big – 350-seat) Chlösterli, a seven-minute car journey out of town, is a popular place to eat and dance. Hotel Rössli's restaurant is reasonably priced. Cheap and sustaining food can be had in the locals' bar of the Olden, but don't stray into La Cave by mistake.

APRES-SKI
Sophistication and informality
During 'the season', nightlife is lively, less so off-peak. Café Pernet, the Apple Pie and Charly's are popular at tea-time, while later Henry's Bar, Richi's Pub and the bars of the Olden and Rialto come alive. People-watching in

ACTIVITIES

Indoor Sports centre (swimming, tennis, sauna), squash, fitness centre, cinema
Outdoor Skating, curling, 50km cleared paths, hot-air balloons, horse-riding, sleigh rides, para-gliding, helicopter flights, excursions, night skiing, salt-water swimming pools, sledging

TOURIST OFFICE

Postcode CH-3780
Tel 010 41 (30) 47171
Fax 45620

the Palace Hotel's GreenGo nightclub is an expensive 'must', but the Olden's La Cave, the Rütti's Keller, and the Viktoria's Taburi are arguably better places to have a bop. The Chlösterli has a live band, and Gstaad's cinema has a change of programme every two days. Nearby Saanen has floodlit skiing three nights a week.

FOR NON-SKIERS
Superb facilities

Gstaad suits non-skiers better than it suits many skiers. The tennis centre and swimming pool complex are particularly impressive, and there is a very wide range of other non-skiing things to do. There are also 50km of pretty, cleared walks, and the buses and MOB make getting around easy, both within the White Highlands and further afield. Montreux and Interlaken are within reach by train. Several attractive mountain restaurants are served by gondolas.

STAYING IN OTHER VILLAGES
Worth considering

Schönried and Saanenmöser are better placed for skiing, and offer slightly cheaper accommodation, but neither has much further appeal. Schönried is a roadside straggle with four hotels, a couple of nightclubs, several restaurants and tea rooms, and one good bar (Sammy's). The 3-star Bahnhof is the third cheapest hotel in the whole area, and the good value it offers is essentially the main reason for staying in Schönried. It is situated next to the railway station, within walking distance of the lifts.

Saanenmöser has very little infrastructure, and two of its three hotels are sufficiently luxurious to be just as expensive as many Gstaad establishments. The 2-star Bahnhof is inexpensive by local standards but is slightly pricier than its 3-star namesake in Schönried.

Saanen is very poorly situated for skiing, being a bus-ride from its nearest lifts and pistes at Rübeldorf. It does, however, have plenty of restaurants and tea rooms, and (as well as slick hotels to match all but the very dearest in Gstaad) has the two cheapest hotels in the whole area. Hotel Boo is an atmospheric, rustic 3-star chalet in the village centre, while the slightly cheaper Landhaus is attractive and well placed for the railway station. Ten minutes out of the village is a youth hostel.

Rougemont is the most attractive village in the whole area – a pretty collection of rustic old chalets. Hotel Valrose is a good-value establishment close to both gondola and railway station. The hotel de Commune is a beautiful old chalet in the centre. The Viva, out of the village, is recommended for its rooms and welcome, but not food. Après-ski centres around the bars of the Valrose and Commune, and the charming, woody Cerf restaurant.

Chateau d'Oex gets more British visitors and is unspoilt, but some of its hotels are very poorly positioned for skiing the White Highlands. The good-value 3-star Beau Séjour is by far the best placed hotel, both for the local skiing and railway station.

Lenzerheide 1470m

HOW IT RATES

The skiing

Snow	***
Extent	***
Advanced	**
Intermediates	****
Beginners	***
Convenience	**
Queues	***
Restaurants	***

The rest

Scenery	***
Resort charm	**
Not skiing	****

Lenzerheide has some decent intermediate skiing and a beautiful setting but little to recommend the resort itself. Its ski area would be worth a visit if you are touring the area.

THE VILLAGE

Lenzerheide is set in a wide, sunny, tree-filled valley with skiable mountains on either side, plus a lake, two pretty churches and a friendly atmosphere. However, it is also an ugly sprawl of traditional and modern buildings, lacking character, with a busy road slicing through it and heading up to its much more glamorous neighbour, St Moritz.

It is not the 'picture book village' sometimes marketed by British tour operators. It used to be popular with British visitors but is now patronised mainly by Swiss and German families. Valbella, at the other end of the lake, is even less attractive.

THE SKIING

150km of piste are spread evenly over two facing mountains, with a circuit possible with a little walking where the valley closes up. The east-facing Danis **ski area** has the greater number of runs and reaches 2430m. Reporters tend to be critical of the high proportion of long T-bars. Ten minutes out of town, towards Valbella, a cable-car and gondola access the more interesting, spacious west-facing Rothorn area, which reaches 2865m.

Sunny slopes, protected by only limited snowguns, are not as snowsure as the altitude would suggest, especially in the trees lower down. However, skiing is usually assured above the mid-station of Rothorn, and plenty of two-stage lifts means lack of resort-level **snow** is not a disaster.

The slopes get steeper with altitude so the few **advanced skiers'** runs have the best snow. The long, beautiful off-piste trail from Rothorn's summit to town is a must. Off-piste excursions to nearby resorts are possible with a guide, including Arosa and Tschiertschen.

The top-to-bottom run of over 1000m vertical from the shoulder of the Weisshorn (on the Rothorn side) to Parpan is a highlight for better **intermediates**. The whole area is ideal for average intermediates. There are long cruises on Danis, and early intermediates will also enjoy the pretty run home through the trees from the middle of the Rothorn cable-car. In general the runs in the trees are

SKI FACTS

Altitude	1230m-2865m
Lifts	38
Pistes	155km
Green/Blue	46%
Red	41%
Black	13%
Artificial snow	1km

PACKAGES

Inghams, Kuoni, Made to Measure, Ski Choice, Swiss Travel Service

Valbella Club Med, Made to Measure

TOURIST OFFICE

Postcode CH-7078
Tel 010 41 (81) 343434
Fax 345383

very easy.

There is an adequate nursery area close to the village and easy runs to progress to. If snow is short here, **beginners** should head for Alp Nova.

With 50km of attractive trails, some on the lake, good tuition and night skiing, Lenzerheide is a leading **cross-country** resort.

There are few **queues** except at weekends, when the cable-car and Parpan lift are jammed. Delays also occur if the lower runs are snowless or the second cable-car stage is closed.

Go for the small, table-service **mountain restaurants**, not the characterless cafeterias, such as the one at Rothorn summit.

The **ski school** has a reputation for small classes but a lack of English-speaking instructors is a problem.

The hotel Schweizerhof and the Soleval apartments have supervised **children's** facilities, open all day on weekdays. There is no public crèche or ski kindergarten.

STAYING THERE

The 4-star Schweizerhof **hotel** is central, with good food, pool, tennis and squash. The Sunstar is a similar standard, next to nursery slopes, with pool. Kurhaus Alpina is cheaper, handy for Danis skiing, with pool. The Dieschen is a family-run 3-star with good health and fitness facilities, near the cable-car. Guarda Val is splendidly rustic, well renovated but out of town.

Soleval **apartments** are high-quality, with health and fitness facilities and free covered parking, 10 minutes from the village but right on the slopes.

Restaurants are mostly hotel-based (the hotels above have good food). Da Elio is a good pizzeria. Hotel Lenzerhorn has dinner dances in a rustic setting.

Après-ski is quiet on weekdays but lively at the weekend. Nino's pub is the liveliest place in town. Café Aurora and the bar of the Sunstar hotel are good spots for a cosy drink. There are two discos.

Facilities for **non-skiers** are good. Apart from sports, there is a cinema, 35km of cleared walks around the lake and along the valley and a bus link to the nearby old town of Chur.

Les Diablerets 1160m

Les Diablerets provokes lots of 'buts'. It is a pleasant village, but lacks a focus. Its skiing is linked to Villars, but the link doesn't suit the intermediate skiers that the resort attracts. There is a glacier nearby, but you have to buy a regional pass to use it, and it doesn't add up to much. But: for limited, amiable skiing in a peaceful, impressive setting, it's worth considering.

HOW IT RATES

The skiing

Snow	**
Extent	**
Advanced	**
Intermediates	***
Beginners	****
Convenience	**
Queues	***
Restaurants	**

The rest

Scenery	****
Resort charm	***
Not skiing	**

SKI FACTS

Altitude	1130m-2970m
Lifts	45
Pistes	120km
Green/Blue	51%
Red	41%
Black	8%
Artificial snow	none

PACKAGES

SkiGower

TOURIST OFFICE

Postcode CH-1865
Tel 010 41 (25)
531358
Fax 532348

THE RESORT

The village of Les Diablerets lies in a broad valley beside the Diablerets massif, towering a neck-craning 2000 metres above the resort. It is a diffuse village – a scattered collection of traditional-style holiday homes and incongruous modern hotels, with some concentration of shops along the main street leading away from the railway station. The road up to the village goes on over the Col du Pillon to Gstaad; Leysin is easily reached by road or railway, and Villars is tenuously linked by lifts and runs.

THE SKIING

Les Diablerets gives access to three separate **ski areas.** Two start from the village, but their base stations are widely separated. Stupidly, the piste map gives no indication of difficulty.

Meilleret is a thickly wooded north-facing intermediate area, served by drags starting a long walk from the village centre. This sector is linked to Villars (covered by the lift pass) but getting to the Villars pistes requires a tiresome walk at the top, and the journey back involves a black run.

Isenau is a small open section of easy runs reached by gondola from the top of the village, with long easy runs back down.

The piste map shows a run down from Isenau to the base station of the third area, at the Col du Pillon (1545m), but it is usually reached by bus. A gondola goes up to Pierres Pointes (2215m) with a black run down. This is the limit of the skiing covered by the Diableretes pass; you need the Alpes Vaudoise pass if you want to go on up by cable-car to ski the Diablerets glacier and the runs from it (see Gstaad, page 337).

The short runs on the glacier would hardly make Les Diablerets a **snow-reliable** resort even if they were covered by the usual lift pass. The skiing is low, and half of it is south-facing, and unsupported by snowmakers.

The long black run down to Col du Pillon is dark and forbidding, but not as super-tough as it looks. There is little else for **advanced skiers.**

The Combe d'Audon piste from the glacier to Olden is one of the great away-from-the-lifts runs of the Alps, and can be tackled by adventurous **intermediate** skiers. Moderate skiers will enjoy the Meilleret and Isenau skiing and would enjoy Villars were it not for the black link on the way back.

There is an adequate nursery slope served by an awkward rope tow at the foot of Meilleret, but the best **beginners'** area is at sunny Isenau. Near-beginners will find Isenau ideal, apart from using drags all day.

There is 27km of **cross-country** skiing, including a pretty trail to Vers l'Eglise and a loop up at Isenau.

During peak season and when snow is in short supply elsewhere, **queues** for the glacier lifts can be serious.

It is not a great area for **mountain restaurants.** The best lunch-spots are at valley level. Vers l'Eglise is popular. The Vioz, close to the bottom of the Meilleret slopes, is a charming chalet.

A regular user of the Swiss **ski school** reports a slight slackening of standards in both organisation and tuition. There is a **kindergarten** by the nursery slopes, with lunch taken at the hotel les Sources, where all-day care is also available.

STAYING THERE

None of the **accommodation** is close to the more important lift station, Meilleret. The Ermitage and Eurohotel are incongruously modern but comfortable 4-star hotels with pools. The 2-star Mon Abri is appealingly rustic, but badly placed. The central, simple Auberge de la Poste is good value and atmospheric.

The Locanda Livia pizzeria and jolly Poste restaurant are relatively cheap places for **eating out.** The Vioz, a cosy wood-panelled chalet on the edge of the village, is more expensive.

Après-ski is very quiet during the week, when the Poste bar is the only place with any animation. Things get livelier at weekends, but the discos remain pretty dead. Car drivers can visit the nearby Gstaad.

There is pretty walking for **non-skiers,** and excursions to Montreux and Gstaad by public transport.

Mürren 1650m

HOW IT RATES

The skiing

Snow	★★★
Extent	★
Advanced	★★★
Intermediates	★★★
Beginners	★★
Convenience	★★★
Queues	★★★
Restaurants	★★

The rest

Scenery	★★★★★
Resort charm	★★★★★
Not skiing	★★★

✔ *Tiny, charming, traditional 'traffic-free' village (reached only by funicular or cable-car) with narrow paths and chocolate-box chalets*

✔ *Stupendous scenery*

✔ *Good sports centre*

✔ *Beautiful, challenging run from the panoramic Schilthorn, with staggering views on the way down*

✔ *Good snow high up even when the rest of the region is suffering – and new lifts make more of the high skiing easily accessible*

✔ *Nearby Wengen offers a big ski area ideal for intermediates*

✘ *Extent of local piste skiing very limited for all grades of skier*

✘ *Little nightlife for club and disco lovers*

✘ *Like all other Swiss 'traffic-free' villages, Mürren is gradually admitting more service vehicles – though it is still about the nearest to truly traffic-free*

ORIENTATION

Mürren is set on a shelf 800m above the Lauterbrunnen valley, opposite Wengen, and is reached by two-stage cable-car from Stechelberg or two-stage railway from Lauterbrunnen. The cable-car arrives at the south end of the tiny village, the railway at the north end, no more than ten minutes' walk away. Two further stages of the cable-car go up to the high skiing of Birg and the Schilthorn. Drag-lifts nearby serve the resort's main lower ski area; an ancient, short funicular halfway along the village gives access to the rest of the skiing.

Wengen can be reached by train from Lauterbrunnen. The skiing (connected with **Grindelwald**) is covered by the Jungfrau lift pass.

Mürren is one of our favourite resorts. There may be other Swiss mountain villages that are equally pretty, but none of them enjoys views like the ones that Mürren gives across the deep valley to the Eiger, Mönch and Jungfrau massifs: simply breathtaking.

But it isn't just the views that keep us going back to Mürren. The Schilthorn run draws us back like a magnet whenever we're driving through the Oberland. The limited ski area doesn't worry us because our visits are normally one-day affairs; holidaymakers, we concede, are likely to want to explore the large intermediate ski area of Wengen and Grindelwald on the opposite side of the valley. Getting there takes time. But who cares, when you've got the most spectacular scenery in the Alps to gaze at?

Others keep going back to Mürren because it's their second home, and that of many other British families. It was here that modern skiing was more-or-less invented by Sir Arnold Lunn, who organised the first-ever slalom race here in 1922. Twelve years earlier his father, Sir Henry, had persuaded the locals to open the railway in winter so he could bring the first winter package tour here (of public school chaps, of course). British families have been coming to Mürren year after year ever since – many of them members of the Kandahar Ski Club which Sir Arnold founded.

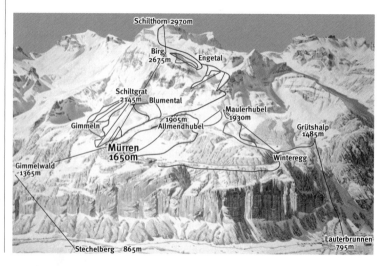

Gimmelwald

↑ Schilthorn

Allmendhubel ↗

down to
Lauterbrunnen →

Stechelberg

1 km

🏠 The resort

Once you get there you can't fail to be
struck by Mürren's tranquillity and
beauty. It really is remarkable how
little development has taken place
over the years. The tiny village is
made up of paths and narrow lanes
weaving between tiny wooden chalets
and a handful of bigger hotel
buildings. The roofs and paths are
normally snow-covered for a long
season, giving the village a really
traditional Alpine feel.

Even in peak season, Mürren feels
peaceful and quiet. And although in
our summary above we've registered a
protest against the gradual increase in
'traffic', Mürren still isn't plagued by
electric carts and taxis as most of the
other traditional 'traffic-free' resorts
now are.

It's not the place to go for lively
nightlife, shopping or showing off
your latest gear to admiring hoards. It
is the place to go if you want
tranquillity and stunning views.

🎿 The skiing

For an internationally known resort,
Mürren has remarkably little skiing –
and much of it is tricky unless you are
a good skier. If you are used to the big
ski areas of most large French resorts
you'll soon be bored here.

But it has one of our favourite runs
in the world. And if intermediates are
happy to travel to the Wengen-
Grindelwald ski area they'll find more
than enough skiing to keep them
happy. This is covered on the area lift
pass, and is easily (though not
quickly) reached.

THE SKI AREA
Small but interesting
There are three interconnected ski
areas on the bottom part of the
mountain. The biggest of these is at
Schiltgrat, served by three drag-lifts
taking you up from behind the cable-
car station. You can also reach these
from the top of an ancient funicular

leaving from near the village centre
and serving the nursery slope area at
Allmendhubel. From there you can
also ski to the third **Maulerhubel**
area, served by a chair-lift up from the
Winteregg stop on the railway. This
lower skiing takes you from the
village's 1650m up to around 2000m.

Much more interesting is the higher
skiing reached by cable-car. The first
stage takes you to Birg at 2675m, from
where you can ski the **Engetal** area.
The final stage takes you up to the
2970m summit of the **Schilthorn**
and the Piz Gloria revolving
restaurant, made famous by the James
Bond film On Her Majesty's Secret
Service. In good snow conditions it's
possible to ski all the way down from
here (via the Engetal skiing and one
drag-lift) to Lauterbrunnen at 795m –
a distance of almost 16km and vertical
drop of 2175m. The annual Inferno
race – open to all comers, but with
roughly 5,000 applicants for the 1,400
available places – takes place in
January over this course. But the
skiing below Winteregg is all pretty
boring paths.

Mürren's high-altitude skiing was
greatly improved last season by the
installation of two new lifts below the
Engetal. Good skiers can now enjoy a
long, testing run from the Schilthorn
without descending all the way to the

SKI SCHOOL

94/95 prices in Swiss francs

Swiss
Classes 6 days
2hr: 10am-noon
6 days (12hr): 123
Children's classes
Ages: from 4
6 days (12hr): 123
Private lessons
Half-day (2hr) or full-day (5hr)
100 for 2hr afternoon

GETTING THERE

Air Zürich, transfer 3½hr. Bern, transfer 1½hr.

Rail Lauterbrunnen; transfer by mountain railway and tram.

---

village, while not-so-good skiers have much more snowsure skiing available than they used to. Plans shown on last year's piste map for a third new chair-lift, up to Birg, have been scrapped in favour of a more ambitious project scheduled for 1996 at the earliest.

SNOW RELIABILITY
Good on the upper slopes
The Jungfrau ski region has struggled for good snow in quite a few recent winters. But when Wengen and Grindelwald (and the lower slopes here) have had problems, the slopes of the Schilthorn and the Engetal have often had packed powder snow because of their height and the north-facing direction of the Engetal skiing. Piste grooming is haphazard, except at Winteregg.

FOR ADVANCED SKIERS
One wonderful piste
The run from the top of the Schilthorn starts off with a steep, but not terrifying, mogul-field for the first few hundred metres. But it soon flattens out into some gentle skiing followed by a schuss to the Engetal skiing below Birg. After this, there's a wonderful wide run with stunning views to the Eiger, Mönch and Jungfrau over the valley. Now that new lifts have been built here you don't feel so far from civilisation, but the views remain staggeringly beautiful and the skiing possibilities have been expanded.

If you ignore the lifts and carry on down, you next hit the Kanonenrohr (or gunbarrel). This is a very narrow shelf with solid rock on one side, and a steep drop on the other (which is thankfully protected by nets). After an open slope and a scrappy zig-zag path, you then have a choice of routes back through the trees into the village or to the lower skiing.

There is a short but serious mogul run from Schiltgrat to the village (the Kandahar), but good skiers are more likely to be interested in the off-piste runs into the Blumental, both in this sector (the north-facing Blumenlucke run) and from Birg (the south-east-facing Tschingelchrachen), or the more adventurous runs from the Schilthorn.

FOR INTERMEDIATE SKIERS
Limited, but Wengen nearby
Keen piste bashers won't find enough skiing in Mürren to keep them happy for a week. You'd have to make a few expeditions to the ideal intermediate terrain of Wengen-Grindelwald.

The best easy cruising run in Mürren is the blue down to Winteregg. The reds in the other lower ski areas can get tough and mogulled, and the snow conditions can be poor. The area below Birg is much more attractive now that there are new lifts – and the snow in this high and fairly shady area is normally good.

Timid skiers should not attempt the top cable-car or the run down through the Kanonenrohr.

FOR BEGINNERS
Go elsewhere
The nursery slopes, at Allmendhubel at the top of the funicular, are fine. But once you get off those, there are no good, easy runs to graduate to. The Winteregg run and the area around Birg are about the easiest.

FOR CROSS-COUNTRY
Forget it
There is one small cross-country loop above the village in the Blumental. And there are extensive loops along the valley floor from Lauterbrunnen or Stechelberg. But snow is unreliable at valley height.

QUEUES
Generally not a problem
Mürren gets much less crowded than Wengen and Grindelwald. There are rarely queues except, occasionally, for the cable-cars. These usually arise when snow shortages bring skiers from less fortunate resorts.

MOUNTAIN RESTAURANTS
Disappointing at altitude
Piz Gloria, at the summit of the Schilthorn, has a revolving restaurant with a fabulous 360° panorama of peaks and lakes. But the service, food and welcome are disappointing and it has a functional atmosphere.

The self-service restaurant at the Birg mid-station is ordinary; there's a big sun terrace but it can get windy.

Lower down, we like the Suppenalp restaurant in the Blumental – rustic and away from the lifts, with good views and a large sun terrace.

It's easy to ski back to Mürren for lunch, where our favourite is the sun terrace at the back of the Bellevue hotel, near the foot of the funicular. The views are stunning and the alcoholic cakes well worth trying.

SKI SCHOOL
Now reliable?
The ski school has had a patchy reputation over the years, and several recent changes of management.

CHILDCARE

The ski school takes children from age 4.

The nursery in the sports centre no longer cares for babies. It now takes children aged 3 or more all day, but those aged 2 to 3 for mornings only. There are few places, so it's advisable to book in advance through the tourist office.

PACKAGES

Chalets 'Unlimited', Inghams, Kuoni, Made to Measure, Plus Travel, Ski Choice, Ski Club of GB, Swiss Travel Service

Lauterbrunnen Ski Miquel, Top Deck

ACTIVITIES

Indoor 'Alpine Sports Centre Mürren' swimming pool, whirlpool and children's pool, library, children's playroom, gymnasium, squash, sauna, solarium, judo, massage
Outdoor Artificial skating rink (curling, skating) free with Visitor's card, toboggan run to Gimmelwald, 15km cleared paths

TOURIST OFFICE

Postcode CH-3825
Tel 010 41 (36)
551616
Fax 553769

According to our most recent reports, the regime of Angelique Feuz, who took over in 1992, is delivering the goods: 'very high standards, very good English'.

FACILITIES FOR CHILDREN
Half-hearted
Mürren doesn't have ideal terrain for infants to find their skiing feet, and the facilities seem to echo this. The ski nursery is open only in the afternoons, and the day-care nursery at the sports centre (now limiting all-day care to children aged 3 or more) has not always met with parental approval, though we lack recent reports.

 # Staying there

Mürren is so small that location is not a concern. Nothing will be more than a few minutes' walk away. But there is something to be said for being based close to one or other of the arrival stations.

HOW TO GO
Mainly hotels, packaged or not
A handful of operators offer packages, but the range of accommodation is not wide.
Chalets As far as we know, there is now only one company offering one chalet – Chalets & Hotels Unlimited.
Hotels There are fewer than a dozen hotels, but they range widely in style.
££££ Mürren Palace Victorian pile close to the railway station – biggest and 'best' in town.
££££ Eiger Plain-looking 'chalet' blocks right next to railway station; good blend of efficiency and charm; swimming pool.
£££ Alpenruh Attractively renovated chalet next to the cable-car station.
££ Alpenblick Simple, small, modern chalet near railway station.
Self-catering There are plenty of chalets and apartments to rent in the village, but they are not packaged on the UK market. There are adequate shops, including a butcher's.

STAYING DOWN THE VALLEY
A cheaper option
See the Wengen chapter for options in Lauterbrunnen and Interlaken. If you want to ski both the Wengen and Mürren areas, Lauterbrunnen in particular is a good budget place to stay. It has a ski resort (rather than town) atmosphere and access to and from both main resorts until late (covered by your ski pass).

STAYING UP THE MOUNTAIN
Two possibilities
Two of the attractive restaurants in the Blumental – the Sonnenberg and Flora-Suppenalp – have cheap dormitory-style accommodation.

EATING OUT
Mainly in hotels
There's not a lot of choice except for hotel restaurants. The rustic Stägerstübli is the main alternative – a popular bar as well as restaurant. The hotels Bellevue, Eiger and Palace have good reputations.

APRES-SKI
Quiet
Mürren isn't a place for party animals. The main haunts are hotel based. The Tachi in the Eiger is the liveliest bar, although the Balloon bar in the Palace and the Belmont are good for a civilised après-ski drink. The Stägerstübli is the place to meet locals. Teenagers fill up the little Blienilichäller disco until it closes at a mere 2am.

FOR NON-SKIERS
Tranquillity but not much else
Other than admiring the peace and beauty, there isn't a lot to amuse inactive non-skiers. It's not the place to go for people-watching. But there is a remarkably good sports centre, with a splendidly set outdoor ice rink.

Meeting up with skiers for lunch is easy – it's no problem for them to ski down to the village and the only problem for non-skiers meeting at the top of the cable-car is the expense – SF52, around £25.

Saas-Fee 1800m

HOW IT RATES

The skiing

Snow	*****
Extent	**
Advanced	***
Intermediates	****
Beginners	*****
Convenience	***
Queues	**
Restaurants	***

The rest

Scenery	****
Resort charm	*****
Not skiing	****

✔ *Good percentage of high-altitude, snowsure skiing*

✔ *Two crucial new lifts for the 1994/95 season will improve access to highest skiing*

✔ *Spectacular setting amid high peaks and glaciers*

✔ *Attractive, traditional, 'traffic-free' village*

✔ *Good amenities including a hillside dedicated to non-skiers*

✘ *Disappointingly small ski area*

✘ *Glacier stifles off-piste potential*

✘ *Much of the area is in shadow in mid-winter – cold and dark*

✘ *Bad weather can shut down the skiing completely*

✘ *Parts of the village are inconvenient for the skiing*

✘ *Rocky home runs need good snow-cover*

Saas-Fee is the kind of place people fall for in a big way. It's got lots of Swiss charm and the setting is just stunning – impressive glaciers and 4000m peaks surround the place.

ORIENTATION

Saas-Fee is a long, narrow, traffic-free village, around 2km from end to end. Visitors arrive at a large car-parking area at the entrance to the resort – close to the village centre and the start of the giant Alpin Express gondola. The other major lifts – two gondolas and a cable-car – start from the far, southern end of the village at the foot of the slopes. Saas-Fee is the main resort of the Saastal – **Saas-Almagell, Saas-Balen** and **Saas-Grund** are a short bus-ride away, down in the valley. The ski areas are not linked but are covered by a single lift pass. Day trips to **Zermatt, Grächen** and **Crans-Montana** are realistic options.

Unfortunately, the dramatic surroundings are also the reason for Saas-Fee's skiing being rather less spectacular than its scenery – the steep terrain and extensive areas of glacier severely restrict the area's development. The tight ring of high peaks can also make the village seem dark and cold for long periods in mid-winter; which is good for the snow, not good for those seeking blue skies and sunshine. It's a place not without its faults and its critics – but it's too good to be ignored, especially if you're taking a late-season holiday. Snow conditions here are often among the best in the Alps when many other resorts are struggling to provide any skiing. That consideration, together with its Alpine charm and wonderful scenery, is enough to continue attracting skiers of all abilities.

 The resort

Like nearby Zermatt, Saas-Fee is car-free but somewhat plagued by electric vehicles. On most other counts, Saas-Fee and its more exalted neighbour are a long way apart in style. Saas-Fee still manages to feel like a village rather than a 'destination resort' – the nearly-9,000 visitor beds are well spread out and have not yet overwhelmed the attractive old chalets, cow sheds and narrow streets. And there's little of the glamour and greed that, for many, spoil Zermatt.

The spread-out nature of the village is a disadvantage – it's a long walk (or expensive taxi-ride) from one end to the other – though for skiing purposes this is less important than it was, because the new Alpin express starts below the centre.

The centre of the village is perhaps a little disappointing – there is the ski school office, the church and a few more shops than elsewhere – but it lacks a feeling of being at the heart of things. The restaurant terraces at the foot of the slopes, however, are anything but disappointing. The views up to the horseshoe of 4000m peaks is breath-taking – you can see exactly

why the village is known as 'The Pearl of The Alps'.

There are some very smart hotels (plus many others that are more reasonably priced) and plenty of good eating and drinking places. During days when the spring sun is beating down, Saas-Fee is a quite beautiful place just to stroll around and relax. It's also a major centre for ski-touring – several nearby peaks can be climbed and the extended Haute Route from Chamonix ends at Saas-Fee.

 The skiing

The main Felskinn-Längfluh area has been improved by recent additions to the lift system. And the skiing is set in classic Alpine surroundings, providing something for everyone but, for some skiers, simply not enough kilometres of piste. It seems to have been a question of fitting in what the mountain allows, rather than designing what might be preferred. For ski-mountaineering and ski-touring, this is one of the top places.

SKI FACTS

Altitude	1800m-3620m
Lifts	26
Pistes	100km
Green/Blue	20%
Red	64%
Black	16%
Artificial snow	2km

LIFT PASSES

94/95 prices in Swiss francs

Saas Fee area
Covers all lifts in Saas Fee only.

Beginners Village area pass covers 3 beginners' lifts.

Main pass
1-day pass 55
6-day pass 255

Senior citizens
Over 62: 6-day pass 235 (8% off)

Children
Under 16: 6-day pass 150 (41% off)
Under 6: free pass

Short-term passes
Single and return tickets on most main lifts. Half-day pass from noon (adult 45).

Notes Discount for groups of 20 or more.

Alternative passes
Separate passes for each of the other ski areas in the Saastal (Saas Grund, Saas Almagell, Saas Balen). Pass for all four villages in the Saastal also available, and includes free ski-bus between them.

THE SKI AREA

A glacier runs through it

Saas-Fee's smallest ski area, **Plattjen**, is reached by gondola from the southern end of the village at the foot of the slopes. This is a small intermediates' hill – frequently used by the ski school 'middle classes' – and has only one chair-lift in addition to the gondola.

The main **Felskinn-Längfluh** area, where most of the skiing is to be found, can be reached in a variety of ways. The Felskinn cable-car, which starts a short drag-lift away from the foot of the pistes, takes you directly to Felskinn at 3000m and the entrance to the Metro Alpin (an underground funicular which hurtles through the rock beneath the glacier and emerges at 3500m). From the top of the Metro, two drag-lifts access the high point of the system – 3620m.

The new Alpin Express 30-person gondola now provides an alternative route to Felskinn. It starts on the fringe of the village, midway between the slopes and parking area, and gets bodies out of the village very efficiently. Its second stage is due to open for the 1994/95 season.

From the same station as the Plattjen lift, another gondola leaves for Spielboden. This is met by a cable-car which takes you up to Längfluh.

Felskinn and Längfluh are themselves almost separate sectors, squeezed out onto opposite fringes of an off-limits glacier area. Connections

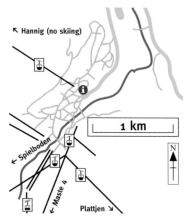

between the two will be vastly improved by a new lift due to open for the 1994/95 season. This will take you up from Längfluh to a point where you can ski down into the Felskinn area. It will replace the old snowcat service and save you the extra SF6 that each ride used to cost. The Längfluh and Felskinn sectors are served mainly by drag-lifts, and you can ski from both all the way down to the village.

The nursery slopes are at the edge of the village and are quite extensive.

SNOW RELIABILITY

One of the best

If Saas-Fee is suffering from lack of snow, it's likely that almost everywhere else has problems too. The village is at 1800m, enough for village-level snow during much of the season.

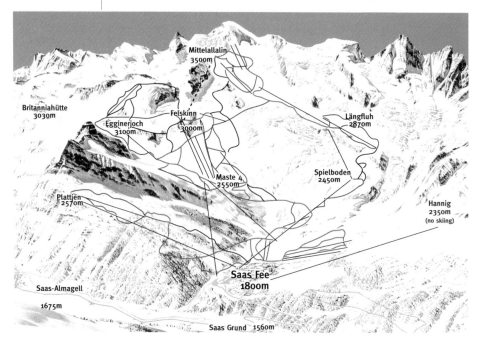

SKI SCHOOL

94/95 prices in Swiss francs

Swiss
Classes 5 days
4hr: 9.45-11.45 and
1.30-3.30
5 full days: 178
Children's classes
Ages: from 5
5 full days: 178
Private lessons
Hourly or daily
54 for 1hr for 1 to 2
people

Most of the skiing is north-facing and much of it above 2500m, which makes Saas Fee one of the most reliable resorts in the Alps for snow. On the glacier there is skiing all year round. Even so, rocks and stones can be a bit of a nuisance on the lower slopes. A short stretch of snow cannons on the nursery slopes normally ensures that they stay in working order.

FOR ADVANCED SKIERS
A few good challenges on-piste
One of the disadvantages of Saas-Fee's glacier is the limitations it imposes on off-piste skiing – crevasse danger is extreme, and good skiers have to content themselves with the pisted areas or take a guide for limited off-piste or extensive ski-touring. Late-season ski-tours are a big feature in this region.

There is not a vast amount of steep skiing, but there's sufficient technical challenge to keep good skiers busy for a while. The highest drag-lift on the left above Felskinn serves two short, steep blacks and one easy one. The lift itself is a bit of a challenge – we've been lifted off the ground here several times. The extremely short Spielboden drag delivers skiers to the top of an equally short, steep and lumpy slope in full view of the terrace below – usually with an audience expecting some entertainment. The slopes around the top of Längfluh often provide good powder skiing. The long return runs to the village from both Längfluh and Felskinn are not easy, with some genuinely black sections which can be especially tricky in icy conditions.

The black runs and the tree-skiing on Plattjen are worth exploring.

FOR INTERMEDIATE SKIERS
Enough to do; plenty to see
Plattjen has a variety of runs down it, all of them skiable by ambitious intermediates. Those looking for long cruising runs should head for the top of the mountain and try all the options from there. The top half of the mountain, down as far as Maste 4 (the end of the first stage of the Alpin Express), is ideal intermediate terrain, with the added advantage of usually excellent snow.

There is a variety of gradient ranging from gentle blue confidence-building slopes to some steeper reds which can build up smallish bumps. We particularly like the runs at the top of the Metro first-thing on a late-season morning – though they can be mind-numbingly cold in early season.

The descent from the top right down to the village is a great challenge for those wishing to prove their stamina. Either way, via Felskinn or via Längfluh, it's a superb descent of 1800m vertical. The runs on the bottom half of the mountain all have some tricky sections, and nervous or tired intermediates would be well advised to take a lift down.

FOR BEGINNERS
A nice place to start
There's a good, large nursery area right at the edge of the village. Three lifts serve an out-of-the-way area without through-traffic of experienced skiers going back to the village. Graduates of the nursery slopes will probably want to head for the gentle blue area on Felskinn just above Maste 4 – the return trip is best completed by Alpin Express. And there are further gentle blues at the very top of the mountain, from where it's possible to ski down the glacier to the Längfluh side – again the lifts would need to be used to return to the village.

There's a useful pass for beginners who aren't ready to go up the mountain, allowing access to all the short lifts at the edge of the village.

FOR CROSS-COUNTRY
A good local trail and lots nearby
There is one short (8km) pleasant, prepared trail at the edge of the village, away from all those noisy downhillers. It snakes up through the woods, providing about 150m of climb and nice views. In the valley there are far more options, including 25km of track and plenty of suitable terrain beyond Saas-Almagell towards Mattmark.

QUEUES
Problems are being sorted
In the past, the main criticism of the skiing has been the appalling queues at the main lifts, particularly late in the season. This problem is now much relieved with the construction of the Alpin Express, the second stage of which goes all the way up to Felskinn and is due to open at the start of the 1994/95 season. Of course, whether this increases queues elsewhere remains to be seen. It will certainly have the effect of increasing piste congestion. It's still possible to find queues at the other departure points in the village, and for some of the higher lifts. Some of these queues can develop into unpleasantly unruly scrums at times.

MOUNTAIN RESTAURANTS
A couple of gems

The main claim to fame belongs to the one at Mittelallalin – at 3500m the world's highest revolving restaurant. It doesn't actually have the best views on the mountain but it does provide 360-degrees-worth each hour. There's a perfectly good café underneath it which doesn't rotate but is cheaper. All the major lift stations have a restaurant – generally functional rather than charming. At Spielboden there's a large terrace with good views of some tricky slopes. At Längfluh the terrace has splendid views of the huge crevasses in the glacier.

The best of the huts are slightly off the beaten track: Berghaus Plattjen (not to be confused with the place at the top of the Plattjen lifts), and the Gletscher-Grotte, half-way down from Spielboden. Both provide excellent food and a lovely old, smoky hut kind of ambience – especially good when the weather's foul. The Britanniahütte is a real mountain hut, awkward to get to but, if you're up to the trek, best for mountain atmosphere and views.

SKI SCHOOL
Attitude problems

It's the Swiss ski school or nothing in Saas-Fee. Unfortunately the lack of competition creates problems – too often classes are overlarge, with a wide range of abilities in a class, and some instructors have limited English.

FACILITIES FOR CHILDREN
Half-hearted

Neither the ski school nor the non-ski kindergarten takes children younger than age 5. One solution for people with younger children is to use one of the hotels that have an in-house kindergarten. Although it has no kindergarten, the hotel Beau-Site has an 'excellent' play-room.

CHILDCARE

The ski school takes children from age 5, and can provide lunchtime care. The Glückskäfer kindergarten also takes children from age 5, from 9am to 5pm.

A couple of 3-star hotels – the Alphubel and the Europa Minotel – have their own kindergartens .

GETTING THERE

Air Geneva, transfer 3½hr.

Rail Brig (34km); regular buses from station.

⬆ Staying there

Staying near one of the lifts out makes most sense. If you do end up at the wrong (north) end of the village – and most of the budget accommodation is there – using the facilities for depositing skis and boots near the lifts will ease the pain. It's worth getting a guest card for miscellaneous discounts.

HOW TO GO
Check the location

Quite a few tour operators include Saas-Fee, providing an excellent range of hotel accommodation, but chalets and apartments are few.

Chalets For a village that looks to be composed almost entirely of chalets, there are surprisingly few offered by UK tour operators – Crystal have the only ones that we know of. Their Feeblick and Schönegg chalets are simple, friendly old places. Viktoria is more modern, and has en suite bathrooms. None is very conveniently placed for skiing.

Hotels 50-plus hotels (the number continues to increase) means lots of choice. The great majority are 3-star, with half a dozen 4-star places and a similar number of 2-star. There are also many lesser-graded but comfortable places.

£££££ Fletschhorn Elegant chalet, a long way out of the village in the wrong direction, but in a lovely tranquil setting – and with fabulous nouvelle food (Michelin star).

££££ Walliserhof Lively, ritzy 4-star – smart but rather brash. Pool.

££££ Schweizerhof Stylish new place in quiet, but not convenient, position just above centre (can leave kit at Saaserhof). 'Excellent' food. Pool.

£££ Beau-Site 'First-rate' but quiet 4-star in central, but not convenient, position. Good food. Pool.

£££ Saaserhof Modern chalet in good position just over the river from nursery slopes.

£££ Ambassador Modern chalet, well placed close to the nursery slopes.

£££ Alphubel At the wrong end of town, but one of the best bets for families, with its own kindergarten.

£££ Hohnegg A more rustic alternative to the Fletschhorn, in a similarly remote spot; only 8 rooms.

££ Belmont The most appealing of the hotels looking on to the nursery slopes.

££ Zur Mühle Rustic restaurant with 3 rooms, well placed by the river bridge.

Self-catering A number of the least attractive looking buildings, at the north end of the village, house apartments which are featured by UK tour operators. Fortunately, the apartments themselves tend to be spacious, clean and well-equipped. Ski convenience is poor, but independent travellers have apartments available in better situated parts of the village. The Residence Hotel Atlantic (Inghams) has unusually comfortable studios, ideal for couples. They come complete with plenty of mod cons, plus a wealth of in-house hotel amenities. Families or groups have a choice between the similarly fair-standard Tobias (Swiss Travel) and Allalin (Inghams, Crystal) apartments.

PACKAGES

Crystal, Enterprise, Inghams, Kuoni, Made to Measure, Plus Travel, Ski Choice, Ski with Julia, SkiGower, Swiss Travel Service, Thomson

Saas Grund
Ski Europe

ACTIVITIES

Indoor Bielen Leisure centre (swimming, jacuzzi, steam bath, solarium, sauna, massage, tennis, gym, whirlpool), cinema, museum, cultural centre at Steinmatte, concerts, badminton **Outdoor** 20km cleared paths, natural skating rink (skating, curling, ice-hockey), ski-bob runs, toboggan run

TOURIST OFFICE

Postcode CH-3906
Tel 010 41 (28)
571457
Fax 571860

EATING OUT

No shortage – some high class

There are 60 restaurants to choose from. Gastronomes will probably want to head for the Michelin-starred Fletschhorn (see Hotels) or the Hohnegg – their high reputations and high prices are widely judged to be justified. Others will no doubt make do with the large selection of hotel restaurants and other eateries in town. Most hotel restaurants welcome non-residents and they usually offer set meals at a good price. The food tends to be traditional – the Belmont and the Tenne are typical; the latter also does charcoal grill specialities. Boccalino is cheap and does pizzas – book or get there early. Alp-Hitta specialises in rustic surroundings and food. The Skihütte is a good bet for both lunch and dinner. The hotel Dom has a splendid restaurant specialising in endless different varieties of rösti.

Locals assure us that the following are all good: Arvu-Stuba, Zur Mühle, the Gorge, the Feeloch and the Ferme.

APRES-SKI

A handful of hotspots

For that tea-time drink the best places are down near the lifts, where it's usually pretty lively for at least a couple of hours. Nesti's ski-bar, Zur Mühle and the little snowbars are all popular.Later on the 'real' bars swing into action – the Tenn's Sissy bar has a good atmosphere but gets terribly cramped; the Fee, Nesti's and the Go-Inn all get busy later on and keep going till 1am. There are three expensive nightclubs with dancing and live bands.

FOR NON-SKIERS

A whole 'mountain' just for you

Non-skiers are likely to enjoy Saas-Fee much better than a lot of places, except perhaps in the middle of winter, when it can seem permanently cold and dark. It's easy to travel around the mountain on the gondolas and cable-cars. There is now a whole mountainside, the Hannig, dedicated to the art of non-skiing. Skiers are banned – eating, drinking, sunning, walking, tobogganing and parapenting take priority. In the village, the splendid Bielen leisure centre has the usual facilities, but also boasts a 25m pool, indoor tennis courts and an unusual lounging area with sunlamps which turn on and off at intervals. Skating and curling are further

possibilities. A close look at the glacier is a must – the views from the terrace at Längfluh are the best; at Mittelallalin there are the added attractions of the rotating restaurant and the ice-cave.

Saas-Grund 1570m

Saas-Grund stretches for 2km along the valley road and the river Vispe below Saas-Fee. The Saas-Fee road turns off from here. It is an ancient farming community which has expanded enormously in recent years, yet has managed to retain some rustic charm. It is Saas-Fee's poor relation, with correspondingly lower prices. The regular bus service means it is an acceptable alternative to staying in Saas-Fee. But don't expect the same charm, beauty or atmosphere.

There are around 15 hotels – mostly 2- or 3-star with 30 or 40 beds each and rooms at between SF50 and SF70 per person per night. The Café Sporting is good value and the hotel Rodania does fine fondues at a good price and puts on a disco.

Saas-Grund has its own pleasant, quiet, small (20km of piste) ski area. A gondola takes you up to the Kreuzboden mid-station at 2400m. A group of short lifts around here do nicely for beginners – particularly later in the season when many lower nursery slopes have already faded away. The second stage goes to 3100m, with glorious views of the Saas-Fee ski area, a couple of nice runs down and a restaurant serving good Swiss food at reasonable prices. The bars near the base station get pretty lively when the skiing stops.

The resort has its own ski school and ski kindergarten, though we suspect lack of English-speakers in both could be a problem. There is no non-skiing crèche.

Saas-Almagell 1670m

From Grund, ten minutes along the valley by bus lies Saas-Almagell, a compact, traditional old village. Its small, wooded ski area comes into its own in bad weather. Walkers are well catered for and the village offers 26km of fine, wooded cross-country trails in both directions through its high snow-reliable valley. Its fair range of accommodation includes 12 hotels and a pleasant, informal pension, the Edelweiss.

St Moritz 1800m

HOW IT RATES

The skiing
Snow	✱✱✱✱
Extent	✱✱✱✱✱
Advanced	✱✱✱✱
Intermediates	✱✱✱✱
Beginners	✱✱
Convenience	✱✱
Queues	✱✱
Restaurants	✱✱✱✱

The rest
Scenery	✱✱✱✱
Resort charm	✱✱
Not skiing	✱✱✱✱✱

ORIENTATION

St Moritz sits in a high valley, reached from the rest of Switzerland by high passes or tunnels.

It spreads around the western end of a lake. Dorf is the main town, built on a steep hillside to the north of the lake, beneath the ski slopes of Corviglia (reached by funicular). Other lifts go up into the Corviglia skiing from **Celerina**, 2km down the valley, and from St Moritz Bad, which spreads up the valley from the the lakeside.

There are several other ski areas. The main one is Corvatsch – up the valley on the opposite side from Corviglia, with lifts at Surlej, on the fringe of **Silvaplana**, and **Sils Maria**. There are hotels and cross-country skiing down the valley, in and around the nearby villages of **Samedan** and **Pontresina**, and 5km from St Moritz up the Bernina valley towards the Lagalb and Diavolezza ski areas. Trips further afield to other resorts such as **Lenzerheide** and **Davos** are possible, but not easy.

✔ Beautiful scenery – St Moritz is set next to a picturesque lake in a spectacular high valley

✔ Non-skiing amenities second to none – including the Cresta run

✔ Big ski area – half a dozen distinct ski areas, each with its own character

✔ High, snowsure skiing

✔ Attracts a 'nice' class of clientele – no hooligan skiers

✔ Good après-ski, catering for all ages from 18 to 80, not just the jet set

✔ Good (but expensive) mountain restaurants

✔ Painless rail access via Zürich

✔ Sunny slopes, particularly at Corviglia (though this can be a minus point late in the season)

✔ One of the most comprehensive snowmaking setups in the Alps

✗ Unattractive towny feel to the resort; little Alpine character

✗ Not many nursery slopes

✗ Poor road access – involving high mountain passes or car-carrying rail tunnels

✗ Long overland airport transfers – over four hours

✗ Lift queues all too frequent

✗ Not much woodland skiing

✗ Expensive; even the Swiss complain that St Moritz is pricey

St Moritz is Switzerland's most famous 'exclusive' ski resort: glitzy, pricey, fashionable and, above all, the place to be seen. But, rather like Aspen in the US, St Moritz is not as snooty as its popular image might lead you to expect. In fact – heaven forbid – they have even opened a half-pipe track for snowboarders on Corviglia. What's more, the skiing – again, rather like Aspen – is superb, with something for everybody. We don't rate it highly for beginners, but there is compensation in the non-skiing diversions, which are unrivalled.

The town of St Moritz itself is surprisingly unattractive. It seems far removed from the chocolate box image of the Swiss mountain resort, all wooden huts and cows with bells round their necks. Here, many of the buildings resemble council flats (extremely neat and clean ones – this is Switzerland, after all).

But if St Moritz is not attractive to look at, it is beautiful to look out from; its setting, beside the lowest in a long chain of lakes at the foot of the 4000m Piz Bernina, is spectacular.

🏔 The resort

St Moritz has two distinct parts. Dorf is the main part, built on a steep hillside above the lake. This is the fashionable St Moritz – a busy, compact town with two main streets lined with expensive boutiques selling Rolex watches, Cartier jewellery and Hermes scarves, a few side lanes and a single small main square. Great big expensive hotels stand guard over the lake, including the famous names – the Palace, the Carlton and the Kulm.

St Moritz Bad is less smart – a spa resort, spread around one end of the lake on the valley floor. There are less prestigious hotels, restaurants and shops, and it is well placed for cross-country skiing as well as walks around the lake. In winter, the lake is used for all sorts of eccentric activities, including various equestrian activities (such as polo), 'ice golf' and even cricket.

SKI FACTS

Altitude	1720m-3300m
Lifts	60
Pistes	350km
Green/Blue	16%
Red	71%
Black	13%
Artificial snow	15km

 ## The skiing

Like the resort, most of the slopes are made for posing. There is the occasional black run, but most pistes are so well groomed that you can easily swoop down with little chance that you'll make a fool of yourself on a rogue mogul. There is tough skiing, but it is dispersed throughout the region. There are lots of long and generally wide runs, with varied terrain including pretty trails through woods to the valley. Beginners' slopes are few and far between. Views in most of the ski area are spectacular.

THE SKI AREA
Large and sprawling
There is a lot of skiing here. With a claimed 350km, the Upper Engadine may not be quite in the Trois Vallées league, but it is definitely in the next division.

The skiing is in several distinct ski areas. The main ones, shown on our piste maps, are Corviglia-Marguns, close to the resort, and Corvatsch-Furtschellas, a bus-ride away. Diavolezza, Piz Lagalb, Alp Languard and a few other bits and pieces more remote from St Moritz make up the rest. If you want to ski these areas (and some of them are well worth an outing) it helps to have a car, although there is an adequate bus service linking to them.

Within half an hour you can be transported by monorail train to Corviglia and on by cable-car to the peak of Piz Nair. Between Piz Nair and Corviglia there is invariably plenty of snow, and this is where the bulk of the lifts in this sector are situated.

From Corviglia you can ski down to both St Moritz Dorf and St Moritz Bad. If there has been little recent snowfall, the lower slopes below Corviglia can be rocky or grassy, and skiers are best advised to take the monorail down from Corviglia to St Moritz. If the snow is plentiful, the more romantic might ski from Corviglia down to Chantarella and hire a horse-drawn open-top carriage to take them all the way back to their hotel.

From Surlej, a few miles up the valley from St Moritz, a two-stage cable-car takes you to up to **Corvatsch**. From there you have a choice of red runs down to Murtel and Alp Margun. From the latter you can work your way across the mountainside to **Furtschellas**, also reached directly by cable-car from Sils Maria. Runs descend to the valley not only to Sils Maria and Surlej, but also to the fringes of St Moritz Bad. The Corvatsch sector has been much improved in recent years by the installation of new chair-lifts, speeding access to the top of Furtschellas and making it possible to get from Furtschellas across to Corvatsch without descending all the way to the valley.

Diavolezza (2978m) and Lagalb (2959m) are the main additional ski areas, on opposite sides of the road to the Bernina pass (a dead end in winter), less than half an hour away by bus. Diavolezza has excellent north-facing pistes of 900m vertical, down under its main cable-car, and a very popular marked off-piste route, off the back of the mountain and down a deserted valley to Morterasch. Lagalb is a smaller area of quite challenging skiing with one main cable-car serving the west-facing front slope of 850m vertical and a couple of drags on the south-facing side.

SNOW RELIABILITY
Excellent snowmaking
St Moritz has a rather dry climate, but the resort's altitude and substantial snowmaking setup, with guns in every sector of the skiing, make it pretty snowsure. (There are glacier areas at the top of some sectors, and some summer skiing.) The most reliable sectors are Corvatsch, across the valley facing back north-west towards the resort, and Diavolezza, which is very high and mostly north-facing.

LIFT PASSES

94/95 prices in Swiss francs

Upper Engadine
Covers all lifts in St Moritz, Celerina, Surlej, Sils Maria, Maloja, Lagalb, Diavolezza, Pontresina, Punt Muragl, Samedan, Müsella and Zuoz, the buses and trains between them, and the swimming pools in St Moritz and Pontresina.

Main pass
1-day pass 51
6-day pass 258

Children
Under 16: 6-day pass 129 (50% off)
Under 6: free pass

Short-term passes
Half-day pass from 11.45 (adult 42).

Alternative periods
5 (adult 248) or 10 (adult 418) days skiing in the season.

Notes Discount for groups of 15 or more. Ski pass also valid in Gstaad Superski region, and gives one days skiing in Livigno.

Alternative passes
Half-day and day passes for individual areas within the Upper Engadine.

FOR ADVANCED SKIERS
Dispersed challenges
Good skiers looking for challenges are liable to find the St Moritz skiing disappointing. Red runs far outnumber the black, and mogul fields are few and far between. There are some serious black runs, but they are dotted about the area in different sectors. (On the positive side, this means that if you want to ski the same area as less adventurous friends, there will always be something challenging to do, not far away.)

Experts head for the toughest parts of the back side of Piz Nair, as well as the Corvatsch summit and the black runs at Lagalb and Diavolezza. The direct Minor run down the Lagalb cable-car may be moguls from top to bottom, while the Schwarzerhang variant on the main red down the front of Diavolezza is seriously steep.

There is considerable off-piste potential in the area, particularly from Corviglia and Corvatsch, all the better for being relatively little exploited by the piste-oriented skiers that the resort mainly attracts.

FOR INTERMEDIATE SKIERS
Good but flattering
St Moritz is well suited to intermediates. 80 per cent of the slopes are for intermediates, and most pistes are easyish reds.

One of the finest runs is the Hahnensee, from the northern limit of the Corvatsch lift system down to St Moritz Bad – a black-graded run that is of red difficulty for most of its 5km length and 1500m vertical drop. It's a five-minute walk from the end of the Hahnensee run to the Signalbahn cable-car, which takes you up to Corviglia.

The skiing at Diavolezza is mostly intermediate. There is an easy open slope beside the drag-lifts at the top, and a splendid long intermediate run back down under the lift, but the great attraction is the popular off-piste runs over the back, across the glacier and through the woods to Morterasch. It includes a 25-minute walk, and there are some tricky narrow passages, but the stunning glacier scenery makes this well worth while.

FOR BEGINNERS
Not much to offer
St Moritz is not an ideal place for beginners. It sits in a deep, narrow valley, which means that there is very little space for nursery slopes at the lower levels. Progression from the nursery slopes to intermediate runs is rather awkward, as these invariably include the odd difficult section that can sap the spirit of the struggling near-beginner.

FOR CROSS COUNTRY
Excellent; go to Pontresina
The Engadine is one of the premier regions in the Alps for cross-country, with 150km of trails of all levels of difficulty, amid splendid scenery and with pretty reliable snow. Pontresina is one of the best locations in the region and also has good skating and curling rinks and swimming pools. There are floodlit loops at Bad, Pontresina and Samedan.

QUEUES
Can be a problem
St Moritz is over-dependent on cable-cars – not of enormous capacity – both for getting up the mountain from resort level and for access to the peaks from mid-mountain, and queues are the inevitable result. The Sils Maria cable-car at the bottom of Furtschellas is relatively queue-free – not surprising, since it is remote from St Moritz and does not give direct access to the most compelling skiing in this sector, on Corvatsch. Like the Valluga cable-car at St Anton, the top cable-car there has a system of pre-allocation of space, so that you can ski around until your number comes up instead of standing in line.

The Cresta Run

No visit to St Moritz is really complete without a visit to the Cresta Run. It's the last bastion of Britishness and male chauvinism (women have been banned since 1929 because the 100mph blows to their breasts were thought unacceptable).

Any man over 18 can pay around £200 for five rides on the famous run (helmet and lunch at the Kulm hotel included). Watch out for the Shuttlecock corner – that's where most people come off, and the ambulances ply for trade. You lie on a toboggan (aptly called a 'skeleton') and hurtle head-first down a sheet ice gully from St Moritz to Celerina. David Gower, Sandy Gall and many others are addicts. Fancy giving it a go?

SKI SCHOOL

94/95 prices in
Swiss francs

St Moritz
Classes 6 days
4hr: 10am-noon and
1.30-3.30
6 full days: 230
Children's classes
Ages: from 5
6 full days: 230
Private lessons
Half-day (2hr) or
full-day (5hr)
140 for half-day

Suvretta
Small groups of 4 to
6 people
Classes 6 days
2hr, 3hr, 4hr or
full-day (5hr)
1 full day: 365
Children's classes
Ages: up to 15
3 days (4hr): 170
Private lessons
Hourly or daily
80 for 1hr between
noon and 1pm

CHILDCARE

The St Moritz ski
school operates a
pick-up service for
children. Both schools
provide all-day care.

Children aged 3 or
more can be looked
after in hotels – there
are nurseries in the
Carlton, the Parkhotel
Kurhaus and the
Schweizerhof, open
from 9am to 4.30
or 5pm.

MOUNTAIN RESTAURANTS
Some of the best in Europe

Mountain restaurants are plentiful,
and among the most glamorous in
Europe. Prices can be high, and
reservations are often necessary,
especially if you want to sit in
particular spots.

On Corviglia, the highlight is the
exclusive Marmite, one of the best
mountains restaurants in the world,
where you may need to keep
expenditure in check by sticking to
the superb cakes and leaving the
gourmet dishes well alone. (Don't be
distracted by the self-service cafeteria
that conceals the sit-down restaurant –
it's almost as pricey and doesn't have
the terrace views.) The Alpina Hutte is
also recommended. On the Corvatsch
side, Fuorcla Surlej is a delightfully
secluded spot – as is Hahnensee, on
the lift-free end-of-the-day run down
to St Moritz Bad.

The restaurant at Muottas Muragl,
between Celerina and Pontresina, is
well worth a visit. It has truly
spectacular views overlooking the
valley, as well as good food.

SKI SCHOOL
Internal competition

The St Moritz and Suvretta schools are
apparently both branches of the
national Swiss school. We lack recent
reports on them.

FACILITIES FOR CHILDREN
Hotel-based nurseries

Children wanting ski lessons have a
choice of the two schools, but others
must be deposited at one of the three
hotels with nurseries. The Parkhotel
Kurhaus is close to the cable-car in
Bad, the other two up in Dorf. Club
Med has its usual good facilities.

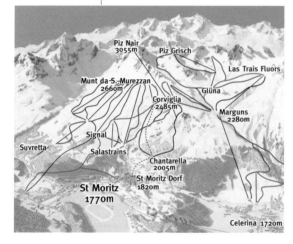

Staying there

If high society is your priority, you
will want to stay in Dorf. If economy
matters, you will probably have to stay
down in Bad – or stay at home. It is
possible to find convenient
accommodation in either part of the
resort, but not easy. Bad has the
advantage that you can ski back to it
from Corvatsch, as well as Corviglia.
Celerina is well worth considering as a
base, as it provides direct access to the
Corviglia skiing.

HOW TO GO
More packages than you expect

Considering how rarely we hear from
anyone who has visited St Moritz, it's
quite surprising to find that more than
a handful of tour operators package
the resort. But there is much more
choice of accommodation open to the
independent traveller. As well as the
many conventional hotels, there are
two branches of Club Med – and going
with an operator like this who does
all-inclusive deals is one way to cut
down the impact of the high prices.
The Roi Soleil Club Med hotel is the
one to go for. It has a good-size pool,
and is conveniently situated in St
Moritz Bad, near the Signal lift.
Hotels Over half the hotels are of 4-star
and 5-star quality – the highest
concentration of high-quality hotels
in Switzerland.
£££££ Badrutt's Palace The top hotel.
Vast place overlooking the lake.
£££££ Carlton Relatively intimate
top-rank hotel, with only 180 beds.
Inconvenient, secluded setting on
fringe of Dorf.
££££ Crystal Big 4-star in Dorf, as
close to the Corviglia lift as any.
£££ Nolda One of the few chalet-style
buildings, close to the cable-car in
St Moritz Bad.

EATING OUT
Mostly chic and expensive

It's easy to spend £50 a head on
dinner in St Moritz, not counting the
wine. Even the Swiss complain about
the prices at St Moritz.

But there are reasonable places. The
Soldanella hotel has a set menu for
SF35 (£17.50) which must be the best
value for money in town; the Steffani
is also inexpensive by St Moritz
standards; and the Belvedere is good
value and has great views of the lake, a
cosy restaurant and a good chef. The
Chesa Veglia is a swanky little
restaurant in Dorf. But the best food is
out at Champfer, at Jöhri's Talvo.

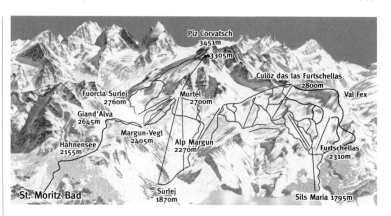

GETTING THERE

Air Zürich, transfer 4¼hr.

Rail Mainline station in resort.

PACKAGES

Alpine Expressions, Club Med, Inghams, Kuoni, Made to Measure, Ski Club of GB, Ski with Julia, SkiGower, Swiss Travel Service

Celerina Made to Measure

Pontresina Club Med, Made to Measure, SkiGower, Swiss Travel Service

Sils Maria Made to Measure

Silvaplana Made to Measure

ACTIVITIES

Indoor Ice skating, curling, swimming, sauna, solarium, tennis, squash, museum, health spa, cinema (with English films), aerobics, beauty farm, health centre, Rotary International club

Outdoor Sleigh rides, ski jumping, toboggan run, hang-gliding, golf on frozen lake, Cresta run, 120km cleared paths, greyhound racing, horse-riding and racing, polo tournaments, cricket tournaments, ski-bob run, para-gliding

TOURIST OFFICE

Postcode CH-7500
Tel 010 41 (82) 33147
Fax 32952

APRES-SKI
Caters for all ages

There is an enormous variety of après-skiing age groups in St Moritz. Kids escape from their parents to Billy's pub, where grunge replaces fur, and the music is loud. At the sedate piano bar there appears to be no-one below bus-pass age.

The fur coat count is high. People come to St Moritz to be seen; and you don't want to make your appearance in an anorak, car coat or Pacamac. The Cresta men have no truck with fashion and all that sissy stuff. So you could adopt their baggy cords and Viyella check shirts. Whatever you do, don't come in your salopettes from Walthamstow market – the raised eyebrows will make you self-conscious for the whole week.

At midnight the streets are full of visitors sampling the nightlife. The most famous is the Kings Disco at the Palace where SF30 gets you in (men need a tie) and buys one drink. The other favourite is the Absolute, near the tourist office.

Others worth trying are the Stubli, with a typical Swiss wood-panelled bar, in the lower level of the Schweizerhof, and the Cave Bar at the Steffani. The Cresta Bar at the same hotel is also a popular place – particularly with the British.

FOR NON-SKIERS
Excellent variety of pastimes

Even if you lack the bravado or masculinity to have a go at the Cresta run, there is lots to do. In winter the great snow-covered lake provides a playground for bizarre events like ice cricket, golf – with red balls on 'white greens' – ice polo and greyhound racing, all of which takes place from Christmas to the end of February. After this the lake starts to thaw.

Some hotels run special non-skiing activities. The hotel Corvatsch offers a 'curling' week; the Carlton a 'health spa week' and the Europa even holds rock and roll dance courses.

Hang-gliding instruction, indoor tennis and even trips to Italy (Milan is four hours away by car) are other non-skiing activities. The public pool in Bad is worth a visit – big, and covered by the lift pass. If you have the time, you could ride the Glacier Express, a spectacular 150-mile journey between St Moritz and Zermatt.

St Moritz has a reputation for being sunny – some 322 days a year according to the Tourist Board statistics – so there are many outside eating facilities even at resort level. Try the Sunny Bar of the Kulm hotel, which is south-facing and overlooks the lake. Many Cresta riders have lunch there.

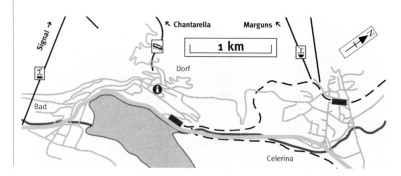

STAYING UP THE MOUNTAIN
Excellent possibilities

Next door to one another at Salastrains, just across the mountainside from Chantarella, are two chalet-style hotels, the 3-star hotel Salastrains, with 60 comfortable beds, and the slightly simpler and much smaller Zuberhütte. Great views, and no queues.

Celerina 1730m

Celerina is a much smaller, more villagey resort, with equally good access to the Corviglia skiing, and well worth considering as a cheaper and less posh base than St Moritz. The 12-room Stüvetta Veglia is a particularly appealing place to stay.

Pontresina 1780m

Pontresina is a small sedate base, in marked contrast to nearby St Moritz. It's a sheltered, sunny village with essentially a single narrow street of traditional old buildings spoilt somewhat by the sanitorium-style of architecture that blights this whole area. Position of accommodation is relatively unimportant – all the skiing involves a bus- or car-ride.

Five minutes away towards Celerina is the Muottas Muragl area, where a mountain railway serves a tiny mountain-top area with marvellous views and a single long run returning to the bottom station. Pontresina's village hill, Languard, has a single long piste.

The sheltered Engadine does not get the amount of snow one might assume from its impressive altitude.

Much is made of Pontresina being a cheaper place to stay than St Moritz, but cheaper doesn't mean cheap – hotels are still very expensive, with little in the way of self-catering options. There is another Club Med here, in addition to the two in St Moritz.

The Collina is one of the better-value luxury hotels, but some of the many 3-star places are more likely to be within the average British pocket. The Steinbock is the most attractive hotel in town, an old inn with an informal atmosphere by local standards and one of only two hotels in the category with a pool. The Rosatch Stummhaus is the other. The ugly Atlas is the best for families, as it houses the village nursery and has some cheaper basic rooms.

Dining is mostly hotel-based, but the Sarazena is an attractive old place with expensive dining on a wooden minstrel's gallery. Hotel Muller has a good stubli, and the Engadinerhof and Bernina restaurants have good reputations.

Nightlife is very quiet. The Sarazena and Engadinerhof have dance floors.

Non-skiers have the numerous facilities of St Moritz close by, while Pontresina has a free skating rink, swimming pool (covered by the lift pass), sauna and massage facilities, sleigh rides, horse-drawn buses and a cinema. Walking is, however, the main pursuit, with 140km of cleared paths throughout the Engadine.

Hotel Atlas has an all-day nursery open to non-residents. There is no ski kindergarten, but ski school starts at 3.

Verbier 1500m

The skiing

Snow	★★★
Extent	★★★★★
Advanced	★★★★★
Intermediates	★★★
Beginners	★★
Convenience	★★
Queues	★
Restaurants	★★★

The rest

Scenery	★★★★
Resort charm	★★★
Not skiing	★★★

✔ Large, challenging ski area with a lot of off-piste potential

✔ Very lively nightlife

✔ Wide range of chalet holidays available

✔ Hardly any drag-lifts

✔ Good off-piste and other advanced-level tuition

✘ Bad queues by today's standards

✘ Overcrowded pistes

✘ Very poor piste maintenance – lack of grooming, marking, safety measures

✘ Very little artificial snowmaking

✘ Long walk or a bus needed to lift from much accommodation

✘ Poorly positioned base from which to ski Four Valleys

✘ Little skiing for novices or early intermediates except paths

✘ Surprisingly little for non-skiers or cross-country enthusiasts

✘ The full lift pass is Europe's most expensive

Verbier has some of Europe's steepest and best off-piste skiing and some of its liveliest nightlife. For these two things its devotees are willing to forgive the resort its many drawbacks. But a lot of first-time visitors are sorely disappointed. They go expecting another Trois Vallées, Val d'Isère or Zermatt – a massive ski area, with varied skiing suiting most skiers from intermediate up, combined with a decent lift system. They come back disillusioned with the resort's expense, the antiquated lifts, the limited and crowded piste skiing and the often poor snow on the lower slopes. A major new lift, due to open for the 1994/5 season, should eliminate one of the major mid-mountain bottlenecks. But it may only succeed in shifting the queues elsewhere and making some of the pistes even more crowded.

To get the most out of Verbier, you really need to party till late and not ski much, or to get up early, beat the lift queues and enjoy the wonderful top-to-bottom of the mountain off-piste adventures with a guide.

ORIENTATION

Verbier sits on a wide sunny balcony, gazing across a junction of valleys below. The resort is an amorphous sprawl, with its main focus 500m (40m vertical) from its main lift station. A notable secondary area, Savoleyres, is accessed from another extremity of town a bus-ride from the centre. The skiing is part of the so-called Four Valleys area, which also includes **Nendaz**, **Thyon**, **La Tzoumaz**, **Siviez** and **Veysonnaz**. **Bruson** is also on the lift pass and reached by bus or by riding a gondola down to **Le Châble** and taking a bus from there. **Argentière** and **Champéry** (which is part of the Portes du Soleil circuit) are other possible road outings.

Verbier grouses

Here is a selection from the unfavourable reports we received from people who told us about their skiing trips to Verbier last season:

'Truly dreadful lift system. I never reached the top of Mont-Fort or Mont-Gelé as I was not prepared to wait for 45 minutes. At one stage I had no option but to wait two hours at Tortin ... Given the price of the lift pass it was a complete rip-off.'

'The piste map is appaling: badly drawn and virtually impossible to find your way around with it.'

'The runs to the resort should have been closed. The lack of cover meant that skiers effectively sandpapered the bases of their skis.'

'One bubble from Medran is almost quaint in its age. It was beaten only by the bubble up from Tortin, which is a disgrace.'

'The piste map is the worst I have seen.'

'My experience of Verbier left a bad taste.'

'The lift system is very badly designed ... an hour's queue for the Tortin gondola was not uncommon.'

'Verbier is grossly overrated and overpriced.'

'Piste skiing, with the exception of Mont-Fort, is a complete waste of time except for unadventurous intermediates. The best skiing for advanced skiers is off-piste.'

But not all of the feedback was negative. For example:

'Very good bus system included in cost of the lift pass.'

'Excellent long challenging runs with beautiful scenery.'

'Huge variety of après-ski.'

'The village has great atmosphere.'

The resort

Verbier is an amorphous, still-expanding sprawl of chalet-style buildings, which retains a certain level of charm by not having too much concrete in evidence, and being impressively set on a wide, sunny, tree-filled balcony beneath spectacular peaks. It's a fashionable, yet informal, very lively place which teems with a young (20s rather than teens) cosmopolitan clientele. But it's no longer exclusive. Sloanes rub shoulders with Essex girls, and the mad Scandinavians often out-party British Hoorays.

The centre of town, where most of the typical touristy ski resort shops and hotels (but not chalets) are, is set around the Place Centrale. A fair proportion of the nightlife is here too, though bars are rather scattered – so there's not much evening street life.

More chalets and apartments are built each year, with much of the recent development inconveniently situated along the bus route to the Savoleyres lifts at the edge of town. There's a good sports centre and an efficient free bus service.

SKI FACTS

Altitude 1300m-3330m
Lifts   92
Pistes   400km
Green/Blue   39%
Red   42%
Black   19%
Artificial snow 30km

The skiing

Verbier is at one end of a long, strung out, interconnected ski area. Its local skiing suits good skiers best because of its steepness and the quality of the off-piste available. Further small ski areas covered by the lift pass are scattered around nearby valleys, reached by bus.

THE SKI AREA
Very spread out

Verbier has two local ski areas. **Savoleyres** is the smaller one, mainly suited to beginners and intermediates and reached by a gondola from the northern end of town. This area is underrated and under-used. It has a pleasant mix of open and tree-lined skiing (and has some of the better mountain restaurants). From the top (2355m) you can ski down to La Tzoumaz. When conditions are good you can also ski back to Verbier on south-facing slopes, but these deteriorate quickly.

Verbier's main ski area is reached by lifts from the opposite end of town, where a double gondola and chair rise to **Ruinettes** and one of the gondolas carries on to **Attelas**. The ancient, small cable-car from Ruinettes to Attelas is due to be replaced for the coming season by a new 30-person jumbo gondola. From Attelas you can ski back down to town or Ruinettes, over to La Chaux or down to Lac des Vaux. The La Chaux area is served by a number of chair-lifts and is the departure point of a huge cable-car up to Col de Gentianes and the glacier skiing area of **Mont-Fort**. A second, much smaller cable-car then goes up to the high point of the Four Valleys skiing at 3330m. All the lifts to and around Col des Gentianes are accessible only if you buy the 'Général' pass. If the weather is doubtful, it may be best to get the basic Four Valleys pass and pay the daily Mont-Fort supplement as needed.

From Mont-Fort you can ski all the

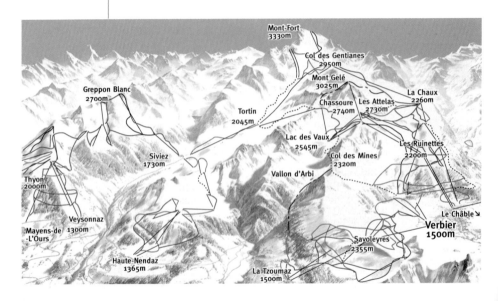

way down to **Tortin**, a run of almost 1300m vertical, which is now defined as off-piste. From here a cable-car returns to Col des Gentianes. An ancient gondola also leaves from Tortin for Chassoure, from where you can ski down to Lac des Vaux. A chair-lift from Lac des Vaux returns to Chassoure and the off-piste mogul run down to Tortin. Other chairs return you to Attelas. From Attelas a cable-car takes you to Mont-Gelé, from where there are only steep off-piste runs.

Tortin is the gateway to the rest of the Four Valleys' skiing. From there you ski down to **Siviez** (previously Super Nendaz). Take the chair up to the left there and you are entering the long, thin **Nendaz** sector.

Take the chair to the right and you are starting the journey to the **Thyon** and **Veysonnaz** sectors, reached by a couple of lifts and a long, easy ski along the mountain. Both these sectors suit intermediate skiers best. The way back from both sectors involves retracing your footsteps to Siviez and then Tortin.

Allow plenty of time for the queues – you don't want to be stranded in the wrong valley because, although it's not far from Verbier to Siviez on skis, it is by road. There is no bus back – and it's a very expensive taxi-ride.

The nearest and most extensive of the small unlinked ski areas is **Bruson**, reached by hourly bus from Verbier or by taking the gondola down to Le Châble and a bus from there.

SNOW RELIABILITY
Limited glacier skiing

The skiing on the Mont-Fort glacier is always on good snow. The runs to Tortin are normally snowsure too. But nearly all this is steep skiing, and much of it is now off-piste. Lesser skiers might well find themselves with a problem because most of Verbier's local skiing is west-facing and gets the hot afternoon sun. Most of it is also below 2500m and the runs to the resort can get very bare indeed. There is hardly any artificial snow.

The north-facing slopes of Savoleyres and Lac des Vaux are normally better than the rest. Veysonnaz's substantial artificial snow facilities can be reached from Verbier when conditions are poor, but the lack of snowmakers around Siviez, and the exclusively tough runs to Tortin, result in many having to take lifts down as well as up – and you don't get much skiing done in a day.

FOR ADVANCED SKIERS
The main attraction

Verbier has some superb tough skiing, much of it off-piste and to be skied with a guide. The very extreme, almost unskiable, couloirs between Mont-Gelé and Attelas are the toughest of all. There are safer, more satisfying off-piste routes from Mont-Gelé to Tortin and La Chaux.

The front face of Mont-Fort is a wonderful, tough mogul field. It is all of black steepness, and the piste map

LIFT PASSES

94/95 prices in Swiss francs

General Four Valleys
Covers all lifts and ski-buses in Verbier, Mont-Fort, Bruson, Champex-Lac, La Tzoumaz, Nendaz, Veysonnaz and Thyon.

Beginners Station pass covers 6 beginner lifts.

Main pass
1-day pass 58
6-day pass 297

Senior citizens
Over 65: 6-day pass 178 (40% off)

Children
Under 16: 6-day pass 178 (40% off)

Short-term passes
Half-day pass from 11am (adult 52) or 12.30 (adult 44).

Alternative periods
10 non-consecutive day pass (excluding Mont-Fort, adult 464).

Notes Reductions for students, families and groups. Children under 6 years 70% off.

Alternative passes
Limited passes for Savoleyres-La Tzoumaz, Bruson-Champex, Thyon-Veysonnaz-Nendez and Four Valleys without Mont-Fort.

no longer shows a red variant, but there is some choice of gradient – from seriously steep to intimidatingly steep. Occasionally you can ski from Mont-Fort all the way to Le Châble off-piste. You can also ski off-piste via one of two spectacular couloirs off the back of Mont-Fort to Siviez.

Both ski routes to Tortin (one from the bottom of the drags below Col des Gentianes and the other under the Tortin gondola) are rewarding and heavily mogulled. But these runs are often spoilt by crowds of intermediates out of their depth yet refusing to take the lift down.

There is often plenty of skiable off-piste powder around the north-facing slope from Gentianes to Tortin. Attelas is also the start of shorter off-piste runs towards the village.

A couple of long, but easy, off-piste routes go from Lac des Vaux via Col des Mines. One is a popular short-cut back to town, but the other is more beautiful, passing through Vallon d'Arbi and the woods before finishing at La Tzoumaz.

The Savoleyres speed-skiing course is open to all, and is a must for all bravos. The World Cup run at Veysonnaz is a steepish, often icy, red, ideal for really fast skiing.

There is also an entertaining off-piste run from Greppon Blanc at the top of the Siviez-Thyon sector down to Leteygeon. An hourly bus service (covered by the lift pass) brings you back to Thyon. Allow a full day for this excursion.

FOR INTERMEDIATE SKIERS
Best for the adventurous

It's for keen piste-bashing intermediates that Verbier is most disappointing. The skiing available to them in the main ski area is concentrated between Attelas and the village, above and below Ruinettes, plus the little bowl at Lac des Vaux beyond Attelas and the skiing served by the chairs at La Chaux. This is all excellent and varied intermediate territory. But there isn't much of it – this whole area is no bigger than the ski area of Alpbach, for example – and it has to accommodate half the skiers staying in what is one of Switzerland's largest resorts. As a result, it is often crowded to a miserable degree.

Savoleyres is a more satisfying and much less crowded section. It is also a good hill for mixed abilities, with variations of many runs to suit most standards of intermediate except the very inexperienced.

The best snow for intermediates is normally on the summer skiing area served by two drag-lifts on the Mont-Fort sector. Early intermediates will probably want to take lifts down as well as to it, though the red run down to La Chaux is not too steep.

A trip across to the Bruson ski area, reached by a bus, is also worthy of a day's excursion.

FOR BEGINNERS
A poor choice

Verbier's nursery slopes are inconveniently positioned (between Savoleyres and town) and tend to suffer from too much sun. Near-beginners and fast improvers have few options, especially if they do not want to pay vast sums for their lift pass. A couple of runs down to La Chaux are easy enough, but get too crowded.

FOR CROSS-COUNTRY
Surprisingly little on offer

Verbier has surprisingly limited cross-country facilities. There is a 4km circuit in Verbier, 4km at Ruinettes-La Chaux and 30km down at Le Châble/Val de Bagnes.

QUEUES
Perhaps the worst in Europe

Verbier has improved its lift system, but so have most other resorts, and by today's standards it is one of the worst places in the Alps for queues. It remains to be seen how much the new jumbo gondola from Ruinettes to Attelas helps. It should help the Medran queues in the morning by encouraging more people to take the six-person gondola or the chair to Ruinettes rather than wait for the old four-person gondola which goes all the way up to Attelas but which is often full, especially at weekends, with people coming up from Le Châble below. It will obviously help the Ruinettes bottleneck enormously, but it is likely to put more pressure on the chair up to Chassoure from Lac de Vaux. And it may make the worst bottleneck, for the ancient Tortin gondola, even worse. Half-hour queues for this are normal and waiting an hour or more is not unusual.

The queues for the Mont-Fort cable-cars can be substantial too. The Greppon Blanc drag and Combatzeline chair out of Siviez are also prone to delays, as is the chair back to Tortin at the end of the day. This can make skiing to and from Thyon-Veysonnaz impractical at times. The main Nendaz lift also gets half-hour queues in high season.

SKI SCHOOL

94/95 prices in Swiss francs

Swiss
Classes 6 days
4hr 45min: 9.15-11.45 and 2.10-4.30
6 half-days: 112
Children's classes
Ages: 3 to 12
6 half-days: 112
Private lessons
Hourly, half- or full-day
55 for 1hr for 1 to 2 people

Fantastique
Small school specialising in private lessons, and adventure skiing.

GETTING THERE

Air Geneva, transfer 2¹/₄hr.

Rail Le Châble (7km); regular buses to resort or gondola.

CHILDCARE

The ski school's Mini Champion-Klub kindergarten, near the sports centre, has its own drag-lift and takes children aged 3 to 10 from 8.45 to 5pm. Apparently it will also accept non-skiing children. There is also a ski playground up at La Chaux, reached by infrequent special bus.

The Schtroumpfs non-ski kindergarten (316585), close to the middle of the resort, takes children of any age up to 4 years (older ones by arrangement), from 8.30 to 5.30.

The Tip-Top kindergarten (316675), in the place Centrale, takes children aged 2 to 5, from 8.45 to 5.30, but only in holiday periods.

MOUNTAIN RESTAURANTS
Very disappointing in main area

There are not enough huts, which creates queues, overcrowding and high prices. Savoleyres is the best area. The hotel by the Tzoumaz chair takes some beating for value and lack of crowds. Chez Simon and Les Marmottes are also worth trying.

In the main ski area, the rustic Chez Dany at Clambin, on the off-piste run down from the La Chaux area, is about the best, but is a bit tricky to get to at times. It is open at night too. Carrefour is popular and well situated at the top of the nursery slopes.

The Tortin has good pasta, and a visit puts off standing in the queue for a while. The Cabane de Mont-Fort, between La Chaux and Les Gentianes, is cheerful, with good food and views, but gets very busy. Violon d'Ingres, at Ruinettes, is a large table-service place popular with several reporters.

SKI SCHOOL
Mixed reports, best for experts

Verbier is an excellent place for advanced skiers, in particular, to get tuition. Several reporters are complimentary about the off-piste lessons. These can be part of a Ski Adventure course (adults only) that takes in local powder and heli-skiing, with video analysis. More than 20 guides are available for heli-skiing, which includes trips to Zermatt and the Aosta valley. The Vallée Blanche at Chamonix, Monte Rosa tours and a trip to Zinal are cheaper excursions. If you prefer fast piste skiing, there are plenty of race competitions organised. Verbier is also quite big on Telemark tuition for those looking for a completely new challenge.

One or two regular visitors reckon the ski school's standards have improved generally in recent years, and we have good reports on beginners' classes. But we've also had reports criticising the children's classes. A 6-year-old was put in a class where no English was spoken, and a 7-year-old had an instructor who was impatient and kept losing her temper.

FACILITIES FOR CHILDREN
Wide range of options

The ski school's facilities in the resort are good, and the resort attracts quite a lot of families. The ski playground up at La Chaux has also received favourable reports. It is used by the ski school but not restricted to them. Bear in mind that space on the bus back is limited, and priority is given to the ski school groups.

The possibility of leaving very young babies at the Schtroumpfs nursery is valuable. British families have the option of travelling with two family-oriented chalet operators – Ski Esprit, who have two chalets with crèches, and Mark Warner, whose Rosablanche chalet-hotel has an 'excellent' crèche.

There are considerable reductions on the lift pass price for families, though it's not clear whether one-parent families qualify.

 # Staying there

Staying at the top of the resort, close to the Medran lift station, is convenient for the skiing and sufficiently distant from nightlife to avoid late evening noise. One reporter mentions New Year's Eve revellers dancing in the main square outside his hotel until 3am to music being blasted out by loudspeakers on hotel balconies – his hotel had to have a bouncer on the door to keep non-residents out. For self-caterers, however, the supermarkets are a tiresome walk from the lift area.

The ski-bus service is mostly good and reduces the inconvenience factor, but there are several routes running around the network of busy (congested at weekends) streets, so it is imperative to study the timetables carefully. Some accommodation has quite an infrequent service.

HOW TO GO
Plenty of options

Verbier is the chalet-party capital of the Alps. It has a higher proportion of chalets than any other resort. Given the size of the place there are surprisingly few apartments and pensions available, though budget skiers have inexpensive B&B options in Le Châble. Hotels are expensive in relation to their grading.

Chalets There are chalets available for most types of holiday-maker. Small ones, ideal for a family or small group of friends to have exclusive use of, are particularly common. There are also large chalets good for groups, ski-to-the-door places, and others bang in the centre of Verbier's nightlife. Prices are generally surprisingly low. There are not, however, many options for luxury lovers. Flexiski's Bouvreuil is the main exception. Owned by a Belgian Count, it's tastefully furnished with antiques and plush sofas. It's also well positioned, mid-way between Place Centrale and the lifts.

FLEXISKI

helped us to compile
the Eating out and
Après-ski sections.
Our thanks to them.

PACKAGES

Bladon Lines, Chalets
'Unlimited', Crystal,
Enterprise, FlexiSki,
Fresh Tracks, Kuoni,
Made to Measure,
Mark Warner, Peak
Ski, Plus Travel, Silver
Ski, Ski Activity, Ski
Beach Villas, Ski
Burnell, Ski Club of
GB, Ski Equipe, Ski
Esprit, Ski Les Alpes,
Ski Weekend, Ski
West, Ski with Julia,
Superski, Swiss Travel
Service, Thomson,
Ultimate, White Roc

Nendaz Travelscene
Ski-Drive

Bladon Lines has the largest
selection, including two of the best in
the resort, the Norma and Mondzeu.
Both of these are comfortable catered
apartments ideal for a small group or
family. The block has a 'very good'
pool. The simple Rendez Vous is one
of the best located chalets available,
with skiing to the door and the main
lifts close by.

Silver Ski has a selection of good-
value, mostly small places, generally
better positioned for the nursery
slopes than the main area. Beach
Villas have some of the cheapest, best-
value places in town, though most are
a fair way from the lifts.

Children specialists Ski Esprit has in-
house crèches with British nannies in
two of their chalets. The little Tai Pan
is perfect for a family wanting
exclusive use, and also has the benefit
of ski-to-the-door convenience. The
Filaos is well placed for the underrated
Savoleyres ski area.

Enterprise has the poorly positioned
but comfortable Les Chirpies; the best
of Crystal's places are the comfortable
chalet Djabo, close to Medran, and the
Sigoget catered apartments well
positioned between the lifts and
centre. The Itroz, close to the nursery
slopes, offers perhaps the best value of
Thomson's range.

Mark Warner leads the chalet hotel
scene. The Mont Fort is close to the
main lifts, whilst the old 2-star
Roseblanche has the benefit of an in-
house crèche, and is well positioned in
a quiet spot close to both centre and
lifts; it's quite simple, with some small
rooms and thin walls.

Hotels

There are half a dozen 4-star places, a
dozen 3-star and a handful of simpler
places.

££££ Rosalp The place to stay if you
can afford it, not least for the food in
Roland Pierroz's restaurant, which is
the best you'll find in a Swiss ski
resort. Good position mid-way
between centre and lifts.

££££ Montpelier Very comfortable
4-star, but out of town (a courtesy bus
is provided).

££££ Rois Mages Smart little B&B
hotel in secluded setting, up near the
Savoleyres lift.

£££ Rotonde Much cheaper, well
positioned 3-star between centre and
lifts; some budget rooms.

£££ Chamois 3-star close to lifts.

£££ Poste Well placed 3-star mid-way
between centre and lifts; 'excellent'
food and the only hotel pool. Some
rooms rather small.

£££ Verbier Central 3-star, popular

with tour operators and their clientele;
renowned for good food; atmospheric,
but 'olde worlde' decor is a little in
need of refurbishment.

££ Auberge Well placed 2-star, mid-
way between centre and lifts.

££ Farinet Central 2-star B&B hotel.

Self-catering Apartments available
through tour operators are extremely
thin on the ground. Self-caterers
usually book direct. The comfortable
Richemont and Troika apartments are
close to the nursery slopes, a trek from
the main lifts. The similar standard
Blizzard is better placed, mid-way
between Place Centrale and lifts.

The Vieux Verbier apartments have
a position second to none for the
skiing, next to the main lift station.
Close to the town centre are the
simple Carina places.

EATING OUT
Very big choice

There is a very wide range of
restaurants. Hotel Rosalp is clearly the
best in town, and among the best in
Switzerland, with an awesome wine
cellar to match its excellent Michelin-
starred food.

Two-star hotel Chalet Phénix has a
surprisingly good Chinese restaurant.
Au Fer à Cheval is a very popular
pizza/salad/breakfast place that's full
of life, though Borsalino's is just as
good and easier to book. Arguably the
best-value Italian food in town,
however, is at Al Capone's out near
the Savoleyres gondola. The Spaghetti
House is another inexpensive place.

The Farinet restaurant is
atmospheric and has good food at
affordable prices. The Vieux Verbier
apartments have a surprisingly good
restaurant that serves huge portions of
Swiss specialities. The Luge is a good-
value, atmospheric place specialising
in steaks. The Crêperie does
everything from snacks to full meals.

L'Ecurie has good but expensive
Swiss specialities. Robinsons and Le
Caveau are others worth trying. Relais
de Neige is one of the cheaper places
in town. Harold's is Verbier's 'fast-
food' outlet – it's less clinical and
more fun than McDonalds.

APRES-SKI
Throbbing but expensive

It starts with a 4pm visit to Offshore,
for people-watching and coffee (no
alcohol sold). Then it's on to the Mont
Fort or Nelson pubs, if you're young,
loud and British. La Luge is good for a
more relaxed drink in a friendly
atmosphere. The Farinet is particularly
good in spring, its live band playing to

ACTIVITIES

Indoor Sports centre (swimming, skating, curling, squash, sauna, solarium, jacuzzi), tennis, fitness centre, cinema, ice hockey, artificial skating rink
Outdoor Ski-bob, 15km cleared paths, para-gliding, hang-gliding, toboggan run, mountaineering, horse riding, jogging tracks, bike paths, tennis, winter walking

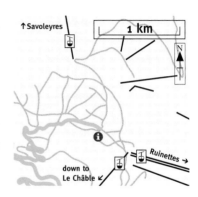

the audience on a huge, sunny terrace. Au Fer à Cheval is a fun place full of locals and regular Verbier-ites.

After dinner the two pubs become very lively pick-up joints, popular with Brits and locals alike. Crock No Name often has live music, and is entertaining for its cosmopolitan crowd. La Luge remains a more relaxed option. Jacky's, under the Grand-Combin hotel, is a classy haunt frequented by big spenders on their way to the Farm Club. This is an outrageously expensive nightclub which nonetheless is very popular – tables are difficult to reserve.

More within the pocket of most Brits is the noisy, glitzy Marshalls Club, which sometimes has live music. Tara Club is less smart but the noise level is more conducive to conversation, and it has a friendly atmosphere. Scotch is a bit of a dive, but it's the cheapest disco in town. It's particularly handy towards the end of your stay, when over-indulgence in the above attractions may have exhausted your flexible friend. Big Ben is another cheaper haunt, popular with teenagers. Harry's Bar is good for a midnight burger.

Something a bit different is to snowmobile up to either Chez Dany or Les Marmottes for an evening meal in the mountains, and follow it with a torchlit descent. The food is good and it's great fun.

FOR NON-SKIERS
No great attraction
Verbier has an excellent sports centre and some nice walks, but otherwise has little for non-skiers. Montreux is an enjoyable train excursion from Le Châble. It's easy for non-skiers to walk to some of the lower mountain restaurants to meet up with skiers for lunch, and there are reachable restaurants at most gondola top stations.

STAYING IN OTHER RESORTS
A lot going for them
There are advantages to staying in the other resorts of the Four Valleys. For a start, you can avoid the worst of the queues if you are not travelling around in the same direction as everyone else (though you're still likely to be clobbered by the waits for the Tortin and Mont-Fort lifts if you want to ski these sections). Secondly,

they are substantially cheaper for both accommodation and incidentals. What you lose is the Verbier ambience and its range of restaurants, bars and nightlife. If you don't care about those, staying elsewhere is well worth considering. Unfortunately only one British tour operator (Travelscene Ski-Drive to Nendaz) offers packages to any of them.

Veysonnaz or Thyon are both small resorts, with mainly apartment accommodation. Veysonnaz is by far the more attractive – an old village complete with church. It has adequate bars, cafés and restaurants, a disco, sports centre with swimming pool, and a ski school. The only hotel is the inexpensive Magrappe, which is situated next to the gondola. Thyon is little more than a functional, ugly, purpose-built place.

Nendaz is a far larger resort, with an enormous number of beds available, mainly in apartments. There are plenty of amenities, including a skating rink, sports centre with swimming, fitness centre and squash, cafés, restaurants, discos, crèche and ski school. The Déserteur is the best-placed of its hotels, all of which are inexpensive, relatively simple 3-stars. Auberge les Etagnes is a very cheap B&B situated next to the gondola. A couple of simple standard chalet parties are also available.

Le Châble is a village just a gondola-ride from Verbier. As changing gondola cars is not necessary for moving on to Ruinettes and Attelas, ski area access can be just as quick (or quicker) from the queue-free valley. Le Châble is particularly convenient for those travelling by train or ski-drivers who want to visit other resorts too. The Giétroz, Poste and Ruinette are all simple, adequate hotels.

TOURIST OFFICE

Postcode CH-1936
Tel 010 41 (26) 316222
Fax 313272

Villars 1300m

With its mountain railway, gentle low-altitude ski slopes and year-round tourist trade, Villars is the kind of place that has been rather overshadowed by modern mega-resorts. But for a relaxing family holiday – perhaps combining skiing with other activities – this formula has clear attractions.

HOW IT RATES

The skiing

Snow	**
Extent	**
Advanced	**
Intermediates	***
Beginners	****
Convenience	***
Queues	***
Restaurants	***

The rest

Scenery	***
Resort charm	****
Not skiing	****

SKI FACTS

Altitude	1130m-2970m
Lifts	45
Pistes	120km
Green/Blue	51%
Red	41%
Black	8%
Artificial snow	none

PACKAGES

Chalets 'Unlimited', Club Med, Kuoni, Made to Measure, Neilson, Ski Esprit, Ski Weekend, Swiss Chalet Company, Swiss Travel Service, Travelscene Ski-Drive

TOURIST OFFICE

Postcode CH-1884
Tel 010 41 (25) 353232
Fax 352794

THE RESORT

Villars sits on a sunny shelf at 1300m, looking south-west across the Rhône valley towards the mountains of the Portes du Soleil. Roads go up from Ollon and Bex, a rack railway only from Bex. A busy high street lined with shops unconnected with skiing gives Villars more the air of a small town than of a ski resort; but a pleasant, reassuring town, with all but two or three of the largest hotels built in chalet style, and fields and woods close at hand. There is further accommodation well outside the main village at Barboleusaz, where a gondola serves the slopes of Les Chaux, and further up those slopes.

There is a tenuous skiing link with Les Diablerets, to the north; outings to Leysin and Champéry are possible by rail or road. Many other resorts (such as Verbier) are within driving distance.

THE SKIING

The railway goes on up into the **ski area**, terminating at Bretaye (1800m); a gondola from the other end of the village goes higher into the skiing.

The col of Bretaye has intermediate slopes on either side, with a maximum vertical of 300m back to the col and a couple of much longer runs back to the village. To the east, easier open slopes (very susceptible to sun) go down to La Rasse (1350m), the meeting point with the otherwise separate Les Chaux sector.

Low altitude and southerly orientation mean that Villars' **snow reliability** is not good. (The top height we quote is for the glacier at Les Diablerets.)

This is not a resort for **advanced skiers**, although there are occasional steep pitches to be found – and small but worthwhile off-piste areas.

For **intermediate skiers** not obsessed by mileage (and not worried about snow reliability), there is an interesting range of pistes. Sadly, the link to the similarly appealing skiing of Les Diablerets involves an awkward (and unpatrolled) black stretch that many will find intimidating.

Beginners will feel comfortable on the village nursery slopes, and riding the train up to Bretaye. There is gentle skiing here, too, but also lots of people charging about in a crowded area.

The **cross-country** trails up the valley past La Rasse are long and pretty, and there are further loops in the depression beyond Bretaye.

It is mainly at weekends that **queues** appear for the lifts at Bretaye.

The **mountain restaurants** are a mixed bag. The main one at Bretaye is characterless and very busy; the du Lac just beyond it is just as busy but more atmospheric; Lac des Chavonnes is worth the walk from the piste (and snowmobile ride back).

It's very unusual for the Swiss **ski school** to have a competitor. Villars' Ecole Moderne was one of the first 'alternative' schools, started in 1974 and still using the ski évolutif or graduated-length method pioneered at Les Arcs. There is also a Bureau des Guides offering heliskiing excursions. The Swiss school nursery takes **children** aged 3 to 12, Monday to Saturday; the Moderne school runs a nursery too. There is also a non-ski nursery in next-door Chesières.

STAYING THERE

Although the centre of Villars is quite compact, the gondola is quite a walk from the railway station. But there is a free ski-bus (reliable but busy at times) and many of the **hotels** are between the two lifts. There are three big 4-star hotels, and several mid-sized and smaller 3-star ones; the Alpe Fleurie and Renardière are our favourites. The huge Palace is now occupied by Club Med. Some UK operators offer self-catering; the Travelscene apartments at Les Chaux are 'first-class'.

For many visitors, **eating out** means regional specialities in the neo-rustic Vieux Villars – though there are numerous alternatives, including a recommended pizzeria in the centre.

There is **après-ski** activity to be found. Charlie's is a very welcoming, pleasantly busy upstairs bar. Le Sporting has great olives. El Gringo is a proper young person's disco.

There is plenty to amuse **non-skiers**, at least active ones; as well as six tennis courts and lots of marked walks there is swimming, skating, curling etc.

Wengen 1275m

HOW IT RATES

The skiing

Snow	**
Extent	***
Advanced	***
Intermediates	*****
Beginners	***
Convenience	***
Queues	***
Restaurants	****

The rest

Scenery	*****
Resort charm	*****
Not skiing	****

✔ Some of the most beautiful scenery in the Alps

✔ Pretty, traditional, 'traffic-free' Alpine village which can be reached only by cog railway

✔ Large ski area ideal for intermediates

✔ Good for non-skiers or part-time skiers who want a relaxing winter break

✘ Limited terrain for experts

✘ Not ideal for beginners – village nursery slopes often short of snow

✘ Snow conditions unreliable, despite some artificial help

✘ Little nightlife for club- and disco-lovers

Wengen, like Mürren across the valley, is one of our favourite resorts. When he was an early intermediate, one of us came to Wengen on holiday for four successive years. It has ideal terrain for someone at that stage. Combine that with the charm of the village, the friendliness of the locals and the beauty of the scenery and you can see why the place entrances many people so completely that they never go anywhere else, whatever their skiing standard.

So it is sad that these days it's a risky bet booking a holiday in Wengen months in advance. It has had a series of very disappointing years for snow. The skiing is not high – there's little above 2000m. And the present investment in snowmaking is insufficient to transform the prospects.

But the old-world charm of the place is difficult to beat. You have to be willing to accept an old-world pace too. Taking the train up the mountain in the morning may be quaint. But quick it ain't. Wengen is a place for relaxing and enjoying winter among Europe's most glorious scenery. It's not a place for skiers who want to maximise mileage, catch the most efficient lifts or find the most challenging skiing. Relax and you'll love it. Stay tense – in working mode – and you'll find it very frustrating.

ORIENTATION

Wengen is set on a shelf high above the Lauterbrunnen valley, opposite Mürren, and can be reached only by cog railway from Lauterbrunnen. The railway arrives at the station at the southern end of Wengen's main street and carries on up, doubling up as the main ski lift out of the village as well as the only access to it. There's also a cable-car up from above the nursery slopes in the centre of the village. The skiing at the top of both lifts is shared with **Grindelwald** in the next valley. **Mürren** can be reached by taking the train down to Lauterbrunnen and a funicular and connecting train up the other side of the valley. The Wengen, Grindelwald and Mürren skiing is all covered by the Jungfrau lift pass.

 The resort

Wengen was a farming community long before skiing became a sport or the first train chugged its way up the mountain. Today it's a charming 'traffic-free' village, much smaller and more unspoilt than you'd expect, given its fame as host to one of the most famous downhill races on the World Cup circuit.

There's really only one main street, which is lined with chalet-style shops and hotels. The focal point of the village is at the southern end where the station and ski school meeting-area are located.

The only traffic you'll see in Wengen are the little electric hotel trucks, which gather at the station to pick up guests, and a couple of Range Rover taxis. But these can be very annoying as they tear past you while you're strolling through the streets.

The views across the Lauterbrunnen valley from the shelf upon which Wengen sits are stunning. They get even better as you travel up the mountain and the Eiger, Jungfrau and Mönch come into view. The Mönch (Monk) is set between the other two and, mythology says, is there to protect the Jungfrau (Girl) from the Eiger (Ogre).

There's a very strong British presence at Wengen. Many Brits have been returning to the same rooms in the same hotels in the same week, year after year. Wengen is home to the Downhill Only Club – so named when the first Brits persuaded the locals to keep the summer railway running up the mountain in winter so they would no longer have to climb up in order to ski down again.

The main street is the hub of the village. Lined with hotels and shops, it also has the ice rink, curling club and village nursery slopes giving it a pleasant open aspect. The nursery slopes double as the venue for floodlit ski-jumping and parallel slalom races on several nights a season.

The main form of transport up the mountain is the regular, incredibly punctual trains to Kleine Scheidegg. There's also a cable-car from above the nursery slopes up to the Männlichen ski area.

SKI FACTS

Jungfrau region –
including Grindelwald
and Mürren

Altitude	945m-2970m
Lifts	45
Pistes	183km
Green/Blue	32%
Red	52%
Black	16%
Artificial snow	10km

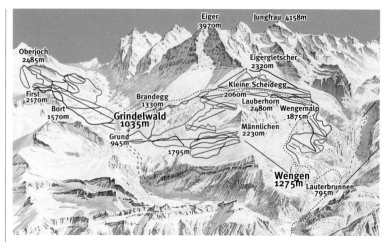

LIFT PASSES

94/95 prices in
Swiss francs
**Jungfrau Top Ski
Region**
Covers all lifts in
Wengen, Mürren and
Grindelwald, trains
between them and
Grindelwald ski-bus.
Beginners Points card
(adult 100 points 46,
lifts cost 4 to 10
points).
Main pass
1-day pass 52
6-day pass 232
Children
Under 16: 6-day pass
116 (50% off)
Under 6: free pass
Short-term passes
Single ascent tickets
for most lifts. Half-day
pass for First (adult
38), Kleine Scheidegg-
Männlichen (adult 40)
and Mürren-Schilthorn
(adult 38).
Notes Day pass price
for Kleine Scheidegg-
Männlichen area only
(98km of piste,
21 lifts), as Jungfrau
Top Ski Region pass
is only available for
3 days or over.
Discounts for
teenagers 16 to 21 (6-
day 186) and groups.
Alternative passes
1- and 2-day passes
avialable for First
(adult 2-day 90),
Mürren-Schilthorn
(adult 2-day 90) and
Kleine Scheidegg-
Männlichen (adult 2-
day 95, child 48).

⚐ The skiing

Although it is famous for the fearsome
Lauberhorn World Cup Downhill
course – the longest and one of the
toughest on the circuit – Wengen's
skiing is best suited to intermediates;
early intermediates at that. There are
no seriously steep pistes and the
scariest part of the Downhill course,
the Hundschopf jump, is shut to
holiday skiers. Most runs are gentle
blues and reds, ideal for cruising. On
the Grindelwald side there are some
long and beautiful runs down to the
village. But the lower parts of these
often suffer from snow shortage or
poor snow conditions – and there is
hardly any snowmaking on the
Grindelwals side of the area.

THE SKI AREA
Picturesque playground
Most of the skiing is on the other side
of the mountain from Wengen. From
the top of the train at **Kleine
Scheidegg** (2060m) you can ski
straight down to Grindelwald or work
your way across the mountain with
the help of a couple of lifts to the top
of the **Männlichen** (2230m). This
area has a lot of skiing, served by drag-
and chair-lifts. It can also be reached
directly by catching the little-used
cable-car up from Wengen.
  On the Wengen side there are a few
runs back down towards Wengen from
the top of the **Lauberhorn** (2470m),
but below Kleine Scheidegg there's
really only one run back to Wengen.
  As well as the Wengen skiing, it's
easy (although a slow process) to get
to Mürren and to the **First** area on
the far side of Grindelwald.

SNOW RELIABILITY
Poor
Most of the skiing is below 2000m,
and at Grindelwald it goes down to
less than 1000m. Very few of the
slopes are north-facing, and Wengen's
snowmaking facilities – 20 mobile
guns – can't deal with more than a
fraction of the shared area. There can
mean severe problems in times of
snow famine or warm weather. We've
experienced wonderful skiing in late
March, but we've also struggled to find
skiable pistes in January.

FOR ADVANCED SKIERS
Few challenges
Wengen's skiing is quite limited for
good skiers. The one genuine black
run in the area takes you from
Eigergletscher to Wixi. The steepest
parts of the famous Lauberhorn
Downhill race course are normally
shut to holiday skiers. The main
challenges are off-piste runs such as
the Oh God from near Eigergletscher
to Wixi and the White Hare from
under the north face of the Eiger.
There are a number of off-piste runs
from the Jungfraujoch late in the
season, but you must ski with a guide.
For more challenging skiing it's well
worth going to nearby Mürren, an
hour away by train and funicular. The
Wengen ski school organises heli-
skiing if there are enough takers.

FOR INTERMEDIATE SKIERS
Wonderful if the snow is good
Wengen has superb intermediate
slopes. Nearly all the skiing is on long
blue or gentle red runs. From Kleine
Scheidegg there's an easy scenic blue
run all the way down through the
trees to Grindelwald – or you can stop
at Brandegg and catch the train back
up. The run back to Wengen is gentle

all the way and is a relaxing end to the day, as long as it's not too crowded.

On the Männlichen there's a choice of several gentle runs down to the mid-station of the gondola up from Grindelwald Grund. If conditions permit, you can ski right down to the bottom. There's a piste from Männlichen to Grindelwald that is marked as black on the map but is perfectly skiable by any competent intermediate skier.

For tougher skiing, head for the runs from the top of the Lauberhorn lift down to Kleine Scheidegg or to Wixi (this piste follows the start of the Downhill course). You could also try the north-facing run from Eigergletscher to Salzegg, which often has the best snow late in the season.

FOR BEGINNERS
Not ideal
There's a nursery slope in the centre of the village – although it's convenient, the snow can be unreliable. There is a beginners ski area at Wengernalp but, to get back to Wengen, you either have to climb up to the train or tackle the run down, which can be tricky in places for novice skiers. There are good, long gentle slopes to progress to – especially the run down by the railway on the Grindelwald side.

FOR CROSS-COUNTRY
There is none
There's no cross-country skiing in Wengen itself. There are tracks down in the Lauterbrunnen valley, but the snow there is unreliable.

QUEUES
Can be bad – but improving
There can be some horrific bottle-necks in peak periods, and daily scrums to board the trains that the ski school generally uses. The weekend invasion of locals and coach parties from Germany can increase the crowds enormously. Particular black spots at these times are the train and gondola from Grindelwald.

However, queues up the mountain have been alleviated a lot in the last few years. Some of the old drag- and chair-lifts have been replaced by new, fast four-person chairs, and the capacity of the Männlichen cable-car has been increased.

MOUNTAIN RESTAURANTS
Plenty of variety
A popular but expensive place for lunch is Wengernalp, where the rösti is excellent and the views of the Jungfrau are superb. The highest

restaurant is at Eigergletscher. If you get there early on a sunny day, you can nab one of the tables on the narrow outside balcony and enjoy some magnificent views of the glacier. The station buffet at Kleine Scheidegg is good value. The Café Oberland, just below Almend, is popular at lunch-time and at the end of the day for those who want to soak up the last of the sun before returning to Wengen. Non-skiers can easily reach all of these places by train.

On the Grindelwald side of the mountain, the restaurants by the Brandegg station and the top of the Aspen drag are recommended.

SKI SCHOOL
94/95 prices in
Swiss francs

Swiss
Classes 6 days
4hr: 2hr am and pm
6 full days: 234
Children's classes
Ages: 4 to 12
6 full days: 234
Private lessons
Half- or full-day
155 for half-day; each
additional person 15

CHILDCARE
The kindergarten on
the first floor of the
Sport Pavilion takes
children aged 3 to 7,
from 8.45 to 4.30.
Children can be taken
to and from lessons
with the ski school,
which starts at age 4.

A couple of 4-star
hotels have their own
kindergartens.

GETTING THERE
Air Zürich, transfer
3¹⁄₂hr. Bern, transfer
1¹⁄₂hr.
Rail Station in resort.

PACKAGES
Bladon Lines, Club
Med, Crystal,
Inghams, Kuoni, Made
to Measure, Plus
Travel, Ski Choice, Ski
Club of GB, Ski
Europe, Swiss Travel
Service, Thomson

SKI SCHOOL
Healthy competition
We have received contrasting reports about the size of classes, from 'too large' to 'reasonable', but good tuition and standards of English are usually praised. The independent Privat school receives praise for good-value tuition of small groups.

Snowboarders are well served, and guides are available for heli-skiing on the Jungfraujoch and powder excursions off the Lauberhorn.

FACILITIES FOR CHILDREN
Apparently satisfactory
Our recent reports on children's facilities are from observers rather than participants, but they are all favourable. It is an attractive village for families, with the baby slope right in the centre, and the train giving warm, easy access to higher slopes.

 # Staying there

Wengen is small, so location isn't as crucial as in many other resorts. The main street is ideally placed for the station and the commuter trains up in the morning. The hotels on the home piste offer ski-in ski-out convenience. Those who don't fancy a steepish morning climb should avoid places set well below the station.

HOW TO GO
Wide range of hotels
Most accommodation is in hotels. Plenty of tour operators organise hotel packages here. But there is only a handful of catered chalets, and self-catering apartments are thin on the ground. There is a Club Med.
Chalets Surprisingly, perhaps, Wengen has no particularly luxurious catered chalets. Bladon Lines' Liane is about the best; a cosy old place eight minutes from the centre. The Boss is a well-located apartment conversion, whilst the Schweizerheim is an old 2-star hotel annexe, comfortable enough but sold as a 'budget' chalet due to its poor position, entailing an uphill trudge to the village and lifts. Crystal has a similar selection, including the comfortable Iris, and attractive Spycher.
Hotels There are about two dozen hotels, mostly 4-star and 3-star, with a handful of simpler places.
££££ Parkhotel Beausite Unattractive block at top of the village, near cable-car; generally regarded as the top hotel. Good pool; kindergarten.
££££ Sunstar Modern hotel on main

street. Comfortable rooms; the lounge has a welcoming log fire. Live music some nights. Large pool with views. Food very good. Friendly staff.
££££ Regina Central position. Smart, traditional atmosphere. Large, chandeliered lounge. 'Best food in Wengen.' Carousel nightclub.
££££ Silberhorn Comfortable modern 4-star in excellent central position.
££££ Caprice Small, new, smartly furnished chalet-style hotel across the tracks from the Regina. Kindergarten.
£££ Alpenrose Long-standing British favourite; eight minutes' climb to the station. Good views; 'first-class' food; friendly staff.
£££ Eiger Very conveniently sited, overlooking the station. Focal après-ski bar. Renovated a few years ago – comfortable modern rooms.
£££ Falken Further up the hill. Another British favourite, known affectionately (and justifiably, apparently) as 'Fawlty Towers'.
££ Bernerhof Wooden chalet on main street; jolly bar.
Self-catering Inghams have an allocation in the hotel Bernerhof's decent Residence apartments, which are well positioned just off the main street, with the facilities of the hotel available to guests.

EATING OUT
Lots of choice
Most of the restaurants in the village are in the hotels. They offer a good standard of food and service, and are open to non-residents. It's worth trying the Eiger which has a traditional restaurant and a stube which has Swiss and French cuisine. There's no shortage of fondues in the village. If all you want is a snack, then try the Pizzeria at the Victoria Lauberhorn, the Silberhorn or the Tanne Bar. You could book a table at Wengernalp's excellent restaurant – the last train back to Wengen leaves at 11.45pm. If you feel a little daring, you could ski or toboggan back.

APRES-SKI
Quietly lively
Wengen has a reputation for quiet nightlife which is rather misleading. Most British guests here want a relaxing time, hence reports tend to minimise what's on offer. But there are a number of places where a lively atmosphere is generated, largely by locals and visiting Germans. A number of reporters have been pleasantly surprised by the action available if you look around. The stube at the Eiger and the tiny Eiger Bar, just round the

ACTIVITIES

Indoor Swimming pool (in Park Hotel), sauna, solarium, whirlpool, massage (in hotels), cinema (with English films), bowling, billiards

Outdoor Skating, curling, 20km cleared paths, toboggan runs, sleigh rides, para-gliding, glacier flights, sledging excursions, hang-gliding

TOURIST OFFICE

Postcode CH-3823
Tel 010 41 (36) 551414
Fax 553060

corner, are popular haunts for skiers at the end of a day on the slopes. If you've still got energy, you could try the tea dancing at the Silberhorn or Belvedere.

The Tanne and Sinaa's are very popular bars, the latter with live music some nights and karaoke the rest. The bowling alley has the cheapest beer in town (SF4 for 0.5l). There are a couple of discos, a nightclub, dancing and live music in some of the hotels.

The cinema often shows English-language films. Sports fans can enjoy floodlit ski-jumping and slalom competitions for the locals on the slopes in the centre of the village. There are also ice hockey matches.

FOR NON-SKIERS
A good choice

Wengen is a superb resort for non-skiers who want a completely relaxing holiday. The unbeatable scenery makes just sitting around and soaking up the sun thoroughly enjoyable. And the train is ideal for non-skiers who want to get up the mountain to meet friends for lunch (there's a special, though expensive, five-day pass for non-skiers). For those who feel the need to take a little exercise there are some lovely mountain walks, ice skating, a curling club and bowling. Excursions to Interlaken and Berne are possible by train, as is the trip to the Jungfraujoch at 3455m for stunning views and a trip to the Ice Palace carved out of the glacier.

STAYING UP THE MOUNTAIN
Great views

You can stay at two points up the mountain, reached by the railway: the pricey Jungfrau at Wengernalp – a favourite lunch spot with great views – and at Kleine Scheidegg, where there's a choice of rooms in the Kleine Scheidegg hotel or dormitory space above the station buffet.

STAYING DOWN THE VALLEY
The budget option

Staying in a 3-star hotel like the Schützen or Oberland in Lauterbrunnen will cost about half as much as similar accommodation in Wengen. Lauterbrunnen isn't exactly throbbing with nightlife, but the train from Wengen runs until 11.30pm and is included in your lift pass. Staying in Lauterbrunnen also has the bonus of improving your chances of getting a seat on the train to Kleine Scheidegg rather than joining the scrum at Wengen. Lauterbrunnen is also much better placed for skiing in Mürren.

You can save even more money by staying further away in the beautiful summer resort of Interlaken. Choose a hotel near Interlaken Ost station, from which you can catch a train to Lauterbrunnen (22mins) or Grindelwald (36mins). Driving takes about as long as the train on weekdays in good weather.

Zermatt 1620m

✔ *Wonderful high and extensive skiing for advanced and intermediate skiers*

✔ *Spectacular high mountain scenery, dominated by the Matterhorn*

✔ *Reliable snow (with summer skiing area)*

✔ *Best resort in the world for mountain restaurants*

✔ *Charming, but rather sprawling, old 'traffic-free' resort*

✔ *Extensive heli-skiing operation for those who can afford it*

✔ *Nightlife to suit most tastes*

✔ *Day-trips on skis to Cervinia in Italy are possible, for a different atmosphere and cheap shopping*

✘ *Car-free village ambience is spoiled by having to dodge impatient electric taxis and carts*

✘ *Getting to main lift stations may involve a long walk, crowded bus- or expensive taxi-ride*

✘ *The three separate ski areas are not well linked*

✘ *Beginners should go elsewhere*

ORIENTATION

Zermatt is reached by mountain railway from Täsch, 6km down the valley, where visitors must leave their cars. The village sprawls along a narrow valley either side of a river, with mountains rising steeply on each side.

From near the main station a separate cog railway takes you up to the Gornergrat ski area. A five-minute walk from here is a fast underground funicular up to Sunnegga. The other main lift is at the far end of town – a brisk 15-minute walk away. From there, gondolas take you the first part of the journey up to the Klein Matterhorn and Zermatt's highest skiing.

From this area you can also ski down to **Cervinia** in Italy. The resorts of **Saas-Fee** and **Grächen** are an easy drive from Täsch.

If you are a keen skier you must try Zermatt before you die. There are few places to match it for its combination of excellent advanced and intermediate skiing, reliable snow, magnificent scenery, Alpine-village charm and (not least) mountain restaurants with an unbeatable combination of superb food and stunning views.

Some people complain that the car-free village is spoiled by the intrusive electric carts and taxis, and that the atmosphere exudes Swiss efficiency rather than friendliness. But the village still has a magical feel to it – with its old buildings and winding paths complementing the modern main street. It is one of our favourite resorts, and we are not alone.

🏠 The resort

Zermatt started life as a traditional mountain village, then developed as a mountaineering centre in the 19th century before becoming a winter ski resort too. Summer is still as important to the resort as winter.

Be warned – Zermatt is big business. Prices are high and courteous service can be lacking. Most of the restaurants and hotels are owned by a handful of families, and their employees don't always seem happy in their work.

The village is a mixture of chocolate-box chalets and more modern buildings – most of them are built in traditional style. The main street runs past the station and is lined with large luxurious hotels and smart shops.

Zermatt doesn't have the same relaxed, quaint feel to it as some other car-free resorts such as Wengen and Saas-Fee. That's partly because the electric vehicles buzzing around the place are more intrusive and aggressive than elsewhere; partly because of the chance of unfriendly service mentioned earlier; and partly because the clientele is more overtly upmarket and jet-set, with large contingents from Japan and the US.

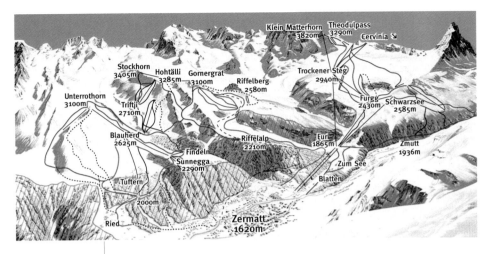

For a resort with such good and extensive skiing, the place has a remarkably high age profile. Most visitors seem to be over 40 and there are very few of the youthful ski bums you get in rival resorts with comparable skiing such as Val-d'Isère, St Anton and Chamonix.

The main street, with the station square near one end, is the focal point of village life. The cog railway to the Gornergrat ski area leaves from opposite the main station, and the underground funicular to the Sunnegga area is just a few minutes' walk away. The gondola to the Klein Matterhorn (and the link to Cervinia) is a 15-minute trek from here.

The ski school office, tourist office and most of the resort's hotels, restaurants, shops, bars and nightspots are on, or a short stroll from, the main street. There's another main thoroughfare a few yards away, along the side of the river. To each side of these main arteries are narrow streets and paths, many of which are hilly and treacherous when icy.

SKI FACTS

Altitude	1620m-3820m
Lifts	36
Pistes	230km
Green/Blue	26%
Red	42%
Black	32%
Artificial snow	17km

 # The skiing

There is skiing to suit all standards except absolute beginners, for whom we don't recommend the resort. For intermediate and advanced skiers Zermatt has few rivals worldwide. There are marvellously groomed cruising trails, some of the best mogul skiing available, long beautiful scenic runs out of view of the lift system, exciting heli-skiing and off-piste possibilities if you hire a guide, as well as the opportunity to ski down into Italy for the day and lunch on pasta and chianti.

THE SKI AREA
Beautiful and varied

Zermatt has three separate ski areas, at best awkwardly linked. The **Sunnegga-Blauherd-Unterrothorn** area is reached by an underground funicular starting about five minutes' walk from the station. This shifts large numbers rapidly but can lead to queues for the subsequent gondola and cable-car. From this area you can ski – south-facing slopes permitting – to and from the second main ski area, **Gornergrat-Stockhorn**, which can also be reached by the cog railway from opposite the main station. New 'high-speed' trains are supposed to cut the 45-minute ride to 25 minutes – but because old trains still operate on the single-track railway, the new ones have to wait long periods to pass and end up taking just as long.

From Gornergrat, if snow-cover permits, you can ski to below Furi to link up with the third and highest ski area: **Klein Matterhorn-Trockener Steg-Schwarzsee**. But you can't do the journey in the opposite direction. Once on the Klein Matterhorn you have to ski down and go from one end of the village to the other to catch a lift up a different mountain. The Klein Matterhorn gives access to Cervinia – you need to buy a daily supplement to your lift pass and the link is frequently shut because of high winds.

In theory you can ski back to the village from all three areas. But in practice the lower runs have often been shut or unpleasant on our visits.

SNOW RELIABILITY
Good higher up, poor lower down

Zermatt has rocky terrain and a relatively dry climate. But it also has some of the highest skiing in Europe,

LIFT PASSES

94/95 prices in Swiss francs

Area Pass
Covers all lifts on the Swiss side of the border.

Beginners Coupon book (100 coupons 136). Pass for Riffelberg-Gornergrat beginner area (adult 6-day 218).

Main pass
1-day pass 60
6-day pass 292

Senior citizens
Over 65 male, 62 female: 6-day pass 219 (25% off)

Children
Under 16: 6-day pass 146 (50% off)
Under 6: free pass

Short-term passes
Single ascent tickets for most lifts.

Notes Daily supplement available to cover all lifts in Cervinia and Valtournenche (31).

Alternative passes
Passes for any period available for each area of Zermatt (Gornergrat-Stockhorn, Sunnegga-Rothorn, Trockener Steg-Klein Matterhorn-Schwarzsee), and combinations of areas. 1-day pass available for Zermatt, Cervinia and Valtournenche (62).

and quite a bit of snowmaking machinery. All three ski areas go up to over 3000m, and the Klein Matterhorn cable-car is the highest in Europe, ending at over 3800m and serving a summer skiing area on the glacier. There is a huge amount of skiing above 2500m, much of which is north-facing, so guaranteeing decent snow except in freak years.

Artificial snowmaking machines serve some of the pistes on both the Sunnegga and Trockener Steg areas from around 3000m to under 2000m. But the runs back to the resort are often closed or tricky, despite the artificial help.

FOR ADVANCED SKIERS
Good – with superb heli-skiing
If you've never been, Zermatt has to be on your short-list. If you have been, we're pretty sure you'll want to return.

For skiers who love long, fluffy mogul pitches the skiing at Triftji below Stockhorn is what dreams are made of. From the top of the Stockhorn cable-car there's a run down to the T-bar which serves another two steep 2km runs – one each side of the lift. The whole mountainside here is skied into one vast mogul field – steep, but not extremely so.

Being north-facing and lying between 3400m and 2700m, the snow here is usually the best around, which makes the huge moguls so forgiving that even we enjoyed them last year. New Year skiers miss out on this area, however, as it doesn't open until January 7th.

You can continue down from here to Gant and catch the gondola up to Blauherd. On that mountain there are a couple of wonderful off-piste 'downhill routes' from Unterrothorn, which used to be official black pistes and have spectacular views down towards the village and over to the Matterhorn.

On the Klein Matterhorn, the best area for good skiers is Schwarzsee, from where there are several steep north-facing gullies through the woods. Unfortunately you can't ski these repeatedly without taking the beautiful, but slightly boring, track they end up on down to Furi and catching the cable-car up again.

There are marvellous off-piste possibilities from the top lifts in each sector, but they aren't immediately obvious to those without local knowledge. They are also dangerous because of the rocky terrain.

We don't recommend anyone skiing off-piste without a guide. But in Zermatt we've found that more of a problem than elsewhere. The ski school doesn't run off-piste groups in the same way they do in resorts such as Val-d'Isère and Méribel. You have to hire a guide privately for a full day, and that's expensive unless you have a fair-sized group. Much better value for individuals and couples is a half-day heli-skiing trip – provided you know what you're in for.

Zermatt is the Alps' biggest heli-skiing centre; the helipad resembles a bus station at times, with choppers taking off every few minutes. There are only three main drop-off points, so this can mean encountering one or two other groups on the mountain, even though there are multiple ways down. From all three points there are routes that don't require great expertise. The epic is from the Monte Rosa at over 4000m down through wonderful glacier scenery to Furi.

FOR INTERMEDIATE SKIERS
Mile after mile of beautiful runs
Zermatt is ideal for adventurous intermediates. Both the blue and the red runs tend to be at the difficult end of their grading.

There are some very beautiful reds down lift-free valleys from both Gornergrat and Hohtälli – we like these first thing in the morning before anyone else is on them. The variant which goes to Riffelalp ends up on a very narrow wooded path with a sheer cliff and magnificent views on the right-hand side.

On Sunnegga, the 5km Kumme run from Unterrothorn to the bottom of the Patrullarve chair also gets away from the lift system and has an interesting mix of straight-running and mogul pitches. On Klein Matterhorn, the reds served by the Hörnli and Garten drags and the fast four-person chair from Furgg are all long and gloriously set at the foot of the Matterhorn.

For the less adventurous intermediate, the best areas are the blues above Riffelberg (on Gornergrat), above Sunnegga, and the runs between Klein Matterhorn and Trockener Steg. Of these, the Riffelberg area often has the best combination of good snow and easy cruising and is popular with the ski school. Sunnegga gets a lot of sun, but the artificial snow here means that the problem is more often a foot or more of heavy snow near the bottom rather than bare patches.

SKI SCHOOL

94/95 prices in Swiss francs

Swiss

Classes 6 days
4hr: 2hr am and pm
6 full days: 215

Children's classes
Ages: 6 to 12
6 full days including
lunch: 255

Private lessons
Half- or full-day
145 for half-day for
1 to 2 people; each
additional person 5

On the Klein Matterhorn, most of the runs, though marked red on the piste map, are very flat and represent the easiest skiing Zermatt has to offer as well as the best snow. The problem here is the possibility of bad weather because of the height – high winds, extreme cold and poor visibility can make life very unpleasant. To get to Cervinia you set off from Testa Grigia with a choice of blue or red routes – even an early intermediate should find the 10km blue route right down to the village manageable.

FOR BEGINNERS

Save your money: learn elsewhere
Zermatt is to be avoided by beginners. The easiest skiing is described above. And there's no decent nursery slope area. Go somewhere else.

FOR EVERYONE

A spectacular cable-car ride
The Klein Matterhorn cable-car is an experience you shouldn't miss if the weather is good. The views down to the glacier and its crevasses, as the car swings steeply into its hole blasted out of the mountain at the top, are stupendous. When you arrive, you walk through a long tunnel to emerge on top of the world for the highest piste skiing in Europe. The top drag-lifts here are for summer skiing and are normally shut in winter.

FOR CROSS-COUNTRY

Fairly limited
There's a 4km loop at Furi, 3km near the bottom of the gondola to Furi, and 12-15km down at Täsch (but don't count on there being snow). There are also some 'ski walking trails' up the mountain – best tackled as part of an organised group.

QUEUES

Still some bottlenecks
Zermatt used to have one of the worst reputations for queues in the Alps. The major problems have now been pretty well eliminated. But there can still be a lengthy scrum for the gondola out of town towards the Klein Matterhorn area at the start of the day. And the lifts above the Sunnegga train can generate queues, especially at peak ski school periods.

To avoid the queues, start out early – really early. If you catch the Gornergrat train before 8.30am or so, you shouldn't encounter queues until late morning at the earliest.

SKI SCHOOL

Bad experiences
The ski school has a poor reputation with a lot of people we've heard from. We're told it's improving under new management. But the transformation clearly has some way to go yet.

The world's best mountain restaurants

We once met a man who had been coming here for twenty years simply because of the mountain restaurants. The choice is enormous (the tourist information says 30 but it seems like more). Most of those we've tried have excellent food and many are in spectacular settings. It is impossible to list all those worth a visit here – so don't limit yourself to those we mention.

At Furi, the Restaurant Furi itself, Aroleid above it and Simi's on the road below, all have large sun terraces and good reputations. The hotel at Schwarzsee is set right at the foot of the Matterhorn at over 2500m, with staggering views of the mountain and the Trockener Steg skiing. On the way back to the village in this area, a couple of popular stopping off points are Zum See and Blatten.

The Kulmhotel at 3100m at Gornergrat has both self-service and table-service restaurants with amazing views of lift-free mountains and glaciers. Further down, the Riffelalp hotel has excellent pot-au-feu and pasta; the chef came from the 5-star Mont Cervin down in Zermatt.

The large terrace of the restaurant at Sunnegga offers decent food and a great view of children's ski school classes falling down the steep ending of one of the favourite blue teaching pistes. Down at Findeln are a couple of rustic restaurants – sadly the owner of Enzo's (thought by many to be the best mountain restaurant in Zermatt) sold up a couple of seasons ago.

Wherever you go, don't miss trying the local alcoholic coffee known as Schlümli Pflümli – but only if you don't fancy skiing in the afternoon!

CHILDCARE

There are nurseries in two upmarket hotels. The Kinderparadies in the Nicoletta (661151) takes children aged 2 to 8, from 9am to 5pm. The Kinderclub Pumuckel at the Ginabelle (674535) takes children from 30 months to 6, from 9am to 5pm, and ski tuition is available on the spot.

The Mini club (674087) takes children from age 2 to 6, from 9am to 5pm.

Ski school lessons start at age 6.

GETTING THERE

Air Geneva, transfer 4hr. Zürich, transfer 5hr.

Rail Station in resort.

Last time we were there the school was advertising powder skiing classes, but when we enquired, they weren't happening. We also asked what would happen if we booked a half-day private lesson for powder skiing the following day and the weather continued to be as appaling as it was then. The surly reply was that if we booked we had to have the lesson as 'you have to learn to ski in bad weather and we have to work to earn'. Things are made slightly worse by Zermatt placing strict limits on tour operator ski guiding.

FACILITIES FOR CHILDREN
Good hotel nurseries
The Nicoletta and Ginabelle hotels have obvious attractions for families who can afford them (though their nurseries are open to others). Despite an exceptionally fat file of skiers' reports on Zermatt, we have no first-hand reports on these facilities. For children of ski-school age, the resort cannot be recommended.

↑ Staying there

Choosing where to stay is very important in Zermatt: the bus service is limited, crowded and not free, and taxis are pricey. The best spot for most people is near the centre and the Gornergrat and Sunnegga railways. Some of the accommodation is inconveniently situated up the steep hill across the river from the centre. The Winkelmatten area can be particularly tedious unless you intend

to ski the Klein Matterhorn area most days (which is unlikely).

The solar-powered ski-buses cost SF2 a go; if you can fill a taxi with your group, that can work out as cheap and more enjoyable. Walking with skis from one end of the village to the furthest ski lifts can take 15 to 20 minutes and can be unpleasant because of icy patches and buzzing electric buggies and taxis.

Getting up to the village from Täsch is no problem. Amazingly, for those of us used to BR, the trains run on time and have automatically descending ramps which allow you to wheel luggage trolleys on and off. You are met at the other end by electric and horse-drawn taxis and hotel shuttles.

HOW TO GO
A wide choice, packaged or not
Chalets Zermatt isn't a major chalet resort; several chalet operators do have places here, but few are in any way remarkable and many are apartments posing as chalets. The Mazot, above the restaurant of the same name, is one of the best, and quite well-placed near the river – booked through Ski Solutions. Bladon Lines has quite a wide selection, including the comfortable Castello. If convenience is not important, the secluded Bambi is a good-value 'real' chalet. Crystal have taken over the Britannia from Mark Warner, who no longer offer Zermatt.
Hotels There are over 100 hotels, mostly comfortable and traditional-style 3- and 4-stars, but including some luxurious and pricey and some more affordable places.

Selected chalets in Zermatt

PACKAGES

Alpine Expressions, Bladon Lines, Chalets 'Unlimited', Crystal, Enterprise, Inghams, Kuoni, Lotus Supertravel, Made to Measure, Plus Travel, Powder Byrne, Ski Activity, Ski Choice, Ski Club of GB, Ski La Vie, Ski Les Alpes, Ski Scott Dunn, Ski Total, Ski with Julia, SkiGower, Swiss Travel Service, Thomson, Trail Alpine

£££££ Mont Cervin Biggest and perhaps best in town. Elegantly traditional inside, despite blocky looks. Central. Good pool.

££££ Alex An established favourite, close to the station: welcoming, charmingly decorated. Good facilities, including a pool.

££££ Ambassador Peaceful position on northern fringe, near Gornergrat station. Large pool, fitness room.

££££ Monte Rosa The original Zermatt hotel, towards southern end of village – full of climbing pictures and mementos, but well modernised. The basement Whymperstube is named after the British conqueror of the Matterhorn, who stayed here.

££££ Ginabelle Smart pair of chalets, over the river not far from Sunnegga lift; great for families – on-the-spot ski nursery as well as day-care.

££££ Nicoletta Bright modern chalet quite close to centre, with nursery.

£££ Julen Charming, modern-rustic chalet over the river, with Matterhorn views from some rooms.

££ Atlanta No frills, but good food; close to centre, with Matterhorn views from some rooms.

££ Alpina Modest but very friendly, and close to centre.

Self-catering There is a lot of apartment accommodation in the village, but not much of it finds its way on to the UK package market – so it sells out early. Inghams and Kuoni have an allocation in the hotel Ambassador apartments, which have excellent facilities. New for 1995, Inghams has the large, comfortable Armina apartments, ideal for large families, plus well-appointed places convenient for Sunnegga. Bladon Lines' Malteserhaus apartments are comfortable, but sell early. Crystal have some simple new accommodation this year, well placed for the Sunnegga lift. Swiss Travel has centrally located studios and apartments.

STAYING UP THE MOUNTAIN
Comfortable ski-in ski-out seclusion

There are several hotels at altitude, of which the pick is probably the Riffelalp, rebuilt from a ruin in 1988 and recommended for good food and a quiet time. It's at the first stop on the Gornergrat railway. The last train up from Zermatt is at 6pm, but if you fancy a night in town and there's room, you can stay at the Seilers' other hotels – the Schweizerhof for no extra charge, or the Mont Cervin or Monte Rosa for a supplement.

STAYING DOWN THE VALLEY
Attractive for drivers

In Täsch, where visitors must leave their cars, there are five 3-star hotels, costing less than half the price of the equivalent in Zermatt. The Täscherhof is next to the station; the City and Bellevue close by. It's a 13-minute ride from Zermatt, with trains every 20 minutes for most of the day; the last train down is 11.10pm.

EATING OUT
Huge choice at all price levels

There are 100 restaurants to choose from, ranging from top-quality haute cuisine to egg and chips. Among the most highly rated restaurants is the

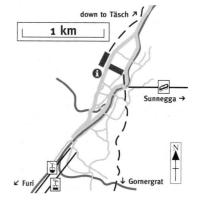

SKI SCOTT DUNN

helped us to compile the Après-ski section. Our thanks to them.

ACTIVITIES

Indoor Sauna, tennis, hotel swimming pools (some open to public) and a salt water pool, keep-fit centre, squash, billiards, curling, bowling, gallery and excellent Alpine museum, cinema
Outdoor Skating, horse-riding, sleigh rides, 30km cleared paths, helicopter flights, para-gliding

TOURIST OFFICE

Postcode CH-3920
Tel 010 41 (28) 661181
Fax 661185

Mazot, which has prices to match the food. At the other end of the scale, Café du Pont has good-value pasta and rösti, and the Bahnhof Buffet offers good food at some of the lowest prices. For its rustic atmosphere and dried meats, try the Whymperstube.

The Chi-Ba-Bou, in the hotel Ambassador, specialises in fondue and has a good reputation. For pizza, Tony's Grotta is hard to beat – we had excellent food but surly service there. Taking the last lift up and strolling down to an early dinner in a mountain hut is worth considering – check their serving times first.

APRES-SKI
Lively and varied
There's something for almost every taste, with a good mix of sophisticated and informal fun, though it certainly helps if you have deep pockets. When you can ski back to the village, there are lots of restaurants on the way back from Furi that are convenient for a last drink and sunbathe.

In town, there are fewer places to have a post-skiing glühwein or hot chocolate than one might expect. The terraces of the Derby and Old Zermatt are two of the most popular. Promenading along the main street is popular in the early evening and gives the village a great atmosphere. Elsie's bar, renowned for its snails and oysters, gets packed early and late.

Later on, the hotel De la Poste

complex is popular for eating, drinking, dancing and jazz – there are parts for each; Zermatt Yacht Club and Pink Elephant are favourite bars.

The Brown Cow is usually full of Brits, as it has some of the cheapest beer in town, but otherwise it's fairly uninspiring. The same can be said of the soulless North Face, which is popular with tour reps. Many of our reporters preferred Grampi's for 'good music, nice decor and fun atmosphere'.

Papagallo's is another popular bar, but the Z'Alt Hischi is more atmospheric and better for a quiet drink. The Hexenbar is a similarly cosy place. The Vernissage Cinema bar is a good, surprisingly trendy haunt that's a far cry from your local multiplex ! Le Village is perhaps the best disco in town, though we have also received recommendations for its rivals, the Pollux and Simi.

FOR NON-SKIERS
Considerable attractions
Zermatt is an easy place for non-skiers to spend time, particularly if equipped with large amounts of cash. And if lunch up the mountain appeals, this is nearly as good a resort for non-skiers as it is for skiers – it's easy to get around and meet skiing friends. The lack of a public swimming pool is no real problem with 15 hotel pools, and there is a decent range of other activities for the energetic.

United States

Views on skiing in the United States tend to be extreme. Most of those who have tried it are captivated by it. What they fall for is partly the USA itself – the famously high standards of customer service, overlaid by the enthusiastic courtesy that is unique to the States. It's partly the snow, which is generally good. It's partly the cute wild-west character of many of the resorts. But a few visitors come away unconvinced. Sometimes it's because they don't like the sense of skiing in a theme park; but more often it comes back to the cost, which is generally higher than going to the Alps, and the nature of the mountains and of the skiing itself, which is different from what we're used to.

Our view? If we had to confine ourselves to the Alps or the Rockies for the rest of our skiing lives, it would be the Alps without a doubt. But, happily, that's not how things are. Between us we've skied practically all the main resorts in the western States, and we love going back.

It was snow that first took British skiers to America in large numbers, during the Alpine snow droughts of the late 1980s. The super-high Rockies had the reputation of getting limitless quantities of super-light snow, and in those crucial years they certainly did better than the Alps. The reputation went slightly beyond the reality, but in practice it doesn't matter – most American resorts have serious snowmaking facilities anyway. What's more, they use them – they lay down a base of artificial snow early in the season, rather than using snow-guns to make up for a lack of the real thing.

This is partly a reaction to the pattern of natural snowfall. A lot of the Rockies' snow arrives relatively late in the season – something that seems to be increasingly true in the Alps, but not traditionally what we expect. When skiing in January or even February, you may encounter signs saying: 'Caution: Early Season Conditions Apply'. What they mean is that you may occasionally encounter a rock.

The state of Utah has staked a claim to the best snow conditions of all by adopting the slogan 'Greatest Snow on Earth'. The Utah resorts – particularly Snowbird and Alta – get very large amounts of snow, and it is by our standards superbly powdery stuff. But measurements of water content have shown that Colorado gets even lighter snow, justifying its 'Champagne powder' label.

Piste grooming is taken very seriously – most American resorts set standards that few resorts in the Alps can match. But this doesn't mean that there aren't moguls – far from it. It's just that you get moguls where the resort says you can expect moguls, and not where you're expecting an easy cruise. Val d'Isère please copy. American resorts are well organised in lots of other respects, too. Many offer free guided tours of the ski area. Lift queues are short, partly because they are highly disciplined, and spare seats on chair-lifts are religiously filled, with the aid of cheerful, conscientious attendants.

US resorts have the reputation of not providing opportunities for off-piste skiing, but this seriously misrepresents the position. It's true that ski areas practically always have a boundary, and that skiing outside it is discouraged or forbidden. But within the ski area there is often challenging skiing that is very much like off-piste terrain in an Alpine resort – with the important advantage that it is much safer because it's patrolled and checked for avalanche risk.

Aside from cost, there are three big arguments against American skiing. One is that it's small-scale. Many big-name resorts have ski areas that are very modest in extent compared with major Alpine areas, whether measured horizontally or vertically. In the Alps, a vertical drop of 1000m is normal, even for a small resort; 1500m is common. For comparison, here are some major American figures: Mammoth Mountain 950m; Vail 1000m; Breckenridge 800m; Park City 900m. Jackson Hole has the biggest vertical that we know of in the States: 1250m. In the horizontal dimension, there are no American ski areas to rival the Trois Vallées, Davos-Klosters or the Sella Ronda. In practice, we and other pro-US skiers don't find this a worry. (When did you last ski 1000m vertical without pausing for breath?) And many US resorts are close to each other, so if you get bored with one you can try some others – easier if you hire a car.

The second criticism – one that we attach more weight to – is that the terrain and the runs are monotonous. You don't get the spectacular mountain scenery and the distinctive high-mountain runs of the Alps. Most of the skiing is below the tree-line, on mountains that, despite their extreme altitude, resemble the Pennines more than the Alps. But there is an upside to this: the skiing is very unlikely to be interrupted by bad weather.

The third weakness is the one that we really have trouble with. We like a good lunch on the mountain, and such lunches are rarely to be had. Monster self-service cafeterias doing pizza, burgers and other fast foods are the norm. Welcoming, atmospheric restaurants on a personal scale with table service are rarities. There are spectacular exceptions – if there is a more civilised lunch spot than Stein Eriksen Lodge at Deer Valley or the Alpenglow Stube at Keystone, we have yet to encounter it – but they are few.

The grading of pistes (or trails, to use the local term) is confusing to European visitors; it has a lot in common with our system but there are important differences. Red runs don't exist. The colours used are combined with shapes: green squares, blue circles, black diamonds. Greens correspond fairly closely to greens in Europe (that is, in France, where they are mainly found). American blues largely correspond to blues here, but also include tougher intermediate runs that would be red here; these are sometimes labelled as double blue squares, although in some resorts a hybrid blue-black grading is used instead. American blacks correspond to steeper European reds and easier European blacks. Many US resorts have double black diamonds, which are seriously steep – often steeper than the steepest pistes in the Alps and including high, open bowls.

Very few British skiers visiting the States seem to go to ski school. This seems rather a shame, since American instruction gets rave reviews from those who do try it. Naturally, the common language helps – particularly with the psychological side of skiing, which many American instructors are well tuned in to. Clear, considerate, fun-oriented instruction is exactly what novices need, and what the States provides. Facilities for children are impressive, too.

The key feature of American resort villages is the quality and sheer spaciousness of the accommodation. The contrast with French apartments, in particular, is incredible. Some package holidays are priced on the basis of four people sharing a room; that probably isn't what you'll want to do, but if you did you'd still have more space than in your usual hutch in Les Arcs. The resorts vary as widely in style and convenience as Alpine resorts. But one thing they have in common (even the smartest) is good, reasonably-priced restaurants.

In the end, your reaction to American skiing may depend mainly on your reaction to America. If repeated cheerful exhortations to have a nice day wind you up, perhaps you'd better stick to the Alps. If you like the idea that the customer is king, give America a try. The resorts with international appeal are concentrated in the Rockies, but visitors to the eastern USA should bear in mind the New England resorts included in our Resort directory.

Alta 2605m

HOW IT RATES

The skiing

Snow	*****
Extent	*
Advanced	*****
Intermediates	***
Beginners	***
Convenience	****
Queues	***
Restaurants	***

The rest

Scenery	****
Resort charm	***
Not skiing	*

SKI FACTS

Altitude	2605m-3215m
Lifts	12
Pistes	2200 acres
Green	25%
Blue	40%
Black	35%
Art. snow	25 acres

Alta's reputation is for remarkable amounts of powder snow to arrive with great regularity, for a stubborn refusal to develop the area as some say it deserves and for one of the cheapest lift passes around. The skiing is classy but the resort is limited.

THE RESORT

Alta sits at the craggy head of Little Cottonwood Canyon, 2km beyond Snowbird and less than an hour's drive from donwtown Salt Lake City. The lovely peaceful location was once the scene of a bustling and bawdy mining town – long since flattened by avalanches and neglect. The 'new' Alta is a strung-out handful of lodges and parking areas that lacks a centre; life revolves around the two separate lift base areas – Albion and Wildcat – which are linked by a bi-directional rope tow along the flat valley floor.

THE SKIING

Alta's **ski area** can't have changed much in the last 20 years; no high-speed lifts here. The dominant feature seen from the resort is the steep end of a ridge that separates the two basins. To the left, from Albion base at the head of the canyon, the skiing stretches away over easy green terrain towards the black runs of Point Supreme; to the right, a more concentrated bowl with blue runs down the middle and blacks either side. There are lift links between the areas in both directions.

A base altitude of 2600m and a vertical drop of 600m are modest statistics for US resorts – but the quantity and quality of snow that falls here, and the northerly orientation of the slopes, put Alta right in the top drawer for **snow reliability**.

Small though it is, Alta is great for **advanced skiers**, who flock to the high ridges after a fresh snowfall. There are dozens of steep chutes through the trees on the front faces leading back to the Wildcat base area, and wide steep slopes around the rim of the Albion basin.

Intermediate skiers with a sense of adventure do pretty well at Alta, too – there's good variety in the standard of runs and the easier blacks offer a gradual progression. But high-mileage piste-bashers will find it very limited.

Timid intermediates and **beginners** need to stick to the Albion side, where most of the lower runs are broad, gentle and well groomed.

There's little provision for **cross-country** skiing but it does go on –

mainly across the road from the downhill slopes – and those experienced enough or willing to hire a guide could certainly venture into the surrounding back-country.

Queues are not unknown at Alta – the snow record, easy access from Salt Lake City and the rather slow chair-lifts see to that – especially in spring and on sunny weekends. At least the lift company limits the tickets sold.

There's a **mountain restaurant** in each sector of the skiing – the Alpenglow on the Albion side has a small, often busy, terrace and a slightly Alpine feel to it and Watson's Shelter on Wildcat has both cafeteria and table-service sections.

The famous Alf Engen **ski school** has been going for over 50 years, which is plenty of time to sharpen-up the powder lessons in which it specialises. All the regular classes and clinics are also available and the small classes, enthusiastic teachers and low prices provide good value.

The ski school does organise **children's** lessons, and day-care for those aged over 3 months is available at the Albion ticket building – but there's little else for kids to do.

STAYING THERE

There are about a dozen places to stay – simple **hotels and apartments**. None of the locations is bad, but for the best ski-in ski-out convenience the smart Alta Lodge and the comfortable modern Goldminer's Daughter take the honours. The latter has a busy après-ski bar. Snowpine Lodge is small and welcoming, between the lift bases. We don't know of any packages.

Eating out in Alta means the Shallow Shaft steakhouse and it's worth a visit if you haven't already paid for your dinner; for most people eating in is the routine. The lodges expect to provide dinner for their guests but not for others.

Après-ski is self-contained in the lodges and rarely goes beyond a few drinks and possibly a ski movie.

Nor is there much to keep **non-skiers** occupied – it's a pleasant location but any distractions other than mountains, snow and skiers will require a trip to Salt Lake City.

TOURIST OFFICE

Postcode UT 84092
Tel 010 1 (801)
7423333
Fax 7423333

Aspen 2420m

✔ A lot of skiing, with terrain to suit all standards

✔ Even better this season, with new lifts making some good skiing more accessible

✔ Attractive, characterful town, with lots of tempting shops

✔ Good for celebrity-spotting

✔ Lively nightlife

✔ Ski-in, ski-out accommodation at Snowmass

✘ Skiing spread over four separate mountains

✘ Rather sprawling town, so choice of accommodation important

✘ Can be very expensive (although Aspen can also be done on the cheap – see page 388)

Aspen is well-known for its rich and famous guests, lots of whom have holiday homes here and private jets parked at the local airport. Jack Nicholson, Martina Navratilova, Jane Fonda and countless more are regulars. But don't let that put you off. Most celebs are keen to keep a low profile and disappear into the crowd, rather than be mobbed by adoring fans.

Aspen has a lot going for it. Its four mountains between them offer a lot of skiing, with enough to keep every standard of skier interested. It has the biggest vertical drop in Colorado. The town is a beautifully restored Victorian silver-mining town, with wide streets built in typical American grid fashion and a huge variety of restaurants, bars and plush shops. And the resort doesn't rest on its laurels – it is always devising new attractions. For this season, for example, there are ski-in, ski-out tours of a mid-mountain silver mine, and free snowcat rides to untracked snowfields.

The main drawback of the place is that you can spend a fortune. But you don't have to: Aspen need not cost more than any other major US resort.

ORIENTATION

Aspen is a compact town with a typical American grid of streets. The skiing is on four separate mountains. Aspen Mountain starts right next to the town. There is more accommodation (and more skiing, in terms of area) at Snowmass, 12 miles to the west. The other two ski mountains – Tiehack and Aspen Highlands – are between these extremes. All the mountains are served by an efficient, free ski-bus.

Day-trips to other resorts are unlikely, but a two-centre holiday is easily arranged, and there's a special lift pass to encourage you to combine Aspen with Vail, including a free transfer between the resorts.

 ## The resort

Just over a century ago Aspen was a booming silver-mining town of 12,000 inhabitants, boasting six newspapers, an opera house and a red light district. But Aspen's fortunes took a nose-dive when the silver price plumeted in 1893, and by the 1930s the population had shrunk to 400 or so. Elegant Victorian buildings – such as the Wheeler Opera House and the Hotel Jerome – had fallen into disrepair.

The historic centre has been beautifully renovated to form the core of what is now the most fashionable ski town in the Rockies. There's a huge variety of shops, bars, restaurants and galleries – though you may find some of the prices a deterrent. Spreading out from this centre, you'll find a mixture of developments, ranging from the homes of the super-rich, on the outskirts, to the mobile homes for the workers who now find it too expensive to buy or rent in Aspen.

Twelve miles away is Snowmass, with its own mountain and modern ski-in, ski-out accommodation.

 ## The skiing

Aspen has lots of skiing for every standard; you just have to pick the right mountain.

THE SKI AREA
Widely dispersed

There are four mountains, only one accessible from Aspen town. Skiing development started in Aspen on a small scale in the late 1930s. The first ski-lift (then the world's longest chair-lift) was opened shortly after the Second World War, and Aspen hasn't looked back since. By 1958, development of Buttermilk (now Tiehack) and Aspen Highlands had started. Snowmass opened in 1967.

Getting around between the areas by free ski-bus is easy. Each is big enough to keep you amused for a full day. All have regular free guided tours.

The Silver Queen gondola takes you from right in the heart of town to the top of **Aspen Mountain** in 15 minutes. The alternative – to take three chair-lifts – is only worth considering if the queues are horrific

SKI FACTS

Altitude 2400m-3600m
Lifts   42
Pistes   4093 acres
Green   17%
Blue   43%
Black   40%
Art. snow   483 acres

for the gondola. A series of chairs including, surprisingly, only one high-speed quad, serve the different ridges – Gentleman's Ridge along the eastern edge, the Ridge of Bell in the centre, and Ruthie's to the west – with valleys or gulches in between. There are no green runs at all. In general, there are long cruising blue runs along the valley floors and short steep blacks down from the ridges. The mountain is ideal for skiers of good intermediate standard or better.

Snowmass is an entirely separate ski resort some 12 miles west of Aspen. It's the largest of Aspen's ski areas – some 2,500 acres in all – fanning out from the purpose-built village at the base. Chair-lifts head off towards four separate peaks, the skiing of which is all interlinked. From left to right looking at the mountain, these are Elk Camp, High Alpine, Big Burn (named after the fire started by Ute Indians protesting against the mining that was ruining their terrain) and Sam's Knob. Many of the runs are wide, sweeping, perfectly groomed highways, providing relaxing and scenic skiing. But it also has some of the toughest skiing in the whole area.

Tiehack – said to be the closest ski area to an airport in the world – is famous as a learning mountain, although a fair proportion of the skiing would suit intermediates too.

The runs fan out from the top in three directions. West Buttermilk, with long, gentle runs through the woods, is ideal for beginners, as is the Main Buttermilk area (though this also has some good intermediate skiing); Tiehack, to the east, is a bit more demanding, but ideal for an intermediate skier to learn or perfect mogul, powder or tree skiing.

Aspen Highlands boasts the greatest vertical drop in Colorado – 1155m. Until 1993, it was separately owned and run, and famous for its antiquated lifts. It is now run by the Aspen Skiing Company, and this season sees two new high-speed quads that will whisk you to the top in under 20 minutes – half the time it used to take. There will also be 45 acres of new tough tree skiing opened up. The skiing is a strange mixture of tough blacks and easy greens and blues. And the views from the top are the best that Aspen has to offer – the famous Maroon Bells that appear on all the scenic postcards.

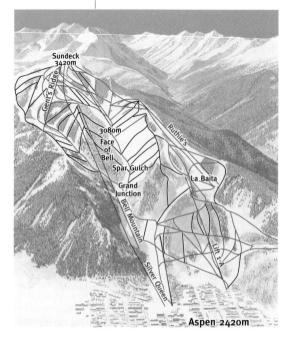

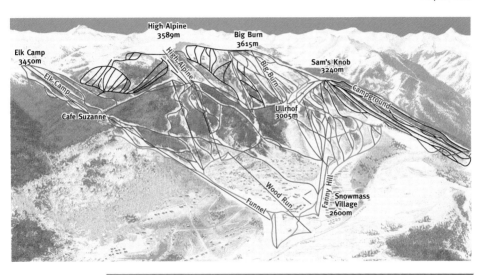

Powder tours

If you can stump up the $200 for the day's tour, this is an experience not to miss – particularly if you hire the revolutionary 'Fat Sticks' to ski on. These are skis about twice as wide as normal ones. The $35 a day ski hire is well worth it for the transformation of your powder skiing ability. If your normal experience of powder is one of continually searching for your skis that have been buried under feet of apparently pristine snow, these are for you.

Your day starts with you signing a form which relieves the Aspen Skiing Company of all responsibility for your safety and welfare, before you climb into the Silver Queen gondola just after 8am (while it is still shut to other skiers). At the top you are armed with an avalanche transceiver and instructed on how to search out your lost colleagues should they be buried under an avalanche (so far there has been no need to use these). You then pile into a heated snow-cat and are driven off onto the 'backside' of Aspen Mountain. Away from the lifts and other skiers, your two guides search out untracked snow.

The cat rejoins you at the end of each run and takes you off for the next. You're likely to squeeze in about 10 runs in all. At midday, you stop for a better-than-average buffet lunch at an old mountain cabin.

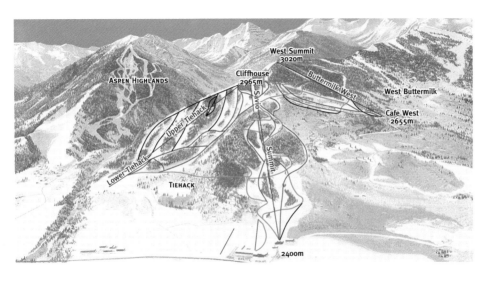

LIFT PASSES

93/94 prices in dollars
Four Mountain Pass
Covers Aspen
Mountain, Aspen
Highlands, Tiehack
and Snowmass, and
shuttle bus between
the areas.
Beginners Included in
price of beginners'
lessons; 129 for 3-day
learn-to-ski or
snowboard lessons.
Main pass
1-day pass 46
6-day pass 240
(low season 186 –
23% off)
Senior citizens
Over 65: 6-day pass
144 (40% off)
Over 70: free pass
Children
Under 13: 6-day pass
144 (40% off)
Under 7: free pass
Notes Single day
passes cover one area
only. All passes over
3 days allow one day
off, eg 6-day pass
valid for 7 days, with
one non-skiing day.
Alternative passes
Premier Passport is
designed for two-
centre holiday. Covers
all Aspen and Vail
skiing and one-way
transfer between the
resorts. Allows from
10 days skiing out of
12 up to 18 out of 21
(38 per day).

SNOW RELIABILITY
Never a problem

Aspen has a good natural snow record.
In addition, all areas except Snowmass
have substantial snowmaking
capabilities. Immaculate grooming
adds to the quality of the piste skiing.

FOR ADVANCED SKIERS
Tiehack is the only soft stuff

There's plenty of skiing to choose
from – all the mountains except for
Tiehack offer lots of challenges.

Aspen Mountain has a formidable
array of double black diamond skiing.
From the top of the Silver Queen
gondola, try Walsh's, Hyrup's or Kristi,
linking up with Gentleman's Ridge
and Jackpot for a combination of steep
slopes, moguls and trees – the longest
black run on the mountain. Or head
for the Ridge of Bell – and a chance to
show off your mogul skills to those
going up in the chair or gondola.
Don't miss the expert tree and bump
slopes running off the International
into Spar Gulch – these are collectively
called the Dumps, because they were
formed out of slag and rubble dumped
by the miners back in the silver-
mining days. There are numerous
other black challenges too – 65 per
cent of the trails are black.

At Snowmass, expert skiers face a
hike to get to the Hanging Valley Wall
and Glades and to most of the Cirque
area runs. But what a reward! Beautiful
scenery, wonderful tree skiing at
Hanging Valley and steep enough
everywhere to satisfy the keenest. The
Cirque area is mainly above the tree-
line, with steep, narrow, often rocky
chutes – Gowdy's is one of the steepest
in the whole area, AMF ('Adios My
Friend') speaks for itself.

The runs back down under the High
Alpine lift offer cruising, bumps and
tree skiing within a small area. And,
lower down, there's a network of long
black trails down from Sam's Knob.

At Aspen Highlands, there are
challenging runs from top to bottom
of the mountain. At the top the
Steeplechase area consists of a number
of parallel natural avalanche chutes,
and their elevation means the snow
stays light and dry. The Olympic Bowl
area, served by Chair 5, has great
views of the Maroon Bells peaks and
some serious moguls. Chair 8 takes
you to more moguls. Chair 6 serves a
nice varied area – you can cream down
Thunderbowl, practice bumps on
Powderbowl and enjoy good snow on
the little-used Limelight.

On top of this there's the 45 acres of
new tough skiing for this season.

FOR INTERMEDIATE SKIERS
More grooming than a male model

Snowmass is the best mountain for
intermediate skiers and the Big Burn is
definitely the first place to head for.
The huge open area is a cruising
paradise. The runs merge into each
other, though there's a satisfying
variety of terrain and some trees to
add interest. This season, free snowcat
rides will take you from the top of the
Big Burn chair to less accessible parts
of the skiing.

The easiest intermediate skiing is
reached from the Elk Camp lift –
there's a choice of runs from the top,
through spruce trees. Naked Lady lift
gives you access to yet more
intermediate slopes – a little trickier
and more varied including some
moguls. The Sam's Knob sector offers
slightly more advanced intermediate
skiing. Finally, Green Cabin, accessed
from the top of the High Alpine lift, is
a magical intermediate run cruising
from top to bottom of the mountain,
with spectacular views on the way.

Most of the intermediate skiing in
Aspen Highlands is above the mid-
mountain Merry-go-Round restaurant.
The most popular slope, Scarlet's Run,
is directly above here. Grand Prix is a
wide cruiser between trees – but watch
out for the path to the right taking
you back to mid-mountain, otherwise
you hit a double black diamond run.
Beyond Grand Prix, you can reach
Picnic Point via Upper Robinson's – a
table and views make it a good place
to pause.

Aspen Mountain has its fair share of
intermediate slopes, but they tend to
be tougher than on the other
mountains. Copper Bowl and Spar
Gulch running between the ridges
making up Aspen Mountain are great
cruises early in the morning but can
get crowded later. Upper Aspen
Mountain, at the top of the Silver
Queen gondola, has a dense network
of well-groomed blues. Ruthie's has
more cruising runs and less in the way
of crowds. Ruthie's Run leads into the
popular Snow Bowl, a wide open area
with moguls on the left but groomed
on the right and centre.

Tiehack may not be the obvious
choice for intermediate skiers – yet it
has quite a lot going for it. The Main
Buttermilk runs offer good, easy slopes
to practise your technique on. And
good intermediates should be able to
handle the relatively easy black runs
in the Tiehack area and gain the
confidence to progress to the
somewhat tougher black pistes on
other mountains.

SKI SCHOOL

93/94 prices in dollars

Aspen Skiing Company
Snowmass and Tiehack for all abilities; Aspen Mountain for intermediate and advanced only
Classes 5 days
5hr: 10.30-3.30;
3hr: 12.30-3.30
3 full days: 126
Children's classes
Ages: 7 to 12
5 5hr 45min days: 210
Private lessons
1½hr, 3hr (am or pm) or 6hr
130 for 1½hr, for 1 to 5 people

CHILDCARE

The childcare possibilities are too numerous to list in detail.

A new children's 'learning center' was opened at Tiehack last season – Fort Frog – with a special children's shuttle bus from Aspen. The Powder Pandas classes there take children aged 3 to 6. At Snowmass, the Big Burn Bears ski kindergarten takes children from age 4, and children aged 18 months to 3 have the Snow Cubs playschool.

There are several all-day non-skiing crèches, taking children from as young as 12 months.

FOR BEGINNERS
Can be a great place to learn

Tiehack is a great mountain for beginners, whether tackling skiing or snowboarding (banned on Aspen Mountain). West Buttermilk has beautifully groomed, gentle and tree-lined runs – ideal for building up confidence. The easiest slope of all, though, is found in the central Main Buttermilk sector – Panda Peak.

The easiest beginner slope at Snowmass is the wide Assay Hill at the bottom of the Elk Camp area. Right next to Snowmass Village Mall is the Fanny Hill high-speed lift and beginners' run of the same name. Further up, from Sam's Knob, a series of runs offer a long, gentle cruise.

Despite its mighty vertical rise, Aspen Highlands boasts the highest concentration of beginners' runs in Aspen, located below the Merry-Go-Round restaurant. Right by the base area, Chair 9 serves Half Inch – the easiest beginners' slope. The biggest problem is meeting up with more experienced friends for lunch – they may be on a different mountain.

FOR CROSS-COUNTRY
Back-country bonanza

There's 80km of groomed trails between Aspen and Snowmass in the Roaring Fork Valley – the most extensive maintained cross-country system in the US. And the Ashcroft Ski Touring Centre maintains around 30km of trails around Ashcroft, a mining ghost-town. Take the opportunity of eating at the Pine Creek Cookhouse, some 2.5km from the Ashcroft trailhead: excellent food and accessible by ski or sledge only. In addition, there are limitless miles of ungroomed trails. Aspen is at one end of the famous 230-mile Tenth Mountain Division Trail, heading north-east and almost linking up to Vail, with 13 huts for overnight stops.

QUEUES
Few problems

There are rarely major queues on any of the mountains. At Aspen Mountain, the Silver Queen gondola can have delays at peak times, but you have alternative lifts to the top.

Snowmass has so many alternative lifts and runs that you can normally avoid any problems. But the long, slow chairs can be cold in mid-winter, and the home slope gets very busy.

Aspen Highlands is almost always queue-free, even at peak times.

The two lifts out of Main Buttermilk sometimes get congested.

MOUNTAIN RESTAURANTS
Good by American standards

Even this smartest of US skiing resorts can't compare with, say, Switzerland for mountain restaurants to seduce you off the slopes. But there are some good places.

On Aspen Mountain try La Baita (an Italian-style restaurant which has replaced Ruthie's), with good views down onto Aspen. Sundeck, at the top, has been taken over by the Little Nell hotel for next season and promises, 'You can't find a better meal on a mountain west of the Alps.' It has has fabulous views and non-skiers can reach it on the gondola.

At Snowmass, Gwyn's is an elegant restaurant serving excellent food. The best views of the mountains surrounding this area are from Sam's Knob restaurant and cafeteria.

Merry-Go-Round at mid-mountain at Aspen Highlands is worth a visit, not just for its good, if fairly basic, cooking (the strudel is famous), but also for the great view of skiers approaching it (including the freestylers on Fridays at noon). At 1pm you could head for the Cloud Nine picnic deck with a snack in the hope that the ski patrollers will do their legendary dramatic ski jump over the 54-foot sun deck.

SKI SCHOOL
Special programmes

There's a wide variety of specialised ski instruction available – bumps, powder, mountain racing and so on – and a four-day Mountain Masters program on Aspen and Snowmass, where small groups of intermediate and advanced skiers ski with the same instructor for five hours a day. Video analysis, NASTAR races, on-mountain picnics and a farewell party are all included.

FACILITIES FOR CHILDREN
Choice of crèches?

There is no shortage of advertised childcare arrangements, but one reporter found care for pre-skiing children at Snowmass was actually in short supply (and very expensive). The broken-up nature of the skiing may present problems for parents who want to get around the whole area. Tiehack's Fort Frog is very impressive – a wooden frontier-style fort, with lookout towers, flags, old wagons, a jail, saloon and native American teepee village outside the fort. But families will probably want to base themselves close to the slopes at Snowmass, and make excursions to Aspen from there.

PACKAGES

American Dream, American Skiworld, Bladon Lines, Crystal, Enterprise, Inghams, Lotus Supertravel, Made to Measure, Ski Activity, Ski Independence, USAirtours

Snowmass American Dream, Crystal, Inghams, Lotus Supertravel, USAirtours

GETTING THERE

Air Aspen, transfer ¹/₂hr. Eagle, transfer 1¹/₂hr. Denver, transfer 3¹/₂hr.

Rail Glenwood Springs (70km).

 # Staying there

In Aspen, by far the most convenient place to stay is near the Silver Queen gondola. Buses for the other ski areas also leave from nearby. For ski-in, ski-out convenience, choose Snowmass. The buses from Aspen run until 1am.

HOW TO GO
Accommodation for all pockets
Aspen Mountain and Snowmass between them have beds for some 16,000 guests in a mixture of hotels, inns, B&Bs, lodges and condos – and now there are one or two catered chalets as well.
Chalets American Skiworld have a very comfortable homestead complete with marble fireplace, just out of town. Crystal also have an attractive place near Aspen Highlands.
Hotels Aspen isn't short of luxury hotels. For cheaper places see Aspen on the cheap, below.
£££££ Ritz-Carlton Opened two seasons ago – opulent city-type hotel, near the gondola. Fitness centre, outdoor pool, whirlpool spas, sauna.
£££££ Little Nell Stylish modern hotel right by the gondola, with ski-in,

ski-out access. Pampers you in a slightly more Colorado style – fireplaces in every room, outdoor pool, hot tub, sauna and more.
£££££ Jerome Step back a century in history in one of Aspen's most famous hotels. Victorian authenticity combined with modern-day luxury; swimming pool, hot tub.
££££ Sardy House Elegantly furnished, intimate little hotel on edge of centre, 10 minutes from the gondola, with comfortable though less captivating modern extension. Small outdoor pool, hot tub.
££££ Lenado Neat modern B&B place with open-fire lounge and cosy rooms, within walking distance of gondola.
££££ Silvertree. Large ski-in, ski-out hotel at Snowmass. Pools, hot tubs.
£££ Innsbruck Inn 'Excellent' Tyrolean-style hotel, a fair walk from centre and lifts.
Self-catering The standards here are high, even in US terms. Many of the smarter developments have their own free shuttle buses. The luxurious Gant (Ski Independence, Supertravel), with impressive communal facilities, is close to the gondola and the centre. The smart Aspen Club complex (Crystal) enjoys a prime position next

---

Aspen on the cheap?

So, your bank balance doesn't match that of Aspen's celebrity clients, but you still want to have a good time in America's trendiest resort? Well, all it takes is a bit of planning.

Accommodation is the major expenditure. If you're prepared to risk slightly inferior snow conditions, you can save up to a third by going either early (mid-Nov to mid-Dec) or late (mid-March to mid-April).

Two favourites among Aspen's lower-cost motels are the Christmas Inn ($100 a double room per night), on the edge of town, and Aspen Manor Lodge, very close to the gondola ($120). Both throw in a big buffet breakfast. The least expensive motel rooms are at the Alpine Lodge ($70 for double with shared bath), but it's a bit of a hike out. Budget options closer to town are the Tyrolean Lodge and the Swiss Chalet, which has kitchenettes (both charge around $80). Finding a two-bed condo for under $200 is increasingly difficult; of the various management companies, Aspen Classic Properties tend to offer the most reasonable prices. There are several decent motels at under $50 in the likeable-enough town of Glenwood Springs, 45 miles north.

Eating and drinking need not cost more than in any other major US resort. Be sure to scan Aspen's two free daily papers for news of dinner specials and happy hours. The town's visitor centre stocks menus and money-saving coupons. The excellent Wienerstube serves delicious Austrian breakfasts for little more than $5. Sno' Beach Cafe in Snowmass does breakfasts from $4. There are plenty of informal dining spots, where a meal can cost less than $10. The Red Onion serves up half-price appetisers in the afternoons and good burritos and burgers. Little Annie's has big platters of trout, chicken or ribs for around $12. Mexican restaurants do good-value meals: try Su Casa or the less expensive La Cocina. Stewpot at Snowmass serves filling meals.

At night, neither the country and western Shooters, nor the rock and dance club, Double Diamond, imposes big cover charges.

to the gondola, with free entry to the excellent health and sports facilities. Chateau Roaring Fork and Eau Claire (several operators), four blocks from the gondola, are spacious, well-furnished and with the largest outdoor pool in Aspen. Supertravel have some luxurious individual houses on offer. American Dream and Supertravel also have good condos in Snowmass.

Lots of restaurants take part in an 'A la Car' scheme: you order from a book of menus, and the meal is delivered.

EATING OUT
Dining dilemma
There is an exceptionally wide choice of styles of eating, including Japanese, Thai and Swiss, as well as the more usual options. The most sophisticated and expensive food is in the top hotels, but there are some excellent upmarket restaurants around the town too. Piñons serves innovative American food in toned-down South-Western surroundings. Syzygy is a suave upstairs place with live jazz. There are some excellent Italian places, including Abetone and Farfalla (where queueing is part of the dining experience). Cache Cache does good-value French with Italian options.

Cheaper places include Ute City Banque, serving grills and seafood in a lively atmosphere; Hard Rock Cafe – part of the famous chain, with one of Madonna's cast-off basques on display; Planet Hollywood – opened here last season, taking over the premises with the famous opening roof – so you can see the stars above you as well as those next to you; Poppie's Bistro Cafe – famous for its breads and puddings; and Su Casa – probably the best Mexican.

Krabloonik, outside Snowmass, reachable by car or cross-country skis, has a rustic log cabin atmosphere.

ACTIVITIES
Indoor Aspen Athletic Club (racquetball, swimming, free weights, aerobics classes, sauna, steam, jacuzzi), skating
Outdoor Ballooning, para-gliding, snowcat tours, snow-shoe tours, sleigh rides, dog-sledding, snow-mobiles, tours of mines

TOURIST OFFICE
Postcode CO 81612
Tel 010 1 (303) 9251220
Fax 9253785

1 km

Silver Queen

APRES-SKI
Party time
Immediately after skiing, Ajax Tavern next to the Little Nell (formerly Shlomo's) is the place to be in Aspen.

There are lots of other bars to move on to, early or late in the evening. The J-bar of the Jerome hotel and the Red Onion still have a local feel to them, attracting a changing crowd throughout the evening. There is the statutory micro-brewery, with the Flying Dog basement bar attached. Shooters Saloon is a splendid country and western dive, with pool tables and (if you're lucky) line-dancing. Legends is a livelier bar, with table football and pool. La Cantina serves the best margaritas in town. The Double Diamond is a big, brash, busy place that has video, good bands and dancing. Tippler is a quite spacious disco-bar, good for meeting people. For exclusive peace and quiet, wangle an invitation to the Caribou club.

FOR NON-SKIERS
Silver service
Aspen has lots to offer the non-skier, especially if you've got a high credit card limit and like shopping. Just wandering around town is pleasant. Getting up the mountains to meet skiers for lunch is easy. Most hotels have excellent spa facilities.

Breckenridge 2925m

HOW IT RATES

Ratings for extent, advanced and intermediates relate to the whole Ski the Summit area, including Copper Mountain, Keystone and Arapahoe Basin.

The skiing

Snow	*****
Extent	****
Advanced	****
Intermediates	****
Beginners	****
Convenience	***
Queues	****
Restaurants	*

The rest

Scenery	***
Resort charm	***
Not skiing	***

ORIENTATION

Breckenridge is based around the long Main Street, with a lot of accommodation towards the top-end where two high-speed quad chairs head up into the skiing. They lead to Peak 9, one of four mountains all linked by lifts and pistes. A regular free shuttle runs around the resort to the Peak 9 and Peak 8 lifts.

Breckenridge was bought in 1993 by the owners of nearby **Keystone** and **Arapahoe Basin**; all three are now covered on the same lift ticket. A Ski the Summit lift pass also covers **Copper Mountain**. These four ski areas are linked by free buses. Those with a car can also try the resorts of **Vail**, **Beaver Creek** and **Steamboat**, all less than two hours' drive.

SKI FACTS

Breckenridge only

Altitude	2925m-3960m
Lifts	17
Pistes	1915 acres
Green	15%
Blue	27%
Black	58%
Art. snow	362 acres

✔ Varied local ski area with something for all standards

✔ Together with Keystone, Arapahoe Basin and Copper Mountain, forms the enormous Ski the Summit ski area, linked by free buses

✔ Efficient lift system means few queues

✔ Lively bars, restaurants and nightlife by US standards

✔ Based on restored Victorian mining town, with many new buildings in attractive 19th-century style

✗ The local ski area is rather small, with few long runs

✗ At almost 3000m it is one of the world's highest resorts, meaning acclimatisation problems for some coming straight from lower altitudes

Breckenridge was the first US resort to market itself aggressively on the British market, and at the end of the 1980s attracted large numbers of British visitors. Many were on their first American skiing trip, and came back impressed. Apparently, Breckenridge still gets more Brits than any other American resort, but we've noticed a rapid decline in the number of skiers reporting on the place – as if many of those first-timers had come back with a taste for skiing in the US, but not particularly for skiing in Breckenridge.

You can't blame them. By European standards, the local ski area is not huge – though it does have some good skiing for advanced skiers. But both they and intermediates will want to explore the rest of the Ski the Summit area on a week or 10-day trip. And if you're looking for the atmosphere of the old West, there are better – rather less Disneyesque – resorts.

Breckenridge is, however, probably the best base for exploration of the whole Ski the Summit area; it's certainly more lively and attractive than the other resorts in the conglomerate (Keystone and Copper Mountain). Between them the resorts offer an enormous amount of skiing – more than enough to keep even the keenest intermediate piste basher happy for a couple of weeks.

The resort

Breckenridge was founded in 1859 and became a booming gold-mining town in the latter part of the century. The biggest ever gold nugget, weighing nearly 14 pounds and named Tom's Baby, was unearthed here. The old wooden and clapboard buildings have been well renovated and form the bottom part of Main Street. Over 250 restored Victorian buildings are included in what is Colorado's largest national historic district. New shopping malls and buildings have been added in similar style – though they are obvious modern additions.

The town centre is attractively lively in the evening, with plenty of shops and over 100 restaurants and bars. Christmas lights and decorations remain on the lamp-posts throughout the season, giving the town an air of non-stop winter festivity. This is enhanced by a number of real winter festivals such as Ullr Fest – a carnival honouring the Norse God of Winter – and Ice Sculpture championships which leave wonderful sculptures for weeks afterwards.

Hotels and condominiums built in more modern style are spread over a wide, wooded area and are linked by a regular Town Trolley. Breckenridge also boasts more ski-in, ski-out accommodation than any other Colorado resort.

The skiing

The local skiing takes place on four separate peaks, linked by lift and piste. Boringly, they are named Peaks 7, 8, 9 and 10 – going from right to left as you look at the mountain. Though there's something for all standards, the keen piste-basher will want to explore the rest of Summit County too – Keystone, Copper Mountain and Arapahoe Basin. If anything, Breckenridge has the least interesting skiing of the Summit County resorts.

LIFT PASSES

94/95 prices in dollars
**Breckenridge-
Keystone**
Covers all lifts in
Breckenridge,
Keystone and
Arapahoe Basin.
Beginners
2 beginners' lifts.
Beginners and
novices have a
reduced area pass in
ski school.
Main pass
1-day pass 40
6-day pass 192
Senior citizens
Over 65: 6-day pass
150 (22% off)
Children
Under 13: 6-day pass
102 (47% off)
Under 6: free pass
Notes Breckenridge,
Keystone and
Arapahoe are all a
ski-bus ride apart.
Discounts for groups
of over 20. Over 70s
have a further
discounted pass
price. All passes
(except day-pass)
allow one non-skiing
day; 6-day pass valid
for 7 days with one
non-skiing day.
Alternative passes
Ski the Summit
coupon booklets
interchangeable for
lift pass at
Breckenridge, Copper
Mountain, Keystone
and Arapahoe Basin
(6 days skiing out of
7 adult 210).

SKI SCHOOL

94/95 prices in dollars
**Breckenridge
Classes** 6 days
4½hr: 10am-12.15 and
1.45-4pm; 2hr 15min:
am or pm
6 full days: 198
Children's classes
Ages: 4 to 12
6 full days including
lunch and ski-pass:
318
Private lessons
Hourly, up to 6hr
70 for 1hr; each
additional person 25

THE SKI AREA
Small but fragmented
Two high-speed quad chair-lifts go
from the top end of town up to
Peak 9, one accessing mainly green
runs on the lower half of the hill, the
other mainly blues higher up. From
there you can ski down to **Peak 10**,
which has a large number of blue and
black runs served by a single high-
speed quad lift.

Skiing down the other flank of Peak
9 takes you to a lift up into the **Peak
8** skiing – tough stuff at the top, easier
lower down. The base lifts of Peak 8 at
the Bergenhof can also be reached by
the town shuttle bus. From the top
T-bar of Peak 8, you can traverse to
the new, all-black **Peak 7** skiing
which has no lifts of its own – you ski
out back to the base of Peak 8.

At the end of the day two trails lead
back down to town from Peak 8 –
Sawmill to the main Peak 9 lifts and
Four O'Clock down towards the centre
of town. Or you can catch a bus.

SNOW RELIABILITY
Excellent
With the village at almost 3000m (the
highest of the main North American
resorts) and the skiing going up to
almost 4000m, it's no surprise that
Breckenridge boasts an excellent snow
record. That is supplemented by
substantial artificial snowmaking
that is mainly intended for pre-
Christmas use.

FOR ADVANCED SKIERS
Quite a few short but tough runs
A remarkable 58% of Breckenridge's
runs are classified as 'Most Difficult'
(single black diamond) or 'Expert'
(double black diamond) terrain. That's
a higher proportion than even in the
famous 'macho' resorts such as
Jackson Hole, Taos and Snowbird. But
remember Breckenridge is not a big ski
area by European standards, so most
good skiers will want to spend a good
proportion of their time exploring the
other Ski the Summit resorts.

Peak 7 is an entirely off-piste skiing
area. It reputedly has some good steep
runs both above and through the
trees. But it opened last season for the
first time, and when we were there in
January there wasn't enough snow.

Peak 8 has some good open skiing in
Horseshoe and Contest bowls, where
the snow normally remains good. But
the runs are short by European
standards and they aren't remarkably
steep despite their double black
diamond rating.

We particularly liked the skiing in

the back bowls of Peak 8. This is
basically ski-anywhere terrain among
a thin covering of trees and bushes.
Lots of runs, such as Lobo, Hombre,
Amen and Adios, are marked on the
trail map. But in practice you can
easily skip between them and invent
your own way down. It's picturesque
and not too steep. Double diamond
black mogul fields lead down under
Chair 4 to the junction with Peak 9.

Peak 9 itself has nothing to offer
advanced skiers except very steep
blacks from the top down under Chair
E on the North Face. These had very
patchy snow covering on each of our
visits, conditions which probably
account for their fearsome names such
as Devil's Crotch and Satan's Inferno.

Peak 10 offers much more interest.
Off to the right of the chair, at the
edge of the ski area, is a network of
interlinking black mogul runs by the
side of the downhill course –
consistently steep and bumpy. To the
left of the chair is a lightly wooded
off-piste area, The Burn.

FOR INTERMEDIATE SKIERS
Nice cruising – but not much of it
Breckenridge has some good blue
cruising runs for all standards of
intermediate. But dedicated piste
bashers will find it very limited and
will want to visit the other Summit
County resorts.

Peak 9 has the easiest skiing. It is
nearly all gentle, wide blues at the top
and greens at the bottom. Timid
intermediates will find it delightful.

Peak 10 has a couple of more
challenging runs graded blue-black,
such as Crystal and Centennial, which
make for good fast cruising.

Peak 8 has a choice of blues down
through trails cut close together in the
trees. We particularly liked the quiet
Claimjumper, which is skied less than
the others because of its position at
the far northern end of the ski area,
next to the boundary.

More adventurous intermediates
will also like to try some of the high
bowl skiing (see above). And Keystone
and Copper Mountain both offer
miles of excellent intermediate terrain.

FOR BEGINNERS
Excellent
The bottom of Peak 9 has a big,
virtually flat area and some good
gentle nursery slopes. There's then a
good choice of green runs to move on
to. Beginners can try Peak 8 too, with
another selection of green runs and a
choice of trails which take you right
back to town.

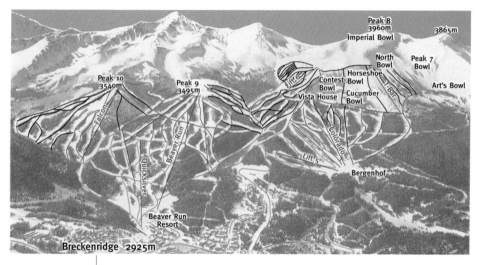

Peak 8
3960m
Imperial Bowl

3865m

North
Bowl

Peak 7
Bowl

Horseshoe

Contest
Bowl

Cucumber
Bowl

Art's Bowl

Vista House

Peak 9
3495m

Peak 10
3540m

Lift 6

Lift 7

Colorado

Falcon

Beaver Run

Lift 5

Bergenhof

Quicksilver

Beaver Run
Resort

Breckenridge 2925m

FOR CROSS-COUNTRY
Specialist centre in woods
Breckenridge's Nordic Centre is prettily set in the woods between the town and Peak 8 (and is served by the shuttle bus). It has 38km of trails.

QUEUES
Not normally a problem
Breckenridge's four high-speed quads (two on Peak 9 and one each on Peaks 8 and 10) make light work of peak-time crowds. We've never come across serious queues and neither have our reporters except in exceptional circumstances, such as after watching a competition.

MOUNTAIN RESTAURANTS
Unexciting
Mountain eating is fairly typical of US resorts: large, efficient self-service cafeterias which serve standard fare of burgers, pasta, chillis in a rather utilitarian atmosphere – and very crowded at peak time.

Vistahaus, at the top of Peak 8, is the best of a poor bunch and known for its soups and pizzas.

SKI SCHOOL
Usual American efficiency
Our reporters were unanimous in their praise for the workings of the ski school: classes of five to eight, doing what the class, not the instructor, wants, special clinics on how to ski bumps or powder or make a quantum leap in your skiing.

A typical comment was 'Standards of tuition were excellent, with instructors showing genuine interest and pleasure in your progress' and 'I went to three special clinics on improving turns, style and skiing bumps. They were all excellent and my skiing leapt ahead as a result'.

CHILDCARE

At each major lift base there is a Children's Center (453 3250), with 'fun facilities' and a complex array of options for all-day care from 8.30 to 4.30. Peak 8 takes children from 2 months, and runs a Snow Play programme for those aged 2 years; both Centers offer this for non-skiers aged 3 to 5. Special ski school classes are held for those aged 3, mornings only. Those aged 4 or 5 have their own junior ski school. Children aged 6 to 12 go into ordinary children's ski school, but all-day care is available at Kid's Castle meeting areas at each lift base.

There is also a separate Kinderhut children's ski school (453 0379) at Beaver Run Resort, with 'magic carpet' ski-lift, offering all-day care.

GETTING THERE

Air Denver, transfer 2½hr.

PACKAGES

American Connections, American Dream, American Skiworld, Bladon Lines, Chalets 'Unlimited', Crystal, Enterprise, Equity Total Ski, Inghams, Made to Measure, Ski Activity, Ski Independence, Ski Val, Snow Cocktail, USAirtours

Frisco Equity Total Ski

FACILITIES FOR CHILDREN
Excellent facilities

We have few reports, but the facilities for infants seem splendid, with the usual American emphasis on having fun. Teenagers have special ski school classes aimed at achieving maximum mileage and fun.

 # Staying there

Breckenridge is quite a spread-out resort. Although there is probably as much ski-in accommodation here as anywhere in the US, there is also a fair amount of accommodation away from Main Street and the lift base-stations. But the efficient free shuttle buses serve most of the accommodation until late.

The area between the base of Peak 9 and Main Street is the best location if you plan to go out in the evening.

HOW TO GO
Lots of choice

Over a dozen tour operators feature Breckenridge in their programme and it's easy to arrange your own holiday there too – Resort Express runs regular transfers from Denver airport to Breckenridge.

Chalets Crystal have various mock-Victorian houses – all as well equipped as you would expect in the US, and all but one close to the lifts. The other tour operators here all have similarly attractive places, though many of them are out of town. American Skiworld's Clearview chalet is centrally positioned, and Ski Independence have an equally well located place. Crystal and Ski Val have some particularly good out-of-town places.

Hotels There's a good choice of style and price range, including several 'resorts' – large complexes which may include self-catering units and shops as well as hotel facilities.

££££ Breckenridge Hilton Prime location, vast rooms (it was built as condos) and good facilities make this recently renovated hotel very popular with British skiers. Pool, tubs.

££££ Lodge at Breckenridge Stylish new luxury spa resort set out of town among 32 acres, with great views. Private shuttle bus. Pool, tubs.

££££ Allaire Timbers Inn Exclusive new B&B (eight rooms, two suites) a little way from lifts and downtown. Good views. Tub.

£££ Beaver Run Huge resort complex with 520 rooms, very convenient for the skiing.

£££ Williams House Beautifully

restored, charmingly furnished four-room B&B on Main St.

££ Fireside Inn Cosy New England-style B&B. Historic part of town. Tub.

££ Breckenridge Mountain Lodge Straightforward, good-value accommodation. Tubs.

£ Breckenridge Wayside Inn Friendly budget place out of town by golf course. Tub.

Self-catering There is a huge choice of

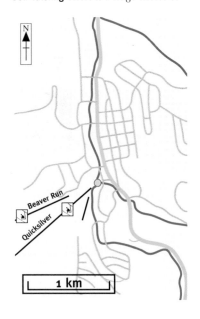

ACTIVITIES

Indoor Sports clubs, swimming, sauna, massage, jacuzzi, cinema, theatre, art gallery, library, indoor miniature golf course **Outdoor** Heli-skiing, horse- and dog-sleigh rides, rafting, fishing, snow-mobiles, snow coach rides, toboggans, scooters, mountain biking

TOURIST OFFICE

Postcode CO 80424
Tel 010 1 (303)
4535000
Fax 4533202

condominiums, many set along the aptly named Four O'Clock run for ski-in (but not ski-out) convenience. Comfortable, well-equipped and conveniently located condos include Liftside Inn (Ski Activity, Enterprise), Tannhaüser, Pine Ridge (both Crystal), River Mountain Lodge (American Skiworld), Sundowner, Wedgewood (both Inghams), Tyra Summit and Wildwood (both numerous operators). The above-mentioned Beaver Run resort (numerous operators) has self-catering as well as hotel accommodation which is probably the most luxurious available on a package.

STAYING DOWN THE VALLEY
Good for exploring Summit County
Staying in Frisco, which is on the route of the Summit Stage shuttle between all the Summit County resorts, is a real possibility for those touring around or on a tight budget. It's a small town based on a Victorian settlement, where the stage-coach used to stop.

There are several cheap motels (including the old stagecoach stop, now the Frisco Inn), some B&B places and a Best Western hotel.

EATING OUT
Over 100 restaurants
There's a very wide range of eating places, with pretty much everything you'd expect, from typical American food to 'fine-dining', and almost every ethnic cuisine you could wish for.

The Brewery is famous for its enormous portions of appetisers such as Buffalo Wings which will fill you up cheaply – as well as its splendid brewed-on-the-spot beers. We particularly liked the Avalanche beer.

The Whale's Tail has been highly recommended for its seafood, lively atmosphere and good, half-price children's portions.

The Cajun Café was recommended by several reporters for its spicy Creole food. The Village Pasta Co serves good fresh pasta and El Perdido 'giant quantities of fantastic Mexican food'. The Red Orchid Chinese was praised. Windy City is 'a simple pizza place but the food is great'. Café Alpine is good for Spanish tapas.

APRES-SKI
The best in Summit County
There's a good, lively after-skiing atmosphere, but things quieten down considerably later. The Breckenridge Brewery, a real working brewery with vats visible from the bar, is the 'in' place at tea-time, though it's not for those who dislike crowds and noise. Its main rival is Jake T Pounders at the Peak 9 base-station, which has live music. Jake is an unusual owner – he's a dog! The Gold Pan dates from Goldrush days, and is reputedly the oldest bar west of the Mississippi. Behind its saloon doors is a good atmosphere, with live music most nights. Shamus O'Toole's roadhouse is good if you want to meet 'redneck' locals straight out of a Burt Reynolds movie. Downstairs at Eric's is a trendy disco bar. Colts Down Under is one of the few lively late bars. Tiffany's is the livelier of the two main discos, especially on the weekly cheap night.

FOR NON-SKIERS
Far from ideal
Breckenridge is a pleasant place to wander around, and not without distractions. But a non-skier staying for a week or 10 days would find it pretty limiting, and the excursion possibilities are few. Skiers should be quite happy to return to one of the base-stations for lunchtime meetings.

Copper Mountain 2960m

HOW IT RATES

Ratings for extent, advanced and intermediates relate to the whole Ski the Summit area, including Breckenridge, Keystone and Arapahoe Basin.

The skiing

Snow	*****
Extent	****
Advanced	****
Intermediates	****
Beginners	****
Convenience	***
Queues	****
Restaurants	*

The rest

Scenery	***
Resort charm	*
Not skiing	*

SKI FACTS

Altitude	2960m-3770m
Lifts	20
Pistes	1330 acres
Green	23%
Blue	36%
Black	41%
Art. snow	270 acres

PACKAGES

American Connections, Club Med

TOURIST OFFICE

Postcode CO 80443
Tel 010 1 (303) 9682882
Fax 9682308

Copper Mountain has little charm but great skiing. It is part of the Ski the Summit region and is well worth a day or two's skiing if you are staying in the more atmospheric resorts of Breckenridge or Keystone.

THE RESORT

Copper Mountain is a functional, purpose-built resort, high on convenience, low on charm – rather like some French purpose-built resorts. The apartment blocks are surprisingly spread out, making the free shuttle bus pretty essential. There is little in the way of shops or ambience away from the area at the base of the skiing. It has a big conference market and the only Club Med ski village in North America. It's good for families, with superb children's facilities, spacious self-catering accommodation and quiet evenings. There's a fine sports club (free entrance to resort guests), with a huge pool and indoor tennis.

Copper is a Ski the Summit resort, and has half-hourly buses to the others: Keystone, Breckenridge and Arapahoe Basin.

THE SKIING

The **ski area** is quite sizeable by American standards, and it is very easy to work out where you want to ski. As you look up at the mountain, the easiest runs are on the the right hand side and the terrain gradually gets steeper the further left you go. Two high-speed quads whizz you up to the tree-line, from where numerous runs head back towards the base. Further lifts serve the resort's open bowls.

Height and an extensive snowmaking operation give Copper very good **snow reliability.**

The 'Extreme Experience' off-piste skiing is superb for experts, and well organised. It's accessed via the Storm King lift up to Copper Peak. Guides are compulsory, avalanche bleepers provided, and a shuttle bus is laid on to return skiers from the end of the trails. 'Mere' **advanced skiers** have fewer options, though Spaulding Bowl offers plenty of choice and there are great bump runs through the trees to the bottom of the two lifts on the left as you look at the mountain.

Good **intermediates** have the benefit of the steepest runs also being the longest. These are in the Copper Peak section. The slightly less proficient can enjoy shorter, gentler runs on the middle section of mountain, while early intermediates have gentle cruising terrain in the Union Peak section.

The nursery slopes are excellent for **beginners**, and there are plenty of very easy green runs in 'slow skiing zones' to graduate to.

Copper is one of the least impressive American areas for **cross-country**, though the 25km of trails through the woods at the base of Union mountain are quite pleasant.

Copper has a lot of skiing served by few lifts, and **queues** are a problem in peak season. However, the uncrowded pistes compensate for delays.

The one **mountain restaurant** is mediocre, and many people prefer to ski back to the base for lunch.

The **ski school** has a fine reputation, especially for teaching children.

The all-day ski kindergarten takes **children** from 3 years, and has its slopes right outside the nursery. The nursery takes children from 2 months old and, as well as the usual facilities, provides cooking and crafts. Evening babysitters are also available.

STAYING THERE

Copper Mountain is essentially a **condominium** resort. All 12 condo complexes are in excellent condition and have all mod cons. The resort has been awarded four diamonds by the American AA for accommodation standards. We have heard rave reports of West Lodge, but other places are also very good.

Copper's only **hotel** is Foxpine Inn. It has well appointed rooms and a swimming pool. There are hotels nearby in Dillon and Frisco on the Ski the Summit bus route.

There are only half-a-dozen **restaurants**, but all are quite good. O'Shea's is an Old West-style barbecue place, Steak Out is good, Pesce Fresco's has an international menu that includes fine fish and the sports club's restaurant does excellent salads.

Nightlife is very quiet. The 'pub' in Copper Commons is a wine bar. A multi-screen cinema is nearby. Evening sleigh rides take people out to a dinner. Other activities for **non-skiers** centre around the The Racquet & Athletic Club and West Lake.

Crested Butte 2855m

HOW IT RATES

The skiing

Snow	****
Extent	**
Advanced	****
Intermediates	***
Beginners	****
Convenience	***
Queues	****
Restaurants	*

The rest

Scenery	***
Resort charm	***
Not skiing	**

✔ *Known for its 'extreme' skiing*

✔ *Enough non-extreme steep runs to amuse advanced skiers for a while*

✔ *Excellent for beginners and for near-beginners, with long easy runs*

✔ *Charming, tiny, restored Victorian mining town with good restaurants*

✔ *Alternative of convenient ski-village*

✔ *Excellent ski school, with a special courses for skiers with disabilities*

✔ *Better-than-average scenery for Colorado*

✘ *Skiing limited for confident intermediate piste-bashers*

✘ *Old town is ten minutes from ski village by shuttle bus*

✘ *Out on a limb, away from mainstream Colorado resorts*

✘ *Only one satisfactory mountain restaurant*

Crested Butte is not yet well-known in Britain, but they're working on it. Among expert skiers who are at home on very steep unprepared runs – and 'extreme' skiers who like their mountains as steep as possible – it enjoys cult status, thanks to the extent and gradient of the slopes on the outer fringes of the ski area. Meanwhile, the commercial success of the place depends on beginners and timid intermediates, for whom the long groomed slopes of the main ski area are ideal. Skiers in these two groups can safely include Crested Butte on their short-lists. Mileage-hungry piste-bashers should stay away.

The resort

Crested Butte takes its name from its mountain – an isolated peak (a butte, pronounced 'beaut') with a distinctive shape. Crested Butte started life as a coal-mining town in the late 1800s; it is now one of the most attractive resorts in the Rockies – just a few narrow streets with beautifully restored wooden buildings and sidewalks, and the tiniest imaginable town jail, straight out of a Western. Elk Avenue, the main street, is a five-minute stroll from top to bottom, and is lined with bars, restaurants and shops. There's even a classic general store, run by an old-timer.

The bars and restaurants are varied in price and character. But wherever you go you'll find genuinely friendly and hospitable locals. And mingled with them you'll find a fair share of down-to-earth celebrities.

The ski village of Mount Crested Butte is a huge contrast to the town of Crested Butte. Nearly all the buildings are modern and characterless, and you can judge the appeal of the place from the fact that its central focus is a bus station and car park – recently reduced in size by the construction of the new Mountain Lair hotel. There is a cluster of bars and restaurants at the foot of the slopes, around the large Grande Butte hotel.

ORIENTATION

Crested Butte is a small resort in a rather inaccessible corner of Colorado, well away from the Denver-Breckenridge-Vail mainstream.

⛷ The skiing

It's a small area, but it packs in an astonishing mixture of perfect beginner slopes, easy cruising runs and the steepest cliff-jumping extreme skiing in North America. The only people who might not be suited by this mixture are piste-bashing adventurous intermediates who like to ski different runs all the time and good skiers who don't fancy extreme terrain.

THE SKI AREA
A Jekyll and Hyde mountain
Two main lifts leave the base area. The Silver Queen high-speed chair-lift takes advanced skiers to black runs and lifts which access the steepest runs. Those just off the nursery slopes will take the Keystone lift to the easiest runs, and intermediates can access cruising blue runs from either.

SNOW RELIABILITY
Excellent – usually
Crested Butte claims to benefit from snowstorms approaching from several directions, and it has a substantial snowmaking installation which covers runs from most of the lifts. We've usually had superb snow here. But in 1994, cover in the early part of the season was thin, keeping the North Face closed until well into the season.

SKI FACTS

Altitude 2775m-3620m
Lifts   13
Pistes   1160 acres
Green   13%
Blue   29%
Black   58%
Art. snow   238 acres

LIFT PASSES

94/95 prices in dollars
Crested Butte
Mountain Resort
Covers all lifts in
Crested Butte only.
Beginners Beginners'
lessons in ski school
includes lift pass.
Main pass
1-day pass 42
6-day pass 222
(low season 153 –
31% off)
Short-term passes
Half-day pass
available (adult 30).
Notes Free lift passes
for first weeks of
season (28/11/94 to
16/12/94), with
reductions on ski hire
and lodgings. All lift
passes over 4 days
allow for one day off,
4 days skiing in 5, 6
out of 7 days.
Children under 13 pay
their age for each
day's skiing.

FOR ADVANCED SKIERS
Some cult terrain

For those up to leaping off cliffs and
skiing steep slopes through the trees,
Crested Butte has an abundance of
double black diamond runs accessed
by two high drag-lifts. The older North
Face lift leads to a series of runs down
the east flank of the mountain, where
there are numerous cliffs, steep
couloirs, rocks and trees to negotiate.
The sign as you enter the North Face
area reads 'This terrain is the steepest
lift-served terrain in North America.
Experts only'.

The High Lift, added a few years ago,
opened up a whole new range of
extreme skiing possibilities previously
reached only by long climbs,
including Paradise Cliffs, Paradise
Headwall and a whole series of runs
on the western side of the ski area.

Not all of the North Face skiing is
extreme; but for the typical black-piste
mogul skier Crested Butte is much
more limited.

FOR INTERMEDIATE SKIERS
Not a lot

Similarly, good intermediate skiers are
likely to find the area limited unless
they enjoy perfecting their technique
on the same few runs each day.

For early, unsure intermediates,
Crested Butte has attractions. The east-
facing runs down the Paradise,
Teocalli and East River lifts are all
wide, fairly gentle, well groomed and
normally uncrowded cruising runs
which can be taken fast or slow. There
are usually several variations to choose
from, ending up back at the same lifts.

A particularly gentle and uncrowded
area is that served by the Gold Link
lift, isolated from the rest of the skiing
and good for near-beginners too.

FOR BEGINNERS
Excellent

There are excellent nursery slopes near
the village. After that you'll be taking
the Keystone chair-lift up to a choice
of several long, easy green runs
leading back down again. Or you can
stop off part-way down to catch the
Painter Boy lift. This has green runs
down again or you can try the easy
blues down the Gold Link lift.

FOR CROSS-COUNTRY
Looks good

There are 30km of cross-country trails
near the Nordic Ski Centre in the old
town of Crested Butte.

QUEUES
No problem

Queues are virtually non-existent
except at peak periods. The trails are
quiet and uncrowded too. Moving
peak-period crowds up the mountain
was speeded up a couple of years ago
by replacing the main Silver Queen lift
with a new high-speed quad chair.

MOUNTAIN RESTAURANTS
Only one worth visiting

Most people ski back to the base-
station for lunch – not a hardship. The
main restaurant at the base of the
Paradise lift is fairly civilised, with a
wooden interior and good choice of
food. There's even a table-service
restaurant inside as well as the large

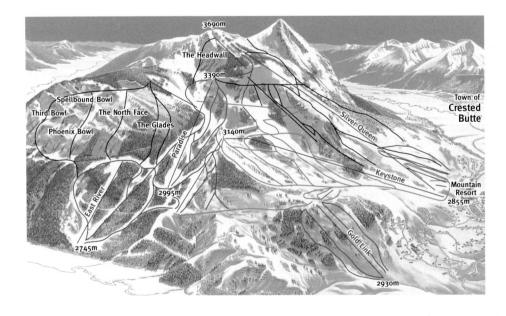

SKI SCHOOL

94/95 prices in dollars

Crested Butte
Classes 5 days
4hr: 10.30-12.30 and
1.30-3.30; 2hr: am or
pm; 3hr: from 12.45
5 2hr days: 116
Children's classes
Ages: 2 to 12
6 8hr days including
lunch: 300
Private lessons
1½hr to 6hr
74 for 1½hr; each
additional person 25

CHILDCARE

The Children's Centre
in the Whetstone
building, at the foot
of the slopes, offers a
comprehensive range
of care for children
aged 6 months to 7
years, from 8.30 to
4.30. There are
separate ski classes
for children aged 2 to
3, 4 to 7, and 8 to 12,
split into beginners
and non-beginners.

GETTING THERE

Air Denver, transfer
4½hr. Gunnison,
transfer 1hr.

PACKAGES

American
Connections,
American Dream,
American Skiworld,
Crystal, Made to
Measure, Ski Activity,
Ski Independence

ACTIVITIES

Indoor Racquetball,
swimming, hot tubs,
weight-training,
aerobic classes,
saunas
Outdoor Snow-
mobiling, sleigh rides,
ballooning, winter
horse riding,
mountain barbecues

TOURIST OFFICE

Postcode CO 81225
Tel 010 1 (303)
3492201
Fax 3492250

self-service and outdoor barbecue
areas. The other restaurant, at the base
of the Twister lift, is accurately
described as a warming house. The
food is primitive, and many callers
bring their own.

SKI SCHOOL
A major asset

Run by French-Swiss Jean Pavaillard,
the ski school has won the Best Ski
School in Colorado vote several times
in recent years. It offers the usual
flexible options you find in US ski
schools of specialised clinics (eg
bumps, powder, racing) as well as
normal group and private lessons.

There are free daily mountain tours
for intermediate or better skiers, and
the ski school has a high reputation
for teaching people with disabilities.

FACILITIES FOR CHILDREN
Comprehensive

Crested Butte takes childcare seriously,
and the facilities look excellent.

Staying there

Most of the accommodation is at the
ski village. From some places you can
stroll to the lifts; but many condos, in
particular, are much further away and
dependent on the ski-bus. There is
some accommodation in the town.

HOW TO GO
Plenty of choice

Practically all the tour operators with
serious US programmes offer packages
to Crested Butte, mainly in hotels.
Chalets We don't know of any.
Hotels You have a broad range of
options, from international-style
comfort to home-like character.
£££ Grand Butte Big, anonymous,
comfortable, convenient (right at the
foot of the slopes) and used by most of
the British tour operators. Small
swimming pool; sauna and hot tub.
££ Nordic Inn B&B The oldest hotel
in the mountain village, only a short
walk from the lifts. It has an outdoor
hot tub, friendly service from Alan
Cox and his staff, and large rooms.
££ Manor Lodge Comfortable modern
hotel close to the lifts, with live
entertainment most evenings.
££ Crested Butte Lodge More
modern, nearer the centre, with an
indoor pool, sauna and outdoor hot
tub – and much more personal than
the Grand Butte.
££ The Inn at Crested Butte Brand-
new non-smoking hotel on the edge
of the old town. Outdoor hot tub.

££ Elk Mountain Lodge Renovated
miners' hotel in old town with good
rooms. B&B only.
££ Gothic Inn Five-room Alpine-style
B&B in the town.
Self-catering There are literally
thousands of apartments available to
rent, mainly in the ski village. Crested
Mountain Village apartments are
perhaps the most convenient and
have pool, hot tubs, saunas and
friendly and efficient reception
facilities. The Buttes, the Gateway and
the Plaza are also recommended. The
Three Seasons condos (American
Skiworld) have plenty of mod cons but
are some way from the lifts.

EATING OUT
Better than you'd expect

For such a small place Crested Butte
has a surprisingly high number of
decent restaurants – nearly all of them
in the old town. Top of the pile is
undoubtedly Soupcon, a tiny place in
an old log cabin just off the main
street, serving refined French food. Le
Bosquet and Timberline run it close.
The Idle Spur is the statutory micro-
brewery, doing satisfying food as well
as a range of beers.

APRES-SKI
Lively bars

The old town of Crested Butte has
plenty of diversions for a short stay,
provided you're not looking for great
sophistication or variety. Kochevar's is
an amusing Wild-West saloon,
complete with shuffleboard (the
American-size version of shove-
ha'penny). Out at the ski village,
Rafters usually has a lot going on.

FOR NON-SKIERS
Limited

Charming though it is, Crested Butte
won't keep most non-skiers amused
for very long.

STAYING UP THE MOUNTAIN
A wilderness retreat

For good skiers, cross-country skiers,
snowmobile fans and those who
simply like to get away from it all,
Crested Butte has something special.

Irwin Lodge is a great wooden barn
of a place in a remote back-country
area, reached in winter only by snowcat or snow-mobile. It has an outdoor
hot tub, great views and fairly simple
rooms above a huge communal sitting
room with open fire. Most people go
there for the guided powder skiing,
with uplift by snow-cat. Heli-skiing is
envisaged, but not yet available.

Jackson Hole 1925m

HOW IT RATES

The skiing

Snow	★★★
Extent	★★
Advanced	★★★★★
Intermediates	★★★
Beginners	★★★
Convenience	★★★
Queues	★★
Restaurants	★

The rest

Scenery	★★★
Resort charm	★★★
Not skiing	★★

✔ One of the toughest ski areas in the US, with some truly radical terrain

✔ Jackson town has more genuine Wild West character than any other US ski resort

✔ People are friendly and hospitable – they want you to have fun

✔ Good variety of cross-country skiing

✔ Beautiful, unspoilt location in a remote part of the US, with several other attractions in the region

✗ There are too few lifts and they're mainly old and slow

✗ Queues, especially for the aerial tram (cable-car), can be bad

✗ It's a long journey from the UK

✗ Primitive mountain restaurants

✗ Snow can be poor on the lower slopes

✗ Limited scope for improving beginners and timid skiers

If you're an adventurous skier and want a real American Wild West atmosphere, Jackson Hole is the place to go. Cowboys – genuine and 'dude' – roam the wooden sidewalks, fall out of saloons, play pool, and dance to country music. The tiny town is the only place for miles around for the ranchers to go. In summer there are staged gunfights every evening, in the town square, underneath the elk antler archways.

But in winter you're more likely to be killed by your own foolishness in the ski area 12 miles away. Jackson Hole has serious skiing for serious skiers – steeps, jumps, narrow couloirs, bumps. Fifty per cent of the skiing is classed as 'expert' terrain – black, double-black and even blacker. It takes a very good skier to get the most out of the area. It takes good snow too – so you've got to be lucky with the weather. Anyone below adventurous and competent intermediate standard may soon get bored with the skiing – the ski area is not huge, and much of it will be beyond their capability. But there's plenty else to see, including the beautiful winter wildernesses of the nearby National Parks of Yellowstone and Grand Teton.

ORIENTATION

The town of Jackson, in the north-west corner of Wyoming, sits at the south-eastern edge of Jackson Hole – the 'hole' being the high, flat valley floor surrounded by mountain ranges. The skiing, 20km north-east, stretches up the eastern flanks of the mountains above Teton Village – a small, modern collection of lodgings, shops and restaurants. The quickest way up is the Tram (cable-car) but there is an alternative chair-lift route which doesn't take you quite to the top. On the fringe of Jackson town is the small Snow King ski area, where night skiing is possible. Within a one-hour drive is Grand Targhee resort, famous for its powder snow – buses run daily.

🏠 The resort

The town of Jackson, a 15-minute drive away from the slopes, is a real 'cowboy' town where skiers and ranchers meet in seemingly perfect harmony. It is small and compact, with characterful western saloons, wooden side-walks and good restaurants. Everywhere there are station-wagons and snow-mobiles, skis and stetsons, saloons and ski-bums – it's a strange mix and the effect is great. In among the cowboys and the log cabins there's now a sprinkling of upmarket galleries and downmarket souvenir shops. But, in winter at least, it retains a genuine Western feel.

🎿 The skiing

The ownership of the ski area area changed a couple of seasons ago, when the founder Paul McCollister finally sold out after a lengthy and costly legal battle. One of the new owners, John Resor, from a local ranching family, now runs the place and has plans for upgrading some of the lifts. He is also working at changing Jackson Hole's image from that of a big, tough ski mountain to one that suits intermediate skiers and family groups as well, but it is still a big, tough ski mountain. Good, experienced skiers will love the challenges on Rendezvous Mountain but, as yet, there's not enough suitable skiing for many intermediates.

THE SKI AREA
One big mountain, one small one
What makes Jackson Hole famous is the one big mountain – **Rendezvous.** The cable-car ('Tram') to its peak provides 1260m vertical drop – the biggest in the US – and serves terrain that's just riddled with chutes, cliffs, bumps and jumps. Signs saying 'experts only' tend to mean it.

Apres Vous mountain is adjacent to Rendezvous. Its peak is 600m lower and it has mainly blue and a few green trails as well as a handful of blacks. There's a half-pipe for snowboarders.

Two double chairs are needed to get from the base area to the summit of Apres Vous – Teewinot and then Apres

SKI FACTS

Altitude	1925m-3185m
Lifts	9
Pistes	2500 acres
Green	10%
Blue	40%
Black	50%
Art. snow	80 acres

Vous. Between the line of these chairs and the Tram there's another couple of chairs serving Casper Bowl and the Amphitheatre. Linking runs connect the Apres Vous and Casper areas. And from there you can work your way over to the two chairs on Rendezvous.

Ski Hosts provide hourly guided tours from the top of Rendezvous. And at 1.30pm on weekdays you can usually ski with Pepi Stiegler, head of the ski school and Olympic gold medal winner.

There's also a small ski area – **Snow King** – on the outskirts of Jackson town, floodlit in the evening.

SNOW RELIABILITY
Steep lower slopes can suffer

The claimed average of between 32ft and 38ft of 'mostly dry powder' snow sounds impressive, and for a core three-month season conditions are likely to be reasonable. But the base elevation here is relatively low for the Rockies, and early- and late-season skiers may well find insufficient cover for the steepish lower slopes like the Hobacks to be open. Snowmaking is limited to the runs on the lower part of Apres Vous mountain.

FOR ADVANCED SKIERS
Best for the brave

After a few runs on Apres Vous to warm up, most capable skiers will want to head for the Tram and take on the best that Rendezvous mountain has to offer. There's no gentle introduction here. So it is worth

pausing at the top to take in the views and pluck up your courage.

You should take the East Ridge Traverse at least once to stare over the edge of the awesome Corbet's couloir – it flattens out to 50° after the vertical entry. Corbet's is the best-known of many thrilling and potentially damaging features on a mountain that needs to be treated with great respect. It's the most famous because the Tram passes right above it and provides a great viewing platform for watching people throw themselves off its lip.

From Corbet's – top or bottom – it's possible to track over to Tensleep Bowl and the tricky Expert Chutes. Tower Three Chute is one of several accessed via the Thunder chair and is a typical example of the many steep, narrow chutes on Rendezvous. Laramie Bowl, which can be reached from the Upper Sublette quad as well as the Tram, has its own series of chutes – the Alta Chutes – and lower down some good bump and tree skiing. Cheyenne Bowl has open bowl skiing and, below it, some lovely runs through the trees.

The lower runs, including the Hobacks, at the edge of the ski area, are generally bumpy and frequently have less-than-ideal snow because of their orientation and altitude.

There are some heli-skiing operations to nearby ranges and some serious back-country routes down from Teton Pass – use a guide. A day's snowcat skiing in the powder of Grand Targhee, just over 40 miles away, is worth the excursion.

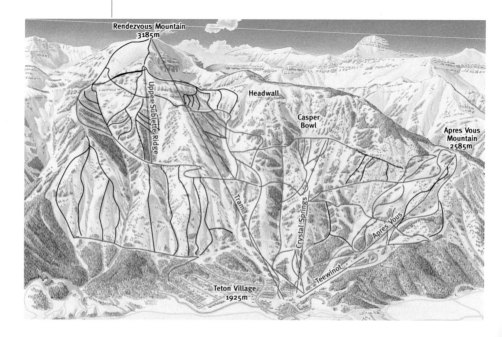

LIFT PASSES

94/95 prices in dollars
Jackson Hole
Covers all lifts and
includes free 'Tram'
tickets.
Main pass
1-day pass 44
6-day pass 240
Senior citizens
Over 65: 6-day pass
126 (48% off)
Children
Under 14: 6-day pass
126 (48% off)
Short-term passes
Afternoon pass from
12.30 (adult 34).
Notes 5 year-olds and
under have free use
on some lifts.
Alternative passes
Chair-lift only pass
excludes Tram (adult
6-day 216). Jackson
Hole Ski Three 5-day
voucher book covers
Jackson Hole, Grand
Targhee and Snow
King resorts (205).

FOR INTERMEDIATE SKIERS
Exciting for some

Most intermediates will be restricted
to Apres Vous for most of the time,
with only the bolder skiers graduating
to, and then enjoying, a few of the
runs on Rendezvous. There are great
cruising runs all over Apres Vous. And
Casper Bowl offers some quite gentle
bowl skiing. There are several black
runs on Apres Vous, many of which
are suitable for improving
intermediates to test their limits.

After that it's a case of checking out
the main mountain by traversing to
Thunder chair and seeking out the few
tough blues among the blacks and
double-blacks. Adventurous
intermediates will want to try their
luck from the top – Rendezvous Trail
is a good starting run and allows you
to take a look at the area.

FOR BEGINNERS
A small number of suitable slopes

There's a choice of two lifts – Eagle's
Rest and Teewinot double chairs – and
four or five runs. These runs are broad
and gentle – fine for getting started.
The problem comes thereafter and the
leap to tackling the runs off either the
Apres Vous or Crystal Springs chairs.
Beginners would really be best served
going to another resort – Jackson is for
experts, and is a long way to go to
learn to ski.

FOR CROSS-COUNTRY
Lots of possibilities

There are six centres in the valley
offering trails of various length and
difficulty and a chance to be mellow
in these beautiful surroundings. The

SKI SCHOOL

94/95 prices in dollars

Jackson Hole
Classes 6 days
4hr: 9.30-11.30 and
1.45-3.45; 2hr: am
or pm
6 full days: 160
Children's classes
Ages: 3 to 14
6 6hr days including
supervised lunch: 274
Private lessons
1hr, 2hr, half- or full-
day
115 for 2hr; 130 for
2 to 3 people

CHILDCARE

The Kids Ranch (739
2691) near the Crystal
Springs lift takes
children aged 2
months to 5 years,
from 8am to 5pm,
with indoor and
outdoor games and
one-to-one ski
lessons from age 3.

Spring Creek Nordic Centre has mainly beginner terrain and also offers moonlight tours. There's a Nordic Centre at Teton Village, with 22km of trails and organised trips into the National Parks.

QUEUES
Can be awful at the Tram

The lengthy legal battle before the ski area's change of ownership held up much-needed modernisation of the lift system. There are frequently long queues for the 30-year-old Tram, despite the extra supplement on top of the basic lift pass for the use of it. But the bad bottleneck in the key link from Apres Vous to Rendezvous should be alleviated this season when the Thunder chair is upgraded to a quad.

MOUNTAIN RESTAURANTS
Ski to the base area

There's only one restaurant on the mountain – at the base of Casper chair-lift – and it's very ordinary. The only other facilities are the snack-bars and toilets at the base of Thunder chair-lift and at the top station of the Tram (being upgraded for the coming season and renamed Corbet's Cabin). For a decent lunch, the best bet is to head to the base area. Nick Wilson's in the Clocktower building, the Alpenhof restaurant and the Mangy Moose are favourites.

SKI SCHOOL
Ski the Big One with confidence

Well that's what the school claims anyway. And it is the Pepi Stiegler ski school so maybe some of that Olympic magic will rub off. Classes are typically small, with only four to six in the group, and the instructors do generate lots of enthusiasm and work hard at the 'inner game' of confidence building. At the higher teaching levels they give an introduction to the wide terrain variations that the area provides and there are clinics for powder and mogul skiing.

All the reports we have are positive, with stress laid on fact that classes operate at all 11 levels regardless of how few pupils there are – two or three in a class is not at all unusual, more than eight exceptional.

FACILITIES FOR CHILDREN
Just fine

The ski area may not seem to be one ideally suited to children, but in fact there is enough easy skiing and the care facilities are as comprehensive as is usual in the US.

Staying there

If you want to be able to ski from the door, choose one of the hotels or condominiums in Teton Village. If you're happy with the idea of a 12-mile drive morning and evening, there's a far better choice of lodgings in the town of Jackson – and lots of other attractions. There is a regular and efficient bus service. Any of the town lodgings are likely to be within a five-minute walk of the town square.

HOW TO GO
Check out the package deals

There's a good variety of lodging styles on offer through UK tour operators – pretty well everything but the guest ranches are covered – and unless you're planning to visit other ski areas, it's likely there'll be a package to suit at a reasonable price. Driving to Jackson from one of the international airports is a long slog; there are now several flights daily to Jackson from Denver, Chicago and Salt Lake City.

Chalets Crystal have a comfortable catered condo five minutes' walk from Jackson town. American Skiworld have a similar style and standard of place close to the Snow King skiing. Both chalets are near stops for the bus to the main ski area.

Hotels From economy motels to expensive hotels and lodges there should be a style and price to suit most tastes. There are a handful of small B&B properties in and around Jackson – they tend not to be cheap, but do give a bit of an insight to the local lifestyle.

££££ Wort Hotel The ritziest place to stay: brick-built hotel right in the centre of town and proud owner of the Silver Dollar Bar. Hot tub.

££££ Inn at Jackson Hole Comfortable, functional Best Western in Teton Village. Pool, sauna, hot tub.

££££ Alpenhof Our favourite in Teton Village. Tyrolean-style, with lots of wood and atmosphere. Good food. Pool, sauna, hot tub.

££££ Rusty Parrot Lodge Another stylish place in Jackson town, with a more rustic feel and handcrafted furniture. Hot tub.

£££ Sojourner Inn At Teton Village. Comfortable and convenient. Pool, sauna, hot tub.

£££ Lodge at Jackson Hole New western-style lodge in Jackson town, with comfortable rooms. Pool, sauna, hot tub.

£££ Parkway Inn Friendly, family-run place in Jackson town; nice pool.

££ Forty-Niner Inn Regular motel; hot-tub and sauna.

Self-catering Condominium beds can be arranged through local agents or central reservations. There are lots at Teton Village, within and around Jackson and some at more isolated locations between the two and elsewhere. The Cowboy Village Resort (Crystal, Enterprise) has neat little log cabins on the edge of town. The Jackson Hole Racquet Club (Lotus Supertravel) has good condos and facilities between town and skiing. Supertravel also has a wide range of other condos and houses. Teton Village Property Management control many of the condos at Teton Village. The Snow King Resort Condominiums (Enterprise) have full hotel service facilities, next to the town skiing. The Mad Dog Ranch has a country location, with great views.

There's only the one large supermarket in Jackson and a number of smaller stores and delis. Teton Village has good small stores but no supermarket.

EATING OUT
It's a pleasure in Jackson

Teton Village can list about ten or so restaurants – there's a pizza place, a Mexican, a Steakhouse and a number of hotel restaurants. They're all OK but most people's favourite is the Mangy Moose and the Rocky Mountain Oyster, downstairs – good value, good fun. In Jackson it's a case of trying as many places as you can in the time available. The Cadillac Grille with it's art-deco interior is the coolest place – and there's a burger bar attached. The Blue Lion is small, cosy and casually stylish. Louie's Steak and Seafood does just that in smart log cabin surroundings. La Chispa is a Mexican cafe attached to the Cowboy Bar and can come in very handy after a hard night on the saddle stools. Italian, Cajun, Chinese and several fast food chains are also represented. The Bunnery is a sound choice for breakfast and fresh-baked things, and for bagels head straight for Pearl Street Bagels.

APRES-SKI
Check out the saloons

The scene is one of bars and occasional live entertainment rather than clubs and discos; this is Wyoming, not Val d'Isère. In Teton Village, Beaver Dick's and the Pub have their fans, but the biggest draw is usually the Mangy Moose – it's a big happy, noisy sort of place and often has good live music. The famous bars in Jackson are JJ's Silver Dollar Bar at the Wort hotel and the Million Dollar Cowboy Bar on the town square. You have to see them both. The Silver Dollar is the classier venue and has over 2,000 silver dollars inlaid into the counter. The Cowboy Bar features saddles as bar stools, a stuffed grizzly bear and is usually the rowdiest place in town. There's quality live music every night (both kinds – country and western). The Rancher and the Shady Lady Saloon might also have some live music; the Rancher is the place to play the pool tables. The Virginian Saloon is a quieter watering hole. It's a good idea for those under 30 to carry their passports – the drinking age is 21 and is zealously enforced.

For a night out, try driving to Wilson where the Stagecoach Inn has live music, cowgirl waitresses and big portions of western food. Or you can go night skiing on the local floodlit Snow King hill on the outskirts of Jackson.

FOR NON-SKIERS
Some great outdoor diversions

There are some big outdoor attractions nearby and plenty of possibilities for trips. Yellowstone National Park is 100km to the north and although most of the roads are closed to traffic in winter, snow-mobile and 'snow-coach' trips are permitted. The park is famous for its geysers, the wildlife and the general beauty of the surroundings. The National Elk Refuge, just outside Jackson, has the largest remaining elk herd in the US – around 8,000 strong. Visits to the Granite Hot Springs and to parts of the Grand Teton National Park are also possible. In town there are some 40 galleries and museums and a number of outlets for Indian and Western arts and crafts. Most of the larger hotels have swimming pools.

Grand Targhee 2440m

This 'resort' 42 miles north-west of Jackson has only 444 beds but is a great place to visit for a day-trip. It has a wonderful reputation for powder snow and has adopted the slogan 'Snow from Heaven not Hoses.' You don't go there for the three chair-lifts but for the snowcat skiing. You ride up in a snow grooming machine converted into a people carrier (10 people plus a couple of guides) and ski virgin slopes. It's a more affordable version of heli-skiing. Book in advance.

Keystone 2835m

✔ *Splendid intermediate ski area with immaculately groomed runs*

✔ *Huge floodlit skiing area with runs open until 10pm*

✔ *Good tough skiing at Arapahoe Basin – Colorado's highest lifts*

✔ *Part of Ski the Summit ski lift pass area*

✔ *Efficient lift system means few queues*

✔ *Luxurious condominiums in woods make for relaxed family holidays*

✗ *Very quiet in the evenings*

✗ *Resort lacks a real centre, so very little ski-village feel*

Keystone has the biggest and best intermediate skiing area of all the Ski the Summit resorts, with miles and miles of immaculately groomed tree-lined runs. It also has Colorado's biggest night skiing operation, with 13 runs operating until 10pm, a huge computerised snowmaking system to supplement the natural stuff, and the best mountain restaurant in the US. Good skiers might find it a bit limited, but with the rest of the Ski the Summit area to explore too, they should find enough to interest them for their stay – especially if nearby Arapahoe Basin is fully open.

The resort best suits keen skiers who aren't seeking lively nightlife. There are some excellent restaurants, but not much in the way of lively bars and dancing. Those who want nightlife would be better off staying in Breckenridge, and making excursions to Keystone.

🏔 The resort

Keystone was the dream of Max Dercum. He gave up his professorship at Pennsylvania State University to drop out with his wife, Edna, to Colorado in the 1940s. Max converted the old stage-coach stop into the Ski Tip Lodge, now the most atmospheric place to stay in the district.

While Max and his wife ran the ski school in Arapahoe Basin, he worked on his plans to convert the wooded mountains in front of his door into one of the best ski areas in the US. He saw his dream open for business in 1969, and it has been growing rapidly ever since. Max sold out long ago, but still lives locally.

Keystone is a sprawling resort of luxurious condominiums spread over

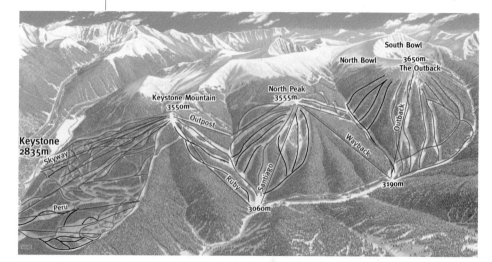

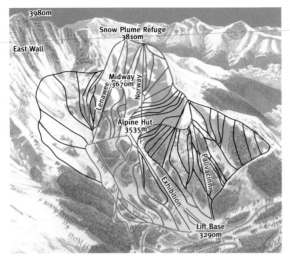

ORIENTATION

Keystone consists mainly of luxurious condominiums spread over a large area at the foot of Keystone Mountain. A high-speed quad chair goes up into the skiing from the Mountain House base, and a gondola goes up from the day-skiers' parking lot out of town.

Nearby **Arapahoe Basin** adds to the skiing of Keystone. In 1993, **Breckenridge** came under the same ownership. All three are now covered on the same lift ticket. A Ski the Summit lift pass also covers **Copper Mountain**. These four ski areas are linked by free buses. With a hire car you can also try **Vail, Beaver Creek** and **Steamboat**, all less than two hours' drive.

wooded countryside. Regular buses transport you between your accommodation and the two main centres, which both have shops, restaurants and bars. The Mountain House area lies at the foot of the main lift, and staying near here is best for ski convenience.

A couple of miles away is the picturesque lake area – a huge natural ice rink in winter. This is the other main resort centre, and includes the large and luxurious Keystone Lodge.

⛷ The skiing

Keystone has expanded rapidly in the last few years, most notably opening up a new $28 million mountain for the 1991/92 season. It now offers the most extensive intermediate skiing in the Ski the Summit area. Nearby Arapahoe Basin (or A-Basin as it's called by the locals) is a complete contrast. Its relatively slow and ancient lift system gives access to steep, high, above-the-tree-line runs.

THE SKI AREA
A keen intermediate's dream
Three tree-lined, interlinked mountains form Keystone's local skiing – Keystone Mountain, North

Peak and The Outback. The only one directly accessible from the resort is **Keystone Mountain**. The quickest way up is by the Peru Express quad chair from the Mountain House centre or by the gondola from the car park.

From the top you can ski down on a choice of 53 runs, or drop over the back and ski down to the foot of **North Peak** and take a chair-lift up. Or you can ride the Outpost gondola which links the top of Keystone Mountain to the top of North Peak (and stays open late into the night to ferry diners to and from the mountain-top restaurants up there).

From North Peak you can ski back to the bases of both Keystone Mountain and the third peak, known as **The Outback**, served by another high-speed quad chair-lift.

Arapahoe Basin is a short shuttle-bus ride away and was developed long before Keystone. In contrast to Keystone's superb modern lifts, A-Basin is still served by a series of slow old chairs. These give it an old-fashioned feel which contrasts remarkably with the large number of young snowboarders you find here. Snowboarders are banned from Keystone's mountains.

SNOW RELIABILITY
Excellent
Keystone rarely suffers from a shortage of natural snow. But in case it does, it has one of the world's biggest snowmaking systems as back-up.

One of the main reasons for the snowmaking is to help form an early season base. Keystone traditionally vies with Killington to be the first US ski resort to open its runs for the season – normally in October.

A-Basin has no need for artificial snow. It has the highest lift-served skiing in the US, at almost 4000m, and the base-station is at an impressive 3285m. The skiing here is normally open well into June.

FOR ADVANCED SKIERS
You'll have to travel
Keystone's own skiing area isn't particularly challenging. There are some good mogul runs, such as Ambush and Geronimo on North Peak. The steepest parts of Keystone's skiing are off-piste, among the trees below the open bowls at the top of The Outback. But most of Keystone's skiing is intermediate cruising.

Arapahoe Basin, down the road, is the best place locally for those looking for a challenge. The East Wall here has some splendid steep chutes. And the

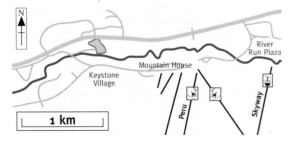

LIFT PASSES

94/95 prices in dollars
Breckenridge-Keystone
Covers all lifts in Breckenridge, Keystone and Arapahoe Basin.
Beginners Beginners and novices have a reduced area pass in ski school.
Main pass
1-day pass 40
6-day pass 192
Senior citizens
Over 65: 6-day pass 150 (22% off)
Children
Under 13: 6-day pass 102 (47% off)
Under 6: free pass
Notes Breckenridge, Keystone and Arapahoe are all a ski-bus ride apart. Discounts for groups of over 20. Over 70s have a further discounted pass price. All passes (except day-pass) allow one non-skiing day; 6-day pass valid for 7 days with one non-skiing day.
Alternative passes
Ski the Summit coupon booklets interchangeable for lift pass at Breckenridge, Copper Mountain, Keystone and Arapahoe Basin (6 days skiing out of 7 adult 210).

SKI SCHOOL

94/95 prices in dollars
Keystone
Classes 6 days
4½hr: 10am-12.15 and 1.45-4pm; 2hr 15min am or pm
6 full days: 198
Children's classes
Ages: 4 to 12
6 full days including lunch and ski-pass: 318
Private lessons
Hourly, up to 6hr 70 for 1hr; each additional person 25

opposite side of the bowl is riddled with steep bump runs – although none of the runs is particularly long.

Copper Mountain and Breckenridge have some good challenging skiing too – Breckenridge opened a new area last season. To get the most out of the region you'll have to be prepared to travel around quite a lot – no real hassle with the free half-hourly shuttles between resorts.

FOR INTERMEDIATE SKIERS
A cruiser's paradise
Keystone's skiing is ideal for intermediates. The front face of Keystone Mountain itself is a network of beautifully groomed blue and green runs through the trees. Keen skiers who want to bash the pistes for as long as possible won't find anywhere better. Over 42% of the mountain's runs are floodlit, and open until 10pm, and the whole mountain is served by snowmaking.

The Outback and North Peak also have easy cruising blues, with The Outback having some of the steepest blue skiing, including a couple of blue-black bump runs through the trees which are pretty much off-piste and unmarked.

On top of that there's the rest of Summit County's skiing to explore. Copper Mountain, in particular, has some great intermediate terrain, and is easily reached.

FOR BEGINNERS
Nice gentle greens
The front face of Keystone Mountain has some excellent easy green runs for beginners to try once they are off the nursery slopes. Schoolmarm goes right from top to bottom of the mountain.

FOR CROSS-COUNTRY
Extensive facilities
There's a special Cross-Country and Touring Center between Keystone and A-Basin which is served by the shuttle bus. There are 29km of groomed trails. And 57km of unprepared trails take you through spectacular scenery in the Montezuma area, with great views of the Continental Divide. Some trails lead to old mining ghost-towns. The Cross-County and Touring Center runs guided tours, including a Full Moon evening tour.

QUEUES
Not a problem
Keystone has an efficient, modern lift system, and except at the morning peak there are usually few queuing problems.

MOUNTAIN RESTAURANTS
Includes the best in the US
There are only two mountain-top restaurant complexes – Summit House at the top of Keystone Mountain and The Outpost at the top of North Peak.

The Outpost, in particular, is streets ahead of most US mountain eating places. Opened three seasons ago, the whole place is beautifully designed in wood, with high ceilings, large picture windows and a big sun terrace. The self-service restaurant is well designed and sells good fresh pizza, pasta, salads and grills. But the real jewel is the table-service Alpenglow Stube, which serves haute cuisine with a Bavarian flavour. It has a luxury atmosphere rarely found in European, let alone American, mountain restaurants – they even swap your ski boots for slippers at the cloakroom.

SKI SCHOOL
Few reports
We have few reports on the Keystone ski school but have no reason to believe it isn't as good as in most US resorts. As well as the normal lessons, there are advanced skiing workshops which specialise in moguls, powder and steep terrain, and five-day courses run by former Olympic medallists Phil and Steve Mahre.

FACILITIES FOR CHILDREN
Excellent
As in so many American resorts, the facilities for childcare are excellent, with programmes carefully tailored to specific age groups, and nursery care going on into the evening. We're not surprised to learn that Keystone has twice been voted Family Resort of the Year by the magazine Family Circle.

↑ Staying there

Keystone is a comfortable place to stay if you're looking for a quiet time with good restaurants but not much other evening atmosphere. The most convenient place to stay is near the Mountain House lift base-station.

But all the accommodation is well served by the shuttle buses. All the condominiums we've seen or heard about are large and luxurious.

HOW TO GO
Independent booking easy
A few tour operators offer packages and booking independently is easy. Resort Express run regular transport from Denver airport to Keystone. There are a few hotels but most

CHILDCARE

The Children's Center at the base of the mountain caters for children aged 2 months to 12 years and is open from 8am to 9pm. They can also provide evening baby-sitting in your own room. From age 3, children can join in the Snowplay programmes.

The ski school's Mini Minor's Camp takes children aged 3 to 4, the Minor's Camp those from 5 to 12.

GETTING THERE

Air Denver, transfer 2hr.

PACKAGES

American Connections, American Dream, Crystal, Getaway America, Made to Measure, Ski Independence, USAirtours

ACTIVITIES

Indoor Swimming, hot tubs, tennis
Outdoor Floodlit ice skating, sleigh and stagecoach rides, snowmobiling, horse-riding, dog-sledding, evening gondola trips

TOURIST OFFICE

Postcode CO 80435
Tel 010 1 (303) 4535000
Fax 4533202

accommodation is in condominiums.
Chalets No tour operators run catered chalets here, as far as we know.
Hotels There isn't a great choice but they're all of a high standard.
££££ Chateaux d'Mont Small luxurious hotel near the lifts; only 15 suites, with private hot tubs and lots of other extravagances.
££££ Keystone Lodge Large, luxurious modern hotel in Keystone Village – a shopping and restaurant complex by the frozen lake. Pool and fitness centre.
£££ Inn at Keystone Modern, comfortable hotel a short walk from the lifts. Outdoor hot tubs. Liked by reporters who stayed there.
£££ Ski Tip Lodge Former stage-coach halt and home of Keystone's founder, Max Dercum, who restored and extended it and used broken ski tips found on the slopes as door handles – hence the name. Atmospheric old rooms, bar and lounge with log fires. Well out of town by the cross-country centre. Good restaurant.
Self-catering There are hundreds of well-appointed condominiums, most with use of a pool and hot tub. The Liftside condos (American Dream, Crystal) are in the heart of the resort, close to the lifts, and come complete with all mod cons and good communal facilities. The equally comfortable and well positioned Frostfire condos have fewer in-house amenities but each unit has en suite whirlpool bath. The Resort condos (Ski Independence) enjoy a pretty location in the woods, a bus-ride from the lifts. The Cinnamon Ridge and Slopeside condos are other comfortable places.

STAYING DOWN THE VALLEY
Possible, good for exploring
A couple of reporters stayed in **Silverthorne**. The Days Inn was thought comfortable but basic. The Alpen Hutte was friendly and had its own private bus transfer. **Frisco** was thought a better centre for skiing the whole of the Summit region.

EATING OUT
Generally very high standard
Whether you want to eat up the mountain or in the valley, there's a good choice.

The Summit House, at the top of the gondola on Keystone Mountain, remains busy at the end of normal skiing because of the night skiing. There's live country and western entertainment and simple food –

hamburgers, ribs and so on.

The Outpost, on North Peak, is a hive of dining activity with the Alpenglow Stube (see Mountain restaurants) open every night for 'fine dining' as well as fondue and raclette and Tyrolean music at Der Fondue Chessel.

In the valley, the Ski Tip Lodge by the cross-country track has good food in a charming restored building that was formerly the stage-coach halt.

The Keystone Ranch has an award-winning restaurant that serves six-course dinners in a building based on a 19th-century homestead built in an area which the Ute and Arapahoe Indians used as their summer campground for buffalo hunting.

There are simpler places in both the lakeside and lift station areas, such as Gassy Thomson's and Ida Belle's for typical American-style burgers, ribs and grills, the Commodore for steak, seafood and pasta, and the Bighorn Steakhouse and Pizza on the Plaza for pizza, soup, salad and sandwiches.

You can get takeaways delivered to your condominium.

Or you can take a dinner sleigh ride to Soda Creek Homestead, or a more unusual 'progressive dinner' – a stage-coach ride where you have each course in a different restaurant, finishing with dessert at the Ski Tip Lodge.

APRES-SKI
Pretty quiet in the evenings
Immediately after skiing can be quite lively. The Summit House at the top of the gondola has live music and caters for night skiers as well as après-skiers. Keysters at the bottom of the gondola has karaoke, Ida Belle ragtime music and a miners' tavern decor, and Montezuma rock 'n roll.

But places empty out quite early and Keystone isn't the place for late-night revellers.

FOR NON-SKIERS
OK if you want a peaceful time
Keystone is one of the best places in Colorado for getting around on the mountain. The gondolas make both mountain restaurant complexes easily accessible, and the Summit Stage shuttle makes getting to Breckenridge and Copper Mountain easy.

There are plenty of other activities, including skating on the frozen lake (the largest outdoor maintained rink in the US).

Lake Tahoe 1890m

HOW IT RATES

The skiing
Snow ★★★★
Extent ★★★★
Advanced ★★★★
Intermediates ★★★★
Beginners ★★★★
Convenience ★
Queues ★★★
Restaurants ★

The rest
Scenery ★★★★
Resort charm ★
Not skiing ★★★

SKI FACTS

Heavenly

Altitude 1995m-3060m
Lifts 24
Pistes 4800 acres
Green 20%
Blue 45%
Black 35%
Art. snow 500 acres

Squaw Valley

Altitude 1890m-2760m
Lifts 32
Pistes 4000 acres
Green 25%
Blue 45%
Black 30%
Art. snow 250 acres

PACKAGES

Lake Tahoe Crystal, Ski Activity, Ski Independence, Virgin Snow

Heavenly American Dream, American Skiworld, Crystal, Getaway America, Ski Activity, Ski Independence, USAirtours, Virgin Snow

Northstar Virgin Snow

Squaw Valley American Skiworld, Ski Independence, Virgin Snow

Set high in the mountains 200 miles east of San Francisco, on the borders of California and Nevada, Lake Tahoe has the highest concentration of ski resorts in the US, with 14 downhill and seven cross-country centres. It is a very beautiful region, ideal for driving around on a tour, visiting a different ski area each day – as well as having two or three areas well worth spending several days exploring. The two areas that are best-known in Britain are Squaw Valley and Heavenly.

THE RESORTS

The main resort of the region is South Lake Tahoe. This spans the California-Nevada border and is certainly the place to stay if you like brash nightlife, 24-hour casinos, fruit machines, live cabaret shows and large hotels. All the gambling is on the Nevada side of the border. It is only five minutes' drive from South Lake Tahoe to the Heavenly ski area, one of the region's biggest and best.

Squaw Valley, venue of the 1960 Olympic Winter Games, is the other main resort on the British package market. This is about 90 minutes' drive, or a cruise across the lake on the Tahoe Queen, from South Lake Tahoe. Until recently there was no accommodation here, but there are now three hotels, including the very luxurious ski-in ski-out Resort at Squaw Creek, complete with leisure complex and heated outdoor pools. And there are lots of B&Bs and motels dotted around the lakeside region away from the ski resort (known as the North Shore).

THE SKIING

The choice of **ski areas** is enormous, with more than enough to keep even the keenest skier happy for a couple of weeks. You just need to be prepared to drive around to the different resorts. Because US lift tickets are priced by the day, with little or no discount for a week's pass, this doesn't add much to the cost of the holiday.

The record for **snow reliability** isn't as good around here as in many other US resorts. But the area does have huge amounts of artificial snowmaking capacity, so lack of snow shouldn't be a problem.

All the resorts have something of interest for every grade of skier.

Heavenly has the greatest vertical drop of the region, with the easiest slopes on the top of the mountain and the more difficult ones lower down. The views – on the Californian side of the skiing over the huge cobalt-blue lake, and on the Nevada side down into the desert – are simply stunning. For the toughest skiing, head over to Mott Canyon which has triple black

Never mind the skiing, feel the nightlife

America's Snow Country magazine rates this area Number One in the USA for nightlife, and it's easy to see why. There are the usual bars and so on, but what makes the area unique is the profusion of casinos across the state line in Nevada. These aren't simply opportunities to throw money away on roulette or slot machines. Top-name entertainers, cabarets and Broadway revues are to be found in them – designed to give punters some relief from 24-hour gambling.

Other entertainments are also on offer – Caesar's has a 'hot buns' night and 'tight jeans' competitions, and an in-house branch of Planet Hollywood; Turtles, at the Embassy Suite, is the place for a bop to the latest hits; the Wild West Country Club has dancing appropriate to its name; you can dine elegantly at Lewellyn's in Harvey's casino, or rise to the challenge of 'all you can eat' in the Forest Buffet on the 18th floor of Harrah's; or, if the slot machines have reduced you to your bottom dollar, try the coffee shop in the Horizon.

A more unusual way to spend the evening after skiing is to dance and dine your way across the lake aboard an authentic paddle steamer. If that's too sedate, there is bungee jumping at High Camp (Squaw Valley) after skiing. And finally: don't miss the pleasure of drinking out of dog bowls at the Naughty Dawg Saloon.

diamond 'Super Expert' runs.

Squaw Valley is celebrating the 35th anniversary of the Winter Olympics by building a new racecourse intended for all standards. Squaw is unusual in having no named runs but acres of open bowl skiing on six linked mountains. Like Heavenly it has its easiest skiing at the top of the mountain. There is plenty for **intermediates** but not that much to interest ordinary **advanced** skiers unless they like steep chutes and cliffs – many extreme skiing movies are made here. Squaw is a big snowboarding centre.

Kirkwood is another ski area renowned for its steep runs, though it has fine intermediate groomed trails too (which in total account for 50% of its skiing).

Alpine Meadows has the longest season and some of the most varied terrain in the Tahoe region.

Northstar is another predominantly intermediate mountain and good for families, with accommodation at its base. Other areas to try include Sugar Bowl, Donner Ski Ranch, Soda Springs, Boreal and Diamond Peak.

There is lots of **cross-country**, with the Royal Gorge Resort having the biggest area – around 300km of tracks.

Queues are rare, with Squaw Valley even refunding your lift pass money if you have to wait more than ten minutes. We have every reason to believe that **ski schools** and facilities for **children** are just as good as elsewhere in the US.

STAYING THERE

The basic choice is whether to stay near the bright, brash Nevada gambling scene or choose somewhere quieter. You might like to spend a few days at the southern end of the lake, skiing Heavenly and Kirkwood, and after loosing your shirt in the casinos move to the northern end, near most of the other ski areas.

TOURIST OFFICE

Heavenly

Postcode CA 95705
Tel 010 1 (702)
5867000
Fax 5885517

Squaw Valley

Postcode CA 96146
Tel 010 1 (916)
5836985
Fax 5835970

Mammoth Mountain 2430m

✔ *One of North America's biggest and best ski areas*

✔ *Impressive snowfall record, and extensive snowmaking*

✔ *Excellent skiing for all standards of skier*

✔ *Extensive skiing both above and below the tree-line*

✔ *Very efficient lift system and piste maintenance*

✔ *Good children's facilities, with particularly caring tuition*

✔ *Extensive, well kept, snowsure cross-country trails*

✘ *Slopes are four miles from town*

✘ *Weekend crowds*

✘ *Town lacks charm*

ORIENTATION

Most people stay in Mammoth Lakes, four miles (7km) from the base of the ski area and linked by efficient shuttle-buses. Lifts go up to the ski area from a few places on the road. The main base area at the far end has the biggest choice of lifts, including a gondola and a high-speed chair. These both connect with other lifts taking you straight to Mammoth's highest skiing.

A separate ski area called **June Mountain** is 30 minutes' drive away and is covered by the lift pass.

California doesn't conjure up skiing in most British people's imagination. They're more likely to think of surfing, beaches, wine and the big cities of Los Angeles and San Francisco. But since Richard Branson decided that Mammoth was his favourite resort and started offering extremely good-value packages there via his Virgin Atlantic flights to LA, more and more Brits have been trying Mammoth.

And they all love it – or at least the ones we heard from do. It's easy to see why. Mammoth is just that – a giant ski area, much bigger than most in the US. It has everything from steep, expert, above-the-tree-line chutes and bowls with magnificent views to easy cruising runs in the trees. Los Angeles residents discovered it years ago and swarm up here for weekends in good weather. But during the week, the slopes are often almost deserted. And on busy days you can always try Mammoth's smaller sister resort of June Mountain, a short drive away.

What it does lack is an atmospheric traditional ski resort at the base of the mountain. The main town is a long string, with pseudo-Alpine rather than traditional US-style buildings. But it does have an excellent selection of restaurants. Mammoth is a resort for keen skiers who want a big ski area, varied terrain and American-style friendliness and efficiency.

 ## The resort

Mammoth Lakes, a small year-round resort town four miles from the ski slopes, is the main accommodation centre. It sprawls for over a mile along an extraordinarily wide road, which is thankfully fairly quiet, at least during the week. Hotels, bars, restaurants and well-stocked ski shops line the roadside. Mammoth is short on European-style Alpine ambience but its setting among trees and its not unattractive buildings give a pleasant enough appearance. Even the ubiquitous McDonald's has been tastefully designed. The town is usually under a blanket of snow, which also helps.

There is accommodation at the base area of the skiing – the Mammoth Mountain Inn complex. And along the road between town and slopes lie several hotels and condos. There is a shuttle-bus between accommodation and lifts, but a car is useful, especially for getting to June Mountain for a change of skiing scenery.

The five- or six-hour drive up from Los Angeles, along a very good road, is spectacular. You pass through the San Bernardino mountains and Mojave Desert before reaching the Sierra Nevada range, of which Mammoth is part. Alternatively you can fly into Mammoth's own airport.

 ## The skiing

Although Mammoth is one of America's largest ski areas, the resort's claim to have 150 trails should not be taken too seriously. The slightest variant of a run is given a separate

SKI FACTS

Altitude 2430m-3370m
Lifts 30
Pistes 3500 acres
Green 30%
Blue 40%
Black 30%
Art. snow 200 acres

LIFT PASSES

94/95 prices in dollars
Mammoth Mountain
Covers all lifts at
Mammoth.
Beginners 1- (54), 2-
(126) and 3-day (206)
learn-to-ski packages
include pass, lessons
and rental.
Main pass
1-day pass 40
6-day pass 210
Senior citizens
Over 65: 6-day pass
105 (50% off)
Children
Under 13: 6-day pass
105 (50% off)
Under 7: free pass
Short-term passes
Scenic ride on
Mammoth Gondola
(adult 10); afternoon
pass available (adult
30).
Notes Passes of 2
days and over also
cover 8 lifts at June
Mountain, 30km
away.

SKI SCHOOL

93/94 prices in dollars
Mammoth Mountain
Classes 7 days
4hr: 10am-noon and
1.30-3.30; 2hr: am or
pm
5 full days: 190
Children's classes
Ages: 4 to 12
5 full days including
lunch: 290
Private lessons
1hr, 3hr or 6hr
60 for 1hr

name and number. Go to the right of a few trees and you're on piste 34, go to the left and it's run 35. Nevertheless, the 30 lifts access an impressive single ski area suitable for all grades. The highest trails, around Huevos Grande, are almost exclusively steep powder bowls and chutes, most of which are for experts only. In general, the lower down the mountain you go the easier the skiing becomes.

Mammoth's ski area is still owned and run by its founder, Dave McCoy, who built the first lift here in the 1940s. He still works actively on the slopes and is immensely proud, yet modest, that his dream of developing the inhospitable mountains of the area into one of the US' top ski resorts has been turned into reality. Many people told him at the outset that it was to high, too remote and too stormy to make it as a ski resort.

THE SKI AREA
Truly mammoth

There are three major lift-stations at regular intervals along the foot of the slopes. An isolated fourth is also reachable by shuttle bus.

All four stations have impressive lifts. Main Lodge, at the far end of the ski area from town, is the main base area and has an array of lifts fanning out over the mountain. One of them links to a triple chair for speedy access to the summit ridge. Once here, skiers not wishing to take on the unpisted bowls have an easy pisted alternative – a run starts just above, at the gondola top-station, and heads along the shoulder of the mountain, all the way down to almost base-station level. The views from the top are stunning, with Nevada to the north-east and the jagged Minarets to the west.

Three of the other Main Lodge lifts, including Gondola 1, move towards the **Mid-Chalet** area, the main mid-mountain base. From this station the second stage of the gondola rises to the top of **Climax**, which at 3370m is the highest point of the skiing.

Beneath the top bowls, lifts serve the whole width of the mountain, some reaching the top of the tree-line, others going above it. It will take you an age to work out the lifts. They are known by numbers and were numbered as they were built , so the system has no geographic logic to it. Lift 28 is between lifts 1 and 19, and so on.

SNOW RELIABILITY
A long season

California had poor years (by US standards) in 1992 and 1994 and is not generally as snowsure as Colorado or Utah. However, 1993 saw a record snowfall of 617 inches, and Mammoth has, over the years, had an impressive snow record. Its season runs from November to June, thanks to its height and its snowmakers.

FOR ADVANCED SKIERS
Some very challenging skiing

The steep bowl that runs the width of the mountain top provides wonderful skiing for experts. The steep chutes either side of Chair 22 also provide very challenging skiing. And above Main Lodge is another steep area ideal for the advanced skier. A quiet little bowl behind the main mountain plunges down to Outpost 14. Many of the lower trails are short, by European standards, but can easily be skied repeatedly. And you can ski virtually from top to bottom all day entirely on black runs. There are plenty of opportunities for couloir-lovers, and some only for the very brave, such as Star Chute and Felipe's.

June Mountain has some steep tree-lined skiing too, and is certainly worth trying for a day. Runs like Matterhorn, Sunset and Powder Chute are as steep as almost anything Mammoth offers.

FOR INTERMEDIATE SKIERS
Lots of great cruising

Mammoth's piste maintenance is such that intermediates can ski runs they might consider too steep in European resorts such as Val-d'Isère and Verbier – where bumps are allowed to build up on even moderately steep pistes. And there is plenty of skiing for all standards of intermediate.

Some of the mountain's longest runs, served by Chairs 9 and 25, are ideal for good intermediates. There are also a couple of lovely, fairly steep, tree-lined pistes running the length of Chair 10 down to Outpost 2.

Many of the tree-lined runs above Outpost 15 and Hut 2 are flattering, while the piste between Mid-Chalet and Outpost 2 is the one real motorway on the mountain.

Less adventurous skiers have some good, wide runs through trees in the triangle between Main Lodge, Outpost 2 and Mid-Chalet, and do not need to fear out-of-control skiers hurtling around the 'slow skiing' areas.

A day out to June Mountain is a must for great intermediate terrain.

CHILDCARE

Children's classes are handled by the Woollywood Ski Academy at the Main Lodge, which 'interfaces' with the Small World Day Care Center (934 0646) based at the nearby Mammoth Mountain Inn. This takes children from newborn to age 12, from 8am to 5pm.

GETTING THERE

Air Los Angeles, transfer 5hr. Reno, transfer 3hr. Mammoth Lakes, transfer 20 minutes.

PACKAGES

American Connections, American Dream, American Skiworld, Crystal, Getaway America, Ski Activity, Ski Independence, USAirtours, Virgin Snow

FOR BEGINNERS
Good tuition

Nursery slopes are no more than adequate. But the excellence of tuition, piste grooming and snow quality usually makes progress very speedy. Hansel and Gretel are a couple of very easy pistes above Hut 2 which wind their way through the trees.

FOR CROSS-COUNTRY
Very popular

There is a fine choice of trails. Two specialist cross-country centres, Tamarack and Sierra Meadows, provide tuition and tours, and there are no fewer than eleven cross-country ski-hire shops. There are 70km of well maintained trails, including some that wind their way through the beautiful Lakes Basin area. There are also many forested areas that have miles of very pretty, ungroomed tracks.

QUEUES
Weekend invasions

During the week the lifts and slopes are usually very quiet, with no queues. But even the super-efficient lift system can struggle to cope with 15,000 skiers arriving from LA on fine weekends. That's the time to try June Mountain.

MOUNTAIN RESTAURANTS
Basic and functional

Mammoth's mountain restaurants are efficient, functional, self-service places lacking charm or atmosphere. They're spotless, but food is uninspiring – burger, pizza, chilli and so on.

SKI SCHOOL
Excellent reports

Mammoth has a high reputation for tuition. We've had particularly good reports of the ski school at June Mountain, where class sizes as small as three don't seem unusual. Advanced

skiers will particularly welcome the opportunity of excellent classes in powder style and 'efficiency' (technique). Heli-skiing is also available.

FACILITIES FOR CHILDREN
Family favourite

Mammoth is very keen to attract families. Children have their own, very caring ski school which works closely with the nearby nursery. There is also a special ski club for teenagers. Night-time babysitting is available. We've had one particularly glowing report of a 3-year-old who had 'a great time' in the Small World nursery and had a private lesson one day which was an unqualified success – she 'came back with a huge smile'.

⬆ Staying there

Staying at the bottom of the slopes is clearly most convenient for the skiing. But there's a much greater choice of bars and restaurants in Mammoth Lakes and the efficient free bus shuttle service means getting to and from the slopes is easy.

HOW TO GO
Some packages, more independent

This year there's a catered chalet available for the first time, and a few condo options, but hotels dominate the scene. Condos tend to be either out near the lifts or along the road to them, rather than in town.
Chalets American Skiworld have a place in a complex of traditional-style townhouses. It's comfortable and has the added benefit of an indoor pool and other leisure facilities on-site.
Hotels Tour operators all use the same few places. Independent travellers have a much wider choice.

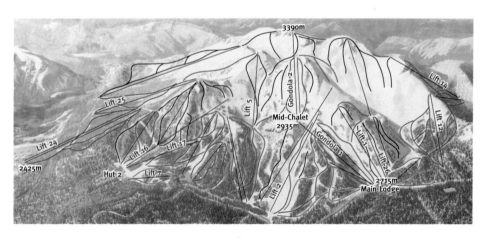

ACTIVITIES

Indoor Mammoth museum, art galleries, theatre

Outdoor Snow-mobiling, ski touring, bobsleigh, dog-sledding, tobogganing, sleigh rides, hot air balloon rides

TOURIST OFFICE

Postcode CA 93546
Tel 010 1 (619)
9340743
Fax 9340603

££££ Mammoth Mountain Inn Motel/hotel/condo complex at the foot of the slopes. Plain but spacious rooms, huge and 'interesting' breakfasts.

£££ Quality Inn Good, main street hotel with the biggest hot tub in town. Shuttle bus outside. Underground car park.

£££ Alpenhof Lodge Comfortable and friendly, in central location. Well liked by reporters. Shuttle nearby.

£££ Jagerhof Lodge British-run, friendly; much praised by reporters. At the edge of town on bus route. Restaurants close by.

£££ Alpine Lodge Refurbished town motel. Bus stop outside.

Self-catering The 1849 condos are spacious, very well equipped and nicely fitted out in pine. The Hut 2 base-station is only a couple of minutes' walk. Other top quality places well positioned for the lifts are Snowbird and Mountainback. The Summit condos (American Skiworld) are similarly convenient; though less luxurious than the above they are still comfortable, with plenty of mod cons. The same can be said of the Sierra Manor and Timberline condos (Crystal). The Aspen Creek condos are other good mid-range places close to the slopes.

EATING OUT
Outstanding choice

There are no fewer than 55 restaurants in town, which between them cater for most tastes and pockets – Japanese, Chinese, Mexican, Italian, Cajun, barbecue steak, and seafood. Roget's and Altitude 9000 are the poshest places in town, serving expensive Continental cuisine. Cheaper good places are the elegant Finicky's, Josh Slocum's and Mogul. Swiss Café is a good cheap, typically American, pancakes and eggs place. Bergers does giant burgers. The Stove and the Mountainside Grill are good places for a hearty breakfast. Roberto's does Mexican food; the Red Rooster Chinese; the Shogun Japanese.

APRES-SKI
Lively at weekends

The liveliest immediate après-ski spot is The Yodler, at the main base area. It's an authentic old Swiss chalet that has been transported across the Atlantic. There is a pleasant evening sleigh-ride and dinner trip, but nightlife is essentially bars which come to life at weekends. Josh Slocum's has a lively piano bar with jazz; Rafters has live entertainment; and Whiskey Creek is an informal eating place with rock 'n roll and country and western bands. Gringo's does the best margaritas in town. Grumpy's and The Cellar are worth trying, the latter with an especially good selection of beers, including draught Newcastle Brown.

Condo dwellers tend to settle down with cable TV. Listening to bar conversation can be an entertainment of sorts – Mammoth's large young hedonistic snowboarder population have made it the 'air head' capital of America. Bill and Ted actually do exist in droves! They talk of 'catching air' while they 'party on'. Eavesdropping can be fun – in small doses!

FOR NON-SKIERS
Mainly sightseeing

There are lots of areas of interest within reach of those with a car. These include the pretty Mono Lake, the beautiful Yosemite National Park, the unique Devil's Postpile National Monument, and the Sequoia and Kings Canyon National Parks (including Mt. Whitney). There's also a gold-mining ghost-town to visit. However, the mountain restaurants aren't especially pleasant places to meet skiers for lunch. Essentially, Mammoth is a place for keen skiers.

Park City 2105m

HOW IT RATES

The skiing

Snow	****
Extent	***
Advanced	****
Intermediates	****
Beginners	****
Convenience	***
Queues	****
Restaurants	**

The rest

Scenery	***
Resort charm	***
Not skiing	***

✔ Atmospheric Wild West-style main street, complete with jail and museum; convenient for the slopes

✔ Good choice of lively bars and restaurants makes nonsense of Utah's image as a puritanical Mormon state

✔ Famous for its light powder snow

✔ Well maintained slopes, and lots of snowmaking

✔ Easy road access to other major Utah ski areas

✘ Rest of town doesn't have same charm as main street

✘ No long runs

✘ Little variation in skiing terrain

✘ Lack of spectacular scenery

ORIENTATION

Park City is in Utah's Wasatch Mountains, 45 minutes by road from Salt Lake City. The resort is spread over a wide area, with chair-lifts and a gondola going into the skiing from the modern purpose-built 'Resort Center' near a big parking lot. This is some distance from Main Street, which is the centre of town. There's a chair-lift from one end of Main Street directly into the ski area. **Park West** and **Deer Valley** ski areas are only a few minutes away, and linked by the free ski-buses. Road connections to other Utah ski areas – including **Snowbird**, **Alta**, **Brighton**, **Solitude** and **Sundance** – are good.

On its own, Park City isn't worth travelling 5,000 miles for. Its ski area is small by European standards, and it has little to offer that hundreds of other resorts don't have too. But there are two compelling reasons to pay it a visit.

First, Utah has some great, tough skiing in what it likes to claim is 'The Greatest Snow on Earth'. Colorado resorts dispute that, but it's Utah that has the phrase on its car number plates. And there is usually no shortage of deep powder snow. Park City and its immediate neighbours don't get the best of it – that's reserved for Snowbird and Alta, in nearby Little Cottonwood Canyon, which have phenomenal snow records and some super-tough skiing. They and other resorts are around half an hour's drive away.

But they have little accommodation, and certainly nothing to match the second reason to visit – Park City's beautifully restored and developed main street, which grew up in the silver-mining boom years of the 1880s and makes it a much more interesting place to stay. It makes a good base for skiing many of Utah's resorts – and here, as elsewhere in the US, buying lift passes by the day rather than the week doesn't add much to the cost.

 ## The resort

Park City was born with the discovery of silver in 1872. By the turn of the century, it boasted a population of 10,000 (largely of Irish origin), a red-light district, Chinese quarter and 27 saloons. All this faded with the crash in the silver price. But careful restoration has left Park City with a splendid historic centre-piece.

The old wooden sidewalks and clapboard buildings of Main Street are now filled with a colourful selection of Park City's 15 art galleries, 100 smart shops and boutiques, a dozen bars and 80 restaurants. New buildings have been tastefully designed to blend in smoothly, but away from the centre the resort lacks the same charm.

The US National Ski Team headquarters is in Park City, and the resort features strongly in Utah's bid for the 2002 Winter Olympics.

The 'Resort Center' is the main base area of the skiing, with its modern buildings and its own bars, restaurants and accommodation.

Deer Valley and Park West are almost suburbs of Park City, but all three retain quite separate identities. Deer Valley is upmarket, ready to pamper its clientele with swish hotels, ski-in, ski-out convenience and some of the most upmarket lunch spots of any US ski resort. Park West is bold and breezy – day passes are cheaper here and snowboarders are welcome (whereas they're banned from the Park City and Deer Valley slopes).

 ## The skiing

Although good enough to host World Cup events, the terrain is generally quite tame – smooth trails cut through the trees on rounded, low mountains. The bite in the system is in the bowls at the top of the resort's skiing.

THE SKI AREA
Nothing spectacular
From the base area, a long 23-minute gondola ride, or a slightly shorter journey on a couple of chairs, takes you up to **Summit House**. Most of

SKI FACTS

Altitude 2100m-3050m
Lifts   14
Pistes   2200 acres
Green   16%
Blue   45%
Black   39%
Art. snow   400 acres

LIFT PASSES

94/95 prices in dollars
Park City
Covers all lifts in Park City ski area, with free ski-bus.
Beginners Beginners' courses (1, 3 or 5 day) includes 1 day free ski pass on First Time Lift.
Main pass
1-day pass 44
6-day pass 240
(low season 138 – 43% off)
Senior citizens
Over 65: 6-day pass 120 (50% off)
Over 70: free pass
Children
Under 12: 6-day pass 108 (55% off)
Short-term passes
Ascent and return on gondola. Half-day passes from 1pm (adult 30). Night skiing pass 4pm-10pm available.
Notes All passes of over 2 days allow 1 non-skiing day; 6 day pass valid for 7 days, with 1 non-skiing day. Reductions for groups and students.
Alternative passes
Multi-area books contain vouchers that can be swapped for day passes in Alta, Brighton, Deer Valley, Park City, Snowbird, Solitude, and Wolf Mountain (adult 6-day 264).

the skiing lies between here and the base area, and spreads along the sides of a series of interconnecting ridges. Virtually all the terrain above Summit House is unprepared, and accessed only by the **Jupiter** chair which takes you to a high point of 3050m.

The Town triple-chair, from the end of Main Street, connects well with the rest of the skiing.

There are a few old, wooden mine buildings left dotted around the slopes, which add extra atmosphere.

Night skiing on the Rockies' longest floodlit run is available until 10pm.

SNOW RELIABILITY
'The Greatest Snow on Earth'
That's what Utah claims on every car number-plate. All the main Utah resorts benefit from their unique position where the Pacific storms hit the Wasatch mountains after crossing over the arid Nevada desert and then picking up moisture from the famous Salt Lake. A season from late November to early April is normally scheduled but, with a bit of luck and use of the extensive snowmaking, the season is frequently extended. Thirty per cent of runs are covered by snowmaking. Snowbird and Alta, a half-hour drive away, have an even better snow record than Park City.

FOR ADVANCED SKIERS
Head for the top bowls
Jupiter Bowl is directly accessible by chair-lift and gets skied-out first after a snowfall. After that it's a case of hiking along the ridge to reach the likes of Puma and McConkey's bowls. All the bowls include some serious terrain – with narrow couloirs, cliffs and cornices as well as easier ways down.

The side of Summit House ridge, serviced by the Thaynes and Motherlode chairs, has some little-used black runs with occasional steep pitches, plus a few satisfying trails in, rather than cut through, the trees. There's a zone of fairly steep runs down into town from further round the ridge, including Willy's Run, which has seen duty as a World Cup men's GS course. And don't miss Blueslip Bowl near Summit House – so called because locals used to ski it although it was out of bounds. If caught, they got a blue slip which meant they were fired.

The Utah Interconnect will interest skiers keen to see a little more of the Wasatch Mountains back-country – it can be completed in a day and links Park City with four other Utah resorts. Advanced skiers will also want to

spend days at the other nearby resorts, notably Snowbird and Alta.

They may even want to try the Utah Winter Sports Park down the road. This is one of the few places where you can learn to ski-jump – starting on a baby jump and gradually working your way up. They have full-scale hills and freestyle jumps here too.

FOR INTERMEDIATE SKIERS
Lots of choice
There are blue runs everywhere, apart from Jupiter. The areas around the King Con and the Prospector high-speed quads have a dense network of great (but short) cruising runs. There are also more difficult trails close by, for those looking for more of a challenge. But there are few opportunities for long cruising runs – most trails are in the 1km to 2km region. The Pioneer chair-lift is slightly off the beaten track and it serves some very pleasant, quiet runs – ideal for warming-up and for those not seeking too many thrills.

Intermediates will certainly want to visit Park West and Deer Valley for a day each. Deer Valley has the best-groomed runs around and offers flattering intermediate cruising.

FOR BEGINNERS
A good chance for fast progress
Novices get started on the short lifts near the base area. The beginners' classes graduate up the hill quite quickly, and there's an 'easiest way down' clearly marked all the way from Summit House. It's easy enough for most beginners to manage after only a few lessons, but it is quite long – both the gondola and the Town chair can be used to descend.

FOR CROSS-COUNTRY
Some trails; lots of back-country
The scope for 'back-country' skiing is enormous – several companies in town arrange trips to some of the nearby National Forests, including overnight stays in log cabins or, for the hardy, snow caves.

There are prepared trails on both the Park City golf course, next to the downhill area, and the Homestead Resort course, just out of town. Both centres can provide lessons and equipment hire – they charge around $5 a day for use of their trails.

QUEUES
Peak period problems only
Lift queues aren't normally a problem. But the slow, old gondola takes an age to get up the mountain and there can

SKI SCHOOL

94/95 prices in dollars

Park City
Classes 5 days
4hr: 9.45-11.45 and
2.15-4.15; 2hr: noon-
2pm or 2pm-4pm
5 4hr days: 187
Children's classes
Ages: 7 to 13
5 6hr days including
lunch: 312
Private lessons
1hr, 2hr, half- or full-
day
74 for 1hr; each
additional person 10

be queues for it at the start of the day. Take the chair-lift alternatives. The Prospector chair can generate queues too, but shifts them very quickly.

MOUNTAIN RESTAURANTS
Nothing exciting

There are three restaurants, all of reasonable quality. The Mid-Mountain restaurant is an old mine building which was heaved up the mountain to its present location near the bottom of Pioneer chair; you may wonder whether it was worth the effort. The food is standard self-service fare. The Summit House is café-style – good for chilli, pizza, soup etc. The Snow Hut is a smaller log building and usually has an outdoor grill sending the smell of burgers half-way up nearby runs.

There's quite a choice of restaurants back at the base area, and that's where many skiers head at lunchtime.

If it's a gourmet lunch you are after, you'd be better-off in Deer Valley.

SKI SCHOOL
Thorough and full of enthusiasm

The official ski school offers all sorts of specialist programmes, and the usual group and private lessons. Group lessons can be excellent value: many skiers choose private lessons, with the happy result that four to six is the normal size for groups.

We've had several glowing reports on the school, but one negative one from a repeat visitor who felt that standards had slipped since 1992.

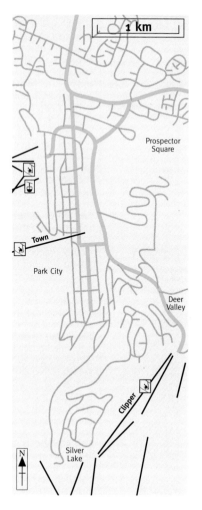

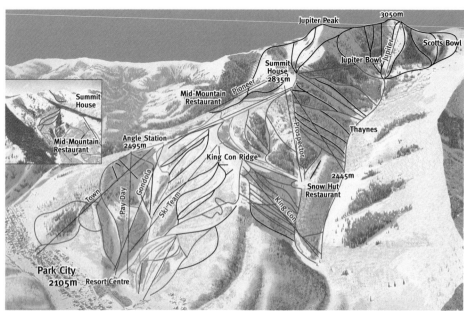

CHILDCARE

The ski school's Kinderschule takes children aged from 3 to 6, from 8.30 to 4.30, mixing tuition with other activities.

There are a dozen different nurseries in the town.

GETTING THERE

Air Salt Lake City, transfer 1hr.

PACKAGES

American Dream, Crystal, Made to Measure, Ski Activity, Ski Club of GB

Deer Valley Made to Measure

FACILITIES FOR CHILDREN
Well organised; ideal terrain
For very young children, even babies, there are a number of licensed carers who operate either at their own premises or at visitors' lodgings. The ski school deals with children under the umbrella of a separate Kinderschule. Book in advance to guarantee a place.

 # Staying there

It's quite practical to stay in Park City and not bother with a car – choose a location that's handy for Main Street and either the Town chair or the free shuttle bus. The bus goes from various locations in town to the base area of the skiing, it's frequent and runs till late. There's also a trolley-bus along Main Street. Regular buses serve Deer Valley and Park West. If you plan to visit resorts such as Snowbird and Alta a few times a car would be useful, though there are buses.

HOW TO GO
Packaged independence
Park City is the busiest and most atmospheric of all the Utah resorts, and a good base from which to visit the others.
Chalets As far as we know, no British tour operators offer traditional catered chalets.
Hotels The mass of chain motels on the fringes of most American towns is missing in Park City; and rooms at typical motel prices are a little scarce.
££££ Silver King Deluxe hotel/condo complex at base of ski area, with indoor-outdoor pool
££££ Washington School Inn Another historic building – there are quite a few around – which doubles as an hotel. Big breakfasts and après-ski snacks. Good location.
£££ Old Miners' Lodge A 100-year-old building next to the Town lift, restored and furnished with antiques.
£££ Radisson Inn Excellent rooms and indoor-outdoor pool but poorly placed for nightlife, out of town.
££ Chateau Apres Close to the ski area: comfortable but slightly faded budget place.
££ Star Hotel On Main Street, cheap, friendly and comfortable.
££££ Homestead Relaxing country resort hotel, with accommodation in houses spread around the grounds. Miles from the downhill skiing, but well placed for cross-country and snowmobiling. Pool.
Self-catering There's a big range of self-

catering units available though only a small selection – typically from the larger condo-complexes – finds its way into the brochures of tour operators. The Shadow Ridge and Park Station apartments (American Dream) and Park Avenue condos (Crystal) are typical. What they lack in character they make up for with their comfort and comprehensive facilities. Silver Cliff Village is adjacent to the skiing and provides spacious, serviced units. It also provides access to the facilities of the Silver King Hotel. Skiers travelling independently have a wider range of smaller places to choose from.

Food shopping in town is good and cheap, especially at Albertson's hypermarket; there are five liquor stores. There are also several take-away outlets – the Park City pizza company is recommended for fresh-made pasta, pizza and sandwiches, and Nacho Mamas for either take-out or stay-in Mexican food.

EATING OUT
Book in advance
Ethnic variation in the cuisine is much greater than might be expected – Szechuan, Cantonese, Japanese, Mexican, Vietnamese and Italian are all represented. Less surprisingly, there are more good steak places than the average digestive system can handle in a fortnight. The Carpetbagger at the

Indoor Park City
Racquet Club (4
indoor tennis courts,
2 racquetball courts,
heated pool, jacuzzi,
sauna, gym, aerobics,
basketball),
Prospector Athletic
Club (racquetball
courts, weights room,
swimming pool,
aerobics, spa,
massage and physical
therapy, whirlpool,
sauna), art galleries,
concerts, theatre,
martial arts studio,
bowling
Outdoor
Snowmobiles,
ballooning, sleigh
rides, ski jumping, ice
skating, bobsleigh
and luge track, sports
and recreation
opportunities for
disabled children and
adults

TOURIST OFFICE

Postcode UT 84060
Tel 010 1 (801)
6498111
Fax 6475374

Claimjumper is worth getting hungry for. Texas Red's does Tex-Mex grub and the Depot Restaurant does steaks and lots of other things – it's also in a fine old renovated railroad building. Cisero's has the best Italian food and gets packed. At the base of the skiing the Baja Cantina does great margaritas and Mexican food. There is a huge number of places to choose from but they all get busy, so book in advance.

APRES-SKI
Plenty of bars

Although there are still some arcane liquor laws in Utah, Park City seems to have adopted a fairly sensible attitude to their application, and – provided you're over-21 and have your ID handy – the laws are never a serious barrier to getting a drink. The Wasatch Brew Pub makes its own excellent ale on the premises and has a good supper menu.

At the bars and clubs which are more dedicated to drinking (ie don't feature food) membership of some kind is required. This may involve handing over $5 to cover a fortnight's membership – one member can then introduce numerous mates – or else there'll be some old guy at the bar already organised to sign a bunch of people in for the price of a beer. The Claimjumper, the splendidly scruffy Alamo and Pop Jenks are the most likely places to be lively and there's usually live music and dancing, at the very least at weekends. Adolph's is a bit smarter.

Steeps Café, in the gondola bottom-station, is the regular happening place straight after skiing – there's a disco and it tends to go on long after your ski clothes ought to have left.

FOR NON-SKIERS
Should be interesting

Salt Lake City has a few points of interest, many connected with its Mormon heritage, and some good shopping – Trolley Square is worth a look, as much for the buildings as the shops. Scenic balloon flights and excursions to Nevada for gambling are both popular. And there are lots of snow-based non-skiing activities – sleigh rides, snow-shoeing, ice-skating; there's even an ice-sculpture festival. Snowmobiling is big – there are 150 miles of prepared trails in lovely countryside. In January there's Robert Redford's Sundance Film Festival.

There are a couple of clubs in town with a pool, gym etc and a fairly up-market range of shops and galleries selling antiques, Western goods, expensive paintings, stuffed animals, Indian artefacts etc. The museum and old jail house are worth a visit.

Park West 2075m

This separate ski area is only four miles down the road, and an easy 15-minute transfer from Park City. It's a little lower, a little less than half the size and less than half the price to ski. Snowboarding is allowed here, unlike Park City and Deer Valley. The layout of the skiing is much like that of Park City, but the bowls are reached only by hiking – no soft-option Jupiter chair here. Ironhorse peak should be avoided by beginners – one side of the ridge has good intermediate runs, the other side has only 'expert' runs. The area is almost always pleasantly uncrowded and there is a collection of lodgings, restaurants and shops at the base area.

But it wouldn't be a particularly exciting place to stay. Buffalo Bob's Paradise Café, at the bottom of Ironhorse lift, is renowned for its après-ski atmosphere – good music, grilled burgers and drinks.

Deer Valley 2075m

Just a mile from the end of Main Street, this is the 'dude' skiing capital of Utah – famed for the care and attention lavished on both slopes and guests. Valets help to unload equipment in the car park, all the chair-lifts are padded and it looks as if stones are hand-picked off the slopes – it's very obviously aimed at people who are used to being pampered and can afford to pay for it. The eating places are particularly upmarket: the Huggery's seafood buffet is spectacular.

Some of the lodgings are similarly top-dollar, including the Stein Eriksen Lodge and Goldener Hirsch at Silver Lake Village at mid-mountain (but reachable by road). The terrace of Stein Eriksen and the Stag, lower down, offer excellent lunchtime cuisine unheard of in most US resorts.

The slopes are immaculate, though not all are easy – there are mogul runs and 'double black diamond' skiing in the top bowls. And some runs are left ungroomed after a snowfall, creating the conditions that incompetent but ambitious intermediates dream about: a foot of powder on a completely smooth base. Deer Valley is a recommended cultural experience.

Snowbird 2470m

HOW IT RATES

The skiing

Snow	*****
Extent	*
Advanced	*****
Intermediates	***
Beginners	**
Convenience	*****
Queues	**
Restaurants	*

The rest

Scenery	***
Resort charm	*
Not skiing	*

ORIENTATION

Snowbird lies 40km south-east of Salt Lake City in the Wasatch mountains, some 10km up Little Cottonwood Canyon – just beyond is **Alta** and the end of the road. The resort area and the slopes are by the road on its south side. Snowbird Centre and the base-station of the main cable-car are towards the up-canyon end of the resort; much of the rest is given over to car-parking areas. From the mouth of the canyon, good road links head for downtown Salt Lake City, the ski areas around **Park City**, and those in Big Cottonwood Canyon – **Solitude** and **Brighton**.

SKI FACTS

Altitude	2410m-3355m
Lifts	8
Pistes	1572 acres
Green	20%
Blue	30%
Black	50%
Artificial snow	none

✔ Quantity and quality of snow unrivalled except by next-door Alta

✔ A lot of skiing crammed into a small area

✔ Some seriously steep stuff

✔ Ski-from-the-door convenience

✔ The nightlife and airport of Salt Lake City are only a short drive away

✘ Ski area is limited, particularly for energetic piste-bashers

✘ Tiny, claustrophobic resort

✘ Uncompromising modern architecture

✘ Main cable-car generates queues, despite its impressive size

There can be few places where nature has combined the steep with the deep better than at Snowbird, and even fewer places where there are also lifts to give you access. So despite the notably charmless appearance of the purpose-built village and the limited extent of the skiing – particularly for keen intermediates – it remains one of the top US locations for hot-shot skiers. For visitors from Britain it is the main destination in Little Cottonwood Canyon, although Alta is if anything more compelling (see separate chapter, page 382) and anyone staying in Snowbird will certainly want to explore it. There is no shared lift pass, but buying passes by the day does not add much to the cost.

 ## The resort

The canyon setting is rugged and grand, and it needs to be: the resort buildings are mainly large and dull – but they do provide decent lodgings and convenient skiing. If function is more important than form, Snowbird Resort, tucked right under some of Utah's most exciting slopes, will do you just fine.

 ## The skiing

The **ski area** covers the north-facing side of the canyon up to Hidden Peak at 3355m. The famed cable-car ('Aerial Tram', with a capacity of 125 persons) takes eight minutes to reach Hidden Peak from Snowbird Centre. The toughest skiing is around the line of the Tram and in Peruvian Gulch, to the east. To the west of the Tram, in Gad Valley, there are five of the seven double chairs and skiing from very tough to nice and easy.

With all the skiing above 2400m, north-facing slopes and Little Cottonwood Canyon apparently acting as the local snowfall magnet, **snow reliability** is very good. Snowbird and Alta typically average about twice the snowfall of the Park City area or of most Colorado resorts.

Snowbird was created for and still appeals mainly to **advanced skiers**. For such a relatively compact area there is a lot of tough skiing. The trail map is liberally sprinkled with double black diamonds, and some of the gulleys off the Cirque ridge are at least that – Silver Fox and Great Scott are very narrow, very steep and frequently neck-deep in powder. Lower down the mountain lurk the bump runs.

Chip's Run provides the only comfortable run down from the top of Hidden Peak for **intermediate skiers** – at 5km it's Snowbird's longest run and is now a designated Family Skiing area. It's a good place from which to enjoy the views, winding down on the east side of the Cirque ridge. Gad Valley is the best area for intermediates to ski – there are some testing runs through the trees off the Gad 2 lift.

Beginners have the Chickadee lift right down in the resort – ideal for getting started – and then there's a small network of suitable trails on the lower slopes of Gad Valley. Big Emma is a lovely smooth trail, broad enough to accommodate the widest of turns.

There are no **cross-country** trails at Snowbird. It's not that far to travel to the likes of Solitude, where there are 20km of trails, but keen cross-country skiers shouldn't really be here.

At Snowbird nearly everyone wants to use the Aerial Tram – for which privilege there's a supplement to pay and probably a queue to endure. The lift system is too reliant on the Tram, and for much of the season **queues** of up to 40 minutes are the result. Some of the chair-lifts can also struggle to meet demand.

PACKAGES

American Dream,
Crystal, Made to
Measure, Ski Scott
Dunn

Choosing a **mountain restaurant** for lunch doesn't take long – there's the Mid Gad self-service cafeteria or else it's back to base. The Taco Bell, at the bottom of the Mid Gad lift, is a slightly off-beat alternative to the usual range of pizza and burger places in the Snowbird Centre. General Gritts has a good take-out deli counter, and lounging over lunch in the plaza is perfectly pleasant when the sun shines.

The **ski school** offers a quite progressive range of lessons and speciality clinics – including disabled skier programmes, women-only clinics and powder lessons using Atomic Powder Plus skis. The school also works to a maximum class size of eight, for all but Christmas and President's Weekend.

Children from age 3 can be handed over to the ski school, and the Cliff Lodge will arrange childcare for those as young as 6 weeks. Camp Snowbird provides non-skiing activities for 3- to 12-year-olds and there are occasional evening distractions like parties, games and movies to keep the kids happy. Seniors also get a good deal at Snowbird – the over-70s ski free – but it's probably not the place to introduce your granny to skiing.

 Staying there

Within Snowbird Resort all the lodgings and restaurants are within walking distance of each other. The Tram station is central and the Gad lifts can be reached mainly on skis. There are shuttle bus services linking the lodgings, the lifts and the car-parks, and a regular service up to Alta.

Choosing how to go depends mainly on which of the other Utah resorts are to be visited. If several are to be tackled, Salt Lake City is probably the most practical base – driving is easy and there are good bus services too. Park City is a more inviting proposition if the extra distance to most resorts isn't a

problem. A few operators feature **accommodation** in Snowbird – typically rooms in Cliff Lodge, a huge hotel and restaurant complex just up the nursery slopes from the Center. The alternative is one of the three smaller condominium properties in the resort or the newer View condominiums on the ridge above Cliff Lodge.

Eating out revolves around Cliff Lodge and Snowbird Center – both house a number of restaurants. It's advisable for at least one member of a party to join the Club at Snowbird ($5) as most of the better restaurants are classed as private clubs. The Aerie and the Wildflower are quite upmarket venues, the Mexican Keyhole and the Forklift are easier on the pocket and better for families. For those not worried about budgets, La Caille, at the mouth of the canyon, provides French food and style right here in the middle of Utah.

Après-ski in Snowbird tends to be a bit muted, though the comedy club may liven things up if you're lucky with the choice of acts. The sunset swim and a few cocktails at the rooftop pool in Cliff Lodge is reputed to be the best way to meet the in-crowd. It's quite feasible to head into downtown Salt Lake City for the occasional big night out – the Rio Grande is a stylish cafe in the Amtrak station, and Squatters Brew Pub is probably the liveliest bar in town. The Zephyr club has live bands, dancing and a distinctly non-Utah feel to it.

Non-skiers will be bored at Snowbird once they've tried the Cliff Spa and it's massages, herbal treatments and the like. Best bet is to head towards the city – the Racquet Club is owned by Snowbird and has superb tennis facilities, and there are some attractions downtown, particularly around Temple Square. And there is, of course, the Great Salt Lake itself. Further afield there are the Utah National Parks – including Bryce Canyon and Arches – and some of the nation's finest scenery.

TOURIST OFFICE

Postcode UT 84092-6019
Tel 010 1 (801) 7422222
Fax 7423344

Steamboat 2100m

HOW IT RATES

The skiing

Snow	****
Extent	**
Advanced	***
Intermediates	****
Beginners	*****
Convenience	***
Queues	****
Restaurants	***

The rest

Scenery	***
Resort charm	**
Not skiing	**

ORIENTATION

Steamboat ski resort is a 20-minute bus-ride from the cattle town of Steamboat Springs, a long drive, or short flight, from Denver.

The main lift into the skiing is a gondola from near the centre of the resort. The accommodation is spread over a fairly wide area – some on the slopes, some a bus-ride away.

If you have a hire car, **Vail-Beaver Creek, Copper Mountain, Keystone, Arapahoe Basin, Breckenridge** and **Winter Park** are all less than a two-hour drive.

✔ Medium-sized ski area with good skiing for all standards of skier

✔ Good restaurants by US standards

✔ Excellent snow record

✔ Ski-in, ski-out convenience if you stay out at the slopes

✔ Famed for its tree-skiing in fresh powder

✘ Western cowboy hype rather overdone

✘ Resort separated from old cattle town, and much less characterful

✘ Ski area rather bland

✘ Although there is some tough skiing, there isn't much

Steamboat markets itself as a real cowboy town. Its brochures usually have horse-riding, stetson-wearing, lassoo-wielding cowboys on the cover. Even Billy Kidd, the head of the ski school (who skis every day with anyone who turns up to meet him at the top of the mountain at 1pm), is decked out in cowboy gear for the brochures. The area does still have genuine working cowboys but the old 'wagon train' atmosphere doesn't permeate the ski resort or old town much. Don't go there just for the Western atmosphere.

A better reason for going is its compact area of largely easy-to-intermediate skiing. And in good snow conditions Steamboat is also one of the best resorts around for skiing off-piste in among the trees. But the skiing has neither the extent of resorts such as Vail, Aspen or the Ski the Summit areas nor the distinctive character of smaller areas such as Telluride. If you are going to travel 5,000 miles across the Atlantic and you're a keen skier, you'd be well advised to combine a visit to Steamboat with a stay at another resort.

🏘 The resort

The ski resort is a 20-minute bus-ride from the old town of Steamboat Springs, and is much the most convenient place to stay. Near the gondola station there are a couple of shop- and restaurant-lined multi-level squares leading to the one main street. The buildings are all modern, but built with some taste and plenty of wooden façades. Much of the accommodation is built up the side of the piste, so the village does have a slightly sprawling feel to it. You couldn't call it ugly but neither is it charming.

The old town is a bit of a disappointment after the hype of the brochures. Its plus-point is that it's a genuine working cattle town. And you're likely to end up chatting to friendly locals if you try some of the bars – we drank with the local on-duty taxi driver. If you go in mid-January you'll catch the Cowboy Downhill, when cowboys pour into town to compete in a fun slalom, lassooing and saddling competition. The rest of the season, there's much less of a real cowboy presence.

The main (and almost only) street is very wide, with multiple lanes of traffic each way – it was built that way to allow cattle to be driven through town. It is lined with bars, hotels and shops, built at various times over the last 120 years, in a wide mixture of architectural styles, from old wooden buildings to modern concrete shopping plazas.

The town got its name in the mid-1800s, when trappers going along by the Yampa river heard a chugging they thought was a steamboat. It turned out to be the sound of a hot spring bubbling through the rocks.

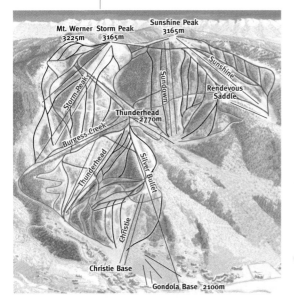

SKI FACTS

Altitude	2100m-3225m
Lifts	20
Pistes	2500 acres
Green	15%
Blue	54%
Black	31%
Art. snow	385 acres

LIFT PASSES

94/95 prices in dollars
Steamboat
Covers all lifts at
Steamboat only.
Beginners Day pass
for beginners covers
two lifts at base
(adult 25).
Main pass
1-day pass 42
6-day pass 240
(low season 210 –
13% off)
Senior citizens
Over 65: 6-day pass
150 (38% off)
Over 70: free pass
Children
Under 12: 6-day pass
150 (38% off)
Short-term passes
Single ascent on
Silver Bullet Gondola
for non skiers only
(adult 11); afternoon
pass from 12.15
(adult 36).
Notes Passes of 4
days and over allow
one day non-skiing,
so 4 days skiing in 5,
6 in 7. Children up to
12 ski free when
parents buy full lift
pass and stay for 5
days or more (one
child per parent).
Discounts for groups.

SKI SCHOOL

94/95 prices in dollars
Steamboat
Classes 5 days
4hr 45min: 10.15-
3pm; 2hr 15min: 9am-
11.15 or 11.30-1.45
5 full days: 137
Children's classes
Ages: 6 to 15
5 5hr days including
lunch: 225
Private lessons
1hr, 2hr, 3hr or full-
day
70 for 1hr

 # The skiing

Steamboat's ski area is prettily set among the trees, with splendid views down to the rolling hills below. Although it claims to be Colorado's second biggest ski area (after Vail), a keen intermediate piste-basher could cover all the marked runs in a day.

THE SKI AREA
Three flanks on a mountain
The skiing divides naturally into three areas and all have runs to suit all abilities. The Silver Bullet gondola from the village rises to **Thunderhead**. One ski area lies on the face of this mountain, with runs back to the village and a variety of chairs to carry you back from various points. From Thunderhead you can ski down to the left to catch a chair up to **Storm Peak** or to the right to go up to **Sunshine Peak**. Each of these has its own runs and lifts and you can ski from one to the other.

SNOW RELIABILITY
Good despite low altitude
Steamboat is relatively low by Colorado standards; it goes from 2100m to 3225m. So its highest skiing is below the height of the base of Arapahoe Basin. Despite this it has an excellent snow record, getting as much in a year as most of the higher resorts. And over 25 per cent of the pistes have snowmaking facilities. We skied there after snow hadn't fallen for a month and, though there were more rocks and icy patches than the other resorts we visited, there was still good skiing to be had.

FOR ADVANCED SKIERS
Tree skiing is the highlight
The main attraction of Steamboat for good skiers is the challenging off-piste skiing in the trees – something which is increasingly banned in Europe for ecological reasons. This is particularly wonderful after a fall of fresh powder. But there isn't much other than that.
   The best area for tree skiing is on Sunshine Peak below the Sundown Express and Priest Creek lifts. There's a huge amount of choice here. You simply take off through the aspens and choose a route where the trees are spaced as you like them – wide or narrow. There are also black pistes marked on the map in this area. The two to the left of the lifts as you go up – Closet and Shadows – are only loosely pistes; basically it's still tree skiing but the trees have been thinned

out a bit. On the right of the lift as you go up the blacks marked are more genuine cleared routes.
   On Storm Peak, experts climb up from the top of the lift to the Chutes – where there's another wide choice of route and the steepest slopes on the mountain. We were told this climb was designed to put less expert skiers off from tackling skiing beyond their abilities – very sensible, having seen the 50-degree slope of Chute 1.
   Elsewhere on the mountain, you'll find other blacks marked. But most are easily skied by good intermediates and make great fast runs if they've been groomed.

FOR INTERMEDIATE SKIERS
Some long cruises
Much of the mountain is ideal intermediate territory, with long cruising blue runs such as Buddy's Run, Rainbow and Ego on Storm Peak and High Noon, One O'Clock and Two O'Clock on Sunshine Peak. Don't ignore the skiing on Thunderhead either – there are a lot of good runs which it's easy to miss out on if you insist on being drawn up to the top of the mountain. At the end of the day, Vagabond is usually less crowded than Heavenly Daze right under the gondola.
   Some of the black runs such as West Side and Lower Valley View also make good challenging intermediate runs when the bumps have been groomed out of them.
   The runs at the far right hand side of the ski area are very gentle – Tomahawk and Quickdraw are marked blue but perfectly skiable by those who normally stick to green. This area is known to locals as 'Wally World' because of the ease of the terrain.
   The main problem for keen intermediates will be the limited extent of the skiing – not really enough to keep you interested for a week unless you enjoy skiing the same runs repeatedly.

FOR BEGINNERS
Excellent learning terrain
There's a big gentle nursery area at the base of the mountain served by four lifts. You progress from this to take the Christie chair-lifts to a variety of gentle green runs such as Yoo Hoo, Giggle Gulch and Right of Way.

FOR CROSS-COUNTRY
Plenty out of town
There's no cross-country in Steamboat itself but a free shuttle service takes you to the Touring Center, where

there are 30km of groomed tracks and lessons available. There are also Forest Service trails on Rabbit Ears Pass.

QUEUES
Not a serious problem
The queues for the gondola up at the start of the day are superbly organised, even by American standards. Two new fast four-person chairs have cut out the worst bottlenecks once you're up the mountain. The one place where significant queues can still develop is at the Sunshine lift serving the easiest top-of-the-mountain runs.

MOUNTAIN RESTAURANTS
Good by US standards
There are two main restaurant complexes on the mountain, both of which include unusually good table-service restaurants by US standards. The biggest is at Thunderhead. You can catch the gondola up from 8am and breakfast while waiting for the skiing to start at 9am. At lunchtime there's a choice of a big self-service restaurant, a barbecue on the sundeck, the Stoker bar and restaurant and Hazie's table-service restaurant.

At Rendezvous Saddle there's a slightly smaller alternative which has a two-floor self-service section including a pizza bar, another sundeck and barbecue and Ragnar's table-service Scandinavian restaurant. You can book for Ragnar's and Hazie's.

There's also a new snack bar and sundeck at Four Points.

SKI SCHOOL
Mixed views
We've had mixed reports of the ski school, some very positive, others rating private better than group lessons. There's plenty of choice in the programme, including a Challenge course aimed at advanced skiers, a Come Smell The Roses course aimed at 'mature' skiers and a Women's Ski Seminar programme.

FACILITIES FOR CHILDREN
Kids Ski Free
Steamboat has a better-than-usual Kids Ski Free scheme – free lift pass and free equipment hire for one child of up to age 12 per parent buying a pass and renting their own gear. Childcare arrangements are comprehensive, including communal evening babysitting in the Vacation Center – an excellent idea that ought to be widely copied. The one weak spot seems to be that ski school ends at 3pm, and there seem to be no facilities for looking after pupils after that time.

CHILDCARE
The Kids' Vacation Center is run by the resort in the gondola station. The Kiddie Coral nursery takes children aged 6 months to 6 years, all day. Those aged 2 can opt for the Buckaroos programme with a one-hour private ski lesson. Older children go on to the Sundance Kids group classes.

The ski school has a Rough Rider programme for children up to 15, with their own skiing skills playground area and lunchtime supervision.

The Adventure Club at Night offers evening childcare in the Vacation Center for ages 2½ to 12, from 6pm to 10.30.

 # Staying there

Staying in the old town of Steamboat Springs is cheaper but much less convenient than staying at the resort itself. And the bus costs 75c each way. Our preference would be to stay on the slopes and make occasional excursions to the town in the evening. In case you're gripped by indecision, there is accommodation between the two – the worst of both worlds.

HOW TO GO
Plenty of packages
More tour operators go here than to many comparable mid-size US resorts. There's accommodation for all tastes, including some more downmarket places than is the US norm.
Chalets Lotus Supertravel have a luxurious private home with open fire, en-suite bathrooms and skiing from the door. Crystal's one chalet is also very comfortable, and has an outdoor hot tub; ten minutes' walk from lifts.
Hotels The smarter hotels out at the resort have less character than some of the in-town options.
££££ Ptarmigan Inn Ideally situated just above the gondola station and right on the piste, with an outdoor pool and hot tub, a sauna and good après-ski bar with a happy hour.
££££ Sheraton Big, anonymous, concrete hotel right on the main square at the foot of the slopes, with a pool and hot tub – just the sort of place we like to avoid in ski resorts.
£££ Harbor The oldest hotel in the old town. All its rooms vary in size and character and there's a sauna, steam room and two hot tubs.
££ Alpiner Lodge Bavarian style economy option in old town.
Self-catering The apartments we have seen have been universally high in quality. The best we saw were the Bear Claw condos (American Dream), wonderfully spacious and individually furnished, and right on the piste at the top of the Headwall chair. The complex has a sauna, outdoor pool and hot tub, and an efficient shuttle bus system. Lotus Supertravel have a wide range of comfortable private homes. Other recommendations include Timber Run (Inghams), a short shuttle-bus ride from the centre with a number of hot tubs kept at different temperatures; the Lodge at Steamboat (Inghams), close to the gondola station, also with good facilities; Thunderhead Lodge (Ski Independence); and the aptly named Ski Inn (Crystal).

GETTING THERE

Air Steamboat Springs, transfer ½hr. Yampa Valley regional airport, transfer 1hr. Denver, transfer 4hr.

PACKAGES

American Dream, American Skiworld, Crystal, Enterprise, Inghams, Lotus Supertravel, Ski Activity, Ski Independence, USAirtours

ACTIVITIES

Indoor hot springs, swimming pools, tennis, weights room
Outdoor Bob-sledding at Howelsen Park, ice driving school, dog-sledding, snow-mobiling, ballooning, bungee jumping, hot springs, dinner sleigh rides, horse-riding, skating, Elk feeding tours

TOURIST OFFICE

Postcode CO 80487
Tel 010 1 (303) 8796111
Fax 8797844

EATING OUT
Huge variety

There's a huge choice of places to suit all pockets. Steamboat specialises in mountain-top eating – there are three places to choose from. You start by going up the Silver Queen gondola (with complimentary blankets). If you're going to Ragnar's, you then take a sleigh hauled by a snowcat for a Scandinavian meal. Or you stay put at Thunderhead. There you can go to BK's (the lunchtime self-service restaurant) for an as-much-as-you-can-eat buffet, accompanied by country and western music and dancing. Or you can try haute cuisine at Hazie's, where the menu goes somewhat upmarket from the lunchtime fare.

Down in the valley you can take horse-drawn sleigh rides to other dinner options, such as down Walton Creek canyon, to eat in heated tents with Western music.

In downtown Steamboat try L'Apogee, for French-style food, or the cheaper Harwig's Grill on the same premises. The Steamboat Yacht Club on the riverbank is recommended for seafood and views of ski-jumping. The Chart House and Coral Grill, on the outskirts of town, are recommended for seafood. For more traditional American fare try the popular Old West Steakhouse or the atmospheric ranch-style Ore House. Gorky Park has good Russian food and live gypsy music. Other options include Japanese, Russian, Chinese and Cajun.

In the resort La Montana, El Rancho and Cantina are recommended for Mexican food, Mattie Silles for seafood, Cipriani's and Cugnino's for Italian and The Butcher Shop for steaks and the like.

APRES-SKI
Fairly lively

The base lodge area has a few noisy bars, but things are much quieter and less brash in the old town. The liveliest place immediately after skiing is usually the Inferno, in the square. This has live music and a happy hour. Buddy's Run, near the gondola entrance, can also be fun, with live music or comedy. Dos Amigos is the place for jugs of margarita. Or try the Tugboat Tavern in the main street. The Conservatory in the Thunderhead Lodge and the Ptarmigan Inn are for those who want a somewhat more sophisticated atmosphere.

The Old Town Pub in Steamboat Springs dates from 1904, often has live music and does Tex-Mex food. Gorky Park has live music and 27 varieties of vodka. The Loft has live country or rock bands.

There are popular micro-brewery bars in both the resort and the old town – the Heavenly Daze and Steamboat Brewery are worth trying. The nearest thing to a disco is Hershey's Bar, but the best place for a bop is the Steamboat Saloon.

There are plenty of evening activities too, including hurtling down a mile-long track in a four-person padded bobsleigh and watching floodlit ski jumping in the old town.

FOR NON-SKIERS
Lots to do

Getting up the gondola to the restaurant complex is easy. Visiting town is too. And you can go and relax in outdoor hot springs seven miles from town or learn to drive on the special ice circuit. There are plenty of other activities too.

Taos 2800m

✔ Some very steep and challenging skiing

✔ Intermediates and beginners surprisingly well catered for, given the apparent general steepness

✔ Small, intimate resort nestled in splendour of New Mexico Rockies

✔ Fascinating contrast between ski resort and Taos town

✔ Has perhaps the best ski school in the US

✘ Taos town a long drive from the resort

✘ Some of the best skiing is a long hike from the top lifts

✘ Relatively small ski area

✘ Very little accommodation in the resort itself

ORIENTATION

Taos Ski Valley is the most southerly mainstream ski resort in North America, not far from Santa Fe in New Mexico. The resort itself is tiny, with little accommodation. Two chair-lifts lead from the centre into the skiing.

Taos town is 18 miles away in the valley. Much of the accommodation is there or on the road between the town and the ski resort. Although there are bus links, having a hire car is convenient.

The Taos experience is unlike any other in the US. For a start it is in New Mexico, with the ski resort set high above the arid valley and the traditional adobe town of Taos, home to many famous artists and writers over the years – including DH Lawrence. The culture is southern and very different from neighbouring Colorado. You'll see many more native American Indians around. You'll be eating spicy southern food as well as burgers and steaks.

The skiing is something different too. If you are after the steep and deep, Taos has it. It has some of the steepest skiing, both above and below the tree-line, of any resort in North America. Much of it is awkward to reach – and made deliberately so in order to keep the numbers skiing it low and the quality of the snow high.

Our main reservation about Taos is that it's such a long drive from other mainstream ski resorts. And because the ski area is not huge and the culture is so different, it would be good to combine it with a stay in a Colorado resort. If you are willing to make the five- or six-hour drive to, say, Telluride or Breckenridge, splitting your holiday between the two would be a very entertaining thing to do.

🏨 The resort

Taos Ski Valley and the town of Taos itself could be on two different planets. The resort is deep in the Sangre de Cristo mountains, some 18 miles from Taos town. Starting on the road from Taos, you travel through the flat, arid desert scenery, with its muted red-brown tones and low-built, adobe buildings, then climb into the wooded splendour of the Rockies, finally reaching the tiny resort. There are regular buses.

The resort is little more than a handful of lodges, built in chalet style at the head of a narrow valley. Space is too restricted to allow the development of a 'fashionable' resort. But there is a huge car park.

It was founded in 1955 by Ernie Blake, who was born in Germany, reared in Switzerland, married an American and fulfilled his vision of building a European-style ski resort in the southern Rockies. The ski resort is still family-run, though Ernie sadly died in 1989.

Taos town, in contrast, is sizeable, spread-out and rich in the many cultural influences – native American, Spanish and classic South-Western – which have shaped it over the centuries. It's full of art galleries, museums, restaurants and bars, as well as hotels and B&Bs.

SKI FACTS

Altitude	2800m-3600m
Lifts	11
Pistes	1100 acres
Green	24%
Blue	25%
Black	51%
Art. snow	496 acres

LIFT PASSES

94/95 prices in dollars
Taos area
Covers all lifts of Taos.
Beginners Yellowbird Program offers 2hr am and pm lessons and 'free' lift pass (adult 44 per day).
Main pass
1-day pass 37
6-day pass 204
(low season 138 – 32% off)
Senior citizens
Over 65: 6-day pass 90 (56% off)
Over 70: free pass
Children
Under 13: 6-day pass 114 (44% off)
Short-term passes
Half-day pass from 12.30 (adult 34).
Notes Discounts for groups of over 25 and tickets bought over 14 days in advance.

 # The skiing

When you hit Taos Ski Valley, the first thing that will strike you is Al's Run, rising sheer out of the resort. Named after a local GP, it's a mogul pitch of formidable length and steepness. As it's virtually the only run you can see from the base, it's no surprise that Ernie Blake felt moved to put up a sign saying 'Don't panic! You're looking at 1/30 of Taos Ski Valley. We have many easy runs too'. They do. The ski area has runs to suit all abilities, but it is best suited to experts nevertheless.

Another of Ernie's ideas was the Martini Trees – burying hand-blown glass bottles of spirits in the snow under blue spruce trees at strategic points. Sadly, when our instructor led us to one, it had already been drained!

Watch out too for Slim, an extremely life-like dummy, spread-eagled, face-down on the snow, boots down the mountain, near the top of lift 6. The sign next to him reads, 'Slim says, know how to stop sliding'. Useful advice on Taos' steep terrain, but unnerving the first time you see it.

THE SKI AREA
Small but expandable

From the top of one of the two chair-lifts out (one of which is a high-speed quad), you can ski back down to the resort or down to two further chair-lifts to take you higher. There is skiing on three separate flanks of the mountain, served by a total of eight lifts. From most of the lifts there are green, blue and black options. A unique feature of the skiing here is that many of the toughest runs (15 of those marked on the trail map) can be reached only by a lengthy climb from the top of the lifts.

SNOW RELIABILITY
Good

Taos has a good snow record (it gets around 300 inches each year). Because of its southerly position, it often gets a weather pattern different from that of the Colorado resorts further north – benefiting from storms which they miss and vice versa. In addition, almost half of the terrain is covered by snowmaking, including 85 per cent of the beginner and intermediate runs.

FOR ADVANCED SKIERS
Hike to the heights

Al's Run is the most obvious challenge for any good skier. In fact, quite often the bottom section is shut – because it's the first thing visitors see, the resort closes it to avoid the snow looking worn.

The best terrain for expert skiers is an energetic hike from the top of the mountain. Highline Ridge and West Basin Ridge both have a collection of steep, steep chutes through the trees and rocks. They're also very narrow so, not surprisingly, they're not always open and are best skied in fresh snow, provided there's no avalanche danger.

The other major challenge is to make the 75-minute-plus hike (not easy at almost 4000m) to Kachina Peak to ski the magical, wide, off-piste bowls and powder after you've stopped to recover and admire the spectacular views.

If you're disinclined to hike, you can still get in some challenging expert skiing – nearly all big bump runs through the trees. Chairs 2 and 6 take you to the best. Walkyries Chute lives up to its name, Castor isn't much easier and Sir Arnold Lunn is long and unrelenting. Our favourite was Lorelei, where the trees are a little thinner and the views superb.

At the eastern end of the mountain, the Kachina lift gives you access to the above-the-tree-line Hunziker Bowl, High Noon and El Funko.

There's yet another area of black runs immediately above the village.

FOR INTERMEDIATE SKIERS
Good but limited cruising

Wherever you go there are easy-cruising, blue-run alternatives to the challenging steeps. But they are limited in extent compared with the variety a bigger resort such as Vail or Aspen has to offer.

At the western end of the skiing, there are lovely long blues such as Lower Stauffenberg, Bambi and Powderhorn, served by three lifts.

To the east, the Kachina lift has more cruising, blue terrain. And adventurous intermediates will enjoy the open skiing of the Hunziker Bowl.

They could also try their luck with some of the tree-lined blacks of Taos. But stick to the single black diamonds until you feel confident!

FOR BEGINNERS
Good facilities

Strawberry Hill at the base is devoted to those who've never been on skis before. This has a nursery area at the bottom, steeper pitches higher up and no through-traffic of better skiers. But the aim of Taos ski instructors is to get their students skiing from the top by the third day. There are easy green tracks all over the mountain.

CHILDCARE

This year Taos has opened a new Kinderkäfig Center, housing all the ski school's children's facilities under one roof. BeBekare takes babies from as young as 6 weeks. Kinderkare takes toddlers not quite ready to ski. Junior Elite I takes pre-school children, introducing them to skiing through games. Junior Elite II does proper classes for children up to age 12, with lunchtime care and indoor supervised play after skiing. The first three schemes run from 8.30 to 4pm, the last from 9.30 to 4pm.

SKI SCHOOL

94/95 prices in dollars

Ernie Blake
Classes 6 days
4hr: 9.45-11.45 and
1.45-3.45; 2hr am or
pm
6 2hr days: 144
Children's classes
Ages: 3 to 12
6 full days including
lunch and lift pass:
330
Private lessons
1hr, half- of full-day
65 for 1hr; each
additional person 30

FOR CROSS-COUNTRY
Not one of the best
There's no formal, groomed cross-country, but skiers with a guide can head off into the Wheeler Wilderness Area and other parts of the Carson National Forest.

QUEUES
Self-imposed limits
The resort restricts sales of ski passes to 4,800 on any one day. This is so that neither the lifts nor the slopes get too crowded. In practice this means queues are rare except for the bottom lifts at peak times.

MOUNTAIN RESTAURANTS
Take a picnic
This is not the place to go to for haute cuisine on the mountain. There are just two restaurants, neither selling the world's greatest food. At the Phoenix, you'll find you get an alcoholic drink only with food, and you're then restricted in the amount you can have. The Whistlestop doesn't sell alcohol at all. You can picnic at both places.

If you want a decent lunch, it's best to ski back to the resort – no great hardship. The large terrace of the hotel St Bernard is a favourite spot.

SKI SCHOOL
Simply the best?
Taos ski school is considered by many the best there is. Their aim is to push all the skiers they teach as far and as fast as possible – but also to have fun. To get the most out of the school, you need to enrol for a whole week, as is normal in Europe but not the US – another result of Ernie Blake wanting to bring European ways to US skiing. As testimony to the school's success, 70 per cent of guests staying in the ski resort for a week take courses.

In addition to straight group classes and private lessons, there are packages designed to encourage skiers to go to school for the whole week. Super Ski Weeks for intermediate and expert skiers provide six days' lift pass and morning and afternoon lessons, video analysis and seminar for $428; Ski-Better-Weeks offer six days' lift pass and six morning lessons, video analysis and race, for all levels, at $348. The Yellowbird Program for beginners includes morning and afternoon lessons for $44 per day, with a free lift ticket thrown in, and cheap ski and boot rental.

Mogul Mastery and special Women's Weekends are among the other special workshops available.

FACILITIES FOR CHILDREN
Childcare from 6 weeks old
The resort takes childcare just as seriously as it takes ski tuition, with programmes tailored precisely to different age groups, and the new Kinderkäfig building brings the various options together. The ability to deposit babies at the age of 6 weeks is more or less unrivalled.

↑ Staying there

The first decision is whether to stay in Taos Ski Valley, in Taos town or in one of the many lodges on the drive between the two. If you stay at the resort, there's a high risk that you won't drag yourself to experience the different culture of Taos town and the surrounding area, which would be a pity. On the other hand, it's a fair old drive up and down a winding road each day to the ski resort.

HOW TO GO
Little choice
Few British skiers have discovered Taos and only a couple of tour operators put it in their brochures – and then not in a big way. But any of the US specialists will be able to put a package together for you.

Hotels There are no particularly luxurious or smart hotels – indeed that's part of the charm of the resort. There are quite a few small B&Bs.
At Taos Ski Valley:
££££ Inn at Snakedance The original Taos ski hotel, this was completely rebuilt in 1993 and now boasts a panoramic, glass-walled bar, large sun terrace and new spa facilities.
£££ Edelweiss Ski-in, ski-out hotel famous for its breakfasts, fine food and live music. No TVs or phones in rooms. Sauna, hot tub.
£££ St Bernard Ski-in, ski-out hotel at the base of Al's Run; fine food, après-ski scene. Also has condos in a separate building.
£££ Innsbruck Lodge and Condos Across from the lifts, combines lodge with self-catering condos. American or Continental cooking, relaxed family atmosphere.
In Taos town itself:
££££ Historic Taos Inn Historic building just off the central plaza, with dramatic two-storey lobby, called 'the town's living room'. Adobe fireplaces, hand-loomed Indian bedspreads and local furniture. Excellent restaurant and stylish Adobe Bar, popular with locals, artists and visitors. Outdoor pool, hot tub.

GETTING THERE

Air Albuquerque, transfer 3hr.

PACKAGES

Chalets 'Unlimited', Ski Independence

ACTIVITIES

Indoor Six local museums, galleries, film theatre and theatre, swimming pools, sauna, hot tubs, tennis, squash, raquetball and basketball courts, weights room, climbing wall, aerobics
Outdoor Day-trips (National Forest, Wild Rivers area, ancient Pueblos-Indian sites, Santa Fe and many others), horse-riding, ice skating, hiking

TOURIST OFFICE

Postcode NM 87525
Tel 010 1 (505) 7762291
Fax 7768596

££££ Casa de las Chimeneas
Charming, romantic B&B with only three rooms.
£££ Sagebrush Inn Built in 1929 in Pueblo-Mission-style adobe. Handmade Mexican furniture and local pottery and antiques. Excellent food, nightly entertainment. Tennis, outdoor pool, hot tubs.
Self-catering There's a wide selection of self-catering condos in the resort.

Kandahar has the highest location on the ski slopes, overlooking the resort and the slopes; hot tub and a steam bath.

Sierra del Sol is in the heart of Taos Ski Valley; each condo has a fireplace; hot tubs and sauna.

Rio Hondo is on the Hondo river and next to the ski slopes; each condo has its own balcony, fireplace, living room; hot tub and sauna.

Between Taos town and the ski valley is Quail Ridge Inn Resort, a large adobe-style complex, with comfortable well-appointed rooms and suites, each with a fireplace. Huge outdoor heated pool, hot tub, sauna, tennis, and fitness centre.

Haçienda del Valdez nestles in the foothills of the Valdez valley, eight miles from resort; South-Western design, wonderful views; hot tub.

EATING OUT
Spoilt for choice if you drive
At the resort, be sure to try Tim's Stray Dog. It specialises in northern New Mexico food – enchiladas, green chilli, tortilla soup – as well as burgers and other US fare, all served in a lively atmosphere, whatever the time of day. At Rhoda's Restaurant, specialities include elk, buffalo and New Mexican dishes – the menu changes daily. The Dolomite has great pizzas and fresh pasta.

Between the town and resort, the locals recommend Chile Connection for the best New Mexican and Spanish food. Brett House is a charming restaurant, serving American and international food.

Another must of a different nature on the road between the resort and Taos, is Casa Fresen Bakery at Arroyo Seco. It sells fantastic bread – wholewheat, cinnamon, nut, rye – as well as mouth-watering cakes, and has a decent deli as well. Useful for those who are self-catering, but worth a visit for those who aren't.

In Taos itself, you practically fall over restaurants. Doc Martin's is so historic that you'd kick yourself if you missed it – and it serves great contemporary South-Western food

too. Lambert's has a different dinner menu each night, specialising in lamb, fresh seafood and steaks. The Historic Taos Inn has good food in beautiful surroundings.

APRES-SKI
Ski hard, sleep early
It's generally quiet, with people skiing hard, then enjoying a meal and quiet and trying to restore their energy for the next day. Some of the hotels do have live music some nights, and there's a jazz festival in the Ski Valley every January.

FOR NON-SKIERS
Plenty of sightseeing
The Taos area is good for sightseeing and a popular summer holiday spot.

The Ski Valley is too tightly packed to feature any activities other than skiing. And non-skiers are likely to prefer skiers to come back to the resort to meet for lunch than walk to the unappealing places on the mountain.

In Taos itself you'll find ice skating and swimming, and you can go on a historic walking tour. The town is rich with art galleries and museums covering the different influences on it. For example, you can visit Kit Carson's home – a 12-room adobe building bought by the famous mountain man and scout in 1843 for his bride.

Taos Pueblo, four miles outside Taos, has been the home of the Tiwa Indians for nearly 800 years and has the largest multi-storied adobe structure in the US.

Excursions to the historic and pretty Santa Fe are possible – and are recommended.

Telluride 2660m

✔ *Charming restored Victorian silver-mining town with a real Wild West atmosphere*

✔ *Skiing for all standards, from beginners to experts, with some of the steepest mogul fields we've seen and some of the longest easy runs in the Rockies*

✔ *Dramatic, craggy mountain scenery – not remarkable by Alpine standards, but rare in the Rockies*

✔ *Some ski-in, ski-out accommodation in newly built Mountain Village*

✘ *Limited amount of skiing for the keen intermediate piste-basher*

✘ *Mountain Village is something of an eyesore when seen from parts of the ski area (but it is well away from the old town)*

✘ *Limited mountain restaurants*

✘ *Access to town from Mountain Village is by a roundabout road, until a new linking gondola is built (for 1995/96 at the earliest)*

Like so many American ski areas, Telluride is rather small; we're in no doubt that high-mileage British piste-bashers used to French mega-resorts would get bored with the skiing if they stayed for a week. But that is our only serious reservation about a resort that, we blushingly confess, we fell for on first acquaintance.

Repeat visits have only confirmed our affection for the place. The scenery is an important factor, as the resort's marketing people are well aware: the San Juan mountains are not remarkable by Alpine standards, but they are impressive enough to set Telluride apart from other resorts in the Rocky Mountains. The town may not be quite as captivating as the more rustic Crested Butte, but it has plenty of character and is pleasantly compact, and has some of the best skiing looming directly above it, so staying in the town is an attractive option even for keen skiers.

The company that runs the mountain has ambitious plans to extend the lift network, almost doubling the skiable area. When they find the money, Telluride will be difficult to beat.

ORIENTATION

Telluride is an isolated resort in a dead-end valley (a 'box canyon') in south-west Colorado, with its own precarious little airport five miles out of town (and a more serious airport at Montrose, 67 miles away). The skiing starts right on the edge of the small town, with chair-lifts close to the centre of town (Oak Street base) and at the west end (Coonskin).

Up in the ski area a separate Mountain Village has been created in recent years specially for skiers and summer golfers. An eight-person gondola linking the town to the Mountain Village and the easiest skiing is under construction.

 ## The resort

Telluride started life in the 1870s as a silver-mining camp; when gold was found, the town boomed. It had a rough reputation for its drinking and whoring; some say its name is a shortened version of 'To hell you ride'. The town slumped in the early 1900s and became virtually depopulated until the skiing was developed in the early 1970s. Since then it has been restored to its former glory, with painted clapboard buildings now turned into friendly, interesting shops and restaurants. It looks like a typical small Wild West town from the movies – except that the main street is busy with pickup trucks, not horse-

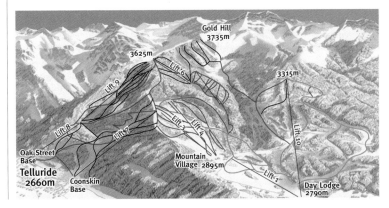

drawn wagons. The inhabitants are a unique blend of ageing hippies, lively young people, old timers who've stuck it out through the bad times, ski bums and a smattering of celebrities who shun the glitter of Aspen.

The new Mountain Village is as different as you could imagine. It is very much the modern American leisure resort, with security guards to keep out the riff-raff, and entirely modern buildings. Most of these have been designed with some regard to appearance, in a sort of post-modern Alpine style, but there is a conspicuous exception – The Peaks, a monster hotel that looks as if it has been imported whole from a housing estate in Poitiers.

⛷ The skiing

The skiing has a macho reputation. It features in many of the extreme skiing videos, and it deserves to – there's some fearsomely steep terrain. But there's ideal beginner and intermediate skiing too. The trouble is that there's not much of it – this is definitely a resort for those who put quality before quantity.

THE SKI AREA
Small but quite complex
Chair-lifts climb the steep, wooded northern flank of the skiing from two points on the edge of town, meeting lifts up from Mountain Village at two points which ought to have names but don't; the higher of the two is the top point of the lift system, at 3625m. Beyond this point is Gold Hill, a lightly wooded area of steep runs reached by hiking up as far as 3735m. The terrain gets flatter down towards Mountain Village; below it is the long, gentle nursery slope, and branching off from the bottom of that the world's longest high-speed quad chair-lift, serving a separate mountain (anonymous, again) with a choice of long, easy runs of 525m vertical.

SNOW RELIABILITY
Good
The height of the isolated San Juan range makes Telluride something of a snow-hole, with an average of 25 feet of snow a year. On top of that (or, in practice, underneath it) there is a considerable amount of snowmaking on the lower half of the mountain. The steep slopes above the town face roughly north, while those in the bowl above Mountain Village range from west- to north-facing.

FOR ADVANCED SKIERS
Extremely steep mogul slopes
Telluride's reputation among the US skiing cogniscenti was made by the double black bump runs directly above the town – a slope of 960m vertical. Aptly named runs such as The Plunge, Spiral Stairs and Kant-Mak-M look terrifying from Lift 9, and only a little less terrifying on the ground. Some of them are now normally half-groomed to make them accessible to less-than-expert skiers – you have the choice of a steep groomed trail or fearsome-sized bumps. There's also some great steep glade skiing on the opposite side of the lift-system high-point. The new Gold Hill area was opened a couple of years ago, and there are plans to build a lift to serve it. It offers tough glade skiing; but Telluride doesn't have the sort of high bowl skiing to set it up as a competitor to Whistler or Vail.

FOR INTERMEDIATE SKIERS
Quality not quantity
Telluride's intermediate skiing is mainly confined to the runs served by the lifts immediately above Mountain Village – runs such as Peek A Boo, Boomerang and Misty Maiden. From the top of the mountain, See Forever is a glorious cruise down the main ridge, with splendid long-range views of mountain ranges in Utah. The other blues from here towards the old town are mainly more difficult double blue squares. But there is one easy way back to town – the winding Telluride Trail.

FOR BEGINNERS
Superb – one of the best
The Mountain Village area has for years had ideal first runs in the Meadows area (served by Lift 1). The opening of the super-long Lift 10 has opened up another three or four excellent beginners' runs. Apart from being shallow and wide, they have the big advantage of being isolated from the rest of the skiing, so beginners aren't worried by better skiers flashing past them.

FOR CROSS-COUNTRY
Very attractive
The scenic beauty of this area makes it splendid for cross-country. The Telluride Nordic Center runs over 40km of groomed trails, and there is plenty of scope for skiing ungroomed trails with a guide. There are even overnight excursions where you stay in back-country huts, and heli-drops are available.

SKI FACTS

Altitude 2660m-3625m

Lifts	10
Pistes	1050 acres
Green	21%
Blue	47%
Black	32%
Art. snow	155 acres

LIFT PASSES

94/95 prices in dollars
Telluride area
Covers all lifts in Telluride.
Beginners Learn-to-ski/shred day course includes lift pass and equipment rental (adult 60).
Main pass
1-day pass 43
6-day pass 222
(low season 174 – 22% off)
Senior citizens
Over 65: 6-day pass 144 (35% off)
Over 70: free pass
Children
Under 12: 6-day pass 144 (35% off)
Under 6: free pass
Short-term passes
Half-day pass available (adult 34).
Notes Passes of over 2 days allow one day non-skiing, eg 6-day pass covers 6 days in 7.

SKI SCHOOL

94/95 prices in dollars

Telluride
Classes 5 days
2hr: 10.50-1pm; 2½hr:
1.20-4pm
6 half-days: 140
Children's classes
Ages: 3 to 12
5 5½hr days including
lunch: 250
Private lessons
1hr, half- or full-day
65 for 1hr; each
additional person 25

CHILDCARE

The ski school runs
special classes for
children aged 3 or
more, provides
lunchtime care and
runs a free Adventure
Club to keep children
occupied before and
after lessons.

The Mountain Village
Nursery takes younger
children from age 2
months, from 8am
to 5pm.

GETTING THERE

Air Telluride, transfer
½hr.

QUEUES
Rarely a problem

Despite many of the lifts being
antiquated by US standards, queues
are rarely a problem because of the
small numbers of skiers using the
resort. Lift 6 can be a bottleneck at
peak weekends because of the large
number of the classic tough runs it
serves and the fact that it's a slow two-
person chair. But the ride is long and
scenic and it makes you feel good
when you see others below you
struggling just as much as you did on
the way down.

MOUNTAIN RESTAURANTS
Could be worse

As in many US resorts, eating on the
mountain is a fairly primitive and
entirely self-service affair – though
both of the two options do have some
merit. The main mountain cafeteria –
Gorrono – is only a few hundred
metres above the Mountain Village.
This is a large, two-storey wooden
barn offering fairly standard American
fare; but it has a big outside terrace
with a barbecue, and a separate bar in
an old cabin. There's also a tiny hut at
the top of Lift 6 – Giuseppe's – which
has tables outside on the snow and
serves sandwiches, chilli, soup and the
like (potato and bean sauté is the
speciality, and it sells out early). There
are good views from up here, with the
chance of the additional spectacle of
Glider Bob's performance (see For
non-skiers). There are alternatives
worth exploring at both the Mountain
Village – the Cactus Cafe, for example,
is close to the lifts – and the town.
Because of the small size of the ski
area, skiing down to the bottom for
lunch is no real problem.

SKI SCHOOL
Seems impressive

The school offers the usual American
range of options, including special
tuition on the resort's amazing mogul
slopes and some very attractive early-
morning starts to get you on the snow
(on- or off-piste) before anyone else.
There are free mountain orientation
tours daily at 10am.

FACILITIES FOR CHILDREN
At the Mountain Village

There is the thorough provision for
children that is usual in the US. The
ski school's Adventure Club provides
indoor and outdoor play before and
after lessons, and for those based in
the town includes transportation to
and from the Coonskin lift for access
to the slopes at the Mountain Village.

 # Staying there

The key decision is whether to stay
down in the town or up in Mountain
Village. But for us, and we guess for
most British visitors, there is no
choice: in the Mountain Village, you
could be anywhere, whereas in the
town you're in no doubt that you're
in Miningville, Colorado. If you stay
close to the centre, you'll be within
easy walking distance of the Oak Street
lift, but beware places on the north-
east fringes. Most of the newer
accommodation at the west end of
town is within walking distance of the
Coonskin lift – but, again, beware
places on the fringes.

HOW TO GO
Fair choice of hotels and condos

Telluride is not among the best-known
American resorts in the UK, but is now
offered by several of the main US
operators.
Chalets We know of no catered chalets
on the British package market.
Hotels With the exception of The
Peaks and one or two others, all the
hotels are in and around the town.
££££ The Peaks The biggest, plushest
and priciest hotel – and the biggest
eyesore in Mountain Village; although
built only a couple of years ago, it
appears to be modelled on the
concrete monstrosities thrown up by
the French in the 1960s. It has already
changed ownership and name (it was
formerly the Doral); and it may by
now have changed colour – it was
painted in drab shades to minimise
the visual impact in summer and
autumn, thus cleverly maximising the
impact in winter. Once you're inside,
of course, all this is forgiven. The new
owners have given the spacious public
areas a warm and inviting ambience,
the bedrooms are big and plush, and it
has a large and very smart health spa
with saunas, steam rooms, pool,
squash courts, a vast range of exercise
machinery and whatever else you
could want. The hotel is conveniently
placed for skiing, on a loop off the
main beginner run (and there is a ski
hire shop in the basement).
£££ New Sheridan One of the town's
oldest and most atmospheric hotels,
about to be entirely revamped when
we visited last season and by now no
doubt irresistible. At the heart of
things on the main street.
£££ Viking Suite New place that
offers luxury suites and couldn't be
more convenient for the Coonskin lift
out of the village.

PACKAGES

American Dream, American Skiworld, Made to Measure, Ski Independence

ACTIVITIES

Indoor Swimming, galleries, Athletics Club (racquetball, aerobics, weights, steam room, massage), health spa, theatre, roller skating, cinema
Outdoor Dinner sleigh rides, ice skating, hot springs, snow-mobiling, glider rides, heli-skiing, climbing instruction, sledding, skating, horse-riding, ballooning, snow-shoe tours

TOURIST OFFICE

Postcode CO 81435
Tel 010 1 (303) 7287404
Fax 7286364

£££ Pennington's Inn Luxy B&B place in inconvenient but secluded setting (with great views) outside the Mountain Village
££ San Sophia Smart, traditional B&B close to Oak Street lift.
££ Alpine Inn Dinky B&B on main street, just west of centre.
££ Skyline Guest Ranch Genuine turn-of-the-century ranch about 15 minutes out of town, with lovely mountain views. Charming rustic rooms, excellent food and a warm welcome from owners Dave and Sherry Farny (it's known to its friends as The Farny Farm – geddit?). There's a minibus service to and from town but only at the start and end of the day and once in the early evening. Cross-country skiing (and snow-mobile) trails start nearby.
Self-catering There are plenty of condos and houses to rent both in town and up at Mountain Village, but none offered by British tour operators. However, the Viking Suite Hotel has self-catering accommodation available through American Dream. It's not particularly luxurious by US standards, but comfortable enough, and is well placed for the town and chair-lift.

WHERE TO EAT
A wide choice
There's pretty much anything you want. La Marmotte is the place for French cuisine, the Athenian Suite for Greek-Italian, Leimgruber's for German-Austrian, Eddie's for pizzas, One World for Chinese and a choice of venues for Tex-Mex and typical American, including the atmospheric Legends Tavern & Grille and T-Ride Country Club, where you can cook your own steaks. About the best food in town is at 221 South Oak – innovative, ambitious food in stylish surroundings. Powderhouse also takes its food seriously. Out of town, the Peaks hotel, at Mountain Village, has two restaurants for formal dining, and the Skyline guest ranch has excellent food and wine in a country setting (where you can combine dinner with snow-mobiling).

APRES-SKI
Plenty going on
Telluride has a lively bar-based après-ski scene. Leimgruber's is popular for immediate post-skiing drinking, replicating an Alpine stube – right down to a Stammtisch reserved for ski instructors and their guests, and Paulaner on draught. The San Juan Brewing Company and Baked and Brewed in Telluride both have good

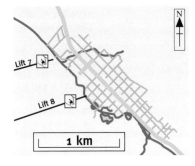

1 km

brewed-on-the-premises beers – the former in the spectacularly restored old railway station known as the Depot (live music on Fridays). Swede-Finn Hall is a relaxed and popular bar and restaurant, with four pool tables downstairs. The Last Dollar Saloon and the bar at the New Sheraton Hotel are traditional drinking venues with lots of old-time atmosphere. Fly Me To The Moon Saloon sometimes has live music, and dancing in its basement may go on into the early hours. The Opera House is a movie theatre, but a thriving amateur rep company performs at the Nugget theatre.

FOR NON-SKIERS
Quite amusing, for a while
For a small resort there's a surprising amount of non-skiing activities to be tried. A glider flight over the ski area is spectacular (ask for Glider Bob. If he has enough altitude left on the home run he'll offer to loop the loop; go for it). The local token cowboy, Roudy, can take you riding. On the whole, though, Telluride is difficult to recommend to non-skiers.

Vail 2500m

✔ *The biggest ski area in the US*

✔ *Superb piste grooming*

✔ *Ideal beginner and intermediate skiing in trails cut through trees*

✔ *Back Bowls offer the biggest area of treeless, go-anywhere skiing for intermediate and good skiers in US*

✔ *Despite its size, Vail is friendly and tastefully-built, largely in Tyrolean-style*

✔ *Excellent reputation for ski school and children's facilities*

✔ *Both Vail and Beaver Creek are largely traffic-free*

✘ *The famous Back Bowls face south, and the snow can suffer in warm weather*

✘ *Tyrolean-style architecture of Vail and modern luxury of Beaver Creek are far from the Wild West atmosphere you might look for on a trip to the US*

✘ *Expensive, especially Beaver Creek*

✘ *Some long lift queues in Vail*

Vail, Beaver Creek and now Arrowhead are all run by the same company. Vail cultivates an exclusive image – but the other two are even more upmarket.

The prices reflect the image. But many are prepared to pay them for the luxurious accommodation, relaxed atmosphere and wonderfully groomed trails you get. They make ideal beginner and intermediate terrain – the biggest in the US. Better skiers will also find runs to interest them in Vail's Back Bowls, if the snow is good, and on the steepest runs of Beaver Creek.

But these aren't the resorts to visit if you're looking for somewhere with a real feel of the Wild West. Vail was developed from scratch in the 1960s, and Beaver Creek opened in 1980. They have no buildings or traditions dating from the gold- and silver-mining days of the movies.

ORIENTATION

Vail is the biggest US ski resort. It stretches for seven miles at the foot of its mountain, beside the freeway. The skiing can be accessed from four main places: by chair from Golden Peak in the east or Cascade Village in the west by high-speed quad from Vail Village centre; and by high-speed quad or gondola from Lionshead. These are easily accessed from all accommodation by frequent free buses.

Sister resort **Beaver Creek** is ten miles to the west, and covered by the same lift pass. It is much smaller and built at the foot of its own skiing, accessed by a high-speed quad. **Arrowhead** is smaller still, and will eventually be linked-in to the Beaver Creek skiing by its own fast quad.

Other resorts within a two-hour drive include **Aspen, Breckenridge, Copper Mountain, Keystone** and **Steamboat**.

🏔 The resort

Standing in the centre of traffic-free Vail, surrounded by chalet-style wooden buildings and bierkellers, you could be forgiven for thinking you were in a top Austrian resort. And that's just how founder Pete Seibert intended it to be when he envisaged it in the 1950s. Vail is now enormous, stretching for seven miles at the foot of the biggest ski mountain in the US. There are hotels, condos, bars, restaurants and night-spots to suit every taste and pocket.

Beaver Creek, a resort developed by the owners of Vail in the 1980s, is ten miles to the west of Vail itself. It is unashamedly upmarket and luxurious, with a choice of top-quality hotels and condominiums right by the slopes. It is pedestrian-only and built around a huge square featuring exquisite bronze statues and even an open-air fire to warm you up on evening promenades.

Arrowhead is the newest addition to Vail's portfolio. A collection of luxury, secluded chalets, it was a tiny exclusive resort until bought by Vail. Arrowhead will be linked to Beaver Creek's skiing for the 1995/6 season.

Between them, Vail and Beaver Creek already have so many 'firsts' it's unbelievable: biggest ski area in the US; most high-speed quad chair-lifts in the world, most snow-grooming machines, and most ski instructors (over 1,100 of them).

SKI FACTS

Altitude	2500m-3490m
Lifts	35
Pistes	5139 acres
Green	17%
Blue	37%
Black	46%
Art. snow	693 acres

LIFT PASSES

93/94 prices in dollars
Vail and Beaver Creek
Covers all Vail and Beaver Creek lifts, and ski-bus around resort.
Beginners Half- (60), 1- (75) and 3-day (210) Learn-to-ski courses include lift pass. 3-day includes equipment rental.
Main pass
1-day pass 42
6-day pass 234
Senior citizens
Over 65: 6-day pass 192 (18% off)
Over 70: free pass
Children
Under 13: 6-day pass 174 (26% off)
Short-term passes
Return trips on some lifts for foot passengers only. Half-day pass from noon available (adult 37).
Alternative passes
Premier Passport is designed for a two-centre holiday. It covers all Aspen and Vail-Beaver Creek skiing, and one-way transport between the resorts. Allows from 10 days skiing out of 12 up to 18 out of 21 (38 per day).

The skiing

Vail and Beaver Creek together have the biggest ski area in the US. It leapt to fame in the UK by hosting the 1989 World Championships and is now the number two US destination for UK skiers (behind Breckenridge). But although big by US standards, it's not by European ones. It can't compare with the likes of Val-d'Isère-Tignes and the Trois Vallées. Its area is more like Wengen, Kitzbühel or St Anton.

The resort's skiing stands out for our reporters' enthusiasm for it. We've had many reports on it, nearly all glowing with praise. 'Brilliant', 'Excellent', 'Grooming exemplary', 'Hazard marking superb' are typical. The main criticism – made by several correspondents – is that some of the runs (especially single black diamonds) are over-graded.

THE SKI AREA
Something for everyone

The Vail and Beaver Creek ski areas are completely separate but linked by bus and covered on the same lift pass. They also feel very different.

Vail gets much more crowded. Its skiing divides neatly into two. The front face is largely north-facing, with well-groomed trails cut through the trees. Efficient chair-lifts and a gondola take you from various points along the long valley floor to mid-mountain, where **Mid-Vail** (3080m) is the main focal point. From here chairs take you to various points along the ridge, which reaches 3430m.

From the top ridge you drop over into the **Back Bowls**; these are largely south-facing and rejoice in names such as Sun Up, Sun Down, China, Teacup and Siberia Bowls. The bowls are mainly open, free of trees, and for the most part unpisted. The story goes that the bowls were denuded of trees by the peace-loving Ute Indians, who were driven from their land by the white men in the 1880s and took revenge by setting fire to their forests before they left.

Beaver Creek is overlooked by many Vail-based skiers. That makes it delightfully uncrowded. There's a high-speed quad from the resort up to **Spruce Saddle**, the mid-mountain focus. From there you can carry on up or ski down to more lifts left and right. Going right takes you to lifts up two separate mountains – **Grouse** (with the best steep skiing) and **Larkspur Bowl**. It also leads to what will be the connection to the

Arrowhead ski area and the newly developed Bachelor Gulch, from where a new lift will bring you back to Beaver Creek's own skiing. These connections have much of their infrastructure already in place.

We love Beaver Creek's skiing and think it is vastly underrated by most visitors who stick to Vail.

SNOW RELIABILITY
Excellent, except in the Bowls

Apart from the exceptional natural snow record, Vail and Beaver Creek both have extensive snowmaking facilities, normally needed only in early season. But one of the biggest disappointments about Vail is that its famous Back Bowls are largely south-facing. That means a fresh snowfall can often get ruined quickly if it's sunny. In three visits we've never hit the champagne powder conditions for which the Back Bowls are ideal.

The steep Grouse Mountain skiing in Beaver Creek can also suffer from thin snow cover.

FOR ADVANCED SKIERS
Enough to keep most people happy

Vail's Back Bowls are vast areas, served by three chair-lifts and a drag-lift. You can ski virtually anywhere you like in their 2,734 acres, trying the gradient and terrain of your choice. There are areas of interesting tree-skiing as well as the more common tree-free mogulled slopes. Some runs are groomed, making it easy for groups of mixed ability to take different routes and ride the lifts together.

The steepest runs are probably Wow and Forever on Sun Down Bowl, which funnel in to the High Noon lift.

On the front face there are some steep, often mogulled, slopes which frequently have better snow than the Back Bowls because of their orientation. The Highline lift on the extreme east of the ski area serves three double black diamond runs – Blue Ox, Highline and Roger's Run. Prima, which comes down from the ridge Summit, is also steep.

The rest of the mountain has a few short black runs and the long Minnies Mile which is a wonderful fast cruise when it has been groomed.

In Beaver Creek, Grouse Mountain is the place for experts to head for. This is almost entirely black run territory. We've twice found this area wonderful but rather bare in parts. Other good steep blacks lead down to the bottom of Grouse from the main mountain summit. This is called the Birds of Prey area because of the runs named after them – Goshawk, Peregrine and Golden Eagle.

The Larkspur Bowl area has three short steep mogul runs worth trying.

The other thing good skiers will love about Beaver Creek is the lack of crowds. Even by American standards, Beaver Creek's runs are often deserted. That means it's normally safe to bomb around the immaculately groomed blue runs at speeds that you couldn't contemplate on Europe's crowded slopes. We've gone flat out with the most responsible of guides every time we've visited.

But the more macho advanced skiers may find too little to challenge them in Vail-Beaver Creek. The Back Bowls, in particular, have disappointed some of our more dare-devil correspondents, because they judge them too tame.

FOR INTERMEDIATE SKIERS
Ideal territory

The majority of Vail's front face is easy cruising, tree-lined blue runs. Particularly on the western side of the area there are excellent long blues such as the easy Born Free and the faster Simba, which both go from top to bottom of the mountain. If you drop over into Game Creek Bowl, you can try Showboat, under the lift, or other blues down from the ridge.

As well, as tackling some of the easier front-face blacks, intermediates will find plenty of interest in the Back Bowls. There are a couple of usually pisted blue runs, Poppyfields and Sleepytime, which both lead down to the Orient Express chair.

And the Silk Road blue leads from the top of the Mongolia drag-lift at the extreme eastern side of the skiing. There are wonderful views from here towards Copper Mountain (much nearer and easier to build a lift-link to than Beaver Creek). The run goes right around the ski area boundary back to the Orient Express lift, with splendid views of the virgin mountain across the river (which Vail has earmarked for expansion into to provide some much-needed north-facing bowl skiing).

All these blues are easily tackled even by early intermediates. More adventurous ones can branch out to try some of the unpisted bowl skiing, much of which is reasonably gentle. In fresh snow this can make the ideal introduction to powder skiing.

Beaver Creek is an intermediate skier's dream. There are marvellous long cruising blue runs almost everywhere you look. Centennial runs from top to bottom of the main

mountain – a vertical drop of just over 1000m. It starts off green and has a black section in the centre (which can be avoided) but is genuine blue for most of its length. Harrier and Red Tail down to the foot of Grouse Mountain and Larkspur Bowl were another two of our favourite long cruises. Larkspur Bowl itself is a huge wide blue run with several variations possible on the lower part of it.

The Arrowhead area is another ideal intermediate area. Served by only one lift, there is a fair variety of runs – our favourites were Golden Bear, Cresta and the black Real McCoy.

FOR BEGINNERS
Difficult to beat

Last season Vail opened a new mountain-top teaching area of five runs, served by six lifts – the Eagle's Nest Beginner Park. It also has separate adult and children areas, a special area to teach safe skiing procedures, an environmental education trail and a native American village.

Combine this dedicated teaching area with Vail ski school's high reputation and you have a very appealing combination. The area is suited to both complete beginners and those trying to make a breakthrough later on in their skiing career.

Once you are off the beginners' slopes, there are plenty of easy greens to progress to – on both the top and bottom parts of the mountain. Cub's Way, Gitalong Road and the lower part of Born Free on the eastern side of the ski area are ideal. Overeasy, Ramshorn and Flapjack on the top part of the mountain are also excellent gentle runs for first-week skiers.

Beaver Creek has good village-level nursery slopes and its fair share of easy greens to progress to. Cinch runs virtually from top to bottom of the main mountain, with Dally the main alternative on the bottom half. There is a good choice of greens on the top half too.

The little-used Strawberry Park lift serves a lot of easy blue run skiing as well as the mountain-top cross-country area.

FOR CROSS-COUNTRY
Some of the best

Vail's cross-country areas are at the foot of Golden Peak and at the Nordic Centre on the golf course. At Beaver Creek, there's a splendid mountain-top network of 32km of tracks at McCoy Park, at the top of the Strawberry Park lift out of the resort.

QUEUES
Can be bad in Vail

Vail has some of the longest lift queues we've come across in the US. Although they move quickly and are well disciplined (as they are everywhere in the US), they come as a shock in comparison with the queue-free environment of most US resorts.

The worst queues (perhaps 20 minutes) build up for the Vista Bahn Express from the middle of town in the morning rush, the Mountaintop Express from Mid-Vail to the top and for the Back Bowl chair-lifts when the snow there is good. Weekends are the worst times because Vail is near enough to Denver to attract weekenders in significant numbers. Reporters thought the traffic-light system at the main lift notice boards was useful for identifying and allowing them to avoid the worst queues.

Beaver Creek, on the other hand, is virtually queue-free – it is amazing that more people don't go there to get away from the Vail crowds.

MOUNTAIN RESTAURANTS
Trying hard

While still far from a gourmet's delight, Vail is trying hard to bring its mountain dining facilities up to European standards.

The Two Elk restaurant was opened for the 1991/92 season. It is huge, and beautifully designed, featuring massive wooden pillars, a high roof and a number of different seating areas.

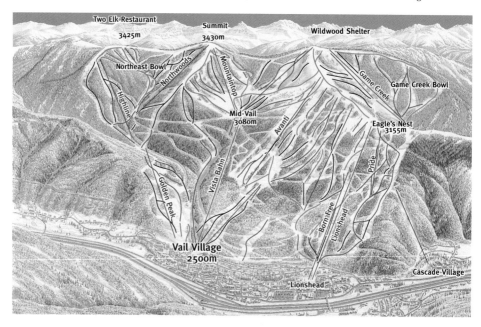

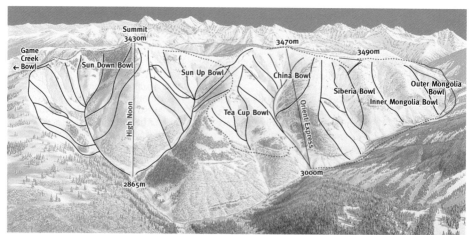

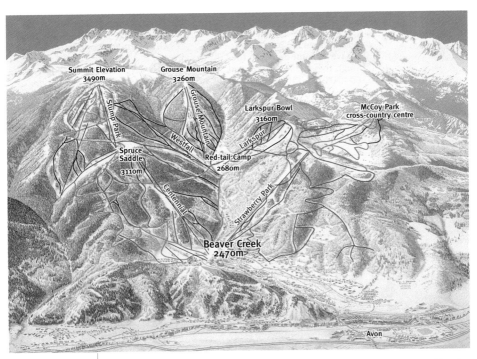

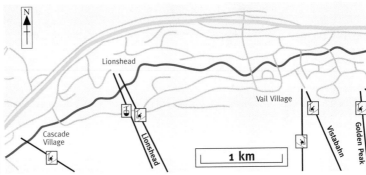

SKI SCHOOL

93/94 prices in dollars

Vail and Beaver Creek
At four locations –
Vail Village,
Lionshead, Golden
Peak and Beaver
Creek

Classes 6 days
5hr: 9.45-3.45 with
1hr lunch; 3hr 15mins:
12.30-3.45
3 full days: 200

Children's classes
Ages: 3 to 12
6 6½hr days including
lunch: 420

Private lessons
1hr, 2hr, half- and
full-day
90 for 1hr, for 1 to 5
people

There's a good choice of food, with salad and pasta bars, and a big selection of grills.

At Mid-Vail there are a couple of large self-service cafeterias and the best table-service restaurant on the mountain in Cook Shack (it's best to reserve a table). The Wine Stube at the top of the Lionshead gondola is also table-service, and there's a self-service restaurant there too.

At Beaver Creek, Spruce Saddle at mid-mountain is the main place for lunch. For last season it was rebuilt along the lines of Two Elk. But the place to go at lunch – if you can get in – is the exclusive Beano's Cabin. This is a private members' club at lunchtime, but it's worth trying to wangle your way in as a guest. It serves superb food in a beautifully-built wooden cabin situated in the woods off the piste near Larkspur

Bowl. At night it's open to all via sleigh-rides – see Eating Out, page 439.

In both Vail and Beaver Creek there are smaller places you can ski into for a swift snack.

SKI SCHOOL
One of the best in the world

The Vail-Beaver Creek ski school has an excellent reputation. All the reports we've had of it have been glowing. It's also one of the biggest, with over 1,100 instructors in high season. This number helps keep class sizes down – as few as four is not uncommon.

We can vouch for the high standard of instruction. We've tried three different instructors, and all have been excellent. Instructors get bonuses for repeat customers, so there's a financial incentive for them to give their clients what they want. In addition to normal classes and private lessons, there are

CHILDCARE

Ski school tuition is based at Children's Ski Centers located at Golden Peak and Lionshead in Vail, and at Beaver Creek resort. There are separate programmes to suit children of different ages and skiing competence – Mini-Mice for children aged 3, Mogul Mice and Superstars for those aged 4 to 6.

Small World Play Schools, at Golden Peak in Vail and at Beaver Creek, take children aged 2 months to 6 years, from 8am to 4.30

GETTING THERE

Air Eagle, transfer 1hr. Denver, transfer 2½hr.

PACKAGES

American Connections, American Dream, American Skiworld, Bladon Lines, Crystal, Enterprise, Go Worlds Apart, Inghams, Lotus Supertravel, Made to Measure, Ski Activity, Ski Independence, Ski Val, Snow Cocktail, USAirtours

Beaver Creek
American Connections, American Dream, American Skiworld, Crystal, Inghams, Lotus Supertravel, Made to Measure, Ski Independence, USAirtours

specialist half-day workshops in, for example, bumps and powder. You can sign up the same day at a choice of mountain-top offices.

FACILITIES FOR CHILDREN
Excellent

The comprehensive arrangements for young children look excellent, and the one report we have on the children's classes says they are 'reliable, safe, kind, fun'. At both Vail and Beaver Creek there are splendid children's areas with adventure skiing trails and themed play areas.

 # Staying there

Vail is vast in ski resort terms. The most convenient – and expensive – places to stay are in Vail Village centre near the Vista Bahn lift or in Lionshead, near the gondola. Of these we prefer Vail Village, which has the best of the mock-Tyrolean architecture and atmosphere. The Lionshead building style – which came later – is more dully modern.

But there is a lot of accommodation further out – the cheapest tends to be across the main I-70 freeway, but lacks the real Vail atmosphere.

The whole resort, however, is connected by a very efficient free bus-service, which brings universal praise from our reporters.

Beaver Creek can be reached by a shuttle bus from Vail. Staying there is an option for the wealthy. It is an unashamedly upmarket resort with a fair choice of luxurious, expensive hotels, all within an easy walk of the slopes. Nightlife and choice of bars and restaurants is much more limited than in Vail; it's not for those who want a wild time.

HOW TO GO
Package or independent

There's a big choice of packages to Vail and a smaller one to Beaver Creek. It's also very easy to organise your own visit, with regular shuttles from Denver airport by Vans to Vail. Hiring a car would be worthwhile if you wanted to visit other resorts such as Breckenridge, but is superfluous in traffic-free Vail and Beaver Creek.
Chalets The widest choice of any US resort. Supertravel have very comfortable places, with all mod cons, in East Vail. In the same area, Crystal have a selection of places, several of which have been praised by our reporters. If you prefer West Vail, the luxurious private homes featured by

Ski Activity are difficult to beat. Ski Val have an impressive, luxurious family home in a secluded spot, best for those with a car. Good apartments out at Gore Creek are also run as catered chalets by Ski Independence and American Skiworld. This season, top-of-the-market operator The Ski Company is opening its first US chalet in Vail.
Hotels Vail has a fair choice of hotels, ranging from luxurious to budget. In the more upmarket Beaver Creek you can go completely overboard.
At Vail:
£££££ Lodge at Vail The best hotel in Vail, owned by Orient Express Hotels. It is right by the Vista Bahn Express, in the centre of Vail Village. Its amazing buffet breakfast features smoked salmon and cold meats as well as hot food, and keeps most people going all day, and its Wildflower restaurant one of the best in town.
££££ Sonnenalp There are various Sonnenalp hotels in town. The most luxurious is the Bavaria House with a large sports complex and splendid piano bar-lounge. Also recommended are Austria House and Swiss House.
£££ Vail Village Inn Condo and hotel complex, recently renovated and rebuilt. Comfortable and cheaper option than many Vail Village hotels. Outdoor pool.
£££ Chateau Vail (Holiday Inn) Not quite as central. Adequate comfort, with a pool.
££ Roost Lodge A popular budget option in West Vail, with comfortable rooms and friendly, helpful staff. Pool, sauna, hot tub, constant free coffee and regular cheese and wine parties.
At Beaver Creek:
£££££ Beaver Creek Lodge All-suite hotel. Luxurious. Health club with pool, sauna and so on.
£££££ Hyatt Regency Standard Hyatt luxury. Lively bar in basement.
Self-catering There are numerous options. For those who want lots of in-house amenities, the Racquet Club at East Vail is superb. American Dream have an allocation of high-standard apartments and town houses available here, with use of pool, health centre and, of course, racket sports. Ski-convenience fans should perhaps opt for Ski Activity's nice places next to the Lionshead gondola. Inghams also have high-quality apartments nearby. Lotus Supertravel have a wide range of condos and private homes. American Skiworld offer a choice of central or East Vail, in less luxurious but perfectly comfortable places. Enterprise have some budget options.

ACTIVITIES

Indoor Athletic clubs and spas, massage, museum, cinema, tennis courts, artificial skating rink, library, galleries

Outdoor Hot-air ballooning, skating, ice hockey, heli-skiing, sleigh rides, fishing, mountaineering, snowmobiles, snow-shoe excursions, snowcat tours, bobsleighing, dog-sledding, para-gliding

TOURIST OFFICE

Postcode 81658
Tel 010 1 (303)
8455724
Fax 8455728

STAYING UP THE MOUNTAIN
Great if you can afford it

Trappers Cabin is a luxurious private cabin up the mountain, which a group can rent by the night ($500 each for a minimum of four people). You ski in at end of the day to a champagne welcome, make a snow-shoe excursion to see the sunset, soak in an outdoor hot tub and enjoy a gourmet dinner. The cabin-keeper then leaves until morning. Splendid isolation.

STAYING DOWN THE VALLEY
Cheaper but dull

Staying out of central Vail is certainly cheaper but not so enjoyable. **East** and **West Vail** both have reasonably priced accommodation.

Another budget option is to stay in **Avon** at the foot of the approach road up to Beaver Creek. Day-trippers have to leave their cars here and take the shuttle bus up to the resort.

It's not a very atmospheric town but it does have a number of reasonably priced hotels and motels. The Comfort Inn is used by a fair number of tour operators.

If you rent a car, staying out of town and visiting nearby resorts makes for an interesting holiday.

EATING OUT
Endless choice

Whichever kind of food you want, Vail has it. Pizza, Burger, Tex Mex, Chinese, Japanese, Moroccan, Italian, Thai and a big choice of European-style fine dining. But expect to pay for it. Vail is not a cheap place for eating and drinking.

The Wildflower, in the Lodge, and Ludwig's, in the Sonnenalp Bavaria House, are two of the best fine-dining places in Vail. The Saddleridge, in Beaver Creek, offers a marvellous night out. It is a luxurious wooden building packed with photos and Wild West artefacts, including old six-shooters and General Custer's hat.

The sleigh-ride to Beano's Cabin in Beaver Creek also makes a fine evening out. The food and setting are several cuts above the average 'dinner sleigh-ride'.

For a budget option we liked the micro brewery in Vail Village, which as well as a choice of local ales has a filling menu of typical American food.

Recommendations from readers include Pepis, Ostello, Ambrosia, Left Bank and Cyrano's.

APRES-SKI
Lively after skiing, but early to bed

A combination of staying at high altitude and the early opening and closing times of lifts, makes Vail's nightlife a short pre-dinner affair. Things are fairly buzzing from three till five, then it's an early evening meal before tiredness sets in for the night.

Many of our reporters have fallen into the convenient, though rather dire, Red Lion after skiing, but there are plenty of better places: the Hong Kong Café is popular for its cocktails; the Swiss Chalet attempts to recreate European 'gemütlichkeit'; King's Club is the place to go for high-calorie cake intake, and becomes a piano bar later; Babau's Café is a piano bar with live jazz; and Los Amigos and the Micro Brewery are other atmospheric places at around four o'clock.

Cyrano's is one of the few places to stay lively throughout the evening, serving good food and becoming a disco later. The Jackalope Café and Cantina is another late joint, and has live entertainment and good food; it's also about the best place in town for rubbing shoulders with the real local 'country boys'.

Cassidy's Hole In The Wall is an Old West saloon reconstruction, with live entertainment including country and western bands. A more authentic Old West scene can be experienced in the 4 Eagle Ranch, a homestead dating from the 1860s, 6km out of town. It has Western-style entertainment such as country and western barn dancing with instructions for the uninitiated.

Nick's and the Club are the main discos in town, but usually only come to life at weekends.

FOR NON-SKIERS
Mainly a skier's resort

Vail and Beaver Creek, like most US resorts, will suit keen skiers best. But there are a lot of other activities to try. Excursions to other resorts and to Denver are feasible.

Canada

Can it really be worth going all the way to western Canada for just a couple of isolated resorts? Well, yes it can, when (in different ways) they are among the most impressive resorts in North America. We'd go back like a shot – and try to visit both main resorts.

Canada combines the best of US skiing with the best of European skiing. It has the service and courtesy that is so striking when you first visit the US – mountain hosts to show you around the slopes, immaculately groomed runs, civilised lift queues, lots of high-speed quad chair-lifts, piste maps available at the bottom of most lifts, and lift operators who seem happy in their job and appear to want you to have a good time. But what distinguishes Canadian from American skiing – at least in the resorts we feature here – is that the mountains resemble those of the Alps. You get spectacular scenery of the kind that is very rare in the US, and very extensive skiing – particularly at Whistler-Blackcomb, which has the biggest vertical drop and highest piste mileage in North America, and a lot of open skiing above the tree-line as well as woodland runs.

Banff-Lake Louise has another big plus-point. It is surrounded by Canadian National Park land and an amazing variety of wildlife that you'd never come across in Europe. Herds of elk and big-horn sheep roam the streets and roadsides. You might even see a moose or bear. Winter is Banff's low season – hotel prices are half their summer levels and the resort offers excellent value for money.

Canada is also home to the world's most famous heli-skiing operations, where you can stay for a week in a luxurious lodge and be whirled up to virgin powder for several runs a day. If you are staying in a resort, you can try heli-skiing for a day if you like.

There are downsides to Canada's skiing though. Whistler suffers from a lot of bad weather coming in from the Pacific Ocean – it is practically on the coast. While this normally means a lot of snow up top, it can also mean a lot of rain at resort level, and days on end without sight of the sun. Banff and nearby Lake Louise have a different problem – especially in early season, temperatures can be bitterly cold (-20°C is not uncommon; -30°C not unknown). Riding a high-speed chair in very low temperatures isn't much fun. Banff also suffers from the fact that there are no villages at the bases of the ski areas – you have to stay a bus- or car-ride away.

Banff-Lake Louise 1340–1660m

HOW IT RATES

The skiing

Snow	*****
Extent	****
Advanced	***
Intermediates	****
Beginners	***
Convenience	*
Queues	*****
Restaurants	*

The rest

Scenery	****
Resort charm	***
Not skiing	***

✔ Three ski areas between them have a large amount of skiing

✔ Excellent snow record over long season (November to May)

✔ Really spectacular high mountain scenery – the best in North America

✘ Can be extremely cold, especially in early season

✘ Separate ski areas are a long drive from each other and there is no accommodation at their bases

There are few ski areas we have such mixed feelings about as Banff-Lake Louise. They are set in the spectacular and unspoilt Banff National Park. The landscape is one of glaciers, jagged peaks and magnificent views. The valleys are full of wildlife that you'll never see in Europe.

The accommodation is tremendous value because winter is their low season. The skiing has something for everyone, from steep couloirs to gentle cruising. The snow is some of the coldest, driest and most reliable you'll find anywhere in the world. And there's a lot of it.

And yet we have mixed feelings? Only because of the 'resorts'. They don't feel like ski resorts as we know them in Europe and the US because they are miles away from their ski slopes. Banff, in particular, feels like what it is – a summer tourist trap trying to earn some extra money from the much quieter winter season.

ORIENTATION

Banff is a summer resort with three separate ski areas nearby, 10 to 45 minutes away by efficient bus – Lake Louise, Sunshine Village and Norquay/Mystic Ridge. **Lake Louise** 'village' is a five-minute drive from the ski area of the same name.

The resort

Most people (including the people who work on the mountains) stay in Banff – which is a 45-minute drive from the largest ski area (Lake Louise), 20 minutes from the Sunshine area and 10 minutes from Mount Norquay/Mystic Ridge.

Banff is spectacularly set with several towering peaks rising up around its outskirts. There is lots of wildlife around. Don't be surprised to find a herd of elk or long-horned sheep outside your hotel. And watch out for black (and even grizzly) bears on the drives to and from the skiing.

Banff gained its independence from the National Park authority in 1990.

Since then it has seen substantial growth and development. But it still consists largely of one long main street and a small network of side roads built in the usual North American grid fashion.

Banff is primarily a summer, rather than winter, resort – hotel prices double for the summer season. The main street is lined with hotels, condominiums, restaurants and tacky souvenir shops – many obviously catering for the Japanese market.

The buildings themselves have been successfully confined to low-rise developments. But despite many wooden clapboard buildings, it lacks genuine charm. It's not another Aspen or Telluride for atmosphere.

The only other place to stay is Lake Louise village, a five-minute drive from the ski area of the same name. But the village is not on the lake; that's another five-minute drive. And 'village' is rather too grand an expression for the tiny collection of hotels, condominiums, petrol station, supermarket, liquor store and few shops. If Banff lacks charm, Lake Louise village lacks it even more. But it does have one excellent hotel.

In marked contrast is Lake Louise itself, site of the Chateau Lake Louise hotel. In terms of scenery, you'd be hard-pressed to find anywhere more beautiful in your skiing travels.

In 1882, Tom Watson, a surveyor for the Canadian Pacific Railroad, was the first white man to set eyes on this lake and the 3564m Victoria Glacier towering above it. On seeing the view Watson exclaimed, 'As God is my judge, I never in all my exploration have seen such a matchless scene.' Neither have we.

SKI FACTS

Altitude 1635m-2730m
Lifts	28
Pistes	5000 acres
Green	25%
Blue	45%
Black	30%
Art. snow	870 acres

 # The skiing

In sharp contrast to our lack of enthusiasm for the villages, we find the skiing hard to beat. Taking account of all three mountains, the ski area is big, and the views are the most spectacular that the Rockies have to offer, rivalling the best in the Alps.

THE SKI AREA
A lot of moving around to do
The biggest of the three ski areas (claimed to be the biggest in North America in terms of skiable acreage, but it certainly isn't in terms of marked pistes) is **Lake Louise**.

Two successive high-speed quads take you to the top of the main mountain. From here, as elsewhere, there's a choice of green, blue or black runs to other lifts. So skiers of varying standards can ski the same lifts together. Almost all the mountain is wooded, good for when it's snowing.

From the top there's a stunning view of some of the high peaks of the Continental Divide (which runs from Canada to New Mexico), including Canada's uncanny Matterhorn lookalike, Mount Assiniboine.

Go over the back of this top ridge and you're into Lake Louise's tree-less back bowl skiing, which is predominantly north-facing and so keeps its snow in good condition.

From the bottom of the bowl runs you can take a lift back to the top again or up to the **Larch** area. This is the area's other mountain and was the original Lake Louise ski area. Served by one double chair, it has a number of pretty, wooded, relatively short runs. From the bottom you can return to the top of the main mountain or ski back to the main base area along a lengthy green path.

There are plans to build a lift up Richardson's Ridge, on the far side of the back bowls, and open up a whole new area of lift-served skiing.

The Lake Louise ski area is owned by Charles Locke, who amassed his fortune in oil and on the stockmarket. He bought the ski area in 1981 through his appropriately named company, Locke, Stock and Barrel. His wife is also appropriately named – yes, she's called Louise!

The second largest ski area is **Sunshine Village**, 20 minutes' drive from Banff, 40 from Lake Louise village. It has the highest skiing and best snow record in the area. It prides itself on not needing any artificial snow – we skied right to the bottom in late April without seeing a bare spot.

Most of the skiing is above the tree-line, up to 2730m. If the weather is bad, it would be best to ski elsewhere. But in good weather this is a great area.

You reach the ski area by taking a long (25-minute) gondola to the main on-mountain base. At the moment there isn't much skiing below this. But there are plans to open up a whole new mountain for skiing, increasing the skiable area by over 60 per cent.

Even without the new area, Sunshine has enough skiing to keep the keenest skier happy for a couple of days, with lifts fanning out in all directions and good snow throughout a long season.

Mystic Ridge-Norquay was Banff's first – and remains its smallest

LIFT PASSES

94/95 prices in Canadian dollars

Tri-area lift pass
Covers all lifts and transport between Banff, Lake Louise and Sunshine Village.

Main pass
1-day pass 40
6-day pass 240

Children
Under 13: 6-day pass 84 (65% off)

Short-term passes
Half-day pass for individual areas of Lake Louise, Sunshine Village or Mystic Ridge/Norquay. Return trips for foot passengers on the Sulphur Mountain Gondola.

Notes Tri-area only available for 3 days or more, and includes a coupon worth 7 dollars towards other services at Mystic Ridge/Norquay.

Alternative passes
Day passes for individual areas of Lake Louise, Sunshine Village or Mystic Ridge/Norquay, with reductions for senior citizens.

– ski area, 10 minutes' drive from town and served by just five lifts. Until a few years ago, this area was known simply as Mount Norquay. It consisted of a tiny area of easy slopes at the bottom, and one lift higher up serving a choice of some of the toughest runs in the area. Then two new lifts were added which serve tree-lined, predominantly intermediate slopes. This area opens for floodlit night-skiing once a week.

SNOW RELIABILITY
Excellent
When we were last there, in late April 1993, there was plenty of snow everywhere on both Lake Louise and Sunshine. And that was at the end of what the locals claim was the worst winter for snow in many years. Mystic Ridge-Norquay was shut due to lack of customers rather than snow. Wherever it's needed, there's artificial snowmaking.

FOR ADVANCED SKIERS
Widespread pleasure
Good skiers will want to spend most of their time at the Lake Louise area. The back bowls offer endless variations of black mogul and powder runs. Many people's favourite is Paradise Bowl – one run is marked on the map but there are at least three commonly skied routes here, and scores of other variants. Others prefer the runs at the far west which take you right away from all signs of lifts. The two steepest are Ridge Run and Whitehorn One. Again, there are endless variations.

Because this is National Park, you can ski anywhere. But the areas outside the boundaries aren't patrolled and there's no avalanche control. A guide is essential.

On the front of the mountain there are more tough runs including Outer Limits, Sunset and the Men's and Women's Downhills.

Sunshine has plenty of open bumps skiing above the tree-line. One particular novelty is a short, steep pitch, near the mid-station, known as the Waterfall run – because you do actually ski down over a snow-covered frozen fall. The proposed extension to the ski area also promises a lot of good advanced skiing.

Norquay has the only double black diamond runs in the region, one a 35-degree bump run, the other a steep gunbarrel. There's a decent selection of other blacks to keep you happy.

FOR INTERMEDIATE SKIERS
Ideal runs wherever you go
On all three mountains, at least 45 per cent of the runs are classified as intermediate. One thing which characterises both Lake Louise and Sunshine is that there is a wide choice of runs from the top of virtually all lifts. Wherever you look there are blue and green ways down – some of the greens as enjoyable (and pretty much as steep) cruises as the blues.

On Louise, Meadowlark is a beautiful tree-lined run from the top of the Eagle chair to the base area. Juniper and Juniper Jungle are wonderful cruising runs on the western side. The Larch area has some short but enjoyable intermediate terrain. And the adventurous should try the blue-graded Boomerang which starts with a hike from the top of the highest lift, the Summit Platter drag. On many runs one side is groomed, the other left to develop moguls.

On Sunshine, we particularly liked the World Cup Downhill run which goes right from the top of the ski area

---

Free ski-guiding

All three areas pride themselves on their free ski-guiding services. Just turn up at one of the two or three meeting times a day and meet your 'snow host' – a volunteer who will show you around the area. You are divided into groups, according to ability and the type of runs you want to ski, and off you go.

You can use the service as many times as you want in order to get the chance to ski with people of similar ability to yourself.

This sort of service is common in the US now – but there it's normally seen as a mountain orientation tour and run once a day for a group of mixed ability. The Banff-Lake Louise service is another step forward – and they claim to have invented the idea which the Americans have copied. Lake Louise alone now has eight volunteer hosts and hostesses available each day. All the reports we've had of the guiding have been very positive.

down to the mid-mountain base. And don't ignore the Wawa T-Bar which gives access to the often quiet Wa-Wa Bowl and Tincan Alley.

The Mystic Ridge area linked to Norquay was developed especially to attract intermediates and has 11 tree-lined blues and a couple of sometimes-groomed blacks served by two high-speed quads. It's worth trying.

FOR BEGINNERS
Excellent terrain

Louise has a good nursery area near the base served by a short T-bar; Sunshine a good area by the mid-mountain base and served by an even shorter hand-tow. And Norquay has a small nursery area but no real runs for progressing beginners.

Recommended graduation runs for improvers on Louise are the gentle, wide Wixwaxy (designated a slow skiing zone, so there are no lunatics bombing past you) and the slightly more difficult Deer Run or Eagle Meadows.

There are even greens round the back bowls and in the Larch area – worth taking for the views.

Sunshine has the beginners-only Meadow Park among other user-friendly greens.

If you're a complete beginner with a party of friends who are experienced skiers and you want to meet up with them regularly, we don't recommend this area as ideal. Each mountain has its own ski school and you'll want to stick to one, whereas experienced skiers will probably want to split their days between the three areas.

FOR CROSS-COUNTRY
High in quality and quantity

It's a good area for cross-country. There are trails near Banff around the Bow River and on the Banff Springs golf course. But the best area is around Lake Louise, which has around 100km of groomed trails of all standards – watch out for the wolf packs!

QUEUES
Deserted during the week

Never a problem except on the busiest weekends. Fifty per cent of the area's skiers are up from cities like Calgary on day passes, rather than holidaying for a week or more. So it's normally quiet during the week. We're told the worst weekend queues can be for the gondola up Sunshine in the morning.

The Lake Louise area is so confident it can handle skier numbers that it offers a full refund of your ski pass on any day you have to queue for more than ten minutes at the base area.

More of a problem than queues is the cold. Temperatures can fall to as low as -30°C. The high-speed chairs can then be extremely unpleasant.

MOUNTAIN RESTAURANTS
Not bad for North America

All three mountains have eating facilities both at the base area and up

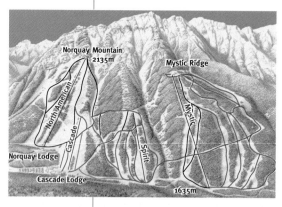

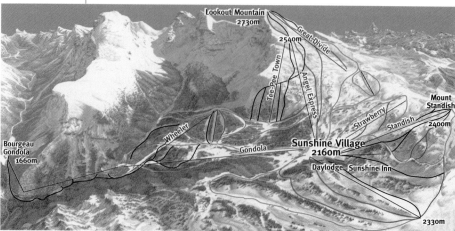

2640m To Back Bowls and Larch ↘

Summit

Top of the World 2530m

To Back Bowls and Larch ↘

Top of the World

Eagle

2090m Whitehorn Lodge

Olympic

Friendly Giant

Olympic Chair

Friendly Giant Chairs

Whiskyjack Lodge 1660m

CHILDCARE

Last year the nursery at Lake Louise took children aged 18 days to 6 years, from 8am to 4.30. The one at Sunshine Village takes children aged 19 months to 6 years, from 8.30 to 4.30. The one at Norquay's Cascade Lodge takes children aged 19 months, from 9am to 4pm. In all three, children aged 3 or more can take short ski lessons.

GETTING THERE

Air Calgary, transfer 2hr.

the mountain. But most are cafeteria-style and serve the usual basics: burgers, hot dogs, sandwiches, soups.

On Louise, Temple Lodge, near the bottom of the Larch lift, is probably the most attractive, built in rustic style with a big terrace and choice of eating venues, including a table-service restaurant. Whitehorn Lodge, near the bottom of the Eagle chair, has excellent views from its balcony. At Whiskey Jack, at the base, the table-service restaurant is much better than the dire self-service cafeteria.

Sunshine Village has a choice of eating places at its mid-mountain base. The Daylodge and Old Sunshine Lodge serve fairly standard food and snacks. The Sunshine Inn (an on-mountain hotel) has the best food – table-service snacks in the Chimney Corner Lounge or a full lunch in the Eagle's Nest Dining Room.

On Mystic Ridge-Norquay, there's a new restaurant-cum-cafeteria at the main base. And the smaller, older Norquay Lodge, at the foot of the North American chair, serves snacks and has good views of skiing – but is only open at weekends and peak holiday periods.

SKI SCHOOL
Caught on film

The Club Ski Program takes adults (16 and over) to all three mountains and offers a mixture of guiding and instruction, including free video analysis. We'd recommend it to anyone who wants to see the whole area while improving their technique too – reporters who've tried say it is superb. All standards are catered for. To ensure continuity, a reporter strongly recommends booking into a four- or five-day ski school course rather than taking odd lessons.

Powder Byrne are running Masterclass packages here this winter.

FACILITIES FOR CHILDREN
Each area has them

As in the US, arrangements for children are thoroughly worked out. We have no confirmation that the Lake Louise nursery's extraordinary facility of taking babies from the age of 18 days will be offered this season.

 # Staying there

Wherever you stay (except at mid-mountain on Sunshine) it will be a drive or bus-ride to the slopes. Lake Louise village is the nearest place to a major ski area. But don't expect any resort ambience or much nightlife.

HOW TO GO
Superb-value hotels

There are no catered chalets available on the British market, but a wealth of hotels give plenty of options.

Hotels Summer is the peak season here. Hotel prices halve for the winter – so you can stay in luxury hotels at bargain rates.

In or near Banff:

£££ Banff Springs The luxury option in Banff, a turn-of-the century, castle-style Canadian Pacific property. It's virtually a town within a town. It can sleep 2,000 people and has over 40 shops, 12 restaurants and bars, Olympic-sized indoor pool and separate outdoor pool.

£££ Caribou Lodge Opened in April 1993, on the main street slightly out of town. It has a variety of wood-clad, interestingly and individually designed rooms, and a sauna and hot tub complex.

£££ Rimrock Also opened in Spring 1993, spectacularly set out of town on Sulphur Mountain, with outstanding views and a fully equipped health club. **££ Inns of Banff** On the way into town, and has been

PACKAGES

Accessible Isolation, All Canada, American Connections, American Dream, Chinook-It, Crystal, Frontier Ski, Inghams, Jean Stanford, Lotus Supertravel, Made to Measure, Neilson, Ski Activity, Ski C & C, Ski Canada, Ski Independence, USAirtours

Lake Louise
Accessible Isolation, All Canada, American Connections, American Dream, Chinook-It, Crystal, Frontier Ski, Inghams, Jean Stanford, Lotus Supertravel, Made to Measure, Neilson, Ski Activity, Ski Canada, Ski Club of GB, Ski Independence, Waymark

Sunshine Village
Frontier Ski, Ski Canada

ACTIVITIES

Indoor Film theatre, museums, galleries, swimming pools (one with water slides), gym, squash, raquetball, weight training, bowling, jacuzzi, sauna, mini-golf, climbing wall
Outdoor Swimming in hot springs, ice skating, heli-skiing, horse-drawn carriage rides, sleigh rides, dog-sled rides, snowmobiles, curling, ice hockey, ice fishing, helicopter tours

TOURIST OFFICE

Postcode TOL oCO
Tel 010 1 (403) 7624561
Fax 7628185

recommended for its large rooms and health club facilities.
££ Banff Park Lodge In the town itself. Used by several British tour operators, large and central,with hot tub, steam room and indoor pool.
At Lake Louise village:
££££ Post A member of the Relais & Châteaux chain, with the best cuisine in the area, wood-panelled rooms and even a few log cabins in the grounds. Indoor pool, hot tub and steam room. Go for a room facing away from the railway to avoid the worst of the hooting trains during the night.
££ Lake Louise Inn The cheaper option in the village, still with pool, hot tub and sauna.
At Lake Louise itself:
£££ Chateau Lake Louise With stunning views over frozen Lake Louise, this 515-room Canadian Pacific-owned hotel has undergone multi-million dollar restoration over the last few years and has a choice of restaurants and a health club with indoor pool, steam room and hot tub.
££ Deer Lodge A simpler, cheaper option with a rooftop hot tub.
Self-catering Condominiums aren't as numerous as hotels but are available. The biggest complex is the Banff Rocky Mountain Resort (Neilson, Crystal), set in the woods on the edge of town, which has a wealth of in-house facilities including indoor pool, squash, hot tubs etc. Inghams have a wide range of places in and around Banff, including luxurious places on the outskirts. Ski Activity have some attractive places, too.

EATING OUT
International choice
The best cuisine in the region is in the Post Hotel restaurant at Lake Louise. The Chateau Lake Louise has two Alpine-style restaurants – the Walliser Stube, serving fondue, air-dried meats etc, and the Edelweiss for more formal dining. It also has the Poppy Room for family-style food. And there are other cheaper options in the village, such as Frankie's Pizza and Pasta Café.
Banff has over 100 different restaurants, from MacDonald's to fine dining in the Banff Springs Hotel. In between you'll find Italian, Greek, Chinese, Japanese, French and Mexican restaurants, steak houses, delis and pub snacks. The Beaujolais and Giorgio's are recommended at the top end of the price range. If you fancy fondued lizard or rattlesnake, try the Grizzly Bear.

APRES-SKI
Liveliest in Banff
One of the drawbacks of the area is that immediate post-skiing après-ski is limited because the villages are a drive from the ski areas.
But things liven up later, especially in Banff. Wild Bill's has live country and western music. The Rose & Crown has music and gets crowded. Barbary Coast often has live music and The Works nightclub and Whiskey Creek Saloon (both in the Banff Springs hotel) are popular.
Lake Louise is quieter. The Glacier Saloon in Chateau Lake Louise, with traditional Wild West decor, often has live music until late. Charly Two's pub in the Lake Louise Inn has dancing until 2am. The Outpost Pub in the Post Hotel is worth trying, as is the Saddleback lounge in Lake Louise Inn.

FOR NON-SKIERS
Beautiful scenery
If you enjoy walking, the area has a lot of attractions. There are museums to visit such as The Whyte Museum of the Canadian Rockies, The Natural History Museum and The Luxton Museum of the Plains Indians. And, of course, there's the wildlife and the natural hot springs. Meeting up with skiers at lunchtime can be a drag.
There are sleigh rides, dog sledding, skating and tobogganing around the Banff Springs hotel area. Lake Louise has ice skating and Broomball games.

STAYING UP THE MOUNTAIN
Worth considering
At Sunshine Village, the Sunshine Village Inn is the only ski-in, ski-out hotel. It has a good atmosphere, a big outdoor hot tub overlooking the slopes, good food, small but attractive rooms with excellent views and is well run. Unlike every other hotel in the area, this one closes in summer, and its winter rates are as high as any.

STAYING IN OTHER RESORTS
The road to Jasper is stunning
An attractive option is to spend a couple of days in Jasper, which has its own small ski area at Marmot Basin. The three-hour trip on the Columbia Icefields Parkway, through the Banff and Jasper National Parks, is one of the most beautiful drives in the world. The nicest place to spend the night here is in the Jasper Park Lodge (Inghams), a collection of log cabins set around a frozen lake. On the walk to breakfast, you are quite likely to encounter a herd of elk grazing outside your cabin.

Whistler 675m

HOW IT RATES

The skiing

Snow	****
Extent	****
Advanced	*****
Intermediates	*****
Beginners	****
Convenience	****
Queues	*****
Restaurants	*

The rest

Scenery	***
Resort charm	***
Not skiing	**

✔ The biggest ski area in North America, with the largest vertical drop of over 1600m

✔ Spectacular 'Alpine' scenery with lots of 'ski-anywhere' above-the-tree-line skiing

✔ Good skiing for all standards

✔ Sea to Sky coast road from Vancouver is one of the most beautiful approaches to any ski resort in the world

✔ Modern pedestrianised resort built in pleasant 'West Coast' style with varied architecture

✗ Proximity to coast and low altitude means it can rain a lot at resort level

✗ Two separate ski areas are linked only at resort level

✗ Mediocre mountain restaurants

Whistler-Blackcomb has come from virtually nowhere in the 1970s to being voted the Number One resort in North America for the last two seasons by Snow Country – the US' best ski magazine.

Billions of Canadian dollars have been invested in developing two separate mountains (linked at their bases), each with considerable attractions, and two separate pedestrianised villages ten minutes' walk apart.

Both mountains have miles of skiing for all standards, the greatest vertical drops in North America, good snow guaranteed on the highest glacier runs, modern lift systems which whisk you rapidly back up the mountain and spectacular 'Alpine'-type scenery so often missing in US resorts. Between them they offer more piste skiing than any other North American resort.

So what's the catch? Only one main one as far as we're concerned. The weather. It's unpredictable in the extreme. It can be mind-numbingly cold. And because it's very near the coast, it can also be damp and dismal as the storms roll in from the Pacific. The rain normally turns to snow as you go up the lifts, but rain low down can dampen your spirits.

ORIENTATION

Whistler village and its smaller neighbour, **Blackcomb**, a 10-minute walk away, are set at the foot of their separate ski areas, a scenic 75-mile drive inland from Vancouver on Canada's west coast.

The main way up Whistler Mountain is by gondola which takes you from Whistler Village, up 1157m vertical, to the hub of the skiing. A high-speed chair-lift from **Whistler Creek**, 10 minutes by bus from the main village, also accesses the Whistler skiing. From Whistler village, a new gondola planned for the 1994/5 season will take you part-way up Blackcomb Mountain, linking with Blackcomb's own lift system which starts with a high-speed quad from the base area. There are pistes linking both villages near the bottom of the ski area.

🏔 The resort

Whistler started life as a ski area in 1965 with the 'village' consisting of a few ramshackle buildings in what is now called Whistler Creek, a few miles down the valley from Whistler proper. It catered largely for day skiers from Vancouver.

Whistler village was built in the late 1970s on the site of what used to be the area's rubbish tip. Blackcomb village was developed in the 1980s. Both are traffic-free.

The architecture is varied and, for purpose-built resorts, quite tasteful. There are lots of chalet-style apartments built on the hillsides. The centres have individually designed wooden and concrete buildings, blended together in a master plan and built around a series of squares. There are no monstrous high-rise blocks. But there are a lot of large five- or six-story hotel and apartment buildings. The Japanese like the resort so much that they've commissioned a replica to be built back home.

Whistler is the main resort, with nearly all the bars, restaurants and shops. It is built around two main squares – one at the base of the gondola and the other, the Village Square, a two-minute stroll away. Whistler North is being developed on the edge of the central area.

Blackcomb is much smaller and quieter with a limited range of shops and restaurants. Its 343-room Chateau Whistler hotel, built in true chateau style, dominates the views down into the village from the mountain.

Whistler Creek, a ten-minute bus-ride from the main Whistler village, is rather out on a limb with limited nightlife and eating and drinking places, though there are plans to develop it further.

There is a free bus service between Whistler and Blackcomb, with fares charged for going further out. But if you're staying centrally it's just as quick to walk between the two.

SKI FACTS

Altitude	650m-2285m
Lifts	28
Pistes	6997 acres
Green	20%
Blue	55%
Black	25%
Art. snow	70 acres

LIFT PASSES

94/95 prices in
Canadian dollars
**Dual Mountain Lift
Ticket**
Covers all lifts on
both Whistler and
Blackcomb
mountains.
Beginners Daily
program for beginners
includes 2hr lesson,
ski rental and pass
(adult 48 per day).
Main pass
1-day pass 47
6-day pass 264
Senior citizens
Over 65: 6-day pass
186 (30% off)
Children
Under 13: 6-day pass
126 (52% off)
Under 7: free pass
Short-term passes
Half-day pass for each
area separately.
Notes Dual mountain
pass of 5 days or
over gives one non-
skiing day; 6-day
pass valid for 7 days
with one day non-
skiing. Further
discounts for 13- to
18- year-olds, (6-day
pass 234).

✱ The skiing

The skiing has acquired a formidable
reputation among good skiers. And
that reputation is well deserved. There
are some fearsomely steep chutes and
lots of off-piste bowls.

But both mountains also have
enormous amounts of well-groomed
intermediate cruising terrain. Together
they have over 200 marked pistes, and
they form the biggest ski area, with
the longest runs, in North America.
But because of the low altitude of the
base villages (less than 700m) it is
often impossible to ski all the way
back, especially in late season.

THE SKI AREA
The best in North America

Both Whistler and Blackcomb
mountains have their own devotees
who choose to ski just one non-stop.
That practice is encouraged by the
mountains being owned and run
entirely separately, though two-
mountain lift passes are now on sale.

The main way up **Whistler
Mountain** is from Whistler Village by
a long two-stage, 10-person gondola
which rises over 1100m from the
village at 650m to Pika's and The
Roundhouse, the main mid-mountain
base at 1810m. From there runs fan
out in all directions back down
through the trees to a series of chairs
which carry you back up again.
There's no need to ski back to
Whistler until the end of the day.

But the jewel in Whistler's crown
only reveals itself when you reach the
top of the gondola. There high above
you lie Whistler's five magnificent

above-the-tree-line bowls which reach
2178m – from left to right, Symphony,
Harmony, Glacier, Whistler and West.
You can ski more or less anywhere in
these, and a few of the ways are pisted
to make areas accessible for
intermediates as well as good skiers.
The nearest we've come across in
Europe resembling Whistler's bowls is
the skiing at the top of St Anton.

Access to **Blackcomb Mountain**
will be greatly improved by the new
Excalibur 8-person sit-down gondola
due to open in November 1994. This
starts in Whistler Village with a mid-
station just above the Blackcomb base
area. It finishes part-way up
Blackcomb Mountain and is met by
another brand-new high-speed quad
chair. This will supplement the
existing route up Blackcomb by a
series of high-speed chairs starting
from the Blackcomb base area. The
1610m vertical rise from Blackcomb
village at 675m to the top of the 7th
Heaven Express at 2285m is the largest
in North America (and impressive
even by European standards).

One of the second-stage chairs, the
Solar Coaster Express, takes you to the
main mid-mountain base and the
Rendezvous restaurant at 1860m. From
here there's a wide variety of
runs through the trees in all directions
and for all standards. Two different
peaks can be reached from a chair
down to the right or a chair and a T-
bar to the left. Both access the summer
skiing area on the Horstman Glacier.
And the T-bar also brings you (with a
short climb) to the Blackcomb Glacier
in the next valley – a beautiful, easy
run which takes you right away from
all lifts and signs of civilisation.

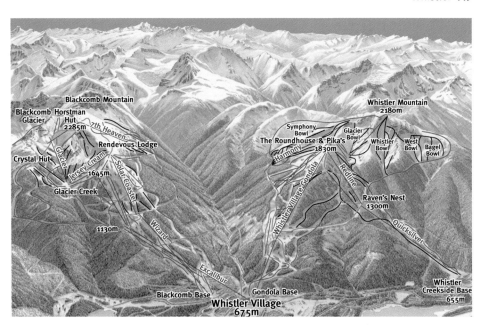

SNOW RELIABILITY
Good high up, poor low down
Snow conditions at the top are usually excellent. But because the resort is low and close to the Pacific, the bottom part of the mountains can be wet or unskiable. Blackcomb has more snowmaking than Whistler Mountain – one of the reasons it shuts later (at the end of May).

FOR ADVANCED SKIERS
Few can rival it
Whistler-Blackcomb has acquired a cult reputation with professional ski bums in the last few years. Whistler Mountain's bowls alone are enough to keep experts happy for weeks. Each of the five has endless possible variations, with chutes and gullies of varied steepness and width. The biggest challenges are around Glacier, Whistler and West Bowls, with runs such as The Cirque and Doom & Gloom – though you can literally ski anywhere in this high and wide area. Access to the bowls will be greatly increased this season by the new high-

speed quad Harmony chair-lift.

Blackcomb has its challenging bowl skiing too. But it's not as extensive or set as dramatically as Whistler's. From the top of the Seventh Heaven lift you can traverse across to the right to Xhiggy's Meadow, where there's good sunny bowl skiing. Or if you're feeling brave you can drop over the ridge behind you down the infamous 41° Saudan Couloir – named after French extreme skier Sylvain Saudan. Amazingly, there's a public race down here each year, late in the season, which attracts entrants from all over the world. Alternatively, you can walk up a little from the run down from the Glacier Express lift and ski down Ruby Bowl, Helterskelter or Spanky's to join the Blackcomb glacier run.

On both mountains there are challenging black mogul runs on the lower part below the tree-line.

If all this isn't enough, there's also local heli-skiing available – something that British Columbia is famous for.

FOR INTERMEDIATE SKIERS
Ideal and extensive terrain
Both mountains are paradise. Good intermediates will enjoy the less extreme variations in the bowls on both mountains in good weather.

One of our favourite intermediate runs is the Blackcomb Glacier from the top of the mountain at almost 2300m down to the bottom of the new high-speed quad at 1130m. This 5km run starts with a short two-minute climb up from the top of the Showcase T-bar over the ridge and into the valley hidden behind. You drop into a wide, wide bowl – the further you traverse, the shallower the slope becomes. A large part of the attraction of the run for us is being away from sight of all lifts.

You are guaranteed good snow on the Horstman Glacier runs too. This is Blackcomb's summer ski area, with typically gentle top-of-the-mountain glacier runs. Lower down there are large numbers of perfectly groomed cruising runs through the trees – perfect when the weather is bad.

On Whistler Mountain, there are easy blue pistes in Symphony, Harmony and the lower part of Glacier bowls, which allow even early intermediates to try the bowls for themselves, always knowing there's an easy way down. And the blue path round the back, which skirts West Bowl, has beautiful views over a steep valley and across to Black Tusk (an apt name for the phallic-shaped top of this famous mountain). The only problem you might have with the top-of-the-mountain paths is an attack of vertigo when you see the near-vertical unfenced drops to one side.

Lower down the mountain there is a vast choice of groomed blue runs with a series of efficient fast chairs to bring you back up to the top of the gondola. It's a cruiser's paradise – especially the aptly named Ego Bowl. A great run to take at the end of the day is the Dave Murray Downhill all the way from mid-mountain to the finish in town. Although marked black on the map, it's a wonderful fast and varied cruise when it has been groomed.

FOR BEGINNERS
A great place to learn
Whistler has excellent nursery slopes by the mid-station of the gondola – and Blackcomb's slopes are down at the base area. Both also have facilities higher up if the snow lower down isn't too good.

On Whistler, Upper Whiskey Jack is a gentle first run from the top of the gondola after progressing beyond the nursery slopes. You can return to its start by various chair-lifts or continue right down to the base area on simple greens. There is a variety of other green runs, and many of the blue runs are only a little steeper or narrower.

On Blackcomb, Green Line goes right from the top of the mountain to the bottom. The top part is a particularly gentle run, with a couple of steeper pitches below the Rendezvous Restaurant and mid-mountain base.

FOR CROSS-COUNTRY
Picturesque but low
There are over 15km of cross-country tracks starting in the valley by the frozen river, on the path between Whistler and Blackcomb, and heading off towards the Lost Lake. And there is more cross-country around the golf courses. But all this is at low altitude, so conditions can be unreliable. Keen cross-country merchants can catch the train to better areas.

QUEUES
Weekend invasions
During the week there's rarely a problem with queues. At weekends, crowds pour in from Vancouver and can create a wait to get up the mountains. But the new Excalibur gondola should help a lot. And once up the mountain, people are moved very quickly by the high-speed quads.

On Whistler, the new Harmony chair-lift will increase the numbers carried to the top of the bowls by 250 per cent, and should eliminate the queues for the slow old Peak chair.

MOUNTAIN RESTAURANTS
Crowded and nothing special
Whistler's main eating venue is Pika's, at the top of the gondola. It is a fairly charmless self-service refuelling stop, which also houses the ski school office. It gets incredibly crowded, has a separate bar and an upstairs Sushi Bar.

The Roundhouse, a few yards up the hill, is much better. It's a circular building with seats round the outside and the serving areas in the centre. There's an attractive salad bar as well as the standard burgers and chilli.

Raven's Nest Café, at the top of the chair up from Whistler Creek, serves the best food on the mountain. It is tiny, with a small terrace with good views down to the creek. Its speciality is pasta, but we've also had great peppery paté and Caesar Salad with Cajun Chicken there.

Rendezvous is Blackcomb's mid-mountain base. It is a massive self-service restaurant, with paper plates and plastic cutlery, which again houses the ski school office. Christine's, at the same location, is the only table-service restaurant around, serving an up-market selection of food (snails, smoked salmon, steaks) and offering an award-winning wine list.

A large, new restaurant, Glacier Creek Lodge, has been built at the bottom of the Glacier Express lift.

The two alternatives are tiny mountain huts built to resemble Alpine refuges. Crystal Hut, at the top

SKI SCHOOL
94/95 prices in Canadian dollars

Whistler and Blackcomb
Guided instruction with Ski Esprit course
Classes 6 days
full-day from 8.45
6 full days: 336
Children's classes
Ages: 3 to 12
5 6hr days including lunch: 185
Private lessons
1hr or full-day
68 for 1hr

CHILDCARE

The Kids' Kamp, at the base of Blackcomb, has a huge dining area and nursery area inside, snow garden and special lifts outside. It takes non-skiing children aged 18 months to 3 years, as well as acting as the base for ski tuition.

Both ski schools have special programmes for young children. Wee Scamps on Whistler and Wee Wizards on Blackcomb take children aged 2 to 3, from 8.30 to 3.30. Super Kids and Ski Scamps take older children, with different schemes for different levels of skiing competence.

GETTING THERE

Air Vancouver, transfer 2hr.

PACKAGES

Accessible Isolation, All Canada, American Connections, American Dream, Chinook-It, Crystal, Frontier Ski, Inghams, Jean Stanford, Lotus Supertravel, Made to Measure, Neilson, Piste Artiste, Ski Activity, Ski C & C, Ski Canada, Ski Club of GB, Ski Independence, Trail Alpine, USAirtours

of the Crystal Ridge chair, has Buffalo Burgers and Buffalo Stew. Horstman Hut, at the top of the mountain, attempts to create a Bavarian feel and does excellent strudels.

SKI SCHOOL
One for each mountain
Whistler and Blackcomb have separate ski schools. The joint programme, Ski Esprit, is as much a guiding service as it is ski instruction. It runs for three or four full days and includes a welcome reception, prizes and après-ski.

As well as standard group and private lessons, both mountains offer specialist courses and clinics such as Bumps, Racing and Parallel Perfection. There is also snowboard instruction.

Children are well catered for with a variety of different programmes for different ages.

There is also a free daily guided tour of each mountain.

FACILITIES FOR CHILDREN
Comprehensive
The facilities are as impressive as usual in North America. Blackcomb's base area has a special, slow-moving Magic Chair to get children part-way up the mountain. Our main reservation about taking young children here would be the weather. Playing in a snow garden in falling snow is one thing; in falling rain, something else.

 # Staying there

The most convenient places to stay are the two main villages. A lot of chalets and apartments are an inconvenient bus-ride from the villages and ski areas. And Whistler Creek, though convenient for Whistler's skiing, is less so for getting to Blackcomb and has much less life than the main villages.

HOW TO GO
High quality packages
A lot of British tour operators have recently 'discovered' Whistler. Between them they offer a wide range of very comfortable accommodation, though catered chalets are thin on the ground.

Chalets Lotus Supertravel have a couple of luxurious places complete with all mod cons. One is convenient for skiing, the other out at Whistler Cay – but it's a beautiful log chalet. Frontier Ski will provide evening meals in their condos on request (see self-catering section).

Hotels There is a very wide range.
£££££ Chateau Whistler The top

hotel, huge and impressive, modern but in traditional Canadian Pacific château-hotel style. Ideally placed at the foot of Blackcomb Mountain. It has an indoor-outdoor pool, exercise machines, saunas etc.
££££ Delta Mountain Inn Big, modern, stylish, in the heart of Whistler village; health club, covered tennis courts, pool.
££££ Nancy Greene Lodge Operated by the 1968 Olympic Gold Medal winner; good reputation, centrally placed in Whistler, 140 rooms, friendly staff, recommended by reporters. Pool.
£££ Timberline Lodge Fairly central Whistler. Pool, hot tub and sauna.
£££ Glacier Lodge In Blackcomb. Pool, hot tub and sauna.
Self-catering There are plenty of condominiums available in both chalet- and hotel-style blocks. Lotus Supertravel's Moose Lodge, out at Whistler Cay Heights, is a luxurious classic mountain retreat with log walls, a stone fireplace and chimney, and a high ceiling. They also have comfortable, central places. American Dream, Frontier Ski, Ski Activity and Ski Independence have a selection of comfortable, spacious places with lots of nice touches. Neilson also have a good range of high-standard condos in various positions, including some on the slopes at Blackcomb and in Whistler village. Crystal have some quite central condos with the bonus of access to the excellent leisure facilities of the Delta Mountain Inn. Inghams have some good apartments at the foot of Blackcomb.

EATING OUT
High quality and plenty of choice
There is no shortage of good places to eat. Whistler is thought expensive by Canadian standards. As a rough guide, expect pasta dishes to be between C$6 and C$10, main course meat dishes C$12 to C$20.

In Whistler Village, Umberto's is highly regarded for Italian cuisine, Val d'Isère for French, Chez Joel for fondue, Myrtle's for international and seafood. Another favourite is the Keg, renowned for great steaks, seafood and its huge salad bar. Try a steak stuffed with crab! Brandy's bar is a popular pre-dinner rendezvous. There are numerous Japanese restaurants catering for the substantial number of Japanese visitors. Sushi Village is good and reasonably priced.

In Blackcomb, the Wildflower restaurant in the Chateau Whistler serves excellent innovative dishes. Rua

PISTE ARTISTE

helped us to compile
the Eating out and
Après-ski sections.
Our thanks to them.

has a good reputation for
Mediterranean cooking, and Monk's
Grill for prime rib and steaks.

But locals reckon the best place to
eat is the Rim Rock Café and Oyster
Bar at Whistler Creek, especially for its
seafood and salmon dishes. Highly
regarded French cuisine is served at
Deux Gros, a beautiful restaurant
which is a five- to ten-minute walk
from the village.

Cheap and cheerful places, popular
with families and youngsters, include
Peter's Underground, Boston Pizza,
Citta's and a good burger joint called
A and W.

APRES-SKI
Something for most tastes
With over 50 bars, night-clubs and
restaurants, Whistler is very lively by
North American standards. The two
favourite bars immediately after skiing
are the Longhorn at Whistler and
Merlin's at Blackcomb, both at the
foot of the slopes. The former has a
huge terrace that is particularly
popular in spring; inside the place
rocks till after midnight. Dusty's Dead
Horse Saloon, at the foot of the
Whistler gondola, is another four
o'clock rendezvous, where huge
quantities of bar snacks are consumed.
Citta 2000 is another popular early
evening bar. Black's Pub in Whistler is
favoured for its supposedly English
decor, but Tapply's is arguably more
interesting – a bit of a dive frequented
by local workers.

The Mallard bar in Chateau Whistler
and Nancy Greene's Piano Bar are
popular for a more relaxed and
sophisticated time.

Later on, Buffalo Bill's normally has
live music and dancing until 2am.
Garfinkel's has occasional live rock 'n
roll and attracts local college students
as well as tourists. Tommy Africa's is
good for a thumpin', pumpin' bop
and comes complete with Go-Go
dancers. The Savage Beagle Club is a
trendy night club popular with
Vancouver yuppies. Waitresses sport
hip-holstered tequila bottles and
crossed shoulder-belts of glasses.

To experience 'redneck' Canada try
the Boot – live music, pool and
seemingly the cast from Thelma and
Louise. Strippers are even brought in
to attract punters in the off-season!
It's a five-minute drive north of the
village.

FOR NON-SKIERS
Not ideal
Whistler is a long way to go if you
aren't going to sample the superb
skiing. The villages are quiet during
the day. Non-skiers can get tickets for
the gondola and main chair-lifts. The
health club in the Delta is open to
non-residents, and there are some
other activities available. Excursions to
Vancouver and to Squamish (famous
for its wild eagles) are easy.

STAYING DOWN THE VALLEY
We wouldn't
Staying out of town basically means
staying at Whistler Creek or along the
road between there and the main
village. There's a regular bus service
until just after midnight.

Accommodation is cheaper but the
ambience is not as nice and the
nightlife not nearly as lively or varied.

ACTIVITIES

Indoor Ice skating,
museum, tennis, hot
tubs
Outdoor Flightseeing,
heli-skiing, para-
gliding,
snowmobiling, snow-
shoe excursions,
fishing, horse-riding,
sleigh rides, guided
tours

TOURIST OFFICE

Postcode VON 1BO
Tel 010 1 (604)
9324222
Fax 9327231

Andorra

More than most skiing countries, Andorra invites generalisations. Perhaps it's because all the resorts are so close to one another that they are so remarkably similar, having almost all the same pluses and minuses. Low prices (including duty-free goods), simple hotels, ugly villages, lively nightlife, good ski schools, fairly reliable snow, a lot of young clientele, small easy ski areas and awful mountain restaurants are all fairly typical of Andorran resorts across the board.

There's an immediate temptation to compare Andorra to Eastern Europe. Many of the above pluses and minuses would be appropriate to Borovets and company, too. Perhaps the main difference is that Andorra is more expensive and attracts a mostly young and lively clientele with more money to spend than the many low-budget families who enjoy Eastern Europe. This difference probably has its roots in the ski boom of over a decade ago. Bulgaria and Rumania suffered the restrictions of the Eastern bloc, while Andorra had duty-free booze. No contest!

Andorra has also proved a tough competitor, on the British market at least, for Austria. Many of the little Austrian resorts where so many of us learned to ski in the 1970s and 1980s are slowly but surely losing British custom, and this is partly because they can't compete with Andorra for providing first-time ski holidays that are not only cheap and cheerful, but also relatively snowsure. Andorra's snow reliability should not be underestimated. A combination of height and heavy investment in snowmakers puts it well ahead of much of Austria. You can book Andorra months in advance with some confidence. And an early reservation is necessary, too: last season, many late bookers had difficulty finding an Andorra package, while many Austrian resorts had plenty of room.

However, two of the apparently crucial elements of Andorra's success – good value and nightlife – do not stand up too well under the microscope. Admittedly prices are low once you arrive, notably for drinks and ski extras such as tuition and equipment hire. But the cost of travel-plus-accommodation packages has crept up considerably over the last few years as demand has exceeded supply. It's difficult to find a half-board package for less than £300 this year, which is not the case in many Italian resorts, never mind Bulgarian ones – and this despite the low standards of Andorran hotels. And although lift pass prices are low, you have to remember they access pretty limited ski areas. For a similar-sized ski area in supposedly more expensive countries, a lift pass may cost much the same as it does here. For example, the French purpose-built resort of Valfréjus has skiing that compares pretty favourably with anything in Andorra, yet it costs only a few pounds more. Many reporters have also been disappointed to find duty-free luxury goods not the super-bargain they had expected. As for nightlife, it certainly is very lively, with lots of throbbing bars to choose from, but it's all rather one dimensional. If you get bored with bar hopping there's little else.

The amount of skiing available can also, in practice , be disappointing. Tour operators are keen to imply that skiing several nearby areas is easily done, but the local buses are so infrequent that few guests bother. Club Cantabrica are a good tour operator for keen skiers, providing their own coach service to a variety of resorts.

It would seem the real secret of Andorra's success may be that it offers a sort of gathering of a particular clan – skiers (mainly young ones) who don't insist on holidays that are really cheap but do insist on their being very cheerful.

Arinsal 1550m

Young people come here for the nightlife, and Arinsal does not disappoint. The numerous lively bars and discos are not as rowdy as in nearby Soldeu. However, some will find the nightlife very one-dimensional. There is little to do outside of bar-hopping and clubbing, and the spread-out nature of Arinsal means there is little village atmosphere but lots of cold walks between 'happening' places. The skiing is very limited, and the resort is difficult to recommend to anyone except beginners.

THE RESORT

Arinsal is a little village of Catalan slate and grey stone, near the head of a narrow walley north of Andorra-la-Vella. It has seen rapid development in recent years, giving the place a building-site appearance. Yet little new accommodation is available near the single resort-level lift, inconveniently situated a kilometre out of town. Most skiers face a long walk or a bus-ride to this chair. Fortunately the village bus service is good. Arinsal is dominated by British holidaymakers.

THE SKIING

The very small **ski area** is a narrow east-facing coomb of mainly open slopes, suitable for beginners, children and unadventurous intermediates. All runs lead straight back towards the mid-station area, ideal for parents to keep a watchful eye on children. Proposed development of the Coll d'Ature mountainside will add not only size, but much needed variety, including some relatively snowsure tree-lined runs. A rarely skied black run or a blue road down to the Arinsal chair are the only options in bad weather.

With almost all skiing above 1950m and a fair number of guns, snow is relatively assured. The **snow reliability** of the nursery slopes is a boon. Most lifts above the mid-station are drags, keeping the mountain open when it's windy.

Advanced skiers and progressive intermediates shouldn't even think about Arinsal. But some of the slopes are not entirely easy and are suitable for **intermediates** who do not mind skiing a very limited area. Piste maintenance is good.

Essentially, Arinsal is a ski area suitable for near-**beginners** or early intermediates. The nursery slopes are gentle, away from the main ski area, and well covered by snow cannons. They do not cover a particularly large area, and as a result can get very crowded in peak season.

Although everyone has to ascend the mountain by a single lift, **queues** are not a problem on weekdays. Spanish weekenders and local children can hit the slopes en masse at times.

If you rate a resort by its **mountain restaurants**, Zermatt this isn't. They're expensive, by local standards, and crowded. And they serve mediocre snacks – hamburgers and so on.

Arinsal's **ski school** is its pride and joy. It offers good technical tuition; patient instruction; English widely spoken; low prices; and lessons that are fun. Class sizes can however be very large in peak season.

There is a ski kindergarten but no non-skiing crèche for young **children**.

STAYING THERE

Arinsal is essentially a cheap and cheerful small hotel resort.

The Crest is perhaps the best **hotel** in Arinsal, and has the advantage of being next to the chair-lift; it offers half-board or B&B terms. The studio-style rooms are geared towards families, sleeping up to five. The Solana has good food but simple rooms. It is much nearer the lifts than the peripheral St Gotthard. Apartments are generally of a higher standard that the hotels. The Velvet (Crystal, Thomson), Poblado (Neilson, Enterprise, Panorama) and Rosa Blanca (Thomson) apartments are all quite comfortable.

There is a fair range of **restaurants** for a small resort. Cisco's is a lively restaurant/bar serving Mexican food, Borda specialises in Catalan dishes and La Calisa has Spanish cooking. Arguably the best in town is Il Neu.

For **après ski**, Arinsal has very animated bars and discos, but if you get fed up with these, there isn't much else to do – a fondue evening is the best bet. Prices are low, but not as low as many expect of Andorra. Red Rock is a focal spot, popular for its large measures, videos and good burgers.

Arinsal has few facilities for **non-skiers**. The main thing to do is shopping in La Vella, half an hour away by infrequent bus.

Soldeu 1800m

Soldeu has a lot in common with other resorts in Andorra – limited skiing, low prices, great ski school, grim-looking village, lively bar-based nightlife. But its ski area is one of the better ones in the region, and is fairly convenient – the walk to the lifts, although irritating, is relatively short.

THE RESORT

The village is a small, though ever-growing, ribbon of ugly modern buildings along a busy road, most of them hotels and bars. Other than sleeping, skiing, eating and drinking, there is nothing to do, and the poor transport facilities make excursions difficult. The ski area lies beyond a long new metal bridge, which is a simple enough walk when there is no ice about, especially if you desposit skis and boots at the chair-lift.

THE SKIING

The **ski area** is shared with El Tarter. There are a few challenges, but the skiing is most suited to timid/early intermediates.

A chair-lift rises over wooded north-facing slopes to Espiolets, a broad, extensive nursery area. From here, a short gentle run to the east takes you to a lift up to Solana (2440m). A longer gentle run in the opposite direction takes you to the foot of the open bowl of Riba Escorxada and the arrival point of the lift up from El Tarter. From here lifts ascend to both Solana and the high-point of Llosada (2560m), with blue and red runs back down. All main routes are very easy skiing options, so all but complete beginners can get around the area.

Soldeu enjoys fairly **reliable snow**. Most of the skiing is north-facing, with artificial snow available on the descents to Soldeu. Should runs to the village be closed, the area as whole is not unduly affected.

It's a limited area for **advanced skiers**. There are short off-piste trails down the bowl beneath Llosada, and you can sometimes play in powder among the trees above El Tarter.

The most direct of the wooded runs down to El Tarter and Soldeu are suitable for good **intermediates**, while moderate skiers will enjoy the relatively long pistes from Llosada. Timid skiers have gentle cruises throughout the area. Riba Escorxada is a fine section for mixed abilities

This is a good resort for **beginners**. The Espiolets nursery area is adequate and relatively snowsure, and there are numerous very easy pistes to move on to. The long run across from Espiolets to Riba Escorxada is flat enough to attract **cross-country** skiers. There is not much else for them.

The lift system is antiquated and inefficient, and free of **queues** on weekdays only because of the high proportion of beginners. When there is an influx at weekends and holiday times, morning queues of 30-45 minutes develop for the village chair.

The **mountain restaurants** are poor. That the top of El Tarter chair is the best of an inadequate bunch.

The **ski school** has a high reputation for standards of English, quality of tuition and friendliness. **Children** aged three to eight can attend a non-ski nursery. Children's ski school starts at six, but lunchtime supervision is not available.

STAYING THERE

The central 3-star Sporthotel is by far the best **hotel** in Soldeu – tastefully designed in local stone and stained pine, with good bedrooms and a pleasant and well equipped sauna/gym. Buffet breakfast is good. The popular Naudi offers good value provided you stay in the main hotel, not the more basis annexe.

The Edelweiss apartments are spacious and generally pleasant, and well placed opposite the Sporthotel, the facilities of which are available.

Though standards are not particularly high, there is plenty of choice of places for **eating out**. The Pussycat is an atmospheric restaurant with reasonable food and good service. The Duc hotel restaurant has arguably the best food in town.

Although **après-ski** is lively, it is very one-dimensional, consisting of bars and rep-organised outings. The Sol Y Nieve bar at the foot of the slopes starts things off after skiing, while later on the Edelweiss, Bruxelles and Bonnel bars are the most popular. The Naudi has a quieter locals' bar. The El Duc is the best disco.

There is virtually nothing to amuse **non-skiers**. There is a very smart sports centre in Canillo (erratic bus service) with 25m pool, ice rink, squash and gym. It is closed in the afternoons. The Sporthotel has sauna and gym, and the only all-day bar.

Spain

The Spanish Pyrenees were a popular British budget destination a decade ago, but they lost out to Andorra and Eastern Europe for such trade. And it's easy to see why. The mass-market resorts often struggled for snow and, even when conditions were good, skiing was far from guaranteed in many places due to the tendency for high winds to close lifts. Furthermore, while prices were low, they were lower elsewhere, and Spain also gained a reputation for low standards – poor hotels, ancient hire equipment, old lifts, limited resorts and so on.

But it's dangerous to generalise about Spanish skiing. There is more to the country than its downmarket image suggests. There is a well equipped Pyrenean resort with fine, snowsure skiing that compares very favourably with the best mid-size places in the Alps. And down in the south, near Granada, lies a resort which is about to host the World Skiing Championships. The two resorts are certainly not downmarket (the King of Spain frequents them both), yet the exchange rate makes them relatively inexpensive. Skiing is also becoming more popular with the increasingly prosperous Spanish themselves, and as a result many of the smaller resorts are now improving their facilities.

Furthermore, the general ambience of Spanish skiing is attractive – not unlike that of Italy. There's plenty of animation, with eating, posing and partying taken seriously. Large families often lunch together, creating much merriment while huge amounts of food are consumed. Dinner starts late after such a blow out, so in turn nightlife doesn't get going before many a British punter has retired disgrunted at the lack of action.

The 1995 World Championships take place in **Sierra Nevada** (2100m) in the extreme south of Spain. Surprisingly, perhaps, snow reliability is a strong point. The resort has state-of-the-art snowmaking, with a refrigeration plant up the mountain to keep the process going in warm weather. Its natural snow arrives via completely different weather patterns from the Alps and Pyrenees. In 1990, when the Alps were disastrously snowless, Sierra Nevada had the best conditions in Europe. The mostly intermediate ski area is very exposed to the elements. When the wind blows, as it does, the skiing stops, and the strong sun makes the pistes either icy or soft in late season. The resort is very ugly but user-friendly, and its restaurants, bars and shops are nicely gathered around a central square. Granada's proximity means good outings, but overcrowding at weekends and holidays. Hotels are comfortable and good value.

Baqueira-Beret (1500m) is atypical of the Pyrenees – a user-friendly resort with high-standard accommodation, modern lifts and a sizeable, fairly snowsure ski area. Spanish prices make it a real bargain. The mountain seems bigger than its claim of 90km of piste would suggest, thanks to its variety. The skiing is mostly above 1800m, much of it northish-facing, backed up by snowmakers. Queues are rare because most of the lifts are high-capacity chairs. There's skiing for all grades including some steep challenges. Ski Miquel have a good chalet and hotels available.

The smaller Pyrenean resorts are best toured by car, spending a day in each, and driving to one of the more sheltered places if the wind blows. **Formigal** is the best-known, and has a good ski school, but it's very windswept. Our favourite is nearby **Panticosa**, a charming old mountain village with sheltered, if limited skiing. **La Molina** has a sizeable ski area. It's an old place, preferable to its dreary purpose-built satellite, **Supermolina**.

Bulgaria

Bulgaria attracts skiers on a tight budget. The initial package, ski extras and other prices are all very low. Drawbacks include limited ski areas, old lifts, and mountain food that has you reaching for the Mars bars. But there are compensations other than simply low prices. All of our reporters have been struck by the friendliness of the local people, the ski schools are excellent, the tour op-organised nightlife is good fun, and from Borovets an excursion to Sofia is recommended. The resorts also try hard to provide the sort of amenities 'Westerners' require from a holiday resort. Many of the hotels have the potential to be perfectly adequate places to stay, and Bulgaria, like the rest of Eastern Europe is struggling to raise standards. Unfortunately the shortages the country is suffering at present have so far limited what can be achieved. Progress is slow, but recognisable. Several old Bulgaria hands have commented on the improvement in food in recent years. Reports of the resorts get more positive each year, and many visitors are return bookings.

The low prices have not attracted huge numbers of young drinkers away from Andorra. Bulgaria receives young and old, families and singles alike. Consequently the atmosphere is nicely cosmopolitan, with people of different ages and walks of life mixing in together.

Bulgaria's two main ski resorts are some way apart, served by different airports, with similarly short transfer times (less than two hours). They are fairly similar places in some ways; both have good tuition ('individuals needs accounted for'), very low prices ('a week's good après-ski for £25') and poor mountain restaurants ('mostly caravans with outside seating'). But the two ski areas suit different levels of skier.

Borovets (see page 458 for a full report) has intermediate skiing that a combination of steepness and poor piste grooming makes awkward for improving beginners and leisurely cruisers.

Pamporovo (1450m) is far better for beginners and early intermediates, with mostly easy skiing. Others may find 25km of short runs too limited. But the skiing is pretty and sheltered, with pistes cut through pine forest. Skiing around is easy, with no bottlenecks or hazards, and getting lost is difficult even in the worst weather. Beginners should book a 'learn to ski' package through their tour operator. It's a good deal, saving up to 80% of the cost of booking ski extras locally. Despite having to bus to the slopes, families praise Pamporovo. Not only is the skiing suitable but the English-speaking crèche is well regarded (only £6.50 a day including lunch), and the purpose-built village has 'everything to hand'. The ski school's instructors are patient, enthusiastic and speak good English, and class sizes are usually quite small. At the heart of the village are the two hotels, Perelik and Mourgaret, both of which are good by Bulgarian standards. The food is monotonous ('it helps if you like pork'), though the buffet offers a fair choice. The Perelik has a large pool, though its 'murky water is rather off-putting'. The organised evening events are popular, and there are some bars, but Pamporovo is generally quieter and less commercialised than Borovets. Late season snowcover is unreliable.

Vitosha (1810m) is no more than a few widely scattered hotels with limited, bland skiing, and on our visit we were unable to find any nursery slopes, which was a surprise given the resort's five-star rating for beginners in one brochure. The hotels are mostly dour, and all but one are a bus-ride from the lifts. Sofia is close by, allowing short transfers and easy excursions, but the slopes get overrun at weekends. Vitosha's main saving grace is its good snow record.

Borovets 1300m

✔ *Very, very cheap*

✔ *A completely different ski holiday, with the chance to experience a fascinating although depressed culture*

✔ *Very good ski school*

✔ *Compact village – little walking to lifts*

✔ *Beautiful setting among thick pine forest*

✘ *Low standards of comfort, particularly food and other things affected by present shortages*

✘ *Archaic airports, airline, coaches can cause long travel delays (We strongly recommend a Sofia flight – Plovdiv airport is a disaster)*

✘ *Not particularly snowsure, yet no artificial back-up*

✘ *Small, yet steep ski area relatively unsuitable for many grades of skier*

✘ *Poor piste maintenance*

✘ *Limited off-slope facilities*

✘ *Ugly hotels*

For visitors who have done some research into what to expect from a Bulgarian ski holiday (other than low prices) Borovets has few nasty surprises and some pleasant ones. It is typically Balkan, with all that implies – kee piste-bashers, gourmets, posers and those wanting creature comforts should look elsewhere. However, it is one of the few resorts to meet the needs of budget skiers seeking a reasonable ski area, pretty scenery, and convenient village lifts. Borovets is also a developing village, with much-needed infrastructure being provided in response to market demands. These assets put it ahead of Bulgarian and Romanian rivals, making it the best all-round ski resort in Eastern Europe.

ORIENTATION

Despite recent development, Borovets remains essentially a compact gathering of hotels. There are two focal points to the resort. The first is a central cluster of large hotels. The main village lift (a gondola) goes from here to two of the three ski sectors. Most of the slopes face north with east-facing runs beneath the top station. A couple of minutes' walk takes you to the top of the resort, where an enormous hotel overlooks the remaining village lifts, all conveniently close to one and other. There are no resorts near enough to justify a ski excursion.

The resort

Borovets is little more than a collection of large, ugly, modern hotels, with most of the essentials of a ski resort – bars, restaurants, shops etc – housed within them. This said, there has been new development apparent every year since the fall of the Communist regime, and some regular guests have come to believe the place is becoming too commercial and is now not as ultra-friendly or cheap as its Bulgarian rival Pamporovo. This is relative of course. It's still very inexpensive and friendly by the standards of most resorts.

The beautiful wooded setting of the place provides a degree of Alpine-style charm, and trees do their best to hide some of the worst architectural excesses.

Despite the very low prices, including cheap beer, Borovets is not overly dominated by young people looking to whoop it up. Many of the visitors are on very low budgets, including a fair number of families. Evening animation is centred mainly within the Rila hotel, leaving the rest of Borovets to have a muted atmosphere.

The skiing

THE SKI AREA
Biggest in Eastern Europe

The 40km of piste are spread over three sectors, two of which are loosely connected. The two largest have fairly steep skiing made more awkward by poor piste maintenance. A gondola rises over 1000m from the edge of town to service both the small, high, easy slopes of the Markoudjika sector, and the mainly long steepish Yastrebets pistes that lead back to the same lift station. A little drag lift and path connect the two. The Baraki sector is within easy walking distance of the gondola bottom station, even in ski boots, starting conveniently in front of the biggest of the village hotels, with several base lifts to choose from. Runs are short, with a ski range of just 550m upto a top station at 1850m.

SNOW RELIABILITY
Not particularly good

The small Markoudjika section is relatively snowsure, but the ski area as a whole is markedly reduced when runs to the village are incomplete –

LIFT PASSES

94/95 prices in
pounds sterling
Borovets area
Covers all lifts in the
resort.
Main pass
1-day pass 11
6-day pass 61
Children
Under 12: 6-day pass
50 (18% off)

SKI SCHOOL

94/95 prices in
pounds sterling

Borovets Ski School
Classes 6 days
4hr: 10am-noon and
2pm-4pm
6 full days: 65
Children's classes
Ages: up to 12
6 full days: 46

CHILDCARE

The kindergarten in
the hotel Rila takes
children aged 2 to 5,
from 9am to 4.30 and
in the evening from
7pm.

GETTING THERE

Air Sofia, transfer
1½hr.

there is little skiing between the top
and middle stations of the gondola,
and Baraki's section is drastically
reduced. Despite advertisements to the
contrary, there is little in the way of
snowmaking machinery.

FOR ADVANCED SKIERS
One run doesn't make a holiday
The long fairly challenging piste, and
its variants, beneath the gondola is
where you'll be practising those turns.

FOR INTERMEDIATE SKIERS
Some variety
Good intermediates will enjoy the red
runs, most of which are fairly tough.
Average performers have a lovely long
blue run, dropping 1000m, from
Yastrebets. Nervous skiers are not well
provided for, although the short easy
runs at Markoudjika at least have good
snow. The lack of good piste grooming
tends to mean there are few leisurely
cruises available.

FOR BEGINNERS
Not ideal
The nursery slopes are conveniently
positioned at the foot of the Baraki
section, but are inadequate. The
excellence of the ski school is some
compensation. Markoudjika is good
for near beginners/fast learners,
though again we have to emphasise
the generally poor grooming does not
make for easy progression.

FOR CROSS-COUNTRY
Not appealing
Officially there are 20 trails but the
area covered is small. Few people
come here to do the sport, so trails are
either pleasantly lonely or lacking
atmosphere depending on your point
of view. Trails are poorly maintained.
Making your own tracks through the
forest is an idea if you like 'off-piste'.

QUEUES
Variable
There are weeks when queues form
only at ski school start and finish
times, but when the resort is full
and/or lacking complete snow cover
lines can be long in places. The
gondola and a single-person chair are
the main bottlenecks. When the
attractions of skiing high are
particularly apparent, delays to reach
Yastrebets can be serious (up to two
hours). At such times skiers bussed in
from Pamporovo have added to the
chaos. Fridays are particularly bad, as
the gondola closes for maintenance
for half the day, and all day on the last
Friday of the month.

MOUNTAIN RESTAURANTS
Basic and inadequate
These are mostly basic little snack bars
with limited seating serving good-
sized portions of very simple fare. It
helps if you like chips. Lunchtime
queues can be more time-consuming
than lift delays. Fortunately, it is not
inconvenient to return to Borovets for
lunch. The Ela hotel is close to the
Yastrebets slopes and has bearable
food. If staying on the mountain, it's
probably safest to stick to pizza.

SKI SCHOOL
A justly high reputation
The Borovets ski school gives caring,
patient, fun tuition four hours per
day. Standards of English are
surprisingly high, and classes not too
large. There is also a new co-operative
school, which offers similar prices and
services.

FACILITIES FOR CHILDREN
Generally approved of
Reports of ski kindergarten have been
highly complimentary, with one
exception which castigated it for
everything including very poor
supervision. This was over New Year,
so perhaps the normally caring staff
were overworked or simply not on
duty. The non-ski nursery is situated
in hotel Rila.

Staying there

The compact nature of the resort, with
everything (including lifts) within
easy walking distance of everything
else, makes location of hotel relatively
unimportant. This said, there is some
accommodation out in the
countryside which relies on quite a
poor ski-bus service and/or taxis (very
cheap). Horse-drawn sleighs also
provide a taxi service around the
village; it is cheap enough to use
frequently, but scarcely needed.

HOW TO GO
On a hotel package, probably
Borovets is essentially a hotel resort.
Apartments are available, but cooking
for yourself is difficult: there are no
supermarkets! There are no catered
chalets.
Hotels The big, modern monstrosities
are conveniently close to the lifts, and
there is also an attractive -style
Scandanavian development out in the
forest.
£ Rila Low marks for virtually
everything, especially food; not
recommended.

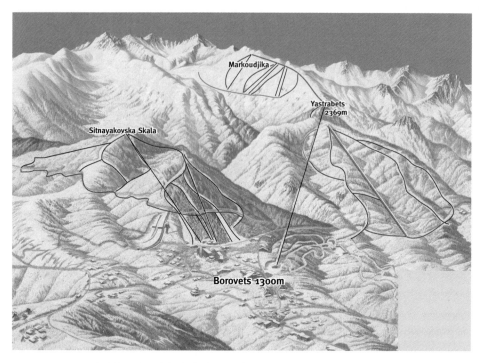

Markoudjika

Yastrabets
2369m

Sitnayakovska Skala

Borovets 1300m

PACKAGES

Crystal, Enterprise, Inghams, Neilson, Ski Ardmore, Ski Balkantours

ACTIVITIES

Indoor Sauna, fitness centre, swimming pools, gym
Outdoor Sleigh rides, helicopter trips, mountain walks, excursions to Samokov, Sofia, Rila monastery and Plovdiv

TOURIST OFFICE

Tel 010 359 (2) 835210
Fax 800134

£ Samokov Much the better of the two enormous conference hotels, though its four-star rating should not be taken too seriously. It has plenty of amenities but little atmosphere or character. The 25m pool is a major asset in a resort with few off-slope facilities.

£ Ela and **Moura** Friendly sister hotels, both with plenty of hot water (an important consideration here) and (at the Moura) particularly good food by local standards.

£ Breza Rather spartan, but small and friendly, with lots of hot water and more rustic character than anywhere else.

£ Bor One of the less well positioned places, and rather basic – but popular for its friendliness.

£ Yagoda Chalets Studio apartments sold on a half-board basis. Part of an attractive Finnish-designed development of log cabins in the forest 3km out of town. Buses every 20 minutes during the morning rush hour, otherwise hourly. Taxis about £2 each way.

Self-catering The Rila studios are clean and comfortable, but hot water can be erratic.

EATING OUT
Organised events best

Food is generally poor. The Maritsa restaurant in the hotel Samokov attempts French cuisine at the bargain price of £5 per head , but the best food of the week is likely to be on the folklore and local village dinner evenings arranged by tour reps. Hotel Moura is the best bet at other times.

APRES SKI
Limited, but a varied range

Events organised by tour operator reps include trips to sample Bulgarian folklore and a visit to a local village for dinner. Sleigh rides and togogganing are available. Many consider the entertaining ski school show the highlight of the week. Others prefer the sumo wrestling! There are three discos – the Rila is the noisiest, the Samokov perhaps the best. The Piano Bar is the best place for a quiet drink, being one of the few bars not to have loud music or MTV. Hotel bars are also generally large and impersonal, with the notable exception of the cosy one in the Breza.

FOR NON SKIERS
Not a lot

There isn't sufficient to keep complete non-skiers happy for long, but part-time skiers have a few intriguing options open to them. Excursions to the Rila monastery by coach and to Sofia, by either coach or helicopter, are very interesting. There may also be an opportunity to see ballet in Sofia. Borovets has little to offer, but the Samokov pool is open to the public. The Piano Bar art gallery has some good works at bargain prices.

Romania

LIke Bulgaria, Romania sells mainly on cost. On-the-spot prices, in particular, are very, very low. Provided you have correspondingly low expectations – and provided you go to Poiana Brasov and not Sinaia – you'll probably come back content. If you have any interest in good living, and particularly good lunching, stay away. It's a place for beginners and near-beginners – the skiing is limited in extent and challenge, but the ski tuition is good (and cheap, of course).

There is another dimension to a holiday in Romania, which is the experience of visiting (and you could say supporting) an interesting and attractive country with an exceptionally traumatic recent history. All of our recent reporters commented on the friendliness of the local people, and most recommended exploring beyond the confines of the ski resorts. Bucharest is 'not to be missed'.

Romania's two ski resorts are in the Carpathian mountains, about 120km north-west of the capital and arrival airport, Bucharest. They are very different places, but do have one or two things in common apart from low prices ('difficult to spend £50 in a week, even if you like to drink a lot,' said one reporter). One is good tuition, with excellent spoken English, small classes of 6 to 10 pupils and a patient, friendly approach. Another is very basic mountain restaurants, with primitive sanitary arrangements that would 'shock the toughest of characters'.

The main resort is **Poiana Brasov** (1020m), near the city of Brasov. It is purpose-built, but not for the convenience of skiers: the hotels are dotted about a spacious, pretty wooded plateau, served by regular ski-buses. There is no village as such.

The main skiing consists of decent intermediate tree-lined runs of about 750m vertical, roughly following the line of the main cable-car and gondola, plus an open nursery area at the top. There are also some nursery lifts at village level. There is a black run that takes a less direct route down the mountain, which means that on average it is gentler than the red run under the lifts; it has one moderately steep pitch towards the end. Adventurous skiers would need to seek opportunities to go off-piste. The resorts gets weekend business from Brasov and Bucharest, and the main lifts can suffer serious queues.

The Bradul and Sport hotels are handy for the lower nursery slopes and for one of the cable-cars, but you can't be certain that it will be operating. None of the hotels is at all special, but the Alpin gets the best reports and the Ciucas is a 'good basic' place. Après-ski revolves around hotels; they have bars and discos which can be 'quite lively' at times. The two nightclubs put on cheap and cheerful cabarets including 'Russian ballet dancers attempting to be erotic – quite good fun'. Non-skiing facilities are limited; there is a good-sized pool, and bowling. Excursions are 'surprisingly expensive'.

One or two companies offer holidays in **Sinaia** – a small town on the busy road from Bucharest to Brasov. When we visited it some years ago we were quite taken by the modest intermediate ski area, on largely treeless hills next to the town. In those pre-revolutionary days the town was a rather depressing place, and to judge by reports it is even more so now – one reporter was shocked and saddened by the evident poverty, and upset by the number of stray dogs around.

The abiding impression we brought back from Romania was one of resources stretched to their limits. To judge by the reports we have received, post-revolutionary Romania has not made much progress. One report tells of the loos at Bucharest airport, where three sheets of toilet paper were issued to each person on entry.

Reference section

Comprehensive listings to help you
fix and prepare for your ski holiday

A classified listing of the names,
numbers and addresses you are
likely to need when fixing a ski
holiday.

Page references for resorts dealt
with in detail in the main part of
the book, and a brief overview of
more than 250 others, all organised
alphabetically.

Dry ski slopes

Let's not beat about the bush: we hate dry ski slopes, and we never go near them if we can possibly avoid it. But we can recall enough about our first skiing trips to know that a few hours on dry slopes got us off to a flying start on the real thing. At the very least, dry slope sessions get you used to the clumpy boots and unmanageable skis. You may even learn the basics of traversing and turning. And it's not unknown for people to develop into dry-slope-skiing enthusiasts – there are lots of good skiers in Britain who hardly ever go near snow. What follows is a full list of the slopes open to the public, arranged by region.

South West

CHRISTCHURCH
Christchurch Ski Centre, Matchams Lane, Hurn, Christchurch, Dorset, BH23 6AW
Tel 0202 499155
Facilities include: one main slope of 110m, two more slopes used for tuition approx 60m in length, and three nursery slopes with opposite counter slopes. The centre is fully floodlit, and all the slopes are served by an integrated mist-sprinkler system. Two Briton buttton lifts serve the main and the training slope.

CHURCHILL
Avon Ski Centre, Lyncombe Lodge, Churchill, Avon CS19 5PQ.
Tel 0934 852335
Facilities include: main run 160m-long through woods, and three nursery slopes each 60m long. All served by misting systems. Also on site: a 60m tobogganing slope, a café, a shop and a hotel.

DORCHESTER
Warmwell Leisure Resort, Warmwell, Near Weymouth, Dorset DT2 8JE
Tel 0305 852911
Facilities include: a 110 metre slope, serviced by a drag lift. Also on site: Crusoes restaurant, with an extensive menu, also serving bar snacks and take-aways.

EXETER
Exeter and District Ski Club, Clifton Hill Sports Centre, Belmont Road, Exter, EX1 2DJ
Tel 0392 211422
Facilities include: a main slope, set at varying angles, and a nursery slope, both floodlit: the main slope is served by a tow.

GLOUCESTER
Gloucester Ski Centre, Robinswood Hill, Gloucester, Gloucestershire, GL4 9EA
Tel 0452 414300
Facilities include: two main ski slopes, 240 and 200m, and a 30m nursery area. All slopes served by a sprinkler system and by four lifts. Also on site: a ski workshop, a bar serving snacks, and a ski shop.

PLYMOUTH
John Nike Leisuresport Complex, Alpine Park, Marsh Mills, Plymouth PL6 8LQ
Tel 0752 600220
Facilities include: a 160m main run, a shorter beginners' run, an intermediate run with moguls half-way, and a licensed bar with bar meals. The main run has a button lift, and the intermediate run has a rope lift. Wax mats are used.

REDRUTH
Ski 1st, Radnor Golf Centre, Radnor Road, Redruth, TR16 5EL
Tel 0209 211059
Facilities include: a revolutionary new revolving belt slope, with variable speed control. The slope is indoors, and beginners are always under close supervision from an instructor.

SOUTHAMPTON
Calshot Activities centre, Calshot Spit, Fawley, Southampton, Hampshire SO45 1BR
Tel 0703 892077
Facilities include: one main slope split into two runs, and a nursery slope. The slopes are all indoors and are floodlit, ensuring all-year round skiing, regardless of weather conditions. Briton ski tows serve both the main and the nursery slopes. The centre stays open until 10pm most nights. Also on site: a fully licensed bar serving drinks and snacks.

SOUTHAMPTON

Southampton Ski Centre, Basset, Southampton, Hampshire SO16 7AY
Tel 0703 790970
Facilities include: three main skiing areas, serviced by two button lifts. The third skiing area is a smaller, gently sloping nursery run. The site is floodlit and stays open late.

TORQUAY

Wessex Ski Club, Barton Hall, Kingskerswell Road, Torquay, Devon, TQ2 8JY
Tel 0803 313350
Facilities include: over 2500 square metres of ski area, a mogul slope for advanced skiers, and an extensive beginners' area. Slopes are served by a button lift and have full floodlighting. Video sessions available. Also on site, a large ski lodge serving hot and cold drinks.

WELLINGTON

Wellington Sports Centre, Corams Lane, Wellington, TA21 8LL
Tel 0823 663010
Facilities include: one slope approx 60m in length, fully floodlit, served by a basic ski tow and serviced by an integrated sprinkler system. Also on site is a small café area furnished with vending machines serving hot and cold drinks and snacks.

YEOVIL

Yeovil Ski Centre, Addlewell Lane, Yeovil, Somerset, BA20 1QW
Tel 0935 21702
Facilities include: one main slope approx 150m long and a nursery slope approx 100m in length. Both the slopes are lubricated by an integrated sprinkler system and served by a button lift which runs between them .

South East

ALDERSHOT

Stainforth Ski Centre, Hurst Road, Aldershot, Hampshire, GU11 2DJ
Tel 0252 25889
Facilities include: a 110m main slope, and two 75m trainer slopes. All three slopes are serviced by ski tows and mist systems. The entire site is fully floodlit. Also on site are vending, snack and bar facilities.

BRACKNELL

Tel 0344 860033
John Nike Leisuresport Complex, John Nike Way, Amen Corner, Bracknell RG12 4TN.
Facilities include: a main 150m run, an 80m nursery run, chairlift, two draglifts, a mist system and a cafeteria.

BRENTWOOD

Brentwood Park Ski Centre, Warley Gap, Brentwood, Essex, CM13 3LG
Tel 0277 211994
Facilities include: five slopes, of which three are main slopes of 70m, 120m and 200m. All are serviced by their own lifts. The entire site is fully floodlit, and open all year round. Ample car-parking is provided.

CHATHAM

Chatham Ski Centre, Alpine Park, Capstone Road, Chatham, Kent ME7 3JH
Tel 0634 827979
Facilities include: 220m slope, 40m wide with mogul run; beginners' slope 40 by 40m. Both slopes floodlit, open until 10pm.

ESHER

Sandown Ski School, More Lane, Esher, Surrey, KT10 8AN
Tel 0372 467132
Facilities include: three slopes, including a nursery slope (approx 90m long), a mogul run (approx 70m long) and a main slope (approx 110m long). The slopes are served by two button ski lifts and the entire centre is floodlit.

FOLKESTONE

Folkestone Sports Centre Ski Centre, Radnor Park Avenue, Folkestone, Kent CT19 5HX
Tel 0303 850333
Facilities include: two slopes. The main slope is 45m and has a learner area down the side, and the other slope is a 38m mogul run. There is a sprinkler system, a Poma lift and a hand tow, and the sports centre's café/bar. In March 1995 permission is expected for a new site with an 80m-long main run and a new mogul run.

GUILDFORD

Bishop Reindorp Ski Centre, Larch Avenue, Guildford, Surrey
Tel 0483 504988
Facilities include: 40m & 20m slopes, served by a rope tow. Specialises in teaching all levels from beginners to BASI. Floodlit, open all year round, car-parking, vending facilities.

HARLOW
Harlow Ski School, Hammarskjold Road, Harlow, Essex, CM20 2JF
Tel 0279 444100
Facilities include: a 160m main slope served by two button lifts, a seperate 90m training slope with button lift, a mogul run for the more advanced skier, and a permanent slalom course. All slopes are served by a mist system, and are fully floodlit. Also on site, a freindly café and licensed bar.

HEMEL HEMPSTEAD
Hemel Ski Centre, St. Albans Hill, Hemel Hempstead HP3 9NH
Tel 0442 241321
Facilities include: a 180m main run, a 40m by 25m training run and a 60m wave run. There are three button lifts.

IPSWICH
Suffolk Ski Centre, Bourne Terrace, Wherstead, Ipswich, IP2 8NG
Tel 0473 602347
Facilities include: one main slope which consists of an improvers' slope (90m), a bumps run (100m), and a graded red run (180m). Slopes are serviced by a button lift to the top of the red run, and a smaller drag lift to the top of the improvers'. There are also two nursery slopes.

LONDON
Alexandra Palace Ski Centre
Tel 081 888 2284
No details of facilities available.

LONDON
Beckton Alp Ski Centre Ltd, Alpine Way, London, E6 4LA
Tel 071 511 0351
Facilities include: two slopes, including a main slope 200m long and a four-lane nursery slope, with gentle gradients ideal for beginners. The main slope is serviced by a ski tow and has a new mist system. Also on site: an Alpine bar and restaurant for Alpine style cuisine.

LONDON
National Sports & leisure Centre, P.O.Box 676, Upper Norwood, London, SE19 2BB
Tel 081 778 0131
Facilities include: a slope measuring 32.3m by 18.3 m, situated on a wooded incline which forms a natural slalom, ideal for beginners, and challenging to the more experienced wanting to brush up on their technique.

LONDON
Hillingdon Ski Centre Ltd, Park Road, Uxbridge, Middlesex, UB10 9NH
Tel 0895 255183/258506
Facilities include: five slopes, with a main slope of 160m, an intermediate slope of 90m that includes a bumps section, two beginners' slopes and a kindergarten area. All slopes are lift-served by three buttons.

NEWHAVEN
Borowski ski centre, New Road, Newhaven, East Sussex, BN9 0EH
Tel 0273 515402
Facilities include: two indoor slopes, one nursery slope, a practice and training slope. The complex contains ski shops, ski workshops, ski rental and a bar for après-ski refreshments.

NORWICH
Norfolk Ski Slope, Whitlingham Lane, Trowse, Norwich, Norfolk NR14 8TW
Tel 0603 662781
Facilities include: 100m main slope, 70m by 40m nursery slope, two Poma lifts, sprinklers. The site is floodlit and has a clubhouse with a bar.

ORPINGTON
Bromley Ski Centre, Sandy Lane, St. Paul's Cray, Orpington, Kent BR5 38Y
Tel 0689 876812
Facilities include: a 120m main slope with a bumps section served by two button lifts, and a nursery slope with a rope tow. Open all year round, floodlit, ample car-parking, bar/cafeteria, shop.

TROWES
Norfolk Ski Club, Whitlingham Lane, Trowes, NR14 8TW
Tel 0603 662781
Facilities include: a 160m main slope and 60m nursery slope, served by three button lifts. Sprinkler system being upgraded. Large tuition set up including teaching the disabled. Racing and junior clubs. Floodlit. Ample car-parking. Open all year round but not daily. Members only some days. Large clubhouse with bar, lounge and satellite TV. Corporate hospitality.

TUNBRIDGE WELLS
Bowles Outdoor Centre, Eridge Green, Tunbridge Wells, TN3 9LW
Tel 0892 665665
Facilities include: an 80m main slope with a moguls section at one side of it. There is also a 50m nursery slope. The main slope is serviced by a button lift. Floodlit. Ample car-parking. Also on site are a chalet

always open for hot and cold drinks, and a licensed bar open after most evening courses. Several group ski holidays organised each year.

Welwyn Garden City

The Gosling Ski Centre, Stanborough Road, Welwyn Garden City, Hertfordshire, AL8 6XE
Tel 0707 391039
Facilities include: one main slope (approx 160m), a nursery slope, and a kindergarten area. The main slope is the widest in the East. All slopes are served by an integrated mist-sprinkler system and by an over-head Poma ski lift. The entire site is floodlit, and open 7 days a week until 10pm. Also on site: a fully licensed bar and cafeteria in the adjacent tennis and bowls centre.

Midlands

Birmingham

The Ackers, Golden Hillock Road, Small Heath, Birmingham, B11 2PY
Tel 021 7714448
Facilities include: one main slope of 100m, two nursery slopes, each approx 50m. All the slopes are served by an integrated sprinkler system. The main slope is served by a button lift and a ski tow. Also on site: a small refreshment area furnished with various vending machines.

Cossall

Ski 2000, Downhill Ski Club Ltd., Solomon Road, Cossall, Notts.
Tel 0602 442870
Facilities include: a 150m main slope and 40m nursery slope, served by two button lifts, and a child's tobogganing area. It has the only Japanese astrogalande (like astroturf – no holes) slopes in the country. Amidst 30 acres of parkland, disabled skiers club and facilities, open all the year round – daily in the winter, floodlit, clubhouse with bar and Sunday carvery, day cafeteria, sports shop, ample car-parking.

Nottingham

Richard Herrod Leisure Centre, Foxhill Road, Carlton, Nottingham NG4 1RL.
Tel 0602 612949
Facilities include: a 60m slope with a pulley system. Café and vending machine.

Rushden

Skew Bridge Ski Slope, Northampton Road, Rushden, Northants
Tel 0933 59939
Facilities include: a 90m main slope with an 85m variant, and a 60m slope, served by two rope tows and one button lift. It shares a complex with a country club which allows its amenities, including restaurants and bars, to be used by skiers. Specialises in children's parties including toboganning. Snowboarding lessons. Open daily all the year round, floodlit, car-parking.

Stamford

Tallington Ski Centre, Tallington Lakes leisure Park, Barholm Road, Tallington, Nr.Stamford, Lincs, PE9 4RJ
Tel 0778 344990
Facilities include: one main slope, (80m) and two nursery slopes, each approx 25 metres long. The slopes are all fully floodlit and served by an integrated sprinkler system and a Briton tow lift.

Stoke-on-Trent

Festival Park Ski slope, Festival Park, Stoke-on-Trent, ST1 5PU
0782 204159
Facilities include: two slopes, served by sprayers, a licensed bar and cafeteria.

Stoke-on-Trent

North Staffs Ski Club, Kidsgrove, Stoke-on-Trent ST7 4EF
Tel 0782 784908

Swadlincote

Swadlincote Ski Centre, Hill Street, Swadlincote, Derbyshire, DE11 8LP
Tel 0283 217200
Facilities include: two ski slopes, serviced by four ski lifts. The main slope is 160m long and 22m wide, constantly maintained for good skiing by a sprinkler system. The Centre also boasts a 650m-long toboggan run. Also on site is an Alpine ski lodge serving traditional Tyrolean dishes.

Tamworth

Tamworth Snowdome, Leisure Island, River Dri
ve, Tamworth, Staffs B79 7ND
Tel 0827 67905
Facilities include: an enclosed dome allowing real snow inside. The main run is 150m by 30m, with a 25m drop.

TELFORD

Telford Ski Centre, Court St, Madeley, Telford, Shropshire, TF7 5DZ
Tel 0952 586862
Facilities include: two ski slopes. The main slope is 85m long and serviced by two ski tows, one of which is a Poma-style button lift. The nursery slope is 30m long. Both slopes are fully floodlit. Also on site: a ski lodge bar, with a purpose-built barbecue on the patio.

Wales

CAPEL CURIG

Plas y Brenin, Capel Curig, Gwynedd, LL24 0ET
Tel 06904 214/280/363
Facilities include: one 60m slope, served by a Briton button lift. The slope has an integrated mist-sprinkler system, and is floodlit.

CARDIFF

Cardiff Ski Centre, Fairwater Park, Fairwater, Cardiff, South Glamorgan, CF5 3JR
Tel 0222 561793
Facilities include: one main slope approx 100m long. The slope is served by a button lift.

GLYNTAWE

Dan-yr-Ogof Ski Slopes, Abercrave, Upper Swansea Valley, Powys SA9 1GJ
Tel 0639 730284
Facilities include: one slope approx 100m long served by an integrated sprinkler system, floodlights and a Poma button lift. The centre has a small cafeteria serving light snacks and soft drinks.

LLANDUDNO

Ski Llandudno, Great Orme, Llandudno, Gwynedd LL30 2QL
Tel 0492 874707
Facilities include: main slope 286m long, nursery slope 50m long, 700m toboggan run, ski lodge serving hot and cold drinks and food. Open 7 days a week except Christmas day. A Briton button lift and a mist system service the runs.

LLANELLI

Pembrey Ski Slope, Pembrey Country Park, Llanelli, Dyfed, SA16 0EJ
Tel 0554 834443
Facilities include: a 130m main slope, a 40m nursery area, a new toboggan run, and an all-new mogul run. All are served by a button lift. Slopes are served by a sprinkler system. Also on site, an Alpine i Lodge and cafeteria.

PONTYPOOL

Pontypool Ski Centre, Pontypool Park, Pontypool, Gwent NP4 8AT
Tel 0495 756955
Facilities include: one main slope, approx 265m in length in a "J" shape, the bottom of which is used as the beginners' area. A second slope is under construction at present. The slope is fully floodlit and served by a high-speed Poma tow lift. A misting system to service the entire length of slope is currently under construction and is expected to be completed for the begining of the 95/96 season. A cafeteria is situated in the nearby sports centre.

TRAWSFYNYDD

Rhiwgoch Ski Centre, Bronaber, Trawsfynydd, Gwynedd, LL41 4UR
Tel 0766 87578
Facilities include: a long wide main run, with two smaller nursery slopes. The main slope and first nursery area are served by two tows. All the slopes are served by a mist system, and all slopes are floodlit.

North

ALSTON

Alston Training and Adventure Centre, High Plains Centre, Alston, Cumbria CA9 3DD
Tel 0434 747000
Facilities include: a 25m nursery slope and a coffee bar. It is a multi-activity centre.

BEBINGTON

The Oval, Wirral, Old Chester Road, Bebington, L63 7LF
Tel 051 645 0551
Facilities include: one 65m ski slope, fully floodlit, but without a ski tow. The site hosts two clubs: the Mersey ski club and the Oval ski club. Also on site, a cafeteria serving snacks and light meals, and a fully licensed bar, for refreshing après-ski.

CATTERICK

Catterick Indoor Ski Slope, Horne Road, North Yorks, Catterick Garrison, DL9 4LE
Tel 0748 833788
Facilities include: a main slope, 35 by 20m with a ski tow, and a smaller slope, 18 by 11m. Small licensed clubroom for refreshments.

CLITHEROE

Pendle Ski Club, Clitheroe Road, Sabden, Clitheroe, Lancs BB7 9HN
Tel 0200 25222

Facilities include: 130m main slope, 35m training slope, two button lifts, misting system, floodlights, and a café in the clubhouse. It is a club but, if pre-booked, non-members may be allowed to ski at weekends.

CROOK
Spectrum Leisure Complex, Hunwick Lane, Willington, Crook, County Durham, DL15 0JA
Tel 0388 747000
Facilities include: a floodlit thematic ski slope with tow and integrated sprinkler system. Also on site: ski repair/maintenance and hire facilities.

DUNSTON
Whickham Thorns Ski Club, Market Lane, Dunston, NE11 9NX
Tel 091 4601193
Facilities include: 40m slope, two rope tows, specialises in improvers classes, mostly for school groups, but also has facilities for the disabled. Open daily, all year round. Weekly ski club. Floodlit, car-parking, vending machines.

FOREST-IN-TEESDALE
High Force Cross-Country Track, High Force Training Centre, Forest in Teesdale, Co Durham, DL12 0HA
Tel 0833 22302
Facilities include: four downhill ski runs, well lubricated by centre staff. All the slopes are floodlit. The centre also boasts a new cross-country track approx 500m in length, perfect for pre-season practice of your langlauf technique.

HALIFAX
Halifax Ski Centre, Sportsman Leisure, Bradford Old Road, Swalesmoor, Halifax, HX3 6UG
Tel 0422 340760
Facilities include: a 90m main slope, 50m intermediate slope and 30m nursery area, served by a button lift and rope tow. Open daily all the year round. Tuition from beginners up to BASI. Floodlit, car-parking.
Pub, restaurant, squash courts, multi-gym.

HARROGATE
Ski Harrogate, Hookstone Wood Road, Harrogate, North Yorkshire, HG2 8PW
Tel 0423 505457/8
Facilities include: a large main slope, extensive separate training slopes. The main slope is serviced by a tow lift. Refreshments are on site, and the site has a friendly atmosphere.

KENDAL
Kendal Ski Club, 24 Michelson Road, Collinfield, Kendal, Cumbria
Tel 0539 733031
Facilities include: one slope approx 70m long, floodlit when required and served by a ski tow. The slope is kept lubricated through an integrated sprinkler system, to allow all-weather skiing.

MIDDLESBOROUGH
Eston Hills Ski Village, Flatts Lane, Eston, Middlesborough, Cleveland, TS6 0NN
Tel 0642 466000
Facilities include: a 120m main slope served by a button lift, and a nursery area. Floodlit, open all year round, car-park.

OLDHAM
Oldham Ski Centre, Oldham Sports Centre, Lord Street, Oldham, OL1 3HA
Tel 061 9114081
Facilities include: a long slope with varying profiles and gradients to suit all abilities, and two training areas, both served by independent tow systems. The main slope is served by a waist-high button tow. A mist system services the entire site, ensuring skiing in all weather.

ROSSENDALE
Ski Rossendale, Haslingdon Old Road, Rawtenstall, Rossendale, Lancashire, BB4 8RR
Tel 0706 222426
Facilities include: a 200m main slope, a 100m intermediate slope, a 40m nursery slope, and a 40m teaching slope. Slopes are served by four ski tows and a sprinkler system, and are fully floodlit. Also on site: a licensed cafeteria and a ski lodge.

RUNCORN
Ski Runcorn, The Ski Lodge, Town Park, Palacefields, Runcorn, Cheshire WA7 2PS
Tel 0928 701965
Facilities include: two runs, one of 100m and one of 30m, a mist system, two button tows, and a café serving drinks and confectionery. Next door to a country club, whose facilities (eg swimming pool) large groups visiting the ski centre are able to use.

SHEFFIELD
Sheffield Ski Village, Vale Road, Parkwood Springs, Sheffield, S3 9SJ
Tel 0742 769459
Facilities include: eight slopes ranging from 150m to 320m in length, and

from easy to very difficult. All the slopes are served by a T-bar lift, a button lift, and mist systems. All slopes are floodlit. Also on site: a continental café and a bar/diner, American style. The centre boasts the most extensive facilities in Britain.

SILKSWORTH

Sunderland Ski Centre, Silksworth Sports Complex, Silksworth Lane, Sunderland SR3 3AN
Tel 091 522 9119
Facilities include: a 165m main slope, serviced by two tows, and a new 55m nursery slope, opened in September 1989.

Scotland

ABERDEEN

Alford Ski Centre, Greystone Road, Alford, Aberdeen, AB3 8JE
Tel 09755 62380
Facilities include: two slopes, 86 and 70m in length. The slopes are floodlit and serviced by a misting system and two Poma lifts. A small pavillion in which there is a café for the use of skiers is situated close to the slopes.

ABERDEEN

Kaimhill Ski Slope, Garthdee Road, Aberdeen, AB1 7BA
Tel 0224 311781
Facilities include: two ski slopes, each 95m long. Served by a Poma and a Button lift. The entire site is floodlit to allow late evening use.

AVIEMORE

Glenmore Lodge, Scottish National Sports Centre, Aviemore, Invernessshire, PH22 1QU
Tel 0479 861256
Facilities include: a 50m floodlit slope served by a Poma drag lift. Open 9am-11pm. There is also a Nordic and Biathlon National Rollerski track for use by clubs and coaches only.

AVIEMORE CAIRDSPORT

The Aviemore Centre, Aviemore, Inverness-shire, PH22 1PF
Tel 0479 810624
Facilities include: an 80 by 10m slope served by a button lift; all amenities within complex.

BALLATER

The Craigendarroch Hotel and Country Club, Braemar Road, Ballater, Royal Deeside, AB35 5XA
Tel 03397 55858
Facilities include: a 75m slope, not generally open to the public.

BANNOCKBURN

Firpark Ski Centre, Tillycoultry, Central Scotland, FK13 6PL
Tel 0259 751772
Facilities include: one main teaching slope, serviced by a button lift. The slope is floodlit and has an integrated sprinkler system. The slope is unfortunately not generally open to the public but, if the visit is pre-arranged, exceptions can be made.

CARRBRIDGE

Lochanhully Woodland Club, Carrbridge, Inverness-shire, PH23 3NA
Tel 0479 841234
Facilities include: one slope of 30m length: the slope is floodlit and served by a button tow. Also on site is a small cafeteria serving drinks and food.

CONNAH'S QUAY

Deeside Ski Slope, Deeside College, Kelsterton Road, Connah's Quay, Deeside, CH5 4BR
Tel 0690 710306
Facilities include: 80m long main run, rope tow, floodlights and hot drinks.

DUNDEE

Ancrum Outdoor Education Resource Centre, 10 Ancrum Road, Dundee, Tayside DD2 2HZ
Tel 0382 643735
Facilities include: one small slope, approx 50m in length. The slope is floodlit, and the centre has a coffee bar serving light refreshments.

EDINBURGH

Hillend Ski Centre, Biggar Road, Edinburgh, Lothian, EH10 7DU
Tel 031 445 4433
Facilities include four slopes: a main slope 440m long, a tow slope 250m long, and two nursery slopes, one 50 by 20m and one 40 by 20m. The two advanced slopes are at varying gradients, averaging 1:2.4. All the slopes are served by a sprinkler system, and all the runs are served by lifts: a chairlift, 400m long, a T-bar tow, also 400m long, and a button lift, 270m long, serve both runs. The site also boasts a restaurant/cafeteria.

GLASGOW

Bearsden Ski Club, The Mound, Stockiemuir Road, Courthill, Bearsden, Glasgow, G61 3RS
Tel 041-943 1500
Facilities include: two slopes, both with tows and both floodlit.

GLASGOW

Glasgow Ski Centre, Bellahouston Park, 16 Dumbreck Road, Glasgow, G41 5BW
041 427 4991/427 4993
Facilities include: one slope, 80m long and approx 60m wide, split into two colour-coded runs; one teaching slope and a free skiing run. The slope is floodlit, serviced by a button lift and equipped with an integrated sprinkler system.

GLENROTHES

Fife Institute of Physical Education, Viewfield Road, Glenrothes, Fife, KY6 2RA
Tel 0592 771700
Facilities include: one small teaching slope, approx 105ft long, made from Dendix ski matting. The slope is floodlit, and drops approx 20ft, ideal for beginners.

JEDBURGH

Jedburgh Sports Complex, Jedburgh Grammar School, Jedburgh, Borders
Tel 0835 862566
Facilities include: 50m slope. Open to the public at evenings and weekends, but bring your own skis.
Alternatively, join the Borders Ski Club for all-day access and skis.

KINLOCH RANNOCH

Loch Rannoch Outdoor Activity Centre, Kinloch Rannoch, Perthshire, PH16 5PS
Tel Kinloch Rannoch 0882 6 32201
Facilities include: one ski slope, approx 70m long, served by a ski tow. The slope is floodlit to allow evening ski sessions.

NEWMILNS

Newmilns Ski Slope, High Street, Newmilns, KA16 9EB
Tel 05603 22320
Facilities include: one main slope, 150m long, served by a button lift: the slope is floodlit to permit late-evening ski sessions. Also on site, a small cafeteria furnished with vending machines and serving light snacks.

POLMONT

Polmonthill Ski Centre, Polmont Farm, Polmont, Nr. Falkirk, Central Scotland FK2 0YE
Tel 0324 711660
Contact also:
Sports Stadium, Kersiebank Avenue, Grangemouth, FK3 0EE
Tel 0324 483752
Facilities include: a 110m slope, floodlit with sprinkler system, served by a button tow. Closed-circuit TV is also used to display recordings of skiers' performances. There is also a small cafeteria with a log fire.

Northern Ireland

BELFAST

Ski Knockbracken, 24 Ballymaconaghy Road, Knockbracken, Belfast BT8 4SB
Tel 0232 795666

LISBURN

Ulster Ski Club, 36 Belfast Road, Lisburn, Co Antrim, BT27 4AG

SILVERWOOD

Craigavon Golf and Ski Centre, Turmoyra Lane, Silverwood, Lurgan, BT66 6NG
Tel 0762 326606
Facilities include: one main slope of approx 100m, and a smaller adjoining nursery slope approx 50m in length. The site is floodlit and served by a sprinkler system. A Poma tow runs adjacent to the slope. Also on site is a clubhouse containing a restaurant, but no bar.

Tour operators

Arranging your own accommodation in a ski resort is not difficult, whether you do it in advance by letter or phone, or do it on the spot. But most people still prefer the convenience of a package holiday, which is what most of the companies listed below are set up to provide. We've also included a few that offer accommodation without travel arrangements.

AA SKI-DRIVEAWAY
Ski drive specialist
PO Box 128, Norfolk House, Priestley Road, Basingstoke, Hampshire RG24 9NY
Tel 0256 493878 **Fax** 0256 493875

ABT SKI
Chalet in St-Martin-de-Belleville
Shepperton Marina, Felix Lane, Shepperton, Middlesex TW17 8NJ
Tel 0932 222002 **Fax** 0932 246140

AGD TRAVEL
Catered apartments in Les Gets
Rails Farmhouse, East Hanningfield, Chelmsford, Essex CM3 8AU
Tel 0245 400684

ACCESSIBLE ISOLATION
Holidays in Canada
Midhurst Walk, West Street, Midhurst, West Sussex GU29 9NF
Tel 0730 812535 **Fax** 0730 812926

AIRTOURS
Fast-growing mainstream tour operator
Wavell House, Holcombe Road, Helmshore, Rossendale, Lancashire BB4 4NB
Tel 0706 260000 **Fax** 0706 229032

ALL CANADA
Holidays in Canada, with some USA
90 High Street, Lowestoft, Suffolk NR32 1XN
Tel 0502 565176 **Fax** 0502 500681

ALP ACTIVE
One luxury chalet in Les Gets
37 Roupell St, London SE1 8TB
Tel 071-401 3030

ALPINE ACTION
Catered chalets in the Trois Vallées
10 Kings Road, Lancing, West Sussex BN15 8EA
Tel 0903 761986

ALPINE EXPRESSIONS
Hotels in big-name French and Swiss resorts
4 Belsize Crescent, Hampstead, London NW3 5QU
Tel 071-794 1480 **Fax** 071-431 4221

ALPINE OPTIONS SKIDRIVE
Self-drive and fly-drive to France
70 Glenwood Way, West Moors, Ferndown, Dorset BH22 0ET
Tel 0202 877148 **Fax** 0202 877148

ALPINE TOURS
Holidays in Austria, Italy and France
54 Northgate, Canterbury, Kent CT1 1BE
Tel 0227 454777 **Fax** 0227 451177

ALTOURS TRAVEL
Wide-ranging programme
41A Church Street, Staveley, Chesterfield S43 3TL
Tel 0246 471234 **Fax** 0246 471999

AMERICAN CONNECTIONS
US and Canadian operator
7 York Way, Lancaster Road, High Wycombe, Bucks HP12 3PY
Tel 0494 473173 **Fax** 0494 473588

AMERICAN DREAM
Major operator to America and Canada
Station Chambers, High Street North, London E6 1JE
Tel 081-552 1201 **Fax** 081-552 7726

AMERICAN SKIWORLD
Specialist American part of Skiworld
41 North End Road, West Kensington, London W14 8SZ
Tel 071-602 7444 **Fax** 071-371 1463

AUSTRIAN HOLIDAYS
Hotel holidays in Austria
5th Floor, 10 Wardour Street, London W1V 4BQ
Tel 071-434 7399 **Fax** 071-434 7393

AUSTRIAN TRAVEL SERVICE
Holidays in Austria and Germany
Bridge House, Ware, Herts SG12 9DE
Tel 0920 487575 **Fax** 0920 487943

BELLE FRANCE
Cross-country specialist
Bayham Abbey, Lamberhurst, Kent TN3 8BG
Tel 0892 890885 **Fax** 0892 890180

BIGFOOT
Variety of holidays in the Chamonix valley
186 Greys Road, Henley on Thames, Oxon RG9 1QU
Tel 0491 579601 **Fax** 0491 576568

BLADON LINES
Major operator, emphasis on chalets
56/58 Putney High Street, London SW15 1SF
Tel 081-785 3131 **Fax** 081-789 8358

BORDERLINE
Specialist in Barèges
Les Sorbiers, Rue Ramond, 65120 Barèges, France
Tel 0963 550117 **Fax** 010 33 62926693

CHALET ALIA
Chalet in Verbier
c/o The Susie Ward Company, Hurling Burrow, Sevenmilestone, St. Agnes, Cornwall TR5 0PU
Tel 0872 553055 **Fax** 0872 553050

CHALET FREESTYLE
Chalet specialist in Les Deux-Alpes
7 Burlington Road, Leicester LE2 3DD
Tel 0533 703063

CHALET SNOWBOARD
Snowboard holidays in Avoriaz
31 Aldworth Avenue, Wantage, Oxon
OX12 7EJ
Tel 0235 767182 **Fax** 0235 767182

CHALETS 'UNLIMITED'
Mainly France and Switzerland
50A Friern Barnet Lane, London N11 3NA
Tel 081-368 4001

CHALETS DE ST MARTIN
A number of chalets in St-Martin-de-Belleville
1-3 Vine Lane, High Street, Christchurch, Dorset
BH23 1AB
Tel 0202 473255 **Fax** 0202 480042

CHINOOK-IT
Adventure holidays in Canada and the USA
30 Sansom Street, Camberwell, London
SE5 7RE
Tel 071-252 5438 **Fax** 071-252 5438

CLUB EUROPE
School and group holidays, mainly Austria
Fairway House, 53 Dartmouth Road, London
SE23 3HN
Tel 081-699 7788 **Fax** 081-699 7770

CLUB MED
All-inclusive holidays in 'ski villages'
106-110 Brompton Road, London SW3 1JJ
Tel 071-581 1161 **Fax** 071-581 4769

COLLINEIGE
Primarily Chamonix valley specialist
32 High Street, Frimley, Surrey GU16 5JD
Tel 0276 24262 **Fax** 0276 27282

COLOR LINE
Holidays in Norway
Tyne Commission Quay, North Shields, Tyne
and Wear NE29 6EA
Tel 091-296 1313 **Fax** 091-296 1540

CONTIKI
Coach-travel holidays for 18-35s
Wells House, 15 Elmfield Road, Bromley, Kent
BR1 1LS
Tel 081-290 6422 **Fax** 081-290 6569

CRESTA SKI FRANCE
French specialist
Cresta House, Victoria Street, Altrincham,
Cheshire WA14 1ET
Tel 061-926 9999 **Fax** 061-953 4444

CRYSTAL
Major mainstream operator
The Courtyard, Arlington Rd, Surbiton, Surrey
KT6 6BW
Tel 081-399 5144 **Fax** 081-390 6378

DAWSON AND SANDERSON
Holidays in Norway
60 Middle Street, Consett, County Durham DH8
5QE
Tel 0207 591261 **Fax** 0207 591262

EAST COAST TRAVEL
Holidays in Eastern Europe
283 Archway Rd, Highgate, London N6 5AA
Tel 081-348 2000 **Fax** 081-348 9938

ENTERPRISE
Major mainstream operator
Groundstar House, London Road, Crawley RH10
2TB
Tel 061-745 7000 **Fax** 0293 525225

EQUITY TOTAL SKI
All-inclusive holidays
Norwood House, 9 Dyke Road, Brighton, East
Sussex BN1 3FE
Tel 0273 203202 **Fax** 0273 203212

FANTISKI
Holidays in France
c/o First Choice Travel Services, Warmlake Estate,
Maidstone Road, Sutton Valence, Kent ME17 3LR
Tel 0622 842555 **Fax** 0622 842458

FINLAYS
Mainly chalets in France
The Green, Ancrum, Borders TD8 6UY
Tel 0835 3562 **Fax** 0835 3550

FLEXISKI
Specialists in flexible breaks
Crogen Stables, Corwen, Clwyd LL21 0SY
Tel 071-352 0044 **Fax** 0490 84446

FRANCE DES VILLAGES
Ski-drive holidays in France
Model Farm, Rattlesden, Nr Bury St Edmunds,
Suffolk IP30 0SY
Tel 0449 737664 **Fax** 0449 737850

FREEDOM
Holidays in Châtel
30 Brackenbury Road, Hammersmith, London
W6 0BA
Tel 081-741 4471 **Fax** 081-741 9332

FRENCH IMPRESSIONS
Mainly self-catering in France
The Broadway, 3-5 Crouch End Hill, London N8
8DH
Tel 081-342 8870 **Fax** 081-342 8860

FRESH TRACKS
Off-piste specialists, mainly France
Argyll House, 1A All Saints Passage, London
SW18 1EP
Tel 081-875 9818 **Fax** 081-874 8827

FRONTIER SKI
Holidays in Canada
3rd Floor, Broadmead House, 21 Panton Street,
London SW1Y 4DR
Tel 071-839 5341 **Fax** 071-839 5761

GETAWAY AMERICA
Package holidays to America, with car hire
The Getaway Group (UK) Inc, 34 The Mall,
Bromley, Kent BR1 1TS
Tel 081-313 0550 **Fax** 081-313 0620

GO WORLDS APART
Small but varied programme
6/8 Church Street, Chesham, Bucks
Tel 0494 793333 **Fax** 0494 792771

HANNIBALS
Holidays in Serre-Chevalier
Farriers, Little Olantigh Road, Wye, Nr Ashford,
Kent TN25 5DQ
Tel 0233 813105 **Fax** 0233 813432

HEADWATER
Cross-country skiing holidays
146 London Rd, Northwich, Cheshire
CW9 5HH
Tel 0606 48699 **Fax** 0606 48761

HUSKI
Holidays in Chamonix
63a Kensington Church Street, London
W8 4BA
Tel 071-938 4844 **Fax** 071-938 2312

ICELANDAIR
Holidays in ... Iceland
172 Tottenham Court Rd, London W1P 9LG
Tel 071-388 5599 **Fax** 071-387 5711

INGHAMS
Major mainstream operator
10-18 Putney Hill, London SW15 6AX
Tel 081-785 7777 **Fax** 081-785 2045

INNTRAVEL
Cross-country skiing holidays
Hovingham, York YO6 4JZ
Tel 0653 628811 **Fax** 0653 628741

INTERHOME
Private property letting agency
383 Richmond Road, Twickenham, TW1 2EF
Tel 081 8911299

INTERSKI
Holidays with tuition
95 Outram Street, Sutton-in-Ashfield, Notts
NG17 4BG
Tel 0623 551024 **Fax** 0623 440742

JEAN STANFORD
Holidays in France and Canada
Ridge House, Chilmark, Salisbury SP3 5BS
Tel 0747 870708 **Fax** 0747 871426

KINGS SKI CLUB
Lively group specialists
1st Floor, Castle Mill, Lower Kings Road,
Berkhamsted, Herts HP4 2AP
Tel 0442 876642 **Fax** 0442 879968

KUONI
Holidays in Switzerland
Kuoni House, Dorking, Surrey RH5 4AZ
Tel 0306 742500 **Fax** 0306 744222

LAGRANGE
Self-catering holidays in France
168 Shepherds Bush Road, Hammersmith,
London W6 7PB
Tel 071-371 6111 **Fax** 071-371 2990

LE SKI
Chalets in Courchevel and Val-d'Isère
25 Holly Terrace, Huddersfield HD1 6JW
Tel 0484 548996 **Fax** 0484 451909

LOTUS SUPERTRAVEL
North America, France and Switzerland
Hobbs Court, 2 Jacob Street, London SE1 2BT
Tel 071-962 9933 **Fax** 071-962 9932

MADE TO MEASURE
Wide variety of tailor-made holidays
43 East Street, Chichester, West Sussex
PO19 1HX
Tel 0243 533333 Fax 0243 778431

MARK WARNER
Chalet holidays in big-name resorts
20 Kensington Church Street, London
W8 4EP
Tel 071-393 3131 Fax 071-393 0093

MARTIN BRODIER
All-inclusive holidays for Christians
Woodside House, 7 Woodside Green, London
SE25 5EY
Tel 081-654 5679 Fax 081-654 5679

MASTERSKI
Christian holidays
Thames House, 63 Kingston Road, New Malden,
Surrey KT3 3PB
Tel 081-942 9442 Fax 081-949 4396

MEDCHOICE
Holidays in Slovenia
Chesham House, 150 Regent Street, London
W1R 6BB
Tel 071-734 7321 Fax 071-439 1720

MERISKI
Mainly chalet holidays in Méribel
The Old School, Great Barrington, Oxon OX18
4UR
Tel 0451 844788 Fax 0451 844799

MOGUL SKI
School and group holidays
Royal Chambers, Station Parade, Harrogate,
Yorks
Tel 0423 569512 Fax 0423 509145

MOSWIN
Small German programme
Moswin House, 21 Church Street, Oadby,
Leicester LE2 5DB
Tel 0533 719922 Fax 0533 716016

MOUNTAIN AND WILDLIFE VENTURES
Nordic ski-touring
The Adventure Traveller, Compston Road,
Ambleside, Cumbria LA22 9DJ
Tel 0539 433285 Fax 0539 434065

NSR TRAVEL
Holidays in Norway
Norwegian State Railways Travel Bureau, Norway
House, Trafalgar Square, 21-24 Cockspur Street,
London SW1Y 5DA
Tel 071-930 6666 Fax 071-321 0624

NEILSON
Major mainstream operator
Iberotravel Ltd, 29-31 Elmfield Road, Bromley,
Kent BR1 1LT
Tel 0532 394555 Fax 0532 393275

OVER THE HILL
Holidays for the older skier
35/37 Moulsham Street, Chelmsford, Essex CM2
0HY
Tel 0245 346022 Fax 0245 354764

PANORAMA
Budget-oriented holidays
29 Queens Road, Brighton, East Sussex
BN1 3YN
Tel 0273 206531 Fax 0273 205338

PASSAGE TO SOUTH AMERICA
Tailor-made holidays to South America
41 North End Road, West Kensington, London
W14 8SZ
Tel 071-602 9889 Fax 071-602 4251

PEAK SKI
Holidays in Verbier and Argentière
White Lilacs House, Water Lane, Bovingdon,
Herts HP3 0NA
Tel 0442 832629 Fax 0442 834303

PISTE ARTISTE
Holidays in Champéry and Whistler
Chalet Mon Travail, 1874 Champéry,
Switzerland
Tel 0800 898604 Fax 010 41 25741344

PLUS TRAVEL
Goes to satellites of major resorts
18 Buckingham Palace Road, London
SW1W 0QP
Tel 071-931 9703 Fax 071-931 9841

POLES APART
Holidays in France
75 Compton Avenue, Plymouth, Devon
PL3 5DD
Tel 0752 257752 Fax 0752 257752

POWDER BYRNE
Small programme of luxury holidays
50 Lombard Rd, London SW11 3SU
Tel 071-223 0601 Fax 071-228 1491

POWDER SKIING IN NORTH AMERICA LIMITED
Heli-skiing holidays in Canada
61 Doneraile Street, London SW6 6EW
Tel 071-736 8191 **Fax** 071-384 2592

PREMIER SKI
Mainly chalet holidays in Tignes
108 Grange Drive, Swindon SN3 4LD
Tel 0793 823667 **Fax** 0793 823667

PRESIDENT
Holidays to Turkey
542, Kingsland Rd, Dalston, London E8 4AH
Tel 071-249 4002 **Fax** 071-923 1856

RAMBLERS
Cross-country holidays
Box 43, Welwyn Garden City, Herts AL8 6PQ
Tel 0707 331133 **Fax** 0707 333276

STS
School group holidays
24 Culloden Road, Enfield, Middlesex
EN2 8QD
Tel 081-367 9090 **Fax** 081-363 4605

SALLY
Self-drive holidays, mainly in France
92-96 Lind Road, Sutton, Surrey SM1 4PL
Tel 081-395 3030 **Fax** 081-395 3008

SALLY FORTT HOLIDAYS
Chalet in Argentière
c/o The Susie Ward Company, Hurling Burrow,
Sevenmilestone, St. Agnes, Cornwall TR5 OPU
Tel 0872 553055 **Fax** 0872 553050

SILVER SKI
Chalet holidays, mainly in France
Conifers House, Grove Green Lane, Maidstone
ME14 5JW
Tel 0622 735544 **Fax** 0622 738550

SIMPLY SKI
Holidays in France and Italy
Chiswick Gate, 598-608 Chiswick High Rd,
London W4 5RT
Tel 081-742 2541 **Fax** 081-995 5346

SKI 3000
Chalets in top French resorts
154-156 Victoria Road, Cambridge CB4 3DZ
Tel 0223 302747 **Fax** 0223 314423

SKI ACTIVITY
Holidays in big-name resorts
23 Blair Street, Edinburgh EH1 1QR
Tel 031-225 9457 **Fax** 031-220 4185

SKI ADDICTION
Chalets in Châtel and Chamonix
The Cottage, Fontridge Lane, Etchingham, East
Sussex TN19 7DD
Tel 0580 819354 **Fax** 0580 819354

SKI AMIS
Chalet holidays in the La Plagne area
Alanda, Hornash Lane, Shadoxhurst, Ashford,
Kent TN26 1HT
Tel 0233 732187 **Fax** 0233 732769

SKI ARAVIS
Chalet in La Clusaz
Les Hirondelles, 74450 Saint-Jean-de-Sixt, France
Tel 010 33 50023625 **Fax** 010 33 50023982

SKI ARDMORE
School group specialists
11-15 High Street, Marlow, Bucks SL7 1AU
Tel 0628 890060 **Fax** 0628 898141

SKI ARRANGEMENTS
Chalets in Val-d'Isère area
Rose Cottage, Milltown, Ashover, Derbyshire S45
0HA
Tel 0773 602194 or 0246 590444
Fax 0246 590654

SKI BALKANTOURS
Holidays in E Europe for schools and groups
37 Ann Street, Belfast BT1 4EB
Tel 0232 246795 **Fax** 0232 234581

SKI BARRETT-BOYCE
Megève and St-Gervais with tuition
14 Hawthorn Road, Wallington, Surrey
SM6 0SX
Tel 081-647 6934 **Fax** 081-647 8620

SKI BEACH VILLAS
Varied programme
55 Sidney Street, Cambridge CB2 3QR
Tel 0223 371371 **Fax** 0223 68626

SKI BEAT
Chalet holidays in La Plagne and Tignes
57 York Road, Montpelier, Bristol BS6 5QD
Tel 0272 557361 **Fax** 0272 412099

SKI BON
One catered chalet in Champagny
Hilldale Radnor, Cliff Crescent, Folkestone, Kent
CT20 2JQ
Tel 0303 241560

SKI BURNELL
Holidays in Verbier
Old Linslade Manor, Old Linslade,
Nr Leighton Buzzard, Bedfordshire LU7 0DU
Tel 0908 281670 **Fax** 0908 281649

SKI C & C
Holidays in Canada
Penwood Lodge, Penwood, Burghclere,
Nr Newbury, RG15 9EX
Tel 0635 255551 **Fax** 0635 255553

BANFF, LAKE LOUISE AND WHISTLER

- Discounts of 10% for booking before January 1st.

- Direct flights with Canadian Airlines International.

- Super hotels, ski passes, car hire.

Contact Ski C & C

TEL 0635 255551
FAX 0635 255553

SKI ÇA VA MONTGENÈVRE
Chalet holidays in Montgenèvre
56 Fourth Avenue, Havant, Hampshire
PO9 2QX
Tel 0705 484189

SKI CAMPUS
Own one hotel near Megève (Le Bettex)
Llangarron, Ross-on-Wye, Herefordshire
HR9 6PG
Tel 0989 770766 **Fax** 0989 770011

SKI CANADA
Holidays in Canada
Cambridge House, 8 Cambridge Street, Glasgow
G2 3DZ
Tel 041-332 1511 **Fax** 041-353 0135

SKI CHALLENGE
La Grave, with guiding and tuition
Airtrack Services Ltd, 16-17 Windsor St,
Uxbridge, UB8 1AB
Tel 0494 670270 **Fax** 0494 676669

SKI CHAMOIS
Holidays in Morzine
18 Lawn Road, Doncaster DN1 2JF
Tel 0302 369006 **Fax** 0302 326640

SKI CHOICE
Mainly hotel and self-catering holidays
27 High Street, Benson, Oxon OX10 6RP
Tel 0491 837607 **Fax** 0491 833836

SKI CLUB OF GB
Holidays for groups of particular standards
118 Eaton Square, London SW1W 9AF
Tel 071-245 1033 **Fax** 071-245 1258

SKI EQUIPE
Upmarket chalet operator
27 Bramhall Lane South, Bramhall, Stockport,
Cheshire SK7 2DN
Tel 061-440 0010 **Fax** 061-440 0080

SKI ESPRIT
Chalet holidays, especially for families
Oaklands, Reading Road North, Fleet, Hampshire
GU13 8AA
Tel 0252 616789 **Fax** 0252 811243

SKI EUROPE
Specialist in school holidays
Brentham House, 45c High Street, Hampton,
Kingston upon Thames, Surrey KT1 4DG
Tel 081-891 4400 **Fax** 081-892 3454

SKI EXPERIENCE
Holidays in Méribel
24 College Road, Clifton, Bristol BS8 3HZ
Tel 0272 745351 **Fax** 0272 731179

SKI FAMILLE
Family holidays in Les Gets
Chesterton Mill, French's Road, Cambridge CB4
3NP
Tel 0223 63777 **Fax** 0223 61508

SKI FRANCE
Chalets and catered apartments
Acorn House, 60 Bromley Common, Bromley,
Kent BR2 9PF
Tel 081 3130690 **Fax** 081 4660653

SKI HILLWOOD
Family holidays in Hopfgarten and Les Gets
2 Field End Road, Pinner, Middlesex HA5 2QL
Tel 081-866 9993 **Fax** 081-868 0258

SKI INDEPENDENCE
Holidays in America and Canada
Osprey Travel, Broughton Market, Edinburgh
EH3 6NU
Tel 031-557 8555 **Fax** 031-557 1676

SKI LA COTE
Chalet holidays in Chapelle d'Abondance
33 Dale Road, Welton, Brough, North
Humberside HU15 1PE
Tel 0482 668357

SKI LA VIE
Upmarket Swiss and French holidays
28 Linver Road, London SW6 3RB
Tel 071-736 5611 **Fax** 071-371 8059

SKI LEOGANG
Leogang specialist
150, Buckingham Palace Road, London SW1W
9TR
Tel 071-730 7234 **Fax** 071-730 1180

SKI LES ALPES
Holidays in Switzerland and France
11 Hillgate Place, London W8 7SL
Tel 071-229 6388

SKI MIQUEL
Unusual resorts in the Alps and Pyrenees
33 High Street, Uppermill, Nr Oldham
OL3 6HS
Tel 0457 820200 **Fax** 0457 872715

SKI MOOSE CHALET CO
Chalet holidays in Morzine
23A High Street, Wealdstone, Middlesex
HA3 5BY
Tel 081-427 4475 **Fax** 081-861 4459

SKI MORGINS
Holidays in Morgins
Raughton Head, Carlisle, Cumbria CA5 7DD
Tel 0697 476258 **Fax** 0697 476258

SKI OLYMPIC
Chalet holidays in France
Pine Lodge, Barnsley Rd, Doncaster, S Yorks DN5
8RB
Tel 0302 390120 **Fax** 0302 390787

SKI PARTNERS
Hotel holidays in Austria
Friary House, Colston Street, Bristol BS1 5AP
Tel 0272 253545 **Fax** 0272 293697

SKI PEAK
Mainly Vaujany (Alpe-d'Huez)
Hangerfield, Witley, Surrey GU8 5PR
Tel 0428 682272 **Fax** 0428 685369

SKI SAFE TRAVEL
Mainly coach holidays to Flaine
Unit 4, Braehead Estate, Old Govan Road,
Renfrew, Scotland PA8 0XJ
Tel 041-885 1423 **Fax** 041-885 2909

SKI SAVOIE
Holidays in France
362/364 Sutton Common Road, Sutton, Surrey
SM3 9PL
Tel 081-715 1122 **Fax** 081-644 3068

SKI SCOTT DUNN
Upmarket holidays
Fovant Mews, 12 Noyna Rd, London
SW17 7PH
Tel 081-767 0202 **Fax** 081-767 2026

SKI TOTAL
European chalet holidays
10 Hill Street, Richmond, Surrey TW9 1TN
Tel 081-948 6922 **Fax** 081-332 1268

SKI VAL
Mainly holidays in France and America
39A North End Rd, West Kensington, London
W14 8SZ
Tel 071-371 4900 **Fax** 071-371 4904

SKI VALKYRIE
Curious travel agent/tour operator hybrid
56 Bower Street, Maidstone, Kent ME16 8SD
Tel 0622 763745 **Fax** 0622 690964

SKI WEEKEND
Weekend and ten-day holidays
Winster, 25 Hambidge Lane, Lechlade,
Gloucestershire GL7 3BJ
Tel 0367 252213 **Fax** 0367 253488

SKI WEST
Cheap chalets and French self-catering
Eternit House, Felsham Road, London
SW15 3SF
Tel 081-789 1122 **Fax** 081-789 8358

SKI WHITE KNIGHTS
Catered apartment in Les Deux-Alpes
10 Woolwich Road, Greenwich, London
SE10 0JU
Tel 081-853 5701

SKI WYATT
Mainly chalet holidays in France
PO Box 260, Shrewsbury, Shropshire
SY1 1WX
Tel 0743 236832 **Fax** 0743 353370

SKI WITH JULIA
Holidays in Switzerland
East Lodge Farm, Stanton, Broadway, Worcs
WR12 7NE
Tel 0386 584478 **Fax** 0386 584629

SKIBOUND
Group holidays specialist
Olivier House, 18 Marine Parade, Brighton,
Sussex BN2 1TL
Tel 0273 696960 **Fax** 0273 676410

SKIGOWER
Schools holidays mainly in Switzerland
2 High Street, Studley, Warwickshire B80 7HJ
Tel 0527 854822 **Fax** 0527 857236

SKIWORLD
Snowsure European programme
Skiworld House, 41 North End Road, West
Kensington, London W14 8SZ
Tel 071-602 4826 **Fax** 071-371 1463

SLOPING OFF
Schools specialist and tailor-made, by coach
31 High Street, Handley, Salisbury, Wiltshire SP5 5NR
Tel 0725 552247 **Fax** 0725 552489

SNOW COCKTAIL
Holidays in selected American resorts
Brunel Road, Hinckley, Leicestershire LE10 0AB
Tel 0455 631022 **Fax** 0455 632774

SNOWBIZZ VACANCES
Holidays in southern French Alps
69 High Street, Maxey, Peterborough PE6 9EE
Tel 0778 341455 **Fax** 0778 347422

SNOWCOACH CLUB CANTABRICA
Coach-based holidays
Holiday House, 146-148 London Rd, St Albans, Herts AL1 1PQ
Tel 0727 866177 **Fax** 0727 843766

SNOWISE
Holidays in Châtel
11A Bridge Lane, Wimblington, March, Cambs PE15 0RR
Tel 0354 740493 **Fax** 0354 740493

SNOWLINE
Holidays in France and Switzerland
PO Box 141, Deal, Kent CT14 6UR
Tel 0304 381551 (Nov-May); 081 810 9484 (Jun-Oct) **Fax** 0304 381546 or 081-810 9690

SNOWTIME
Holidays in Méribel
96 Belsize Lane, London NW3 5BE
Tel 071-433 3336 **Fax** 071-433 1883

STENA SEALINK
Ski-drive to France and Austria
Charter House, Park Street, Ashford, Kent TN24 8EX
Tel 0233 647033

SUNQUEST SKI
Holidays in Turkey and Eastern Europe
9 Grand Parade, Green Lanes, London, N4 1JX
Tel 081 800 8030 **Fax** 081 809 6629

SUPERSKI
Mainly chalets in big-name resorts
The Barns, The Old Rectory, Snetterton, Norfolk NR16 2LG
Tel 0953 498078 **Fax** 0953 498077

SWISS CHALET COMPANY
Family chalets in Villars, with nanny
10 Westwood, Cofton, Star Cross, Exeter EX6 8RW
Tel 0626 891989 **Fax** 0635 35434

SWISS TRAVEL SERVICE
Mainly hotels in Switzerland
Bridge House, 55-59 High Road, Broxbourne, Herts EN10 7DT
Tel 0992 456123 **Fax** 0992 448855

THE SKI COMPANY
Off-peak holidays in Tignes, with tuition
13 Squires Close, Bishop's Park, Bishop's Stortford, Herts CM23 4DB
Tel 0279 653746 **Fax** 0279 654705

THE SKI COMPANY LTD
Luxury chalets mainly in France
c/o Abercrombie & Kent, Sloane Square House, Holbein Place, London SW1W 8NS
Tel 071-730 9600 **Fax** 071-730 9376

THE SKI FIRM
Holidays to Norway
44 Charles Street, Leicester LE1 1FB
Tel 0533 515111 **Fax** 0533 537536

THOMSON
The market leader
Greater London House, Hampstead Rd, London NW1 7SD
Tel 021-632 6282 **Fax** 071-387 8451

TIMESCAPE
Budget-priced holidays by coach to Austria
581 Roman Road, London, E3 5EL
Tel 081-980 7244 **Fax** 081-980 7157

TOP DECK
Lively, informal holidays
131-133 Earls Court Rd, London SW5 9RH
Tel 071-370 4555 **Fax** 071-373 6201

TRAIL ALPINE
Small but varied programme
Papertree House, 68 Mostyn Street, Llandudno, Gwynedd LL30 25B
Tel 0492 871770 **Fax** 0492 872437

TRAVELSCENE SKI-DRIVE
Self-drive holidays, mainly in France
11/15 St Ann's Road, Harrow, Middlesex HA1 1AS
Tel 081-863 2787 **Fax** 081-861 3674

UCPA
All-inclusive budget trips for under-40s
c/o Action Vacances, 30 Brackley Road, Stockport, Cheshire SK4 2RE
Tel 061-442 6130 **Fax** 061-442 6130

USAIRTOURS
Holidays in America
1 Raven Road, London E18 1HD
Tel 081-559 7700 **Fax** 081-559 7722

ULTIMATE
Modest but wide-ranging programme
Ultimate House, Twyford Business Centre, London Road, Bishop's Stortford, Hertfordshire CM23 3YT
Tel 0279-755527 **Fax** 0279 655603

VIRGIN SNOW
Holidays to America
Virgin Holidays Limited, Galleria, Ground Floor, Station Road, Crawley, West Sussex RH10 1HY
Tel 0293 617181 **Fax** 0293 536957

WAYMARK
Cross-country skiing holidays
44 Windsor Rd, Slough SL1 2EJ
Tel 0753 516477 **Fax** 0753 517016

WHITE ROC
Weekends and short breaks
69 Westbourne Grove, London W2 4UJ
Tel 071-792 1188 **Fax** 071-792 1956

WINTERSKI
Holidays mainly in Italy
31 Old Steine, Brighton BN1 1EL
Tel 0273 626242 **Fax** 0273 620222

YSE
Variety of holidays in Val-d'Isère
The Business Village, Broomhill Rd, London
SW18 4JQ
Tel 081-871 5117 **Fax** 081-871 5229

Black-and-White Pages

Starting opposite: a classified listing of the names, numbers and addresses you are likely to need when preparing for a skiing holiday. Tour operators and dry ski slopes are covered in their own special sections immediately before this one.

Airlines

Air Canada
7/8 Conduit Street, London W1R 9TG
Tel 081-759 2636 Fax 081-564 7644
Linkline number from outside London
0345 181313

Air France
Colet Court, 100 Hammersmith Road, London
W6 7JP
Tel 081-742 6600 Fax 081-750 4391

Air UK
Stansted House, Stansted Airport, Essex
CM24 1QT
Tel 0345 666777 Fax 0279 680012

Alitalia
205 Holland Park Avenue, London W11 4XB
Tel 071-602 7111 Fax 071-602 5584
Linkline number from outside London
0345 212121

American Airlines
23/59 Staines Road, Hounslow TW3 3HE
Tel 081-572 5555 Fax 081-572 8646
Linkline number from outside London
0345 789789

Austrian Airlines
5th Floor, 10 Wardour Street, London
W1V 4BQ
Tel 071-434 7300 Fax 071-437 0343

British Airways
PO Box 10, London Heathrow Airport,
Hounslow, Middlesex TW6 2JA
Tel 0345 222111

Canadian Airlines
1st Floor, Rothschild House, Croydon
CR9 3HN
Tel 0345 616767 Fax 081-688 2997

Continental Airlines
Beulah Court, Albert Road, Horley RH6 7HP
Tel 0800 776464 Fax 0293 773726

Delta Airlines
Ground Floor, Oakfield Court, Consort Way,
Horley RH6 7AF
Tel 0800 414767 Fax 0293 821374

Lauda Air
Units 1 and 2, Colonnade Walk,
123 Buckingham Palace Road, Victoria, London
SW1W 9SH
Tel 071-630 5924 Fax 071-287 8140
Freephone number 0800 767737

Northwest Airlines
Northwest House, Tinsley Lane North, Crawley
RH10 2TP
Tel 0293 561000 Fax 0293 574537

Swissair
Swiss Centre, 1 Swiss Court, London W1V 4BJ
Tel 071-439 4144 Fax 071-439 7375

United Airlines
United House, Southern Perimeter Road, London
Heathrow Airport, Middlesex
TW6 3LP
Tel 081-990 9900 Fax 081-750 9429
Freephone number 0800 888555

Virgin Atlantic Airways
Ashdown House, High Street, Crawley
RH10 1DQ
Tel 0293 747747 Fax 0293 561721

Airports

Aberdeen Airport Ltd
Dyce, Aberdeenshire AB2 0DU
Tel 0224 722331 Fax 0224 725724

Belfast International Airport
Belfast BT29 4AB
Tel 0849 422888 Fax 0849 452096

Birmingham International Airport
Birmingham B26 3QJ
Tel 021-767 5511 Fax 021-782 8802

Bournemouth International Airport
Christchurch BH23 6SE
Tel 0202 593939 Fax 0202 590647

Bristol Airport
Bristol BS19 3DY
Tel 0275 474444 Fax 0275 474099

Cardiff-Wales Airport
Rhoose, South Glamorgan CF62 3BD
Tel 0446 711111 Fax 0446 711675

Dublin Airport
Dublin, Eire
Tel 010 353 1 8444900
Fax 010 353 1 7044643

East Midlands International Airport
Castle Donington, Derby DE74 2SA
Tel 0332 810621 Fax 0332 850393

Edinburgh Airport
Edinburgh EH12 9DN
Tel 031-333 1000 Fax 031-335 3181

Exeter and Devon Airport
Exeter, Devon EX5 2BD
Tel 0392 367433 Fax 0392 364593

Glasgow Airport
Paisley PA3 2ST
Tel 041-887 1111 Fax 041-848 4859

Leeds-Bradford International Airport
Leeds LS19 7TZ
Tel 0532 509696 Fax 0532 505426

London Gatwick Airport
Gatwick, West Sussex RH6 0NP
Tel 0293 535353 Fax 0293 503794

London Heathrow Airport
Hounslow, Middlesex TW6 1JH
Tel 081-759 4321 Fax 081-745 4290

London Luton Airport
Luton LU2 9LY
Tel 0582 405100 Fax 0582 395313

Manchester Airport
Wythenshawe, Manchester M90 1QX
Tel 061-489 3000 Fax 061-489 3813/3647

Newcastle International Airport
Woolsington, Newcastle-on-Tyne NE13 8BZ
Tel 091-286 0966 Fax 091-271 6080

Stansted Airport
Enterprise House, Stansted, Essex CM24 1QW
Tel 0279 680500 Fax 0279 662066

Teesside International Airport
Darlington, Co. Durham DL2 1LU
Tel 0325 332811 Fax 0325 332810

Breakdown Insurance

AA Five Star Service
AA Five Star Postlink, Freepost, PO Box 128,
Basingstoke, Hants RG21 1BR
Tel 0800 800555 Fax 0256 460750

Autohome
202-204 Kettering Road, Northampton
NN1 4HE
Tel 0604 232334

Britannia Continental
St Georges Square, Huddersfield, West Yorkshire
HD1 1JF
Tel 0484 514848 Fax 0484 518961

Europ Assistance
Sussex House, Perrymount Rd, Haywards Heath,
West Sussex RH16 1DN
Tel 0444 442211 Fax 081-680 8992

International Assistance Services
32 High Street, Purley, Surrey CR8 2PP
Tel 081-763 1550 Fax 081-668 1262

Leisurecare Insurance Services
Shaftesbury Centre, Percy Street, Swindon, Wilts
SN2 2AZ
Tel 0793 514199 Fax 0793 481333

Mondial Assistance UK
Mondial House, 1 Scarbrook Rd, Croydon, Surrey
CR0 1SQ
Tel 081-681 2525 Fax 081-688 0577

National Breakdown
PO Box 300, Leeds LS99 2LZ
Tel 0800 800600

RAC Travel Services
RAC Enterprises Ltd, Travel Services, P.O. Box
499, Croydon CR2 6ZH
Tel 0800 550055 Fax 081-681 8710

Car Hire

Alamo
Alamo House, Stockley Close, Stockley Rd, West
Drayton, Middlesex UB7 9BA
Tel 0895 443355 Fax 0895 441133

Avis
Trident House, Station Road, Hayes, Middlesex
UB3 4DJ
Tel 081-848 8765 Fax 081-561 2604

Budget
41 Marlowes, Hemel Hempstead HP1 1XJ
Tel 0800 181181 Fax 0442 230757

Eurodollar
Beasley Court, Warwick Place, Uxbridge
UB8 1PE
Tel 0895 256565 Fax 0895 256050

Europcar Interrent
Interrent House, Aldenham Road, Watford, Herts
WD2 2LX
Tel 0923 811000 Fax 0923 811010

Hertz
Radnor House, 1272 London Road, Norbury,
London SW16 4XW
Tel 081-679 1777 Fax 081-679 9931

Holiday Autos
25 Saville Row, Mayfair, London W1X 1AA
Tel 071-491 1111 Fax 071-355 4352

Suncars
Sandrocks, Rocky Lane, Haywards Heath RH16
4RH
Tel 0444 456446 Fax 0444 441234

Cross-Channel Travel

Brittany Ferries
Millbay Docks, Plymouth PL1 3EW
Tel 0705 827701 Fax 0752 661308
Route: Portsmouth–Caen
Hoverspeed
International Hoverport, Western Docks, Dover
CT17 9TG
Tel 0304 240241 Fax 0304 240099
Routes: Dover–Calais, Folkestone–Boulogne
Le Shuttle
Cheriton Parc, Cheriton High Street, Cheriton,
Folkestone, Kent CT19 4QS
Tel 0303 271100 Fax 0303 850360
Channel Tunnel service, reservations not required
North Sea Ferries
King George Dock, Hedon Road, Hull
HU9 5QA
Tel 0482 77177 Fax 0482 706438
Routes: Hull–Zeebrugge, Hull–Rotterdam
P & O European Ferries
Channel House, Channel View Road, Dover,
Kent CT17 9TJ
Tel 0304 203388 Fax 0304 223223
Routes: Dover–Calais, Portsmouth–Le Havre,
Portsmouth–Cherbourg, Felixstowe– Zeebrugge
Sally Lines
Argyle Centre, York Street, Ramsgate, Kent CT11
9DS
Tel 0843 595522 Fax 0843 589329
Routes: Ramsgate–Dunkerque, Ramsgate– Ostend
Stena Sealink Line
Charter House, Park Street, Ashford TN24 8EX
Tel 0233 647047 Fax 0233 646024
Routes: Dover–Calais, Harwich–Hook,
Newhaven–Dieppe, Southampton–Cherbourg

Insurance Companies

Accident and General
ISIS Building, Thames Quay, 193 Marsh Wall,
London E14 9SG
Tel 071-512 0022 Fax 071-512 0602
Apple Booking Company
Apple Barn, Smeeth, Ashford, Kent
Tel 0800 414141 Fax 0303 812893
BUPA Travel Cover
Sussex House (Ground Floor), 58-62 Perrymount
Road, Haywards Heath, West Sussex RH16 1BR
Tel 0444 442400 Fax 0444 459292
Cover provided by Europ Assistance
Bishopsgate Insurance
Bishopsgate House, Tollgate, Eastleigh, Hants
SO53 3YA
Tel 0703 313030 Fax 0703 644614
British Activity Holiday Insurance Services
Security House, Frog Lane, Tunbridge Wells, Kent
TN1 1YT
Tel 0892 534411 Fax 0892 511980
For groups of 10 or more only
Columbus Travel Insurance
17, Devonshire Square, London EC2M 4SQ
Tel 071-375 0011 Fax 071-375 0022
Commercial Union
PO Box 420, St Helens, 1 Undershaft, London
EC3P 3DQ
Tel 071-283 7500 Fax 071-662 8140
Cork, Bays & Fisher
66 Prescot Street, London E1 8BU
Tel 071-481 0707 Fax 071-488 9786
Derek Ketteridge & Associates
Ketteridge Vaughan, New Loom House Suite 8,
101 Back Church Lane, London E1 1LU
Tel 071-702 1912 Fax 071-702 1909
Douglas Cox Tyrie
Central House, 32/66 High Street, Stratford,
London E15 2PF
Tel 081-534 9595 Fax 081-519 8780
Europ Assistance
Sussex House, Perrymount Rd, Haywards Heath,
West Sussex RH16 1DN
Tel 0444 442211 Fax 081-680 8992
Extrasure Holdings
6 Lloyd's Avenue, London EC3N 3AX
Tel 071-480 6871 Fax 071-480 6189
General Accident
Pitheavlis, Perth PH2 0NH
Tel 0738 621202 Fax 0738 621843
Hamilton Barr Insurance Brokers
Bridge Mews, Bridge Street, Godalming, Surrey
GU7 1HZ
Tel 0483 426600 Fax 0483 426382
JS Insurance
196-197 High Street, Egham, Middlesex
TW20 9ED
Tel 0784 430043 Fax 0784 472601
Jardine Insurance Brokers
23rd Floor, Sunley Tower, Piccadilly Plaza,
Manchester M1 4BT
Tel 061-228 3742 Fax 061-228 6475

MATTHEW GERARD TRAVEL INSURANCE SERVICES
MG House, Westminster Court, Hipley Street,
Old Woking, Surrey GU22 9LQ
Tel 0483 730900 Fax 0483 730969

MCLEAN, KENT AND COOMBER
Priory Lodge, School Lane, Wickford SS12 9JL
Tel 0268 590658 Fax 0268 590860

P J HAYMAN & CO
Forestry House, New Barn Road, Buriton,
Nr Petersfield, Hants GU31 4AU
Tel 0730 260222 Fax 0730 266655

PERRY, GAMBLE & CO
Tuition House, 27/37 St George's Road, London
SW19 4XE
Tel 081-879 1255 Fax 081-879 1767

SNOWCARD
Lower Boddington, Daventry, Northants
N11 6BR
Tel 0327 62805 Fax 0327 62805

SURETRAVEL
The Pavillions, Kiln Park Business Centre, Kiln
Lane, Epsom, Surrey KT17 1JG
Tel 0372 749191 Fax 0372 749701

TRAVEL INSURANCE SERVICE
Rowlandson House, 289/293 Ballards Lane,
London N12 8NP
Tel 081-446 8431 Fax 081-445 9085

VISASPORTS U.K.
62 Prince Street, Bristol, Avon BS1 4QD
Tel 0272 226222 Fax 0272 221666

WHITELEY INSURANCE CONSULTANTS
Kingfisher House, Portland Place, Halifax
HX1 2JH
Tel 0422 348411 Fax 0422 330345

NATIONAL TOURIST OFFICES

ANDORRAN DELEGATION
63 Westover Road, London SW18 2RF
Tel 081-874 4806

ARGENTINIAN TOURIST BOARD
Trevor House, 5th Floor, 100 Brompton Road,
London SW3 1ER
Tel 071-589 3104 Fax 071-584 7863

AUSTRALIAN TOURIST COMMISSION
Gemini House, 10/18 Putney Hill, Putney,
London SW15 6AA
Tel 081-780 2227 Fax 081-780 1496

AUSTRIAN NATIONAL TOURIST OFFICE
30 St George Street, London W1R 0AL
Tel 071-629 0461 Fax 071-499 6038

BULGARIAN NATIONAL TOURIST OFFICE
18 Princes Street, London W1R 7RE
Tel 071-499 6988 Fax 071-499 1905

CANADIAN TOURIST OFFICE
62-65 Trafalgar Square, London WC2N 5DY
Tel 071-839 2299 Fax 071-258 6387

CHILE – CONSULATE GENERAL
12 Devonshire street, London W1N 2DS
Tel 071-580 1023 Fax 071-436 5204

FRENCH GOVERNMENT TOURIST OFFICE
178 Piccadilly, London W1V 0AL
Tel 0891 244123 Fax 071-493 6594

GERMAN NATIONAL TOURIST OFFICE
65 Curzon Street, London W1Y 7PE
Tel 071-495 3990 Fax 071-495 6129

ITALIAN STATE TOURIST OFFICE
1 Princes Street, London W1R 8AY
Tel 071-408 1254 Fax 071-493 6695

NEW ZEALAND TOURISM BOARD
New Zealand House, Haymarket, London SW1Y
4TQ
Tel 071-973 0360 Fax 071-839 8929

NORWEGIAN TOURIST BOARD
Charles House, 5/11 Lower Regent Street,
London SW1Y 4LR
Tel 071-839 6255 Fax 071-839 6014

ROMANIAN NATIONAL TOURIST OFFICE
83A Marylebone High Street, London
W1M 3DE
Tel 071-224 3692 Fax 071-224 3692

SCOTTISH TOURIST BOARD
23 Ravelston Terrace, Edinburgh EH4 3EU
Tel 031-332 2433 Fax 031-343 1513

SLOVENIAN TOURIST OFFICE
Moghul House, 57 Grosvenor Street, London
W1X 9DA
Tel 071-495 4688 Fax 071-355 4828

SPANISH TOURIST OFFICE
57/58 St James's Street, London SW1A 1LD
Tel 071-499 0901 Fax 071-629 4257

SWEDISH TRAVEL AND TOURISM COUNCIL
73 Welbeck Street, London W1M 8AN
Tel 071-935 9784

SWISS NATIONAL TOURIST OFFICE
Swiss Centre, Swiss Court, London W1V 8EE
Tel 071-734 1921 Fax 071-437 4577

UNITED STATES TRAVEL AND TOURISM ADMINISTRATION
PO Box 1EN, London W1A 1EN
Tel 071-495 4466 Fax 071-495 4377

RAILWAYS

BRITISH RAIL INTERNATIONAL
Victoria Station, London SW1V 1JY
Tel 071-834 2345 Fax 071-922 9874
FRENCH RAILWAYS
179 Piccadilly, London W1V 0BA
Tel 0345 300003 Fax 071-409 1652
Timetable: 0891 515477
Motorail: 071 409 3518
GERMAN RAIL
Suite 4, 23 Oakhill Grove, Surbiton KT6 6DU
Tel 0891 887755 Fax 081-399 4700
SWISS FEDERAL RAILWAYS
Swiss Centre, Swiss Court, London W1V 8EE
Tel 071-734 1921 Fax 071-437 4577

SKI EQUIPMENT DISTRIBUTORS

BLUE RIDGE
The Gate Studio, Station Road, Borehamwood,
Herts WD6 1DE
Tel 081-207 6775 Fax 081-207 5650
Pre skis, Tecnica, Geze
EUROPA SPORT
Ann Street, Kendal, Cumbria LA9 6AA
Tel 0539 724740 Fax 0539 726314
*Nordica boots, Kastle skis, Marker bindings, Gipron
poles*
EUROSKI
66/67 North Road, Brighton BN1 1YD
Tel 0273 688258 Fax 0273 608758
Alpina
GLACIER IMPORTS
74 Prospect Road, Southborough, Tunbridge
Wells, Kent TN4 0EH
Tel 0892 543952 Fax 0892 535464
*Atomic, Koflach, Ess, Oxygen (snowboarding
equipment)*
MAST CO
24 Albert Road, Caversham, Reading RG4 7PE
Tel 0734 471735 Fax 0734 461213
Fischer, Dynafit, Tyrolia, Raichle
OUTDOOR LEISURE
Moac House, Demmings Road, Industrial Estate,
Cheadle, Cheshire SK8 2PE
Tel 061-428 1178 Fax 061-428 1243
K2
SALOMON
Annecy House, Gastons Wood, Reading Road,
Basingstoke, Hants RG24 OTW
Tel 0256 479555 Fax 0256 465562
ULTRA SPORT
Acton Grove, Acton Road Industrial Estate, Long
Eaton, Nottingham NG10 1FY
Tel 0602 731001 Fax 0602 461067
Rossignol, Look bindings
VENTURA
Hall House, New Hutton, Kendal, Cumbria LA8
OAH
Tel 0539 728386 Fax 0539 741165
Lange, Dynastar, Kerma ski poles

SKI ORGANISATIONS

ARTIFICIAL SKI SLOPE INSTRUCTORS (ASSI)
The English Ski Council, The Area Library
Building, The Precinct, Halesowen, West
Midlands B63 4AJ
Tel 021-501 2314 **Fax** 021-585 6448
BRITISH ASSOCIATION OF SKI INSTRUCTORS (BASI)
Grampian Road, Aviemore, Inverness
PH22 1RL
Tel 0479 810407 **Fax** 0479 811222
BRITISH SKI CLUB FOR THE DISABLED
Springmount, Berwick St John, Shaftesbury SP7
0HQ
Tel 0747 828515
BRITISH SKI FEDERATION
258 Main Street, East Calder, West Lothian,
Scotland EH53 0EE
Tel 0506 884343 **Fax** 0506 882952
BRITISH SNOWBOARDING ASSOCIATION
6 Sedley Place, London W1R 1HG
Tel 071-408 1187 **Fax** 071-493 4317
ENGLISH SKI COUNCIL
Area Library Building, The Precinct, Halesowen,
West Midlands B63 4AJ
Tel 021-501 2314 **Fax** 021-585 6448
SCOTTISH NATIONAL SKI COUNCIL
Caledonia House, South Gyle, Edinburgh EH12
9DQ
Tel 031-317 7280 **Fax** 031-339 8602
SKI CLUB OF GREAT BRITAIN
118 Eaton Square, London SW1W 9AF
Tel 071-245 1033 **Fax** 071-245 1258
THE UPHILL SKI CLUB
12 Park Crescent, London W1N 4EQ
Tel 071-636 1989 **Fax** 071-436 2601
Ski organisation for the disabled
ULSTER SKI COUNCIL
8 Abercorn Park, Hillsborough, County Down,
Northern Ireland
Tel 0846 683243
Ring in evenings only
SKI COUNCIL OF WALES
240 Whitchurch Road, Cardiff, CF4 3ND
Tel 0222 619637 **Fax** 0222 619637

SPECIALIST SKI TRAVEL AGENTS

ALPINE ANSWERS
The Business Village, 3-9 Broomhill Road,
London SW18 4JQ
Tel 081-871 5100 **Fax** 081-871 9676
CHALET CONNECTIONS
1st Floor, 79 Street Lane, Roundhay, Leeds LS8
1AP
Tel 0532 370371 **Fax** 0532 693305
Deals only with smaller operators
SKI OPTIONS
Hobbs Court, Jacob Street, London SE1 2BT
Tel 071-962 9940 **Fax** 071-962 9932
SKI SOLUTIONS
84 Pembroke Road, Kensington, London
W8 6NX
Tel 071-602 9900 **Fax** 071-602 2882

SKI TRAVEL CENTRE
1100 Pollokshaws Road, Glasgow G41 3NJ
Tel 041-649 9696 **Fax** 041-649 2273
SKIERS TRAVEL BUREAU
79 Street Lane, Roundhay, Leeds LS8 1AP
Tel 0532 666876 **Fax** 0532 693305
SNOW LINE
1 Angel Court, High Street, Market Harborough,
Leics LE16 7NL
Tel 0858 433633 **Fax** 0858 433266
SUSIE WARD
Hurling Burrow, Sevenmilestone, St Agnes,
Cornwall TR5 0PG
Tel 0872 553055 **Fax** 0872 553050

Resort directory / Index

As well as the resorts we've covered in detail there are literally hundreds more in the Alps and North America, most of them much smaller than those we've given full coverage to. Here we give brief details on another 250-plus; many of these are well worth exploring, especially if you're in the area already or touring around. We also list the pages on which you'll find the in-depth coverage of the main resorts.

Key

🚡 *Lifts*
🎿 *Pistes*
✉ *Tour operators*

Abetone Italy
Resort in the exposed (and as such fairly reliable for snow) Appenines, less than two hours from both Florence and Pisa. Good for a ski/culture trip.
1390m; skiing 1390m–2160m
🚡 *27* 🎿 *50km*

Achenkirch Austria
Unspoilt, low-altitude Tyrolean village close to Niederau and Alpbach, in a beautiful setting overlooking a lake.
930m; skiing 950m–1780m
🚡 *14* 🎿 *25km*
✉ *Winterski*

Adelboden Switzerland **306**

Akakura Japan
Old spa of some oriental charm, 150km from Tokyo, with a modern lift system serving mostly easy skiing.
770m; skiing 770m–1500m
🚡 *41* 🎿 *85km*

Alagna Italy **281**

Alba Italy
Picturesque Dolomite village with a small, quiet ski area, and well placed for access to the Sella Ronda at nearby Canazei.
1515m; skiing 1515m–2430m
🚡 *5* 🎿 *10km*
✉ *Crystal, Simply Ski*

Alleghe Italy
Dolomite village in a pretty lakeside setting close to numerous ski areas. Cheap base from which to ski nearby Cortina.
980m 🚡 *24* 🎿 *80km*

Alpbach Austria **54**

Alpe-d'Huez France **137**

Alpendorf Austria
Hamlet cum base station 4km from St Johann im Pongau, with immediate access to the Salzburger Sportwelt ski area.
800m; skiing 800m–2185m
🚡 *59* 🎿 *200km*

Alpine Meadows USA
Ski area (there's no resort) best for intermediate cruisers, with the most reliable snow in the Lake Tahoe area.
2125m; skiing 2125m–2625m
🚡 *13* 🎿 *2000 acres*

Alta USA **382**

Altenmarkt Austria
Unspoilt village well placed just off the Salzburg-Villach autobahn for skiing numerous resorts including snowsure Obertauern and pretty Wagrain.
855m; skiing 855m–1675m
🚡 *9* 🎿 *30km*
✉ *Alpine Tours, Made to Measure, Mogul Ski*

Aminona Switzerland **316**

Andalo Italy
Atmospheric Dolomite village near Madonna with low wooded skiing well supported by snowmakers, best for novices and leisurely intermediates.
1050m; skiing 1040m–2125m
🚡 *17* 🎿 *40km*
✉ *Crystal, Enterprise, Equity Total Ski, Winterski*

Andermatt Switzerland **307**

Les Angles France
Characterless Pyrenean resort with a good sports centre and varied skiing worth a day-trip from nearby Font-Romeu.
1600m; skiing 1650m–2375m
🚡 *19* 🎿 *40km*

Annaberg-Lungötz Austria
Peaceful village in a pretty setting, sharing a sizeable ski area with Gosau, in the Dachstein region close to Filzmoos.
780m; skiing 780m–1700m
🚡 *34* 🎿 *50km*

Anzère Switzerland
Sympathetically designed modern resort set on a lovely sunny balcony near Crans-Montana, with slopes suited to leisurely skiers but not beginners.
1500m; skiing 1500m–2460m
🚡 *12* 🎿 *40km*
✉ *Made to Measure*

Aprica Italy
Ugly, straggling, characterless village between Lake Como and the Brenta Dolomites, with bland skiing, limited facilities, and no real atmosphere.
1175m; skiing 1175m–2575m
🚡 *30* 🎿 *60km*
✉ *Equity Total Ski, Kings Ski Club*

Arabba Italy **292**

Arapahoe Basin USA **404**

Arcalis Andorra
Andorra's most interesting ski area (there's no resort), 15km from La Massana, with varied, scenic and, in places, steep skiing uncharacteristic of the region.
skiing 1940m–2600m
🚡 *12* 🎿 *20km*

Les Arcs France **144**

Ardent France **149**

Åre Sweden
Traditional village 650km by train (driving not recommended) from Stockholm, with by far the best Alpine skiing in Scandanavia.
550m; skiing 550m–1240m
🚡 *29* 🎿 *100km*

Argentière France **153**

Arinsal Andorra **454**

Arosa Switzerland **308**

Artesina Italy
Limited south Piedmont resort, a short car-trip from Nice or Monte Carlo, though neighbouring Limone is a more attractive day-trip.
1500m
🚡 *25* 🎿 *90km*

Aspen USA **383**

Auffach Austria **90**

Auris-en-Oisans France **137**

Auron France
Pleasant village with varied, sheltered skiing; a stark contrast to nearby Isola 2000.
1600m; skiing 1600m–2450m
🚡 *27* 🎿 *130km*

Avoriaz France **149**

Axamer Lizum Austria **69**

Badgastein Austria **56**

Bad Hofgastein Austria **56**

Bad Kleinkirchheim Austria **55**

Banff Canada **441**

Baqueira-Beret Spain
Smart, convenient resort. Fine skiing and lift system, and more snowsure than the rest of the Spanish Pyrenees. Plenty of good accommodation.
1500m; skiing 1500m–2510m
🚡 *22* 🎿 *90km*
✉ *Ski Miquel*

Barboleusaz Switzerland **366**

Bardonecchia Italy **262**

Barèges France
Cheerful old Pyrenean spa village that shares an intermediate ski area with La Mongie. Good ski school. Unreliable snow.
1220m; skiing 1220m–2350m
🚡 *56* 🎿 *100km*
✉ *Borderline, Thomson*

Les Barzettes Switzerland **316**

Bear Mountain USA
Southern California's main ski area, in the beautiful San Bernadino National Forest region, with snowmaking on all 25 runs.
skiing 2170m–2675m
🚡 *11* 🎿 *174 acres*

Beaver Creek USA **433**

Berchtesgaden Germany
Pleasant old town close to Salzburg, known for its Nordic skiing but with several little Alpine areas nearby; the Jenner is the best.
560m; skiing 1105m–1640m
🚡 *33* 🎿 *65km*
✉ *Moswin*

Bergun Switzerland
Traditional, quiet, unspoilt, virtually traffic-free little family resort on the rail route between Davos and St Moritz.
1455m; skiing 1455m–2490m
🚡 *5* 🎿 *21km*
✉ *Kuoni*

Berwang Austria
Unspoilt village nestling in a spacious valley, close to Lermoos. Best visited in snowy years due to unreliable cover.
1340m; skiing 1270m–1640m
🚡 *11* 🎿 *40km*

Le Bettex France **190**

Bettmeralp Switzerland
Central village of the sizeable Aletsch ski area near Brig, perched high above the Rhône valley, surrounded by spectacular glacial scenery.
1940m; skiing 1925m–2710m
🚡 *26* 🎿 *90km*

Biberwier Austria
Limited little village with a small ski area, best as a quiet Brit-free base from which to ski the Zugspitz area resorts such as Lermoos.
990m; skiing 1000m–1840m
🚡 *7* 🎿 *25km*

Bichlbach Austria
Smallest of the Zugspitz villages with very limited skiing of its own, suitable as an unspoilt base from which to tour the area.
1070m; skiing 1070m–1260m
🚡 *4* 🎿 *5km*

Big Mountain USA
Family ski area close to Montana's Glacier National Park, with lots of skiing accessed by few lifts.
1400m; skiing 1400m–2055m
🚡 *8* 🎿 *3000 acres*
✉ *Chinook-It*

Big Sky USA
Great skiing near Yellowstone and Little Big Horn, with plenty for all grades accessed by few lifts, including renowned powder.
2055m; skiing 2055m–3310m
🚡 *10* 🎿 *2400 acres*
✉ *American Connections*

Big White Canada
Convenient purpose-built family resort six hours east of Vancouver, renowned for huge dumps of fluffy powder.
1660m; skiing 1660m–2320m
🚡 *8* 🎿 *1000 acres*

Bivio Switzerland
Quiet village near St Moritz with a fair amount of easy skiing opened up by a few drag-lifts.
1780m; skiing 1780m–2600m
🚡 *4* 🎿 *30km*

Blackcomb Canada **447**

Blatten-Naters Switzerland
Ski area amidst stunning glacial scenery, immediately above Brig, with the larger Aletsch skiing nearby.
675m; skiing 1325m–2880m
🚡 *9* 🎿 *60km*

Bled Slovenia
Beautiful lakeside base from which to drive to several nearby ski areas. Its own skiing is very limited but OK for a ski-cum-sightseeing day-trip from Austria.
500m; skiing 880m–1265m
🚡 *5* 🎿 *16km*
✉ *Medchoice*

Blue River Canada
Town 200km north of
Kamploops, from where you
can heli-ski the famous
Monashees and Cariboos
without being incarcerated in a
remote mountain lodge.
☒ *Fresh Tracks, Ski Scott Dunn*

Bohinj Slovenia
Lakeside village near Bled set in
a beautiful valley, with lovely
views from its plateau ski area
of short runs high above.
540m; skiing 1535m–1880m
🚡 *6* 🚠 *20km*
☒ *Medchoice*

Bonneval France
Unspoilt old village near
Modane with much of its
skiing above 2500m. There are
future plans to link to Val
d'Isère over the Col de l'Iseran.
2000m; skiing 1800m–3000m
🚡 *10* 🚠 *40km*

Bormio Italy **263**

Borovets Bulgaria **458**

Bourg-St-Maurice France **144**

Brand Austria
Old family favourite,
unpopular these days, perhaps
because it lacks the charm to
compensate for its small, low
ski area. A nice outing from
Lech or St Anton.
1035m; skiing 1035m–1920m
🚡 *13* 🚠 *50km*
☒ *Made to Measure*

Breckenridge USA **390**

Briançon France **230**

Brides-les-Bains France **199**

Brixen Austria **124**

Bromont Canada
Purpose-built resort an hour
east of Montreal, with one of
the best small ski areas in the
East, popular for its night
skiing.
🚡 *6* 🚠 *140 acres*

Bruck Austria
Low, one lift 'learn to ski'
resort, but might suit
intermediates looking for a
small, quiet base from which to
ski nearby Zell am See.
560m; skiing 560m–600m
🚡 *1* 🚠 *1km*
☒ *Neilson*

Bruson Switzerland
Relaxing respite from Verbier's
crowds, on the other side of Le
Châble. Well placed for car
trips to Chamonix and
Champéry.
1080m; skiing 820m–2200m
🚡 *7* 🚠 *15km*

Campitello Italy **292**

Canazei Italy **292**

Les Carroz France **177**

Caspoggio Italy
Attractive, unspoilt village
north-east of Lake Como, with
novice/leisurely skiing and
similar slopes at neighbouring
Chiesa.
1100m; skiing 1100m–2155m
🚡 *9* 🚠 *22km*

Cauterets France
Historic Pyrenean spa town
with easy/intermediate open
bowl skiing high above it.
Particularly suitable for
families.
935m; skiing 1400m–2500m
🚡 *15* 🚠 *29km*
☒ *Thomson*

Cavalese Italy
Unspoilt medieval town with
its own pretty skiing and
proximity to the Sella Ronda.
You need a car to make the
most of the scattered ski areas.
1000m; skiing 1000m–2260m
🚡 *11* 🚠 *70km*
☒ *Enterprise, Thomson*

Celerina Switzerland **353**

Cerler Spain
Very limited purpose-built
resort with a compact
amphitheatre ski area similar to
that of nearby Andorra's
Arinsal.
1500m; skiing 1500m–2355m
🚡 *11* 🚠 *35km*

Cervinia Italy **266**

Cesana Torinese Italy **207**

Le Châble Switzerland **359**

Chamonix France **153**

Champagny France **217**

Champéry Switzerland **311**

Champex Switzerland
Lakeside hamlet tucked away in
the trees above Orsieres. A nice
quiet, unspoilt base from which
to ski Verbier's Four Valleys
area if you have a car.
1470m; skiing 1470m–2190m
🚡 *4* 🚠 *8km*

Champfèr Switzerland **353**

Champoluc Italy **281**

Champoussin Switzerland **311**

Chamrousse France
Functional two-centre family
resort near Grenoble, with
good, sheltered ski to the door
slopes suitable for all grades.
*1650m–1750m; skiing
1650m–2255m*
🚡 *26* 🚠 *70km*

Chantemerle France **230**

La Chapelle-d'Abondance France
160

Château d'Oex Switzerland **337**

Châtel France **160**

Chiesa Italy
Attractive 'learn to ski' venue
with a fairly high plateau of
easy runs way above the resort.
Neighbouring Caspoggio adds
to the skiing available.
1000m; skiing 1700m–2335m
🚡 *8* 🚠 *25km*
☒ *Enterprise*

Le Chinaillon France
Modern, chalet-style village at
the heart of the pretty,
intermediate Le Grand Bornand
ski area, close to La Clusaz.
1300m; skiing 1000m–2100m
🚡 *40* 🚠 *60km*

Churwalden Switzerland **342**

Clavière Italy **207**

La Clusaz France **164**

Les Coches France **217**

Colfosco Italy **292**

Colle di Tenda Italy
Dour modern resort that shares
a good, though far from
snowsure, ski area with much
nicer Limone, not far from Nice
or Monte Carlo.
1400m; skiing 1005m–2060m
↥ *33* ↧ *100km*
✉ *Altours Travel, Winterski*

Combelouvière France
Quiet hamlet tucked away in
the trees at the foot of
Valmorel's skiing, well placed
for day-trips to the Trois
Vallées, La Plagne and Les Arcs.
1250m; skiing 1250m–2550m
↥ *48* ↧ *163km*

Combloux France
Quiet, unspoilt alternative to
Megève, with which it shares a
ski area. Best for car drivers,
who can easily reach the rest of
the local skiing.
900m; skiing 1100m–2350m
↥ *82* ↧ *300km*

Les Contamines France **168**

Copper Mountain USA **395**

Le Corbier France
Relatively inexpensive purpose-
built resort that shares an
extensive, underused
intermediate ski area with La
Toussuire, east of Grenoble.
1550m; skiing 1500m–2265m
↥ *41* ↧ *200km*
✉ *Made to Measure, Sally*

Cortina d'Ampezzo Italy **271**

Corvara Italy **292**

Courchevel France **170**

Courmayeur Italy **276**

Crans-Montana Switzerland **316**

Crested Butte USA **396**

Les Crosets Switzerland **311**

La Daille France **241**

Damüls Austria
Scattered but attractive village
in the snowsure Bregenzerwald
area close to the German and
Swiss borders. Quiet ambience
and leisurely skiing.
1430m; skiing 1430m–2005m
↥ *7* ↧ *40km*

Davos Switzerland **321**

Deer Valley USA **414**

Les Deux-Alpes France **177**

Les Diablerets Switzerland **343**

Dienten Austria
Quiet village at the heart of one
of Austria's largest low-altitude
ski areas, close to Zell am See. A
high proportion of drag-lifts is
a drawback.
790m; skiing 790m–1900m
↥ *42* ↧ *160km*

Disentis Switzerland
Unspoilt old village in a pretty
setting on the Glacier Express
rail route near Andermatt.
Scenic ski area with lovely long
runs.
1150m; skiing 1215m–2905m
↥ *9* ↧ *60km*

Dolonne Italy **276**

Dorfgastein Austria **56**

Ehrwald Austria
Friendly, relaxed, pretty village
with several nicely varied ski
areas, notably the Zugspitz
glacier, nearby. Poor bus
services make having a car
desirable.
1000m; skiing 1000m–2950m
↥ *9* ↧ *13km*
✉ *Crystal, Enterprise*

Ellmau Austria **62**

Encamp Andorra
Unattractive town, 20 minutes
by bus from the Soldeu slopes,
popular for its nightlife and
particularly low prices.
skiing 1680m–2560m
↥ *22* ↧ *50km*
✉ *Enterprise, Top Deck*

Engelberg Switzerland **327**

Entrèves Italy **276**

Essert-Romand France **211**

Etna Italy
Scenic, uncrowded, short-
season ski area on the volcano's
flank, 20 minutes from
Nickolossi, with a couple of fair
runs and some easy off piste.
1800m; skiing 1800m–2350m
↧ *5km*

Falera Switzerland **328**

Falls Creek Australia
Euro-style modern on-
mountain family resort, 5
hours from Melbourne, with a
fair network of short
intermediate runs.
1600m; skiing 1180m–1780m
↥ *20* ↧ *20km*

Fernie Canada
Pleasant old lumber town three
hours south of Banff, renowned
for huge dumps of fluffy snow
and superb deep powder bowl
skiing.
1065m; skiing 1065m–1800m
↥ *7* ↧ *800 acres*
✉ *Chinook-It*

Fieberbrunn Austria **66**

Fiesch Switzerland
Traditional Rhône valley resort
close to Brig, with special
facilities for school trips, and a
lift up into the beautiful
Aletsch ski area.
1050m; skiing 1925m–2710m
↥ *26* ↧ *90km*
✉ *SkiGower*

Filzmoos Austria
Charming, unspoilt, friendly
atmospheric village with pretty
skiing ideal for novices and
leisurely skiers. Good snow
record for its height.
1060m; skiing 1060m–1645m
↥ *16* ↧ *32km*
✉ *Inghams, Made to Measure*

Finkenberg Austria **85**

Fiss Austria
Nicely compact, quiet traditional village with a sun-kissed ski area well protected by snowmakers that's linked to Serfaus.
1435m; skiing 1200m–2685m
⛷ *38* 🚡 *150km*

Flachau Austria
Quiet village in a pretty setting, well situated at the heart of the large Salzburger Sportwelt ski area.
925m; skiing 800m–2185m
⛷ *59* 🚡 *200km*
✉ *Austrian Holidays, Club Europe, Made to Measure, STS*

Flachauwinkl Austria
Well placed within the Salzburger Sportwelt ski area, but no more than a ski station with the Salzburg-Villach autobahn carving through it.
930m; skiing 800m–2185m
⛷ *59* 🚡 *200km*

Flaine France **177**

Flims Switzerland **328**

Flumserberg Switzerland
Collective name for Tannenheim and Tannenbodenalp, villages sharing a varied ski area an hour south-east of Zurich.
1220m-1400m; skiing 1220m–2220m
⛷ *16* 🚡 *40km*

Folgarida Italy **287**

Font-Romeu France
Family resort set in woodland, with the biggest snowmaking set-up in the Pyrenees protecting its easy pistes from the mild climate.
1800m; skiing 1750m–2250m
⛷ *31* 🚡 *30km*
✉ *Inntravel*

Foppolo Italy
Relatively unattractive but user-friendly village, a short transfer from Bergamo, best for families on a budget seeking fairly reliable snow.
1510m; skiing 1105m–2300m
⛷ *15* 🚡 *47km*
✉ *Crystal, Equity Total Ski, Ski Partners, SkiBound*

Formigal Spain
Cheap Pyrenees resort with a reputation for good tuition, and lift closures due to high winds. Sheltered Panticosa is a nearby failsafe.
1520m; skiing 1510m–2250m
⛷ *20* 🚡 *50km*
✉ *Thomson*

Le Fornet France **241**

La Foux-d'Allos France
Purpose-built resort that shares a good, large intermediate ski area with Pra-Loup in southern French Alps.
1800m; skiing 1500m–2600m
⛷ *63* 🚡 *230km*

Frisco USA **390**

Fügen Austria
Unspoilt village with limited skiing best suited to beginners, poorly placed for skiing other Zillertal resorts.
560m; skiing 560m–2050m
⛷ *9* 🚡 *21km*
✉ *Ski Partners, Sloping Off*

Fulpmes Austria
Sizeable village in a beautiful valley, with a small ski area of its own, close to Neustift and the Stubai glacier.
960m; skiing 960m–2260m
⛷ *8* 🚡 *30km*
✉ *Alpine Tours, Crystal*

Fuschl Austria
Attractive, unspoilt lakeside village close to St Wolfgang and Salzburg, 30 minutes from its ski slopes. Best suited to part-time skiers cum sightseers.
670m; skiing 750m–1570m
⛷ *8* 🚡 *10km*
✉ *Crystal, Inghams*

Galtür Austria **67**

Gargellen Austria
Charming, secluded village over the hill from Klosters, highly regarded by families and older guests. Madrisa hotel well-liked by reporters.
1425m; skiing 1425m–2150m
⛷ *9* 🚡 *25km*
✉ *Made to Measure*

Garmisch-Partenkirchen Germany
Large twin resort; unspoilt traditional Partenkirchen much the prettier. Disjointed skiing, with superb main area of wooded runs when the unreliable snowcover allows; great glacier views from another section when it doesn't.
720m; skiing 750m–2965m
⛷ *43* 🚡 *109km*
✉ *Moswin*

Gaschurn Austria
Attractive, unspoilt, Brit-free village with the largest of the pretty Montafon ski areas south of Lech, well suited to intermediates.
1000m; skiing 900m–2370m
⛷ *26* 🚡 *100km*

Geilo Norway
Pleasant but limited resort, with mainly Nordic skiing, and some short Alpine pistes.
770m; skiing 800m–1170m
⛷ *18* 🚡 *25km*
✉ *Crystal, Dawson and Sanderson, Inntravel, NSR Travel, The Ski Firm*

Gerlos Austria
One of Austria's few inexpensive but fairly snowsure resorts, tucked away near Zell am Ziller. Queue-free, varied intermediate ski area with old lifts.
1245m; skiing 1245m–2300m
⛷ *18* 🚡 *52km*

Les Gets France **211**

Glaris Switzerland
Hamlet base station for the uncrowded Rinerhorn section of the Davos skiing. Well placed for an excursion to St Moritz.
1455m; skiing 1455m–2490m
⛷ *5* 🚡 *30km*

Going Austria **62**

Gosau Austria
Straggling village with plenty
of pretty, if low, skiing.
Snowsure Obertauern and
Schladming are within reach by
car if local conditions are poor.
750m; skiing 750m–1600m
⛷ *35* 🚡 *50km*
✉ *Ski Europe*

Gostling Austria
One of Austria's easternmost
resorts, midway between
Salzburg and Vienna. A
traditional village in a pretty,
wooded setting.
550m; skiing 550m–1900m
⛷ *12* 🚡 *50km*

Gotzens Austria **69**

Gourette France
Most snowsure resort in the
French Pyrenees. Very popular
with local families, best
avoided at weekends.
1400m; skiing 1400m–2550m
⛷ *21* 🚡 *30km*

Grächen Switzerland
Uncommercialised, quiet little
family village, a contrast to its
bigger, higher near-neighbours
Zermatt and Saas-Fee, but with
similarly beautiful, if less
extensive, skiing.
1615m; skiing 1615m–2865m
⛷ *14* 🚡 *50km*

Le Grand-Bornand France
Pleasant, atmospheric 'real'
provincial village with a pretty,
varied intermediate ski area,
close to Annecy and La Clusaz.
1000m; skiing 1000m–2100m
⛷ *38* 🚡 *60km*
✉ *Headwater*

Grand Targhee USA **399**

La Grave France **188**

Gray Rocks Canada
Very popular family resort,
120km north of Montreal,
renowned for its ski school and
fun-filled all-inclusive (Club
Med style) 'ski weeks'.
⛷ *4*
✉ *Accessible Isolation*

Gressoney-St-Jean Italy **281**

Gressoney-la-Trinité Italy **281**

Grimentz Switzerland
Captivating, unspoilt rustic
village with high, varied skiing
served by modern lifts; near the
Rhône valley town of Sierre,
with Crans-Montana quite
close by.
1570m; skiing 1570m–2900m
⛷ *10* 🚡 *50km*

Grindelwald Switzerland **333**

Grossarl Austria
Secluded village tucked away
over the mountain from the
Gastein valley. It shares a good
sizeable intermediate ski area
with Dorfgastein.
920m; skiing 850m–2010m
⛷ *23* 🚡 *70km*

Grünau Austria
Attractive, spacious riverside
village in a lovely lake-filled
part of eastern Austria. Nicely
varied, but very low, ski area.
530m; skiing 600m–1600m
⛷ *13* 🚡 *45km*

Gstaad Switzerland **337**

Gudauri Georgia
Austro-Soviet Glasnost attempt
at a good ski hotel complex
near Tbilisi; its potential,
notably for cheap heli-skiing,
inhibited at present by
Georgia's problems.
2005m; skiing 2005m–3010m
⛷ *5* 🚡 *5km*

Hainzenberg Austria **134**

Haus in Ennstal Austria **114**

Heavenly USA **408**

Heiligenblut Austria
Picturesque village in beautiful
surroundings with mostly high
skiing. Its remote position west
of Badgastein ensures crowds
don't invade when snow is
scarce.
1300m; skiing 1300m–2900m
⛷ *14* 🚡 *52km*

Hemsedal Norway
Pleasant, friendly little family
resort, midway between Oslo
and Bergen, with limited but
varied intermediate skiing.
Reliable snowcover.
650m; skiing 650m–1450m
⛷ *17* 🚡 *35km*
✉ *Crystal, NSR Travel, The Ski
Firm, Waymark*

Hermagor Austria
Carinthian village below the
Sonnenalpe ski area. Franz
Klammer rates this one of the
best mid-sized ski areas in
Austria.
590m; skiing 1210m–2005m
⛷ *24* 🚡 *80km*

Hinterstoder Austria
Quiet, unspoilt traditional
village, 80km east of Salzburg,
with a good snow record for its
height. A fair proportion of its
skiing is above 1400m on short
easy runs.
600m; skiing 600m–1860m
⛷ *17* 🚡 *38km*

Hintertux Austria **68**

Hippach Austria
Hamlet near a queue-free lift
into Mayrhofen's main skiing.
An astute choice if Mayrhofen's
on-slope merits are more
important than its off-slope
ones.
625m; skiing 625m–2250m
⛷ *23* 🚡 *65km*

Hochgurgl Austria **91**

Hochsölden Austria **120**

Hochybrig Switzerland
No village as such, but a
purpose-built complex only 64
km south of Zurich, with skiing
and facilities for families.
1050m; skiing 1050m–2200m
⛷ *16* 🚡 *50km*

Hopfgarten Austria **124**

Hospental Switzerland **307**

Les Houches France **153**

Igls Austria **69**

Inneralpbach Austria **54**

Innerarosa Switzerland **308**

Innsbruck Austria **69**

Ischgl Austria **70**

Isola 2000 France **189**

Itter Austria **124**

Jackson Hole USA **399**

Jasper Canada
Friendly railroad town, 30 minutes from its small ski area, best suited to intermediates. Best as a two-centre holiday with Lake Louise, Banff or Whistler.
skiing 1720m–2415m
≟ 7 ➤ 2400 acres
✉ *All Canada, Frontier Ski, Inghams, Made to Measure, Ski Canada*

Jochberg Austria **75**

Jouvenceaux Italy **288**

June USA
Recipient of rave reports from all that have visited from nearby, lift pass-sharing Mammoth. Quiet slopes and superb ski school.
2295m; skiing 2295m–3080m
≟ 8 ➤ 500 acres

Juns Austria **68**

Kaltenbach Austria
Village with one of the larger, quieter Zillertal ski areas. With plenty of skiing above 1800m it's a good outing from lower Tyrol resorts when snow is scarce.
560m; skiing 560m–2265m
≟ 15 ➤ 32km
✉ *Ski Europe*

Kandersteg Switzerland
Good cross-country base amidst beautiful scenery near Interlaken. Limited Alpine skiing but Adelbolen and the Jungfrau resorts are nearby.
1175m; skiing 1175m–2000m
≟ 6 ➤ 10km
✉ *Inntravel, Kuoni, Made to Measure, Waymark*

Kaprun Austria **130**

Les Karellis France
Resort with a ski area that offers more scenic, challenging and snowsure skiing than nearby Valloire, which has a weekly lift pass that allows one free day there.
1650m; skiing 1600m–2520m
≟ 17 ➤ 40km

Keystone USA **404**

Killington USA
Eastern America's biggest and best ski area, with skiing for all standards and an impressive snowmaking facility. Lack of any real village and intense cold are drawbacks.
320m; skiing 320m–1295m
≟ 19 ➤ 829 acres
✉ *American Dream, Crystal, Ski Activity, Ski Independence, Virgin Snow*

Kimberley Canada
Mining town turned twee mock Austro-Bavarian-English Tudor ski resort. It's not as tacky as it sounds, and being in a beautiful setting is well worth the two-hour drive from Banff.
1280m; skiing 1280m–1980m
≟ 7 ➤ 450 acres

Kirchberg Austria **75**

Kirchdorf Austria **110**

Kitzbühel Austria **75**

Kleinarl Austria
Secluded traditional village up a pretty side valley from Wagrain, with lifts into the Flachau section of the Salzburger Sportwelt.
1015m; skiing 800m–2185m
≟ 59 ➤ 200km
✉ *Club Europe, Made to Measure*

Klosters Switzerland **321**

Kolsass-Weer Austria
Dated resort; low, inconvenient, limited skiing which used to suit those more concerned with partying than skiing, but now loses out to cheaper, more snowsure Andorra.
555m; skiing 555m–1850m
≟ 8 ➤ 9km
✉ *Airtours*

Königsleiten Austria
Quiet resort that has the more interesting half of the pleasantly varied, fairly snowsure ski area shared with Gerlos.
1600m; skiing 1245m–2315m
≟ 26 ➤ 52km

Kopaonik Bosnia
Modern, sympathetically designed family resort in a pretty setting, with the best ski area of the regions that used to make up Yugoslavia. Off-limits at present.
1650m; skiing 1270m–2005m
≟ 20 ➤ 45km

Kössen Austria
British schools destination near St Johann in Tirol with little to attract others; very low, scattered, limited skiing.
600m; skiing 600m–1700m
≟ 8 ➤ 20km
✉ *STS*

Kranjska Gora Slovenia
Slovenia's leading resort, close to Austria/Italy, good for cheap, fun, convenient holidays for beginners but limited (despite its World Cup status) for others.
805m; skiing 805m–1500m
≟ 19 ➤ 20km
✉ *Inghams, Medchoice*

Kühtai Austria
Huddle of good hotels with a small, snowsure ski area suited to leisurely skiers. Similar to Obergurgl, but with far fewer Brits, and only 35km from Innsbruck.
2020m; skiing 2010m–2655m
≟ 10 ➤ 50km
✉ *Alpine Tours, Inghams*

Laax Switzerland **328**

Le Laisinant France **241**

Lake Louise Canada **441**

Lake Placid USA
Attractive lakeside winter sports
resort 15km from the small but
varied Whiteface ski area. 93%
snowmaking and low
temperatures ensure good
snowcover. Plenty of things to
do off the slopes.
975m; skiing 975m–1340m
9 ⏚ 150 acres

Lake Tahoe USA **408**

Lanersbach Austria **85**

Lauterbrunnen Switzerland **344**

Le Lavancher France **153**

Lech Austria **80**

Las Leñas Argentina
Up-market, Euro-style modern
resort, three hours south of
Mendoza, with varied, beautiful
skiing. Peak season crowds and
queues.
2240m; skiing 2255m–3400m
11 ⏚ 65km
⊠ *Passage to South America*

Lenk Switzerland
Traditional, though relatively
unexceptional village by local
standards, that shares a sizeable
area of easy, pretty skiing with
Adelbolen.
1070m; skiing 1070m–2200m
47 ⏚ 130km
⊠ *Made to Measure, Swiss
Travel Service*

Lenzerheide Switzerland **342**

Leogang Austria **97**

Lermoos Austria
Focal resort of the Zugspitz
area, a delightful base for cross-
country enthusiasts and novice
Alpine skiers.
1005m; skiing 1005m–2200m
10 ⏚ 18km
⊠ *Crystal, Enterprise, Made to
Measure, Thomson*

Leukerbad Switzerland
Major spa resort of Roman
origins, with spectacular cable-
car rides to mostly high skiing
including a World Cup
downhill course.
1410m; skiing 1410m–2700m
17 ⏚ 60km

Leutasch Austria
Traditional cross-country
village with limited Alpine
skiing but a pleasant day-trip
from nearby Seefeld or
Innsbruck.
1130m; skiing 1130m–1600m
9 ⏚ 7km
⊠ *Inntravel*

Leysin Switzerland
Large winter sports resort near
Aigle, with a good range of
facilities, but its low sunny
skiing is often very limited due
to lack of snow.
1255m; skiing 1255m–2200m
19 ⏚ 50km

Lienz Austria
Pleasant town cum ski resort in
pretty surroundings, ideal for a
skier/non-skier couple. Cortina
and Badgastein are very good
excursions for both parties.
730m; skiing 730m–2280m
13 ⏚ 45km
⊠ *SkiGower*

Lillehammer Norway
Cultural fjordside town, two to
three hours north of Oslo by
train/car, with its two Olympic
ski areas 15km and 35km away,
poorly served by bus.
180m; skiing 180m–1500m
11 ⏚ 35km
⊠ *NSR Travel*

Limone Italy
Pleasant old railway town not
far from Turin, with a pretty, if
far from snowsure, ski area.
Good for independent skiers
seeking the 'real' Italy.
1010m; skiing 1010m–2150m
33 ⏚ 100km

Livigno Italy **282**

Lofer Austria
Quiet, traditional Brit-free
village close to Salzburg with a
small ski area of its own, and
Waidring's relatively snowsure
Steinplatte nearby.
640m; skiing 900m–1745m
14 ⏚ 35km

Longchamp France **250**

Loon Mountain USA
New Hampshire's premier ski
area (there's no resort as such),
set amidst scenic wilderness,
renowned for immaculately
groomed intermediate slopes.
290m; skiing 290m–910m
9 ⏚ 234 acres
⊠ *Virgin Snow*

Macugnaga Italy
Two pretty villages, 1km apart,
set amidst stunning scenery.
Staffa has high intermediate
skiing and an off-piste route to
Saas-Fee, Pecetto has sheltered
novice runs.
*1330m–1390m;
skiing 1390m–2900m*
12 ⏚ 40km
⊠ *Crystal, Neilson*

Madesimo Italy **286**

Madonna di Campiglio Italy **287**

Malbun Liechtenstein
Quaint, civilised, user-friendly
little family resort, 16km from
the capital, Vaduz. Many guests
are regulars. Limited skiing,
with short easy runs.
1595m; skiing 1595m–2100m
6 ⏚ 16km

Malga Ciapela Italy
Well positioned resort sitting at
the foot of the Marmolada
glacier massif, with a link into
the Sella Ronda, and Cortina
nearby.
1445m; skiing 1445m–3340m
8 ⏚ 18km

Mallnitz Austria
Village in a pretty valley close
to Slovenia, with two varied ski
areas providing a fine mix of
wooded and open intermediate
skiing and good off-piste.
1200m; skiing 1300m–2650m
8 ⏚ 30km

Mammoth Mountain USA **410**

Maria Alm Austria
Charming unspoilt village east
of Zell am See with a varied ski
area that stretches impressively
over five linked mountains.
Highly recommended by
several reporters.
805m; skiing 790m–1900m
⚊ *42* ⛷ *160km*
✉ *Mogul Ski, Ski Partners*

Mariazell Austria
Traditional Styria village with
an impressive basilica, that has
a real antiquated feel to it.
Limited ski area.
870m; skiing 870m–1625m
⚊ *19* ⛷ *15km*

Marilleva Italy **287**

La Massana Andorra
Lively village with no slopes of
its own, but the best base if you
want to ski several areas,
notably Pal, Arinsal and Arcalis.
skiing 1545m–2590m
⚊ *44* ⛷ *60km*
✉ *Snowcoach Club Cantabrica*

Mayens de Riddes Switzerland
359

Mayrhofen Austria **85**

Megève France **190**

Meiringen Switzerland
Conan Doyle's deathplace for
Sherlock Holmes. A sightseeing
centre with varied skiing, a
good outing from the nearby
Jungfrau resorts or Interlaken.
595m; skiing 1050m–2245m
⚊ *15* ⛷ *60km*
✉ *Made to Measure, Ski Europe*

Les Menuires France **195**

Méribel France **199**

La Molina Spain
Cheap, limited resort near
Andorra with a fair amount of
quite varied skiing served by a
poorly conceived lift system.
1700m; skiing 1600m–2535m
⚊ *29* ⛷ *85km*

Monêtier France **230**

Montalbert France **217**

Montchavin France **217**

Mont-de-Lans France **177**

Monte Bondone Italy
Essentially a Trento
weekenders' ski area (there's no
resort and some of the lifts are
closed weekdays). A possible
outing from Andalo or
Cavalese.
skiing 1300m–2100m
⚊ *9* ⛷ *10km*

Montgenèvre France **207**

Mont Orford Canada
Cold, windswept lone peak
(there's no resort) with skiing
worth a trip from nearby
Montreal on a fine day.
⚊ *8*

Mont Ste Anne Canada
Largest ski mountain in Eastern
Canada (there's no resort) with
an impressive night skiing
facility. Being only 40km from
Quebec city, it gets very
crowded at weekends and some
evenings.
⚊ *12* ⛷ *390 acres*
✉ *All Canada*

Mont St Sauveur Canada
Perhaps the prettiest ski village
in Canada, popular with
Montreal (60km) day-trippers
and luxury condo owners.
⚊ *9*
✉ *All Canada*

Mont Sutton Canada
Varied area with perhaps the
best glade skiing in the East,
including some negotiable by
novices. Quaint Sutton village
nearby. Highly rated by a
reporter.
⚊ *9*

Mont Tremblant Canada
Eastern flagship due to huge
recent investment, with a
charming new pedestrian
village and upgraded
mountain. Good but exposed,
cold skiing.
265m; skiing 265m–910m
⚊ *10* ⛷ *425 acres*
✉ *All Canada*

Morgins Switzerland **311**

Morillon France **177**

Morzine France **211**

Les Mosses Switzerland
Uninteresting resort and ski
area, best for a day-trip if
staying in nearby Leysin, Les
Diablerets or Villars.
1450m; skiing 1450m–2350m
⚊ *12* ⛷ *60km*

Mottaret France **199**

Mount Bachelor USA
Interesting 360 degree ski area
(there's no resort) on an extinct
volcano in central Oregon.
Pacific sends a lot of rain.
1825m; skiing 1825m–2755m
⚊ *10* ⛷ *6000 acres*

Mount Buller Australia
Largest resort in Oz, built on
the mountain, 3 hours from
Melbourne, with a 360 degree
network of short runs on its
isolated massif.
1600m; skiing 1375m–1790m
⚊ *26* ⛷ *80km*

Mount Cook New Zealand
Superb heli-skiing in the Mt.
Cook National Park/Tasman
Glacier area (South Island),
with intermediate as well as
expert descents.

Mount Hutt New Zealand
Steepest, most snowsure ski
area in NZ, with ocean views,
but prone to bad weather;
100km from Christchurch, a
tricky drive up from Methven.
skiing 1420m–2075m
⚊ *10* ⛷ *902acres*

Mount Lyford New Zealand
Limited but developing ski area
close to the superb whale- and
seal-watching centre, Kaikoura,
140km north of Christchurch.
⚊ *6* ⛷ *803acres*

Mount Snow USA
Twin Vermont ski areas (there's
no village as such), only 340km
from New York City, that total
the second highest mileage in
the US East.
575m; skiing 575m–1095m
⚊ *24* ⛷ *643 acres*

Mühlbach Austria
Village near Bischofshofen, a short bus hop from one end of an impressive five-mountain ski area that stretches for miles towards Maria Alm.
855m; skiing 790m–1900m
⬧ *42* ⬧ *160km*

Mühltal Austria **90**

Mürren Switzerland **344**

Mutters Austria **69**

Nasserein Austria **103**

Nauders Austria
Attractive village near Samnaun and Serfaus with a high, sunny intermediate ski area supported by a good artificial snow set-up.
1400m; skiing 1400m–2750m
⬧ *15* ⬧ *55km*

Nendaz Switzerland **359**

Neukirchen Austria
Quiet, pretty beginners resort with a fairly snowsure plateau at the top of its mountain. Intermediates have the Ziller valley nearby.
855m; skiing 855m–2130m
⬧ *13* ⬧ *25km*
✉ *Waymark*

Neustift Austria **89**

Niederau Austria **90**

La Norma France
Traffic-free purpose-built resort near Modane and Val-Cenis, with mostly easy skiing, popular for cheap British school trips.
1350m; skiing 1350m–2750m
⬧ *18* ⬧ *70km*
✉ *UCPA*

Northstar USA
Limited Lake Tahoe family resort with a scenic, varied ski area.
1925m; skiing 1925m–2615m
⬧ *11* ⬧ *1800 acres*
✉ *Virgin Snow*

Nôtre-Dame-de-Bellecombe France
Pleasant village spoilt by the busy Albertville-Megève road. Inexpensive base from which to ski Megève, though it has fair skiing of its own.
1135m; skiing 1035m–2070m
⬧ *40* ⬧ *120km*

Oberau Austria **90**

Obergurgl Austria **91**

Oberlech Austria **80**

Oberndorf Austria **110**

Oberstdorf Germany
Attractive winter sports town with famous ski jumping hill, near the Austrian border, with three small ski areas. The Fellhorn is the most noteworthy.
840m; skiing 810m–2245m
⬧ *26* ⬧ *30km*

Obertauern Austria **96**

Okemo USA
Worthwhile intermediate ski area (there's no resort) above the old Vermont town of Ludlow, close to Killington.
395m; skiing 395m–1010m
⬧ *14* ⬧ *310 acres*

Orcières-Merlette France
Good family resort; convenient snowsure nursery slopes, longer runs mostly funnel safely back to town, useful village facilities – eg large pool and kindergartens.
1850m; skiing 1850m–2655m
⬧ *29* ⬧ *100km*
✉ *Sally*

Les Orres France
Friendly modern resort that enjoys great views and varied intermediate skiing, but snow is unreliable in this area, a very long transfer south of Lyon.
1600m; skiing 1550m–2770m
⬧ *23* ⬧ *50km*
✉ *Club Europe, Ski Ardmore, SkiBound*

Ortisei Italy **292**

Oukaimeden Morocco
Ski area 75km from Marrakesh that can have a surprisingly long season. A few simple hotels and ski hire are available. Pistes are marked but grooming is perfunctory.
2630m; skiing 2630m–3310m
⬧ *6* ⬧ *15km*

Ovronnaz Switzerland
Pretty village set on a sunny shelf above the Rhône valley, with a good pool complex. Limited ski area but Crans-Montana and Anzère are close by.
1350m; skiing 1350m–2425m
⬧ *8* ⬧ *25km*
✉ *Ski Ardmore*

Owl's Head Canada
Steep ski mountain rising out of a lake that affords superb views, in a remote spot bordering Vermont, away from weekend crowds.
⬧ *7*

Oz-Station France **137**

Pal Andorra
Andorra's prettiest ski area (there's no resort), near La Massana, laid out amidst pine trees, best suited to beginners/early intermediates.
skiing 1780m–2360m
⬧ *15* ⬧ *30km*
✉ *Panorama*

Pamporovo Bulgaria
Great value, family/fun resort in a pretty setting, with skiing for beginners and early intermediates, good tuition and a few decent hotels (unusual for Bulgaria).
1620m; skiing 1600m–1935m
⬧ *13* ⬧ *25km*
✉ *Crystal, Enterprise, Ski Balkantours, Sunquest Ski*

Panorama Canada
Pretty, convenient family resort, two hours west of Banff, renowned for its big vertical drop, top tuition, and superb heli-skiing.
975m; skiing 975m–2135m
⬧ *8* ⬧ *300 acres*
✉ *All Canada, Chinook-It, Frontier Ski*

Panticosa Spain
Charming old Pyrenees village
in a sheltered spot good for
calm weather, bad for
snowcover. Limited ski area
best for novices.
1165m; skiing 1165m–1885m
⸸ 7 ⸷ 25km

Park City USA **414**

Park West USA **414**

Parpan Switzerland **342**

Pas de la Casa Andorra
Sprawling mess popular with
French duty-free shoppers, in a
bleak setting with Andorra's
largest, highest skiing.
2095m; skiing 2095m–2820m
⸸ 29 ⸷ 75km
*✉ Airtours, Enterprise, Neilson,
Panorama, Thomson, Top Deck*

Pass Thurn Austria **75**

Peisey-Nancroix France **144**

Pejo Italy
Unspoilt traditional village in a
pretty setting, with a limited
ski area. A cheap base from
which to ski nearby Madonna
di Campiglio.
1340m; skiing 1340m–2800m
⸸ 5 ⸷ 15km
✉ Winterski

Perisher/Smiggin Holes
Australia
Twin ski areas 30km from their
dormitory town, Jindabyne, 6
hours from Sydney, which
between them offer plenty of
short, intermediate runs.
skiing 1675m–2055m
⸸ 30 ⸷ 75km

Pettneu Austria **103**

Piancavallo Italy
Uninspiring yet curiously
trendy purpose-built village
with a mediocre ski area of
short runs, an easy car outing
from Venice.
1830m; skiing 1300m–2000m
⸸ 17 ⸷ 45km
✉ Equity Total Ski, Ski Europe

Piau-Engaly France
User-friendly St-Lary satellite
similar in appearance to Les
Arcs 1600, in one of the best ski
areas in the Pyrenees.
1850m; skiing 1420m–2500m
⸸ 32 ⸷ 70km

Pico USA
Low-key little family ski area
(there's no resort) with fine
views, close to Killington, in
central Vermont.
605m; skiing 605m–1215m
⸸ 9 ⸷ 160 acres

Pila Italy
Old village with a modern
section that has varied, fairly
snowsure skiing that shares an
area lift pass with nearby La
Thuile, Cervinia and
Gressoney.
1790m; skiing 1370m–2650m
⸸ 13 ⸷ 60km
✉ Interski

Pinzolo Italy
Atmospheric village with a life
outside skiing, that has its ski
area well supported by
snowmakers, and is a cheap
base from which to ski nearby
Madonna.
900m; skiing 900m–2100m
⸸ 9 ⸷ 30km
✉ Equity Total Ski

La Plagne France **217**

Poiana Brasov Romania
Cheap, informal user-friendly
resort amidst lovely Carpathian
scenery. Fine ski school and
limited skiing make it best for
novices.
1165m; skiing 1165m–1885m
⸸ 10 ⸷ 15km
*✉ Airtours, Crystal, East Coast
Travel, Enterprise, Inghams,
Neilson, Ski Balkantours,
Sunquest Ski*

Pontresina Switzerland **353**

Portillo Chile
Little more than a luxury hotel
150km north-east of Santiago,
with more snowsure, less
crowded skiing than Las Leñas
in Argentina.
2850m; skiing 2850m–3685m
⸸ 7 ⸷ 25km
✉ Passage to South America

Pozza di Fassa Italy
Pretty Dolomites village with
its own skiing, three other
small ski areas on its doorstep,
and access to the Sella Ronda at
nearby Campitello.
1320m; skiing 1320m–2215m
⸸ 13 ⸷ 20km
✉ Crystal

Pra-Loup France
Convenient, purpose-built
family resort with an extensive,
varied intermediate ski area in
a rather isolated position south
of Gap.
1600m; skiing 1500m–2600m
⸸ 63 ⸷ 230km
*✉ STS, Ski Europe, Snowcoach
Club Cantabrica, Thomson*

Pralognan-la-Vanoise France
Unspoilt traditional Savoie
village with skiing overlooked
by spectacular peaks.
Champagny (La Plagne) and
Courchevel are closeby.
1410m; skiing 1410m–2355m
⸸ 14 ⸷ 25km

Le Praz France **170**

Les Praz France **153**

Praz-de-Lys France
Little known snow-pocket ski
area near Lac Leman, that can
have good snow when nearby
resorts (eg La Clusaz) do not.
1500m; skiing 1200m–1740m
⸸ 21 ⸷ 50km

Praz-sur-Arly France
Traditional Haute Savoie village
in a pretty wooded setting just
down the road from Megève,
with its own varied ski area.
1035m; skiing 1035m–2030m
⸸ 33 ⸷ 100km

Purgatory USA
Limited Colorado resort with
enough good skiing to make it
a useful day out from nearby
Telluride.
2670m; skiing 2670m–3290m
⸸ 9 ⸷ 692 acres

Puy-St-Vincent France
Modern apartment complex
above an old village south of
Briançon; convenient access to
a modest but quite varied ski
area. Relatively inexpensive
and popular with families.
*1400m–1600m; skiing
1400m–2750m*
🚡 15 ✦ 50km
*✉ Alpine Tours, Ski Ardmore,
Snowbizz Vacances*

Queenstown New Zealand
NZ's only large resort, in a
stunning lakeside setting
overlooked by one of its two ski
mountains, the aptly named
Remarkables.
skiing 1215m–1955m
🚡 11 ✦ 1235 acres

Radstadt Austria
Interesting unspoilt medieval
town near Schladming that has
its own small ski area, with the
Salzburger Sportwelt accessed
from nearby Zauchensee or
Flachau.
855m; skiing 855m–1675m
🚡 9 ✦ 30km
✉ Club Europe, Made to Measure

Ramsau Austria
Charming village overlooked
by the Dachstein glacier.
Renowned for cross-country, it
also has Alpine skiing locally,
on the glacier and at nearby
Schladming.
1200m; skiing 1100m–2700m
🚡 22 ✦ 40km
✉ Waymark

Rauris Austria
Old roadside village close to
Kaprun and Zell am See, with a
long narrow ski area that has
snowmakers on its lower
slopes.
950m; skiing 950m–2210m
🚡 11 ✦ 25km
✉ Club Europe

Ravascletto Italy
Resort close to Carinthian
Austria in a pretty tree-filled
setting, with most of its skiing
high above on an open plateau.
920m; skiing 920m–1735m
🚡 12 ✦ 40km
✉ Equity Total Ski, Ski Europe

Red Mountain Canada
Ski area renowned for its steep
and deep powder, eight hours
east of Vancouver, 3km from
Rossland, a charming old
mining town.
1185m; skiing 1185m–2040m
🚡 4 ✦ 2500 acres
✉ Chinook-It

Reutte Austria
500-year-old market town with
many suitably traditional
hotels, and rail links to nearby
Lermoos, Garmisch and
Innsbruck.
855m; skiing 855m–1900m
🚡 11 ✦ 10km

Revelstoke Canada
Town from which you can heli-
ski the Monashees without
staying in a remote mountain
lodge, with local skiing on Mt
McKenzie for bad weather days.
460m
*✉ Powder Skiing in North
America Limited*

Rhêmes-Notre-Dame Italy
Unspoilt village in the beautiful
Rhêmes valley, south of Aosta,
with skiing of its own and that
of Courmayeur and La Thuile
nearby. Hotel Granta Parey is
recommended by one reporter.
1800m; skiing 1800m–2200m
🚡 2 ✦ 5km

Riederalp Switzerland
Pretty car-free village perched
high above the Rhône valley
amidst the glorious scenery of
the Aletsch ski area. Access by
cable-car from Mörel, near Brig.
1925m; skiing 1925m–2710m
🚡 26 ✦ 90km

Rigi-Kaltbad Switzerland
Resort on a mountain rising
straight out of Lake Lucerne,
with superb 360 degree views,
accessed by the world's first
mountain railway.
1440m; skiing 1195m–1795m
🚡 9 ✦ 30km

Riksgränsen Sweden
Unique Arctic Circle Alpine ski
area not open until late
February. Skiing under the
midnight sun (lift-served) from
mid-May to June 30. 20 hours
by train from Stockholm.
600m; skiing 600m–910m
🚡 7 ✦ 10km

Risoul France **225**

Rohrmoos Austria **114**

La Rosière France **226**

Rougemont Switzerland **337**

Saalbach-Hinterglemm Austria
97

Saanen Switzerland **337**

Saanenmöser Switzerland **337**

Saas-Almagell Switzerland **348**

Saas-Fee Switzerland **348**

Saas-Grund Switzerland **348**

Sahoro Japan
Ugly purpose-built Hokkaido
Island complex with a limited
ski area, but one of the most
exotic destinations available on
a package.
400m; skiing 400m–1100m
🚡 10 ✦ 15km
✉ Club Med

St Anton Austria **103**

St Cergue Switzerland
Limited resort less than an
hour from Geneva, good for
families with young children.
1185m; skiing 1185m–1700m
🚡 9 ✦ 20km

St Christoph Austria **103**

Sainte-Foy France **229**

St-François-Longchamp France
250

St Gallenkirch Austria
Smaller, less attractive village
than Gaschurn, with which it
shares a sizeable intermediate
ski area near Schruns.
900m; skiing 900m–2370m
🚡 26 ✦ 100km

St-Gervais France 190

St Jakob in Defereggen Austria
Unspoilt traditional village in a
pretty, sunny valley close to
Lienz and Heiligenblut, with a
good proportion of its skiing
above 2000m.
1390m; skiing 1390m–2520m
⚡ 14 ⚡ 25km

St Jakob in Haus Austria
Snowpocket village with its
own skiing, and a shared lift
pass with charming nearby
Fieberbrunn, Waidring and St
Johann. Good for leisurely
skiers with a car.
855m; skiing 855m–1442m
⚡ 7 ⚡ 25km

St Johann im Pongau Austria
Bustling, lively town with a
small ski area of its own, but
the impressive Salzburger
Sportwelt skiing starts only
4km away at Alpendorf.
650m; skiing 800m–2185m
⚡ 59 ⚡ 200km
✉ *Enterprise, Kings Ski Club,
STS, Ski Europe*

St Johann in Tirol Austria 110

St-Lary France
Well preserved old stone
Pyrenean village, a lift-ride
below its fine intermediate ski
area. Not unlike a downmarket,
Brit-free Courmayeur.
890m; skiing 1420m–2500m
⚡ 32 ⚡ 70km

St Leonhard in Pitztal Austria
Village beneath a fine area of
glacier skiing in the Oetz area,
accessed by a fast new
mountain railway.
1250m; skiing 1735m–3440m
⚡ 12 ⚡ 40km

St Luc Switzerland
Quiet unspoilt rustic village on
the south side of the Rhône
valley, with plenty of high easy
skiing.
1650m; skiing 1650m–3025m
⚡ 16 ⚡ 75km

St-Martin-de-Belleville France
195

St Michael im Lungau Austria
Quiet unspoilt village in the
Tauern pass snowpocket with
an uncrowded but disjointed
intermediate ski area. Close to
Obertauern and Wagrain.
1075m; skiing 1075m–2360m
⚡ 29 ⚡ 60km
✉ *Alpine Tours, Club Europe, Ski
Partners*

St Moritz Switzerland 353

St-Nicolas-de-Véroce France 190

St Oswald Austria 55

St Stephan Switzerland
Unspoilt, relatively inexpensive
old farming village at the foot
of the largest ski area in the
Gstaad Super Ski region.
995m; skiing 950m–2155m
⚡ 69 ⚡ 250km

St Wolfgang Austria
Charming lakeside resort near
Salzburg, some way from any
ski slopes, best for a relaxing
winter holiday with perhaps
one or two days' skiing
included.
540m; skiing 665m–1350m
⚡ 9 ⚡ 6km
✉ *Austrian Holidays, Crystal,
Inghams, Neilson, Thomson*

Les Saisies France
Traditional-style Albertville
Olympics cross-country venue
in a pretty setting, surrounded
by a wonderfully varied four-
mountain Alpine ski area.
1650m; skiing 1150m–1950m
⚡ 24 ⚡ 100km
✉ *Over the Hill*

Samnaun Switzerland 70

Samoëns France 177

San Bernadino Switzerland
Pretty resort south of the road
tunnel of the same name, close
to Madesimo, with a fair
amount of skiing opened up by
its few lifts.
1595m; skiing 1595m–2515m
⚡ 7 ⚡ 50km

San Carlos de Bariloche
Argentina
South America's only year-
round community cum ski
resort, with five ski areas
nearby. Cerro Catedral is the
best but gets crowded in
August.
790m; skiing 1045m–2045m
⚡ 7 ⚡ 26km
✉ *Passage to South America*

San Cassiano Italy 292

San Martino di Castrozza Italy
Plain village in the southern
Dolomites with varied skiing in
four disjointed areas, none of
them very extensive.
1465m; skiing 1450m–2385m
⚡ 25 ⚡ 50km

Sansicario Italy 299

Santa Caterina Italy
Pretty, user-friendly village near
Bormio, with which, along
with Livigno, it shares an area
lift pass. It has a particularly
snowsure novice and
intermediate ski area but the
slopes are dark and cold in
early season.
1740m; skiing 1740m–2725m
⚡ 7 ⚡ 25km
✉ *Airtours, Enterprise, Thomson*

Santa Cristina Italy 292

San Vigilio Italy
Charming, atmospheric
Dolomite village with a
delightful, sizeable ski area well
covered by snow cannon.
1200m; skiing 1200m–2275m
⚡ 35 ⚡ 40km

Sappada Italy
Isolated resort close to the
Austrian border below Lienz.
1215m
⚡ 22 ⚡ 50km
✉ *Ski Europe*

Sauze d'Oulx Italy 288

Savognin Switzerland
Pretty village with one of
Switzerland's best mid-size ski
areas, and a good base for
skiing top nearby resorts – St
Moritz, Davos/Klosters, Flims.
1200m; skiing 1200m–2715m
⚡ 17 ⚡ 80km

Scheffau Austria **62**

Schladming Austria **114**

Schönried Switzerland **337**

Schröcken Austria
Bregenzenwald area village close to the German border with an amazingly good snow record. Good day-trip from Lech, St Anton or Brand.
1260m; skiing 1260m–2050m
⬥ *14* 🚡 *40km*

Schruns Austria
Pleasant little town at the heart of the Montafon ski region; a collection of charming unspoilt Brit-free villages and ski areas south-west of Lech.
700m; skiing 700m–2250m
⬥ *16* 🚡 *50km*
✉ *Alpine Tours*

Schüttdorf Austria **130**

Scuol Switzerland
Year-round spa resort midway between Davos and Samnaun, with an impressive ski range.
1245m; skiing 1245m–2800m
⬥ *16* 🚡 *80km*

Sedrun Switzerland
Charming unspoilt old village on the Glacier Express rail route close to Andermatt, with fine on- and off-piste skiing amidst glorious scenery.
1400m; skiing 1215m–2905m
⬥ *13* 🚡 *60km*
✉ *Waymark*

Seefeld Austria **118**

Sella Nevea Italy
Limited but developing resort in a beautiful setting on the Slovenian border, with skiing amidst dramatic scenery. Summer glacier skiing nearby.
1140m; skiing 1190m–1800m
⬥ *11* 🚡 *8km*

Selva Italy **292**

Semmering Austria
Long established, civilised wintersports resort amidst pretty scenery, 100km from Vienna, towards Graz. Mostly intermediate skiing.
985m; skiing 985m–1340m
⬥ *13* 🚡 *33km*

Les Sept-Laux France
Ugly, user-friendly, family resort near Grenoble, reminiscent in some ways of a small Avoriaz. Pretty skiing for all grades.
1350m; skiing 1350m–2400m
⬥ *35* 🚡 *60km*
✉ *Altours Travel*

Serfaus Austria **119**

Serre-Chevalier France **230**

Sesto Italy
Dolomite village on the road to Cortina surrounded by nice pretty little ski areas.
1310m
⬥ *31* 🚡 *50km*

Sestola Italy
Appenine village a short drive from Pisa and Florence with its skiing, starting some way above, almost completely supported by snowmakers.
900m; skiing 1280m–1975m
⬥ *23* 🚡 *50km*
✉ *Winterski*

Sestriere Italy **299**

Shiga Heights Japan
Largest ski area in Japan, site of Nagano's 1998 Olympic skiing events, 150km from Tokyo. Happo One is a pretty pseudo-European resort in the area.
930m; skiing 1220m–2305m
⬥ *74* 🚡 *130km*

Sierra Nevada Spain
Very ugly but user-friendly resort near Granada, with superb snowmaking facilities and great-value hotels. Suitable for beginners and intermediates but strong late season sun causes icy/soft pistes.
2100m; skiing 2100m–3470m
⬥ *19* 🚡 *55km*
✉ *Crystal, Enterprise, Thomson*

Sils Maria Switzerland **353**

Silvaplana Switzerland **353**

Silver Star Canada
Newly developed resort built on an 1890's theme, with snowsure skiing above the town of Vernon, midway between Banff and Whistler.
1150m; skiing 1150m–1915m
⬥ *8* 🚡 *850 acres*
✉ *All Canada, Made to Measure*

Sinaia Romania
Depressed and depressing main-road town with a modest, open ski area.
795m; skiing 795m–1995m
⬥ *9* 🚡 *15km*
✉ *Crystal*

Siviez Switzerland **359**

Smokovec Slovakia
Spa town near Poprad, with three small ski areas on its doorstep, known collectively as North Tatras.
1020m; skiing 850m–2005m
⬥ *21* 🚡 *10km*

Smugglers Notch USA
Pretty, quiet purpose-built Vermont resort near Stowe, with award-winning children's services, voted best US family ski resort by Family Circle magazine.
315m; skiing 315m–1110m
⬥ *7* 🚡 *246 acres*
✉ *American Dream, Virgin Snow*

Snowbird USA **419**

Snowmass USA **383**

Sölden Austria **120**

Soldeu Andorra **455**

Solitude USA
On the Utah Interconnect route from Park City to Snowbird. More suited to intermediates than neighbouring Alta and Snowbird.
2430m; skiing 2430m–3190m
⬥ *14* 🚡 *1950 acres*

Söll Austria **124**

Sorenberg Switzerland
Popular weekend retreat
between Berne and Lucerne,
with a high proportion of
steep, low skiing.
1165m; skiing 1165m–2350m
⛷ *18* 🚡 *50km*

South Tatras Slovakian Republic
A ski area (there's no resort)
covering both sides of Mount
Chopok near Poprad.
skiing 1240 1240m–2005m
⛷ *19* 🚡 *20km*

Spital am Pyhrn Austria
Limited village east of
Schladming, 4km from its easy
intermediate skiing. Nearby
Hinterstoder is more
interesting.
650m; skiing 810m–1870m
⛷ *10* 🚡 *18km*

Spittal/Drau Austria
Historic Carinthian town with
a limited ski area starting a
cable-car ride above it. A good
day-trip from Bad
Kleinkirchheim or Slovenia.
555m; skiing 1650m–2100m
⛷ *10* 🚡 *20km*

Sportgastein Austria **56**

Squaw Valley USA **408**

Srinagar India
Himalayan resort in trouble-
torn Kashmir, best ignored at
present, with a small pisted
area but excellent heli-skiing.
2720m; skiing 2645m–3645m
⛷ *7* 🚡 *5km*

Stafal Italy **281**

Steamboat USA **421**

Steinach Austria
Pleasant village in picturesque
surroundings, an easy outing
from Innsbruck, just off the
autobahn near the Brenner
Pass.
1045m; skiing 1045m–2005m
⛷ *9* 🚡 *18km*
✉ *Alpine Tours*

Stoneham Canada
Leading Quebec resort, better
equipped and more sheltered
then most neighbours, with
skiing across four mountains,
including the largest night
operation in Canada. 92%
snowmaking.
⛷ *10*

Stowe USA
Probably North America's
prettiest resort; a beautifully
preserved and restored old
Vermont village, 10km from a
mostly intermediate ski area
which also has some very
challenging slopes.
395m; skiing 395m–1115m
⛷ *11* 🚡 *487 acres*
✉ *American Dream, Crystal, Ski
Independence, USAirtours, Virgin
Snow*

Stratton/Bromley USA
New York City weekend retreat
that has two ski areas, with
Bromley reputedly the warmest
place to ski in chilly Vermont.
515m; skiing 515m–1175m
⛷ *18* 🚡 *458 acres*

Stuben Austria **103**

Sugar Loaf USA
Developing Maine resort, five
hours from Boston, with US
East's best open skiing.
405m; skiing 405m–1260m
⛷ *15* 🚡 *433 acres*

Sugarbush USA
Resort in upper Vermont near
Montpelier, trendy in the
1960s, now a more low-key
place with a well designed ski
area.
455m; skiing 455m–1235m
⛷ *16* 🚡 *497 acres*

Sundance USA
Robert Redford-owned,
tastefully designed family resort
set amidst trees in snowsure
Utah, with a fair amount of
mostly intermediate skiing
opened up by few lifts.
2505m; skiing 2505m–3160m
⛷ *4*

Sunday River USA
One of the more attractive
resorts in the East, four hours
from Boston, best for
intermediate cruisers.
245m; skiing 245m–840m
⛷ *12* 🚡 *411 acres*

Sunshine Village Canada **441**

Sun Valley USA
America's original glamour
resort, spread over disjointed
developments, most a bus-ride
from the slopes. Skiing suitable
for all.
1755m; skiing 1755m–2790m
⛷ *12* 🚡 *2000 acres*
✉ *American Connections,
American Dream, Ski Activity,
Ski Independence*

Superbagnères France
Little more than a particularly
French-dominated Club Med,
best for a low-cost, low-effort
family trip to the Pyrenees.
1880m; skiing 1450m–2260m
⛷ *15* 🚡 *15km*
✉ *Club Med*

Superdévoluy France
Ugly, purpose-built, user-
friendly family resort, an hour
south-east of Grenoble, with a
sizeable intermediate ski area.
1500m; skiing 1470m–2470m
⛷ *32* 🚡 *105km*
✉ *STS, Sally*

La Tania France **170**

Taos USA **425**

El Tarter Andorra
Relatively quiet, convenient
alternative to Soldeu, with
which it shares a ski area.
Having a chalet package is a
boon given the poor hotels.
1680m; skiing 1680m–2560m
⛷ *22* 🚡 *50km*
✉ *Panorama*

Tarvisio Italy
Interesting, animated old town
bordering Austria and Slovenia.
A major cross-country centre
with fairly limited Alpine
skiing.
750m; skiing 750m–1860m
⛷ *12* 🚡 *15km*
✉ *Ski Europe*

Täsch Switzerland **372**

Tauplitz Austria
Traditional village at the foot
of an interestingly varied ski
area north of Schladming, close
to Salzburg.
895m; skiing 895m–1965m
🚡 *18* 🎿 *25km*
✉ *Club Europe*

Telluride USA **429**

Terminillo Italy
Purpose-built resort 100km
from Rome with a worthwhile
ski area when its lower runs
have snowcover, but not
surprisingly this isn't assured.
1500m; skiing 1500m–2700m
🚡 *13* 🎿 *40km*

Thredbo Australia
Oz's best, six hours from
Sydney; with
uncharacteristically long (and,
in places, testing) runs,
snowmaking, lots of
accommodation and active
nightlife.
1365m; skiing 1365m–2035m
🚡 *15* 🎿 *70km*

La Thuile Italy **300**

Thyon 2000 Switzerland **359**

Tignes France **235**

Tonale Italy
Ugly resort in a bleak setting
with little to offer except the
not inconsiderable guarantee of
snow at a bargain price. Pretty
Madonna is nearby.
1885m; skiing 1885m–3015m
🚡 *28* 🎿 *80km*
✉ *Altours Travel, Crystal,
Enterprise, Equity Total Ski, Ski
Europe, Winterski*

Torgon Switzerland
Old village in a pretty tree-
filled setting, with a nearby lift
connection to the Portes du
Soleil.
1095m; skiing 975m–2275m
🚡 *224* 🎿 *650km*

Le Tour France
Charming unspoilt hamlet at
the head of the Chamonix
valley with much easier skiing
than its near neighbours.
1465m; skiing 1465m–2185m
🚡 *9* 🎿 *40km*
✉ *Bigfoot, Poles Apart*

La Toussuire France
User-friendly modern resort
east of Grenoble, with a large
uncrowded intermediate ski
area that deserves to be better
known.
1800m; skiing 1450m–2265m
🚡 *41* 🎿 *180km*
✉ *Enterprise*

Trafoi Italy
Quiet, traditional (Austrian-
style) South Tyrol village near
Bormio, worth a day-trip if you
can ski down to the resort; not
if you can't.
1570m; skiing 1570m–2550m
🚡 *6* 🎿 *10km*

Troodos Cyprus
A good outing from Greek
sector coastal resorts, with
interesting old villages en-
route. Pretty, wooded pistes
and fine views.
🚡 *4* 🎿 *5km*

Tschagguns Austria
Village with a varied little ski
area of its own and the skiing
and town life of Schruns a
stone's throw away.
700m; skiing 655m–2085m
🚡 *12* 🎿 *50km*

Tulfes Austria **69**

Turoa New Zealand
Arguably North Island's best ski
area, on a volcano's flank with
superb views of its classic cone.
350km south of Auckland, near
Ohakune.
🚡 *10* 🎿 *914 acres*

Turracher Höhe Austria
Tiny, unspoilt lakeside resort
on a mountain shelf with
varied intermediate skiing
above and below it. A good
outing from Bad
Kleinkirchheim.
1765m; skiing 1400m–2205m
🚡 *12* 🎿 *40km*
✉ *Alpine Tours*

Uludag Turkey
Surprisingly suave, laid-back,
well equipped, purpose-built
resort near Bursa, south of
Istanbul, popular with poseurs.
1800m; skiing 1800m–2225m
🚡 *12* 🎿 *15km*
✉ *President, Sunquest Ski*

Untergurgl Austria **91**

Vail USA **433**

Valbella Switzerland **342**

Val-Cenis France
Ramshackle old twin villages
over the Iseran pass (closed in
winter) from Val-d'Isere that
have varied skiing, with the
best runs above 2000 metres.
1400m; skiing 1400m–2800m
🚡 *23* 🎿 *60km*
✉ *Sally, Ski Valkyrie, UCPA*

Val-d'Isère France **241**

Valfréjus France
Underrated, pleasant modern
family resort near
Bardonecchia, with a cheap lift
pass and varied, interesting,
snowsure skiing.
1500m; skiing 1500m–2730m
🚡 *13* 🎿 *52km*
✉ *Made to Measure, Neilson,
Thomson*

Vallandry France **144**

Valloire France **249**

Valmeinier France **249**

Valmorel France **250**

Val Senales Italy
In the Dolomites near Merano,
this isn't so much a resort as a
top-of-the-mountain hotel
that's the ultimate in snowsure
skiing from the door.
3250m; skiing 2005m–3250m
🚡 *10* 🎿 *24km*

Val-Thorens France **255**

Valtournenche Italy **266**

Vars France **259**

Vaujany France **137**

Vent Austria
High, remote Oztal village with just enough skiing to warrant a day-trip from nearby Obergurgl.
1900m; skiing 1900m–2680m
⛟ *4* ⛷ *15km*
✉ *Sloping Off*

Verbier Switzerland **359**

Veysonnaz Switzerland **359**

Vigo di Fassa Italy
Best base from which to ski the Fassa valley, with the Sella Ronda also close via neighbouring Campitello.
1390m; skiing 1320m–2215m
⛟ *13* ⛷ *20km*
✉ *Crystal*

La Villa Italy **292**

Villard-Reculas France **137**

Villard-de-Lans France
Unspoilt traditional village west of Grenoble, full of life and character with animated canopied cafés etc. It's also snowsure thanks to very extensive snowmaking.
1050m; skiing 1110m–2170m
⛟ *36* ⛷ *130km*
✉ *Alpine Options Skidrive, Headwater, Inntravel*

Villaroger France **144**

Villars Switzerland **366**

Vitosha Bulgaria
A few widely scattered dour hotels (there's no resort) with very limited skiing. Low budget skiers have far better options – eg Borovets, Pamporovo or Poiana Brasov.
1810m; skiing 1515m–2200m
⛟ *8* ⛷ *20km*
✉ *Enterprise, Sunquest Ski*

Vorderlanersbach Austria **85**

Voss Norway
Well equipped winter sports resort attractively set on a lake, with relatively limited Alpine skiing.
60m; skiing 150m–945m
⛟ *10* ⛷ *40km*
✉ *Color Line, Dawson and Sanderson, NSR Travel, The Ski Firm*

Wagrain Austria
Traditional village at the heart of the extensive Salzburger Sportwelt intermediate ski area linking Flachau and St Johann im Pongau.
900m; skiing 800m–2185m
⛟ *59* ⛷ *200km*
✉ *Club Europe, Made to Measure, Mogul Ski, STS*

Waidring Austria **110**

Wanaka New Zealand
Village in what must be one of the most beautiful lakeside mountain settings in the world, with two ski areas each half an hour away.
skiing 1200m–1860m
⛟ *9* ⛷ *2223 acres*

Wengen Switzerland **367**

Westendorf Austria **129**

Whakapapa New Zealand
NZ's largest ski area, on a volcano close to Turoa with similarly superb views. The Grand Chateau is a lovely old hotel in the tiny village 6km away.
skiing 1625m–2300m
⛟ *22* ⛷ *988 acres*

Whistler Canada **447**

Wildhaus Switzerland
Undeveloped farming community in stunning scenery, near Liechtenstein, popular with families and good serious snowboarders.
1050m; skiing 900m–2260m
⛟ *21* ⛷ *50km*

Winter Park USA
Perhaps the best Colorado resort yet to be widely 'discovered' by Brits. Good, snowsure skiing. World leader for disabled skier facilities.
2745m; skiing 2735m–3665m
⛟ *22* ⛷ *1300 acres*
✉ *Made to Measure, Ski Independence*

Yong Pyeong Korea
Largest resort in Korea, 200km east of Seoul, with snowmakers on all 19 of its exclusively short runs. Much less crowded than Japanese resorts.
750m; skiing 750m–1460m
⛟ *15* ⛷ *20km*

Zakopane Poland
An interesting old town near charming medieval Cracow and moving Auschwitz. Mostly intermediate skiing.
685m; skiing 685m–1990m
⛟ *7* ⛷ *10km*

Zauchensee Austria
Purpose-built resort with lifts fanning out into the Salzburger Sportwelt skiing that surrounds it.
855m; skiing 800m–2185m
⛟ *59* ⛷ *200km*
✉ *Alpine Tours, Made to Measure, Mogul Ski*

Zell am See Austria **130**

Zell am Ziller Austria **134**

Zermatt Switzerland **372**

Zinal Switzerland
Rustic village, pretty but for some incongruous modern building, with plenty of high skiing and a striking, unusual Matterhorn view.
1700m; skiing 1660m–2895m
⛟ *9* ⛷ *70km*
✉ *Club Med*

Zug Austria **80**

Zürs Austria **80**

Zweisimmen Switzerland
Limited but inexpensive base from which to ski nearby Gstaad, with its own delightful little easy skiing area too.
950m; skiing 950m–2005m
⛟ *6* ⛷ *25km*

Ordering more copies of Where to Ski

Where to Ski is available by post at the bookshop price of £14.99, post and packing included. You don't have to use this form, but it helps us and it may help you.

Where to Ski order

TO
WHERE TO SKI, THE OLD FORGE, NORTON ST PHILIP, BATH BA3 6LW

Please supply   copies of Where to Ski at £14.99 per copy including post and packing. I enclose a cheque for   made out to Where to Ski.

Name

Address

Pre-publication offers on the next edition

The second edition of Where to Ski will be published in early September 1995. If you would like the opportunity to buy a copy in advance of publication at a special discount price, send in this form to reach us before 31 July 1995.

Where to Ski pre-publication offers

TO
WHERE TO SKI, THE OLD FORGE, NORTON ST PHILIP, BATH BA3 6LW

Please send me details of special pre-publication discounts available on the next edition of Where to Ski. I understand that I am under no obligation to buy.

Name

Address

Get your money back

it couldn't be easier

Book your 1994/95-season skiing holiday through the specialist travel agency Ski Solutions, and the price of this book will be knocked off the cost of your holiday.

Ski Solutions are Britain's longest-established and most respected ski travel agency. You can book more-or-less any ski holiday through them, whether you want to go independently or on a tour operator's package.

To book your holiday, ask their advice, or just get hold of some brochures, phone them on 071-602 9900. When you make your booking, tell Ski Solutions you're claiming a refund and send Part 1 of the voucher opposite to them with your booking form. Send Part 2 to us at Where To Ski. The price of this book will then be deducted from your final invoice.

MONEY BACK VOUCHER – PART 1

TO BE SENT TO
SKI SOLUTIONS, 84 PEMBROKE ROAD, LONDON W8 6NX
ALONG WITH YOUR BOOKING FORM

Name _____

Address _____

_____

_____

_____

Tour Operator (if applicable) _____

I have bought a copy of Where to Ski and claim a refund of the £14.99 cover price. I understand this amount will be deducted from the cost of the holiday I am booking through Ski Solutions. Offer valid for bookings for 1994/95 season holidays made before 30 April 1995.

Departure Date _____

MONEY BACK VOUCHER – PART 2

TO BE SENT TO
WHERE TO SKI, THE OLD FORGE, NORTON ST PHILIP, BATH BA3 6LW

Name _____

Address _____

_____

_____

_____

Ski Resort(s) to be visited _____

I have booked a 1994/95 ski holiday through Ski Solutions and claimed a refund of the price of Where to Ski.

Departure Date _____

Have you booked any other holiday through Ski Solutions in the last two seasons?   Yes ☐   No ☐

Where did you hear about Where to Ski (please tick all that apply)?

Daily Mail Ski magazine ☐

The Independent newspaper ☐

The Independent on Sunday ☐

Other magazine or newspaper ☐

Saw in book shop ☐

Where to Ski mailing ☐

Reports on resorts help us make Where to Ski as useful and up-to-date as possible. Please tick here if you would be willing to fill in a questionnaire about your holiday and about how Where to Ski could be made even more useful to you. We will then send you one shortly before your departure date.

Yes, please send me a questionnaire ☐

CUT ALONG DOTTED LINE

WHERE *to* SKI

WHERE *to* SKI

WHERE *to* SKI

WHERE *to* SKI

WHERE *to* SKI

WHERE *to* SKI

WHERE *to* SKI

WHERE *to* SKI